John Quincy Adams

John Quincy Adams

A Man for the Whole People

Randall Woods

DUTTON

DUTTON

An imprint of Penguin Random House LLC
penguinrandomhouse.com

Copyright © 2024 by Randall B. Woods
Penguin Random House supports copyright. Copyright fuels creativity, encourages diverse voices,
promotes free speech, and creates a vibrant culture. Thank you for buying an authorized edition of this
book and for complying with copyright laws by not reproducing, scanning, or distributing any part of it
in any form without permission. You are supporting writers and allowing Penguin Random House to
continue to publish books for every reader.

DUTTON and the D colophon are registered trademarks of Penguin Random House LLC.

Map by Jack Critser

LIBRARY OF CONGRESS CATALOGING-IN-PUBLICATION DATA

Names: Woods, Randall Bennett, 1944- author.
Title: John Quincy Adams : a man for the whole people / Randall B. Woods.
Description: [New York] : Dutton, [2024] | Includes bibliographical
references and index.
Identifiers: LCCN 2023038729 (print) | LCCN 2023038730 (ebook) |
ISBN 9780593187241 (hardcover) | ISBN 9780593187258 (ebook)
Subjects: LCSH: Adams, John Quincy, 1767-1848. | Statesmen—
United States—Biography. | Founding Fathers of the United States—Biography. |
Presidents—United States—Biography. | Adams family. | United States—
Politics and government—1783-1865.
Classification: LCC E377 .W663 2024 (print) | LCC E377 (ebook) |
DDC 973.55092 [B]—dc23/eng/20231109
LC record available at https://lccn.loc.gov/2023038729
LC ebook record available at https://lccn.loc.gov/2023038730

Printed in the United States of America
1st Printing

BOOK DESIGN BY NEUWIRTH & ASSOCIATES

For Jeffrey Randall Woods, son, friend, and colleague

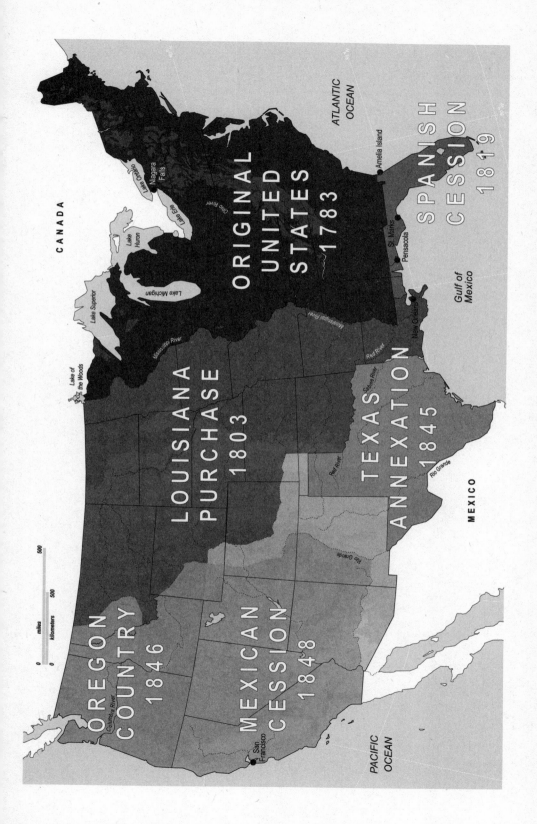

ORIGINAL
UNITED
STATES
1783

LOUISIANA
PURCHASE
1803

SPANISH
CESSION
1819

TEXAS
ANNEXATION
1845

OREGON
COUNTRY
1846

MEXICAN
CESSION
1848

CANADA

MEXICO

ATLANTIC
OCEAN

PACIFIC
OCEAN

Gulf of
Mexico

Lake Superior

Lake Michigan

Lake Huron

Lake Erie

Lake Ontario

Lake of
the Woods

Niagara
Falls

Ohio River

Mississippi River

Mississippi River

Red River

Red River

Sabine River

Rio Grande

Rio Grande

Columbia River

Amelia Island

St. Marks

Pensacola

New Orleans

San
Francisco

miles

kilometers

0   500

0   500

Contents

1

The Adamses of Braintree

JOHN QUINCY ADAMS WAS a child of the Enlightenment, of the American Revolution, and, perhaps most important, of John and Abigail Adams. Highly intelligent, public-spirited, intellectually curious, and intensely ambitious, the Adamses were a formidable couple. Born British, they would play a leading role in the Revolution and then in imagining and shaping the republic that emerged from it. John and Abigail would become among the best-known Americans of their generation: he the coauthor of the Constitution and second president of the United States, and she—through her voluminous correspondence—a voice for women's rights and a noted commentator on life and letters. They knew virtually every American of prominence during the Revolutionary Era and the Early Republic.

John Quincy would both reflect and transcend his famous parents. While they were alive, they would be their eldest son's most intimate confidants. Their formidable moral and intellectual universe would be his touchstone. John Quincy was molded by his parents' fierce patriotism; by their religious beliefs, which were both fundamental and discerning; and by their devotion to the country that they helped bring into being. Their history was his, their friends and enemies his. Especially their enemies. In the Adams clan, public service took pride of place only after God and family. When, in 1812, the younger Adams was serving as U.S. minister to Imperial Russia, he experienced profound doubt about a life in politics and diplomacy. He and his family were in extremis, suffering physically from the Russian winter and emotionally from separation from their two eldest sons. An inadvisable and potentially disastrous war between the United States and Great Britain loomed. Perhaps, John Quincy wrote his father, it would be best for him to return home to a life of law and literature. Do not deceive yourself, John wrote back. You are a patriot, both architect and servant of the republic of which you are a citizen. Often, I wish it were not so, the father confided, but it is undeniable that your very soul is intertwined with that of America's. Your country will never leave you be; it will continue to seduce you, disappoint you, thrill you, but, above all, demand everything that you have until your dying day.

The lives of fathers and sons are typically inextricably intertwined, for better or worse. In the case of John and John Quincy Adams, it was surely for the better. From the time he was eleven until he was sixteen, while his father served as minister plenipotentiary to the Netherlands and France during the American Revolution, John Quincy was John's bosom companion. The motherless boy and wifeless man were a solace to each other. During their travels and travails, the boy seemed absolutely secure. When he was not in school, John Quincy accompanied his diplomat father to theatrical performances, dinners, receptions, and even official functions. Given their transience, the only constant in the education of John Quincy was his father, one of the major intellects of his time and a leading figure in the American Enlightenment. As they lived their lives, John and John Quincy nourished each other emotionally and intellectually as one and then the other took his place at the center of national politics and diplomacy. Theirs was a relationship unique in American history.

JOHN ADAMS WAS BORN on October 19, 1735, in Braintree, Massachusetts, to John and Susanna Boylston Adams. John the elder was a farmer and cordwainer by vocation, and a prominent member of the community, serving as a deacon in the local Congregationalist church and holding several offices in the civil government and militia. His great-grandfather Henry Adams had immigrated to Massachusetts Bay Colony from Braintree, Essex, England, around 1638. Susanna, twenty years younger than her husband, was the daughter of a prominent Massachusetts family. The Adamses revered their Puritan forefathers but embraced a more liberal theology that rejected notions of predestination and irredeemable sin. But as John later recalled, his parents "held every species of libertinage in contempt and horror," continually warning their children against the evils of sexual promiscuity, drunkenness, and sloth.[1]

Young John relished the outdoor life he experienced as a child on the family's fifty-acre farm, but his parents envisioned a larger world for their eldest son. His father found farming laborious and monotonous; both of his grandfathers had attended Harvard College, and they intended that John would follow in their footsteps. The boy attended Braintree's Latin School until his tutors deemed him ready for admission to college. At age fifteen, terrified, he survived the grueling admission interview.[2] Steeped in the classics and in moral and natural philosophy, John graduated in 1755, ranked fourteenth out of his class of twenty-five.[3]

John's parents wanted him to become a minister. He thought otherwise. The ordeal of the Reverend Lemuel Bryant, whose liberal theological views had prompted his conservative congregation to put him on trial in Deacon Adams's parlor, was burned into John's memory. Bryant's persecution aside, the younger Adams had on his own come to have grave doubts concerning the received Calvinist doctrines of New England's Congregationalist establishment. The doctrine of innate human depravity and predestination struck him as spiritually absurd and contrary to the teachings of the New Testament. By his early twenties, he had embraced Unitarianism, whose followers rejected both the trinity and the divinity of Christ. This is not to say that he was not a believer; he was, and his faith in a loving God sustained him through incredible trials and tribulations. The very existence of the universe, its "surprising diversity" amidst "Uniformity," was in itself proof of a Grand Design. He believed that humans were born with an innate moral sense, and that the function of religion was to cultivate and sharpen that sense. "Without religion this world would be something not fit to be mentioned in polite company," he would observe to Thomas Jefferson.[4]

But if not the ministry, what then? The law seemed a likely means to achieve a decent living and to play a prominent role in the public life of the colony. But the elder Adams, like many of his class and vocation, regarded attorneys as either shysters or predators, so John accepted a position teaching Latin in Worcester, a town some fifty miles west of Boston. He took an immediate dislike to his new life, and in 1756, he persuaded James Putnam, Worcester's leading lawyer, to tutor him for two years.[5]

Adams's studies completed, his father invited him to return home to Braintree, where at the time there was no practicing attorney. The town was part of the greater Boston legal district, and it was there that the younger Adams would have to be admitted to the bar. The dean of Boston's legal community, Jeremiah Gridley, agreed to examine him. John passed with flying colors. He was duly admitted and hung out his shingle.[6] During 1759 and 1760, John barely scraped by, but he was persistent and so ambitious that his friends could not but laugh at him sometimes. He watched and mimicked Putnam and the renowned James Otis; he read; he observed; he practiced rigid self-discipline, a trait that would remain with him for the rest of his life.[7] He was driven by a "passion for superiority," he once observed of himself, while at the same time he was determined to "subdue every unworthy Passion and treat all men as I wish to be treated by all."[8] Gradually, the professional tide began to turn, and the cases came.

Initially Adams was as unlucky in love as he was in the law. Somewhat shy and socially awkward, he twice fell in love and was twice rejected. But then, in late 1759, he met Abigail Smith. It was not love at first sight. Abigail's father, "a crafty and designing man," put him off. He observed in his diary of Abigail, then barely fifteen, and her sister Mary that they were "Not fond, not frank, not candid."[9] Apparently the Smith sisters had found the young barrister somewhat pompous and had cut him down to size. It would be two years before they met again, but that next time John found Abigail Smith increasingly irresistible.

Abigail was born to the Reverend William Smith and his wife, Elizabeth Quincy Smith, in 1744 at her father's parsonage in Weymouth, a rustic community some fourteen miles southeast of Boston. Smith had married well. The Quincys were among Massachusetts Bay's most distinguished families, their arrival dating back to 1633. Abigail's grandfather had served as the speaker of the colony's House of Representatives during her childhood. The Reverend Smith augmented his meager clerical salary by working two farms, one of which was apparently supplied by the affluent Quincys. To assist him in his labors, he bought four slaves. William and Elizabeth were serious about their religious calling. In 1751, Weymouth was devastated by a diphtheria epidemic that in a year killed a hundred fifty of the town's twelve hundred residents. Elizabeth, accompanied by her six-year-old daughter, Abigail, made the rounds of the bereaved, providing not only consolation but food and clothing.[10]

As she grew, Abigail, an intelligent and intellectually restless girl, became increasingly aware that she was not receiving the same education as the young men of her age. A few Massachusetts academies admitted female students, but William and Elizabeth were not willing to send their daughter away to school. Most young women of the time were educated by their families and received tutelage in nothing more than reading, writing, and simple arithmetic.

As she approached young womanhood, Abigail immersed herself in a group of like-minded and education-hungry peers; she and her companions learned French and discussed contemporary literature. But it was not until the arrival of Richard Cranch that her horizons really began to expand. While courting Mary, Cranch introduced the Smith sisters to fine literature—Shakespeare, John Milton, Alexander Pope.[11] It was Cranch who would reintroduce his good friend John Adams to Abigail.

By the spring of 1763, the two were finding it increasingly difficult to be separated. A physical attraction on his part was understandable. At seventeen, Abigail, with olive skin and dark hair and eyes, was growing into a beauty. John, on the other hand, was plain with a round face and an equally round body. But Abigail sensed a kind heart and a noble spirit, sufficient, apparently, to trump his annoying pomposity. In later life she observed that her paramour "confirmed my taste and gave me every indulgence that books could afford."[12] She also perceived in him a common outlook on what it meant to be a human being.

Abigail and her friends were deeply influenced by a new cultural movement known as sensibility. Superficially it meant developing a taste for fine art, fine literature, and fine wine. At a deeper level, it meant acknowledging the universality of empathy as a human trait. A "man of feeling" (the title of a popular novel published in 1771 by Henry Mackenzie) was incapable of hearing about another person's distress and desires without being moved. In part, sensibility was a reaction to John Locke's depiction of infants as clean slates upon which the world wrote their life stories. During the eighteenth century, other thinkers—Adam Smith, for example—insisted that human beings were born with an innate moral sense. This notion would constitute the base upon which John and Abigail Adams's moral and political philosophies would rest. "Humanity obliges us to be affected with the distresses and miseries of our fellow creatures"—even those with whom one was not personally acquainted, Abigail wrote.[13] She and John became not only lovers and friends but soulmates.

In public the couple talked of every subject under the sun. In private they kissed and caressed. Forced to be away on business, John longed for "her fair complexion, her crimson blushes and her million charms and graces."[14] John wanted to propose, but he feared he could not yet support a wife and children. His patron, Jeremiah Gridley, had advised him to "Pursue the law itself rather than the gain of it. . . . I advise you not to marry early." John took the counsel to heart. "[A]lthough my propensity to marriage was ardent enough, I determined I could not indulge it, till I saw a clear prospect of business and profit to support a family without embarrassment."[15] Nevertheless, after some prompting from Abigail, he proposed. There was a short delay while John recovered from the effects of a smallpox inoculation, and the two were married on October 25, 1764. John was twenty-eight and his bride nineteen. Parson Smith presided and completely changed John's earlier bad opinion of him by endowing the couple with a generous sum of money, enough, John later recalled, to purchase "an orchard and very fine piece of land near my paternal house and homestead."[16]

The newlyweds' first residence was a traditional New England saltbox-style structure featuring two stories in front and a single story in back, all covered by a roof sloping from front to rear. The clapboard-sheathed structure boasted two bedrooms on the top floor and a kitchen and a parlor on the bottom. A massive fireplace used for heating and cooking was situated in the middle of the house. The single story in back could accommodate two additional bedrooms. The steeply pitched roof protected the house from the region's heavy snowfalls. On July 14, 1765, Abigail gave birth to the couple's first child, also named Abigail but known henceforth within the family as "Nabby." The baby girl was born eight and a half months after the couple took their wedding vows, meaning that Abigail might have been pregnant at the time of her marriage. In this she was not alone. Despite Puritan New England's frequently expressed fears about sexual licentiousness, fully one-third of the region's brides were with child when they wed.[17] On July 11, 1767, just days before Nabby's second birthday, Abigail delivered a boy, whom she and John named John Quincy, the middle name honoring Abigail's grandfather, who at the time lay dying.[18] John was a bit overwhelmed at the prospect of raising two children in the manner he and his wife thought appropriate. "But what shall we do with this young fry?" John wrote his brother-in-law, Richard Cranch, whose wife, Mary, had also just given birth. "In a little while Johnny must go to college, and Nabby must have fine clothes, aye, and so must Betcy [the Cranch child] too. . . . And very cleverly you and I shall feel when we recollect that we were hard at work . . . and Johnny and Betcy at the same time raking and fluttering away our profits. Aye, and there must be dancing schools and boarding schools and all that, or else, you know, we shall not give the polite education—better not have been born you know than not have polite educations."[19]

Meanwhile, the ties that bound Britain's thirteen American colonies to the mother country were fraying. In 1760, Britain crowned a new king, George III. He and his supporters in the Tory Party managed to maneuver the Whigs, champions of representative government, out of control of Parliament. In 1763, the king named George Grenville, a Whig, his new prime minister. Under his leadership, the British government took the position that the American colonists existed solely for the benefit of the mother country. Whatever rights they enjoyed were the product of Britain's tolerance and generosity. This marked a sharp reversal of policy. Under previous ministries, which had believed that giving the colonial governments and economies the freest possible hand would lead to the prosperity of all, the provincial governments had grown increasingly independent and at times defiant. The French and Indian War—1754 through 1763—had effectively put an end to France's North American empire but had nearly bankrupted Britain. King George and his prime minister—and the Parliament they controlled—believed that the American colonies had benefited most from the war and ought to be taxed to refill the exchequer's coffers. The colonists resisted, declaring that they had done most of the fighting in the Anglo-French conflict, and insisted that they were English citizens. Thus, "no taxation without representation."

In 1764, Parliament passed the Sugar Act, which levied a tax on sugar and related products such as molasses and rum. Then came the Stamp Act the following year. That measure imposed a tax in the form of a stamp on virtually all paper products—newspapers, legal documents, pamphlets, even decks of cards and dice. The tariff affected Americans of all classes and regions; the inclusion of newspapers and tavern licenses offended those who were most responsible for molding public opinion. In the fall of 1765, readers of the *Boston Gazette* were treated to a series of articles denouncing the Sugar and Stamp Acts as unconstitutional and oppressive. They were signed "Humphrey Ploughjogger," the first pseudonym adopted by John Adams.[20]

In the spring of 1766, Parliament, under pressure from British merchants suffering from the effects of the American boycott, repealed the Stamp Act but replaced it with the Declaratory Act, reaffirming Britain's right to levy taxes on the colonies, colonial assemblies notwithstanding. Then in 1767 came the Townshend Duties, taxes on imports of certain commonly used commodities, such as glass, lead, paint, and tea. Parliament established boards of customs commissioners to collect the taxes and dispatched contingents of troops to protect them and help enforce the tariffs.

By 1768, John's legal practice was flourishing. In April, he moved the family to Boston, where he rented a white clapboard house on Brattle Street. The move would spare him the endless trips in from Braintree and provide more time with his growing family. It was not his intention to place himself near the center of the gathering storm in Anglo-American relations, but that was certainly the result.[21]

In May 1770, Abigail gave birth to another son, Charles. His arrival helped the couple recover from the loss of a daughter, Susanna, who had been born shortly after the Adamses moved to Boston. A sickly child, she expired when just thirteen months old. Charles, like Nabby and John Quincy, thrived, however. On April 13, 1771, the Adamses departed Boston and returned to Braintree. Their stay was brief; both Abigail and John found life there a bit stultifying and certainly inconvenient. In August 1772, John purchased a commodious brick house in Boston. The family delayed moving until Abigail could give birth to their third son, Thomas Boylston.[22]

There was obviously nothing amiss with John and Abigail's sex life, and for two such strong-minded individuals, they got on remarkably well outside the bedroom. John found his mate bright, attractive, stimulating, and amazingly capable as a manager of the household. Though John could be vain and self-centered, Abigail was content with her spouse. Not so much with her status as a woman in colonial America. Every wife in America was a *feme covert*—a covered woman. "The husband and wife are one person in the law," the English legal theorist William Blackstone had proclaimed in 1765; "that is, the very being or legal existence of the woman is suspended during the marriage."[23] The right to vote was out of the question, but in addition, everything that the wife possessed belonged to the husband and was subject to his disposal. Abigail would accommodate herself to existing law and custom only to a degree. She exhibited a lifelong interest in the status of women and sought the company of other intelligent and educated females.

She was a great admirer of Catharine Macaulay, England's renowned female historian.[24]

Despite the tensions created in Britain and the American colonies by the Boston Massacre, the years from 1770 to 1772 were relatively tranquil. Trade revived at last, following a long postwar depression. British customs agents and the Sons of Liberty showed restraint. But then, the relative calm was broken by Parliament's passage of the Tea Act of 1773 and Boston's violent reaction to it. In an effort to save the British East India Company, then facing bankruptcy, Parliament removed all duties on tea imported to America from India and authorized the company to sell directly to retailers. The colonial merchant class was outraged. Was Britain going to grant monopolies to British concerns on every other product, thus putting thousands of American importers and wholesalers out of business? In May, mobs gathered in a number of ports, but they merely prevented the East India Company's tea from being landed or sold. In Boston, on the night of December 16, 1773, a hundred fifty Sons of Liberty, led by Sam Adams and loosely disguised as "Mohawks," boarded a British vessel and threw overboard some twenty thousand pounds worth of tea.

For the British, the so-called Boston Tea Party was the proverbial last straw. The government of Lord North pushed through Parliament a series of punitive measures: the Boston Port Act, which closed the port to all commerce until the tea was paid for; the Massachusetts Government Act, which forbade town meetings without Crown approval and made the colony's upper house appointive rather than elective; a measure providing that British officials accused of capital crimes could be tried only in British courts; the Quartering Act (applied to all colonies), which required colonial communities to furnish housing at their expense to British troops within twenty-four hours of their arrival; and the Quebec Act, which detached the territory south of the Great Lakes that had been claimed by various colonies and merged it with the Canadian province of Quebec. To make sure that Massachusetts buckled under the "Intolerable Acts," as Adams and his fellows termed them, the North ministry dispatched four regiments of redcoats under the command of General Thomas Gage.

During the summer of 1774, each of the thirteen colonies established committees of correspondence to discuss a common response to the Intolerable Acts. This led to an agreement to hold elections for delegates who would attend a Continental Congress. On September 5, 1774, fifty-six of America's most articulate and respected citizens assembled in Philadelphia. John Adams was among them.

The troubles with Great Britain had prompted John to move the family back to Braintree. Living there would be cheaper and probably safer. The honor of being chosen to go to Philadelphia was somewhat dimmed by the threat it posed to the family's financial well-being. There would be no legal fees coming in. The family would have to depend on income and food from the farm. Suddenly, Abigail was cast in the role of farm manager and businesswoman.[25] Thus began a separation that would last off and on through the Second Continental Congress in 1776. Abigail seemed more than willing to bear the burden. "Our country is as it were a secondary God," she wrote Mercy Otis Warren months after independence was declared, "and the first and greatest parent. It is to be preferred to parents, to wives, children, friends, and all things, the gods only, excepted. These are the considerations which prevail with me to consent to a most painful separation."[26]

John's most pressing concern upon his departure other than the farm was the education of their offspring. "Make your children hardy, active, and industrious. . . . Strength, activity and industry will be their only resource and dependence."[27] Abigail could tutor them in French, but what of the rest of their education? Braintree boasted an elementary school whose sole instructor was Nathan Rice, one of John Adams's former law clerks. But she decided not to send seven-year-old Johnny. Instruction was not the problem; it was the example that might be set by the other children that worried Abigail. She was determined that her children would grow up to "chill with horror at the sound of an oath, and blush with indignation at an obscene expression."[28] So she arranged for a private tutor, John Thaxter Jr., one of her cousins and another former law clerk of her husband's.

Compared to some of the wealthy plantation owners from the Mid-Atlantic and Southern colonies, Adams was somewhat provincial, never having traveled west of New Haven, Connecticut. He certainly could not match their wealth. What monies he possessed were mostly tied up in his extensive library. Few could match his mind and education, however. A voracious reader and book collector, the New Englander was steeped in the classics (Cicero, Herodotus, Plotinus) and in political and moral philosophy (from Locke to Rousseau to Voltaire), grounded in the sciences (Newton, Diderot, Bacon), well-read in Shakespeare, and conversant with current literature. Not surprisingly, Adams found Thomas Jefferson, almost ten years his junior, a particularly stimulating companion. The first few days of the Congress found Adams euphoric: "There is in the Congress a collection of the greatest men upon this continent, in point of abilities, virtues and fortunes. The magnanimity, and public spirit, which I see here, makes me blush for the sordid venal herd, which I have seen in my own province."[29] After a month of speechmaking and posturing by his colleagues, he had changed his tune: "This assembly is like no other that ever existed," he declared. "Every man in it is a great man—an orator, a critic, a statesman, and therefore every man upon every question must show his oratory, his criticism, and his political abilities."[30]

"The great distance between us, makes the time appear very long to me," Abigail wrote John in August 1774. "The great anxiety I feel for my country, for you and for our family renders the day tedious and the night unpleasant. The rocks and quick sands appear upon every side." The children seemed fine, however. And there were books aplenty: "I have taken a very great fondness for reading Rollin's *Ancient History* [Charles Rollin]. . . . I find great pleasure and entertainment from it, and I have persuaded Johnny to read me a page or two every day."[31] Fear not, John wrote back: "Resignation to the will of Heaven is our only resource in such dangerous times. . . . Remember my tender love to my little Nabby. I am charmed with your amusement with our little Johnny. Tell him I am glad to hear he is so good a boy as to read to his Mamma . . . and to keep himself out of the company of rude children."[32] But John continued to worry about the child's education; for example, who was to teach him Latin? At Abigail's urging John Quincy wrote, attempting to reassure his father: "I have been trying ever since you went away to learn to write you a letter. I shall make poor work of it, but Mamma says you will accept my endeavors. . . . I hope I grow a better boy and that you will have no occasion to be ashamed of me when you return. Mr. Thaxter says I learn my books well."[33]

In their efforts to effect a complete separation from England, the New England delegations faced an uphill battle initially. The Mid-Atlantic and Southern colonies were not actually in the embrace of British power and had a great deal to lose in case of an open breach with the mother country. But gradually John and Sam Adams and their colleagues won them over, persuading them to endorse the Suffolk Resolves, resolutions passed by Suffolk County, Massachusetts, calling upon the colonies to resist British coercive measures with force. The delegates also agreed to the formation of a Continental Association to enforce an embargo against Britain until Parliament repealed the Intolerable Acts. They pledged to meet again if the crisis was not resolved.

It would not be resolved, of course. Upon learning of the goings-on in Philadelphia, King George declared that "the line of conduct seems now chalked out. . . . [The] New England Governments are in a state of Rebellion; blows must decide whether they are to be subject to this country or independent."[34]

In April 1775, six months after the adjournment of the Continental Congress, General Thomas Gage, acting on intelligence that the Massachusetts militia was stockpiling arms in Concord, dispatched a column of troops to uncover and destroy the cache. The redcoats succeeded in finding only a few scattered weapons. On their way back to Boston, while marching through the village of Lexington, they were fired on by militiamen. A running battle ensued until what was left of the British contingent reached Boston. The encounter left ninety-five colonists and 273 redcoats dead, wounded, or missing. John Quincy later remembered that just after the clash at Concord "a company of militia . . . came down from Bridgewater and passed the night at my father's house and barn . . . and in the midst of whom my father placed me, then a boy between seven and eight years, and I went through the manual exercise of the musket by word of command from one of them."[35] A month later New England militia laid siege to Gage's forces by occupying the crests of two hills, Bunker and Breed's, which overlooked Boston Harbor.

Meanwhile, on May 10, 1775, the Second Continental Congress convened in Philadelphia. Once again John Adams was elected a delegate. His separation from his family would be even more stressful this time because there was no telling how long this conclave would stay in session—for the duration of the looming conflict, probably. Moreover, John was leaving his wife and four children in a war zone. In a letter to Joseph Sturge written in 1846, John Quincy recalled those perilous days: "The year 1775 was the eighth year of my age. . . . Boston became a walled and beleaguered town garrisoned by British Grenadiers. . . . For the space of twelve months my mother with her infant children dwelled; liable every hour of the day and of the night to be [murdered] in cold blood or taken and carried into Boston as hostages by any foraging or marauding detachment of men."[36]

Realizing that her correspondence with her husband was subject to capture by the British or the American loyalists supporting them, Abigail adopted the pseudonym Portia. Brutus was known best as the lead assassinator of Caesar and he had enjoyed the unflagging support of his wife, Portia. A year after Caesar's demise, upon hearing that her husband had been killed in battle, she died by suicide.[37]

In the early hours of June 17, 1775, Abigail and her children were awakened by the sound of artillery fire coming from the north. There was nothing new about this, but the barrages continued unabated and seemed to increase in intensity. The Adams abode lay at the foot of Penn's Hill, one of the taller promontories in the Braintree area. At sunup, Abigail and John Quincy, hand in hand, climbed to the top of the hill. There they would witness what became known as the Battle of Bunker Hill. At ten miles, it was difficult to follow the course of the engagement, but from the amount of smoke and noise, it was clear that the battle was major.[38] "The day; perhaps the decisive day is come on which the fate of America depends," Abigail wrote John. "The battle began . . . a Saturday morning about 3 o'clock and has not ceased yet and 'tis now 3 o'clock Sabbath afternoon. . . ."[39] The British managed to dislodge the Americans but at great cost, suffering 1,054 casualties to the colonists' 450.

The encounter demonstrated that the infant Continental Army could hold its own in battle against one of the more seasoned armed forces in the world. Following the battle, General Gage observed that the Americans had displayed "a conduct and spirit against us, they never showed against the French."[40] One of the Americans who died that day was Dr. Joseph Warren, Mercy Otis Warren's brother-in-law and a close friend of both John and Abigail. "He had been our family physician and surgeon," John Quincy later recalled, "and had saved my forefinger from amputation under a very bad fracture." For the Adams family, the fallen Warren would come to personify patriotic valor. Every morning upon rising, Johnny was required, after saying the Lord's Prayer, to recite from William Collins's "Ode Written in the Beginning of the Year 1746":

> How sleep the brave, who sink to rest,
> By all their Country's wishes blest? . . .
> By Fairy hands their knell is rung;
> By forms unseen their dirge is sung:
> Their Honor comes a pilgrim grey,
> To . . . the turf that wraps their clay;
> And Freedom shall awhile repair
> To dwell a weeping hermit there.[41]

In the weeks that followed, British raiding parties sallied forth from Boston, and local militias fought to defend Braintree and surrounding villages. Abigail, Johnny, and their neighbors labored to feed the refugees who streamed out of Boston and to nurse wounded militiamen.[42] In September, John Quincy, barely eight years old, became a "post-rider" carrying mail by horseback to and from Boston.[43]

From Congress John wrote that he deeply regretted not wearing a uniform and bearing a musket. It was he who nominated George Washington to be commander in chief of the Continental Army and it was he who led the way in funding an army and navy. Many of his Northern colleagues disapproved of his choice of Washington, not because of any doubts about him personally, but because they thought it improper that a Virginian should command New England troops. When, subsequently, Washington and his soldiers drove the British out of Boston in the Battle of Dorchester Heights, all murmurings ceased.[44]

As the weeks passed, the Adams cousins became increasingly impatient with delegates like John Dickinson of Pennsylvania who continued to preach conciliation. But time and events were on the New Englanders' side. In July, the Crown rejected the so-called Olive Branch Petition. Then Lord Dunmore, governor of Virginia, offered freedom to any enslaved man who would agree to fight for the British. Suddenly, delegates from the Southern and Mid-Atlantic colonies were as militant as the New Englanders.

Finally, in May 1776, Congress authorized the various colonies to form their own governments. More than those of any other person, it was John Adams's moral and political philosophies that would shape the constitutions that emerged. He would almost single-handedly draft Massachusetts's state constitution of 1780, which became a model for many others.[45]

Curious about all things in the physical, social, and spiritual realms, John Adams was both a product and an architect of the American Enlightenment. Like his Harvard mentor, John Winthrop, Adams became an ardent supporter of the "new learning." Winthrop was a devotee of Francis Bacon, who in *The New Organon* had predicted that the emerging scientific method of empirical observation, experiment, and induction would allow mankind not only to penetrate the secrets of nature, but literally to master and manage the natural world with the object of satisfying human needs.[46] American Enlightenment figures like John Adams believed that empiricism—the scientific method—should also be applied to humanity's ongoing search for the best possible political system. Indeed, they believed that there was an inextricable connection between political liberty and education. "Wherever a general knowledge and sensibility have prevailed among the people, arbitrary government, and every kind of oppression, have lessened and disappeared in proportion," Adams wrote.[47] Humanity's struggles for liberty and enlightenment were mutually reinforcing. In *Novanglus*, Adams insisted that it was ancient Rome's rejection of monarchism and embrace of republicanism that had produced "the great Roman orators, poets, and historians, the greatest teachers of humanity and politeness . . . the delight and glory of mankind of seventeen hundred years."[48]

But none of this was inevitable. By the time he traveled to Philadelphia to attend the First Continental Congress, Adams had developed a healthy skepticism about the notion of the perfectibility of humankind, both intellectually and morally. The scientific method was the best and only method for exploring the physical universe and devising just government, but human beings were less predictable. "The faculties of our understanding are not adequate to penetrate the Universe," he would write Jefferson in retirement.[49] Moreover, Adams's passion for enlightened learning was tempered by the realization that not all men were equal in their capacity to seek and receive truth and that, in fact, "bad men increase in knowledge as fast as good men," and that "science, arts, taste, sense and letters" could be employed to spread "injustice and tyranny" as well as "law and liberty."[50]

John Adams was one of the foremost social psychologists of his time. He was convinced that the springboard of all human action was the desire for the approval and esteem of one's fellow human beings. "There is none among them [human propensities] more essential or remarkable, than the passion for distinction," he would write in *Discourses on Davila*.[51] This universal search for distinction and esteem could produce individuals who were committed to the welfare of the community and to the good opinion of others that comes from doing virtuous deeds. Or it could lead to avarice, deceit, manipulation, demagoguery, and exploitation of one's fellow human beings.

Adams understood that those who fled Europe for America were seeking opportunity, social mobility, and the chance to better their lives and the lives of their children. To a remarkable degree that dream was being realized. Adams wrote and thought at a time when society in America was rapidly liberalizing, when everyone from merchants, bankers, and shipowners to farmers and mechanics seemed to be rebelling against traditional constraints imposed by deference and community norms. He was both fascinated and repelled by the avarice that seemed to be blooming all around him. "The labor and anxiety, the enterprises and adventures, that are voluntarily undertaken in pursuit of gain," he declared, "are out of all proportion to the utility, convenience, or pleasure of riches."[52]

John Adams knew classical political theory as well or better than anyone in America. Unlike Jefferson, who dismissed the writings of the ancients as nothing more than ongoing justifications of privilege, the New Englander saw in them eternal truths about society and politics. He was an ardent student of history, ancient and modern. At the time of the Second Continental Congress, the members of the Adams family including John Quincy had read or were reading Tobias Smollett's *A Compleat History of England*.[53] Adams would argue in his *Defence of the Constitutions of the Government of the United States of America* that there were only three basic forms of government available to human societies: monarchy, aristocracy, and democracy. Of these three "simple" systems of governance, he asserted, pure democracy was the worst. At least monarchs and aristocrats had a vested interest in maintaining order if for no other reason than to preserve their privileges and property. But a world composed only of these two forms of government would lead to constant social turmoil and war because a large portion of the population would be shut out, powerless, and exploited.

The best form of government, the New Englander asserted, was a "mixed republic" that combined all three forms. Building on John Locke's ideas, Adams insisted that government would have to be representative. In a republic of any size, direct democracy was out of the question. Adams had read Thomas Paine's *Common Sense* on his way back to Philadelphia in early February. He acknowledged the value of Paine's tract in rallying public opinion, but he expressed disgust at his advocacy of a unicameral legislature.[54] In the government of a republic, the aristocracy, the middling kind, and the common man would all have to be represented, with powers divided and balanced. What he envisioned was a three-branch government composed of an executive, a bicameral legislature, and an independent judiciary. In order that the aristocracy and the masses both be represented, legislatures would have to be bicameral. The executive would administer the government, the legislature would make laws, and the judiciary would apply them. The executive would execute the laws and wield a veto over all measures proposed by the legislature.[55]

There was at Philadelphia little formal discussion of slavery despite the obvious contradiction of colonial delegations crying out for freedom and independence when a substantial portion of their population was in chains. John and Abigail were aware of the hypocrisy. "I wish most sincerely there was not a slave in the province," she opined to John on September 22. "It always appeared a most iniquitous scheme to me—fight ourselves for what we are daily robbing and plundering from those who have as good a right to freedom as we have."[56]

Abigail was also concerned about the status of women in the republic that was aborning. "I long to hear that you have declared an independency—and in the new Code of Laws which I suppose it will be necessary for you to make, I desire you would Remember the Ladies and be more generous and favorable to them than your ancestors," Abigail famously wrote John on March 31, 1776. "Remember all men would be tyrants if they could. If peculiar care and attention is not paid to the ladies we are determined to foment a rebellion and will not hold ourselves bound by any laws in which we have no voice, or representation."[57] Two weeks later John rebuked her: "As to your extraordinary Code of Laws, I cannot but laugh. We have been told that our struggle has loosened the bands of government everywhere," he wrote. "That children and apprentices were disobedient—that schools and colleges were grown turbulent—that Indians slighted their guardians and Negros grew insolent to their masters. But your letter was the first intimation that another tribe more numerous and powerful than all the rest were grown discontented . . . you are so saucy. . . . Depend upon it, we know better than to repeal our masculine systems. Although they are in full force . . . we dare not exert our power in its full latitude."[58] As time would tell, John would accord his wife and daughter the greatest possible latitude in the private and public spheres—but there were limits. All very well and good, declared Abigail, but "you must remember that arbitrary power is like most other things which are very hard, [they are] very liable to be broken."[59]

As if life in wartime Massachusetts were not difficult enough, by early 1776, Boston and its environs were in the grip of a smallpox epidemic. Abigail had been waiting for an opportunity to have herself inoculated against the disease ever since John had done so just prior to their marriage. She decided to seize the opportunity for both herself and her children. By the time they departed for Boston on the morning of July 12, Abigail's unmarried sister, Betsy, and her older sister, Mary, had decided to take the plunge. Fortunately, Abigail's wealthy uncle, Isaac

Smith, had offered the use of his commodious house. In order to acquire immunity, one had to actually contract smallpox. The process turned out to be more drawn out than expected. "The infection has been extremely slow in its progress, from inoculation to eruption," Cotton Tufts, another of Abigail's uncles, wrote John.[60]

It was not until July 22, eleven days after she had been inoculated, that Abigail began to show signs of the disease. Several days later John Quincy broke out, but she had to have Charles and Tommy inoculated twice. "We are ordered [to take] all the air we can get," Abigail wrote John, "and when we cannot walk, we sleep with windows open all night, and lay upon the carpet or straw beds, mattress, or anything hard; [we must] abstain from spirit, salt, and fats."[61] Nabby required a third injection of the virus under her skin. Finally, Abigail could report to John that his daughter had broken out with a vengeance, her body covered with more than a thousand pustules, each "as large as a great green pea."[62]

While Abigail and the children were risking their lives in Boston, John and his colleagues in Philadelphia were moving toward a declaration of independence. Adams, Jefferson, and Benjamin Franklin, along with Robert R. Livingston of New York and Roger Sherman of Connecticut, were named to the committee to draft a document of separation. All agreed that Adams and Jefferson were intellectually and stylistically the best qualified to prepare the document. Adams recalled how Jefferson was decided upon. The Virginian proposed Adams.

"I will not," the New Englander declared.

"You should do it," Jefferson said.

"Oh! No."

"Why will you not? You ought to do it."

"I will not."

"Why?"

"Reasons enough."

"What can be your reasons?"

"Reason first, you are a Virginian, and a Virginian ought to appear at the head of the business. Reason second, I am obnoxious, suspected, and unpopular. You are very much otherwise. Reason third, you can write ten times better than I can."

"Well, if you are decided, I will do as well as I can."[63]

The document that Jefferson prepared was a concise summation of Enlightenment thought concerning the sanctity of the individual and the right of human beings to govern themselves. The original draft called for the emancipation of slaves. Adams was well pleased. "I was delighted with its high tone and flights of oratory with which it abounded," he wrote in his diary, "especially that concerning Negro slavery, which though I knew his Southern brethren would never suffer to pass in Congress, I certainly would never oppose."[64] Congress did indeed eliminate the clause repudiating human bondage. The signers of the Declaration of Independence proclaimed that all white males had a natural, God-given right to "life, liberty, and the pursuit of happiness." Adams played a leading role in the intense debate over the contents of the document, which culminated in a vote of approval on July 2. The Declaration was ratified and signed on July 4, 1776. One of the signers, Richard Stockton of New Jersey, proclaimed to his family upon his return home, "The man to whom the country is most indebted for the great measure of independence is Mr. John Adams, of Boston. I call him the Atlas of American independence. He it was who sustained the debate, and by the force of his reasoning demonstrated not only the justice, but the expediency, of the measure."[65]

In October 1776, John Adams asked Congress to grant him a leave of absence. He missed his family terribly. "I will never come here again without you, if I can persuade you to come with me," he had written Abigail in December 1775. "Whom God had joined together ought not to be put asunder so long with their own consent."[66] He needed to make some money, and he felt he had neglected his children.

Neither war, nor disease, nor financial insecurity, nor prolonged separation could divert John and Abigail Adams from the task of educating their children. Like many of their class, the couple was obsessed with the task. They were, of course, primarily influenced by Enlightenment thinkers like John Locke, whose *Some Thoughts Concerning Education* was their primer on the subject.[67] He and his peers argued that children were born with an innate moral sense but were also deeply influenced by the environment in which they grew up. Thus, responsibility for the moral, intellectual, and emotional well-being of the child lay primarily with the parent. "It should be [our] care," John wrote his wife, "to elevate the minds of our children and exalt their courage to accelerate and animate their industry and activity; to excite in them a habitual contempt of meanness, abhorrence of injustice and inhumanity, and an ambition to excel in every capacity, faculty, and virtue. If we suffer their minds to grovel and creep in infancy, they will grovel all their lives." But there could be no intellectual acumen or moral probity without physical health. "Their bodies," he declared, "must be hardened, as well as their souls exalted. Without strength and activity and vigor of the body, the brightest mental excellencies will be eclipsed and obscured."[68]

In the absence of sound institutions and eminent tutors, John and Abigail would have to operate their own virtual school for their children. An educated young gentleman of the late eighteenth century would have been steeped in the classical languages, French, moral philosophy, history, literature, and rhetoric. An authentic child of the Enlightenment would also have been conversant with the natural sciences: astronomy, physics, and mathematics. And then there were the fine arts to be explored—music, art, and theater. Girls were viewed differently from boys, of course. Reading, writing, simple mathematics, expertise in voice and/or a musical instrument, and some knowledge of the fine arts were all that were expected. As an Adams, Nabby was treated to a cut above this.

Increasingly, John and Abigail's formidable ambitions for themselves and their country were focused on John Quincy. "I hope that you will . . . remember how many losses, dangers and inconveniences have been borne by your parents and the inhabitants of Boston in general for the sake of preserving freedom for you, and yours," John wrote John Quincy, "and I hope you will . . . follow the virtuous example if, in any future time, your country's liberties should be in danger, and suffer every human evil rather than give them up."[69] If Johnny, then ten years old, was going to be a statesman, he was going to have to immerse himself in history, beginning with Herodotus and Thucydides and going through the moderns. Upon learning that his eldest son was reading the third of the sixteen volumes of Smollet's *History of England*, John sent him a reading list. Among the recommendations were three books by the Abbé René-Aubert de Vertot d'Aubeuf: *The Revolutions of Portugal*, *The History of the Revolution in Sweden*, and *The History of the Revolutions That Happened in the Government of the Roman Republic*. Then there was *The History of the Wars of Flanders* translated into English by Henry Carey, Second Earl of Monmouth. (All of these had been purchased by John Adams and were in his library at Braintree.)[70]

John Quincy had sense enough to leave these volumes of higher learning for later, but he nevertheless was reading his little heart out. "I have been reading the history of *Bamfylde Moore Carew*," he wrote his father. "He went through the greatest part of America twice, and he gives a very pretty description of Maryland and Philadelphia and New York but though he got a great deal of money, yet I do not think he got his living either credibly or honestly for surely it is better to work than to beg and better to beg than to lie."[71] Carew, the "King of the beggars," was the son of a Devonshire clergyman who had run away from home as a boy and led a career devoted to "swindling and imposture, very ingeniously carried out."[72] In truth, what young Johnny liked best was Shakespeare: *The Tempest*, *As You Like It*, *The Merry Wives of Windsor*, *Much Ado About Nothing*, and *King Lear*. "The humors of Falstaff scarcely affected me at all. Bardolph and Pistol and Nym were personages quite unintelligible to me," he later recalled. "But the incantations of Prospero, the loves of Ferdinand and Miranda, the more than ethereal sprightly loveliness of Ariel, and the worse than beastly grossness of Caliban, made for me a world of revels and lapsed me in Elysium."

He had heard his mother and father mention Milton with great admiration. There was a small two-volume edition of *Paradise Lost* in Abigail's closet. He tried some ten times to master the text but never could get though "half a book." "I was mortified even to the shedding of solitary tears, that I could not even conceive what it was that my father and mother admired so much in that book."[73] To console himself he took up smoking. "After making myself four or five times sick with smoking, I mastered that accomplishment . . . but I did not master Milton."[74] Not until he was forty, some thirty years later, did he come to appreciate what had so enthralled his parents.

2

Innocence Abroad

THE SECOND CONTINENTAL CONGRESS might have declared independence, but making it a reality would depend upon Washington, the Continental Army, and the fledgling republic's success in securing aid and recognition from Britain's European enemies. Following Gage's expulsion from Massachusetts, the British ministry replaced him with General Sir William Howe.

Quick victories in New York and New Jersey prompted predictions of an early and easy peace. Washington's forces retreated into Pennsylvania. His army lacked arms, ammunition, and other basic supplies. Many of his troops had signed up only for short-term enlistments and intended to return to their farms and families as soon as their stint was up. But then a glimmer of light. In the summer of 1777, General John Burgoyne descended from Canada in command of a seven-thousand-man army. At the Battles of Bennington and Saratoga, a combined force of regular continental troops and New England militia cut Burgoyne's forces to pieces. The haughty Englishman was forced to surrender his fifty-eight hundred surviving troops to American general Horatio Gates on October 17, 1777. The war was far from over, but American patriots were hopeful that Bennington and Saratoga would persuade France to come out in full support of the infant republic in its struggle for independence.

Louis XVI had no interest in promoting republicanism; France's monarchy was one of the most autocratic in the world. But he and his ministers longed to gain revenge for their country's expulsion from North America in the French and Indian War. Indeed, in 1775, Louis's foreign minister had dispatched an agent to Philadelphia to report on the course of the Revolution. For its part, Congress appointed a Committee of Secret Correspondence to explore the possibilities of foreign aid and dispatched Connecticut businessman Silas Deane to Paris with instructions to purchase arms and ammunition for Washington's army.

Burgeoning republicans that they were, American leaders had frequently expressed disgust with Europe's cynical balance-of-power politics, but as independence dawned, they plotted to turn Europe's rivalries and vested interests to their advantage. At the same time, the delegates to the Continental Congress were determined not to become politically or militarily entangled in the machinations of the Old World. No one was more adamant on the subject than John Adams, who was the principal author of the so-called Model Treaty, or Plan of 1776. Whatever agreements America entered into, it must not expose the country to involvement in future European wars, of which there were sure to be many. Adams recommended specifically that in dealing with France, U.S. commissioners should not enter into a military alliance. They should secure aid and recognition if possible but never agree to receive French troops. France would have to pledge not to attempt a restoration of its North American empire; in return Congress would agree not to stand in the way of French conquest of the British West Indies or to make a separate peace with Great Britain in case of a general war.[1] In September 1776, Congress adopted the plan and selected Benjamin Franklin to join Deane and his colleague Arthur Lee in Paris to bolster their efforts to obtain aid and recognition.

On November 17, 1777, Congress adjourned, having completed work on the nation's first constitution, the Articles of Confederation. John Adams, accompanied by his cousin Samuel, set out on horseback for Massachusetts. Even before John arrived home, letters for him from the president of Congress had reached Braintree. Two weeks after his departure, that body had named him to replace Silas Deane in France. Deane had indeed negotiated arms sales with the French but had raked off a substantial part of the payment for himself. In addition, he had managed to employ a British spy and had granted commissions in the Continental Army to several French officers. Dr. Franklin was elderly, and Arthur Lee was proving ineffective.[2] "We want a man of inflexible integrity" among the American commissioners in Paris, James Lovell wrote Adams on behalf of Congress.[3]

As soon as John arrived in Braintree, he and Abigail began discussing the most momentous decision of their lives. For his part, he could not resist the call of his country and, not coincidentally, the notoriety that would accompany his new diplomatic post. But he allowed his wife to absorb the news and, he hoped, bring herself to make the sacrifice—which she did. What made her decisive in her decision to acquiesce, she wrote John Thaxter, was the conviction that her husband's country, in dire straits, was in need of his service. "I resign my . . . felicity and look for my satisfaction in the consciousness of having discharged my duty to the public."[4] Initially, John and Abigail thought that both she and John Quincy should accompany him. "My desire was you know to have run all hazards and accompanied him," Abigail wrote Thaxter, "but I could not prevail upon him to consent. The dangers from enemies were so great, and their treatment to prisoners so inhumane and brutal, that in case of a capture my sufferings would enhance his misery."[5]

Reluctantly, Abigail agreed to allow John Quincy to accompany his father. The decision was not as outrageous as it appeared. Indeed, Silas Deane's son was to be a passenger aboard the ship that carried the Adamses to Europe. John desperately wanted his son's companionship if he could not have that of his wife, and exposure to Paris, the cultural capital of the Western world, would transform Johnny's life, he believed. Still, separation from son as well as husband was an almost unbearable prospect to Abigail. To Thaxter again: "And now cannot you imagine me seated by my fireside bereft of my better half and added to that a limb lopped off to heighten the anguish."[6]

On Friday, February 13, 1778, John and John Quincy rendezvoused at Moon Head with Captain Samuel Tucker, commander of the frigate *Boston*. The day was windy and frigid, the seas rough even in the harbor. "But by means of a quantity of hay in the bottom of the boat and good watch coats with which we were covered . . . we arrived on board the *Boston* about five o'clock, tolerably warm and dry," John recorded in his diary.[7] The shortest Atlantic crossing one could expect at that time was around twenty-five days. The Adamses' voyage would last six mostly hellacious weeks.

John Adams was pleased with the captain, his civilian shipmates, and the ship's surgeon, a Mr. Nicholas Noel. Johnny had Jesse Deane as a companion, and Noel, who had with him the latest work on translating English to French, agreed to tutor John Quincy in the language. The Adamses spent their first night pleasantly enough. "My lodging was a cot, with a double mattress, a good bolster, my own sheets, and blankets enough," John recorded in his diary. "My little son, with me—We lay very comfortably, and slept well." But then ominously, "A violent gale of wind in the night."[8] The *Boston*'s departure was delayed for two days due to a snowstorm, and the entire voyage would be marked by one tempest after another. At such times, John found their existence almost unbearable: "To describe the ocean, the waves, the winds, the ship, her motions, rollings, wringings, and agonies . . . No man could keep upon his legs, and nothing could be kept in its place—an universal wreck of everything in all parts of the ship, chests, casks, bottles &c." He complained of the "inexpressible inconvenience of having so small a space between decks, as there is in the *Boston*." In stormy weather the ship rolled violently, with the main deck being almost constantly submerged. If the hatch was opened, the Adamses' quarters would have been flooded immediately. If they were left sealed, the compartment became airless and overheated. Part of the problem was that the *Boston* was carrying an excess of armament: five twelve-pound cannons and nineteen nine pounders. This made the ship top-heavy, and to make matters worse, the constant threat of engagement with a British man-of-war led the captain to sail with the ship's guns run out, which allowed seawater in through the gunports "so as to oblige us to kee[p] the chain pumps as well as the hand pumps, almost constantly going." During one of the storms, the main top-mast was carried away, almost causing the helmsman to lose control of the vessel. During all of these trials, Adams recorded, "Mr. Johnny's behavior gave me a satisfaction that I cannot express—fully sensible of our danger, he was constantly endeavoring to bear it with a manly patience, very attentive to me, and his thoughts constantly running to a serious strain."[9]

Militarily, the *Boston* was a work in progress. Adams observed in his diary early in the voyage that among the 172 souls aboard the frigate, there were very few able seamen: "All is as yet chaos on board. His [the captain's] men are not disciplined. The Marines are not. The men are not exercised to the guns. They hardly know the ropes."[10] Initially, in times of action, only the threat of the officers' pistols kept the sailors at their stations. But rather quickly the *Boston*'s crew began to round into shape. A week into the voyage, the Americans encountered three British frigates, one of which pursued them an entire day until giving up. In mid-March, the *Boston* captured a British transport, the *Martha*, out of London. The merchantman fired a single shot and then struck its colors after seeing the *Boston*'s massive broadside. Captain Tucker estimated the prize value to be seventy thousand pounds sterling. Shortly thereafter, the American frigate encountered another potential prize, an armed British brig. Captain Tucker demanded its surrender, whereupon the brig fired a broadside into the *Boston* and then struck its colors before the Americans could respond. In the midst of the action, Tucker discovered John Adams clad "in the uniform of a marine on deck with musket in hand."[11] Just prior to the British ship's salvo, First Lieutenant Barron of the *Boston* had attempted to fire a warning shot, but the cannon burst, shredding his lower leg. "I was present at this affecting scene," John Adams recorded in his diary, "and held Mr. Barron in my arms while the doctor put on the tourniquet and cut off the limb."[12] The young man died several days later.

On March 30, 1778, the *Boston* made land at the port of Pauillac, not far from the city of Bordeaux. "Europe thou great theatre of arts, sciences, commerce, and war, am I at last permitted to visit thy territories?" John Adams exulted.[13] At dinner aboard the *Julie*, a commodious French vessel bound for Saint-Domingue, the

Adamses learned that Benjamin Franklin and the French foreign minister, the Comte de Vergennes, had signed a treaty of alliance in which France recognized American independence and the two nations agreed to fight as one in case of a general war. Both parties promised not to make a separate treaty with Great Britain. So much for the Model Treaty and no entangling alliances.

John and John Quincy spent four days in Bordeaux being wined and dined by local dignitaries. They then set out by chaise for Paris, traveling up to a hundred miles a day going by way of Poitiers, Tours, and Orléans. Father and son entered the city on April 8. They found the streets jammed with carriages. With some difficulty, they secured a night's lodging at the Hôtel de Valois on Rue de Richelieu. "My little son has sustained this long journey of near 5000 miles . . . with the utmost firmness," John noted in his diary.[14] The next morning John and John Quincy set out for Franklin's residence in Passy, a suburb of Paris on the road to Versailles.[15]

Franklin and John Adams greeted each other warmly, and the author of *Poor Richard's Almanack* showed his guest to the well-furnished apartments just recently vacated by Silas Deane. John set out immediately with Franklin and Arthur Lee for a luncheon engagement with the Comte de Vergennes. "I am pleasantly situated at Passy," John subsequently wrote Abigail, "a fine airy, salubrious situation, in the same house with Dr. Franklin, with whom I make one family. The Dr. is in fine health and great reputation."[16]

Within the week, John had installed John Quincy in a Passy boarding school run by a Monsieur Le Coeur. There was instruction in Latin and French, the classics, and history. Also fencing, dancing, drawing, and music.[17] Johnny was not the only American. In addition to Jesse Deane, twelve-year-old Benjamin Franklin Bache, Franklin's grandson, and another boy, the son of a merchant, were in attendance. Johnny described a typical day in a letter to his mother: "At 6 o'clock in the morning we get up and go in to school and stay till half after 8 when we breakfast . . . after dinner we play till 2 when we go in & stay till half after 4 when we come out and play till five when we go in and stay till half after 7 when we sup; after supper we go up and stay about an hour and go to bed."[18] Weekends and holidays Johnny spent with his father.

Both Adamses were swept off their feet by Paris, its architecture, art, and high society. Europe's second-largest city, with a population of some six hundred fifty thousand, Paris was a maze of boulevards crisscrossing the Seine, churches, mansions, and beautiful gardens such as those surrounding the Tuileries Palace. The eighteenth century had witnessed the construction of the Place Vendôme, the Place de Louis XV, the Champs-Élysées, the Hôtel des Invalides, and the Panthéon. Impoverished neighborhoods there were, but Paris's magnificence could not be denied. It was in that city that John Quincy began his lifelong love affair with the theater. "My Pappa & I went to the theatre called the Italian Comedy where we had the women & the secrets of which we see but very little," Johnny wrote his cousin Lucy Cranch.[19] What the Adamses saw at the Comédie-Italienne included *Les femmes et le secret*, a comedy by Antoine-François Quétant; *Silvain*, a comedy by Jean-François Marmontel; and *Les nymphes de Diane*, a comic opera by Charles-Simon Favart. During one performance, the pair found themselves seated next to Voltaire, who would die shortly thereafter.[20] Meanwhile, John was writing Abigail, extolling the cultural and architectural splendor of the city. He was swept along from ball to ball, dinner to dinner, soiree to soiree. "The delights of France are innumerable. The politeness, the elegance, the softness, the delicacy, is extreme."[21] "To tell you the truth," he wrote injudiciously, "I admire the ladies here. Don't be jealous. They are handsome, and very well educated. Their accomplishments are exceedingly brilliant. And their knowledge of letters and arts, exceeds that of the English ladies much, I believe." Adding fuel to the flames, he reported, "My venerable Colleague [Franklin] enjoys a privilege here, that is much to be envied . . . the ladies not only allow him to buss them as often as he pleases, embrace as often as he pleases, but they are perpetually embracing him."[22]

Abigail Adams was no prude—one of her favorite plays was *School for Scandal*. Both she and John were fans of Laurence Sterne's *A Sentimental Journey Through France and Italy*, a semi-autobiographical, humorous, sometimes bawdy account of the author's travels.[23] Abigail was not concerned with John; he could fend for himself, but Johnny was another matter altogether. Shortly after her husband and son departed for Europe, she had written John Thaxter: "There are many snares and temptations [in France]; I hope some of the worst [of] which on account of his age he will be likely to escape. Yet there are many, very many which may stain his morals even at this early period of life . . . the only method which can be pursued with advantage is to fix the padlock upon the mind."[24] Her first letter to her son in Europe created a virtual prison: "Improve your understanding for acquiring useful knowledge and virtue, such as will render you an ornament to society, an honor to your country, and a blessing to your parents." And then, "I had much rather you should have found your grave in the ocean you have crossed, or any untimely death crop you in your infant years, rather than see you an immoral profligate or a graceless child. . . . You must keep a strict guard upon yourself or [an] odious monster will soon lose its terror by becoming familiar to you."[25]

A remarkably severe admonition, but Abigail believed she had reason. European society was infamous for its licentiousness, and alcoholism and profligacy ran through the Smith family. One of her brothers abandoned his wife and children and drank himself to death. "The Smith blood seems to have had the scourge of intemperance dreadfully applied to it," her grandson Charles Francis would later observe.[26] Two of Abigail's three sons would succumb to alcoholism. Perhaps it was not just the family's blood that was stained but the very soil from which it sprang. Indeed, Mount Wollaston, the site of Abigail's grandparents' farm, was something of a symbol of debauchery and licentiousness in the minds of New Englanders. In 1625, Thomas Morton arrived in Massachusetts Bay from England. He immediately established a lucrative trade with the local Indians that involved supplying them with guns and whiskey. In 1627, he set up his famous (or infamous) Maypole on Mount Wollaston. He was twice arrested and deported by Massachusetts authorities for promoting immorality among both Indians and whites. Merry Mount was on his farm, John later reported to Thomas Jefferson, where "Englishmen and Indians—sannups and squaws—danced and sang and reeled around the Maypole till Bacchus and Venus, I suppose were satiated."[27] In warning her son against the dangers of immorality and debauchery, Abigail perhaps feared that debauchery was rooted in the soil of Mount Wollaston and had seeped into the family tree.

Both John and John Quincy read Abigail's admonitory letter. Their response was to hold her at arm's, or rather pen's, length. Between June and November of 1778, Abigail received only a handful of missives from her husband and son. When she pressed, John replied that he was loath to write because his correspondence might very well fall into British hands.[28] But there was more to it than that; after the first letters praising Paris and its culture, John's infrequent letters read like reports, like business correspondence. "You have changed hearts with some frozen Laplander or made a voyage to a region that has chilled every drop of your blood," she complained to John.[29] He replied indignantly: "This moment I had, what shall I say? The pleasure or the pain of your letter of 25 of Oct. . . . What course shall I take to convince you that my heart is warm?" he asked. He was not above deploying his son in the tiff with his wife. "It really hurts him [John] to receive such letters," the eleven-year-old wrote his mother. "If all your letters are like this my papa will cease writing at all."[30]

FRANCE DID NOT SIGN a treaty of alliance with America in the fall of 1778 out of sympathy for republicanism. Louis XVI's monarchy was one of the most absolute in the world. Vergennes and his king wanted to do anything they could to damage their perpetual enemy, who had humiliated France in the Seven Years' War. The regime viewed America as a mere pawn in the great game of European power politics. Nevertheless, in recognizing American independence, the government of Louis had crossed the Rubicon; France and Britain drifted into war in

June of 1778. But John Adams was right to congratulate both Franklin and Vergennes on the Treaty of 1778 upon his arrival in Paris. America could not have won its independence without French aid. Altogether, France would supply Britain's rebellious colonists with nine million dollars in aid, a huge sum at the time. A major portion of the Continental Army's muskets, cannon, powder, and shot was supplied by France or bought with French money. French volunteers fought alongside Washington's soldiers, and the French navy would provide invaluable support in the decisive Battle of Yorktown in 1781.

Nevertheless, John Adams's initial interview with Franklin proved somewhat troubling. The American delegation had been racked by deep divisions. Deane, now recalled, had continually overstepped his charge, even commissioning French officers to serve in the Continental Army and pushing for Washington's removal as head of the Continental Army. Arthur Lee, Franklin reported, was more hindrance than help. Haughty, aloof, suspicious that his colleagues were shouldering him to the sidelines, he had opposed virtually every move Franklin had wanted to make. The French thought Lee to be secretly pro-British.[31] Franklin and Adams did not discuss the matter explicitly, but it was clear that with the conclusion of the Franco-American Treaty, Adams's role had been rendered superfluous. There would be only one American minister to France, and that would surely be Franklin.[32] Adams considered returning home immediately, but then quickly rejected the idea. He and his son were fresh off a harrowing sea voyage. There should be some payoff, some opportunity to experience and enjoy European culture. Moreover, the conclusion of the Franco-American Treaty would most assuredly touch off a general European war, requiring his country to establish relations with nations other than France. He would certainly be the first choice for another diplomatic post. So, for the next ten months, Adams chose to live in a kind of diplomatic limbo; he served as the de facto administrator for the U.S. mission in Paris while Johnny attended school. Father and son habituated the theater and traveled when they could.

The task confronting Franklin, Adams, and Lee was to keep the pressure on the government of Louis XVI to maintain the flow of supplies and troops to North America while it was simultaneously fighting Britain on numerous other fronts. On the surface, Adams and Franklin seemed to work well together. But the two men were so different that clashes were inevitable. John Adams was a proud and, at times, vain man. When he arrived in France, some mistook him for *"le fameux"* Adams—that is, Samuel. Others mistook him for the author of *Common Sense*. When the French were disabused of these notions, Adams was reduced to playing a distant second fiddle to Franklin.

In truth, the journalist-inventor-diplomat cast a large shadow. Learned but

unpretentious, Franklin listened more than he spoke. He was affable, companion-
able, and deferential; "all jollity, and pleasantry," as one friend put it.[33] His method
of dealing with the French was to flatter and cajole rather than to confront. He
was by this point in his life a hedonist and womanizer. His dinners were on a par
with the best that the French could offer, his wine cellar reportedly filled with a
thousand bottles of the finest vintages. Women seemed to throw themselves at
him.[34] Franklin had left his wife, Deborah, behind in Philadelphia in 1764. She
died ten years later, having never seen her husband again.[35]

Privately at first and then more publicly, Adams became increasingly critical of
his colleague. He deplored what he perceived to be Franklin's frivolous and de-
bauched lifestyle. He declared the doctor's methods of dealing with Vergennes
unmanly and dangerous.[36] In his opinion, Franklin was willing to concede control
of America's fate to the French. He believed that France needed America as much
as America needed France. His elderly colleague had become a tool of the French,
Adams wrote Robert Livingston, a member of the Continental Congress, "because he was always easy, quiet, never proposing anything." Part of the problem,
the New Englander insisted, was that Franklin "has been actuated and is still by
a low jealousy and a meaner envy of me."[37] A clear case of projection if there had
ever been one. Franklin was something that Adams could never be. His onetime
friend Jonathan Sewall observed that in undertaking a career as a diplomat, Adams was "quite out of his element. He cannot dance, drink, game, flatter, promise,
dress, swear with the gentlemen, and talk small talk or flirt with the ladies." A
shame in Sewall's eyes, because there was not one American abroad who possessed the New Englander's intelligence, learning, or integrity.[38]

During their first stay in Paris, John was not willing to leave the task of educating his son entirely in the hands of the tutors at the Passy boarding school. The
elder Adams was much impressed with James Harrington's *Commonwealth of
Oceana* (1656), which declared it incumbent on those who were fortunate enough
to travel to report all that they saw and heard in order to enlighten their fellow
human beings.[39] He persuaded John Quincy to preserve copies of his letters and
to begin a diary, which by the end of a long life would become one of the most
significant memoirs in the English language. Of this, of course, the young man
had no inkling. "A journal book & a letter book of a lad of eleven years old cannot
be expected to contain much of science, literature, arts, wisdom, or wit," he wrote
his mother, "yet it may serve to perpetuate many observations that I may make &
may hereafter help me to recollect both persons, & things that would otherwise
escape my memory."[40]

Out of school for an extended period in 1778, John Quincy amused himself by
perusing his father's burgeoning collection of books on French grammar, orthog-

raphy, rhetoric, prosody, lexicography, and the philosophy of language. Later that month he wrote his brothers, Charles and Thomas: "The grammars in common use in America are Boyer Chambaud & Tandamm every one of which is imperfect and inaccurate." Far preferable were "a Volume intitled *Principes Generaux et raisonnés de la Grammaire Francoise*[,] . . . *Les vrais Principes de La langue Francoise*[,]" and a work by Antoine Court de Gébelin that "contains a collection of almost everything which has ever been written in whatever language upon the subject of philosophical grammar."[41] Altogether John Quincy's bibliography came to more than twenty citations. This from a boy of eleven to his brothers aged eight and six. Emotionally, however, Johnny was still a child. The diary he would soon begin was illustrated with crude drawings of soldiers in formation and fighting ships. He constantly berated himself for his tendency to play, but play he did.

In February 1779, word arrived in Paris that to no one's surprise Congress had named Franklin as America's sole representative to the French government. Adams did not know what would become of himself. Despite having advised Congress shortly after his arrival in Paris that America did not need and could not afford more than one representative to France, John was somewhat bitter about his recall. To add to his unhappiness, he had heard, correctly as it turned out, that in America Silas Deane was demeaning him at every opportunity.[42]

John and John Quincy departed Passy for Nantes on Monday, March 8. They expected to set sail for America aboard the Continental Navy frigate *Alliance* sometime in April. The month was spent pleasantly in the beautiful city on the Loire situated some thirty-five miles inland from the Atlantic. Part of the time was whiled away with John supervising Johnny as he translated Cicero's first *Philippic Against Catiline* and Horace's *Carmen Saeculare* from the Latin.[43] "My son has had a great opportunity to see this country," John wrote Abigail, "but this has unavoidably retarded his education in some other things. He has enjoyed perfect health from first to last and is respected wherever he goes for his vigor and vivacity both of mind and body, for his constant good humor, and for his rapid progress in French, as well as his general knowledge which for his age is uncommon."[44] Among the Americans in Nantes with whom John and John Quincy passed time were the Joshua Johnsons. Joshua was the brother of the prominent Maryland patriot and delegate to Congress, Thomas Johnson. He had established himself as a leading merchant and shipping agent in London. With the coming of the Revolution, which had his total support, Joshua had moved his wife and eight children to Nantes. The Johnsons entertained the Adamses several times in their elegant apartments at the Temple du Goût. John Quincy, then eleven, would marry Louisa Catherine Johnson, age four, some twenty years later.[45]

Finally, on April 28, John and John Quincy made the trip to the port of Lorient and boarded the *Alliance*, but just as it was ready to sail, word came from Paris that the Americans were to disembark and wait for the French frigate *La Sensible*, which had been designated to transport the first French minister to America, the Chevalier de la Luzerne, and his secretary, François Barbé-Marbois.[46] "This is a cruel disappointment," John wrote in his diary. "To exchange May for July and the *Alliance* for another frigate is too much."[47] He suspected that the devious and vengeful Franklin was responsible for the switch to *La Sensible* and the resulting delay. The doctor, he confided to his diary, was afraid of what he, Adams, would tell Congress about the American minister's kowtowing to the French and his rumored peculation.[48] In truth, the request had come from Commodore John Paul Jones, then in Lorient, who wanted the *Alliance* attached to his squadron.

Waiting for *La Sensible*, John and John Quincy spent several enjoyable evenings aboard the *Bonhomme Richard*, being wined and dined by Jones. "We practiced the old American custom of drinking to each other, which I confess is always agreeable to me," John wrote in his diary.[49] Adams believed Commodore Jones to be a man of destiny. "This is the most ambitious and intriguing officer in the American Navy," he said of him. "Jones has art, and secrecy, and aspires very high."[50]

At long last La Luzerne and his party arrived in Lorient, and *La Sensible* set sail on Thursday, June 17. The ship's officers, La Luzerne, and Adams were housed aft on the quarterdeck; the minister and the captain were on the starboard side in two back-to-back eight-by-six compartments, and Adams and the second-in-command on the port side. The hallway separating them opened up into a large cabin that stretched the width of the afterdeck. Here was the ship's common room, where John Quincy and Barbé-Marbois hung their hammocks at night. "The Chevalier de la Luzerne and M. Marbois are in raptures with my son," Adams reported. One morning he entered his cabin to find Johnny stretched out on the cot, La Luzerne seated on a cushion at one end, and Barbé-Marbois standing at the other. La Luzerne was attempting to read aloud in English from one of Blackstone's discourses, with John Quincy correcting his grammar and pronunciation. "He shows us no mercy, and makes us no compliments," Barbé-Marbois told the father. "We must have Mr. John."[51]

La Sensible arrived in Boston on August 3, following a relatively uneventful eight-week journey. The last Abigail had heard of husband and son was that they had departed France aboard the *Alliance* sometime after their arrival in Nantes in March.

Imagine her surprise and joy when man and boy crossed her threshold unannounced in Braintree.[52]

* * *

JOHN AND JOHN QUINCY hadn't been home for three months when on October 20, 1779, the elder Adams learned from the president of Congress, Samuel Huntington, that he had been named minister plenipotentiary to "confer, treat, agree and conclude a treaty of peace with representatives of King George III."[53] By the fall of 1779, Great Britain was fighting with its back to the wall. Earlier in the year, Spain had entered the war on the side of France by means of the Treaty of Aranjuez (which did not, by the way, provide for Spanish recognition of American independence). For the first time since 1588, Britain's naval supremacy in the English Channel was in jeopardy, and she was faced with the grim prospect of invasion. Catherine the Great of Russia would form the Scandinavian countries into the League of Armed Neutrality. Its objective was to keep British warships and privateers from preying on their merchant vessels as they traded with France and its allies, including America. If and when the government of George III indicated that it was inclined toward an armistice and/or peace treaty, Congress wanted to have a man like Adams on the spot.

Elated at what he regarded as his redemption and a repudiation of Franklin, John accepted immediately. Abigail was deeply conflicted. Was it her fate to be forever separated from her husband? Was their marriage to consist of intermittent correspondence only? In the days before John's departure, she began to think of herself as a widow. Patriotism extracted a high price, but in the end, she acquiesced. But what of John Quincy?

The previous month, Barbé-Marbois, certain that Adams would return to France in one capacity or another, had written: "I desire very much, Sir, that you would carry with you again to Europe, the young gentleman your son . . . he will learn of you the means of being, one day, useful to his country."[54] In truth, Johnny was reluctant to go. He had his heart set on enrolling at Phillips Academy in Andover, where he would prepare himself for Harvard. One Sunday after church, Abigail counseled her eldest son: "In all human probability," she said, "it will do more for your education to go back to France with your father than to prepare for college at Andover."[55] Later, after John Quincy had departed, Abigail wrote that she was convinced he was destined to be a great man, but that would not just happen on its own. "Great necessities call out great virtues. When a mind is raised and animated by scenes that engage the heart, then those qualities, which would otherwise lay dormant, wake into life, and form the character of the hero and the statesman."[56]

The family decided that Charles, then nine years old, should accompany his brother and father. Charles was a gentle, likable child, but far less resolute and mature than John Quincy. Perhaps Abigail thought him in need of toughening up. The party also included John Thaxter—Abigail's cousin and Johnny's former tutor, who would serve as John's private secretary—and a servant, John Stevens. Francis Dana, a former delegate to the Continental Congress, would go as secretary to the legation, that is, John's diplomatic lieutenant.[57] From the port side of the ship as he prepared to depart, John wrote Abigail, "Let me entreat you, to keep up your spirits and throw off cares as much as possible. . . . We shall yet be happy."[58]

To John and John Quincy's gratification, they would be returning to Europe aboard *La Sensible*. As the Americans' barge approached, the ship's crew turned out en masse, shouting huzzahs in English and *"Vive le roi"* in French.[59] *La Sensible*, accompanied by the brig *Courier de l'Europe*, departed Boston on Monday, November 15. *La Sensible* would make the Atlantic crossing in a swift twenty-three days, but the voyage was fraught. John occupied his old quarters, bunking with Charles. John Quincy and Thaxter shared a cabin. Also on board was Samuel Cooper Johonnot. The eleven-year-old son of Lieutenant Colonel Gabriel Johonnot, a merchant of Boston, was being sent to Europe to further his education.[60] "Sammy Cooper . . . is a very agreeable young gentleman and makes the passage much less tedious to me than it would have been if he had not come with us," John Quincy recorded in his diary.[61]

Intelligence reports indicated that there were two British frigates hovering off the American coast, but *La Sensible* managed to elude them and make the Grand Banks on November 17, 1779. Attempting a winter crossing of the North Atlantic was a hazardous undertaking. On the twentieth, the seas roughened, and by the twenty-fifth, the two vessels found themselves in the midst of a full-blown gale. For three days men and matériel were thrown about the ships, causing several serious injuries and much seasickness. The *Courier* lost its foremast and *La Sensible* had to leave its sister ship behind. "There were about thirty souls on board . . . one a woman," Francis Dana recorded in his journal. "Heaven protect them from further harm."[62]

La Sensible itself had been damaged, its hull springing two large leaks. Amidst a relentless series of squalls featuring heavy rain and lightning, the passengers had to man the ship's pumps four times a day, at eight a.m., twelve noon, four p.m., and eight p.m. Eventually the captain announced that the ship was so compromised that he was going to have to take the shortest route to the Continent and seek a landing in Spain. On December 7, 1779, *La Sensible* entered the port city of Ferrol.[63] Later, John Quincy would write his mother, "It was well for us that we arrived as we did; one more storm would very probably have carried us to the bottom of the sea."[64]

The passage into the port was very narrow, no more than one mile wide. The approach bristled with fortifications, John Quincy counting no fewer than 365 gunports in one castle.[65] The city itself seemed prosperous enough, with a number of stone houses under construction. Ferrol teemed with Spanish and French officers, all of whom treated Minister Adams with the utmost respect. He, however, was consumed with anxiety. Perhaps chances for peace were slipping away while he was trapped on the coast of Spain, hundreds of miles from Paris, the epicenter of diplomacy. The party could wait for *La Sensible* to be repaired, but he was told that the necessary work could take up to two months. The alternative was an arduous land journey over the Pyrenees. Adams opted for the second choice, but then which route to take—a longer but easier trip by way of Madrid, or a more direct passage due eastward through the countryside? He settled on the latter. "What accommodations I can get upon the road, how I can convey my children, what the expense will be, are all questions that I cannot answer," he lamented to his diary.[66]

Early in the morning of Tuesday the fourteenth, the party of thirteen Americans, "like so many Don Quixote's and Sancho Panza's or Hudibras's and Ralpho's" climbed atop a like number of mules and set out for La Coruña, some twenty miles inland.[67] The road, at times treacherous, took them over mountains higher than the New Englanders had ever seen. Upon arriving in La Coruña, they were greeted by the governor with open arms and secured lodging in a respectable tavern. La Coruña was the capital of the province of Galicia, and as such filled with dignitaries who wished to pay homage to Spain's new tacit allies.[68] The festivities forced the party to delay for a few days, giving John Quincy time to make some observations. He was struck with how Catholic the town was, with its numerous churches and nunneries. He was mystified by the latter, by the willingness of young women who chose "to be shut up in convents and never see any men except the friars." Perhaps it was the prevailing marriage customs, he mused. In Europe marriages were generally arranged. Perhaps nunneries were for those young women who could not abide the matches that had been made for them, he speculated.[69]

Michel Lagoanère, "a gentleman who has acted for some time as an American agent at Corunna," provided invaluable assistance in arranging for guides and transportation. He advised Adams and company on the best routes and provided a published travel guide. For the trip Adams was forced to hire mules, muleteers, and three carriages, or "calashes," at an exorbitant price.[70] On the twenty-seventh of December, the travelers arrived in Castellano, where they lodged in conditions that were mind-boggling in their primitiveness. The posthouse was a two-story stone structure with a floor of dirt covered with straw, mud, and animal feces. A stable adjoined the main room on the first floor; the door separating the two was always open. In the center of the common room was a fire built upon a mound of dirt. There was no chimney and only two small holes in the roof to draw off the smoke. Against one wall was a grime-covered stove and against another a lean-to "where I suppose the Patron del Casa, i.e. the Master of the House, his wife, and four children all pigged in together," Adams recorded.[71] John, John Quincy, and Charles were assigned a chamber on the second floor. As they ascended, the Adamses encountered a pig ensconced on the straw-covered landing.

Slowly, laboriously, the Americans made their way across the countryside of northern Spain. John and the boys rode in one calash, Dana and Thaxter in another, and Mr. Allen and Samuel Cooper in a third. The servants rode on mules. Sometimes the servants and gentlemen switched places. Sometimes everyone walked. The roads were terrible, at one point breaking the axletree of one of the carriages. The travelers had to supply their own food, drink, and bedding. "We have not met with any place so bad as [Castellano]," John Quincy recorded in his diary, "but we have come very near it. They show us chambers in which anybody would think a half a dozen hogs had lived there six months."[72] The poverty and wretchedness of the common people were appalling. "As for the people, they are lazy, dirty, nasty . . . their clothes are commonly of a dirt color and their breeches are big enough for them to put a bushel of corn in besides themselves." Young as he was, Johnny understood that the wretchedness of the Spanish peasants was not their fault. "Near three quarters of what they earn goes to the priests. Thus is the whole of this Kingdom deceived and deluded by their religion. I thank Almighty God that I was born in a country where anybody may get a good living if he please."[73]

When the Americans reached Bilbao, John traded in their mules and chaises for several postilions for travel over the icy roads to Bordeaux. The party arrived in Paris late in the afternoon of February 9. The journey from Ferrol had consumed two months, twice the duration of an average Atlantic crossing.[74] John, John Quincy, and Charles took up lodgings at the Hôtel de Valois in the Rue de Richelieu. John would remain there until he and the boys left for another assignment in the Netherlands in July 1780.[75]

3

Revolutionary Diplomacy

JOHN ADAMS ARRIVED IN Paris with an explicit set of instructions from
Congress—sine qua nons for a peace with Great Britain. In addition to recognizing the independence of the United States, the former mother country
would have to cede all territory between the Appalachian Mountains and the
Mississippi River and between the Great Lakes and the thirty-first parallel. The
peace accord would have to guarantee the right of New England fishermen to
continue to harvest the abundant cod of the Grand Banks off the coast of Newfoundland.[1] Initially, there was little for Adams to do in his official capacity. Vergennes forbade him from making public the nature of his mission, and the Treaty
of 1778 prohibited America from making a separate peace with Britain. During
this first five-month stay, the minister plenipotentiary spent his time filing voluminous reports with Congress, writing pro-American pieces for French newspapers
and journals, and buying books.[2] The relationship between Adams and Vergennes
quickly deteriorated. The foreign minister complained to Franklin and La Luzerne
that the New Englander was unmanageable. For his part Adams was convinced
that Vergennes would make a separate peace with Great Britain and sacrifice America's interests without a qualm.

Shortly after the Adams party arrived in Paris, John installed his three charges—
John Quincy, Charles, and Sammy Johonnot—in school at Passy. It was a boarding
school run by a M. Pechigny and his wife. Although its formal name was the
École de Mathématiques, it was often called, simply, the Pension.[3] In attendance
were two of John Quincy's former schoolmates at Le Coeur's, Jesse Deane and
Charles Cochran. Johnny wrote his mother that he and Charles were quite con-
tent with their situation—"Brother Charles begins to make himself understood in
French."[4] After a month, however, he complained to his father that the curriculum

was onerous: Latin, Greek, geography, geometry, fractions, writing, and drawing: "A young boy cannot apply himself to all those things and keep a remembrance of them."[5] He enjoyed his classes in dancing and fencing. But alas, John responded by writing Pechigny and instructing him to remove his sons from these two frivolous enterprises and have them concentrate on Greek, Latin, and French, "which will be more useful for them in their own country, where they are to spend their lives."[6] The boys were able to spend weekends with their father, during which they saw the sights of Paris and became habitués of the theater.

As always when John Quincy was abroad, there were frequent messages from his mother intended to keep him on the straight and narrow. She wrote in March, "You my dear son are formed with a constitution feelingly alive; your passions are strong and impetuous." He must base his conduct on three pillars: religion, reason, and self-governance. "Passion unrestrained by reason cooperating with power has produced the subversion of cities, the desolation of countries, the massacre of nations, and filled the world with injustice and oppression."[7]

At the same time Congress had commissioned Adams to be its plenipotentiary for peace, it had named Henry Laurens as its envoy to the Netherlands. His mission was to sign a treaty of amity and commerce and to obtain a loan of $10 million. Unfortunately, Laurens's brigantine was captured by a British frigate while he was en route to Europe. He would spend the next fifteen months as a prisoner in the Tower of London.

The Netherlands was then a confederation of seven semiautonomous states ruled by a national parliament, the States General. Small though the country was, it presided over a vast empire that included Indonesia, Ceylon, the Dutch West Indies, and colonies in North Africa. As Dutch power faded, the country was increasingly drawn into the orbit of Great Britain. The Dutch were a seafaring people and adamantly opposed to restrictions placed on neutral shipping such as those imposed by the British orders-in-council. Nevertheless, in the Wars of the American Revolution, the States General was determined to remain neutral.

In France, Adams was aware only that Laurens had not arrived in the Netherlands, that his country was in desperate need of funds, and that Vergennes and Franklin had checkmated him for the time being. So he decided on his own to remove himself and his family to Amsterdam to see what could be done. He and the boys arrived in the city in mid-August after visiting Antwerp, Rotterdam, and the Hague. They took an immediate liking to Amsterdam and the Netherlands in general. New England–like in their frugality and sobriety, the members of the Dutch intelligentsia were freethinkers, and the country's cafés and salons were thriving centers of Enlightenment thought. John leased a large, comfortable house on the Keizersgracht, with an ample kitchen, an elegant dining room and parlor, and a drawing room for entertainment. He hired three servants and a chef, and began wining and dining influential Dutchmen and their families. Toward the close of the year, John was gratified to learn that in view of Laurens's plight, Congress had named him commissioner of the United States to the United Provinces.[8]

Throughout his stay in the Netherlands, John Adams relied heavily upon the advice and service of Charles Guillaume Frédéric Dumas. Dumas had been born in Germany of French parents. In 1750 he had settled in the Netherlands. Inherited wealth and a keen intellect had allowed him to make a name as a scholar of the classics and to become an outspoken advocate of Enlightenment values. The republican experiment in America fascinated him. Dumas had traveled to Paris, then introduced himself to Franklin and subsequently served the distinguished American as an intelligence gatherer. He and Adams resonated, and when John departed for the Netherlands, Dumas offered to accompany and assist him. Once they settled in, he introduced the Adamses to Dutch society, especially to its intellectuals. He advised the minister on all things Dutch, and Madame Dumas acted as a hostess at diplomatic functions.[9]

Worried as always about his children's education, John enrolled John Quincy and Charles in the prestigious Latin School located on the Singel canal just across from the Bloemenmarkt (flower market). The Latin School had been established in 1631; its curriculum was so rigorous that graduates found it unnecessary to attend university. Each boy had his own room. A servant awoke the pupil at six a.m., and the rhythm of the day was very much like that at Le Coeur's school. But the Latin School featured a distinguished faculty and a first-class library.[10] At first things went well: "John [Quincy] has seen one of the commencements when the young gentlemen delivered their orations and received their premiums and promotions which set his ambition all afire," John wrote Abigail. "Charles is the same amiable, insinuating creature. Wherever he goes, he gets the hearts of everybody especially the ladies. One of these boys is the sublime and the other the beautiful."[11] But then clouds appeared on the horizon. "Brother Charles and myself study in a little chamber apart because we don't understand the Dutch," John Quincy wrote his father.[12] John complained to the preceptor of the Latin School, H. Verheyk, that boys were being discriminated against. Verheyk sent back a blistering reply: "The disobedience and impertinence of your older son who does his best to corrupt his well-behaved brother . . . can no longer be tolerated as he endeavors by his bad behavior to bring upon himself the punishment he deserves in the hope of leaving school as a result."[13] John withdrew both boys immediately. He did not intend to have his children educated in Dutch schools "where a littleness of soul is notorious. The masters are mean spirited writches [*sic*], pinching, kicking, and boxing the children upon every turn. There is besides a general littleness arising from the incessant contemplation of stivers and doits [money]."[14]

At this point, John decided to seek the advice of Dr. Benjamin Waterhouse, a fellow son of New England. Waterhouse had pursued medical studies at universities in Edinburgh, London, and Leyden, earning his medical degree at Leyden in 1780. He had elected to stay on for a bit to attend some additional lectures; he was thus engaged when Adams's letter reached him. Leyden would be perfect for the boys, he advised. Education would be much cheaper and of higher quality than in Amsterdam. He and Thaxter could procure private tutors for Latin and Greek, and John Quincy and Charles could attend lectures on virtually every subject under the sun at the university. On December 18, John bade farewell to Thaxter and his sons after depositing them in Leyden.

John Quincy would regard the next six months as one of the most stimulating and enjoyable periods of his early life. Waterhouse invited his fellow Americans to take lodgings in the same house in which he was dwelling.[15] Thaxter succeeded in hiring a tutor to instruct the boys in Greek and Latin. They attended lectures on medicine, chemistry, and philosophy at the university, in the process becoming acquainted with some of the finest scholars in the Netherlands. "Mr. Waterhouse says that for riding I must have a pair [of] leather breeches and a pair of boots," thirteen-year-old Johnny wrote his father. "I should be glad to have a pair of Scates [sic]," as well.[16] John visited his sons at school and was well pleased. "Was present from twelve to one o'clock when the preceptor gave his lessons in Latin and Greek to my sons. His name is Wensing. He is apparently a great master . . . besides which he speaks French and Dutch very well. He is pleased with [his pupils] and they with him."[17] Needless to say, Johnny got his riding apparel and skates. In January 1781, Thaxter and John Quincy were officially admitted to the university.[18]

In Braintree, Abigail's loneliness was turning to bitterness. John had been absent from her for approximately 90 percent of the time for the past seven years. Between December 1780 and the end of September 1781, she received only six letters from her husband. Shortly after John departed for Europe the second time, Abigail wrote her intimate friend James Lovell that this separation might "destroy a tabernacle already impaired."[19] As the weeks and months passed, her correspondence with Lovell, who had long been in love with her, increased in volume and sometimes intimacy. Abigail lived in a world where rumors were rampant, and no letter was safe from prying eyes. Yet she was lonely and found Lovell's attentions flattering. Soon he was referring to "Portia" as "lovely woman" and even as a "Saucy-box." She admonished him: "[W]icked man."[20]

But instead of having an affair (Lovell was in Philadelphia, then the nation's capital), she immersed herself in business. She loved John Adams; she could not help herself. "How fondly can I call you mine, bound by every tie, which consecrates the most inviolable friendship . . . ," she wrote in December 1780. "The busy Sylphs are ever at my ear, no sooner does Morpheus close my eyes, than 'my whole soul, unbounded flies to thee.'"[21]

Although John remained committed to the notion of male supremacy within the family structure, particularly when it came to suffrage, he was more than happy to turn over management of the family's farm and finances to Abigail. She collected the rent, hired and fired tenants and laborers, purchased supplies, and paid the bills. It was up to her to make ends meet. It was against the law during the Revolutionary period for married women to own property. But with John away in Europe, Abigail decided to subvert the system. Earlier, when her husband was in Philadelphia, she'd had him send her packets of needles, which were in short supply in Massachusetts and which she sold for a handsome profit. Later, when John was in Paris and Amsterdam, Abigail had him supply her with lace and other European finery, which she also sold at a good markup. By 1781, Abigail had squirreled away enough money to begin investing. She placed it "in the hands of a friend."[22] That friend and financial adviser was her uncle Cotton Tufts. The connection and ensuing transactions were initially concealed from John. Abigail made the most of the "money which I call mine." She speculated in government securities that Revolutionary War soldiers had been forced to part with for pennies on the dollar. Once she offered to use some of her money to purchase an additional farm for the family, but only if John would quit "running away to foreign courts" and return to Braintree.[23]

In July 1781, word reached the Adams party in the Netherlands that Francis Dana had been appointed American minister to Russia. He was to convince Catherine the Great and her advisers that it was in Russia's interests to recognize America's independence and to sign a treaty of commerce and friendship. Congress believed, and Dana concurred, that Catherine—with her leadership in forming the League of Armed Neutrality, which was directed largely against Great Britain—would respond favorably. There was also the prospect of lucrative trade ties: American tobacco, rice, indigo, naval stores, flax, and iron for Russian hemp, sailcloth, tallow, lumber, and salted meat. Dana was well qualified for his task. A Harvard-educated lawyer and former delegate to the Continental Congress, he was intelligent, judicious, and dedicated to furthering his country's interests. His one great problem was that he spoke no French, the lingua franca of European diplomacy. He cast about for individuals willing to serve him as a secretary and interpreter, but the only person to volunteer was John Quincy, then just short of fourteen years old. His father was conflicted, at once proud that Dana would consider his son and fearful of the dangers of such an arduous journey to such a faraway place. Ever the man of public affairs, however, he assented.[24]

Dana and John Quincy set out from Amsterdam by boat for Utrecht at one o'clock on the afternoon of July 7, 1781, a perfect time of the year for travel. The morning after their arrival in the city, Dana purchased a new coach. From Utrecht it was on to Nijmegen; during the trip, they crossed the Rhine by means of what was called a rope ferry. A series of boats bound together side by side by cables stretched across the river; the small craft were covered with a layer of timber, and then upon that, planking was laid. Several hundred travelers could be ferried across in a relatively short time. John Quincy found the mechanism intriguing.[25] From Nijmegen the Americans traveled through the fortress cities of Kleve, Xanten, and Rheinberg and the villages in between on their way to Cologne. There they took note of a village opposite the city inhabited entirely by Jews. It was not John Quincy's first encounter with the Chosen People. Soon after his arrival in Amsterdam, he had written in his diary: "They say there are a hundred thousand Jews in this town, I am sure they are all wretched creatures for I think I never saw in my life such a set of miserable looking people, and they would steal your eyes out of your head if they possibly could."[26] John Quincy and Dana discovered a similar situation in Cologne. "Like all other places that they [the Jews] inhabit," wrote young Adams in his diary, "[it] is most shockingly offensive to every person who has a nose."[27]

On July 25, the travelers arrived in Berlin, "the capital of the King of Prussia." Because their carriage had overturned and been damaged on the road between Leipzig and Berlin, the Americans—unscathed—were forced to spend nine days in the city.[28] John Quincy was charmed with the tree-lined boulevards and magnificent architecture. He reported to his father that the king [Frederick the Great] was not particularly popular with his people, but as long as dissent consisted of words and not action, it was tolerated. Prussia was then a military state with its entire adult male population subject to conscription. Indeed, in this respect, John Quincy observed, the king treated the common people like slaves. "Among other things if a farmer has two or more sons the eldest inherits all the land, and all the others (when of age) are soldiers for life for . . . about two pence sterling a day."[29] But then came Eastern Europe, and to the young American, Prussia seemed a social paradise in comparison. "In that province [Courland, near Riga, the capital of Livonia], all the farmers are in the most abject slavery; they are bought and sold there like so many beasts and are sometimes even changed for dogs or horses. Their masters," he reported, "have even the right of life and death over them, and if they kill one of them, they are only obliged to pay a trifling fine."[30]

As he would throughout his life, John Quincy thanked his parents for having the good grace to bear and raise him in a land of opportunity, social mobility, freedom, and democracy. He must have been aware of his parents' abhorrence of American slavery, but there is no record of his thought on the matter at this point in his life.

Dana and his secretary arrived in St. Petersburg on August 27, 1781, completing a journey of fifty-one days. Somewhere between Cologne and Coblenz, John Quincy had acquired and read Voltaire's two-volume *Historie de l'empire de Russie sous Pierre le Grand*, a flattering history of Russia paid for by Catherine the Great.[31] Voltaire had described the city built by Peter the Great on the marshy delta of the Neva River, but nothing prepared the two Americans for the graceful canals, the baroque mansions, the Hermitage, or the magnificent public buildings built on commission by a collection of distinguished French, Italian, and Scottish architects. A number of the palaces boasted "*jet d'eaus*, or water-works, far superior to those of Versailles."[32] "This is the finest city I have seen in Europe," Dana wrote John Adams. "Alone, it is sufficient to immortalize the memory of Peter the first."[33] The would-be minister and his secretary secured temporary lodgings at the Hôtel de Paris, the name belying the modesty of the abode. Dissatisfied, they then made arrangements to room and board with a Monsieur Artaud, a man who would be a companion and guide to young Adams during his nearly yearlong stay in St. Petersburg.[34]

Dana's mission to Russia was an exercise in frustration. America's first envoy to the Court of St. Petersburg was never officially received. He had been instructed to consult closely with the French ambassador, the Marquis de Vérac (Charles Olivier de Saint-Georges de Vérac). Vérac informed the American that it was "too soon" to expect recognition.[35] It would remain too soon for the remainder of Dana and John Quincy's stay. Catherine was then attempting to mediate the conflict between France and Great Britain. Recognizing Britain's rebellious colonies would not be conducive to that end. Dana reported that "favoritism and blackmail" played an important part in the routine of Russian official life, "while bribery offered a golden key to every negotiation."[36] As good republicans, he and his secretary believed themselves bound not to participate in such corruptions. In truth, it did not matter what the Americans did or did not do. Diplomatically their situation was hopeless.

John Adams had allowed his son to accompany Francis Dana only because he believed that in St. Petersburg, John Quincy could continue his education unabated. As with the diplomatic aspect of the American mission, father and son were deeply disappointed. "I can't get here any good dictionary either French and Latin or English and Latin," John Quincy reported to his father in October. "Indeed, this is not a very good place for learning the Latin and Greek languages, as there is no academy or school here, and but very few private teachers who demand at the rate of 90 pounds sterling a year for an hour and a half each day."[37] In truth, there were no schools to speak of because the Russian aristocrats sent their children abroad for their educations. So Dana and John Quincy set about the task themselves.

Fortunately, Dana was able to obtain a subscription to an English-language library, and Johnny proceeded to immerse himself in English history; in succession, he read David Hume's *History of England* in eight volumes; Catharine Macaulay's *History of England from the Accession of James I to That of the Brunswick Line*, also in eight volumes; and William Robertson's three-volume *History of the Reign of the Emperor Charles V.* He copied the poems of Dryden, Pope, and Addison. By early 1782, John Quincy had obtained a Latin dictionary, and he began translating the sketches of Cornelius Nepos and several of Cicero's orations. And he began to take German lessons from a tutor.[38]

St. Petersburg might have been pleasing to the eye, but it was brutal to the other senses. As the Russian winter closed in, daylight was reduced to a few hours a day. The Neva River froze over, and it snowed and snowed. The temperature could plunge to twenty degrees below zero. Walls were thick and windows were double paned, but the average indoor temperature hovered around fifty degrees Fahrenheit. Primitive though the medical arts were in the 1780s, people knew enough to recognize the value of fresh air. Dana and John Quincy threw open their windows for thirty minutes each morning to air out their quarters.[39] Nevertheless, they were constantly ill with colds.

Socially, John Quincy made do the best he could; the diplomatic corps and his Russian hosts were generally friendly and welcoming. He visited the Hermitage and Peterhof Palace, and in a party of three sleighs, he traveled to Oranienbaum, which contained one of the tsarina's more opulent palaces. Writing from Braintree, Nabby observed that he was the luckiest boy in the world to be experiencing such sights and sounds. Channeling her mother, she instructed him to be grateful and to learn as much as he could and write about it.[40] But John Quincy was lonely; he missed his father, and he missed America. He did not complain, but there were days and days when he did not leave the house.

In April 1781, Charles Adams had become seriously ill. John referred to his malady as "seizures," but it is possible the boy fell victim to a strain of malaria present in Northern Europe, a disease that would afflict his father for nearly six months beginning in August. Charles had recovered physically within a month but was painfully homesick. With John Quincy gone to Russia, he had only his father, who was frequently absent on official business, for company. Reluctantly, John decided to send Charles back to Braintree to his mama and siblings. In August he placed his eleven-year-old son in the care of an American physician who was returning to America. The ensuing voyage would stretch over five months.[41]

THE REPUTATION OF CATHERINE the Great and the beauty of St. Petersburg did not blind John Quincy to the evils of the Russian political and social systems. "The government of Russia is entirely despotical," he wrote his mother. "The Sovereign is absolute in all the extent of the word." The persons and property of the nobility were subject to her caprice. The common people, the vast majority of whom were illiterate and impoverished, were equally dependent upon the nobility. Serfs were bought and sold with the land they tilled. They were compelled to work exclusively for their lord for a number of days each week and were required to pay a tax of two or three rubles a year to him. The estates were vast; rumor had it that one nobleman collected tax from no fewer than six hundred fifty thousand serfs for an annual income of a hundred thousand pounds sterling. One out of every five hundred serfs was pledged to the empress for military service. The system, John Quincy observed to Abigail, was not only unjust and immoral, but unstable, there having been four revolutions during the previous century.[42]

As early as December 1781, John began to think about recalling his son from Russia; he did not care so much about loneliness or physical difficulties; but education mattered. "You had better be [or rather, would be better] at Leyden where you might be in a regular course of education," he wrote in December 1781. "You might come in the spring in a Russian, Swedish, or Prussian vessel, to Embden [*sic*] or perhaps Hamburg, and from thence here in a neutral bottom."[43]

On September 4, 1782, John Quincy finally received the call from his father to return to him at the Hague, to which he had moved from Amsterdam. "I want you with me," he wrote. "Mr. Thaxter will probably leave me soon and I shall be alone. I want you to pursue your studies too at Leyden."[44] Dana's secretary, who had turned fifteen in July, immediately began preparations. During the summer months, the quickest and easiest route would have been by sea, but winter was approaching—John Quincy would not be able to depart St. Petersburg until October—and by then the gales and ice of November might make a sea route impossible.

In company with "Count Greco an Italian gentleman with whom I was acquainted," John Quincy set out for Stockholm, the first leg of his journey. The eight-hundred-mile trip proved arduous—and lengthy. Along the way John Quincy stopped off at Helsinki and dined with the commander of Swedish forces in Finland. Then, alternating between boat and carriage, Count Greco and he island-hopped across the Åland archipelago in the Baltic Sea. He finally arrived in

Stockholm at midnight on November 22. Finding all of the taverns closed, he had to spend the night in his carriage. The following day the young American secured suitable accommodations; he would spend the next five weeks in Stockholm, one of the most pleasant experiences of his life. His intention was to take sail for Copenhagen, the next leg of the trip, but every attempt was foiled by wind or ice. In truth, John Quincy was in no hurry to leave the Swedish capital. "[I] was much pleas'd with the polite manner in which the people of the country treat strangers," he subsequently wrote Abigail. "Sweden is the country in Europe which pleases me the most."[45]

John Quincy had in his possession numerous letters of introduction, which opened all kinds of social doors. One of his first acquaintances was Carl Bernhard Wadström, a mechanical and mining engineer who offered to be his guide and with whom he lodged during part of his stay. As he toured Northern Europe, John Quincy was rounding into a mature young adult. He felt free for perhaps the first time in his life, and he blossomed into the socially charming and intellectually stimulating person that his family and friends would come to revere. Johnny, a handsome youth with fine features, was of average height and stocky. He found the women of Sweden particularly alluring; they were, he later recalled, "as modest as they were amiable and beautiful." Sweden would always be "the land of lovely dames," he would write his friend Alexander Hill Everett in 1811, "and to this hour I have not forgotten the palpitations of heart which some of them cost me."[46] When John Quincy and Nabby were reunited and living together in Paris in 1783, she would tease him, because she had learned of his amorous exploits from a woman who had known him in Stockholm: "Now what think you young man. Does not your heart go pitapat, now bounce, as if it would break your rib. Nor do you know how many of your adventures she confided to me."[47]

Aware that his father would be worrying about him, John Quincy slipped the embrace of Stockholm society and set off for Copenhagen, a trip of some six hundred miles. He broke up the journey with a three-week stay at Gothenburg, Sweden's second-largest city. On the eve of his departure, John Quincy attended a masked ball and stayed until four a.m., whereupon, as he recorded in his diary, "I return'd to my lodgings threw myself upon a bed and slept till about 7 o'clock then pack'd up my trunks and set away for Copenhagen about half past 8."[48] He arrived in the Danish capital on February 15 and subsequently reported that the people were welcoming, polite, and civil but "not with the same open-heartedness which they do in Sweden."[49] There he was reunited with his friend Count Greco, who had taken a different road from Stockholm. The two arranged for berths aboard a vessel that would transport them to Hamburg, but the port froze over, and they were obliged to make the trip overland. John Quincy spent a month in Hamburg before setting off again.

In February 1783, John, at long last, heard from his wayward son, then in Copenhagen. "You cannot imagine the anxiety I have felt on your account," he wrote John Quincy. "When you arrive at the Hague, you may take your choice, either to remain there and follow your studies under the direction of Mr. Dumas or go to Leyden to your former tutor."[50] His son arrived in the Hague on April 21 and immediately informed his father that he would stay there and study with Dumas.

DURING JOHN QUINCY'S MISSION to St. Petersburg and his tour of Northern Europe, the course of the Revolutionary War had changed drastically. Britain's campaign to seize the South had begun well but then gradually deteriorated as elements of the Continental Army and bands of guerrilla fighters harassed Lord Cornwallis's army, compelling him to take refuge in the sleepy tobacco market town of Yorktown, Virginia, on a peninsula between the York and James Rivers. Smelling blood, Washington marched south from New Jersey while a French fleet under the Comte de Grasse entered the Chesapeake and blocked Cornwallis's retreat. On October 19 the entire British force of 7,241 men surrendered while a British band allegedly played a march entitled "The World Turned Upside Down."[51]

Gradually the pieces of the puzzle began to fall into place. In the Netherlands, the States General, under growing pressure from France, recognized American independence and acceded to Minister Adams's request for a large loan. In Britain, the North ministry fell in the wake of Yorktown, and the House of Commons adopted a resolution declaring that anyone who in any way continued to wage war or to urge that the war against America be continued was an enemy of the king.[52] In April 1782, Lord Shelburne, the British home secretary, dispatched an unofficial emissary, Richard Oswald, to Paris to explore the possibility of a treaty of peace with Franklin. As Adams followed these events from his post in the Netherlands, he received word that he had been appointed peace commissioner. He believed that Shelburne could be dealt with, but he did not trust Franklin and Vergennes. He had good reason. The two, working through La Luzerne and pro-French solons in America, had persuaded Congress to revise Adams's commission. In future negotiations, he was to be guided always by the French foreign ministry. In addition, three new peace commissioners were named: Franklin; Henry Laurens, recently freed from the Tower; and the distinguished New York lawyer John Jay, then representing American interests in Spain.

Jay was first to reach Paris. Realizing that he and Adams were of like mind regarding the reliability of the French, Jay urged his colleague to join him as soon as possible. But though Adams continued to be concerned about Franklin's willingness to allow Vergennes to dictate the course of American foreign policy, he was in the midst of negotiating a series of loans from Dutch bankers that eventually totaled $3.5 million.[53]

As a result, Jay decided to take matters into his own hands. Without informing Franklin and Vergennes, he opened secret talks with Oswald. It was in the midst of these negotiations that Adams finally arrived in Paris on October 26. In the days that followed, he fought for the transmontane West and the right of New Englanders to fish the Grand Banks. On these matters as well as several others, including, of course, independence, he and Jay prevailed, and a preliminary treaty of peace was signed on November 30, 1782. It was left to Franklin to inform Vergennes. The French foreign minister expressed mild indignation that his ally was negotiating with the enemy behind his back, but he was secretly pleased. France was committed by its treaty with Spain to fight until Britain agreed to cede Gibraltar to the Spanish. The conclusion of a separate peace between Britain and America would allow the government of Louis XVI to avoid that virtually impossible task.

ABIGAIL HAD LONG WANTED to visit Europe, and in the winter of 1782, she began to press her husband to allow her to come to him. In December, John wrote her that their reunion was his most cherished desire, but that he had just written the president of Congress offering his resignation.[54] Congress received but refused to act on Adams's proffered resignation, leaving him in diplomatic limbo. In truth, Adams had no intention of abandoning the field. He was determined to be part of the negotiations of a permanent peace with Great Britain, and he harbored an intense desire to be named the first U.S. minister to the Court of St. James's. "I am soberly of the opinion," he wrote Abigail in February 1783, "that for one or two years to come, I could do more good in England . . . [for] the United States of America, than in any other spot upon earth."[55]

John Quincy had remained behind in the Hague while his father negotiated peace in Paris. He later remembered his time with the Dumas family as among the most pleasant experiences of his life. The young man and what he came to consider his second family lived in the "large, roomy and handsome" house that John had rented the previous April. Located in the Fluwelen Burgwal (the Street of Velvet Makers), the mansion, following Dutch recognition, would serve as the first American embassy; it came to be known as the Hôtel des États-Unis—"or if you will 'L'Hotel de Nouveau Monde,'" John Adams reported.[56] In Dumas, John Quincy could not have chosen a better tutor. In addition to being a spy for and adviser to representatives of the United States, Dumas was one of the most learned men in Europe. John would describe him as a "walking library, and so great a master of languages ancient and modern [that] is rarely seen."[57] Under the scholar's supervision, John Quincy began translating Suetonius's *Life of Caligula*; he read the works of Plautus and Terence in Latin; he started translating Horace's *Odes* into French; and for good measure, he read and translated part of the New Testament in Greek. For "amusement" young Adams turned to Virgil, perusing a hundred verses of the *Aeneid* at a time with Dumas, who "explain[ed to] me everything which regards the ancient rites and ceremonies."[58] All was not cerebral; he began a mild romance with Dumas's daughter, Nancy, the two playing the flute and piano and singing duets. Beginning what was to become a fetish for physical exercise, John Quincy walked several miles a day and rode horseback twice a week. The father was in general pleased with his son's education but could not refrain from offering advice. Study some mathematics, he wrote, and above all do not forget moral philosophy; he recommended particularly William Wollaston, who had become famous for his widely read *Religion of Nature Delineated* (1724).[59]

On July 22, John arrived back in the Hague. He wanted to consult with Dumas and his banker friends and collect his son. He had decided to make John Quincy his secretary. "He is grown to be a man," John wrote to Nabby, "and the world says they should take him for my younger brother, if they did not know him to be my son. His knowledge and his judgment are so far beyond his years as to be admired by all who have conversed with him. He is very studious and delights in nothing but books which alarms me for his health; because, like me, he is naturally inclined to be fat."[60] Father and son arrived in Paris on August 9, 1783, and lodged at the Grand Hôtel du Roi in the Place du Carrousel. "The first thing to be done in Paris," John wrote in his diary "is always to send for a tailor, peruke [wig] maker, and shoemaker for this nation has established such a domination over the fashion that neither clothes, wigs, nor shoes made in any other place will do in Paris."[61]

The next three months were a whirlwind of social and diplomatic activity for John Quincy. Shortly after their arrival, father and son journeyed to Passy to pay their respects to Dr. Franklin and introduce the younger Adams to John Jay. "They were at breakfast and had a great deal of company," John Quincy remembered.[62] The younger Adams was able to renew his friendship with Benny Bache, Franklin's grandson. He was also introduced to Peter Jay Munro, John Jay's nephew and his secretary. Peter, like John Quincy, was sixteen and perhaps the only American of that age who could match his countryman in travel and learning. The two became fast friends, meeting often at Franklin's house in Passy and, among other things, reading Samuel Johnson's *Life of Pope* together.[63]

One morning the British minister to France, David Hartley, called to see John, but he was out. Hartley proceeded to hold an extended discussion with John Quincy on the prospects for a final peace. Another morning, with his father gone to Versailles, John Quincy rendezvoused with the Vertot d'Abeuf, an old acquaintance, and as they strolled the gardens at the Tuileries, the Frenchman, who had just returned from Poland, provided some interesting observations on Europe's Jewish population, information that partially corrected John Quincy's previous negative impressions. Poland could not have existed without the Jews, the abbé observed. It was they who carried on the commerce of the country; the nobility was too proud for business and the serfs were incapable of it.

Every night possible, father and son, together with a party of French notables, attended the theater—Italian and French comedies mostly; the French were not inclined to tragedy, John Quincy observed. There was the obligatory visit to the Louvre: "There are some good paintings there amongst a great number of indifferent ones."[64]

In Paris, the Adamses were able to witness the first public showing of "the flying globe." The device itself, John Quincy recorded in his diary, "was of taffeta glued together with gum and lined with parchment." Its operators pumped heated air into the device from a gondola suspended beneath, enabling the balloon to "rise up to an immense height of itself." On the appointed day a crowd, including the two Americans, gathered on the Champ de Mars, an open military field. "Great guns fired from the Ecole Militaire were the signal given for its going; it rose at once, for some time perpendicular, and then slanted," before disappearing into the clouds.[65] This first crude device was the creation of the Montgolfier brothers, Joseph-Michel and Jacques-Étienne. This would be the first of many hot-air balloon ascents the Adamses would witness in Paris, some ending not as happily.

News of these amusements did not sit well with Abigail. "My anxieties have been, and still are great lest the numerous temptations and snares of vice, should vitiate your early habits of virtue, and destroy those principals, which you are now capable of reasoning upon," she wrote John Quincy.[66] In truth, Abigail Adams was a brilliant, brave, principled person, but she was also domineering and controlling, particularly when it came to the family. In many respects, the Adams clan was a matriarchy. According to her future daughter-in-law, Abigail was determined to be "the guiding planet" around which family members conducted themselves according to "the impulse of her magnetic power."[67] And Abigail was always a little jealous of her husband and son. For a woman of her intelligence, being forced to the political and intellectual sidelines amidst world-shaking events was at times more than she could bear.

4

Paris

THE FINAL TREATY OF Paris ending the war between Great Britain and its former colonies was signed on September 3, 1783. The same day a general peace was concluded among the warring European powers. The previous September, John had been notified that Congress had appointed him, Franklin, and Jay to negotiate treaties of commerce with the states of Europe and Africa. At the insistence of the Southern states, Thomas Jefferson was later added to the group while Jay decided to return home in 1784. To Adams's immense gratification, Congress named him head of the commission.[1] "I must stay another winter," he wrote Abigail. "But what shall I do for want of my family? Please come with Nabby," he pleaded. Even if they were ordered back to the United States in the spring, it would be worth it. "The moment I hear of it [your arrival], I will fly with post horses to receive you at least, and if the balloon should be carried to such perfection in the meantime as to give mankind the safe navigation of the air, I will fly in one of them at the rate of thirty knots an hour."[2]

On September 22, John and John Quincy moved from the Grand Hôtel du Roi in Paris to Auteuil, a western suburb of Paris located on the right bank of the Seine near the Bois de Boulogne. They were the guests of Thomas Barclay, another American who was renting a large and elegant house from the Comte de Rouault. John was at the time recovering from the prolonged fever he had contracted in the Netherlands and welcomed the relative peace and quiet in which to convalesce.[3]

On October 20, 1783, the Adams men departed Auteuil for England. John wanted his son to see the sights of London and experience the delights of the English countryside. In addition, at the urging of friends who were alarmed by his gaunt, emaciated appearance, John intended to sample the healing waters at the resort town of Bath.[4] The travelers arrived in London on Sunday, October 26, and booked rooms at Osborn's Hotel, Adelphi, in the Strand. Although John and John Quincy had just undergone a painful separation from the mother country during which their homeland had experienced seven years of sometimes savage warfare, they were, themselves, still English. Despite his distrust of various British ministries and their intentions toward his country, John still regarded the English as the freest of all European peoples. The Adamses, like most other Americans, would continue to identify with British culture and history.

The pair could not wait to see the sights they had heard so much about. They were struck by Westminster Abbey, its architecture and monuments. They visited St. Paul's Cathedral, which John Quincy appreciated for its history if not for its style.[5] As a sixteen-year-old, John Quincy found the historical weapons display at the Tower of London particularly interesting. The American-born painter Benjamin West managed to obtain entrance for them to Buckingham Palace, where they marveled at the van Dycks, the Rubenses, and West's own *Death of General Wolfe*. And there was the London theater. Nary an evening passed that John and John Quincy were not at Drury Lane or Covent Garden. They got to see the incomparable Sarah Siddons play the title role in *Isabella, or The Fatal Marriage*. John Quincy was ecstatic over witnessing the "wonderful, wonderful, wonder of wonders Mrs. Siddons," he wrote his friend Peter Jay Munro. "The most capital performer upon the stage, not only of Europe, at present, but that ever was seen."[6] "A young lady, in the next box to where we were, was so much affected by it as to be near fainting and was carried out," Johnny noted in his diary.[7]

The Adamses renewed their acquaintance with the Joshua Johnsons, the Maryland family they had met in Nantes. Louisa Catherine Johnson, John Quincy's future wife, was then eight years old.[8] The Adamses made the obligatory trip to Bath to take the waters. John and John Quincy were back in London on December 28. Five days later they boarded a packet headed for Hellevoetsluis, a Dutch port some twenty miles south of the Hague.[9]

What ensued was one of the most harrowing journeys of the two Americans' lives, which, given their Atlantic crossings, was saying something. It was the dead of winter. "In this channel, on both sides of the island of Great Britain," John wrote in his diary, "there is in bad weather a tremulous, undulating, turbulent kind of irregular tumbling sea that disposes men more to the *mal de mer* than even the surges of the gulph [*sic*] stream."[10] For three days their ship was blown about until the captain and crew, exhausted from work and sleep deprivation, decided to abandon the attempt to reach Hellevoetsluis and land on the southern tip of the island of Goeree. John and John Quincy were simply dumped on the beach; the only structure in sight was a fisherman's hut. The Americans learned from its inhabitant that they were some four miles from the town of Goodereede. John, still weak from the remnants of his illness and further depleted by the voyage, nearly despaired, but John Quincy bore him up. The elder Adams noted later in his diary, "My young companion was in fine spirits; his gaiety, activity, and attention to me increased as difficulties multiplied."[11] Braving sleet, snow, and bone-chilling wind, the two walked to Goodereede. There they put up in the local tavern and learned that they would have to cover the whole distance of the island from south to north, cross an arm of the sea to the island of Overflakkee, and then traverse another, wider arm of the sea to reach a point on the continent where they would still be five or six miles distant from Hellevoetsluis.

Rested, the travelers set out overland, their transportation a simple peasant's wagon with no springs or cushions. Eventually they reached the ferryboat port. Two days' rest at the local inn, and they were off again. Their transportation was a large iceboat mounted on runners. The captain and eight-man crew would row the vessel until it reached solid ice. After the passengers disembarked, the crew would leap out of the boat and draw it up on the ice. The passengers would then climb aboard with the crew advancing the vessel by towropes. This process was repeated again and again for a day and a night. "The weather was cold—we were all frequently wet," John recalled. "I was chilled to the heart."[12] But the iceboat eventually reached the mainland, and the Adamses were able to make their way to Hellevoetsluis. Following a few days' rest, they went on to the Hague and the comfort of their commodious house.

In April, the Adams men learned that Abigail and Nabby, in lieu of specific instructions from John, had decided to take matters into their own hands. Abigail wrote her son that they had booked passage on a Yankee merchantman but that the weather was so unpredictable that she could not give a departure date.[13] John, still busy with his Dutch bankers, dispatched John Quincy to London to wait for his mother and sister. He arrived in the city on May 18 and took temporary quarters at the Imperial Hotel in Suffolk Street. Never one to let grass grow under his son's feet, John wrote from the Hague, instructing John Quincy to visit Parliament and witness the debates in the British House of Commons, that "great and illustrious school."[14] The last week in May, a family friend, Benjamin Vaughan, secured a seat in the galleries for John Quincy. For the next month, he attended parliamentary sessions on a regular basis; there he observed the historic and stirring debates between William Pitt the Younger, who at age twenty-four had recently been elected prime minister, and his archenemy, Charles James Fox, ten years his senior.[15] On June 15, young Adams witnessed Edmund Burke's powerful challenge to King George III, who had dissolved the previous Parliament. That body, Burke declared, was the protector of the people's liberties, and the Crown must defer to it.[16]

During a visit to the Temple, London's historic legal district, John Quincy met a young Marylander, William Vans Murray. "We dined there together. Had an interesting conversation upon the merits of the Christian and Mahometan *Paradise*, and went in the evening to hear a debate at Coachmaker's Hall."[17] The two would meet again when both were American diplomats in Europe in the 1790s. Their friendship and collaboration would do much to shape the foreign policy of the United States during the presidency of John Adams.

On May 24, Abigail booked passage on the American merchantman *Active*. "It is said to be a good vessel [with a] copper bottom, and an able captain," she wrote John. She entrusted the care of Charles and Thomas to her sister and placed her uncle Cotton Tufts in charge of the farms. The upcoming voyage elicited mixed feelings—anxiety at the dangers and anticipation at seeing her husband and eldest son again. "I am embarking on board a vessel without any male friend, connection, or acquaintance, my servant excepted, a stranger to the Capt. and every person on board," but she and Nabby would have their own stateroom. "Please come to London in July to meet us. I cannot wait to see you," she wrote her husband.[18]

Abigail had never been to sea before, and she was violently seasick the first ten days of the trip. But then the mal de mer subsided, and the rest of the voyage proved uneventful. The ladies arrived in London the evening of July 21 and checked into Low's Hotel in Covent Garden. Still in the dark as to Abigail and Nabby's arrival date, John had recalled John Quincy to the Hague; the women would have to wait at least a week to see their menfolk. Members of the American community in London had been forewarned of Abigail and Nabby's coming, and on the morning of the twenty-second, they received no fewer than five visitors. "I had always dreamed of seeing the land of my forefathers," Abigail had written John Quincy before departing Boston. Now her wish had come true. Thomas Jefferson arrived later in the week and called but was too late; he and Abigail had met briefly in Boston as she awaited her ship, but their paths would not cross again until both were in France.[19] After several days of sightseeing and clothes buying, Abigail made the decision not to leave her rooms until one or both of the Adams men arrived on the scene. On the morning of the twenty-ninth, she was in her suite at the hotel when a servant rushed in.

"Young Mr. Adams is come," he declared.

"Where is he?" she demanded.

"In the other house, Madam; he stopped to get his hair dressed."

At last John Quincy appeared. Mother and daughter were stunned. When Johnny had departed America in 1779, he had been a boy of twelve. He was now a young man of seventeen. "Oh, my Mamma! And my dear Sister," he exclaimed, and the three embraced.[20] Shortly thereafter, John arrived, and the reunion was complete.

Somewhere along his diplomatic journey, John had secured an income stream. He departed for Europe a middling sort—a farmer and lawyer. As he later observed, unlike Washington and Jefferson, he had not been born to wealth. Congress was famously stingy in funding its overseas representatives. But he and John Quincy had traveled extensively, sometimes on official business and sometimes not. The family would crisscross the Atlantic several times. Upon John Quincy's return from his Northern European travels, he had submitted a bill for his expenses. Costly, his father had declared, but well worth it. John responded similarly to Abigail and Nabby's shopping spree in London: "[A]s to clothes for yourself and daughter, I beg you to do what is proper; let the expense be what it will."[21] Abigail and Nabby's suite at Low's Hotel was one of the finest in the establishment.[22] What was the source of this largesse? Early American diplomats sometimes doubled as commercial agents for U.S. trading firms. In addition, there were, perhaps, some commissions to be earned from floating loans with the Dutch bankers. The Amsterdam bank of Willinks and Sons would serve as financial agents first for John and then for John Quincy. Whatever the case, as the Adams family prepared to embark for the Continent, money was not a pressing concern.

By the time John Adams reached London, Thomas Jefferson had already passed through and was well on his way to Paris. There was not a moment to be lost, the elder Adams informed his family. At John's direction John Quincy had already purchased a slightly used coach suitable for four people.[23] On Sunday, August 8, the entire family set off for Dover. The servants followed behind in a rented post chaise. John Quincy had purchased a copy of Samuel Johnson's *Lives of the Poets*, from which the family took turns reading aloud to pass the time. On Monday the ninth the Adamses arrived in Dover and immediately boarded a packet for Calais. From there it was another two hundred miles to Paris, but the trip provided the ladies an opportunity to take in some of the French countryside.[24] The party arrived in Paris on the thirteenth, and after a four-day stay in the city, the Adamses made their way to their new home in Auteuil.

Situated on the right bank of the Seine some four miles west of central Paris and one mile south of Passy, Auteuil was home to some of the most elegant residences in France. Such luminaries as Boileau and Molière had built houses there. The Adamses took up residence in the Hôtel de Rouault, where John and John Quincy had stayed in the fall of 1783. This time John and his family would have the run of the entire forty-room hôtel particulier. The structure had belonged to the Comte de Rouault, a wealthy French nobleman who had frittered away his wealth. Among other amenities, the hôtel particulier boasted a full-fledged theater, where the comte and his young wife had hired troops of actors to stage tragedies and comedies at two hundred pounds a performance.[25] "I am situated at a small desk in an apartment . . . [that] opens into my lodging chamber which is handsome and commodious," Abigail wrote her niece Elizabeth Cranch. Her apartment and bedroom were elegantly furnished in leather, marble, and velvet. Her apartment looked out upon the magnificent garden surrounding the hôtel particulier. "The garden Betsy! Let me take a look at it. . . . It is square and contains about 5 acres of land . . . laid out in oblongs, octagons, circles &c. filled with flowers; upon each side are spacious walks with rows of orange trees and pots of flowers."[26]

With Paris in particular and France in general, Abigail was not so well pleased. She found managing the household onerous. There were eight servants, but because of the medieval custom of craft separation, each would only perform his or her allotted task. The cook would prepare the meals but not deign to clean the kitchen. "Your Coiffer de femme, will dress your hair . . . but she will not brush out your chamber," she wrote. Abigail believed that Parisian society was immoral and superficial, obsessed with dress and licentious to the core. A friend of John's, an abbé, informed her that there were fifty-two thousand registered prostitutes in the city. Marriage vows were frequently considered an inconvenient formality. But, she noted, "you can wander around the French capital with perfect security to your person and property, but in London, at going in and coming out of the theatre, you find yourself in a mob; and are every moment in danger of being robbed."[27]

At Auteuil, Nabby and John Quincy grew to know and love each other. The nineteen- and seventeen-year-olds were near constant companions, reading to each other, attending plays and dinners, and sharing secrets. Nabby was, as her mother described her, "tall, large, and majestic," if not beautiful; "she was handsome with an attractive figure and elegant manners."[28] Her mother thought her at times haughty, but as her letters to her brother and friends showed, Nabby was intelligent, witty, playful, and thoroughly charming.

From the Adamses' arrival in Paris in August 1784 until John Quincy's departure for America in mid-1785, he continued to serve as his father's secretary. Where John dined, John Quincy dined; whom his father saw, he did also. When not so engaged, the young man was frequently in Paris with the ladies, attending the French and Italian theaters and the opera, of which he was most fond. He and his father continued to be avid book buyers, frequenting Froulle on the Quai des

Grands-Augustins.[29] Soon after his arrival, John Quincy had dined with Jefferson and John Paul Jones, who was in Paris on orders from Congress to collect prize money owed American vessels from actions during the past war. There he also met Jean-Pierre-François Blanchard, the French aeronaut who had recently crossed the English Channel from Dover to Calais. His balloon had suffered such an acute descent during the flight that he and his companion had had to throw everything, including their clothes, overboard.[30]

Every Monday evening the Marquis de Lafayette and his wife gave a dinner for all the members of the American community in Paris. "Madame is a very agreeable woman," John Quincy noted in his diary, "and has a pleasing countenance: She is extremely fond of her husband and children, which is a most uncommon circumstance; especially as when they were married, neither of them was more than 12 years old."[31] Indeed, the marriage customs of the European aristocracy proved to be a topic of some interest to him. On another occasion, he and "the ladies," as he referred to Abigail and Nabby, paid a visit to the queen's milliner, Mademoiselle Bertin, who was one of the richest commoners in the kingdom. At that time she was turning out dozens of dresses for the ten-year-old Infanta of Spain, who was engaged to be married to one of the princes of Portugal, age seventeen.[32] On the twenty-seventh of March, the queen of France delivered a son. "'Tis one of the most important events that can happen in this kingdom," John Quincy confided to his diary, "and every Frenchman has been expecting it as if the fate of his life depended upon it. They would prefer being governed by a fool or a tyrant, that should be the son of his predecessor, than by a sensible and good prince, who should only be a brother."[33]

The Adamses were frequent guests at Dr. Franklin's table. John had publicly reconciled with the philosopher-diplomat, while continuing to rail against him privately. John Quincy and the ladies found him most amiable and engaging. "The old gentleman, is perfectly well," John Quincy wrote, "except the [kidney] stone, which prevents him from riding in a coach and even from walking."[34] Young Adams was both dismayed and amused that William Temple Franklin, the elder man's grandson and secretary, had become a follower of Frederick Anthony Mesmer. Mesmer was a Viennese-trained physician who claimed to have discovered a property he called animal magnetism, which he claimed he could capture and use to cure a variety of diseases.[35]

John Quincy had a front-row seat at the Cathedral of Notre-Dame to witness the king and queen singing the Te Deum during Lent. What piety! he thought as the king approached the altar on his knees. "What a charming sight: an absolute king of one of the most powerful empires on earth, and perhaps a thousand of the first personages in that empire, adoring the divinity that created them, and acknowledging that he can in a moment reduce them to the dust from which they sprung." But what evils lurked beneath the surface? he wondered. What monstrous acts of cruelty, oppression, and exploitation had been authorized by Louis?[36]

During their stay at Auteuil, the Adamses spent more time with Thomas Jefferson and his young daughter Martha than with any other Americans. In conducting the business of his country, John enjoyed a rapport with the Virginian that he had never had with Franklin. Abigail would declare him to be "one of the choice ones of the earth."[37] Little did they know at the time that their lives would be forever intertwined.

Thomas Jefferson, born in 1743, was destined to become a Southern gentleman, benevolent planter, and educated benefactor of his colony, his commonwealth, and eventually his country.[38] He was educated by private tutors until old enough to enroll at William and Mary.[39] Jefferson was admitted to the bar in Virginia in 1767 and quickly assumed a prominent role in the life of the commonwealth. In the summer of 1774, he published *A Summary View of the Rights of British America*, in which he linked the colonists' struggle for freedom and self-government to the advance of democracy in English society. Elected to the First and Second Continental Congresses, Jefferson was, like Samuel Adams, crucial to converting the rebellion against British tyranny into a mass movement. In the House of Burgesses, he championed private manumission and then, of course, proposed a clause in the Declaration calling for abolition of what John C. Calhoun would subsequently refer to as "the peculiar institution." Jefferson served somewhat ingloriously as governor of Virginia during the war. He was sitting in Congress as a delegate from Virginia in 1783 when that body selected him as one of three commissioners to negotiate a commercial treaty with Great Britain.

Thomas Jefferson, six feet two with red hair and rugged good looks, was an authentic member of the Republic of Letters. When not engaged in politics or public business, he immersed himself in botany, archaeology, astronomy, and meteorology. Monticello was, famously, both plantation and laboratory. He read Greek and Latin and spoke French, Spanish, and Italian. Personally, he was charming, empathetic, and, at least early in life, unassuming. Women loved him and he loved women. Devoted to his first wife, Martha (Patty) Wayles Skelton, he had promised her on her deathbed never to remarry. But he then conducted an affair with Maria Cosway, a married woman, and famously fathered several children with his slave and concubine, Sally Hemings, who was also his deceased wife's half sister.[40]

Of all the Adamses, Jefferson made the greatest impression on John Quincy.

"Paris afternoon, alone . . . Mr. Jefferson, at Paris, in the forenoon . . . Dined at Mr. Jefferson's," he recorded in his diary.[41] On January 29, 1785, he was with the Virginian when Jefferson learned of the death of his two-year-old daughter, Lucy Elizabeth. "He looks much afflicted," John Quincy noted. "He has a great deal of sensibility." Jefferson treated him as his intellectual equal, something that the younger man found intoxicating. "Spent the evening with Mr. Jefferson whom I love to be with, because he is a man of very extensive learning, and pleasing manners."[42]

As for Jefferson's opinion of John Quincy Adams, "This young gentleman is I think very promising. To a vast thirst after useful knowledge, he adds a facility in acquiring [it]," he wrote his friend James Monroe. "What his judgment may be, I am not well enough acquainted with him to decide, but I expect it is good, and much hope it [is so], as he may become a valuable and useful citizen."[43]

In the winter of 1784–1785, talk around the Adamses' dining table turned to the question of John Quincy's future. Abigail was very much of the opinion that he should return to America and complete his education at Harvard and from thence proceed to the study of law. He had been in Europe too long already and was possibly becoming infected with its pretensions and licentiousness, she declared.[44] John Adams was conflicted. His friend Elbridge Gerry had written that he, John, was to be appointed American minister to the Court of St. James's. He would very much have liked to keep his son by his side as secretary and confidant, but he also knew that if John Quincy was to become an "ornament" to his country, he would have to establish himself as an authentic American. Like his father, John Quincy was of two minds. As he noted in his diary, he had spent seven years immersed in the glories of Europe: its incomparable art, music, and theater; its intelligentsia; and its sexual freedom. He was now faced with the prospect of returning to his socially and artistically primitive homeland, where he would exchange the sophistication of Leyden for the rusticity of Harvard. "[T]o return and spend one or two years in the pale of a college subjected to all the rules which I have so long been freed from," he confided to his diary, "then to plunge into the dry and tedious study of the law for three years, and afterwards not [to] expect . . . to bring myself into notice under three or four years more, if ever; it is really a prospect somewhat discouraging for a youth of my ambition (for I have ambition, though I hope its object is laudable)."[45] There was finally a romantic regret: he would be forsaking the company of the lovely and charming Nancy Dumas. Later, he would confide to his aunt Cranch that his heartstrings had been severely plucked.[46]

But John Quincy recognized that his and his family's status in European society was something of an anomaly; there was a financial if not cultural disconnect.

His father had been received and feted because of his intellect and his diplomatic status. On his own he could never have maintained a European lifestyle. Young Adams was well aware that he and his siblings would not be heirs to a great estate; they would have to make their own way in the world. "My father has been so much taken up all his lifetime with the interests of the public that his own fortune has suffered by it; so that his children will have to provide for themselves; which I shall never be able to do if I loiter away my precious time in Europe."[47] Financial independence above all else! he told himself. In truth, while John Quincy sometimes dreamed of a life of letters, he had also been bitten by the bug of public acclaim. His parents had labored to convince him that he was a person of destiny, and he had come to believe it. "My country has over me an attractive power which I do not understand," he confided to his cousin Billy Cranch.[48]

In due course, John Adams wrote Harvard president Joseph Willard, proposing that the college admit his eldest son. John Quincy's attainments at the University of Leyden should have entitled him to be admitted—after passing the appropriate examinations—as a junior or senior, his father argued. He expressed the hope that his son would be tested in French, "with which language he is more familiar than his own," but he understood that that was probably not possible.[49] John admitted to the irregularity of his son's education. "He will be found awkward in speaking Latin . . . [but] I know not where you would find anybody his superior in Roman and English history," he wrote. "Despite translating in Aristotle's *Poetricks* [sic] and Plutarch's *Lives*, he is deficient in Greek. For mathematics and physics, he has had to depend on me," John wrote. "He is studious enough and emulous enough, and when he comes to mix with his new friends and young companions, he will make his way well enough."[50] At the same time, John sought to enlist the aid of Benjamin Waterhouse, his young friend from his and John Quincy's days in Leyden. Dr. Waterhouse had been named Harvard's first Hersey Professor of the Theory and Practice of Physic at the recently founded Harvard Medical School. In due course, Willard wrote back that the Board of Overseers had agreed that John Quincy should be admitted upon examination "into one of the higher classes in this University free from all extra expense to you." The offer of free tuition was, Willard wrote, in acknowledgment of John Adams's contributions to his college and his country.[51]

In April 1785, on the eve of John Quincy's departure for America, Abigail wrote her sister Mary, "I must request you to take care to provide whatever is necessary for him and to have the same care of him that I would take for yours." To cover any and all expenses associated with John Quincy's education, Mary should draw on Cotton Tufts. She then wrote Tufts, notifying him that when not at Harvard, her son was to reside with the Shaws in Haverhill, and he was to cover all expenses. Though John Quincy "has been a witness to the pomp and splendor of courts, he is I hope republican enough to leave these ideas in their native soil and to exhibit an example of prudence and frugality which he knows to be very necessary."[52]

5

Harvard

John Quincy departed Paris on May 12, 1785, for Lorient, where he booked passage on a French packet headed for America. On the twenty-first, the *Courier de l'Amérique*, ninety-six feet at the keel and two hundred tons in weight, set sail. Comfortably situated in the roundhouse—an apartment on the captain's deck—young Adams had had to bring with him only pillows and sheets plus his own wine. Passengers were allowed one mattress and two trunks. He was eligible to dine always at the captain's table.[1] The voyage proceeded smoothly.

Later, John Quincy would reflect on his European experiences as a youth: "There is a character of romantic wildness about the memory of my travels in Europe from 1778 to 1785 which gives to it a tinge as if it was the recollection of something in another world. Life was new, everything was surprising, everything carried with it a deep interest. It is almost surprising to me now that I escaped from the fascination of Europe."[2] On another occasion, however—perhaps haunted by the ghosts of his Puritan ancestors—he wrote Abigail: "If you or my father had known the *moral* dangers through which I passed, and from which by the mercy of Providence I escaped, I think neither of you would have had the courage to expose me to them."[3]

While John Quincy was making ready to traverse the Atlantic, John, Abigail, and Nabby prepared to cross the English Channel. In May the patriarch of the family had finally received his commission as America's first minister to Great Britain.[4] The debate in Congress over Adams's nomination had been stormy. Southerners expressed doubt that he would work to secure compensation for enslaved people seized by the British during the war. Several of his letters castigating Franklin and Vergennes had been published. The pro-French faction in Congress did not trust him. One of its leaders, James Madison, wrote to Jefferson that the New Englander's correspondence was "not remarkable for anything unless it be a display of vanity, his prejudice against the French Court, and his venom against Doctor Franklin."[5] At this point, Madison had never met Adams. The best Jefferson could do was provide a backhanded compliment: "He [Adams] hates Franklin, he hates Jay, he hates the French, he hates the English." Jefferson conceded Adams's vanity and "want of taste." But "[n]otwithstanding all this he has a sound head on substantial points. . . . His dislike of all parties, and all men, by balancing his prejudices, may give the same fair play to his reason as would a general benevolence of temper."[6] The Virginians were being somewhat unfair. In 1783, Adams had recommended either John Jay or Francis Dana for the British post. Jay had in turn recommended Adams.[7]

The Adamses reached London in late May and rented a large town house on a corner of Grosvenor Square; among their neighbors was Lord North. Just a short walk from Hyde Park, the house featured three floors for the family, a kitchen in the basement, and quarters for the servants on the fourth floor. To her immense gratification, Nabby was asked by her father to act as his personal secretary. In due course John was presented to the king. Nervous and stiff, he proffered his credentials and expressed the hope that, despite the hostilities just ended, there could be peace and amity between America and its former mother country. George III expressed a similar wish and then bowed stiffly, indicating that Adams was dismissed.[8] Abigail accompanied her husband and was presented to the king and Queen Charlotte. She subsequently wrote John Quincy that she could not compete with any of the company "in richness of attire," but that "I know I will not strike my colors to many of them."[9]

No sooner had they parted than John Quincy and Nabby began an intense six-month correspondence that revealed how close they had become. Having just taken the road to Lorient, John Quincy wrote his sister: "You know by experience what it is to leave, for a long, we know not how long, a time those we love . . . you will . . . imagine, that I shall never set down this day as one of my happy days."[10] "Every day, hour, and minute, your absence *mon cher frere*, pains me more and more," Nabby wrote John Quincy in July. "I have got settled . . . in our own house in this place. . . . But then, I would walk, my brother is gone. I would ride, my brother is gone. I would retire to my chamber. Alas, I meet him not there. I would meet him in his apartment—but where is it?"[11]

In London, John busied himself trying to make contacts with influential government figures and merchants. He had to look after the day-to-day concerns of American citizens living in and trading with Great Britain. He hoped to sign a commercial treaty with his host country, but the newly formed government headed by William Pitt the Younger was in no mood to allow the rebellious Americans to once again taste the fruits of empire trade. Everyone Adams encountered, whether government officials or private citizens, treated him with the "same uniform tenor of dry decency and cold civility."[12]

John and Abigail continued their close relationship with Thomas Jefferson, who had been named U.S. minister to France at the same time Congress had selected Adams for the British post. Adams and Jefferson's correspondence was cordial; both men seemed to see eye to eye on the major issues of the day. Abigail's letters to Jefferson and his to her were warm, affectionate, and gossipy.

They exchanged gifts and even shopped for one another. Jefferson was good enough to procure some French corsets for Nabby.[13] In March 1786, Jefferson spent six weeks in England, summoned there by Adams to cosign a treat of commerce with Portugal. In 1787, John and Abigail played host to Jefferson's eight-year-old daughter, Mary, or Polly as she was called, until Jefferson could come from Paris to fetch her. The little girl arrived frightened and disoriented, her only companion a fourteen-year-old black servant girl named Sally Hemings. Abigail took the child under her wing, caring for her as one of her own.[14]

"What a rage for painting has taken possession of the whole family," Nabby wrote John Quincy in late 1785. John Singleton Copley had painted John Adams's portrait in 1783, when the latter had been in England recuperating. He was a frequent visitor at Grosvenor Square and would depict Adams again. The young American artist Mather Brown actually lived with the Adamses for a time. He rendered portraits of both Abigail and Nabby. Both women—Abigail in her early forties, and Nabby barely twenty—appear attractive and intelligent. In his Copley portrait, John appears as he wished: serious, respectable, intelligent—the essence of a diplomat. Nabby wrote her brother that the portrait was "a very tasty picture . . . whether a likeness or not."[15]

In the wake of Nabby's breakup with her suitor Royall Tyler, Colonel William Stephens Smith, her father's secretary at the American legation, was paying her marked attention. The thirty-year-old soldier, a genuine hero of the Revolutionary War, cut a dashing figure; he was literally tall, dark, and handsome. The ladies found him polite, charming, and self-effacing. Smith seemed happier walking with Abigail and Nabby, reading to them, and accompanying them to the theater than in doing anything else, Abigail reported. Both she and John became his advocates. By early 1786, Nabby and Smith were engaged. Married that spring, they presented John and Abigail with their first grandchild, William Steuben Smith, eleven months later.[16]

Abigail missed John Quincy—his wit, his intellect, his worldliness—though she would never admit the last. But she had reasons other than her eldest son's education for wanting to him return to Massachusetts—namely the care and feeding of her two other sons. Before she and Nabby had departed for Europe, Abigail had despaired of their education. There was no doubt about their determination to achieve. Braintree, however, was unable to maintain a schoolmaster in wartime, and there was not a boarding school that suited Abigail. Her brother-in-law John Shaw was reputed to have had great success in preparing boys for entry into Harvard. She did not like Shaw, a Calvinist minister, but she felt she had no choice. So prior to her departure for Europe, she had agreed to terms and deposited fourteen-year-old Charles and twelve-year-old Thomas at the Shaw home in Haverhill. "I have done the best I could with them," she told John.[17]

Thomas seemed a reserved, conventional boy, Aunt Shaw wrote, "and he never thinks of setting down out of his school room, but with us." Charles was another matter. Aunt Shaw again: "They have been two quarters to dancing school, and they both dance excellently, but Mr. Charles exquisitely. You know what an ear he has for music. . . . I find the misses all like to have him for a partner."[18] And then subsequently Abigail learned from her sister that Charles had fallen in love. She was horrified. No son of hers would form any attachment to a member of the opposite sex "until years have matured their judgment, and learning has made them wise. . . . No passion but for science, and no mistress but literature."[19] Subsequent reports from the Shaws and the boys themselves reassured Abigail, but there was nothing for Charles and Thomas like immediate family. John Quincy could reconnect with his brothers at Haverhill and, after enrolling at Harvard, pave the way for them.[20]

On the eighteenth of July, the *Courier de l'Amérique* deposited John Quincy Adams and his trunks on the docks at New York Harbor. The city was then the seat of American government under the Articles of Confederation. Johnny spent the next month basking in the attention of the most prominent figures in American politics and society. He delivered letters to Secretary of Foreign Affairs John Jay and Elbridge Gerry, a member of the Massachusetts delegation to Congress and a fast friend of the Adamses. The president of Congress, Richard Henry Lee, invited John Quincy to lodge with him while he was in New York and introduced him to fellow Virginian James Monroe. One ball and soiree followed another. At a dinner at Governor George Clinton's, John Quincy met Don Diego de Gardoqui, the Spanish minister to the United States. Johnny credited all this attention to the reputation and influence of his father, but he was flattered. And, in truth, his manners, knowledge, and travel experience were as responsible for his reception as his father's reputation, which in some cases was actually a minus.[21]

In the middle of John Quincy's visit to New York, a friend from his days in France arrived from Philadelphia. Jacques Le Ray de Chaumont, the son of Franklin's landlord at Passy, was in the United States on a personal tour of the country. In mid-August, the young Frenchman proposed that they travel together by horseback to Boston. John Quincy agreed and soon learned that the Dutch ambassador, Pieter Johan van Berckel, had an animal for sale. The asking price was an intimidating fifty pounds. John Quincy considered taking the stage but decided against it. He would not get to see as much of the countryside, and American coaches were notorious for overturning.[22]

Adams, Chaumont, and a servant made their way slowly northward in the summer heat through the Hudson Valley and into Connecticut. In New Haven the president of Yale, Ezra Stiles, played host and gave them a tour of the college. The institution's library, of which Stiles was inordinately proud, "was neither as large or as elegant as your Pappa's," John Quincy subsequently wrote Nabby.[23] He recalled with amusement Jefferson's comment on Stiles that he was "an uncommon instance of the deepest learning without a spark of genius."[24] In Hartford, John Quincy found the poet, lawyer, and leading light of the Connecticut Wits, John Trumbull. Trumbull, who had studied law with John Adams from 1773 to 1774, presented his young guest with a copy of *McFingal*, an epic poem satirizing the blunders of the British during the Revolutionary War. In a local bookshop, John Quincy purchased *The Conquest of Canäan*, an epic poem celebrating the birth of America by Timothy Dwight, who would succeed Stiles as president of Yale. Adams was thrilled with these examples of an emerging American literature. "These are the two pieces in which Americans have endeavored most to soar as high as European bards," he noted in his diary.[25] Late on the night of August 25, Adams and Chaumont finally reached Boston.

"No person who had not experienced it can conceive how much pleasure there is in returning to our country after an absence of 6 years, especially when it was left at the time of life that I did," John Quincy noted in his diary. He sought out his great-aunt and -uncle, Elizabeth and Isaac Smith. He dined with his uncle Richard Cranch and was united with his cousins Betsy and Lucy.[26] "We sat and looked at one another," he subsequently reported to Nabby. "I could not speak, and they could only ask now and then a question concerning you. How much more expressive this silence, than anything we could have said."[27] Charles came down from Cambridge; the fifteen-year-old had been admitted to Harvard as a freshman some six weeks earlier. One of John Quincy's duties was to deliver a letter from his father to Samuel Adams. The old patriot was deeply affected. "The child whom I led by the hand with a particular design, I find is now become a promising youth," he subsequently wrote John. "God bless the lad! If I was instrumental at that time of enkindling sparks of patriotism in his tender heart, it will add to my consolation in the latest hour."[28]

John Quincy's aunt Mary and his cousin Betsy were entranced with him. "I am pleased when I look at him to trace the features of both his parents so plainly in his face and more of yours my dear Aunt than either of your other children," Betsy wrote Abigail. "When we hear him converse, we think 'tis the language of experience."[29] Aunt Cranch found her nephew somewhat intimidating. "He enters into characters with a penetration that astonished me," she wrote Abigail. "If I had anything in my disposition that I wished to hide, I would not be acquainted with him. He is formed a statesman. I shut him out of the room when I want to work. I can do none when he is in it. I can do nothing but look at him."[30]

As it turned out, President Willard was not as impressed with the young man as either the members of Congress or his family. On the last day of September 1785, John Quincy made his way to Cambridge. Before keeping his appointment with Willard, he toured the Harvard campus. The library, he recorded in his diary, was singularly unimpressive. Indeed, the best the college had to offer physically, it seemed, was a series of portraits painted by John Singleton Copley. His meeting with the president was disappointing. After testing him briefly in Latin and Greek, Willard declared the young man deficient in both. It was decided that he would spend the winter months in Haverhill, studying with his uncle, the learned reverend. He could be examined again in the spring, and if he passed, he would be enrolled as a third-year student in the session beginning in April. In truth, John Quincy and his parents had anticipated as much.[31]

John Quincy dallied in Braintree for a period, visiting friends and relatives. He was overcome with nostalgia at the site of the saltbox house in which he had been born and raised. And then it was on to Haverhill, a veritable metropolis compared to Braintree. A bustling town of some twenty-four hundred souls, Haverhill hosted a shipyard, several tanneries, and a thriving market. His home for the next six months was the parsonage of the First Parish Church (Congregationalist) of Haverhill, a substantial white-columned house situated at the top of the main street. The first thing Reverend Shaw did was to take John Quincy to see his thirteen-year-old brother, Thomas. John Quincy subsequently described the scene in a letter to Nabby. "Here's somebody wants to see you," Shaw announced. Tommy, six years old when John Quincy had departed for Europe, looked up but said nothing. "Don't you know this person?" his uncle asked. "I believe I do," said Tom. "I guess it's brother John."[32]

By mid-October, John Quincy was settled in and deep into his studies. Over the next four months, he would translate the entire New Testament from the Greek and several volumes of Xenophon's *Cyropaedia*. He felt more versed in Latin, so he translated four books of Horace's poetry. His favorite, however, was Virgil. The Reverend Shaw's expertise was not limited to the classics. He had his nephew pursue Isaac Watts's *Logic: or the Right Use of Reason in the Enquiry After*

Truth (1725), John Locke's *Essay Concerning Human Understanding*, and a selection of works on astronomy.[33] His aunts thought their nephew obsessed and expressed concern about his health. John Quincy never retired before one o'clock in the morning, Aunt Shaw observed to his sister. "His candle goeth not out by night," Aunt Shaw wrote Nabby; "I really fear he will ruin his eyes."[34] Aunt Cranch, to Abigail: "He has not I believe one vacan[t] moment. . . . Neither the gaieties of life nor the most pressing invitations can allure him from the grand object he has in pursuit. I was almost afraid to let our children visit Haverhill this vacancy [vacation] least it should interrupt him."[35]

John Quincy was indeed studious, but not unusually so. He labored well into the night, but he slept into the late morning because he found the household too restless and noisy for him to study earlier in the day. "I would warn you against the danger of keeping much company," John had written his son. "It consumes one's time insensibly, and young as you are, you will have none to spare."[36] But keep company he did and plenty of it. Judging from his diary, John Quincy became a veritable fixture in the social life of the town's upper-class youth. When Haverhill's Baptist minister launched a campaign against dancing, John Quincy led the counterattack. There were teas, horseback rides, and fishing during the days and socials and dances in the evenings. The winter months featured unchaperoned sleigh rides, although, as he later recalled with amusement, these outings were generally chaste, as the participants were wrapped in layers of clothing against the cold. In truth, it was the company of Haverhill's young women that drove him out of doors and not the need for stimulating conversation. Of that, he found little: "The way we have here of killing time in large companies appears to me most absurd and ridiculous," he confided to his diary. "All must be fixed down in chairs looking at one another like a puppet show and talking some commonplace phrases."[37]

It was in Haverhill that young Adams first fell hard in love. Anna (Nancy) Hazen had been boarding with the Shaws for the previous twelve months when John Quincy arrived on the scene. The seventeen-year-old was attractive if not beautiful, charismatic, and fine figured.[38] Her uncle and guardian, General Moses Hazen, was frequently away on business, and the Shaw household served as a home for his niece when he was away. Alternately repelled and attracted by what he saw in Nancy, young Adams soon found he could think of nothing else. "She seems to have engrossed the attentions of almost every youth in Haverhill," he wrote. "The girl has surely something bewitching in her, for she treats them all very ill."[39] He soon found every excuse to be in her company.

Not surprisingly, John Quincy Adams's diary began to paint a more generous portrait of Miss Nancy: "She is not a regular beauty, but has one of the most expressive countenances, I have ever seen; her shape is uncommonly fine, and her eye seems to have magic in it."[40] There was no denying that the young lady was at times a coquette. "She asserts in the most positive manner that . . . [she] is entirely free from any engagement," but left the constant impression that she was on the verge of forming a connection. "Yet her heart is kind, tender and benevolent; and was she sensible of the pain she causes, she would be the first to condemn herself." Best of all to a young man of such self-importance, Nancy Hazen stood instruction and correction without complaining.[41] John knew that he was in no position to support a wife, but his hormones raged. "When our reason is at variance with our heart, the mind cannot be in a pleasing state," he observed to his diary.[42] When Nancy was absent, John Quincy pined for her; when she was present, he could barely control himself: "Does not reason alone suffice to show that when the passions are high and the blood is warm, it is impossible to make a choice with the prudence necessary?"[43] To make matters worse, the object of his desire continued to flirt. "I have never seen Nancy coquet it quite so much," he complained in early December; "she seemed really determined to outstrip herself."[44] He became increasingly embittered and misogynistic. "Most of our damsels are like portraits in crayons, which at a distance look well, but if you approach near them, are vile daubings," he complained.[45] His cousin Betsy was repelled. "He is monstrously severe with the follies of mankind, upon our sex particularly, but 'tis not only our follies he condemns."[46] His sister was equally outraged. When he wrote Nabby commenting on the vacuousness of Haverhill's damsels, she rebuked him. Young women were not afforded the same educational and travel opportunities as young men, she observed. "A gentleman who is severe against the ladies is also on every principle impolitic," she replied. "His character is soon established for a morose, severe, ill-natured fellow."[47]

The Shaws eventually put an end to their nephew's sufferings by sending Nancy to board at another Haverhill household in early February 1786. Their young guest was fond of keeping late hours, which disrupted the routine of the household, Elizabeth explained to Nabby. She was a very attractive girl, too attractive, but she lacked "those sentiments of sincerity, delicacy, and dignity of manners essential to the female character." And as for John Quincy, "His time is not yet come."[48] "Her going away, has given me pleasure with respect to myself," he recorded in his diary, "as she was the cause of many disagreeable little circumstances to me."[49] He was nevertheless moved to write "An Epistle to Delia" as he struggled to accept that he could not be Nancy Hazen's lover: "Let Poets boast in smooth and labored strains / Of unfelt passions and pretended pains / To my rude numbers, Delia now attend / Nor view me, as a lover, but a friend."[50]

Just after the New Year, Adams received word from Harvard that he should make an appointment as soon as possible to be examined because the new term would commence in March rather than in April. "Since the first of January, I have not, upon an average, been four hours in a week (Sundays excepted) out of Mr. Shaw's house," he wrote Nabby in March.[51] He was in truth not sad to leave Haverhill. He admired the Shaws but found the life they led monotonous and unrewarding. "The family I am in," he wrote, "presents as perfect a scene of happiness as I ever saw. . . . A life of tranquility is to them a life of bliss. It could not be so to me. Variety is my theme." He craved a life of adventure, he confided to his diary, the valleys and mountains, the pains and pleasures of it.[52] There was another reason to part company with the Shaws; he had discovered that his aunt Elizabeth and cousin Betsy had secretly been reading his diaries and reporting back to his mother. "Upon my word," Elizabeth wrote Nabby, "I was never so afraid of any young man in my life. These journals of [h]is are a continual spy upon our action and your brother is exceedingly severe upon the foibles of mankind."[53] When John complained that his relatives had violated his privacy, Elizabeth retorted that the journal he kept was a constant spy on them. The mutual accusations did not lead to an open breach, however. John Quincy and the Shaws would part on good terms. Elizabeth reported to Abigail that her nephew was kind, generous, loving, and charming. He had his eccentricities: "He had imbibed some curious notions and was rather peculiar in some of his opinions, and a little too decisive, and tenacious of them. Mr. Thomas said to him one day, 'I think, brother, you seem to differ most always from everyone else in company.'" But he seemed to know his faults and weaknesses and was engaged in a constant struggle to control them. "His father is his (Delphic) Oracle. There never was a son who had a greater veneration for a father." And never was there a closer or more astute student of the customs, peoples, laws, and manners of the places he visited. "In him I see the wise politician, the good statesman, and the patriot in embryo."[54]

John Quincy made the journey from Haverhill to Cambridge on March 14, 1786. The next morning, he presented himself to President Willard at his house to be examined. Willard, four tutors, three professors, and the college librarian—the redoubtable James Winthrop—put the questions. He was called upon to parse Latin and Greek verbs. He was compelled to translate several stanzas of Homer, which, according to his own account, he did very indifferently. There were questions on geology and inquiries as to the principal theses in Watts's *Logic* and Locke's *Understanding*. Thereupon, President Willard ushered him into an adjoining room and disappeared for a quarter of an hour. Upon his return, he declared, "Adams, you are admitted."[55] John Quincy was then required, as all entering students were, to sign a contract with a bondsman who agreed to pay two hundred ounces of silver if Adams did not meet the expenses of his room and board.

Upon learning that his eldest son had been admitted to his alma mater, an elated John Adams wrote from London: "You will find a pleasure and improvements equal to your expectations. You are now among magistrates and ministers, legislators and heroes, ambassadors, and generals. . . . You are breathing now in the atmosphere of science and literature. . . . Every visit you make to the chamber or study of a scholar, you learn something."[56] This would generally be true, but his first night at college, John Quincy experienced another side of life at Harvard. "The sophomore class had what is called [in] College, a high-go," he recorded in his diary. This involved all the students gathering in one of the member's chambers and getting as drunk as they could. Several "then sallied out and broke a number of windows for three of the tutors." They then staggered back to their chambers and fell into their various beds. "Such are the great achievements of many of the sons of Harvard; such the delights of many of the students here," Adams declared.[57]

President Willard had been informed by John Shaw and Cotton Tufts that their nephew wished to reside in the college. On the twenty-second, he summoned John Quincy and informed him, "Adams, you may live with Sir Ware, Bachelor of Arts." John Quincy was pleased with the pairing; Henry Ware, studying for his master's degree, had an excellent reputation in the college and occupied commodious chambers on an upper-floor corner apartment in Hollis Hall. With President Willard himself, John Quincy was less pleased—pompous, rigid, and unsociable, young Adams found him. Underclassmen were to be called by their surname alone, no exceptions. Tutors who dared employ the prefix "Mr." were severely reprimanded. Postgraduates were rewarded with the title "Sir." Willard had two students boarding with him, John Quincy reported, but he did not condescend to speak with either of them.[58]

Although no sufferer of fools, John Quincy was generally a hail-fellow-well-met at Harvard. As his aunt noted, he kept his curmudgeonly self to his diary, letters, and confidential conversations. During his last year at Harvard, he would enjoy the security and companionship of family. John Quincy left Henry Ware's lodgings to room with his contemporaries. His cousin Billy Cranch lived with him in Hollis Hall during his senior year. "Master John's chamber is on the south side of the entry next to Harvard," Richard Cranch wrote Abigail, "and commands a fine prospect of Charlestown and Boston and the extensive fields between. Master Billy's chamber is on the other side of the entry fronting the common and has a fine view of the country towards Watertown." Charles Adams resided on the first floor, his room next to Holden Chapel.[59] Thomas would join them as a freshman in the fall term of 1786. Mary Cranch furnished John Quincy's quarters with furniture from his parents' house. "Four more promising youth are seldom seen," she wrote her sister.[60]

Soon after he was situated at Harvard, John Quincy wrote his father that his time at the Shaws' had been well spent. It wasn't so much that he had been deficient in Latin and Greek as that he had not read the same books as the members of the junior class he was to enter. At his examination, the only author whom he had read before returning to America and on whom he was questioned was Horace.[61] In a separate letter to Nabby, he described his course of studies and a typical weekday. Every minute of every Monday, Tuesday, and Wednesday was filled to the moment. "The rest of the week, any person that chooses may loiter away doing nothing. But a person fond of studying will never want for employment." Every morning the students were called to prayers by the college bell. One minute late and they were fined. They would then recite in Greek and Latin to the appropriate tutors and follow up with lectures on geometry, astronomy, and natural philosophy.[62] "The next year we shall be confined to mathematics, natural philosophy, and metaphysics; we shall finish Locke on the understanding and begin in Reid on the mind." (Thomas Reid, *An Inquiry into the Human Mind on the Principles of Common Sense* [1764]).[63] On Friday and Saturday there might be divinity lessons or scientific experiments. One evening each week, there was some activity outside the confines of the campus, such as dinner in Boston.

John Quincy was generally disappointed in Harvard's faculty. James Winthrop, the librarian and son of his father's tutor when he had been at Harvard, was learned and intelligent, a man "who for genius and learning, would make a figure in any part of Europe," but he was such a misanthrope that he was often unapproachable. John Quincy's favorite was Samuel Williams, Hollis Professor of Mathematics and Natural Philosophy. Indeed, algebra, geometry, and the experimental sciences, in which he had been tutored only by his father, soon became young Adams's favorite subjects.[64] The rest of the lot, he observed to his sister, were mediocre or worse. His four tutors were a disgrace to the institution: "They appear all to be in a greater necessity of going to school themselves than of giving instruction." The only one who did not try to put on airs and intimidate his students was simple-minded.[65] His Greek tutor, a Mr. Jennison, was only twenty-four and "so ignorant in Greek, that he displays it sometimes in correcting a scholar that is right, and other times suffering the most absurd constructions to go unnoticed." Mr. Hale, the tutor in metaphysics, was "equally morose, surly and peevish to all; he has got the nickname of 'the cur.'" The tutors, who had the power to impose fines on their students, were notorious for playing favorites.[66]

The students would often retaliate by stamping their feet and hissing when the tutors' backs were turned or by breaking the windows in their quarters. "It seems almost to be a maxim among the Governors of the College, to treat the students pretty much like brute beasts," John Quincy noted in his diary.[67] Both Abigail and Nabby begged him to show proper respect to President Willard, his professors, and his tutors. It was not in his nature, John Quincy replied: "I could never bring my countenance or my actions to oppose the sentiments which I possessed."[68] Nevertheless, he managed to hold his tongue, at least in public, and seems to have avoided attracting the ire and ill will of his tutors and professors.

As was true of most liberal arts colleges, Harvard's real strength lay with its student body. Since 1636 the institution had been producing the cream of New England society—its clergymen, its politicians, its merchants, its teachers, and its medical doctors, or rather its scientists. For in truth medicine was so primitive in colonial and revolutionary America that an imbecile could master its so-called precepts. On June 21, John Quincy, along with William Cranch and Josiah Burge, was inducted into Phi Beta Kappa. His classmates and friends James Bridge and Nathaniel Freeman would follow soon thereafter. He characterized what would become America's preeminent fraternity of scholars as an organization "established to promote friendship and literature."[69] Members met regularly in one another's chambers to debate the major issues of the day, read poetry they had written, and socialize. In addition, he joined the AB Club, a literary society before which he regularly read essays. Among the subjects it fell to John Quincy to discuss were whether humans were born with innate reason (yes) and whether there was a connection between democracy, freedom, and education (emphatically yes). In addition, he had to support or denounce absolute democracy (echoing his father: no) and a mixed government and natural aristocracy (emphatically yes).[70]

At Harvard, John Quincy first evidenced his fascination with *Othello*, which for the Adams family as a whole was something of an obsession. The tragic and to them horrific combination of love, jealousy, sex, race, and murder was irresistible. The play itself in terms of language and acting was close to perfection, he declared, but its premises were too absurd to countenance. That Venice would grant governance to one of its island possessions to a Moor was unimaginable. That a young lady so virtuous and chaste as Desdemona would, as Brabantio expressed it, "Run from her guardage to the sooty bosom / of such a thing as him, [Othello], to fear, not to delight'" was inconceivable. The character of Iago was dramatically necessary to produce such jealousy in Othello to murder his wife, but "I never could conceive what induced the poet to take a negro for an example of jealousy."[71] After attending a performance of *Othello* in London, Abigail admitted her "disgust and horror" at seeing the "sooty" title character "touch the gentle Desdemona." (Othello was actually being played by Sarah Siddons's heavily made-up brother John Philip Kemble.)[72]

During his year and a half at Harvard, John Quincy's best friend next to Billy Cranch, whom he loved like a brother, was James Bridge. A native of Maine, Bridge was simultaneously unassuming and ambitious. He and John Quincy shared a love of literature and philosophy, and both were set on a career in the law. "As a scholar and as a gentleman, he is inferior to no one in the class, and with no one have I contracted since I entered the university, so great a degree of intimacy," the younger Adams wrote in his diary.[73]

Initially, John Quincy looked upon the members of the student body as unified in their identities as scholars of Harvard. "This evening, there were, it is said, upwards of 100 scholars out on the common, armed with clubs, to fight the people belonging to the town," he recorded in his diary the first week of classes. It seems that several evenings before, at a local tavern, a junior named Lovell had gotten into a dispute with a townsman over a girl. Blows had ensued, and both parties swore revenge. Though the student had reportedly been at fault, "this Society [Harvard's student body] . . . thinks that an insult offered to one member must be resented by all, and as in a well ordered Republic . . . immediately upon a foreign insult, they all united."[74] But he was soon disabused of the notion of Harvard as an "orderly Republic." In August he wrote his father lamenting that the four classes were virtually sealed off from one another. It was unheard of for a sophomore to associate with a senior, for example. There was every variety of young man at the college. Some, he said, did not study twelve hours in twelve months, while others were at their books almost that much in a day. Nevertheless, the coin of the realm at Harvard was scholarly attainment. Even the slackers had contempt for other slackers. Within each class there was much maneuvering for ranking and the honors to be bestowed at commencement. "In these peaceful mansions there is the same spirit of intrigue and party and as much inclination to cabal as may be discovered at courts."[75]

John Quincy's hormones were in continual conflict with his commitment to self-governance, the latter buttressed regularly by admonitions from Abigail. There was no absence of female companionship for the young men of Harvard. Dances, sleigh rides, dinners, and teas abounded. After dinner in Boston at Judge Francis Dana's, John Quincy's former mentor and companion in St. Petersburg, he wrote in his diary: "Miss Almy informed us . . . that Bridge was deeply smitten with a Miss Hall . . . and I forsooth, am the humble admirer of Miss Dixey. If personal beauty was my only object of admiration, I should certainly be in this predicament, but I must look a little further before I surrender my liberty entirely."[76] The charms of Cambridge's young ladies prompted John Quincy to versify—"You know I am now and then addicted to the rage of rhyming," he wrote Nabby.[77] In fact, poetry would become an intermittent obsession for the rest of his life.

Shortly before commencement in 1787, John Quincy's second and final year, he read an essay on the question of the propriety of forwardness in a young woman. Since the beginning of time, women had been considered inferior and subject to the will of their lord, but in turn their husbands were held responsible for their well-being in all respects. Of this, the young man approved. He noted without comment that members of the fairer sex were denied advancement in public and military affairs, their education limited to matters domestic. What he considered unfair was that they were saddled with the notion that all virtue was concentrated in their ability to protect their chastity. "If a woman preserves that, she claims esteem and respect, though [in] her mind, [it] should be corruption itself. From this system has arisen the maxim that no woman should first disclose affection for a man." Absurd! It was common knowledge that every woman "was formed with a deeper sensibility and with warmer passions than [men]."[78] In love, men and women should be perfectly equal. Surrounded by romances that were coming to fruition, John wrote his sister that he was being "supplanted" by another suitor in his attentions to a particular young lady. "[I]t is against the law for me to look at a young lady till the 20th of July 1787 [commencement], and then I suppose it will be too late."[79]

Early in the first term, Billy Cranch had bought his cousin a flute. John Quincy was delighted. He immediately joined the musical society at Harvard and began lessons. Music had always attracted him, he wrote Nabby, but he had never been settled long enough in one place to give an instrument the attention it required. Harvard's musically inclined students gathered regularly in one another's chambers to play, but the flutes and violins were so frequently out of tune, John complained, that they could play only three or four pieces at a setting. When Nabby learned that her brother had taken up the instrument, she was horrified. Charles Warren, a close family friend, had recently died of consumption, and the idea had somehow taken hold that his addiction to the flute had been responsible. "I must beg of you to lay it aside and to persuade your brothers, should they be so unwise as to [pur]sue it, to do so likewise."[80] Undaunted, he wrote back that he had found that the flute was his "greatest amusement and the chief relaxation after study, and indeed it affords me so much pleasure that I cannot think of giving it up."[81]

Harvard's senior class commenced on July 20, 1786, whereupon John Quincy, Charles, and Billy Cranch retired to Haverhill for vacation. Then, in mid-August, it was back to Cambridge. "Very busy all day in papering Charles's study," John Quincy noted in his diary on the seventeenth, "and part of mine but before we finished the paper failed us." That evening a deranged student tried to beat down

John Quincy's door. Failing in that, he jumped out a second-story window and broke his leg.[82]

While John Quincy and his classmates were struggling with their recitations, translations, and scientific experiments, the country under the Articles of Confederation was falling apart. Between 1784 and 1787, the United States experienced a severe depression. Spending by Congress and state governments dropped sharply, Britain refused to allow its former colonies to resume trade with the West Indies, the country lacked a national currency, and Congress did not have the power to regulate trade between the states, which proceeded to erect tariff barriers against one another. Congress did not even have the authority to tax, and as a result, the national government was constantly in danger of bankruptcy. Dominated by debtor groups, some state governments issued paper money, and currencies become so inflated as to be virtually worthless. In foreign affairs, the United States proved unable to enforce the terms of the Treaty of Paris. The British held on to their posts and forts in the Old Northwest and continued to intrigue with their Indian allies against America. In 1784, Spain had closed the Port of New Orleans to American farmers and merchants who had been shipping goods from the trans-Appalachian West to the East Coast via the Mississippi River. The nation even lacked a permanent capital, and Congress drifted from Philadelphia to Princeton to Annapolis to New York, prompting one humorist to suggest that the government purchase a hot-air balloon to facilitate travel.[83]

"The Commonwealth [of Massachusetts] is in a state of considerable fermentation," John Quincy reported to his diary on September 7, 1786. "Last week at Northampton, in the County of Hampshire, a body of armed men to the number of three or four hundred, prevented the Court of Common Pleas from sitting, and bruised the high-sheriff dangerously."[84] Thus began what became known as Shays' Rebellion. Massachusetts was economically, socially, and geographically divided between merchants, shippers, bankers, and professional people living mostly in the state's eastern cities and subsistence farmers residing in the rural interior. In the mid-1780s, debt-ridden farmers and artisans began flooding the state legislature with petitions demanding tax relief and the issuance of paper money. The violence at Northampton erupted when the Massachusetts General Court adjourned without taking any action on the debtors' demands. Revolutionary War veteran Daniel Shays emerged as the leader of the spreading rebellion. The governor denounced the uprising but initially refused to call out the militia. In September and October, the rebels succeeded in shutting down courts in Great Barrington, Concord, and Taunton. "We are now in a perfect state of anarchy," young Adams declared. "No laws observed, and no powers to punish delinquents; if these treasonable practices, are not properly quelled, the consequences must be fatal to the Constitution [the Articles] and indeed to the Commonwealth."[85]

"This evening just before prayers about 40 horsemen, arrived here under the command of Judge Prescott [General Oliver Prescott] of Groton, in order to protect the court to-morrow, from the rioters," John Quincy noted. "There have been in the course of the day fifty different reports flying about, and not one of them true."[86] He later recalled that "a military mania seized upon the undergraduates." The juniors and seniors formed themselves into a militia and named it the Marti-Mercurian Band, the name of a similar troop that had been formed during the Revolutionary War. Despite his revulsion at the insurrection, John Quincy deigned to join. Hearing that Shays and fellow conspirator Job Shattuck were in the area, the student-soldiers demanded to be let in on the hunt. They were refused.[87]

Shattuck was captured and sent to Boston for trial, but Shays escaped. At the head of several hundred rebels, he advanced on the arsenal at Springfield. Blocked by a local militia force, the insurrectionists turned north and east. On the night of February 4–5, 1787, Shays's forces were surprised and routed by an army of some three thousand men commanded by Continental Army general Benjamin Lincoln. Shays and his followers fled to neighboring states.[88] Over the course of the next two years, Shays, Shattuck, and four thousand of their followers were pardoned.

John Quincy's mother, who was speculating in depreciated government promissory notes to Revolutionary War veterans, was horrified at Shays' Rebellion. "I could not refrain shedding tears over . . . my countrymen who had so nobly fought and bled for freedom, tarnishing their glory, loosening the bands of society, introducing anarchy, confusion, and despotism," she wrote her eldest son upon learning of the insurrection. History taught, she declared, that popular tyranny was always followed by a dictatorship.[89] John Quincy was equally horrified, initially placing most of the blame on what he termed the lazy, shiftless, ignorant mob that could not live within its means.

In September, in the midst of the crisis, he and Billy Cranch had engaged in a debate in the Harvard Yard attended by some four hundred people. The topic was "Whether inequality among the citizens, be necessary to the preservation of liberty of the whole." Absolutely, John Quincy declared. Echoing his father, he asserted that some individuals were more virtuous than others; that was why America was a nation of laws. If every scoundrel were allowed to ignore and alter the law at his whim, chaos would ensue: "Too great a degree of equality among the citizens is prejudicial to the liberty of the whole; the present alarming situation of our own country will, I think, afford us a sufficient proof."[90] In time, the conservative hotspur modified his views. Protests against injustices, real or perceived, were inevitable in a democracy and probably healthy as long as they were kept within bounds, he would observe. Mirroring other nationalists of the time, including his father, Alexander Hamilton, and James Madison, John Quincy concluded that the Articles of Confederation were fatally flawed. There must be a stronger government in place capable of making and enforcing the laws of the nation and one strong and yet flexible enough to mediate between the haves and have-nots.[91]

In early October, the Adams boys and their cousin Billy departed Cambridge for Braintree to spend their fall break. "'But' ask you, 'how did you spend your time at Braintree during that fortnight?'" he wrote Nabby. "Why Madam, I read three or four volumes of history, and Burlamaqui upon law [Jean-Jacques Burlamaqui's *Principals of Natural and Politic Law* (1763)]; I wrote a few letters. . . . I went fowling once or twice. . . . I picked off a few tunes and played them on the flute." About this latter activity, she should not worry, he told his sister, who together with Abigail continued to insist that playing the flute would damage his lungs. He had consulted "several persons used to that instrument," and they had told him that unless an individual was of a "very slender constitution," moderate use would have no ill effects.[92]

The young gentlemen began the winter term on November 1, but it was short-lived. Cambridge and environs endured several snowstorms so massive that no firewood could be brought in from the countryside for three weeks. On Wednesday, December 13, all students were dismissed for the remainder of the term. John Quincy and his friend Bridge decided to stay in Cambridge and continue their studies on their own. They kept their chambers in the college and boarded with the Hollis Professor of Divinity, Edward Wigglesworth. "This gentleman is equally free from the supercilious frown of the President, and the distant reserve of a tutor."[93] Even better, there were two interesting young women in the household—the professor's niece, Katherine Jones, and his daughter, Margaret "Peggy" Wigglesworth.

In February 1787, Adams and Bridge's classmates began to drift back into town, and their final term at Harvard got underway. Determined to finish at the top of his class and to garner as many awards as possible at commencement, John Quincy studied himself into ill health. His aunt Cranch duly reported to Abigail: "He looked so pale & wan when he came home this spring that I was not a little alarmed about him. He has lost so much flesh within these nine months that I have been obliged to take in his waistcoats a full quarter of a yard."[94] Abigail in turn wrote him with a diagnosis and a remedy. It was reported that he was suffering from "a swimming in the head." She had suffered the same malady when she was in Holland, she said. "I would advise you upon the approach of spring to lose some blood; the headaches and flushing in your face with which you used to be troubled was occasioned by too great a quantity of blood in your head." And he should get out and get some exercise "as you and I both are inclined to corpulence."[95] John ignored her initially, but then decided he needed to do something—to get some exercise if not to lose some blood. "I have begun to take much exercise, from 9 to 1 and from 3 to 6, I was rambling about with my gun [fowling]," he reported to his diary.[96]

In late January 1787, John Adams submitted his resignation as U.S. minister to the Court of St. James's. He was stuck in diplomatic and social gridlock; British merchants and their representatives in Parliament were quite satisfied with the status quo. Cheaply produced English manufactured goods flowed into America and dominated the market. What incentive was there to open the British West Indies to the avaricious Yankees? All of his and Abigail's sons were in America. Charles was eleven when he had last seen John. He was now sixteen and in his sophomore year at Harvard. Thomas had been separated from his parents for four years. There were also career considerations. John believed that his political destiny lay in the United States.

Even before Shays' Rebellion, he had like other American nationalists come to the conclusion that the Articles of Confederation had to be fundamentally altered or even replaced by a new federal charter. Soon after taking up his duties in Great Britain, John had begun work on his *A Defence of the Constitutions of the Government of the United States of America*. The first of two volumes would be published in the spring of 1787 on the eve of the Constitutional Convention. Since arriving in Europe in 1778, Adams had been following the debate among French philosophes concerning the best methods to move France away from monarchism toward some form of republican government. In part, the *Defence* was a response to the political theories of French minister and reformer Anne Robert Jacques Turgot, Baron de l'Aulne, to the political philosopher Marie-Jean-Antoine-Nicolas de Caritat, Marquis de Condorcet, and indirectly to their friend Benjamin Franklin.[97] All were advocates of a government composed of a one-house legislature—a form of government, they argued, that was closest to a pure democracy. All men, argued Condorcet, "were endowed with sensation, capable of reasoning upon and understanding his interests, and of acquiring moral ideas."[98] In 1778, Turgot, in a public letter addressed to the British radical Richard Price, had criticized the state constitutions then being constructed in America for their insistence on adopting the British model of a bicameral legislature and a system of checks and balances. In doing so they were thwarting the "general will."[99] In his treatise, Adams sided with the more conservative French reformers who looked to England with its bicameral legislature as a model. In essence, Adams argued that the United States should adopt a constitution that closely resembled that of the Commonwealth of Massachusetts, a document largely of his own creation.

Adams also disagreed with those like Turgot, Franklin, and James Madison who believed that a political consensus could be achieved and maintained in a republic. "I am not . . . of [the] opinion that the independence of our country entirely depends on a harmony and unity of sentiment," he declared.[100] He agreed with Condorcet that all human beings were endowed with an innate moral sense, but that did not mean they would always be guided by it. Indeed, in the wake of the Revolution—as individuals, states, and vested interests had repeatedly acted contrary to the common good—his optimism had waned. Human beings were selfish and self-interested, and societies would forever be divided between the haves and have-nots, Adams believed. There should certainly be one house based on direct representation, but also a second chamber representing the interests of the social and economic elite. In Adams's view, this separation was more to protect the common man from the aristocracy rather than the reverse. Natural though that aristocracy might be, "The rich, the well-born, and the able acquire an influence among the people that will soon be too much for simple, honest, and plain sense, in a house of representatives." In a unicameral legislature the wealthy and powerful would overwhelm representatives of farmers and artisans.[101]

Departing from the English Whigs, Adams argued for a strong executive armed with an absolute legislative veto. The president, the one official elected by all the people, would be able to discern and act on the interests of the nation as a whole. A strong executive would be the country's last, best hope for preventing tyranny by one class or another, one constellation of interests or another. If somehow a tyrant were chosen chief executive, the legislature would have the power of impeachment. Finally, there would be a third branch, an independent judiciary to administer the laws.[102]

The delegates who met in Philadelphia from May 25 through September 17, 1787, would produce a constitution that closely resembled the one outlined in Adams's *Defence*. Ironically, it was Adams's old colleague/adversary Benjamin Franklin who informed him of the impact the *Defence* was having. The book, he wrote, was in "such request here" that it had been "already put to press and numerous editions will speedily be abroad." As a populist, James Madison disagreed with many of Adams's arguments and conclusions, but he admitted to Jefferson that the treatise would be "a powerful engine in forming the public opinion."[103] John Quincy would have his own ideas about the new Constitution, but they would have to wait until after commencement.

* * *

JOHN QUINCY'S AUNTS FOUND him much restored in June. The trials of the winter and spring terms were over. As he had admitted to his diary, he had little to do until graduation except exercise, visit his friends and family, and read according to his interests. His aunt Shaw found him not only restored in body but altered in disposition. "Upon my word, I know not a likelier youth," she wrote Abigail. "He is much thinner than he was in Europe, but what he loses in flesh, he gains in beauty. . . . He behaved in so modest, agreeable, & pleasing a manner as if he wished to convince us that the only error which we ever suggested to him [his bullheadedness] was entirely removed."[104] In May, John Quincy learned that he was to be given a choice spot at the commencement exercise: "An English Oration, upon the importance and necessity of public faith to the well-being of a community."[105] It was one of two English orations, the highest honors to be given out. John Quincy was thrilled but apprehensive. The second had been awarded to the very talented Nathaniel Freeman. This was just the sort of exercise at which his friend so excelled. "I shall rejoice to see him perform his part with universal approbation and unbounded applause," he wrote in his diary, "yet I cannot help fearing that contrasts may be drawn which will reflect disgrace upon me."[106]

In the interim before graduation, the Adams boys stayed with the Cranches in Braintree. Billy had also been given a part, and he and John Quincy busied themselves with their respective orations. Mary was surprised and amused by John Quincy's intense anxiety at speaking before such a large and distinguished crowd. John Quincy and Billy's class had previously petitioned the Harvard Corporation to permit a private rather than a public commencement, citing the expenses involved with the latter. "My nephew walks about with his hands hung down crying 'Oh Lord! Oh Lord—I hope it will rain hard that all their white wigs may be wet who would not let us have a private commencement,'" she wrote Abigail. "Be composed said I, perform your parts well and you will find that the honor you will gain & the pleasure you will give your friends will over balance all the anxieties you have experienced."[107]

At eleven o'clock on the appointed day, several hundred invited guests and dignitaries gathered to witness the graduation ceremonies. Freshmen, sophomores, and juniors processed in first, followed by the seniors and the faculty, and then the governor and council of the commonwealth. A company of light cavalry was drawn up before the meeting hall. Everyone in his place, the orations, recitations, and syllogisms began.

John Quincy used the topic of public faith and credit to address the prevailing political and social climate in the country: "To every reflecting mind the situation of this Commonwealth for some months past must have appeared truly alarming.

On whatever side we turn our anxious eyes, the prospect of public affairs is dark and gloomy . . . the violent gust of rebellion . . . sullen discontent . . . luxury and dissipation." Principle among the causes of this state of affairs were disregard for the sanctity of contract and failure to maintain the public credit. America's economy was inescapably global. Those who argued for default on foreign debts and the wanton printing of public money were threatening the very existence of the republic, the young orator declared. Throughout history from ancient Greece and Rome to the present, states that ignored their fiscal obligations had inevitably declined and disappeared. "Shall we draw upon our country the execrations of injured foreigners? Shall we deprive the man who nobly fought and bled to establish our freedom of that subsistence which he can no longer procure. . . . [M]ay national honor and integrity distinguish the American commonwealth till the last trumpet shall announce the dissolution of the world."[108] Alexander Hamilton could not have said it better.

An amazing address from a man whose mother was speculating in depreciated government bonds. But hypocrisy aside, the speech, which was printed and widely distributed, established young Adams as a nationalist committed to the establishment of a federal government capable of vigorously conducting foreign policy, enforcing the rule of law, and promoting domestic prosperity. All of those things, he understood, would require a degree of coercion. Not all citizens of the republic were willing to sacrifice for the common good.

The Cranches had rented several rooms in a Cambridge hotel to celebrate John Quincy and William's graduation. They had food and drink brought up from Braintree and served dinner to a hundred persons, including the governor and the members of the council, and then dessert to nearly four hundred.[109]

If John Quincy shared his father's political philosophy, he also shared his vanity. His graduation oration was published with accompanying plaudits in Jeremy Belknap's *Columbian Magazine*. It was reviewed less favorably in other Massachusetts newspapers. The *Columbia Centinel* opined that more should have been expected of the son of a prominent American diplomat and observed that the honor bestowed on John Quincy more than likely stemmed from the favoritism shown him by the college authorities. The consensus was, as Johnny had feared, that Nathaniel Freeman had done a much better job. The memory of that speech and his perceived humiliation would stay with John Quincy Adams for the rest of his days.[110]

6

Law and First Love

THAT JOHN QUINCY WAS to take up the law had never been in question despite his forebodings and misgivings. It was decided that following graduation from Harvard, he would place himself in the hands of the distinguished jurist Theophilus Parsons at Newburyport. His uncles Cranch and Tufts made the necessary inquiries and settled on a fee. On July 23, John Quincy learned that Parsons had agreed to take him. "It is not without many melancholy reflections that I bid a last adieu to the walls of Harvard!" he wrote in his diary. The institution had succeeded in completing his liberal education and he had made several close friends. Perhaps the greatest benefit had been to reduce "my opinion of myself, of my acquirements, and of my future prospects, nearer to the level of truth and reality," he wrote. "I hope that in two or three years more I shall have taken down, without any violence, all the elegant castles which my imagination had built in the air over my head."[1] During the next few difficult years, those castles would indeed come crashing down, doing some violence to their architect. Two weeks before commencement on July 11, his birthday, John Quincy had confided to his diary: "This day completes my twentieth year; and yet I am good for nothing . . . three long years I have yet to study in or to qualify myself for business: and then . . . how many more years to plod along mechanically if I should live. . . . I sicken at the very idea."[2] Ah, for the glories of Europe!

In mid-August, John Quincy traveled to Newburyport to meet his new mentor and to make living arrangements. A bustling town of some five thousand souls, Newburyport was located on the south bank of the Merrimack River just a few miles inland from the ocean. It was one of the busiest entrepôts in Massachusetts, receiving shipments of wine, cloth, and gunpowder from Europe and sugar and molasses from the West Indies. The city sprawled downward from High Street to the harbor, which was generally a sea of masts. The streets in between were lined with a number of fine mansions, both brick and wood frame, belonging to the town's shipowners and merchants.[3] After meeting with Parsons and agreeing to begin his studies three weeks hence, John Quincy arranged for room and board at the home of Mrs. Martha Leathers, widow of Newburyport shipwright Joseph Leathers.[4] He found her "civil and obliging" and, most important to his studies, silent.[5]

John Quincy had as his companions in the study of law in Newburyport two former classmates, Thomas Thompson and Horatio Townsend. Another college mate, Moses Little, was living in town, studying medicine. Lawyer Parsons had John Quincy begin with William Robertson's *History of the Reign of the Emperor Charles V* to acquaint him with the feudal institutions on which much of European law was based. Then came Emmerich de Vattel's *Le droit des gens*, which proposed a system of international law rooted in natural-rights philosophy and the Golden Rule. Then followed William Blackstone's multivolume *Commentaries on the Laws of England*, a work John Quincy found well constructed and enlightening, far more than he did Edward Coke's *First Part of the Institutes of the Lawes of England*. John Quincy was well pleased with his mentor. Theophilus Parsons was a major figure in Massachusetts law and public life. "He was," the younger Adams wrote his mother, "in himself a law library and proficient in every branch. . . ." Parsons would go on to become chief justice of the state's Supreme Judicial Court. "I could not possibly have an instructor more agreeable than this gentleman."[6] At one point he asked Parsons for suggestions for nighttime reading. John Quincy should peruse the best writers on ethics, Parsons told his pupil, and consult classical philosophers such as Quintilian, but above all the leading Christian theologians. "It was necessary," he advised, "for a person going into the profession of the law to have principles strongly established: otherwise, however amiable and however honest his disposition might be, yet the necessity he is under of defending indiscriminately the good and the bad, the right and the wrong would imperceptibly lead him into universal skepticism."[7] When he was not reading, John Quincy attended the court of common pleas to listen to the area's most prominent lawyers argue their cases.

While John Quincy was studying law in Newburyport, Massachusetts, the United States was deciding whether to ratify the new Constitution. Predictably, it pitted the farmers and artisans of the interior (debtors) against the bankers, merchants, and shipbuilders of the Eastern towns (creditors). The struggle in Massachusetts was crucial, for if the state did not approve of the new national charter, it would fail. John Quincy had thought a bit about the new Constitution while at Harvard. Initially he had been somewhat skeptical. There was not enough difference between the proposed Senate and House of Representatives, he believed; both would be dominated by the rich and wellborn. He feared, he wrote his cousin

William Cranch, the birth of a new "aristocratic party." It seemed that the impression left by Shays' Rebellion had been fleeting.[8] In August 1787, John Quincy had read Jefferson's *Notes on the State of Virginia* (1784–1785) and expressed his admiration. It displayed "a great deal of learning shown without ostentation and a spirit of philosophy equally instructive and entertaining."[9] Following a conversation with Parsons, who strongly favored ratification, John Quincy noted in his diary, "Nor do I wonder at all that he should approve of it, as it is calculated to increase the influence, power and wealth of those who have any already." There would be no titles of nobility in America, but "there will be great distinctions; and those distinctions will soon be hereditary."[10] When the Massachusetts General Court—the Anti-Federalists having been placated with a promised bill of rights— ratified the Constitution, John quickly reconciled himself. "It is hard to give up a system which I have always been taught to cherish [democracy] and to confess that a free government is inconsistent with human nature," but he supposed it would all work out for the best.[11] Men on both sides of the argument seemed to be high-minded. Whatever the case, the Constitution had become the law of the land, and "I should view a man who would now endeavor to excite commotions against this plan as no better than an insurgent who took arms last winter against the courts of justice."[12]

With its five thousand inhabitants, Newburyport was not Boston, but neither was it a burg like Braintree. John Quincy was immediately welcomed into the town's thriving social life. Its young people danced, sleighed, drank tea, attended dinners, played cards and parlor games, and romanced. September 29: "In the evening I took something of a long walk with Townsend, and as I returned stopped to sup with Amory and Stacy. . . . There were three other gentlemen there; We got to singing after supper and the bottle went round with an unusual rapidity until around dozen had disappeared."[13] October 15: "At about 7 o'clock we met at the dancing hall, and from that time 'till between 3 and 4 in the morning we were continually dancing; I never saw a collection of ladies where there was comparatively so much beauty."[14]

But then with the onset of winter, with the continual snow and ice and darkness settling in by late afternoon, the black dog of depression settled upon John Quincy Adams. In truth he hated the law, but duty compelled him to spend most of his waking hours reading Blackstone and *Coke on Littleton* or attending court. The twenty-year-old was blessed/cursed with an insatiable curiosity and a very large brain. "A thousand subjects call my attention and excite my curiosity," he confided to his diary; "most of them I am obliged to pass from without noticing them at all; and the few to which I can afford any leisure, only lead me to regret that I cannot go deeper."[15] He despaired of his future. He was not at all sure that he could stay the course that his parents had set out for him. But to defy them was unthinkable. And if not the law, how would he support himself to the point where he could marry and have a family? "You know that we shall return poor," his mother had written him from London. "After college you are on your own." (At the time Abigail had just purchased five three-hundred-acre tracts of land in Vermont.)[16]

Increasingly, John Quincy became a recluse, spending night after fitful night alone in his room at Mrs. Leathers's. The Adamses' sense of purpose, destiny, and duty dissolved into nihilism. "I look forward and ask what am I to do, what am I to expect . . . nothing is the only answer. In the physical world, what are sensual gratification, what is the earth, and all it contains, what is life itself—nothing."[17] The dawn of the New Year found him positively suicidal. "All my hopes of going through the world in any other than the most contemptible manner depend upon my own exertions, and if I continue thus to trifle away my time, I shall become an object of charity or at least of pity. God of Heaven! If those are the only terms upon which life can be granted to me, oh! Take me from this world before I curse the day of my birth."[18] Nabby sensed from her brother's correspondence that something was wrong. "I am sorry to find by your letter that your spirits are so low," she wrote. Persevere! Be not afraid! "[B]ear this belief in mind—that you were designed for some high and important station upon the stage—qualify your-self to fill your part with reputation—and then aspire to that station which you esteem desirable."[19] As his sister and aunts continued to nurture him, John Quincy began to right his mental ship—at least temporarily. He finally finished Coke and returned to Blackstone. "[T]he contrast," he observed, "was like descending from a rugged, dangerous, and almost inaccessible mountain into a beautiful plain."[20] And at last, with the approach of spring, the days began to grow longer and warmer.

ONCE JOHN ADAMS SUBMITTED his resignation as minister to the Court of St. James's, he and Abigail decided to spend the rest of their time in England seeing the sights and learning what there was to learn. Abigail attended a series of lectures on electricity, magnetism, hydrostatics, optics, and pneumatics—and was thrilled. "It was like going into a beautiful country," she wrote her niece Lucy Cranch, "which I never saw before, a country which our American females are not permitted to visit or inspect."[21] In due course, John received notice that he was officially relieved of his duties. He and Abigail enjoyed a relatively uneventful Atlantic passage aboard the *Lucretia*.[22] To Adams's surprise and intense gratification, he was received as a returning hero. When the *Lucretia* docked at Boston

Harbor, it was met by a representative of Governor John Hancock, who insisted that the Adamses take temporary lodgings with him. During the next six weeks, John Adams had virtually every political and judicial post—save that of president, which had been reserved for George Washington—offered to him.[23]

John and Abigail stayed at the governor's mansion until their new house was ready for occupancy. Six months before leaving Great Britain, the couple had purchased an eighty-three-acre estate known as the Vassal-Borland place. The property had been abandoned by loyalists fleeing to Canada during the Revolution. It had passed through the hands of several owners, the most recent Nabby's jilted fiancé, Royall Tyler. The house, which became known as Peacefield, was located about a mile north of the saltbox abode in which John Quincy and his siblings had been born. Besides a large house, the property included a coach house, gardens, and an orchard. The residence, renovated and enlarged after the couple's return from Europe, was an elegant two-story structure with tall windows and a Honduras mahogany–paneled interior. John and Abigail paid six hundred pounds for the place.[24] In his instructions to Cotton Tufts, John had told him not only to purchase the Vassal-Borland estate but "every other [property] that adjoins upon me. . . . My view is to lay fast hold of the town of Braintree and embrace it with both my arms and all my might. There to live, there to die . . . and there to plant one of my sons in the profession of the law and the practice of agriculture like his father."[25]

While they were still lodging with Governor Hancock, the Adamses were reunited with their children. Charles and Thomas, both still at Harvard, came down from Cambridge and John Quincy made the trip from Newburyport. Nabby and her family had returned from England and settled in Jamaica, New York. "I was up early in the morning, and mounted my horse at about seven," read John Quincy's diary entry for June 20, 1788. He arrived in Boston about ten and found his mother at the governor's mansion. John had gone to Braintree but returned that evening. John, Abigail, and their three sons were all together for the first time in nine years. John Quincy spent the next few days helping his father unpack his books, whose purchase had in reality been a joint undertaking by both father and son. "There are a great many books which I wish very much to peruse," John Quincy lamented, "but I have not the time at present, and must certainly for some years be separated from them."[26]

In due course, John Quincy returned to Newburyport to continue his studies in Lawyer Parsons's office. He was subsequently buoyed by the arrival of his old friend James Bridge, who had persuaded Parsons to take him on as a student. The two immediately arranged to lodge together. The first week in May, they made their way to Cambridge, where John was scheduled to deliver the annual Phi Beta

Kappa address, which had evolved into one of the most prestigious intellectual events in New England. The crowd was large and distinguished. The governor was in town and attended, as did the French consul.[27] Adams read a rather insipid, self-pitying speech on the need for young men to persevere in the pursuit of their chosen professions.

No sooner had John Quincy arrived back in Newburyport than his depression descended upon him again. Sleepless nights, anxiety, feelings of worthlessness were more acute than ever. In desperation he retreated to the Shaws' house in Haverhill for some tender love and care from his aunt Elizabeth. To avoid hurt feelings, she wrote Abigail that her eldest son had come to Haverhill rather than return to Braintree because it was closer. But in truth he believed, probably correctly, that he would receive more sympathy from his aunt than from his mother. A few years earlier, Abigail had written John Quincy warning against the dangers of excessive mirth: "In your early days you had a great flow of spirits and quick passions . . . never suffer the natural flow of your spirits to degenerate into noisy mirth. . . . I never knew a man of great talents much given to laughter."[28] The local doctor in Haverhill plied him with "Bark, and Mary with valerian Tea." (The tea was made from a root that naturally induced sleep.) His aunt soon reported that her charge was sleeping through the night and feeling much better. "He thinks he is half cured because he has got somebody to care for him," she observed to Abigail.[29]

On October 3, Elizabeth wrote Abigail again. Her son had departed for Newburyport but was as ill as when he came. "If I had not felt too great a tenderness for the *Parent*, I would have told you that your son was here very sick, & had alarming complaints. . . . But I did not want to decoy you here in this way, & make you travel the road with an aching heart."[30] She was well aware of the strains that existed between Abigail and John Quincy. When her own son Billy left home, she had begged him not to throw her letters away, "as your cousin John used to do to his mother's."[31]

Abigail Adams was not an insensitive person. She cared deeply about her eldest son, but he was the vehicle for her formidable ambitions. Charles was weakminded and flighty, and Thomas at this point in his life—long neglected by his parents—was withdrawn. To her mind John Quincy had enjoyed every advantage, had had opportunities and experiences that would never be open to her. Her son was destined for greatness, and she was determined that he would realize that destiny whether he liked it or not.

John Quincy returned to Newburyport, but finding it impossible to study, he removed to Braintree, where he remained until the close of March 1789. For much of this time, Abigail was absent. In November and December, she would spend three weeks in Jamaica, New York, attending Nabby as she recovered from a difficult childbirth.[32] But he had his father, who had always been the emotional nurturer in the family. John Quincy read in Peacefield's library, rode, hunted, attended court occasionally in Boston, and reveled in the events leading up to his father's election as the first vice president of the United States under the new Constitution.

John Adams was one of the best-known public figures of his time. If not well-liked, he was almost universally respected for his integrity and patriotism. The *Defence* had resonated strongly among the conservative nationalists who wanted to establish a strong federal government capable of curbing the democratic excesses spawned by the Revolution. There were other aspirants for the vice presidency, however—Secretary of Foreign Affairs John Jay and New York governor George Clinton, for example. But as fellow New Yorkers, Jay and Clinton effectively canceled out each other. The Constitution did not then provide for separate ballots for president and vice president, and influential Federalists—most notably Alexander Hamilton, who disliked Adams personally—worked behind the scenes to deprive the New Englander of a ballot here and a ballot there in the hope that the election would be thrown into the House of Representatives. When the electoral votes were all counted, Washington was elected unanimously, with sixty-nine tallies, but, although victorious, Adams received a mere thirty-four, less than half the total cast. He felt humiliated.[33]

Following the election, John Quincy returned to Newburyport. Except for the possibility of sex, the conduct of the town's young continued to bore him. The community's eligible population would regularly gather at the home of one or another to socialize. Following one particularly inane soiree, John Quincy expressed his disgust: "When one game was finished," he recorded in his diary, "another equally stupid succeeded." One of the worst was "playing pawns" in which "a number of pledges were given all round, and kissing was the only condition upon which they were redeem'd." The young sophisticate, who had been exposed to the sexual mores of a variety of European countries, was repelled. "'Tis a profanation of one of the most endearing demonstrations of love. A kiss unless warm'd by sentiment and enlivened by affection, may just as well be given to the air."[34]

In time, his latent misogyny reappeared. Between January 1789 and June 1790, John Quincy secretly penned a series of savage satirical sketches of eight of Newburyport's most prominent young women. Unfortunately for John Quincy's reputation, the "Vision" did not remain secret. Billy Cranch subsequently reported meeting a young lady of their acquaintance in Boston. "She did not know any person she should be so afraid of as you," he reported. Cranch asked her what on earth had produced such a reaction, and she pulled from her pocket a copy of the "Vision." She said that she was both charmed by the elegance of its imagery and repelled by the savagery of its satire.[35]

Finally, however, John Quincy met a girl who approached his standard; she was Mary Frazier, the fifteen-year-old daughter of Moses Frazier, a wealthy ship-owner and local official. John Quincy was taken not only with the young woman's blond, blue-eyed beauty, but also with the elegance of her manners and the substance of her conversation. By the summer of 1789, John Quincy was a regular caller at the Fraziers' elegant three-story frame house situated on Green Street.[36] John Quincy struggled to keep his infatuation from his parents and succeeded for a time. Charles had been an admirer of Mary and eventually got wind of the affair. He duly reported the news to Nabby. "There is nothing so like perfection in human shape appeared since the world began," he had declared according to Nabby.[37] Nabby wrote John Quincy reassuringly. Of what she had heard of Mary, "you may worship without idolatry."[38]

The last sketch in the "Vision" was entitled "Clara"; standing in stark contrast to the other portraits, it was clearly an ode to Mary Frazier and a declaration of Adams's love for her: "The partial god's presiding at her birth / Gave Clara beauty and yet gave her worth / Kind nature formed of purest white her skin / An emblem of her innocence within / And called on cheerful health her aid to lend / The roses' colors in her cheeks to blend / While Venus added, to complete the fair / The eyes blue languish and the golden hair / But far superior charms exalt her mind / Adorned by nature, and by art refined / Hers are the lasting beauties of the heart / The charm which virtue only can impart." He then confessed: "On the thy ardent lover's fate depends / From the evil or the boon descends / Thy choice alone can make my anxious breast / Supremely wretched, or supremely blest."[39]

In early September 1789, John Quincy traveled from Newburyport to New York—the temporary seat of government of the United States—to visit his parents and enjoy the fame of being the vice president's son. His father was delighted to see him. In an earlier letter John Quincy had expressed interest in a state judicial post should Theophilus Parsons and other Massachusetts legal luminaries be promoted to federal judgeships. John did not discourage him: "A few months will produce changes that will easily settle that question for you."[40] Upon his arrival in the city, the younger Adams was immediately swept up in the intoxicating world of a new government establishing itself. There was plenty of room for him in Richmond Hill, the vice presidential residence, which was located on the west side of Manhattan, facing the Hudson River, in what is now Greenwich Village. The elegant mansion, with its columned portico and eleven-foot ceilings, had previously served as George Washington's headquarters during the early stages of the Revolutionary War.[41]

In May 1789, the family decided to bring Charles to New York to live with them even though his graduation from Harvard was still several weeks away. Charles's tenure at the college had not been as problem-free as his older brother's. He had become embroiled in the Thanksgiving Day riot of 1787, during which a group of students had turned on their tutors, pelting them with food and then breaking out some of their windows. Charles, a dining room waiter, had not been directly involved, but he had angered the authorities by refusing to name any of the perpetrators. Cotton Tufts found that "some imprudences (at least) had given countenance to suspicion" concerning Charles's character. Among other things he seemed to have been a frequent visitor to Cambridge's and Boston's taverns, news of which aroused in his parents' minds fearful memories of Abigail's alcoholic brother, William Smith, who had died broken and alone in September 1787.[42]

While Abigail was in Jamaica in the fall of 1790 attending to Nabby, who had just given birth to her and William Stephens Smith's third child, she expressed the hope that the couple would postpone bearing additional children, for they were having trouble supporting themselves as it was. It seems that Colonel Smith, heroic soldier and accomplished diplomat, was simply waiting around for a lucrative federal appointment. President Washington eventually named him federal marshal for the New York district in which he resided, but the income from that position was paltry.[43] In December 1790, Smith left his family and set sail for England, where he hoped to establish himself as a go-between for British and American shippers and merchants.[44]

John Quincy spent a month in New York, dining several times at President Washington's home. He visited the House of Representatives, then housed in the old city hall on the corner of Wall and Nassau Streets. He listened to James Madison and other luminaries orate. He was impressed not so much with the rhetoric of the congressmen as with their practice of the art and science of political compromise. It showed "the difficulty of men living in different climates and used to very different modes of living" reconciling their interests.[45]

No sooner had John Quincy Adams arrived back in Newburyport than he was swept up in the festivities surrounding a visit by none other than the president himself. Washington arrived in town on October 30 and was greeted with a parade and fireworks. John Quincy kept constant company with the father of his country until he departed for Portsmouth, New Hampshire, the next morning. "I had the honor of paying my respects to the President, upon his arrival in this town," he boasted to his mother, "and he did me the honor to recollect that he had seen me a short time before at New York." The young law student breakfasted with Washington and presented him with an address from the citizens of Newburyport commemorating the occasion, a speech that John had written himself.[46]

In truth, John Quincy was delighted to be back in Newburyport, where he could resume his courtship of Mary. They walked, talked, danced, and grew ever more intimate. He was conflicted, however, because he well understood that it would be quite some time before he could support a wife and children. A request to his father to augment his allowance had been rejected. On April 7 he wrote Billy Cranch that his feelings for Mary had grown only stronger with time. He spoke of the battle "between my sentiments and my opinions," and confessed to the urge to run from temptation: "Flight, and speedy flight too is the only resource that is now left me."[47] But then, in the spring of 1790, John Quincy decided he could not live without Mary Frazier, who that year had turned sixteen. It was then that he penned his ode to "Clara." He wrote his father, suggesting Newburyport as an alternative site for setting up a law practice. He had established, he said, an "agreeable circle of acquaintances" there, and as for Boston, "I cannot say I am pleased with the manners of the town"; the city was rife with "the opportunities and temptations of dissipation."[48] Both John and Abigail, still in the dark about their son's love life, were adamant. It must be Boston both for professional and political reasons.

JOHN QUINCY ADAMS WAS admitted to the bar on July 15 and opened his law office in Boston on August 9, 1790. The romance continued, however, with him visiting Newburyport but more often Medford, because Mary had relatives there and it was much closer to Boston. "All my hopes of future happiness in this life center in the possession of that girl," he wrote miserably to Billy Cranch.[49] Shortly thereafter, Abigail got wind of the liaison and moved at once to quash it. She wrote her son: "Common fame reports that you are attached to a young lady. I am sorry that such a report should prevail." For weeks she kept up a drumfire: "Never form connections until you see a prospect of supporting a family. Never take a woman from an eligible situation and place her below it." It was cruel to lead a young lady on so. Too early a marriage (John was twenty-eight when he and Abigail had wed) would lead to a life of unhappiness for both parties.[50]

So strong was his attachment to Mary Frazier that John Quincy decided to defy his mother, a step fraught with emotional and psychological danger if ever there was one. Between October 11 and November 2, he and Mary met in Medford to try to work out a solution. He proposed that they privately acknowledge their love and commit to marry as soon as his financial circumstances permitted. No, she said; her parents insisted on a formal public commitment or none at all.

Whether that was her wish or not is uncertain. What is clear is that Moses Frazier, one of the wealthiest men in Newburyport, could have subsidized the union. Such a thing was not uncommon. And, after all, his future son-in-law would be the son of the vice president of the United States. It might very well have been that when copies of the "Vision" began to circulate in Newburyport, John Quincy acquired a reputation as something of a woman hater, the "Clara" having not yet been written. At the time, John Quincy had admitted to his cousin Cranch that the collection of poison-pen poems "has made me enemies."[51] And so it was that Mary and John Quincy decided to go their separate ways.

A week after Mary and his final meeting, John Quincy wrote his mother, "I conjure you, my dear Mamma, not to suffer your anxiety on my account": she should forget "the report of my attachment." And subsequently: "I am perfectly free, and you may rest assured I shall remain so."[52] To his aunt Shaw, however, he poured out his broken heart, telling her that he feared he would never be able to love again. "I could have sat by your side and counted out tear for tear," she wrote back. Never fear, you are a most worthy young man with a fine heart; you will find another.[53] In 1838, John Quincy Adams, seventy-one years old, came across a headstone marking the burial spot of Mary's daughter while visiting a Boston graveyard (Mary had wed Daniel Sargent in 1802). He would later receive in the mail a tattered copy of "Clara" that was in Mary's hand. "Dearly! How dearly did the sacrifice of her cost me, voluntary as it was," after she "insist[ed] upon a positive engagement or a separation." He recalled that "four years of wretchedness followed . . . nor was the wound in my bosom healed till the Atlantic Ocean flowed between us."[54]

WHEN JOHN QUINCY SETTLED in Boston, his prospects were desperate. "I am very much in want of fifteen or eighteen pounds," he wrote Billy Cranch. "I have about six dollars remaining of 20 that Dr. Tufts last supplied me when I was in Boston."[55] His office was a room in a house that his father owned on Court Street. John readily agreed to let him utilize his law library. He roomed and boarded with two distant Adams relatives, Dr. and Mrs. Thomas Welsh.[56] The couple duly reported to Abigail that their guest was a fine young man but deplorably attired. He had arrived without a pair of undamaged stockings, and his tunics were so filthy that they had to be washed in buttermilk. John Quincy wrote his parents that as far as the Boston bar was concerned, he felt himself at sea with a school of sharks. "Mr. [Christopher] Gore is one of those men whom Cardinal Richelieu would have employed in public affairs," he wrote his father. Two of his contemporaries, Harrison Gray Otis and William Wetmore, were making money hand over fist by using the assets of their clients to speculate in government bonds and private stocks.[57] In mid-October, John Quincy tried his first case before the court of common pleas in Boston. Given the case only three hours before the first hearing, he promptly lost to Harry Otis. He wrote of his miserable failure to his parents. Cheer up, replied John; read some Suetonius, Cicero, and the Scottish philosophers. Brother Charles was more solicitous. "I think an harangue of fifteen minutes is by no means despicable for a first essay [speech]," he wrote John Quincy, adding that "you could persuade yourself to take the world a little more fair and easy."[58] John Quincy was predictably inconsolable. "I have now the advantage of being three hundred miles distant from every member of the family; alone in the world, without a soul to share the few joys I have or to participate in my anxieties and suspense which are neither few nor small."[59]

In July 1790 the federal government had moved from New York to Philadelphia. Under the Residence Act, which was part of the deal that had reconciled the South to Hamilton's financial schemes, the permanent seat of government was to be in Maryland at a site upon the Potomac River. During the ten years it would take to build a capital city, the seat of government would remain in the City of Brotherly Love. Early in 1791, John Quincy's worried parents decided to invite him to visit, luring him with descriptions of Philadelphia's libraries and learned scientific societies and, of course, of the political life of the nation's new capital. He left Boston on January 22 and, after traveling by stagecoach, reached his parents' residence at Bush Hill a week later. The city turned out to be as exciting as promised. It was intoxicating to be a person of interest among some of the most important people in the country. John Quincy attended sessions of Congress and dined with George and Martha Washington on the evening of February 22, the president's birthday.[60] Abigail was still worried about him as he left to return to Boston. "He appears to have lost much of his sprightliness and vivacity," she reported to Nabby. "He wishes sometimes that he had been a farmer, a merchant, or anything by which he could earn his bread, but we all preach patience to him."[61]

Cases continued to come into John Quincy's office at a trickle, but in April he received news that improved his financial situation markedly. John agreed to increase his allowance to twenty-five pounds a quarter and authorized him to manage the family farms and other property in Boston and Braintree, a task for which he would receive a commission. "Power from my father," he wrote across the top of the document placing him in charge.[62] John Quincy began participating more actively in Boston society. He cofounded the Crackbrain Club, which included many of the city's rising legal and political stars, some of them his former classmates at Harvard. One of the reasons for the younger Adams's improved mental state was that he had begun to indulge his intellectual interests again, renewing particularly his lifelong communion with Cicero and taking up Tacitus. "Fully persuaded that the clearest and most copious streams of science, flow only from the fountains of antiquity," he wrote in his diary, "I have often determined to make myself a complete master at least of all the Latin classics."[63]

Shortly after his return from Philadelphia, John Quincy and some of his cohorts from the Crackbrain Club mounted Bunker Hill to observe a total eclipse of the sun. He neglected to take with him the eyepieces made of smoked glass that were required for safe viewing of such an event. As a result, he burned his eyes most severely. "Hurt my eyes much," he reported to his diary.[64] Then in August, "almost blind." The damage would plague him for the rest of his life, one eye or another becoming swollen and inflamed, especially after overuse.

7

Taking the Stage

WHILE THE UNITED STATES was moving during the late 1780s toward a stronger, more centralized government, France was going in the other direction. Between 1700 and 1789, the French population had increased from eighteen million to twenty-six million, leaving large numbers of people unemployed. The government of Louis XVI had incurred huge debts fighting the Wars of the American Revolution, which in turn had led to tax increases borne largely by the middle class. A series of bad harvests culminating with the extremely severe winter of 1788–1789 led to wheat and bread shortages. Though a divine-right, absolute monarch, Louis had been unable and sometimes unwilling to suppress the circles of French philosophes who were determined to transform France into a democratic republic. As was the case in other European countries, the "public sphere"—which included newspapers, journals, Masonic lodges, coffeehouses, and literary societies—increased dramatically and provided locales where partisans of all stripes, from royalists to anarchists, could debate. Public unrest became so intense that Louis was compelled to call elections for delegates to the States General, a three-branch legislature that had last met in 1614. Voters for the Third Estate were all French males twenty-five years or older who paid taxes. The First represented France's hundred thousand clergy and the Second some four hundred thousand nobles.

Because the first two estates could always outvote the third, social and economic injustices remained unaddressed. On June 17, 1789, Abbé Emmanuel-Joseph Sieyès, a friend and adviser to the Adamses when they had lived in France, proposed that the Third Estate should meet separately. It did and immediately renamed itself the National Assembly, which proclaimed that it and it alone represented "the People." When Louis ordered the building that housed the Assembly closed, representatives gathered on a tennis court outside Versailles and promised not to disband until France had a constitution (the Tennis Court Oath). The Salle des États was reopened, but delegates noted with alarm a military buildup in and around Paris; among the troops were a number of foreign mercenaries. On July 14, famously, a Paris mob, joined by some sympathetic regular troops, stormed the Bastille, a royal fortress housing large stores of arms and ammunition. The governor of the Bastille was executed, and his head paraded around the city on a pike. Alarmed, Louis appointed the Marquis de Lafayette commander of the National Guard and accepted a new governmental structure for Paris that invested all legislative and advisory power in the National Assembly. In August 1789, the Assembly abolished feudal privileges, including the institution of serfdom. On the twenty-sixth, the body adopted the Declaration of the Rights of Man and of the Citizen, France's statement of independence from royal absolutism. The American ambassador, Thomas Jefferson, author of the Declaration of Independence, helped draft the Rights of Man.[1]

All of these events, of course, were followed closely in the United States by men and women interested in international affairs. Virtually everyone applauded the formation of the National Assembly and the storming of the Bastille, declaring them to be nothing less than the fruits of the American Revolution. But in a very short time, the increasingly radical turn of events in France was exacerbating an already deepening divide in the United States over the country's political future: what policies should its executive pursue, what laws should Congress enact, and in what manner should the Constitution be interpreted? How much democracy was sufficient to ensure that America remained a republic without descending into chaos and mob rule?

As HE SURVEYED THE scene in New York in the wake of his inauguration, John Adams had reason to be pleased. He and Washington respected and, at that point at least, trusted each other. Jefferson, the secretary of state, had long been his friend and fellow patriot. The secretary of the treasury, Alexander Hamilton, he knew less well but his nationalist ideas resonated with Adams. John Jay, the first chief justice of the Supreme Court, and he had been fellow laborers in the vineyard of American diplomacy.

America was born a republic, in the minds of its creators a form of government eminently suited to a free people. But as the events and debates leading up to the abolition of the Articles of Confederation and subsequently the adoption of the Constitution indicated, republicanism could be interpreted in vastly different ways. As the new government took hold in the years 1789 to 1791 and Congress debated legislation that would give definition to the vagueness of the Constitution and hopefully fulfill the promise of the Declaration, two very different paths were laid out by Washington's two most prominent cabinet members, Alexander Hamilton and Thomas Jefferson.

Hamilton, thirty-four years of age in 1789, had been born in Nevis in the West Indies, the illegitimate son of a Scottish merchant. A precocious, intelligent youth, he was hired as a clerk in a commercial house in Saint Croix. Powerful patrons who recognized the young man's potential paid to send him to a preparatory school in New Jersey and subsequently to King's College (Columbia) in New York. Hamilton wrote a series of pamphlets in support of independence while he was still in college. In truth, he was possessed of a martial spirit and longed for a war in which he could give it full rein. When fighting broke out, he was commissioned as an officer in the Continental Army, and through his intelligence and valor soon came to Washington's attention. The general promoted him to the rank of lieutenant colonel and made him his aide-de-camp. As a brigade commander at Yorktown, Hamilton had led a successful bayonet assault on a British redoubt. Out of uniform, he published an impressive series of essays on how to strengthen the national government. In 1782, New York elected him to be one of its delegates to Congress. There he met James Madison and the two would begin a collaboration that would result in *The Federalist Papers*.[2]

Hamilton, physically slight but brilliant and charismatic, viewed himself as a kind of prime minister in Washington's cabinet, and he was determined to use the wide-ranging but rather vague powers granted to the Treasury Department to create the kind of republic he envisioned. His political philosophy, like Adams's, stemmed from a view of human nature that was distinctly gloomy. He feared the ignorant and semi-educated masses. He believed that the common man was often incapable of acting in his own best interests, much less those of the nation as a whole. He feared pure democracy, certain that it would lead to anarchy. "The truth," he claimed, "unquestionably is that the only path to a subversion of the republican system of the country is by flattering the prejudices of the people and exciting their jealousies and apprehension to throw affairs into confusion and bring on civil commotion."[3] Control of the government should be entrusted to its moneyed classes—its bankers, shipowners, merchants, and manufacturers. If they were given a major stake in the future of the republic, they would be committed to its survival. Hamilton envisioned a strong national government and argued for a broad, or loose, interpretation of the Constitution to bring that sort of government into being. He believed that to survive, the United States would have to become a modern, developing country with a balanced, independent economy and vigorous foreign trade. To defend its interests, America should construct a strong army and navy. Central to all of this were a national banking system and stable currency.

Following a bitter struggle with James Madison and his followers in the House, Hamilton's supporters succeeded in 1790 and 1791 in enacting his Reports on the Public Credit into law. These created a national bank, funded Revolutionary War bonds at full value, and provided for a protective tariff to shield American manufacturers from having to compete directly with more cheaply produced foreign goods.

Jefferson and his ideological soulmate, James Madison, did not believe in a weak government. Contrary to the claims of some of his critics, the Virginian did not advocate for agrarian self-sufficiency or long for a bygone golden age dominated by simple, virtuous yeomen. Unlike Hamilton, however, Jefferson was optimistic concerning the human condition. Human beings were innately virtuous and, if provided with a modicum of education and not corrupted, would unfailingly act in their own and the commonwealth's best interests. He feared that an unrestrained federal government would inevitably encroach on the liberties of the people, hence his advocacy of a strict construction of the Constitution. The primary threat to the young republic, he argued, came from Hamilton's plutocracy, which would always value "property over persons," civil order over "liberty." He despised speculators who encouraged "the rage of getting rich in a day"; these "coupon-clippers" were not real producers of wealth but scavengers who profited from the labor of others.[4] He and Madison fought Hamilton's financial plan tooth and nail. Payment of continental and state securities at face value would create a large national debt—a threat to the liberties of the people if ever there was one, they argued. Jefferson and Madison agreed on the need for commerce and manufacturing but saw land as the truest source of wealth. They viewed a protective tariff as a scheme by merchants and manufacturers to benefit themselves at the expense of agriculturalists, who favored free trade.

The differences between Jefferson's and Hamilton's political philosophies, particularly when it came to specific policies and actions, should not be exaggerated. They were both committed to a republican form of government. Hamilton was frequently referred to as a royalist, but he remained true to the principles of the American Revolution articulated in the Declaration of Independence. Both believed in an activist federal government that would protect the liberties of the people and promote the general prosperity. The conflict between Jefferson and Hamilton, and the political parties that they fathered, had more to do with personal animosity and the ongoing influence that Britain and France had on American politics than philosophical differences. Hamilton believed that Jefferson, one of the drafters of the Declaration of the Rights of Man, secretly favored direct democracy in spite of the anarchy that would result, and that he was willing to sacrifice America's interests to those of France. Jefferson saw Hamilton not so much as a monarchist but as a plutocrat and a stalking horse for the British government and British interests. Brilliant though he might have been, the New Yorker was, Jefferson believed, a Machiavellian and a would-be man on horseback who would not shy away from establishing a military dictatorship.

Where did John Adams stand in the midst of this mounting political and personal controversy? On the sidelines mostly, and when he did enter the fray, he was pummeled by both sides. In truth, Adams had probably been too long in Europe. Shortly after the inauguration, Senator Richard Henry Lee, a personal friend of Washington's, brought up the issue of a title for the nation's new chief executive. Some favored the republican simplicity of "the president of the United States." Adams, who presided over the Senate, objected vociferously. "President" was too common a title; for heaven's sake, the heads of "fire companies and the Cricket Club were called presidents. . . ."[5] In order to gain and keep the respect of the international community, the chief executive must have a tonier title; he suggested "His Highness, the President of the United States of America, and Protector of the Rights of the Same." For short, the president would be called "His Highness." The vice president's folly opened him to accusations that he was a closet royalist. It did not help that he insisted on wearing a white powdered wig to preside over the Senate, decorated himself with a sword on ceremonial occasions, and rode to work in an expensive carriage driven by a servant in livery. Capital wits began referring to him as "His Rotundity" and the "Duke of Braintree."[6]

Much more damaging to Adams's reputation, however, was a series of newspaper articles he published in 1790 and 1791 under the title *Discourses on Davila*. (Historian Henrico Caterino Davila had written several essays on the French civil wars of the sixteenth century.) In truth, John Adams had been a late convert to republicanism. During the early stages of the Revolution, he had favored simple separation but was radicalized by his cousin Samuel and the whole process of organizing and advocating for independence. He had always harbored a rather dark view of human nature. He had expressed hope that mankind's universal appetite for distinction and acclaim could be harnessed for the good of the commonwealth, but he had his doubts. The notion of human perfectibility struck Adams as nonsense. So too did Whiggish notions of inevitable progress. He had been deeply affected by the historical approaches of Hume, Gibbon, and William Robertson, who brought a more ironic, detached approach to their subjects. They eschewed Whiggish historicism, which had framed the story of England as a passion play in which the heroes of liberty and reason were pitted against the forces of tyranny and superstition. The new history was more nuanced and embraced the irony that the expressed intentions and goals of historical actors and the actual long-term consequences of their actions were often quite different.[7]

Adams believed in representative government, in the rule of law, in the notion of equality of opportunity (for white males, at least), and in a political society that advocated and rewarded public virtue. Shays' Rebellion and the earthshaking events in France, however, had obliterated whatever political radicalism he had espoused during the Revolution. Indeed, *Discourses* was deeply pessimistic, even reactionary. In the *Defence* he had warned against the inevitable dangers of wealth and hereditary privilege; in *Discourses* he railed against the threat posed by unbridled democracy. He still believed with Locke that human beings were born with an innate moral faculty, but he had become convinced that it was too easily corrupted. Adams was troubled by the avarice he saw all around him. The Revolution had spawned a "liberalizing society," one in which opportunity abounded and the accumulation of individual wealth was touted as a public virtue. Some like Hamilton argued that the primary task of government should be to promote trade, manufacturing, and finance.[8] Americans had grown selfish and self-indulgent in the years after the Revolution, Adams believed. Prosperity was a cancer gnawing away at the guts of the virtuous republic.

To protect America from the seeds of disorder that had plagued Massachusetts in 1787 and France in 1789, its natural aristocracy should be given a special, privileged place in the political system. Adams proposed nothing less than a new branch of government composed of the educated and well-to-do. The chief executive, he wrote, should be someone with "an illustrious descent." Hereditary monarchy was attended by "fewer evils" than a republican chief executive.[9] Adams would subsequently oppose any extension of the franchise in Massachusetts to non-property-holding males. "Depend upon it, sir," he wrote an acquaintance, ". . . there will be no end of it—new claims will arise—women will demand a vote—lads from twelve to twenty-one will think their rights not enough attended to—and every man who has not a farthing will demand an equal voice with any other in all acts of states."[10]

In truth, Adams's views coincided with the conservative, nationalist bent of mind that had developed among many public figures in the 1780s and produced the Constitutional Convention. The nationalists included New England shipowners, bankers, and manufacturers disgusted with a government that could not open British markets and protect them from cheap imports, and slave owners dismayed at Congress's inability to open the trans-Appalachian West to allow them to find acreage to replace their exhausted soil. They included property owners of all classes in the North and South who were alarmed by the inflationary policies of some debtor-controlled state legislatures. "Good God," George Washington had exclaimed upon hearing of the disorder associated with Shays' Rebellion, the people involved apparently believing the lands of America "to be the common property of all!"[11] But even if Adams's fellow nationalists harbored some sympathy for a heredity nobility and life-tenured chief executive, they, unlike him, had the good sense not to splash their views across the front pages of the nation's newspapers. James Madison wrote Jefferson that Adams was "getting faster and faster into difficulties" for his "unpardonable" ideas and "obnoxious principles," which had "produced . . . a settled dislike among republicans everywhere."[12]

John Quincy's emerging political views were not as reactionary as his father's; in his letters and diary, there was no praise for "monarchy" or hereditary nobility. But he was just as much a conservative nationalist as his father and Alexander Hamilton. Indeed, both father and son regarded Jean-Jacques Rousseau as a dangerous radical. "In France it appears to me the National Assembly, in tearing the lace from the garb of government, will tear the coat itself into a thousand rags," he wrote his father in October 1790. "A nobility and a clergy, church and state levelled to the ground in one year's time . . . are inauspicious omens for the erection of an equitable government of laws."[13]

The Adamses' fears extended to the cultural as well as the political sphere. There were aspects of the Enlightenment that frankly frightened John and John Quincy. In the eighteenth century, philosophes on both sides of the English Channel had embraced materialism and sensuality as absolute goods. According to one British radical, there was no such thing as the soul, and the workings of the mind were determined purely by experience and passion. In 1748 an anonymously pornographic novel entitled *Thérèse philosophe* had taken the French intellectual community by storm. Its English equivalent was John Cleland's immensely popular *Fanny Hill; or, Memoirs of a Woman of Pleasure* (1749). Pure democracy, atheism, and licentiousness were all linked together in the minds of people like the Adamses.

In many ways Thomas Jefferson's political ear was as tinny as that of John Adams. In March 1789 his friend Francis Hopkinson had observed to Jefferson that most Americans viewed him as an Anti-Federalist. "I am neither a Federalist nor Anti-Federalist," the Virginian replied. He refused to be bound by factional interest, he declared. "If I could not go to heaven but with a party, I would not go there at all."[14] But Jefferson found the French Revolution and his role in it intoxicating. The chaos, bloodshed, paranoia, and hysteria that gripped France after the beginning of the Reign of Terror seemed not to faze him. "We are not to expect to be translated from despotism to liberty in a feather-bed," he declared to Lafayette.[15] And, famously, "The tree of Liberty must be watered with the blood of tyrants from time to time." He seems during his time in France to have become untethered from his previous commitment to a permanent, written constitution with a strong executive, a bicameral legislature, and a system of checks and balances.

Jefferson had met Thomas Paine in Paris in 1787 and expressed admiration for the author of *Common Sense*. In 1791, Paine, ever the radical, published *The Rights of Man*, a paean to the French Revolution. He went on to declare that the British constitution, which was unwritten, was no constitution at all, and he called on the British people to establish a new political order rooted in direct democracy and programs of social welfare. Jefferson publicly praised *The Rights of Man* and declared that it was especially welcome, given the "political heresies" that had recently been circulating in the United States. This was a clear reference to John Adams and his *Discourses on Davila*.[16] Thus opened a breach into which John Quincy would insert himself and come to public prominence.

THOSE SEEKING TO INFLUENCE public opinion and make a name for themselves during the Early Republic did so by publishing essays in the nation's many newspapers. In 1790 the United States boasted only ninety-two newspapers, a mere eight of them dailies. By 1800 that number had more than doubled to 235, including twenty-four dailies. In 1810 Americans bought more than twenty-two million copies of issues published by 376 newspapers, the largest aggregate circulation of newssheets of any country in the world.[17] Newspapers in the Early Republic consisted generally of a single folded sheet with international news on the first page, national and local news on the second and third, and advertisements and poetry on the fourth.[18] When a two-party system emerged in America, its lifeblood was the national postal system, both as a means of distributing highly partisan newspapers and as a source of patronage for the winners. Alexis de Tocqueville observed that the American postal system was a "great link between minds" that penetrated into "the heart of the wilderness."[19] Perhaps so, but there was almost no such thing as impartial news when it came to domestic matters. Local postmasters were shameless in their partisanship; they shared mail from political foes with political allies; they were not above opening the mail and printing damaging, even scurrilous letters disparaging their political enemies. "There is not one of them whose friendship is worth buying, nor one whose enmity is not formidable," John Quincy complained to his diary. "They are a sort of assassins who sit with loaded blunderbusses at the corner of streets and fire them off for hire or for sport at any [passerby] whom they select."[20] But if John Quincy was to have a future in public life, he was going to have to hold his nose and enter the journalistic lists.

The controversy aroused by the publication of John Adams's *Discourses* would serve as a launching pad for John Quincy Adams's political and diplomatic career. After conferring with his father, who was then in Braintree, he published a series of articles in Boston's *Columbia Centinel* under the pen name Publicola that ran from June 8 through July 27, 1791.[21] What were these "political heresies" that Mr. Paine spoke of? John Quincy asked as Publicola. There were political heresies about, but they were not to be found in the *Defence* or *Davila*. It was rather Paine's efforts "to convince the people of Great Britain that they have neither liberty nor a constitution—that their only possible means to produce these blessings to themselves is to 'topple down headlong' their present government and follow implicitly the example of the French" that were heretical.[22] There was no liberty without the protection of inalienable rights, John Quincy insisted. "If, therefore, a majority thus constituted are bound by no law human or divine and have no other rule but their sovereign will and pleasure to direct them, what possible security can any citizen of the nation have for the protection of his inalienable rights?"[23] The citizenry of England, like the people of the United States, "have no right to demolish their government unless it be clearly incompetent for the purposes for which it was instituted."[24] Manifestly, John Quincy proclaimed, this was not the case with either. He, like Paine, did not blame the Paris mob for its excesses. They were but an unthinking force that educated, calculating, and ambitious men had incited and manipulated to serve their own interests: "As they [the mob] have nothing to lose by the total dissolution of civil society, their rage may be easily directed against any victim which may be pointed out to them . . . the rights of man to life, liberty, and property, opposed but a feeble barrier to them."[25] Only a constitution, either written or unwritten, could ensure the rule of law, political participation by men of some means and education, and a strong national government simultaneously protecting the rights of the individual and promoting the general welfare. Absent a constitution, nothing could prevent a return to anarchy and the law of the jungle.

To John's and John Quincy's delight, the Publicola letters were widely reprinted in newspapers throughout the United States. They were reissued in London under the mistaken title of "An Answer to Paine's Rights of Man. By John Adams esq." and in Edinburgh under a still different title. The prosecutor in Paine's subsequent trial for seditious libel quoted liberally from John Quincy's essays. Vice President Adams was immensely proud. "I am well informed that the Speaker of the House of Commons, Mr. Pitt and several other characters high in office besides the Attorney General have pronounced it one of the ablest things of the kind they ever read," John exulted to his son Charles.[26] The editor of the *Columbia Centinel* denied that John Adams was the author of Publicola, but Jefferson did not believe it. "The stile [*sic*] and sentiments raise too strong a presumption," he wrote James Monroe.[27] His friend disagreed. He had intelligence indicating that it was John Quincy and not his father who was the author. Madison agreed: "There is more of method also in the arguments, and much less of clumsiness and heaviness in the style that characterize [John's] writings," he observed in a letter to Jefferson.[28] Jefferson, Madison, and their supporters noted with some dismay that there were no compelling refutations of the ideas contained in Publicola.

Jefferson subsequently wrote Adams, apologizing and denying that the "political heresies" mentioned in his correspondence referred to Adams. "That you and I differ in our ideas of the best form of government is well known to us both: but we have differed as friends should do, respecting the purity of each other's motive and confining our difference of opinion to private conversation."[29] John replied civilly but remained unconvinced, and deservedly so. Privately Jefferson declared that the only way Adams could redeem himself was to publicly disavow both *Davila* and the *Defence*. He wrote Paine again, congratulating him on the publication of *Rights*: "A sect here, large in names but small in numbers . . . had flattered themselves that the silence of the people under the 'Defence' and 'Davila' was a symptom of their conversion to the doctrine of king, lords, and commons. They are checked at least by your pamphlet."[30]

John Quincy was not immediately aware of how the *Rights*/Publicola controversy would change his fortunes. Legal cases still came to him very intermittently. He tried to distract himself with Cicero, Spinoza, Shakespeare, and the flute, but to no avail. He attended the usual rounds of parties, suppers, and dances but found "conversation sentimental & insipid." He stopped writing in his diary: "And why should I write in my diary [about] events perfectly trivial."[31] He was twenty-five; many of his contemporaries at the bar had distinguished themselves and were earning a handsome living. "Support me," he pleaded in his diary, "ye powers of patience, through these sandy deserts of legal study from whence I am to pick up a scanty subsistence by forcing an unnatural cultivation." His morals began to erode. He began frequenting the Mall, a walking area near what today is the Tremont Street side of Boston Common, and looking for prostitutes. As he observed in 1791, he no longer felt drawn to women who were cautious and correct, conceding that "my taste is naturally depraved." No longer did the female qualities of "prudence and discretion" win him. "I revere them as virtues; I should be sorry to find them strangers to the object of my affections. Yet freely must I confess it, never can they rouse those affections, never can they deeply interest me."[32] "Walk in the Mall this eve. Could not procure a chamber at Vila's."[33] "Walking in the Mall all the evening. Fortunately, unsuccessful."[34] "Resisted seduction in the afternoon." In early October, following dinner with friends: "Late home Oh! Shame where is thy blush!"[35] His prowling the seedier districts of Boston, sometimes on a nightly basis, continued into 1793. "Walking with Frazier this evening, met Gardner and two ladies, but made a lamentable mistake again. There is a fatality in it, I think."[36]

By the fall of 1791, John Quincy's law practice was showing some signs of life. He argued and won two consecutive cases in the court of common pleas. "I found my confidence in myself growing much stronger," he confided to his brother Thomas, "and acquitted myself more to my satisfaction than I had ever done before."[37]

Of great benefit to him, personally and professionally, was his budding relationship with Harrison Gray Otis, a member of one of Boston's most prominent families and a rising star in its legal profession.[38] The Adamses might have been successful politically but they were never part of Boston's social elite. The Otises were, but never condescended to their friends from Braintree. In December 1792, John Quincy and Harry found themselves linked together defending a troop of actors.

John Quincy had only one constant mistress—the theater. He had read the plays of Shakespeare at age ten, but it was not until the following year, when he traveled to Europe with his father, that he had actually witnessed a stage production; he could not get enough. In Paris, in London, in every village and town that boasted a stage, John Quincy was in attendance. He had written swooning letters about Sarah Siddons to his adolescent chum Peter Jay Munro. Ironically, Massachusetts sported a long history of opposition to the theater. In 1750 the General Court had passed "An Act to Prevent Stage-Plays and Other Theatrical Entertainments." In 1767 the court beat back an attempt to repel the measure, declaring that "a majority of the members of the legislature believed that such exhibitions had a tendency to corrupt the morals of the people and were inconsistent with the sober deportment which Christians ought to maintain."[39] In 1792, Adams and Otis, representing the theater lovers of Boston and environs, approached the General Court to request relief for them but were rebuffed. Undaunted, a group of thespians and their supporters built an illicit theater, the New Exhibition Room, in a converted stable in Board Alley. It staged its first performances on August 10, 1792.

Provoked to action—perhaps by the spirits of their Puritan forebearers—the antitheater party appealed to Governor John Hancock, and on December 5, he ordered the New Exhibition Room closed. Two days later, in the midst of a performance of Sheridan's *School for Scandal*, Sheriff Jeremiah Allen and his deputies stormed onstage and arrested the lead actor, Joseph Harper. The disappointed theatergoers rioted, trampling a portrait of Governor Hancock in the process.[40] Two days later an antitheater mob attempted to tear down the New Exhibition

Room but was prevented by the justice of the peace, who read them the Boston Riot Act.[41] At this point, John Quincy leapt into the fray, penning two articles for the *Columbia Centinel* defending the right of Boston's citizens to patronize dramatic productions. Writing under the pen name Menander—the Athenian general and poet—he admitted that those who staged productions at the house on Board Alley had violated the law but insisted that they had had every right to defy a statute that was unjust and unconstitutional. Harper was subsequently charged with violating the 1750 antitheater statute and a trial date was set. Harry Otis agreed to represent the thespians. So great was public interest that the proceedings were held in commodious Faneuil Hall. The crowd in attendance was clearly pro-theater, and the court ruled that the arresting officer had not properly secured a warrant for Harper's arrest. The case was dismissed. Upon exiting the hall, the spectators "closed the business with three huzzas." Discretion being the better part of valor, however, Harper and his fellow players temporarily left town.[42]

IN MARCH 1792, NABBY; her husband, William Stephens Smith; and their children departed New York for England. Colonel Smith intended to further develop the business connections he had made during his 1790–1791 trip.[43] The family arrived safely in London and during the next ten months kept John, Abigail, and John Quincy abreast of the dramatic events unfolding in France.

In the summer of 1792, the revolutionary fervor that had led to the storming of the Bastille but that had been temporarily dammed up by moderates in the National Assembly burst into full-scale, armed revolution. In 1789 radical deputies had formed an anti-royalist debating society, the Society of the Jacobins, Friends of Freedom and Equality—or Jacobins. By 1792 what had begun as a political club had grown into a loosely organized national movement dedicated to converting France into a republic. In the National Assembly the Jacobins split into two factions, the Girondists, or moderates, and the Montagne, or Mountain, who advocated a radical sweeping away of the past by means of violence if necessary. On August 10, spurred on by radical Jacobins, National Guard soldiers, joined by armed volunteers from the provinces and the impoverished masses of Paris, marched over the bridges of the Seine to attack the Tuileries Palace. Following a siege of several hours, the Swiss Guards hired to protect the royal residents surrendered, and according to the *National Gazette*, "the justice of the people displayed itself in all its horror."[44] The National Guardsmen and their sansculotte (peasants and workers, literally "without knee breeches") cohorts proceeded to murder several hundred people, including palace domestics and royal functionaries. Soldiers who had dared to rally to the king were hunted down in the streets and killed.

Meanwhile, Louis had sought refuge in, of all places, the Salle du Manège, the meeting place of the National Assembly. The deputies in attendance voted to "temporarily relieve the King of his duties."[45] A week later the insurgents set up a guillotine in front of the Tuileries Palace, and the Reign of Terror began in earnest.

In residence in London with her family, Nabby wrote that "the accounts from Paris are shocking to every human mind and too dreadful to relate," and she enclosed newspaper accounts of the massacres. She warned her mother not to assume that the English press "exaggerate[s] in their accounts. . . . I fear they do not, for I saw, on Sunday last a lady who was in Paris . . . and she heard and saw scenes as shocking as are related by any of them; they [the Jacobins and the mob] seem to have refined upon the cruelties of the savages."[46]

In January 1793, French revolutionaries beheaded Louis XVI. The following month, either as a preemptive strike or out of revolutionary fervor—or both—France declared war on England, Spain, and the Netherlands. The Wars of the French Revolution had begun, and the United States would be in constant danger of being drawn in on one side or the other. Not surprisingly, the Hamiltonians sided with Great Britain and the Jeffersonians with France. The outbreak of war in Europe, in turn, helped precipitate the emergence of political parties in the United States. In 1791, Jefferson and Madison had established a newspaper—the *National Gazette*—that was edited by Philip Freneau and served as a platform to attack the ideas and assumptions in the Reports on the Public Credit. Earlier, Hamilton and his supporters had founded the *Gazette of the United States*, edited by John Fenno, to articulate their conservative, nationalist views. During Washington's second term, the Hamiltonians would coalesce into the Federalist Party and the Jeffersonians into the Democratic-Republican Party.

Both John and John Quincy deplored the emergence of political parties in the United States. The latter quoted David Hume: "It is no wonder that faction should be productive of such calamities [partisan strife and enmity, demagoguery, and Machiavellian maneuvering] since no degree of innocence can protect a man from the calumnies of the other party, & no degree of guilt can injure him with his own."[47] Washington shared their fears. "Why," he wrote Jefferson, "then, when some of the best citizens in the United States—men of discernment—informed and tried patriots, who have no sinister views to promote, but are chaste in their ways of thinking and acting are to be found, some on one side, and some on the other of the questions which have caused these agitations should either of you be so tenacious of your opinions as to make no allowances for those of the other?"[48] Almost by default, the Adamses, like Washington, found themselves lumped in with the Federalists. In truth, the ideas expressed in *Davila* were congenial to Hamilton's way of thinking, but John and John Quincy disagreed with a number of Federalist tenets. They distrusted Great Britain just as much as they did France. They feared equally the excesses of the mob and the ambitions and avarice of the elite. They did not like rubbing shoulders with former loyalists who seemed to flock to the Federalist Party with the same enthusiasm and in the same numbers as immigrants, especially French and Irish, did to the Democratic-Republican Party.[49]

In the election of 1792, the Republicans were not ready to challenge Washington, but they ran New Yorker George Clinton against Adams. The father of his country was of course elected unanimously, while Adams prevailed over Clinton in the Electoral College by a margin of only twenty-seven votes, 77 to 50.

On April 8, 1793, revolutionary France's first minister to the United States, Citizen Edmond Genêt, arrived in America. Instead of disembarking at Philadelphia—the nation's temporary capital—he landed at Charleston, South Carolina, and proceeded in triumph through the backcountry, where support for revolutionary France had reached a fever pitch. The Treaty of 1778, committing France and the United States to come to each other's aid should one or the other find itself at war, was still in effect. Genêt's instructions did not direct him to invoke the alliance, but he was to do everything in his power to tilt the United States toward the French cause. Aided by South Carolina's governor, he set up prize courts and outfitted privateers to raid British shipping. He also commissioned George Rogers Clark to lead an army of frontiersmen against New Orleans, then in possession of Britain's ally, Spain. Writing from Philadelphia, Charles reported: "We daily expect a French fleet in this port. I dread the moment. We have many turbulent people in this city, who would wish to take advantage of such an event."[50]

As Genêt made his way to Philadelphia—at a leisurely pace in order to enjoy the dinners and large crowds of Francophiles singing "La Marseillaise"—the Washington administration debated the proper course of action in case France should indeed invoke the Franco-American Treaty. The president asked Jefferson and Hamilton to prepare position papers. Not surprisingly, the secretary of the treasury argued against coming to France's aid. The treaty, he declared, had been made with the government of Louis XVI, and that government was no more. Jefferson replied that agreements such as the 1778 pact were concluded between the sovereign peoples of the United States and France, not simply their governments, and hence were binding on the Washington administration. But both men concluded that the United States was under no obligation to take military or diplomatic action that would endanger its peace and safety. On April 22, President Washington issued a Proclamation of Neutrality. In it, he insisted that both France and Great Britain recognize America's right as a neutral to trade freely with both nations. Because the Royal Navy was much stronger than France's fleet and better able to seize shipping headed for French ports and to protect vessels destined for British ports, neutrality favored Great Britain.

On April 24, 1793, two days after Washington issued his Neutrality Proclamation, John Quincy published the first of two letters in the *Centinel* under the pseudonym Marcellus. In them he penned an eloquent defense of the president's foreign policy. He repeated Hamilton's argument that treaties were made between governments and that that of Louis XVI had ceased to exist. Had not the French National Assembly itself declared all compacts made by the monarchy null and void? Neutrality was the proper course for the United States in the midst of the burgeoning European conflict, but it must be impartial neutrality. Taking a swipe at Genêt without mentioning his name, John Quincy denounced those in America who would hire themselves out as privateers. Privateering by nations at war was a questionable practice, he wrote, but by a neutral, it was inexcusable. If America allowed itself to be dragged into war with France, it would be scourged by Britain and its allies. He then stated what would become one of the first principles of American foreign policy: "[A]s the citizens of a nation at a vast distance from the continent of Europe; of a nation whose happiness consists in a real independence, disconnected from all European interests and European politics, it is our duty to remain the peaceable and silent, though sorrowful spectators of the sanguinary scene."[51] Either his father or someone else had briefed him on the cabinet debate that preceded the Neutrality Proclamation. John Quincy was the first to write about it; Hamilton's Pacificus would not appear until July.

Genêt, whom John Adams had met in France, was outraged by the Neutrality Proclamation and the chilly reception he received from President Washington. He believed that a large majority of the American people wanted at the very least a pro-French neutrality. In defiance of federal law, Genêt outfitted a captured British ship, the *Little Sarah*—renamed *La Petite Démocrate*—in Philadelphia and sent her to sea as a French privateer to attack British shipping. He demanded that the United States provide advance payments on its debt to France and began financing anti-administration newspaper articles. Finally, even Jefferson had had enough: "Never in my opinion," he declared, "was so calamitous an appointment made as that of the present Minister of F[rance] here. Hot headed, all imagination, no judgment, passionate, disrespectful & even indecent towards the P[resident] in his written as well as verbal communications, talking of appeals from him to Congress, from them to the people, urging the most unreasonable & groundless proposition."[52] Finally, on August 23, the secretary of state wrote asking the French government to recall Genêt. As it happened, there had been a change of leadership in the National Assembly, and Genêt had fallen out of favor. The French

Committee on Public Safety appointed a new envoy and dispatched a four-person commission to arrest and return Genêt to France.[53] But in the end the firebrand was allowed to retire to New York, where he married a daughter of the governor. He would spend the rest of his life in America. "You have never felt the terrors excited by Genet in 1793," Adams later wrote Thomas Jefferson, "when 10,000 people in the streets of Philadelphia, day after day, threatened to drag Washington out of his house and effect a revolution in the Government, or compel it to declare war in favor of the French revolution and against England."[54]

As pro-French mobs in Philadelphia and other cities took to the streets denouncing the father of their country, John Quincy published a vigorous defense of the president and his actions in the *Columbia Centinel*; it appeared in five parts, which ran from November 30 through December 14. Writing as Columbus, he excoriated Genêt as nothing less than a cancer threatening the American body politic. In appealing to the people to overthrow their elected representatives, Genêt had violated every international norm. His "[l]etters . . . addresses . . . [and] remonstrances" were nothing less than a call to armed insurrection; how else would a populace in a democracy force its will on its constitutional offices?[55] Most despicable were Genêt's personal attacks on Washington, "the patriot, whose disinterested virtues and superior talents had been employed in their [the American people's] service through all the vicissitudes of fortune . . . the glory of their war, and the ornament of their peace." Diplomatic recall was too simple a punishment for the "petulant stripling," John Quincy proclaimed.[56]

Perhaps more alarming to John and John Quincy than Genêt's specific crimes was his fostering of "democratic societies" in America. These dangerous associations were composed of American Jacobins, who were nothing less than French Trojan horses, they believed. Political parties were an unfortunate necessity in a republic, John Quincy observed, and they were appropriate when they represented regions, classes, and interests—purely domestic concerns—but became poisonous vines when they were linked to the interest of a foreign nation. "The interference of foreigners upon any presence whatever in the dissensions of fellow-citizens must be . . . inevitably fatal to the liberties of the State."[57]

John was ecstatic at the reception that Columbus received. "I have read all the numbers with attention, and consider them a valuable present to the public," John Quincy's father wrote. "The President . . . with the unanimous concurrence of the four offices of state has formed the same judgments with Columbus, and I hear no members of Congress who profess to differ from them."[58] "I dare not repeat the observations which have been reported to me lest you should suspect the author of vanity beyond the limits of common extravagance." John Quincy replied that he was aware of the seductions of public adulation: "The public is a lady having so many admirers that a favor is not to be obtained from her by one of them with impunity . . . she cannot grant it without exciting all the evil energies of those whose ardor aims at much more familiar caresses."[59] He was, of course, ecstatic.

Genêt's demise, John wrote his son, did not mean that the danger America faced from the French Revolution was over. The Jacobins were still triumphant in France, and they would attempt to spread their political poison to the New World and influence U.S. politics as much as possible. Washington was sure to experience a backlash for his commitment to neutrality; partisanship was on the rise in America. "A party spirit will convert white into black and right into wrong," John wrote Abigail.[60] "When Junius said the opinions of the people were always right and their sentiments never wrong, I wonder what world he lived in."[61]

When Thomas Boylston Adams wrote congratulating his brother on his acclaim and suggesting that he assume a larger role in public life, John Quincy replied that politics held no allure for him: "If those writings have done any service to the cause of real liberty and of my country, I am amply rewarded."[62] God forbid that an Adams should admit to personal ambition.

8

A Diplomatic Education

ON NOVEMBER 6, 1793, orders went out from the British Admiralty to all ships of the line and privateers to seize and prize all vessels "laden . . . with the produce of any colony belonging to France or carrying provisions or other supplies for the use of any such colony."[1] Within weeks more than a hundred New England merchantmen had been captured and brought before British Admiralty courts in Halifax and the British West Indies. The orders-in-council were a direct challenge to the American principle of "free ships make free goods." "I fear we shall have no alternative but war," John Quincy wrote his father; "indeed it is of itself a state of war to have everything that passes under the denomination of supplies liable to capture."[2] France might be in a state of constant political upheaval, "a nation of fanatical atheists, all warriors," but he had to admit that in its decrees and policies "the French ruling powers have been constantly favorable to us, and . . . the British government, acrimonious, jealous and, under the guise of fair pretensions, deeply malignant."[3]

Depressed and frightened by the growing partisan divide in America, John wrote Abigail in a moment of weakness. "Let him [John Quincy] listen to the charge of a father to mind his private business and keep himself forever independent of the smiles or frowns of political parties." His focus should be on his law practice, the accumulation of wealth, and, eventually, the life of a gentleman farmer.[4] In truth, the vice president was feeling the first pangs of despair that would plague every person who held that office. He was frequently excluded from Washington's inner councils, particularly when it came to domestic affairs. After two years in office, he was spending three-quarters of every year in Quincy, as Braintree was now called. "My sons according to all appearances, must be content to crawl into fame and be satisfied with mediocrity of fortune like their father."[5]

But then, sometime toward the end of April 1794, John must have had a premonition or heard rumors that the powers that were in Philadelphia were considering John Quincy for an important post. "You must hustle in the crowd to make speeches in town meetings and push yourself forward," he wrote his eldest son.[6] "But I am afraid of these things," John Quincy wrote back. A life of politics would subject him to every passing whim of the electorate and lead to a "life of dependence."[7] Nonsense, said John. "You come into life with advantages which will disgrace you if your success is mediocre.—And if you do not rise to the head not only of your profession but of your country it will be owing to your own *laziness, slovenliness,* and *obstinacy.*"[8]

Apparently, sometime in early to mid-May 1794, Secretary of State Edmund Randolph (Thomas Jefferson had resigned his post in January 1793) had informed John Adams that President Washington was thinking of naming his son minister resident to the Netherlands, but he pledged the vice president to secrecy until the process was further along. Then, on the twenty-sixth, Randolph made it official. He called on Adams and informed him that John Quincy's name would be submitted to the Senate. The president wanted to know if he would accept. I think so, the elated Adams replied; he would certainly advise John Quincy to accept. As soon as Randolph departed, John dashed off a note to his son, informing him of the conversation and urging him to accept the position. "Your knowledge of Dutch and French, your education in that country, your acquaintance with my old friends there, will give you advantages beyond many others."[9]

"This intelligence was to me very unexpected and indeed surprising," John Quincy confided to his diary. He had determined early on not to solicit the government for any office, and he was not sure that his father had not done so on his behalf. The appointment, if he accepted, would certainly smack of nepotism. "I was very sensible that neither my years, my experience, my reputation, nor my talents could entitle me to an office of so much respectability."[10] A week later, on June 10, he met with his father, who had just arrived in Quincy from Philadelphia, and was reassured. "I found that my nomination had been as unexpected to him as to myself, and that he had never uttered a word upon which a wish on his part could be presumed that a public office should be conferred upon me."[11]

Some years later John confided to a friend that "Washington was indeed under obligation to him [John Quincy] for turning the tide of sentiment against Genet," and he was sensible of it and grateful for it. Neither Hamilton nor Timothy Pickering nor any other cabinet member could have written with such effect, he declared. Adams claimed that Washington had taken great pains to discover the identity of the author of Marcellus and Columbus, and when he did, he had Randolph sound out members of Congress on their views on confirming John Quincy to a diplomatic post.[12]

John and Abigail were, of course, over the moon. "It [the appointment] will be a proof that sound principles in morals and government are cherished by the executive . . . and that study, science, and literature are recommendations which will not be overlooked." It was also a signal from the president and the cabinet that "they are not hurried away by a wild enthusiasm for every unremitting cry of liberty, republicanism, and equality."[13] Abigail wrote Martha Washington, expressing her profound gratitude and promising that her son would never do anything to bring discredit on himself or the country that he represented.[14]

John Quincy departed Boston for Philadelphia on June 30 to receive his instructions from the secretary of state. On the way he stopped in New York and spent three days with Nabby and her family, who had recently returned from England. On one of the evenings of his visit, the Smiths hosted a dinner that included Charles-Maurice de Talleyrand-Périgord, Bon-Albert Briois de Beaumetz, and Louis Saint-Ange Morel, Chevalier de La Colombe. Talleyrand, Bishop of Autun, was assistant to the French ambassador in England, Beaumetz a prominent member of the National Assembly, and Colombe aide-de-camp to the Marquis de Lafayette during the American Revolution. All had been promoters and subsequently victims of the French Revolution and were then exiled to the United States.[15] Talleyrand and Beaumetz were in New York seeking business opportunities, which might have explained their presence at the Smiths'. The colonel was then heavily engaged in land speculation, having purchased a hundred fifty thousand acres in central New York the previous year.[16] Following his dinner with the distinguished Frenchmen, John Quincy speculated, "Perhaps there never has been a period in the history of mankind, when fortune has sported so wantonly with reputation as of late in France. The tide of popularity has ebbed and flowed with nearly the same frequency as that of the ocean, though not with the same regularity."[17]

On July 10, John Quincy arrived in Philadelphia. He immediately paid his respects to Randolph, who brought him into the president's office to exchange greetings with Washington. Time was of the utmost concern, the secretary of state told the new minister. America remained one of the Netherlands' largest debtors; negotiations regarding repayment and the extension of new loans were ongoing. John Quincy asked if he would have time to return to Boston to take care of his business affairs and some personal matters. He wasn't sure at that point, Randolph replied, but John Quincy should spend the next ten days in the capital getting up to speed on past negotiations and receiving additional instructions from Secretary of the Treasury Hamilton.[18] His salary was to be five hundred dollars annually.

The following day, John Quincy's twenty-seventh birthday, he received his commission from the secretary of state and at Washington's invitation attended a reception for Piomingo, a chief of the Chickasaw. The Native American dignitary was accompanied by four other chiefs and seven warriors. "There was nothing remarkable in their appearance," John Quincy recorded in his diary. "Some of them were dressed in coarse jackets and trousers and some in the uniform of the United States. Some of them had shirts and some none. They were none of them either painted or scarified and there were four or five who had rings in their noses. One or two had large plates apparently of silver hanging upon the breast." Servants brought in a large East Indian pipe made of leather and measuring some fifteen feet in length. The president and the chiefs took turns puffing. Adams noted that the instrument seemed to have been as foreign to the Indians as it was to the whites.[19]

Among the diplomatic papers that John Quincy perused during his time in Philadelphia were the six volumes of his father's correspondence while he was special envoy in Paris during the Revolution. Like his father, John Quincy viewed international relations as a matter of realpolitik. Jefferson and Madison believed that it was sufficient to demand that the United States be treated as a juridical equal in the community of nations. In so arguing, they cited the writings of Hugo Grotius and Emmerich de Vattel, whose central thesis was that international relations ought to be conducted according to the Golden Rule.[20] John Adams's cynicism concerning human nature spilled over into his views on the conduct of nations. Monarchies were by nature selfish and avaricious. Colonialism was an inevitable appendage of all monarchical systems. For republics—advocates of free trade and peaceful coexistence—this was not necessarily so, but as ancient history demonstrated, even republics could degenerate into empires. America's dependence upon international trade meant that it could not avoid economic entanglement with the nations of Europe, thus opening it up to the Old World's intrigues and avarice. To survive in this dangerous world, the United States would have to play one power off against another and use the leverage of its vast store of raw materials and its merchant marine to protect the nation's independence and ensure respect for its neutral rights. No one in America had had greater experience as a diplomatist than John Adams. He might not have been liked by those who prowled the halls of power, but he was respected for his learning and his impartiality. In early 1797, the French ambassador to the United States, the Comte de Moustier, reported back to the Quai d'Orsay following his first audience with Adams. "Overall, I had reason to be satisfied with the comments of the Vice President," he wrote, "and it seemed to me that the little success he had had in England had served as a corrective for the bad inclination he has had toward France in the past. If he were to come to be impartial, we could not but be satisfied. I think it is wise to humor him not so much due to his influence in the Senate as because of the influence he can have on the President who unfortunately can scarcely avoid recourse to him, to Mr. Jay or to both of them together in foreign policy as they are the only two who have any knowledge or experience in matters related to this."[21]

At dinner on the evening of his first night in Philadelphia, John Quincy sat next to the French minister plenipotentiary to the United States, Joseph Fauchet. During the course of the conversation, the French envoy observed to him that William Pitt and the British had as their goal the complete and total destruction of French power. This, he argued, would certainly not be in America's interest. If Britain were the sole remaining superpower, it would be free to sweep American merchant shipping from the seas, close all of its ports to American trade except on conditions most favorable to it, retain its military posts in the Northwest Territory, continue to intrigue with the Indians living south of the Great Lakes, and side with Spain in denying use of the Mississippi, thus blocking America's further westward expansion. "I believe it [Fauchet's reasoning] has too much foundation," John Quincy subsequently recorded in his diary.[22] As events would reveal, both of the Adams men were able to rise above their ideological sympathies and conduct foreign affairs with a view to protecting American interests, strategically and economically. They and their approach would become the cornerstone of American foreign policy during the Early Republic.

In Philadelphia, while waiting for Hamilton to return from the countryside, John Quincy suffered a severe case of buyer's remorse. He did not see much importance in the post he was to assume, he wrote his father. Holland was America's banker, and he was no banker. The negotiation of debt repayment and a proposed new $800 million loan (part of the proceeds of which were to be used to ransom Americans held captive by the Barbary pirates in Algiers) would be tedious at the least, he complained to John. The prospect of a long separation from family and friends he regarded with deepening anxiety. And what of his law practice? It was just then gaining traction. An absence of two to three years would place him well behind his contemporaries.[23] Nonsense, his father replied. The importance of the post in the Netherlands lay not primarily in its financial nature but in its value as a source of intelligence. Holland was still neutral. The Hague was the perfect listening post, a window into the scheming and strategizing going on in London, Paris, and other European capitals. He could report firsthand on the course of the war then raging. In a matter of two or three years, John Quincy would certainly be promoted to the rank of minister plenipotentiary.[24] John was right, of course. In his instructions to John Quincy, Randolph stressed the importance of intelligence gathering.[25] It was not clear at the time that Washington and Randolph appreciated the younger Adams's aptitude for gaining the trust of those who would be in the know in Europe or his astounding skills at information gathering and analysis, but they would soon come to do so. Whatever the case, from that point on, John Quincy kept his reservations concerning his new post to himself.

While he was in Philadelphia, John Quincy persuaded his brother Thomas to accompany him as his secretary. Tom was at first reluctant, expressing the same concerns about his law practice as his brother had about his. But he was the only Adams who had not yet experienced Europe. Immersion in new cultures, learning a new language, and admission to the Adams fraternity of cosmopolites proved irresistible.[26] His salary was to be a hundred thirty-five dollars a year. Both John and Abigail were delighted.

John Quincy and Thomas were allowed to return to Boston to gather their belongings and say their goodbyes. Having attended to his domestic chores, John Quincy was anxious to get away. He did not want to test Secretary of State Randolph's patience. But the only ship to be had was the *Alfred*, an "old, crazy and leaky" vessel. His and Tom's friends warned that they were endangering themselves by booking passage on such an "eggshell." They did, nonetheless, and on September 17, 1794, the Adams brothers—accompanied by Nathan Frazier, Mary's brother, and Daniel Sargent, her future husband—sailed to the Boston lighthouse, where Frazier and Sargent were put ashore. "The pain of separation from my friends and country was felt as poignantly by me at the moment when these two young men left the ship as it ever has been at any period of my life," John Quincy confided to his diary. "It was like the severing the last string from the heart. . . . I did not, but I could have turned my eye and wept."[27]

The *Alfred*'s crew totaled eleven, including two of the captain's brothers and "a black fellow who is the cook." With fall coming on, the passage grew increasingly stormy. During one tempest the passengers were treated to Saint Elmo's fire, "a ball of fire which in these heavy gales sometimes comes on board and moves upward by the side of the mast until it reaches the top . . . and it afterwards descends again and disappears."[28] More by chance and favorable winds than anything to do with the qualities of the ship and its crew, the *Alfred* hove in sight of the white cliffs of Dover on October 14. The passage had taken a remarkably short twenty-eight days. The *Alfred* made land at Deal, a squalid little town full of would-be thieves, situated some ten miles north of Dover. John Quincy, Thomas, and their servant, Tilly Whitcomb, stowed their numerous trunks on two chaises and climbed aboard for the eighty-mile trip to London. The little party reached the city at midnight. Just as the two carriages were crossing over London Bridge, John Quincy heard a thump and ordered the drivers to halt. When he and Thomas got out to inspect the noise, they found that two of the trunks, one holding a mass of dispatches for Minister Plenipotentiary John Jay, had fallen off. Another was wedged under Tom and John Quincy's chaise and a fourth beneath the one that followed them. They were duly retrieved and loaded inside the brothers' carriage. By the light of a streetlamp, they discovered that the ropes and straps securing the trunks had been cut. "I cannot but attribute it to an extraordinary degree of good fortune that in the noise and bustle of a London street in the darkness of the night, I was enabled to save the trunk which had fallen [during] the full drive over the pavements and which in a half a minute more would have been irretrievably gone," John Quincy wrote his father.[29]

The Americans booked a room at the Virginia and Baltick Coffee House on Threadneedle Street: fearful of another "accident," John Quincy proceeded the next morning to John Jay's suite at the Royal Hotel in Pall Mall. He had arrived in London just as Jay and his fellow envoy Thomas Pinckney were concluding negotiations on what would become known in the United States as the Jay Treaty. Following the British orders-in-council of November 1793 mandating the seizure of any and all merchantmen attempting to trade with metropolitan France or its colonies, Anglo-American relations had reached a breaking point. By the summer of 1794, British cruisers had seized two hundred fifty unsuspecting American merchantmen operating in the Caribbean and dozens more in the Atlantic. American shipowners and the owners of their cargoes demanded redress. In 1794 the Washington administration dispatched the widely respected Jay to London to partner with Pinckney, then U.S. minister to the Court of St. James's. Jay's instructions, drafted primarily by Alexander Hamilton, authorized the American envoys to negotiate on a whole host of questions, not only neutral rights but the continued occupation of the British posts in the Northwest Territory, incitement of the Indians, indemnities to the shipowners victimized by the orders-in-council, and boundary disputes between Canada and the United States in the Northeast and Northwest.

The negotiations had not gone well for the Americans. Their British counterparts declared that their country, in its war with revolutionary France, was fighting for its very survival and refused to make any concessions regarding its maritime restrictions. Hamilton, in the driver's seat following Jefferson's resignation from the cabinet on January 31, 1793, had secretly informed the British minister in Philadelphia that the United States would concede to the British positions on virtually every issue except the posts. By the time John Quincy came calling, Jay and Pinckney had in fact surrendered on one issue after another. The text that they were considering, and that was eventually approved, recognized Britain's right to seize goods aboard American ships headed for French ports if they were paid for. This included both contraband—that is, arms and ammunition—and nonmilitary items like food. This amounted to a total abandonment of the "free ships make free goods" principle, which had been established in 1776. The British agreed to evacuate the Northwest posts by June 1796. No mention was made of the Indians, of slaves seized by the British during the Revolutionary War, or of the American seamen impressed into British service. The U.S. government committed itself to the payment of all prewar colonial debts owed by Americans to British creditors. The treaty established mixed commissions that would meet later and address various border disputes.[30]

Jay greeted John Quincy as an equal, and for the next three days, he was an active participant in discussions with the chief justice and Minister Pinckney. "My observations were made with the diffidence which naturally arose from my situation," he wrote his father, "and were treated with all the attention that I would expect or desire."[31] John Quincy recognized that the treaty would not be popular in the United States, but he, like his colleagues, concluded that it was the best that could be obtained. "The national honor will be maintained; the national interest will suffer infinitely less than it would by the most successful war we could wage," he subsequently observed.[32] Many of his countrymen would disagree.

The pro-French Republicans were predictably outraged when a copy of the agreement reached America. James Madison termed the Jay Treaty "a ruinous bargain." Robert R. Livingston observed to Washington: "I see in it not the slightest satisfaction of our wrongs. . . . I dread in the ratification an immediate rupture with France. . . . I dread a war with France as a signal for a civil war at home."[33] Word of the treaty also aroused the hitherto politically inert. Mobs gathered in Philadelphia and other cities to denounce the agreement as a dishonorable surrender of American interests to the former mother country. Rural dwellers burned so many effigies of Jay that he would jokingly remark that he could find his way across the country by the light of his flaming likenesses.[34] So conflicted was President Washington that he submitted the agreement to the Senate without a recommendation. It was ratified by the barest of margins, a two-thirds majority.

John Quincy and Thomas took time to revel in London's social life. There were the obligatory visits to the theaters at Covent Garden and Drury Lane, where John Quincy took special delight in Sarah Siddons's portrayal of Queen Katharine in Shakespeare and Fletcher's *Henry VIII*.[35] Thomas was deliciously scandalized. "The stage has never been reputed a school for morals behind the scenes, however it may have been preservative of them by its influence upon the public," he wrote in his diary. Indeed, the prevailing opinion was that "the theater and morality are incompatible," and that "every actress by definition had prostituted their virtue."[36] As Adamses the two young men were granted access to many of the best American expatriate households: "dinner at 5 pm, followed by the theater, dancing and cards and then retirement at 2 am." One evening Thomas supped alone with the Joshua Johnsons. He was "particularly pleased with the middle sister," he recorded in his diary.[37] This would have been nineteen-year-old Louisa Catherine Johnson. One of the final evenings in London was spent with the family of John Singleton Copley, the American expatriate artist. John Quincy and Thomas found the Copley daughters extremely attractive. Afterward, John Quincy noted in his diary that there was "something so fascinating in the women I meet with in this country, that it is well for me I am obliged immediately to leave it."[38] He wrote his mother that Tom was so entranced with the eldest Copley daughter that he thought he might have to leave him behind.

The brothers departed London for the Netherlands on the morning of October 28, 1794. They arrived safely at the Hague three days later. The only misstep was a thoroughly drunken ship's captain who managed somehow to steer their packet successfully from Harwich to Hellevoetsluis.[39] Like most Dutch cities, the Hague was well laid out, orderly, and generally welcoming. Although it was the capital, it paled in comparison to the commercial hub, Amsterdam, and the cultural and intellectual center of Leyden. The brothers rented an apartment on the Hoogstraat, near the Binnenhof, the huge stone building that housed the Dutch national government. The first order of business was to call on Monsieur Dumas, John Quincy's former tutor. The old gentleman, then "between 70 & 80 years of age," did not immediately recall his former pupil. But when John Quincy refreshed his memory, he welcomed both the Adamses with open arms.[40] As he explored the city and the surrounding countryside, Thomas was charmed by the physical beauty but repelled by the plight of the common people. There was a great disparity of wealth, and at least one in ten Dutchmen he encountered was physically deformed. "Some with humpbacks, & distorted bodies, some with crooked hands, cloven feet, and disproportionate limbs, & many whose visages are marked with unnatural traits."[41]

When the Adams brothers arrived in the Hague, the Netherlands was deeply divided and under siege by the armies of the French Republic. By the late eighteenth century, the Dutch were still Europe's leading bankers and in possession of a sprawling empire that included the Dutch East Indies. Between 1780 and 1787, the middle class and some of the minor nobility had grown restive under the authoritarian rule of the stadtholder, William V, prince of Orange. In 1781, Joan Derk van der Capellen had published a pamphlet entitled "To the People of the

Netherlands," in which he advocated the formation of civil militias on the American model to restore the country's republican constitution. The result was a civil conflict that pitted the newly formed Patriots against the Orangists, the backers of Prince William. When the Patriot militia managed to gain control of Holland and a number of cities in the west, William fled to his palace in Nijmegen in the east. At this point Princess Wilhelmina appealed to her brother, Frederick William II of Prussia, and on September 13, 1787, a Prussian army crossed the border into the Netherlands and restored the stadtholder to power. Many of the Patriots fled into exile in France. But many remained, as did the grievances that had caused them to take up arms.

The French Revolution infused the Patriots with new life. William had made the mistake of joining the First Coalition, which was arrayed against France. That error led to an invasion of the Netherlands by a French army under the command of General Jean-Charles Pichegru. The winter of 1794–1795 was particularly harsh, turning the great rivers that traditionally protected the Netherlands into highways of ice facilitating the French advance. The Patriots, of course, were ready to welcome Pichegru with open arms, and by the time Thomas and John Quincy arrived in the Hague, two provinces were once again in open revolt against the stadtholder.[42]

"The successes of the French armies in every quarter have exceeded all the powers of calculation," John Quincy wrote his father. Pichegru had taken Nijmegen and Maastricht and was advancing on Amsterdam. The British troops stationed in the Netherlands to defend the stadtholder were fleeing in disarray. Two of the Patriot leaders presented to the government a petition requesting that all resistance cease; they were thrown into prison for their efforts. Prince William ordered troops of cavalry into the Hague and placed cannon around the Stadthouse in an attempt to intimidate the populace. He then issued a decree promising instant death to any person showing the slightest sign of opposition to the government or sympathy for the French.[43]

On November 5, John Quincy presented his credentials to the government. After some delay, he was notified that their High Mightinesses received communications only in Dutch, French, and Latin. English was the language of his country, the American envoy replied, and that was that. He quickly retreated, however, and translated his credentials into French. On the fourteenth, Prince William officially received the new American minister. John Quincy found him "civil enough."[44]

The new American envoy understood that there were available to him two channels of communication with his own government. His direct superior was Edmund Randolph, but his father was vice president. There were things he could include in his correspondence to John that he did not feel comfortable putting in his official reports. "I can depend upon you," he wrote his father, "to provide the Secretary of State with whatever additional information he requires."[45]

The Patriots, John Quincy reported, expected to be treated as comrades by the French, their rights and property respected. And indeed, there were some grounds for this expectation. Since Maximilien Robespierre's beheading on July 28, 1794, and the ascension of "le Plaine" (the Plain), or moderates in the National Convention, there had been a marked change in both the domestic and foreign policies of France. The new regime had declared that the horrors of the past two years—"the sinking of thousands of boat loads in the Loire; the shooting of thousands by Parisians at Lyons and elsewhere, the murdering of thousands . . . by the guillotine"— lay dead and buried with Robespierre. And, in truth, large numbers of political prisoners had been released from prison, and moderates were offering reconciliation with the royalists not only in Paris but in the provinces as well.[46] In the field, France's conquering armies had begun extending the olive branch to those they mastered. Private property was respected and local and regional governments left intact as long as they did not resist.[47]

In desperation, the stadtholder dispatched an envoy to London in an effort to persuade the British government to redouble its efforts to defend the Netherlands. It was hopeless. George III was receiving reports from the Duke of York, commander of the redcoat contingent in the Netherlands, that the Dutch were doing almost nothing to defend themselves. Tell the stadtholder to make the best treaty of peace he could with the French, George instructed his diplomats. Truthfully, even the Orangists hated the British troops who had been dispatched to defend them. "It is hardly possible to conceive how much their assistance is dreaded," John Quincy wrote his father. "The cities shut their gates against them; all ranks of people equally detest and shun them."[48]

On January 18, William and Wilhelmina abandoned their country and went into exile in Great Britain; they were forced to make the journey in a humble fishing boat. "The Stadtholder himself is well disposed with a good heart and a feeble mind," the younger Adams observed in his diary. "He is the man of his councils [advisers] and not his own energy." The princess was thoroughly detested, however. She was haughty and domineering, almost totally lacking in grace. Traumatized by having to flee in such humiliating circumstances in the dead of winter, she "broke out into transports of rage until she was totally exhausted and sank into a state of sullen apathy."[49]

The looming occupation of the Netherlands confronted John Quincy with something of a diplomatic quandary. If the National Convention in Paris allowed the Dutch to retain some semblance of sovereignty, his credentials would still be valid. But if France annexed the country outright, he would have to return home unless otherwise instructed.

The first French troops entered Amsterdam on January 19, 1795. The States General had ordered its commanders throughout the country to lay down their arms. Prominent Orangists went into hiding. That evening tricolored cockades begin appearing in the streets, and a tree of liberty was erected before the state-house.[50]

Members of a revolutionary committee subsequently appeared in front of the government building and read the names of twenty-one members of a newly con-stituted Provisional Representatives of the People of Holland. The following day the committee received the commissioners dispatched by the French National Convention as friends and allies. By late February, the government of the occu-pied country was in place; its first chairman, Peter Paulus, was an old friend of John Adams. All hereditary privileges and titles were abolished. The French troops were perfectly well-behaved, John Quincy reported. Their exceptional dis-cipline was based on the severest punishment for the most minor violation.[51]

The French delegation received John Quincy warmly and assured him that they would treat him with the respect due a representative of an independent and powerful nation; after all America and France were still connected by the twin links of equality and fraternity.[52] General Pichegru, a former sergeant of the ar-tillery, seemed judicious and unassuming. The change of government in Holland was very much in America's short-term interests, John Quincy wrote the vice president. The Orangists were mercantilists; the Patriots now in power would be much more amenable to open and free trade. It might now be possible for the $800 million loan the United States had been seeking to go through.[53]

But America and the Netherlands were, of course, fools to trust their fate to the course of French politics. "The violent party [in France] are far from being crushed," John Quincy wrote his father in October 1795. The Jacobins were still a force in the Convention, as were the democratic societies scattered across the countryside that supported them.[54] And then, during the spring and summer, John Quincy began to receive alarming reports of the spread of French political radicalism to the United States. The "Jacobine societies established in Europe have taken flight to America," his mother warned. If every man was allowed to go his own way, "we might then form ten or twenty thousand democracies. . . . What could prevent the whirlwind, and fires of discord, internal & foreign, from scat-tering and consuming these fritters and rags of the society?"[55]

It soon became apparent that the French had come to the Netherlands as con-querors, not as allies; that the Patriots, their fellow democrats, were in power mattered not. On May 16 a treaty of peace was signed between France and the Batavian Republic, the new name the Convention had bestowed on the Netherlands. Under its terms, the Dutch were to pay an indemnity of a hundred million florins, to contribute twelve ships of the line and eighteen frigates to aid in the planned invasion of the British Isles, to cede the territories of Maastricht, Venlo, and Dutch Flanders, and to pay for the support of a French army of occupation comprising some twenty-five thousand soldiers.[56]

John Quincy and Thomas found their official life somewhat uncomfortable. As royalists, the Orangists did not trust their republican visitors. When John Quincy refused to openly side with the Patriots—he was even solicited to join the local democratic society—they too turned a cold shoulder. "My situation has indeed been as you suspected, difficult and embarrassing," he wrote Charles. He had acted strictly neutral and proper, as was called for under the situation; he had not lost his temper despite numerous provocations, and he had done nothing to impair his country's status as a neutral. And yet there was opprobrium on every side.[57]

LIFE OUTSIDE POLITICS AND diplomacy was most congenial, however. "My mind [is] very easy," John Quincy wrote his friend James Gardner back in Boston. "I have found here exactly what I wanted and feel myself to be once more my own man again."[58] John Quincy and Thomas were still young men, attractive and sociable; they were welcomed into high society in both the Hague and Amsterdam. There were the usual soirees, dances, and dinners. Amsterdam was then one of Europe's intellectual meccas. Enlightenment philosophies of all stripes were discussed in the city's innumerable coffeehouses and its Masonic lodges. It was this culture that had produced Baruch Spinoza's *Three Impostors* (Moses, Jesus, and Mohammed), in which he rejected religion altogether, insisting that reason and the passions, if left to themselves, could lead to the establishment of relatively just and equitable societies (Spinoza was a good Dutch republican).[59] This was certainly a bit much for John Quincy, but he found the discussions of Diderot's and Spinoza's works stimulating and perhaps titillating. There were interesting characters among the diplomatic corps, particularly Baron de Bielfeld, the Prussian minister. He and his American counterpart took frequent walks in the city's parks and the surrounding countryside. "Our conversation was political, literary, and critical, without sliding, as it often does, into the bottomless pit of metaphysics," John Quincy wrote.[60] During one of their exchanges Bielfeld observed that there was no situation, no dilemma, that could justify a violation of the truth. An extraordinary assertion coming from a diplomat, John Quincy retorted.[61]

There was plenty of time to read and buy books. "Obliged to finish reading *Les liaisons dangereuses*," he recorded in his diary; "the book is very well written, but it is a portrait of human depravity which one would fain hope is exaggerated." It lacked the moral stringency of Shakespeare's works, he sniffed. The female character's calamities did not match her crimes. It was true that "rain falls and the sun shines equally upon the just and the unjust," but the role of literature was to provide a moral lesson. "Guilt," he observed, "is followed generally by punishment, and . . . the misery inflicted upon vice can be just only as it proceeds from it."[62]

By all accounts, young Adams's performance as a diplomat was earning plaudits from all quarters in America. "No public minister has ever given greater satisfaction, than Mr. Adams has hitherto," John wrote Abigail. "His prudence, caution, and penetration are as much approved as the elegance of his style is admired."[63] The young man was still not convinced that his post in the Netherlands was of much importance. He was getting paid to read and analyze newspaper articles, he complained to Charles.[64] He might as well put his free time to good use. He was planning to write four books, he told Thomas one morning at breakfast; one a "Treatise Upon Government," another on the history of the American Revolution, a third comparing the reign of the Roman emperor Augustus and the French Revolution, and a fourth refuting Voltaire.[65]

On August 22, 1795, the French National Convention approved the Constitution of the Year III. It was then endorsed overwhelmingly in a plebiscite. The new government was composed of an executive—a five-person Directory—and a bicameral legislature. The first chamber, the Council of Five Hundred, would initiate laws, and the second, the Council of Elders (two hundred fifty members), would approve or disapprove legislation passed by the lower house.[66] As events would quickly demonstrate, the Directory did not understand the country that it governed. Its members proved to be entirely self-interested. Though ruling in the name of the French people, the new regime distrusted the masses. The Directory tended to equate religion with royalism and reaction. Local administrators knew better. One wrote to the minister of the interior: "Give back the crosses, the church bells, the Sundays, and everyone will cry 'vive la République!'"[67] The new regime proceeded to split into two factions, the Brissontin party on the one hand and the Thermidorian on the other. The principal difference separating them was the extent to which they were willing to go to discredit and, indeed, exterminate the followers of Robespierre.[68]

The Directory was deeply offended by the Jay Treaty, regarding it as a violation of the Treaty of 1778 and a stab in the back by a fellow republic. Outwardly, John Quincy reported to the State Department, the French remained friendly and congenial but secretly they were plotting to involve the United States in a war with Great Britain. Their reasoning was that Britain was so dependent upon trade with America that its cessation would lead London to immediately sue for peace with France on its terms.[69]

Surveying the scene from the Hague in 1795, John Quincy Adams feared the worst. Not only were both the British and French plotting to undermine American independence and make the United States into their pawn, but the values of the Enlightenment and Western civilization were under assault. Britain and France were waging war beyond all reason and self-interest. The populations of both countries were suffering extreme hardships. The government of George III was motivated purely by hatred of France, and the French were caught up in a perpetual cycle of revolution and war, the former used to justify the latter. In truth, he opined, the new moderate consensus in France would not long survive. Both the Jacobins and the Royalists detested it. The democratic societies and the committees—the ghosts of Robespierre and Georges Danton—were still lurking in the shadows. "The arts and sciences themselves . . . are liable to become objects of prescription to political fanaticism . . . and if the principle is finally to prevail which puts the scepter of sovereignty into the hands of the European sansculottes, they will soon reduce everything to the level of their own ignorance."[70]

In October 1795, John Quincy wrote his father concerning his future. He hated the law: "I shall . . . always consider the Bar as a resource, but I shall certainly consider it as the last." His diplomatic post at the Hague, "insignificant as it is," he found personally satisfying. It placed him in a position to monitor, analyze, and report on the period's earthshaking events. There were stimulating companions and ample time for reading and study. Society and culture in Amsterdam could not equal those of London and Paris, but there was nothing to compare with them in America. In short, he found the life of scholar-diplomat most satisfying.[71] John reassured him that a brilliant future awaited him in the foreign service. "I have reason to think that your whole correspondence, public and private, has been as much esteemed as that of any former American Minister, and more admired for a brilliancy of style and a freedom, independence, and boldness of sentiment. . . . Go on my worthy son in your glorious career and may the blessing of God crown you with success."[72] His only request was that John Quincy would take an American wife.

In truth, President Washington had written the vice president on August 20, "They [John Quincy's letters] contain a great deal of interesting matter and No. 9 [May 22] disclosed much important information and political insight." His son must not think of retiring from the way of life he was in. "His prospects, if he continues in it, are fair, and I shall be much mistaken if . . . he is not found at the head of the diplomatic corps, let the government be administered by whomever the people may choose."[73]

By the time he penned his encouraging words, John had no doubt learned that the administration had decided to name John Quincy special envoy to Great Britain to exchange ratifications of the Jay Treaty. On August 25, Acting Secretary of State Timothy Pickering had written, instructing John Quincy to proceed to London no later than October 20 to supervise the proceedings. The regular minister to Great Britain, Thomas Pinckney, was then in Spain negotiating the momentous treaty that would bear his name.

On October 14, John Quincy recorded in his diary, "Received this morning [orders] to repair without delay to London where I shall find directions and documents from my government." He added presciently, "This business is unpleasant and unpromising, but I have no election [choice]."[74] He took the boat for Delft the morning of October 21 and reached Hellevoetsluis a day later; he would languish there for three weeks, all ships to England being bottled up by the westerly winds that blew constantly at that time of year. John Quincy finally boarded the schooner *Aurora* on November 9 and, after a pleasant voyage of twenty-four hours, arrived in London via Margate and Canterbury. He took lodging at Osborn's Hotel. The next morning, he made contact with the American chargé d'affaires, William Deas, and learned that he was too late for the exchange. The process had already been completed. Deas asked him to step in and continue the negotiations that Minister Pinckney had initiated with the British government concerning a number of still outstanding issues between the two countries. He would, Adams replied, but he would have to step lightly, very lightly, he thought to himself.

John Quincy Adams possessed a genius for gathering intelligence and separating the wheat from the chaff. He also had a strong sense of self-preservation. He had approached the assignment in Great Britain with much trepidation because he would be associated from then on with the hugely unpopular Jay Treaty. Francophile Republicans with their democratic societies were scheming to overthrow the government, Abigail had written her eldest son. Led by Benny Bache, Franklin's grandson, Republican newspapers were portraying the Jay Treaty as nothing less than a betrayal of American independence; "the President and Mr. Jay are treated like the vilest tyrants and greatest traitors of the age."[75] Meanwhile, the new ambassador to France, James Monroe—a protégé of Jefferson and Madison—was adding fuel to the fire. Arriving in Paris a week after John Quincy took up his post in the Netherlands, Monroe had addressed the Convention, assuring the deputies that if he could establish a permanent bond between France and the United States, it would be the "happiest event of my life."[76] In truth, the Quai d'Orsay looked upon the United States as "the Holland of the New World." Washington must go, declared the Directory's first minister to the United States. "[A] friend of France must succeed him in that eminent office. . . . We must raise up the people and at the same time conceal the lever by which we do so."[77] Thus, despite the comings and goings of various factions in the Council of Five Hundred and the Council of Elders, the goals and methods of French foreign policy toward the Early Republic remained strikingly consistent.

John Quincy shared his mother's apprehensions regarding French designs on American independence, but he believed that Britain posed no less a threat. The Glorious Revolution and British common law aside, he viewed Britain as a proud, imperious, ruthless power, its foreign ministers masters of realpolitik, and its populace still unreconciled to American independence. Indeed, he reported there were many in Britain who secretly hoped to see President Washington deposed even though this would play into the hands of the French. From his outpost in the Hague, it was John Quincy's duty to report on the threat posed to the United States by the French Revolution and its supporters in America. In London, his task would be to ensure that the British abandoned their forts and their Indian allies in the Old Northwest, and to persuade them to cease further depredations against American merchantmen.

During his negotiations in London, Minister Adams feared being used by the British. "I have been accustomed all my life to plain dealing and candor and am not sufficiently versed in the art of political swindling to be prepared for deficiencies of which on this occasion I am strongly sensible," he declared. "I have not the experience which the proper performance of the duty would require." He was intimidated, he wrote his father, by "the magnitude of the trust and my own incompetency."[78]

During the ratification exchange, Deas had stoutly protested ongoing British seizures of American ships loaded with grain and other foodstuffs, items then recognized under international law as noncontraband. The British Foreign Office let it be known that henceforward the American chargé d'affaires was persona non grata. John Quincy called on the British undersecretary for foreign affairs, thirty-two-year-old George Hammond, on November 25. The meeting did not go well. Adams had met Hammond when both were in Paris in 1783, John Quincy serving as secretary to his father and Hammond acting in a similar capacity to David Hartley, the chief British negotiator. Perhaps as an insult, perhaps not, Whitehall had subsequently sent Hammond, then twenty-seven, to be its first minister to the United States. He was completely outmaneuvered by Secretary of State Jefferson over interpretations of the treaty of peace, and although the Englishman would marry a Philadelphia girl, he would remain deeply anti-American.[79]

Hammond greeted John Quincy cordially enough, welcoming him and re-
marking that he wished he had come sooner. Deas's communications were too
"violent and fractious," he remarked. No more insulting and offensive than some
British officers in America, Adams replied. Yes, said Hammond, and those men
had been recalled. Two days later John Quincy called again at the Foreign Office
and Hammond introduced him to William Wyndham Grenville, Lord Grenville,
the minister of foreign affairs. "He said he heard the democrats [Republicans]
were quite cock-a-hoop—talked [the] very thing of impeaching the President."
People speak of overthrowing the government here, Adams replied. Yes, said
Grenville. The best method is to let them talk. We let them talk, Adams thought
to himself; you hang them. You should become minister to the Court of St.
James's, Grenville observed. We would like it, and you would like it. It would be
fitting for you to follow in your father's footsteps. "That may be very well for you,"
John Quincy remarked; "but in my country, you know there is nothing hereditary
in public affairs." After the meeting the young American wrote in his diary that
if he stayed on for a period, he might learn not to be "quite so impertinent."[80]

Minister Adams met with Hammond, alone, again on December 5. The undersecretary's tone was far less cordial than during their initial meeting. Hammond insisted on discussing party politics in America. The Republicans—Jacobins
to the core—are our enemies and yours (meaning the Federalists), he declared.
They speak ill of your father. "'Why,' said I, 'all Governments have their opposition who find fault with everything. Who has better reason to know that than you
have in this country?'" In America everything comes out: "We have no lurking
disaffection that works in secret and is not seen; nothing that rankles at the heart
while the face wears a smile." You should know, Adams said, that when I or any
other American diplomat speaks, it is for the whole people, not just one political
faction. All American citizens are political equals. (John Quincy's definition of
"all" was of course limited to propertied white males.) Why do you not make common cause with us? Hammond asked. We are your best customer. Yes, but on
your terms, Adams replied. You take our raw materials at what you choose to pay
and charge us for your manufactured goods at whatever price you choose to set.
All the specie the United States earns from its trade with other countries is drained
off into your coffers. Hammond abruptly turned to the question of John Quincy's
pending reception by the king.[81]

Thus did John Quincy Adams demonstrate the diplomatic techniques that he
would employ during the remainder of his remarkable career. No one was more
intelligent, well-read, or better informed than he, and with that knowledge came
great confidence. He would not give an inch on substance and form unless it was
reciprocated. Demanding and gaining respect for American independence were

to him far more than a matter of pride, however. Though growing daily in power and prosperity, the United States was still a military dwarf compared to the nations of Europe. In the midst of the world war then raging, both sides would do everything in their power to bend America to their will or, failing that, to cripple it. Both the French and the British were deeply involved in American party politics. "The public opinion in America concerning European affairs is in a considerable degree formed from the representations of the Americans arriving occasionally from Europe or writing Americans from some part of it [Europe] to their friends," John Quincy observed to the vice president. "Our political dependence upon France, and our commercial dependence upon Britain," he wrote his brother Charles, "have both been great and heavy clogs upon us from the time of the Peace to this day. Every hour of neutrality now has a tendency to extricate us from both these shameful dependencies and to make us a really & completely independent people."[82] America's only refuge—the key to its independence—was neutrality; indeed, the two were inseparable. That was one reason Adams was so defensive of George Washington. "At the present moment, if our neutrality be still preserved," he wrote a colleague, "it will be due to the President alone. Nothing but his weight of character and reputation, combined with his firmness and political intrepidity, could have stood against the torrent that is still tumbling with a fury that resounds even across the Atlantic."[83]

John Quincy's support for the Jay Treaty had alienated Francophile Republicans at home and abroad. His efforts to compel John Bull to respect American neutrality sat no better with pro-British Federalists. Shortly after his arrival in London, John Quincy met with Gouverneur Morris, a thoroughgoing Anglophile then in the process of being recalled as minister to France because of his open hostility to the country to which he was accredited. "You will find, I think," Morris said, "the Cabinet here well-disposed to America." Really? replied young Adams. Then why don't they respect our neutrality? Why don't they agree to a reasonable trade agreement? Why do they plot continually to divide us?[84] Writing of Adams in his diary two months later, Morris declared: "Mr. Adams . . . in his wrath and indignation at the conduct of the British Government seemed absolutely mad. He breathed nothing but war and was content to run into it at the hazard of our finances and even of our Constitution."[85] Morris, who had made a fortune financing the Revolutionary War, was deeply involved financially and politically with the Bank of England.

Adams continued to believe that the British Foreign Office would, if it could, make him their pawn, that they believed he would be full of "complaisance," as he put it. It was certainly true that Grenville and Hammond did everything in their power to convince the corps diplomatique that John Quincy was the American minister in Pinckney's absence. In truth, they believed Thomas Pinckney to be no less hostile to Britain than Deas.

John Quincy was under no illusion as to the lengths the Foreign Office would go to discover his most secret conversations and communications. During their second interview, Hammond had asked if the American's lodgings at Osborn's Hotel were not too noisy. Perhaps he should move to one of the private houses in the neighborhood of Whitehall. "Does he [Hammond] wish to have facilities for keeping spies over me greater than my present lodgings give," Adams speculated in his diary, "or does he fear I shall change, and by advising me to it, think it will deter me from changing?"[86] For his part, Adams, like every other American official in London, had standing instructions to gather intelligence by whatever means necessary. His most important task, John Quincy wrote the vice president, was to obtain copies of the top secret orders-in-council issued by the British government to the commanders of British naval vessels.[87]

Following several delays, John Quincy was scheduled to be presented to the king on January 9. Shortly before the audience was to take place, Adams had a premonition that a trap was being set for him. He immediately sent to Grenville a note declaring that in no case was he to be presented as the minister plenipotentiary for the United States. His credential letter named him as minister resident at the Hague and nothing more. If that precluded him from being received, then so be it. "It suited their purposes to convert me into a Minister at this Court," John Quincy wrote the vice president, "and . . . they have persevered in this intention with such a supple obstinacy, that one of my principal cares has been to disclaim . . . a rank to which I have no title, and to avoid every act that could make me accessory."[88]

To his great relief, the American minister was informed that the king would receive him according to his credentials. Following a stiff formal exchange, George III launched into small talk. From where in the United States did Mr. Adams hail? Massachusetts, sir. Were all the Adamses from Massachusetts? he asked Grenville. I believe so, he replied. Is your father the governor? asked the monarch. No, that would be our cousin, Mr. Samuel Adams. My father is vice president of the United States.[89]

Eventually, Thomas Pinckney returned to assume his duties as minister to Great Britain in February 1796. Yet John Quincy lingered; he would not return to the Hague until he received his official instructions to do so in April 1796. His decision to stay on had largely to do with matters of the heart.

9

Louisa

IN THE FALL OF 1795, John Quincy learned from Nabby that their brother Charles had married Sarah (Sally) Smith, the sister of William Stephens Smith. "After all the hair breadth scrapes and imminent dangers he has run," Nabby declared, "he is at last safe landed—and I believe is very happy."[1] John and Abigail had had some premonitions regarding the heartache that the commingling of the Adams–Smith clans would produce, but they gave their approval. John Quincy was happy for his brother, but the more he thought about the different ways that his parents treated his love life and Charles's, the angrier he became. Charles was his junior; he was flighty, impulsive, and certainly not financially independent. All of the pent-up bitterness John Quincy felt toward his parents over the Mary Frazier affair poured out in a letter to his mother. "Can a widowed heart, a heart which . . . has offered up at the shrine of worldly prudence the painful sacrifice of an ardent affection," ever be able to love again? "When all the pleasing illusions which youth, beauty, and real merit have implanted in the breast . . . when they have been radically torn from the bosom by voluntary violence," could they ever be replaced? His love for Mary could never be duplicated, but perhaps there was room for someone else. Whatever the case, he told his mother, if another opportunity arose, he was determined to be ruled by the heart and not the head. "As to a marriage of convenience, it will be time enough to think of that at five and forty." His love life, if the subject of a novel, could not end but with "a pistol or a bowl [of poison]." Then "I hope you will not think me romantic." (A definite character flaw in the ideal person as far as the Adams family was concerned.)[2]

Adams's first evening in London found him at the home of Joshua and Catherine Johnson, where he dined with the couple, their three daughters, and the distinguished American painter John Trumbull.[3] The Adamses had socialized with the Johnsons previously, in London and then in Nantes. In 1795, Joshua was chief U.S. consul to Great Britain, and his mansion on Cooper's Row near Great Tower Hill—both Roman and medieval in its design—was a frequent site for dinners and balls. John Quincy found the Johnson sisters "pretty and agreeable." Nancy was adept at the piano, Carolina at the harp, and Louisa, the middle sister, at singing. Louisa recalled that when John Quincy sat at their table that November evening, "he was in high spirits [and] conversed most agreeably." After he departed, the family expressed its approval but made fun of his appearance—he was attired in heavy Dutch clothing with a white greatcoat. "His dress did not impress us agreeably as it made his person appear to very great disadvantage." (In fairness, John Quincy had just stepped off the boat from Hellevoetsluis.) Colonel Trumbull remarked that young Adams (he was twenty-eight) was a most eligible bachelor, Louisa later recalled. But she would subsequently deny that there was a family plot to ensnare him; the sisters were "too entirely happy to make marriage a want, and we only looked forward to it as . . . evidence that we were not devoid of those attributes which generally are the operating causes of affection."[4]

Joshua Johnson was descended from a distinguished Maryland planting family. His brother Thomas had been a delegate to the First Continental Congress, where he became an intimate of John Adams. He would go on to serve as wartime governor of Maryland and, after the new Constitution was adopted, was named an associate justice of the Supreme Court. The eighth of eleven children, Joshua had been destined for a career in business. He was apprenticed to the countinghouse of a Scottish émigré merchant from whom he learned the rudiments of accounting and other instruments of commerce. While still in his early twenties, he entered into a partnership with the well-established trading house founded by Charles Wallace and John Davidson. In 1771 the three agreed that Johnson would go to London and establish connections directly with British importers and exporters and thus enable the firm to avoid paying commissions to middlemen. At first, household goods and then all sorts of British manufactures flowed across the Atlantic to Annapolis, there to be purchased by wealthy planter families. Johnson expanded the business to include insurance, and he speculated in tobacco and other commodity futures on his own.[5]

In December 1773, Joshua Johnson fathered a daughter whose given name was Ann but who went by Nancy. The mother was his mistress, Catherine Young Nuth, then fifteen or sixteen. She was no chambermaid; her origins were obscure, but her manners, speech, education, and confidence indicated that she was probably the illegitimate daughter of a nobleman and a commoner, or perhaps the daughter of a family of literati. It would be twelve years before Joshua and Catherine were formally married. He made no mention of her in his correspondence to America, but they lived as man and wife and evidently were fully accepted as such in the community of American officials and businessmen living in London. Nancy was duly baptized, as were Louisa and Carolina, who followed in quick succession. By the time the couple was formally wed, they had produced six living children. They took their vows in St. Anne's, Soho.[6] Significantly, Soho was a district notorious for its bohemian culture, a dense network of brothels, music halls, and pubs.

Catherine Johnson was petite, pretty, vivacious, and, in her maturity, a charming conversationalist and accomplished hostess.[7] "My father seemed to hang on every word she uttered and gazed on her with looks of love and admiration 'as if an increase of appetite had grown by what it fed on,'" Louisa recalled in her memoir *Adventures of a Nobody*.[8] In their various residences in London and France, Catherine would play hostess to some of America's most distinguished citizens. In London she would manage a household that included eleven servants. Later, in America, Mrs. Johnson would be received at both Monticello and Mount Vernon. Abigail and John would find her a stimulating correspondent. "I shall be happy to learn from your pen whatever occurs worthy of observation, for though retired from the world, I like to know what is passing in it—especially if I can obtain it from one who is so capable of describing life & manners," Abigail would later write Catherine.[9]

Louisa Catherine was born in the midst of the widening rift between Great Britain and its American colonies. Joshua Johnson made no effort to hide his sympathy for the revolution blooming on the other side of the Atlantic. Indeed, between 1774 and 1777, he might have acted as an intelligence agent for the Continental Congress. The British secret service thought him worth spying on. With the outbreak of hostilities, Anglo-American trade began to dry up, and the firm of Wallace, Davidson, and Johnson decided to close their London office. Joshua was able to make a tidy profit for his partners and himself on some last-minute shipments of tobacco, the price of which had skyrocketed. He expressed his determination to take himself and his family away to America, but meanwhile two additional daughters, Carolina Virginia Marylanda (1776) and Mariane Ann (1777), had been born. Joshua and Catherine now had four daughters all under the age of five. An Atlantic crossing was out of the question. After the signing of the Franco-American Treaty of 1778, Johnson moved his family to Nantes, a thriving center of commerce situated on the Loire.[10]

The Johnsons rented a suite of rooms in the Temple du Goût (the Temple of Taste, a nickname bestowed by the locals), one of the most elegant residences in the city. Built in 1750 by a successful slave trader, the six-story mansion featured a vaulted staircase, decorated wrought iron balustrades, the finest draperies, and numerous objets d'art, some of them African themed. Nantes at the time was a major entrepôt for the Franco-American trade that helped support the Revolutionary War. It also served as a haven for American ships and as a jumping-off spot for Franco-American naval expeditions against the British. The five years that Joshua Johnson spent in Nantes were among the most profitable of his life. Shortly after the Franco-American Treaty of 1778 was signed, Maryland named him its commercial agent in France. He served in a similar capacity for Congress for a period of time. Johnson, his former partner Wallace, and John Muir, another Annapolis merchant, formed a new company to take advantage of the burgeoning trade opportunities.[11] It was in Nantes that John and John Quincy really became acquainted with the Johnson family.

Catherine enrolled six-year-old Nancy and four-year-old Louisa in a convent school run by the Ursuline nuns on the top floor of the Temple du Goût. Such a practice was not at all unusual for aristocratic families or even members of the bourgeoisie. The girls received instruction in music, dancing, the social graces, needlework, and French. And of course, there was religious instruction. "I perfectly remember . . . the strong impression made upon my imagination by the Roman Catholic Church, the heartfelt humility with which I knelt before the image of the tortured Jesus, and the horror I felt at the thought of mixing with heretics," Louisa later recalled.[12] She would claim that by the time the Johnsons left Nantes when she was eight, she had forgotten almost all of her English. Certainly this was an exaggeration because her diary was filled with detailed descriptions of the parties and dinners at the Temple du Goût. Louisa remembered her beautiful mother being completely occupied with household affairs and the social duties of the wife of the American consul.[13]

In the aftermath of the signing of the Anglo-American Peace of 1783, Joshua, anxious to take advantage of the new trade opportunities that he anticipated, packed up the family and headed back to London. No sooner had Joshua and Catherine settled in their new home on Cooper's Row, just footsteps from the Tower of London, than they shipped Nancy, Louisa, and Carolina off to an English boarding school run by a Mrs. Carter in the village of Shacklewell in the nearby London borough of Hackney. Though sometimes bordering on the inhumane, the practice was customary. Jane Austen was sent off to a similar establishment at a similar age; thinking of the experience later in life, she wrote, "One's heart aches for a dejected mind of eight years old."[14] The experience was particularly difficult for the Johnson girls. "[I]n consequence of our extraordinary dress [much too fashionable and elegant] and utter ignorance of English, we became objects of ridicule to the whole school which consisted of forty young ladies from the ages of seven to twenty."[15] Louisa recalled her horror at being taken by Mrs.

Carter with other girls to attend the nearby Anglican church in Hackney. Forced to kneel down among "heretics," she fainted forthwith.[16]

Louisa would later claim that her experience at the English boarding school scarred her for life. She was singled out and punished for doing things that she had been taught to do and of which she had been proud in Nantes. Her French was so much better than her instructor's that the teacher constantly persecuted her. "It was excruciating," Louisa observed, to be "untaught the language which I had acquired in its native elegance and purity" and forced to learn the "execrable jargon" of the English schools. "To this cause I am convinced I owe the haughtiness and pride of character which it has been impossible for me to subdue."[17] While at school the girls counted the days to vacation.[18]

A busy social schedule was only one reason for Catherine's neglect of her three daughters; she continued to give birth on a regular basis: Catherine Maria in 1784, Eliza Jennet in 1786, and Adelaide in 1788. There would eventually be three more sisters to Louisa Catherine. In raising their children, the Johnsons relied heavily on the advice of their friends Elizabeth and John Hewlett. John was a biblical scholar and private tutor, Elizabeth a no-nonsense woman who believed firmly in the virtues of an English boarding school education.[19] When Louisa fell ill with typhus or a typhuslike illness, however, it was Catherine who nursed her. "My Mother while the tears ran down her cheeks sat by my bed anxiously noting every change, seemingly busy in dressing my doll and making its clothes to amuse me." Apparently, Louisa, then nine, hungered for the attention. Every time Harriet, her three-year-old sister, would appear at the door seeking her mama, the patient would throw a fit.[20] "The weakness and delicacy which ensued in consequence of this . . . illness left me for serval [sic] years very weakly, and I became a pet as is usual in such cases."[21] A lesson was subconsciously learned that would lead to a life of hypochondria punctuated periodically by actual illness.

By the time Louisa returned to school, her English had improved and with it her confidence. If the other students did not love her, they respected her, she recalled. The child possessed perfect pitch, which drove her instructors trying to teach her to read music to distraction. She heard a piece and then performed it flawlessly. Nancy proved adept at the piano, and she frequently accompanied Louisa as they performed duos. But Louisa wanted more than music, dancing, social skills, and rudimentary learning. In this, she was joined by a new friend, a Miss Edwards. They became inseparable, rooming together, taking their meals together, and sharing secrets. "She was an East Indian, very dark, with long black Indian hair," Louisa wrote in her memoir, "not handsome, but looked up to by all the teachers and scholars as a girl of uncommon talents."[22] The head teacher, a Miss Young, recognized in the two girls an intellectual yearning that was absent from most of the other students. Miss Young, a masculine, forbidding figure to most of the girls, had managed to acquire an education usually reserved for males. She knew Latin and a bit of Greek and was steeped in the classics and in modern literature. "She took much pains to improve us and conversed freely with us upon the books we read, pointing out and selecting the most beautiful and striking passages and cultivating our taste by her judgment."[23]

Louisa's appetite for learning, which turned out to be lifelong, was one of the things that would connect her to John Quincy. Another was the theater. She recalled her joy at being cast to perform in Hannah More's *The Search After Happiness*, her first role. "It was universally admitted that the haughty Euphemia [*sic*] *was* exactly suited to me." During school holidays the Johnson girls were allowed to attend performances at Drury Lane and Covent Garden, where they saw Sarah Siddons and "the elegant Miss [Elizabeth] Farren."[24]

In 1789 the Johnsons and the Hewletts decided that Louisa had had enough formal education. She returned to her parents' house at Number 8 Cooper's Row to serve as an ornament to the household and await, hopefully, a proposal of marriage. If she or any of her sisters were attracted to a suitor, they could count on a five-thousand-pound dowry to augment their natural charms.[25] Louisa had claimed shortly after meeting John Quincy that she and her sisters were in no way desperate to find husbands. If she really believed that, she was engaging in massive self-deception. Life for an unmarried woman in late-eighteenth-century Britain was daunting indeed. There were no social safety nets. On the death of a daughter's father, all property devolved on the brothers unless she had been singled out in the will for a bequest. Unmarried women, especially as they increased in years, were exploited as unpaid nursemaids or caregivers in the houses of relatives who generally regarded them with either pity or scorn. One could teach, but that paid little or nothing, and it lacked security. The most popular refuge for spinsters was the position of governess. But that meant a life of dependence lived in the midst of children who were often spoiled and unruly. Life "midway between the servants' hall and the drawing room" could be trying to say the least.[26] Witness the characters in *Emma, Vanity Fair*, and *Jane Eyre*. No wonder Jane Austen would describe marriage as "the only honorable provision for well-educated young women of small fortune, and however uncertain for giving happiness, must be their pleasantest preservative from want."[27]

Nancy's, Louisa's, and Carolina's formal education might have been at an end, but Joshua was determined that they should continue to learn. He hired a full-time governess and tutors in music, drawing, and dancing. He understood that Nancy, Louisa, and Catherine, when married, would each have to learn to run a household. Despite his hope that they wed Americans, he prepared them to run an upper-class British domestic operation. Each girl was required to supervise the Johnson household for one week at a time. Louisa learned the culinary arts from the cook, sewing (at which she later excelled) from the seamstress, and, most important, financial management from her mother. The lady of the house was required to keep accounts, pay the servants and tradesmen, and order food and other supplies. She was also the family nurse and as such would have had to become familiar with treatments for everything from colds to typhus. Unfortunately, Louisa would have to make a home in America, not England. Household management, as typified by Abigail's experience, was much more fraught, requiring constant adjustments and hands-on work. The Johnsons' servants were well trained and generally accepting of their roles. Servants in America tended to be rawer and less accommodating. They came and went as opportunities arose. Most American wives worked alongside their cooks and gardeners rather than just supervising them.[28]

In the summer of 1790, Secretary of State Thomas Jefferson appointed Joshua Johnson U.S. consul in London, an important post given that the city was the commercial and financial center of the Atlantic world. There were two probable reasons for the appointment. Johnson knew more important people in Britain and France than perhaps any other American. Aside from his business acumen, there were his exploits during the early stages of the Revolutionary War. Johnson had worked for the release of both Henry Laurens after he was captured and imprisoned in the Tower and then John Trumbull, who was charged with treason and incarcerated at Tothill Fields Bridewell.[29] Moreover, he had performed intelligence duties for his country when he was consul in Nantes. Jefferson's 1790 instructions were revealing. Not surprisingly the new consul was to report on the movements of the British mercantile and naval fleets, to represent American seamen who had been impressed into the Royal Navy, and to see that the rights of American merchants were protected. But in addition, Johnson was to act as an intelligence gatherer.[30] Consular positions were unpaid, but Johnson made it clear to Jefferson from the outset that spying cost money. "You who have been in Europe . . . know how difficult it is to obtain information that can be depended on without . . . spending considerable sums of money."[31]

In August 1792 the new U.S. minister to Great Britain, Thomas Pinckney, and his family arrived in London. Pinckney was an English-educated planter and prominent political figure from South Carolina. The Pinckneys and the Johnsons, both Southerners, quickly hit it off.[32] As wealthy Southern aristocrats, the Pinckneys had access to Anglo-American high society. At the center of this community were the British businessman and MP John Barker Church and his American-born wife, Angelica, a member of two of New York's wealthiest and most politically influential families, the Van Rensselaers and the Schuylers. She was the sister-in-law of Alexander Hamilton. The three eldest Johnson girls became frequent ornaments at the fabulous Church parties.[33] By the time she was seventeen, Louisa had had a suitor or two, one of them being David Serett, an employee of Joshua's who boarded with the family, but nothing came of it.[34] William Vans Murray, then a law student at the Temple, was a frequent guest at the Johnson residence. He paid Louisa some attention, but the romance fizzled before it began. Nancy, Louisa, and Carolina's social circle shrank dramatically after their father received a letter from his renowned brother Thomas. He had heard much of his charming nieces, he wrote, and urged Joshua to be sure that they became engaged only to "men of note and distinction in his own country."[35] "I cannot pretend to mention all the gentlemen with whom we were acquainted," Louisa wrote in her diary. "I can only say that in consequence of my Uncle's silly letter . . . we were kept almost entirely out of English society."[36] "If I ever had any admirers, no woman I can assure you ever had fewer lovers than your Mother," she would later tell her children.[37]

Louisa Catherine was by all accounts a keen observer of the human condition—her nickname in the family was Cassandra. She read the romance novels of the time that featured heroes in disguise and heroines in constant danger of losing their virtue. She understood that the conventions of the time required women to be graceful, artistic, and ornamental in order to attract men who were strong and romantic. But her reading in the serious and substantive, introduced to her by Miss Young, continued. She used a New Year's Day cash gift from her father to purchase John Milton's *Paradise Lost* and *Paradise Regained,* and John Mason's *Treatise on Self-Knowledge.*[38] She enjoyed the company of older, learned men. She had spent two months with the Hewletts at their country house and remembered being enthralled with John Hewlett's learned conversation. John Trumbull, who had served as secretary to John Jay during the final negotiations on the Anglo-American Treaty of 1783 and who had studied art in London and Paris, was a constant visitor at the house on Cooper's Row. By that time, he was already famous for his historically themed paintings such as *The Death of General Warren at the Battle of Bunker's Hill* and *The Declaration of Independence.* Although he was only thirty-nine at the time, Louisa described him as old enough to be her father. Their conversations were wide-ranging, and Trumbull attempted, unsuccessfully, to teach her to paint. "Once in his life he said he wished he was a young man for then he should certainly pay his addresses to me; and this was the utmost that ever passed between us," Louisa later recalled.[39]

Joshua and Catherine were well acquainted with the Adams family, having entertained John and Abigail frequently during John's stint as minister to Great

Britain. But Louisa and her sisters had been away at school during most of that period. When William Stephens Smith made his solo foray to England in 1790–1791, he was a constant visitor.[40] When, in early 1793, Smith returned from America with his family in tow, the bonds between the two families grew even stronger. "The Colonel's manners . . . were irresistible and we seldom sat down to our favorite suppers without him." When Smith was away on business, Nabby and the children would go and spend the day at Cooper's Row. "It was my delight to dress her [Nabby]," Louisa later remembered, "and I was often employed in making up articles of millinery which I used to insist upon her wearing and in which she looked beautiful. She was one of the most placid, quiet beings I ever saw; very cold in her general manners, but when she laughed or entered into the spirit of our gaiety . . . she seemed to be the life of the party—she would romp or dance and partake of all the jokes like one of us, and she was perfectly adored by the family."[41]

It would be a month after the dinner at the Johnsons'—his first night in London—before John Quincy saw the family again. But when he did call, it became the first of many visits. Indeed, barely an evening passed during the next four months that he was not at Cooper's Row. He would dine with the family and then return later in the evening for the night's entertainment, which included musicals by Louisa, Nancy, and Carolina and games of whist. Over time he began accompanying the ladies on some of their daily outings and escorting them to assorted balls.[42] His diary was a chronicle of life with the Johnsons: "Danced with Miss Church, with Louisa & etc. After three in the morning before we retired."[43] "Evening at Drury Lane Theatre, Mrs. Johnson and her Daughters at Mrs. Church's box."[44] "Evening at Mrs. Johnson's . . . playing cards . . . Some music . . . Louisa 21."[45]

Soon, however, John Quincy sensed that his presence was creating tension in the household. Louisa would later recall that her mother was enchanted with her prospective suitor, her father not so much. "He always had a prejudice towards the Yankees and insisted that they never made good husbands."[46] But Joshua managed to conceal his feelings. After all, there were seven daughters to be married off, and John Quincy was the son of the vice president of the United States. Initially, the family believed that the object of young Mr. Adams's interest was their eldest, Nancy, as she was pretty, vivacious, and an accomplished pianist. Louisa was convinced that was the case, so much so that she relaxed with John Quincy, "rattling on," as she put it.[47] The first indication that it was Louisa and not Nancy in whom John Quincy was interested came when he would pick up his hat and coat and leave in a huff when Louisa sang particular tunes. It seems that those were favorites of Colonel Trumbull, whom Adams had come to see as a rival. A year later, long after they were engaged, John Quincy wrote Louisa that in his jealousy, he had raged at Trumbull: "by my Gods—Wished him . . . D[ead], innocent as he was of all I feared."[48]

Aware that John Quincy was something of a poet, Louisa insisted that he compose her a song. At an ensuing dinner, he handed her a piece of paper and declared, "Here is your song." The unsuspecting Louisa began reading the lyrics aloud. Miss Henning, the governess, snatched the sheet and whispered in her ear that such an intimacy was not to be shared. "This as you may believe caused me to blush and behave like a fool," Louisa recorded in her diary.[49] As it dawned on the family that John Quincy had his sights set on Louisa, a momentary chill settled over the household. Nancy was furious.[50] Shortly afterward, John Quincy, Catherine, and the girls went to Covent Garden to hear Handel's *L'Allegro* and *Il Penseroso* performed. "Sullen and silent the whole time," he recorded.[51] A week later: "Dined at Mr. Johnson's; Nancy very much affected I know not at what; Louisa pretended a headache for the privilege of being cross."[52]

In truth, at the outset, Louisa and John Quincy's romance made them both uncomfortable. Louisa might have perceived some condescension in John Quincy's attitude toward her. Though she excelled in the feminine arts, she viewed herself as more than an ornament. She read serious literature and participated in conversations about art, philosophy, and politics with her father, Trumbull, and other accomplished male visitors. In truth she was not yet in love. Rather than being swept off her feet, "my vanity was enlisted and without an article of affection at the time, I suffered myself to be coaxed into an affection."[53] For his part, John Quincy was both attracted to and repelled by the Johnsons' lavish lifestyle. How could he ever hope to afford the fine houses, dinners, balls, and other accoutrements of those members of the upper-class society in which Louisa had been raised? And he had still not gotten over Mary Frazier. Both Louisa and John Quincy felt they were being forced into a relationship by social convention.

There were more than societal norms at work, however. Joshua Johnson was in financial free fall, making it economically as well as socially imperative for him to marry off his daughters. Louisa would claim that life at the Johnson mansion was not extravagant, but she was wrong. Joshua, believing that evidence of material success attracted business, had never been one to scrimp. Their house featured eleven servants; there was a carriage house, which required a stable boy, a blacksmith, and a coachman. Given the abundance of hackney cabs in London, owning a carriage in the city was an extravagance. There were a wife and seven daughters to dress and dinners and balls to be paid for. Since his return to London from Nantes, Johnson had walked the razor's edge with prosperity on one side and bankruptcy on the other. In 1784 his partners in Wallace, Johnson and Muir learned that he had not collected twenty-four thousand pounds owed to them by another firm, and had continued to extend credit to the other business's customers. In 1787, Johnson brought his firm's thirteen principal creditors together and turned the books over to them, thus temporarily avoiding arrest for fraud. In December 1789, bankruptcy was declared, and the company was dissolved. Johnson thereupon formed his own mercantile trading business and somehow managed to stay afloat for the next six years.[54] But by the time John Quincy came calling, the end was near.

When, exactly, John Quincy and Louisa became engaged is unclear. During March, the two saw each other nearly every day—at dinner and afterward, at the theater, touring London's art galleries, walking its parks. After an evening at Cooper's Row on March 2, there came a strange entry in John Quincy's diary: "ring from Louisa's finger. Tricks play'd . . . Placed in a very difficult dilemma. Know not how I shall escape from it."[55] Perhaps the sisters had played a trick on the couple; perhaps John Quincy was the prankster. Louisa was not pleased; the next night, he and she had "some conversation. Did not close well."[56] Throughout the spring, John Quincy's diary was filled with self-loathing. He complained of being unable to concentrate, to read little else but the newspapers, but he was drawn to the Johnsons', fraught or not, like a moth to a flame. Finally, Catherine had had enough: "Card this morning from Mrs. Johnson desiring to see me. Partly apologetical, and partly spirited. Went accordingly."[57] What exactly were his intentions toward her daughter? Catherine asked. Finally, he was compelled to cross the Rubicon. "Came to a full explanation of my views and intentions with Madam upon the subject which was interesting to her. She declared herself well-satisfied."[58] Neither party, it seemed, had bothered to consult Louisa or Joshua. At dinner the following evening, John Quincy found his betrothed smoldering with rage and resentment. But over the next few days, the couple talked it out, and Louisa resigned herself to becoming Mrs. Adams.

Understanding or not, when in the days that followed, the Johnsons pressed John Quincy to set a marriage date; he adamantly refused. "Upon one point . . . the only one to which I must adhere, neither of them was satisfied. The right and the reason of the thing are however indisputably with me, and I shall accordingly persist."[59] He must return to his post in the Netherlands, he declared. It was still unclear whether the French would leave the Batavian Republic its pseudo-independence or annex it outright, in which case John Quincy would have to withdraw. He could not yet assure the family that he had the means to support a wife and children. Louisa and her parents felt trapped. As long as Louisa remained engaged and unmarried, she would live in social limbo. Attending balls and dancing with unattached young men were out of the question. Joshua, of course, was increasingly uncertain concerning his own financial future. Later, when John Quincy and Louisa were alone, she begged him to marry her before he left for the Netherlands, to give her his name, and then she could join him at a mutually agreeable time. He refused.

As the courtship continued into May, resentments on both sides grew apace and at one point threatened to end in an open breach. On May 10, John Quincy wrote in his diary: "At Mr. Johnson's in the evening. The usual asperities arose. . . . I must get away."[60] The next day he and two other young men were to escort Catherine and her daughters to Ranelagh, a twenty-three-acre wooded park in the fashionable Chelsea district of London. The park included English gardens, numerous fountains, walking paths, and a wooden rotunda at its center. Earlier that night, Louisa had told John Quincy that if he accompanied the ladies, he must dress himself handsomely and "look as dashy as possible."[61] John Quincy, notoriously neglectful of his appearance, had since his courtship began spending a full hour each day dressing and grooming himself. To her delight, when the ladies picked him up at Osborn's Hotel, John Quincy "was very handsomely dressed in blue [and] he had a large napoleon hat and altogether looked remarkably well." She herself had dressed "very becomingly."[62]

The party rode to Ranelagh in high spirits, and Louisa anticipated a gay time. After stepping down from the coach, the party separated, and she took John Quincy's arm for a stroll. Louisa then made the mistake of complimenting him on his dress. He immediately "took fire and assured me that his wife must never take the liberty of interfering in those particulars [of dress] and assumed a tone so high and lofty and made so serious a grievance of the affair that I felt offended and told him that I resigned all pretensions to his hand and left him as free as air to choose a lady who would be more discreet."[63] She then dropped his arm and joined her mother. John Quincy and Louisa made up on the carriage ride home, but the incident had planted in Louisa's mind a seed of doubt that would grow over time. John Quincy's only mention of the affair was a note in his diary: "More lessons of dress."[64]

At this point, John Quincy had not informed his parents of his engagement, but they knew from Thomas Boylston and Thomas Baker Johnson, Louisa's brother, who was then in the United States, that John Quincy was a constant guest at Cooper's Row.[65] In May, Abigail and her niece Lucy Cranch received two cloaks made by the Johnson girls. The previous February, Abigail had requested a long cape as a present for her niece. "The cloaks were chosen by Mrs. Johnson, and by her second daughter, a very amiable young lady bearing the name of Louisa Catherine," John Quincy wrote his mother.[66] Abigail's response was encouraging. "The young lady who undertook the commission shews that she inherits the taste of elegance which her Mamma is conspicuous for." She sensed a romance. "Some fair one has shewn you its sophistry. . . . Youth and beauty have penetrated through your fancied apathy. . . . I would hope for the love I bear my country, that the Siren, is at least *half blood*."[67]

In April, John Quincy finally received instructions from Secretary of State Pickering to return to his post at the Hague. As the time for his departure neared, his relationship with Louisa improved dramatically. There was and always would be a strong sexual attraction between the two; indeed, part of the rancor of April and May might have been the result of sexual frustration. Dinners at the Johnsons' became once again warm and gay. John Quincy booked passage on a small Prussian schooner due to depart on May 28. One last dinner the night before: "Evening at Mr. Johnson's, an evening of delight and of regret. Took my leave of all the family with sensations unusually painful."[68]

John Quincy was late in reaching Gravesend the next morning and found that his ship had sailed. He prevailed upon some local boatmen—for an exorbitant fee—to take him on board and catch up to the packet. This they did, rendezvousing with the vessel some six miles beyond Gravesend. John Quincy arrived safely in Rotterdam three days later.[69]

The minister resident was relieved to be back in the Hague, where he felt he could gain some perspective both on his love life and his future as a public man. He had missed Thomas and was much comforted by their reunion. The stimulating walks and talks with Baron de Bielfeld were resumed, and after a few weeks, John Quincy began taking Italian lessons under his direction.[70] There was time for Smith's *Wealth of Nations*, with which John Quincy declared himself to be well pleased. On July 11, John Quincy turned twenty-nine. "The irresistible dissipation of London is done," he observed in his diary.[71] He reveled in Dryden and Pope, he walked several miles a day, but Louisa was never far from his mind—nor was she from Abigail's.

As the drama of John Quincy and Louisa Catherine's engagement unfolded, Abigail sensed a threat to the independence of the vehicle of her ambition. On February 29 she wrote her eldest son a letter that on its face was comforting and reassuring but was in fact a dagger aimed at his romantic heart: "I do not wonder that it [the news of Charles's marriage] awakened the dormant feelings of your soul and uncovered the fire, which though smothered, gleamed up again. . . ." But duty called and the destiny laid out for him required "a single, [rather] than a married state. . . . Let the consciousness of having acted right console you." As for Mary Frazier, Abigail was sure that she would not marry as long as he remained single. "She may not appear to you in a few years with all those outward attractions which the bloom of 18 gave her," because after all, looks were not everything.[72]

John Quincy did not receive the letter until May and did not reply until July, but when he did, it was with conviction. "You enquire whether Maria [Mary Frazier] has no claims?—She has none but to my fervent and cordial good wishes for her welfare. I have often assured you that we had parted forever." No doubt, he would have liked to have added, *How dare you!* Instead, he declared that he and Louisa had entered into "an attachment which has now become irrevocably fixed." Their bonding was not without sacrifice, he reminded his mother, in that they had agreed to separate and delay their marriage until the future more clearly defined itself. "Prudence is a sorry match-maker," and a life of celibacy was not for him. "I . . . am with unceasing duty and affection, your son."[73]

In early August 1796, John Quincy learned that he had been appointed minister plenipotentiary to Portugal. He greeted the news with mixed emotions. In truth he liked the diplomatic life, and the difference in salary between a resident and a plenipotentiary was huge: five thousand dollars per annum for the former and nine thousand dollars for the latter. But he feared that he and John would be accused of nepotism. Never, never would he accept a post through the influence of his celebrated father. Abigail reassured him that the appointment had been one of Washington's last, and John had been at home in Quincy when John Quincy's name was submitted to the Senate.[74]

Although John Quincy did not learn of his new appointment with its accompanying largesse until August, his parents had known about it since June. They realized that a minister plenipotentiary's salary was more than enough to support a family, but they continued to heap guilt on their son for planning to marry before he returned to America.[75] Abigail to John Quincy: "I approve of the young lady's discretion in sending you to the Hague without her . . . you should learn to accumulate some solid property before you take upon you the charge of a family."[76] John observed to his son that a young woman coming from a background like Louisa's, "of fine parts and accomplishments, educated to drawing, dancing, and music," would "when she comes to shine in a court among the families of ambassadors and ministers of state . . . be in danger of involving you in expenses far beyond your appointments. . . . I give you a hint and you must take it," he admonished.[77] It seemed that John and Abigail would not be reconciled to a union between John Quincy and Louisa even if he were to retire from the diplomatic corps and return to America. It was very doubtful, Abigail wrote, that a young woman of such refined manners could adapt to the simple republican ways of America. It would not be fair to expect it of her![78]

John Quincy's first letters to Louisa following his return to the Hague were affectionate, almost lyrical. He found his mind constantly returning to life at Cooper's Row, now remembered blissfully. "I see you sitting on the sofa with the table before you, working at a Vandyke, and Caroline at the other end with her silken network pinned before her while Nancy calls the very soul of harmony from the forte-piano. I place myself between you. . . . From thence we pass to the opposite room where the humorous additions to the dictionary from one sister, and the unfilled outlines of imprecation from another, delight, and charm."[79] He told her that he believed that his time at the Hague and in Europe was drawing to a close and he was planning a life for them in America. Two weeks later: "I am at this moment looking at Mr. Birch's young lady [Louisa had presented him with a miniature painting of herself upon his departure] and using all my little eloquence to solicit a smile from her countenance."[80]

Hidden away in a cottage in Clapham Common—a parklike area in southern London—and separated from the intense, stimulating social life of Cooper's Row and its environs, Louisa set about conquering a rather intimidating reading list that John Quincy had presented to her just before their separation. Louisa was overcome with self-doubt to the point that writing to her lover frightened her near to death. "I shall never forget the anxiety with which I awaited a letter from Mr. Adams and the terror which assailed me at the idea of answering it."[81] Her first offerings were the stilted, saccharine work of Miss Henning, the governess and her companion at Clapham. John Quincy grew impatient, and upon learning from his betrothed of the reason for her brief and stale letters, he admonished her. Your mother is one of the most accomplished letter writers in England, he wrote. Surely the apple falls not far from the tree. Eventually Louisa cut Miss Henning out of the loop, and her correspondence became more substantive and revealing.

On August 6, John Quincy wrote Louisa to inform her that he had been named minister plenipotentiary to Portugal. He did not refer to the large increase in salary; it was his intention to stop off in London on his way to Lisbon so they could marry. But in a post a week later, John Quincy began to voice the doubts that were being implanted in him by his parents. It could very well be months before he was relieved of his post at the Hague. He warned Louisa that the sheltered life she had led had not prepared her for life as the spouse of an American diplomat. There would be arduous sea voyages, rough overland travel, uncomfortable lodgings, and strange people.[82]

Louisa responded with spirit. She was not a slave to pomp and splendor, she wrote; the prospect of dangerous sea passages and arduous land travel held no dread for her. John Quincy and she would, after all, be bearing the burdens together. As to Portugal, she had no objection, but told him that if she had been consulted, she would have opted for them to marry and repair immediately to America.[83] He backtracked: "As to the subject of pomp or parade, I will henceforth be totally silent upon it." But he would not, he told Louisa, raise false hopes or paint overly rosy pictures.[84] During this period, John Quincy repeatedly wrote his betrothed to be prepared to marry on short notice. "Several letters came on the same subject," Louisa recalled in her memoir, "and my Mother began to prepare my wedding finery, which was all got ready for the expected occasion. Weeks rolled on, however, without any further intelligence and considering it as a false alarm, everything was locked up and all the preparations concealed with as much care as if I had committed some crime in having made them."[85]

By September, Joshua had become increasingly worried about his second daughter's well-being. She had lost her usual vivacity and zest for life; she complained of various physical ailments. After allowing her to return to Cooper's Row, the father decided to break the marital logjam. With the dissolution of Wallace, Johnson and Muir, life in England was no longer tenable. It had become imperative that the Johnsons return to Maryland, where, they hoped, the family's fortunes could be recouped. "Unless I go to America soon, I may lose everything that I have been laboring for during my life & leave my family unprovided for & even unprotected," he wrote John Quincy. He offered one of his ships—sailing under a neutral flag—to fetch John Quincy to London or, if that was not convenient, to come to Holland and explain.[86] When John Quincy waffled, Joshua wrote again, this time proposing that on their way to America the Johnsons stop off at the Hague so that Louisa and John Quincy could be married."[87] At the time unaware that her father had contacted her betrothed with his proposal, she wrote John Quincy that she hoped to visit Holland so that they could see each other for the last time before a long and perhaps final separation.[88] He responded to these initiatives by accusing father and daughter of attempting to ensnare him. Adding insult to injury, he declared, "You will be sensible what an appearance in the eyes of the world of you coming here would have; an appearance consistent neither with your dignity, nor my delicacy."[89]

In an act of indignant defiance that, ironically, probably saved their relationship, Louisa wrote back, "I regret most sincerely ever having expressed a wish to see you in Holland since it appears to have given you so much uneasiness. . . . I never really mentioned it to my father. You tell me that our visit would neither have been consistent with your delicacy or my dignity. I rather think you ought to have reversed it and said it would have been inconsistent with your dignity and my delicacy."[90] Had you only given some encouragement, some idea when we might be united, I could bear it, she wrote. But no, and as a result, "the die is cast, I go to America, you to your embassy, where I ardently pray the great disposer of events to grant to your bosom the peace that mine has."[91] "The broken ice is not likely to be repaired," John Quincy noted tersely in his diary.[92]

But these bitter exchanges were interspersed with expressions of love, affection, and commitment. The couple was physically and intellectually attracted to each other. Louisa proved that she had the spirit to survive as an Adams. John Quincy was lonely. There was his avidity for study, with which he felt marriage would interfere, but that did not explain his obstinacy, sometimes morphing into cruelty. By this time he had at long last received permission from his mother to marry Louisa. "I think you ought not to go to Portugal alone. Your brother means to return to us. You whose chief delight is in domestic life, must feel yourself in a desert without a companion. . . . I advise you to marry the lady before you go to Portugal. Give my love to her and tell her I consider her already as my daughter."[93] There is an entry in John Quincy's diary at the close of January 1797 that is revealing: "A profound anxiety has taken possession of my mind. The situations of two objects the nearest to my heart, my country and my father, press continually upon my reflections. They engross every thought and almost overpower every faculty."[94]

ONE OF THE THINGS that had made John Quincy's six-month stay in England so fraught was the prospect that the House of Representatives would not appropriate the funds necessary to give effect to the Jay Treaty. The Democratic-Republicans in America, in league with the Francophile American community in Paris, were doing everything in their power to torpedo the treaty. The British, in continuing to seize scores of American commercial vessels, were not helping matters. But then in late June 1797 word came that the Senate had ratified the Jay Treaty by a vote of twenty to ten, the barest of victory margins. The House fell in line by voting to fund America's obligations under the agreement. In June, the British would in fact surrender their forts in the Northwest Territory to American forces. Though John Bull continued to violate America's neutral rights and to impress its seamen, a war that seemed almost inevitable two years earlier had been averted. John Quincy was under no illusions regarding the impact of ratification on Franco-American relations. "France must consider us henceforth as an infallible ally of Britain against her," he wrote his father. He believed that the Directory's minister to the United States, Pierre Adet, acting in league with American Jacobins, had been plotting the overthrow of the Washington administration and even amending the Constitution so as to replace the office of president with an American directory.[95]

The previous year, in August 1796, Benny Bache, Franklin's Francophile grandson, had published a copy of a philippic by Tom Paine vilifying George Washington. Shortly after, the Washington administration recalled James Monroe as minister to France on the grounds that he was not doing enough to defend America's interests, especially its neutrality. When his replacement, General Charles Cotesworth Pinckney, a staunch Federalist, arrived in Paris, the Directory declared him persona non grata and refused to accredit him.[96] Among other things, Pinckney had refused to provide bribes to the members of the Directory and their minister of foreign affairs, Charles-Maurice de Talleyrand-Périgord. "They really think the American people not only as ignorant of Europe as they themselves are of America," an outraged John Quincy wrote to his father in January 1797, "but moreover idiots and cowards upon whom tinsel can with the utmost facility be palmed for bullion." John Quincy hoped that the future president of the United States, "whoever he may be," would continue the "same wisdom, firmness and moderation" exhibited by the immortal Washington.[97]

When he penned this letter, John Quincy knew that his father was a leading candidate to become Washington's successor. He loved his father and wished the very best for him, but the next president was sure to be caught between the Scylla of French depredations and the pro-French party in America, and the Charybdis of British orders-in-council and the pro-British High Federalists. John's election to the presidency would mean the end of public life for his eldest son for at least the next four years. In his mind and in his diary, John Quincy was telling himself that he would never accept an appointment from his father and expose both of them to the crippling and humiliating charge of nepotism.

Washington announced his intention to retire from public life and, on September 19, 1796, published his famous Farewell Address. That document, a paean to nonpartisanship and neutrality, owed much to the thought and writings of John and John Quincy Adams. Indeed, on the eve of his departure, Washington informed the vice president that John Quincy's views on foreign affairs coincided exactly with his own. John Adams's long and meritorious service to his country as delegate to the Continental Congresses, peacemaker, minister to Great Britain, and vice president eminently qualified him for the presidency in the eyes of many Americans. But, despite his independence of mind, he was widely associated with the Federalist Party. Madison and the Democratic-Republicans continued to suspect him of being a closet monarchist and reviled both him and his son for their support of the Jay Treaty.

Alexander Hamilton had grown used to exerting a strong influence over the executive, and the prospect of Adams as president made him vaguely uneasy. But it was clear that if matters rested, he would be the Federalist nominee. Thomas Jefferson, somewhat against his will, had become the choice of the Democratic-Republicans. Indeed, it was Hamilton's constant attacks on Jefferson in the press that had thrust him into the limelight. Thomas Pinckney was the Federalists' choice for vice president while the Republicans selected Aaron Burr for second place on their ticket.[98]

The architects of the U.S. Constitution did not anticipate (or perhaps did not want to accept) the emergence of political parties. As a result, the members of the Electoral College were to vote for two persons, one of them a resident of a state other than their own, without declaring a preference for president or vice president. The individual receiving the most tallies would be chief executive and he who came in second would be vice president. Thus did the Founders unknowingly open the door to political intrigue that would threaten the very fabric of the infant democracy. The differences between Alexander Hamilton and John Adams were not so much matters of policy as attitudes toward power. For Hamilton, it was to be gotten by whatever means necessary. For Adams, the acquisition of power by less-than-honorable methods was abhorrent, as was its exercise for other than what he considered virtuous ends.[99] Hamilton wanted to control the next chief executive, and Adams would not be controlled. Behind the scenes, the New Yorker maneuvered to have Pinckney elected president. He assumed that New Englanders to a man would vote for Adams and Pinckney. He urged Southern Federalists to submit Pinckney's name only. Adams's loyalists got wind of the scheme, however, and dropped Pinckney from their list.[100] Some electors voted for Jefferson and Pinckney and others for Adams and Jefferson. In the end Adams triumphed, receiving seventy-one electoral votes, mostly from New England, New York, and New Jersey. Jefferson was second with sixty-eight, all from Pennsylvania and the states to the south. Pinckney garnered fifty-nine votes and Burr thirty.[101]

There was never any question that Thomas Jefferson would serve under Adams. Indeed, while the electoral votes were being tallied and with a chance of the election being thrown to the House of Representatives, he instructed Madison to "fully solicit on my behalf that Mr. Adams may be preferred. He has always been my senior from the commencement of our public life."[102] When it became clear that Adams had won, Jefferson again wrote Madison, indicating that he would be happy to be the vice president in an Adams administration. It would be "for the public good to come to a good understanding with him."[103] For their part, both John and John Quincy had expressed their view that the republic would be in good hands with Jefferson at the helm. "As to the decision upon the presidential election," John Quincy wrote to a colleague, "I am not alarmed about it at all but have the most unequivocal confidence that in either of the probable alternatives, the chief magistracy of the union will be administered with wisdom and integrity, with moderation and spirit."[104]

John Adams took the oath of office as second president of the United States in the House of Representatives before a joint session of Congress, members of the Supreme Court, and the ministers of the diplomatic corps. In his inaugural address, he expressed friendship for both France and Great Britain, denounced foreign meddling in American politics, and promised to adhere to strict neutrality in his foreign policy.[105] Abigail did not join her husband in Philadelphia until June. They had hoped that he would have a respite in the aftermath of the election, she wrote John Quincy, but that was not to be the case. "The critical state of our country as it respects France, the daily and increasing depredations made upon our commerce, and refusal to receive our minister" required his immediate and full attention.[106]

The Hague continued to be one of the most important listening posts on the Continent. On March 2, 1797, two days before Washington left office, the Directory declared that the Jay Treaty had invalidated the Franco-American commercial treaty of 1778 and that France would no longer recognize the principle of free ships make free goods; henceforward, all U.S. vessels found bearing cargo for Britain or British colonial ports were subject to seizure by French naval vessels and privateers. "That *arrêté* is equivalent to a declaration of war," John Quincy wrote Joseph Pitcairn.[107]

John Quincy subsequently reported—accurately—that Talleyrand was secretly negotiating with Spain for the retrocession of Louisiana. The French plan was to use New Orleans as a base to link up with disgruntled frontier farmers in the American West and split the Union.[108] With France's new proconsul, Napoleon Bonaparte, rampaging through Italy and beating up on the Austrians, the French were feeling invincible. If America was prepared to stand up to France as one people, matters might have been less disturbing to John Quincy. Political dissent in the United States was one thing, but there were Americans in Europe actually participating in France's maritime war against the United States. U.S. citizens living in France, John Quincy reported to Philadelphia, were paying visits to Britain, gathering information on the comings and goings of American merchantmen, and then returning to France, where they outfitted privateers sailing under the French flag. These marauders then sallied forth from the ports of Brest, Le Havre, and Dieppe to lay waste to the American merchant fleet.[109]

IN THE MIDST OF this looming crisis, John Quincy was unwilling to name a date for his and Louisa's marriage. Following the angry exchanges of December 1796, both had drawn back from the brink. In truth, they loved each other. Both wanted to have a family, and Louisa desperately needed a suitable marriage. "No sooner were those letters gone," she wrote her betrothed, "than I repented my folly and was convinced my conduct was weak and ridiculous. . . . Let me again assure you, my best friend, that you shall never more be offended by an assertion of spirit that I in reality do not possess."[110] For his part, John Quincy confessed that he had walked the three miles that separated the Hague from the sea so that he could cast his gaze toward the coast of England. "An instant of illusion transported me to you."[111] The letters that followed were full of expressions of love and affection but were at the same time a subtle struggle for power. Louisa would affect the role of a submissive wife, but when John Quincy's condescension and pretentiousness became unbearable, she would assert herself. In response to her letter of apology, John Quincy wrote back: "Let me now assure you that I never thought your disposition deficient in spirit, and that I am fully convinced you have as much of it as can be consistent with an amiable temper, but let me earnestly entreat you never to employ it in discussion with me, and to remember that it is in its nature a repellent quality."[112] When they seemed to draw too close, he sought to thrust patriotism between them. "I may . . . own [confess] to you that my duty to my country is in my mind the first and most imperious of all obligations; before which every interest and every feeling inconsistent with it must forever disappear."[113] Louisa could not help pricking that balloon: "I think as you do respecting your attachment to your country; it is certainly a virtue, but like all other virtues may be carried to too great a height."[114]

During his six-month stay in London, John Quincy, distracted by an intense courtship and nagging self-doubt, had had little or no time for intellectual endeavors. In this regard, his return to the Hague brought respite. Unfortunately, in his correspondence with Louisa, he had the gracelessness and insensitivity to compare the life of the heart unfavorably with the life of the mind. "In my books I can return with pleasure, even from the most pleasing excursions of the fancy. They leave no languor, no satiety, no listlessness of indolence upon the mind."[115] In perhaps her most audacious sortie into the formidable environs of John Quincy's world, Louisa Catherine wrote back: "You are I think too young a man to devote all your time to your books and solitude . . . what will you do some years hence, even after we are married? Even your Louisa's [company] may then become irksome . . . you know I think it [overindulgence of the life of the mind] prejudicial to your health . . . and hurtful to your temper."[116] He let her know that she had trod on hallowed ground: "I believe that my temper never was and never will be hurt by my devotion to study or to solitude—There is another thing which never failed to hurt it . . . and that is any attempt by those whom I love to cross the current of my character, or control my sentiments or manners."[117] Perhaps this was a reaction to his parents' constant efforts to shape his character, direct his intellect, and control his will, but it was sheer hypocrisy. His letters to Louisa were packed with instructions on reading, the virtues of self-control, the importance of morality, and the exercise of virtue in all things.[118]

In late March, Louisa notified John Quincy that her father could no longer delay returning to America and that the whole family would be departing in July.[119] The following month, he learned that Congress had approved President Adams's choice of William Vans Murray to be the new minister to the Netherlands; at last he was free to go to Lisbon to take up his new post. "I have in some of my former letters mentioned several circumstances which seem to render inexpedient your going to Lisbon; yet the moment when the possibility that you may presented itself to me, all those objections lost much of their force in my mind."[120] The problem was reduced to logistics. John Quincy could not travel in a British ship from Holland to Lisbon via London for fear of it being seized by a French privateer. Apprised of the situation, Joshua Johnson wrote John Quincy, offering one of his vessels, either the *Mary* or the *Holland*, to transport him to London and from thence, with Louisa as his bride, to Lisbon. Johnson also informed him that he intended to name his son; Thomas Baker, his nephew; and John Quincy executors of his estate.[121]

Here matters lay until John Quincy learned in June that the previous month Congress had approved his father's nomination of him to be minister plenipotentiary to Prussia rather than to Portugal. He was predictably conflicted. Prussia was a much more important post than Portugal, but how could the Adams family avoid charges of nepotism sure to be flung in the overheated political atmosphere that prevailed in the United States? He need not have worried. John Quincy was indeed, as his father claimed, the most esteemed and respected member of the U.S. diplomatic corps. In late February, John, still vice president, had forwarded one of his son's dispatches to President Washington. "Mr. Adams is the most valuable public character we have abroad," Washington had written John. ". . . and if my wishes would be of any avail, they should go to you with a strong hope that you will not withhold merited promotion from Mr. J Q Adams because he is your son."[122]

The vote in the Senate to confirm was nineteen to nine. Benny Bache and his *Philadelphia Aurora* immediately cried nepotism. John Quincy subsequently dashed off to his father a letter full of self-righteous indignation, a missive that looked suspiciously as if it had been prepared with a mind to publication. John poohpoohed his son's objections. The national interest always trumped personal interest, he wrote John Quincy. His objections "were the worst founded opinion I ever

knew you to conceive." He would make no more money as minister plenipotentiary to Prussia than he would have as America's man in Lisbon. Even if he had
gone to Portugal, he would still be part of the Adams administration. What was
the difference?[123] His son readily surrendered.

The new post simplified the logistical problems facing John Quincy and Louisa. John Quincy and Thomas immediately booked passage on a Prussian schooner,
the *Alexander*; Prussia was as yet nonaligned. Incredibly, John Quincy offered his
betrothed one last chance to bail out of their engagement. The correspondence of
the previous year had given Louisa a more perfect picture of the type of man she
was choosing to spend her life with, he wrote. "He has disguised to you none of
his feelings and weaknesses. . . . Choose, Louisa, choose for yourself, and be assured that his heart will ratify your choice. . . . You have put too much gilding
upon your prospects, you have promised yourself too much, and I regret already
your disappointment." *You are not getting off that easily*, she must have thought.
"Why, my beloved friend did you tell me to choose what I have always declared,
[it] requires not a moment's hesitation to determine."[124]

The Adams brothers were detained in Rotterdam for twelve days due to contrary winds. The pair did not reach London until July 12, arriving at midday and
then booking rooms at Osborn's Hotel.[125] John Quincy and Louisa Catherine were
married on a warm summer's morning, July 26, 1797, at the Church of All Hal-
lows, Barking, just west of the Tower of London. In addition to the Johnsons, John
Quincy, and Thomas, two of the groom's London friends, James Brooks and Joseph Hall, were in attendance. The couple was joined together by the Reverend
John Hewlett—preacher, theologian, Oxford don, and an old friend of the Johnsons.[126] Small weddings were customary in Georgian London. Catherine had
brought out Louisa's wedding finery—a white Empire-style dress made of fine
muslin with three-quarter-length sleeves accompanied by a new bonnet and elegant shawl.[127] "On the Wednesday 26 of July 1797 I became a bride under as everybody thought the happiest auspices," Louisa recorded ambivalently in her
memoir.[128] She was twenty-two, the groom thirty.

That afternoon the party traveled by carriage some ten miles southeast of London to tour Tilney House, "one of the splendid country seats which this Country
is known for." Then it was back to Cooper's Row for a private dinner. "The day was
a very long one and closed about 11," John Quincy recorded in his diary.[129] The
following morning found the bridegroom walking the two and a half miles to
Osborn's, where he and Thomas had retained their rooms; he spent the day reading, writing, and greeting friends. This would become his daily routine while he
and Louisa remained in London; the evenings were a blur of dinners, dances, and

entertainments put on by members of the American merchant community and friends of the Johnsons. Sundays were spent with the family at the chapel at the Foundling Hospital, where Mr. Henning was the preacher.[130]

Two days after their nuptials, John Quincy and Louisa, in accompanying notes, notified John and Abigail that they had tied the knot. "I have now the happiness for presenting to you another daughter . . . the day before yesterday united us for life," John Quincy wrote. "My recommendation of her to your kindness and affection I know will be unnecessary." Louisa wrote that "to meet the approbation of my husband and family is the greatest wish of my heart."[131] Abigail responded graciously, addressing Louisa as "My Dear Daughter" and expressing sympathy over the pending separation from her family.[132] If John Quincy found the social rounds that followed his marriage tedious, he did not so find his wife. "Since I wrote you on the 24th, my brother has been married and has given me an amiable and accomplished sister," Thomas Boylston, who had accepted John Quincy's offer to accompany him to Berlin as his secretary, wrote his parents. "He is very happy at present, and I doubt not will continue so, for the young lady has much softness of temper and seems to love as she ought."[133]

ON SEPTEMBER 9 THE Johnsons departed for Maryland aboard Joshua's ship *Holland*. Their parting from the Adamses was painful for more than emotional reasons; Joshua's financial house of cards was about to collapse. On August 25, he had learned that he would not be able to deliver the five hundred pounds that he needed to tide over his creditors until he could recover his fortunes in America. John Quincy was not unaware of the precipice upon which his father-in-law teetered. "I should feel it more had I expected less," he noted in his diary. "Mr. Johnson ill—the cause an unhappy one," he wrote two nights later. On September 2, John Quincy and Louisa moved into a suite of rooms at Osborn's Hotel and shortly thereafter to a rented house. "Mr. Johnson and all his family dined with us at our house into which we have just moved. . . . After supper we had a distressing scene while the whole family took leave of Louisa."[134]

Later that month John Quincy received a letter from Frederick Wichelhausen, a Bremen merchant and the U.S. consul there, a man to whom Joshua was indebted. Mr. Johnson, he wrote, had fled to America, leaving his debts and his honor behind. He demanded that Johnson's misdeeds be made public and that John Quincy make good on his father-in-law's debts. John Quincy replied that he was married to Louisa Catherine and not her father. Mr. Johnson's financial affairs were his and his alone to settle. Wichelhausen was just one of many; in the days following the family's departure, tradesmen, merchants, and even former servants came calling on the Adamses, seeking redress. "Every tap at the door made me tremble as every rap produced a dun to my father; and to me they appealed for payment believing that my father had left the means with me to settle them," Louisa lamented. [135] It fell to John Quincy to try to explain. He gave assurances that Johnson would reestablish himself in America and pay his debts. "Find the affairs of Mr. J. more and more adverse," he recorded in his diary on October 9. "This trial is a strong one. More so indeed than I expected. And I expected it would be strong. I have done my duty, rigorous, inflexible duty."[136]

It quickly became apparent that Joshua Johnson would not be able to pay a penny toward the five-thousand-pound dowry both Louisa and John Quincy had come to expect. She would never admit that her father was capable of the least wrongdoing. It was he who was being falsely accused and defrauded by unscrupulous creditors. Her protestations did not sit well with John Quincy, who could not help but recall Joshua's efforts to make him coexecutor of his estate with the motive, perhaps, of making his new son-in-law responsible for his debts. He did not reproach Louisa directly, but she could not help being stung when he turned over management of their house's financial affairs to their servant, Tilly Whitcomb, rather than to her, as was the custom. Louisa would never recover from the humiliation. She was convinced that the whole Adams clan believed she and her family had ensnared John Quincy in marriage and then swindled him.

10

Berlin and the XYZ Affair

JOHN QUINCY RECEIVED HIS official commission and instructions as minister plenipotentiary to Prussia on September 22, 1797, and immediately began preparations for his little family's departure. With some difficulty, he managed to book passage on the Prussian merchant vessel *Frans*, bound from Gravesend to Hamburg.[1] He bought a heavy English carriage that would be stowed in the hold of the ship. The schedule called for the party to depart London for Gravesend on October 18, but they were delayed when John Quincy's passport was temporarily lost in the British bureaucracy. Upon reaching Gravesend, they found that the *Frans* had already departed and was anchored some ten miles downriver at Lower Hope Point. John Quincy, Louisa, and Tom were forced to make the trip of two hours to catch up in an open rowboat; fortunately their carriage and other heavy baggage had already been taken aboard the *Frans*. "Mrs. Adams was sick immediately upon our getting on board the vessel," John Quincy recorded in his diary.[2] In truth, she was suffering from the early stages of her first pregnancy.[3]

The eight-day passage from Gravesend to Hamburg took place in a constant gale; even John Quincy, an experienced seagoer, was brought to the verge of mal de mer. The *Frans* anchored at Hamburg on the morning of the twenty-sixth. The American consul there—an old friend of the Adamses—secured them lodgings at the King of England Hotel.[4] The party departed Hamburg on November 2, Louisa and John Quincy in their English coach and Thomas and Whitcomb following in a post chaise. The sand roads, turned into a bog by the fall rains, were almost impassable. The carriages were able to make only two German miles every hour. "We proceeded . . . by land I was going to say; but it is rather an ocean of a different description, or what Milton would call a windy sea of land," John Quincy wrote his mother.[5]

Exhausted from the trip, the Americans managed to secure rooms at the Hôtel de Russie at the end of Berlin's principal avenue. The following day John Quincy called at the Prussian foreign ministry. He was greeted warmly but informed that the king, Frederick William II, was too ill to receive him. Indeed, when in Hamburg, John Quincy had heard that the monarch was on his deathbed. Because he was accredited to Frederick William II and not to his heir, John Quincy assumed that it would be several months before his credentials were officially accepted.[6] "Upon my return home, found Mrs. Adams very unwell. A very distressing evening and night."[7] The crisis continued throughout the following week. "She was in the most excruciating pain," he recorded in his diary for the twelfth. Either John Quincy or Louisa's maid or both sat with her around the clock. All the while Thomas lay abed with what the hotel physician feared was diphtheria. Louisa was suffering from a prolonged miscarriage. Fortunately, the physician to the royal family, Dr. Charles Browne, a Scottish émigré, lived close by and was summoned. On the nineteenth, Louisa at last delivered the fetus. Throughout this ordeal, her only female companion was her seventeen-year-old maid, Elizabeth Epps, who was as frightened as her mistress. Only four months married, Louisa found herself far from her family in a foreign land and at death's doorstep after a miscarriage. "[There I was] lying in the most helpless condition from sickness and disappointment with every sense of delicacy shocked by the disgusting and to me indecent manners of the people who attended me and in a noisy and public hotel."[8]

John Quincy shared Louisa's sense of alienation, if not her pain. "In a strange country, not understanding the language, and having no friend to consult, I find imposition of every kind recurring at every moment; [it] is enough to weary and disgust me with such a life."[9] The crisis had seemed to dissipate the anxiety and resentment that had plagued John Quincy and Louisa's marriage since its inception, however. "My wife and brother thanks be to God, are now both recovered, though with regard to the former a remainder of anxiety must rest upon my mind until time shall discover whether her constitution has suffered any injury," John Quincy wrote his mother. "I assure you that I find her every day more deserving of all my affection."[10]

On December 3, Count Finckenstein, the Prussian foreign minister, informed John Quincy that the new king, Frederick William III, had agreed to receive him as if his credentials were addressed to him rather than to his father. He informed the American minister that he was expected to send cards and call upon the dowager queen and other members of the royal family. On the fifth, "in full dress mourning," John Quincy made his appearance at the palace. In due course he was ushered into the new monarch's apartments, where he was received cordially. The two men, who were almost the same age, exchanged pleasantries. Frederick William observed that the commercial interests of the two countries almost exactly complemented each other and invited the American envoy to initiate negotiations on a new treaty.[11] The visits to the dowager and to the king's brothers and sisters went equally well. Prince Friedrich Heinrich Karl—Prince Henry—observed to John Quincy that America was a rising star in Western civilization while Europe was on the decline; in the course of two or three centuries, he said, "the seat of arts and sciences and empire would be with us [the United States]."[12] "The King though quite a young man is not without some experience, and is said to have a very military turn. This indeed can hardly be otherwise here," John Quincy wrote his father. "His habits of life are domestic, distinguished by great simplicity, and a laborious activity. There is in his manners a gravity approaching to harshness, but nothing that betokens weakness, indolence, or dissipation."[13]

Eventually, the three Adamses and Whitcomb secured apartments over the guardhouse at the Brandenburg Gate. It was a beautiful location, just a short walk to the Tiergarten. The only drawback was that the soldiers stationed there were continually drilling and assembling to salute with cannonades every passing royal, noble, or foreign diplomat. One morning a Mademoiselle Dorville, apparently one of the princess's ladies-in-waiting, dropped by and after small talk asked when Louisa intended to present herself at the court. It had been almost two months and people were beginning to talk. Perhaps she was the American minister's mistress and not his wife. Horrified, Louisa had John Quincy make the necessary arrangements. She borrowed a dress from her new friend Countess Pauline Neale. The princess named January 20 in the early evening, prior to a dinner and dance she was giving. Louisa appeared at the palace at the appointed hour, alone, "frightened almost out of my senses at the idea of entering upon a stage so new."[14] But the princess met her almost at the door, graciously inquired after her health, and invited her into her court circle. She was then ushered into the drawing room, where she found other relatives of the royal family and members of the diplomatic corps including John Quincy. Louisa, with her humor, charm, beauty, and self-effacing manners, proved an instant hit.

The Prussia that John Quincy and Louisa visited in 1797 had been transformed into a major European power by Frederick II (Frederick the Great). His nephew and heir, Frederick William II, had built on that foundation, strengthening the military and infrastructure even further. At the time the scepter was passing from Frederick William II to Frederick William III, Prussia had just participated in the partition of Poland in league with Austria and Russia. It had survived being a member of the First Coalition formed to defeat revolutionary France, but had kept its military at full strength as a guard against future French aggression.

As John Quincy noted, Prussia seemed to be a nation of soldiers, but it was not a military dictatorship. There was some press censorship, but citizens of all ranks enjoyed equality under the law. Berlin was a cultural jewel in a crown of military garrisons. There were innumerable coffeehouses and salons where ideas were exchanged; even at court Berliners freely discussed politics, religion, and moral philosophy.[15]

December, January, and February marked the height of the social season in Berlin. There were dinners, balls, and soirees almost nightly. For John Quincy these were business affairs during which he could glean valuable information from Prussian officials and other members of the corps diplomatique. Louisa was on his arm when her health permitted, but she soon developed her own circle of friends. The Brownes lived just a few doors down, and she immediately became intimate with Dr. Browne's three daughters, Margaret, Isabella, and Fanny. There she could relax and speak English. Her adviser and link to Berlin court society was Pauline Neale, maid of honor at the court of Princess Louise. "She was not handsome, but full of animation and esprit, and perfectly amiable, with all the bonhomie and sincerity of the German character," Louisa observed.[16]

IN WHAT HE LATER described as the greatest political mistake of his life, John Adams chose to keep Washington's cabinet on almost intact. Secretary of State Timothy Pickering, Secretary of the Treasury Oliver Wolcott, and Secretary of War James McHenry were all High Federalists and minions of Alexander Hamilton. Although officially retired from public life in New York, Hamilton was determined to control the domestic and foreign policies of the Adams administration through these three men. They regularly briefed Hamilton on the inner deliberations of the cabinet and passed on to him secret state papers. He in turn wrote policy recommendations that the three submitted to President Adams under their own names. It wasn't as if Adams had not been forewarned. Jefferson and Madison had written the incoming president, pledging their allegiance and advising him to beware "your arch-friend from New York." Jefferson subsequently wrote Elbridge Gerry, a Massachusetts Republican, that the Hamiltonians were "only a little less hostile to [Adams] than to me."[17]

Despite his revulsion at the excesses of the French Revolution, John Adams wanted peace with France, just as he had desired it with Great Britain. He, like John Quincy, was a great admirer of French culture and customs. He realized that a war with the Directory would be popular with many within his own party, especially the members of the notorious Essex Junto, the core of High Federalism in New England. It was composed chiefly of tough-minded merchant shipowners and lawyers who had moved to Boston from Essex County: Timothy Pickering,

Theophilus Parsons, John Lowell, and Fisher Ames. The Essex men were rigid ideologues, determined that Massachusetts and the United States should be controlled by its propertied, educated classes. Pro-British for economic and ideological reasons, they had by 1797 come to wish fervently for war with France in hopes of destroying the Democratic-Republican Party once and for all. Ames was a classicist who cited numerous incidents from antiquity to prove that democracy would inevitably lead to mob rule, anarchy, and, finally, tyranny. Unlike their political allies—the fire-breathing New England preachers who equated Jefferson, Madison, and the French Jacobins with the Antichrist—they were, except for Pickering, men who could dance, rhyme, and flirt with the ladies.[18]

John Adams believed that overseas trade constituted the lifeblood of the republic. It earned specie that backed the nation's currency and generated prosperity among manufacturers and agriculturalists alike. Foreign trade, the president believed, would fuel America's growth to the point at which the country could defy one and all of its rivals. But that would take time and, above all, peace. Like his eldest son, John Adams was able to differentiate between the different dynamics of domestic and foreign policy. "There is one point upon which we have committed many great errors," John Quincy would write William Vans Murray. "It is in confounding the principles of internal government with those of external relations."[19] Ideology had no place in diplomacy. The United States must treat all nations as juridical equals and assume, unless otherwise demonstrated, that they would act in their own national interests, strategically and economically defined. In their foreign policies, the Jeffersonians expected other nations to live up to their ideal of peaceful negotiation; if they did not, the United States could turn to economic coercion to preserve its interests. Republicans feared a powerful executive and a standing army and navy as threats to their liberties, but Adams and the Federalists believed that a strong military was absolutely essential to protecting the nation's independence.

Shortly after taking office, Adams learned that the Directory had issued a degree abrogating the Franco-American Treaty of 1778. This, together with continuing ship seizures (316 in 1795 and 1796 alone) and the humiliation of Charles Cotesworth Pinckney, who had been rejected as U.S. minister to France, demanded action. Several choices were available to the new president: he could embargo all trade with France; he could arm American merchantmen; he could license privateers to prey on French shipping; he could even declare war. Adams convened his cabinet on March 14 and informed them that he was calling Congress into a special session in two months, and would recommend a course of action. It was his intention to request permission to appoint a special commission to negotiate a peace accord with France. The three High Federalists immediately informed

Hamilton, who in his imagination was already taking his place as Washington's second-in-command in the American army that would defend the United States against a French invasion. Surprisingly enough, he advised his lieutenants that one more effort at peace was necessary. It would inevitably be rejected, thus unifying the country in its putative war with France.[20]

When Congress convened in May, Adams submitted his recommendations. He began indignantly and militantly, denouncing the Directory for its rejection of Pinckney and its ongoing maritime depredations in the Caribbean. He urged Congress to strengthen the navy, authorize the arming of American merchantmen, and consider establishing a permanent army. The president finished with an olive branch, however. He had learned from John Quincy and William Vans Murray that the new French foreign minister, Charles-Maurice de Talleyrand-Périgord, desired peace with the United States. It seemed that Talleyrand was planning to attempt a resurrection of French North America in which Spain would retrocede Louisiana to France in return for the cession of the Caribbean island of Saint-Domingue, which was then racked by a slave rebellion. In such a scheme, peace with America was preferable to war. Thus informed, President Adams had already been mulling over the names of individuals for the peace commission. He settled on two staunch Federalists—Charles Cotesworth Pinckney, then in the Hague, and the distinguished Virginian John Marshall—to team up with Elbridge Gerry, an old friend of the Adams family. Federalists screamed bloody murder at Gerry's nomination; he was, they declared, a New England Jacobin who had opposed the Constitution. But Adams was determined. He wanted political balance on the commission, and Gerry was a man of integrity.[21] In the end President Adams had his way.

The Americans' instructions, almost entirely written by Alexander Hamilton, called for the negotiation of a new treaty that would suspend the Franco-American accord of 1778. The U.S. commissioners were to bring up the claims of Americans for ships seized by the French, but this was not a sine qua non. As with the Jay Treaty, the United States would be willing to forfeit the principle of free ships make free goods. The French navy and privateers would be free to seize noncontraband goods headed for British ports. Hamilton reasoned that this apparent equity would favor Britain because the Royal Navy was much more powerful and pervasive than the French fleet. In the new accord, the United States would be relieved of the burden of having to defend French possessions in the New World in case of war. It should be noted that John Quincy objected strongly to surrendering the principle of free ships make free goods. "Every instance . . . in which these principles are abandoned by neutral powers . . . is to be regretted as furnishing argument, or at least example, to support the British doctrines," he wrote Secretary of State Pickering.[22]

As soon as Congress adjourned, John and Abigail abandoned Philadelphia for Quincy. The president would not return to the capital until October.

IN APRIL 1797, WILLIAM Stephens Smith left his wife and three children on their farm in Eastchester, situated some twenty miles from New York City. He would not return until February 1798. In his new role as a real estate speculator, Colonel Smith visited lands he had purchased in Chenango County, New York, and then moved on to Detroit in the Northwest Territory. He spent some time at Fort Stanwix, New York, before returning home. During his travels he rarely if ever wrote Nabby (there are no extant letters), and the family began to assume Colonel Smith had abandoned them. Abigail was a frequent visitor at Eastchester and became more and more anguished over her daughter's plight. In truth, it seemed that Colonel Smith might have been an officer and a gentleman but also something of a scoundrel. Several years earlier, he had purchased a hundred fifty thousand acres in central New York for £24,375. The land was organized into eight townships. Smith kept four and sold the other four to two Englishmen and agreed to act as their agent. They subsequently accused Smith of refusing to pay them for acreage he had sold on their behalf and for keeping sixty thousand pounds they had advanced him. As of October 1797, Smith was in debt to the two Englishmen to the tune of $230,000, a sum that was never repaid.[23] Shortly after his return to Eastchester in mid-February, the colonel received a scorching reprimand from his father-in-law. "It is reported not much to the advantage of your reputation or mine that you have been to Detroit . . . to speculate in lands . . . and that to cloak your real purposes you gave out that you had been sent by me for ends of government of some sort or other."[24]

Meanwhile, alarming news arrived from another front. Charles's wife, Sally, began to hint in her correspondence at prolonged absences and excessive visits to the tavern by her husband. In December 1796, John Quincy had directed Charles, his business representative, to invest two thousand dollars of his money "to good advantage in a proper and legal manner." He inquired repeatedly as to the fate of his money. "I have never received any answer to it [his latest letter] whatever," he wrote Charles in August 1797.[25] The president and his diplomat son had to put concerns about children and siblings on the back burner, however, because the crisis with France had reached a turning point.

PINCKNEY, MARSHALL, AND GERRY arrived in Paris to begin negotiations at an inauspicious time. Napoleon, the young Corsican general in command of

French armies in the East, had humbled Austria in the Treaty of Campo Formio and was continuing his rampage through the Italian principalities. The coup d'état of 18 Fructidor (September 4, 1797) had produced a hard-line majority on the Directory.[26] "Since the affair of 4 September . . . , I have lost all hopes of any possible accommodation," John Quincy wrote Murray in November. "[I]f we openly and unequivocally were at war with them, they could not injure us externally in our commerce so much as they do."[27] The three Americans presented their credentials on October 8, 1797, and were told that conversations would begin in a few days. While they waited in their quarters, Pinckney, Marshall, and Gerry were paid a series of visits. A Swiss banker named Jean Hottinguer, acting in his "private capacity," asked according to "diplomatic usage" for a $250,000 gift for the Directory and a contribution to the French treasury of several million dollars. Then a Mr. Bellamy, a merchant of Hamburg, turned up, claiming to be a confidant of Talleyrand, and announced that negotiations could not begin until the Americans committed to a $12 million loan to France. At this, Pinckney blurted out his famous "It is no; no not a sixpence."[28] Hard upon Bellamy's heels came a mysterious and attractive Frenchwoman, adding her voice to her predecessors, in urging a loan. "We have a very considerable party in America who are strongly in our interests," she had the indelicacy to say.[29] Finally, a gentleman calling himself Lucien Hauteval appeared and urged the three Americans to meet privately with Talleyrand. Pinckney and Marshall refused, but Gerry agreed. He returned from his interview to inform his colleagues that the foreign minister, whom Napoleon would later refer to as shit in silk stockings, had said that if the sums were not forthcoming within a week, war would be declared. The three Americans were not naive; they knew that bribes and sex were a regular part of the diplomatic business in Europe. And despite Pinckney's indignation, there was not really a moral issue. The United States had been paying thousands annually to the Barbary pirates to keep them from raiding American shipping in the Mediterranean. But they had no authority to make such large payments to the French. Moreover, if they agreed to loan France money, it would compromise the United States' status as a neutral and provide Britain with a casus belli. They considered asking for their passports but delayed, hoping for a change in French attitudes and policy.

On January 15, 1798, John Quincy informed the secretary of state that the Council of Five Hundred and Council of Elders had unanimously approved a law "declaring that a neutral flag shall no longer protect the enemy's property and that every vessel laden wholly or in part with articles for British produce or manufacture shall with its cargo be lawful prizes, be that property whose it may." This was surely "war proclaimed," he observed.[30]

* * *

MEANWHILE, LOUISA WAS ADAPTING to Berlin high society quite nicely. She had been singled out by the recently crowned Queen Louise for special attention. Indeed, she and Louise, famed for her beauty and grace, would become quite close. That Louisa had been thus privileged was duly noted by the other members of the Hohenzollern family and the lesser nobility.[31] Her minister husband was frequently so busy that she was left alone, but in this regard her rod and staff were Thomas Boylston, whom everyone called "the Judge" after a minor post he had occupied before accompanying his brother to Europe. They were constant companions, laughing at the foibles of courtiers, visiting the Brownes at their country house at Charlottenburg, and attending the theater in Berlin. "He soothed me in my afflictions, corrected gently my utter want of self-confidence; flattered me judiciously. . . . I never saw so fine a temper or so truly and invariably lovely a disposition. . . . I have always believed that he both respected and loved me and did me justice in times when I needed a powerful friend," Louisa would later write in her autobiography.[32] But eventually Thomas felt the need to return to America and make his own way in life. He was replaced as his brother's secretary in September 1798 by Thomas Welsh Jr., the son of a family friend.

By this point, however, Louisa had learned to make her own way. She admitted with some embarrassment that she had become something of a "belle." The two princes had made her promise to dance with them at any and every ball they should all find themselves attending. She was a guest at card parties given by female members of the royal family. "I was seized upon by two old Ladies and an old Officer to play Whist," she recalled of one outing. John Quincy had furnished her a purse with some gold coins, which they soon relieved her of. "[A]fter fleecing me unmercifully, they made me pay for the lights and cards. . . . Mr. Adams was quite dismayed when I showed my purse and we agreed that I should go as seldom as possible to Princess Henry's."[33] Neale and the Browne sisters were now her constant companions: "We amused ourselves with the scandal of the town, or satirizing the vagaries of the Court belles, or the follies of the Court dowdies."[34] In April she and John Quincy went to see Gotthold Ephraim Lessing's tragedy *Emilia Galotti*. In the middle of the first act, Louisa fainted and tumbled out of her seat. She was pregnant again. "My ill health was a perpetual tax upon Mr. Adams' feelings—but his kindness was unremitting in promoting my comfort."[35]

After six months at the Brandenburg Gate apartments, John Quincy and Louisa moved to another suite of rooms just three blocks away. In comparison to the baroque palaces and grand government buildings that surrounded them, their quarters were modest indeed. The front two rooms were furnished elegantly so that John Quincy could receive visitors and the couple could host small parties. The rest of the apartment was bare bones. "My bedchamber had no carpet, a bedstead with white cotton curtains of the coarsest quality bordered with a strip of calico . . . and made by myself, with window curtains to match; a toilet, glass-nook fire in the winter and half a dozen chairs."[36] When Louisa was presented to the dowager queen on short notice, she and Pauline Neale had to make her a dress out of whatever scraps of cloth and curtain they could find.

On July 17, Louisa suffered her second miscarriage. "A dreadful night. Mrs. A. soon after going to bed was taken extremely ill," John Quincy recorded in his diary. By midnight, his wife was in such excruciating pain that John Quincy sent for Dr. Browne and a colleague who were then at Charlottenburg. They arrived between three and four a.m. Shortly thereafter, Louisa delivered her unborn child. "The anticipation of evils that we cannot prevent is itself a great misfortune," her husband wrote in his diary. "I have these 8 months been convinced, with scarcely the shadow of a doubt what this event would be. Yet now that it happens, I feel it with no less poignancy than if it had been unexpected."[37]

DESPITE THE DEMANDS OF nursing Louisa through her failed pregnancies, mining court society for intelligence that would be valuable to his country, and writing dispatches, John Quincy, as always, found time for his intellectual pursuits. There were Shakespeare and the classics but also German literature. He began taking German lessons in 1798 and the following year hired the distinguished teacher Samuel Heinrich Catel as his personal tutor.[38] He read Gotthold Lessing's dramatic poem, *Nathan der Weise*, in German and then Friedrich Schiller's unfinished novel, *Der Geisterseher*, with which he was delighted. He chose as his first translation exercise Friedrich von Gentz's *Origin and Principles of the American Revolution Compared with the Origin and Principles of the French Revolution* and then moved on to Christoph Martin Wieland's classic *Oberon: A Poetical Romance in Twelve Books.*[39] "The stagnation of political events during the winter months . . . induced me at first, to undertake the work as an amusement for myself," John Quincy wrote his mother, "but what I had taken as a pleasant companion soon mastered me so completely that for months together I could scarcely snatch from it here and there an hour for any other purpose whatsoever."[40]

And, of course, Adams read Immanuel Kant's *Project for a Perpetual Peace*. In a letter to his father, he paid homage to Kant's brilliance. "His writings are all moral or political" and of such "profound obscurity" that "it required at least two years of steady application to understand him." Much of this opaqueness stemmed from political necessity. Kant's prediction that "all the governments of Europe should become Republican" was such a dangerous forecast, especially when proclaimed in the capital of the Kingdom of Prussia, that it was necessary for his survival to shroud his ideas in a "cloak of metaphysical subtleties."[41] John Quincy reveled in his new language and would come to see himself as its principal advocate in America.

DURING THE QUASI-WAR BETWEEN France and the United States, which raged on the high seas from 1798 to 1800, John Quincy Adams was his father's principal foreign affairs adviser. The previous year, on the eve of his departure for Prussia, the president had written his son: "You have wisely taken all Europe for your theatre. . . . Send us all the information you can collect. I wish you to continue the practice of writing freely to me and cautiously to the office of State."[42] Second only in importance to John Quincy was his compatriot William Vans Murray. Born in Maryland in 1760, Murray had been elected to the House of Delegates in 1788 and then to the House of Representatives in 1791, serving there until his nomination to be minister to the Netherlands in 1797. Murray had come to know the Adamses while he was in London studying law at the Temple in the early 1780s. When he was still in private law practice, Murray and the elder Adams, then minister to the Court of St. James's, corresponded regularly, discussing moral and political philosophy. In time, Murray became something of a disciple and protégé of John's. With John Quincy situated in Berlin and Murray at the Hague, the two could share intelligence and explore ideas in, for them, what was real time. Like Minister Adams, Murray was invited by the president to report to him separately and directly.

In truth, John Adams could not trust his secretary of state, Timothy Pickering, an Anglophile who seemed determined to embroil the United States and France in a declared war. Both Adamses continued to see revolutionary France—its ideals and armies—as the principal threat to American independence. It was not only that the Directory and Talleyrand, its mendacious minister of foreign affairs, were avaricious and completely lacking in integrity, but in addition, they seemed to be perched atop an ongoing revolution that they could not control. France exported insurrection out of not only ideological zeal but necessity. In all of the countries they had conquered, the French government would station tens of thousands of troops—in Holland alone twenty-five thousand. "Still, they have immense numbers upon their hands which they cannot support at home, and this is undoubtedly the principal foundation of the necessity under which they are to spread their revolution over Europe," John Quincy observed to John.[43] At the same time, father and son recognized that the Jay Treaty had earned only a temporary respite in America's ongoing feud with Great Britain. Various orders-in-council continued to expand the powers of the Royal Navy and British privateers to seize American merchant vessels, impressment continued unabated, and reports that Canadian officials were intriguing with the Indians of the Old Northwest were pouring into Washington.

In April 1798, in the wake of the French government's failed attempt to extract bribes from the American peace commission, Pinckney and Marshall decided to break off negotiations and return home. Elbridge Gerry, who had been singled out and courted by Talleyrand, decided to stay. His colleagues were appalled. "I have made great sacrifice of my feelings to preserve unity but in vain," Pinckney wrote Rufus King, a fellow Federalist. "I never met with a man of less candor and so much duplicity as Mr. Gerry."[44] Secretary of State Pickering did everything he could to discredit Gerry short of declaring the New England Republican a traitor to his country. All of this was very painful to the Adamses, who considered Gerry a friend and a man of principal. For his part Gerry insisted to Talleyrand that he remained in Paris as a private citizen only, with no powers to negotiate. He later wrote the president that if he, Gerry, had not decided to remain in order to keep open a line of communications, a declaration of war would have certainly ensued.[45] John Quincy sympathized with his father over the Gerry predicament. "That one [who chose to stay] is your particular friend and acquaintance," he wrote John, "the special object of your choice against whom even the warmest promoters of the American cause objected at the time of his appointment."[46] But in agreeing to stay on indefinitely, Gerry was playing into the hands of Talleyrand and the Directory.

Their object was to drag out the maritime war then raging between France and the United States and to continue to sow discord in Congress and among the American people. Talleyrand hoped by cultivating Gerry and giving the appearance of conciliation to throw American Republicans a bone in their conflict with the Federalists. "The policy of temporizing will not answer with men of such character as those with whom he has to deal [Talleyrand and the Directory]," John Quincy advised his father. "It was tried by Venice, by Genoa, Geneva, but most especially by the Swiss republics—they trusted to professions of friendship and gave up one point of controversy after another without making adequate preparations for defense until the enemy was at their very gates."[47]

Word of the attempted subornation of his envoys in Paris reached President Adams on March 4, 1798. Pickering, an "Essex man" to the core, was furious and demanded an immediate declaration of war. The president was incensed at the Directory's treatment of Pinckney, Marshall, and Gerry, but he did not want to go that far. In his message to Congress on the nineteenth, he announced that he was recalling the three envoys and asked for funds to further strengthen America's defenses. To his chagrin, his message was met with open hostility by the Republicans—Jefferson would refer to Adams's "insane message" to Congress—and they demanded that Adams reveal the content of Pinckney, Marshall, and Gerry's dispatches to Congress and to the public. They were joined in this by certain High Federalists who had read the dispatches and knew what was in them. Adams complied but insisted on substituting the letters "W, X, Y, and Z" for the names of the French agents. The Republicans looked on aghast as public opinion turned sharply against France and cries for war echoed throughout the land. Abigail was overjoyed. At last her fellow countrymen had come to realize that "we did not break from the shackles of our parent to become slaves of our sister, a venal depraved corrupt and profligate wretch, who has rejected our proffered terms of reconciliation and calls for bribes."[48] John Adams was truly popular for the first time in his administration.

John Quincy initially had mixed feelings about publication of the XYZ dispatches. It set a dangerous precedent and would constrain American diplomats in their future correspondence with the executive. Indeed, in the short term, the revelations might expose America's envoys to imprisonment or bodily harm.[49] But upon learning that release of the dispatches had created widespread outrage against France in America and put the pro-French Republicans on the defensive, he rejoiced. Young men from the ages of eighteen to twenty-one were flocking to enroll in the army and the navy, even in the Francophile stronghold of Philadelphia, he wrote Murray.[50] And he sensed a turning point in Franco-American relations. Talleyrand, he wrote his friend at the Hague, "has come forth foaming and snarling," denouncing the American envoys and attacking President Adams personally. But all indications were that "they do not wish an open rupture now, and that they are alarmed at the spirit which the publication roused in our country."[51]

During the summer of 1798, Congress approved a war loan, voted to create a "Provisional Army" of some ten thousand men to supplement the thirty-five hundred regulars scattered along the nation's frontiers, authorized the creation of a Department of the Navy, and appropriated funds to increase the fleet from three to twenty-seven vessels. At George Washington's insistence, Adams reluctantly named Alexander Hamilton inspector general and second in command of the new force. The administration declared the Treaty of 1778 null and void and authorized the licensing of privateers. America and France were at war—undeclared though it might have been—on the high seas.

The Federalists, sensing an opportunity to break the backs of their Republican opponents, pushed through Congress a series of measures that on their face were designed to prevent subversion and sabotage by French agents. The Alien Friends

Act empowered the president to arrest and deport "dangerous" aliens; the Alien Enemies Act authorized the deportation of citizens of enemy countries during wartime; and the Sedition Act prohibited "any false, scandalous and malicious writing" against the government. The Naturalization Act raised residency requirements for citizenship from five to fourteen years; the Republican Party then teemed with French and Irish immigrants.

Jefferson, Madison, and their colleagues did not suffer these abuses in silence. After repeatedly failing to block passage of the offending measures, the two secretly authored the Kentucky and Virginia Resolutions, in which the legislatures of those two states declared the Alien and Sedition Acts null and void and invoked the principle of "interposition"—that is, the right of a state to block the enforcement of any federal measure or act that allegedly infringed on the constitutional rights of its citizens. In truth, the Alien and Sedition Acts, especially the law on sedition, constituted one of the greatest infringements on civil liberties in American history. It would not be the last time America would engage in civil conflict while waging a foreign war.

John Quincy Adams thoroughly approved of the Alien and Sedition Acts. "In these times the traitors from bribery are nothing in comparison with the traitors from principle," he wrote Murray. Speaking of the "American Jacobins," he declared, "Treachery is organized into a system, rooted into every passion that actuated the species, and preached into the conscience as a moral and political obligation . . . every third man is at the bottom of his heart at war with every two others. In that war his countrymen are his enemies, and France is his ally."[52] He thought the Kentucky and Virginia Resolutions nothing less than calls to armed rebellion. But he did not believe it would come to that: "Desperate men indeed sometimes fly to violent measures impelled by passion rather than policy. . . . But things appear to me very far from being ripe for the serious struggle which must, indeed, some day happen between the Ancient Dominion [Virginia] and the Union."[53]

John Quincy was ready to turn Europe's distress to America's advantage. European empire in the New World could not last much longer, he wrote Murray in March 1798: "Turgot [Anne Robert Jacques, French economist and statesman], one of the fathers of the revolution, saw this so clearly more than twenty years ago, that he wrote a long memorial to prove that all the powers of Europe must lose their colonies, and the sooner they reconciled themselves to it the better." Why should they not be replaced by an empire of liberty with the United States leading the way? America, John Quincy declared, should at every opportunity be ready to catch the falling fruit.[54] If war should be declared formally between France and the United States, America should extend its protective arm over the French West

Indies. "Our newspapers say that their generals of color are decidedly with us and in case of war will declare for us," he wrote his friend at the Hague. "[S]uch a connection as I have in my mind [is] a more natural connection than that of metropolis and colony, or in other words, master and servant. In close alliance, leaving them as to their government totally to themselves, we can protect their independence, furnish them with necessaries, and stipulate for the exclusive carriage of their produce."[55] So much for free trade.

On August 2, 1798, Murray informed John Quincy that he had gained access to a captured French dispatch. It reported that "a Mr. Droghan has just arrived here from the U.S. on his way to Paris. He brings letters to m. de La Fayette, to Merlin [Philippe-Antoine Merlin de Douai, president of the Directory] and Talleyrand from Mr. Jefferson and others, with the hope of averting war between France and the U.S."[56] "Droghan" was in fact Dr. George Logan, a Philadelphia Quaker whom Jefferson, Madison, and Monroe had dispatched as an unofficial peacemaker. Logan had applied to Lafayette, who used his influence with the French agent at Hamburg to obtain a passport. Murray approached the French consul at the Hague, Louis-André Pinchon, and sought to have Logan arrested but failed. He did discover the kernel of Logan's message: that a war between France and the United States would destroy the Republican Party in America. Pickering, when he learned of the initiative, was beside himself at Logan's audacity. At his behest Congress passed legislation imposing a fine and imprisonment on any person acting as an unauthorized diplomat, a law that came to be known as the Logan Act.[57]

At this point France launched a peace offensive. Pinchon informed Murray that "a great change had taken place in the mind of his government on American affairs, that it was now clear to them that they had been deceived by men who meddled on both sides of the water." The Directory and Council of Five Hundred and Council of Elders now understood that war would only drive America into the arms of Great Britain and lead to the loss of France's New World colonies.[58] John Quincy reported to his father that events indeed "have produced a great and important change in the conduct towards us . . . no longer an overbearing and insolent minister of external relations . . . no longer a self-imagined conqueror, dictating apologies and prescribing tribute." But be not deceived, he warned. France's willingness to conciliate would depend upon America's control of its own internal discords and its determination to prosecute the war on the high seas with vigor.[59]

Throughout the summer and fall of 1798, the High Federalists in the cabinet continued to press for a formal declaration of war; all the while, Hamilton was encamped with his new army, plotting John Adams knew not what. Rumors that Hamilton was scheming to attack the French and Spanish on America's western frontiers continued to circulate; Abigail even suggested that he was plotting a military coup to oust her husband from office. Hamilton did indeed dream of leading an army of conquest that would expel Spain from North America, thereby expanding and securing America's western frontier. Nine years earlier, he had urged Washington to recognize the necessity of the United States securing control of the Mississippi. Upon being named inspector general of the army in 1798, he had remarked to a subordinate that "tempting objects" would "be within our grasp" should war with France be declared.[60]

In response to these machinations, the president decided to plot his own course, relying on intelligence and advice from his son and Murray. He realized that British naval victories over the French at Camperdown (October 11, 1797) and Aboukir Bay (August 1, 1798) had made an invasion of the United States virtually impossible. Domestically, the country was still deeply divided. The public was beginning to groan under the burden of the new taxes required to fund preparedness measures. And finally, Adams feared that American democracy was being threatened by a burgeoning plutocracy nurtured by Hamilton's nationalist financial policies and the massive profits being reaped through trade with Great Britain.

In recalling the three American peace commissioners from Paris, Adams had declared, "I will never send another minister to France without assurances that he will be received, respected, and honored as the representative of a great, free, powerful, and independent nation."[61] In September 1798, Talleyrand sent a message to Pinchon and requested that it be conveyed directly and confidentially to President Adams through American diplomatic channels. In it, the French foreign minister promised that any plenipotentiary the president chose to nominate to settle the differences between their two countries would be "received with the respect due to the representative of a free, independent, and powerful country."[62] Pinchon conveyed the message to Murray. Neither Murray nor John Quincy trusted the mail and were willing to convey diplomatic correspondence only through a few trusted intimates. "Our government has in fact no more retention than a sieve," John Quincy lamented to his friend.[63] It just so happened that Thomas Adams was then passing through the Hague on his way home. He arrived in New York on January 12, 1799, and made his way immediately to Philadelphia to deliver to his father the secret dispatches offering peace.[64]

The president remained suspicious of Talleyrand, but he trusted his son and William Vans Murray, both of whom urged him to accept the offer and appoint a

new peace delegation. He bypassed his cabinet but consulted with other prominent Federalists, such as Marshall, John Jay, and even Washington. All agreed
that the country needed peace rather than war with France. They urged him to
appoint John Quincy and Rufus King to join Murray in a peace commission. But
the nomination of either "would probably defeat the whole measure," John wrote
Abigail. On February 25, the president submitted to the Senate the names of
Murray; Oliver Ellsworth, chief justice of the Supreme Court; and William R.
Davie, governor of North Carolina. The whole enterprise was outrageous, even
treasonous, exclaimed Pickering, McHenry, and Hamilton. Some of the High
Federalists were opposed on principle, others on method. Bypassing the cabinet
violated "established practice," McHenry declared. Boston Federalist George Cabot
branded those who supported the commission "federal hypocrites with Jacobin
hearts." But moderate Federalist newspapers voiced approval of the move as, of
course, did Republican sheets like the *Philadelphia Aurora*.[65] In due course, the
Senate voted to confirm Murray, Ellsworth, and Davie.

THREE DAYS AFTER CHRISTMAS 1798, Abigail, still in Quincy, wrote John that
she was depressed and distressed about her children. She had reason to be. Nabby's husband, William Stephens Smith, was in the headlines once again. No one
questioned his valor or competence as a soldier. Earlier that month General
Washington had submitted Smith's name to the secretary of war to be commissioned as lieutenant colonel, commandant of New York, provided he could clear
himself of allegations of "very serious instances of private misconduct."[66] Smith
had since his return from Detroit proclaimed his innocence to all who would listen. It was he who was the victim of unscrupulous land agents and speculators, he
declared. The whole thing "has embarrassed me," the president wrote Smith. He
was loath to submit his nomination to the Senate, for fear it would be rejected.
"Your pride and ostentation which I myself have seen with inexpressible grief for
many years have excited among your neighbors so much envy & and resentment
that if they have to alledge [*sic*] against you any instance of dishonorable and dishonest conduct it will never be forgiven or forgotten. . . . They are now taking
vengeance on you with a witness."[67] Smith again protested his innocence and expressed his desire to put his land-speculating past behind him and become a soldier once again.

Abigail had used the plural because the family was as distraught over Charles
and Sally as they were over Nabby and her husband. John Quincy had continued
to entrust management of his assets, now totaling some four thousand dollars, to
Charles. He had instructed his brother to invest half of the money and offered a

generous commission. He had not heard from Charles in nearly two years, he complained to his parents. "I have written to him over and over again requesting him to inform me regularly of its [the investment's] situation—I have written in vain."[68] He finally gave up. Before Thomas left Berlin, John Quincy had authorized him to take control of his affairs; invest my money as you think best, he instructed Thomas, but not with Francophiles. "I should think my property just as safe in the hands of a Jacobin as in those of a convicted thief."[69] When he arrived in Boston from Philadelphia, Thomas found matters in total disarray. On her own Abigail had tried to sort out what was going on but with little result. Charles refused to answer her inquiries. She learned from Sally that he was drinking heavily and absented himself from her and their two children for long periods of time. "I will write you whatever I can collect," she reported to John Quincy, "but the poor child is unhappy . . . he is not at peace with himself."[70] A man could not ask for a more amiable wife or loving children; Charles was his own worst enemy. "I wish . . . some means could be devised to save him from that ruin and destruction with which he must soon be overwhelmed, if he is not already," she wrote John Quincy in February 1799.[71]

Thomas Boylston seemed headed in an entirely different direction. Abigail's third son had profited immensely from his time in Europe, John Quincy wrote Abigail. He had become fluent in French and gained a reading knowledge of Dutch and German. As John Quincy's secretary and temporary chargé d'affaires in the Netherlands, Thomas had met many of the principal figures of European politics and acquired hands-on knowledge of diplomatic negotiation.[72] He had proven an amiable companion and comfort to both John Quincy and Louisa. "I fear it will be a long time before he becomes reconciled to your departure," Louisa had written Thomas. "He seldom mentions you without tears in his eyes."[73] Thomas disliked the law less than his brother, and it was his intention to return to its practice in either Philadelphia or Boston and then perhaps stand for office. Six years earlier, while studying law in Philadelphia, Thomas had met Sarah "Sally" Wister while boarding in Germantown, Pennsylvania, to escape yellow fever. The daughter of a Quaker family, she was, Thomas wrote his mother, not only attractive, but "very intelligent . . . too, whose mind is as chaste as her person, and whose understanding has been cultivated by an intimacy with the choicest books." In 1793 she had presented Thomas with a volume of her poems, one of which, "Lucius," was dedicated to him. Now back in Philadelphia, Thomas sought out his old friend, and they renewed their courtship.[74] In Boston, Annapolis, and Philadelphia, Thomas utilized his family's broad and influential network of acquaintances to establish himself as an up-and-coming lawyer and prospective candidate for office; he attended sessions of the local and federal courts and applied for admission to the Pennsylvania bar. A bit of John Quincy had rubbed off on him. "I converse with Cicero, Tacitus, Ovid, Horace," he reported to his cousin William Smith Shaw.[75]

IN BERLIN, LOUISA CONTINUED to flourish. Indeed, from being an isolated flower sheltering within the bosom of her family, she had become quite the cosmopolite. "Blessed be the person who was able to travel and experience the cultures of other nations," she wrote in her memoir. "[K]nowledge of the world . . . gives the last polish to man by curing him of the narrowness of local prejudices and teaching him that liberality of opinion which is acquired by travel through different countries."[76] She remained a particular favorite of the king and queen. At one court ball she had worn a train, not intending to dance. She politely refused the two princes when they asked and seated herself, only to be approached by the queen's secretary, who informed her that the king had selected her to be his partner for the first dance. Abashed but unable to decline, she gathered her train and took her place. "The King walked up and spoke to me and the Queen with her usual loveliness took my hands and stood and talked some minutes until I recovered myself."[77]

During her conversation with the queen, the latter commented upon Louisa's wan appearance and pale complexion. I will send you a box of rouge, she said. Later, Louisa mentioned the offer to John Quincy. No wife of mine will wear rouge on her face, he declared. As her health continued its ups and downs, Louisa became very self-conscious about her appearance. She secretly acquired some artificial color for her cheeks and appeared with painted face before her husband just as they were leaving for a performance of *The Marriage of Figaro*. No, he declared, this will not do. He sat down, pulled his wife on his lap, and wiped off the rouge with his handkerchief. "A kiss made the peace," Louisa noted in her diary, "and we drove to the [opera] where I showed my pale face as usual."[78] But the affair of the rouge was not yet over. Sometime later, tired of being teased at court for her bloodless countenance, Louisa again painted her face. "I walked boldly forward to meet Mr. Adams—as soon as he saw me, he requested me to wash it off which I with some temper refused; upon which he ran down and jumped into the carriage and left me *plante la*! Even to myself appearing like a fool, crying with vexation."[79]

Kind though the royal pair were, the Hohenzollern court was just as licentious as any other in Europe. The king had just recently fathered twins with one of his wife's beautiful maids of honor; her husband, a military officer, had been promoted and given a post near the palace. Though his was an improvement on Uriah the Hittite's situation, the Adamses were shocked. John Quincy was not unaware of his wife's charms. When Louisa was selected to perform in a quadrille in honor of the marriage of the Duke of Gloucester and Edinburgh and Princess Mary of England, he ordered her to decline with the excuse of ill health. Rehearsals were scheduled to take six weeks: "The constant rehearsals would have thrown me into a constant association with the gay persons of the court, not agreeable to him, and perhaps hazardous to me."[80] Louisa was expecting at the time. She had suffered from ill health throughout the month of April 1799. And then disaster struck. "While standing at the window in the library, I saw a child run over by a cart— He was taken up dreadfully injured, and I fainted and fell—the consequence was a sudden illness full of disappointment and ruinous to my constitution."[81] She had again miscarried.

So concerned with his wife's health was John Quincy that he arranged for an extended vacation. From late July through early October, the couple would reside in Toeplitz and Dresden. Toeplitz, situated on a lake surrounded by dense forests high up in the Alps, was a favorite watering hole for European royalty and nobility. Among other things, the city was famed for its hot springs, which provided water for curative baths. "Toeplitz itself is on the side of a hanging hill," Adams wrote his friend Murray, "& just before reaching it we had to descend a mountain called the Geyersberg which is so excessively steep & rocky that nobody ever thinks of coming down in a carriage. Ladies are carried down in chairs borne by two men, like sedans. . . . I myself came down on foot.[82] John Quincy and Louisa took lodgings at one of the city's most elegant hotels, and she began a series of baths prescribed and supervised by a local physician. He also advised frequent walks, music to John Quincy's ears. "The country round Toeplitz is magnificent," Louisa recorded in her memoir.[83] There was, not surprisingly, an intense social life at the resort, and the Adamses participated fully.

Louisa was struck by the breadth and depth of superstition among the local inhabitants—of all classes. On the way up the mountain, they had passed the ruins of a castle that, their coachman had told them, once was the abode of a notoriously wicked count who had sold his soul to the devil; for his sins, he was eventually thrown, shrieking, from the parapets of his castle. Every season Satan reappeared to oversee a reenactment of the count's orgies and subsequent demise. "I have often remarked that the traditions and superstitions which you hear related by the uneducated and ignorant produce a much stronger effect upon the mind than the varnished tales depicted by writers of eminence," Louisa observed. "[They] awaken feelings of which we are ashamed but which influence the imagination . . . despite . . . reason and resolution."[84] Nor was superstition limited to the common folk. Her husband had noted when in Berlin that even the most sophisticated and highly placed persons believed in ghosts and spirits. "The press both in Germany and England has for many years turned with novels, romances, and plays formed upon mysteries, and goblins, and incantations, always connected with some tale of horror," he wrote John.[85]

In their correspondence, his father asked John Quincy if rumors of the existence of the Illuminati were widely credited. The term referred specifically to a Bavarian order founded in 1776 consisting of enlightened intellectuals who dedicated themselves to creating a more just and humane society through influence, persuasion, and behind-the-scenes political machinations. More generally it referred to a network of secret societies bent on controlling world affairs. John Quincy replied that he had heard rumors of "the idea of a sect of Illumines" that included such diverse groups as the followers of Mesmer, the Freemasons, and the Jacobins. But he did not believe in its existence. The more one pressed believers to elucidate, the vaguer they became.[86]

WHILE JOHN QUINCY AND Louisa were taking the waters at Toeplitz, matters were coming to a head in the struggle between the president and his cabinet of adversaries in America. Soon after his March message to Congress, John had decamped for Quincy; he would not return to Philadelphia until October. As the weeks passed, the High Federalist press became increasingly shrill in its accusations of executive negligence. The *Philadelphia Gazette* printed an unsigned letter from a citizen of Northampton County, Pennsylvania, alleging that "Congress have empowered the President to borrow as much money as he pleases and to mortgage any, or all of the states for the payment!" It was further alleged that the president planned to use the money to escape to England, purchase a lordship, and marry one of his daughters into the royal family.[87] To Thomas, who was then living in the "hotbed of sedition [Philadelphia]," Abigail wrote begging him to give the lie to all of this calumny. "The President will never desert his station when the exigencies of government require his presence, but he will not stay from his wife. Tell them so."[88] In truth, John would remain at Peacefield far beyond the time the exigencies of government required his presence. Even his supporters suspected him of trying to hide.

Meanwhile, the president continued to receive from John Quincy and William Vans Murray encouraging words concerning France's desire for peace. Murray passed on a direct message from Talleyrand assuring Adams again that peace emissaries would be received with open arms and treated with dignity. In response the president ordered Pickering to prepare instructions for Murray, Davie, and Ellsworth and announced that the latter two would soon set sail to join their colleague. Following a monthlong delay, Pickering provided Adams with a draft while urging him to postpone the mission indefinitely. Adams intended to remain in Quincy until November, but then in August he received an urgent message from Benjamin Stoddert, the secretary of the navy and an Adams ally. He must come at once to foil the "artful, designing men" who were plotting to take control of American foreign policy and preempt his peace initiative.[89] Indeed, the High Federalists were circulating rumors that Adams intended to resign, and they were already discussing a replacement. (This apparently originated from a message from Adams to Pickering in which Adams declared that he would rather resign than have his foreign policy dictated by a foreign government [Great Britain].)[90] At long last, Adams decided to act.

The cabinet was then ensconced in Trenton, New Jersey, Philadelphia being then still under a plague watch. The president arrived on October 10 and immediately huddled with his "advisers." For five days Adams listened as Pickering, McHenry, and Wolcott railed against the mission to France. In the end, however, he prevailed, and the instructions to the peace mission were approved. Adams insisted that Davie and Ellsworth leave before the end of the month. At this point, Hamilton, informed of the virtual certainty of a peace mission, left his troops at Newark and after a two-day gallop arrived in Trenton. Granted an audience with the president, he inveighed against a new peace mission to France. It would certainly be viewed as a hostile act by Great Britain. Instead of kicking Hamilton back to his barracks as he deserved, Adams listened patiently and then refuted every one of his arguments. He later observed that the "[over]wrought . . . little man" had exhibited a "total ignorance . . . of everything in Europe, in France, England, and elsewhere."[91] Having daunted Hamilton at last, Adams was gratified to see Davie and Ellsworth depart for Europe on November 3; they arrived in Lisbon a month later.

ON HIS WAY BACK to Quincy, John stopped off in New York to visit Charles and his family. He found that his middle son had succumbed completely to drink, leaving his wife and children abandoned and miserable. Charles had squandered six thousand dollars of John Quincy's money and, more important, all of the opportunities a distinguished family and a Harvard education could offer. John reported to Abigail that Sally had "opened her mind" to him. "I grieved, I mourned but could do no more." He is "a madman possessed of the devil. . . . I renounce him."[92] Abigail could not yet bring herself to abandon Charles. In early 1800 she would visit New York, where she found that Sally and her two young daughters had taken refuge with Nabby and her family. In time, however, she too gave up, confiding to William Stephens Smith that she considered Charles "a miserable man whom I can no longer consider as my son."[93]

At long last, John, with Abigail accompanying him, departed Quincy for Philadelphia. Just after they arrived in the capital, they learned that George Washington had died, probably of a streptococcus infection. The first couple attended memorial services at a nearby Anglican church and then held a commemorative dinner for selected guests. Despite Washington's support of Hamilton, the Adams family forgave and forgot. "Death, thou art no Respecter of Persons," Abigail wrote Mary Cranch. "Washington is no more! A great man has fallen."[94] Washington deserved every accolade, John and Abigail believed. He had never misused the unparalleled power invested in him, he had never been tainted by a hint of corruption, he had been an exemplar of nonpartisanship in domestic affairs and of neutrality in foreign, and he had borne the insults of his foes with quiet dignity. John Quincy fully shared this approbation, and he would throughout his public life use Washington as an icon to rally support for his nationalist domestic programs and a foreign policy rooted in continental expansion and nonalignment.

HAVING PUT ASHORE AT Lisbon in late December 1799, Davie and Ellsworth made their way to the Hague to rendezvous with William Vans Murray. The three arrived in Paris in February 1800, where they were warmly greeted by Talleyrand. The Americans encountered a French government and political culture profoundly changed since their appointment. In July 1798 a French force under the command of General Napoleon Bonaparte had landed at Alexandria. His mission was to defeat Egyptian forces under the thumb of Great Britain and secure Egypt as a base to disrupt British communications with its Asian colonies. He was successful on land but was unable to match the Royal Navy at sea. Learning of French defeats in Europe, he departed Egypt with what remained of his force on August 24, 1799. He returned to Paris to find the Directory virtually paralyzed. Napoleon was greeted as a conquering hero. In cooperation with two directors, Abbé Emmanuel-Joseph Sieyès and Joseph Fouché, Napoleon had staged a coup d'état on November 9, 1799 (the eighteenth of Brumaire, according to the revolutionary calendar). A new constitution replaced the Directory with a Consulate, Napoleon being appointed First Consul for a term of ten years. The Council of Elders and the Council of Five Hundred were replaced with new legislative bodies whose members were either appointed or controlled by the First Consul.[95] In June 1800, Napoleon, at the head of twenty-four thousand troops, would defeat an Austrian army of approximately equal size in the Battle of Marengo. It once again secured French control of the Italian Peninsula and solidified Napoleon's political position in France.

John Quincy Adams was not a fan of military dictatorship, but he believed Napoleon and the Consulate a great improvement over the Reign of Terror and the Directory. French and American Jacobins were much dissatisfied with these developments, John Quincy wrote his mother, but there was little they could do about them as long as the First Consul continued to be a victorious general. "The state of France has been very much ameliorated in every respect by this change. Internally a dangerous rebellion has been suppressed and externally victory has returned in every quarter to their banners." It was true that unprecedented power had been invested in the office of First Consul, "but his character improves by success; he has done very few importune things since he attained his present station, and many wise things." France's posture and policies toward neutrals like the United States were completely altered. "All their plundering and barbarous decrees against neutral navigation have been rescinded and they have established a court of final appeal in admiralty cases."[96]

Meanwhile, the congressional elections of 1798 had brought to the House and Senate a group of moderate Federalists whose views were more in tune with those of John Adams and John Marshall.[97] In May 1800, in the midst of the peace negotiations in Paris, the Federalist caucus in Congress nominated John Adams and Charles Cotesworth Pinckney for the presidency and vice presidency, although without specifying their preference for the higher office. Once again, the door was left open for Hamilton to try to rig the election against Adams. At this point the president decided to at last purge his cabinet of the Essex men. On May 5, he summoned Secretary of War McHenry and vented all of his pent-up wrath. McHenry was nothing less than a traitor. Adams knew quite well, he declared, that McHenry had acted as Hamilton's Trojan horse, that he was plotting with the New Yorker to deny him reelection, and that he had done everything in his power to sabotage the peace mission to France. How McHenry could attach himself to such a man as Hamilton, "a man devoid of any moral principle,—a bastard, and . . . a foreigner," was beyond him. "Mr. Jefferson is an infinitely better man, a wiser one, I am sure," Adams declared. "You cannot, Sir, remain longer in the office."[98] McHenry submitted his resignation the next day.

Pickering was another matter. Four days after his tête-à-tête with the secretary of war, the president requested the secretary of state's resignation. Pickering refused, declaring that he had unfinished business to attend to. Whereupon Adams promptly fired him. "Pickering mistook Mrs. Reynolds' paramour [Hamilton] for President of the United States and surrendered up his official virtue to that gay deceiver as fondly as the lady did her conjugal virtue," John Quincy would later observe to Thomas.[99] Incredibly, Wolcott survived. The president named a former Federalist senator from Boston, Samuel Dexter, to replace McHenry and John Marshall to take Pickering's place.

IN BERLIN, THE WELCOME news from Paris and Philadelphia did much to ease John Quincy's mind concerning public affairs, and it was with much pleasure that he immersed himself in the translation of Wieland's *Oberon*. His wife's health, however, continued to trouble. While attending a large party given in honor of the marriage of two members of the Prussian nobility, Louisa suffered another trauma. In turning to speak to Louisa, the wife of the Spanish minister caught her foot in the carpet and fell, breaking her ankle in two places. Louisa knelt and supported the woman's head on her knee while a surgeon was being summoned. When the physician arrived, he asked Louisa to assist him, and she complied, cutting the stocking off the other lady's very swollen ankle. "I tried to find Mr. Adams that I might get home but ere I could succeed, I fell down in a deep fainting fit and was carried home."[100] Shortly thereafter Louisa miscarried for a fourth time. "These violent, long continued and frequently repeated shocks from the state of my wife's health must at last have an effect upon mine," John Quincy noted in his diary.[101]

With the prospect of peace with France looming, John Quincy decided that for Louisa's health and his own an extended vacation was called for. The region selected was Silesia, situated on Prussia's eastern frontier. The area included portions of Bohemia and Moravia and ran along both banks of the Oder River. Silesia consisted mostly of plains and rolling hills until one approached the southern border, where the Sudeten Mountains loomed. It was Prussia's primary manufacturing area, specializing in broadcloth and porcelain. The couple departed Berlin on July 16 and did not return until mid-September.

Adams kept a detailed journal of the trip, which he posted to his brother Thomas in a series of forty-two letters. He might have been considering publication in some form or another; travel literature was very popular at the turn of the eighteenth century, and a literate description of the social and physical landscape of the infrequently visited Silesia would certainly enhance his reputation as a man of letters. In many ways the province was stuck in the feudal past. John Quincy's letters described the lives led by all conditions of men—nobility, peasants, soldiers, innkeepers, mountain guides, and merchants. His accounts of the forests, waterfalls, and sunsets were lyrical.

Thomas was so struck with his brother's letters describing Silesia that he suggested that they be published in a new magazine, the *Port Folio*, which had been established in Philadelphia by his old Harvard classmate Joseph Dennie Jr. Murray also urged publication, and in December John Quincy gave his permission, writing Thomas that he trusted him to edit out anything that was personal or offensive. Dennie began publishing the letters in January 1801 under the title *Journal of a Tour Through Silesia.* "It will be obvious to every intelligent reader," he wrote in the preface to the first installment, "that it has been made by no vulgar traveler but by a man of genius and observation."[102] The letters were subsequently published in London as *John Quincy Adams, Letters on Silesia* (1804) and appeared in translation in Germany (1804) and France (1807).[103] John Quincy was obviously flattered by the publication and acclaim, but he took special pleasure in supporting the *Port Folio*, the first literary journal of its kind to go to press in America. "The plan of this undertaking has given me more pleasure than I can express," he wrote Thomas. "The object is noble. It is to take off that foul stain of literary barbarism which has so long exposed our country to the reproach of strangers and to the derision of her enemies."[104]

11

The Election of 1800

I N SEPTEMBER 1800, JOHN's and John Quincy's arduous labors to establish a
lasting peace between the United States and France finally came to fruition.
Bonaparte had eagerly embraced Talleyrand's scheme for reestablishing New
France in the trans-Mississippi West. The plan was to persuade/intimidate Spain
into retroceding Louisiana to France. The agricultural bounty of the Mississippi
Valley could be used to feed Saint-Domingue and France's other sugar colonies in
the Caribbean. For this, peace rather than war with America was required. After
Murray, Ellsworth, and Davie arrived in Paris, the French foreign office negotiated in good faith. The Treaty of Mortefontaine was signed on September 30,
1800. In it, France and the United States pledged undying friendship. The pact
endorsed the principle of free ships make free goods. Bonaparte anticipated res-
urrecting the League of Armed Neutrality, which would be capable of resisting
British maritime depredations, and he wanted America to be part of it. The
French agreed to the abrogation of the Treaty of 1778 if the United States would
assume the claims of its citizens against France for ship seizures before and during
the Quasi-War. It was so agreed.

Napoleon hosted a magnificent fete at his brother Joseph's estate to celebrate
the accord. Unbeknownst to the peace commissioners and the Adams administration, the French had simultaneously concluded the Treaty of San Ildefonso
with the Spanish Crown in which Madrid agreed to cede Louisiana to France in
return for the Italian province of Tuscany. In mid-December, John Quincy wrote
Murray to congratulate him on his singular achievement: "If ever a mariner in the
midst of a furious tempest, with a long ridge of rocks under their lee, found an
opportunity to slip by a narrow passage into a snug little harbor sheltered from
every blast, their situation in my opinion highly resembled that of our country."[1]

News of the signing of the Treaty of Mortefontaine was greeted with appropriation by both the Federalist and Republican presses. "No possible advantage could have been derived from the consideration of perpetuating the difficulties which had embarrassed and deranged the national peace of France and America," opined the *Philadelphia Aurora*.[2] But John Adams's difficult decision for peace with France was not sufficient to secure his reelection. The Republicans had put up a slate of Thomas Jefferson and Aaron Burr to challenge Adams and Pinckney. The parties appeared evenly matched, so the election would be determined by the outcome in one or two battleground states. On his way to inspect the new federal city being built in Maryland, President Adams delivered several speeches defending his policies and highlighting his role in the American Revolution. A most un-Massachusetts thing to do, it signaled Adams's desperation. He had learned that New York had cast its ballots for electors pledged to Jefferson and Burr.[3] James McHenry had reported to Hamilton in detail the dressing-down he had received from the president, including the slanderous comments about Hamilton himself. In October, the former treasury secretary published "Letter from Alexander Hamilton Concerning the Public Conduct and Character of John Adams." He admitted to supporting Pinckney over Adams in 1796; he had done so, he said, because the South Carolinian was a man of honor, moderation, and judgment— all the things Adams was not. The New Englander's personality was, Hamilton charged, composed of "disgusting egotism . . . distempered jealousy," and "ungovernable indiscretion." In claiming that a cabal against him existed within his cabinet, Adams was being paranoid and delusional. "Against me his rage has been so vehement as to have caused him, more than once, to forfeit the decorum which in his station, ought to have been an inviolable law."[4] Hamilton's broadside appalled Federalists and delighted Republicans. It created a fissure in the Federalist Party that could possibly sound its death knell.

The campaign was bitter. This was a contest between "democracy" and "republicanism," declared Federalist orators. It was Adams who would be guided by reason, moderation, and judgment, opined one editor, while Jefferson and Burr would be but tools of the mob.[5] Rumors abounded concerning Jefferson's alleged atheism and his licentious behavior with Sally Hemings. Republicans denounced the Federalists as monarchists, pawns of Great Britain, and relics of the past. The Alien and Sedition Acts were nothing more than barefaced attacks on the country's civil liberties; their support for a standing army and a powerful navy was proof that the Federalists were determined to turn American into a modern-day Sparta. December 4 was the date set for the assembly of the Electoral College in Washington. When the votes were tallied, Jefferson and Burr tied with seventy-three apiece. Adams finished third with sixty-five, one more than Pinckney. Not a single Republican elector had broken ranks or thrown his vote away.[6]

With Jefferson and Burr tied, the election would be determined by the House of Representatives, with each state having one vote. To the dismay of many Republicans, Burr refused to withdraw. The vote stood eight for Jefferson, six for Burr, with two delegations divided. The deadlock lasted for thirty-six ballots, until Federalist James Bayard representing Delaware switched his vote from Burr to Jefferson.

Both Abigail and John Quincy had anticipated defeat, Abigail as early as August. "Brittania & Gallia" were the two rivals that were dominating American politics, Abigail had written Catherine Nuth Johnson. "One party is making love to one, and another party to another—and they are ready to sacrifice some of their friends and their chief [John Adams] into the bargain because he insists that he will not quarrel with either if they are willing to be friends. But choose, they say, or we 'will certainly pick your eyes out.'"[7] In November, John Quincy had written his father a letter of condolence and support. The prevalent opinions in Europe bolstered by American newspaper reports "leave scarce a doubt, but that a change will take place at the ensuing election which will leave you at your own disposal. Do not grieve, do not let this rejection affect your health; do not think more hardly of your country than she deserves." The ultimate consolation, John Quincy declared, was that you were rejected for doing the right thing.[8]

John Quincy, not surprisingly, began to worry about his own future. He dreaded returning to the law. At heart, he believed, he was a man of letters and in this regard occupying diplomatic posts abroad had served him well. Life in the foreign service consisted of long stretches of free time punctuated by crises and bursts of frenzied activity. "My leisure has indeed been so considerable," he wrote his father, "that I could follow the bent of my own inclination or caprice in the choice of my studies. . . . I am persuaded that upon the whole, my hours of application have been more useful to the culture of my own mind and heart than they would have been in the dry and drudging study of legal questions."[9] Abigail wrote bidding him to return to the land of his birth. She and John missed him intensely; in view of Charles's imminent demise, having him and Louisa at hand would prove a great comfort. You have been abroad these six years, she wrote. You are destined to be a great man, but for that to happen you must return to America and appear upon its public stage. "Our countrymen are very apt to suspect, and not without reason that a man cannot be long absent from the place of his nativity without contracting foreign manners, tastes, and habits, which are ill calculated to assimilate with theirs."[10] And there was Louisa's health to consider. A settled existence would be of great benefit. None of this could John Quincy deny. The pull of family was very strong. In December 1800, John Quincy wrote Thomas, instructing him to place all his—John Quincy's—assets at the disposal of their father. "[H]e has been so far from growing rich in the service of the public that it is not improbable he may in his retirement have occasion for money. I therefore authorize and direct you to consider all and every part of my property in your hands, whether of principal or interest, as subject at all times to his disposal for his own use . . . you will not mention to him that I have given you this instruction."[11]

On January 31, President Adams directed Secretary of State Marshall to prepare letters recalling John Quincy from his post in Berlin. He told Marshall that his son certainly deserved another diplomatic post, but that would have to be up to his successor. In truth, the Jeffersons and the Adamses parted ways on the most cordial of terms. As John and Abigail were taking their leave of Philadelphia, the new president called. He told Abigail that he would keep on any and all of the household staff she would recommend and "begged me to be assured nothing would so much contribute to his happiness as to be able in any way to be serviceable to Mr. Adams, myself, or any of my family," Abigail wrote Thomas. "[He] inquired particularly after Mr. JQA—whether he liked his residence at Berlin . . . he never sees me but he inquires with affection after him."[12]

Whether or not Jefferson would have kept John Quincy on is not clear—his new secretary of state, James Madison, did not like the Adamses at this point in his career. It was irrelevant. Abigail, John, and his country had called John Quincy home, and he was going to obey.

ON THE DAY THE electors met to cast their votes, John and Abigail learned that Charles had died. Abigail had visited him in New York early in November. She discovered him living at the house of a friend. "I found my poor unhappy son laid upon a bed of sickness . . . a distressing cough, an affection of the liver, and a dropsy will soon terminate a life which might have been ma[de] valuable to himself and others," she wrote Mary Cranch. "Sally was with him, but his physician says he is past recovery."[13] Upon learning that Charles had died on November 30, Abigail took some comfort that he had expired at the Smith residence, with Nabby at his bedside. John Quincy had found it in his heart to forgive Charles; John could not. "There is nothing more to be said," he declared upon learning of his son's demise.[14]

After Abigail and John retired to Quincy, Sally and both children would come to live with them. In truth, John and Abigail were devastated by Charles's death. In the weeks that followed, John mused about happier times when he, John Quincy, and Charles were exploring life together in the Netherlands and France, a time when the beautiful, whimsical child had been "the delight of my eyes and a darling of my heart."[15] He would never admit that his exalted standards and long absences had had anything to do with the death of his son.

* * *

JOHN ADAMS'S DEFEAT COMPELLED John Quincy to ponder its consequences—consequences that would surely have a profound impact on his own political future. He trusted Thomas Jefferson personally, but there were forces at work that transcended the individual. The Virginian had been elected with the votes of Northern backcountry farmers and urban workingmen as well as those from the slaveholding South, but John Quincy believed, correctly, that it was the slavocracy that was calling the shots in this coalition. In the immediate aftermath of the election, he speculated that the triumph of the slaveholding South might lead to the dissolution of the republic. "[T]he planters have not discovered the inconsistency of holding in one hand the rights of man, and in the other a scourge for the back of slaves," he wrote Thomas.[16] Then to Murray, "[I]f, they [the Jeffersonians] will break us up, in God's name, let the Union go. I love the Union, as I love my wife. But if my wife would . . . insist upon a separation, she should have it, though it broke my heart."[17]

Of one thing Adams was certain—the Federalist Party was doomed. Always more charitable than his parents—at this point at least—he believed that Alexander Hamilton was a brilliant but misguided and overly ambitious man. He was a nationalist who had put the country on a sound financial footing, but he was also—most alarmingly—a militarist. With Bonaparte as a constant example, John Quincy worried that partisan strife encouraged by France and Great Britain coupled with the presence of would-be men on horseback like Hamilton would turn America into a garrison state. "[If] you [the national government] maintain the war for the army while you tell them [the American people] you maintain the army for the war, you lose their attachment forever . . . then your army will be the sole support you have."[18] Whatever the case, the Federalist Party would not be able to recover from the machinations of the Essex men. "I shall have no hesitation in quitting them, be the consequences what they may."[19] Then to the crux of the matter. "Let us knit our system of policy so closely with their [the people's] interests that they cannot tear one without rending the other," he wrote Murray.[20] If civil war was inevitable, it would be on the basis of slavery and slavery alone, a crusade of good versus evil.

UPON RETURNING TO BERLIN from Silesia, John Quincy once again turned to his German translations. Louisa was now pregnant again. The fires of his passion for Mary Frazier were at last banked. "From the wounds I was never entirely healed," he wrote Murray, "but by the balm of a second & more auspicious attachment after an interval of five years," he was on the mend. He had nearly been driven mad by passion, John Quincy confessed, at a time "when the verses of Catullus were so applicable," but they were now but a poignant memory. During their return voyage to the United States, Louisa would first learn of Mary's existence. She pressed her husband for every detail: "My curiosity was much excited to see her; the elaborate but just account which I heard of her extreme beauty; her great attainments; the elegance of her letters; altogether made me feel little, and though I was not jealous, I could not bear the idea of the comparison that must take place. It was true I had every confidence in my husband's affection, yet it was an affair of vanity on my part."[21]

Not much was known in late-eighteenth-century medicine about hypochondria. But Louisa Catherine Adams was at times her own worst enemy. She had become convinced that the least shock, nervous agitation, or emotional distress would affect her physical health, and so they did. This vicious cycle was interrupted for a time by Louisa's friendship with Lady Elizabeth Carysfort, the remarkable wife of the recently named minister to Prussia. A woman of will, intellect, and academic achievement, Lady Carysfort took an immediate liking to Louisa. Their friendship had a long social bridge to cross. Elizabeth, twenty years older than Louisa, was the daughter of one prime minister and the sister of Lord Grenville, a future one. But there was something compelling in the American girl—the daughter of a bankrupt Maryland merchant and a woman of dubious lineage. Louisa was frequently summoned to Lady Carysfort's boudoir, where the older woman shared her innermost secrets. "Her conversation [was] so instructive, so interesting, and at times so delightful, I clung to her as if she had been my own mother and love her with equal sincerity."[22]

As Louisa struggled with the discomforts of her latest pregnancy, Elizabeth would not allow her to take to her sickbed, to dwell on past miscarriages, to become morbid. She insisted that her American friend take walks, go for carriage rides, and enjoy the company of her friends. Louisa recalled that one morning she was so ill, she could not sit up. Throughout the day, Lady Carysfort sent notes insisting that Louisa come to her. Finally, at eight in the evening, Louisa gathered her strength and found Elizabeth ensconced on a sofa in her private apartment and surrounded by amusing friends. Soon Louisa was conversing and laughing, so invigorated that she stayed to dinner. Sandwiched between her and another young woman was the Duke of Darmstadt, "a German lump of obesity" who kept the pair in "a perfect gale" of laughter with his witty and ribald stories.[23] Elizabeth's nurturing was rewarded. On April 12, 1801, John Quincy recorded in his diary, "I have this day to offer my humble and devout thanks to almighty God for the birth of a son at half past three o'clock this afternoon."[24] The birth had nearly killed Louisa. She was attended by a "drunken Accoucheur" [obstetrician], and the delivery was so poorly managed that she was left temporarily paralyzed on the left side from the waist down.[25] Two weeks after her son's birth, she was too weak to stand or even turn her body. But Louisa managed not only to nurse her babe but that of a "kindly English woman." Dr. Browne believed that an excess of milk would lead to a fever of the brain and so Louisa suckled two newborns.[26] So concerned were the king and queen over Louisa's health that Frederick William had the entrance and exit to the street on which the Adamses lived barricaded so that the noise from passing carriages would not disturb the new mother. Illness prevented Louisa from attending the christening of her son on May 4. Lord and Lady Carysfort served as godparents at the baptismal service, which was performed by the Anglican chaplain attached to the British embassy. "The child's name is George Washington, and I implore the favor of almighty God that he may live and never prove unworthy of it," John Quincy recorded in his diary.[27] Upon learning of the baby's christening, Abigail wrote Thomas that the naming of her grandson for George Washington was "ill judged"; she knew because she and John had made the same mistake. "I am sure your brother had not any intention of wounding the feelings of his Father, but I see he has done it—had he called him Joshua, he would not have taken it amiss."[28]

Though George was less than three months old and Louisa still nursing, John Quincy decided to head for home. If he waited any longer, the season would become unfavorable, and he was eager to start their new life in America. With their servants Epps and Whitcomb in tow, the Adamses departed Berlin on June 17. A week later at Hamburg, John Quincy booked passage for them all on the ship *America* bound for Philadelphia; the fare was a hundred guineas.

Three days into the voyage, John Quincy noted in his diary: "I enter upon my thirty-fifth year with a grateful heart to a kind Providence for its great indulgence through the course of my life and with a supplication for the means of making my future days, days of usefulness."[29] Louisa had rarely been shipboard except to cross the English Channel; both she and George immediately became ill, he with diarrhea and she with seasickness. Both soon recovered, however; the sea air seemed to agree with the baby. John Quincy subsequently reported in his diary that soon the crew was passing him from arm to arm.[30] The voyage, he recalled, was tedious but not unpleasant.

The little party landed at Philadelphia on September 4, 1801; Thomas was dockside to greet them. He was shocked at Louisa's wan and emaciated appearance but found John Quincy little changed—a bit fatter, but pleasingly so. Thomas accompanied his brother and sister-in-law to the home of a Mrs. Roberts, a private room and board situated at North Walnut Street. John Quincy immediately wrote to the secretary of state, announcing his arrival. It was decided that the family would separate, Louisa and George to travel to Washington to visit with the Johnsons, and John Quincy to Boston. He had not seen his parents for seven years. "At eight o'clock in the morning, Mr. Adams put me into the stage for Baltimore with Epps, my baby, and Whitcomb to visit my poor father and my family in Washington," Louisa recorded in her journal. "We had never been parted before, and though this country was to be my home, I was yet a forlorn stranger in the land of my Fathers."[31]

Following a rough-and-tumble journey by stagecoach, Louisa, George, and the servants arrived in the nation's new capital and appeared unannounced on the Johnsons' doorstep. Louisa later recorded that her father, who was then in declining health, did not at first recognize her. But when he did, "It was sometime before he could calm his feelings and talk with me." Louisa was once again swept into the bosom of her family. Predictably she fell ill from the stresses of the trip and by subsequently being forced to wean George "by absolute compulsion, against my will, and with great bodily suffering."[32]

Meanwhile, John Quincy was moving in the opposite direction toward Quincy but at a deliberate pace, stopping to visit with family and dignitaries. He was amazed by the prosperity he witnessed as he made his way. "I find everywhere the marks of peace within our walls, and prosperity within our palaces," he wrote Rufus King, "for palaces they may truly be called, those splendid and costly mansions which since my departure seem to have shot up from the earth by enchantment."[33] He stopped in New York to reunite with Nabby. There he dined with the new vice president, Aaron Burr, and other dignitaries. On September 17, John Quincy sailed from Crane's Wharf to Providence and from there took the stage to Boston.[34] He immediately rented a horse and chaise and set off for Quincy, arriving at nine in the evening. "Here I had the inexpressible delight of finding once more my parents."[35] He spent the next few days getting reacquainted with family and friends, roaming the farm with his father, and writing letters. "I have resumed the practice of bathing and taking exercise before breakfast which I found so beneficial last spring."[36] Abigail fretted about her son and his family's future. John was out of a job, so they could not help financially. John Quincy had not practiced law for seven years; there was a hostile administration in Washington and so there was little or no hope of appointment to office. And she had enough insight to worry about how Louisa would cope. Abigail had warned her son, "Mrs. Adams is going to a place different from all she has ever yet faced and among a people where it is impossible for her to be too guarded." Her every utterance would be examined under a political magnifying glass: "such is the spirit of the party."[37]

Enthralled though she was to see her family, Louisa was soon pleading with John Quincy to come and visit. The family is all extremely eager to see you, she wrote, and he must witness the charms of the new capital. "I am quite delighted with the situation of this place and think would it be finished, it will be one of the most beautiful spots in the world. The President's House and the Capitol are two most superb buildings and very well worth coming to see."[38] John Quincy responded with surprising ardor. "Our dear George—how I long to kiss even his slavering lips!—As for those of his mother I say nothing. . . . This day week—the 15th—I propose to take the wings—alas! Not of the wind, but of that very earthly vehicle, the Providence Stage and thence by land or by water creep or wade or swim with all that motion give to this sluggish lump of matter, my body, until I can more than in wishes and imagination fly to the arms of my best beloved."[39]

John Quincy made the trip from Boston to Washington in a remarkably brief six days. The Johnsons did indeed embrace him, and the two weeks that followed were a whirl of engagements, both social and official. He called on Jefferson, Secretary of State Madison—who saw to it that he was fully compensated for his diplomatic duties—and Secretary of the Treasury Albert Gallatin. The Adamses were invited to a dinner party at the executive mansion, where the atmosphere, described by one in attendance, was of "chilling frigidity."[40] Jefferson and Madison were bitter over John Adams's last-minute appointment of as many Federalists to the federal bench as possible. Among these "midnight judges" was John Marshall, Jefferson's archenemy, who would serve as chief justice of the Supreme Court for thirty-four years.

Soon John Quincy announced that it was time to depart for Massachusetts; winter was setting in and he wanted to embark before snow and ice made the trip more difficult. On November 3 the entire family set out for Frederick, Maryland, to gather at the estate of Thomas Johnson before splitting up. On the way, Joshua fell ill—he was already in frail health. John Quincy observed that he was suffering from "the gravel"—that is, kidney stones—but it was more than that. On the eighth, he, Louisa, George, and the two servants departed for Boston. Louisa's sister Caroline was scheduled to accompany them, but she decided to stay behind to nurse her ailing father. Predictably, Louisa became ill before the journey had completed its first day. In Philadelphia, "I was so severely ill that Mr. Adams sent for Dr. Rush [the renowned physician Benjamin Rush] who administered a few drops of laudanum." Her husband surmised that it was her spirits that were more afflicted than her body. "She is under great apprehensions," he wrote, "and still more depressed in her spirits than really ill."[41]

Adams allowed his wife and child, who was sick with dysentery, one day's rest and then it was on the road again. On the eighteenth, the party reached Paulus Hook on the New Jersey side of the Hudson. A winter storm had blown up and, in a hail of sleet and frozen rain, John Quincy, Louisa, George, and the servants had to make the crossing to New York in a pirogue, a sort of oversize canoe with a sail. Louisa was spectacularly unprepared—"without even an umbrella, dressed in a blue satin pelice [pelisse—a woman's cloak reaching to the ankles] trimmed with black lace, and without one particle of covering"; she was drenched to the skin and numb with cold by the time they reached the New York side. Fortunately, Nabby and her family were there to greet them. "[W]ithout stopping to ask any questions, she led me into a bedroom, tore off my things and insisted upon nursing me in the kindest and most affectionate manner."[42]

Revived, the Adamses proceeded on to Quincy and arrived on November 25, 1801, Thanksgiving Day. John and Abigail had gathered the extended family at Peacefield, the large, comfortable home they had remodeled and expanded following their return from Great Britain. The former president and First Lady greeted their daughter-in-law warmly and cooed over George.[43] Louisa was appalled at the rusticity of Quincy and the inelegance of both her surroundings and her new relatives. "What shall I say of my impressions of Quincy! Had I stepped into Noah's Ark, I do not think I could have been more utterly astonished," she recorded in her diary. "Dr. Tufts! Deacon French! Mr. Cranch! Old Uncle Peter! And Capt. Beale!!! It was luck for me that I was so much depressed and so ill, or I would certainly have given mortal offence—even the church, its forms, the snuffling through the nose, the singers, the dressing, and the dinner hour, were all novelties to me."[44] In truth Louisa was an English-bred Southern belle plunked down in the midst of a group of staid, starchy, and hardheaded Yankees.

While he was in Boston and getting reacquainted with his parents, John Quincy had bought for six thousand dollars the house in which he had previously resided at 39 Hanover Street. He moved his family into their new residence and put Tilly Whitcomb in charge of the household. In December, Louisa developed what John Quincy referred to as a "very distressing" and "incessant" cough. At length he summoned Dr. Thomas Welsh, an old family friend, who bled and blistered her. He confided to John Quincy that he expected her not to survive. "Her frame is so slender & her constitution so delicate that I have many fears that she will be of short duration," Abigail wrote Thomas.[45] The only things that seemed to bring Louisa some comfort were the small doses of laudanum that Dr. Welsh prescribed.

But Louisa did not expire and she gradually began to take her place as wife and daughter in one of New England's most influential families. "In Boston I met with the most decidedly flattering reception. . . . All the elite of Boston called on me and entertained me most handsomely."[46] She was soon deprived of the service of her nurse and servant, Elizabeth Epps. John Quincy declared that he could no longer afford her and offered to pay her way back to England. She declined, and

in 1804 she and Tilly Whitcomb married; he became the proprietor of Concert
Hall on the corner of Hanover and Court Streets. "The charge of my darling boy
then devolved upon me," Louisa lamented, "and the sleepless nights of Mr. Adams soon taught him to regret the loss of his loving and faithful nurse."[47]

Not surprisingly, Louisa's initial relationship with her mother-in-law was tense.
They were very different people. Louisa and her family were gay, warm, fun loving. Abigail was a mother who had once warned her sons against excessive mirth.
Abigail tried to conceal her instinctive dislike for his son's bride by being overly
solicitous. When Louisa visited Quincy, everyone hovered, lavishing her with
attention and special dishes of food. By her own admission, Louisa "became cold
and reserved, and seldom spoke at all." In truth Abigail thought Louisa a spoiled,
weak European woman unfit for the rigors of American life. Her daughter-in-law
did not seem to be able to manage her own household, much less a farm. For
Abigail, being a loving, dutiful wife meant immersing oneself in work—cooking,
gardening, mending, hiring and firing servants, managing accounts, and, in her
own case, overseeing tenants. Her ambitions for John Quincy knew no bounds,
and here he had gone and married a young woman who apparently would be an
albatross rather than a helpmate. Louisa, of course, sensed all of this. "The qualifications necessary to form an accomplished Quincy lady, were in direct opposition to the mode of life which I had led. . . . I tried by every means in my power
to work, as they call it; but my strength did not second the effort—Mrs. Adams
gave me instruction and advice, but I did not readily learn. . . . I was literally and
without knowing it a *fine* lady." In her mind she was constantly being compared
with Mary Frazier and unfavorably so. The only bright spot for Louisa was John:
"The old gentleman took a fancy to me, and he was the only one."[48]

On January 5, 1802, John Quincy moved into his first-floor office on State
Street in Boston. Upstairs were the offices of the *Columbia Centinel*, edited by
the ardent Federalist Benjamin Russell. "The commencement of my old profession again is attended with difficulties somewhat embarrassing and prospects not
very encouraging," John Quincy confided to his diary.[49] The newly retired diplomat suffered from three disadvantages. He lagged far behind his peers in building
up a client base. It had been years since he had studied the law; with little enthusiasm, he had begun again on Blackstone in late December. Most important,
jurisprudence bored him. John Quincy was not without means. He had while
abroad succeeded in living on his salary. His "Waste Book and Journal" begun on
January 1, 1802, listed his total assets at $43,702.54. They included two houses in
Boston—the Hanover Street residence at six thousand dollars and another at five
thousand dollars. There were eleven thousand dollars in 8 percent U.S. stocks and
his magnificent library valued at five thousand dollars. He had begun investing in

insurance companies and municipal bonds as well as in various infrastructure projects. A respectable estate despite some nine thousand dollars in uncollectible debts incurred by his deceased brother and Dr. Welsh.[50]

In a fit of fancy, John Quincy suggested to Thomas that they abandon Boston and seek their fortunes in central New York on lands then held by William Stephens Smith. The real estate, he asserted, comprised "the most promising spot on the continent for enterprise and industry." "What say you to joining me in the plan and going with me . . . Why should we wither away our best days and sneak through life pinched . . . for the sake of a few luxurious indulgences in a large town?" Thomas, who was no more fulfilled by the practice of law than his brother, responded enthusiastically. "I am your man for a new country & manual labor. Head-work is bad business, and I never was fond of it. My capital is chiefly in my hands & feet, and they are at your service."[51] It was all a pipe dream, of course. John, Abigail, and the call to their eldest son to serve his country would never permit it.

Though he denied any interest in politics, John Quincy knew intuitively that the time and call would come. He was an Adams and as such a man of renown and destiny. In the short term, however, he decided to focus on intellectual endeavors. "During the course of the present year, I shall undertake to do little or nothing. My object will be to *learn*."[52] He and nine other intellectuals formed the Society for the Study of Natural Philosophy, dedicated to the investigation of the physical world. The plan was to read deeply in the literature of chemistry, physics, and geology, to conduct experiments, and to present the findings in evening lectures. "I broke two of our Leyden jars by charging them too highly," he recorded in his diary in February. "I took several shocks and a succession of sparks [while] standing on the insulating stool, applied to my shoulder, which for several days past has suffered considerable with the rheumatism."[53]

Boston Federalists knew that, like his father, the son was an independent man. Before John Quincy's return to America, Thomas had speculated on his brother's political future: "If he does discuss his opinions openly, he will by the Federalists be called a Jacobin and by the Jacobins a Federalist."[54] But Massachusetts was fast becoming a bipartisan state. Republican Elbridge Gerry would make a respectable showing in the gubernatorial election in April. The Essex men were in temporary eclipse. Following the election of 1800, Harry Otis and his colleagues had realized that they would have to develop some sort of party organization to compete with the Democratic-Republicans. The Federalists could not sustain themselves by "writing private letters to each other," as James McHenry put it.[55] But the mechanism that Otis and his colleagues created was highly centralized. There were caucuses at the local level, but they were mere rallies during which party leaders told the rank and file whom to vote for. Nominations were published in the local newspapers prior to an election. Scurrilous articles abounded, but electioneering by the candidates was strictly forbidden. Stump speeches could lead to personal confrontations and then to violence.[56] The system perfectly suited the Adamses, who continued to believe in a virtuous republic in which virtuous men were called to duty by the populace. Electioneering, they were convinced, was undignified and inevitably degenerated into demagoguery.

Not a week passed that one of the local Federalist leaders didn't approach John Quincy about accepting a nomination to this post or that. "Walked in the mall just before night," he wrote in his diary on January 28. "I feel strong temptation and have great provocation to plunge into political controversy. But I hope to preserve myself from it. . . . A politician in this country must be the man of a party. I would fain be the man of my whole country."[57] In April he was elected to the Massachusetts Senate by the voters of Suffolk County, which included Boston. He immediately proceeded to bite the hand that had fed him.

Following each election, the members of the state legislature chose some of their number to serve on the Governor's Council. John Quincy pushed to have members of the minority Republican delegation included. "In May 1802," the *Independent Chronicle and Boston Patriot* reported, "Mr. Adams attended a federal caucus called to nominate counsellors. At this meeting Mr. Adams proposed that four of the counsellors should be of the Republican party. The federal leaders said 'this man is not our friend, but against us.'"[58]

BOSTON WAS NOT LONDON or Berlin, nor was it the small provincial community of wooden houses, churches, shops, and warehouses clustered together and connected by winding, narrow streets that it had been during John Quincy's youth. The city had grown from some six thousand during the Revolutionary War to twenty-five thousand by the turn of the century. Its native son and most famous architect, Charles Bulfinch, had returned from his studies abroad to transform Boston. Under his direction, stone-and-brick mansions, churches, and public buildings sprang up. Most notable was the brick-and-marble Massachusetts Statehouse in Beacon Hill, whose golden dome would dominate the city's skyline for decades to come.[59]

John Quincy Adams was a former ambassador and the son of a president. He and Louisa were welcomed into the parlors of Boston's first families: the "Amory's, the Codmans, the Russells, the Shaefer's, the Sergeants, the Cushings . . . and many more which formed a very large circle of acquaintance and made me as dissipated as I had been in Berlin," Louisa wrote.[60] And she met Mary Frazier, then engaged to Daniel Sargent; she claimed to be much impressed with her husband's first love.[61] John Quincy and Louisa's particular friends were Harrison Gray Otis and his wife. Harrison and John Quincy had been pro-theater allies, and the histories of the Otises and Adamses had long been intertwined. "Their house at this period was the very center of fashion and they were so calculated to shine by the ease of their manners, their distinguished minds, and their liberal hospitality; it was impossible to know them without feeling . . . admiration," Louisa later recorded.[62]

In April 1802, Joshua Johnson died, and the following October, Catherine and Caroline Johnson arrived in Boston for an extended stay. Louisa was delighted to see her mother and sister. John Quincy was, it seemed, rarely at home. He left Hanover Street every morning for the office and spent at least one day every weekend at Peacefield visiting his parents, generally without Louisa, who claimed illness, or George. George's first birthday went uncelebrated in Quincy—a snub resulting from his naming, Louisa believed. She and John Quincy did not even attend the same churches. Louisa was a devout Anglican. She found the Congregationalist services that her husband preferred austere and depressing compared to the music, liturgy, and pageantry of the Episcopalians. Out of respect, she would sometimes accompany him to services at First Church, Boston, where the Reverend William Emerson, the father of Ralph Waldo Emerson, held forth. When she could, however, she joined friends at Christ Church (the Episcopal Old North Church).[63]

Louisa continued to disappoint the Adamses and herself on the domestic front. Caroline, a favorite of Abigail and John's, had grown into an attractive, self-confident young woman. "My kind sister took upon herself the cares of housekeeping and released me from a thrall heavy enough to break the spirit of a tyrant," Louisa wrote in her memoir.[64] Servants in America were far different from those in Europe. The latter were trained to their calling, which usually lasted a lifetime. Servants in Boston were girls fresh off the farm or ne'er-do-well men who could find no other work. Many of them were thieves and/or drunkards and prone to rebelliousness.

Louisa found it humiliating to deal with them but at the same time she shrank from performing the household tasks herself—the cleaning, cooking, and washing in great copper vats filled with dirty laundry. Her husband did the shopping and kept her on a strict allowance, which she attributed to his resentment over not having received a marriage dowry.[65] In truth, Louisa was both repelled and attracted by the quintessential American woman as embodied by Abigail and the doyennes of Boston. "There is generally a want of feminine grace and sweetness in these showy, strong-minded women which produce fear in us lesser lights; and this has always been my first impression on becoming acquainted with them—yet they always appear to me to be *what God intended woman to be*, before she was carved by her *master,* man."⁶⁶ With her husband gone most of the time, Louisa was relieved to have her mother and sister to entertain and chaperone her.

Meanwhile, John Quincy busied himself with Senate affairs, his scientific experiments, translations of Juvenal's "Seventh Satire," and the comedies of Plautus. Much of this had to be done while standing because the thirty-five-year-old had begun what would become a lifetime struggle with hemorrhoids. He continued his program of vigorous exercise, swimming in the bay off the Common or behind Mr. Black's wharf between five and six every morning, weather permitting. He often walked an hour in the morning and an hour in the afternoon, occasionally traversing the six miles from Hanover Street to Peacefield in Quincy. He delivered two public addresses, one to the Massachusetts Charitable Fire Society on the virtues of brick and stone over wood as a building material and the other to a Plymouth Rock memorial gathering, in which he praised the Pilgrims for taming a savage wilderness and subduing the local aborigines.⁶⁷

Financially, John Quincy was having to survive on the meager dividends coming in from his investments. His seat in the Massachusetts Senate was hardly remunerative. Confident in his own good repute, he waited like some ripening political fruit to be plucked for higher office. In November 1802, he was nominated to represent his congressional district in the House of Representatives. John Quincy lost by fifty-nine votes to Dr. William Eustis, the Republican incumbent, carrying Boston but falling short in the surrounding counties. He blamed his loss on a low turnout caused by rainy weather. "This is one of a thousand proofs how large a portion of federalism is a mere fair-weather principle, too weak to overcome a shower of rain."⁶⁸

There was, however, a silver lining to this proverbial cloud. In early February, John Quincy learned that his name had been placed in nomination for election to the U.S. Senate seat then held by Jonathan Mason, who had decided not to stand again. At that time in Massachusetts, senators were elected by the state legislature. His chief rival for the post was Timothy Pickering, the ultimate Essex man and an inveterate foe of John Adams. The Adams and Pickering factions proceeded to cut a deal. Whoever won would agree to support the other for the unexpired term of Massachusetts's second senator, Dwight Foster, who had decided to resign. Because Mason's seat would be for a full term, it was the more desirable. The Adams men agreed that Pickering, by far the elder of the pair, would have first shot, but after two ballots in the House if he had not captured a majority, the Pickering men would switch to Adams. John Quincy gave his personal assurance that he was perfectly willing to work with Pickering and would vote for him for either post. There were, of course, other candidates, both Republicans and independents. In the House eighty-six votes constituted a majority. On the first ballot Pickering scored sixty-seven and Adams ten. Pickering was well short of a majority. On the fourth ballot, John Quincy was elected with eighty-six votes. In the Senate he won a clear majority. Shortly thereafter Pickering was elected to fill Foster's unexpired term although by a margin of only one vote.[69] Though both nominally Federalists, Massachusetts's two new senators could not have been more different in philosophy and disposition.

ON APRIL 1, JOHN Quincy received word that the British banking house of Bird, Savage & Bird had failed. This was of some immediate concern to him because he had on deposit with the bank some thirteen hundred dollars. Much more significant were the losses to be incurred by his father. While minister plenipotentiary to the Netherlands during the latter stages of the Revolutionary War, John had, with his own funds, purchased American bonds underwritten by Dutch bankers, a mechanism used to make loans to the Continental Congress. When the bonds were redeemed, the elder Adams had deposited the proceeds with Bird, Savage & Bird. "I went out to Quincy . . . in the evening and had the task to perform of giving notice to my father and mother of this misfortune," he wrote in his diary; "they felt it severely but bore it with proper firmness and composure."[70] John's losses would come to just under £2,872—more than ten thousand dollars. As he had previously assured Thomas, John Quincy was determined to keep his parents out of poverty; he immediately sold his shares in a fire-and-marine insurance company and the house on Hanover Street, and gave his parents the proceeds. In return, John and Abigail deeded him 275 acres from their Peacefield estate; the parcel included John Quincy's ancestral home on Penn's Hill. The saltbox would be John Quincy and Louisa's Massachusetts residence throughout his tenure in the Senate.[71] Bird, Savage & Bird and their executors eventually repaid the debt, but the last installment would only arrive twenty-three years later.

John Quincy and Louisa might not have seen much of each other in the daytime, but nighttime was a different matter. In the fall of 1802, Louisa was pregnant again; perhaps because of the presence of her mother and sister, she managed rather well. On July 3, 1803, John Quincy walked to Quincy to visit his ailing mother, leaving Louisa in Boston with her sisters and three maids. Louisa was having tea with Charlotte and Harriet Welsh and Caroline when her contractions began. Dr. Welsh soon appeared, and under his care, Louisa gave birth to a healthy six-pound boy at three a.m. "He was laid upon the carpet and took a violent cold, the young women in our service not thinking it delicate to afford assistance to a fellow creature in such circumstances," Louisa wrote, "but Caroline jumped out of bed and ran into the room almost undressed to assist and took the child immediately."[72] John Quincy did not learn of the birth until he arrived home the next morning. "For this new blessing, I desire to offer my humblest gratitude to the throne of Heaven."[73] The babe was christened on Sunday, July 17, at the Congregationalist church by William Emerson. To appease the "old gentleman," the couple's second born was named John. Though too weak to attend, Louisa was happy: "He was beautiful, and I fear I was too proud of being the mother to two fine children."[74]

THE EIGHTH CONGRESS WAS not scheduled to convene until November, so John Quincy had ample time to close his law practice and transfer the family's furniture and his books to Quincy. He was able to sort and categorize the papers, diaries, and letter books he had accumulated during seven years in Europe. It was decided that the Adams family while in Washington would room and board with Louisa's sister Nancy and her husband, Walter Hellen. Hellen, a successful tobacco merchant, had built a spacious, elegant mansion in Georgetown, some two miles from the Capitol. The Hellens proved gracious and welcoming hosts. In addition to John Quincy and his family, the couple would take Catherine Johnson and her unmarried daughters under their roof.

On October 4, 1803, John Quincy, Louisa, George, baby John, Caroline, and their servant Patty boarded the packet *Cordelia*, destined for New York. It was to be a miserable trip. Louisa, George, and John were crowded into one cabin, Caroline and Patty in another, and John Quincy in a third. The storms of October were setting in, and the *Cordelia* faced a constant headwind and heavy seas. Everyone except John Quincy became intensely seasick. "We continued beating between Fisher's Island and Long Island the whole night which was extremely boisterous," he recorded in his diary. On the sixth the ship at last docked at New London; the family disembarked, expecting a brief respite at a comfortable tavern, but they were summoned back on board in the middle of the night because of favoring winds.[75] Following a fifteen-hour run, the *Cordelia* landed at Paulus Hook, and John Quincy secured lodgings at Gifford's tavern in Newark. Unfortunately, George, while playing in his and his mother's cabin, had thrown his shoes and the keys to the family's trunks out an open portal into the sea. The trunks had to be prized open. Gifford's was crowded with New Yorkers driven from the city by a yellow fever outbreak. Louisa herself was ill when they arrived at the inn. Fearing the worst, the proprietor isolated the family and sent for a Dr. Johnson, who came and administered a dose of opium, which allowed Louisa to sleep.[76]

From New York the little party traveled by stage to Philadelphia. The city being also under quarantine, John Quincy was forced to find lodgings in a northern suburb. Thomas came out with a carriage and horses, which enabled John Quincy and his family to make their way to Baltimore and from thence to Washington. At every stop the entire family was forced to sleep in one chamber for fear that Louisa was contagious with the fever. "[We] arrived safely at Washington then a scene of utter desolation," Louisa recorded in her journal. "The roads were almost impassable, and Mr. Hellen's house lonely and dreary and at least two miles from the capitol."[77] The trip from Boston had consumed twenty harrowing days.

12

"A Foolish Consistency . . ."

THE NEXT MORNING, AS would become his custom, John Quincy walked to the Capitol, where he was sworn in and proudly took his seat in what future generations would refer to as "the nation's most exclusive gentlemen's club." Between the time he was elected and sworn in, Adams had had time to take stock of what Thomas Jefferson and his followers referred to as the "Revolution of 1800." Jefferson and his new secretary of state, James Madison, had had their doubts about the Constitution. They believed—and to their minds the Alien and Sedition Acts proved it—that it provided too much leeway for the creation of a massive federal establishment that would be controlled by the rich and powerful and that would steadily encroach on the rights of the individual. The architects of the Revolution of 1800 came into office determined to rule through persuasion and consensus, reducing or eliminating many of the agencies of power available to the executive. They dared to imagine that the common man was willing and able to see that his welfare was tied to that of the larger community and would gladly sacrifice for the greater good. The Republicans were willing to trust their political fate and the future of the country to public opinion—"that invisible guardian of honor—that eagle-eyed spy on human actions—that inexorable judge of men and manners—that arbiter whom tears cannot appease, nor ingenuity soften and from whose terrible decisions there is no appeal," as a Phi Beta Kappa orator described it.[1]

The Republicans had ridden into power on the backs of a vastly expanded electorate. The participation of eligible voters went from 20 percent in the 1790s to 80 percent or more in the elections of 1800 and 1804. Unlike the Federalists, the Republicans embraced electioneering and sought to get out the vote. At the same time, more and more states were expanding the franchise by eliminating property qualifications, requiring merely payment of taxes; the franchise, of course, was denied to free Blacks, even in states where it had formerly been granted, and women were still considered beyond the political pale.[2] John Adams's construct of the family as a political unit with the husband and father as head continued to prevail. In reality, as John Quincy had noted, the country would continue to be ruled by a slavocracy preaching democracy. This was not the only irony of the Revolution of 1800. Jefferson and his successor, Madison, when faced with the opportunity for territorial expansion and the danger of foreign war would violate many of their Republican principles by vastly increasing the power of the federal government.

John Quincy Adams recognized the methods and appeal of the architects of the Revolution of 1800. "The strength of the present administration is continually increasing," he wrote Rufus King. "It has obtained and preserves an irresistible preponderance in thirteen of the sixteen state legislatures." In Pennsylvania, the Federalists were so weak that it was probable that they had not even put up a slate in 1802. If the Federalists continued to simply talk among themselves and wait for the populace to realize that they must defer to their betters, they were doomed, John Quincy declared. There were new young leaders who were trying to organize at the local and state levels, but the Essex men and their mentality still dominated the party. How long the Republicans—the "American Jacobins"—would be able to safely sail the ship of state was the great question of the day. "The base of it all is democratic popularity, and the leaders are all sensible how sandy a foundation it is." Public opinion was indeed a weak reed to lean on, but politicians and parties from this point on had no choice. "It [the Federalist Party] never can and never will be revived," John Quincy declared. "The experiment, such as it was, has failed and to attempt its restoration would be as absurd as to undertake the resurrection of a carcass seven years in its grave."[3]

The newly elected senator was, of course, right. The Federalist political philosophy, which arrogated power to the wealthy and educated few, and its Hamiltonian financial system, which promoted hard money and restricted credit to the wealthiest merchants and manufacturers, were anachronistic and irrelevant to an America that was increasingly democratic and entrepreneurial. There was little or no room in the Federalist Party for commercial farmers, small manufacturers, master artisans, and self-made merchants, who were multiplying and gaining strength in the Northern and Mid-Atlantic states.[4] John Quincy continued to have his doubts about the innate virtue and wisdom of the common man, but he believed that his political future and the welfare of the country consisted of binding the various sections and interests of the country together so tightly that the bonds could not be broken. What was called for, he believed, was "a man of the whole people."

Adams took his place in the Senate four days after the session had opened. To his great regret, both houses of Congress had voted to approve the Louisiana Purchase without him. During the Adams administration's peace initiative that would end the Quasi-War with France, John Quincy had speculated that one of the reasons Talleyrand and Bonaparte craved rapprochement with America was that they were planning to revive the French empire in North America, which had been lost as a result of the Seven Years' War. Writing from Berlin on April 25, 1801, he had reported that rumors were "circulating all over Europe" that Spain had ceded the Floridas and Louisiana to France. John Quincy had advised his father, "We must be on our guard," lest France pursued such a course "in order to obtain a powerful influence over us."[5] But neither he nor any other American diplomat had actual knowledge of the Treaty of San Ildefonso, signed the day after the Treaty of Mortefontaine, in which Spain had in fact agreed to retrocede Louisiana to France in return for the Kingdom of Etruria (Tuscany) in Italy. The Spanish had found it increasingly difficult to garrison and finance their vast territory west of the Mississippi. And they feared that the avaricious frontier farmers who were pressing against their borders were but the advance guard of American empire. Talleyrand had promised Madrid that Louisiana in French hands would serve as an impenetrable barrier protecting Spanish holdings that stretched from Mexico to California from U.S. expansionism. And so, the deed was done. Word of the retrocession began circulating in the United States some six months later.

Jefferson and Madison were alarmed, but they could not prevent the retrocession by force of arms without British help, and in that case, they believed, the cure would be worse than the disease. But the Republican Party was increasingly dependent upon the yeomen farmers of the West and the land speculators who lurked in the shadows behind them. When on October 16, 1802, the Spanish intendant closed the port of New Orleans to the hundreds of American riverboats that floated raw materials down the Mississippi for transshipment to the East Coast and Europe each year, Westerners threatened to take matters into their own hands.

At this point an old friend of Jefferson's, Pierre Samuel du Pont de Nemours—who was also close to Lafayette—suggested that the United States attempt to purchase what it could not take by force. Jefferson and Madison leapt at the idea. They were willing for France to take possession of the Louisiana Territory if it would sell New Orleans and the Floridas to the United States. (Jefferson and de Nemours both mistakenly believed that the retrocession had included the Floridas). They persuaded Congress to approve instructions to the U.S. minister to France, Robert Livingston, to begin negotiations. Jefferson appointed James Monroe, a Francophile, land speculator, and longtime spokesman for the West, as special envoy to assist Livingston. Just before Monroe arrived in Paris, Talleyrand asked Livingston, What will you give for the whole? In truth, by the spring of 1803, the First Consul and his foreign minister had come to see Louisiana as an albatross rather than an ornament. Despite dispatching an army of some fifty thousand seasoned troops to Saint-Domingue, Napoleon had been unable to quell the slave rebellion there led by the Black general Toussaint L'Ouverture. Moreover, France and Britain were once again drifting toward war. For the looming conflict, Napoleon needed American friendship, not hostility.

Monroe arrived in Paris and the deal was quickly done. On April 30, 1803, the two American envoys signed the Louisiana Purchase agreement, in which the United States agreed to pay $15 million in cash and claims for some 828,000 square miles of land west of the Mississippi. What exactly were the boundaries of the territory the United States had purchased? Livingston asked. "I can give you no direction," Talleyrand replied; "you have made a noble bargain for yourselves, and I suppose you will make the most of it."[6]

John Quincy was ecstatic over the Purchase. He had witnessed the weakness of the Netherlands and other European countries that had been unable to resist the might of either Britain or France. He longed for the day when America would be strong enough to hold its own with any European power. Control of the Mississippi and the vast acreage west of it would prevent either France or Spain from blocking U.S. expansion and add millions of acres of fertile soil that would attract immigrants from all over Europe.

Like John Quincy Adams, Jefferson recognized that nowhere in the Constitution was the federal government given the power to acquire new lands or to incorporate the citizens of a foreign country into the Union. He briefly considered proposing a constitutional amendment but was dissuaded. Napoleon was in a hurry for his money; France had reneged on its promise to Spain never to alienate the Louisiana Territory to a third party; and New England was up in arms over the whole transaction, fearing the dilution of its power by the addition of numerous Western states. And so, declaring that he would not be deterred by "metaphysical subtleties," Jefferson submitted the treaties with France naked.[7]

To the newly minted senator from Massachusetts, the issues involved were neither metaphysical nor subtle. Logician to the core, he believed that a constitutional amendment was essential. America was not an imperial power like Britain, France, or the Netherlands—which viewed the world as nothing more than a field for conquest. A week after he was sworn in, Adams called on Madison and asked if he did not think an amendment essential. The secretary of state said that he did not; "the magnitude of the object" eclipsed every other consideration.[8] Undeterred, Senator Adams submitted the draft of an amendment empowering the United States to acquire territory from a foreign power through treaty and

purchase. "A desperate and fearful cause in which I have embarked," John Quincy
wrote in his diary. "It is another feather against a whirlwind. But I must pursue it
or feel myself either a coward or a traitor."[9] Assuming that the Adams proposal
would require a lengthy debate, the Senate soundly rejected it. Adams subsequently voted for the bill to fund the Purchase, but the whole affair troubled him.
"We could not wield with too prudent and wary a hand the rod of empire and
dominion which we had assumed over a foreign people," he wrote.[10]

In the weeks that followed, Senator Adams joined his fellow Federalists in
voting against every other Louisiana bill: the measure creating the District of
Louisiana and the Territory of Orleans and extending the laws of the United
States, including taxation statutes over them; the measure enabling the president
to take possession and provide a temporary government composed of officials
solely appointed by him; and the Mobile Act, which authorized the president to
seize West Florida as part of the Louisiana Purchase transaction. Pickering, who
voted similarly, and his ilk were concerned about weakening the political power
of New England. Adams, it seemed, was focused on no taxation without representation and on the peaceful assimilation of more than a hundred thousand
French- and Spanish-speaking citizens into the Union. He even called for a plebiscite to be held among the inhabitants of the Louisiana Territory on the question
of annexation. "We can have no right of conquest over a people who have never
injured us," he wrote. "The law of conquest is a law of slavery, and the people of
Louisiana whose liberty we are solemnly bound to protect are not slaves."[11] Adams voted against an amendment to the funding bill proposed by Connecticut
Federalist James Hillhouse providing for the gradual emancipation of slaves. The
institution was immoral and abhorrent, John Quincy declared. But this was an
issue for the people of Louisiana to decide.[12] Throughout the controversy, which
stretched from November 1803 through January 1804, the senior senator from
Massachusetts read and reread the *Federalist Papers*.[13]

Politically, it was John Quincy's vote for funding the Purchase and admitting
the territory to the Union that attracted the most attention. The *Philadelphia Aurora*, Benny Bache's old paper, was full of praise. Quoting Adams, who justified
overcoming his constitutional scruples by declaring, "'I consider the object as of
the highest advantage to us,'" the paper declared, "Such language . . . is gratifying,
coming from a New England federalist; it will have more weight than columns of
the declamations of the *Essex-junto*."[14] The High Federalists denounced John
Quincy as a traitor to his native region. "Like a kite without a tail," declared the
Boston banker and Essex man Stephen Higginson. "He will be violent and constant in his attempts to rise and will pitch on the one side and the other as the
popular currents may happen to strike. . . . His views are ambitious even to the

Chair of State [presidency] . . . he will besides be often misled by his visionary scheme of building up a third and independent party."[15] Theodore Lyman wrote to Timothy Pickering, "[H]e inclines to be preemptory. Those who have known the father will readily 'Curse on the stripling, how he apes his sire.'"[16] Even his parents had misgivings. Abigail observed that she might have voted differently but probably did not have all of the information that was available to her son. "I do not disapprove of your conduct in the business of Louisiana," John wrote, "though I know it will become a very unpopular subject in the Northern states."[17] Their offspring, however, was satisfied with himself: "The county is so totally given up to the spirit of party that not to follow blindfold the one or the other is an expiable offense. . . . I see the impossibility of pursuing the dictates of my own conscience without sacrificing every prospect of advancement. . . . Yet my choice is made, and, if I cannot hope to give satisfaction to my country, I am at least determined to have the approbation of my own reflections."[18]

But John Quincy was shrewder and more calculating than that. He was also more ambitious than he or his diary would have one believe. It was clear from the outset that the Jefferson administration was willing to sacrifice principle—strict construction of the Constitution, among other things—to what it perceived to be an overriding national interest. In voting for the appropriations to fund the Louisiana Purchase, Adams demonstrated that he fully concurred. And as far as the political consequences, the old Federalist Party was dying, and he did not intend to die with it. The man for the whole people wanted to ingratiate himself with both Republicans and moderate Federalists. It was risky, but he was willing to take that chance. Significantly, he chose to attend a Republican feast to celebrate the acquisition of Louisiana.[19]

IN 1790 SOUTHERN CONGRESSMEN and senators had traded their acquiescence in Hamilton's plan for the federal government to assume the revolutionary debts of the states in return for Northern agreement to locate Washington, DC, on the border between Maryland and Virginia. Jefferson, Madison, and their followers rejoiced that the seat of government would be far removed from the countinghouses and power brokers of Boston, New York, and Philadelphia. The new capital was "like no other in the world," a British visitor noted. It was not a compliment. The town in which John Quincy and Louisa settled in 1803 comprised some four thousand inhabitants including seven hundred slaves. Pierre L'Enfant had laid out a city plan that would link the Capitol and the President's House—situated a mile and a quarter from each other—with broad boulevards that crisscrossed elegant gardens and parks. That vision was years away from realization. The tiny settlement that was then Washington was surrounded by woods and pastures and located squarely in the middle of a mosquito-infested swamp. The streets, dotted with large stumps, turned to rivers of mud when it rained. Travel by carriage in early Washington could be extremely dangerous. Cows grazed on the Mall. There were small advantages. "[E]xcellent snipe shooting and even partridge shooting was to be had in each side of the main avenue and even close under the wall of the Capitol," reported one visitor.[20]

The President's House was, as Washington had intended, designed to be the largest abode in the country, but it would not be finished for years. The grounds surrounding the building site were home to blacksmiths' forges, workmen's shacks, brickkilns, and outdoor privies. The Capitol itself lay unfinished and was encircled by "seven or eight boarding houses, one tailor, one shoemaker, one printer, a washing woman, a grocery shop, a small dry-goods shop, and an oyster house."[21] The village of Georgetown, which lay some two miles to the northwest of the White House and some four miles from the Capitol, featured boarding-houses, taverns, and a few mansions similar to the one built by Walter Hellen.

For her part, Louisa was glad to be back in the South, living in the bosom of her family. Despite the fact that she was residing in an iniquitous swamp, her health improved. She took up horseback riding, an exercise that John Quincy encouraged. There were dinners at the President's House, at the residences of cabinet members, and at the tables of the British and French ministers. A number of magnificent plantations were within riding or carriage distance. John Quincy continued to rise early to read and write. Breakfast was served between nine and ten, after which he embarked on the forty-five-minute walk to the Capitol, usually arriving after the Senate was in session. Unless there was special business to attend to, Congress adjourned around four. Then it was back to the Hellens' for supper. When not attending one social function or another, John Quincy preferred to stay in and read to the ladies. Bedtime was around eleven. There were then no churches in Washington. Nondenominational services were held in the Capitol and the Treasury Building on Sundays. Walter Hellen would not name a price for sheltering the Adamses, so John Quincy took it upon himself to pay a hundred dollars a session.[22]

As the date for adjournment of the Eighth Congress approached, John Quincy and Louisa discussed their living arrangements during the six-month interregnum before the next session began. The decision they made nearly wrecked their marriage. He was determined to return to Quincy to be with his parents. "The duties of filial, of conjugal, and of paternal tenderness are all equally sacred, and I wish to discharge them all with equal fidelity," he would write her.[23] He wanted the children and her to accompany him, but Louisa decided to stay in Washington to continue living with her mother and sisters at the Hellens'. But she was embittered by the separation; days after John Quincy departed, she wrote him an angry letter accusing him of "coldness and unkindness" and of preferring his parents over his own wife and children. He received her broadside while in New York waiting to board the packet *Cordelia* for Providence. Your letter was "painful and unexpected," he replied, and it had wounded him deeply. It was your choice to remain in the bosom of your family, he reminded her. "Thinking as I do that my home is the proper and only proper home of my wife and children, I shall always feel the sweetest satisfaction in having them with me and shall ever lament your determination to abide elsewhere." It was you, Louisa, who chose to privilege your family over me.[24]

Louisa refused to back down. I had no choice, she retorted. "You have repeatedly told me that it was not in your power to take me with you after the first winter [and] that we must therefore be separated one half of the year for six years: the only thing left for me was to endeavor to make our separation as easy to myself as possible." Then the deepest cut of all: "I preferred passing the summer months with my family to living alone at Quincy through five dreary winters."[25] Apparently, John Quincy had wanted Louisa and the children to move in permanently with his extended family at Peacefield while he boarded at a rooming house in Washington when Congress was in session.

The dispute was particularly bitter because it went to the root of both Louisa's and John Quincy's insecurities. The Bird, Savage & Bird failure had depleted much of John Quincy's resources. He had to live on the meager return from his remaining assets and the six dollars per diem allotted to senators. He no longer owned the house on Hanover Street. If they lived by themselves when both were in Quincy, it would have to be in the little saltbox house on Penn's Hill. "My situation and circumstances, since we married have very materially declined," he wrote. "It has taken from me the means of contributing every comfort and enjoyment that your heart could wish; it is a perpetual source of anxiety to me."[26] That might have been true, but Adams did not lift a finger to earn extra income while in Quincy and Boston; rather he spent his time planting a fruit tree orchard, gamboling over the countryside with his father, and talking politics and literature with both his parents. He did send Louisa bits of money, fifty dollars now and then. Whether John Quincy knew of his mother's wealth is unclear. She was not supposed to own property—Dr. Tufts was her "trustee"—and she and John went to great lengths to keep that secret. The previous fall Abigail had persuaded a grudging Thomas to come with his family and live at Peacefield. She and John would turn over one of their farms (they owned six thousand acres) to his management, and he would receive all of the profit.[27]

Louisa felt her dependency deeply. Her mother had received a payment of a hundred pounds from Joshua's estate, raising hopes, but it turned out to be a one-time distribution. Louisa, her mother, and her sisters continued to depend entirely on the generosity of Walter Hellen. He could not have been more gracious about it, but Louisa was abashed by her indebtedness. And of course, there was the eternal dowry issue. Joshua's inability to deliver the promised five thousand pounds created an indelible suspicion throughout her life that the Adams family believed that the Johnsons had deceived John Quincy into marrying her. "I brought you nothing and therefore have no claim on you whatever," she wrote her husband; "my life ever has been and ever must remain a life of painful obligation."[28]

But then, both John Quincy and Louisa backed away from the brink. She was the first to offer the olive branch. "I fear I have made you depressed and anxious," she wrote on May 12; although "my absence [cannot] have produced this effect as we are less together at Quincy than at any other time [one last barb]. However, be what it may, I am ready and willing to return home immediately . . . if you will send the means of return, I will with pleasure take charge of the children, provided you will let me bring one of my sisters." Where they lived was of no consequence. "As for the house [the saltbox] . . . I believe I never made any objection to it. I only said that in the state you represented your affairs to be that it would be both imprudent and inconsistent to build."[29]

"I feel myself greatly obliged to you for your kind offer to come on here," he replied. "But the summer [it was then May 20!] is already running so fast away that by the time you could get well here it would be necessary to think of returning." Oh, and by the way, I am not depressed: "[M]y health has been very good and were it not for my absence from you and our two darlings, I should enjoy a greater tranquility of mind, than I have known for some years."[30]

Interestingly, both Louisa and John Quincy began reading at the same time Madame Germaine de Staël's new novel, *Delphine* (1802), which featured a liberated heroine trying to make a life in a France that was moving rapidly from hidebound convention to a revolutionary new order. "The language is most beautiful, but the morals appear to me detestable," Louisa wrote her husband. The author, that famous intellectual and infamous libertine, argued that if God were merciful and good, then "how could one make a vow as in marriage pledging to adhere to it for life come what may. [S]he recommends everybody to divorce as soon as they upon trial find that their dispositions do not accord." Louisa observed that fashionable society seemed to have been taken by storm by the idea. But it "appears to me calculated to destroy every moral principle, to destroy every tie which binds society together."[31] John Quincy agreed. Madame de Staël was just trying to justify her own licentiousness, he replied. She was, in *Delphine*, repeating one of the heresies produced by the French Revolution. "I remember . . . when the great regenerating French National Convention passed their law to make divorce just as easy as marriage. . . . Honest and virtuous minds can promise to love for life, and can perform the promise."³² It was an Adams way to say, "I love you whatever your faults and promise to search for only the best in you."

There was one more dimension to this domestic drama, however. By this point Louisa had become almost as ambitious for her husband as John and Abigail. "However painful a separation must ever be to me, your interest alone must be my consideration and everything else must give way." And she meant it. "Formed for domestic life, my whole soul devoted to you and my children yet ambitious to excess, my heart and head are constantly at war."³³

Peace restored, at least for the time being, John Quincy and Louisa's subsequent correspondence focused on children, gossip, and agriculture. "George is very well, grows very tall and is so intolerably mischievous, I hardly know what to do. He destroys all Mrs. Hellen's chickens, drives the ducks to death, gets down to the wharf & plays such pranks, I am obliged to keep a person constantly running after him," she wrote the last week in May. "I am obliged to make him fear me; he laughs at everybody else, and nobody can do anything with him."³⁴ Jérôme Bonaparte, the youngest brother of Napoleon, was then conducting a scandalous and very public affair with Elizabeth Patterson, the beautiful daughter of a wealthy Baltimore shipowner. Louisa reported seeing her "almost naked" on the arm of her paramour at a Washington ball.³⁵ Jérôme and Elizabeth were married on Christmas Eve 1803. (The couple sailed for Europe but upon arrival learned that Napoleon had persuaded the Pope to annul the marriage.) In another letter Louisa reported that an Irish gardener had attempted to burn Mount Vernon to the ground, one of five attempts at destroying the structure since Washington's death. Another talk of the town was the French ambassador General Louis-Marie Turreau, infamous for the mass murders he had overseen in the Vendée during the uprising there. It seems that he was in the habit of beating his wife black-and-blue and locking her up in their house when he was away.³⁶ John Quincy's attempts at farming, so hopefully begun, were a failure, he reported. In late April, he had planted more than a hundred peach trees in a would-be orchard on his little farm. He grafted, inoculated, and fertilized, but by May nearly all of the saplings were dead of the "worm."³⁷ He comforted himself by perusing a three-volume edition of Thucydides.

In September, John Quincy was given an opportunity to choose between academia and politics. On the twenty-fifth, Joseph Willard, Harvard's longtime president, died; John Quincy's cousin Josiah Quincy, a member of Harvard's

Board of Overseers, called at Peacefield and urged him to accept the presidency
of the college. John Quincy was noncommittal, but both he and his father attended Willard's funeral. On October 4, two of John Quincy's oldest friends and
supporters, Judge John Davis and the Reverend John T. Kirkland, called and took
up where Josiah Quincy had left off. But Adams wanted to be a statesman more
than he did a man of letters, and so he declined.[38]

In John Quincy's and Louisa's efforts to outsacrifice each other by staying separated, it was John Quincy who broke first. He was increasingly sex starved. Louisa's comments about Betsy Patterson seemed to have titillated him. "A very little
clothing you know, upon a Lady, will answer all my purposes," he wrote Louisa
at the end of May. "I am still of opinion that a lady when she goes to bed at night
should have something to do besides opening the sheets."[39] Later, he transcribed
a love poem that John Donne had written after being compelled to go to France
and leave his wife behind in England. Lovely, she replied, but I would much
rather have original verses authored by you.[40] Louisa did not say so, but she probably thought, with some angst, that her husband was much more romantic and
engaged when they were apart than when they were together.

In the late summer of 1804, Louisa felt confident enough in her relationship
with her husband to rebuke him over his reaction to the death of Alexander
Hamilton. In the spring of 1804, Aaron Burr had decided to stand for the governorship of New York. Though he ran as a Republican, he retained his ties with the
High Federalists, several of whom were then plotting to have New England and
New York secede from the Union. Invited to a secret meeting in the autumn of
1804 in Boston, he attended, but refused to participate in the scheme and urged
the preservation of the Union.[41] Hamilton, still a powerful figure in New York
politics, campaigned vigorously against Burr, declaring that he was "a dangerous
man who ought not to be trusted with the reins of government."[42] When he lost
to the little-known Morgan Lewis, an enraged Burr challenged Hamilton to a
duel. On July 11, 1804, on a field at Weehawken, New Jersey, the vice president
shot and killed the former secretary of the treasury. Two weeks later, a memorial
service for Hamilton was held in Boston. Harry Otis delivered the eulogy. John
Quincy refused to attend. "[H]is base treatment of more than one of my connections would [not] permit me to join in any outward demonstration of regret which
I could not feel at heart," he wrote Louisa.[43] She wrote back, reproving him: "I
wonder you were not there. Whatever a man's faults may have been, we should not
carry resentment beyond the grave. Remember my beloved friend that as we forgive so shall we be forgiven, and the opinion of the world must be favorable when
we act up to the true principles of our religion."[44] Louisa, of course, had her husband's public reputation in mind as much as his spiritual well-being.[45]

John Quincy and Louisa had come a long way from that day in 1796 in Ranelagh when John Quincy had warned his fiancée that he would not tolerate any strictures on his dress and appearance. Louisa had successfully walked the fine line between offending her husband and standing up to him. In this, the seventh year of their marriage, each had come to believe in their devotion to the other. Louisa was no longer the "faded thing" as she had described herself upon their arrival in America from Prussia, but rather the proud mother of two sons and the wife and helpmate of a rising star in American public life.

The long and complicated separation came to an end in late October, when John Quincy returned to Washington. "This is the last time I shall write you from this place for the present," John Quincy wrote on October 14. "I have determined to accelerate my departure and not wait until the 22d. . . . On Wednesday next it is my intention to take passage in the Stage to Providence." He would stop briefly in New York and Philadelphia but would arrive on the twenty-ninth or thirtieth.[46]

THE ISSUE THAT DOMINATED the opening days of the Eighth Congress's second session was the impeachment trial of Samuel Chase, an associate justice of the Supreme Court. Republicans, it will be remembered, had been enraged by the Judiciary Act of 1801, which had made possible John Adams's "midnight judges." On January 22, 1802, the Republican-dominated Congress had repealed the Judiciary Act of 1801, but Jefferson and Madison were still not satisfied. Their partisans in Congress insisted that federal judges should be made more responsive to the will of the people. They argued that Congress could impeach sitting judges for acting against the will of the majority although the Constitution stipulated that the process be limited to those convicted of only high crimes and misdemeanors. The Republicans' first target was John Pickering, a New Hampshire federal judge and a Federalist. Pickering was clearly incompetent, being both an alcoholic and mentally unstable. The Senate voted nineteen to seven to convict on March 12, 1804; John Quincy, elected as a Federalist, was among those who voted to acquit. He told a colleague that "the whole proceedings had been contrary to law." The subserviency of the Senate when acting "as a Judicial Court to a few leading members of the House of Representatives" was appalling. So was the precedent set "that insanity, sickness, any trivial error of conduct in a judge must be construed into misdemeanors, punishable by impeachment."[47]

Following the Senate's vote to convict, John Quincy walked over to the House of Representatives and watched as it voted to impeach Samuel Chase, an associate justice of the Supreme Court. Chase was neither an alcoholic nor insane, but he was an ardent Federalist. In May 1803 he had denounced the Republican majority in Congress for repealing the Judiciary Act of 1801, observing that it would "take away all security of property and personal liberty, and our republican constitution will sink into a mobocracy."[48] He had enforced the Alien and Sedition Acts with vigor, acting more as a prosecutor than a judge. When Jefferson read of Chase's comments to the grand jury in a Baltimore newspaper, he was enraged. "Ought the seditious and official attack on the principles of our Constitution go unpunished?" he wrote a leading Republican congressman.[49]

On December 6, 1804, the House approved eight articles of impeachment against Chase. The team of House prosecutors was to be led by the brilliant but erratic Republican congressman from Roanoke, Virginia, John Randolph. The Senate committee that would review and recommend was chaired by the equally ardent and partisan Republican senator from Virginia, William Branch Giles. Senator Adams listened incredulously as the trial unfolded. "According to him [Giles] impeachment is nothing more than an enquiry by the two houses of Congress whether the Office of any public man might not be better filled by another. . . . He treated with the utmost contempt the idea of an independent judiciary."[50] John Quincy noted that Randolph and Giles seemed to be in constant consultation, conspirators rather than impartial officiators. His description of Randolph's presentation was devastating: "On the re-opening of the Court, he began a speech of about two hours and a half with as little relation to the subject-matter as possible. Without order, connection, or argument, consisting altogether of the most hackneyed common-places of popular declamation, mingled up with panegyrics and invectives upon persons, with a few well expressed ideas, a few striking figures, much distortion of face, and contortion of body, threats, groans, and sobs, with occasional pauses for recollection and continual complaints of having lost his notes."[51] John Quincy wrote his father, "[T]he assault upon Judge Chase was unquestionably intended to pave the way for another prosecution, which would have swept the supreme judicial bench clean at a stroke."[52] Adams spoke only once during the proceedings; it was sufficient. He and the other Federalist senators, of course, voted to acquit on the second and seventh articles of impeachment; so did fifteen of twenty-five Republicans, although to a man they detested Chase. No one voted in favor of the fifth article.[53]

To John and John Quincy, disaster had been averted, but the threat remained. For father and son, the very life of the republic depended upon the preservation of a three-branch government, each independent but constrained by a system of checks and balances. Shortly after the Chase trial, John Adams wrote John Quincy, "That in all ages and countries, liberty, property, and safety have been in proportion to the perfect[ness] of the balance [among the branches of government and] that without some balance, there never was or can be any liberty but such as depends upon mere will, either of a prince, a senate or a multitude, and we know that neither prince, senate, nor multitude, ever willed liberty long."[54] Both men were reminded by the diatribes of Randolph and Giles of the early stages of the French Revolution, when the Mountain in league with the Paris mob swept away the recently adopted constitution in favor of direct democracy. The result was mobocracy and the Reign of Terror. John still believed that French Jacobins and their Irish immigrant allies were plotting to overthrow republican government in America.[55]

In November 1804, John Quincy wrote his father that the Revolution of 1800 would continue, and Republicans would sweep the upcoming elections, including those in that stronghold of Federalism, Massachusetts. He had argued for fairness toward the Republican Party when he had been in the state senate and had supported the Louisiana Purchase, but he still did not trust Jefferson and the Republican leadership. Witness the House's recent attacks on an independent judiciary. But he could not continue to support or even be identified with the Federalists. At this point John Quincy was probably aware of the machinations of the Essex men to separate New England and perhaps New York from the United States and form a new, separate confederation. In October he made a desperate effort to draw support away from the secessionists by proposing a plan that would satisfy New England's anxieties over being reduced to a powerless minority. He then published a series of essays in the Boston magazine *The Repertory* under the name Publius Valerius. (Publius Valerius was one of four Roman aristocrats who overthrew the monarchy in 509 BC and converted Rome into a republic.) I understand your misgivings over the addition of a vast new territory that would most assuredly be divided into a collection of Republican states and your resentment over the fact that the Northeast was going to have to foot most of the bill, he wrote. But westward expansion was inevitable, and in that it strengthened the Union economically and strategically, it was to the good. The real threat to New England was the disproportionate power that the slaveholding states were able to wield under the three-fifths clause in the Constitution. He pointed out that Virginia, with a free population only slightly less than that of Massachusetts, had five more congressmen and electoral votes than the Bay State. Earlier that year in the Massachusetts General Court, William Ely of Springfield had offered an amendment to the federal Constitution that would have abolished the three-fifths clause. The Federalists then being still in the majority in Massachusetts, the measure passed by a straight party vote.[56] Publius enthusiastically endorsed Ely's proposed amendment. The three-fifths clause, he wrote, violated the Declaration of Independence and made the United States less than a republic. Massachusetts must make common cause with the other eight states in which slavery was prohibited and, indeed, with freemen throughout the Union. "At present the people of the United States consist of two classes. A privileged order of slave-holding lords, and a race of men degraded to a lower station, merely because they are not slavehold-ers."[57] Questions of sectional power, shared interest, and republican ideology all hung in the balance. "The amendment, when proposed in Congress, will be ad-opted or rejected. If adopted, it will have a greater tendency to cement and per-petuate the Union than anything since the adoption of the Constitution itself."[58]

Congress did not, of course, repeal the three-fifths clause, and Republicans swept the Massachusetts elections as well as the national contests in November–December 1804. John Quincy Adams would be one of seven Federalists remaining in the Senate. He was, not surprisingly, uncertain about his country's future and his own. The United States was prospering, but Adams understood that America was still young and weak, its political institutions only recently established and its politics increasingly at the mercy of public opinion. The Peace of Amiens had not held, and in 1803, France and Great Britain had once again drifted into war. Westerners would not be satisfied with just New Orleans. They wanted the Flor-idas as well, but Spain, angry over Napoleon's betrayal in selling Louisiana, was hostile and intransigent. America's hope, John Quincy believed, lay in cling-ing firmly to republican principles at home and pursing a pragmatic balance-of-power policy abroad. Perhaps he could better serve his country by becoming a Republican—by inculcating his views in what promised to be the majority party in America for the foreseeable future—than by working to change the Federal-ist Party.

LOUISA WELCOMED HER HUSBAND back to Washington with open arms: she would soon be pregnant again. John Quincy read to the ladies at night, he and his wife strolled together on weekends, and he joined her in her new passion, horse-back riding. It was not always the safest of recreations. In November while they were riding on High Street in Georgetown, Louisa's saddle turned, and she was thrown to the ground. She was barely saved from the plunging, bucking horse's hooves by a gentleman bystander who dragged her into a nearby store. "He [the steed] was soon caught and saddled and though still a little restive, we took a long ride and returned home safe."[59] Louisa accompanied John Quincy to various soirees and state dinners. Her observations on the great men of the day were keen if not unbiased. She was harsh toward Jefferson primarily because upon his elec-tion, Joshua had lost the small patronage job he had enjoyed under the Federalists. "His countenance indicated strongly the hypocrisy of his nature and all about him was smile and his actions indicated a sort of tricky cunning, the sure attendant of a sophisticated mind devoid of a strong basis of substantial principle," she wrote in her memoir. "Showy, prosperous and backed by a strong party, his character was exactly adapted to lead restless demagogues and turbulent politicians."[60] Perhaps she was an Adams after all.

Louisa was kinder to the Madisons. "Mr. Madison was a very small man in his person with a very large head—his manners were peculiarly unassuming and his conversation lively, often playful, with a mixture of wit and seriousness. . . . I never saw a man with a mind so copious, so free from the pedantry and mere classical jargon of university scholarship." The incomparable Dolley "was tall, large, and rather masculine in personal dimensions; her complexion was so fair and brilliant as to redeem this objection."[61] Not surprisingly, given her European upbringing, one of Louisa's favorites was Albert Gallatin, the Swiss-born Pennsylvania Republican who was then serving as Jefferson's secretary of the treasury. Although he had had little to do with the Adamses during John's presidency, he and his wife became quite friendly with John Quincy and Louisa after their arrival in Washington. "[H]e is one of the most charming, talented, nay gifted men that I ever knew in any country," Louisa declared. "This was a mind of the highest order; blended with a brilliant wit and keen observation; which with a woman's intuitive readiness seemed to seize the characteristic traits of his fellow men with quick perception. Shrewd, subtle, and penetrating, few could cope with him."[62] The eccentric John Randolph of Roanoke was a study in contrast: "Ever in extremes, he was at times a delightful companion or an insolent bully. . . . Surrounded by admirers who loved the excitement produced by his waywardness and his brilliant rhapsodies, he appealed to the great men of his day, for he ruled the timid and amused the weak."[63]

John Quincy did not find Thomas Jefferson quite as repugnant as did Louisa. He regarded him as intelligent, learned, well-meaning but possessed of a flawed political philosophy and questionable morality. In August 1804 the president was compelled to admit that he had, beginning in 1768, attempted to seduce the wife of a close friend, Colonel John Walker. As part of his campaign to discredit his former hero, journalist James Callender had written of the youthful indiscretion two years earlier, but it had generally been dismissed as libel. But when publicly confronted by Colonel Walker, Jefferson was forced to write to him a letter admitting his transgression and asking for forgiveness. Adams was appropriately scandalized, but he did not proceed to pile on like other Federalists.[64] In truth Adams and Jefferson had too much in common—their learning, their sophistication, their devotion to their country's interests, especially in the area of foreign policy—not to be drawn to each other. In late August 1804, John Quincy and the president engaged in a typically candid conversation. The course that the French

Revolution had taken since he helped draft the original Declaration of the Rights of Man in 1789, Jefferson remarked, had crushed all of his expectations and hopes. It seemed as if everything in that country for the past twelve or fifteen years had been a "dream" and a bad one, Adams recalled him saying. "He thought it very much to be wished that they [the French] could now return to the Constitution of 1789, and call back, *the Old Family* [that is, the Bourbons]. For although by that constitution the government was much too weak, and although it was defective in having a legislature only in one branch, yet even thus it was better than the present form, where it was impossible to perceive any limits," John Quincy recorded in his diary. "This is one of the most unexpected phases, in the waxing and waning opinion of this Gentleman concerning the French Revolution." The president had not lost his talent for exaggeration; he claimed, for example, to have learned Spanish with the help of a grammar book and a copy of *Don Quixote* while on a sea voyage lasting only nineteen days. But again, John Quincy was kind. "You never can be an hour in this man's company without something of the marvelous like these stories. His genius is of the Old French School."[65]

13

Cicero's Acolyte

ON THE WHOLE LOUISA found European court life preferable to Washington society. In Paris or Berlin, everyone knew their place; in democratic Washington, everyone was jockeying for position and ever ready to take offense. "In the courts of princes you get written instructions to teach you the forms and etiquettes—you are therefore seldom liable to give offence by erring," she wrote in her diary. "In a democrat government where all are monarchs, although one yourself, there is a perpetual struggle for position, which gives rise to constant feuds and demands utterly impossible to satisfy."[1] Socializing could also be dangerous in the literal sense: "[T]he city not being laid out; the streets not graduated; the bridges consisting of mere loose planks; and huge stumps of trees recently cut down intercepting every path; and the roads intersected by deep ravines continually enlarged by rain."[2]

To say that Washington society was truly cosmopolitan would have been a stretch, but it had its exotic aspects. The president's receptions were sometimes attended by Indian delegations clad in a variety of costumes. The emissaries included the semicivilized Creeks and Cherokees of the Southeast, but also the more exotically attired Sauk, Sioux, and Osage chiefs sent to the capital by Lewis and Clark. Rivaling even them was the ambassador from the bey of Tunis, Sidi Soliman Mellimelli. Upon his arrival, Mellimelli presented Arabian steeds and other presents to Jefferson and Madison. The State Department accepted the Eastern custom of bearing the expenses of visiting delegations, which in this case included paying for concubines. In his records Madison listed the expenditures as "appropriations for foreign intercourse."[3]

Life at the Hellens' was as close to life at Cooper's Row as it could be. Louisa lived with her mother and sisters in a large, comfortable house where they conversed, sang, gossiped, and played with their babies. John Quincy spent most of his evenings at home in his study, reading and writing. Louisa managed to make some progress in her relationship with Abigail. She charmed the matriarch of Peacefield with colorful descriptions of Washington social life. But when Abigail attempted to bully her, she stood up for herself. The previous spring, her mother-in-law had written how alarmed she was at John Quincy's appearance when he had arrived at Peacefield. He was pale, thin, and subdued. Abigail attributed his condition to overwork and a tendency to "engage in any service but with his whole attention, and the labors and anxiety of the mind are a weariness to the flesh." The inference was that his wife was not able to take care of him. Six months later, shortly after John Quincy had arrived back in Washington, Louisa wrote Abigail: "I was much surprised and grieved to see him look so ill when he returned. I thank God he is now better."[4] Touché. Despite her sniping, Abigail was gratified to see that her daughter-in-law had come to share her ambitions for John Quincy. "His talents are so superior and he is so perfectly calculated for the station in which he is placed," Louisa wrote. "His manners are so perfectly pleasing and conciliating, and his understanding is so refined even his enemies envy and admire him."[5] Another thing that the two women agreed upon was John Quincy's shortcomings in the fashion department. Louisa wrote that she had tried without much success to have him copy the fashions of the time. Abigail expressed her sympathy: "It is in vain to talk of being above these little decorums—if we live in the world and mean to serve ourselves and it, we must conform to its customs, its habits, and in some measure to its fashions."[6]

TOWARD THE END OF the short congressional session, John Quincy grew increasingly frustrated at the antics of the Senate and with his political prospects. Despite the Republican Party's attempt to subvert an independent federal judiciary, Jefferson had won reelection overwhelmingly in 1804, 162 electoral votes to his opponent's 14. Even Massachusetts had gone for him. "My political prospects have been daily declining," Adams wrote in his diary in late December.[7] He had been admitted to the bar of the Supreme Court and participated in a few cases, but he continued to find the practice of law unsatisfying. Stung by the lack of support he had received for his Louisiana resolutions and contemptuous of his colleagues' apparent preference for the horse races over Senate business, Adams began to make a nuisance of himself. He managed to make another new and potentially powerful enemy—General Andrew Jackson, head of the Tennessee state militia. Jackson chaired the committee on military affairs, which had presented to the Senate forty-three new Articles of War. John Quincy did not suffer average people, much less fools, and he thought Jackson a fool and a backwoods barbarian.

After reading the articles the Tennessean had written, he remarked to friends that it contained "the most barbarous English that ever crept through the bars of legislation." It was "grossly and outrageously defective and blundering," and he declared his intention not to allow this "mockery of legislative deliberation" to go unchallenged. To Jackson's enragement, Adams insisted that the clerk of the Senate read the entire piece of legislation out loud.[8] It was fortunate that the second session ended in March before the senior senator from Massachusetts could do any more political damage to himself. He was not unaware of his shortcomings: "I am afraid that the pride of opinion, and a paltry vanity mingles itself with my judgment," he confessed to his diary. "I know how often this happens to me and it often ends in mortification as is most just."[9]

The Adamses departed Washington on March 19, 1805, soon after Congress had adjourned. John Quincy and Louisa had decided that their marriage could not bear another separation. The little party included them, George, baby John, and Louisa's younger sister Eliza. The most memorable part of the trip for Louisa was Aaron Burr, who was their companion on the packet from Baltimore to Philadelphia. At this point the former vice president was under indictment for murder (for having killed Hamilton in their duel) in both New York and New Jersey. Unbeknownst to the Adamses, Burr was headed west to the Northwest Territory to set in motion a vaguely conceived plan to detach the trans-Appalachian states and territories from the Union and form them into a new country. As did most people, Louisa immediately fell under his spell: "He was a small man, quite handsome, and his manners were strikingly prepossessing, and in spite of myself I was pleased with him—He appeared to fascinate everyone in the boat down to the lowest sailor, and he knew everybody's history by the time we left—He was politely attentive to me, devoted to my sister—At table he assisted me to help the children with so much ease and good nature that I was perfectly confounded. . . . At about twelve at night we landed and it was diverting to see Mr. Burr with my youngest child in his arms, a bundle in his hand and [me] leaning on his other arm to walk from the wharf while my sister, Mr. Adams, and George followed. . . . He talked and laughed all the way and we were quite intimate by the time we got to Philadelphia."[10]

Two weeks after they arrived in Quincy, the Adamses and Eliza moved into the little house on Penn's Hill. "Returned to my father's with the chaise and early in the evening came home to the house in which I was born," John Quincy wrote in his diary, "but in which I have not before passed a night for upwards of twenty-five years." The saltbox-style house would be the family residence during the summer recesses for the remainder of John Quincy's tenure in the Senate. Their abode was beneath both him and his family, but because of the failure of Bird, Savage &

Bird, there was no alternative.[11] The two sisters set about their domestic chores in good humor, cooking, gardening, and even milking the cows. "I confess with all my labor for want of knack I could not get a drop of milk," Louisa later recalled.[12] Their burdens diminished considerably with the arrival of a young boy and two farm girls hired to help with the chores. Quincy was a far cry from Washington in every way possible. Louisa again felt the comparative chill of New England society. She lamented the remoteness of their cottage and found the neighborhood "in many respects unpleasant, there being [among other things] two or three insane persons under no control of whom we were very much afraid."[13] Once again, close proximity to her mother-in-law seemed to diminish her. As in the past, John Quincy spent more time at Peacefield than at his house on Penn's Hill.

The senator seemed at loose ends. He roamed the countryside with John and Thomas, who had married and been elected to the state legislature. He also fiddled with his indifferent orchard and read Juvenal. His massive intellect craved stimulation and focus. "I have been a severe student all the days of my life," he observed of himself. "I have been tempted to abandon my books altogether. This however is impossible. For the habit has so long been fixed in me as to have become a passion, and when once severed from my books, I find little or nothing in life to fill the vacancy of time."[14] But then, on the morning of June 24, 1805, his cousin Josiah Quincy called to inform him that the Harvard Corporation had elected him the first Boylston Professor of Rhetoric and Oratory at the school.[15]

IN 1771, NICHOLAS BOYLSTON, a first cousin of John Quincy's grandmother, had left fifteen hundred pounds to endow a professorship in rhetoric and oratory. The gift lay forgotten, gathering interest, until 1801, when Ward Nicholas Boylston, Nicholas's nephew and a kinsman of John Quincy's, filed suit to recover the $23,200 that had accumulated. The Corporation immediately created the chair, but Ward Boylston agreed to withdraw the suit only on the condition that his cousin John Quincy be named to the position. Adams was intrigued, but there were questions to be answered, conditions to be met. Would Harvard allow him to teach solely when he was between sessions of Congress? Would it permit him time to prepare the lectures he would have to deliver? Would he be required to be in residence at the college? Negotiations continued through July and August. The Corporation eventually agreed that John Quincy would be required to teach only during the months from March to October. He would deliver two morning lectures a week to seniors and graduate students. Senior declamations would take place in the afternoons; he could live anywhere he wished whether in Boston or Cambridge. Harvard wanted the power to appoint a substitute instructor when the chair holder had to be absent. Only a person of my choosing, Adams insisted. College regulations called for a religious declaration by every faculty member on the day of his inauguration. "With the most perfect deference and respect for the legislature of the college," Adams declared, "I must question their authority to require my subscription to a creed not recognized by the Constitution or the laws of the state." Confession of faith must always be something private between man and his Maker, he declared.[16] Finally, John Quincy insisted, he would need up to two years to prepare his lectures. Harvard agreed to everything.

The Adamses departed for Washington and the opening of the Ninth Congress on November 11, 1805. John Quincy and his parents had decided with no input from Louisa that George and John would stay behind in Quincy. George would board with Aunt and Uncle Cranch at $2.50 a week, while toddler John would live with Grandmother Adams. Perhaps John Quincy hesitated to expose his two young children to another long and arduous journey; perhaps he felt the Hellen household already overcrowded, and he wanted to be free of distractions to concentrate on writing his Boylston lectures. Most likely he was bullied into the decision by his mother. If she had been in Washington, Louisa might have stood up to her mother-in-law, but six months in Quincy had once again eroded her confidence and self-esteem.

Louisa gloried in her two sons; throughout the winter she bombarded Abigail with instructions for their care and feeding, the letters from Washington tinged with regret. Abigail was characteristically unsympathetic—she was then addressing Thomas's wife as "Dear Nancy" but Louisa still as "Mrs. Adams." "They are much better off than they could have been at any boarding house in Washington where they must have been confined in some degree or other [and] have mixed with improper persons," she wrote. "I should suppose that your own judgement, experience, and good sense would have convinced you of the propriety of the measure without compulsion. I have experienced separations of all kinds of children equally dear to me . . . but I considered it the duty of a parent to consult the interest and benefit of their children."[17] Louisa would never be reconciled to the separation. "No substitute on the face of this Earth can be found for the mother's attachment or the mother's devotion if she is virtuous." And what of the mother whose children were her ultimate consolation?[18] Abigail had begrudged Louisa her son and was now trying to steal her children!

WHEN JOHN QUINCY RETURNED to the Senate in the fall of 1805, Britain and America were teetering on the edge of war. With the collapse of the Peace of Amiens in May 1803, Britain and its allies had once again faced off against Bonaparte and his vassal states, which by this time included Spain. For the first two years of the war, America managed to dodge both British orders-in-council and French maritime decrees. France and Britain were happy at first to open the carrying trade between their West Indian colonies and their home ports to American merchant vessels. In the end, however, John Bull could not resist the temptation to use his domination of the high seas to sever Bonaparte's transatlantic lifeline. The British Board of Trade declared that U.S. trade with France and its colonies violated the Rule of '56, which held that trade closed in time of peace could not be opened in time of war. American shippers initially got around this obstacle by "breaking" the voyage—that is, landing their cargoes in American ports, paying nominal duties, and reloading them, thus making the goods American or "free." In the *Polly* decision of 1800, the British government approved this stratagem. Between 1803 and 1805, the value of goods transshipped by American vessels increased from $13 million to $53 million. The U.S. merchant fleet ballooned into the largest in the world, and American shipowners, manufacturers, and commercial farmers prospered.

Not surprisingly, the *Polly* decision did not sit well with either British manufacturers and shipowners or with the Admiralty. The damned colonists were growing rich by supplying Britain's enemy. All that came to an end with the infamous *Essex* decision of 1805. In the spring of that year, a British cruiser seized the American merchant vessel *Essex*, which was transporting cargo from Havana to Barcelona. The ship stopped in Charleston and paid a duty totaling $198 prior to clearing the harbor and heading for Spain. The *Essex* was subsequently intercepted by a British cruiser and hauled before the Admiralty court in Newfoundland. The magistrates promptly overturned the *Polly* decision. Simply landing cargo in a neutral port did not make it neutral cargo. In the wake of the *Essex* decision, British warships and privateers began seizing and prizing dozens of U.S. merchant vessels.

Shortly after his arrival back in Washington, Senator Adams called on Jefferson. Madison and the secretary of the navy were also present. The four men held a far-ranging discussion on the state of American foreign affairs.[19] On December 3, the president delivered his fifth annual message to Congress. It was surprisingly belligerent, condemning Great Britain for its violations of American neutral rights and not so subtly threatening its ally, Spain. Expansionist to the core, Jefferson coveted not only the Floridas but Cuba as well. The "piratical" activities of Spanish subjects against the merchant vessels of the United States would serve as justification enough for seizure, the president declared. "Our coasts have been infested and our harbors watched by private armed vessels, some of them without commissions, some with illegal commissions, others with those of legal forms . . . they have carried them [U.S. merchantmen] off under pretense of legal adjudication; but not daring to approach a court of justice, they have plundered and sunk them by the way, or in obscure places."[20] John Quincy expressed his support for the strongest possible measures. "[I]f we submit to them without resistance, it will be equivalent to a total abandonment of all rights of neutral commerce," he wrote his father.[21]

Both John and John Quincy, however, feared that a Republican administration shackled by its small-government, antitariff, strict-constructionist, and no-standing-army principles would not be sufficient to the task. Their anxiety was well-founded. Jefferson and Madison were hampered by a group of ideological purists spearheaded by John Randolph of Roanoke and John Taylor of Caroline. They referred to themselves as the "Old Republicans." The newspapers labeled them the "Tertium Quids," the third way. They were agrarian radicals who deplored commerce and banking, particularly a national bank, and who argued that America could defend its rights with a militia and coastal gunboats. Randolph summarized the views of the Quids as a "love of peace, hatred of offensive war, jealousy of state governments toward the general government; a dread of standing armies; a loathing of public debts, taxes, and excises; tenderness for the liberty of the citizen; jealousy, Argus-eyed jealousy, of the patronage of the President."[22] John Quincy wrote his father, "The effect of Mr. Randolph's having thus suddenly turned upon his party is violent and has thrown them [the administration] into the greatest consternation."[23] The merchants and shipowners of New England, New York, and Pennsylvania who had voted Republican should not have been surprised, John Adams wrote his son. "To commit the command of their commerce to Virginians was to commit the lamb to the guardianship of the wolf."[24]

Jefferson and Madison, like the Adamses, were nationalists first and partisans second. In truth, the American presidency during the Early Republic and the Era of Good Feelings was occupied by individuals who believed that they ought to operate above party, although they were of party. All had read and expressed admiration for Lord Bolingbroke's *Idea of a Patriot King*. Indeed, John Adams insisted that he had perused all of Bolingbroke's works at least five times. His 1738 treatise warned against the dangers of faction, avarice, and political opportunism. It was naive, Bolingbroke wrote, to expect patriotism and public virtue—which required the individual to sacrifice for the common good—to spring spontaneously from the people. He advocated for a balanced government, but one headed by a hereditary king who would reject both divine right and direct democracy. But such a monarch was "responsible for the moral health of the body politic" and must be held accountable, constrained by statute, and judged by his actions. A ruler who abused his subjects and ignored the common good was nothing more than a tyrant and unchristian to boot. Washington fit the mold of patriot king to perfection. He had been nominated commander in chief by a New Englander, had personally led his troops in the field, had surrendered his sword to Congress at the close of the Revolutionary War, and had refused a salary. He had deplored the emergence of political parties. But the American Revolution had ruled out the possibility of a hereditary executive in the United States.[25]

The idea of a hereditary executive was, of course, an abomination to Jefferson and Madison, but they embraced Bolingbroke's portrait of an activist executive devoted to furthering the general welfare. Upon becoming president, Jefferson, the author of the Declaration of Independence and the coauthor of the first draft of the Declaration of the Rights of Man, proposed federally funded internal improvements—by constitutional amendment if necessary—in order to bind the various parts of the Union together with "new and indissoluble ties."[26] He reached out to moderate Federalists like John Quincy; he pursued policies designed to strengthen the nation domestically and assert its rights internationally. The American executive, he believed, was constrained by natural law and the Constitution but had a clear obligation to lead, to formulate a domestic program, to set a moral example, and to have the nation be a model for the rest of the world. The principal differences between Jefferson and John Quincy, then, were their view of human nature—with the Virginian being an optimist and the New Englander a pessimist—and their personal ambitions. But Jefferson had to deal with the Quids.

In the wake of the *Essex* decision, Senator Adams, in consultation with Secretary of State Madison, helped prepare in committee three resolutions denouncing the British seizure of American vessels under the Rule of '56 and proposing measures of retaliation. The first resolution accused Britain of "unprovoked aggression upon the property of the citizens of these United States, a wanton violation of their neutral rights, and an encroachment upon their national independence." The second requested the president to "demand and insist upon" restoration and indemnity. And the third recommended a policy of nonimportation of British goods until the Admiralty should cease and desist. Pickering and the Essex men were appalled. Adams was the only Federalist in the Senate to vote for nonimportation, a measure detested and denounced by New England's financial and commercial interests.[27]

At this point, Jefferson dispatched James Monroe and William Pinkney to London to join with U.S. minister Rufus King in negotiating a new Anglo-American treaty that would respect American neutral rights. Not surprisingly, they ran into a brick wall.

* * *

ON APRIL 7, 1806, Colonel William Stephens Smith, Nabby's husband, was arrested in New York and charged with the "high misdemeanor" of violating the Neutrality Act of 1794 by helping to outfit a military expedition against a nation with which the United States was nominally at peace—Spain. When John Quincy arrived in New York on May 1 on his way home, he visited the Smiths and to his distress found them planning to move that same day into a cottage on prison grounds (probably Newgate in Greenwich Village).[28] It seems that Colonel Smith had fallen in with General Francisco de Miranda, a former officer in the Spanish army who had become an independence leader in his native Venezuela. Miranda, like Jefferson and the Adamses, was a child of the Enlightenment. The scion of a prominent Caracas family, he had traveled widely in Europe, where he learned several languages and studied art and architecture. He enlisted in the Spanish army and fought in the Revolutionary War for royalist Spain, but then in the French revolutionary army during the Reign of Terror. Attacked by the Inquisition for his liberal views, Miranda took refuge in America, where he made the acquaintance of Washington, Jefferson, and Hamilton. When and how Smith met Miranda—"his very intimate friend"—is unclear, but the colonel proceeded to help the Venezuelan organize a marine military expedition to free his homeland from Spanish rule. Smith raised money from American enthusiasts for the cause of Latin American independence and even persuaded his son, William Steuben Smith, to leave Columbia College and become one of Miranda's volunteers. On February 2, 1806, a small flotilla consisting of the merchant vessel *Leander* and several schooners sailed from New York and headed for Venezuela. They were intercepted by Spanish warships in the Caribbean. A number of conspirators were sent to Caracas, where they were subsequently hanged. The *Leander* managed to flee to Aruba, a safe harbor. Young Smith was imprisoned but later managed to escape.

Upon hearing of this outrage against his country, the Spanish minister to the United States, Marquis de Casa Carlos Martínez de Yrujo, struck the State Department like a thunderbolt. Everyone assumed at the time that young William Steuben had been captured and was languishing in a Caracas cell. Yrujo wrote Colonel Smith, demanding that he confess to aiding the revolutionaries and threatening his son with execution if Smith did not provide the names of everyone involved in the plot.[29] "The Col. returned a very spirited, indignant, and proper answer," John Quincy wrote Louisa. "I wish William was at home—I wish neither he nor his father ever had any concern with this knight-errant expedition. But I had rather tremble, nay I had rather weep, for my friends than blush for them."[30]

Colonel Smith's trial opened on July 14, 1806, and was widely covered in the newspapers. His principal defense was that both President Jefferson and Secretary of State Madison had met with Miranda and given their approval for the expedition. He had written John Quincy repeatedly, asking him to confirm this, but his brother-in-law refused. Miranda might have met with the Virginians, but he doubted seriously that they had consented to an attack on Spanish territory in the Americas. Their policy was and would continue to be strict neutrality in the burgeoning conflict between Spain and its New World colonies. "That he [Miranda] misunderstood or misrepresented their real intentions I have no doubt."[31] Nevertheless, Stephens testified at his trial that Miranda's expedition "was set on foot with the knowledge and approbation of the President."[32] The jury believed him, and he was acquitted. Filibustering expeditions in which Americans participated or even led attempts to overthrow French and Spanish colonial regimes in the Americas were quite popular with large sections of the public. Louisa, an astute observer of her fellow human beings, wrote of Smith: "He was always the gay deluded toy, that wanton'd with the wind, and good fortune was to him but the ebb and flow of a changing idea—He was a delightful companion; one of those beings who are born to be the charm, and the plague of doting woman." He was generous to a fault: "What he possessed he shared too liberally with all that he loved . . . until repeated follies turned the scale and left him nearly friendless. . . . Mrs. Smith [Nabby] loved this man with the purest devotion under all circumstances."[33]

WITH THE FIRST SESSION of the Ninth Congress drawing to a close, John Quincy prepared to depart for Quincy—alone. Louisa missed George and John terribly, but she was then well into another pregnancy. Shortly after his arrival at Peacefield, John Quincy wrote Louisa that her sons were thriving; both spoke of her often and affectionately. She was properly appreciative but lamented that their child would be born without its father present and that she would miss his inauguration as Boylston Professor.[34] As her time approached, Louisa suffered from abscesses in her throat and a swelling of her legs so severe that she could wear only her husband's stockings. She gave birth to a stillborn boy in June. "I can safely assure you that this misfortune was not caused by any imprudence on my part," she subsequently wrote John Quincy. "Dr. Weems is satisfied that the child had been subject to violent convulsions sometime before he died and had he lived, the probability is that he would have been all his life subject to fits."[35]

John Quincy received the news on the thirtieth while in Cambridge. He went about his business and then took supper at Dr. Waterhouse's, where he was boarding. "I retired to my chamber after dining by myself and there yielded to the weakness which I had so long struggled to conceal and restrain. I endeavored to reason myself into resignation to the will of Heaven," but he could not, and he wept bitterly.[36] Louisa's letter, he wrote in his diary, had "affected me deeply by its tenderness, its resignation, and its fortitude." He urged her to come to him as soon as her health would bear it.[37] Soon thereafter, Adams bought two houses from John Lowell: one a comfortable abode at the corner of Nassau Street and Frog Lane in which the family would live, and another at Half-Court Square, which would be rented at nine hundred dollars per year. Once again, Louisa would be able to have the children with her, enjoy Boston society, and live a life more like the ones that she had enjoyed at Cooper's Row or in the Hellen household in Washington.[38]

On the afternoon of June 12, 1806, John Quincy Adams was installed as the Boylston Professor of Rhetoric and Oratory at Harvard College. John, Abigail, Thomas, and assorted cousins, nieces, and nephews came down from Quincy to attend the ceremonies. The members of the Corporation and the Overseers, of which the governor was chairman, presided. It was oppressively hot in Cambridge that afternoon, and the ceremonies had to be delayed for two hours due to a violent thunderstorm. Finally, the proceedings commenced. Adams's inaugural address was a survey of the central role rhetoric and oratory had played in the history of Western civilization. "Sons of Harvard!" he proclaimed, do you dream of becoming a clergyman, a jurist, or a public official? If so, "let him catch from the relics of ancient oratory those unresisted powers which mold the mind of man to the will of the speaker and yield the guidance of a nation to the dominion of the voice."[39] Press reviews were generally favorable. "This address was in the highest degree elegant, classical, and energetic; abounding in fertility of illustration, force of delivery, and originality of remark," declared *The Repertory*.[40]

John Quincy's interest in oratory stemmed not only from his historical studies but from his own sense of inadequacy. During the debates over his proposal to amend the Constitution to allow for the Louisiana Purchase, he confided to his diary, "I felt most sensibly my deficiency as an extemporaneous speaker. No efforts, no application on my part can ever remove it. It is slowness of comprehension. An incapacity to grasp the whole compass of a subject in the mind at once. . . . An incapacity to form ideas properly, precise and definite. My manner therefore is slow, hesitating, and often much confused."[41] This was most certainly an exaggeration, but in truth, speaking to persuade in a deliberative body was foreign to Adams; his stay in the Massachusetts Senate had been brief. His written reports as a diplomat and his letters both public and private were models of their kind, and he was an accomplished conversationalist and negotiator. But the skills needed for those were quite different from the ones required for congressional and public debate.

As soon as he learned that he was to be appointed Boylston Professor, John Quincy began delving deeply into the literature on oratory and rhetoric, and sampling the speeches of the greatest speakers the Western world had to offer. He perused Charles Huit's writings on the history of languages, *Les origines greques du stoïcisme*, and, most important, Cicero's *De claris oratoribus*, in which Cicero describes, in dialogue form with the fictional Brutus and Atticus, the substance and techniques of Rome's greatest orators.[42] Like his father, John Quincy had long looked to Cicero as a role model and teacher.

He would later observe that "living without Cicero at hand would be as [to deprive me] of one of my limbs."[43] *Oratoribus* was just the beginning, however. John Quincy's bible was *De Oratore*, written in 55 BC amidst the moral and political decline of the city-state. In this tract Cicero attempted to describe the ideal orator and expanded on the methods employed by Marcus Antonius and other great influencers of public opinion. Cicero's orator was more than just a skilled mechanic, a means to an end to be used by one political faction or another. He was to be the moral compass of the republic. In *De Oratore*, Book I, Chapter V, which Adams committed to memory, Cicero declared, "There is to my mind no more excellent thing than the power, by means of oratory, to get a hold on assemblies of men, win their goodwill, direct their inclinations wherever the speaker wishes. . . . What function is so kingly, so worthy of the free, so generous as to bestow security, to save the free from peril, to maintain men in their civil rights?" The effective orator must be grounded in the liberal arts, especially the ethics and ideals of the Greek philosophers. "In an orator we must demand the subtlety of the logician, the thoughts of the philosopher, a diction almost poetic, a lawyer's memory, a tragedian's voice, and the bearing of the consummate actor."[44]

Both John and John Quincy detected some similarities between Cicero and themselves. He, like they, came from an old and distinguished but not aristocratic family. All were called to a life of public service and inherited common notions about what constituted statesmanship: personal integrity, a moral compass, a commitment to serve the common good—and, above all, an abiding belief in the virtues of a liberal education. Cicero, like John and John Quincy, was given to fits of self-doubt and depression. When out of office, he wrote long commentaries in an attempt to keep Rome from destroying itself. The consul's wife, Terentia, managed the family property and household while her husband was absent on business.[45] John Quincy would observe of Cicero that he was "not only the orator but the moral philosopher of Rome and the Latin language. Greek civilization abounded with statesmen, orators, and philosophers. In Rome there was none prior to Cicero."[46] "Every one of the letters of Cicero," John Quincy would write his son Charles, "is a picture of the state of the writer's mind when it was written. It is like an evocation of shades to read them. I see him approach me like the image of a Phantasmagoria—he seems to be opening his lips to speak to me and passes off, but his words as if they had fallen upon my ears are left stamped deep upon my memory."[47]

By the time he was inaugurated as the Boylston Professor, John Quincy had already begun writing his lectures. From his rooms at Dr. Waterhouse's, he could be near Harvard's library. He went at the task with typical single-mindedness. "Your mother writes me that you apply so closely to this, permit me to say, strange occupation of yours that she is fearful you will materially injure your health," Louisa wrote. "Mon Amie I grant as you have undertaken the business that it is necessary to attend to it, but your family have some call on you as well as the public, and the place you fill will become more odious than ever if it is to occasion you to neglect your [wife and children]."[48]

By the end of August, the Boylston Professor had completed seven lectures. The first was delivered in June 1806, the last not until the summer of 1809. Adams's course of instruction, following the classical model, identified three kinds of oratory: political, judicial, and ceremonial. "The object of the first was utility, the second justice, and the third virtue." Ceremonial speakers were called on to appeal to the prevailing opinions and prejudices of their audience; legal or judicial speakers to their listeners' knowledge of the law and of precedents; but orators operating in deliberative bodies had to use every technique to affect the will of their colleagues and produce concrete action.[49] In 1810, Adams's treatises were published as *Lectures on Rhetoric and Oratory, Delivered to the Classes of Senior and Junior Sophisters in Harvard University.*

As a writer, John Quincy Adams had always considered his primary audience the English-speaking world. He was fluent in French—he loved the language—but he did not compose his prose and poetry in it. At the time, among the literati in America, there was an ongoing debate concerning what was and what was not proper English. Adams was part of the discussion. In 1806, Noah Webster had set about creating the first American dictionary, and he consulted John Quincy as to which benchmarks to use. Webster had published an excerpt from his dictionary and been excoriated by one critic for too slavishly following the British model. America had its own vocabulary and pronunciation that had evolved over time, and they should be privileged. John Quincy disagreed. Both he and Webster were apprehensive about trying to force something new on what was already generally accepted regarding both vocabulary and pronunciation. Voltaire had tried imposing a vernacular on traditional French usage, and it had not worked. Certainly, there were words purely American, and they should be included, but Adams's advice to Webster was to rely on British grammarian John Entick's *English Grammar*

(1771) as his guide. "Where we have invented new words, or adopted new senses to old words, it appears but reasonable that our dictionaries should contain them. Yet there are always a multitude of words current within particular neighborhoods, or during short periods of time, which ought never to be admitted into the legitimate vocabulary of a language. A very good proportion of the words of American origin are of this description."[50]

While Louisa was away, John Quincy spent much of his free time with members of the Boston Philosophical Society. According to their calculations, a rare solar eclipse would take place on June 16, 1806. John Quincy and his colleagues gathered to witness the event, which began at three minutes past ten in the morning and ended at twelve forty-eight in the afternoon. The sky was perfectly cloudless. As the moon gradually eclipsed the sun, several stars came out, and an eerie darkness descended over the land. "The colors of natural objects appeared to the eye with a tinge different from anything I had ever seen," John Quincy recorded in his diary.[51] "A feeble luminous circle, not equally light in every part, surrounded the edge of the moon. The darkness was about equal to . . . that which I have witnessed in June at St. Petersburg. But the most striking appearance was the first returning beam: it was about two seconds supportable to the naked eye, and in brightness far exceeding anything I ever beheld," he wrote his wife.[52]

In early August Louisa departed Washington for Quincy. She traveled by packet from Baltimore to Philadelphia, then spent a day in the City of Brotherly Love.[52] At last, she arrived in Quincy, where "my children received me as a stranger, and I was almost forgotten."[53]

Before she departed Washington, John Quincy had written his wife of his plans for the future. The prospects of continuing in public service were slim to none, he wrote. Politics had reached a "state of things in which merit of any kind whatsoever will be no consideration at all . . . and when the only essential qualification for Office will be party." The Republicans had already swept from office every man who smelled even faintly of Federalism. He had considered resigning his seat in the Senate at once but had decided not to, he wrote. He would fill out his term and then retire to private life, in which he'd split his time between Cambridge and the Boylston Professorship, and his law practice in Boston.[54] Louisa wrote back, urging him not to give up. He was destined for greatness: "Nature [has] produced very few really great men. Interest and the world corrupt many of those few." She admitted that her ambition for him would come at great personal cost. Nevertheless, "If I know my own heart, it springs from the purest motives which banish every interest but the public welfare. . . ."[55] Later in life Louisa would claim that devotion to public life had warped her husband, damaged their relationship, and scarred their children. But in truth she was as ambitious for John Quincy as Abigail and John.

In mid-November, John Quincy set off, alone, for Washington to attend the second session of the Ninth Congress, which would last from December 1, 1806, to March 3, 1807. Louisa, her sister Eliza, and George stayed behind in Boston. Both of the houses he had purchased were being rented at the time, so he had moved his family into apartments on Poplar Street.[56]

BY THE TIME JOHN Quincy rejoined his colleagues in the Senate, the Napoleonic Wars had entered a new stage. On October 21, 1805, Lord Nelson had crushed a combined French and Spanish fleet at the Battle of Trafalgar. Soon after, Napoleon had defeated a combined Russian–Austrian force at the Battle of Austerlitz. He was master of the Continent while Britannia ruled the waves. On November 21, 1806, Bonaparte issued the famous Berlin Decree, declaring the entirety of the British Isles blockaded. Neutral ships seeking to enter British ports did so at their peril. Then on December 17, 1807, came the Milan Decree, proclaiming that any neutral vessel allowing itself to be stopped and searched by a British cruiser was subject to seizure by French warships. The Berlin and Milan Decrees were the foundations of Napoleon's Continental System, a plan to isolate Great Britain commercially and starve it into submission. At the same time a series of British orders-in-council declared that all Continental ports closed to British merchant vessels were off-limits to neutrals. These measures were designed by Britain and France not necessarily to choke off all trade with the enemy but to control what commerce there was and tax it to the hilt. If the conflict between the United States and Great Britain had been limited to trade issues, it might have been contained, but it was not.

When hostilities were renewed between Britain and France in 1803, the Royal Navy was desperately short of able-bodied seamen. One did not normally enlist in that branch of the service; the pay was low, the food terrible, and the discipline brutal. The symbol and instrument of coercion was the cat-o'-nine-tails, a lead-tipped rawhide whip. Lord Nelson reported that as of the end of hostilities in 1801, forty-two thousand sailors had jumped ship. Some naval vessels had become so undermanned that they sank in the first storm they encountered after leaving a neutral port. The British government subsequently took the position that in time of war every able-bodied man owed military service to the Crown. It sent out press-gangs to scour British ports for likely seamen and then abducted them. The Admiralty also reserved the right to raid merchant vessels in search of able-bodied seamen. Britain did not claim the right of impressment on foreign soil or of American citizens. But it did insist on the right to search American vessels for deserters. Of these there was an abundance. Given the chance, most British seamen would jump ship in an American port and then sign on to an American merchant vessel. The pay was better, living conditions superior, and discipline lighter. U.S. ship-owners even offered bounties, and "naturalization" papers could be obtained in an American port for as little as a dollar. When a British man-of-war stopped an American vessel to search for deserters, the boarding party would line up the merchantman's crew, and anyone who vaguely resembled an Englishman was im-pressed. All told, British press-gangs seized between eight thousand and ten thousand American seamen during the Napoleonic Wars. Many were killed in action or died of mistreatment.

Outrage over impressment cut across sectional and commercial interests. The notion that the rights of the individual were coterminous with the rights of the nation was deeply rooted in republicanism. Secretary of State Madison summoned the British minister David Erskine and told him that, except for military person-nel, "We consider a neutral flag on the high seas as a safeguard to those sailing under it. Great Britain on the contrary asserts a right to search for and seize her own subjects." Please inform your government that we will not tolerate such vio-lations of our sovereignty. British foreign secretary Lord Harrowby's reply was sharp and to the point: "The pretension advanced by Mr. Madison that the Amer-ican flag should protect every individual sailing under it on board of a merchant ship is too extravagant to require any serious refutation."[57] The view of one British naval commander was typical: "It is my duty to keep my ship manned, and I will do so wherever I find men that speak the same language with me."[58] John Quincy was unequivocal in denouncing the practice. "Is not the impressment of a native-born American citizen from an American vessel in point of principle precisely the same thing as if a British recruiting officer from Canada should come within our lines and forcibly take away a man to make him a British soldier?" he would ask his father rhetorically. "And is not this forcible levying of recruits by the officer of one nation within the jurisdiction of another the offence against the laws of na-tions know by the name of *plagiat* [*sic*] or man-stealing? And is not that offence by the universal usage of civilized nations punished with death?"[59]

Congress fumed and fussed at French and, particularly, British depredations but took no concrete action. The bulk of American foreign trade continued to be with Britain and its colonies, and with the Royal Navy in control of the Atlantic and Mediterranean, that commerce flourished. But the impressment issue would fester.

* * *

MEANWHILE, THE NATION WAS much distracted by the trial of Aaron Burr. During the spring and summer of 1805, the former vice president had traveled through Kentucky, Tennessee, and Ohio, cultivating local politicians and attempting to recruit soldiers of fortune willing to join a filibustering expedition against Mexico as part of his larger plan to detach the West from the Union. Among his converts was General James Wilkinson, commander of the U.S. Army in the Mississippi Valley. John Randolph would describe Wilkinson as "the only man that I ever saw who was from bark to the very core a villain."[60] In the late summer of 1806, as Burr was on the verge of taking concrete action, Wilkinson betrayed him in a series of letters to President Jefferson. The attorney general issued warrants for Burr's and his associates' arrests, charging them with treason. As the former vice president was attempting to escape to the Spanish Floridas, he was arrested and brought to Richmond for trial. "The Burr conspiracy," John Quincy wrote Thomas, "the object of which nobody yet seems to understand, is the only thing which appears to agitate our political nerves."[61]

Adams was, of course, aghast at Burr's machinations, and in the Senate he supported any and all efforts to apprehend him and his fellow conspirators, even going so far as to propose suspending the right of habeas corpus temporarily. He was given pause when rumors reached him that Colonel Smith had been part of the Burr plot and had been planning to join him in the West. But those rumors turned out to be false, or at least the plot was revealed before the swashbuckling Smith had had time to play a role. Burr was eventually acquitted in September 1807 in a trial presided over by Jefferson's archenemy, Chief Justice John Marshall. That fall, John Quincy was named to head a committee to investigate his colleague Senator John Smith of Ohio, who had been implicated in the Burr affair. The report that Adams authored accused Smith and his coconspirators of raising the specter of "a war of the most horrible description . . . a war at once both foreign and domestic," and recommended expulsion. Smith survived by a margin of one vote.[62]

BY THE DAWN OF the New Year, John Quincy was once again lusting for his wife. After attending a ball in Washington at which he had encountered a young lady "rather more than usually undressed," he sent Louisa a piece of doggerel entitled "To Miss in Full Un-Dress at a Ball." He recounted how in the Garden of Eden nakedness had been a symbol of innocence; "Dear Sally! Let thy heart be kind— / Discover all thy charms— / Fling the last fig-leaf to the wind / And snatch me to thy arms!"[63] His wife was amused by these, some of the "sauciest lines I ever perused." Perhaps she would have them published, Louisa teased. Then in mid-February, John Quincy penned a poignant poem to her entitled "A Winter's Day." It closed with these lines: "Louisa! Thus remote from thee / Still something to each joy is wanting / While thy affection can to me / Make the most drear scene enchanting."[64]

The second session of the Ninth Congress ended in early March 1807. On March 5, John Quincy boarded the stage and headed for Massachusetts. On the way he stopped in New York to find that Colonel Smith had literally abandoned his family. At her brother's insistence, Nabby and the children joined him on his journey. When the travelers arrived in Boston, John Quincy had to search for Louisa. She had abandoned the rented apartments and moved into the house her husband had bought on Nassau Street when it had become vacant.[65] She was soon found, however, and the couple was reunited.

John Quincy dispatched Nabby and her children to Peacefield, where they were to live until Smith turned up, if he ever did. He then set about getting the Nassau Street house in order—he found it so smoky and leaky that some of the rooms were uninhabitable. He retained two servants to help run the household: "Theodore French as man servant, and Sally Hayden, a girl of about thirteen, who is to live until eighteen with Mrs. Adams if they should mutually suit." It was not long until John Quincy recorded in his diary: "Mrs. Adams continues very ill, confined to her chamber."[66] While supervising repairs on the house and caring for Louisa and little John, who was also ill, Adams prepared his twelfth lecture as Boylston Professor. On the twenty-seventh, he made the trip to Cambridge to find only four of his twelve students in attendance. Harvard was then experiencing a major rebellion as a result of which a large portion of the student body faced expulsion. The Boylston Professor determined to walk to Cambridge for his classes, but on the next appointed date, the area was hit by a spring snowstorm, forcing Adams to make the trip "half-leg deep in mud and in the face of a violent gale."[67] Weather and student unrest were not the only problems with which Professor Adams had to deal. When he received his pay for the term from June 30 to September 30, it was $117.20 instead of the $348 to which he was entitled. Only with great difficulty did he wheedle the remainder of his salary from Ebenezer Storer, Harvard's treasurer.[68] The student rebellion was soon quelled, and John Quincy's lectures were fully attended. One of those in attendance was Ralph Waldo Emerson, who wrote that "not only the students heard him with delight, but the hall was crowded by professors and unusual visitors."[69]

14

The Russian Assignment

IN FEBRUARY 1807, A boat's crew from a British man-of-war moored in the harbor of Norfolk, Virginia, fled to shore, and subsequently signed on as able-bodied seamen aboard the American frigate U.S.S. *Chesapeake*. When word reached Halifax, Nova Scotia, headquarters of the British Admiralty in North America, the impetuous commander, Vice Admiral Sir George Berkeley, ordered British ships in the vicinity of Norfolk to seize the deserters no matter what the cost. On June 22, 1807, the *Chesapeake* set sail for the Mediterranean. Some ten miles outside U.S. territorial waters, H.M.S. *Leopard* hailed the *Chesapeake*. Thinking that the Briton just wanted him to carry mail to Europe, Commodore James Barron ordered his ship to heave to. When the British commander demanded permission to search the American frigate for the deserters, Barron quite correctly refused. At this point the *Leopard* fired three broadsides point-blank into the American vessel, killing three and wounding eighteen. After firing a single shot in defiance, Barron struck his colors. A British boarding party secured their prey, who were found hiding in the hold. Thereupon, the *Chesapeake* limped back into Norfolk.

When news of the *Leopard*'s attack on the *Chesapeake* spread up and down the Eastern Seaboard, outraged mobs took to the streets, crying for blood. British officers on shore leave fled to their ships in fear for their lives. Jefferson confided to his friends that the British "had their foot on the threshold of war" and that the United States "has never been in such a state of excitement since the battle of Lexington."[1] Under a provision of the Jay Treaty, British warships were entitled to call at American ports to secure water and provisions. Jefferson canceled that privilege, and he asked the states to activate their militias, with the goal of creating a volunteer army of some hundred thousand men. He ordered the strengthening of coastal defenses and called a special session of Congress to meet in October.

In Boston, Republican leaders convened a public meeting to denounce what had clearly been an unprovoked attack by a British warship on an American naval vessel. Adams attended and served on the committee that drafted a resolution declaring "that though we unite with our government in wishing most ardently for peace on just and honorable terms, yet we are ready cheerfully to support them with our lives and fortunes" (echoing, of course, the Declaration of Independence).[2] Federalists were enraged by what they perceived to be John Quincy's betrayal. At the Insurance Offices, he encountered John Phillips, an old friend, who "told me I should have my head taken off for apostasy."[3] John Lowell, one of the original Essex men, even went so far as to justify Berkeley's actions. Moderate Federalists quickly realized that to remain silent was to commit political suicide. They called their own meeting. John Quincy and Harry Otis attended, and Adams helped draft resolutions of protest, though none pledged the attendees' lives and fortunes. Essex men like Lowell, Theophilus Parsons, Timothy Pickering, and George Cabot were noticeably absent.[4]

Shortly afterward Senator Adams became privy to a secret correspondence between members of the Essex Junto and the governor-general of Canada, Sir James H. Craig. In the exchange the British official warned that Jefferson was conspiring with the French to foment war with Great Britain, a conflict that, if realized, would allegedly reestablish New France and reduce the United States to the status of one of Napoleon's vassals. The Essex men assured Craig that they would not permit New England to participate in a war against Great Britain and hinted at secession.[5] This was only the latest chapter in a story that had begun with Jefferson's election and the Louisiana Purchase. In 1804, with Republicanism sweeping the country, Pickering, Uriah Tracy, and other Essex men, together with Roger Griswold of Connecticut, had approached Aaron Burr about joining New York with the states of New England to create an independent federation.[6] "The principles of democracy are everywhere what they have been in France," wrote arch-Federalist Fisher Ames in 1803. "The fire of revolution . . . when once kindled, would burrow deep into the soil, search out and consume the roots, and leave after one crop a *caput mortuum*, black and barren, for ages. . . ."[7]

MEANWHILE, LOUISA HAD BECOME pregnant again. She and John Quincy prepared themselves for the worst, but as her date drew near, she was uncharacteristically healthy. On August 17 they took their usual stroll through Boston Common. At two the next morning, she called for the doctor but had to do with just a nurse. Her labor was severe. "My nurse towards morning was so alarmed at my situation that she burst into tears and was sent away," Louisa later recalled in her diary. For the first time, John Quincy was pressed into service. "Mr. Adams was with me at the birth to see another apparently dead child." But no, "in about half an hour the child had recovered the play of his lungs, and my husband had witnessed sufferings that he had no idea of."[8] A month later Charles Francis Adams was christened at First Church in Quincy. His name, John Quincy noted, was given "in remembrance of my deceased brother" and "as a token of honor to my old friend and patron Judge [Francis] Dana."[9]

While he waited for the special session to begin, Adams worked on his lectures in the newly established Athenaeum, destined to become one of America's great libraries, and attended sessions of the Society for the Study of Natural Philosophy. In August he reopened his law office in one of the downstairs rooms in the Court Street house. To beat the summer heat, he swam in the bay off Alms-House Wharf. One day, after a plunge with George, John Quincy and Louisa noticed that while their son was changing clothes, he was unable to use his right arm and sported a large bruise on a hip. As it turned out, several days earlier, the six-year-old had been playing on a swing with friends and had fallen off. "But as he complained little of it and has been cheerful as usual, we apprehended nothing more than a bruise," John Quincy recorded in his diary. The next day he took the boy to "Mr. Hewes, the bone-setter," who declared that George had a dislocated shoulder and a broken collarbone. He put the joint back in place and plastered the broken bone.[10] The boy remained stoic throughout.

Louisa's illnesses continued intermittently and were sometimes severe. Upon one such bout, John Quincy observed, "Doctor gave her laudanum, which he had avoided as long as possible, but which we have found on such occasions the only thing that could procure relief for her."[11]

In early October, John Quincy began preparations for the trip to Washington and the opening of the special session. Only Louisa and the baby would accompany him. Son John would again live with Aunt Cranch in Quincy while George was to attend Atkinson Academy in Atkinson, New Hampshire, a school run by Aunt Elizabeth and her second husband, the Reverend Stephen Peabody.[12] John Quincy made no secret of his belief that the children had been overindulged when under Louisa's care. At eight o'clock on the morning of October 10, husband, wife, and newborn baby boarded the stage to Providence. The entire trip was difficult: heavy seas, contrary winds, seasickness, crude lodgings, crowded stages and chaises, rough roads, and illness for both mother and child. During the layover in New York, Louisa was walking with her maid and Charles to catch a carriage when a man snatched the baby out of the maid's arms; the two women ran screaming after the culprit. Louisa followed him into a building and was about to mount the stairs when the man appeared with Charles in his arms, apologizing, "saying that

the child was such a perfect beauty, he thought he must show him to his wife—
The apology was irresistible to a mother," Louisa wrote in *Adventures of a Nobody*,
"and we turned back and met Mr. Adams who was in great agitation looking for
us."[13] Why the Adamses did not contact the authorities and charge the individual
with attempted child stealing is a mystery. At last the party arrived safe and
sound at the Hellens' in Georgetown on the twenty-fourth.

As he prepared once again to take his seat in the Senate, Adams reflected, with
typical gloom, upon his legislative achievements. "Of the very little business
which I have commenced during the four Sessions, at least three-fourths has
failed with circumstances of peculiar mortification," he wrote in his diary. "The
very few instances in which I have succeeded have been always after an opposition
of great obstinacy, often ludicrously, contrasting with the insignificancy of the
object in pursuit." Frequently his proposals had been passed easily when sponsored by others. But he had sense enough to realize that the problem was not
personal but political.[14] He was a Federalist who found himself repeatedly supporting a Republican administration.

By the time Congress had convened, Great Britain had disavowed Berkeley
and the attack on the *Chesapeake*. Whitehall apologized and offered to make
amends but refused to budge on the principle of impressment. Senator Adams felt
the steam go out of his colleagues and the members of the administration. "The
great sentiment which appears to me predominating in the minds of congressmen
at present is the dread of their own valor," he wrote Abigail. "Every man seems to
tremble least he should do something rash."[15] It was not just the shipowners, merchants, and manufacturers who were opposed to conflict with Great Britain; it
was "the Cotton of the South" as well.[16] John Quincy was himself conflicted. He
was under tremendous pressure from his Massachusetts constituents to vote to
end nonimportation. He admitted to Joseph Hall, editor of *Port Folio*, that the
measure was proving to be ineffective. He wrote that British promises not to
search for deserters aboard American naval vessels had made that issue moot. He
hoped and believed, he said, that war with Great Britain could be avoided.[17] But
the larger issue of impressment of merchant seamen remained. "Yet for this we
must wage war now if for anything," John Quincy observed to his brother. He was
all for standing up for American rights but not if the Jefferson administration was
unwilling to assume the military and financial burden necessary to defend the
country. And he saw no prospect of that happening—not as long as the parsimo-
nious Albert Gallatin was secretary of the treasury and Randolph and the Quids
were nipping at Jefferson's and Madison's heels.[18]

The president and the secretary of state had long believed in the efficacy of
economic coercion as a diplomatic tool. On December 21, 1807, at Jefferson's

urging, Congress passed the Embargo Act. That measure cut off all trade with foreign countries; American vessels were forbidden to leave port, and ships engaged in coastal trade were compelled to post large bonds ensuring they did not bolt for Europe. The administration insisted that the embargo would weigh equally upon France and Britain. The latter would allegedly "feel it in her manufactures, in the loss of naval stores, and above all in the supplies essential to the colonies." France would suffer from the loss of sugar, molasses, and other raw material imports from its Caribbean colonies. In truth, because the Royal Navy ruled the waves, Jefferson's prohibition on trade bore most heavily on Great Britain. "Mr. Jefferson," a Boston Federalist exclaimed, "has imposed an embargo to please France and to beggar us."[19]

The Embargo proved indeed to be a perfect complement to Napoleon's Continental System. Upon learning of the measure, the emperor ordered all American ships then in Continental ports seized. He was just helping the American president enforce his own legislation, he declared.

John Quincy Adams voted for the Embargo, one of the few Federalist senators to do so. As they left the committee room where the measure had first been considered, he remarked to his colleague and fellow Embargo supporter from Vermont, Stephen Row Bradley, "This measure will cost you and me our seats, but private interest must not be put in opposition to public good."[20] Bradley was a Republican, but he was also a New Englander and hence would be the object of outrage by commercial interests injured by the Embargo. John Quincy subsequently wrote his father that he viewed the Embargo as a purely defensive measure, but it was the only step the administration was willing to take. He favored the arming of American merchantmen, but Jefferson and Madison were not even willing to go that far. The Embargo had better have a powerful, immediate effect because it could not long endure, the younger Adams observed; if it remained in place for any period of time, it might very possibly wreak more havoc with America's economy than Britain's. "My situation here at the moment is singular and critical. My view of present policy, and my sense of the course enjoined upon me by public duty are so different from those of the Federalists that I find myself in constant opposition to them." He was not a confidant of Jefferson and Madison, he told his father. "Yet since the commencement of the present session I have [by the Republican majority] been placed upon every committee of national importance."[21]

On January 23, 1808, Senator Adams, at the express invitation of Stephen Bradley, attended the Republican congressional caucus, which was meeting to select candidates for president and vice president for the forthcoming elections. William Branch Giles had been cultivating his Massachusetts colleague since the opening of the session. The administration was well aware of where the talent and moderation lay in the Federalist Party, and was eager to make common cause with it, he whispered in Adams's ear.[22] At Jefferson's urging, the caucus nominated James Madison for the highest office in the land and George Clinton for the second place. John Quincy voted in favor of the proposed ticket.[23] Abigail was aghast: "I have considered it as inconsistent both with your principles and your judgment to have countenanced such a meeting by your presence," she fumed. Caucuses were both undemocratic and unconstitutional. "If you were present, I can only say, thinking as I do, I can never cease to regret it."[24] Constitutional considerations aside, Abigail was smarting over the broadsides being fired against her son by New England Federalists. One paper in western Massachusetts declared that John Quincy Adams was "one of those amphibious politicians, who lives on both land and water and occasionally resorts to each, but who finally settles down into the mud."[25] John wrote his son, "I am not of her [Abigail's] opinion." The Romans held caucuses; the history of Federalism in Massachusetts was but one long series of caucuses. "I blame not your attendance nor your vote. Proceed with your plan to support your system [the Republican Party] . . . though its measures have not been wise, nor its morals pure, nor its religion divine." It is the only system we have at present and we "have no other way to defend ourselves against the sharks and panthers."[26] John Quincy recorded in his diary, "I received this morning letters from my father and mother. [They] contain a test for my firmness, for my prudence; and for my filial reverence."[27]

Although Senator Adams still claimed to be a man without a party, he was in effect now a Republican. In terms of his own constituency, the switch could not have come at a worse time. By the summer of 1808, the Embargo was taking a dreadful toll on the seaports of the Northeast and the Mid-Atlantic states. A British traveler described New York at the time: "the port indeed was full of shipping, but they were dismantled and laid up; their decks were cleared, their hatches fastened down, and scarcely a sailor was to be found on board. The coffee-houses were almost empty; the streets near the water-side were almost deserted; the grass had begun to grow upon the wharves."[28] The economic situation was bad enough, but the Jefferson administration also received fire for the draconian measures used to enforce the Embargo. It was, opponents declared, a sweeping exercise of federal power and included violations of individual rights not seen, ironically, since the Alien and Sedition Acts. And, in truth, Jefferson, a strict constructionist in theory, interpreted the commerce clause of the Constitution in ways that gave Washington control over virtually every aspect of the nation's economic life.[29] Adams might have retained his seat in the Senate, had the Republicans kept control of the Massachusetts legislature, but they were swept from office by the Federalists in the election of 1808. "The present time and the prospects of the nation are such that a seat in the public councils cannot be an object of my desire," he wrote his father. "My literary profession and the education of my children will occupy all my time. . . . I shall also resume the practice of the law as far as that will resume me."[30]

John Quincy was being a bit disingenuous. As early as the fall of 1805, Jefferson and Madison were sending out peace feelers. In November of that year, Benjamin Rush had called on Adams. "The object . . . was to inform me of a conversation which he had with Mr. Madison the Secretary of State in the course of the last summer respecting me. Mr. Madison, he said, had expressed himself in very favorable terms, of me and had told him that the President's opinion of me was equally advantageous and that it was his wish to employ me in some mission abroad, if I was desirous of it."[31] Throughout 1805 and 1806, rumors had circulated through Washington that John Quincy was to be appointed minister to the Court of St. James's. Party aside, the Napoleonic Wars showed no signs of abating, and Adams had been the most astute and influential reporter of European affairs during the crucial decade of the 1790s. But at that point, he was still in the Senate.

His own political fortunes notwithstanding, Senator Adams's greatest fear was that the Embargo would so strengthen the hand of the Essex men that they would succeed in effecting a permanent schism of the republic. His old law tutor, Theophilus Parsons, now chief justice of the state supreme court, made no secret of his Anglophilia. "I called on Chief-Justice Parsons," John Quincy confided to his diary. "I found him as I expected totally devoted to the British policy and avowing the opinion that the British have a right to take their seamen from our ships, have a right to interdict our trade with her enemies. . . . He also thinks the people of this country corrupted, already in a state of voluntary subjugation to France, and ready to join an army of Bonaparte if he should send one here to subdue themselves. The only protection of our liberties, he thinks, is the British Navy."[32] Adams believed that he was now forever beyond the Federalist pale. "Because a certain portion of Federalists have thought fit to connect the fortunes of their cause with that of Admiral Berkeley and with that of Emperor Burr, I have thought it my duty not only to abandon them [the High Federalists] but to take a part active and decided against them. . . . [T]he only reason upon which I have supported or may support the Administration is a conviction that they are struggling to maintain the best interests and rights of the country."[33] In early February, Josiah Quincy—John Quincy's cousin, a sitting congressman from Massachusetts, and an Essex man—asked for an explanation of John Quincy's recent actions. "I fully opened to him my motives for supporting the administration at this crisis," John Quincy wrote, "and my sense of the danger which a spirit of opposition at this time is bringing upon the Union. I told him where that opposition in case of war must in its nature end. Either in a civil war or in a dissolution of the Union with the Atlantic States in subserviency to Great Britain. That to resist this I was ready if necessary to sacrifice everything I have in life, and even life itself."[34]

The first week in March, Senator Adams told Giles and former representative John Nicholas of Virginia, Madison's campaign managers, of the letter he had seen the previous year in which the governor-general of Canada had proposed to certain New England Federalists cooperation between the Northeast and Great Britain in case of war with the possibility of secession and the creation of a new republic. They understood the import of this information, coming as it did from an Adams, and arranged for an audience with Jefferson. The Essex men were then charging that the president was planning an alliance with France. Jefferson assured Adams that the administration was determined to maintain strict neutrality.[35] John Quincy then proceeded to describe the conspiracy being hatched to separate the Northeast from the rest of the nation. The New Englander confided to Jefferson "that propositions had been made by certain British agents to many leading Federalists in the eastern states [that] in the event of war between the U.S. and Great Britain to separate New England from the rest of the states and to enter into an offensive and defensive alliance."[36]

William Branch Giles, who was present at the meeting, later recalled that Adams himself had been "consulted on its feasibility and urged to unite with the approving Federalists" but due to "his love of country became shocked at the proposition, and he had resolved to abandon a party who could be induced to countenance the treasonable prospect." John Quincy assured Jefferson that he expected no "official preferment" or "personal aggrandizement in any form."[37] In ensuing discussions with various administration officials and Republican congressmen, Adams would urge modification or repeal of the Embargo in order not to drive moderate Federalists into the arms of the Essex men.

Shortly thereafter, Timothy Pickering, one of the secessionist conspirators, published his "Letter from the Honorable Timothy Pickering . . . Exhibiting to His Constituents a View of the Imminent Danger of an Unnecessary and Ruinous War."[38] In it he attacked the Embargo as one of the most ill-conceived pieces of legislation ever passed by Congress. In proposing it, the Jefferson administration was giving aid and comfort to Napoleon. The Embargo was nothing less than a declaration of war by the Jacobin-controlled federal government on the seafaring states of the Northeast. He called for New England and New York to "interpose" their will, declare the Embargo unconstitutional, and refuse to obey it.[39]

Seventy thousand copies of Pickering's "Letter" were printed and distributed throughout New England. Although John Quincy Adams's name was not mentioned in the broadside, its intention was clear—not only to rally the Northeast to obstruct Jefferson's foreign policy but also to oust Adams from the Senate. The pamphlet appeared on the eve of the elections of delegates to the Massachusetts General Court, the outcome of which would determine whether John Quincy remained in the Senate.[40] "You may depend on it then that your fate is decided. . . . You will be supported by neither Federalists nor Republicans. In the next Congress Dr. [William] Eustis will be chosen senator and you will be numbered among the dead . . . return to your professorship, but above all to your office as a lawyer," John Adams advised his beleaguered son.[41]

But John Quincy did not intend to go quietly into the night. He received a copy of Pickering's pamphlet on March 16. "It may cost me my eyes," he wrote in his diary, "but I cannot remain silent."[42] On March 31 he penned an open letter to Harrison Gray Otis refuting Pickering. In his references to the Essex man himself, Adams was quite restrained, but he attacked the concept of interposition with gusto. "The interposition of one or more state legislatures to control the exercise of the powers vested by the general Constitution in the Congress of the United States, is at least . . . questionable." By definition the concerns of state legislatures were parochial, those of Congress and the executive national. "If the commercial states are called to interpose on one hand, will not the agricultural States be with equal propriety summoned to interpose on the other? If the East is stimulated against the West, and the Northern and Southern sections are urged into collision with each other . . . in what are these appeals to end?" No quarter could be expected from Great Britain amidst these divisions. The Whigs, who were reconciled to American independence, were out of power, and the Tories, who were not, were in.[43]

"These two gentlemen [Pickering and Adams] have lately excited so much attention throughout the union that there is scarcely a newspaper on the continent which has not their names starring in broad capitals," declared the *Albany Gazette*.[44] "The step I have this day taken of publishing my letter to H. G. Otis will be to me of the first importance. It will not be without importance to the nation," John Quincy wrote proudly in his diary. "It was taken from a strong sense of duty. That it will increase the difficulties and dangers of my [political] situation I am fully aware."[45] In the short run, perhaps, but not in the long. Adams was acting out of a sense of duty, but he was also convinced that an unwavering commitment to union at home and neutrality abroad would generate large and long-lasting political capital.

John Quincy, Louisa, and baby Charles Francis returned to Boston to a hostile reception. "Dr. Osgood of Medford attacked me in a rude and indecent manner on the subject of my letter to Mr. Otis," Adams reported.[46] At the end of May, members of the General Court voted 248 to 213 to appoint James Lloyd Jr. to succeed John Quincy even though his term was not set to expire until 1809. It also instructed the state's congressional delegation to vote to overturn the Embargo. On June 8, John Quincy submitted his letter of resignation to the Massachusetts legislature; the notification, which politely defended his decision to support measures of economic retaliation against both Britain and France, was printed in the Boston newspapers and subsequently in sheets throughout the nation.[47]

Soon after his ouster from the Senate, Adams met Harry Otis's father, Samuel Allyne Otis, in the street. He apologized to John Quincy and insisted that his son, who was then the presiding officer in the General Court, "was mortified at the electing of another person in my place; that his son had done everything in his power to prevent it but could not; that the tide ran too strong; that 'the Essex Junto were omnipotent.'"[48] Louisa, for one, was not convinced. "Otis was, is, and ever has been his custom playing a double game talking one way and acting another."[49] In fairness, Harry, a moderate Federalist, was engaged in a political balancing act of his own. He would observe of all the Adams men that they were "a peculiar species of our race exhibiting a combination of talent & good moral character with passions and prejudices calculated to defeat their own objects & embarrass their friends."[50]

Just prior to his departure from Washington in April, John Quincy had been approached by a group of Republican legislators "with intimations to bring me forward in some active and distinguished station." But there were still lingering rumors that in his earlier writings John Quincy, like his father, had expressed a preference for a monarchical form of government. Would it be possible, they asked, for Senator Adams in a speech or pamphlet to make clear his devotion to democracy and republicanism? He would consider it, John Quincy replied, but his record was clear. He had sworn an oath to support the Constitution. He had alienated his party by voting for the Embargo and the ouster of Senator Smith. "But I had not set one party at defiance in this conduct for the purpose of making myself the instrument of another. I would not speak ten words nor write two lines to be President of the United States." Nicholas Gilman, senator from New Hampshire and the group's spokesman, declared that he was satisfied, and then asked John Quincy which post he would prefer, secretary of state or secretary of the treasury. If he were president, Gilman declared, it would be State.[51] John Quincy was, of course, much gratified.

As the relatively close vote in the General Court regarding John Quincy's ouster indicated, he still had friends and supporters in Boston. During the summer, the former senator busied himself with his teaching duties at Harvard, attended meetings of the Society for the Study of Natural Philosophy, and bathed in the bay with George. He found time to read Demosthenes in the original.[52] An hour each day was devoted to instructing George, "whose mind is opening rapidly."[53] One morning in July, the seven-year-old suffered a near fatal accident. Dr. Waterhouse had come to visit John Quincy, and as he was leaving, George went with his father to say goodbye. He fell through the venetian blind door, tumbled down the steps, and struck his head on the stone sidewalk. John Quincy and Louisa feared a fractured skull, but George's injuries turned out to be a severe contusion and concussion, from which he soon recovered.[54]

Officially, John Quincy was retired from public life; unofficially he was not. He maintained a steady correspondence with his Republican friends in Congress, particularly William Branch Giles in the Senate and Orchard Cook in the House. He was, he said, now in a "private station," but a man like him, residing in a democracy, "cannot cease to feel a concern for the affairs of the public."[55] Through letters to prominent Republican figures in Congress, John Quincy offered a running commentary on American foreign policy. He urged the administration to substitute a simple nonintercourse bill with Britain and France for the Embargo in an effort to tamp down secessionist talk in New England. His preference, he said, was to arm American merchant vessels; this surely would lead to war with Great Britain, but it would be purely defensive in nature. The Essex men did not give a damn about U.S. property rights. "For among themselves, I know that they chuckle and exult as much at the operation of the Embargo, as in public they whine and rave against it."[56] At any rate the notion that economic coercion might sway either British or French policy was an illusion. "[N]ations which sacrifice men by the hundred thousand, and treasure by the hundred millions in war for nothing, or worse than nothing, pay little attention to their real interests."[57] Cook wrote him in December that Gallatin and Madison had taken his advice; their plan was to replace the Embargo with nonintercourse no later than June 1809.[58]

In September, Massachusetts Republicans approached Adams about running for Congress. He was tempted but refused because such a contest would have pitted him against his old friend and relation Josiah Quincy.[59] In December they offered him the Republican nomination for governor, but he again declined. In the midst of all this activity, Louisa wrote in her diary, "My three children were all dangerously ill of fever and the dreadful restless anxiety of my husband almost made me crazy."[60] And, in truth, John Quincy was like a caged animal during the winter and spring of 1808–1809. Great events were transpiring both domestically and internationally, and he—a man of destiny, a man for the whole people—was being relegated to the sidelines.

John Quincy arrived back in Washington on February 3; he immediately made the political rounds, visiting Jefferson, Madison, and Robert Smith, who would become the new secretary of state. On March 4, John Quincy, in company with Josiah Quincy, traveled to Capitol Hill to witness James Madison's swearing in as president of the United States. With Catherine Johnson and the Hellens, John Quincy made the rounds of the dinners and balls that followed.[61] At one of the fetes, he and Jefferson were able to have a private word. "[H]e asked me whether I continued as fond of poetry as I was in my youth—I told him yes . . . though my taste for . . . amatory verses was not so keen as it had been when I was young."[62]

On the morning of the sixth while he was at breakfast, Adams received a note requesting him to call upon President Madison either on Capitol Hill or at his residence. He complied and found Madison at his official residence. In thirty minutes, the president told John Quincy, he was going to submit a list of nominations to the Senate; among those was John Quincy's to be America's first minister to Imperial Russia. Madison apologized for not giving more notice, but the press of business had been great. The emperor, Alexander, was very desirous of establishing formal relations with the United States for both commercial and strategic reasons. John Quincy thanked Madison and asked what specific negotiations would be expected of him. None beyond a commercial treaty, Madison replied, but Russia was then the most powerful neutral in Europe. Washington and St. Petersburg had coinciding interests when it came to the great conflagration then raging. Moreover, like Berlin in the 1790s, St. Petersburg would be a most advantageous listening post. His salary would be that which he had enjoyed as minister plenipotentiary to Prussia—nine thousand dollars. When would I be expected to depart? When it is convenient, the president replied, but the sooner the better. Adams told Madison that "I could see no sufficient reason for refusing the nomination, though from the circumstances, the confirmation by the Senate might be uncertain."[63] And, in fact, on March 7, the Senate voted seventeen to fifteen that it was inexpedient "at this time" to appoint a minister to Russia. Most of those voting no went out of their way to make it clear that their opposition had nothing to do with the nominee.[64]

The first Louisa heard of all this was in a letter dated March 9. "I believe you will not be much disappointed at the failure of a proposition to go to Russia—In respect to ourselves and to our children it would have been attended with more troubles than advantage. I had as little desire as expectation of that or any other appointment," John Quincy wrote disingenuously.[65] She later recalled, "I had the satisfaction to learn that the Senate had rejected Mr. Adams's nomination to Russia, a thing perfectly abhorrent to me and which I hoped was done with forever."[66]

Her husband was in fact intensely disappointed. He returned to Boston in a

foul mood. Between April and June a series of essays appeared in the newly established *Boston Patriot*, reviewing the recently published *Works of Fisher Ames*. Ames,
who had died in 1808, was the "pope of the Federalists," as one wag had termed
him. An accomplished classicist, Ames was all Sparta and no Athens. He distrusted democracy, despised "the mob," and spied a Jacobin under every bed. Like
Parsons, he defended British maritime restrictions and even impressment. The
commentaries on Ames's *Works* were not signed, but that John Quincy was the
author was common knowledge. In particularly compelling prose, John Quincy
used the occasion to reaffirm his diplomatic and political principles: nation above
party; neutrality and independence peacefully obtained, but if not, through force
of arms. "While we drop a tear of compassion upon the political weakness of Mr.
Ames's declining days, let us rejoice that the maintenance of our national rights
against Great Britain has been committed to men of firmer minds."[67]

"The [Essex] Junto are now haunted by an evil spirit that will require all the
abilities of all the clergy . . . ," Henry Dearborn wrote Madison. Some Federalist
pastors of Congregationalist churches, such as David Osgood of Medford, were
continuing to deliver hysterical rants against Republican "Jacobins" and their apos-
tate supporters such as John Quincy. "[S]ome incantations have been attempted,
but the diabolical spirit of Quincy continues to appear to them so frequently as to
render it doubtful whether it can be [destroyed], even with the aid of Salem
witches and Northampton deacons."[68]

IT SEEMED TO MANY, especially to the man himself, that the nation had forgot
about John Adams. Neither the Republicans nor the Federalists, especially the
Essex men, had reason to honor his contributions. Critics suggested that he and
the nation would have been better off had he retired from public life following his
vice presidency. But then in 1809, with the United States caught between the
rocks of the Continental System and the shores of the British orders-in-council,
two leading citizens of Boston called on the former president and asked him to
provide the American people with the fruits of his wisdom. "Thousands will hear
your voice," they told him, and suggested that he utilize the *Boston Patriot* as his
forum.[69] Adams leapt at the opportunity, intending not only to showcase his sig-
nature foreign policy of balance and moderation but to defend his record. "I will
either throw off that intolerable load of obloquy and insolence that they [his ene-
mies] have thrown upon me, or I will perish in the struggle," he wrote a friend.[70]
What ensued was three hundred letters, with two printed each week over a period
of three years.

In mid-June, William Eustice, the Massachusetts Republican whom Madison had named secretary of war, wrote John Quincy, urging him to have his father cease and desist. He was attacking men (Republicans) who were in a position to help or hurt his son.[71] John Quincy showed the letter to his father, who was infuriated. "He [John] advised me, if I should be nominated to St. Petersburg, to refuse the appointment," he noted in his diary. "He declared his determination to continue his publications, which I had supposed he meant to suspend for the present."[72]

On July 4, 1809, while John Quincy was attending Independence Day celebrations with his father, his cousin Billy Shaw brought him letters from Washington. It seemed that the Senate of the United States had confirmed him as minister plenipotentiary to Russia; the vote had been nineteen to seven. Five Federalist senators, including Pickering and Lloyd, had voted in the negative. Two Republicans still thought the mission a waste of money.[73] On July 5, without consulting either Louisa or his father, John Quincy accepted the post. "This day the news arrived of Mr. Adams's appointment to Russia," Louisa lamented in her diary, "and I do not know which was the most stunned with the shock, my Father [John Adams] or myself—I had been so grossly deceived every apprehension lulled— and now to come on me with such a shock! Every preparation was made without the slightest consultation with me."[74] Abigail was also opposed to the appointment, if for different reasons. She observed to her sister Elizabeth Peabody, "A man of his worth ought not to be permitted to leave the country," although she admitted that he had been so "traduced and vilified" that a public career in the United States might be out of the question for the time being.[75]

John Quincy Adams and James Madison would make a good team. Both were nationalists who in the breach would sacrifice political considerations to the country's larger interests. Internally there was more agreement than disagreement. Like Jefferson, both Madison and Adams had publicly supported internal improvements and moderate tariffs to bind the various sections of the country more closely together. Madison had taken an extreme states' rights position only to counterbalance Hamilton's schemes. In truth, the president believed that Randolph and the Old Republicans were either naive or wickedly perverse. Madison and his new minister to St. Petersburg were appalled by the New England Essex men and their secessionist schemes. France, they perceived, posed a threat to American independence and would do everything in its power to block further westward growth. But Britain was the more immediate threat; its control of the seas brought the Royal Navy into much more frequent contact with American citizens and their property than France.[76]

The prominent Republican congressman Ezekiel Bacon wrote John Quincy that his friends would have preferred that he played some large role on the domestic scene, but the temporary eclipse of the Republicans in Massachusetts and, perhaps, John Adams's newspaper articles had made that impossible. "A mission to the Court of St. Petersburgh [*sic*] is to a man of active talents, somewhat like an honorable exile . . . though your friends will not probably accede to the position that it was the best thing, yet they will very readily agree that it was a very good thing."[77]

In his diaries, John Quincy could sometimes be nauseatingly self-righteous, frequently displaying a martyr complex and being disingenuous concerning his motives. Once again, he was sacrificing all his personal consideration for his country, he wrote. He was abandoning his aging parents, leaving his professorship and law practice. "It is with a deep sense of the stormy and dangerous career upon which I enter, of the heavy responsibility that will press upon it, and of the unpromising prospect which it presents."[78] In truth he exulted at the prospect of being a Massachusetts Yankee at a major European court. While he was politically and philosophically a Republican to the core, he was culturally a European. Art, literature, science, and philosophy were so far advanced in the Old World that living in the New left him feeling starved. As he had learned at the Hague and in Berlin, a diplomatic post offered much leisure time for study and frequent opportunities to interact with the great scientific and creative minds of Europe.

On June 28, John Quincy delivered what would be his last lecture as Boylston Professor. He was uncharacteristically warm and personal. Since his return, John Quincy's enemies had been attempting to poison his students' minds against him—"Sophistry pining for envy"—or so he thought.[79] But they had failed. Praising their loyalty, he told the class that they must always sacrifice personal interest to public service if the call should come. He advised, "In a life of action, however prosperous, there would be seasons of adversity and days of trial but at no hour of your life will the love of letters ever oppress you as a burden or fail you as a resource. . . . Seek refuge, my unfailing friends . . . in the friendship of *Laelius [de Amicitia*, a work by Cicero] and Scipio; the patriotism of Cicero, Demosthenes, and Burke."[80]

Although Madison had told Adams that he could depart at his convenience, the window of opportunity weather-wise was closing quickly. If the new minister did not depart by the end of July, he would arrive in Scandinavia to find portions of the Gulf of Finland swept by storms that would hold any vessel at bay and prevent it from reaching St. Petersburg. On July 7, John Quincy met with William Gray, a wealthy Boston merchant and shipowner, and inquired whether one of his vessels might be preparing to sail for Russia. Gray, from Lynn, Massachusetts, had risen from a working-class family to become one of the richest men in New England. At its largest, his merchant fleet comprised sixty four-masted vessels.

Gray told Adams that he had available the *Horace*, which could be loaded with cargo in five days and assigned to deliver it to St. Petersburg. Adams and his family were welcome to travel on board as passengers. Gray's only request was that the newly named minister take along his son Francis, recently graduated from college, so he could spend some time in the nations bordering on the Baltic and learn the import-export business. John Quincy readily agreed.[81]

Against his better judgment, John Quincy employed his nephew William Steuben Smith—he of Miranda expedition fame just recently returned from Aruba—as his personal secretary. The appointment put young Smith on the public payroll, much to the relief of his parents. One of Adams's protégés and law clerks, Alexander H. Everett, had asked to serve in that capacity; John Quincy would have preferred him, but blood trumped reason. Adams agreed, however, that Everett could come along at his own expense, joining Gray and another young man, John Spear Smith, the son of Senator Samuel Smith of Maryland (the elder Smith was the brother of the secretary of state).[82]

Again, without consulting Louisa, John Quincy and his parents had decided that George and John—eight and six years old, respectively—would stay behind. On July 23, he called on Mary and Richard Cranch in Quincy and arranged for the boys to board with them. He understood from the president and the secretary of state that the mission would last a minimum of three years. John Quincy would not have to worry about Charles's education for some time to come, but George's and John's were a different matter. There were no boarding schools in St. Petersburg and scarce few tutors, as John Quincy well remembered from his previous stay. He would not have the time to instruct the two boys himself. John Quincy could not summon the courage to tell Louisa; he left that to Thomas, who did so on the twenty-sixth during a visit from Louisa and Catherine. Five days later John Quincy traveled to Quincy to say goodbye to his sons. On the third of August, two days before their departure, Louisa went out for a last farewell; John Quincy did not accompany her. She was, of course, in great distress. I was "not . . . permitted to speak with the old gentleman [John] alone lest I should excite his pity and he allow me to take my boys with me."[83] It would be six years before John Quincy and Louisa would see their sons again. She would never forgive him.

On the morning of Saturday, August 5, 1809, the couple departed their house on the corner of Frog Lane and Nassau Street, bound for William Gray's wharf in Charlestown. With them were Louisa's sister Catherine; one-year-old Charles Francis; a maid, Martha Godfrey; and a recently acquired manservant, a free Jamaican known only as Nelson. There they found waiting the *Horace*, Captain Bickford in command, and the three young gentlemen who were to accompany them.[84] A host of friends and relatives had gathered to see the diplomat and his entourage off. Abigail was not among them. "My dear Children," she had written, "I would not come to town today because I knew I should only add to yours and my own agony. My heart is with you, my prayers and blessing attend you. The dear children you have left will be dearer to me from the absence of their parents."[85]

As the *Horace* got underway, the church bells of Boston and Charlestown were ringing the one o'clock hour. There were salutes from the navy yard and all the ships in Boston Harbor, including the now famous *Chesapeake*. The garrison at Fort Independence paraded in the new minister's honor. Thomas and longtime family friend Dr. Thomas Welsh stayed on board until the *Horace* reached the open sea, then returned to Boston by cutter. John Quincy remained on deck until darkness finally obscured his native land. He would not see it again for eight years.[86] Unbeknownst to Adams, the secretary of state, fearing that the minister to Russia would "not now be able to proceed to any port in Russia in a private vessel," had ordered the American frigate *Essex* to undertake the task. But the *Horace* had already sailed.[87]

As the ship reached the open sea, John Quincy was seized with a fit of remorse. "The separation from my family and friends has always been painful," he lamented in his diary, "but never to the degree which I feel it now. The age of my parents, weakness both in them and me, the hopes of our meeting again; and I now leave two of my own infant children behind . . . the ties which bind me to my country have multiplied with the increase of my years."[88] Yet duty called. And so did ambition, a thirst for adventure, and, last but not least, the stimulation of European culture and society. Burdens would just have to be borne.

Louisa considered herself nothing less than a martyr. She had been compelled to abandon two of her sons, she faced the trials of another transatlantic voyage—the mal de mer set upon her almost at once—and she had to chaperone the notoriously flirtatious Catherine "Kitty" in the midst of three hormonal young men.[89] The only bright notes were that she was leaving behind the rusticity of Quincy and the smothering presence of her mother-in-law. Like John Quincy—and even more so—she was as much European as American.

Off the Grand Banks, Adams spied a flotilla of six New England cod fishing vessels at work. They were hauling in each day a catch of a thousand fish. Thus did John Quincy witness firsthand the maritime gold mines that his father had fought so hard to preserve for the fishermen of New England. The *Horace* beat on briskly, but the weather soon chilled to the point that being on deck was uncomfortable. The new minister to Russia occupied himself reading Plutarch's *Lives* and playing cards with the ladies. On the sixteenth of September, the ship, having passed through the North Sea, came in sight of the Norwegian coast. The *Horace* was immediately stopped by an armed brig, Norway then being under British blockade. Where to? Russia. Where from? Boston. The captain of the Norwegian vessel did not identify himself but demanded that Captain Bickford come aboard. The seas being very rough, he refused, whereupon a musket shot was fired across the *Horace*'s bow. Bickford then attempted to cross over, but his small boat threatened to swamp at every wave, and he returned. After firing another shot, the brig retreated.[90]

That evening the *Horace* entered the Skagerrak, known as "the Chart of the Sleeve," a stretch of calm water separating Norway from Jutland. The next day, the Americans were once again accosted by an armed brig, this one flying British colors. The captain came aboard, examined the Americans' passports, and granted permission to proceed. The *Horace* was lucky it had not encountered his ship at night, the captain said; he was in pursuit of two Danish commerce raiders and would have fired a broadside without asking questions. Captain Bickford decided to put in at Christianssand on the southern tip of Norway for provisions and some respite from the stormy seas. Denmark and Norway had been joined in 1380 to create the Dano-Norwegian Kingdom. It was then allied with France and at war with Sweden, which was allied with Great Britain. The *Horace* had just taken a Norwegian pilot on board when it was hailed by a Danish "two-mast boat with swivel." Its boat crew commanded by a Danish lieutenant came alongside. He boarded and demanded to escort the *Horace* into port, supposedly as its prize. Bickford refused to cooperate. The lieutenant directed his crew, about twenty in number, all armed with swords, to board the *Horace*. "[Bickford] ordered his men to keep them off, and pikes, swords, and axes were in immediate opposition to each other. The lieutenant finding himself the weakest, made a signal to his men to stop, and none of them came aboard," Adams wrote home.[91]

At last, the *Horace* made port. John Quincy found at Christianssand some four hundred stranded American seamen: "the masters, supercargoes, and crews of thirty-six American vessels captured by Danish privateers between the months of April and August, and still detained for trial in the Admiralty courts."[92] Since Denmark–Norway had become part of the Continental System, Danish privateers had been seizing neutral vessels and their valuable cargoes and bringing them into Danish and Norwegian ports to be sold as prizes of war. Officers and crews were left stranded. "These unfortunate sufferers," John Quincy wrote his brother Thomas, "have requested some interposition on my party which, though without authority, I shall hazard if I land at Copenhagen."[93] The *Horace* sailed southward from Christianssand into the Kattegat Sea, which separated Denmark from southern Sweden. As the vessel neared the head of the strait separating the Danish island of Zealand from Sweden, it encountered a picket line of British warships. The *Horace* approached the flagship, the sixty-four-gun H.M.S. *Statley*, Rear Admiral Thomas Bertie commanding. Bertie received Bickford and Adams coolly and told them they could not pass because the coast of Sweden was under strict blockade. They would have to take the western route, the Great Belt, running between the island of Zealand and the rest of Denmark. That would take much longer, Bickford protested; the weather was worsening, and the danger that the waters around St. Petersburg would be frozen over by the time the *Horace* arrived increased by the day. Bertie refused to budge, whereupon John Quincy reminded Bertie that he was the representative of a sovereign nation and that the law and custom of nations provided for the free passage of diplomats. Besides, he had family aboard. Grudgingly, Bertie allowed the *Horace* to proceed. "Of the most ordinary of civilities," John Quincy noted in his diary, "he either neglected or purposely omitted . . . during the whole time we were with him, he never offered us a seat."[94]

The *Horace* then proceeded to the port of Elsinore, situated on the northern tip of Zealand. It was boarded by the commander of a Danish gunboat but immediately given permission to land. The local authorities proved quite hospitable, and the Americans were hosted by agents representing the U.S. vessels that had been seized. With the *Horace* bottled up in port by adverse winds, John Quincy decided to make the twenty-eight-mile overland trip to Copenhagen to appeal to the Danish government for a quick release of the American merchantmen stranded in Danish ports. He was given assurances but could not wait to see them fulfilled, lest the weather at Elsinore improve. It had, and the *Horace* weighed anchor on the morning of October 5.

As the American merchantman proceeded northward into the Baltic, a winter storm engulfed it. While the *Horace* attempted to shelter off the island of Bornholm, the governor sent invitations to John Quincy and his entourage to come ashore and allow him to extend his hospitality. Louisa noted the ludicrousness of the situation: "In the midst of sickness, distress of mind, weariness of body, constant alarm, & not daring to put [in] our last anchor for fear we should lose it—we received an invitation to a ball at the Governor's for eight o' clock in the evening while the vessel was rocking, rolling, and pitching as if she would go to pieces— We were obliged to decline the honor."[95]

Every time the *Horace* attempted to penetrate the Baltic, it was blown backward; the vessel tacked back and forth into the howling easterly but no avail. "[D]uring ten days and nights we were beating to and frow in sight of it [the Baltic], without advancing so much as a league upon our voyage [in] a constant succession of violent squalls of rain, hail and snow, flat calms and strong gales." Captain Bickford, who had completed eleven voyages to St. Petersburg, despaired. He "dreaded the Gulf of Finland infinitely more than the Baltic and a harbor closed against us by the ice at Kronstadt [the naval base guarding the entrance to the Russian capital] still more than the Gulf of Finland," John Quincy subsequently wrote Thomas.[96] The pilot on board, a veteran of thirty-six passages, was even more pessimistic. The two men told John Quincy that it was imperative that the *Horace* retreat to Kiel in the north German province of Holstein, where it would sit out the winter. Once there the Adams party would face a fifteen-hundred-mile overland journey to St. Petersburg amidst unrelenting snow, ice, and wind. Against his better judgment, the new American minister gave in with the stipulation that between Bornholm and Kiel if the winds should turn favorable, the *Horace* would reverse course and head north. Two days later, miraculously, the prevailing winds shifted from the northeast to the southwest, and the ship was able to resume its journey. It took a week to reach the mouth of the Gulf of Finland, where additional terrors waited. The body of water, as John Quincy noted, was formidable in the summertime, but by late October, the Russian winter had settled in and it was dark most of the time; the *Horace* had to contend with narrow passages between unlighted islands and floating ice. But at last, the Americans reached Kronstadt, arriving on the afternoon of October 22, 1809.[97] The voyage had consumed eighty days.

A Russian officer came on board—fortunately he could speak German with John Quincy—and declared that the entire party would have to present itself to at the residence-headquarters of the admiral of the fleet. After a walk of a mile from the wharves, the Adams party reached their destination only to discover a number of other Americans waiting to be "examined." When the admiral discovered who John Quincy was, he had the Adamses ushered into his private quarters, where he and his lady received them most graciously. They would have to wait until the morrow to navigate the final eighteen miles to the capital. Their host summoned the American agent representing U.S. ships arriving at Kronstadt and asked him to find lodgings. None were available, so the party spent the night most comfortably at the agent's—a Mr. Sparrow. Louisa recalled that the first impression they made on Russian society was something less than stunning: "My sister and myself wore hats which had been chosen at Copenhagen that we might appear fashionable—and we could scarcely look at one another for laughing; immense brown beaver . . . as much too large as our American bonnets were too small. Thus accoutered [we were] ushered into an immense Salon at the Admiral's House full of elegantly dressed ladies and gentlemen staring aghast at the figures just introduced to them."[98]

The next morning, as they prepared to depart by cutter for St. Petersburg, John Quincy and Louisa were informed that the *Horace* had been blown back down the gulf several leagues and would probably not be able to return for ten days. All of the party's trunks were on board. Thus were the Adamses singularly ill-equipped as they prepared to call at the imperial court: "Myself a white cambric wrapper; my sister the same; A child of little more than two years old with only the suit on his back, and the Minister with the shirt he had on."[99]

The Americans landed at the quay where the Neva River emptied into the Gulf of Finland at four in the afternoon. The plaza they entered was dominated by the magnificent equestrian statue of Peter the Great. The U.S. consul Levett Harris was on hand to meet them; he had arranged for temporary quarters at the Hôtel de Londres on Nevsky Prospect. It was, John Quincy recorded in his diary, "said to be the best in the city." The next day Harris wrote the tsar's imperial chancellor, Count Nikolai Petrovich Romanzoff, asking him to set a date for Adams to present his credentials. The chancellor appointed seven o'clock in the evening of the following day and observed that the minister was to appear in full court dress. What ensued were frenzied, expensive sessions "with tailors, hatters, wigmakers, shoemakers, milliners and the like description," Louisa wrote. She thought her husband looked "very handsome all but the wig. O horrid! Which entirely disfigured his countenance and not to his advantage."[100] John Quincy made his appearance at the appointed time and was cordially received. Romanzoff accepted a French translation of John Quincy's credentials but informed him that the emperor was temporarily indisposed with inflammation in both legs. He would grant the minister and his wife an audience at the earliest opportunity. The chancellor confided to the American minister that Alexander was much pleased with the appointment and the person who filled it.[101] Three days later John Quincy dined at Count Romanzoff's palatial residence and was introduced to the other members of the diplomatic corps, two of whom he knew. "The rest of the company were strangers to me," he noted in his diary. "But they were all covered with stars and ribbons beyond anything that I had ever seen." The dinner was "magnificent in every particular."[102]

15

Alexander

On November 3, John Quincy received written notice from Count Romanzoff that the emperor would receive him the following day at the imperial palace following mass. That evening the master of ceremonies arrived at the Hôtel de Londres to brief him on the etiquette to be followed. "The formalities of these court presentations are so trifling and insignificant in themselves and so important in the eyes of prince and courtiers, that they are much more embarrassing to an American than business of real importance," John Quincy wrote in his diary. "It is not safe or prudent to despise them nor practicable for a person of rational understanding to value them."[1]

Adams arrived at the palace at one o'clock and was ushered into the royal cabinet, where he found Alexander I alone. The emperor greeted the American minister in French. I am very pleased and charmed to meet you, Alexander said. Veteran that he was, John Quincy responded with all the graciousness due the occasion. The president sent his greetings and desired the emperor to know how much he valued his person and his past expressions of friendship for the United States. It was hoped that the establishment of relations would prove of benefit to both countries both economically and strategically. Indeed, replied Alexander, both the United States and Russia shared common interests as neutrals in the great conflicts in which the rest of Europe were involved. Russia had made peace with France, and although his people suffered from the Continental System, it was the British orders-in-council that bore on his country most heavily. It was the Royal Navy that was sweeping neutral shipping from the seas and that was blockading the Baltic, thus depriving Russia of much-needed raw materials and finished goods. His country fully supported the American principles of free ships make free goods, no paper blockades, and the right of neutrals to trade freely with belligerents. "In the midst of this conversation, he had taken me by the arm and walked from near the door to a window opening upon the river," John Quincy later recorded in his diary, "a movement seemingly intended to avoid being over-heard."[2] Adams carefully avoided expressing an opinion on the comparative op-pressiveness of the Continental System and the orders-in-council but declared that Russia, as the European guardian of neutral rights, would have the full sup-port of the United States "consistent with their peace and their separation from the political system of Europe."[3]

At this point Alexander slipped easily into small talk. How had John Quincy and his family borne the stresses of a transatlantic voyage? He had heard they were considerable. Had John Quincy ever visited Russia before? Yes, as an adoles-cent, the minister replied. Alexander confided that he was fascinated by republi-canism and at a later date wished to hear more about how it worked. What was America like? Did it boast large cities? The two largest were New York and Phil-adelphia, Adams replied; each featured handsome public buildings and private homes, some three and four stories high, but nothing in America could compare with the architectural magnificence of St. Petersburg; to the American eye it ap-peared as a "city of princes." St. Petersburg was indeed a modern city, the tsar replied, and as such devoid of the slums and urban decay that were a feature of other European capitals. But architecture was relatively insignificant. "That a re-publican government whose principles and conduct were just and wise was re-spectable as any other."[4] How did American and Russian winters compare? One of the few blessings of the Russian winters, he said, was that once the roads and rivers froze over, it was possible to reach even the most remote provinces more easily, a matter of no small importance in the vastness of an empire like Russia. Alexander politely dismissed the new minister, and thus began one of the most important relationships in the diplomacy of the Early Republic.

From the cabinet Adams went to be presented to the empress, the beautiful and accomplished princess of Baden. "The Empress, who was dressed in a gown of lace without a hoop, with a necklace of rubies, and a chain of the like precious stones around the head, connected the utmost simplicity with the costliest orna-ment, addressed me by saying she was happy to see me here and inquired about Louisa's health." As he departed, Adams bowed and kissed the empress's hand, an endearing gesture that she did not forget.[5]

Alexander was born in St. Petersburg, a son of the Grand Duke Paul Petro-vitch, later Emperor Paul I. Alexander and his brother Constantine were the fa-vorites of their grandmother Catherine the Great, who considered cutting her son Paul out of the succession and naming Alexander as her successor, but she died before taking that step. In truth, as John Quincy had noted to his friend William Vans Murray in 1800, Paul was as mad as a hatter. He alternated between waging military war against France and economic war against Great Britain. While embracing Denmark and Prussia as allies against France, "he Embargoes all English ships in his ports, sequesters all English property in his dominion, & proclaims the English not to be a race of human beings, but a vermin that infests the sea." His principal adviser, one Ivan Dutzov, was a Turk by birth who had risen from being a servant in the palace to become one of the most powerful men in Russia.[6] By the spring of 1801, Paul had so alienated the Russian nobility and officer corps that a plot was hatched to remove him from the throne. The plan called for key officers and nobles to persuade Paul to step down or to forcibly deport him, putting Grand Duke Alexander on the throne. In March the conspirators confronted the emperor, but Paul resisted and he was beaten and then strangled to death. Alexander had been aware of the plot and acquiesced but on the condition that his father not be killed.[7] Paul's murder would haunt him for the rest of his life.

Catherine had dreamed of transforming herself into an enlightened autocrat. She failed in the attempt, but her vision was imparted to her grandson Alexander. Throughout his life he would be torn between this liberalizing impulse on the one hand and loyalty to the Russian nobility and officer corps on the other. He and his brother had been taught English by their tutor, a thing very unusual for a Russian tsar. In 1804, Alexander had begun a correspondence with President Jefferson in which he asked for recommendations for readings that would further inform him about republicanism and democracy. He was, he wrote, considering granting his subjects a constitution and finding a way to liberate the serfs. When Adams first met the young tsar, he found a handsome, unassuming man who was absorbed in maintaining a balancing act between France and Great Britain during the Napoleonic Wars. He would alter Russia's posture toward France four times between 1804 and 1812, and engage in low-grade naval warfare with Great Britain between 1807 and 1812 as the Royal Navy enforced its blockade of the Baltic.

When Adams arrived, Russia was looking for a trading partner to substitute for, or at least compete with, Great Britain. On March 1, 1809, Congress passed the Non-Intercourse Act as a replacement for the Embargo, an option long advocated by John Quincy. It prohibited American ships from calling on both British and French ports. If one or the other relaxed its maritime restrictions, the president was authorized to open trade with that nation while continuing to embargo trade with its enemy. The measure was intended to elicit concessions from one or both of the belligerents while giving American merchant ships access to European markets through the few remaining neutrals like Russia. For its part Russia lacked both the merchant fleet and the middlemen to conduct trade. For that, it had been almost completely dependent upon Great Britain. Russia exported raw materials—primarily naval stores and iron ore from the Urals—for the finished goods that the Russian nobility depended upon for their lavish lifestyle. Count Romanzoff observed to the American minister "that the English exclusive maritime pretensions and views of usurpation upon the rights of other nations made it essential to . . . Russia that some great commercial state should be supported as their rival . . . the United States of America were such a state and the highest interest of Russia was to support and favor them."[8]

At this point, trade with Russia constituted a small portion of the whole of American overseas commerce. Most of it ran through Great Britain, which allowed it but only after charging exorbitant customs fees. The Jefferson and Madison administrations were as eager as the Russians to nurture direct trade.[9] Most of the merchants in St. Petersburg and other Russian ports were consigners who bought the cargoes of foreign vessels and sold the owners of those vessels raw materials from the interior. They were almost exclusively British and German, the former dealing primarily with Americans because of the common language. They were, as John Quincy wrote an American friend, accountable to almost no one, charging both importers and exporters all sorts of fees and commissions.[10] In the summer of 1807, Alexander had ended hostilities with France by signing the Treaty of Tilsit on a raft in the middle of the Niemen River. In it he committed Russia to enforcing the Continental System; in retaliation Britain blockaded the mouth of the Baltic. In truth, France and Britain were in desperate need of overseas products, Britain from the Continent and France from the New World. Each permitted trade with its enemies but only if they could profit from it. The Napoleonic Wars were as much commercial and financial as military. The British became experts at posing as Americans. In London, Liverpool, and other British ports, the counterfeiting of American ships' papers was a veritable underground industry. Forgers become so accomplished at reproducing the seal of the United States and the signatures of Jefferson and Madison that even the most trained eye could not tell the difference.[11] It fell to John Quincy as U.S. minister to encourage and support Russian neutrality and to maximize U.S. trade with his host country while separating the wheat of authentic American merchants from the chaff of British impostors.

After settling in, John Quincy approached Count Romanzoff and requested Russia's aid in forcing Denmark to release the thirty-six American merchant vessels being held at Christianssand and Bornholm. The chancellor was not unfriendly to the interests of the United States, but he was decidedly pro-French. There was nothing his government could do, he told John Quincy. The French were at Denmark's gate and Napoleon was determined to compel that country to become part of the Continental System. The French-declared blockade of the European Continent was not only onerous to neutrals; it was not working, Adams observed. It leaked like a sieve and the British were growing rich by running it. If the intent of Napoleon's system was to turn British opinion against its government and the war, it was having the opposite effect, he observed. Romanzoff remained unmoved but agreed to raise the matter with Alexander. Several days later an abashed chancellor reported to John Quincy "that the Emperor had judged differently upon the subject from him. He had ordered immediate representations to the Danish Government expressing his wish that the examination might be expedited, and the American property restored as soon as possible, which order he had already executed."[12] By early 1810, Minister Adams was receiving letters of thanks from various American ship captains recently released by the Danes.[13]

Meanwhile, Louisa, Catherine, and their male companions struggled to settle in. Their first accommodation was the Hôtel de Londres on Nevsky Prospect opposite the admiralty—five rooms to accommodate the entire party. The abode did not live up to its reputation. "The chamber I lodged in was a stone hole entered by stone passages," Louisa recalled in her memoir, "and so full of rats that they would drag the braid from the table by my bed side which I kept . . . [for] the child and fight all night long—and my nerves became perfectly shattered with the constant fright lest they should attack the child."[14] The entire party became immediately and violently ill from drinking water drawn from the Neva. Several days later, Consul Harris's assistant found new rooms at the Ville de Bordeaux: "We entered our new lodgings today—somewhat better but very bad."[15]

Shortly after the move, two messengers from the Department of Ceremonies called and informed Louisa that she was to be presented to the empress and the empress mother at the imperial palace the following day. The news propelled Kitty and her into a frenzy of activity. They quickly put together an ensemble from available materials. Her husband was already at court when she departed the hotel. "I was left alone to go through all the fears and frights of the presentation perfectly alone at the most magnificent court in Europe. Off I went with a fluttered pulse."[16] She was attired in a hoop skirt of silver with two trains, one of heavy crimson velvet and another, longer white one with body and sleeves. She and Kitty had managed to procure white satin shoes and a fan. When Louisa arrived at the palace, the empress's lady-in-waiting instructed her to stand in front of a pair of folding doors through which her mistress would enter. Curtsy, but be careful not to touch her person, she was instructed. "Two Negros dressed a la Turk with splendid uniforms were stationed at the doors with drawn sabers with gold handles."

The doors opened and both Alexander and the empress entered. Polite small talk ensued, and the presentation ended. From there it was on to the dowager empress's apartments. If the old lady expected an unpolished provincial, she was surprised. In fluid French, Louisa raved about the beauties of St. Petersburg but then described her experiences in London, Paris, and Berlin. "Ah mon dieu, vous avez tout vue [My God, you have seen everything]!" the dowager exclaimed.[17] Two days later the Adamses attended a grand ball at Count Romanzoff's at which the royal family was in attendance. Alexander made polite conversation with Louisa after which supper was served on fifteen tables, the emperor's ornamented and equipped with solid-gold dishes. Louisa was introduced to the entire diplomatic corps. "[One of the ambassadors told] me I was too serious for a pretty woman and that when 'we were at Rome we must do as Rome'—I told [him] if I should go to Rome perhaps I might." The gentleman was there with his mistress.[18]

The Adamses found St. Petersburg a jarring combination of elegance and severity. In early December they visited the incomparable Hermitage. "Here is one of the most magnificent collections of masterpieces in many of the arts that the world can furnish," Adams wrote. "Pictures, antique statues, medals, coins, engraved stones, minerals, libraries, porcelain, marble . . . the catalogue seems without end." It would take him three months to appreciate the paintings alone.[19] In mid-December John Quincy and Louisa took Charles to a *bal masqué d'enfants* at the French ambassador's sumptuous residence. Some forty children ranging in age from two to twelve were in attendance, all in costume. "We took Charles who I had dressed as an Indian chief to gratify the taste for savages, and there was a general burst of applause when he marched in at which he was much surprised."[20] The boy was then two and a half. With the aid of their mamas, the children danced a polonaise, Charles escorting the daughter of the ambassador.[21] At the same time, most of St. Petersburg's streets were not safe to traverse. "I walked out in the morning and visited the shops," John Quincy noted in his diary. "But it is dangerous to walk the streets and quite out of fashion. The immense number of carriages constantly driving, and the violence with which they drive keeps the walkers in perpetual hazard of being run over."[22] The sun rose at nine thirty a.m. and set at two p.m.; the city was covered in ice and snow from late October through April. Poverty and ignorance among the general population were pervasive and extreme.

As in most Catholic countries, John Quincy reported to Abigail, the royal family and nobility were devout. Mass every Sunday and Te Deums on special occasions. Also, as in other Catholic societies, whether Roman or Greek Orthodox, the clergy served the aristocracy by keeping the common people ignorant and continually fearful of eternal damnation. During Lent the general populace, if not the nobility, remained abstinent. But once Easter mass was celebrated, it seemed that the entire population of St. Petersburg was inebriated for days. Drunkenness, John Quincy observed, was a Russian characteristic; it was the only indulgence available to the masses. "But there is a singular character of harmlessness in the [in]ebriety of this people—Among the multitudes whom I daily meet stagger[ing] and sprawling about the streets, I have never witnessed anything like a fray and scarcely anything like a brawl." This seeming anomaly was, he observed, due to the natural docility of the populace and the ubiquity of the gendarmerie. "Every police officer of the lowest class has the privilege of using the cudgel over the backs of the populace at discretion." At the least sign of disorder by a muzhik in the streets, "the culprit received the immediate admonition of a severe bastinade from some little, spare, green-coated beadle, who seems as if to start out of the ground for that single purpose."[23]

As in Berlin, the Adamses were sparrows among peacocks, but even more so. The European members of the diplomatic corps were equipped financially to match the grandeur of the Russian court. Napoleon encouraged his ministers and officers to spend lavishly. His representative in St. Petersburg, the Duc de Vicence, spent a million rubles a year ($350,000) with the Dutch minister coming in last at fifty thousand rubles ($17,500) per annum. The American minister's salary was nine thousand dollars a year plus another nine thousand dollars for travel and expenses. The first house that the American minister considered leasing cost ten thousand rubles a year—excluding servants.[24] Adams complained bitterly to his parents about the costs of being a New England Yankee at Alexander's court. It appeared, he wrote, that he was going to have to tap his meager personal resources. If John Quincy was distressed, Louisa was distraught. "[T]he expenses of this country are insupportable," she wrote her mother-in-law. The price of a decent house in St. Petersburg was prohibitive. She and Kitty made many of their own clothes, and Louisa was constantly self-conscious about their appearance. "Mr. A has been totally unused to this expense, and every bill that I am forced to bring in makes [provokes a] ruing stare in the face; he has borne it very patiently, but I cannot. It has ever been a maxim with me knowing I brought him no fortune to make my expenses as light as possible, and I am under necessity of relinquishing society here altogether."[25] She could not and did not, of course. Louisa did offer to return to America to spare John Quincy the expense of her and Kitty's wardrobes, but he would have none of it.

Finally, after eight months, John Quincy was able to rent a house for six thousand rubles a year in the Novy Pereulok (New Place) on the Moika Canal. But the rent was only the beginning. To maintain a ministerial household, John Quincy had to retain a steward, a cook, two scullion maids, two footmen, a porter, a coachman, a postilion, a housemaid, and a laundry maid. Then there were John Quincy's manservant, Nelson, and Louisa's maid. Several of the servants had children who lived in the house. And there were bills, bills, bills: "I have baker's, milkman's, butcher's, greengrocer man's, poulterer's, fishmonger's and grocer's bills to pay monthly, besides purchases of tea, coffee, sugar, wax and tallow candles," Adams recorded in his diary. "On all these articles of consumption the cook and steward first make their profits on the purchase, and next make free pillage of the articles. The steward takes the same liberty with my wines."[26] He subsequently discovered that he was missing 373 bottles from his cellar.

Alexander was not insensitive to the American minister's situation. In the spring of 1810, he and John Quincy encountered each other as they walked on the city's main boulevard. The emperor inquired wither Adams and his family planned to rent a residence in the country for the summer, as was the custom among the Russian nobility. He was considering it, John Quincy replied, but did not think it possible. "Why so?" Alexander asked but then seeing John Quincy's embarrassment answered himself: "Financial considerations, perhaps?"

"Well yes, Sire, in large part," Adams had to admit.

"Well enough," the tsar replied. "You are quite right. We must always balance income and outgo."[27]

Adams saw Emperor Alexander at official functions and at various balls and masses, but their burgeoning friendship grew out of chance meetings when the two men took their frequent walks on the Fontanka Embankment, the promenade bordering the Fontanka River. Despite the frigid weather, John Quincy persisted in his obsession with taking long walks as a health measure, averaging six miles most days. It was also part of Alexander's daily routine when he was in St. Petersburg both to maintain fitness and in part to feel the pulse of his people. "It is the Emperor's daily practice to ride or walk," John Quincy noted in his diary, "and when walking he stops and speaks familiarly to any of his acquaintance and often to people whom he does not know, even the most common person. He walks entirely alone."[28]

During their encounters the two men discussed the weather, dress, architecture, and travel. Adams observed that the windows of the upper floors of the palace were often left open. Did not the emperor suffer from the cold? No, it was deliberate, Alexander replied. During the time of his grandmother, it was the custom to be shut up in hot, stuffy apartments. He was convinced it was bad for one's health.[29] During another conversation, Alexander observed that John Quincy often wore a fur cap, a headdress then out of fashion in the capital. Did the fur not irritate his head? No, sire, I have not enough hair for it to matter, the minister replied.[30] Alexander remarked on the arrival of a young American in St. Petersburg; he seemed to be neither businessman nor public official. "He is a young man of fortune who travels for his pleasure and to acquire instruction," Adams told him. His thirst for these must indeed be great for crossing the Atlantic was not like crossing the Neva. "My countrymen, Sire, are so familiarized with the ocean that they think not much more of crossing it than of going over a river."³¹ "It seems you are a great favorite here," France's ambassador, Armand-Augustin-Louis de Caulaincourt, the Duc de Vicence, told John Quincy.³²

Louisa was equally taken with the emperor. She had "had the honor of dancing with [him] a short time ago at a splendid ball given by the French ambassador in honor of the late, great marriage of Napoleon to eighteen-year-old Marie-Louise of Austria," she wrote Abigail. Alexander was "remarkably unaffected in his manners and dislikes very much the forms and etiquette of his court. He is remarkably handsome and very mild and amiable."³³ Alexander reciprocated her estimation; Louisa's beauty, charm, and informality disarmed him. At one ball, Alexander, having learned that Louisa was pregnant, assigned her a special escort so that she would not be jostled by the crowd. Later in the evening, "he again accosted me and insisted that I should go and sit by the Empress who sat on an elevated seat attended by her ladies," Louisa later recalled. "I thankfully declined the honor—when he insisted and said Don't you know that no one says Nay to the Emperor—I laughed and replied but I am a republican—He smiled and went on his way."³⁴ But it was really Kitty who had captured the tsar's imagination.

Like John Quincy and Alexander, the sisters were fond of walks along the banks of the Fontanka. There they encountered the emperor on one of his daily jaunts. Louisa he found disarming, but the vivacious and beautiful Kitty mesmerizing. In truth Catherine was more than a coquette; she had impressed even the formidable person of Abigail Adams, who had written Catherine Johnson, "I do love Kitty sincerely. I think her a charming girl and though not the most beautiful [a nod to Louisa, perhaps] of your family, she is not the less amiable [because of it] . . . ; the wit . . . the easy affability of her manners . . . I think she has stronger marks of her descent from you than any of your other daughters."³⁵ When Louisa and Kitty failed to appear for a period, the next time Alexander saw them, he told the sisters not to miss a day at the quay. "This was a real imperial command in its tone and manner," Louisa observed.³⁶

Kitty was amused; the men of the Adams entourage were not. Alexander was notorious for his infidelities. His longtime mistress, Maria Naryshkina, was a fixture at the court and did nothing to conceal her pregnancies. The empress had lost two daughters and was unable to have more children. You must rebuff the tsar, the three young men insisted. John Quincy looked on gravely but made no comment. Deliberately avoiding the tsar "diplomatic usage did not permit," Louisa wrote in her diary, "and we continued our walks occasionally taking Charles with us who always had a kind greeting from his Majesty and a shake of the hand."³⁷

What ensued was a shell game in which the Adams women were continually invited to the court, where they duly appeared while John Quincy and Louisa worked to make sure Kitty and Alexander were never alone by moving her from one room to another. In May, at another grand ball at the French minister's, Alexander danced the opening polonaise with Louisa, a singular honor, and then he declared that he was off to find Kitty. "[He] took her out himself to dance and she not knowing the etiquettes began laughing and talking to him as she would have done to an American partner, herself beginning the conversation contrary to all *usage du monde*—and he was so charmed with the novelty that he detained Caulaincourt's supper twenty-five minutes to prolong the Polonaise."[38]

The rumor mills of St. Petersburg began to grind in earnest; Louisa and John Quincy were granted a temporary reprieve when the royal family departed for their summer residence. The following October, however, with the resumption of the winter social season, the game was on again. The tsar invited the Adamses—and Kitty specifically—to a private performance at his personal theater at the Hermitage. Louisa had mixed feelings; their inclusion was exceptional and indicated "the great partiality of the Emperor for my husband."[39] But she took alarm when Alexander announced that henceforward Kitty should be accepted at court as if she had been formally presented.[40]

Shortly thereafter, while Louisa and her sister were out for their daily promenade, they spied the emperor hurrying to meet them. Louisa summoned a carriage and whisked the object of his desire away. Alexander was highly insulted, and the next time their paths crossed, he refused to meet the two women's gaze. Louisa feared that her husband would be shunned by both the court and the diplomatic corps, and for a time he was. But Alexander soon relented, letting it be known that he hoped the American ladies would resume their walks—for their health. When subsequently Kitty became engaged to William Steuben Smith, the tsar backed off.

John Quincy was not unhappy in St. Petersburg, despite the emperor's amorous eye and the cold winters. There was in the Adamses' new house a study to which he could retreat to read and write. In October, as winter was setting in, Adams had double windows installed in their residence. The outer panels, twenty-five inches long and nineteen inches wide, were attached to the exterior walls and the inner to the interior walls with about an inch of sand at the bottom to seal cracks. The walls of the house were of stone, two to three feet thick: So well insulated was the Adamses' abode that a fire was required only intermittently. John Quincy observed that during one of the coldest stretches of the year, "We have never . . . had the fire made more than once a day in our chambers. In our bedchamber, it has not been made more than five times this winter, and in the adjoining chamber often not more than three or four times a week."[41] "Double windows, double doors, and stove fires keep our apartments at the exact temperature that we choose to have them."[42]

The threat to one's health in the Russian capital came from moving from indoor heat to outdoor cold. Frequently, members of the diplomatic corps had to stand for hours outside in temperatures that hovered near zero, waiting for the royal family to pass or to witness a military review. St. Petersburg high society delighted in midnight sledding on man-made ice hills. It was not unusual for John Quincy and Louisa to return from one of these dinner/sledding parties at four or five in the morning. John Quincy suffered from intermittent colds; those he could bear, but in the spring of 1810, he was afflicted with twin disorders of the eye and leg. "I had a violent inflammation in my left eye," he reported in his diary in early March, "which continued increasing the whole of this day and was severely painful. At night the eye was almost closed, much swollen, and deeply inflamed." This, of course, was a legacy of his viewing the solar eclipse of 1791 without eye protection. "At the same time, I find myself with a wound on my right leg; how or when received I know not"; it was also inflamed. His eye improved but his leg did not. For two weeks he could barely rise from his bed, the limb so swollen that he could not get a stocking over it. The minister's English doctor applied "a continual fomentation of lead-water mixed with brandy" but to no avail. John Quincy was suffering from an infection later discovered to be caused by a streptococcus bacterium. Eventually his immune system came to the rescue, and by the end of the month, he was out and about.[43]

During the years of his Russian sojourn, John Quincy Adams rarely if ever attended church, save for required Te Deums at the Catholic cathedral to celebrate a birth or an anniversary in the royal family or a military victory. There were a couple of English churches that he chose not to frequent, in part because the British merchants imposed levies on all neutral shipping to support them. Throughout most of his life, John Quincy had read the Bible in its entirety every year, either in Latin, French, or English.[44] He continued to do so in St. Petersburg, supplementing his Bible study with sermons and essays from the famous French Catholic cleric Jean-Baptiste Massillon. During the early eighteenth century, Massillon had headed the Oratorian Seminary of Saint Magloire and preached on numerous occasions for the royal family. He was much praised by Voltaire and his fellow Encyclopedists, primarily because he deplored disputes over dogma and instead chose to speak and write on moral subjects—poetically at times—and about both human passions and human reason. He focused on the universal grace of God and the glory of his creation.[45] The former Boylston Professor of Rhetoric and Oratory admired Massillon as much for his language as for his theology. The French cleric was to religion what Cicero was to statecraft, Adams declared.

Like his father and mother, John Quincy was a believer, but a searching, discerning one. Not surprisingly, his religious convictions were both a complement and a reaction to those of his parents. "You Sir, and my ever dear and honored mother took care to give me a pious education," he wrote his father in 1814, "and although at the same time you sent me upon the theatre of an infidel world . . . the morals or the hopes which I derive from my religion—I have seen nothing in the glories of this world, nothing in the pride of human learning which should make me ashamed of the cross of Christ."[46] But he would come to dissent sharply from his father's Congregationalist-cum-Unitarian beliefs. John Adams was throughout his life a theological quester. He rejected the predeterminism of his Calvinist ancestors although he, like them, believed that it was in the power of individual congregations, and indeed of the rational individual, to find the true path. But John could never convince himself that human beings were innately good. Historical events like the coming of Protestantism and the American Revolution were divinely inspired events intended to get human beings back on the right track, but then, most fell back into error. John remained a disciple of the Scottish philosophers throughout his days. The way to authentic faith lay through reason and study.[47] "I perceive you are a great student of the Bible," he wrote John Quincy in 1813. "But have you studied the Canon of Scriptures? Its history? Its evidence? Its authority? In what sense do you understand the inspiration, the infallibility, and the sanctity of the books of the Old and New Testaments? Have you considered what is to be understood in a literal sense and what in a figurative?"[48] As a Unitarian, the elder Adams rejected the notion of the trinity, taking his stand in one of the greatest and most divisive debates among Christians of the early nineteenth century. Jesus was but a man, a very good man and an instrument of God, but not divine himself.

John Quincy had not delved as deeply into the history of Christian theology as had his father, he declared. He did not say it but implied that a close examination of a thousand years of quibbling over doctrine was hardly conducive to a healthy spiritual life. "My own opinions on this subject have resulted solely from the impression of the scriptures upon my own mind," he wrote Abigail. "The very little of controversy that I have read . . . had rather tended to confirm than weaken that impression."[49] How could a rational believer consider Jesus as just another man? "[Joseph Priestley's] *Socrates and Jesus Compared* is a wretched performance," he wrote John. "Socrates and Jesus! A farthing candle and the sun!"[50] True Christianity was based on faith. At the core of everything was the Sermon on the Mount, in which Christ commanded "me to lay up for myself treasures not upon earth but in Heaven. . . . You think it blasphemous to believe that the omnipotent Creator could be crucified," John Quincy wrote his father. "God is a spirit. The spirit was not crucified. The body of Jesus of Nazareth was crucified. The Spirit, whether eternal or created, was beyond the reach of the cross."[51]

Ever the rationalist, John was skeptical concerning the notion of divine inspiration. His son was certain of it. "I am not sure individuals like Homer, Virgil, and John Milton were visited by the Holy Spirit," John Quincy told his father, but he was certain their works were part of God's creation.[52] "My father has so strong and reflecting a mind," he confided to his diary, "that I always distrust my own judgment when it differs from him. But I think he overrates some of the books which he first read in early life and which opened to his mind philosophical views of nature . . . which struck him most forcibly because they were new to him."[53] He assured his parents that he, like them, believed in a loving, forgiving deity whose grace was open to all men and women. "Exhortations to righteousness and truth, brotherly kindness and charity," he wrote in 1830, "have more prevalence over me than unceasing denunciations of vengeance and punishment." He could not help but observe to his mother, however, that Unitarianism seemed much too nebulous to sustain Christian belief over any length of time.

The origins of republicanism, the Adamses believed, were to be found in the Bible. Like his father, John Quincy was convinced that every individual had been created with a moral component and that every person had the capacity, if not the inclination, to place the interests of society as a whole above their own personal well-being. That capacity was a gift from God. "There is no such thing [morality]," John had written, "without a supposition of a God. There is no right or wrong in the universe without the supposition of a moral government and an intellectual and moral governor."[54] Both Adams men believed that no government was valid that was not based on the consent of the governed. The Declaration of Independence was a covenant entered into by the people of the newly created United States; the notion of coveted communities originated with the Bible. In conversation with a Unitarian divine in 1827, John Quincy observed that "the covenants of the Old and New Testaments . . . seem to me to sanction the political principle that by the law of nature all legitimate government is founded in compact."[55]

Both Adams men believed that Roman Catholicism was a greater perversion of Christianity than Calvinism. John Quincy had witnessed the spiritual and material exploitation of the Spanish peasantry by bishops and priests firsthand during his travels through rural Spain as a youth. Both men reserved special scorn for the Jesuits, who, they were convinced, concealed their worldliness beneath a cloak of piety and who used their intellect and education to perpetuate a manifestly unjust world. The younger Adams was particularly offended by the doctrine of transubstantiation. Christ's offerings of wine and bread on the eve of his betrayal as his blood and body were symbolic. But even if the Savior could perform such a miracle, it did not follow that every priest and bishop could do the same. It was a scheme by the Catholic hierarchy—"corrupt and fallible men like ourselves"—to "enslave the human mind." One's salvation depended upon the "Disposer of All Events" and not on some parish priest or even the Pope.[56]

Despite his fervent belief in the existence of a loving God, John Quincy was troubled by the seeming insensitivity of the Almighty to the injustices of the world. There must, he reasoned, be a hereafter in which "a balance of virtue and of vice" were to be accounted for. If the righteous were rewarded and the wicked punished in this world to the full extent of justice, there would be no need for judgment in the hereafter, he reasoned.[57] In truth, John Quincy could never escape the notion that his personal travails were God's punishment for the sins he had committed. He would comfort himself with the belief that the misery suffered by him and his family was atonement for his transgressions and a guarantor of their well-being in the next world.[58]

Salvation, John Quincy asserted, depended upon faith and works. "That the execution, as a malefactor, of one person, the Creator of all worlds, eighteen hundred years ago, should have redeemed me, born nearly eighteen centuries after his death, from eternal damnation is . . . too shocking for my belief. . . . A melancholy monument of mental aberration and impotence."[59] Like his father, he questioned the notion that Jesus was literally the Son of God. "It is often obscurely intimated," he commented on the latter; "sometimes directly, and sometimes indirectly, asserted; but left, on the whole, in a debatable state."[60] But John Quincy had too much of his parents' rationality in him to leave well enough alone. He would observe to a Congregationalist cleric "that my faith must be subject to my judgment, and that I could believe nothing contrary to my reason and not intelligibly revealed."[61] Indeed, Adams rejected the accounts of Jesus's miracles in Mark, Luke, Matthew, and John as absurd: "The miracles in the Bible furnish the most powerful of all the objections against its authenticity, both historical and doctrinal: and were it possible to take its sublime morals, its unparalleled conceptions of the nature of God, and its irresistible power over the heart, with the simple narrative of the life and death of Jesus, stripped of all the supernatural agency and all the marvelous incidents connected with it, I should receive it without any of those misgivings of unwilling incredulity as to the miracles."[62]

When John Quincy's rationality threatened to overwhelm his faith, he made himself read again the Ten Commandments and the Sermon on the Mount. "I have at all times been a sincere believer in the existence of a Supreme Creator of the world, of an immortal principle within myself, responsible to that Creator for my conduct upon earth, and of the divine mission [not necessarily the divinity] of the crucified Savior, proclaiming immortal life and preaching peace on earth, good will to men, the natural equality of all mankind. . . ." But, he admitted, "I entertain involuntary and agonizing doubts which I can neither silence nor expel. . . . I need for my own comfort to be fortified and sustained by . . . frequent opportunities of receiving religious admonition and instruction."[63]

THE RUSSIAN SUMMER, WITH its long hours of daylight, provided John Quincy with abundant leisure to pursue his intellectual interests and spend time with his family. The internecine warfare with his steward and cook over pilfered supplies led him to an interest in weights and measures. He set about comparing various methods used to quantify precious metals and raw materials from antiquity to the present. He compared an apothecary's scale and weights brought from America with Russian, British, and French instruments of measure.[64] Most mornings were devoted to tutoring the three-year-old Charles in French. "His eyes fly over the page, and when I am pointing to one letter, he insists upon looking at another; upon turning over the leaf; upon hunting for a picture; upon anything but naming the letter to which I point," John Quincy lamented. "The sugar-plums yet serve as a guard against the sentiment of toil, but to dispense them with efficacy is a delicate task."[65] He received a published copy of his Boylston lectures and stayed up all night reading them. They were, he confided to his diary, "the measure of my powers, moral and intellectual. . . . I shall never . . . accomplish any work of higher elevation."[66]

Throughout 1810, John Quincy and Louisa continued to complain about their impecuniousness and the humiliations to which it constantly exposed them. It was ironic, John Quincy wrote his brother Thomas, that he was being attacked in the American press for the lavish expense of his mission while at the same time he was being ridiculed in St. Petersburg for his poverty. The lowliest of European representatives made twenty thousand dollars annually compared to his paltry nine thousand dollars. "He [the U.S. minister] cannot associate upon terms of equality either with the other foreign ministers or with the court nobility of the country or even with the merchants who are making enormous fortunes by American consignments of sugar and coffee." To make matters worse, the members of each of these three classes were showing him and his family every courtesy and attention without any possibility of reciprocation.[67] "[T]he climate does not agree with Mr. A.

so well as America," Louisa wrote Abigail, "and the horror he has of the expense which even with the utmost care he must live at preys upon his spirits and will I fear prove injurious to his constitution."[68] At this point, the redoubtable Abigail decided to take matters into her own hands. Without consulting John Quincy, she wrote President Madison a private note requesting that her son be immediately recalled. The family was much honored by John Quincy's appointment to the Russian imperial court, she declared, but it was threatening to impoverish him both materially and psychologically.[69]

Madison was, to say the least, taken aback. In a handwritten note composed while he was at Montpelier, he declared that it was never his intention to impoverish Mr. Adams and that he would not stand in the way of his immediate return.[70] But he did wonder if Abigail was speaking more for herself than for her son. Both Secretary of State Robert Smith and Secretary of War William Eustis were aghast. Minister Adams's return after only a year would start the rumor mills in America and Europe churning. "Opposition will again and again illiberally repeat what it has before grossly asserted—namely that the mission was devised merely as a provision for certain favorites," Smith wrote Madison.[71] The president was more concerned about the diplomatic implications. A sudden recall might signal to some a break in Russo-American relations; at the least, John Quincy's return would leave the United States unrepresented at the court of Alexander I at a crucial time. Madison instructed the secretary of state to draft a letter agreeing to Adams's recall if that was his wish, but at the same time asking him to reconsider. You have been granted leave, he wrote, but "as no communication of your wishes . . . has yet been received from yourself, I cannot but hope that the peculiar urgency manifested in the letter of Mrs. Adams, was rather hers, than yours."[72]

John Adams was conflicted. "You and your family are never out of my thoughts," he wrote in January 1811. "Your friends often wish you in America . . . but when you return you will find as I did [that] they will not know what to do with you. To make you a great man will be dangerous and to make you a little one will be impossible."[73]

Without having heard from Minister Adams, Madison on February 11 submitted his name to the Senate for confirmation as an associate justice of the Supreme Court. John Quincy did not receive official notification until July, but he read about the nomination, which was unanimously confirmed, in the English newspapers in late May.[74] Both John and Abigail were gratified by the news. The appointment would place their son above partisan politics and provide him a platform from which he could comment upon the great issues of the day. The elder Adams observed that John Quincy "did not love the law so well as other studies," but the Supreme Court was a different kettle of fish from schlepping for clients as a civil attorney.[75] "You will be at home with your children," he wrote Louisa, "to oversee the education of your sons. . . . Both your sons here are fine children, but George is a treasure of diamonds. He has a genius equal to anything, but like all other geniuses requires the most delicate management to prevent it from running into eccentricities."[76]

After John Quincy received official notice of his appointment to the Supreme Court, it required just one sleepless night for him to make a decision. He promptly turned the appointment down, notifying Smith and Madison that he intended to complete his mission to Russia, to stay and look after his country's interests until his services were no longer required. He wrote his parents that Louisa was then well into another pregnancy and that nothing could tempt him to trust the lives of mother and child to the dangers of the Gulf of Finland and the Baltic in late October, the earliest they could depart. Later, he wrote John that he did not trust himself to observe the impartiality that a position on the high court required. "If my own passions would allow me to stand aloof from all politics as much as every judge ought to, the passions of others would involve me in them."[77] A remarkable bit of introspection.

ADAMS CONTINUED TO BE one of the most influential members of the corps diplomatique. Alexander was as aggressive as ever in keeping Russian ports open to American shipping. When rumors of John Quincy's recall reached him, the emperor went out of his way to assure the American envoy "that they had a very great and sincere esteem for me," and expressed the wish that John Quincy would stay on as long as possible.[78] With France and Russia on a collision course and the United States and Great Britain on one of their own, the ministerial post in St. Petersburg became ever more important.

There was another, unspoken reason for John Quincy's decision not to return home. By 1811 his financial situation had improved dramatically. It was not uncommon for U.S. diplomats to act as protectors of and even commercial agents for American merchants trading with their host countries. Adams was no exception. During his stay in St. Petersburg, he served as the guardian of William Gray's immensely profitable business dealings with Russia and through that country with the rest of Europe. Gray—the master of a worldwide shipping network, a man whose net worth was estimated at $2.5 million in 1808—had like John Quincy abandoned the Federalist Party for the Republican during Jefferson's second term. He had supported the Embargo because there were plenty of opportunities for a superrich merchant like himself to cheat on it. Many an American vessel involved in coastal trade fled to Europe with its cargo at the first opportunity. Gray and

Adams had grown close during the summer of 1808, when John Quincy was in political exile in Boston. In early 1810, Adams had written Gray that his meager salary prevented him from representing the interests of his country properly. Gray promptly extended the minister a thirty-thousand-dollar line of credit and ordered his representative in St. Petersburg, C. L. Woodward, to be guided in every instance by the minister's advice. Among other things, Adams counseled Woodward and Gray on the various devices English and Russian middlemen employed to cheat American importers. Many of the ships Adams had freed from Danish admiralty courts belonged to Gray. The *Horace*, which had borne the Adamses to St. Petersburg, sold its cargo of coffee and sugar for $115,000.[79]

In 1811, John Quincy acquired another powerful patron: John Jacob Astor. In that year Astor's Pacific Fur Company had established a fort and trading post—Astoria—at the mouth of the Columbia River in present-day Oregon. The settlement gave Astor and his company control of the river valley up to the fifty-first parallel, where they had come into conflict with Russian fur traders. Several years earlier Paul I had granted a hunting and commercial monopoly on the northwest coast to the Russian-American Company. In 1799 the enterprise established a trading post called Novo Arkhangelsk (present-day Sitka, Alaska).[80] Indeed, at the time, the tsar had claimed all of the northwest coast of North America, including Nootka Sound and everything down to the mouth of the Columbia. Astor dispatched one of his agents, William B. Adams, to St. Petersburg to settle differences with the imperial government before they could get out of hand, and Secretary of State Smith instructed John Quincy to assist him. American citizens had every right to trade with the Indians of the Pacific Northwest, Adams insisted, and under no circumstances would the United States recognize Russian sovereignty over Nootka Sound and the Strait of Juan de Fuca, he informed Romanzoff. John Quincy subsequently worked out a modus vivendi in which the count agreed to respect Astor's interests in return for him providing merchant ships to aid in the burgeoning trade between China and Russian America.[81]

But there were limits to the support John Quincy would accept from American merchants with interests in Russian–American trade. He and Louisa could not help but notice the opulent lifestyle the U.S. consul, Levett Harris, was enjoying when they arrived in St. Petersburg. He had been most attentive, introducing them to the city's social elite and attempting to shower Louisa and Kitty with expensive gifts. Louisa found him unctuous but not entirely repellant.[82] In September an American merchant called on Minister Adams and informed him that Harris was selling the services of his office to the highest bidder. He regularly charged American vessels entering Russian ports up to twenty-five thousand rubles, a sum that he would subsequently split with Count Romanzoff's secretary.

John Quincy was appalled, but he had to tread carefully before accusing Harris because in doing so he would implicate the chancellor's office.[83] Adams later learned that American merchant houses alone had paid the U.S. consul more than one hundred fifty thousand rubles for the privilege of doing business for one year while a single vessel seeking entry in 1809 had been forced to cough up seventy thousand rubles.[84]

16

The Republic in Peril

IN APRIL 1809, SECRETARY of State Robert Smith and the British minister to the United States, David Erskine, signed an agreement in which Britain committed to rescinding its orders-in-council in return for continued U.S. enforcement of the Non-Intercourse Act against France. Shortly thereafter, six hundred American ships laden with desperately needed raw materials sailed for England. When British foreign minister George Canning learned of the Smith–Erskine Agreement, he immediately repudiated it. The pro-American Erskine had failed to compel the United States to accept the Rule of '56 and to allow British warships to enforce the Nonimportation Act. Madison immediately reimposed nonimportation on Britain, but the damage—diplomatically and psychologically—had been done. Frustrated by the ineffectiveness of the Non-Intercourse Act, Congress replaced it in May 1810 with Macon's Bill No. 2, which reopened U.S. trade with all the world but decreed that if either Britain or France would repeal their oppressive maritime orders, the United States would enforce nonintercourse with the other. Duplicity was not the best path to follow in dealing with Napoleon, a master of double-dealing. On August 5, 1810, the Duc de Cadore notified the American minister in Paris that as of November the Berlin and Milan Decrees would be rescinded, thus compelling the United States to reimpose an embargo on British trade.

In August 1810, John Quincy reported to the secretary of state that the Berlin and Milan Decrees had been repealed in name only. It was true that American and other neutral vessels were to be admitted to Continental ports but "upon the payment of duties so enormous that one would think they must be equivalent to prohibitions. . . . In short, sir, . . . the continental system . . . appears terminating in a tax levied upon commerce by France, equal or more than equal to that which Great Britain has levied by the superiority of her naval power."[1] The French revocation "was a trap to catch us into a war with England; a war which England most richly deserves but which would on our part be more than ever impolitic at this time."[2] Despite Adams's warnings, Madison invoked Macon's Bill No. 2, and on February 11, 1811, after Whitehall refused to fall for the French ruse and kept its orders-in-council in place, the president embargoed American trade with the former mother country.

Humiliation from the Erskine affair was only one of the factors responsible for Madison's decision. A new Congress had been sworn in, and it featured freshmen legislators from the Western states who joined hands with hard-liners from other regions to combine into a faction that the press dubbed the War Hawks. Led by Henry Clay of Kentucky and John C. Calhoun of South Carolina, these congressmen and senators were militant nationalists outraged over depredations on the western frontier committed by British-armed Indians, by impressment, and by the refusal of London to cancel or modify its orders-in-council.

Meanwhile, throughout 1810 and 1811, Adams struggled with the powerful French minister to the court of Alexander I, Caulaincourt, to shape the course of Alexander's foreign policy. Adams, aided by a series of French diplomatic blunders, prevailed. Caulaincourt, a close adviser to Napoleon and a fellow soldier, had been dispatched to Russia in 1807 to ensure that the tsar lived up to the terms of the Treaty of Tilsit. When John Quincy arrived, Caulaincout was first among equals in the diplomatic corps. He had found an ally in Count Romanzoff, the Russian foreign minister. Personally, John Quincy was impressed with the Frenchman. "He has a family of sixty-five persons and keeps fifty-six horses in his stables," he noted in his diary, "but in his manner is modest and unassuming. There is a becoming gravity in his manners, and something in his countenance and eye which indicates hardness as well as polish."[3] Caulaincourt seemed similarly enamored of Adams. In the spring of 1811, the French minister in several private and confidential conversations with Adams indicated that if he, Adams, were America's minister to France, a rapprochement could easily be achieved. The previous minister, General John Armstrong, had been "morose, captious, and petulant." He had little or no interaction with the foreign minister, the Duc de Cadore. But John Quincy smelled a trap, and merely replied that he would report France's request for a new representative to the State Department.[4]

It was Caulaincourt's task to counter the considerable English influence in St. Petersburg and to see that Alexander enforced the Continental System. The first week in November 1810, the French minister—at dinner with the tsar—complained that not only were American ships funneling goods into Continental Europe, but English vessels were sailing under forged American papers as well. Alexander replied that the Continental System had so devastated Russia's foreign commerce that the United States remained almost its only trading partner. He informed Caulaincort that he would not close Russian ports to American vessels. Minister Adams was doing an excellent job ferreting out impostors.[5] In truth, the tsar ordered every vessel flying the American flag to be admitted to Russian ports if certified by John Quincy.[6] As of March 1811, when Caulaincourt was recalled, not a single American vessel had been detained by Russian officials.[7]

Alexander's refusal to enforce the Continental System against American shipping was perhaps the crowning achievement of Adams's mission to St. Petersburg. It would play a direct, though unintended, role in precipitating war between Russia and France. On December 2, Napoleon wrote Alexander and complained that "of the 2,000 ships which entered the Baltic this year, not one was neutral; all were sent by the English; all were loaded in London. . . . If one went on appearance, one would think that they came from America, but they all came from England."[8] (Most did come from America.) Alexander recognized that Napoleon was tightening a noose around his neck. During the previous two years, France had annexed the Netherlands, put a French general in line to succeed to the Swedish throne, and provided clandestine aid to the Ottoman Empire with which Russia was then at war.[9]

EVER CURIOUS, JOHN QUINCY used some of his leisure to explore Russian society outside the walls of the imperial court and the mansions of noblemen and merchants. He and a Russian guide visited the Aleksandrovsk Manufactory located some five miles upriver on the banks of the Neva. The facility produced vast amounts of fabric: "There are four or five hundred carding, spinning, and winding machines which are kept at work by three steam engines. The machinery was operated by five hundred orphans taken at the ages of eight, nine, and ten from the foundling hospitals of St. Petersburg and Moscow." The children, who were required to work twelve hours a day, were bound to remain at Aleksandrovsk till the age of twenty-one for boys and twenty-five for girls. For the older ones, there was some encouragement to marry, and squalid apartments were provided for those who chose to do so. The American minister noted that almost all of their children died in infancy because of "the want of cleanliness, and the almost pestilential air. . . . The working foundlings themselves look for the most part wretchedly and very unwholesome."[10] Boys and girls ate and slept in separate dormitories, the windows of which were virtually never opened. Their dinner was thin turnip soup, a dish of boiled buckwheat, and a piece of rye bread. Here then was a perfect example of the coming industrial age: human squalor and exploitation in the midst of ingeniously designed machinery.

Adams was fascinated by new inventions and technology in general. In October and November 1812, he would succeed in securing a fifteen-year monopoly for Robert Fulton for the operation of his steamboats in Russia. Fulton offered to pay him, but John Quincy refused. Such representations were part of his duties, he wrote. Besides, such grants were by special decree of the emperor, and as his personal relationship with Alexander probably had had something to do with the charter, he did not want to profit from it.[11] The advent of the steamboat and other marvels, of course, led John Quincy—being an Adams—to speculate on the origins of human creativity. Some argued that inventions such as Fulton's were products of divine intervention into human history. Nonsense! Creativity might have been a gift from God; machines were merely a by-product of that gift. How creativity itself, artistic or scientific, worked was, however, beyond him, he wrote his father.[12]

In October 1809, John Quincy and Louisa escorted young Charles to another masked ball; this time he was costumed as Bacchus. Charles, it seemed, "has been the admiration of Petersburg and has had the honor of being presented to their Imperial Majesties who played with him near an hour, the Empress on her knees looking at some prints with which Charles was very much pleased," Louisa wrote Abigail.[13] But what the child really wanted was to witness the peasant circuses that were held in St. Petersburg's public squares during holidays. His parents relented, and he and John Quincy visited the stalls at the Square of St. Isaac in the spring. "At the first was a dromedary and two monkeys, a dancing bear, and a couple of poor tumblers." There was a man "whose leg was deformed and seemingly jointed like an arm." He used his foot like a hand to eat, drink, and play the violin. There were tumblers, tightrope walkers, puppet shows, and Chinese shadow performances. "On each side of the church [were] a number of swings and whirligigs filled by a succession of men, women, and children who keep them in perpetual motion. The whirligigs are cross bars something like the wings of a windmill with a large chair, or bucket, suspended at the ends of each bar in each of which two or three persons are seated, and which are swung around perpendicularly by machinery."[14] John Quincy thought them all the "lowest order of public amusements." The grotesqueries were at first too much for the two-and-a-half-year-old, but by his next birthday, he and his father had become regular attendees.[15]

The members of the aristocracy were not without their own physical eccentricities. While attending a fete at the country estate of one prominent nobleman at which there were a number of counts and dukes, Adams was introduced to Princess Woldemar Galitzin, "venerable by the length and thickness of her beard. This is no uncommon thing among the ladies of the Sclavonian breed [she was a descendent of the Sclaveni, a Slavic tribe that had invaded and settled the Balkans in the Early Middle Ages] but of all its examples, she was "the one who most resembles a Grecian philosopher."[16]

In August 1810 the grand marshal of the imperial household, Count Tolstoy, approached Minister Adams concerning an unusual matter. It seemed that the emperor wanted the Adams family's black servant, Nelson, to enter his service. It was the custom of the royal household to employ twelve to fourteen black males clad in Turkish costume to serve meals and perform other menial duties. Those so employed were compelled to sign on for life but were very well treated. "They have a handsome table [and] a carriage and four at their service," Louisa noted in her diary.[17] When one of these servants died, it was, of course, quite difficult for the grand marshal to replace him. Nelson had been approached and wanted to accept the position, but Tolstoy assured Adams that he would not take the man into service unless the minister agreed. John Quincy and Louisa were sorry to lose Nelson's services, but as he wrote his mother, "However, as it was making him a fortune for his life, and as I had neither the inclination, nor in my own mind the right, to keep him against his own will . . . I gave him his discharge and a recommendation to the Grand Marshall."[18] When, subsequently, Nelson expressed the wish to be joined by his wife and children, both Alexander and John Quincy worked to make it happen.[19]

John Quincy and Louisa missed George and John terribly and were periodically guilt-ridden. Louisa wrote her absent boys tender, intimate letters; their father, not surprisingly, was more concerned with their education, especially George's, as he was approaching adolescence. When the two were much younger, John Quincy had written Abigail, "I am afraid there is too much truth in an observation of Lady Mary Wortley Montagu's that the most extravagant and groundless of all castles in the air are those we build on the hopes of our children's virtues or happiness in the world—After all the pains we can take, nature and fortune ninety-nine times in a hundred contrive to disconcert all our purposes."[20] He did not believe a word of it. He was an Adams, for whom molding their children's minds and morals was an obsession.

Like his parents, John Quincy was much influenced by Adam Smith's *Theory of Moral Sentiments*, which argued that human beings were naturally imbued with a sense of their own self-interest and comfort but also with a natural sympathy for their fellow beings that made them feel pain and sorrow of others as their own. The Adamses believed that education should accentuate the value of empathy because it led not only to personal morality but public virtue as well. In a long letter to George written in September 1812, John Quincy urged his eldest son to immerse himself in the classics, "for the lessons of literature, of wisdom, and virtue" that might be collected from them. Read history beginning with Goldsmith's

History of England, for it will acquaint you with the culture and society from which you sprang. Initially you will be drawn in by the narrative, the adventure, and the "character of distinguished personages," but as you grow older, you will come to see much more in the chronicles of the past and be able to assume the ironic, detached perspectives of Hume and Gibbon. Learn Greek and Latin so well that you will be able to read Homer, Demosthenes, and Thucydides, Lucretius, Horace, Livy, Tacitus, and all Cicero with as much ease as if they were written in English. Finally, for insight into human nature, its passions, prejudices, and paradoxes, there is Shakespeare. As you progress through preparatory school and college, John Quincy advised his eldest, do not use your contemporaries as your model but strive always to fulfill your own unique potential. And, above all, make learning a lifetime affair—not for pride of accomplishment but for the thing itself.[21]

In the fall of 1810, it was decided that George and John would leave the Shaws, who were by then quite elderly, and move in with Thomas Boylston and his family. "[W]hile he [George] is made to pursue his sedentary studies with all the assiduity which he can bestow upon them, I wish him also to be inured to bodily fatigues and even hardships," John Quincy wrote his brother. "Let him have no effeminate indulgencies, no cockering, no encouragement to the anticipations of a life of indolence, and ease, and enjoyment. Let his sports and amusements ever be for the hard kind. . . ." He suggested hiking, horseback riding, hunting, and fencing; he was especially adamant about "the use and management of firearms . . . which no man can teach him better than you."[22] But then his feminine side kicked in. My boys should not be devoid of manners and sociability, he wrote Thomas. "As the Graces are ladies, they generally recommend those who pay them the most attention. . . . And as Montesquieu observes, the ladies are the best judges of many qualities very essential to a man's success in the world."[23]

MEANWHILE, RUSSO-FRENCH AND ANGLO-AMERICAN relations continued to deteriorate. The bilateral relationships would have a major impact on each other. If Napoleon invaded Russia, as was increasingly likely, he would drive the tsar into the arms of Great Britain. The specter of war between Russia and France in turn freed London to be much more aggressive with the United States, more resistant to lifting its orders-in-council and modifying impressment. War between the United States and Britain would mean that the Royal Navy would be able to sweep American commercial shipping from the high seas, thus placing St. Petersburg at the mercy of British exporters and commercial regulations.[24] Russia and America would be left to face their enemies without benefit of trade with each other. It was left to John Quincy Adams to fend off the inevitable, then clean up the diplomatic debris when he could not.

On December 2, 1810, Alexander issued a ukase (imperial decree) that effectively barred French overland imports into Russia and that opened the country's ports to all neutrals. He had at long last rejected the Continental System in its entirety.[25] "The frontier of Russia on the side of Poland has been strengthened by additional fortifications, troops, and artillery," John Quincy reported to the secretary of state in January 1811. "[T]he levy of 90,000 to recruit [reinforce] the Russian armies has been followed by a conscription of 120,000 to reinforce those of France."[26] American ships were best positioned to take advantage of the tsar's decree. "Nearly two hundred American vessels laden with valuable cargoes have already entered the ports of Russia since the commencement of this season's navigation—and as many more are expected," John Quincy wrote his father in July 1811. But he expressed the fears that the Russian market would be flooded with sugar, coffee, cotton, and indigo and that the hordes of American merchantmen and their owners would be bankrupted.[27]

John Quincy need not have worried; the desire for American imports caused the Continental System to be outflanked in the late summer of 1811. Food and fiber from the New World poured into Europe as the Prussian and Austrian borders began leaking like sieves. Adams was exultant. "The Emperor Napoleon has been preaching abstinence of sugar and coffee to the people of Europe, with as much zeal as the hermit Peter once preached the recovery of the Holy Sepulcher from the infidels," he wrote. "Finding his eloquence less persuasive than that of Peter, he has invaded, conquered, incorporated . . . half a dozen sovereignties, merely to teach the people abstinence of sugar and coffee . . . he has taxed these delicious dainties beyond all endurance, and he has threatened fire and sword against whoever would not proscribe them." But the commodities were so much in demand and the profits so great in trading them that even the walls of France had been breached and the appetites of her citizens satisfied.[28]

The economic bonanza that Americans were enjoying as they navigated between British and French restrictive maritime decrees would not, could not last long. The outbreak of Franco-Russian hostilities would only embolden the British to crack down on American trade. Meanwhile, Anglophobia was growing fiercer by the day in the United States. On May 16, 1811, the forty-four-gun American frigate the *President* engaged the British sloop of war *Little Belt* off the coast of Virginia. It was unclear who fired the first shot but not the last. The *President* virtually blasted the smaller vessel out of the water. Americans cheered what they saw as revenge for the *Chesapeake* affair, and British tabloids called for blood. Then, on November 7, 1811, three days after the convening of the Twelfth Congress, an

American militia force of a thousand men under the command of General William Henry Harrison clashed with a confederation of Indian warriors led by Tenskwatawa at Tippecanoe Creek in the Indiana Territory. The Indians inflicted two hundred casualties on the whites but then retreated. Harrison subsequently reported to Washington that he and his men had found numerous rifles bearing the stamp of British manufacturers left on the battlefield by Tenskwatawa's fallen warriors. On April 1, 1812, Madison recommended, and Congress imposed, a ninety-day embargo on all foreign commerce, giving time to American merchant vessels to return to port before they could be seized by British warships. It was a clear signal that hostilities were impending.

Not surprisingly, Adams was torn. He believed that British maritime depredations, especially impressment, justified a declaration of war. Impressment was nothing more or less than seagoing slavery, he confided to his diary. But America was ill prepared to fight a war against Great Britain. "Upon the ocean we could do nothing," he confided to Count Romanzoff. How could a handful of American warships compete with the Royal Navy's six hundred men-of-war? Congress had passed a measure calling for the creation of an army of twenty-five thousand. But as there was no provision for conscription in the U.S. Constitution, that would take time. We should not, he declared, "commit the folly of commending or declaring war before we could do something to maintain it."[29] The Republican administration in Washington, constrained by habit of mind and the extreme small-government, no-tax philosophy of the Quids, was leading America into a conflict that it was disastrously unprepared to fight. Upon hearing of the encounter between the *President* and the *Little Belt*, John Quincy wrote Thomas, "A war appears to be inevitable, and I lament it with the deepest affliction of heart and the most painful anticipation of consequences."[30]

The American minister had another reason to dread war with Great Britain. The Embargo and Nonimportation Acts had paved the way for a Federalist comeback in New England, thus rejuvenating the Essex Junto. The party with which he once identified, John Quincy wrote William Plumer, former governor of New Hampshire, had abandoned all its principles and given itself over entirely to the British faction in America.[31] All of Britain was following the elections of 1811 in Massachusetts, hoping for a sweeping Federalist victory, Adams subsequently observed. "However hostile a British ministry may feel against us, they will never venture upon it [war], until they can depend upon active cooperation with them within the United States," he wrote Abigail in June 1811. "It is from the New England Federalists alone that they can expect it, and from them they will doubtless receive it."[32] "If that party are not effectually put down in Massachusetts . . . the Union is gone." All his and his family's dreams for their country would be shattered. "Instead of a nation, coextensive with the North American continent, destined by God and nature to be the most populous and most powerful people ever combined under one social compact, we shall have an endless multitude of little insignificant clans and tribes at eternal war with one another for a rock or a fishpond, the sport and fable of European masters and oppressors."[33]

But if the United States could somehow defend its interests and survive a war with Great Britain, the path to national greatness would be open. John Quincy exulted at the country's population growth. The censuses of 1800 and 1810 showed an increase of between 36 percent and 37 percent for both decades. "It is a phenomenon which the world never witnessed before and which probably will never be seen again," he declared in his diary. The prosperity that the United States had enjoyed during the previous two decades was also unexampled in history. "Blessed be God for it," he wrote; "and may he still protract it, notwithstanding the ingratitude and other vices by which we have forfeited almost the right to ask his favour."[34]

As it was attempting to navigate between the Continental System and the British orders-in-council, the Madison administration continued with its program of continental expansion. In 1808, Napoleon's armies had invaded Spain and taken Ferdinand VII captive. The emperor's brother Joseph assumed the throne. Spain's New World colonies took advantage of the chaos in the mother country to make bids for independence. By 1810, there were armed insurrections ongoing in several provinces; the revolutionaries dispatched agents to Washington to seek diplomatic recognition. Madison was far from ready to take that step, but the Spanish empire appeared to be a piñata ready to be smashed. Washington did move to occupy West Florida, the area between New Orleans and the Perdido River. Encouraged by agents of the U.S. government, the sizable American population there rose in revolt, proclaimed independence, and asked for annexation to the United States. In October, Madison ordered the American commandant in New Orleans to take control of the territory.

These developments were most gratifying to Adams. During one of his strolls with Alexander, the emperor observed, "I hear you have lately made an acquisition." Yes, replied Adams. The Floridas had come to the United States in the Louisiana Purchase but Spain had insisted that they had not. The acquisition of West Florida was just the first step in the inevitable. "One keeps growing bit by bit in this world," quipped Alexander.[35] Adams's vision of an empire of liberty extended far beyond the Floridas, however. "It appears not improbable that one ultimate result of the present war will be the total dissolution of the European colonial system," he wrote Ezekiel Bacon in November 1810. "Spain has every prospect of being irrevocably severed from all her transatlantic possessions." In a conversation with Count Romanzoff around the same time, Adams declared that Ferdinand VII was now a cipher, impotent, unable to exert any influence in metropolitan Spain, much less in its dependencies. "[W]ithout hesitation I do give it as my opinion that all the Spanish colonies will be either independent, or at least have an existence totally different from that which they have been under from the discovery of Columbus to these times."[36] The implication was that independent Central and South Americas would eventually be drawn into the orbit of the United States.

LOUISA FOUND HERSELF PREGNANT once again early in 1811. She suffered from morning sickness and dreaded having another child in a foreign land. She continued to pine for George and John.[37] Then in May came news that Nancy Hellen had died during childbirth and her infant with her. "Mr. Adams and my sister were reading letters just received from America in his study. . . . I immediately saw by their distressed countenances that bad news had come to us," Kitty wrote.[38] "The shock was sudden, unexpected and violent," John Quincy recorded in his diary. "Mrs. Adams was alarmingly ill."[39] Fearing for the health of both his wife and unborn child, he summoned Dr. Galloway, who administered two successive doses of laudanum. As in the past, that seemed to do the trick.

Personal crises seemed to draw John Quincy and Louisa closer together. In late July, on the fourteenth anniversary of their marriage, John Quincy confided to his diary: "There are many differences of sentiment, of tastes and of opinions in regard to domestic economy and to the education of children between us." Indeed, there were. No one would ever have described the Adams clan as merry or gay. Had not Abigail warned her boys against excessive mirth? Noting that there was no biblical reference to Christ laughing, John Quincy declared in his diary after he witnessed a clergyman making light that "the pulpit is not for laughter."[40] The Johnsons, conversely, teased, joked, gossiped, and generally enjoyed themselves at every opportunity. "There are natural frailties of temper in both of us," John Quincy continued his marriage retrospective. "But she has always been a faithful and affectionate wife, and a careful, tender, indulgent and watchful mother to our children . . . my lot in marriage has been highly favored."[41]

In July, Adams's landlord called and announced that the family must be out of their house within two weeks because it had been purchased by the chancellor to be used for public offices. John Quincy replied that "unless he sent me a police officer to turn me out, I could not engage to go at so short notice." He reminded the man that his lease was not due to expire until June 1812. The landlord said that he had expected resistance and that he had been sent only "to inquire whether it would be convenient."[42] The American minister was not willing to risk his relationship with the emperor or any member of his government, however, so he informed his visitor that they would vacate the premises as soon as possible. Fortunately, the Adamses were able to rent a comfortable summer home on Apothecary Island for four months. The house had been listed for a year but remained unsold, so they were able to secure it for a very reasonable sum.

Apothecary Island was situated in the middle of the Neva, north of the capital, some four and a half miles from the city's Garden Gate. It got its name from a garden of medicinal herbs on its southern tip. During the time of Paul and Alexander, it had become a resort, and several members of the nobility had built country estates there. "Our situation is very pleasing . . . in sight of the Emperor's Palace at Kammenoi-ostroff, and nearly opposite Count Stroganoff's garden," John Quincy wrote. "From my cabinet windows I see all the boats passing up and down the river and am as quiet and undisturbed as if it were a hermitage a hundred miles from the city."[43] Two imperial bands performed twice daily aboard yachts moored in the river south of the summer palace so that "with the open doors and windows of warm weather we heard [the music] . . . as if it had been before our own door."[44] In the winter, when the Neva was frozen over, inhabitants of the island could travel to and from the mainland by means of sleighs. In the summer there was a "bridge of boats" that could accommodate both pedestrians and carriages.[45]

On August 12, 1811, after twelve hours of difficult labor, Louisa gave birth to a healthy baby girl. John Quincy was ecstatic. "[O]n this twelfth day of August at seven o'clock in the evening, she [Louisa] had the wisdom to produce me a charming daughter, to you a granddaughter," he wrote his mother. "I think this will convince you that 'the climate of St. Petersburg is not too cold to produce an American,'" he added, quoting one of Abigail's earlier letters.[46] "It is so patriarchal to have sons and daughters," he wrote Thomas. It was "the great end of human existence." He rejected, he declared, St. Paul's dismissal of marriage and family as "a mere indulgence to frailty." If it had not been for its approval of polygamy, he would have much preferred the Koran to the Bible on marriage because it declared procreation to be a moral duty.[47] The baby, named Louisa Catherine at John Quincy's insistence, was christened in an Anglican ceremony on September 9 at the English Factory Chapel by the Reverend Loudon King Pitt. A number of friends, both American and Russian, attended, including Magdalen Astor Bentzon, the daughter of John Jacob Astor. Little Louisa's three godparents were Levett Harris; Madame Bezzara, the wife of the Portuguese minister; and Louisa's close friend Annette Krehmer. "That a Quaker and a Portuguese Roman Catholic should join a Church of England clergyman to baptize the child of a New

England Congregationalist at St. Petersburg, the capital of Russia, is an incident rather extraordinary in the annals of the world," John Quincy wrote his mother.[48]

The emperor and empress had expressed a wish to be the baby's godparents, but Adams, worried about the political fallout in America when it was learned that the child of a republican had royal sponsors, politely declined. Alexander was miffed. Two months after little Louisa's birth, he encountered John Quincy on one of his walks. Had Louisa had her confinement yet? "Yes sire, more than two months ago."[49] The emperor knew, of course, that Louisa had given birth. It was his way of expressing his displeasure, but the rift was temporary, and he and John Quincy resumed their cordial relationship.

Louisa was besotted with her new baby: "Oh, she grows lovely—such a pair of eyes!! I fear I love her too well."[50] When little Louisa's vaccination festered and she became very ill, her mother was filled with foreboding. In her diary she recorded that everyone she met on the street stopped them to admire the child, declaring, "'She is born for Heaven.' The Russians are very superstitious, and I fear that with the impressions already made upon my weak mind during my four years [sic] residence in Berlin, I may be too ready to fall into this [same] error."[51] In January 1812, Louisa received word that her mother had died in a yellow fever epidemic the previous October, as had Caroline's husband, Andrew Buchanan. More bad omens.

The Adams family moved back into town from Apothecary Island to a house John Quincy had rented on Little Officers' Street. The winter of 1811–1812 was one of the most severe on record; during January the thermometer rose above zero for just a single day.[52] "When I walked out yesterday at 4 in the afternoon, Reaumur's thermometer was at about 5 degrees below zero . . . but the heat in the palace halls was almost insupportable."[53] Not surprisingly, John Quincy suffered from one cold and bronchial infection after another. He fought his illnesses with exercise. "Rose before full day-light, and walked my six miles round before breakfast," he recorded in his diary on February 5, 1812. The French ambassador suggested tennis, but John Quincy confided that he had neither the time nor the inclination to learn. He tried cold-water baths after his walks and then hot-water and steam immersions at the city's public baths. Miraculously, he survived these treatments and subsequently limited himself to his walks.[54]

On August 12, 1812, John Quincy noted proudly that his daughter had just celebrated her first birthday.[55] Louisa weaned the baby, which seemed to disturb the child's constitution. She developed dysentery and began to run a dangerously high fever. On the evening of the twenty-second, John Quincy became so alarmed that he sent for Dr. Galloway, only to learn that he was out of town for four or five days on vacation. John Quincy then dispatched a messenger to another physician, a Dr. Simpson, who sent back word that he would come in the morning. Frantic over the child's deteriorating condition, John Quincy went to the man's house, roused him out of bed, and persuaded him to come at once.[56] All he could do was "apply an emetic." When Galloway returned, both he and Simpson advised the frantic parents to move little Louisa out of the city to the countryside; John Quincy duly secured a suite of rooms in a house on the outskirts of St. Petersburg. "The physicians do not expect she will be . . . better until the teeth come through, the breeding and cutting of which they think the occasion of her disease."[57] Nothing seemed to help.

On September 4, John Quincy and Louisa brought their daughter back to their house on Little Officers' Street. "The child is exceedingly ill and who appears every day weaker," Adams wrote. "I endeavor to brace my mind by reason and reflection to an event which I cannot disguise to myself to be probable. But reason has little if any more control over the pains to the mind than over those of the body."[58] In desperation, the parents summoned a surgeon, who lanced the child's gums. On the twelfth she was seized with violet convulsions; Louisa and Kitty attended her night and day. On the evening of the thirteenth, Louisa "was forced to quit the side of the cradle which for three days and nights she [had] scarcely left a minute and remove to another chamber to be spared witnessing the last struggles of her expiring life."[59] "The Lord gave, and the Lord hath taken away. Blessed be the name of the Lord. At twenty-five minutes past one this morning, expired my daughter, Louisa Catherine, as lovely an infant as ever breathed the air of Heaven."[60]

Louisa's death devastated her parents. "She was precisely at the age when the first dawn of intelligence begins to reward the parents' pains and benefits," John Quincy lamented. "When every gesture was a charm, every look a delight, every imperfect but improving accent at once rapture and promise. To all this we have been called to bid adieu."[61] He tried to console himself with the knowledge that the child had been spared the miseries of human existence, but he found himself unconvincing. Why had God taken her away? And why had she been allowed to suffer so? Perhaps as punishment for his sins. Perhaps the toddler's trials guaranteed her bliss in heaven. "And if her long and racking agonies were an atonement for my offences," he wrote Abigail, "I may be permitted to hope that her happiness in immortality will be proportioned to the rigor of her destiny upon earth."[62] Louisa's thoughts turned to suicide. "[M]y babe's image flits forever before my eyes and seems to reproach me with her death," she wrote in her diary a month later. "I feel that all my wishes centered in the grave . . . surely it is no crime to pray for death . . . my heart is buried in my Louisa's grave and my greatest longing is to be laid beside her."[63] She was not alone in her mother's suffering.

Infant mortality in the early nineteenth century was rampant, but no less traumatic for its frequency. The demise of her infant would prompt Mary Wollstonecraft Godwin Shelley to begin writing *Frankenstein* in 1817, two years following the death of her first baby and while she was pregnant with her second. "I awoke in the night to give it suck," she wrote of the first, "[but] it appeared to be sleeping so quietly that I would not awake it," and then in the morning, "Find my baby dead." In the days that followed, "Dream that my little baby came to life again; that it had only been cold, and that we rubbed it before the fire, and it lived," she wrote in her diary. "Awake and find no baby."[64]

Louisa too dreamed of death and resurrection. In one she was back in London at the house on Cooper's Row playing with her little daughter in the full bloom of health. Her father, entertaining gentlemen in the next room, bade her fetch three bottles of wine from the cellar. She and Nancy "descended a flight of steps which appeared to lead to a deep vault, and at the bottom of the stairs I stumbled and fell over a body newly murdered from which the blood still appeared to stream." In another she was playing with little Louisa when a terrific storm with thunder and lightning obscured the sky: "I was left alone in indescribable terror [and] I fell upon my knees and implored the mercy of Heaven when suddenly the thunder ceased and I raised my eyes and beheld . . . a stream of fire which extended completely across the Heavens in which was distinctly written, 'Be of good cheer thy petition is granted.'" She awoke, of course, to find her baby still dead and gone.[65]

By October, John Quincy had apparently grown impatient with his wife's grief and self-pity. He began reading Thomas Gisborne's *An Enquiry into the Duties of the Female Sex*.[66] When he upbraided Louisa for neglecting Charles's education, particularly his "prayers and commandments," she stormed out of the room and sought solace in her diary. "[H]e complains of my being suspicious and jealous; these were faults once foreign to my nature, but they are insensibly acquired by a perpetual coldness and restraint operating on a naturally warm and affectionate disposition." She wished she were home in Quincy, where "in Mrs. Adams I should have found a comforter and a friend who would pity sufferings which *she* would have understood."[67] Once ambitious for her husband, Louisa now not only disavowed it as a trait in her own character—"my heart decidedly assures me that for this great end [attachment to one who aspired to greatness] I was [not] made"— but concluded that ambition was the greatest weakness of her husband and his family.[68] In her memoir, she would warn her children against associating with anyone who would come "to presume that everything that surrounds him must live for him. . . . No sacrifices however great and painful in those who are so unfortunate as to belong to him can satisfy, for he is too much absorbed in himself."[69]

During her and John Quincy's sojourn in Russia, Louisa's relationship with

Abigail had grown warmer. George and John's grandmother wrote detailed and loving accounts of their activities to their mother, whom she had begun addressing as "My dear daughter" rather than "Mrs. Adams."[70] She attempted to reassure Louisa concerning the absence of a dowry: "The subject which preys upon your mind . . . is surely no fault of yours. It was well known to Mr. Adams before he was connected with you and can never be a complaint against you."[71] She could sympathize with the personal travail caused by little Louisa's death. Abigail had herself lost an infant daughter, Susanna. And death was stalking her adult daughter. In 1811, Nabby had noticed a lump and irritation in one of her breasts. She concealed the news for several months but then consulted a physician, who declared that it was just an obstruction of a gland. But Nabby's condition worsened, and she traveled alone to Quincy, where, at the insistence of Dr. Benjamin Rush, she went under the knife. Nabby spent most of the following year at Peacefield recuperating.[72] Louisa was effusive in her sympathy.

In February 1812, John Quincy had received official notification from President Madison that he had selected another man for the Supreme Court and expressed the hope that the minister would remain at his post until the present crises abated. John Quincy, of course, was gratified. That October he wrote his mother that he and the family had become quite comfortable in St. Petersburg, the severe climate and the illnesses that accompanied it notwithstanding. "I know too well my native land and its inhabitants and all the passions that are working and will work among those of my own neighborhood to believe that I shall go home to the personal tranquility that I am enjoying here." But he admitted that whether at home or abroad, he would not be able to abstain from public affairs. "[O]ur ship is in the midst of the tempest and in undertaking any part of her management, it is an inevitable necessity not only to share in all her dangers, but to be made responsible for her fate."[73]

John Adams understood his son and the fate that awaited him. "This nation will not cease to irritate and torment you, both with flattery and reproach till they force you out, that they may have the pleasure of insulting and abusing you." But for you there is no escape. To voluntarily retire from public life would be impossible. "Your nature cannot bear it."[74]

17

War

O N THE MORNING OF September 15, 1812, as John Quincy and Louisa were still mourning the loss of their daughter, a victorious Napoleon Bonaparte at the head of his six-hundred-thousand-man army rode into a deserted Moscow, the ancient capital and cultural heart of the Russian empire. Everyone, including John Quincy, had been predicting war between France and Russia since the fall of 1810. Napoleon had concluded that in the end war was necessary to compel Russia to acquiesce to the Continental System. He would just before invading proclaim to his armies, "At the end of 1810, Russia changed her political system; the English spirit recovered its influences; the ukase on commerce was the first act."[1]

In the autumn of 1811, Russia had begun peace negotiations with Turkey, and Alexander ordered large contingents of troops moved from the battlefront in the Near East to Russia's Polish frontier. John Quincy had reported to Washington that there were two factors prompting these moves: Russia's dependence on income from its exports and Alexander's friendship with the United States. "The Russian commerce of exportation is an object of such importance not only to the nation but to the crown and the nobility who compose the imperial councils and command in the armies that they can never consent to sacrifice it," he had written the secretary of state in the fall of 1811. But if Russia went to war with France to escape the Continental System, it risked throwing itself into the arms of the British government and the avaricious merchants it represented. Alexander and his councilors hoped desperately that the United States and Great Britain would not go to war in order for Russia to be able to depend on American merchant vessels as neutral carriers. But as John Quincy pointed out to Count Romanzoff, the closer Russia and France came to war, the more arrogant and brutal the British became in enforcing their maritime restrictions and in snatching American sailors from their ships.[2]

Minister Adams made it clear to the imperial government that the United States hoped very much that hostilities between France and Russia could be avoided, but he could hardly press the Russians on the matter because he had been instrumental in getting the tsar to resist the Continental System. In a very frank conversation with John Quincy on February 12, Count Romanzoff declared that Napoleon did not understand the complex system of trade that sustained the nations and peoples of the world; even if he did, he wouldn't give a damn! He made war for war's sake and to nourish his dreams of world conquest. "I can say to you in confidence that he once told me so himself," the chancellor confessed to Adams. "I was speaking to him about Spain and Portugal, and he said to me, 'I must always be going after the peace of those, so where could I go but to Spain? I went to Spain because I could not go elsewhere.' He may intend to turn against us from the same want of any other place where to go."[3] In truth, Napoleon's conquest of Russia was part of a grand scheme to surpass Alexander the Great as history's most successful empire builder. Six d'Oterbeck, then minister to the imperial court from the Netherlands, told Adams that "Napoleon had conceived the opinion that he was possessed of supernatural power; that he was more than a human being; and that this phantasy had taken possession of all his family . . . he would finish by establishing a western empire embracing the whole continent of Europe, and that he would claim to be the prophet of God and enact over again the tragedy of Mahomet."[4] Napoleon's army of invasion included auxiliaries from nations he had conquered—the Netherlands, Prussia, Italy, and even Austria. After Russia, he planned to ravish Persia and India, his forces bolstered with Russian auxiliaries.

As was their wont, John Quincy met Alexander as they strolled along the Fontanka embankment in March 1812. "And so, it is that, after all, war is coming which I have done so much to avoid—everything," the tsar blurted out. "He [Napoleon] keeps on advancing. He began by taking Swedish Pomerania—now he has just occupied Prussia—he can't advance much further without attacking us."[5] The following month Alexander departed for the frontier to be with his generals as they prepared for battle. On May 9, Napoleon left Paris to take personal command of his army in Poland. On June 24, 1812, France invaded Russia, and the battle commenced. Alexander declared that he would never make peace as long as there was a single Frenchman on Russian soil.[6]

At the head of his Grande Armée, the largest force ever assembled in the history of European warfare, Napoleon executed a series of long marches, pushing deep into western Russia. He won a number of minor engagements and a major one, the Battle of Smolensk, in August. The French hoped these defeats would demoralize the Russians, but Alexander's forces retreated in an orderly fashion, burning crops, destroying bridges and livestock, and evacuating towns. This scorched-earth policy left Napoleon's huge army to struggle with provisioning. On September 7, the Grande Armée fought a pitched battle against the Russian forces at Borodino some seventy miles from Moscow. With seventy-two thousand casualties, it was the costliest single-day battle of the Napoleonic Wars. Napoleon prevailed but only by the narrowest of margins. When the French entered Moscow, they found it deserted. Bonaparte and his men lingered there for six weeks, waiting for a Russian peace feeler that never came. In October, the French departed, marching southwest toward Kaluga after leaving much of Moscow in ashes.

Most observers predicted an eventual French victory, but not John Quincy Adams. "A more extraordinary phenomenon is here unfolding itself before my eyes," he wrote his father in November 1812. "With a standing army [of] at least five hundred thousand men, the Emperor of Russia by a simple summons to his people has called forth in less than three months three hundred thousand more; who with the caftan, and the beard, and the hatchet, are mingled in among the regiments of smooth-faced, uniformed veterans. . . . Napoleon has taken Moscow, but it is doubtful whether he or his army will ever get back from it."[7] The Grande Armée made side thrusts at St. Petersburg and Riga but was rebuffed.

With the outbreak of hostilities, the French ambassador as well as those emissaries from nations Napoleon had subjugated departed St. Petersburg, leaving the British and Turkish ministers as John Quincy's sole diplomatic companions. There was a chance, he wrote his mother, that the imperial family and its court would have to flee into the interior, but not much of one. Even if that happened, he would remain at his post.[8]

Following the inconclusive Battle of Maloyaroslavets, Napoleon gave up and headed for the Polish border. But he and his men were eight hundred miles from the frontier "with a starving and almost naked army . . . exposed to all the rigors of a Russian winter, with an army before him superior to his own, and a country behind him already ravaged by Himself, and where he had left scarcely a possibility of any other sentiment than that of execration and vengeance upon himself and his followers." John Quincy reported that two Russian armies were converging on Napoleon as he retreated while bands of Cossacks harassed his columns. His auxiliaries, pressed into service against their will, were deserting in droves. But the real threats to the Grande Armée were "General Famine and General Frost."[9] By December, John Quincy was reporting that the road from Moscow to Prussia was strewn with Napoleon's artillery, baggage wagons, ammunition chests, and dead and dying men. By the time the Grande Armée crossed the Berezina River in late November, only twenty-seven thousand out of 685,000 men remained.

John Quincy hailed his friend Alexander as the prince of peace and the savior of European civilization. "It may well be doubted whether in the compass of human history since the creation of the world a greater, more sudden and total reverse of fortune was ever experienced by man," he wrote his mother. For the previous twelve years, Napoleon had bestridden Europe like a colossus, drenching it in blood as he piled on victory after victory. "There has been something so fascinating and so dazzling in the fortunes of this military adventurer . . . that it has kindled into tenfold fierceness all the flames of individual ambition throughout Europe. It has made millions of hearts pant for war which in ordinary times would have beaten only pulsations of tranquility."[10] There was only one drawback to Alexander's magnificent victory; it left John Bull free to turn his full wrath against the United States.

John Quincy had hoped until the very last moment that war between the United States and Great Britain could be avoided. Not that he didn't think that there were compelling casus belli. "Every particle of argument that can bear against the slave trade bears with equal force against impressment."[11] But he recognized how disproportionate the power relationship between the two parties was. "They [the British] are in point of naval force scarcely ten to five hundred," he wrote Abigail, "and our principal object to contend with is unfortunately on the sea."[12] In conversation with John Quincy, Count Romanzoff—desperately hoping that Russia's new ally, Great Britain, would not go to war with Russia's old one, the United States—asked if armed conflict was inevitable. I am afraid so, Adams replied; even without impressment, the United States must defend its rights as a neutral. (He said nothing, of course, about the expansionist schemes of the War Hawks.)[13]

In mid-June, Adams learned that Parliament had on the sixteenth revoked its offensive orders-in-council. The Nonimportation Act of 1811 and Madison's embargo imposed in the spring of 1812 had had the desired effect. By the summer of 1812, Britain was in the grip of a two-year-long depression. Denied American cotton and wheat, British workers were without jobs and food; their protests and demonstrations were shaking the British government to its foundations. British planters in the West Indies as well as shipowners, formerly stalwart supporters of their country's system for maritime restrictions, had flipped. Then Prime Minister Spencer Perceval was murdered in the lobby of the House of Commons by one of His Majesty's deranged subjects. In doing so, the assassin removed one of the government's staunchest defenders of the orders-in-council. But Madison had recalled his minister to the Court of St. James's and so was without useful intelligence during the weeks leading up to the repeal. John Quincy, for one, believed that it would not have made any difference. The abrogation of the orders-in-council was so laden with provisos—the United States would have to furnish proof that France had indeed revoked the Berlin and Milan Decrees—that Madison and Congress would have continued on course anyway. And there was the matter of impressment, a practice that the new foreign minister, Lord Castlereagh, made clear Britain would never relinquish.[14]

Thus did John Quincy Adams's ongoing struggle to preserve American neutrality come to an unsuccessful end. Perhaps it was inevitable, he wrote William Plumer, "that we should be destined to enjoy a perpetual peace, however ardently humanity may desire it, cannot reasonably be expected. If war is not the natural state of human society at all times, it is that for the age upon which we have fallen."[15]

America's minister to Russia was certainly correct about his country's unpreparedness for war. Republican foreign and defense principles emphasized economic coercion, opposition to a standing army and navy, low taxes, a strictly balanced budget, and states' rights. On the eve of the conflict, Treasury Secretary Albert Gallatin wrote Jefferson, "With respect to the war, it is my wish . . . that the evils inseparable from it should, as far as practicable, be limited to its duration, and that at its end the United States may be burdened with the smallest possible quantity of debt, perpetual taxation, military establishment, and other corrupting or anti-republican habits or institutions."[16]

At the outset of hostilities, the War Department issued a call for fifty thousand one-year volunteers. A mere ten thousand responded. Moreover, the country continued to be deeply divided. Though New England would profit mightily from the war until the fall of 1814, the state governments of the region withheld taxes from the federal government; Massachusetts refused to place its militia under command of the War Department. Though specie flowed into the banks of the Northeast, financial leaders in Boston and Philadelphia conspired to withhold subscriptions to government loans until and unless the Madison administration sued for peace. A few days after Congress declared war, a prominent Federalist journal opined, "For the government of a country, without armies, navies, fortifications, money or credit, and in direct contradiction to the voice of the people, to declare war against a power which is able in a few months' time to sweep from the ocean millions of property belonging to the people of that country, is an act of imprudence, not to say wickedness, such as perhaps, was never before since civil government was established."[17]

But the war also had its rabid supporters. Not only the Western War Hawks and their expansionist, Indian-obsessed constituents but the numerous Anglophobe Irish, German, and French immigrants who had flocked to New York and other Eastern cities. Six weeks after the war started, an incident occurred in Baltimore that confirmed the Federalists' worst fears about the threat posed by "American Jacobins." Anti-war editorials in the Baltimore *Federal Republican* had so enraged the city's immigrant population that an armed mob gathered outside its editorial offices threatening violence. Among those inside were former Revolutionary War generals James Lingan and "Light-Horse Harry" Lee. Local authorities spirited the Federalists away to the county jail, where they were imprisoned for their own protection. Undeterred, the mob broke down the doors of the lockup, dragged the men out, and proceed to beat and dismember them. Lingan was killed and Lee crippled for life.[18]

There was much talk among the War Hawks of an easy romp through a thinly defended Canada; in the summer of 1812, the British still had to worry about a rampaging Napoleon even though his attention and armies were then focused on Russia. After taking Canada, American jingoes predicted, militia from the Southwest would complete the conquest of the Floridas. John Quincy was among the most enthusiastic expansionists. "Our means of taking the British possessions upon our continent are so ample and unquestionable," he wrote his brother Thomas, "that, if we do not take them, it must be owing to the want of qualities without which there is no independent nation and which we must acquire at any hazard and any cost."[19]

It soon became apparent that perhaps the United States had not acquired those traits necessary to maintain its independence. Invasion attempts through Lake Champlain, Niagara, and Detroit ended in failure because of the incompetency and inexperience of American officers and the unwillingness of militiamen to fight in an extended campaign. British forces under General Isaac Brock, the governor of Upper Canada, laid siege to Fort Detroit, which was commanded by General William Hull, governor of the Michigan Territory. When Brock sent word that his troops and Indian allies would kill every man, woman, and child in Detroit if Hull did not surrender, the American yielded without a fight, and this to a force half the size of his own. Hull was subsequently relieved of his command, court-martialed, and sentenced to hang. But Madison pardoned him, citing Hull's service during the Revolutionary War. In August, Captain Issac Hull's U.S.S. *Constitution* defeated the H.M.S. *Guerriere* in a fierce battle; the fleet of sixteen American warships went on to win a series of other engagements, but they were drops in the bucket.[20] When, in October, John Quincy learned of Hull's surrender of Detroit, he lamented to his diary, "[T]he honor of my Country! Oh! God! Suffer it not to go unredeemed."[21]

John Quincy began to fear the worst. "Upon a late debate in the House of

Peers," he wrote Abigail, "something having been said of the American Navy, Lord Bathurst, one of the Ministers, told their Lordships that the American Navy consisted of five frigates—and the House burst into a fit of laughter."[22] In the wake of Perceval's assassination, a more moderate government under Lord Liverpool had taken office. It was that regime that had been responsible for the revocation of the orders-in-council, but once hostilities began, pressure on Liverpool from the Tories led by the Marquess Wellesley and George Canning to affect the complete destruction of the United States became intense. "The real object of the present war," John Quincy wrote his father, "is the dismemberment of the American Union."[23] Britain's blind attachment to the practice of impressment was corrupting the country's values and its judgment. "The cause of the press-gang is doubly atrocious as a British cause," he declared. "Impressment as a practice upon their own subjects and within their own territory not only brands the nation with the mark of the most odious despotism but gives the lie to even pretense of freedom in their constitution."[24]

Although he would continue to speak and write bravely concerning America's prospects, John Quincy believed that the only hope for averting disaster was a negotiated peace—the sooner the better—and he was determined to do everything in his power to facilitate that process. With minister to France Joel Barlow's death in December 1812, Adams remained the only accredited minister of the United States in Europe.[25]

On September 12, 1812, Count Romanzoff summoned Adams and informed him that Russia and Great Britain had just signed a treaty of amity and commerce. It was of deep concern to the emperor and to himself that the United States had seen fit to go to war with Russia's new ally. Adams observed that the situation did not have to lead to a disruption in the friendly relations between Russia and the United States. He agreed, the chancellor replied. The two nations were natural allies; their economic and strategic interests exactly complemented each other's. Alexander had instructed him to say that in his relations with third countries, "he would assent to nothing which could interrupt or impair his relations of friendship with the United States."[26] The tsar wondered if the Madison administration would be amenable to an offer of Russian mediation? Adams replied that he could not speak for his government, but he knew that the president longed for peace, as did he. "I knew the [Anglo-American] war would affect unfavorably the interest of Russia," Adams declared. "I knew it must be highly injurious both to the United States and England. I could see no good result as likely to arise from it to anyone." Excellent, Romanzoff replied. He would immediately write the Russian minister in Washington, Andrei Dashkov, instructing him to put the mediation proposal before the president.[27] Russia would make the same offer of mediation to the

British government. Could he in the meantime assure the emperor that despite the existing hostilities between Britain and the United States, Washington would do nothing to provide aid and comfort to Napoleon? Yes, John Quincy replied. To do so actually might discourage Britain from coming to the negotiating table.[28]

When word of Alexander's offer of mediation reached Washington, Madison and his new secretary of state, James Monroe, grasped at it as drowning men would at a life buoy. The president had wanted to declare war on Great Britain as a show of defiance and to preserve the nation's honor, but he was not prepared to and did not want to fight the war he had asked Congress to declare. He immediately submitted the names of Secretary of the Treasury Albert Gallatin, a staunch Republican; former senator James Bayard of Delaware, a Federalist; and John Quincy Adams to Congress as a three-person commission to negotiate a peace with Great Britain under the auspices of Tsar Alexander. Although as yet unaware of these developments, John Quincy sensed that more diplomatic glory lay in store for him. On April 7, 1813, he wrote Abigail that if the offer of mediation was received and approved both in Washington and London, as he hoped it would be, "the measures adopted in consequence of them may make it my duty, as it will be my inclination, to postpone my return home."[29] Also unbeknownst to him, three days after the administration had proposed its peace mission, Monroe wrote John Adams that both he and President Madison heartily approved of his son's negotiating and reporting. It was the intention of the administration to appoint him minister to the Court of St. James's when peace should be obtained. In the meantime, he would be asked to serve on the three-man commission that would negotiate that peace. "His knowledge of the subject in relation to both makes it of great importance that his country should have the advantage of his services in those important transactions."[30] A week later, Monroe wrote directly to John Quincy, outlining his new duties.

EARLY IN 1813, JOHN Quincy and Louisa discovered that Kitty had become pregnant by John's secretary and nephew, William Steuben Smith. "I had a long and very serious conversation with Mr. Smith," Adams wrote in his diary, "who finally avowed a disposition to do right"; shortly thereafter he proposed and Kitty accepted.[31] They were married on February 15 at the Adams household by an Anglican minister. John Quincy was loyal to his kinsmen—sometimes to a fault. There was every evidence that William Steuben was as irresponsible as his father. Indeed, by the spring of 1813, the young man was a thousand dollars in debt to his uncle, a debt neither he nor his father would ever be able to repay.[32]

Servants continued to be a problem. Not only did they persist in stealing from

John Quincy, but he also discovered that one had been keeping a prostitute in the house for several months. Then, in January 1813, the police arrested his coachman "for going into the streets in a woman's dress."[33]

Meanwhile, Louisa had become pregnant again with all of the physical, emotional, and psychological travails that that involved. When a member of the American community died and was buried in the city cemetery, she confided to her diary her fears that she would not be buried on the plot of ground next to little Louisa. "I cannot describe the terror I feel lest they should usurp the little spot of earth which I have set my heart on . . . in vain I reason with myself; the desire is uncontrollable, and my mind is perpetually dwelling upon some means to procure this desired blessing." John Quincy began reading Benjamin Rush's *Medical Inquiries and Observations upon the Diseases of the Mind* published the previous year. "I feel myself called by a duty to devote as much of my time as I can spare to soothe and comfort my wife in her distressed [sic] state."[34] Abigail was not quite so sympathetic: "Despond not my dear daughter, be cheerful [and] submissive. . . . God loves a cheerful Christian."[35] In desperation, John Quincy gave Rush's treatise on the human psyche to Louisa to read. "I confess it produced a very powerful effect upon my feelings and occasion'd sensations of a very painful kind," Louisa subsequently wrote in her diary. "[S]ince the loss of my darling babe I am sensible of a great change in my character, and I often involuntarily question myself as to the perfect sanity of my mind."[36]

But then, after miscarrying, Louisa's physical and mental health improved. "With a grateful heart I return my thanks to Heaven for the restoration of my health and a new sense of the blessings which are still within my power, and I trust in the mercy of my God to pardon the weakness of his creature," she wrote in her diary on March 27.[37] The winter of 1812–1813 was particularly harsh. Everyone in the Adams household suffered continually from colds and fever. (Indeed, few members of the diplomatic corps could last more than a year or two in St. Petersburg. Most reported that it took a year or more after returning home to recover from the effects of the climate.) "The health of your son my dear Madam is a source of perpetual anxiety to us all," Louisa wrote Abigail, "and I myself believe it absolutely essential to remove him to a milder climate."[38] The sicker Adams became, the more diligently he stuck to his regimen of a six-mile walk before breakfast. At one point, he feared that the severe cold had frostbitten his feet, but it turned out to be just prolonged numbness.[39]

One of the primary reasons John Quincy continued exposing himself and his family to the rigors of the Russian climate—in addition to protecting the interests of his country—was the opportunity to meet and converse with Europe's literati. In the spring of 1813, he learned that Madame de Staël had taken up temporary residence in St. Petersburg. Anne-Louise-Germaine de Staël-Holstein was the daughter of Jacques Necker, Louis XVI's director-general of finance. She had been a voice of moderation during the early stages of the French Revolution, attending both the States General in 1789 and sitting in on the drafting of the Declaration of the Rights of Man. During the 1790s she wrote internationally acclaimed novels, travelogues, and treatises on politics and culture. In 1795 she took up with Benjamin Constant, the Swiss-French political activist and writer, and for the next ten years, the couple dazzled the Republic of Letters. She was of the romantic school, her writings privileging the role of feeling and passion in human existence. The lady became a bitter enemy and public critic of Napoleon, for which she was persecuted and forced to flee into exile.

John Quincy wanted to call on Madame de Staël, but with the decline in Anglo-American relations and her avid support of Great Britain in its struggle with Napoleon, he thought it unwise. But then, in mid-March 1813, he received an invitation to attend her salon. When he arrived, the hostess was in the midst of a monologue, heaping praise on the British minister Lord Bathurst and on Great Britain in general. "The lady insisted that the British nation was the most astonishing nation of ancient or modern times, the only preserver of social order, the exclusive defenders of mankind," Adams later reported to his father. When Bathurst replied that Britain's greatness lay in its public and private morality, John Quincy could barely contain himself. But in time all of the other guests retired, leaving the American minister and the madame tête-à-tête. Was he the son of the famous John Adams? she inquired. The very one, he replied. Both she and her father had read and much admired both the *Defence* and *Discourses on Davila*. Madame de Staël wanted to know why America, one of the seedbeds of liberty and equality, had not joined with the allies in taking up arms against Napoleon? It was complicated, Adams replied. She invited him to return the next morning, which he did, and for three hours they discussed moral and political philosophy, and religion. The lady went out of her way to inform John Quincy that she was not a believer. In referring to her observations and arguments, he wrote, "There was neither disguise nor veil to cover their naked beauties, but they were expressed with so much variety and vivacity that the hearer had not time to examine the thread of their texture."[40]

In September 1813, John Quincy and Louisa received word from America that Nabby had died of cancer the previous month. She had decided to embark for Quincy even though she was so racked with pain that she could hardly stand.[41] At last Nabby and her two children had arrived at Peacefield. "Emaciated, worn down with pain, still she appeared delighted to again embrace her parents," Abigail wrote John Quincy. "[O]pium was the only palliative, the only relief she could obtain. . . .

When she had a temporary ease, she was cheerful, conversing . . . [with] her friends abroad and wishing that she might have seen him [John Quincy] again."[42] Abigail Adams the younger died on August 15, 1813, "in the arms," her father wrote Thomas Jefferson, "of her husband[,] her son, her daughter, her father, and mother, her husband two sisters [in-law], and two of her nieces in the 49th year of her age."[43] A week after Nabby's death, Abigail received a very gracious note from Thomas Jefferson. "I will take time now to ask you how you do, how you have done? And to express the interest I take in whatever affects your happiness."[44]

Louisa and Abigail exchanged condolences; unfortunately, the mother-in-law could not refrain from a little grief one-upmanship. "Bitter is the loss of a sweet infant, but how much increased are the pangs which rend the heart of a mother when called to part with the Head of a Family, in the midst of her days and usefulness."[45]

IN JUNE 1813, in one of his conversations with Count Romanzoff, John Quincy expressed gratitude for the emperor's offer of mediation. But from all he could discern from the newspapers and his intelligence sources in London, the Liverpool government would turn it down. In terms of public opinion, this would be all to the good, placing the onus of unreasonableness on the British. He had heard, he continued, that Albert Gallatin and James Bayard had been appointed to join him in a three-person negotiating team. He doubted that this was true. Secretary Gallatin was too valuable to be sent abroad, and, besides, John Quincy's and Bayard's views on international affairs were diametrically opposed. But could the latter not be the very reason they were appointed? the chancellor queried perceptively.

Gallatin and Bayard, as it would turn out, were both willing to compromise even on the question of impressment if doing so was necessary to secure peace with Britain. As a sweetener, prior to the anticipated negotiations, Congress had passed a measure in the summer of 1813 prohibiting the enlistment of foreign seamen in the American navy and merchant marine. In his instructions to Gallatin, Secretary of State Monroe declared that if Britain would not agree to forswear the practice of impressment in return for the foreign seamen's act, the commissioners should hold the line. Bayard had immediately huddled with Gallatin. Both men wanted peace with Great Britain, if for different reasons: Bayard because he was a Federalist and Gallatin because he feared that a prolonged war would bankrupt the republic and destroy everything for which Jefferson, Madison, and he had been working. If the American commissioners were not granted some leeway on impressment, Bayard observed to his colleague, the negotiations would surely fail.

Gallatin agreed. When apprised of the two men's opinions, Madison and Monroe replied that they cared not what form an agreement on impressment might take, but it must provide absolutely for its discontinuance.[46]

On July 22, Romanzoff informed Adams that Great Britain had politely but firmly rejected the offer of mediation because "their differences with the United States of America, involving certain principles of the internal government of England, were of a nature which they did not think suitable to be settled by a mediation."[47] In other words, Britain still considered the United States its colony. Romanzoff recalled that at the time Alexander had first proposed extending Russia's good offices, he, Romanzoff, had speculated that Britain would decline because America was her former possession. The tsar had replied that that mattered not a whit to him. The United States was a sovereign, independent nation, and he was determined that it be treated as such.

Gallatin and Bayard arrived at last in St. Petersburg on July 23 and were presented to the chancellor the next morning. News that London had rejected mediation plunged the Americans into confusion. Was their commission still valid? Would Alexander take another stab at persuading the Liverpool government? Did Gallatin and Bayard have any diplomatic standing at all?[48] In mid-August, Adams informed Romanzoff that his colleagues wished to return home as soon as possible, because they had no powers to negotiate peace outside the bounds of Russian mediation. But then, on the seventeenth, Gallatin gathered his colleagues and informed them that he had received from Alexander Baring of the Barings Bank in London a letter stating that although the British government would not accept a mediated peace, the firm would be willing to enter into direct negotiations with the three American commissioners either in London or in Gothenburg if that was their preference and hinted that there might be some accommodation possible on the issue of impressment.[49]

The Gallatin–Baring pipeline would continue to be a major factor in the ensuing Anglo-American negotiations and a source of intermittent frustration to John Quincy. Albert Gallatin was a Swiss émigré who had risen quickly through the ranks of the Republican Party. He had been elected successively to the House and Senate from Pennsylvania before assuming control of the Treasury. Intelligent, sophisticated, and grounded in the world of international finance, Gallatin was the Republican Party's Alexander Hamilton. The House of Baring was famous, or notorious if you were British, for its American sympathies. One of the partners had married an American, and the bank actually furnished the Madison administration with capital during the War of 1812.

The tsar, then at Toeplitz, headquarters of the Russian–Austrian–Prussian coalition, offered to propose mediation a second time. Meanwhile, on September

19, the American commissioners learned that the U.S. Senate, by a margin of one vote, had rejected Gallatin's nomination on the grounds that he could not simultaneously serve as minister plenipotentiary and treasury secretary. He was out of the diplomatic picture, at least formally, but the three Americans agreed that because Adams's and Bayard's nominations had both been approved, they could carry on. Their official position, conveyed to both the Russians and informally to London through the British minister, was that they were not empowered to enter into direct negotiations; Gallatin was not so bound and began privately communicating with Whitehall through the Barings. Castlereagh made it clear to the Russians that mediation was out of the question before they even had a chance to offer it again.[50]

At this point Gallatin and Bayard informed Minister Adams that they were going to go to Allied headquarters and discuss mediation directly with the tsar. He immediately objected. They did not have the diplomatic standing necessary for such a mission. He and he alone was America's accredited representative to the imperial court. "Both the gentlemen appeared to be very strongly affected by this expression of my opinion," John Quincy recorded in his diary. "They both started instantly from their seats and walked to and fro in the chamber in directions crossing each other and in great apparent agitation."[51] His colleagues thereupon abandoned their plan but informed Adams that they were both going to London. If Gallatin wanted to go to England and conduct himself as a private citizen, that was his business, John Quincy declared. To Bayard, in a separate conversation: you may go and sign whatever agreement you wish, but it will be invalid without authorization from Washington.[52] Adams subsequently confessed that he trusted Gallatin far more than he did Bayard. The treasury secretary and would-be envoy could be presumptuous, but he was intelligent and shrewd, and he had the best interests of his country always in mind.[53] And as Adams well knew, Gallatin had the absolute confidence of Madison and Monroe.

Almost absolute. Gallatin might have been part of the Republican Party's inner circle, but it was Adams who was diplomatic first among equals. John Quincy did not say it, but it was he and he alone of all the Americans who enjoyed the confidence of Emperor Alexander, the man who had driven Napoleon out of Russia and who now headed the Sixth Coalition, which was in the process of bringing France to its knees. And both Madison and Monroe realized it.

At this point Bayard in his official capacity and Gallatin as a private citizen departed for England determined to discover just how much Whitehall would be willing to give on the issue of impressment. Gallatin was uncertain; Bayard was not. He insisted that Castlereagh had already given sufficient assurances of modification such that a treaty was now possible, and he intended to conclude one if he could.[54] With his colleagues' permission, John Quincy reported all of this to Monroe; in his letter Adams expressed the opinion that the British and American positions on impressment were irreconcilable.[55] But it probably did not matter. Unspoken but lurking in the back of everyone's minds was the likelihood that during the following year Napoleon would be finally and utterly defeated, and the global conflict that had made impressment an existential issue for the British would be over. "[A] peace in Europe will leave the war between us and England without any object but an abstract principle to contend for," John Quincy wrote his father in February 1814. "Neither of the parties will be disposed to continue the war upon such a point, and I hope that [this] will make the peace not very difficult to be accomplished."[56]

John Quincy had been a staunch supporter of the war, but he was not willing to risk his country's survival over a point of honor, despite all his rhetoric to the contrary. A rational position, but Adams himself had previously observed that Britain seemed to be fighting France and the United States out of passion and blind hatred; indeed, the former mother country seemed at times to be acting against its own best interests. Gallatin and Bayard departed St. Petersburg on January 25 aboard the *Neptune*. John Quincy sat back and waited for the future to define itself.

Like his patriotism, John Quincy's intellect would give him no rest. "I find it easy to engage my attention in scientific pursuits of almost any kind," he wrote in his diary. Astronomy was particularly compelling: "The day and evening were perfectly clear and gave me a good opportunity to survey the parts of the skies that can be seen from my windows. I recognized the Hydra's head and heart. The two Aselli of Cancer with the nebula between them, the little Lion; the paws of Ursa Major."[57] The only instrument available to him for his survey of the heavens was an "Opera-Glass of Amsden."[58] John Quincy dabbled in comparative anatomy and read Malthus on the overwhelming and irreversible pressure of population on the means of existence. "His pictures of the checks upon population [famine, pestilence, war] are precise, specific, drawn from the most authentic accounts, and turn the stomach with disgust and horror."[59]

18

Ghent

THE FIRST WEEK IN January 1814, Secretary of State Monroe wrote Adams and Bayard, informing them that the president had accepted the Liverpool government's offer of direct negotiation and ordering them to Gothenburg to await further instructions. Later that month, he submitted the names of both emissaries plus those of Henry Clay and Jonathan Russell to be ministers plenipotentiary to negotiate a treaty of peace with Great Britain. Russell's appointment was something of a mystery. He had played a minor role in Massachusetts politics as a Republican. John Quincy had corresponded with him when he was chargé d'affaires, first in France and then in England. In 1814, Madison had nominated Russell to be the United States' first minister to Sweden. But he was not a major figure in American politics nor a particularly distinguished diplomat.[1]

Henry Clay, who was then emerging as one of America's signal political figures, was a natural choice not because of any diplomatic experience but because he was Speaker of the House of Representatives and the preeminent spokesman for the American West. Born into a prosperous tobacco plantation family in 1777 near Hanover Courthouse in Virginia, Clay had been educated initially by an itinerant English tutor. At age fourteen he moved to Richmond to study the law. He soon came to the attention of George Wythe, who had taught jurisprudence to Jefferson, John Marshall, and Monroe. For the next four years, Clay would serve as Wythe's secretary and protégé. When he was ready to stand for the bar, Richmond was saturated with lawyers, so Clay decided to join his mother and her family, who had removed to Kentucky. By the time Clay arrived, a large number of Virginians had settled in the state and created a cultural enclave designed to replicate the society they had enjoyed back home. Clay hung out his shingle and immediately entered politics as a Jeffersonian Republican. He was elected to the Kentucky General Assembly in 1803. In 1810, Kentucky sent Clay to the House to fill an unexpired term where he soon became leader of the War Hawks. In 1811 he was elected Speaker, the youngest in the nation's history until 1839.

Henry Clay, "Harry of the West," was a natural politician, charismatic, socially adept, and pragmatic. Like the Adamses and the members of the Virginia dynasty, he was a democrat and an expansionist; like the Adamses, he was a nationalist and a natural aristocrat. Unlike John and John Quincy, he could boast, brag, exaggerate, and charm the opposite sex. He was an inveterate gambler, winning and losing large sums in a single sitting.[2] From his first gavel to order, the Speaker used his rhetorical talents and power over committee appointments to push the country toward war with Great Britain if it did not relent on the issues at hand. He had insisted on the creation of a twenty-five-thousand-man army and the enactment of the taxes to pay for it. This, of course, flew in the face of Republican frugality. When John Randolph of Roanoke, leading the Quids, moved to block the War Hawks, Clay brought him to heel. Randolph was fond of appearing on the House floor clad in his riding clothes—whip in hand—with his hunting dogs trailing behind. When one member dared to complain, the Virginian assaulted him with his cane. Shortly after becoming Speaker, Clay ordered the sergeant at arms to remove the beasts. When Randolph protested, the Speaker ruled him out of order and threatened to expel him along with his dogs.[3] Clay and John Quincy would lock horns initially, but it became apparent over time that despite their differences in temperament, circumstances and their philosophies of government would draw them ever closer.

Madison needed to put a War Hawk on the peace commission in part to mollify the militants in case the treaty should include significant concessions to the British. Clay was the logical choice. He would defend the interests of the West, but he had already admitted that the United States might have to give up on impressment and that the shape of the peace settlement would depend upon the course of the war. Russell and Clay traveled to Europe together. During their five-week sail across the Atlantic, Clay mesmerized Russell with his charm and force of personality; from thence forward Russell would serve as the Kentuckian's loyal acolyte.[4]

James Bayard, longtime U.S. senator from Delaware, was a moderate Federalist. He had supported Jefferson over Burr in 1801, and then, like John Quincy, he became a vigorous defender of the war after initially opposing it. Federalists, especially Essex men, denounced Bayard as a traitor for agreeing to join Madison's peace mission. He was unmoved, writing that he was compelled by "a solemn duty not to refuse . . . any means in my power which could aid in extricating the country from its embarrassments."[5] Both Gallatin and Adams considered Bayard a true and disinterested patriot. Unfortunately, the Delaware Federalist contracted dysentery from drinking water from the Neva. Despite bleeding, emetics, and leeches, he would die of the disease within a week of his return to the United States in 1815.

Adams regretted the exclusion of Albert Gallatin from the mission. "His desire to accomplish the peace was sincere and ardent," he wrote Abigail. "I had several opportunities of observing his quickness of understanding, his sagacity and penetration, and the soundness of his judgment."[6] Gallatin seemed to reciprocate the sentiment. "I will ever retain a grateful sense of yours and Mrs. Adams's civilities and kindness at St. Petersburg," he wrote John Quincy from England, "but I fear that bad health and worse spirits made me still more dull than usual."[7]

Who would be first among equals in the American delegation was unclear. It seemed, however, that John Quincy, by dint of his experience and acumen, would serve as chief negotiator. In April 1814, Richard Rush, Madison's attorney general, wrote John Adams concerning his eldest son: "[H]is diplomatic correspondence on file in the Department of State exhibited . . . a fullness, an elegance, an accuracy, an extent of observation, a sagacity, a profoundness of political knowledge and forecast not equaled by any other similar dispatches to be seen from the pen of a foreign minister appointed under the present Constitution." That same month John Adams sent to Rush a copy of John Quincy's long letter on the Russian offer of mediation and the British government's motives in rejecting it. "The President and Mr. Monroe have read it with the greatest interest and pleasure," Rush responded.[8]

In March 1814 the American commissioners received their instructions from Secretary of State Monroe. The president was adamant concerning impressment, he wrote. "This degrading practice must cease; our flag must protect the crew or the United States cannot consider themselves an independent nation." Congress's action in barring British seamen from service on American ships should have been more than sufficient to induce the Admiralty to give up the practice. On British maritime restrictions, Monroe declared, you shall have ample room to compromise, although the practice of paper blockade was most offensive. Press for disarmament on the Great Lakes; the continued presence of British–Canadian naval vessels there would be invitations to another war. If possible, settle the prewar territorial disputes along the Canadian–American boundary in the Northeast and the Northwest. Enslaved people who had been carried off to the West Indies during the Revolutionary War should be returned or paid for. No mention was made of either party's right to navigate the Mississippi River. In a separate, confidential note to the commissioners, Monroe instructed them to obtain Canada from Britain if they could, on the grounds that there could never be peace as long as this outpost of British imperialism existed to intrigue with the Indians and threaten American sovereignty.[9] All parties involved recognized that impressment would be the be-all and end-all of the negotiations. "The only way of coming to terms of peace with England . . . at this time," John Quincy wrote his father, "is to leave the question just where it was, saying nothing about it. But I know such a peace would not satisfy the people of America, and I have no desire to be instrumental in concluding it."[10]

On April 27, John Quincy learned that Napoleon had abdicated and been sent into exile on the island of Elba. The Allies were united in victory for the time being, he wrote his father, but unity could not last. There were issues that would inevitably divide them. The most immediate problem was what to do with France. "The Bourbons are to receive France and France is to receive the Bourbons as presents from the allies." French power would have to be hedged in but not to the point that the restrictions imposed would sow the seeds of a future war.[11] The key to a peaceful future, John Quincy declared, lay with Russia. "The real part for the Emperor Alexander now to perform is that of the umpire and arbitrator of Europe. [H]e must lay aside all his own passions and resist all the investigations of his co-operators."[12] Adams hoped to make the forthcoming Anglo-American peace negotiations a piece of the larger picture, a component of the negotiations that would transpire at the forthcoming Congress of Vienna. "I do not consider the questions at issue between the United States and Great Britain as questions in which the continent of Europe has no interest—not even the question of impressment."[13] His hope that Russia and the other maritime nations of Europe would make common cause with America against the British would prove to be a pipe dream, however.

On March 20, John Quincy learned that Clay and Russell would not be able to set sail from America until April 1 at the earliest. Nonetheless, he immediately began preparing for his trip to Gothenburg. Louisa and Charles were to be left behind in St. Petersburg with chargé d'affaires Levett Harris serving as their protector. Adams's plan was to travel overland to Reval (Tallinn in present-day Estonia) and from thence by sea to Gothenburg, which was situated on the west coast of Sweden. "At half past one o'clock in the afternoon I left my house. . . . My dear wife and Charles came with me to Strelna, the first stage, where we dined together at the Post-house opposite the Grand Duke Constantine's Summer Palace. At half past four I embraced them and committed them to the protection of a kind and gracious Providence."[14] It would be a little over a year before he would see his wife and youngest son again. "I have become once more a wayfaring man," he wrote in his diary, "and am separated from every part of my family."[15]

The trip to Reval was marred by a carriage mishap in which the tongue attaching the harnessed horses to the coach was broken in two. With the help of some local peasants, the postriders lashed the broken parts together until the next town could be reached and repairs made. When Adams reached Reval, the city was celebrating Napoleon's defeat. Business acquaintances had arranged apartments for Adams; no sooner was he settled in than a delegation from the Young Merchants Club showed up and invited him to their festivities. He accepted, and they headed to the club amidst parades, serenades, fireworks, and the ringing of city bells.

Due to contrary winds and ice floes blocking the harbor, John Quincy would remain bottled up in Reval for nineteen days. He complained to Louisa that he had never felt so lonely in his life. His thoughts turned to death. "Among the papers which I ought and intended to have left with you, but which in the hurry of departure I took with me . . . is my will of which you are constituted the sole executrix for all my affairs out of the United States." He promised to send a copy by the next post.[16] Louisa wrote back that she was overwhelmed by John Quincy's trust in her. It did much to relieve the guilt that had been haunting her since they were first married. John Quincy in reply: "[L]et me repeat the wish I have so often expressed to you that if ever a suspicion, tending to give you disquietude should again obtrude itself upon your mind, you would disclose it at once and give me the opportunity of proving to you not only my confidence in you, but how much I have at heart the comfort and happiness of your life."[17]

On April 19, John Quincy boarded the *Ulysses*, a German vessel sailing under Russian colors bound for Stockholm. No sooner had the ship cleared harbor than it encountered an endless chain of ice islands. The captain spent the night attempting to find a passage, but after the *Ulysses* struck one of the ice floes, he ordered a return to port. John Quincy chose to remain on board in case a more favorable wind sprang up and an opening appeared in the ice fields. "In the cabin where I sit, there is no fire," he wrote Louisa. "The thermometer is between 8 and 9 degrees, and my fingers are so benumbed that I can scarcely hold a pen." On the twenty-first, the *Ulysses,* propelled by fresh winds from the northeast, managed to clear port. "We have been nearly 36 hours coasting along the ice-fields to and fro across the gulf with calms and light breezes," he wrote on the twenty-first. Slowly, carefully, the *Ulysses* steered along the rocky coast of Finland with a floating ice island to starboard. Finally, on May 25, the vessel reached Stockholm.[18]

Adams took lodgings at the English Tavern and the next day rendezvoused with Jonathan Russell, who was in the city with his secretary and fourteen-year-old son. From him John Quincy learned that Albert Gallatin had been added to the American delegation and that Gallatin and Bayard, still in England, had agreed to the transfer of negotiations from Gothenburg to Ghent in Belgium. Of this move John Quincy did not approve; Ghent was then garrisoned by British troops. So disturbed was he by this news and Monroe's instructions insisting on British renunciation of impressment that he briefly considered returning to St. Petersburg. But duty called, and the Russell party and he made their way overland to Gothenburg, where the corvette U.S.S. *John Adams* waited to transport them to the Netherlands.[19]

On June 11, 1814, Adams, along with Russell and his entourage, boarded; they were greeted by the ship's marines standing at arms and by a thirteen-gun salute. John Quincy had considered leaving his heavy Swedish carriage behind but changed his mind, and it was loaded aboard from a tender. As the *John Adams* waited to depart, a Frenchman appeared onboard and begged to be taken to America. Adams considered the request briefly, but then dismissed the petitioner when he found that he was a royal hairdresser by trade; he "menaced me with a wig," Adams chuckled.[20] The six-day trip from Gothenburg to Amsterdam proved to be a balm. The officers of the *John Adams* were all veterans of previous naval engagements: "Here, I am in a manner at home; surrounded by my countrymen— and have as much society as I could wish."[21] John Quincy's worries were mostly logistical. His Swedish servant, Axel, had chosen to remain behind. When Adams landed in the Netherlands, he would hire Antoine Guista, a Piedmontese and veteran of Napoleon's army who had been set adrift by the peace. Guista would remain a faithful and valuable employee for the next fifteen years. Amazingly, Adams's appointment as minister plenipotentiary to the American peace delegation did not provide for a secretary. John Quincy had issued a plea to the State Department because in the forthcoming negotiations there would be hundreds of pages of documents to be copied and recopied; he could hardly accomplish the task by himself. But as of his departure from Stockholm, there had been no word from Washington.[22]

The *John Adams* arrived safely at Texel roads on the afternoon of June 17. John Quincy in his heavy Swedish carriage and the Russells in a light two-wheeled chaise made the fifty-mile journey to Amsterdam easily in a day. They had hoped to find the other members of the American delegation there but were disappointed. Adams and Russell learned that Clay had left Copenhagen for Hamburg on the eighth; Gallatin was still in England and Bayard in Paris.[23] Russell left his son in Amsterdam to attend school and joined Adams in his dormeuse for the journey to Ghent via the Hague. As he neared his old stomping grounds, John Quincy was overcome with nostalgia. "I can scarcely account to myself for the sensations which I felt on approaching the Hague where I resided at several of the most interesting periods of my life. I dwelt at the Hague on my first public mission from the United States. . . . It was here that the social passion first disclosed itself with all its impetuosity in my breast. . . . It was here, that ten years later, I made my entrance in the political theatre as a public man. . . . It was a confusion of recollections so various, so melancholy, so delicious, so painful . . . that if I had been alone, I am sure I should have melted into tears."[24]

On the twenty-eighth, Adams and Russell had arrived in Ghent and booked rooms at the best public house in the city, the Hôtel des Pays-Bas situated on the Place d'Armes. Bayard arrived on the twenty-seventh, Clay on the twenty-eighth also. Although Gallatin was still in transit, the American commissioners held their first formal meeting on the thirtieth.[25] Serving as secretary to the legation was the adroit and genial Christopher Hughes. John Quincy in particular delighted in his companionship. Their secretary was, Adams wrote in his diary, "lively and good-humored, smart at . . . repartee, and a thorough punster [in] theory and practice."[26] At last, on July 6, Gallatin with his son in tow arrived from Paris.

Madison and Monroe had intended Gallatin to head the delegation, but after his initial rejection by the Senate, they named John Quincy to sit first chair. There were his experience and his capacity for observation and analysis, and besides, he alone knew where in Martens's definitive *Receuil des Traités* to find the proper procedure for conducting negotiations with an enemy. As head, John Quincy would present the delegation's formal statements and proposals to the British; he initially assumed the duty of preparing all first drafts but quickly abandoned the task when his colleagues proceeded to gut and rewrite every one of his offerings. In truth, Albert Gallatin considered himself the true head of the delegation. A champion of the Revolution, a cofounder of the Republican Party, and a cabinet member, he believed that he was the delegate possessing the most gravitas. A European by birth, Gallatin saw himself in a unique position to understand and negotiate with his fellow Europeans (a belief shared and encouraged by the Duke of Wellington). Although the Pennsylvanian proved restrained and amiable in negotiation, both with the British and his colleagues—he often broke the tension in talks with his fellows with a joke or a pun—he possessed an enormous ego. Gallatin requested his own diplomatic cipher and corresponded directly and privately with Madison and Monroe. As a Republican ideologue, he wanted peace, but he was also a patriot who was determined to see his country accorded the respect it was due. Gallatin's ideal was an armed truce in which the United States could grow strong enough to defend its interests.[27]

Before he left London, Gallatin wrote Monroe and Madison and painted a bleak but accurate picture of the diplomatic-military situation. There had been a "total change in our affairs produced by the late revolution [in France, restoring the Bourbons to power] and by the restoration of universal peace in the European world from which we alone are excluded. A well organized and large army is at once liberated from any European employment and ready, together with a super-abundant naval force, to act immediately [against the United States]." No one, he declared, knew better than the president and the secretary of state how ill prepared the United States was to bear the brunt of all this. He agreed with Adams that America's greatest albatross was anti-war feeling in New England. The British hoped not for total conquest, Gallatin advised, but a dissolution of the Union, which would leave their former colonies weak and vulnerable. "They [the British people] do not even suspect that we had any just cause of war and ascribe it solely to a premeditated concert with Bonaparte at a time when we thought him triumphant and their cause desperate."[28] In the wake of Bonaparte's departure for Elba, the British press and public were indeed demanding their pound of flesh. "No quarter," declared the *Times* of London. "Oh, may no false liberality, no mistaken lenity, no weak and cowardly policy, interpose to save [the United States] from the blow! Strike! Chastise the savages for such they are. . . . With Madison and his perjured set, no treaty can be made. . . . Our demands may be couched in a single word: Submission."[29]

On June 27, Monroe wrote John Quincy, paraphrasing Gallatin's report and informing him that the administration had learned that in Vienna Britain had extracted a promise from the other allies not to interfere in the Anglo-American war. In light of all these circumstances, the president had decided that "you may omit any stipulation on the subject of impressment."[30]

While they waited for their British counterparts, the Americans attempted to settle in. Everyone anticipated a prolonged and difficult negotiation lasting at least through the winter. Initially, John Quincy kept some social distance from his colleagues: "I dined again at the table d'hôte, at one. The other gentlemen dined together at four," he recorded in his diary. "They sit after dinner and drink bad wine and smoke cigars which neither suits my habits nor my health [Adams had just recently given up smoking] and absorbs time which I cannot spare." Nor did their nocturnal habits suit him. Rising at his usual hour of five a.m.: "I heard Mr. Clay's company retiring from his chamber. I had left him . . . at cards."[31] But at Clay's urging, John Quincy soon warmed to his colleagues, agreeing to dine with them at four each afternoon. None of the other members of the delegation had had much experience with the New Englander. They initially found him distant, stiff, and somewhat condescending. Russell would later write that he and the others viewed John Quincy as "a kind of laborious pedant without judgment enough to be useful or taste sufficient to be admired."[32]

On July 21 the American commissioners quit the Hôtel des Pays-Bas on the

Place d'Armes and took up residence in an elegant neoclassical villa, the Hôtel Alcantara, on the Rue des Champs.[33] "We had drawn lots for the choice of apartments," John Quincy noted in his diary. "My lot was the third and gave me the chamber I should have taken with the first."[34] There was only one drawback: "One of our troubles you must know," Adams wrote to Louisa, "was that this house was haunted, and its ill-fame in this respect was so notorious that the servants and the children of our party were very seriously alarmed before . . . we first came in. The perturbed spirits have all forsaken the house since we entered it, and we hope they are laid [by] forever."[35]

The British delegation arrived at last in Ghent the second week of August. Compared to the Americans, they were an undistinguished lot. Lord Castlereagh was in Vienna. Liverpool and his secretary for war and colonies, Henry Bathurst, Third Earl Bathurst, would, in consultation with the Duke of Wellington, be making all of the decisions. Nevertheless, the trio that Whitehall dispatched to the Netherlands would be the faces and personalities that Adams and his colleagues would have to deal with for the next three months. Heading the British delegation was Lord Gambier, an experienced naval officer who, according to one observer of the ensuing negotiations, was "a testy firecracker always sputtering but never going off."[36] Then there was the thirty-year-old Henry Goulburn, an undersecretary in the Colonial Office. In that post he had become familiar with and sympathetic to Canada's desire to push their boundary with the United States far to the south, giving them undisputed control over the Great Lakes and protecting them from Yankee filibustering expeditions. The third member of the British delegation was Dr. William Adams, an expert on international and maritime law. Of the three, the most aggressive and offensive to the Americans was Goulburn, who, like Gallatin, communicated independently with his home government. The undersecretary quickly became convinced that Adams and company had no intention of making a satisfactory peace, and he continually assumed positions more extreme than Liverpool and Bathurst supported. Of the three, John Quincy got on best with Gambier. When they met, the Englishman told him that he had known his father and that he was vice president of the British and Foreign Bible Society, which had collaborated with its sister organization in Boston.[37] John Quincy described Dr. Adams as a "blunderbuss of the law" with "pretentions to wit."[38] His view of Goulburn reflected the Englishman's perspective on the Americans. The British delegation, John Quincy was convinced, did not want a reasonable peace and would throw up any and every object to prevent one being concluded. James Gallatin, the commissioner's son, recorded in his diary that his father was not "impressed with the British. . . . [They were] men who have not made any mark and have no influence or weight . . . but puppets of Lords Castlereagh and Liverpool." Albert "felt quite capable of dealing with them."[39]

In truth Liverpool and Bathurst did not share their countrymen's thirst for Cousin Jonathan's blood. A continuation/escalation of the war would add to Britain's enormous debt, which had already swollen from 240 million pounds to 861 million pounds by the Napoleonic Wars. Bathurst, who also had responsibility for supervising military operations in America, hoped that successes on the battlefield would put Adams and company on the defensive, but he did not want capitulation. He did not envision a breakup of the Union and realized that even if crippled, America would grow only stronger.[40]

As the American and British delegations prepared to meet in Ghent, thousands of British troops, veterans of the Napoleonic Wars, were preparing to board transports headed for America. Bathurst planned to use them in three operations: one an invasion of New York via the shores of Lake Champlain to be commanded by Sir George Prevost; the second a landing at Chesapeake Bay followed by an attack on Washington to be led by Admiral Alexander Cochrane and General Robert Ross; and the third an assault on New Orleans under the command of Lord Hill.[41] Liverpool's instructions to the British delegation were to reject all mention of impressment or maritime rights, to demand the creation of an Indian enclave south of the Great Lakes, to put an end to American access to the fisheries off Newfoundland, and to establish boundaries in the Northeast that would give Britain control of both banks of the St. Lawrence.[42]

When presented with these demands at the initial meetings, John Quincy and his companions expressed astonishment. They had assumed that negotiations would center on issues previously discussed between the two countries. The Treaty of 1783 had settled questions regarding the Old Northwest and the fisheries. The Americans did not even have instructions regarding those two issues.[43] On the evening of August 18, Castlereagh stopped off at Ghent on his way to Vienna. He met with the British commissioners, who informed him that the Americans had made no great protest over the proposed Indian homeland and the fisheries question. They were as well willing to concede a permanent British naval presence on the Great Lakes. Thus misinformed, he instructed Goulburn and company to make the Indian enclave a sine qua non.[44] They did, and the Americans indignantly rebuffed them. On this "there has not been a shadow of difference of opinion between any one of my colleagues and me," John Quincy reported to Louisa.[45]

The evening prior to sending their written rejection of the British terms, the Americans and their counterparts attended a banquet hosted by the intendant of Ghent at his palatial home. Bayard took Goulburn aside for a private conversation.

What in the world are you doing? he asked; the terms Britain had laid down would do nothing but unite America and lead to a long and sanguinary war. Did they really expect the United States to surrender large and important portions of its territory? If America had gone to war over impressment and neutral rights, think what it would do to defend its sovereign soil. It seemed, Bayard declared, that the Liverpool government was doing everything in its power to destroy the Federalist Party in America, hitherto its strongest advocate.[46]

The Americans prepared to pack their bags and ask for their passports. "I fully expect that the negotiations here will be terminated before the first of next month—I believe it to be substantially terminated already," John Quincy wrote Louisa.[47] When the negotiators met again, the British informed their counterparts that they would have to send the American response to London and wait for instructions. Adams and Goulburn had a heated exchange. An Indian buffer was necessary to protect Canada from an American invasion, the undersecretary declared. Failing to mention Monroe's earlier secret instruction to the U.S. delegation to press for the cession of Canada, John Quincy declared that the American probes into Canada had been merely a function of the war and had no long-term objectives. The real object of the British demand for an Indian homeland was to block further westward expansion by the United States, Adams declared. "If Great Britain meant to preclude forever the people of the United States from settling and cultivating those territories," she was tilting at a windmill. "It was opposing a feather to a torrent." He then accused Admiral Cochrane of encouraging slaves to desert their masters and flock to the British banner, which was true. How dared he impugn the integrity of a British naval officer? Goulburn replied. "I found the more I conversed with him, the more the violence and bitterness of his passion against the United States disclosed itself," Adams recorded in his diary."[48]

When Liverpool and Bathurst received copies of the American responses, especially those concerning the Indians and the Great Lakes, they were taken aback. The American note was "impudent," Liverpool wrote Wellington, then in Vienna with Castlereagh, but "[o]ur commissioners had certainly taken an erroneous view of the line to be adopted." Goulburn had told Adams that the talks must surely fail and said "we must fight it out."[49] The Madison administration was sure to publish this exchange, and the onus for breaking off negotiations would fall on Great Britain, something Liverpool very much wanted to avoid. Keep the Americans on the line, he ordered Goulburn and company, and stop issuing ultimatums. They complied, dropping the Indian sine qua non. "It appears to me," John Quincy wrote Louisa on September 27, "to be the policy of the British government to keep the American war as an object to continue or to close according to the events which may occur in Europe or in America. If so, they will neither make peace nor break off the negotiation, and the circumstances may be such as to detain us here the whole winter."[50]

LIFE FOR THE AMERICAN delegates in Ghent assumed a not-unpleasant routine. They were wined and dined by the intendant and accorded access to the city's balls and soirees while the British were almost completely ostracized.[51] At one of the entertainments, the hosts asked the Americans if there was not "some American national air." Oh, yes, they replied, "Hail, Columbia." Could anyone sing or play it? their hosts asked. Embarrassed, John Quincy and his colleagues said no, but Peter, Gallatin's Black servant, stepped forward and declared that he could whistle the song and proceeded to do so with Hughes accompanying him on the fiddle. "And from those elements the tune was made out," John Quincy wrote Louisa, "and announced as *l'air national des Américains* . . . and now is everywhere played as a counterpart to God Save the King."[52] He continued to dine with his colleagues, but while they gambled and drank wine in the evenings, he took long walks around the town and its environs. In the delegation's meetings a pattern emerged. Adams and Gallatin would both prepare drafts of notes to the British delegation. Bayard, Clay, and Russell would discard almost all of what John Quincy had written but just a fraction of what Gallatin had penned. "He is always perfectly cool, and I, in the judgment of my colleagues, am often more than temperately warm," John Quincy wrote Louisa. "There is much more verbal criticism used with me too than with any other member of the mission."[53]

During the nine months they were separated by John Quincy's mission to Ghent, he and Louisa wrote each other at least twice a week. When not discussing personal matters, John Quincy's missives included detailed descriptions of the negotiations, the issues involved, and the players in the drama. It was clear from this correspondence—which resembled his exchanges with Abigail—that he had come to regard his wife as his intellectual equal. "You will now, my Dearest friend, receive in the mos[t] exclusive confidence whatever I shall write you on this subject—say not a word of it to any human being until the result shall be publicly known."[54] On her part, Louisa felt the vicissitudes of war and diplomacy as deeply as her husband. She was appalled by her country's misadventures early in the conflict. After attending a fete at the palace, she remarked to John Quincy that in Levett Harris's absence, she was the sole American diplomatic presence at court, but "considering how we go on in Canada, an old woman or a child would answer the purpose."[55] But like her husband, she expressed the hope that adversity would make America stronger. She deplored the burgeoning separatist sentiment in

New England. "[O]ur internal factions have hitherto in a great measure high-lighted [undermined] the efforts of our Government, and if by strong measures it can by any means crush them, we must still remain a great and independent nation."[56]

Louisa managed household affairs with aplomb during her husband's absence. She dealt successfully with drunken manservants, a cook given to strokes, and various other disasters, and she purchased a new carriage when hers broke in pieces. She took it upon herself to rent a summerhouse in the country so that Charles could recover some of the health he had lost during the winter.[57] "As . . . your removal into the country was considered by Dr. Galloway as absolutely nec-essary for Charles, I cannot scruple or disapprove of the expense," Adams wrote his wife.[58]

When in July, Kitty and William Steuben Smith together with their young son departed St. Petersburg intending to take ship to America, Louisa was devastated. "[M]y spirits were so much depressed at the parting with my sister and the dear babe, and the house is so dull and gloomy without them that I roam about like a spirit without knowing what to do with myself."[59] Her loneliness and frustration led her to lash out at Abigail: "Mr. Adams as you probably know has left me in Petersburg and it is very uncertain when we shall meet again; did I not fear to indulge my feelings, I could make bitter complaints of the cruel separation I am obliged to endure."[60] To John Quincy again: "I am almost astonished myself to see the painful effect [my tears] produce in him [Charles]; he leaves no means un-tried to soothe me, and his little heart seems swelling with feelings too big for expression—he is affectionate, kind, and attentive, but at the same time highly resentful to those who he imagines have been the cause of my sorrow."[61]

Adams chose to ignore this last barb, and during his absence, he and Charles, then six years old, exchanged letters. "Went to a Ball at Mrs. Krehmers and Danced eight Country Dances," Charles wrote his father. "Mr. Betancourt has taken away my gun and has given me another, a smaller and a lighter gun; but I hope to learn to handle my gun in such a way as to be able to defend both my Country and the ladies in case of need."[62] Shortly after his arrival at Ghent, John Quincy wrote his youngest that he wished he and his mother could see the coun-try in which he was residing. "It is all smooth and level as the floor of a house; a constant succession of green-pastures, covered with multitudes of sheep and cat-tle; I am sure it would be a pleasure to you to see the little boys in large breeches, big enough to make you two suits of clothes, and wooden shoes, and black round wigs, and pipes of tobacco in their mouths; and the little girls, with petticoats stuffed out like an umbrella . . . and blue stockings, and slippers without heels, flapping at their feet as they walk along."[63] He had gone to see a living rhinoceros, John

Quincy reported to his son, "one of the most uncommon and ugliest animals that my eyes ever beheld—He is six feet high, ten feet long, and weighs nearly five thousand pounds; his skin is so thick and hard that you could not shoot through it with your gun."[64]

IN JULY, ALEXANDER RETURNED from Vienna, and the social season in St. Petersburg kicked off with its usual energy and gaiety. Louisa was once again a favorite at court. After dinner at a fete at Pavlovski (Pavlovsk Palace, one of the imperial residences in St. Petersburg), "we joined the Empress in the garden and walked with her to the theater where we were seated in the front row close to the Empress and Grand Duchess. Her Majesty was as usual extremely gracious more particularly so to the corps diplomatic [by] whom I [was] never treated with so much distinction since I have been in Russia."[65] A month later she attended another celebration at Pavlovski, this time a two-day affair. She danced with Alexander and was her usual vivacious self.[66]

Life in Ghent was not nearly so glamorous, John Quincy wrote his wife. "The theatrical season has . . . commenced from the first of this month," he wrote in November. "The company is, for French players, without exception the worst I ever saw. There is but one tolerable actor and not one actress in the whole troop. Occasionally they have had one good singer, male, but he had a figure like Sancho Panza, and one female, but she was sixty years old and had lost her teeth."[67] He missed Louisa terribly. "There was a rose-bud of your own drawing enclosed in one of your last letters." He hoped it was not by accident, he wrote. "If a bunch of flowers may pass in Persia for a message of love, why may not a rose just-blooming be taken in Russia for a token of affection and its image be received by me as an emblem of yours?"[68]

John Quincy and Louisa had their differences and their similarities; two of the less admirable traits thy shared were oversensitivity and a martyr complex. I am more miserable than you, Louisa wrote shortly after John Quincy had departed St. Petersburg. "You *Mon Ami* are blessed with one of those characters which can mold itself almost without a struggle to the different circumstances which are perpetually occurring and are therefore incapable of judging of the pangs which are endured by those who are not so happily gifted." Not so, retorted her husband: "So far from it, that my natural disposition is of an over-anxious cast, and my struggles to accommodate myself to circumstances which I cannot control have given my constitution in less than fifty years the wear and tear of seventy."[69] Following Louisa's account of one of the royal entertainments she had attended, John Quincy could not resist a small guilt trip: "That you are reconciling yourself to the inconveniences and troubles of a separation from me cannot give me pain; on the contrary I hear it with pleasure. . . . But I should deeply lament if the time should ever come that you would like to live absent from me. I certainly never shall like life absent from you."[70] She rushed to reassure him. "I should never even in jest have hinted that I could live happily without you."[71] But then: what makes you think domestic life with you is always a bed of roses? "I confess my ideas of happiness extend to something beyond the pleasure of passing every evening one hour together, the one party sleeping and the other sinking into absolute silence or gaping for want of something better to do."[72] But in truth, Louisa's and John Quincy's piques and barbs were frequently due to illness, loneliness, severe weather, and depression. Louisa had been left alone to fend for herself in a remote, inclement foreign city, and John Quincy had to bear the weight of his country's future on his shoulders.

IN SEPTEMBER 1814, ADMIRAL Cochrane extended the British blockade northward from the Chesapeake to include all of New England. Abigail wrote that Boston was like a city under siege; a British force actually invaded and occupied Maine north of the Penobscot River. At the same time two of the three planned British land offensives got underway. Prevost's thrust southward from Lake Champlain was thwarted when a naval squadron under Captain Thomas McDonough defeated a British flotilla guarding Prevost's line of supply at Plattsburgh Bay. But Cochrane and Ross's assault on Washington proved much more successful. On August 16 a British flotilla of fifty ships carrying a force of nearly five thousand regulars appeared at the mouth of the Potomac. Secretary of War John Armstrong had convinced Madison that Cochrane's real target was Baltimore; consequently, the seven thousand combined American regulars and militia were taken by surprise when the redcoats marched on Washington. They fled in disarray. General Ross and his force entered an almost deserted town and proceeded to set fire to the White House, the Capitol, and other public buildings. The British then wheeled and assaulted Baltimore but were repulsed by the American garrison at Fort McHenry. During the British bombardment of Baltimore, Washington lawyer Francis Scott Key penned "The Star-Spangled Banner."

In the Northeast, an American force of some thirty-five hundred regulars and volunteers defeated a combined British–Indian force at the Battle of the Thames in Ontario. In the melee, Tecumseh, who had spent the past five years putting together an Indian confederacy capable of defending its homelands against the incursions of American frontier farmers, was killed. The following year General William Henry Harrison and Governor Lewis Cass signed the Treaty of Greenville with the tribes of the Old Northwest in which the tribes ceded some of their lands; some even switched sides and fought with American forces as auxiliaries. From this point on, the whole question of an Indian enclave designed to protect Canada was a dead letter.

News of the sack of Washington was, not surprisingly, greeted with jubilation by the Liverpool government and despondency and anger by Adams and his colleagues. "The destruction of the Capitol, the President's House, the public offices, and many private houses is contrary to all the usages of civilized nations and is without example even in the wars that have been waged during the French Revolution," John Quincy wrote his wife. (Untrue, of course.) "The *Times* and the *Courier* rave and foam at the mouth about it." Adams had learned that in their haste to leave Washington to assault Baltimore, the British "had left their own dead unburied and on the fields and their own wounded as prisoners at the mercy of the very people whose public edifices . . . and private habitations they had been consuming by fire." If those wounded prisoners have not been gibbeted on the trees between Bladensburg and Washington to fatten their region's kites and to swing as memorials of British valor and humanity, it was because "it belongs to our national character to relent into mercy towards a vanquished and defenseless enemy."[73]

The last week in October, Liverpool and Bathurst authorized Goulburn and his colleagues to drop the Indian homeland demand as a sine qua non, but they were to insist upon a peace based on uti possidetis (that which you possess), which would leave portions of Maine and upstate New York in British hands. The Americans replied that under no circumstances would they sign a peace that ceded an inch of American soil. "The doctrine of the American government is a very convenient one," Liverpool wrote Wellington, "that they will always be ready to keep what they acquire, but never to give up what they lose. . . . We still think it desirable to gain a little more time before the negotiation is brought to a close."[74]

On October 4, 1814, Madison and Monroe wrote the American delegation in Ghent, authorizing them to abandon the issues of impressment and neutral rights. The end of the war in Europe had rendered them moot. John Quincy and his colleagues were instructed to seek a peace based on the status quo ante bellum. During the second week in November, Adams and his colleagues received word of the new course that they were to follow. Meanwhile, on November 3, the entire British cabinet had convened to discuss the American question; they decided to approach the Duke of Wellington and persuade him to take command of British forces in North America and deal the United States a series of punishing blows. Such was his prestige that no one in the Liverpool government dared order him into action. "The . . . idea which had presented itself to our minds is that you should be appointed to the chief command in America and that you should go out with full powers to make peace, or to continue the war, if peace should be impracticable, with renewed vigor."[75] The Iron Duke demurred; the state of things in Europe was too unsettled for him to go to America. Furthermore: "In regard to your present negotiations, I confess that I think you have no right from the state of the war to demand any concession from America . . . from particular circumstances such as the want of the naval superiority on the Lakes, you have not been able to carry it [the war] into the enemy's territory . . . and you have not even cleared your own territory of the enemy. . . . You can get no territory; indeed the state of your military operations, however creditable, does not entitle you to demand any."[76]

In truth, Wellington was never much of a supporter of the war with America. He was an admirer of Albert Gallatin and wrote him while the negotiations were ongoing, "In you I have the greatest confidence. . . . You are a foreigner with all the traditions of one fighting for the peace and welfare of the country of your adoption."[77] Matters were indeed unsettled in Europe. Cracks had appeared in the coalition that had defeated Napoleon, and there were rumblings of anti-Bourbon discontent in central France. Ironically, the sack of Washington had taken some of the steam out of the British public's demand for American blood. A week after the exchange with Wellington, the Liverpool government decided to make peace with America on the basis of the status quo ante bellum.

The British knew that their Canadian brethren were going to give them absolute hell when they signed a treaty that they would see as leaving them again at the mercy of the avaricious Yankees. In an attempt to throw them a bone, the British negotiators at Ghent decided to demand the right to navigate the Mississippi. They declared that the outbreak of war had canceled the provisions of the Treaty of 1783 including that granting to the United States the "liberty" to fish the Grand Banks and to dry their catches on designated shorelines. Goulburn and his fellows proposed a trade-off: we get to traverse the great river and you get to mine our fishing grounds. The proposal at once set Adams and Clay at each other's throats. Clay declared that he would not sign any treaty that granted the right of navigation to British citizens. "Mr. Clay lost his temper, as he generally does whenever this right of the British to navigate the Mississippi is discussed," John Quincy recorded in his diary. "He was utterly averse to admitting it as an equivalent for a stipulation securing the contested part of the fisheries. He said the more he heard of this [the right to fish] the more convinced he was that it was of little or no value."[78] Adams responded that for his part, he would not take pen in hand unless the fishing privileges were preserved. Gallatin intervened on his behalf. There were elements in New England then plotting to secede from the Union on the grounds that the war had been initiated and prosecuted over the region's opposition and against its interests, he declared. "If we should abandon any part of the territory [or its rights], it would give a handle to the party there now pushing for a separation from the Union and for a New England confederacy . . . and to pretend that by a separate confederacy they could obtain what is refused to us." Clay retorted that it was useless to try to appease people who would not be appeased.[79]

In his diary and letters, Adams would admit the rancorous differences that existed within the American delegation, but he insisted that it always presented a common front when dealing with the British. He was generous in his description of Henry Clay. There were many similarities between him and the Kentuckian, he wrote Louisa. "There is the same dogmatical, over-bearing manner, the same harshness of look and expression, and the same forgetfulness of the courtesies of society in both. An impartial person judging between them I think would say that one has the strongest, and the other the most cultivated understanding; that one has the most ardency, and the other the most experience of mankind; that one has a mind more gifted by nature, and the other a mind less cankered by prejudice. Mr. Clay is by ten years the younger man of the two, and as such has perhaps more claim to indulgence for irritability."[80]

Though he knew how committed his father was to the fisheries issue—indeed, he still seemed obsessed with it—John Quincy gave way, and on the afternoon of December 23, the British and American delegations agreed to omit any mention of either the Mississippi or the fisheries from the final draft of their treaty of peace. By this point, John Quincy had become thoroughly disgusted with his native New England. Despite Massachusetts furnishing more volunteers for military service per capita than any other state, the Essex men were in control of the state government. On October 17, 1814, the Massachusetts legislature had issued a call to all other New England states to send delegates to a convention to be held at Hartford, Connecticut, to air the region's grievances. Vermont and New Hampshire refused, but Connecticut and Rhode Island accepted. The stated purpose was to draft amendments to the U.S. Constitution to protect the region's interests. Extremists like Timothy Pickering, however, talked openly of secession.[81] "[A]t this moment how fearfully does this mad and wicked project of national suicide bear upon my heart and mind . . . if we now fail to obtain peace, it will be owing entirely to this act of the Massachusetts legislature," John Quincy wrote Louisa.[82] Perhaps, when Massachusetts came to its political senses, and he was still in the diplomatic corps, he could fight the fisheries fight to a successful conclusion. "We have obtained nothing, but peace and we have made great sacrifices to obtain it," John Quincy declared. "But our honor remains unsullied. Our territory remains entire. The peace in word and in deed has been made in terms of perfect reciprocity and we have surrendered not one right nor pretension of our country."[83]

The icing on the American cake came with Andrew Jackson's victory over General Sir Edward Pakenham at the Battle of New Orleans some two weeks after the signing of the Treaty of Ghent. In December 1814 a British combined naval and land force of some 14,450 under the command of Admiral Cochrane anchored off the coast of Louisiana. James Monroe, now secretary of war, ordered General Andrew Jackson and his twenty-five-hundred-man force to proceed at once to New Orleans and mount a defense. In the predawn hours of January 8, a superior force of redcoats staged an ill-conceived frontal assault on the earthen works Jackson's men had erected along canals four miles south of the city. In a battle that lasted twenty-five minutes, the British lost 2,084 dead, wounded, or captured; American losses were thirteen killed and thirty wounded. News of Jackson's victory rolled up the Mississippi and traveled across the Appalachians, reaching Washington the first week in February. Collective intoxication over the Battle of New Orleans obliterated any domestic opposition to the Peace of Christmas Eve.

John Quincy would rightly describe the War of 1812 as America's second war for independence; this was particularly true in psychological terms. That a militarily weak and politically divided nation could stymie one of the world's great military powers was something of a miracle; perhaps, Americans thought, the United States had been singled out by the Almighty or, at least, by destiny to play a unique role in world affairs.

AT THE SAME TIME the United States was beating back efforts by the former mother country to reclaim its strayed child, it was succeeding in breaking the back of Native American resistance to white incursions into Indian lands. The Washington administration had recognized the Indians as legitimate inhabitants of their tribal territories. Land could only be taken from them in a "just war" or through a treaty-making process in which the Indians consented to sell parts of their territory for fair compensation. Members of the American Enlightenment like Thomas Jefferson and John and John Quincy Adams embraced the picture of Native Americans later painted by James Fenimore Cooper in his novels: "noble savages" exhibiting the same virtues of courage, independence, and integrity that whites had had in their primitive state. But civilization, they believed, was passing the Native Americans by. Virtually all Americans in positions of influence agreed that only two alternatives existed for American Indians as they faced the march of civilization: assimilation or removal to lands beyond the western frontier. If the red man would embrace Christianity, white education, private ownership of property, and the agricultural life, they could be admitted to full citizenship. If they insisted on clinging to their religion, language, and commitment to open land use, they would have to move. Some tribes, most notably the Cherokee, decided to accommodate those demands, but others led by Tecumseh and his younger brother Tenskwatawa (the Prophet) chose to resist.[84]

In 1808, at Tecumseh's urging, Tenskwatawa had persuaded representatives from the Kickapoos, Potawatomi, Winnebago, and Wyandotte to send representatives to a gathering on the banks of the Tippecanoe River in Indiana with the intent of establishing an intertribal confederacy. In a letter to the territorial governor, William Henry Harrison, the Prophet proposed a modus operandi: "That we ought . . . to live agreeably to our several customs, the red people, after their mode, and the white people after theirs."[85] But he made it clear that the land that his people occupied was theirs—given to them by the Great Spirit—and always would be.

Harrison, with the support of the federal government, rejected the Prophet's proposal. At the Battle of Tippecanoe on November 7, 1811, he soundly defeated the braves of the tribal confederation, burning Prophetstown to the ground. Tecumseh subsequently worked to rebuild the shattered coalition, and when the War of 1812 erupted, the tribes allied themselves with the British. The brothers' dream of an autonomous, independent Indian nation situated in the Old Northwest came to an end with the Battle of the Thames when an American force again under Harrison's command drove off the British and defeated the Indians. Tecumseh died in the fighting.

In the South it appeared initially that the powerful Creeks would go the way of the Cherokee, but young nationalists, incited by Tecumseh, decided on armed resistance. Civil war erupted between the accommodationists and the militants called Red Sticks. In August 1813, a group of militants attacked and overran Fort Mims, a poorly guarded settlement comprising some five hundred accommodationists, slaughtering some two hundred fifty men, women, and children. Swearing vengeance, General Jackson and his army of regulars and militiamen descended on the Creek militants. At the Battle of Horseshoe Bend in March 1814, his forces crushed the Creek Red Sticks and their Cherokee allies. In all, a thousand Creeks—15 percent of the population—were killed. In the subsequent Treaty of Fort Jackson, the Indians surrendered without any compensation twenty-three million acres of their land and forswore any further contact with the British or Spanish. No foreign nation would ever again intercede on behalf of Native Americans.[86]

In the midst of negotiations with the British concerning the establishment of an

Indian enclave, John Quincy observed that the nations of Europe were different from America in origin and makeup. Britain, France, and Prussia emerged from feudalism to become nation-states, monarchies defined by fixed borders established through negotiation or war. The United States was a voluntary confederation of thirteen original states with an open frontier to the west. The British, he argued, wanted to treat the American Indian tribes as nation-states; whether they clung to their native ways or assimilated, this would not be possible, Adams observed. "To condemn vast regions of territory to perpetual barrenness and solitude [in order] that a few hundred savages might find wild beasts to hunt upon it, was a species of game-law that nations descended from Britain would never endure—It was as incompatible with the moral as with the physical nature of things."[87] The Indians, he insisted, were much better off as wards of the United States than as slaves to the Europeans—the only way they knew how to deal with them. The War of 1812 might have been a second war for independence but only for white Americans. Slaves remained slaves, free Blacks led lives of relative unfreedom, and Native Americans, it seemed, were doomed to perpetual removal or extinction.

19

A Winter Odyssey

THE CONCLUSION OF THE treaty [of Ghent] was officially communicated by the British plenipotentiaries to the Intendant on Christmas day, "the day of all the year most congenial to the proclamation of peace on earth," John Quincy wrote Louisa. "We received his congratulations the same evening at a large party." The secretary to the British delegation departed immediately for London with a copy of the pact. Christopher Hughes left the next day for Bordeaux, there to sail for America with additional copies of the treaty. Adams's colleagues intended to rest and recuperate in Pairs, and he decided to join them. To Louisa: "I therefore now write you to break up altogether our establishment at St. Petersburg . . . and to come with Charles to me at Paris where I shall be impatiently waiting for you. . . . I suppose you will not be able to make all the necessary arrangements to leave St. Petersburg no later than the middle of February. If the season should still be too severe, I wish you to wait until it shall be milder."[1]

Louisa was concerned not so much with the daunting prospect of a two-thousand-mile journey in the dead of winter through territories recently ravaged by war as she was with disposing of their property and arranging for the passports and letters of introduction, which were prerequisites for her trip. "I know not what to do about the selling of the goods, and I fear I shall be much imposed upon," she wrote her husband, "this is a very heavy trial, but I must get through it at all risks and if you receiving me with the conviction that I have done my best, I shall be amply rewarded."[2] She reported that there was a shortage of cash in the city. "I find it almost impossible to dispose of the things to any sort of advantage. Nobody has ready money."[3] But as the date she had set for her and Charles's departure—February 15—drew near, she began to have some success. Louisa managed to sell their carriage and most of their furniture. All told she was able to bring in $1,693, which would cover 90 percent of the cost of the trip. As always, the judgment of her husband hung heavy on her: "If I do wrong, it is unintentional, Mon Ami," she wrote John Quincy. "I am so afraid of cold looks."[4]

Both the Russian Foreign Office and the French ambassador made out passports for her. On her way to Paris, she would be traveling through the provinces of Livland and Kurland in Russia, Poland, Prussia, and the Confederation of the Rhine. Russian, Prussian, German, and French officials and merchants in St. Petersburg provided her with letters of introduction while bankers furnished letters of credit. A deputy foreign minister sent word ahead to Russian provincial officials to watch for her arrival and "on pain of punishment" to provide her with the best horses for her carriages.[5] Louisa's friends and members of the corps diplomatique showered her with gifts as she made the rounds to say her goodbyes.

When Louisa called on the tsarina, Elizabeth greeted her warmly and remarked afterward that she had never seen a woman "so alter'd in her life for the better."[6] Indeed, during the six weeks of preparation for her departure, Louisa did not even contract a cold. Despite her fear of John Quincy's recriminations concerning her business dealings, she longed to be reunited with him. She was thrilled upon receiving some love poems from him. "I think Mr. Jefferson would say you have not lost your talent for amatory verses," she wrote back. "Your lines are beautiful and even comparing them with those I used to receive, I can trace no diminution of either the fire or the tenderness which rendered them so beautiful and flattering."[7]

Two nights before her scheduled departure, Louisa called upon her young friend Countess Marie Colombi to say goodbye. To her consternation they were joined by the Countess Apraxin, "a fat, course woman, very talkative, full of scandal, and full of the everlasting amusement so fashionable in Russian society, the *bonne aventure* [fortune-telling]." Though Louisa had never even met the woman before, Countess Apraxin insisted on forecasting her future. Louisa, she declared, was getting ready to depart on a long journey to be reunited with her husband. Approximately halfway through she would be engulfed by a major political upheaval that would threaten to plunge the Continent into war once again and present all sorts of difficulties for the travelers. The cause of all of this would be "some extraordinary movement of a great man." "I laughed and thanked her and said I had no fear of such a circumstance . . . as it was a time of peace."[8]

For the journey Louisa purchased two conveyances; one was a berline, a heavy, enclosed, Russian-built carriage pulled by six horses. There was room for a small bed to accommodate Charles, but she would have to sleep sitting upright. The second was a kibitka, which most resembled a tent on sleds. Then there was the matter of hiring servants, no easy task given the length of the journey and the unlikelihood of ever returning to Russia. Eventually, through Countess Colombi, Louisa procured a maid, a Frenchwoman who had been a nanny to several royal families and who desired to return to her homeland to end her days. Madame Babet was, Louisa later recalled, "a quiet and respectable person, older than myself and very plain in her person and manners, and very steady." To do the heavy lifting and guard the women and child, Louisa hired two men: John Pulling, an unprepossessing man who had once served William Steuben Smith, and an individual known simply as Baptiste who was a recently released prisoner of war from Napoleon's army. Baptiste was by far the rougher and more aggressive of the two; Louisa would never entirely trust him. "I had contrived to conceal the bags of gold and silver which I carried in such a manner [probably sewn into the lining of her voluminous cloak] that neither of my men servants supposed that I possessed any."[9] She would cash small letters of credit along the way and keep her hard currency hidden for emergencies.

"On the 12th day of February at five o'clock in the evening of Sunday, I bade adieu to the splendid city of St. Petersburg where I had resided upwards of five years," she recorded in her diary. "To avoid the disagreeable and painful feelings of parting with friends with whom I had formed a friendship of some standing, I chose the above hour while they were engaged at their dinner."[10] In a letter to John Quincy written shortly before her departure: "I could not celebrate my birthday in [a] manner more delightful than in making the first step toward that meeting for which my soul pants and for which I have hitherto hardly dared to express my desire."[11] Louisa, Madame Babet, and Charles occupied the coach, the two menservants the kibitka. The carriages were driven by postilions. Under the European post road system, the thoroughfares were divided into posts usually six to twelve miles apart. At each station, there would be new postilions and horses, and an opportunity for food and rest if so desired. The passengers paid per horse and postilion at each stop.[12] The weather was bitterly cold when the Adams party departed, and would remain so for the next two weeks. When they reached their first rest stop at Narva, Louisa found that the bottles of Madeira she had packed had frozen solid.

Louisa secured lodgings at the best inn in town, but just as she was settling in, she was visited by a messenger, who informed her that apartments had been prepared for her at the governor's mansion. She declined but was subsequently visited by the dignitary himself, who paid his respects. Louisa was determined not to pause on her journey for several reasons: she missed her husband, from whom she had been separated for nine months; she feared that she would be seduced by the dinners, theater visits, and soirees that would be offered and of which she was so fond; and she dreaded the expense of a prolonged trip. So, at dawn, it was up and into the carriage and on the road to her next stop, Riga.[13]

By the time Louisa and her entourage reached Riga, the roads had begun to thaw, and she had to pause for several days while laborers at the post attempted to fit the kibitka with wheels. Their efforts proved fruitless and the tent on sleds was sold. Four days out of St. Petersburg, the group had covered three hundred fifty miles, nearly ninety miles a day.[14] The lodgings in Riga were adequate but nothing more. One evening Louisa made the mistake of leaving on the table in their sleeping quarters a silver cup presented to Charles by the Westphalian minister. When she awoke in the morning it was gone. "Here for the first time, I had some reason to doubt the honesty of my servant [Baptiste]; there was little doubt that he had made free with it."[15] But she had no proof of the theft, and she needed the protection that both her menservants, heavily armed, provided. During their layover, she was the guest of the governor and his lady—"All the most distinguished persons in town were invited to meet me."[16]

On the nineteenth, the heavy carriage with the menservants and their baggage perched on top departed for Mitau. On the road through what is present-day Latvia, winter returned with a vengeance. Several times the berline became stuck in the snow, whereupon the postilions would ring a bell and the local peasants would come and for a few coins dig the coach out. Mitau was a charming town with a thriving cultural life, but Louisa was determined to sleep a few hours and then proceed to another stop some four German miles down the road to spend the night. Before she could retire, the innkeeper Monsieur Morel came knocking. He closed the door after glancing furtively around. "He again examined the doors with an appearance of great anxiety and then sat down close to me, who felt not a little uncomfortable at all this apparently terrible preparation—I however assumed an air of great calmness and patiently awaited the [direction the conversation] might take which was to thrill my nerves with horror."[17] She must delay her departure until morning, Morel declared; there had been a heinous murder the night before on the very road she intended to travel. It was a public thoroughfare with many postilions about, she replied. They would be fine. The innkeeper paused and then confided that there was another matter about which he wished to speak. Her servant Baptiste had been a soldier in Bonaparte's army and had resided for some two years in Mitau, where he had earned a reputation as "a desperate Villain of the very worst character . . . he did not consider my life safe with him."[18] Louisa replied that she did not particularly like or trust Baptiste, but she had no other choice but to rely on him, there being no proof of impropriety. Then, advised Morel, you must defer to him, convince him that you would rely on his good judgment unconditionally. Precisely, Louisa replied. Please, Morel pleaded, do not tell Baptiste of their conversation, "as it would certainly endanger us both."[19]

Louisa would make light of Morel's warnings in her diary, but in fact she was most apprehensive as she, Charles, and Madame Babet boarded the berline in the dark. "I got into the carriage and began my ride under the most uneasy impressions." In pitch darkness, with the road becoming rougher and rougher, the postilion suddenly announced that he had lost his way. "Until eleven o'clock at night, we were jolted over hills, through swamps, and holes, and into valleys into which no carriage had surely ever passed before," Louisa later recalled in her diary. She was terrified for her small son, then sleeping innocently on his little pallet. At midnight, with the horses exhausted and not a star out to serve as guide, it was decided that Baptiste would take one of the steeds and ride for help. Fifteen minutes later, the two women were alarmed by the sound of horses' hooves and voices. They feared highwaymen, but it was Baptiste in company with a Russian officer. The Frenchman had come upon the officer's house situated only a short distance away, and the man had offered his services as a guide. "We proceeded at a fast pace and arrived at the inn at half past one." Louisa ordered drinks for the men and coffee for herself. She rewarded the Russian officer with a small sum of money; thereupon, he instructed the innkeeper to do Louisa's every bidding. She was relieved not only to find shelter but to see that she could trust Baptiste.[20] We have passed through "the greatest difficulties and even dangers," Louisa subsequently wrote her husband.[21]

WHILE LOUISA WAS PREPARING for her departure from St. Petersburg, John Quincy was packing up and getting ready to head for Paris. At last, he and his servant Antoine Guista departed Ghent—"My residence in the city has been of seven months and two days, and it has been the most memorable period of my life"—and traveled by sledge to Brussels, where they took lodgings at the Hôtel de Flanders, one of the finest in the city. His large and luxurious quarters fronted on the Grand Place, Brussels's main square. The evening before his departure, the citizenry celebrated the "deliverance of Brussels." "The firing of cannons and ringing of bells at intervals the whole day through, and the illumination of the city in the evening," he wrote Louisa, reminded him of St. Petersburg in the aftermath of the triumph of Russian forces over Napoleon's invading armies.[22] And then it was on to Paris, with its memories of life with his father when the elder Adams had been negotiating the Treaty of Paris in 1783, and of the family idyll at Auteuil. At Gallatin's recommendation, John Quincy took a suite of rooms at the Hôtel du Nord, on the Rue de Richelieu.

As soon as he was settled in, Adams called on the U.S. minister to France, William H. Crawford, who arranged to have Adams presented at court several days later. "The king, princes, and princess seldom speak to any person presented to them," John Quincy noted in his diary. "The king however asked me if I 'was any [way] related to the celebrated Mr. Adams.'"[23] The days that followed were filled with visits with old acquaintances: Lafayette; Count Barbé-Marbois, who had been secretary of the French Legation in Philadelphia thirty years before; Madame de Staël; and the Count de Tracy. William Steuben and Kitty Smith were then in Paris, and John Quincy found them rooms in the Hotel du Nord. On their way home from St. Petersburg in the summer of 1814, the Smiths had become stranded in Amsterdam. John Quincy had had them come to Ghent, where Smith had served as one of his secretaries. "I saw the gloomy court of Louis XVIII and the splendid circles of the Duke of Orleans," he later wrote his mother. "I frequented the unparalleled assemblage of the masterpieces of art in the Museum of Napoleon and . . . the French monuments, the meetings of the National Institute, the Courts of Law, the theatres, the collections of mechanical models, the Gobelin tapestry manufacture, and even the deserted churches and the subterraneous catacombs."[24] "The tendency to dissipate at Paris seems to be irresistible," he wrote in his diary. "There is a moral incapacity for industry and application; a *molesse* [a Voltairean word for softness] against which I am as ill-guarded as I was at the age of twenty."[25]

On March 7, 1815, word came to John Quincy that Napoleon had broken out of captivity in Elba and returned to France. "He landed on the first of this month near Cannes in the Department of the Var," he wrote in his diary. "[T]hey say with 1200 men and 4 pieces of cannon."[26] It was true. With the Congress of Vienna quarreling over the spoils of war, Napoleon had boarded the French brig *Inconstant* with some thousand men and slipped through the British blockade. He landed on the coast between Cannes and Antibes on March 1. As he made his way through the countryside, his former solders flocked to his banner.

Returning from the theater on March 12, John Quincy encountered "numerous patrols of soldiers, National Guards, and sentinels at the corner of the streets; news [of the crisis was] placarded upon the pillars and clusters of people collecting and attempting to read them by the light of the lamps."[27] "In the streets, at all the public places," he subsequently wrote Abigail, "in all the newspapers, one universal sentiment is bursting forth of fidelity to the King and of abhorrence and execration of this firebrand of civil and foreign war . . . the National Guards, the marshals, generals, and officers and garrisons of almost every city in the kingdom, are flocking to the Tuileries with addresses of inviolable attachment for Louis XVIII and of their readiness to shed their blood in his cause."[28] But it was all a sham. The Frenchman with whom John Quincy conversed all predicted that none would fire on Bonaparte and that he would enter Paris without opposition.[29] On March 15 one of Louis XVIII's top commanders, Marshal Ney, defected, taking with him some six thousand troops. Promising constitutional reform and direct elections to a national assembly, Napoleon entered Paris in triumph. On the twenty-first, the king and his family fled the capital. "If the people of Paris had been seriously averse to his [Napoleon's] government," John Quincy wrote his mother, "the National Guards of the city alone would have outnumbered five times all the troops that had then declared in his favor."[30]

OF THESE MOMENTOUS DEVELOPMENTS Louisa was yet unaware. Following their harrowing nighttime experience outside Mitau, she and her party set out for Tilsit. At four in the afternoon on February 19, they arrived at the Windau River, where it ran into the Baltic. There was no bridge, but the river appeared to be frozen over. Louisa could choose a long detour to a safer passage or risk the ice. She chose the latter. With help from several men hired from a nearby hamlet, her servants unharnessed the horses from the carriage and reattached them with long poles so as to better distribute the weight on the ice, which was in the midst of a spring thaw. With the locals ranging ahead, tapping the ice to determine its thickness, Louisa and her entourage made their way slowly. Just short of the west bank, they encountered a narrow stretch of open water. The horses were reharnessed, and they and the carriage plunged into the river, barely making it up the bank to dry land.[31]

Eventually Louisa reached the last posthouse in Russia. Customs officials delayed her three hours, going through her baggage and asking endless questions. The landlord of the posthouse ignored her request for food and horses. "[T]he people were so much inclined to be impudent," she recorded in her diary, "I was obliged to produce my letter [passport] and to inform the master of the house that I should write immediately to the Minister of the Interior and complain of his conduct . . . the man appeared to be much alarmed, made a great many apologies and said the horses should be ready immediately and very politely obliged me to take a couple more than the usual compliment, as he thought the carriage very heavy."[32] Louisa ordered the postilions to travel on through the night, and the next day the berline arrived in Tilsit.

At this point the travelers' route merged with that of Napoleon's devastated forces as they had retreated before the rampaging Cossacks of the Imperial Russian Army. Everywhere there were burned-out houses, abandoned carriages and artillery, and bone fields: "a very thin population; women unprotected, and that dreary look of forlorn desertion which sheds its gloom around on all the objects announcing devastation and despair."[33] From Tilsit the Adams party made its way to Königsberg, which had in 1812 served as the assembly point and procurement base for the Grande Armée. It had also been a funnel through which the army's

shattered ranks would retreat in 1814. The battle tested Prussian general Friedrich Wilhelm von Bülow, who later wrote that nothing he had ever witnessed
could match the carnage in Königsberg during the winter of 1814.[34] Louisa spent
the day in the city acquiring letters of credit and exploring.

On the way to Küstrin, a fortress city on the road to Berlin, one of the carriage's wheels shattered. Baptiste went ahead to the next village and returned
with a peasant and a farmer's cart, in which the two women and Charles were
obliged to ride to the posthouse. That dwelling, Louisa recorded, was nothing
more than a hovel with two rooms and a blacksmith's shop. "One woman made
her appearance—dirty, ugly, and ill natured, and there were two or three very
surly ill-looking men" loitering about. The blacksmith set to work making another
wheel for the berline, and one of the rooms was made available to Louisa, Madame Babet, and Charles. Baptiste and Pulling, fully armed, took turns guarding
the door. Still, the two women refused to sleep and sat up watching over Charles.
The next morning it was on the road again with the carriage bumping along on its
crude new wheel. At Küstrin the party secured accommodations in a tolerable
house; the town and its fort still bore the marks of battle. Louisa was surprised to
find the populace very pro-French. Memories of the Cossacks who had raped and
pillaged were still fresh in their minds. "The Cossacks! The dire Cossacks! were
the perpetual theme, and the cheeks of the women blanched at the very name."[35]

At last, on March 4, after a fourteen-year absence, Louisa arrived in Berlin.
Memories flooded in, but she noticed that war and occupation by the French had
changed the city. It was still charming but had lost some of its luster, its confidence. The principal source of Prussia's pride had been its army, which had been
crushed by Bonaparte's forces at the Battles of Jena and Auerstedt in 1806. Under
the Treaty of Tilsit, signed in 1807, the king had been compelled to surrender his
remaining forces to Napoleon to serve as auxiliaries to the Grande Armée. Prussia had lost all its lands west of the Elbe and was forced to pay a heavy indemnity.[36]

Louisa booked rooms for a week at the Hôtel de Russie, which would allow
time for the carriage to be fully repaired and for her to visit old friends. As soon
as she heard of Louisa's arrival, Countess Pauline Neale, her dearest friend from
her first stay in Berlin, rushed to greet her. Like the king and the queen, Pauline
had suffered from the Napoleonic occupation. Before the French conquest, she
had visited Paris and written home about some of Napoleon's plans. The letters
were intercepted, and she became famous. When, upon entering Berlin, Napoleon had learned that she had fled, he declared, "Well, if I had caught her here,
I should have had her hair cropped and sent her to Bicêtre"—the asylum near
Paris—"for her interference in having political opinions and expressing them

publicly."[37] The two women visited Princess Radziwill, who invited Louisa to spend every evening with her. "My friends greeted me with the most unaffected warmth, and my reception was that of a long separated and beloved sister." She left the city both exhilarated and saddened. "I missed many objects which had formerly excited my admiration, and the perfect stillness seemed to cast a gloom over all the scenes which had once been so gay and brilliant."[38]

At this point Louisa had received not a single letter from her husband. "I am cruelly disappointed," she wrote on March 5.[39] For his part, John Quincy had received three letters from Louisa and was anticipating her arrival any day. He had in fact written twice, but his correspondence missed their mark, arriving at their addresses after she had departed.

After bidding her friends a fond farewell, Louisa, Charles, and Madame Babet climbed into the heavy carriage, and her two armed menservants took their places in the coachmen's seats. They headed west toward Frankfurt am Main. Following a particularly long day, the party stopped overnight at an inn. Tired from the trip, Louisa left a bag of gold coins on the table in their bedchamber. In the morning the money was gone. Remembering distinctly that Madame Babet had locked their door, she thought: Baptiste again?[40] But she had no proof.

As they approached the fortified city of Hanau, the scene of a ferocious battle between the French and Austro-Bavarian troops on October 30, 1813, which took the lives of ten thousand soldiers, the party came across a horrifying scene. "We entered on a wide extended plain over which was scattered remnants of clothes, old boots in pieces, and an immense quantity of bones laying in the ploughed field." Louisa shielded her young son's eyes from the "sight of such butchery. I could with difficulty keep from fainting." Waiting for fresh horses at Hanau, she heard rumors of Napoleon's return. The natives were ecstatic. "The renowned cruelties and barbarities of the Cossacks seemed to have white-washed all other crimes from their minds. Soldiers were mustering in every direction," she reported to her diary.[41]

The berline managed to make its way safely to Frankfurt. Still no word from John Quincy. Louisa had several letters of credit addressed to a prominent Frankfurt banker, Simon Moritz von Bethmann. At her request, he called on her at the hotel where she and the others were staying. After conducting their business, Bethmann insisted that she avoid the most direct route to Paris because soldiers on both sides were mustering up and down the road. She agreed to take a more circuitous route through Strasbourg. The next morning Baptiste and Pulling appeared and announced that they must quit her service and hide themselves in Frankfurt in order to avoid conscription by one side or the other. She protested but to no avail. Bethmann promised to find replacements, but the best he could come up with was a fourteen-year-old boy. Louisa retained him in order to have someone to help Madame Babet and herself in and out of the carriage, to run errands, and to load and unload the baggage. From then on, she would proceed without armed protection. Bethmann pleaded with her to tarry in Frankfurt until the situation around Paris became more settled, but she refused. Once the two sides coalesced, there would be fighting and battle lines to cross. "At present the panic itself proves advantageous," she told him.[42]

As Louisa made her way to Paris, it was crucial that she avoided being identified either with the Bonapartists or the Bourbons. Although only fourteen years old, her adolescent companion had served as an aide to a Prussian officer attached to the Grande Armée. He was a great admirer of Napoleon as it turned out. The party stopped at Karlsruhe for dinner, in the midst of which the innkeeper rushed in and declared that Napoleon had been captured and shot. "I heard an exclamation of horror," Louisa wrote in her diary, "and turning round, saw the boy who I had hired as pale as a ghost and ready to faint—he looked piteously at me saying, 'O that great Man! I did not expect that!'" Fortunately, the innkeeper had left the room.[43]

Mrs. Adams's berline passed through the Duchy of Baden without incident, but everywhere there were "wagons of every description full of soldiers . . . continually rushing toward the frontier roaring national songs and apparently in great glee at the idea of a renewal of hostilities."[44] Louisa and her entourage finally arrived at Kehl, the last Prussian station on the German side of the Rhine opposite the city of Strasbourg. Immigration officials questioned her, examined her papers, and went through her luggage but eventually allowed her to proceed. In Strasbourg she found lodgings at a respectable inn recommended by a French immigration officer. The landlord proved to be an amiable person who advised that she again alter her route and proceed by way of Château-Thierry. She thanked him and lamented that she would have to proceed without a guide or guards. The master of the house replied that he would see what he could do. Meanwhile, Louisa and Charles toured the city, which was famed for its beauty. In the district called le Petite France, they passed by timber-and-plaster buildings dating from the sixteenth and seventeenth centuries, a replica of the Strasbourg Cathedral, and numerous bridges linking the shaded banks lining the River Ill.[45] On returning to her lodging, Louisa found that the keeper had secured the services of a Monsieur Dupin, whom Louisa found "a most respectable looking person." They must be circumspect, he told his new employer. The boy must be kept quiet and hidden if possible. She should let him, Dupin, do the talking.[46]

From Strasbourg to Paris, it was still three hundred miles. With Dupin added to her party, Louisa departed at the crack of dawn the next morning. She insisted on traveling into the night, but around one o'clock in the morning, her postilions declared that they could go no farther. The only structure in sight was a lonely and dilapidated inn. "We drove up to a miserable place in which we found a long room with pine benches to sit on—Here I was obliged to sit while they procured us a little milk, the only thing we could get."[47] Several rough-looking customers attempted to interrogate Charles; Dupin intervened and asked if there was a chamber where the women and child could pass the night. The woman of the house showed them into an adjoining squalid room in which Louisa, Charles, and Madame Babet barricaded themselves. By this time the dignified nanny was hysterical, wringing her hands, weeping, and declaring that she would never live to see Paris. Throughout the night rowdy customers, including Louisa's postilions, drank noisy toasts to Napoleon. With the approach of dawn, the women's terror began to abate. Dupin, whom Louisa would praise for handling a dangerous situation with "a quiet smoothness of manner which enforced respect and defied suspicion" told Louisa that the weather was propitious and the roads ahead smooth.[48] It was quite possible that they would reach Paris ahead of Napoleon.

The final leg of their journey took them through Nancy, Épernay, and Château-Thierry.[49] About a mile and a half outside Épernay, the carriage was engulfed by a troop of Imperial Guards deserting to Bonaparte. "The first notice I had of my danger was hearing the most horrid curses and dreadful language from a number of women who appeared to be following the troops," Louisa would write in her memoir. They were, of course, camp followers. "Presently, I heard these wretches cry out, 'tear them out of the carriage; they are Russians; take them out [and] kill them.'"[50] At this point several of the soldiers turned their rifles on the postilions and seized control of the carriage. Terrified but composed, Louisa pulled out her passports, and when a general officer approached, she presented them to him. He was General Claude-Étienne Michel, who had fought Toussaint L'Ouverture and his rebel slaves in Haiti. The lady, he announced, was not Russian but American on the way to Paris to join her husband. "Vive les Americans," shouted the crowd, which then awaited Louisa's reply. "Vive la Napoleon," she shouted in perfect French, waving her handkerchief. A contingent of soldiers took their places in front of the carriage. If the Americans attempted to bolt, the soldiers' orders were to shoot at once. The general and his lieutenants bracketed the berline as it proceeded. "My poor boy seemed to be absolutely petrified and sat by my side like a marble statue."[51] Michel advised Louisa that she was in a very precarious situation; the soldiers were completely undisciplined and would take orders from no one. He promised to find them lodgings at the first posthouse and complimented Louisa on her French, which, he said, would stand her in good stead. "In this way we journeyed; the soldiers presenting their bayonets at my people with loud and brutal threats every half hour—the road lined on each side for miles with intoxi-cated men ripe for every species of villainy."[52]

General Michel was as good as his word, persuading the landlady at the next posthouse to take in the weary travelers. She proved apprehensive and reluctant at first but then warmed to the American lady and her son. They must hide the car-riage, she declared, and agree to be shut up in a darkened room for the duration of their stay. Louisa readily consented and was then surprised and delighted when "I was put into a comfortable room, a wood fire was made and a very kind old gentleman came to me and encouraged me with the hope that we should get through the night without further molestation."[53] The lady of the house brought coffee and apologized for not being more attentive. Throughout the night, Louisa and Ma-dame Babet were treated to the shouts and commotions of drunken soldiers. When morning came, their hostess informed Louisa that she had opened several casks of spirits to appease the drunken Bonapartists.

At Châtillon, some guests at the posthouse warned Louisa not to proceed any farther. There were forty thousand troops massed before the gates of Paris, and a great battle was about to begin. Believing that John Quincy would appear at any moment to guide and protect her, Louisa insisted that they press on. Dupin spread the rumor that Louisa was actually Napoleon's sister, who was proceeding incog-nito to Paris to be reunited with him. "The mistress of the house told me the most dismal tales of the atrocities of the Cossacks . . . and she showed me the graves of six of the most beautiful young girls of the place who had fallen victims to the murderous horrors of savage war with all its detestable concomitants," she re-corded in her diary. The last leg of the journey took the berline through the Forêt de Bondy "so long celebrated for Banditti exploits."[54] But in due course Louisa and her companions arrived safely at the Hôtel du Nord.

John Quincy had gone to the theater that evening. "I expected to have found my wife's carriage in the yard and was disappointed," he recorded in his diary, "but had scarcely got into my chamber when she arrived—It was eleven in the evening." He found Louisa and Charles well and "was delighted after an absence of eleven months to meet them again. They have been exactly forty days in com-ing from St. Petersburg."[55] Louisa wrote of their reunion, "I was once more happy to find myself under the protection of a husband who was perfectly astonished at my adventures as everything in Paris was quiet, and it had never occurred to him that it could have been otherwise in any other part of the country."[56] (How could this have been true?)

If John Quincy's diary was any guide, he had not given his family's journey, which he must have known would have been arduous and dangerous, more than a passing thought. The morning following Louisa and Charles's return, he bundled them into a carriage to tour the Bois de Boulogne and to see the house he had lived in as a teenager with his parents and Nabby. That evening he and his wife attended the opera. Louisa soon adopted the nonchalant attitude of her husband. "[M]y journey from St. Petersburg," she wrote Abigail in June, "was performed with as little uneasiness and as few misfortunes as could possibly have been anticipated, and I have really acquired the reputation of a heroine at a very cheap rate."[57] But apparently Louisa did indeed consider herself a heroine. Though she would not say so until years later when she wrote "Narrative of a Journey from Russia to France, 1815," Louisa was justifiably proud of herself. She had managed men and money, war and weather, weakness and treachery, and, most important, her own doubts about herself. The two-thousand-mile journey from St. Petersburg to Paris did not transform Louisa Catherine Adams so much as reveal once again the spirit and resilience she had demonstrated when her back was to the wall. Was John Quincy's seeming dismissal of his wife's achievement due to jealousy, distraction, or inattention simply because of his role as diarist? Whatever the case, Louisa Catherine was now back under the shadow of the Adamses—their brilliance, their ambitions, and their egos—and of the institutionalized misogyny of her age.

20

Minister to the Court of St. James's

JOHN QUINCY HAD REASON to believe that he would be appointed U.S. minister to Great Britain, but he would not receive official confirmation until May 7. In the meantime, the other American peace commissioners and he assumed that they would be instructed to proceed to London and begin negotiations with the British government on a treaty of commerce and other issues left unresolved by the Treaty of Ghent. Questions relating to impressment and neutral rights were dead letters and would probably remain so. Europe was then at peace; if another war erupted, it was likely to be fought primarily on land. Hopefully, in the interim, the United States would enlarge its naval establishment to the point at which it could successfully resist a foreign blockade. But there were dangerous Anglo-American boundary issues to be resolved. British and American soldiers still occupied their enemy's territory. Then there was Britain's claim of the right of its citizens to navigate the Mississippi and to trade with the Indian tribes of the Old Northwest. The most dangerous outstanding issue, however, was the fisheries. John Adams had no intention of letting his son off the hook on this question. "Neither nature nor art have distributed the sea into empires, kingdoms, republics, or states as they have the land," he wrote his son. The Europeans "were all indebted to us and our ancestors for all these fisheries. We had discovered them; we had explored them. We had settled the country at our own expense, industry, and labor without assistance from Britain." It was American colonial troops who had conquered Cape Breton and Nova Scotia during the Seven Years' War. "We must not yield an iota."[1]

While he waited in Paris for his commission from Secretary of State Monroe, John Quincy paid his respects to the newly named French minister of foreign affairs, the Duc de Vicence, Armand de Caulaincourt, an old acquaintance. He congratulated Caulaincourt on his appointment and asked what the future held with Napoleon now back in power. "The Emperor had renounced all ideas of an extended empire," the Frenchman declared. He wanted peace with all the world and intended to rule by means of a constitution and a limited democracy. Surely the nations then assembled at Vienna would declare war, Adams observed. Perhaps, Caulaincourt replied, but it would be for France a war for national survival and not empire. Adams labored under no illusions concerning the emperor. "Napoleon Bonaparte was a man of great genius for military combinations and operations, whose head was turned by success, who had magnificent imaginations and some generous purposes, but was under no control for moral principle," he would later write.[2] But he detested the Bourbons. He wrote the secretary of state that Louis XVIII had restored feudalism to France, with all its aristocratic privilege and religious bigotry. The real power in the country following Napoleon's defeat had been the Duke of Wellington.[3]

The first week in May, John Quincy, Louisa, and Charles visited the Marquis de Lafayette at his country estate. "His residence is in the midst of a very beautiful country in an ancient castle, internally fitted up to modern taste and convenience surrounded by a garden and park in the English style and a large farm which he cultivated himself," John Quincy wrote his mother.[4] The general was, predictably, in agony at the recent turn of events. As John Quincy put it, Lafayette was motived by "an ardent love of his country"; he wanted Napoleon to defend France if it was attacked by the Quadruple Alliance, but he feared the consequences if he were successful.[5]

At last, on May 7, John Quincy received his commission as minister to Great Britain. On the twenty-third, John Quincy, Louisa, and Charles embarked from Le Havre aboard the *Gilliote Olga* out of Riga. The trip was short—twenty-four hours—but extremely unpleasant; the ship was in ballast—that is, unloaded—and as a result, it was blown about like a leaf on the surface of the ocean. The Adamses were crowded into a tiny cabin with Louisa and Charles in the bunk while John Quincy slept on the floor with only the Danish flag as a comforter. Mother and son became acutely seasick; John Quincy came closer to suffering the mal de mer than he had in twenty-four years. But in due course, the cliffs of Dover hove into view, a familiar sight to Adams.[6]

At eight in the evening, the trio arrived at their temporary quarters at 67 Harley Street near Cavendish Square, which had been booked by the U.S. consul. They were delighted to find there George and John; the boys had made the Atlantic crossing in an easy twenty-seven days in the company of two American scholars, one of whom was Edward Everett, the brother of Alexander, John Quincy's young protégé in St. Petersburg. John Quincy and Louisa did not recognize George, now fourteen. A tall, gangly youth, indeed a bit taller than his father, he was full of words and nervous energy. Abigail had written earlier to try to prepare the parents for the reunion. Please excuse George's "rusticity": both body and mind had outgrown themselves. "[H]e hardly knows what to do with himself." His mind, she wrote, was "a casket which contains jewels that only want culling, refining, and burnishing in his father's crucible to render them bright."[7] John, six when his parents had last seen him, was now eleven and precocious. He could use a little discipline, his grandmother had advised. The captain of the ship upon which they had sailed reported back to John's grandparents that before the voyage was over, John could name every sail and every rope in the rigging, earning him the title of "the Admiral" among the ship's crew.[8] The sophisticate of the trio of Adams brothers was seven-year-old Charles. He was conversant in French and German and had a bit of Russian. The former apple of Alexander's and Elizabeth's eyes was fresh from Paris, where he had attended the theater and various fetes with his parents.[10]

With unconscious irony, Abigail had written John Quincy to take it easy on the boys. "It is an observation of a judicious writer that if we expect boys should make valuable men, they must continue sometime in the state of boys or they will never make men worth forming."[9] John Quincy would heed the advice to an extent, but he could not help worrying about George, who was fast approaching the time when he would apply to Harvard. His father found him deficient in Greek and Latin and his handwriting deplorable. John Quincy quickly hired tutors in mathematics and penmanship for the boys, and he personally set about improving George's skills with the ancient languages. To their parents' dismay, George talked of a life in the army while John was entranced with the navy. Neither career, their parents advised them, would contribute to either their education or their prosperity.[10]

The day following his arrival in London, Minister Adams sent notice to Lord Castlereagh, asking for an inaugural interview. He visited Henry Clay, who was preparing to return to the United States; Gallatin, who had been named minister to France; and Bayard, who had turned down John Quincy's old post in St. Petersburg due to ill health. The foreign secretary received Adams on May 29. John Quincy was initially chilled: "His deportment is sufficiently graceful, and his person is handsome. His manner was cold, but not absolutely repulsive."[11] John Adams had warned his son that he was lying down in a bed of thorns: "There are secret correspondences, theological, ecclesiastical, philosophical, democratical Jacobinical, aristocratical, and monarchical between Europe and America by the players in which games you will be watched and represented in a manner that you never can discover."[12] In truth, public opinion in Britain continued to be virulently hostile to the United States. Shortly after the close of the War of 1812, a group of British students had written and performed an anti-American play. The tale featured a misguided youth who planned to emigrate to America. "What!" his friend exclaimed, "to that country which is beyond the ocean; a country barbarous in itself and inhabited by barbarians."[13] The *Port Folio* obtained a copy of the script and published it in its entirety.

The course of British foreign policy during Adams's stay in Britain would not be determined by the tabloids or public opinion, however, but by Robert Stewart, Viscount Castlereagh. The foreign secretary was a wealthy aristocrat with a common touch. He was also a sensible man. The war with America was over; it had served no useful purpose, he believed. Rapprochement with Britain's former American colonies—on Britain's terms, of course—was clearly in his country's interest. When John Quincy had his initial meeting with Castlereagh, the Englishman had just returned from Vienna, where he had secured everything Britain coveted, and prevented others from having what Britain did not want them to have. His initial iciness toward Adams soon melted away. On June 11, he hosted a dinner for the American diplomats in London. "Lord Castlereagh treated us with the politest attention," John Quincy recorded in his diary. "He seated me at his right hand and Mr. Clay at his left."[14] Then came news of Napoleon's defeat at Waterloo. "Shortly after rising this morning, I received a note from Lord Castlereagh's office announcing the splendid and complete victory of the Duke of Wellington and Marshal [Gebhard] Blucher over the French Army commanded by Buonaparte in person."[15] How exactly this would affect Britain's posture toward the United States, Adams was not quite sure.

Britain might have been the undisputed Mistress of the Seas and the flywheel of Continental diplomacy when the Adamses arrived, but the country was suffering from a severe depression and the social unrest that accompanied it. With the close of hostilities, some three hundred thousand sailors and soldiers had been cashiered and thrown upon the streets. The manufacturers and shipbuilders who had prospered during the war were suddenly without government purchases; many had to close their doors and turn out their workers. During the war, the price of British agricultural products had soared because the Continental System had closed the door to the import of cheap cereals grown on the Continent. In 1815, Parliament, dominated by wealthy landowners, had passed the Corn Law, which barred European grain from British ports. To top it all off, the Liverpool government kept high wartime taxes in place in an effort to reduce the enormous national debt. "People are suffering from actual famine," John Quincy wrote his mother, "and a very large portion are struggling with the extremity of want; if the severity of cold were added to their calamities, they would be perishing by the thousands."[16] Louisa wrote Abigail, "I am positively assured that the poorer classes of society do not taste meat once in several months and it is hardly possible to [take] five steps from your door without being surrounded with . . . beggars who assure you they have not a bit of bread."[17]

Much of the blame for these woeful circumstances was laid at the doorstep of the prince regent, the future George IV, who was ruling in his father's stead. George III had gone quite mad. The prince and his coarse and scandal-prone wife, Princess Caroline, pursued a lifestyle whose extravagance was worthy of a Bourbon. In early 1817 a mob pelted the prince regent's carriage with stones, breaking out the windows.[18] Rumor had it that the missiles were bullets, not stones. "Princes may perhaps be more willing to be shot at with bullets than stoned," John Quincy observed. "[A]ssasination is more likely to prove the existence of a plot than mere mobbing."[19]

The Treaty of Ghent, which merely restored the status quo ante bellum, would seem to have demonstrated that the War of 1812 was a draw. Such was not the case, John Quincy insisted. Any American who had visited Europe in 1811 would find his country viewed in a much different light, were he to cross the Atlantic in 1815. "The importance of the United States in the general scale of civilized Nation, increases in the estimation of all Europe," he wrote Abigail. "Their naval exploits throughout the late war had made an impression profound and universal . . . the issue of the last campaign by land, both in the North and South, has still deepened and confirmed that impression."[20] Except for Russia, virtually no nation in Europe had been able to resist domination and subordination by either France or Great Britain—not only the weak and irresolute Dutch, but the proud and mighty Prussians as well. America had demonstrated both the spirit and the will to resist the ships of the Royal Navy and the soldiers of the Iron Duke. The Federalist Party was on the verge of extinction, Adams predicted, and he looked forward to a period of bipartisanship and nationalism. Castlereagh's accommodating posture toward Adams and his country was more than simply a product of his amiability, the American minister observed.

Shortly after news of Waterloo arrived, Adams, Clay, and Gallatin signed a commercial convention with Great Britain. There was no mention of impressment or neutral rights; there was no need, as John Quincy had already observed. "The world of Europe is in a glassy calm," he wrote his father. "Not a breath of wind or a ripple of water is moving."[21] Goulburn, William Adams, and Frederick John Robinson, vice president of the British Board of Trade, negotiated for His Majesty's government. The convention provided for reciprocal free trade between the United States and British ports in Europe plus Calcutta, Madras, and Bombay in the East Indies. The much-coveted trade with the British West Indies was denied to Americans. The names of His Majesty's negotiators came first on the document. Adams insisted on the practice of alternat—that is, in the various copies that needed to be made of the commercial convention, the British and American signatures would take turns occupying the place of honor. Unheard of, declared Goulburn and company. If they would check with their foreign office, John Quincy interjected, they would find it common international practice. Both Clay and Gallatin thought the matter trivial. "Oh, that [the demand for alternat] is entirely wrong," Gallatin declared; "it will throw the business into confusion." John Quincy was adamant: "Indeed, sir," declared the new minister to Great Britain, "I will not sign the treaty in any other form. . . . I think it by much the most important thing that we shall obtain by this treaty. The treaty itself I very much dislike, and it is only out of deference to you and Mr. Clay that I consent to sign it at all."[22] Adams had his way both with the British and American delegations. The copies featured alternating signatures.

During 1815 and 1816, Castlereagh and Adams negotiated almost continuously on matters of mutual interest to their two countries. Throughout their talks the two men proved civil and restrained in their arguments; each came to respect the other, and that mutual respect was as important to the First Rapprochement as the interests that were discussed. At Ghent, the American commissioners had proposed mutual disarmament on the Great Lakes, but nothing had come of it. Indeed, during the spring and summer of 1815, British military authorities in Canada had steadily enlarged their freshwater naval squadron. When Adams brought the subject up, Castlereagh declared that Britain favored disarmament on the inland lakes; that was why at Ghent Goulburn and company had proposed that all the shorelines should be placed under Canadian control. America had not and would not agree to any such thing, Adams declared. Finally, Castlereagh conceded that time and geography were on America's side, and agreed to propose mutual disarmament without condition to his government. The upshot of these negotiations was the Rush–Bagot Agreement of April 28–29, 1817, the first instance of reciprocal naval disarmament in the history of international relations.[23]

In the aftermath of Waterloo, the restored monarchy of Ferdinand VII lay completely under the control of Great Britain. Castlereagh boasted that the Spanish royal household would literally starve to death if it were not for British aid.[24] In one of his initial reports to the secretary of state, Minister Adams repeated rumors that Madrid had been forced to cede the Floridas—which the United States had been coveting virtually since its birth—to Britain. This was not true, but a British adventurer, Lieutenant Colonel Edward Nicolls, had remained in Florida after the close of hostilities and was then intriguing with the Indian tribes of the Southeast, arming and encouraging them to resist American incursions. Declaring that the Treaty of Ghent had invalidated the Treaty of Fort Jackson, he, without authorization from London, concluded an agreement with the Red Stick Creeks, recognizing them as an independent nation to be defended and commercially supported by Great Britain.[25] When Adams protested to Lord Bathurst, who was still in charge of military operations in North America, the Englishman declared, "Why to tell you the truth Colonel Nicholls is, I believe, a man of activity and spirit, but a very wild fellow. He did make and send over to me a treaty, offensive and defensive, with some Indians, and he is now come over here and has brought over some of those Indians." Bathurst assured Adams that the Liverpool government had rejected both the treaty and Lieutenant Colonel Nicolls. The Foreign Office was going to aid the Creek delegation, which was in a very bad way, but then send it home, advising their guests to make the best agreement they could with the government of the United States.[26]

In discussing the fisheries, John Quincy did not, of course, reveal his disgust with New England but pressed U.S. claims with vigor. There was a sense of immediacy in these talks, as Captain Nagle Lock, commander of the British naval squadron operating out of Halifax, had warned American vessels not to approach closer than sixty miles to the coasts of Newfoundland and Nova Scotia. He had in fact boarded several Yankee fishing vessels that had ignored the order. The War of 1812 and the Treaty of Ghent had not invalidated the Treaty of 1783, as the British were claiming, John Quincy insisted. The Treaty of Paris was not between two nations. "It was not simply a treaty of peace; it was a treaty of partition between two parts of one nation, agreeing thenceforth to be separated into two distinct sovereignties." Britain had no more right to deny the United States access to the Grand Banks than the United States did to deny Britain access to the West Indies.[27] Whitehall ordered Lock to rescind the sixty-mile decree and agreed to extend the "privilege" of fishing and drying to American vessels on a year-to-year basis; that was as far as Castlereagh and Bathurst would go.[28]

Perhaps the most vexing topic in the 1815–1816 negotiations had to do with runaway slaves who had been taken in by the British during the War of 1812. Following the ratification of the Treaty of Ghent, several thousand remained aboard British warships, a number of which were still in American waters. Washington had demanded the return of the slaves, but Britain had refused. His Majesty's government had not provided indemnification for "carrying away any Negroes" during the Revolutionary War, and they were determined not to do so in the wake of the War of 1812. The Monroe administration estimated that around thirty-six hundred human chattels had taken refuge with the British at a cost of several hundreds of thousands of dollars to their masters.[29] John Quincy pointed out that the Treaty of Ghent required the mutual return of all private property. Liverpool himself entered the conversation: "I do not think," he declared, "they can be considered precisely under the general denomination of private property. A table or a chair, for instance, might be taken and restored without changing its condition; but a living and a human being is entitled to other consideration." William Wilberforce and his abolitionist cohorts in Parliament were pressing their campaign to outlaw the slave trade, and the government was under some pressure. "I do readily admit the distinction suggested by you," Adams said, but he pointed out that slavery was legal in several states of the Union, and insisted that the owners of the runaways deserved compensation.[30] He added, slyly, that there were rumors that several British commanders sold their runaways in the slave markets of the West Indies, which was true. To this, Liverpool had no answer. The negotiators agreed in the end to refer the matter to a mixed commission. In 1826, Britain agreed to pay $1.2 million in compensation to American claimants.[31]

IT QUICKLY BECAME APPARENT to the Adamses that they could not afford to maintain a residence in London. John Quincy had called at the banking house of Baring Brothers, and they had readily agreed to extend him a twenty-five-thousand-dollar line of credit. But both John Quincy and Louisa wrote home complaining of the lack of financial support from Congress. "Jonathan [the United States] chooses to live snug and at small cost," Adams wrote Congressman George Joy. "He chooses to have no useless servants at great expense. When you talk to Jonathan about the necessity of maintaining his dignity, he laughs, casts a sly look across the waters at Brother John [Bull] and says, there's dignity enough for both of us."[32] It quickly became apparent that Washington was not going to provide him with an "outfit."[33]

On August 1, the Adamses moved to Little Ealing, a hamlet situated some ten miles west of London. With John Quincy busy from dawn to dusk with official business, it was Louisa who had found a country home for them. "The family were engaged the whole day in packing and loading two carts and a wagon with our baggage, furniture, and wines to remove to this place," John Quincy recorded in his diary.[34] Adams was well pleased with their new abode, which was named Little Boston House; it was a "dower" situated on the grounds of Boston Manor House, a magnificent Jacobean mansion. In England, when the eldest son took possession of the manor house, he often built a smaller home for his mother—a dower. The three-story structure was "not large but neat and elegant and fitted up with all that minute attention to comfort which is characteristic of English domestic life."[35] The dower came with a coach house and stables, as well as walled-in flower and vegetable gardens. Little Boston House was situated at the entrance to the grand estate, and the Adamses would have access to the beautiful gardens and woodlands that it comprised. The rent also included two pews at St. Mary's Anglican Church in Great Ealing, a mile away.

The Adamses' landlady was Mary Clitherow, the sister of the lord of the manor, Colonel James Clitherow IV. The weekly rent was five guineas, less than half what a very modest abode in London would have cost. Louisa herself was elated. "The situation is beautiful, the house comfortable, and the distance from the great city supportable. . . . We are within an hour's ride of Kew, Richmond, Twickenham, Harrow, and a variety of other beautiful places, and the situation is said to be perfectly healthful."[36]

As soon as they were settled, John Quincy and Louisa began to look about for a suitable boarding school for John and Charles. They first visited Orger House, situated about two miles away in Acton, but found it unsatisfactory. John Hewlett, the Johnsons' old friend and adviser, recommended the Great Ealing School, whose headmaster, Dr. George Nicholas, was a fellow graduate of Oxford. Everything about the institution, only a mile from Little Boston House, pleased John Quincy and Louisa. They found Nicholas both genial and progressive. In truth, Great Ealing was considered one of the premier boarding schools in England, the academic equivalent of Harrow or Eton. The school's two hundred fifty students, ranging in age from six to seventeen, came from the ranks of the country's upper-middle class—the sort of boys with whom John Quincy and Louisa intended their sons to associate and identify. John and Charles would not be allowed to return home for two weeks; after that, they could visit Little Boston House on weekends. No exceptions, please, Dr. Nicholas declared. But parents could visit the school each morning if they wished.[37] Initially John and Charles were quite discontented. "They have never before been accustomed to the restraints of an English school; and both of them have been several months released from all study so that a return to it is irksome," their father confided to his diary.[38] But they soon settled in.

John Quincy intended to tutor George himself and focus on the Harvard entrance examinations. The fourteen-year-old was roused out of bed at six a.m. and put through his paces. "He read three chapters in the French Bible, while I had the Latin Bible to follow him as he read," John Quincy recorded. "After which we exchanged books, and I read three chapters of the French while he held the Latin Book to compare with it."[39] A week later John Quincy assigned Cicero's *Second Philippic* for his son to translate. "He has not been used to the exercise and performs it very indifferently."[40] Cooped up with his father's intellect and intensity, George was no doubt miserable. In late September, in company with his parents, the teenager attended a dramatic performance at Great Ealing School. The chance to mix and mingle with youths of his own age and background was intoxicating.

The young man begged his parents to enroll him, and they reluctantly acceded. John Quincy insisted, however, that he continue to live at home, rise at five for instruction in Latin and Greek, and then walk the mile to school, where classes began at seven a.m. During the next year and a half, George was perhaps never happier in his life. To Louisa's delight he began bringing his friends home to dinner and assumed his place among the more socially and intellectually active students. He appeared in several stage performances and was elected to "the Spy Club," a select group of older boys that included John Henry (later Cardinal) Newman. The club put out a literary magazine, the *Portfolio*—the name having been suggested by George, as Newman later recalled.

John was even happier at Great Ealing School than George. Charles, not so much. He was still young and had grown used to private instruction either from his father or tutors. The tumult of two hundred fifty boys in close association with one another overwhelmed and distracted him. John was a naturally social being, inquisitive and adventurous. He proved popular both with his teachers and his mates. "John remains much as he was as to height," Louisa wrote her mother-in-law, "but in fine health and grown extremely fat . . . he is a great arithmetician, and the rapidity with which he learns quite surprises his master."[41] John had always been the apple of his grandfather's eye. The young man wrote boasting of his athletic exploits; John the elder responded, "I approve your . . . playing football, cricket, running, climbing, leaping, swimming, skating and have no great objection to your play at marbles. . . . These are good for your health; but what do you do for your mind?"[42]

John Quincy took care to see that his sons did not neglect the martial arts. He hired a fencing master and bought a brace of pistols so that George and John could learn to shoot. One mild October afternoon with the fencing master, a Mr. Barberi, at the house, John Quincy decided to give the pistols a test. He would go first, he decided. Barberi unfortunately doubled John Quincy's powder charge, and when he pulled the trigger, the pistol exploded, flying some ten feet over his left shoulder. The misfire left John Quincy's right hand severely burned.[43] The wounds festered, making it impossible for Adams to write; he compensated by reading incessantly, which led to inflammation and swelling of his left eye, previously damaged by his unguarded viewing of a solar eclipse. The hand began to heal slowly, but not the eye. "The pain became intensely severe and almost without interval," he recorded in his diary on October 26. The doctor was called in and prescribed dieting and elderflower tea. He also recommended leeches. "I was so averse to the use of leeches that he consented to wait a day or two longer."[44] Two days later, John Quincy gave in. "I accordingly consented and about noon he brought and applied six of them to the swelling round the lower eyelid. Two of them, would not effectually bite, but dropped off within five minutes. The other four bit keenly and were nearly an hour on my face. After they dropped off, the wounds they had made were kept bleeding . . . between four and five hours."[45] The cure initially proved worse than the disease. "I went to bed about eight in the evening," John Quincy reported on the twenty-ninth, "and the pain soon after became so violent, that I was nearly delirious. It seemed to me as if four hooks were tearing that side of my face into four quarters."[46] Soon after, with the eye continually draining tears and "purulent matter," the swelling and pain began to subside. The first week in December, John Quincy was able to walk from his London offices to Little Boston House, making the eight-mile-plus trip in two and a half hours.

Twice a week Minister Adams journeyed into London, usually by carriage, to attend to official business, sometimes spending the night. The American minister had rented several rooms in a house near Downing Street. A private secretary came to the offices every day to open and send letters, to copy papers, and to deal with distressed American seamen stranded in Britain by the ending of the Napoleonic Wars. John Quincy was due a paid secretary of legation. John Adams Smith, brother of William Steuben Smith, had applied for the job, but the minister refused to consider him. In truth he was sick and tired of the Smiths. He was glad to learn, he wrote his mother, that William and Kitty had reached America safely. "I have occasionally made you acquainted with many of the incidents which made his residence and political relation with me unpleasant to us both." Smith was deficient in "prudence," and John Quincy assumed his brother was similarly afflicted. Besides, he had had enough of nepotism.[47] John Quincy had nominated his protégé Alexander Hill Everett to be secretary of legation. But with Abigail, blood was thicker than water, and she used her influence to see that Monroe named her grandson to the post. The younger Smith arrived in December just as John Quincy was recovering from his eye infection. He proved intelligent, honest, and diligent and became a welcome member of the family.[48]

Between negotiations with Castlereagh and Bathurst, Minister Adams spent much of his time dealing with stranded and impoverished American seamen. "When I got to the office," Adams recorded in his diary for December 2, "I found there an official note from him [Castlereagh] stating that the Lord Mayor of London had made a representation to the home department that a number of American seamen were wandering about the streets in a most wretched and distressed condition and that several of them were supported at the police establishments and hospitals of the city at a considerable expense." Could the American minister please arrange for their repatriation?[49] Some of the destitute Americans had been impressed into the Royal Navy and dismissed along with British seamen when the fleet was reduced. Some were former prisoners of war. The task of caring for the stranded sailors really belonged to the U.S. consul general, R. G. Beasley. Adams found the man completely indifferent; indeed, sailors lined up on his doorstep to complain of Beasley's callousness. A particular victim of his neglect was one Thomas Nelson, a Black sailor who had been jailed at St. Albans on the suspicion that his papers had been forged. "I have the fullest conviction that this man is no impostor," Adams wrote the consul, "and was improperly left by his captain at Havre." Whether the unfortunate individual was ever released is unclear. Adams did his best for the stranded sailors, but, as he wrote Beasley, "I can neither turn them from my doors nor afford them the relief which they so eminently need."[50]

ONE OF THE ADAMSES' dinner guests in the spring of 1816 was Prince Saunders ("Sanders" in John Quincy's diary), an African American educator who had been hired by the king of Haiti, Henri Christophe, to create a nationwide system of public education. He had arrived in England aboard the same ship as George and John, whom he had befriended. Saunders, born in Lebanon, Connecticut, in 1775, was raised by the prominent attorney George Oramel Hinckley and educated at Dartmouth College. Upon graduation he devoted his life to furthering Black education. With the support of Dartmouth president John Wheelock and Unitarian minister William Ellery Channing, Saunders was able to establish several schools devoted to teaching Black youth. Through his friendship with British abolitionists William Wilberforce and Thomas Clarkson, Saunders came to the attention of King Henri, who dispatched him to England in 1815 to drum up support for the Haitian school system he envisioned. "Mr. Sanders, the Black Gentleman came for the purpose of spending the day with my sons," Adams recorded in his diary on April 17, 1816, "and being disappointed by not finding them at home, he stayed and spent it with me." Over dinner the two had a long discussion about "Hayti, as he calls it, or St. Domingo, and found he was in the highest degree delighted with his new connection there."[51] Saunders praised the king and confided to Minister Adams that Henri Christophe was determined to expel the Catholic Church from his country and establish Anglicanism. The Church, it seemed, was in league with the French and Creoles in Haiti in a scheme to relegate Blacks to an inferior place in the nation's society. John Quincy was wont to view Henri Christophe as a "gilded African," as Napoleon had Toussaint L'Ouverture. "I believe he [Saunders] is a well-meaning man but stronger heads than his have been turned by such a change of circumstance."[52] Before he left to return to Haiti, Saunders became the toast of London society, hosted by the great patron of science Sir Joseph Banks and the Countess of Cork. He returned to Haiti, where, with the help of several English educators, he established the Royal College of Haiti in Cape Henry. In later life as a congressman, Adams would introduce legislation providing for diplomatic recognition of Haiti, a move that brought the full ire of the slave power down on his head.

John Quincy and Louisa found their treatment by the Court of St. James's far different from their receptions in Berlin and St. Petersburg, where Louisa had danced with both King Frederick William and Tsar Alexander. Though they were invited to every official reception at Carlton House, the prince regent's official residence, the head of state never deigned to speak to her. "I confess I feel very awkward under such circumstances and never know how to behave," Louisa wrote Abigail. "I do not like to find myself in a house where I am not acknowledged as an acquaintance." John Quincy was received by the queen, and though he had been presented to her twenty years earlier, "She asked me whether I was related to the Mr. Adams who had been formerly the minister to this country and appeared surprised when I answered that I was his son."[53] At one soiree, Adams encountered the Duke of Wellington. Though they had been introduced twice before, Adams had to remind the Iron Duke who he was. "This is one of the many incidents from which I can perceive how very small a space my person or my station occupy in the notice of these persons and at these places."[54] Though he was the minister plenipotentiary representing the United States, John Quincy and his wife were republicans and therefore commoners and thus, in Britain's rigid class system, inferior. Though they lived just down the road from Boston Manor, the Clitherows never even bothered to offer the Adamses a cup of tea. Even Lord and Lady Carysfort, George's godparents and intimate friends of the Adamses when they all were in Berlin, remained aloof.

So John Quincy and Louisa embraced their upper-middle-class status and made a life for themselves at Ealing. They held frequent dinners to which they invited prominent locals. Among the guests were Dr. Nicholas and his wife; Major Alexander Morrison, a retired East India army officer; and Alexander Copeland, a wealthy developer.[55] In February 1816, John Quincy and Louisa were introduced into a new, more prestigious social circle when John Quincy was befriended by Matthew Wood, a chemist and hop merchant and the lord mayor of London. John Quincy was invited to "a splendid dinner and ball" given in honor of the two visiting Austrian archdukes. To his surprise he was called upon to offer up a toast in response to one made in honor of the president of the United States. He performed admirably; his elegant offering was printed in the London newspapers to much acclaim. "He [Wood] invited me within ten days afterwards to another great entertainment which he gave to the wardens of his fishmongers' company. I was the only foreigner invited to that party, and there I met the Duke of Kent again and the Duke of Sussex, whom I had formerly known in Berlin"; the crème de la crème was a cruise on the lord mayor's barge from Westminster Bridge to Richmond.[56] "The barge was elegantly ornamented with streamers, and the Duke of Kent's band of music were on board. . . . The weather was fine, and the barge was surrounded all the way down by . . . perhaps twenty boats filled with company, ladies and gentlemen, as witnesses of the scene; about five o'clock near Richmond Bridge . . . the whole company sat down to an elegant cold dinner."[57]

Occasionally John Quincy and Louisa would stay overnight in London to attend the theater. One could reserve seats with the boxkeeper but did not have to pay in advance. However, for a shilling theatergoers could secure a man to hold their seats for them until the end of the first act. Then it was every person for themselves. The first row of boxes was called dress boxes and those immediately behind, the first row. The Adamses saw Charles Kemble play Orlando in *As You Like It* and Sarah Siddons as Queen Katharine in *Henry VIII*. During the performance of *As You Like It*, "There arose a brawl in the pit just before our box in which there was an attempt to turn a man out, some pulling and hauling, and one or two fisty-cuff blows given; but the man kept his seat."[58]

In the year 1816, Europe experienced winter in the middle of summer. "There were several sharp frosts in July and August," John Quincy reported to his mother, "and the newspapers are filled with accounts of snow in harvest and of ice an inch thick in dog-days [of summer] within a hundred miles of London." Scarcely a night passed that the residents of Little Boston House did not have to light a fire. Astronomers and astrologists blamed the absence of a summer on sunspots. However, Adams wrote, "There has scarcely been seen enough of the sun to know whether it was spotted or not."[59] In fact, the "Year Without a Summer" was the result of the massive volcanic eruption of Mount Tambora on the island of Sumbawa in the Netherlands East Indies. The outpouring reached its climax on April 10, 1815, and continued for the next six months, emitting a cloud of smoke that spread over much of the globe, obscured the sun, and drastically lowered temperatures.[60] As usual, John Quincy refused to allow the weather to deter him from his exercise routine. "I left the Office and walked home in two hours and twenty minutes," he recorded in his diary for April 12. "I was twice overtaken with heavy showers of hail, sleet, and snow, the first in Hyde Park and the second at Turnham Green. The last soaked me through and through."[61]

That September, John Quincy visited the American expatriate artist Benjamin West at his residence. He found him in the midst of painting *Death on the Pale Horse* from the Book of Revelation. John Quincy was a bit shocked: "the two pictures of Christ healing the sick, and Christ rejected are more to my taste."[62]

John Quincy and Louisa had their portraits painted by the twenty-one-year-old artist Charles Robert Leslie. Both paintings, rendered in vivid detail, portray the couple elegantly dressed and at their handsomest.[63] In truth, in England, John Quincy seemed to have been overtaken by unaccustomed serenity, even to the point of softening his ambitions for his sons. "I must and do leave them to their teachers and masters," he wrote Abigail. "They are all, thanks to God, boys of good tempers and good dispositions. But the great and constant effort of them all, including George, is to escape from study, and to this effort I have given up all opposition as vain. I comfort myself with the reflection that they are like other children and prepare my mind for seeing them, if their lives are spared, get along in the world like other men."[64] He even eased up on himself. Instead of spending evenings exploring a new language or analyzing texts composed by the ancients, John Quincy entertained, read novels aloud to Louisa, or stargazed with George and Ellen Nicholas, one of the headmaster's daughters.

By the fall of 1816, Miss Nicholas was a constant companion to the Adamses, living at Little Boston House for weeks at a time. John Quincy became infatuated with the charming girl and began a platonic relationship that had him composing romantic verse in every spare moment. Louisa was as pleased with Ellen's companionship as her husband. The eighteen-year-old might have served as a surrogate for the daughter she had lost. The two women rode horses together, shopped in London, and embarked on fishing expeditions. In the evenings Ellen accompanied Louisa on the pianoforte as she sang Handel's arias and other selections. In mid-October Ellen and Louisa exchanged some verses they had written and urged John Quincy to respond. "I pleaded the barrenness of my imagination as long as I could but in return for Ellen's poetry, something was become indispensable. I strained from hard bound brains two stanzas of eight lines in the amatory style."[65] He composed several more stanzas on a carriage ride to London the next day and finished the following morning as he was rising from bed. "But there is an incongruity in the lines," he reported to his diary, "because the additional stanzas . . . are too serious and even solemn, written as if from a youthful and ardent lover, and expressing sentiments which I neither do nor ought to feel for her. The love is all merely poetical but has so much the appearance of reality that I scruple to show the lines now they are written."[66]

In early December, Ellen returned to her parents' house, having spent nearly three months with the Adamses. "I have totally ceased writing verse," John Quincy recorded in his diary. But then, at her request, he penned a fifty-six-line ode to his young admirer entitled "To Miss Ellen Nicholas on Her Birth-Day, 14 December 1816." In her complexion, "the lovely Ellen" had joined the "Snows of December to the lilies of June."[67] "The poetic fountain spouts through all its pipes," he exulted.[68] Louisa feigned jealousy; Ellen's verses far surpassed anything he had ever written for her, she teased. After John Quincy and Louisa returned to the United States, Ellen wrote to "my sweet Mr. Adams," requesting that he correspond so that she could continue to be enlightened by his wisdom.[69] Ellen Nicholas would die prematurely in 1818. "She was only 20, a lovely and accomplished girl," John Quincy would lament in his diary.[70]

21

Secretary of State

IN JANUARY 1817, JOHN Quincy wrote his father: "About the middle of November last [year] Mr. George Boyd arrived here and . . . told me it was said by some that the State Department would be offered to me by the next President. Since then, numerous suggestions to the same effect have reached me, and the report has finally been distributed throughout this country by the paragraphs of newspapers extracted from those of the United States."[1] The rumor was true. In the wake of the Treaty of Ghent, the Federalist Party had become irrelevant. The party of Jefferson, now known simply as the Republicans, was everywhere dominant. The Federalists' demise was due both to the Hartford Convention and to the Republicans' virtual abandonment of the philosophy of states' rights and limited government. In December 1815, President Madison had proposed to Congress the reestablishment of a national bank, passage of a protective tariff to encourage domestic manufacturing, and creation of a program of federally financed internal improvements to bind "more closely together the various parts of our extended confederacy."[2] Madison, like Jefferson, handpicked his successor.

James Monroe was the fourth in the line of the Virginia dynasty. He had crossed the Delaware with Washington and been wounded leading a charge against the Hessians at the Battle of Trenton. A lawyer and states' rights Republican, he had opposed ratification of the Constitution. Monroe had challenged Madison for a seat in the House of Representatives in the First Congress and lost. In 1808, the Quids ran him against Madison for the Republican nomination for president. He lost again. But then, in March 1811, Jefferson engineered a rapprochement between the two men, and Madison named his former rival secretary of state. Monroe emerged from the War of 1812 a convert to nationalism and Madison's chosen successor.[3]

There were three candidates for the post of chief diplomat in the new Monroe administration: Albert Gallatin, Henry Clay, and John Quincy Adams. The urbane Swiss émigré was both diplomatically and politically qualified. He was respected in virtually all of Europe's foreign ministries, and he had been a stalwart and prominent Republican. But Gallatin had supported Daniel Tompkins of New York rather than Monroe for the presidency. He was also foreign-born, so he would require special dispensation from Congress. Exhausted by his exertions as secretary of the treasury and a participant in the Ghent negotiations, Gallatin did not covet the job. Conversely, Henry Clay wanted desperately to be secretary of state, then considered a stepping stone to the presidency. But Monroe believed that he needed a New Englander in a prominent place in his cabinet—very Adams-like, he intended to be president for the whole nation. He offered Clay the War Department, but Harry of the West insisted that it was State or nothing; he actively opposed Adams's nomination. He was not the only one. The arch-Federalist Rufus King wrote a political friend, "Your J.Q.A., it is said, is to be recalled to be made Monroe's secretary of state, either to disgrace, or to promote him. But rather any Southern or Western democrat than J.Q.A. for president . . . If J.Q.A. becomes president, all of New England that is virtuous or enlightened will be persecuted and degraded; manners, laws, principles will be changed and deteriorated."[4] Gallatin, however, supported Adams. "After the explanation of his views to me, he [Monroe] could not for a moment have thought of Mr. Clay for the State Department without having previously made up his mind to lose my good opinion and, of course, my services," Gallatin wrote a friend.[5] "I shall take a person of the Department of State from the eastward," Monroe wrote Andrew Jackson, "and Mr. Adams by long service in our diplomatic concerns appearing to be entitled to the preference [and] supported by his acknowledged abilities and integrity, his nomination will go to the Senate." For his part, the Hero of New Orleans was enthusiastic: "I have no hesitation in saying you have made the best selection to fill the Department of State that could be made."[6]

Whether Monroe intended to anoint the New Englander as his successor was a matter of much speculation. Adams seemed a safe choice for the Republicans, a party that was turning from states' rights to nationalism. His only real political enemies were the High Federalists, more and more of whom were expiring literally or figuratively. Clay argued that his rival was not a true Republican, but given Adams's actions and rhetoric since the Louisiana Purchase, that was a hard case to make. Still, there were doubts, particularly concerning his personality. "Some think there is a *bona fide* intention to designate him for the next presidency and that Colonel Monroe believes this the best way of securing his next four years' term," Gallatin wrote a friend. "Others suppose the only object is to afford A. a fair chance of hanging himself which they say he will certainly do in a short time."[7]

John Quincy received official word of his appointment in April. Monroe wrote that he had submitted Adams's name to the Senate, and the nomination had been confirmed. "I have done this in confidence that it will be agreeable to you to accept, which I can assure you will be very gratifying to me."[8] The offer came from a man whom Adams had once derided as a fervid Jacobin who as minister to France had conspired to betray his country's interests. An intimate of Thomas Paine, Monroe had openly plotted with Francophiles in Congress to undermine Adams's father, in his view. But times had changed, and John Quincy's ambition burned as hot as ever. Louisa noted in her diary that her husband had been on pins and needles since rumors of his appointment surfaced. "Every man knows the plague of his own heart," John Quincy wrote in his diary. "Mine is the impossibility of remaining where I am and the treacherous project of the future. Let me hope."[9] Ambition aside, Adams had enthusiastically embraced the Republican Party's swing to nationalism, and Monroe's stated determination to be a president above party appealed to him. He accepted immediately and "with . . . no hesitation," as he wrote the president.[10] Louisa was delighted. Her ambition for her husband was as strong as his and more overt.[11]

By April 28, the family had packed their belongings and was ready to depart Little Boston House. After taking one last walk around the manor grounds, Adams wrote in his diary, "I have perhaps never in the course of my life resided more comfortably than at the house which we now quit, and which I shall probably never see again."[12]

The previous year John Quincy had attempted to make contact with the radical reformer and philosopher Jeremy Bentham, but they had missed each other. In early May, while the Adamses waited in London for a ship to carry them to America, John Quincy and Bentham had dinner. During the days that followed, they took three-hour walks around Hyde Park and Kensington, discussing moral and political philosophy. The British radical was an advocate of public welfare, the separation of church and state, absolute freedom of expression, equal rights for women, the right to divorce, and the decriminalization of homosexuality. Bentham was also an abolitionist and an opponent of the death penalty. Among his disciples were John Stuart Mill and Robert Owen, one of the founders of utopian socialism. Bentham was the author of "utilitarianism," the notion that the object of all government—indeed, of society itself—was the greatest good for the greatest number. The overriding goal of his life was to create a "Pannomion," a comprehensive utilitarian code of law. He had outlined his plan in *The Principles of Morals and Legislation*, copies of which he sent to both Madison and Jefferson. "Mr. Bentham is a man of 70 somewhat eccentric in his deportment but of great ingenuity and benevolence," John Quincy observed noncommittally.[13]

At the time Adams and Bentham conducted their series of ambulatory conversations, the British philosopher, then sixty-nine, had just published *A Catechism of Parliamentary Reform*, in which he urged converting the British monarchy and House of Lords into mere figureheads and investing virtually all power in the House of Commons, whose members would be chosen by universal suffrage, including women. You reject, then, the notion of a government balanced between a monarchy, an aristocracy, and a democracy—the three estates? Adams asked. I do, Bentham replied; the Crown and the British nobility had so circumscribed the power of the people entrusted to the House of Commons that "the liberties of the country were utterly gone."[14] The Whigs were no better than the Tories, Bentham declared. "I considered him as having conceded that reform with democratic ascendency would lead to the abolition of the crown and peerage," John Quincy noted in his diary. "But these institutions were too powerful and too deeply rooted to perish without a struggle; and what would be the consequences of that?"[15] "The real object of the radical reformers was revolution," was it not? Adams asked the philosopher. "And what if they [the people] should put down the crown and the peerage?" Bentham asked. Is your government in America the worse for having neither king nor lords? "Or are you exclusively entitled to the enjoyment of good government, and must you begrudge it to others?"[16] Still haunted by the excesses of the French Revolution and the machinations of Thomas Paine and other American "Jacobins," Adams replied that Americans had taken up arms not to establish a pure democracy but a balanced, three-branch federal government that would represent the interests of all the social classes. Evil would always lurk in the hearts of men, especially the immoral and uneducated, he declared.

From statecraft, the two philosophers moved on to the issue of religion, with Bentham, the atheist, pitted against Adams, the discerning Christian. No movement there either. Jeremy Bentham was the quintessential materialist. At the root of his political philosophy was the notion that human society is governed by pleasure and pain very broadly defined. He doubted the existence of a divine Creator, he told Adams, because such a being had never been experienced by any of the five senses. All human knowledge was either positive or inferential. Only that confirmed by the senses could be trusted. Moreover, "all inferential knowledge was imperfect and uncertain, depending upon a process of the human mind which could not in its nature be conclusive. That our knowledge of the physical world was positive while that of a Creator of it was inferential . . . [a] deduction from a syllogism, a mere probability from the combinations of human reason."[17] Nonsense, Adams replied. There were numerous instances in which the senses transmitted false information. "Did not our eyes tell us that the sun and the heavens rotated daily around the earth, and yet astronomy and mathematics had revealed that the opposite was true?" Everywhere there were examples of human intellect molding and controlling matter, but had anyone ever seen, heard, or smelled that intellect? "He [Bentham] replied little to this argument, apparently because he saw that my opinions were decided, and he did not wish for controversy."[18]

Bentham and his philosophy were part of a reform movement that took root and flourished following the end of the Napoleonic Wars. David Ricardo led a crusade to repeal the Corn Laws, those immovable obstacles to free trade. The Chartist movement argued and demonstrated for the expansion of male suffrage. Abolitionism was gaining political strength. Those in Britain seeking change frequently looked to the United States both as an inspiration and a laboratory to test their ideas. As they parted, Bentham presented Adams with twenty-five copies of *The Principles of Morals and Legislation* to be delivered to each governor in the United States. John Quincy would dutifully comply but without enthusiasm.[19] Other reformers approached Adams as he prepared to depart, one being the communitarian Robert Owen. The Welshman called and presented his pamphlet *A New View of Society* and subsequently brought additional copies to Adams to be gifted to all in authority in America. Adams was dismissive; what Owen was advocating was "a community of shared goods and of industry; projects which can never succeed, but with very small societies and to a very contracted extent. Mr. Owen however seems to think that it is of universal application and destined to give a new character to the history of the world."[20]

Later in the month, the prominent abolitionist William Wilberforce came calling on the secretary of state designate. He was spokesperson for the "Saints," a term applied derisively to the growing abolitionist contingent in Parliament. He had been the driving force behind the Slave Trade Act of 1807, which prohibited traffic in human chattel. According to Adams, Wilberforce was one of the most influential members of the House of Commons, a man who had both Liverpool's and Castlereagh's ears. He had noticed in the papers, Wilberforce said, a movement in Congress to abolish the slave trade. He urged adoption of a scheme already broached by Castlereagh to Adams—the conclusion of an international treaty under which the warships of any signatory could seize a slave-trading vessel no matter what flag it was flying. John Quincy observed that the only ships in a position to do this belonged to the Royal Navy. The slave trade was already prohibited in America. His compatriots would view the proposal as nothing more or less than an effort by the Mistress of the Seas to establish the arbitrary right of visit and search in peacetime.[21]

The week before the Adamses' departure, the American minister made his last official rounds. Castlereagh greeted him warmly and expressed regret at his recall. In truth the two men had come to respect and even admire each other. Not so Adams with the prince regent. The future George IV received him cordially enough, but Adams found the prince both obtuse and frivolous. "He is a Falstaff without the wit and a Prince Henry without the compunctions. His only talent is that of mimicry which he exercises without regard to dignity or decorum. . . . His supreme delight is to expose persons dependent upon him to ridicule."[22] Before John Quincy departed Carlton House, the assistant master of ceremonies asked him if he was ready to receive the parting gift that all foreign emissaries received— in this case a hundred pounds. The Constitution forbade emoluments, he replied. Had his predecessors accepted a gift? John Quincy could not help but inquiring. Some had and some had not, the other man replied. John Quincy and Louisa found time to visit the spot where Ranelagh, the fashionable garden and promenade where they had courted, used to be. "Instead of the splendid company, the song, the dance, the festive banquet, the walls are down and removed, the spot is covered with grass and the cattle are feeding upon it," Adams recorded in his diary.[23]

On June 11, 1817, John Quincy and Louisa together with George, John, Charles, Louisa's two maids, a manservant, and Antoine Guista, the household manager, departed London for Cowes, where Adams had booked passage on the *Washington,* Jacob Forman master. The ship was commodious—1,008 tons—and John Quincy had secured the use of the entire aft cabin; the fare was thirty-seven guineas a head, with Charles and the three servants traveling at half price plus two pounds per ton of baggage.[24] The *Washington* departed the roads at Cowes with a favoring wind on June 15. It would be the last time any of the party would see Europe. Louisa nearly did not make the trip. At forty-two, she was midway through what would be her last pregnancy. There was a serious risk of losing the baby on a transatlantic voyage. But Louisa dreaded facing what promised to be a difficult delivery in a foreign country alone. And so she was with her family when the *Washington* sailed.

By the twenty-fifth, the weather had turned foul. "The day was the most uncomfortable one that we have yet had on board ship," John Quincy recorded in his diary. "[A]ll the morning steering her course but as close upon the wind as possible with a heavy swell and a breeze almost equivalent to a gale of wind." By nightfall the ship was being drenched by squall after squall. "The motion of the vessel

was of the worst kind." Louisa retched without pause, her seasickness accompanied by fever and cramps. One of the passengers, a Dr. Tilley, attended and bled
her but to no good effect. On the twenty-eighth, John Quincy was called to her
side from dinner. "She thought she was dying," he wrote. Tilley administered a
substantial dose of laudanum. Then at sunset she miscarried, and the pain subsided.[25]

During the first part of the voyage, the weather continued so rough that Adams
could neither read nor write. Somehow, he and one of the passengers managed to
play chess. John Quincy quickly became obsessed. He recorded in his diary that
he had taken up the game in St. Petersburg, but it had come to absorb so much of
his time, he had had to give it up. A game was never just a game with the Adamses; when his opponent, Otis by name, bested him time and again, the secretary of state designate could not contain himself. "I sometimes lose the calmness
of my disposition to a degree bordering upon rudeness," he confided to his diary.
". . . it mortifies my pride beyond endurance . . . a single blunder throws me so
completely off my center that I scarcely ever can redeem the game. There is a capacity of combinations in chess which is a painful test of intellect. It occupies the
understanding and works upon the feelings too powerfully for sport."[26]

On July 11, John Quincy entered his fiftieth year. Louisa and the boys had
alerted the ship's crew and passengers, and a general celebration ensued. "Mr.
Davis, the poet of the steerage, had written yesterday three complimentary stanzas which he proposed to have sung with chorus at their dinner," Adams recorded
in his diary. Word was sent belowdecks to send a deputation to have a glass of
wine with the distinguished passenger. It arrived and the crew was gifted an extra
ration of grog.[27]

On August 4, 1817, the lookout on the *Washington* spied the eastern shore of
Long Island, and the ship landed safely at New York Harbor two days later. John
Quincy was overcome with both nostalgia and a sense of trepidation. "The sentiments with which after an absence of eight full and eventful years I touched once
more my native land were of a mingled nature," he wrote. "Of the deepest gratitude to the Supreme Disposer for all the enjoyments and preservations of that
long period . . . together with an anxious forecast of the cares and perils of the new
scene upon which I am about to enter."[28] The family took lodgings in New York
City and was immediately swamped with visitors and invitations. Governor De-
Witt Clinton presided over a dinner in John Quincy's honor at Tammany Hall.
His escort to that event was John Jacob Astor, who hoped to win the new secretary of state's support for his schemes of empire in the Pacific Northwest.[29] After attending church on the ninth, the family went down to the harbor to see the newest
and most modern of America's steamboats, the *Chancellor Livingston*, just arrived

from Albany. "It is a travelling city," Adams noted in his diary.[30] It was now possible to make the trip from New York to Boston by steamboat and stage in forty hours—a trip that twenty years earlier could have consumed several days.

John and Abigail had, meanwhile, learned of their family's arrival; they were in raptures. "Yesterday was one of the most uniformly happy days of my whole long life," the ex-president wrote his eldest son. I was "in a kind of trance of delight the whole day. Kiss all the dear creatures for me, Wife, George, John, and Charles. I hope to embrace them all here in a few days. God Almighty bless you all. So prays John Adams." And Abigail: "God be thanked. We now wait in pleasing expectation of welcoming you, one and all, to the old habitation, altered only by the depredations of time like its ancient inhabitants. Come then all of you; we will make you as comfortable as a cup of cold water, tempered with love and affection, can render you."[31]

The plan was for the family to book passage on one of the new steamboats to New Haven and a second from there to New London and Providence. The last leg of the trip would be by stage. On the appointed date, John Quincy rose before dawn to write in his diary. Three hours later he was distracted by his sons pounding on his door; they had missed their boat and had to wait until the evening and take a packet to New London. The remainder of the trip went well, though, and John Quincy and his brood were soon reunited with the rest of their family. For George and John, it was a sweet reunion with grandparents who had spent as much time raising them as their mother and father. While they rushed to embrace John and Abigail, Charles, just turned ten and without his brothers' memories, held back. Abigail greeted Louisa without reservation. Her admiration of her son's wife had grown exponentially, particularly in the wake of the hardships she had endured during the wintertime journey from St. Petersburg to Paris.[32] That evening relatives flooded into Peacefield. Uncharacteristically, John Quincy ignored the call of duty for a month, lingering in Quincy, Boston, and Cambridge to renew old acquaintances and witness the changes time had wrought. He was astonished at the growth and prosperity of Boston. There were the new Central Wharf and dozens of new houses and shops on Cornhill and Common Street.

Much to his gratification, John Quincy found that the political animosities held against him by some of his fellow Bostonians had virtually disappeared. Republicans were in ascendency in Massachusetts, but there was also reconciliation with former Federalist adversaries such as Harry Otis. John the elder had already made up with the Otises a year earlier while John Quincy was still in Britain, and he had written urging his son to follow suit. It was Harry Otis who had ridden out to Quincy to inform John Adams that his son had been confirmed to be the next secretary of state. John Quincy proved willing to reconcile. "His

[Harry Otis's] person while in youth, his graceful deportment, his sportive wit, his quick intelligence, his eloquent fluency, always made a strong impression upon my mind," John Quincy responded to his father; "his domestic affections, his active friendship, and his generosity always commanded my esteem." Otis's one great flaw was to support public policies that "from the want of mental energy" he knew to be wrong.[33] Otis was one of the organizers of a huge testimonial dinner given on John Quincy's behalf upon his return to Boston.

It was not all bonhomie; there were family issues that needed attending to. Thomas Boylston, who had married—unhappily, as it turned out—Ann Harrod in 1805 and settled in Quincy, had begun drinking heavily. John Quincy had to rescue what was left of the business he had entrusted to his brother.[34] Then there was George's admission to Harvard. As his father had before him, John Quincy attempted to use his connections with President Kirkland and the Board of Overseers to gain entry to the sophomore class for his sixteen-year-old. Also, as had happened in John Quincy's case, a faculty committee examined George and found him woefully unprepared. At that point John Quincy hired a tutor, a Mr. Gillman, at two dollars per week to prepare his eldest. The goal would be entry following the winter break, "but he [Kirkland] intimated that it would be difficult and would require very close application from George." While preparing himself, young Adams was to board at Holworthy Hall on the Cambridge campus. On the advice of President Kirkland, John Quincy and Louisa enrolled John and Charles at the Boston Latin School. They would board with old family friends Dr. Thomas and Harriet Welsh.[35]

On September 9, 1817, John Quincy and Louisa departed Quincy for Washington. They traveled by steamboat to New London and from thence to New Haven and New York City. "We have arrived safely at this place [New York City] after a fatiguing journey owing to the dust and extreme heat of the weather," Louisa wrote Abigail. "We then exchanged boats and took in so numerous a company that during the night we were almost suffocated by the heat which I think can only be exceeded by the black hole at Calcutta . . . the squabbling for beds . . . would have been exceedingly amusing to a disinterested spectator."[36] The new secretary of state and his wife arrived in the nation's capital on September 20 and took temporary lodgings with Louisa's sister Caroline and her second husband, Nathaniel Frye Jr.

The Adamses found Washington much changed since they had last lived there in 1807. The city was still recovering from the destruction wrought by British invaders during the War of 1812. The rebuilding of the President's House had just been completed, indeed so recently that President Monroe and his wife dallied at

Ash Lawn–Highland until the paint could dry. The Capitol would not be fully restored for another seven years but work on its two wings was nearing completion. Washington still had the air of a boomtown, but it was a far cry from the muddy building site the Adamses had encountered when John Quincy had been elected to the Senate. The population had quadrupled to over thirteen thousand. Both sides of Pennsylvania Avenue were lined with milliners' shops, bookbinders, dry goods stores, and boardinghouses. The street itself, intended by Pierre L'Enfant to be both a link to and a barrier between the executive and legislative branches, was still unpaved and so heavily rutted that every carriage ride was a dangerous adventure. Members of the diplomatic corps and wealthier natives had constructed handsome three-story town houses on long rectangular lots near the executive mansion. Some single representatives and senators boarded in Washington City and Georgetown, but most married men now brought their spouses with them to the capital, which in turn had spawned a flourishing social scene. Mothers visiting Washington soon realized that the city was a virtual paradise for daughters seeking marriages and sons searching for careers. The presence of the young people who flocked to the capital served to enliven the nightly dinners, balls, soirees, and weekly presidential receptions called "drawing rooms."[37] John Quincy selected as their first house a rental halfway between the President's House and Capitol Hill. Louisa found it most unsatisfactory. She hosted her first dinner party for twenty there and had to cope with "a French cook very drunk and a house without an indoor oven."[38]

John Quincy called on President Monroe the day after his arrival in Washington and immediately assumed his duties as secretary of state, the first of the new administration's cabinet to take his place. Monroe, plagued by the still lingering paint fumes in the White House, again retired to his plantation in Virginia, but over the next few days confirmed the other members of his inner circle. Of these the most congenial to John Quincy was the new secretary of war, John C. Calhoun of South Carolina. Tall and erect with blue eyes and dark hair, Calhoun was an educated, cultivated man. The scion of a wealthy plantation family, he had been classically educated at Yale and then, after studying law, had been admitted to the bar in Connecticut. No one who knew him at this point in his life could have anticipated the fire-breathing states' righter that he would become in the 1830s and 1840s. Slavery would not emerge as a national issue pitting region against region and Free-Soilers against the slave power until the Compromise of 1820. Like Adams and Monroe, Calhoun at this point was a nationalist who supported a national bank, internal improvements, and a strong military. Like Adams, Calhoun believed that public policies whenever possible ought to be morally based. Possessed of a subtle, inquiring mind, he was ambitious and assertive without being pretentious. John Quincy saw much of himself, or what he hoped was himself, in the South Carolinian.[39]

The new secretary of the treasury was William H. Crawford, an accomplished and charismatic Georgian, a plantation owner and lawyer who had captured every office for which he had run except the presidency. He was a former U.S. senator and most recently the American minister to France. Crawford was an imposing figure, tall, heavily built, and handsome. Like Henry Clay, he was at home in any gathering no matter how humble or exalted. Also like Clay, he was charming and ingratiating. But Crawford possessed a streak of violence. In 1802 he had killed a man, Peter Van Allen, in a duel; in a subsequent confrontation in 1806 with John Clark, a Georgia political rival, he had gotten the worst of it, receiving in the wrist a pistol ball that crippled his hand. Crawford not only wanted to be president; he believed it to be his destiny to hold the highest office in the land. He had come close, barely losing to Monroe in the Republican caucus in 1816. Politically, there was no substance to the man. Crawford managed to avoid taking a clear-cut stance on the principal issues of the day and his penchant for political maneuvering and manipulation would have put Burr and Hamilton to shame. Working through his supporters in the press, Crawford proved an expert at character assassination. Initially the target of his barbs was General Andrew Jackson, who because of his enormous popularity figured to be his principal rival for the presidency. Adams did not trust Crawford from the outset, and with good reason as it turned out.[40]

Monroe had hoped to recruit a Westerner for the post of attorney general but failed to find a suitable candidate willing to take it. He then turned to his old friend William Wirt, a prominent Baltimore attorney and man of letters. Among his achievements was a well-received biography of Patrick Henry and a gentle satire on American foibles and manners, *The Letters of the British Spy*.[41] In the free-ranging cabinet discussions that ensued, Wirt tended to stick to issues that were clearly in his bailiwick. A pleasant man and a good conversationalist, he quickly became friends with Adams.

In the Monroe cabinet, John Quincy would be first among equals. He saw the president almost every day, and Monroe solicited his opinions on a wide range of issues both foreign and domestic. Monroe viewed the cabinet not as a decision-making body but as a collection of individuals representing different interests and regions among whom he would try to build a consensus in support of a course he had already settled on. In his *Letters of the British Spy*, William Wirt had painted a famous and much-cited portrait of Monroe: "Nature has given him a mind neither rapid nor rich, and therefore he cannot shine on a subject which is entirely new to him. But to compensate him for this, he is endued with a spirit of restless emulation, a judgment strong and clear, and a habit of application which no difficulties can shake, no labors can tire."[42] John Quincy was at first put off by what he believed was the excessive deliberation with which Monroe made decisions, but he soon came to appreciate the president's integrity and judiciousness. His chief was willing to listen and take advice, a trait "which in so high a place is an infallible test of a great mind."[43] The Virginian shared Adams's dislike of Crawford. He was a self-controlled, civil man who did not like confrontation; the secretary of the treasury, when opposed, tended to bluster and bully.

Both the president and his secretary of state were nationalists. In his inaugural address, Monroe had articulated the program that had come to define the Republican Party: an active federal government including a national bank and funding for a system of highways, canals, and ports that would link the various sections of the country to one another, thus creating a national, self-sufficient economy. In cooperation with Henry Clay, who had once again been elected Speaker of the House of Representatives, Monroe would push through Congress a series of laws that would dramatically increase the power of the federal government. The administration and its allies in Congress proposed a standing army of ten thousand men and a network of military roads and canals to support them. In April 1816, Congress passed the Tariff of 1816, the nation's first experiment with protectionism. Manufacturing had flourished in the United States during the War of 1812. With the coming of peace, European competitors were sure to recover and offer stiff competition. With great difficulty Republican nationalists succeeded in establishing a national bank. The Second Bank of the United States would be headquartered in Philadelphia with branches in other major cities. It would be capitalized at $35 million with the federal government subscribing one-fifth of the amount and the investing public the other four-fifths. Five of the twenty-five members of the board of directors would be chosen by the national government, the remainder by the bank's principal stockholders.[44]

Adams, Clay, and Monroe truly believed that in a republic the government of the people existed for the people—the third of the six objectives listed in the preamble to the Constitution was "to provide for the General Welfare"—but their view of how this should be achieved was distinctly Hamiltonian. The bank, the tariff, and the internal improvements were by design intended to benefit the businessmen, manufacturers, shippers, and bankers—the country's haves. But at this point the agriculturalists of the South and the West—represented by Calhoun and Clay—also believed that their interests were enhanced by federal programs and subsidies. The war had created an unparalleled demand for American-produced food and raw materials both at home and abroad. The population of the Old Northwest and Old Southwest, the territory between the Appalachians and the Mississippi, had doubled every ten years since the first census was taken in 1790. In both the rural North and South, young tenant farmers could expect to own their own places by middle age.[45] They were no less businessmen than the merchants and bankers of the Northeast.

On September 22, 1817, Adams was officially sworn in as secretary of state by Daniel Brent, a justice of the peace of the District of Columbia who was also the chief clerk of the State Department. In attendance was Richard Rush, John Quincy's longtime friend and supporter who had been acting secretary. The United States' diplomatic headquarters was located in a three-story brick building on Seventeenth Street opposite G Street NW where the present Eisenhower Executive Office Building stands. Adams's support staff would consist of Brent—chief clerk and translator—and seven assistant clerks. At this point the entire budget for the Department of State, domestic and foreign, was $123,062, less than the British government spent on just its secret service. Adams's salary was set at thirty-five hundred dollars a year, increased by an act of Congress to six thousand dollars in 1819. By contrast Castlereagh earned seventy-two thousand dollars a year at the 1817 exchange rate. It was an old story for the Adamses; there was no way a secretary of state could perform his duties, social and official, on that stipend. During his eight years in office, John Quincy would have to draw continually on his own resources. Fortunately, they were substantial; including property and stock, his estate was estimated at a hundred thousand dollars upon his return from Europe—this in spite of Thomas's neglect.[46]

Initially John Quincy continued the practice he had adhered to when he was a minister abroad; he would see everyone who wanted to see him—congressmen, senators, members of the diplomatic corps, newspapermen, intellectuals, and even tourists—as many as fifty a day. He personally composed two sets of instructions, one general and one specific for all American ministers serving abroad. "Business crowds upon me from day to day requiring instantaneous attention and in such varied [ways] that unless everything is disposed of just as it occurs," he wrote his mother, "it escapes from the memory and runs into the account of arrears . . . the session of Congress is at hand . . . and until I shall have gone through that ordeal it will be impossible for me to ascertain whether my strength will be equal to my task or will sink under it."[47] John Quincy continued his practice of rising between five and six to take an hour or more of exercise. One day, Adams and Josiah Quincy, then president of Harvard and also an early riser, attended a law lecture delivered by a distinguished jurist. To honor the two, the speaker called them up to sit beside him on the dais. Within moments Adams and Quincy were snoring away. Dismayed, the judge paused a moment and, pointing to the two sleepers, declared, "Gentlemen, you see before you a melancholy example of the evil effects of early rising." This remark was followed by a shout of laughter, which effectually roused Adams and Quincy from their naps.[48]

WHEN JOHN QUINCY ADAMS became secretary of state, the United States seemed politically united as never before—the Era of Good Feelings was at hand. Republicans controlled every state government but that of Massachusetts; the economy was booming, and the nation's self-image had never been better. The diplomatic skies were less clear, however. There were still issues to be settled with the British, including the fisheries and control of the Pacific Northwest as well as the pending slave trade convention. Much more important was the question of whether the United States would extend diplomatic recognition to Spain's New World colonies, which were then in revolt. The issue had profound implications not only for America's relationship with Spain but with the rest of the world as well. Closely intertwined with this issue was the Monroe administration's determination to take advantage of Spain's decline to expand the nation's continental empire to include East Florida at a minimum and the trans-Mississippi West at a maximum. Then there was the issue of America's native peoples, who were being driven out of their tribal lands in both the Southeast and the Northwest. Finally, it would be up to Adams and Monroe to define and articulate exactly what role the United States intended to play in world affairs, and to construct compelling justifications for that role.

James Monroe did not, as some other presidents, attempt to be his own secretary of state. Both Jefferson and Madison had felt free to discuss matters directly and privately with the ministers and ambassadors accredited to them. Monroe refused to do that. He insisted that when the members of the diplomatic corps had business, they should deal first with John Quincy. The president told Adams to inform the foreign diplomats that he would grant audiences to them but would not tolerate back channels.[49] Foreign lobbying of individual cabinet members and congressmen had been the plague of American foreign relations during the Revolutionary Era and the Early Republic. The secretary of state was, of course, quite pleased. John Quincy made it clear to his parents and associates that he understood that his role was to advise and not to decide. Yet he did not hesitate to disagree with the president and to press him to alter course. Supported by the weight of his education, experience, and judgment, he often carried the day. Following his first interview with Lord Castlereagh, Richard Rush, John Quincy's successor as minister to the Court of St. James's, observed, "First of his [Monroe's] cabinet as regard everything foreign stood Mr. Secretary Adams; a statesman of profound and universal knowledge. . . . He had received the best education that Europe and his own country could bestow. . . . Minister at several of the courts of Europe, favorable opportunities were before him of studying their policy, and a superior capacity enabled him to improve his opportunities . . . he was accomplished as a scholar, fervent as a patriot, and virtuous as a man."[50]

"'Political calms' cannot be of long duration in this country," John Adams wrote his son in October 1817. "As our constitutions of government, general and particular, are greenhouses and hotbeds of ambition, eternal and incalculable competitions will grow out of them as naturally and necessarily as grass and corn grow in a rich deep soil well sunned, watered, and cultivated."[51] And so it was in America in 1817; the Era of Good Feelings did not apply to the Republican Party, which, in the first year of Monroe's first term, threatened to splinter under the machinations of the president's aspiring successors. There was the disappointed and embittered Henry Clay, who would from his post as Speaker of the House wage war on the Monroe administration on almost every front not only because the president had passed him over for secretary of state but because the cabinet included his three principal rivals. First among these was Secretary of the Treasury Crawford. The charismatic, ubiquitous Georgian would strive to undermine his rivals while portraying himself as the friend of the common man, local government, and states' rights. Then there was Calhoun, Southern nationalist and secretary of war—dynamic and ambitious, if a bit young. The third member of the aspiring triumvirate was John Quincy, whose diary expressed contempt for those who would openly seek office, but who burned with ambition. The presidency would fulfill his parents' dreams for him and the family, and demonstrate that the citizens of a virtuous republic, left to themselves, would select as their leader a man of integrity, education, judgment, and patriotism. To many observers, however, Adams's chances seemed slim. He had no domestic following or political organization, and as he readily admitted, he was lacking in charisma. His reputation for aloofness was only reinforced by the "Washington etiquette wars" of 1817 to 1819.

As THE CAPITAL OF an infant republic, Washington, DC, lacked the long-established social norms that governed life in Europe's capitals. The Washington administration's relative formality had been replaced by the easy sociability of the Jefferson and Madison regimes. No one did more to shape the capital's social scene than the woman Louisa referred to as "dear Dolley."[52] Her political skills more than matched her husband's. She had presided over weekly drawing rooms, called "squeezes" because they were standing room only. Virtually anyone with a letter of introduction could gain access. Her soirees were in line with the democratic ethos of the Republican Party but also a mechanism to enhance James Madison's political power. Dolley also set the precedent of calling personally on every new congressman, senator, and diplomat who arrived in Washington during her husband's eight-year term. Calling cards were the political coin of the realm in early Washington. They opened doors and established relationships—between members of Congress and the executive branch, between members of political and personal factions, between new arrivals and permanent residents, between job seekers and those in control of the jobs. Who called on whom first bestowed political status and power. The Madisons had expected cabinet wives to follow Dolley's lead in making first calls.[53] Elizabeth Monroe was no Dolley Madison. Indeed, during Monroe's years as secretary of state, the couple had largely held themselves aloof from Washington's social scene. Personal preferences aside, the practice of First Ladies calling on any and every personage of importance was quickly becoming a physical impossibility. The rapid increase of population, and with it the admission of new states, meant more and more legislators and their families were crowding into Washington. The steamboat had rendered travel along the East Coast much easier, paving the way for relatives of officials, tradesmen, lobbyists, and tourists who wanted to visit the capital. Thus, at the opening of Monroe's first term, he and his wife announced that the presidential mansion would be open mornings to visitors, but the First Lady would not be making first calls.

Though some traditionalists were outraged, both John Quincy and Louisa thoroughly approved. John Quincy described the now discarded practice of first call as "torture" in a city with deeply rutted streets, rickety bridges, and collapsed culverts.[54] In December 1817, after three months of "torture," Louisa with her husband's support decided to renounce the practice herself. She had had enough of the "usual business of visiting," she wrote in her diary. "All the ladies appear to think that they must visit me about once a week so that I have no sooner got through [making the return calls] than I am compelled to begin again, and even this perpetual slavery to which I seem to be doomed does not prevent censure and [a] little jealousy. Mrs. Monroe never did a wiser thing than give it up altogether."[55]

Shortly after New Year's Day 1818, Senators John Gaillard and William Smith of South Carolina called on John Quincy at the State Department and inquired politely why he and his wife had not yet left their calling card. It was the custom, they declared, for cabinet members to pay first call to members of Congress, with senators being privileged. "I told them this was the first intimation I had ever

received of the existence of such a rule," Adams recorded in his diary. During his
five years in the Senate, it had been his experience that members of Congress paid
first calls on department heads; in truth he thought the practice of first visit by
residents on either end of Pennsylvania Avenue a waste of time.[56]

All of this precedent breaking was too much for Washington society. The outraged wives of congressmen and senators, led by Mrs. William Crawford, went on
the warpath. Daunted by the possible political fallout from criticizing the Monroes, they turned their fire on the Adamses. In truth James and Elizabeth Monroe had intended their action to be the exception and not the rule. Inconvenience
aside, it was part of a plan to reintroduce a degree of formality and distance in the
relationship between the first family and other Washingtonians. But cabinet members and their wives were expected to take up the slack. In late January, Elizabeth
Monroe invited Louisa to call. Was it true that she, the wife of the secretary of
state, was refusing to make first calls? Was this not a violation of established etiquette? Louisa replied, It did not have anything to do with etiquette. It was a practical matter, even one of personal safety. "I told her that the distances were so great
and the difficulty of finding the different parts of the city where ladies thought
proper to take up their abode such as to make it impossible to devote the time to
it." Later in her diary: "It is really laughable to see in our boasted republic how
much may be gained or lost by the failure of a morning visit between two ladies,
particularly if those ladies are the wives of members of Congress."[57]

The Adamses held firm; no first visits—only returns. Four days after Louisa's
conversation with Elizabeth Monroe, she and John Quincy hosted a ball for which
she had sent out three hundred printed invitations; the turnout was excellent, she
reported to Abigail, but the wives of U.S. senators had boycotted the affair. At
Quincy, old John Adams—kept abreast of developments by lively accounts from his
daughter-in-law—chortled at the scenes she described. He had visions, he wrote
her back, of Speaker Clay bringing to the floor of the House "a bill to settle the etiquette of the United States. The debates in Congress upon that important subject
will amuse, divert, instruct, and edify me to the end of my life." The lesser people of
Washington were probably better off not to be overly exposed to you, he wrote lov-
ingly. "Experience in Berlin, Petersburg, & St. James [and] your sense, wit and perfect fluence and purity in the French language" would show them in a very poor light.[58]

Later that year a group of John Quincy's political supporters called, warning
that he was widely perceived as "cold and unsocial" and that he might "serve the
public and himself better than by remaining all this time in his closet."[59] John
Quincy was stung by their depiction of his reputation. Shortly thereafter, he admitted in his diary that he was "a man of reserved, cold, austere, and forbidding
manners." It was child's play for his rivals to portray him as a "gloomy misanthro-

pist" and "a universal savage."⁶⁰ Louisa tried to comfort him. "Had some chat with Mr. A. after dinner," she recorded in her diary. "He is continually reproached for want of sociability and for pride, hauteur, and foreign manners—these are so absurd that I cannot listen to them without laughing, and they really are too ridiculous to merit the most trifling attention." She lamented that politics had changed dramatically since their return from Europe. Previously, election to office had hinged more on a man's achievements and integrity than his ability to glad-hand.⁶¹ Still, the first calls issue aside, Louisa seemed to understand the importance of social life to political advancement better than her husband. During the tumultuous early months of 1818, John Quincy sent Louisa alone to attend balls and receptions. She went willingly.

Which John Quincy Adams was authentic—the cold and effete intellectual or the warmhearted bon vivant and poet? Both. At court in Europe, except in his relations with the members of the governments to which he was accredited, he could be aloof to the point of rudeness. One of his young aides while he was in St. Petersburg painted a stark portrait. John Spear Smith, a nephew of then Secretary of State Robert Smith and son of Senator Samuel Smith from Maryland, referred to him as the "mute in Siberia." "He has no manners as such, never was intended for a foreign minister. . . . You would blush to see him in any society, and particularly at court circles walking about perfectly listless speaking to no one and absolutely looking as if he were in a dream."⁶² Another observer of Adams while he was representing the United States at the court of Alexander I was Lord William Henry Lyttleton. "Of all the men whom it was ever my lot to accost and to waste civilities upon, [Adams] was the most dogged and systematically repulsive. With a vinegar aspect, cotton in his leathern ears, and hatred of England in his heart, he sat on the frivolous assemblies of Petersburg like a bull-dog among spaniels."⁶³ Given the state of Anglo-American relations at the time, Lyttleton was hardly an impartial observer. John Quincy was conflicted concerning social life in Europe. He worshipped European art, theater, literature, and science. He was appalled by the superficiality and licentiousness of court society. In 1815 he had advised his young protégé Alexander Hill Everett, then at the Hague, to return to America as frequently as possible to cleanse himself of Europe's "sensuality, dissipation, indolence, pride, and, last . . . but not least, avarice."⁶⁴ But Adams, the master intelligence gatherer, could not have held himself that aloof.

But then there was the other John Quincy Adams, when he was in the bosom of his family or at dinner with people he respected; his inhibitions softened by wine, he was a witty, charming raconteur, toasting, singing, rhyming, and dancing. In London on private business during the period when Adams was minister to the Court of St. James's, Richard Rush had had a chance to observe the latter edition. "Under an exterior of, at times, almost repulsive coldness, dwelt a heart as warm, sympathies as quick, and affections as overflowing as ever animated any bosom. His tastes too were all refined. Literature and art were familiar and dear to him. At his hospitable board, I have listened to disquisitions from his lips on poetry, especially the dramas of Shakespeare, music, painting, sculpture. . . ."[65]

If zest for politics and politicians was a primary qualification, neither John nor John Quincy should have held elective office. Father and son thoroughly loathed both. John Adams was a patriot and master constitution maker; John Quincy was a patriot, a superb diplomat, and a gifted orator. Both were public intellectuals. They considered the give-and-take of politics—favor trading, cultivation of both rivals and supporters, and playing to the galleries—beneath them. No wonder this disdain, coupled with the ambition that it threatened, made them grumpy.

The etiquette wars continued unabated through 1819; there were personal pique and offended senses of honor involved, but the matter had devolved into a power struggle between the Congress and the executive. Disgusted and fearful that the etiquette wars would affect his chances for reelection, Monroe called a cabinet meeting to discuss what John Quincy observed with contempt was "the important question of etiquette in visiting."[66] The president was inclined to humor members of Congress and their wives, but his cabinet balked. At this point the secretary of state decided to seize the proverbial bull by the horns. On Christmas Day 1819, he wrote the president a statement of policy on the matter. There would be no first calls by the First Lady or the wives of cabinet members. He accompanied it with a stouthearted defense of Louisa: "She has received with pleasure and returned the visits of all ladies who have called upon her whether connected with members of Congress or otherwise . . . she has invited to her house, without waiting for formal visits, every lady of a member of Congress to whom she had no reason to believe such an invitation would be unwelcome."[67] Four days later Vice President Daniel Tompkins, who presided over the Senate, distributed a copy of the no-first-visit memo to all members of Congress.

By this point John Quincy's political star was ascending because of his diplomatic accomplishments, and he had become a leading contender in the presidential race of 1824. No member of Congress, not even Clay, was willing to cross him on the matter of first visits. Despite the boycott imposed by congressional wives, Louisa had continued to host dinners and dances, and by the close of 1819 she had acquired a reputation as one of the most gracious hostesses in Washington. In the end, the prestige of being invited to one of her soirees was too great for the wives of senators and representatives—many of whom came from rustic backgrounds—to resist. "I shall really think I have rendered an essential service to the nation,"

Louisa wrote her father-in-law, "if I am the cause of establishing such a decent and regular system as will enable people to go on smoothly in [the] future."[68]

In the fall of 1817, the Adamses had moved into a spacious rental situated at the northeast corner of 4½ Street NW that was owned by his chief clerk. It was located a mile and a half from the State Department offices. John Quincy completed the walk every day in twenty-two minutes. The new abode was suitable for dinner parties but not larger venues. In 1820, John Quincy and Louisa bought a house previously lived in by James and Dolley Madison located at 1333 F Street NW.[69] It was here that Mrs. Madison had hosted her many soirees, but the structure had been neglected after the Madisons moved into the President's House, and it was in disrepair. Without really consulting her husband, Louisa embarked on a massive renovation and expansion that eventually doubled the size of the house. "On going to my office as I passed by the house, I have purchased in F Street, I was surprised to find workmen employed in pulling down the wooden shed adjoining it," John Quincy recorded in his diary. "Mrs. Adams has made a contract with [a] mason named Van Cable to build an addition to the house, a measure I have acquiesced inasmuch as I have not expressly prevented it."[70]

Gradually, with Elizabeth Monroe choosing to sit on the sidelines, Louisa became the doyenne of Washington's social scene. Interspersed between balls to which anywhere from two to three hundred people were summoned by handwritten invitations were intimate dinner parties of from ten to twenty. At the latter Louisa was frequently the only female in attendance—something she rather enjoyed. Her balls were increasingly the talk of the town. Putting them on was arduous and expensive; furniture had to be removed and the carpets rolled up for dancing. There were extra servants to be hired and an orchestra booked. She described one exceptionally successful dance she put on in January 1820: "We had about three hundred, perhaps more, and the evening was more than commonly animated—I could give them no supper but substituted as well as I could all sorts of refreshments, and all my guests were apparently satisfied, but what was best of all, Mr. A was so pleased with my success that [afterward] he joined in a reel with the boys and myself."[71] Later that year she launched a new platform—"sociables"—held every Tuesday evening when Congress was in session. These popular gatherings included music, dancing, cards, and dinner. Louisa's triumphs as a Washington hostess had, as she well knew, important political implications. John Quincy seemed incapable of making himself personally popular; her balls and sociables were the next best thing. Through all of this, the wife of the secretary of state had to operate on a shoestring. She made her own dresses. For one event, she "brought out a gown which I have had seven years and which I have never made up and taking some trimmings from one nearly worn out, I put the materials together and produced a dress so splendid that it created great admiration. The truth is that Mr. A furnished my wardrobe very handsomely in Paris, and I have nursed it so as to make it answer my wants for seven years."[72]

ONE OF THE REASONS that John Quincy seemed in a perpetual fog was that he was deeply engrossed in a study of weights and measures. He had delved into the subject while in Russia but had only just begun when called to other duties. Intellectual that he was, Adams was delighted to discover while settling in at his offices at State that Congress had mandated the nation's chief diplomat to prepare a report on the weights and measures used by the various states and foreign nations and to recommend a uniform system for the United States. Most secretaries of state would have assigned the task to a clerk, but not John Quincy Adams. For him nothing was too arcane. In truth he was dedicated to the proposition that government could improve society by supporting scientific inquiry. Soon he was discovering how many English ounces constituted a French liter and measuring the impact that atmospheric conditions had on those measurements' use in human commerce. In the summer of 1819, he recorded in his diary: "I plunged deeper and deeper into my enquiries concerning coins, currencies, and exchange. The deeper I go, the deeper and the darker appears the deep beneath, and although the want of time will soon force me to break away from the subject without even finding its bottom, yet it now fascinates and absorbs me to the neglect of the most necessary business." The *Report upon Weights and Measures* was submitted to Congress on February 22, 1821. His father, irked that John Quincy had skipped his annual vacation in Quincy to work on the report, observed wryly to Louisa that the document was a "mass of historical, philosophical, chemical, metaphysical, and political knowledge" that even he could not wade through. She wrote back, "[T]hank God we hear no more of Weights and Measures."[73]

Young John Quincy Adams

Braintree Farmhouse, John Quincy's birthplace and later home

Portrait of John Adams
by Gilbert Stuart

Portrait of Abigail Adams
by Gilbert Stuart

Franklin's reception at the court of France by John Smith

Nabby Adams at nineteen
ADAMS NATIONAL HISTORIC PARK

Portrait of Thomas Jefferson
LIBRARY OF CONGRESS

"The Ascent of the Charles's Balloon from the Champ de Mars"

Wonderful Balloon Ascents (1870)

Portrait of John Quincy at twenty-nine by John Singleton Copley

Louisa Catherine Johnson Adams

Portrait of
George Washington
by Edward Savage

ADAMS NATIONAL HISTORIC PARK

Alexander Hamilton by
John Trumbull

NATIONAL PORTRAIT GALLEY

Portrait of Grand Duke
Alexander Pavlovich
(Tsar Alexander I) of
Russia by George Dawe

WIKIPEDIA

Portrait of Henry Clay

NATIONAL PORTRAIT
GALLERY

"Signing of the Treaty of Ghent" by Sir Amédée Forestier

Portrait of James Monroe

"President's House, Washington," by Anthony St. John Baker

Opothle Yoholo

Portrait of Andrew Jackson by Ralph E. W. Earl

Portrait of Martin Van Buren by George Healy

Portrait of Charles Francis Adams by Anson Dickinson

Joseph Cinquez addressing his compatriots on board the
Spanish schooner *Amistad*

SLAVERY IMAGES

Sarah M. Grimké

Wood engraving
of Sarah Moore
Grimké

LIBRARY OF CONGRESS

A E Grimké

Wood engraving
of Angelina Emily
Grimké

LIBRARY OF CONGRESS

Explosion on the U.S. steam frigate *Princeton*

Portrait of John Tyler

22

The Politics of Empire

JOHN QUINCY ADAMS'S FIRST great policy task was to complete the Anglo-American rapprochement that Castlereagh and he had initiated. The man he would negotiate with in Washington was thirty-six-year-old Charles Bagot, the son of a peer and husband to one of Wellington's nieces. He had been named minister plenipotentiary to the United States in July 1815 but had had to delay his departure for several months to allow for the birth of his and his wife's second child. During the interim, he and Minister Adams had become acquainted.[1] The new ambassador's introductory interview with President Monroe went well. Bagot conveyed his government's pleasure with "the conciliatory conduct of Mr. Adams" and assured his host of the prince regent's desire for the best possible relationship with the United States.[2] In truth, Bagot shared George Canning's antipathy for America. "[T]he question is not so much how you will treat them," declared the former foreign secretary, "as how they will treat you, & that the hardest lesson which a British Minister has to learn in America is not what to do, but what to bare [sic]."[3] Following a year in Washington, Bagot would write that he had dutifully fulfilled the social obligations required of him and his wife from the opening of Congress until "the wild and hairy deputies of which it is composed are gone back into their woods and wigwams."[4] Adams would say of Bagot on the eve of his departure in 1819 that he possessed the "qualities of a good negotiator, but neither his intellectual power nor his acquisitions . . . [are] striking. . . . No English Minister has ever been so popular, and the mediocrity of his talents has been one of the principal causes of his success . . . it has staggered my belief in the universality of the maxim that men of greatest talents ought to be sought out for diplomatic missions . . . a man of good breeding, inoffensive manners, and courteous deportment is nearer to the true diplomatic standard than one with the genius."[5]

John Quincy was still ready to claim Britain as the parent who had birthed and bred his country. Could there be any doubt that Great Britain was the greatest nation that Europe had yet produced? he asked his protégé Alexander Hill Everett. Witness the productivity of her manufacturing and agricultural sectors, her naval might, but above all her institutions of government. What other nation could have spawned a country like the United States? "If England had no other claim to reverence than that of having founded the colonies which are now your country and mine, her solid and unquestionable glory would transcend all Greek, all Roman fame. France, Spain, Portugal, and Holland have founded colonies as well as England—look at them, and look at the United States, and what is the cause of the difference between them? English institutions, principles, and manners."[6]

But the War of 1812 was only six years in the past. Public feeling against John Bull was still running high. The Adamses were invited as honored guests to the christening of Bagot's latest child, and they readily accepted. But when rumors began circulating that the prince regent was to be one of the infant's sponsors and that John Quincy was to stand in for him, the public outcry was so great that Monroe intervened. How could the chief diplomat of the United States consider such a thing? he inquired; the Adamses should not even attend. John Quincy reluctantly agreed but recorded in his diary that he was amazed at "seeing the President thrown into such a state of trepidation for fear that I was about to commit an enormous indiscretion which might ruin the popularity of his Administration . . . without waiting to ascertain the facts."[7]

During the summer and fall of 1818, Anglo-American negotiations in Washington and London produced the Convention of 1818, the next great step in the ongoing Anglo-American rapprochement. The issues addressed were the fisheries, slaves seized during the late war, boundaries between the Lake of the Woods and the source of the Mississippi, and Anglo-American trade. While John Quincy had still been minister to the Court of St. James's, Castlereagh had offered to "renew" the "liberty" granted to the citizens of the United States to fish the Grand Banks. Adams, of course, wanted to substitute the word "right" for "liberty." The real sticking point, however, was the ability of American fishermen to dry and cure their catch along designated stretches of shoreline in Labrador and Newfoundland. If no agreement could be reached and the British naval commander at Halifax ordered the seizure of American fishing vessels, there would be war, John Quincy warned Bagot. "I am afraid we shall have to fight for this matter in the end," he told the Englishman in one of their first conversations, "and I am so confident of our right that I am for it."[8] Perhaps John Quincy's bellicose language was intended as a homage to his father, perhaps not. Whatever the case, James Monroe was not going to war for the fisheries. In London, British and American negotiators reached a compromise whereby Americans would enjoy forever the liberty to fish along certain areas on the coastlines of Canada's two Atlantic provinces in return for giving up inshore fishing along other parts of the North American coast. Drying and curing were to be confined to unsettled areas along the coasts of Newfoundland and Nova Scotia.

On the matter of trade, the British proved characteristically unyielding. What incentive did His Majesty's government have to open either direct trade with its West Indian possessions or the carrying trade between the mother country and its colonies? Bagot and Goulburn, who was assisting in the negotiations, asked. All the Liverpool government would agree to were some trial openings in India and South Asia.

Also in dispute was the Canadian–American boundary west of the Lake of the Woods to the source of the Mississippi. The treaty of peace and independence signed in 1783 had stipulated that the boundary would run due west from the northwest tip of the lake directly to the mouth of the Mississippi. Some years afterward the Canadian explorer and fur trader David Thompson discovered that the source of the great river lay some 152 miles south of the northwest extremity of the lake. British negotiators pressed to shift the latitude southward in order that their citizens might have access to the Mississippi. Richard Rush declared the point nonnegotiable, and the British gave in. It was agreed that the Canadian–American boundary should run along the forty-ninth parallel from the lake to the Rocky Mountains.[9] That left the Oregon Territory as the last issue to be settled.

When he had been minister to Imperial Russia, John Quincy had used his influence to protect the fur-trading magnate John Jacob Astor's interests in the Pacific Northwest from Russian encroachment. In 1818, as secretary of state, he would act to shield Astoria and its environs from Britain and its avaricious North West Company. In their quest to expand America's continental boundaries, expansionists like Adams and Monroe were tacit partners with explorers like Lewis and Clark, frontier farmers, and entrepreneurs like Astor. Astor, despite his struggles with the English language, was not a man to be denied. In 1810, the German American businessman had established his Pacific Fur Company and begun building trading posts along the route mapped out by Lewis and Clark. His grand scheme culminated with the establishment of a fortress/post on Puget Sound—Astoria. Thus began a very lucrative trade in which Astor's trappers and traders would deliver their pelts to Astoria, where they would be loaded onto seagoing vessels bound for China. There they would be exchanged for silk, teas, spices, and nankeen (a lightweight cotton fabric). One of Astor's ships exempted from the embargo during the War of 1812 earned a profit of two hundred thousand dollars on a single voyage.[10]

In December 1813 the British sloop of war *Racoon* arrived at Astoria with orders to take the fort and destroy the American settlement. Finding no one there but Canadians, the captain merely hauled down the Stars and Stripes and departed. As it turned out, Astor wanted his fortress/post back and so did the Madison administration. Thus, at Ghent, John Quincy and his colleagues were instructed to insist upon a mutual return of property seized during the war.[11] Two years later, Monroe and Adams ordered the U.S.S. *Ontario* and Captain James Biddle, with American commissioner J. B. Prevost on board, to sail around Cape Horn, make its way to Puget Sound, and raise the American flag over Astoria once again. But Biddle and company should do so without harming British subjects: "no force is to be employed."[12] Both the president and the secretary of state were determined to secure the Pacific Northwest for their countrymen for both strategic and economic reasons, but at this point not at the risk of renewed hostilities with the former mother country.

At the same time, Adams wrote Rush that he should assert to his British hosts that American occupation of the Pacific Northwest was inevitable. Destiny aside, the United States' land-hungry population and money-hungry entrepreneurs would over time pour into the area and overwhelm the North West Company. "[I]t can scarcely be supposed that Great Britain would find it useful or advisable to resist their claim to possession by systematic opposition. If the United States leave her in undisturbed enjoyment of all her holds upon Europe, Asia, and Africa, with all her actual possessions in this hemisphere, we may very fairly expect that she will not think it consistent either with a wise or a friendly policy to watch with eyes of jealousy and alarm every possibility of extension to our natural dominion of North America which she can have no solid interest to prevent."[13]

Unfortunately, in all the confusion, the Monroe administration neglected to inform the British minister of the *Ontario* and its mission. When he learned of the voyage, Bagot descended on the State Department in high dudgeon. Was it true that an American naval vessel had been dispatched "for the purpose of disturbing the British settlement at the northwest coast of America"?[14] The United States had no intention of dismantling any British settlement or trading post, but only to assert sovereignty over what was rightfully hers, Adams responded. Failure to inform was a mere oversight. This would not stand, Bagot declared. But it would. Castlereagh had no intention of risking war with the United States over the Oregon Territory. At the meeting of the Quadruple Alliance né Holy Alliance at Aix-la-Chapelle, the foreign minister had become alarmed at a rumored plan by the Continental powers to send an armada to the New World to restore Spain's and Portugal's rebellious colonies to them. Like the Monroe administration, the Liverpool government was not ready to extend diplomatic recognition to the self-proclaimed republics of South America, but it was busily building lucrative trade relationships with them. Liverpool and Castlereagh envisioned a common Anglo-American front to fend off intervention by the Continental powers in the affairs of the New World. Thus did Castlereagh send orders to the commander of the British naval squadron at Valparaíso, Chile, to anticipate the *Ontario*'s arrival en route to Puget Sound and to offer every cooperation. Then to Bagot: you should concede the right of the United States to the fortress at Astoria but go no further.

Meanwhile, in London, negotiations on an Anglo-American boundary in the Oregon Territory were coming to a head. Rush and Albert Gallatin, who had been sent to assist him, had proposed extending the line of forty-nine degrees all the way to the Pacific. That would be too great a surrender of British interests, Goulburn replied. Let's extend it to the Columbia River, then southward to the point where it emptied into the sea. The Americans replied that they were not authorized to concede anything south of the forty-ninth parallel. And so the commissioners compromised. The Convention of 1818 provided that the area between the forty-ninth and forty-fifth parallels was to be free and open to settlement of citizens of both nations for a period of ten years, the agreement being subject to renewal.[15]

The Convention of 1818 served the interests of both the United States and Great Britain. It freed Castlereagh to deal with his European partners-cum-rivals, and it enabled the Monroe administration to proceed with the dismantlement of much of Spain's empire in North America. Indeed, when John Quincy received a copy of the convention and delivered it to Monroe, he was deep in discussions with the Spanish minister Don Luis de Onís that would bring Florida into the Union and extend America's western boundary all the way to the Pacific.

THE MONROE ADMINISTRATION'S COMMITMENT to continental expansion was but the continuation of a phenomenon that had begun with the Treaty of 1783. In that agreement Great Britain not only recognized the independence of the thirteen original colonies but granted them sovereignty over the trans-Appalachian West. In the years that followed, the Jefferson, Madison, Monroe, and the two Adams administrations justified their expansionist policies on economic, strategic, and ideological grounds. Of these the most powerful perhaps was the last. The term "manifest destiny" was not officially coined until 1845, when a New York newspaper editor invoked it to justify occupation of the Oregon Territory, but the concept was as old as Plymouth Plantation. The notions of chosenness and predestination were an integral part of the Puritan dissent from the established

Church of England. The Pilgrims used as their guide the Book of Exodus, in which God's select were promised a land of milk and honey—a specific territorial pledge—in return for obedience. America's first-generation settlers saw themselves as people of the covenant: there was the promise but also the obligation. By the time of the American Revolution, most New Englanders had abandoned the notion of predestination as an article of personal faith and salvation, but in the wake of the war for independence, many Americans applied the concept to their new nation, which they viewed as an island of republican virtue in a sea of political absolutism and tyranny. Members of the American Enlightenment like the Adamses, Jefferson, and Madison were much more New Testament than Old. Republicanism was the political manifestation of Christ's invocation to "love thy neighbor."[16] A new covenant had emerged: in return for practicing republican virtue, the Almighty had singled out the United States for special treatment.

In view of this new compact, middle- and working-class Americans came to believe that they had a "right" to settle the West. Waves of immigration coupled with a burgeoning birth rate led to a population explosion in the United States. Driven by dreams of a better life, frontier farmers poured over the Appalachian Mountains, flowing inexorably toward the Mississippi Valley. Exemplars of enterprise and self-reliance, they squatted on public and foreign lands alike, building rough wooden houses and barns, planting and raising crops, and clamoring for roads and access to rivers in order to get their produce to markets. In 1799, Daniel Boone moved his extended family from Kentucky to what is now Missouri—then claimed by Spain—without a thought that doing so threatened to compromise his American citizenship. Boone later observed that he would never have settled outside the United States "had he not firmly believed it would become a portion of the American republic."[17] The Old Southwest had its frontier farmers, but the driving force behind settlement there was plantation owners from the slave states who migrated with their human chattel in search of fresh soil in which to grow cotton, sugar, and indigo. "Empire, learning, and religion," the Reverend Thomas Brockway declared in 1784, "have in past ages, been traveling from east to west, and this continent is their last western state. . . . Here then is God erecting a stage on which to exhibit the great things of his kingdom."[18] As John Quincy observed several times to the European governments to which he was accredited, any attempt to block this surge would be like trying to prevent rivers from emptying into the ocean.

The goal that the Monroe administration set for itself was to acquire East Florida from Spain, peacefully if possible, through subversion and military action if necessary. America's campaign to secure control of the Gulf Coast and expand its western frontier was complicated by the issue of whether to recognize Spain's rebellious Central and South American colonies and by the Quadruple Alliance's attitude toward both U.S. expansion and the independence of the emerging republics.

The Adams men believed that republicanism, carefully restrained by a constitution and the rule of law, represented the best effort by a flawed humanity to give substance to Christ's kingdom on earth, but they certainly did not believe that all of this was preordained. John Quincy would invoke the notion of destiny both temporal and spiritual to justify the drive for continental expansion, but like his father, he took far too dim a view of human nature to believe that an empire of liberty in North America was inevitable. God helped those men and nations who helped themselves. Secretary of State Adams was determined to ensure that his beloved country would become strong enough to resist the machinations of the European monarchies and survive the internal divisions that threatened to rend the fabric of the Union. It was imperative, in his view, that the western boundary of the United States should extend to the Pacific to include the Oregon Territory and as much of Spanish North America as possible. To obtain these ends, he was willing to tolerate the expansion of slavery into newly acquired territories, sacrifice those Native Americans who stood in his way, and violate the provision in the Constitution giving Congress and Congress alone the power to declare war. Leadership, Adams recognized, required the setting of priorities. And, of course, John Quincy Adams very much wanted to become president of the United States, despite innumerable disclaimers in his diary to the contrary. The secretary of state was an astute reader of political tea leaves, and his instincts told him that the man who was able to appeal to America's sense of mission and exceptionalism while serving its strategic and economic interests would win the prize. Monroe and Calhoun among others shared Adams's thirst for continental empire, but it was he who would be willing to take the risks to accomplish the deed; it was he who would successfully read the motives and predict the actions of America's enemies and victims.

If John Quincy did not believe in predestination and inevitability in this world or the next, he recognized the appeal the notion would have to his fellow Americans as they considered the issue of continental expansion. He also believed it could be useful in bullying Spain and the members of the Quadruple Alliance into acquiescing in America's drive for empire. During a cabinet discussion in which Crawford observed that Europe had come to see America as an avaricious, overweening bully, Adams replied, "Nothing that we could do or say would remove this impression until the world shall be familiarized with the idea of considering our proper dominion to be the continent of North America. From the time when we became an independent people, it was as much a law of nature that this should become our pretension as the Mississippi should flow to the sea." That Spain's possessions to the south and Britain's to the north should become part of the burgeoning American empire was inevitable. It was absurd that sovereigns situated some three thousand miles away should continue to lay claim to lands into which American frontier farmers and entrepreneurs were bound to spread. Until Europe should recognize that "the United States and North America are identical," any attempt to argue that Americans were not indeed ambitious would be regarded as pure hypocrisy. "If the world do not hold us for Romans, they will take us for Jews, and of the two vices, I had rather be charged with that which has greatness mingled in its composition."[19]

The nexus of the Transcontinental Treaty of 1819 was the intersection of the United States' determination to acquire Florida, the desire of Spain's rebellious New World colonies to make an ally out of the burgeoning republic to the north, and the possibility that the members of the Holy Alliance would intervene on the side of Spain to help it retain Florida and its colonies in Central and South America. By 1817 the United Provinces of the Río de la Plata had sustained their independence for four years. José de San Martín's victory at Chacabuco in February of 1817 had decided the issue in Chile, while in the north, the revolutionary forces commanded by Simón Bolívar were eroding the will of the Spanish and their loyalist allies.[20]

Meanwhile, in Madrid the government of Ferdinand VII was struggling to come to terms with reality. Most Spaniards had cheered the restoration but soon soured on their king. Ferdinand, ignored by his father and mistreated by his mother and her lover, was a weak reed who bent easily to the forces of reaction. He frequently chose to ignore the advice of the *consejo de estado*—the council of ministers—and his capable and realistic foreign minister, Don José García de Léon y Pizarro. Instead, he relied on a secret cabinet, the *camarilla*, a collection of noblemen, courtiers, and reactionary clergy. Wallowing in denial, they insisted that Spain could recover its past glory, putting down the revolutions in Central and South America and stemming the American expansionist tide through a combination of military force and support from members of the Quadruple Alliance. The *camarilla* and Ferdinand dreamed of a new Spanish Armada that would sail to the New World and restore the ancien régime as it had been restored in the Old World following Napoleon's final defeat. To this end, the Spanish navy purchased eight warships from Russia, but it failed to inspect the vessels before they were delivered. Two sank on the way from St. Petersburg to Cádiz, and the remaining six were declared unseaworthy. Eventually two were refurbished and set sail for the Americas. One sank before it reached its destination, and the other was promptly seized by Chilean revolutionaries.[21] None of this came as a surprise to

John Quincy. "The first touch of the talisman of Ferdinand was to restore the Inquisition—The Constitution he dissolved before he reached Madrid," he had wryly observed to Louisa in 1814.[22]

There was, not surprisingly, a great deal of popular support in the United States for the insurgents of Latin America. They were, many agreed, seeking to emulate the American Revolution. The tide of history begun at Lexington and Concord was now running its inevitable course in the remainder of the New World. The leading advocate for U.S. recognition of Spain's revolted colonies was Speaker of the House Henry Clay. The year 1817 saw the Kentuckian at the height of his power; he dominated the House of Representatives through his ability to appoint the members of every committee and through his eloquence and force of personality. Clay genuinely believed it was in the interests of the United States to recognize the emerging republics of Central and South America. He represented the trans-Appalachian West, a region whose inhabitants detested Europeans, especially the British and the Spanish, whom they saw as threats to their interests because they blocked further westward expansion and incited the Indian tribes of the South and Southwest to wage savage war against the settlers. Westerners benefited little from transatlantic trade and considered themselves an economic colony of the Northeast. Manufactured goods were made very expensive by high freight rates, and transporting raw materials produced in the West to markets on the East Coast was still difficult. Clay's people looked to South America as their natural trading partner.[23] "What I would give . . . could we appreciate the advantages which may be realized by pursuing the course which I propose!" Clay declared in a speech to Congress. "It is in our power to create a system for which we shall be the center and in which all South America will act with us. In respect to commerce, we should be the most benefited: this country would become the place of deposit of the commerce of the world. . . . We should become the center of a system which would constitute the rallying point of human freedom against all the despotism of the Old World."[24] It was a compelling address, which was translated into Spanish and read to the armies of the South American republics in the field.

There was, of course, more than sectional interest behind Clay's championing of the Latin American cause. Denied the stepping stone to the presidency, he decided to make war on those responsible. There was emerging in Washington, John Quincy noted in his diary in January 1818, "a new system of opposition to the administration with Clay at its head. Crawford told me the other day that Clay, Saturday evening before last, being gay and warm with wine, told him he meant to follow up his attack; 'and I'll beat you, by the by.'"[25] In March, Harry of the West would introduce legislation demanding that the executive recognize the newly independent government of Buenos Aires, and he railed against administration efforts to tighten the nation's neutrality laws. Agents of various South American revolutionary parties were then busy in American ports from Baltimore to New Orleans, fitting out privateers to prey on Spanish shipping and raising money and enlisting volunteers to aid their cause. At a dinner party hosted by the Crawfords and attended by the Clays, Calhouns, and Adamses, the Speaker, again warm with spirits, delivered a diatribe against the administration's Latin American policy. "Clay is as rancorously benevolent as John Randolph," John Quincy subsequently observed.[26]

AT A SERIES OF cabinet meetings that took place in October and November 1817, Adams took the lead in shaping administration policy. He argued, and Monroe and his colleagues agreed, that the United States should follow a policy of strict neutrality toward the conflict between Spain and her New World colonies. As a corollary, federal authorities should suppress as far as possible activities by agents of the patriot movements, both real and bogus. It seemed that hordes of buccaneers, adventurers, pirates, and slave traders were passing themselves off as Latin American revolutionaries. Lurking in the background was the issue of Cuba. The Ever-Faithful Isle was still firmly under Spanish control but was the apple of America's expansionist eye. Upward of fifty U.S. merchant vessels called at Havana each month, most of them based in New York or one of the New England states. The slave power was terrified that Cuba would fall into the hands of the British and be ravaged by Wilberforce and his abolitionists. Rumor had it that Ferdinand was willing to transfer Cuba to any European power that would help Spain retain its empire in Central and South America. In 1820, Calhoun would write Andrew Jackson that Cuba "is in my opinion, not only the first commercial and political position in the world but is the key stone of our Union. No American statesmen ought ever to withdraw his eye from it, and the greatest calamity ought to be endured by us rather than it should pass into the hands of England."[27]

In December 1817, Adams wrote a series of letters published in the *National Intelligencer* under the pen name Phocion. In them he attempted to pour cold water on Clay and his fellow crusaders. There was not an iota of similarity between the American Revolution and the uprisings in Central and South America, he wrote. The first had been driven by principle; the second was a matter of circumstance. It was neither the duty nor the destiny of the United States to revolutionize the rest of the world. The secretary of state warned his countrymen that Great Britain was conspiring to convert the United States into its cat's-paw, a stalking horse to facilitate Latin American independence without risking its relationship with Spain and the other Continental powers. Turning to the slave states, he asked rhetorically if they were willing to stand by and see a series of Haitis erected in Central and South America. Adams had carefully chosen the pseudonym Phocion; it was the name of an Athenian leader of the fourth century BC renowned for his public virtue, his aesthetic lifestyle, and his fear of the mob.[28]

Privately, the secretary of state was even more outspoken. The American Revolution had been fought by Englishmen who were attempting to realize the ideals of the Glorious Revolution. The Latin Americans came from a very different background, which included Roman Catholicism, Jesuitical casuistry, and political absolutism. "The struggle in South America," John Quincy wrote his brother Thomas, "is savage and ferocious almost beyond example. It is not the tug of war between Greek and Greek, but the tiger-conflict between Spaniard and Spaniard. . . . Ours was a war of freemen for political independence—This is a war of slaves against their masters—It has all the horrors and all the atrocities of a servile war . . . the South-Americans have occasionally fabricated and are now fabricating constitutions, but in the whole history of their revolutions, there is not an instance in which the patriot commanders have shown the slightest respect for individual rights or personal liberty [of their people]—There is no more liberty of the press at Buenos Ayres than at Madrid."[29]

For tactical reasons, Adams was deliberately painting as negative a picture of Latin culture as possible. His sympathy for Latin American independence increased in direct proportion to his perception that it would serve the national interest of the United States, economically and strategically defined. One step at a time. He wanted to put off the recognition issue until his country had successfully concluded a treaty with Spain that would bring East Florida and as much of the trans-Mississippi West as possible into the Union. In addition, he felt it necessary to defend himself against what he considered Clay's political grandstanding. "That Clay should have taken pains to prevent my appointment is as natural as that he should have coveted [it] himself," he confided to his diary, "but in his management of his opposition to me, there is a total disregard, not only of generosity, but of fairness."[30]

Looming always in the background was the threat that one or another of the European powers would intervene and in the name of legitimacy help Spain regain control of its revolted colonies. By the Treaty of Chaumont of March 1814, renewed in the Treaty of Paris of November 1815, Austria, Russia, Prussia, and Great Britain had bound themselves to the future convocation of diplomatic congresses to ensure the preservation of peace and the status quo. Thus was formed the "Concert of Europe"—the Quadruple Alliance—and, following the formal entry of France in 1818, the Quintuple Alliance. At Vienna in 1815, Tsar Alexander, firmly under the influence of the Christian mystic Baroness Barbara von Krüdener, proposed the creation of a "Holy Alliance." The signatories would pledge themselves "both in the administration of their respective states and in their political relations with every other government to take for their sole guide the precepts of that Holy Religion, namely, the precepts of justice, Christian charity, and peace."[31] The pact eventually was signed by all the rulers of Europe except the sultan of Turkey, the Pope, and the prince regent of Great Britain. It was impossible for the sultan, a Muslim; the Pope presumably did not need to sign; and the prince regent replied that the principles of the alliance already guided his reign. Although the flywheel of the Quintuple Alliance, Prince Klemens von Metternich, initially decried the Holy Alliance as a "resounding nothing," he would subsequently make use of it as part of a larger campaign to suppress democracy, revolution, and secularism throughout Europe. Although Great Britain would attempt to moderate its excesses, the confederation established at the Congress of Vienna was and would remain profoundly reactionary.

John Quincy well understood the nature of the Concert of Europe and the threat it posed to the United States and its interests. The Holy Alliance was a most unusual pact, he wrote the new American minister to Imperial Russia, George Washington Campbell. The tsar might have believed it possible for the international community to be guided by the precepts of the New Testament in their dealings with one another, but for the rest, the pledge was cynical cover for a concert of powers dedicated to protecting thrones and altars and suppressing democracy. In June 1818, the secretary of state got wind of a scheme put forward by Great Britain to effect a mediation between Spain and its New World colonies that would end with the restoration of Spanish sovereignty in return for the opening of Latin American markets to the trade of the entire world. Castlereagh had successfully endeavored to keep this initiative secret from Washington; Adams learned about it only by accident. When he did, he instructed America's European ministers to inform their host governments that "the interests of this nation are so deeply concerned, and the feelings of the country are so much excited on this subject that we have a just claim to be informed of the intentions as well as the acts of the European alliance concerning it." Furthermore, "we will not participate in and cannot approve any interposition of other powers unless it be to promote the total independence, political and commercial, of the colonies."[32]

What a contrast to the Phocion letters! John Quincy's editorials and his note to his brother probably represented his true feelings toward Latin America and its revolutionaries, but he was determined, as he had been since the beginning of his public career, to diminish European influence in the New World. That crusade was, of course, the flip side of the coin of continental expansion. Adams labored under no misconceptions concerning the Holy Alliance's attitude toward the United States. "[T]here is a vague and general sentiment of . . . fomenting jealousy against us prevailing all over Europe," he had written William Plumer in January 1817. "We are considered not merely as an active and enterprising but as a grasping and ambitious people. We are supposed to have inherited all the bad qualities of the British character," particularly "British rapacity."[33]

The State Department would complain bitterly to the governments of Europe that the disintegration of Spain's New World empire had opened the door for all sorts of scoundrels to prey upon American commerce, conduct a clandestine slave trade, and threaten the neutrality of the United States. Their base of operation was East Florida. In February 1817, a Scottish adventurer named Gregor McGregor enlisted some fifty-five volunteers, most of them from Charleston and Savannah, and attacked the Spanish outpost on Amelia Island, situated at the mouth of the St. Mary's River just a stone's throw from the Georgia border. To bolster his forces, he had formed an alliance with the notorious pirate Jean Laffite. The Spaniards fled without firing a shot. McGregor, who styled himself "Brigadier General of the United Provinces of New Granada and Venezuela and General-in-Chief of the Armies of the two Floridas," raised a white flag with a green cross over Fort Carlos and declared Amelia to be the capital of the "Republic of the Floridas." Who was he and in whose stead was he acting? Rumors abounded. He was British and a clandestine agent of the Crown. He had been sent by Simón Bolívar to create an outpost from which the Latin American revolutionaries could attack Spanish shipping in the Caribbean. Acting either for himself or for his Latin American sponsors, McGregor intended to seize East Florida and sell it to the United States for a million and a half dollars.[34] Whatever the case, he had gotten the attention of the Monroe administration. Amelia Island soon became a haven for smugglers, slave traders, and pirates. The general-in-chief of the Floridas set up an admiralty court that for a fee would condemn vessels and their cargo captured by marauding "privateers."[35] In the summer, anticipating a multinational effort to oust him, McGregor gave way to the Venezuelan patriot Louis Aury, who had previously occupied Galveston Island.[36]

Monroe convened a series of cabinet meetings in October 1818 to discuss a wide range of policy options for dealing with the disintegration of Spain's New World empire. Adams dominated the proceedings. He insisted that the United States should refrain for the time being from recognizing any of the Latin American republics but should do everything possible to foil British mediation schemes. The pirates of Amelia Island and Galveston Island must be suppressed by force. The last week in December, President Monroe dispatched two naval squadrons, one to Galveston and the other to Amelia Island—the latter commanded by General Edmund P. Gaines—with orders to occupy the territories and put an end to smuggling, slave trading, and piracy.[37] On December 23, 1817, Gaines and his forces occupied Amelia without opposition.

In the weeks that followed, the cabinet divided, sometimes rancorously, over the question of whether to retain Amelia Island or return it to Spain.[38] The deadlock continued through the month of January. To Adams, Monroe seemed paralyzed, unduly frightened by the prospect of a war with Spain in which she would be supported by one or more of the members of the Holy Alliance. The rumor that Madrid had offered to cede East Florida to Great Britain in return for favorable mediation of Spain's dispute with its rebellious Central and South American colonies surfaced again. Monroe pointed to various reports that claimed that British agents were then active in Florida, stirring up the Seminoles to resist U.S. encroachment. There was nothing to fear, the secretary of state declared. He pointed out that the United States and Great Britain were then negotiating the Convention of 1818, which would cement the First Rapprochement. For reasons of his own, John Bull would not allow any of the Continental powers to come to Spain's aid, certainly not to help her retain Amelia Island and East Florida. And in fact, in the wake of Gaines's occupation of Amelia Island, Charles Bagot assured Adams that Britain would not support Madrid "in any extravagant pretensions."[39] John Quincy reminded the president of the Secret Act of 1811, in which Congress had endorsed the no-transfer principle.[40] But Monroe would not be calmed. "I took the President's direction upon several other objects," Adams noted in his diary, "but his mind is so absorbed with Amelia Island that he can scarcely bear to have any other presented to him."[41] Taking matters into his own hands, the secretary of state informed the Spanish minister that the United States would continue the occupation until Madrid demonstrated a willingness and capacity to prevent its territory from being used by smugglers and pirates.[42]

John Quincy saw the occupation of Amelia and its justification as an opening wedge that would push Spanish–American negotiators off dead center and pave the way for the acquisition not only of East Florida but much of the trans-Mississippi West. In Madrid, Pizarro recognized what the secretary of state was up to. Alarmed by the American occupation of Amelia and Galveston, he remarked to Spain's minister of war, "The difficult negotiation based on the cession of the Floridas will be useless as we shall not have them to cede." It was Pizarro's intention to sell the Floridas to the United States in return for Washington's acceptance of the Mississippi as its western frontier and a pledge not to recognize the independence of Latin America. In January 1817, Bagot had written the Foreign Office that those matters were on the verge of settlement, that the U.S.

minister to Spain had been instructed to offer five million dollars for the Floridas and that the Spanish government, teetering as always on the edge of financial ruin, was ready to accept.[43]

Unfortunately, Ferdinand VII and the *camarilla* were not ready to throw in the towel on East Florida. For its part, the Monroe administration would never accept the Mississippi as the nation's western boundary. At this point the Adams–Onís negotiations bogged down in a mire of obfuscation and delay. On January 9, Monroe instructed Adams to summon Onís and ask him what his country would take for East Florida. He did but to no avail. "I urged him for a full hour to make me a proposition . . . but he absolutely declined."[44] Reflecting the lack of reality in Madrid, the Spanish ambassador insisted that the tide was turning in Central and South America: "They [the Patriots] had been subdued in Mexico and New Granada," he insisted to Adams, "and would be soon subdued in Buenos Ayres and Chile."[45] Nothing could have been further from the truth. What was needed, Adams thought to himself, was for Spain to be administered a dose of reality. Little did he know that the doctor and the medicine were about to arrive.

When General Andrew Jackson had defeated the Creek Red Sticks at the Battle of Horseshoe Bend and forced the Treaty of Fort Jackson on them, many had fled into Spanish Florida, there merging with the Seminoles and joining in their desperate effort to fend off the avaricious white settlers who coveted their lands. During the War of 1812, British agents had armed and provisioned a combined force of Seminoles, Creeks, and runaway slaves. Then, in 1814, a company of Royal Marines, commanded by the redoubtable Lieutenant Colonel Edward Nicolls, had begun building a fort on the Apalachicola River at Prospect Bluff. Jackson had during the war been able to drive the British and their Indian allies out of the provincial capital, Pensacola, but the stronghold at Prospect Bluff remained intact. Following the signing of the Treaty of Ghent, Lieutenant Colonel Nicolls remained in Florida, stocking the storehouse at Prospect Bluff with cannon, muskets, and ammunition. Before departing in 1815, he turned the stronghold over to the Seminoles and their Black allies. The following year Jackson demanded that Spanish authorities in Florida dismantle what was now referred to on the American frontier as the Negro Fort. The Spanish commandant in Pensacola replied that he lacked the power. Thereupon, Jackson assigned General Gaines to take control of the fort. In July 1816, two American gunboats took up positions opposite Prospect Bluff and began a bombardment. One hot shot landed in the stockade's magazine, causing a tremendous explosion that killed two hundred fifty men, women, and children instantly.

Low-level hostilities simmered along the Florida–Georgia border for the next several years. Runaway slaves continued to flock to the Seminoles; Indians and white militias conducted cross-border raids. Matters came to a head in November 1817 when a group of Indians attacked a U.S. riverboat commanded by Lieutenant Richard W. Scott. The vessel was carrying supplies up the Apalachicola River to Camp Crawford, a stockade situated on the banks of the Flint River in southern Georgia. Aboard were twenty ill soldiers, seven women, four children, and a guard of twenty healthy soldiers. One woman and six soldiers swam to safety as the Red Sticks overwhelmed the craft. The survivors subsequently reported that the children were killed by having their heads bashed against the hull of the boat. When news of the Scott Massacre reached Washington, Secretary of War Calhoun ordered General Gaines to invade Florida and subdue the hostiles, but to avoid attacking Spanish outposts. When Gaines replied that he was too occupied with Amelia and Galveston to take on another task, Calhoun ordered General Jackson to proceed directly to the Georgia–Florida frontier and prepare for action against an estimated twenty-seven hundred hostile Seminoles.

The Hero of New Orleans eagerly embraced his new assignment. Indeed, on January 6, 1818, just days before he received his new orders, he had written Monroe, approving of the occupation of Amelia Island. The United States, he suggested, should move on from there and take all of East Florida to be "held as indemnity for the outrages of Spain upon the property of our citizens."[46] If the United States did not seize this opportunity, it was likely that one or another of the European powers would take the prize themselves. He was aware of the diplomatic delicacies involved in the situation. "This can be done," he proposed, "without implicating the government. Let it be signified to me through any channel, (say Mr. J. Rhea) [Congressman John Rhea of Tennessee, a Jackson protégé] that the possession of the Floridas would be desirable to the United States, and in sixty days it will be accomplished."[47]

When Jackson's letter reached the capital, Monroe was indisposed with an illness, and the matter was referred to Calhoun. Both the secretary of war and Crawford read the letter and sent it to the president for his action. Monroe would later claim that Jackson's missive was misplaced and that he never had a chance to read it until a year later. On January 30, 1818, Monroe instructed Calhoun to order Jackson during his campaign against the Indian–runaway slave force "not to attack any post occupied by Spanish troops from the possibility it might bring the allied powers on us."[48] Both Monroe and Calhoun would later deny that they knew that Jackson planned to shatter Spanish rule in Florida and let the diplomats sweep up the debris. Calhoun at least knew, and it is inconceivable that he did not inform his chief, but the president wanted plausible deniability in case the situation soured. He had been secretary of state when the Madison administration had in 1811 given to George Mathews just such a sign regarding East Florida, and then disavowed him. Moreover, had not Jackson invaded Florida without permission in 1814 as part of the War of 1812? God only knew what excesses the Hero was capable of. All of Washington was familiar with his reputation for impetuousness if not disobedience.[49] "His passions are terrible," Thomas Jefferson recalled. "When I was President of the Senate, [and] he was Senator . . . he could never speak on account of the rashness of his feelings. I have seen him attempt repeatedly and often choke with rage. His passions are, no doubt, cooler now; he has been much tried since I knew him, but he is a dangerous man."[50]

Following a forty-six-day march, Jackson and his command reached Fort Scott on March 9, 1818. His army consisted of three thousand regulars and volunteers and two thousand Indian allies, most of them accommodationist Creeks.[51] A week later the combined forces crossed the border into Florida and established a base at the remains of the Negro Fort, which Jackson renamed Fort Gadsden. From there his forces began to sweep through the Seminole villages, black and red, that lined the Apalachicola. By the first week of April, Jackson and his men had reached the Spanish fort and Indian settlement at St. Marks. An American gunboat flying the British flag weighed anchor in the river. Two Red Stick Creeks—Hillis Hadjo (who had accompanied Lieutenant Colonel Nicolls on his trip to England when John Quincy was minister) and Homathlimico (who had commanded the Red Sticks in the Scott Massacre)—paddled out to meet it. Hadjo, also known as "Francis the Prophet," and his comrade were the Seminole versions of Tenskwatawa, dedicated to preserving their people's lands and way of life. The crew of the gunboat subdued the two, put them in chains, and, following Jackson's arrival, summarily hanged them.[52] The Hero of New Orleans and his men then proceeded to occupy St. Marks.

Among those taken into custody in the process was an elderly Scottish trader named Alexander George Arbuthnot, who had been working out of the Bahamas. The Americans found on him correspondence pleading the case of Florida's Indians sent to British and American officials. It was clear that Arbuthnot had been selling guns to the Seminoles; he insisted that they were for hunting purposes, but the invaders were certain they were meant for war.

Operating out of St. Marks, Jackson and his command attacked native villages along the Suwannee River, most of which were inhabited by Black Seminoles. At one Red Stick village, they found Elizabeth Stuart, a white woman captured by the Indians during their raid on the supply boat in the Apalachicola the previous November. Having destroyed every major settlement along the Apalachicola and Suwanee, Jackson declared victory and sent his volunteers and his Lower Creek allies home. He and his regulars then returned to St. Marks. Shortly thereafter, American troops captured Robert Armbrister, a former Royal Marine, in possession of arms he intended to provide to the Seminoles and their Red Stick allies. He denied acting as a secret agent for the British government, but his papers belied him. Jackson ordered both Armbrister and Arbuthnot court-martialed (an activity usually reserved for the members of one's own armed forces). The soldier threw himself on the mercy of the court while the trader pleaded his innocence. Arbuthnot was sentenced to death and Armbrister to fifty lashes and a year at hard labor. But Jackson intervened, and the court changed Armbrister's sentence to death. The marine was executed by firing squad on April 29, 1818, and Arbuthnot was subsequently hanged from the yardarm of his own trading schooner.

In the days that followed, Jackson received intelligence that the governor of East Florida was sheltering and arming hostiles at Pensacola. When the general demanded that the official live up to Spain's commitments to restrain Indians menacing the American frontier, the magistrate ordered the Americans to leave his province at once. On May 7, Jackson departed St. Marks at the head of a thousand men. When he reached Pensacola, the hundred-seventy-five-man Spanish garrison traded artillery rounds with the Americans and then surrendered, with the governor fleeing to Havana. At this point, Jackson—his health broken by old wounds, malaria, and chronic dysentery—departed for Tennessee. Gaunt but erect on his mount, the Hero reminded an observer of one of the Four Horsemen of the Apocalypse.[53]

23

The Transcontinental Treaty

WORD OF JACKSON'S EXPLOITS reached Washington in May, precipitating the first great crisis of the Monroe administration. On the fourth the cabinet gathered at the President's House. "The dispatches from General Jackson were just received containing the account of his progress in the war against the Seminole Indians, and his having taken the Spanish Fort of St. Mark's in Florida where they had taken refuge," the secretary of state recorded in his diary. "They hung some of the Indian prisoners, as it appears, without due regard to humanity. A Scotchman by the name of Arbuthnot was found among them, and Jackson appears half inclined to take his life. Crawford some time ago proposed to send Jackson an order to give no quarter to any white man found with the Indians. I objected to it then, and this day avowed that I was not prepared for such a mode of warfare."[1] Several days later the president read in the newspapers that the general had in fact executed two British citizens for running guns to the Indians. Monroe was beside himself with anxiety, Adams reported. Jackson had committed an act of war against a friendly government without either the permission of the executive or a congressional declaration—and this in the midst of the burgeoning rapprochement with Great Britain.

Not surprisingly, Onís, when he arrived back in the capital from vacationing in Bristol, descended upon the State Department exuding righteous indignation. Jackson was a dangerous adventurer and an inveterate enemy of his country, he declared. His assaults on St. Marks and Pensacola were totally unjustified and were clearly acts of war. In light of the execution of Arbuthnot and Armbrister, Great Britain would surely side with Spain even to the point of hostilities. What a shame, Onís declared; his government had been willing "to give us the Floridas for nothing," but now all bets were off, Adams recorded Onís as saying in his diary. John Quincy's lengthy diplomatic career had convinced him that the best defense was a good offense. If there had been acts of war, they had been committed by Spain, he retorted. In Pinckney's Treaty, Madrid had pledged to prevent hostile Indians based in Florida from raiding American settlements in southern Georgia and Alabama. Clearly its civilian and military officials in North America had been unable or unwilling to fulfill that commitment. The United States, Adams countered, "could not suffer our women and children on the frontiers to be butchered by savages . . . and when the governor of Pensacola threatened General Jackson to drive him out of the province by force, he left him no alternative."[2]

Monroe returned to Washington from Ash Lawn–Highland, his Virginia estate, on July 12, and for the next ten days he and his cabinet met almost continuously to discuss the Florida–Jackson crisis. Only Adams was willing to defend Jackson. Hero of New Orleans or not, Monroe declared, the general had exceeded his instructions. Not only had he not been authorized to attack Spanish garrisons in Florida; he had been expressly forbidden to do so. Unless the United States repudiated the Tennessean and returned Pensacola and St. Marks immediately to Spain, war would ensue, probably with one or more members of the Holy Alliance siding with Spain. Privateers and European warships would sweep American commercial shipping from the high seas. Crawford leapt to Monroe's support, asserting "that if the Administration did not immediately declare itself and restore Pensacola, it would be held responsible for Jackson's having taken it and for having commenced a war in violation of the Constitution."[3] For his part, Calhoun, viewing Jackson's actions as nothing less than insubordination, was personally offended. "Thinks Jackson's object was to produce a war, for the sake of commanding an expedition against Mexico," Adams confided to his diary.[4]

Presidential aspirant Henry Clay viewed Jackson's Florida escapades as an opportunity to deliver another hammerblow, perhaps a fatal one, to the Monroe administration in general and John Quincy in particular. Throughout 1817, the Speaker had continued to lambast Monroe and Adams's Latin American policies, denouncing the occupation of Amelia and Galveston as unwanted interference with the patriots as they sought to establish bases from which they could harass their Spanish masters. He pushed for repeal of the nation's neutrality law and, in March 1818, moved an appropriation of eighteen thousand dollars to support an American minister to Buenos Aires, a measure that administration supporters managed to defeat.[5] Mistakenly believing that the American people would support him, Clay denounced the Hero of New Orleans as a man on horseback, an adventurer who would involve his country in a needless foreign war just for the sake of his own glory.[6] Crawford and he mobilized John Randolph and the Old

Republicans to denounce and thwart what they believed was sure to be seen as a flagrant violation of the Constitution. "The *Richmond Enquirer* which is the Voice of Virginia," John Quincy wrote in his diary, "speaks to him [Monroe] like a master to his slave."[7] The administration, he observed, was wilting under the pressure.

John Quincy was well aware that Monroe was caught between Scylla and Charybdis. "The Administration were placed in a dilemma from which it is impossible for them to escape censure by some and fractious crimination by many. If they avow and approve Jackson's conduct, they incur the double responsibility of having commenced a war against Spain and of warring in violation of the Constitution. . . . If they disavow him, they must give offence to all his friends, encounter the shock of his popularity, and have the appearance of truckling to Spain."[8] But he believed that there were larger—much larger—issues involved; the Constitution authorized the executive to fight a defensive war without express congressional approval, and Jackson was defending the southern borders of the United States against bloodthirsty savages operating from a derelict territory—Florida. Besides, with the threat of a Spanish cession of the province to Great Britain, the no-transfer principle approved by the House and Senate in 1811 provided sufficient legal justification for Jackson's actions. Politics aside, it would be "weakness, and a confession of weakness," to disavow Jackson and return St. Marks and Pensacola to Spain in the absence of any evidence that Madrid had either the will or ability to restrain the Seminoles and Red Sticks. Britain, Adams was convinced, was not going to intervene and risk the ongoing rapprochement with America. Finally, and most important, a repudiation of Jackson would put the United States on the defensive in its negotiations with Spain to acquire Florida and extend America's western frontier to the Pacific.[9]

Undaunted by the president and other cabinet members, Adams insisted that Jackson's violation of his orders was apparent rather than real. He had been instructed to pursue the hostile Indians to their villages and sources of support. This he had done, and then finding that Spanish and British agents were aiding the Seminoles and Red Sticks, he had taken action against them. The assault on Pensacola was entirely justified because the governor had threatened to expel the general and his soldiers by force, thus threatening his mission to destroy or pacify the hostiles. There was no question whatsoever that the executive had the power to take military action in response to an attack on the country. Would the administration treat Jackson as Elizabeth had Sir Walter Raleigh, have the benefit of his services and then abandon him?[10] "I admitted that it was necessary to carry the reasoning upon my principles to the utmost extent it would bear to come to this conclusion," John Quincy noted in his journal. "But if the question was dubious, it was better to err on the side of vigor than on the side of weakness."[11] The president listened patiently to everything his secretary of state had to say but remained unmoved.

IF MONROE AND HIS cabinet officers' obduracy was not enough, John Quincy had to deal with the sweltering Washington heat. "There was not a spot in the house where I could stand or sit ten minutes in quiet, and I sauntered about the house from room to room like a ghost in Tartary [Tartarus, the deep abyss in Greek mythology used as a prison for the Titans]. . . . The thermometer at the hottest part of the day was at 95 and all day above 90," he recorded on July 12. The secretary of state's only relief was swimming. "Bathed in the Potomack [*sic*] immediately after rising. The river is within a few yards of two miles from my house, and I was two hours engaged upon this operation."[12] His manservant, Antoine Guista, usually accompanied him, and the two located a raft from which they could dive and swim. But relief was only temporary. The heat produced uncomfortable side effects. "I passed the night without closing my eyes under a perpetual irritation of the skin over my face and almost every part of the body which I supposed to be the effect of what is called prickly heat. But on changing my linen this morning, I discovered it was caused by a nest of spiders just from the egg-shell, so small that most of them were perceptible only by their motion. . . . How this horrible creeping nation got upon me, I could not exactly ascertain."[13]

On July 17, Monroe submitted to his colleagues the draft of a letter to Onís that neither justified Jackson nor repudiated him. It largely followed the line of reasoning Adams had taken in previous cabinet meetings. Jackson's incursion had been triggered by Spain's refusal to live up to its pledge to restrain "its Indians from committing murders upon the aged and the infirm, the woman and children of the United States." Indeed, from forts built by the British during the War of 1812, Spain had given aid and comfort to the savages. General Jackson had discovered this during his pursuit of the Seminoles and Red Sticks, and taken actions that, if not previously authorized, were perfectly justified. But the United States recognized that the seizure of the two Spanish forts was a temporary expedient. It would turn over Pensacola to any representatives Spain might designate. So too would Washington return St. Marks as soon as Madrid demonstrated the intent and capacity to control the hostile Indians operating out of the Floridas.[14]

Monroe and Adams then turned to the unenviable task of appeasing Jackson, Congress, the British, and Europe in general. On July 19 the president wrote his general: "In transcending the limits prescribed [in your] orders you acted on your own responsibility, on facts and circumstances which were unknown to the Government when the orders were given many of which . . . occurred afterward and which you thought imposed on you the measures as an act of patriotism, essential to the honor and interests of your country."[15] There were times when officers of the United States were justified in exceeding instructions, and this was one of them. But the seizures of St. Marks and Pensacola were acts of war; they must be returned to Spain. To retain them would mean armed conflict, and only Congress had the power to declare war, Monroe wrote Jackson. Hopefully, restoration of the forts would open the way for a peaceful acquisition of the Floridas. Nothing was said of Arbuthnot and Armbrister.

Monroe rather indelicately offered Jackson the chance to alter his dispatches to show himself in the best light, but then insisted that in the future he must communicate with the president through the secretary of war. Thank you, but no, the Hero of New Orleans replied. He would continue to correspond directly with the commander in chief, and there was no need to alter dispatches since his actions had been in perfect accord with the orders and intentions of the government.[16]

Turning to Europe, Adams penned a sweeping defense of Jackson and his exploits in Florida in the form of a letter to Minister George Erving in Madrid in November. "The task is of the highest order," John Quincy observed in his journal; "may I not be found inferior to it!"[17] In Pinckney's Treaty, Spain had given a solemn pledge to restrain Indians residing in their territory from attacking the United States. It had failed utterly to do so. In August 1814, when America was at war with Great Britain, Madrid, having declared its neutrality, had stood by while a British military force invaded Florida, "a thousand miles from any British territory," seizing Pensacola and enlisting "all the runaway negroes—all the savage Indians—all the pirates and all the traitors to their country" to wage merciless war against America's southeastern border.[18] At the close of the conflict Lieutenant Colonel Nicolls had remained, telling the Seminoles and Red Sticks that the Treaty of Ghent had restored their claim to all their lands not only in Florida but in the southern part of the United States. He had established Prospect Bluff, or the Negro Fort; all the while, Spain had done nothing to prevent these outrages. Cruel as war was when waged by civilized nations, it was "doubly cruel when waged with savages [who take] no prisoners but to torture them; that they give no quarter; that they put to death, without discrimination of age or sex."[19]

But it was those Europeans who incited and armed the hostiles who were the real culprits, Adams declared. Arbuthnot and Armbrister, licensed by Spanish authorities to trade with the Indians but disavowed by the British government, had gotten just what they deserved. And whether they were acting out of impotence or malice, so had the Spanish at St. Marks and Pensacola. At the very least, Spain had demonstrated that it could not control the Florida territories and the savage barbarians who resided there. General Jackson had not been acting under orders when he executed the Englishmen together with Hillis Hadjo and Ho-mathlimico, but in uncovering this "narrative of dark and complicated depravity, this creeping and insidious war," he had been entirely justified in his actions.[20] Adams's message was clear. The Floridas were derelicts and should be ceded at once to the United States.

Several weeks before sending this missive to Minister Erving, Adams had it leaked, with supporting documents, to the American press. Monroe took care to send a copy of Adams's defense of Jackson and indictment of Spain to Jefferson. The Sage of Monticello suggested that the administration have Adams's letter to Erving as well as his July 23 note to Onís staking America's claim to Spanish territory north of the Río Grande translated into Spanish and French and distributed throughout the capitals of Europe. "The paper on our right to the Rio Bravo," Jefferson wrote Monroe, and the letter to Erving of November 28 "are the most important and are among the ablest compositions I have ever seen, both as to logic and style."[21]

Adams's defense of Jackson was received by the Liverpool government with some relief. It could be used to quiet public outcry over the execution of two British citizens. Castlereagh had previously observed to Richard Rush that the country was so outraged over the executions that a declaration of war would have ensued had the ministry but "held up a finger." John Quincy's letter to Erving gave Liverpool some cover. "There has been scarcely a pistol flashed since the great gun from Washington to Madrid," John Adams Smith wrote his uncle from his position in the American legation in London.[22] In the aftermath of John Quincy's broadside, Castlereagh wrote Bagot that "it is impossible not to admit that the unfortunate sufferers [Arbuthnot and Armbrister], whatever their intentions, had been engaged in unauthorized practices of such a description as to have deprived them of any claim on their own Government for interference on their behalf."[23] For his part, Bagot declared the executions to be nothing less than extrajudicial murders, a "crying outrage," but he dutifully informed Adams that Arbuthnot and Armbrister had been acting entirely on their own and that the Liverpool government would not take any action on the matter.[24]

Meanwhile, in Congress, Clay and Calhoun continued to misplay their hands. In January 1819, the House Committee on Military Affairs, which had been packed with Clay supporters, issued a report condemning the executions of Arbuthnot and Armbrister. A Crawford lieutenant added a codicil prohibiting the invasion of foreign territory without the express consent of Congress.[25] The following day the Speaker stepped into the well of the House and delivered a diatribe against the Monroe administration in general and Jackson in particular. The speech was vintage Clay, bitingly sarcastic, wickedly humorous. It would end any

chance he had of ever becoming president. "Whenever did conquering and deso-
lating Rome fail to respect the altars and the gods of those who she subjugated!"
he exclaimed. The two Englishmen, whatever their transgressions, had been executed illegally. The assaults on St. Marks and Pensacola were unauthorized acts of
war. "Remember that Greece had her Alexander, Rome her Caesar, England her
Cromwell, France her Bonaparte, and if we would escape the rock on which they
spilt, we must avoid their errors."[26] What hypocrisy! John Quincy wrote his father. "That General Jackson should be [called] a murderer . . . and then [for him
to] express profound gratitude to [Old] Hickory for his services to the country"
was contemptible.[27]

When Clay's speech produced a motion of censure against the general, an infuriated Jackson descended upon Washington determined to foil the dastardly
plot being hatched against him. Some observers predicted a duel between the
general and the Speaker, but when, on February 8, the House rejected a motion
of censure by a vote of sixty-three to 107, Jackson declared that he was ready to
forgive and forget the members of that body—except for Clay. The Speaker called
upon Jackson following the failed censure vote and assured him that his barbs
were political and not personal. Jackson was far from assuaged. "The hypocrisy &
baseness of Clay," he wrote an acquaintance, "in pretending friendship to me &
endeavoring to crush the executive through me, make me despise the villain. . . .
You will see him skinned here, & hope you will roast him in the West."[28]

THE OCCUPATION OF AMELIA Island and Jackson's rampage through Florida
were but pieces in the larger puzzle that when fitted together would become the
Adams–Onís Treaty of 1819. Adams's opposite number in these negotiations was
Don Luis de Onís, then fifty-six years old, a diplomat with a long and distinguished career. Like Talleyrand, he had political principles that were extremely
flexible. He had come to the United States in 1809 as the unofficial representative
of the constitutionalist junta that was allied with Great Britain against the occupation regime of Joseph Bonaparte. But when Ferdinand VII was restored, Onís
declared himself a monarchist and was appointed minister to the United States.
The scion of a distinguished Salamanca family, Onís was classically educated,
fluent in four languages, and trained as a lawyer. His diplomatic specialties were
obfuscation and obstruction. Adams thought him the epitome of an unprincipled
European diplomat: "Cold, calculating, wily, always commanding his own manner, proud because he is a Spaniard, but supple and cunning, accommodating the
tone of his pretensions precisely to the degree of endurance of his opponent, bold
and overbearing to the utmost extent at which it is tolerated, careless of what he

asserts . . . his morality appears to be that of the Jesuits as exposed by Pascal."[29] The acerbity of this portrait was a testament to the degree to which Onís was able to frustrate the secretary of state. Onís knew exactly what and with whom he was dealing. "The Americans believe themselves superior to all other nations of Europe," he would observe in his *Memoria sobre las Negociaciones entre España y los Estados Unidos de América*, "and see their destiny to extend their dominion of the isthmus of Panama and in the future to all of the New World."[30]

John Quincy had hoped that Jackson's exploits had so demonstrated Spain's weakness that Madrid would be forced to sign a transcontinental treaty on U.S. terms. Adding to his optimism were the goings-on at the Concert of Europe's gathering at Aix-la-Chapelle in October. The Russians and the Austrians wanted to invite Ferdinand to attend in order to demonstrate the alliance's solidarity with a fellow monarch who was fighting both revolution and democracy. Castlereagh blocked that invitation and made it clear that Great Britain would not support the Holy Alliance's efforts to stem the tide of popular sovereignty and quell movements for national self-determination whether in the Old World or the New. Clearly isolated, Madrid, it seemed to Adams, would have to give in. He was to be bitterly disappointed.

In April 1818, Onís had received best-case instructions from Pizarro. Spain would cede the defenseless Floridas but only in return for United States' acceptance of the Mississippi as its western frontier and a pledge not to recognize the Central and South American republics. Onís had already advised Madrid that a nonrecognition pledge was out of the question. Spain should concentrate on protecting Texas and its vast holdings to the west. "That is the sole object of the sacrifices which His Majesty is disposed to make of the Floridas," Onís told Adams, "and I will not advise His Majesty to make any settlement unless it fixes . . . permanent limits west of the Mississippi."

Perfect, John Quincy replied. "If that's the way it is, we can take the Rio Bravo [Rio Grande, the present-day western boundary of Texas] del Norte for a frontier."

Onís: "And what are your plans from there on?"

Adams: "From there on a line might be drawn to the source of the Missouri, thence straight to the Pacific Ocean."

Onís: "So you are trying to dispossess us also of the whole Pacific Coast, which belongs to us and which Juan de Fuca took possession of in the king's name up to fifty-six degrees!"

"Nonsense," declared Adams. "The English pretend the Columbia River is theirs. The Russians have possessions north of it, which you have never disputed, and we have more right than anybody else to the River Columbia. We have establishments on its banks, and we need it to keep open our communications with the interior."

"Here are their views, clear enough," Onís subsequently wrote to Pizarro, "and the truth is they are less exaggerated than their real ones. . . . If His Majesty can't get the support of any power and hasn't sufficient forces to make war on this county, then I think it would be best not to delay making the best settlement possible seeing that things certainly won't be better for a long time."[31]

Pizarro agreed, but he was still a prisoner of Ferdinand, and Ferdinand of the reactionary *camarilla*. As a result, Onís was forced to resort to delay and misdirection. He would have to obtain a new set of instructions, he told Adams. Perhaps it would be best to transfer the negotiations to Madrid. Either place would suffice, the secretary of state replied. The Río Grande was not an acceptable border with Texas, the Spaniard declared. What about the Sabine [the eastern boundary of present-day Texas]? No, declared Adams. They might compromise on the Colorado from its source in the Rocky Mountains to its mouth on the Gulf of Mexico.[32] He would have to write Madrid for new instructions, Onís replied. Frustrated, Adams informed the Spaniard in mid-April that President Monroe had observed to him that he "thought it utterly useless either to write or to talk any more upon the subject as there never had been a negotiation so completely exhausted, and upon which there was so little prospect that the parties would ever come to an understanding with each other." To Adams's consternation, the Spanish minister responded by proposing a Spanish–American alliance directed against Great Britain, the object of which would be to break John Bull's control over international trade.[33]

At this point the French minister Hyde de Neuville stepped forward to offer his services as mediator. France's motives here were somewhat obscure. As an absolute monarch Louis XVIII would have been expected to support his fellow royal in Madrid, but France feared that Great Britain would then take advantage of the situation to broaden its base in the Americas. British schemes could be nipped in the bud if a peaceful settlement of the issues at dispute between Spain and the United States could be worked out.[34]

Jean-Guillaume, Baron Hyde de Neuville, had never been a thoroughgoing royalist, but during the French Revolution, he had remained a consistent supporter of the Bourbons and served them in a number of diplomatic capacities. The Hyde de Neuville sat out the Napoleonic era in comfortable exile in the United States. With Louis XVIII's return, he was immediately named minister to the country of his exile. Quixotically, the Frenchman was an unabashed admirer of the republican experiment in America. A large, open, pleasant-faced man, gracious and engaging in society, Hyde de Neuville was one of the Adamses' favorites.[35] John Quincy chose to overlook his friend's devotion to the Bourbons. "[I]n all the intercourse that I have had with European statesmen, I have not met with a man of higher sentiments of honor, of kinder and more generous feelings, or of a fairer and more candid mind," he later wrote Richard Rush.[36]

Tell Onís, Adams instructed the French minister, that if Spain did not come to the point, it was most likely that Congress at its next session would unilaterally vote to annex the Floridas, and Spain would lose whatever leverage it had in negotiations. In December, Adams informed Hyde de Neuville that the Monroe administration was on the verge of extending diplomatic recognition to Buenos Aires and perhaps Chile and other of the American republics as well.[37] At the same time, the secretary of state wrote Richard Rush in London, instructing him to inform Castlereagh and the rest of the diplomatic corps "how important it is to them, as well as to us, that the newly found[ed] states should be . . . recognized." The period is fast approaching, he confided to the American minister, when the independence of Buenos Aires "will be so firmly established as to be beyond the reach of any reasonable pretentions of supremacy on the part of Spain."[38] An agitated Hyde de Neuville subsequently called on Adams on December 28. Could not the United States hold off on recognition? It would only play into Britain's hands. "Events were placing the affairs of South America quite out of our control," Adams replied. But if Spain would agree to a reasonable treaty, "there would probably be much less ardor in this country against Spain and consequently less in favor of the South Americans."[39]

Adams had cleared the message with Monroe, but his colleagues in the cabinet were taken aback. Heretofore administration policy had been staunchly against recognition. Would this not appear to be an unjustified reversal of course? Conditions had changed, Adams exclaimed—in South America, in Europe, and in the ongoing negotiation with Spain. "I added," he observed in his diary, "that I had always considered and declared the question of acknowledging the South American Governments as a question of time."[40]

Despite these moves, John Quincy remained pessimistic. In September the realist Pizarro had been replaced by the Marquis de Casa Yrujo—"former Minister to this country, and a very obnoxious one," Adams observed of him.[41] However, unbeknownst to Adams, Onís in January 1819 received a new set of instructions from the foreign ministry. Cede the Floridas. If necessary to forestall U.S. recognition of the Latin American republics and to prevent a formal break with Washington, which could very well lead to an invasion of Mexico, Onís should settle the western boundary as best he could. He should, if possible, persuade the

Americans to accept the line of the Missouri River to its source. In extremis, the minister was authorized to cede Texas.[42]

IN SEPTEMBER, JOHN QUINCY and Louisa departed Washington for a month-long vacation in Massachusetts. For him it promised a much-needed respite from the political and diplomatic tensions of his office, not to mention Washington's heat. He visited with his parents, was wined and dined in Boston, and went with the family on an excursion to West Point. The beauties of the Hudson Valley were more striking than he remembered, he noted in his diary. And he escaped to his father's library at Peacefield to immerse himself in Plato's *Phaedo*. He and Louisa departed for Washington in mid-October. This would be the last time John Quincy would see his mother.

"There was a letter came from my son John to my wife dated the 22d and saying that my mother was very dangerously ill," John Quincy recorded in his diary on October 26.[43] Indeed, Abigail had contracted typhoid fever. John Quincy was momentarily paralyzed by the news, unable to write either to his mother or his father. "In the agitation of my own heart," he later explained to John, "I knew not how to order my speech."[44] As the disease progressed—and with her doctors knowing only to bleed and blister her—the matriarch suffered through extreme pain. "I wish I could lay down beside her and die too," her husband wrote Harriet Welsh. "I cannot bear to see her in this state."[45] Amidst reports of his mother's declining health, John Quincy lamented to his diary, "I am endeavoring to prepare my mind for submission to the divine will. Might this cup, Oh God pass from me!"[46] Abigail Adams died at one p.m. on October 28, three days after her fifty-fourth wedding anniversary. "I am advised that you have endured the agony of her illness with the fortitude that belongs to your character," John Quincy wrote John on November 2. "Let me hear from you, my dearest father, let me hear from you soon."[47] John wrote a week later: "The bitterness of death is past. The grim specter so terrible to human nature has no sting left for me. My consolations are more than I can number."[48] Among hundreds of letters of condolence that poured into Peacefield was a kind and empathetic note from Thomas Jefferson.

Long forgotten were the days of John Quincy's youth, when his mother had declared to her eleven-year-old son that she would rather see him sink to the bottom of the sea than stray from the path of righteousness and morality. Abigail had spoiled one romance after another, holding her eldest son to almost unattainable standards and looking down on his "European" wife. John Quincy never doubted her love for him even though it frequently manifested itself in unremitting ambition. Abigail had drawn the extended Adams clan to Peacefield, and to her bosom as Charles and then Thomas succumbed to dissipation. "My Mother as an angel upon earth. She was a minister of blessing to all human beings within her sphere of action. . . . She had no feelings but of kindness and beneficence."[49]

THE PRESS OF OFFICIAL business would admit John Quincy only a brief period of mourning. During the next five weeks, Adams and Onís via Hyde de Neuville bickered over the exact boundary that would separate the two empires west of the Mississippi. The unfortunate Onís was caught between the stubborn and aggressive secretary of state and the *camarilla*, which had apparently countermanded Casa Yrujo's instructions giving him leeway to negotiate the best western boundary he could under the circumstances. "[H]e insisted much upon the infinite pains he has taken to prevail upon his Government to come to terms of accommodation with us," John Quincy recorded in his diary, "but the King's Council was composed of such ignorant and stupid Grandees of Spain and Priest, that I could have no conception of their obstinacy and imbecility."[50] For his part Adams had to deal not only with Onís but with Monroe and the rest of the cabinet. So anxious was the president to have Florida, Adams recalled, that he was willing to grant a boundary much farther north and east of the Rocky Mountains than his secretary of state believed advisable.[51] In the end Adams prevailed. Onís and he settled on a border consisting of the Sabine River due north to the Red River until it intersected the hundredth meridian, then north to the Arkansas River, west to the hundred fifth meridian, north to the forty-second parallel, and from thence to the Pacific Coast. The Adams–Onís, or Transcontinental, Treaty would effectively exclude Spain from the Oregon Territory.

The first week in February, Monroe, with an eye to the presidential election of 1820, asked Adams to run the treaty past Andrew Jackson, then in town putting down the movement in Congress to censure him. On February 3, Jackson, at Adams's invitation, dropped by his house to examine the treaty map. In his opinion, the Hero declared, "The possession of the Floridas was of so great importance to the Southern frontier of the United States and so essential even to their safety that the vast majority of the nation would be satisfied with the Western boundary as we propose."[52] There could be no security for the southern part of the United States as long as the mouths of the rivers emptying into the Gulf of Mexico were in foreign hands.

The Transcontinental or Adams–Onís Treaty ceded the Floridas to the United States in return for it assuming the claims of American citizens against Spain to a maximum of five million dollars; it established a stepping-stone boundary separating American and Spanish territory from the Gulf of Mexico to the Pacific. The Senate gave its assent unanimously, and the document was signed on February 22, 1819.

John Quincy tried to be humble but could not. "It was near nine in the morning when I closed the day with ejaculations of fervent gratitude to the Giver of all Good. It was, perhaps, the most important day of my life. . . . Let no idle and unfounded exultation take possession of my mind as if I could ascribe my . . . exertions [to] any portion of the event."[53] He then proceeded to do just that. Completion of the Transcontinental Treaty was an event unparalleled in American history, Adams crowed in his diary. Neither the authors of the Treaty of 1783 nor the managers of the Louisiana Purchase had dreamed of an empire stretching to the Pacific. "I record the first assertion of this claim for the United States as my own."[54] There was no doubt that the signing of the treaty made the secretary of state not only respected but popular with his countrymen. "The Treaty has produced a wonderful sensation and is another proof that real unassuming ability will confound intrigue," Louisa—admittedly not an unbiased observer—wrote in her journal. "My husband now stands on the highest pinnacle of elevation. . . . May my children walk in his steps and may their greatest ambition be to 'go and do likewise.'"[55]

The Adams–Onís Treaty was a signal achievement, but it contained the seeds of the Union's destruction, and Adams and Monroe knew it. "From this view," Monroe observed, "it is evident, that the further acquisition of territory to the West and South, involves difficulties of an internal nature which menaces the Union itself."[56] The Transcontinental Treaty in opening up new, fertile lands west of the Mississippi served to ensure the survival of slavery and perpetuate the rancorous division between free states and the slave power.

The Transcontinental Treaty came with a price both monetary and moral. During his first year and a half as secretary of state, John Quincy had justified undeclared acts of war by one of his country's general officers. He had utilized Jackson's incursion to bully Spain into ceding the Floridas and a huge portion of their territory west of the Mississippi and abandoning any claim to the Oregon Territory. In so doing he had abridged Congress's constitutional right to declare war and confirmed the nations of Europe in their opinion that the United States was just another avaricious empire. The only difference between them and America was the latter's self-righteousness. They had a point.

Both John Quincy and his father had turned up their noses at what they believed to be the rank cynicism of Niccolò Machiavelli's *The Prince*, but during his bullying of Onís and his reversals concerning U.S. recognition of the rebellious Latin American republics, John Quincy proved to be the essence of Machiavellianism. While privately condemning the Central and South American revolutionaries as incapable of forming and sustaining representative democracies, he publicly declared them to be sons and daughters of the American Revolution. "[M]ay our country be always successful, but whether successful or otherwise always right," John Quincy had written John while minister to Great Britain. But he believed that by virtue of its republican institutions and its democratic ideals, it could not, in the end, be wrong.[57] Without strength, the Union could not survive. If the United States could not endure, the cause of republicanism was lost. Therefore, any action that strengthened the Union was justified. It would take time and perhaps a civil war, Adams believed, for America to convert the ideas expressed in the nation's founding statement of purpose into reality: "The seeds of the Declaration of Independence are yet maturing," he wrote in 1819; "the harvest will be what West the Painter calls the terrible sublime."[58] In the meantime, America, the great experiment—the next stage in the story of the English-speaking people's quest for liberty, justice, and equality—must be protected and nourished at all costs. But if, once impregnable, America did not live up to its ideals, it was damned, Adams declared. "May they [future Americans] be armed in thunder for the defense of right and self-shackled in eternal impotence for the support of wrong."[59]

24

Empire and Slavery

DURING HIS CONVERSATIONS WITH Adams, Jackson warned that Clay and Crawford had entered into an unholy alliance to discredit the administration and the secretary of state in particular. The Georgian was a Trojan horse within the administration. The problem was, the general continued, that "Mr. Monroe was of an open, fair, unsuspecting character . . . and would not believe human nature capable of the baseness which Crawford, while holding a confidential office under him, was practicing against him."[1] This was hardly news to John Quincy. He knew that as secretary of state, the putative stepping stone to the highest office in the land, he had a political target on his back.

In January 1820, Clay took to the floor of the House to condemn the Transcontinental Treaty as the product of "the blunders of a most ill conducted negotiation"; the secretary of state had not acquired all that he could have, and he had given up much more than he should have. The Speaker proceeded to offer two resolutions. The first declared that Congress and Congress alone had the power to dispose of public lands and insisted that "no treaty, purporting to alienate any portion thereof is valid without the concurrence of Congress."[2] The second proclaimed that the "cession" of Texas without an equivalent was unacceptable and ought to be repudiated. Both motions failed; the Senate's subsequent unanimous approval of the treaty provided further proof of Clay's increasingly tin ear.

Of his two principal rivals, John Quincy found Crawford the more insidious. "[H]is ambition swallows up his principle," he wrote in his diary. "This Government is . . . assuming daily more and more a character of a cabal . . . working . . . with many of the worst features of elective monarchies."[3] Then there was Jackson, who at this point was Adams's ally, but who also coveted the White House. In Adams's view the problem was not only the overarching ambition of the contenders but the congressional caucus as a nominating mechanism. "The only possible chance for a head of department to attain the presidency," he observed, "is by ingratiating himself personally with the members of Congress, and as many of them have objects of their own to obtain, the temptation is immense to [establish] corrupt coalitions and tends to make all the public offices objects of bargain and sale."[4]

In March 1819, a gleeful Clay called at the White House and informed the president that Adams had made a huge blunder. Under pressure from the *camarilla*, Ferdinand had granted most of East Florida to three court favorites: two on December 17, 1817, and one on January 25, 1818. Adams had unwittingly agreed to January 24, 1818, as the effective date of the treaty, leaving the first two grants, comprising hundreds of thousands of acres of East Florida, in the hands of Spanish grandees. Adams instructed the new minister to Spain, John Forsyth, to demand that Ferdinand withdraw the grants. He eventually did but not until after much wrangling and a large share of political embarrassment for the secretary of state.[5]

Despite Clay's machinations, the Adamses were willing to credit the Kentuckian when he insisted that there was nothing personal in his political attacks. Following a wedding reception at the President's House for one of Monroe's nieces, Louisa encountered the Kentuckian: "The Speaker was in high spirits," she recorded in her diary, "and came and spoke very graciously to me and offered his hand which I immediately accepted—we meet but to *War* and each of us are ready with a jest on all occasions."[6] A close and insightful student of the human condition, Louisa remarked of Clay: "There is something about Mr. Clay that pleases me in spite of reason—and it is this; that if you watch his character, you almost immediately discover that his heart is generous and good and that his first impulse is almost always benevolent and liberal—But a neglected education, vicious habits, and bad company, united to overweening ambition, have made him blush to act the better part and covered with foul blots that which might have been made perfect."[7]

JOHN QUINCY'S PRESIDENTIAL AMBITIONS were not without hope. The country was intoxicated with manifest destiny, and he was chief dispenser of the spirit. The more Monroe came under assault from rivals within and without his cabinet, the more favorably he viewed his secretary of state. In January 1818, Jeremiah Mason wrote his fellow Federalist Rufus King: "It is reported here that M. Monroe intends *bona fide* to make his Secretary of State his eventual successor and that he will in due time give evidence of such intention."[8] But others thought presidential anointment would not suffice. "Already there is considerable stir and whispering as to who is to be the next President," Supreme Court justice Joseph Story wrote a friend. "It is thought here that J.Q. Adams will not be a successful candidate. It seems that the great objection to him is that he is retiring and unobtrusive, studious, cool, and reflecting; that he does nothing to excite attention or to gain friendships. He contents himself with doing his duty without seeking any reward. . . . 'God helps those who help themselves.'"[9] It was not that Adams was unaware: "My friends earnestly urge me to mingle more in society and to make myself more extensively known," he wrote in his diary, "but I am scarcely ever satisfied with myself after going into company, and always have the impression that my time at home is more usefully spent."[10]

John Quincy's reputation for unsociability was offset by his wife's growing reputation as one of Washington's accomplished and most amiable hostesses. By the summer of 1819, her balls and dinners were the talk of the town; indeed, the Adams house on F Street had become the social center of official Washington in lieu of Elizabeth Monroe's abdication. At the same time that she was shoring up her husband's political fortunes, Louisa was caring for an ever-extending family. The eldest of the seven Johnson daughters, Nancy, had died eight years earlier, leaving behind three children. Her husband, Walter Hellen, had subsequently married the youngest Johnson daughter, Adelaide. When he died in 1815, Adelaide was left with Walter and Nancy's three surviving children plus one she had borne Walter. The youngsters split time between Quincy and Washington; Adelaide remained in the capital and was a regular guest at the dinner parties hosted by John Quincy and Louisa. In September 1818, she gave birth to a baby girl, Georgiana Adelaide Hellen, a child fathered by George Boyd, the husband of her sister Harriet. In 1817, Louisa's sister Caroline moved to Washington from Baltimore with her second husband, Nathaniel Frye. Frye, who came from a slaveholding family, was chief clerk in the War Department. Caroline was in charge of four stepchildren from her first marriage and she bore Frye a son, Thomas. Louisa presided over two of Caroline's stepdaughters' comings-out. Both young women proved to be charming, gracious, and socially adept.[11] Not so Mary Catherine Hellen, Nancy's daughter, whom Louisa and John Quincy virtually adopted when she was eleven. She proved to be a spoiled, headstrong child. "I have taken [Mary] from school as I was not satisfied with the progress she made there. She now studies with me and I hope will improve more rapidly. . . . [She] is a very fine girl but a little wild."[12] A little wild indeed. Resistant to any sort of book knowledge, she in her adolescence seemed interested only in torturing her many suitors.

Louisa's bond with her father-in-law, always strong, grew even stronger during her years in Washington. She had inherited her mother's talent for description, social criticism, and character sketching, and she continued to write John long, vivid, and amusing letters describing the Washington social scene.[13] She and the old boy shared an affection for and tolerance of George, John, and Charles that frequently paired them against John Quincy and his enormous and frequently disappointed expectations. The elder Adams always chose to see the best in his grandsons, reporting that all three were bound to distinguish themselves as sons of Harvard.

In the fall of 1817, John, fourteen, and Charles, ten, had been enrolled in the Boston Latin School. They boarded with Dr. and Mrs. Thomas Welsh, John Quincy apparently having forgiven the doctor for squandering much of his wealth on reckless speculation during the St. Petersburg years. George was placed with a tutor in Cambridge to prepare for entry into Harvard as a member of the sophomore class in the spring of 1818. He did indeed make the grade, although dread of failing the entrance examination brought the seventeen-year-old to the verge of a nervous breakdown.[14] His father had been brutal: "I cannot but acknowledge my surprise and mortification," he wrote his son in the run-up to the dreaded examination, "to learn that you have been wasting your time with Mr. Gilman upon the Greek Testament and Collectanea [brianova] and other books with which you was already perfectly familiar instead of applying to those particular studies in which you was deficient. . . . I can attribute it to nothing but a propensity to skulk from real study and idle away hours upon what was no study at all."[15] Nor was John Quincy's second son spared the rod. When John dared to write complaining of the harshness of his uncle Thomas (who had been entrusted with paying the expenses of all three boys) and the difficulty of his lessons at the Latin School, John Quincy blasted the child: "You boast of your studying hard and pray for whose benefit do you study? Is it for mine or for your uncle's? Or are you so much of a baby that you must be teased to spell your letters by sugar plums? Or are you such an independent gentleman that you can brook no control and must have everything you ask for? If so, I desire you not to write for anything to me."[16] Not surprisingly, George, John, and Charles spent as much time as possible in Quincy, where George consumed books in his grandfather's library, John roamed the woods, and Charles played under his grandmother's adoring eye.

John Quincy would continue to be the scourge of his sons through their college years. What had happened to the warm, tolerant father of Little Boston House in Ealing? Adams was, of course, under intense stress in his official life, much more so than in England. But he bore that trait that his father had identified as defining in human beings—the need to be recognized and respected by others. John Quincy was jealous of his reputation and determined that his sons would do nothing to tarnish it. He like many of his generation regarded child-rearing as a vocation. He had always been easier on Charles—his youngest was naturally more disciplined and self-controlled than his brothers—but it was John Quincy who had abandoned his two elder sons for six years while he burnished his diplomatic reputation in Europe. His guilt over this neglect could go either of two ways—lowering the bar or raising it. He was driven to raise it—to absurd extremes as it turned out.

JOHN QUINCY'S ELATION OVER the conclusion of the Transcontinental Treaty soon turned to dismay. The document he and Onís concluded had bound Ferdinand "on the faith and word of a king to approve, ratify, and fulfill whatsoever might be stipulated and signed" by his envoy. But after reading its terms, the reactionaries on the *camarilla* pressured His Most Catholic Majesty to delay ratification. Onís had ceded too much territory, and he had failed to extract a pledge from the Monroe administration that it would not recognize the Latin American republics and that it would strictly enforce its neutrality laws.[17] Clay was ecstatic; he demanded that the administration seize the Floridas, annex Texas, and recognize the insurgent republics. "[O]ur relations with Spain and the peace of the country are thrown into a more dangerous and fearful crisis than they ever have been," the secretary of state lamented in his diary. "A responsibility is again cast upon me, under which all my natural powers would sink, and the issue of which may be the worst possible."[18]

In mid-August 1819, Monroe returned to Washington from a tour of the South and summoned his cabinet to discuss the new crisis. Remarkably there was instant consensus. If Spain did not ratify the treaty before the House and Senate convened in November, everyone agreed that the administration should request Congress to authorize the occupation of Florida—"not as an act of hostility to Spain but as an assertion of our own right."[19] Monroe declared, "[If] we should not act with promptitude, decision, and vigor, we should lose consideration in the eyes of the world; it would be taken for a symptom of weakness and all the other Nations whose respect it is important to us to command would immediately take advantage of it against us."[20]

Then, on November 25, Adams received word from the American minister in Madrid, John Forsyth, that instead of ratifying the treaty, Ferdinand had decided to send a new envoy to America to negotiate "modifications." Before Monroe could order Florida to be taken by force, Gallatin, then U.S. minister to France, reported that both the French foreign minister and the Russian ambassador had approached him to ask that the United States hold its hand and wait for the diplomatic process to run its course.[21] Shortly thereafter, the Russian minister in Washington, Pyotr Poletika, called on the secretary of state. Adams's old friend Tsar

Alexander wished for a peaceful solution to the simmering Spanish–American dispute, he said. His preference was for Spain's New World colonies to be restored to his brother monarch, Ferdinand. Demonstrating just how out of touch Alexander was, Poletika conveyed his sovereign's wish that the United States join the Holy Alliance. John Quincy remained unmoved, but suddenly Monroe began waffling. "I found the President extremely anxious at this state of things," he reported, and Monroe was evidently unwilling to recommend to Congress the course that had been decided upon.[22] Why not, the secretary of state suggested, simply describe the situation to Congress and the American people, and declare that in response to requests from European powers friendly to the United States, the administration would allow Spain more time to see the error of its ways, while at the same time stating that the terms of the treaty would be executed one way or another?[23]

For two days the president wavered. Then, on the twenty-sixth, the cabinet unanimously approved a stratagem whereby the executive would merely ask Congress for contingent authority to unilaterally occupy Florida, a compromise suggested by the secretary of state. Actually, this was the only course open to the administration. "Congress will do nothing," Adams observed in his diary, "because to do anything they must assume the responsibility of consequences, because they must incur at least the hazard of a war . . . and, after all, the Executive would get the principal credit of all that Congress would do. One of the most remarkable features of what I am witnessing every day is a perpetual struggle in both houses of Congress to control the Executive, to make it dependent upon, and subservient to them."[24]

At long last, in mid-April 1820, following a leisurely tour of Paris and other European capitals, the new Spanish minister, Governor-General Francisco Dionisio Vives, arrived. Vives boldly declared that there would be no ratification unless and until the U.S. satisfied Spain in regard to enforcing its neutrality laws, committed to nonrecognition of the republics, and agreed to legitimize the land grants the king had made to his courtiers. No, absolutely not, Adams told Vives. The United States had negotiated in good faith, Spain had pledged its troth, and Madrid had no alternative but to live up to the terms of the treaty. Vives, who was merely following orders, conceded Adams's points and agreed to advise his government that ratification of the treaty was not only inevitable but in Spain's interests. Before Madrid could respond, Monroe called a cabinet meeting and suggested that since the six-month deadline for ratification had long since passed, the United States should seize Texas as indemnity. No less a personage than Thomas Jefferson had written, advocating such a move. Adams immediately declared his opposition. Give Vives's recommendations a chance. Seizure of Texas would only give Madrid an excuse for further delay.[25]

The president was persuaded. In May 1820, Monroe wrote to Jefferson (the draft had almost certainly been prepared by Adams) that Spain's ongoing weakness and a looming civil war in Mexico did indeed invite further expansion. "It would be easy to arrange the boundary in the wilderness so as to include as much territory on our side as we might desire. No European power could prevent it. . . . But the difficulty does not proceed from these sources. It is altogether internal and of the most distressing and dangerous tendency."[26] The nation was then in the midst of the Missouri controversy. Opinions had hardened both in the slaveholding South and the "free" states of the Mid-Atlantic and the Northeast. Only after Missouri was admitted as a slave state and Maine as free did tempers cool. Acquisition of Texas, almost certain to become one or more slave states, would once again upset the delicate and hard-won balance.

Patience proved to be the best course. As so often happened, Europe's misfortunes turned to America's advantage. News arrived that the constitutionalist movement in Spain had forced Ferdinand to restore the Constitution and recall the Cortes of Cádiz.[27] A new council of state advised ratification of the Transcontinental Treaty as it stood and recommended cancellation of the land grants. On September 30, 1820, the Cortes give its assent. The U.S. Senate voted to approve the pact on February 19, 1821.[28] "Let my sons, if they ever consult this record of their father's life," John Quincy wrote subsequently in his diary, "meditate upon all the vicissitudes which have befallen the treaty and of which this diary bears witness. . . . Let them remark the workings of private interests, of perfidious fraud, of sordid intrigues, of royal treachery, of malignant rivalry, and of envy masked with patriotism playing to and fro across the Atlantic into each other['s] hands, all combined to destroy this treaty. . . . Under the petals of this garland of roses the Scorpion Onyx had hidden a viper [the land grants]. Clay and his admirers here were snickering at the simplicity with which I had been bamboozled by the crafty Spaniards. The partisans of Crawford were exulting in the same contemplation of a slur upon my sagacity." But "the goodness of that inscrutable Providence which entraps dishonest artifice in its own snares" intervened.[29]

THE DEBATE OVER WHETHER Missouri was to be admitted to the Union as a slave or free state in 1819–1820 brought the paradox of America to a head; how long could the nation continue half slave and half free? How long could the promise contained in the Declaration of Independence—a society rooted in equality, opportunity, and the rule of law—be denied to several millions of its citizens? Prior to this, issues other than chattel slavery had pitted the Northeast against the South and the West: the tariff, sectional struggle for power in Congress, internal improvements, free versus tight money, and manufacturing versus agricultural interests. Hitherto, various administrations had managed to balance the admission of slave and free states, avoiding a national debate on the institution as a moral issue. Everything changed with Missouri's application for statehood in 1819. Thomas Jefferson had written that slavery was a moral and political evil, that the master class was a collection of tyrants, and that the continued existence of the institution gave the lie to the promises of the Declaration of Independence. And yet, when the United States gained its independence, slavery was an established institution, extant in every state but Massachusetts and Vermont. The seven hundred thousand bondmen had become integral to the colonial-cum-national economy and were an accepted part of the culture. Slaveholders dominated national politics for the first thirty years of the country's existence. The Constitution did not explicitly mention slavery, but through the three-fifths clause, the provision prohibiting the federal government from interfering with the slave trade for twenty years, and the fugitive slave clause, which forbade runaways ("person held to service or labor") from gaining citizenship in free states, the national charter institutionalized chattel slavery.

In the Northern states, a handful of crusaders steeped in natural rights philosophy had called for emancipation, but most people were either indifferent to the plight of Black bondsmen or openly hostile to emancipation. There was widespread respect for the rights of property in New England, and the slave economy produced many of the raw materials that Yankee shipowners exported. Racism was endemic. Emancipation, Northerners feared, would flood their neighborhoods with free Blacks. Prejudice aside, a number of educated Northerners expressed doubt that those who had never known freedom or literacy could ever become responsible citizens.[30] But slavery was a human institution with a human face, a fact that could not be denied.

By the time Missouri applied for statehood, the plantation economy had exhausted much of the soil in the Old South, especially in Virginia, the state with the largest slave population. Slave owners had coveted the fertile lands acquired through the Louisiana Purchase not only for economic reasons but for considerations of personal safety as well. In the wake of the successful 1804 slave rebellion in Saint-Domingue, which had established Haiti as an independent country, slave owners in the United States, remembering Gabriel's attempt to seize Richmond four years earlier, were increasingly worried that their bondsmen would some night break into their homes and murder them in their beds. Expansionist slaveholders like Jefferson argued that the spread of slavery into the Western territories would thin out the slave population, thus reducing the threat of an organized, armed uprising. By the time Adams and Onís were negotiating their treaty, thousands of slave owners, old and new, had moved into Louisiana, Alabama, and Mississippi. They found that the global market for cheap calicos and muslins made of cotton was insatiable.[31] By 1822, Northern merchants and bankers were purchasing one-third of the South's cotton. Much of the fiber was transshipped to Europe, but a substantial amount went to the burgeoning textile manufactories of New England.[32] Slavery was truly a national institution.

On February 13, 1819, James Tallmadge, a first-term congressman from New York who had been working for years to remove the last vestiges of slavery from his home state, introduced an amendment to the Missouri statehood bill providing "that the further introduction of slavery or involuntary servitude [into the territories] be prohibited . . . ; and that all children of slaves, born within the said state, after the admission thereof into the Union, shall be free at the age of twenty-five years."[33] What ensued was a year-and-a-half-long debate on the meaning of America and whether the nation could survive partially free and partially slave. The census of 1820 would enumerate a slave population of 1,538,038 with some nineteen thousand still living above the Mason–Dixon Line. Most Americans shared John Quincy Adams's view of America as an island of republicanism in a sea of despotism, nothing less than the hope of the world. Hitherto the nation had been able to finesse the question of whether slavery could be abided in the land of the free. Many prominent antislavery advocates in the South—Washington, Jefferson, Madison, and Monroe among them—had condemned the institution and predicted its inevitable but gradual decline. Northerners, for economic and racial reasons, had been willing to remain silent. But no longer. After Tallmadge had finished speaking, Thomas W. Cobb of Georgia rose to warn of the Pandora's box about to be opened: "You have kindled a fire which all the waters of the ocean cannot put out, which seas of blood can only extinguish."[34] Tallmadge was undaunted. "Sir," he responded, "on this subject the eyes of Europe are turned upon you. You boast of the freedom of your Constitution and your laws; you have claimed in the Declaration of Independence, 'that all men are created equal'; and yet you have slaves in your country. . . . If a dissolution of the union must take place, let it be so. If civil war must come . . . I can only say, let it come!"[35]

With the slave-driven economy booming and fears of "a servile war" increasing by the day, the slave power was forced to abandon talk of eventual emancipation. Any notion of defending slavery on moral grounds was now impossible. The Missouri debate forced Southern leaders to choose: abandon the ideals of the Declaration of Independence or reject slavery and the society that it underpinned.

Spokesmen for perpetual Black bondage resorted to two tactics. One was to deny the humanity of Blacks, to claim that they were genetically inferior, beyond the pale. The other was to take an extreme states' rights position, insisting that each state had the sole right to decide the issue, and beyond that every citizen had the inalienable right to move with his property freely throughout the country.[36] "The slave drivers, as usual, whenever this topic is brought up, bluster and bully, talk of the white slaves of the Eastern states, and the dissolution of the Union, and oceans of blood," John Quincy wrote in his diary. "And the Northern men as usual pocket all this hectoring, sit down in quiet, and submit to the slave-scourging Republicanism of the planters," he wrote Louisa.[37] He believed that the pro-slavery clause in Missouri's application for statehood did not represent the will of the people. He insisted that if the free white voting population of the territory was actually polled, "a majority of the suffrages [votes] would appear against the admission of slavery"; the prospective state would prosper if "the middling class of people" knew they would not have to compete with "great hordes of Black serfs."[38]

In the House the Committee of the Whole approved the Tallmadge Amendment by a vote of seventy-nine to sixty-seven. The Senate, largely unaware of the storm gathering in the chamber next door, approved Missouri's application for statehood, striking out the antislavery addendum, and sent the bill back to the House, which promptly rejected it. Shortly thereafter, Congress adjourned, leaving the issue unresolved. During the months that followed, the fires ignited by the Tallmadge Amendment would sweep the nation, bringing it, at least rhetorically, to the brink of civil war. On February 6, General Armistead T. Mason, a former Virginia senator, and Colonel John M. McCarty, also of Virginia, met on the Bladensburg Dueling Grounds in Maryland. The two were bitter political enemies. Following an extended debate over the terms of the duel, which included hand-to-hand combat and seeing who could blow themselves up first while sitting on casks of powder, they settled on muskets at ten feet. Mason was killed instantly while McCarty was severely wounded in the arm.[39]

With tensions rising, prominent Americans such as James Monroe and Henry Clay looked to the American Colonization Society as a safety valve that might just be able to preserve the Union. The ACS had been founded in 1816 in Washington, DC, by Robert Finley, a Presbyterian minister. The stated objective of the organization was to establish a homeland for free Blacks somewhere on the coast of Africa. The Colonization Society attracted some strange bedfellows. Southerners who were philosophically opposed to slavery—James Madison, James Monroe, Henry Clay, and John Randolph among them—became enthusiastic supporters. Transporting freeborn Blacks and emancipated slaves out of the United States would, they believed, reduce opposition to emancipation both in the South and the North. Clay, among others, argued that with the passage of time, the population of the United States would become increasingly white, driving down the cost of labor to the point at which white workers would be cheaper than slaves.[40] They were joined by some hard-line pro-slavery figures who believed—rightly so—that free Blacks were a constant source of support and encouragement for runaways. They were, moreover, living proof that Blacks were human beings fully able to function and prosper in a democratic society. In the ACS's early years, it attracted Quakers, evangelicals, and abolitionists who were convinced that racial prejudice in America would never permit Blacks to enjoy full citizenship. By 1820 the Colonization Society could claim a powerful lobby in Washington.

In a March 1819 meeting, President Monroe lectured his cabinet on the benefits of colonization. Virginia was committed to gradual emancipation. The problem was that free Blacks had proven to be "a class of very dangerous people . . . who lived by pilfering and corrupted the slaves." As a result, the Virginia legislature had passed legislation prohibiting emancipation. But with a homeland in Africa to which they could be removed, the menace would cease, and Virginia could gradually free its slaves, the president enthused. Afterward, John Quincy poured out his contempt: "There are men of all sorts and descriptions concerned in this Colonization Society: some exceedingly humane, weak-minded men, who have really no other than the professed objects [of the organization] in view and who honestly believe them both useful and attainable. Some speculators in official profits and honors which a colonial establishment would of course produce. Some speculators in political popularity who think to please the abolitionists by their zeal for emancipation and the slaveholders by the flattering hope of ridding them of the free colored people at the public expense. Lastly some cunning slaveholders who see that the plan may be carried far enough to produce the effect of raising the market price of their slaves."[41] John Quincy believed that those people of color who were born free or had managed to purchase their freedom were entitled to every right of American citizenship. The ACS would return them to a life of barbarity and the ongoing danger of reenslavement.

The Constitution stipulated that after January 1, 1808, the external slave trade was to be abolished. Congress had subsequently passed legislation making it a federal crime to import slaves into the United States. But the House and the Senate did not address the question of what should be done with chattel seized from the illegal trade. In 1819 the ACS decided to fill the void. Monroe, Clay, Crawford, and other leaders of the Colonization Society declared that it was unthinkable to resell those Africans who were seized. Nor could they just be dumped on the west coast of Africa. At the president's urging, Congress passed on March 2, 1819, "the Act in Addition to the Acts" passed previously prohibiting the slave trade. It authorized the executive to dispatch U.S. war vessels to search for and seize ships engaged in the illicit trade. The president was further empowered "to make such regulations and arrangements as he may deem expedient," including the purchase of land in Africa and the appointment of agents to receive those Blacks who had been illegally enslaved.[42] The Act in Addition included an initial appropriation of a hundred thousand dollars. In cabinet, the secretary of state observed that Congress and the ACS had no idea of the problems that the Act in Addition would lead to, and he pushed for a full review. Monroe ignored him.[43] In truth, neither the slave power nor advocates of the Tallmadge Amendment viewed African colonization as the solution to the Missouri controversy.

For James Monroe—who, like Madison, was fond of viewing the republic as a puzzle in which clashing sectional, class, and economic interests were reconciled and the pieces fitted together—the Missouri question was a nightmare. From the outset he was determined to veto any measure that placed restrictions on Missouri. He cited the constitutional provision requiring that new states be admitted on an equal footing with the old; in other words, the slavery question was up to the Missourians to decide. This from a man who had labeled slavery a cancer that had to be excised from the body politic. But 1820 was an election year, and the Virginian was walking a political tightrope. Crawford and Randolph were already labeling him a neo-Federalist for his nationalist domestic policies, while many of his Republican supporters in the free states were determined to rein in the slave power. A compromise was clearly in order, and when Congress reconvened in December 1819, Monroe and Clay temporarily buried the hatchet and set to work finding a solution. In June 1819, the Massachusetts legislature had agreed to allow the "District of Maine" to separate and become a sovereign state. James Barbour of Virginia, one of the president's closest allies in the Senate, apparently came up with the idea of linking the admission of Maine, a free state, with that of slaveholding Missouri. But the logjam continued. Further complicating matters, the delegates to Missouri's constitutional convention added to its statehood application a new proviso barring "free negroes and mulattoes from coming to and settling in this state."[44] At this point—January 1820—a number of Northern solons were still determined to hold out for the Tallmadge Amendment, but then Senator Jesse Thomas of Illinois offered a sop in the form of an amendment prohibiting slavery not in Missouri itself but north of thirty-six degrees, thirty minutes—that is, the southern boundary of Missouri. When asked his position on the pending legislation, John Quincy declared that forbidding chattel slavery north of the thirty-six-degree, thirty-minute parallel and balancing Maine off against Missouri were the only ways to prevent a constitutional crisis.

But the more Adams thought about the proposed compromise, the more troubled he became. He was outraged at the provision in Missouri's constitution prohibiting the immigration of free Blacks. The article was a direct violation of the provision in the Constitution of the United States guaranteeing the rights and immunities of every citizen wherever he might live or move in the Union. The Missouri charter contained the seeds of disunion, he wrote. If acquiesced in, it would rob thousands of citizens of their rights. "And which citizens?—the poor, the unfortunate, the helpless. Already cursed by the mere color of their skin—already doomed by their complexion to drudge in the lowest offices of society, excluded by their color from all the refined enjoyments of life . . . excluded from the benefits of a liberal education; from the bed, from the table, and from all the social comforts of domestic life; this barbarous article deprives them of the little remnant of right yet left them—their rights as citizens and men."[45] If he had been a member of the Massachusetts legislature, Adams declared in his diary, he would have voted for a law barring any citizen of Missouri from entering the commonwealth.

Natural rights philosophy aside, Adams's humanitarian hackles had been aroused by an incident that had recently occurred in the capital. "A shopkeeper by the name of Holmes dropped yesterday from his pocket in the street a check upon one of the banks for 100 dollars and 150 dollars in bank bills. A mulatto boy of 14 or 15 years of age found the check and not knowing how to read took it to a shop to enquire what it was. He was then called upon for the bank-bills and denying that he had found them was tortured, thumb screwed, and beaten to extort confession from him. He finally named several persons to whom he said he gave the bills."[46]

In February, Adams had a long conversation with John C. Calhoun, at this point still his respected friend. "I do not think it [slavery] will produce a dissolution of the Union," the secretary of war observed, "but if it should, the South would be from necessity compelled to form an alliance, offensive and defensive, with Great Britain." But this would be nothing less than a return to colonial status, Adams declared. "Yes, pretty much," admitted Calhoun, "but it would be forced upon us." Adams then asked, "If by the effect of this alliance . . . the population of the North should be cut off from its natural outlet upon the ocean [by means of a British blockade], do you think it would fall back upon its rocks bound hand and foot to starve, or would it not retain its powers of locomotion to move southward by land?" "Then," declared Calhoun, "we shall find it necessary to make our communities all military."[47] The two men parted amicably, but the next day John Quincy observed in his diary, "Slavery is the great and foul stain upon the North American Union." On the possibility of emancipation/abolition, he wrote that "this object is vast in its compass—awful in its prospects, sublime and beautiful in its issue. A life devoted to it would be nobly spent or sacrificed."[48]

   Like Monroe and Clay, however, John Quincy hoped that the proverbial can could be kicked down the road. Whatever his private views, Adams was determined to maintain as low a public profile as possible. "Your son requests me to beg of you as a particular *favour to* him should you be addressed on the subject (which he has no doubt you will be)," Louisa wrote her father-in-law, "to refrain from giving any opinion whatever as he does not think the time has arrived in which he can with propriety take a part in the business."[49] If the secretary of state were to take a harsh public stance against Southerners who were breathing the fire of secession, they would throw the Hartford Convention in his face, ignoring his role in exposing the scheme. In fact, at the same time the nation was writhing in the coils of the Missouri serpent, Massachusetts was demanding compensation for the state's payment of the salaries of its militia during the War of 1812 and asking the secretary of state for support. Adams told Governor John Brooks that he would do what he could, but "the difficulty there would be that the Union cannot assume those expenses without sanctioning the principle of its own dissolution."[50]

   With Clay orchestrating, the House moved toward compromise on the Missouri question. The Speaker answered Missouri's prohibition against the immigration of free Blacks with a resolution declaring that nothing in Missouri's constitution could be construed as infringing upon the privileges and immunities that citizens of the United States enjoyed under the U.S. Constitution.[51] In the end, eighteen Northern representatives voted for Missouri's admission without any restriction on slavery, thus enabling passage. John Randolph labeled those Northerners who facilitated Missouri's entry into the Union as a slave state as "doughfaces," a sobriquet that stuck. When the Lion of Roanoke rose, ready to filibuster the Missouri Compromise, Clay declared him out of order and, during the melee that followed, snuck the bill into the Senate, where it was approved by a vote of twenty-four to twenty.[52] "I have been convinced from the first starting of this question that it could not end otherwise," Adams wrote in his diary. "The fault is in the Constitution of the United States which has sanctioned a dishonorable compromise with slavery; there is henceforth no remedy for it but a new organization of the Union to effect which a concert of all the white [free] States is indispensable. Whether that can ever be accomplished is doubtful."[53] In conversation with Senator Ninian Edwards, a committed Free-Soiler from Illinois, Adams insisted that if he were a member of either house, he would be a straight-line restrictionist, voting against the admission of a new state if its constitution did not prohibit slavery. That would include both Florida and Texas if it were acquired.[54]

   Northerners regarded the Missouri Compromise as a resounding defeat and Southerners an unqualified victory, John Randolph notwithstanding. Newspapers north of the Mason–Dixon Line listed the names of those who had voted for the measure and demanded that they be turned out of office at the next elections. But in time citizens of both sections would breathe a sigh of relief that a mechanism for balancing slave and free states had been established, thus ensuring peace for the foreseeable future. For all intents and purposes, antislavery sentiment as a political force in the South was dead. From 1821 on, Dixie would defend slavery not as a necessary evil but as a positive good, an economic necessity and the only safe and proper haven for members of the subhuman Black race. During the Missouri debates, Charles Pinckney of South Carolina declared that Africa was the only region of the globe whose peoples had remained unaltered from their creation to the present. Inhabitants of the Dark Continent were "still as savage as ever . . . as unchanged as the lion or the tiger which roams in the same forests with himself."[55] John Quincy did not realize it, but the Missouri Compromise and its aftermath sounded the political death knell for nationalists like him. Both North and South would gravitate toward a states' rights, individualist political philosophy, because, among other things, doing so would hopefully keep the debate over slavery off the table and thus, ironically, preserve the Union.

Adams recognized that the South would have to abandon the ideals of the Declaration and insist on an absurdly narrow definition of the Constitution, and because of this, he was deeply saddened. Following a cabinet meeting in which the secretary of state argued that Congress did indeed have the power to prohibit slavery in the territories, Calhoun and he had another discussion. "The principles which you have avowed," the South Carolinian declared, "are just and noble, but in the Southern country whenever they are mentioned, they are understood as applying only to white men. . . . menial labor [was] the proper work of slaves. No white person could descend to that. And it was the best guarantee to equality among the whites."[56] Later, in his diary, Adams mused, "It is among the evils of slavery that a man of Calhoun's intellect and moral character could be induced to grant the right to life, liberty, and happiness to one man and deny it to another on account of the color of his skin." There was no excuse for the deal the Constitution had made with the devil regarding human bondage. It was "morally and politically vicious, inconsistent with the principles upon which alone our Revolution can be justified by riveting the chains of slavery; by pledging the faith of freedom to maintain and perpetuate the tyranny of the master; and grossly unequal and impolitic by admitting that slaves are at once enemies to be kept in subjection, property to be secured or restored to their owners, and persons not to be represented themselves but for whom their masters are privileged with nearly a double share of representation." Perhaps, Adams wrote, he had erred in supporting the Missouri Compromise. Perhaps the free states should have taken a stand. "If the Union must be dissolved, slavery is precisely the question upon which it ought to break."⁵⁷ Adams itched to take the bit in his mouth: "Oh! If but one man could arise with a genius capable of comprehending, a heart capable of supporting, and an utterance capable of communicating those eternal truths that belong to this question, to lay bare in all its nakedness that outrage upon the goodness of God— human slavery—now is the time, and this is the occasion upon which such a man would perform the duties of an angel upon Earth."⁵⁸ But, of course, John Quincy had supported the compromise; there was a presidential election to be won. Martyrdom would have to wait.

Louisa and her friends readily recognized the existential nature of the Missouri debates, but they also regarded them as great theater. "The Senate chamber in which they now admit ladies on the floor, has been occupied quite early every day," she recorded in her diary. For decorum's sake, women were supposed to be escorted to their visitors' seats by a member of the upper house, but, Louisa noted, "Ladies of a very public character did get in and take seats on either hand of the Vice President; he has been subjected to some jests for having been thus supported."⁵⁹ The elegant and eloquent Charles Pinckney of South Carolina was a prime attraction. Before one widely advertised speech, the pro-slavery advocate kept the throng waiting but eventually appeared "in all the elegance of dress with his hair nicely oiled and curled 'shedding odors round.'" He paid his respects to the presiding officer and "glided gently into the most flowery, elegant, and splendid compliments to the state of Massachusetts I ever heard with the intention I presume of giving a 'sop to Cerberus.'" The antihero of the debates was John Randolph. After listening to the Virginian rant and rave for several hours, Louisa observed, "Poor man; he has so entirely sunk in the public estimation that he is by many thought to be partially insane and a mere wreck for what once was great in intellectual power—there is a sort of painful consciousness about him of this fact which excites compassion."⁶⁰

25

The Holy Alliance

J OHN C. CALHOUN'S NOTION that Great Britain would rush to the South's aid if it seceded from the Union was a pipe dream. Emancipation sentiment was growing apace in the former mother country; indeed, at the very time Secretary of State Adams was negotiating the Transcontinental Treaty and America was embroiled in the Missouri controversy, London was pressuring the Monroe administration to sign an international slave trade agreement that would authorize the warships of member nations to board and seize any vessel engaged in transporting human beings for sale. The last week in September 1820, a new minister from Great Britain, Stratford Canning, arrived in Washington. No sooner had Adams and Monroe received him than he began to press the secretary of state on the slave trade issue. His government had recently signed treaties with Portugal and the Netherlands authorizing the war vessels of each nation to stop and search their respective merchant vessels suspected of engaging in the slave trade. Not possible, Adams declared. As he had informed Lord Castlereagh when he, Adams, had been minister to the Court of St. James's, such a treaty would violate the U.S. Constitution. The federal government could not grant authority to a judge who was not liable to impeachment by Congress. Moreover, it had been less than a decade since the United States had fought a war with Great Britain over the latter's insistence on the right to board and search neutral (American) vessels in time of peace with the intention of impressing able-bodied seamen. "[T]hey may spare themselves . . . the trouble of applying to us to unman our independence by trusting them to search our ships for black slaves to emancipate," John Quincy had written Richard Rush the previous year. For the United States to even consider such a proposition, John Bull would have to renounce the right of impressment.[1] Moreover, American participation in a European treaty would violate the two-spheres doctrine that the United States had adhered to since the

Washington administration. But the international slave trade issue was far from dead; the rising abolitionist tide on both sides of the Atlantic would breathe life into it.

Monroe and Adams had shied away from including Texas in the Transcontinental Treaty because of the Missouri controversy. They could afford to wait, they believed. The continent would be ripe for the taking for the foreseeable future. Spain posed no threat to American ambitions in the Southwest, and with the passage of time, both Russian and British claims to the Northwest would weaken. But what to do about the emerging republics of Central and South America? To what extent could the United States rely on the British navy to protect the colonies in revolt from being restored to Spain by an armada assembled by the Holy Alliance? Beginning in 1818, the Continental powers had sent troops into the field to suppress movements for national self-determination and representative government in several European hot spots. Ferdinand's reluctant embrace of constitutional government in Spain was deeply troubling to his fellow monarchs and their minister of reaction, Prince Klemens von Metternich of Austria. Dedicated as it was to preserving the prerogatives of altar and Crown, the Holy Alliance was determined to suppress popular uprisings in the New World as well as in the Old. Metternich and the Bourbons saw republicanism and movements for national self-determination as existential threats. The United States was a reality, but perhaps its contaminating role in world affairs could be limited—contained, as it were. Adams and Clay had differed profoundly over the nature of the Latin American revolutions and the direction they would take, but both agreed that the United States could not permit the region to allow Spanish hegemony to be replaced by French, Russian, Austrian, or even British rule. But the very act of American recognition might precipitate European intervention. It fell to Secretary of State Adams to discern the fine line to be walked and to see that his country walked it.

Early in 1818, Great Britain had simultaneously offered to mediate the dispute between Spain and the United States and between Spain and its New World colonies. John Quincy was opposed to the first option and ambivalent concerning the second. He had explained to Charles Bagot that the very news of the first offer would "tend to excite ill-will and irritation in the minds of our people."[2] Bagot replied that His Majesty's government would never proceed without the unqualified agreement of both parties. His government was much more interested in the offer of mediation between Spain and the Latin American republics. Britain was willing to allow the Holy Alliance to impose their reactionary policies on the Continent but not on the New World. Situated ideologically between the United States and the Holy Alliance, dependent as always on foreign markets, and possessed of the world's greatest navy, John Bull was determined to control the course of events. "The revolution in South America had opened a new world to her commerce which the restoration of the Spanish colonial dominion would close against her," John Quincy wrote to George W. Campbell, U.S. minister to Russia, in June 1818. "Her Cabinet therefore devised a middle term, a compromise between legitimacy and traffic; a project by which the political supremacy of Spain should be restored, but under which the Spanish colonies should enjoy commercial freedom, and intercourse with the rest of the world."[3]

The secretary of state would accept British mediation only to the point that it served U.S. interests. As to Clay's notion of an "American System," a coalition of like-minded republicans acting together to guard their independence and advance the causes of republicanism and reciprocal free trade, Adams remained skeptical if not cynical. "So far as they [the Latin American republics] were contending for independence, I wished well to their cause; but I had seen as yet no prospect that they would establish free or liberal institutions of government. They are not likely to promote the spirit either of freedom or of order by their example. They have not the first elements of good or of free government. Arbitrary power, military and ecclesiastical, was stamped upon their education, upon their habits, and upon all their institutions. Civil dissension was infused into all their seminal principles; war and mutual destruction was in every member of their organization—moral, political, and physical. I had little expectation of any beneficial result to this country from any future connection with them, political or commercial," he confided to his diary in 1821.[4] Every people had a right to national self-determination, but the United States was not, as some in the Holy Alliance believed, ready to embark on a crusade to spread its republican ideals across the globe. His country, John Quincy famously said, would not look abroad for monsters to slay.[5] But as long as he was secretary of state, America would do everything in its power to defend its "city upon a hill" and its burgeoning continental empire. In their independence the new republics of Central and South America were much less a threat to the security of the United States than they had been when they were dominions of a European power. "[W]e will not participate in and cannot approve any interposition of other powers unless it be to promote the total independence, political and commercial, of the colonies," he wrote George Campbell.[6]

All the while Adams was trying to fend off the Holy Alliance, manage British efforts at mediation, and hold the Latin American Republics at arm's length, Clay and his supporters were providing ideological and political cover for hordes of Latin American agents and their American collaborators who were outfitting privateers in American ports from New York to New Orleans to prey upon Spanish and Portuguese shipping.[7] The situation in Baltimore was particularly egregious.

There, General José Artigas, whom Uruguay would recognize as one of its Founding Fathers and who had been ousted from his base in Montevideo by the Portuguese, was busily outfitting privateers to raid both Portuguese and Spanish shipping. Adams, whose duty it was to defend U.S. neutrality, subsequently complained that the Baltimore pirates had "brought the whole body of European allies upon us."[8] The commissioner of customs was thoroughly corrupt, allowing privateers commissioned by Artigas and other revolutionary agents to come and go as they pleased. So tempting was the vocation of legitimized piracy that American adventurers disguising themselves as South American patriots manned privateers and raided Spanish and Portuguese shipping on their own. There was on the books a congressional act passed in 1817 prohibiting insurgent groups from purchasing and arming vessels in American ports (American citizens who did this were guilty of piracy), but Clay and Senator Charles Pinckney of South Carolina, who was on retainer as counsel to a group of South American agents, succeeded in having the measure watered down until it was virtually meaningless.[9] When the federal district judge in the city announced that he was going to put some of the pirates on trial, one of them publicly threatened to murder him. There was no trial.[10] "The officers of the United States have been the principal causes by connivance . . . of all the piracies which for these three or four years have issued from that city," the secretary of state noted in his journal. "The only remedy yet devised is that . . . the commanders of our armed vessels are ordered to bring their prizes to ports other than Baltimore."[11]

Onís, the Spanish minister, complained of the American-based privateers, but he was principally occupied with hanging on to as much of Spanish North America as possible and preventing the United States from recognizing the Latin American republics. Not so the Portuguese minister, the Abbé Correa da Serra. Correa was something of a fixture in the American diplomatic corps, serving during both the Jefferson and Madison administrations. "[He] is a man of extensive and general [learning in] literature [and] of science, [a man] of brilliance with . . . inexhaustible powers of conversation," John Quincy said of him. He was so renowned as a philosopher on the Iberian Peninsula "as to have incurred the vindictive pursuit of the Inquisition." Though sixty-eight years old, he seemed to possess the energy and charm of a man of twenty-five. "His temper, however, is not remarkable for equanimity. It is quick, sensitive, fractious, hasty and when excited obstinate." The Portuguese minister liked to drop in on presidents and secretaries of state unannounced for impromptu conversation and a bit of official business. Fond of informality themselves, Jefferson and Madison did not discourage the practice. Monroe did. "[H]aving no relish for literature and philosophy and no time to listen and laugh at jokes, he always kept the abbe . . . at arm's length," Adams observed.[12]

In October 1818, Correa descended upon the State Department in a fit of indignant rage. How dared the United States allow a man like Artigas to fit out privateers to ravage his country's shipping; were not Portugal and the United States at peace? The secretary of state chose to play defense. If the abbé could produce evidence, the attorney general would instruct the U.S. attorney for the District of Maryland to bring charges. The Portuguese minister replied that "he could have no confidence in any judicial prosecution . . . the Sheriff of Baltimore . . . was himself concerned in the fitting out of these privateers." Was he impugning the integrity of the U.S. legal system? Adams asked. No, no, said Correa; he was certain of the good intentions of the Monroe administration, but the officials in Baltimore were obviously "a most unmanageable crew."[13] In the fall of 1818, when the members of the Quintuple Alliance gathered at Aix-la-Chapelle, Portugal presented a list of grievances against the United States and charged it with failing to enforce its own neutrality laws. Thereupon, France, Great Britain, Austria, Prussia, and Russia unanimously passed a resolution condemning the Monroe administration.[14]

Though he could not say it, John Quincy sympathized with Correa and the Portuguese. He was disgusted with Monroe for kowtowing to Clay—the president refused even to issue a statement condemning the pirates of Baltimore—and he was disgusted with the Latin American revolutionaries. "We have done everything possible in their favor and have received from them little else than injury in return. . . . They have been constantly endeavoring to entangle us with them and their cause."[15]

Perhaps angry over the Holy Alliance's condemnation of the United States at Aix-la-Chapelle, Adams none too subtly put Europe on notice that if it continued to stick its collective nose into the affairs of the New World, it could not expect the United States to remain aloof from European politics. When he arrived in the United States, the new minister from Imperial Russia, Pyotr Poletika, had called on John Quincy and informed him that Alexander had instructed him "to use whatever influence he might possess to dissuade us from the adoption of this measure [recognition of Buenos Aires], as [it would be] an act of hostility against Spain, the Emperor's ally."[16] He was also instructed to compel the United States to cooperate with the Concert of Europe, "hinting that a contrary course of policy could not be carried in effect and that the United States, whether willing or not, must follow the impulse of Europe combined."[17] The secretary of state curtly informed the Russian that the United States had not decided the matter but reserved its right to act as it deemed fit. Recognition should be forthcoming "when the independence is established as a matter of fact so as to leave the chance of the opposite party to recover their dominion utterly desperate." In his government's opinion, Adams said, that time had arrived for Buenos Aires and perhaps for several other of Spain's revolted colonies.[18] Speaking of revolutions, he added, the Holy Alliance seemed to have enough to worry about on its own doorstep. Liberals in Spain had forced Ferdinand to accept the Constitution of 1812. Napoleon's occupation of Portugal in 1808 had compelled the king to move the seat of his government to Brazil. Naples had taken up arms against Austria. "[B]efore the European Sovereigns should resolve upon any system for the treatment of the Spanish malady," the secretary of state advised Poletika, "they would do well to consider the whole case." Taken aback, Poletika promised that Russia would not interfere with the revolution in Spain unless, like the French, it became aggressive and turned outward.[19]

Still in high dudgeon at Europe's pretentions, Adams turned his fire on Stratford Canning. "The scepters of all the European continental Monarchs were turning to ashes in their hands," he declared. "Their crowns were dropping from their heads; the very instruments of power upon which they were leaning pierced their hands and sides. [In certain areas of unrest, government troops had thrown down their arms and joined the rebels.] Government was melting into its original elements." Was Great Britain, the home of the Glorious Revolution, going to continue to side with the forces of reaction? Canning replied that his country "had never taken part against liberal institutions . . . but it was scarcely possible to foresee what would be the course of the present agitations in Europe."[20]

BY THIS TIME, JOHN Quincy Adams was one of the most famous and revered figures of his time. The rich, the famous, the influential competed for his attention. But none of his admirers could capture the fullness of the man. The famed travel writer Anne Royall met Adams when he was secretary of state and painted this portrait: "Mr. A received me with the ease of manner which bespeaks him what he really is, the profound scholar. . . . I had heard much of Mr. Adams . . . while beholding this truly great man, I was at a loss how to reconcile such rare endowments with the meek condescension of the being before me. He neither smiled nor frowned but regarded me with a calmness peculiar to him [and] awaited my business. . . . His complexion is fair, his face round and full, but what most distinguished his features is his eye, which is black; it is not a sparkling eye, nor yet dull, but of such keenness that it pierces the beholder. He has the steadiest look I ever witnessed; he never smiled while I was in his company; it is a question with me whether he ever laughed in his life, and of all the men I ever saw, he has the least of what is called pride both in his manners and dress."[21] But of course in the bosom of his family and friends, John Quincy laughed, rhymed, and even danced. His famous depiction of himself—"I am a man of reserved, cold, austere, and forbidding manners"—was written in sarcasm in the wake of Louisa's chastising him for looking "ill-tempered" while listening patiently to yet another office seeker. As a young man he had swooned over his favorite actresses, and he was a connoisseur of fine wines. A walker, swimmer, and horseback rider, the New Englander was an advocate for and exemplar of physical vigor. He was a man of both science and letters. While immersed in his study of weights and measure, he dreamed of becoming one of America's first great writers. "Literature has been the charm of my life, and could I have carved out of my own fortunes, to literature would my whole life have been devoted," he confided to his diary. "The summit of my ambitions would have been by some great work of literature to have done honor to my age and my country and to have lived in the gratitude . . . [of] future ages."[22]

Adams's ability to determine character and discern motives in his fellow human beings was seemingly unparalleled. "He is sedate, circumspect, and cautious," George Watterston of the Library of Congress wrote of him in 1818. "Reserved, but not distant; grave but not repulsive. He receives, but seldom communicates, and discerns with great quickness motives however latent and intentions however concealed by the contortions of cunning or the drapery of hypocrisy. This penetration seems to me intuitive and natural. . . . It is the operation of native judgment and not the exercise of acquired cunning."[23] Above all, John Quincy seemed born to public service: "I fear that he could not live long out of an active sphere of public life," Louisa wrote in her diary, "and that it is absolutely essential to his existence."[24] And like many intensely ambitious public men, Adams could be a brute to his family.

John Quincy expected his sons to follow in his and his father's footsteps. Because he believed liberal education to be the foundation of a virtuous republic and an absolute necessity for the men who served it, he demanded that his offspring distinguish themselves at Harvard. Louisa shared her husband's expectations to an extent, but her vision was of young men well-rounded, educated, socially adept, compassionate, moral but fun loving—"ornaments to society." As it became clear that neither George nor John would ascend to the heights reached by their grandfather and father, she assumed the role of buffer between her elder sons and their increasingly angry and humiliated father.

George was spectacularly ill-equipped for the future John Quincy had planned for him. A sensitive, romantic youth fond of poetry, history, and literature, he had spent almost as much time in his grandfather's library at Peacefield as his father. He and the former president were particularly close. When at Quincy, George would occupy many an evening reading to the old man from the classics or history or Shakespeare and discussing the arts and human nature. George's younger brother Charles would later refer to the "pleasant kindness of his nature" and the "light yet ornamental cultivation of his mind."[25] Of her eldest, Louisa wrote, "Easily distressed, he equally magnifies his joys and sorrows until the real world in which he moves vanishes from his sight like the baseless fabric of the visions which continually beat his imagination where all is poetry, fiction, and love."[26] Clearly, the eldest son was made to live the life of a novelist or poet, not that of a lawyer and politician.

Soon after George returned to Harvard in the fall of 1818, his parents learned that he faced suspension for participating in a student riot in the dining hall. George's class had been campaigning for a change in the restrictive rules of the college and against the virtually unlimited power the tutors exercised over their students. Louisa was beside herself with worry that her husband would disown their eldest. "I am waiting with extreme anxiety to know whether I am to consider him [George] as an affectionate son or as a castaway—Whether seeing the error of his ways, he has promptly resolved to redeem as far as he yet can the character that he has lost; or whether by persevering in folly he is prepared to set his father as he has the guardians and teachers . . . at defiance."[27] George wrote his parents a disjointed, almost hysterical letter of apology. In this instance, John Quincy proved uncharacteristically forgiving. You got caught up in the passions of the moment, John Quincy wrote his son. "My purpose at present . . . is not to reproach you with what is past and irredeemable . . . [I] look forward with the most cheering hopes to the promise of your usefulness hereafter in the world."[28]

During the year that followed, Louisa received numerous reports of George's poor health. "Mr. Appleton when he returned from Cambridge told me he thought you looked pale and thin, but he believed it was only the effect of hard study, but then they wrote me from Quincy that in consequence of having been to serenade Dr. Kirkland on his return home you had taken a very bad cold which had much affected your lungs."[29] Quit smoking and cut down on your flute playing, Louisa advised. She suspected, however, that George's infirmities resulted in no small part from late nights at the tavern and the hangovers that inevitably followed.[30]

John Adams the younger seemed more robust than his elder brother; the middle son, unlike his father, believed that there was a time for work and a time for play and never should the twain meet. Rather than reading in the library at Peacefield,

John spent his vacation riding, hunting, and fishing. His family had remarked with some mirth on his susceptibility to the charms of the opposite sex. And, in truth, John seemed continually infatuated. Nevertheless, he performed well enough at his studies at the Boston Latin School and was in due course admitted to Harvard. His mother thought him far too attached to novels and freethinkers. "Vice is so loathsome in its nature, its gratifications are so inefficient to promote happiness, its enjoyments . . . are so gross, and its consequences so degrading . . . that could we for a moment admit the possibility of the theory of what are termed free thinkers, a reflecting mind must immediately perceive that . . . it is our interest to practice virtue."[31]

Charles, the only sibling to have lived with his parents during their stint in St. Petersburg, was still studying at the Boston School and living with the Welshes. He seemed to his family more serious than his elder brothers, more literal-minded, and, as it would turn out, more emotionally robust. Strangely, John Quincy seemed to think that Charles was capable of the same intellectual achievements as his brothers although they were several years older. "There are many boys," he wrote the eleven-year-old, "with no better advantages than you enjoy, who enter younger than you will then be [fourteen], and I know your capacity is equal to attaining in that time the necessary proficiency for it. If you will [only] have the ambition to undertake it."[32] That the child was under some stress was evidenced by the fact that he had become a regular smoker. "[Y]ou are too young to smoke!" Louisa admonished him. "It is a wretched and disgusting habit of the most pernicious tendency as it produces a constant thirst which inevitably leads to that most dreadful and loathsome one of inebriety, sinking whole families in shame and ruin."[33]

In September 1819, John Quincy and Louisa departed Washington for Quincy for a monthlong vacation. The secretary of state found his father, then eighty-three, frail and in low spirits: "I endeavored as well as I could to cheer him," he wrote in his diary, "and hope that he will yet long enjoy support from a higher source." John and Charles came out from Boston for a visit. "I examined my sons . . . upon their progress in the Greek and Latin Languages with which I was well satisfied."[34] Shortly after their arrival, Thomas Boylston bolted, following an argument with his father over the terms of John's will. "When I came home, I found the family in great distress; my brother having this morning left the house in consequence of having given offence to my father. He went away taking most of his personal effects with him and without telling his wife or any other person where he was going."[35] Since the Adamses' return from Europe, Thomas had continued his downward spiral. Among his duties was management of the farm on Mount Wollaston. In that, he was failing miserably. Charles later recalled that his uncle had degenerated into "one of the most unpleasant characters in this world in his present degradation being a brute in his manners and a bully in his family."[36] At the time Thomas was deeply in debt to John Quincy, and they had had a row when John accused him of gambling away his family's money. His lack of success compared to his brother's was a torture to him. Thomas had written Louisa that her husband was "a faultless monster that the world ne'er saw."[37]

Cousin and lawyer Josiah Quincy told John Quincy not to allow his brother to return and above all to keep him away from his father. "He explicitly declared that he thought my father's life depended upon it and that it was my duty to make the necessary arrangement to prevent it."[38] But in that case, what was to become of Thomas's wife, unlikable though she might have been, and their six children? Distraught, John Quincy visited his mother's grave. He prayed for her wisdom, "and I implored the divine blessing that the cup of affliction might be administered in mercy." Finally, the wayward brother and son reappeared. John Quincy was out at the time; when he returned home, Louisa took him aside and told him that Thomas was ill and distraught. He had taken refuge at the "Farm house" (apparently John Quincy's birthplace) and asked that her husband wait until the following morning to meet with him. It was subsequently decided that Thomas and his family were to take up residence at the old family home permanently. John had changed his will, bequeathing to his youngest son several small parcels of land he had acquired over the years. To compensate for the loss of income, John Quincy agreed to buy Mount Wollaston from his father, paying him a thousand dollars a year for the rest of his life.[39] The crisis had passed, but John Quincy knew that it was but a chapter.

The boys passed the extended Christmas holiday of 1819–1820 with their parents in Washington. "You and George may get whatever is necessary for you to have to enable you to appear as you ought here as to clothing," Louisa wrote John.[40] It proved a pleasant interlude. Remarkably, the secretary of state seemed more interested in his two elder children's social graces than in their intellectual development. Louisa and he took pains to introduce them into Washington society. "There is a bashfulness in young persons first coming into general society very painful to themselves and disadvantageous to their estimation with others which their parents and friends should assist them in throwing off," Adams observed in his diary. Most important was dancing, which led to "an easy but respectful and delicate familiarity . . . with women [and] is essential to the perfection of good breeding." John Quincy was convinced, he wrote, that waltzes were "favorable to the usefulness both physical and moral . . . of both sexes." He recalled that he had been taught to dance as a child but "having no fund of conversation adopted to the taste and feelings of the sex, I have always been reserved and cold in my intercourse with them."[41] How he could have so misremembered his youth is astounding. Whatever the case, John Quincy was now a dancing enthusiast, and by the time his sons departed, so were they.

The seas in the Adams household were never entirely calm, however. Feeling neglected, Louisa, in the midst of a dinner dance at the Adamses', ostentatiously retired to her chamber. To her immense irritation, no one paid any attention to her sulk, and the dancing and laughter continued unabated. "The noise, the sense of neglect, and unkindness which this conduct indicated proved too much for me, and I believe I was thrown into a state of delirium almost amounting to madness. . . . Mr. Adams found me in this state."[42] Louisa would extract her revenge. During the entire week that followed, every member of the household tiptoed around in virtual silence while the mistress of the house lay swooning. "Since God in his wisdom took my daughter on whom I madly doted, I have never found a thing which could fill the void made in my heart, and tho' I fondly love my sons, I have always considered them more as subjects born to gratify my pride or ambition than as being calculated . . . [to elicit] my feelings of affection or sympathy."[43]

Yuletide festivities were further marred by the ongoing effort of thirteen-year-old Mary Catherine "Fanny" Hellen to seduce George. Louisa had done her best to smooth Fanny's rough edges. "I wish to purify a little the natural tendency to grossness which she ever displays and, if suffered to grow, will make her what I most thoroughly despise—a woman of low conversation and impure mind."[44] But to no avail. "She is beautiful and fascinating, but heartless," John Quincy confided to his own journal, "absorbed in selfishness and has the appetite of a shark for lovers merely to display her power. Mere coquetry is only ridiculous, but hers is mischievous."[45]

One evening after dinner, the family was gathered by the fire when there was a loud knock at the door. A servant entered bearing a note for George and declared that its bearer was insisting on an immediate response. The message was from one R. N. Martin, one of Fanny's most ardent admirers; it demanded that George come immediately to his quarters at Strother's Hotel to make explanations. George considered arming himself but then thought better of it. When he arrived at Martin's rooms, he found the irate young man standing behind a table with a horsewhip lying on it. "I see you have been riding," George quipped. Martin accused him of mistreating Fanny, shunning her, and spreading rumors concerning her liaisons with other young men. Where he chose to place his affections was his business and his business alone, young Adams replied. Fanny was a guest

in his father's house and would be treated with every respect. Martin quickly
cooled down, accepted George's explanations, and bade him not to chastise "Miss
Hellen." The last week in January, Fanny took leave of the Adams household to
visit other friends and relatives. "I am heartily glad to have her out of the house,"
John Quincy confided to his diary.[46]

George and John departed Washington on February 6 aboard the six o'clock
stage. Both parents gave them a fond adieu. The next day, a chagrined John appeared on their doorstep. On the road to Baltimore, the bindings restraining the
passengers' luggage had broken. Of the seven trunks dumped in the road, four
were recovered. George's was among them; John's was not. Sensing her husband's
irritation, Louisa rushed to buy John some essentials and sent him on his way.[47]

Back at Harvard, George did his best to soldier on. In his junior year he captured one of Harvard's two Boylston Prizes for Elocution. The other winner was
Ralph Waldo Emerson. John Quincy was pleased, all the more so because "I am
well aware of the petty prejudices against his name [Adams] and connections
which sway among the Learned Thebans of Harvard."[48] John was not so fortunate. The class of 1823, of which he was a member, would achieve renown as one
of the most rebellious in the institution's history. According to one historian of
Harvard, John and his classmates were given to "forbidden dinners, battles in
commons, bonfires and explosions in the Yard, cannonballs dropped from upper
windows."[49] In November, Louisa and John Quincy heard rumors that John along
with a number of his classmates had been expelled. "Your father and I are in a
state of great anxiety for the consequences of your fault and impatiently wait for
the result which must fix your future destiny," Louisa wrote her middle son.
Somehow John and his classmates survived, ironically, no doubt, because President Kirkland was loath to incite the wrath of the powerful Adams family.[50] "My
Children seem to have some very intemperate blood in them, and are certainly not
very easy to govern," Louisa lamented to her diary.[51]

Life in Washington during these years seemed to John Quincy and Louisa a
combination of elegance and sophistication on the one hand and primitiveness
and barbarity on the other—sort of like St. Petersburg but with an opposite climate. "[T]he heat of the weather is almost unremitted," John Quincy wrote in his
diary in August 1819, "with myriads of flies, bats, and vermin of all filth. . . . This
morning Antoine killed a brownish snake two feet long in the house at the foot of
the staircase in the entry."[52] The city's streets continued to be as dangerous as ever.
Returning from a party at the Bagots', the Adamses encountered two overturned
carriages. "I am surprised we got home safe as our horses were so frightened at
seeing one of these . . . laying [sic] in the road it was scarcely possible to make
them pass it."[53] Visitors to the secretary of state's house included three Osage In-

dian chiefs—Big Bear, Big Road, and Black Spirit—who arrived unannounced and possessing not a word of English. "They sat with us about half an hour and particularly noticed the glass lamp in the entry [and] the luster in the drawing room. . . . One of them spanned Mary Hellen round the waist, and then applying the same span of his fingers to himself marveled how she could be so small . . . they are of the dark copper color, all three men above the middle size, with countenances strongly expressive of the effect of hardship and passion upon the muscular organization," Adams recorded.[54]

Politicians, soldiers, and other gentlemen continued to slaughter one another on the dueling fields at Bladensburg. In March 1820, Commodore Stephen Decatur and Commodore James Barron shot each other, with Decatur suffering a stomach wound and Barron taking a bullet in the leg. Barron had commanded the ill-fated *Chesapeake* in 1807 and been decommissioned. Decatur had blocked his reentry into the service. Decatur "expired at eight o'clock last evening to the grief of the whole nation who will long mourn the loss of a favorite hero whose amiable qualities as a private citizen entitled him to the esteem of all," Louisa wrote in her diary. "Mr. A. was anxious to have some law passed with a view to check this fatal practice [dueling], but the people of our country still seem to possess a little of their original barbarism, and I fear he will have few supporters, more especially as our Chief Magistrate seems to approve the spirit."[55]

Northern visitors to the capital were struck by its several slave markets. Abuse of the city's Blacks, both free and enslaved, was a daily occurrence. In November, Louisa reported to her father-in-law a most bizarre event. All of the bells in John Taylor's famed Octagon House had begun ringing alternately or all at once without any apparent cause. The structure's wiring was inspected and then shut off, but the clamor continued. "Some recommended a general whipping of all the Blacks and even suggested the torture to force confession." Fortunately, cooler heads prevailed.[56]

26

Political Caballing

THE PRESIDENTIAL ELECTION OF 1820 was anticlimactic. Monroe encountered no serious opposition, and newspaper columnists spent more time speculating about the 1824 contest, which, they predicted, would most likely feature Crawford, Calhoun, Jackson, and Adams. To Adams's embarrassment, his friend Governor William Plumer of New Hampshire cast a sole electoral vote for him.[1] Monroe took the oath of office in the House Chamber. "A quarter before twelve, I went to the President's House and the other members of the administration immediately afterward came . . . the President attired in a full suit of black broad cloth of somewhat antiquated fashion, with shoe and knee buckles, rode in a plain carriage with four horses and a single, colored footman. The Secretaries of State, the Treasury, War, and the Navy followed, each in a carriage and pair; the House and galleries were as thronged as possible. There was much disorder of loud talking and agitation in the gallery not altogether ceasing even while the President was reading his address."[2]

No sooner had the dishes for the inaugural banquets been put away than Monroe and Adams had to deal with another Jackson crisis. During the previous year, in the wake of the economic downturn following the Panic of 1819, Congress had passed an economy act that among other things reduced the size of the officer corps in the army. Despite his heroics at the battle of New Orleans and his campaigns against the Seminoles and Red Sticks, there was no room for Old Hickory. As a consolation prize, Monroe named him governor of the Florida Territory. "This office of governor of Florida presented itself as a fortunate occasion to save the nation from the disgrace of even appearing to discard . . . a man to whom they are so deeply indebted," John Quincy wrote in his diary.[3] That the president and he could not have foreseen that the Hero's reign would quickly become mired in controversy is a mystery.

In the summer of 1821, Jackson and his wife, Rachel, sailed in fashion aboard a steamboat from Nashville to New Orleans and proceeded from thence to Pensacola. There they rendezvoused with a company of American troops under the command of Colonel George Mercer Brooke. Old Hickory insisted on remaining outside the walls of the city and communicating with the departing Spanish governor, Colonel José María Callava, by note until the Spanish flag was ready to be lowered and the Stars and Stripes raised. When the appointed day arrived, Jackson and Callava met and exchanged pleasantries; then the Spaniard got about the business of evacuating his troops and officials from Pensacola to Havana.[4] But he would not be allowed to go into that good night quietly.

The issue that gave birth to the ensuing dispute was incredibly banal. A female resident of Pensacola had filed a lawsuit to validate her claim to some land she had inherited. To make the case, she required documents in possession of Callava's administrative assistant, Domingo Sousa. She appealed to Jackson, who decided her request was a reasonable one. He sent men to collect the papers, but Sousa declared he could not turn them over without Callava's authorization. When U.S. soldiers reported back to headquarters, Old Hickory, who was suffering from distemper of the bowels, exploded. Callava had absolutely no authority in Florida; he was there as a guest of the United States until he could depart for Cuba. Immediately Jackson dispatched a detachment of troops to the ex-governor's house, where they found Callava just returned from a dinner party. The Spaniard could not speak English (nor Jackson Spanish), but according to Callava, who subsequently published his account of the affair, "A party of troops with the commissioners assaulted the house, breaking the fence and the commissioners entered my apartment. They surrounded my bed with soldiers with drawn bayonets in their hands. They removed the mosquito net; they made me sit up and demanded the papers or they would use the arms against my person."[5] The Americans then proceeded to haul an indignant Callava before Jackson. The two shouted at each other, one in Spanish, the other English. He had diplomatic immunity, Callava declared. No, he did not, Jackson replied; the six-month time period for the Spanish evacuation had long since expired. According to one Spanish observer, Jackson with "blows on the table, his mouth foaming, and possessed of the furies, told the Spanish commissary to deliver the papers" or go to jail.[6] Callava refused and was duly locked up.

News of the incident soon reached Washington, sending the press into a frenzy. Crawford and Clay's partisans revived their charges that Jackson was nothing more than an American Caesar. Beaten down though it was, the Spanish government howled. Monroe and his cabinet met in almost continuous session during the last week in October. Adams and his colleagues were intensely aware that virtually every action they took during these days of the Early Republic was precedent setting. Jackson had previously insisted that his powers as governor were both military and civilian. In this, John Quincy had supported him. Monroe and William Wirt argued that to give the governor of Florida military powers would violate the principle of civilian control of the military. Jackson was, moreover, undermining the principle of strict separation of executive, legislative, and judicial powers. All this appeared to me to be very sound reasoning, Adams wrote in his journal. But it was beside the point. Jackson was operating in a vacuum, the secretary of state asserted. He was charged with guaranteeing the property, rights, and welfare of the inhabitants of Florida until Congress could provide for them. The only recourse available to him was to continue to administer the province as it had been administered when it was under Spanish control, exercising both full military and civilian powers.[7]

In cabinet, Calhoun complained that Jackson inevitably exercised every power available to him and then some. He ignored both "the nature of our institutions" and public opinion. In short, Old Hickory needed to be reined in. "I said with too much warmth," Adams wrote in his diary, "that I could not and would not consider the nature of our institutions, the transient popular opinion, or the factious comments of newspapers as having any weight in the case. The enquiry was of justice and of power."[8] Pragmatism should rule the day, he insisted. Had that not been true during earlier administrations? Jefferson and Madison had invoked states' rights and a narrow construction of the Constitution merely to attract the votes of farmers and laborers. "They argued and scolded against all implied powers and pretended that the government of the Union had no powers but such as were expressly delegated by the Constitution. . . . Mr. Jefferson was elected president and the first thing he did was to purchase Louisiana. An assumption of implied power greater in itself and more comprehensive in its consequences than all the assumptions of implied power in the twelve years of the Washington and Adams administrations put together."[9]

When, subsequently, Jackson's men retrieved the relevant papers from Callava's house, the ex-governor was released from jail. In due course he and his men departed for Havana. Several months later Jackson took leave of Pensacola and headed for the Hermitage. No doubt the secretary of state breathed a large sigh of relief. Had the Hero lingered, he might have been tempted to invade Cuba, and the secretary of state, for a variety of reasons, very much wanted the Ever-Faithful Isle to remain in Spanish hands for the time being.

IN THE WAKE OF Monroe's inauguration, the presidential campaign of 1824 began in earnest. Adams believed that his two principal rivals were Crawford and

Clay. Of the two, Crawford seemed stronger. He had come close to besting Monroe in the 1816 Republican caucus, he was then using his position as secretary of the treasury and the immense patronage it controlled to spread his influence throughout the Union, and he was a Southerner and slaveholder at a time when the slave power dominated Congress. Though a member of Monroe's cabinet, Crawford had schemed at every opportunity with members of Congress to discredit the administration's foreign policy and John Quincy with it. Both he and Clay were instigators of the etiquette controversy, which had done much to alienate members of Congress and their wives from the Adamses. Clay was a man of more substance than the Georgian, in the secretary of state's view, but no less ambitious and unscrupulous. He had used the speakership and his opposition to the administration to endear himself to political figures and journalists who felt snubbed by the administration and who wanted to fish in troubled waters. The Kentuckian was a slaveholder and perceived by many to be the champion of the West.

To everyone's surprise, Henry Clay, early in May 1820, announced his intention to retire from the House. He was at the time some twenty-five thousand dollars in debt. The Second Bank of the United States had offered to name him as its agent for Kentucky and Ohio under a "very liberal arrangement."[10] In March 1821, Clay approached Representative Henry Brush of Ohio, an administration supporter, and assured him that he harbored no "unfriendly or disrespectful sentiment" toward Adams.[11] Brush then approached the secretary of state and proposed a rapprochement. Adams declared that "there had never been between him and me any ill understanding of my seeking," although he did find it hard to overlook the "sneers and sarcasms" leveled at him by the Speaker when he, Adams, had had no means to defend himself. Undeterred, Clay asked Adams if he could call on him, and John Quincy agreed. The two exchanged pleasantries, and seemingly out of the blue, the secretary of state asked his visitor if he would accept a ministerial post abroad. Suspecting, correctly, that his rival hoped to remove him from the field of political battle, Clay demurred. He must spend three or four years tending to business affairs and his family, and then, possibly, he might return to public life. The Kentuckian then got to the point of his visit. "He [Clay] said he considered the situation of our public affairs now as very critical and dangerous. . . . Mr. Monroe had just been reelected with apparent unanimity, but he had not the slightest influence in Congress. His career was considered as closed. . . . Looking at Congress, they were a collection of materials, and how much good and how much evil might be done with them, accordingly, as they should be well or ill directed."[12] He regretted their differences over U.S.–Latin American relations, but predicted, presciently, that their views would soon align. Clay then proceeded to sketch his vision of a strong national government dedicated to reconciling the interests of the country's regions and classes, a liberal government committed to internal improvements and the creation of an inter-American community that would make common cause, if necessary, against the Holy Alliance. The political void Clay referred to would be filled; were they to be friendly rivals or bitter enemies? "I make no sacrifice of principle for any man's political friendship," Adams pompously declared in his diary following the meeting.[13] John Quincy later observed that Clay was a man of a "large and liberal view of public affairs" but if he became president, the West and the South would continue to control the destiny of the nation.[14]

Throughout the spring of 1821, a stream of Adams supporters called at the State Department or at his home to urge him to launch his own campaign—to use his influence to have his supporters appointed to office, to secure the endorsement of key newspapers, to cultivate members of Congress. Daniel P. Cook of Illinois, a longtime Adams booster, urged him not to break his own political neck. He should have known that John Quincy's neck was too stiff to be broken. He was perfectly conscious, he told Cook, "of my inability to make interest by caballing, bargaining, place-giving, or tampering with members of Congress. Upon the foundation of public service alone must I stand, and when the nation shall be called to judge of that, by the result, whatever it may be, I must abide."[15]

But in his own fashion, Adams did campaign. His colleagues did him the honor of inviting him to deliver the annual Fourth of July address to the House and Senate assembled together. For the occasion, he donned his academic robes. The Boylston Professor of Rhetoric and Oratory outdid himself. The address was an eloquent attack on authoritarianism, both civil and religious. Adams repeated the Whiggish argument that the United States was but the next phase in the history of the Anglo-Saxon struggle between liberty and democracy on the one hand and oppression and tyranny on the other. (The *Edinburgh Review* had recently published an article entitled "What Has America Done for Mankind?") The Pilgrims had fled British tyranny, political and ecclesiastical. They had tried to remain loyal to the Crown, but the Crown would not allow it. "The first settlers of the Plymouth colony at the eve of landing from their ship . . . bound themselves together by a written covenant and immediately after landing purchased from the Indian natives the right of settlement upon the soil. Thus was a social compact formed upon the elementary principles of civil society in which conquest and servitude had no part."[16] What ensued was unique—the birth of a City on the Hill, a beacon to the rest of mankind. "The tie which binds us to our country . . . is more deeply seated in our nature, more tender and endearing, than that common link which merely connects us with our fellow-mortal, man. It is a common government that constitutes our country . . . in that association all the sympathies of domestic life and kindred blood, all the moral ligatures of friendship and of neighborhood, are combined."[17] America was destined to feel sympathy and empathy for those other peoples who were struggling for freedom, but "[s]he goes not abroad in search of monsters to destroy."[18] It was this, among other things, that made the French and American Revolutions so different.

As Adams had hoped, the speech created a sensation and was reprinted and discussed in more than a hundred newspapers. Admirers of the Glorious Revolution were offended; so were devotees of the French Revolution. The British were insulted; so were the Russians. Both Stratford Canning and Pyotr Poletika boycotted the speech, sensing, correctly, that the histories and institutions of both of their countries would be disparaged. The Russian, however, obtained a copy and made some telling editorial remarks: "How about your two million black slaves," he asked rhetorically, "two million black slaves who cultivate a great expanse of your territory for your particular and exclusive advantage? You forget the poor Indians who you have not ceased to [de]spoil. You forget your conduct toward Spain."[19] But the vast majority of Americans loved Adams's speech. "We had an Orator here on the Fourth which will produce a sensation," Joseph Gales, editor of the *National Intelligencer*, wrote a friend. "It was Demosthenes *redivivus* in substance and manner. I have never witnessed anything superior to the *tout ensemble*."[20] In truth, the address marked Adams out in the public mind as one of the age's great patriotic orators. Of course, John Quincy Adams's Fourth of July address was both a sweeping statement of American civil values and an electioneering document. Like Cicero, Adams believed that political rhetoric could inspire, persuade, and, he hoped, transcend patronage, demagoguery, favor trading, and other less attractive elements of democratic process.

In October 1821 one of John Quincy's supporters called on him at the State Department to report that Crawford was already handing out cabinet posts in his putative administration. Adams acknowledged the Georgian's "superior talent for political management," but observed that "there were ten [persons] promised or more for every office and the disappointment would be so much more numerous than the fulfilment, that ultimately there would be more enemies made than partisans."[21] Newspapers loyal to Clay continued to blast the secretary of state for his seeming indifference to the independence movements in Latin America; Adams was nothing less than a closet monarchist. "He has already publicly christened the Emperor of Russia the 'Titus of the Age.'"[22]

Shortly before Christmas, Adams's former intellectual soulmate, John C. Calhoun, declared his candidacy for the presidency. "[L]ast Friday evening a deputation from a small number of members of Congress waited upon Mr. Calhoun at his house and invited him to stand as a candidate at the next presidential election to which he assented," Adams recorded in his diary. "The next day in a gazette of this city a piece of three columns [that poured] the vilest and foulest slander upon me was published, and from that day, no conclave of Cardinals was ever more belabored with caballing than Congress have been."[23] Subsequently, former governor William Plumer of New Hampshire, a mutual friend of Adams and Calhoun, called on the secretary of state. Calhoun wanted Adams to know that he actually favored a Northern man for the presidency—John Quincy specifically— but that he perceived that Adams's refusal to raise a hand on his own behalf was costing him support even in New England. Calhoun could not stand by and watch Crawford, "whose principles and character he could not approve," sweep into office.[24] Adams was unappeased. As usual, John Quincy equated political opposition with personal animosity. A breach had opened between the South Carolinian and him that would never be closed.

The only real politician in the Adams family, Louisa, was beside herself at her husband's obtuseness. "I will take the liberty of expressing my doubts as to the propriety of shrinking thus forever from any manifestation of the public feeling which it is natural to expect." Our "institutions are entirely popular," she wrote her husband from Quincy. People do not view your "natural coldness and reserve of . . . manners as modesty but . . . [as] pride."[25] John Quincy did not deign to reply.

Despite Adams's reticence, Henry Clay continued to view him as his chief rival for the presidency. In December 1821 one of Clay's acolytes, Congressman John Floyd of Virginia, demanded that President Monroe submit to Congress all correspondence involved in the negotiation of the Treaty of Ghent. His intent was to reveal that Adams had been willing to sell out Western interests—neglecting to secure clear title to the Columbia River basin, allowing the British to continue trading with the Indian tribes residing south of the Great Lakes, and granting British citizens the right to navigate the Mississippi—in return for New England's right to fish the Grand Banks. Central to this attempt at character assassination was John Quincy's old colleague Jonathan Russell. Though newly elected to the House from Massachusetts, Russell was still under the sway of Clay. It was he who would be the driving force behind the charge that Adams had been willing to sacrifice the Mississippi for the fisheries.

Monroe was averse to turning over the diplomatic correspondence underpinning the Treaty of Ghent—he understood that Floyd's request was nothing more or less than an electioneering tactic on behalf of Clay—but he felt he had no choice. At the president's direction, Adams had his chief clerk, Daniel Brent, scour the State Department's files and compile the requested documents. Much of the correspondence had already been published, but some of it had not. Among that lot was a private letter from Jonathan Russell to James Monroe, then secretary of state, informing him of Clay's and Russell's opposition to a proposal made to the British delegation offering to grant British citizens the right to navigate the Mississippi in return for American fishermen's right to mine the scaly treasures that lay off the coasts of Newfoundland and Nova Scotia. In truth no such offer had been made, at least not directly. As Adams informed his friend Charles J. Ingersoll, the British plenipotentiaries had insisted that the War of 1812 had nullified the Anglo-American Treaty of 1783 and with it the "liberty" of fishing the Grand Banks. The outbreak of hostilities had done no such thing, the American delegates had replied; to admit as much would invalidate America's independence. In conference Clay had declared that he would not sign any treaty granting Britain access to the great Western waterway; Adams had replied that he would not agree to give up the fisheries; Gallatin had predicted rightly that the British did not really care much about either issue, and the final document had made no mention of the two matters.[26]

Technically, the Monroe administration did not have to turn over Russell's letter of December 25 because it was private, but Adams and the president realized that it was precisely this document that Clay's minions wanted made public. If Adams did not include it, his enemies would accuse him of trying to conceal the truth. What particularly galled the secretary of state was that he would have to ask Russell's permission. Russell agreed, of course, and while at the State Department looking over related correspondence, he reminded Brent that he had also written Monroe a letter dated February 11, 1815, that further "implicated" Adams in the plot to betray the West. Because a copy of the second letter was not among the official Ghent correspondence, it was not included in the documents submitted to Congress on February 23, 1822. Thereupon, Floyd persuaded the House to ask specifically for the second letter. At this point Brent called on Russell and asked for a copy and requested that it be labeled "duplicate" to indicate that it was official. Russell agreed and promised to deliver the letter in a few days. "It is a letter of seven folio sheets of paper," Adams subsequently reported to his diary, "and amounts to little less than a denunciation of the majority of the Ghent Mission. . . . Russell wrote this Letter at Paris, where we all were, without ever communicating it to me or letting me know that he had any intention of writing such a letter." Its object, John Quincy declared, was "to decry my chances of popular favor in the Western country."[27]

As Adams read and reread the February 11 letter, he became suspicious; there were passages containing information that Russell could have gained access to only recently when he had called at State to review the Ghent document. He had also predicted that Britain would surrender on the fisheries question without an equivalent as had happened in the Convention of 1818. "I have strong suspicions that the duplicate is not a true copy of the original," Adams wrote. "There is particularly one paragraph, which on the 11th of February 1815 would have been prophetic."[28] Adams called on Monroe, to whom the original letter had been sent, and asked him to examine his private papers for the original. The president subsequently located it and provided it to the secretary of state. When Adams read the original, his suspicions were confirmed. Pointing out the discrepancies, Adams informed the president that he intended to submit the original and the duplicate with some accompanying remarks to the House. Monroe recoiled at the suggestion. "As I pressed him to communicate the letter, he said it would utterly ruin both him and me." Perhaps so, Adams replied, but not to submit the documents would most assuredly ruin him.[29]

On April 29, Adams confronted Russell personally. You included information that was incorrect and excluded information that placed the controversy in context, he declared. Russell was conciliatory. If that is your memory of events, then it is undoubtedly correct, Adams's fellow New Englander declared. "I have not acted in this case in concert with your enemies, and I have never written or published a word against you in the newspapers. I have acted from no motive of hostility to you."[30] I have no way of discerning your motives, the secretary of state said. I will not lift a finger to seek revenge. But the truth will out, and you must take the consequences. "I wish you well," Russell declared as he departed. Two hours later, the secretary of state called on Monroe and encountered Russell leaving. It seems, Monroe declared, that Mr. Russell no longer wished his correspondence communicated to Congress. Let us forget the whole thing. No, said Adams, the Clay cabal had started the controversy and the administration must finish it. He intended to press forward with his report. Monroe exploded: "Your report . . . 'tis my report." John Quincy stood his ground: "Sir, it is your report to do what you please with it when received, but so far as I understand the Constitution of this country, it is my report to make." The whole transaction, Monroe declared, was intended to influence the next presidential election, "elections in [which] he felt it his duty to take no part." By doing nothing you are taking part, John Quincy rejoined. He had been accused of violating the public trust. By not revealing Russell's perfidy, Monroe was decidedly taking sides against him, John Quincy Adams. Monroe replied that he would think on the matter.[31]

On May 4, Monroe informed Congress that in regard to Congressman Floyd's resolution requesting a copy of Russell's February 11, 1815, letter, no copy had been found in the State Department's files; Russell had provided a duplicate, but then Monroe had discovered the original in his papers. Nevertheless, said the president, he had decided not to send the duplicate and the original unless the House specifically requested them. Not surprisingly, Floyd experienced a sudden change of heart. He was now perfectly satisfied that the American negotiators at Ghent had not surrendered a single American interest.[32]

The cabal had underestimated Mr. Adams, however. One of his supporters in the House, Timothy Fuller of Massachusetts, introduced a resolution calling for the submission of both letters. It passed on a voice vote, and the duplicate and the original were published both in the *National Intelligencer* and in the *Philadelphia National Gazette*, which was edited by John Quincy's friend and supporter Robert Walsh Jr. Russell was undone. Clay and Floyd both repudiated him, and he was not reelected to Congress by his Massachusetts constituents. Even the Adamses' old enemy, Essex man Timothy Pickering, was appalled. At a dinner party in Philadelphia, the old man declared, "Sir, I regard Mr. Russell as a man fairly done over. Mr. Adams will be exalted in the estimation of New England by his remarks and ought to be exalted to any part of the world."[33] Ever the dilettante, John Quincy published a lengthy defense entitled *The Duplicate Letters, the Fisheries, and the Mississippi*.[34]

JOHN FLOYD'S PRIMARY OBJECTIVE had been to indict Adams for not only surrendering Texas but sacrificing U.S. interests in the Pacific Northwest. A native of frontier Kentucky and a friend to the newly elected senator from Missouri, Thomas Hart Benton, Floyd in December 1819 had proposed the creation of a select committee of the House to investigate the possibility and necessity of establishing an American settlement in the Columbia River Basin.[35] In truth, since the signing of the Convention of 1818, the British had been busy consolidating their control of the Oregon Territory. The convention had thrown open the door to both countries to claim and occupy whatever part of the territory they could. The only restraint imposed was that one signatory could not discriminate against the citizens of the other in areas that it staked out. In 1821 the Hudson's Bay Company absorbed the British North West Company, and His Majesty's government granted the new entity a trade monopoly over the entire area from Hudson Bay to the Columbia Basin.

In the Oregon Territory the chief factor for the Hudson's Bay Company, Dr. John McLoughlin, ruled like an oriental potentate. He administered justice to British subjects and Native Americans alike, although not in equal portions. McLoughlin supervised the lucrative fur trade and all other aspects of the region's economy. In 1823, Hudson's Bay moved its headquarters from Fort George, the British name for Fort Astoria, southward to Fort Vancouver, situated on the north bank of the Columbia. To discourage intrusion from American fur trappers, Hudson's Bay employees worked assiduously to keep a wide belt of territory south of the Columbia trapped out.[36] Although the United States had as much right as the British to claim territory, establish settlements, and trade with the Indians, there were not many Americans who wished to see the United States challenge the former mother country over a wilderness thousands of miles from the country's population center. But those who did were most influential.

Massachusetts and New York shipowners and merchants made fortunes buying furs from both Indian and white trappers, and trading them in China for silks and porcelain. Then there were the whalers operating out of Boston, Nantucket, and other Massachusetts ports who plied their trade in the North Pacific. As a Massachusetts man and friend to both William Gray and John Jacob Astor, John Quincy had defended American commercial interests in the Pacific Northwest from Russian encroachments when he was minister to the court of Alexander I. Monroe was not much interested in the trans–Rocky Mountain West. Adams was, but he did not want to risk the burgeoning rapprochement with Great Britain over an issue that he believed time and demographics would settle to America's advantage.[37]

Yet when Britain and Russia dared challenge America's right to trade and settle the vast area west of the Rocky Mountains from the forty-ninth parallel to the fifty-fifth parallel, the secretary of state was ferocious in his defense of U.S. claims present and future. In January 1821, after listening to remarks by Hugh Nelson of Virginia in the House of Representatives and reading Tennessee senator John H. Eaton's article in the *National Intelligencer* calling for the immediate settlement of the Northwest Territory, Stratford Canning called at the State Department. What were his government's intentions? Canning asked Adams. "It was very probable that our settlement at the mouth of the Columbia River would be increased," the secretary of state declared. Canning bridled. When he declared that any expansion of the American community on the Columbia would be a direct violation of the Convention of 1818, Adams rose from his chair, pulled down from his shelves a volume containing the text of the agreement, and read it. The Anglo-American convention provided that all of the Oregon Territory was to be open and free to settlement by the citizens of both nations. If you have anything further to say on the matter, please put in writing. Canning then said with great vehemence, "and do you suppose, Sir, that I am to be dictated to in the manner in which I may think to communicate with the American Government." Then, "in a louder and more passionate tone of voice, Am I to understand that I am to be refused henceforth any conference with you on the business of my mission?" Of course not, Adams replied, but an exchange of notes would prevent any confusion. He then took the offensive. The executive was not responsible for what the members of the legislative branch might say. Surely, his foreign minister and he had read the U.S. Constitution. Moreover, communications between members of the administration and individual congressmen were not any of Britain's or any other nation's business. Adams recounted the conversation Bagot and he had had concerning the voyage of the *Ontario* shortly before the latter departed for England; Mr. Bagot and he had parted on the friendliest of terms. "I will stop you there," Canning shouted. "I know very well what transpired between you and Mr. Bagot. . . . I am treated like a schoolboy."[38]

Canning called again the next day. Was it the position of the United States that Britain had no claim to the Oregon Territory? "I do not know what you claim nor what you do not claim," Adams replied testily. "You claim India—you claim Africa—you claim—" Canning interjected, "Perhaps a piece of the Moon?" Perhaps not the moon, Adams said, "but there is not a spot on this habitable globe that I could affirm you do not claim." Do you refuse to recognize our outpost at Fort Vancouver? Canning inquired. "No, there the boundary is marked, and we have no disposition to encroach upon it. Keep what is yours but leave the rest of this continent to us." But this affects the rights of Spain as well as Britain. That is no concern of yours, the secretary of state declared. "Do you wish me to report this conversation to my government?" Canning asked. Do as you please, Adams replied.[39]

Canning did in fact convey the substance and tone of Adams's and his conversation to the foreign minister, who commended his zeal but told him to stand down. Adams had once again correctly read the diplomatic tea leaves. "They are anxious to prevent our acquiring a firm footing on the shores of the South Sea [Pacific]" he wrote, "and yet they dare not take a fixed unequivocal stand against it."[40]

By early 1822 the secretary of state had decided that the time had come for U.S. recognition of the Latin American republics. In Colombia, Chile, and Buenos Aires, any semblance of Spanish authority had evaporated. Mexico and Central America had also made good their bids for independence. Monroe's cabinet met almost continually during January. Rumors were circulating that the Colombian representative in Madrid was offering his country to the highest bidder and that the members of the Holy Alliance were plotting to use the newly established monarchy in Mexico City to spread the ideals of the ancien régime throughout the Americas. Buenos Aires was said to be considering a limited monarchy and an appeal for British protection. If the American eagle did not spread its wings, Central and South America might very well degenerate into European outposts or at the very least become a collection of jealous and warring sovereignties, Adams argued.[41] There was also the political angle, of course. Adams's rival Henry Clay had banked a great deal of political capital by championing the Latin American cause. Adams's arguments at last convinced Monroe and his cabinet colleagues.

In a message to Congress delivered on March 11, 1822, the president declared that Colombia, Chile, Peru, the United Provinces of the Río de la Plata, and Mexico had all established their independence from Spain. He asked for authority to appoint ministers to the five new states, and Congress responded with a hundred-thousand-dollar appropriation to fund the positions. The vote was 167 to one in the House and thirty-nine to three in the Senate. Adams drafted the first sets of instructions to the new ministers. They were to do everything in their power to encourage republicanism, negotiate most-favored-nation trade pacts, help fend off European efforts to meddle in the respective countries' affairs, and promote political and economic concert among the newly independent American states.[42]

Recognition gained Adams some political capital in the West, but if he had any hope of capturing the presidency in 1824, he was going to have to have some support from the slaveholding states of the South. In November 1822 the *Washington City Gazette* published a story claiming that during the Missouri controversy, Adams and the former Federalist luminary Rufus King had plotted to create a new Free-Soil political party; the two, according to the article, had intended to appeal to "the benevolent feelings of the New England States, of New York, Pennsylvania, and Ohio" to block the elevation of "any Southern citizen to the presidency." John Quincy's supporters in the press issued fervent denials.[43]

Adams was determined to avoid the slavery issue altogether if he could. The American Colonization Society had succeeded in persuading Congress to appropriate twenty thousand dollars for the purchase of land on the west coast of Africa where free Blacks and Africans confiscated from illegal slave ships could be settled. Monroe went so far as to appoint a commissioner to supervise whatever colony was established. Privately, Adams argued that nowhere in the Constitution was there a provision authorizing the federal government to establish overseas colonies to house free Blacks. The whole scheme was a travesty. Like it or not, he wrote, the economy of the United States at that point depended upon the labor of Blacks, both free and enslaved. He observed to George Hay, President Monroe's brother-in-law, that "there was no such weak and absurd reasoner in the world as humanity. It never looked but at one side of a question."[44] At the same time, he beseeched abolitionists and other supporters of the ACS not to force him to take a public stance on the issue.[45] For the sake of the republic and his own political future, Adams believed, the day of reckoning on the inextricably intertwined issues of race, freedom, and slavery had to be postponed.

* * *

As GEORGE'S COMMENCEMENT APPROACHED in the late summer of 1821, John Quincy seemed confident that his eldest would distinguish himself. He went so far as to invite the governor of Massachusetts as well as President Kirkland to the family's postgraduation celebration. The ceremonies, when the day appointed arrived, were uncommonly brief. George spoke for three minutes. Louisa was exuberant in her praise: "George spoke as I wished a son of mine should speak. . . . His voice is fine, his manner easy, at times even graceful and his emphasis, modulation, and action perfectly natural."[46] John Quincy was less impressed: "My eldest son, George Washington Adams, was one of those who graduated and had a part in the second conference," read his terse diary entry.[47] John fared no better in his father's eyes. Following the graduation ceremonies, the secretary of state served as one of the judges for the 1821 Boylston Prizes for Elocution. "My son John was among the unsuccessful candidates," John Quincy noted in his diary. "He spoke . . . without sufficient force and animation."[48]

Charles, of course, came out from Boston for the festivities. He had been admitted conditionally for the fall term, having been deemed insufficient in Latin. His father was indignant, for once blaming the institution rather than his son. Charles had been required to translate passages from Sallust, the Roman historian. John Quincy had his youngest read from the same text and saw nothing amiss. The fault lay not with Charles but with his examiner, he insisted, a "Mr. Channing, the professor of Rhetoric and Oratory, a man himself quite incompetent to the office of which he holds. . . . Hated and despised by the students," he had "never yet delivered a public Lecture."[49] Adams confronted Kirkland in the president's office and bullied him into granting Charles a second examination, this time with his father present. Charles passed and was admitted without condition.

Afterward, in private conversation with Kirkland, John Quincy asked where exactly George and John ranked in their respective classes. He was bitterly disappointed to learn that George had placed thirtieth in a class of fifty-nine and John ranked a mere forty-fifth in a class of sixty-four students.[50] When his distinguished visitor proceeded to question the college's ranking system, Kirkland showed him proof that John had earned abysmal grades in Greek and was one of a number of students "to avail themselves of every indulgence and relaxation which could escape from actual punishment."[51] The father—would-be man of letters, Phi Beta Kappa, president of several learned societies—spent a sleepless night. "I had hoped that at least one of my sons would be ambitious to excel," he moaned. Instead, they were "coming into manhood with indolent minds—flinching from study whenever they can. The blast of mediocrity is the lightest of the evils which such characters portend."[52]

John Quincy, Louisa, and George were scheduled to depart Quincy for Washington on October 3. Neither John nor Charles was to be allowed to come to Washington for the winter holiday, he informed his sons before they left. They were to reside in Quincy with their grandfather and uncle Thomas, studying and reflecting on their future. In the meantime, until the end of term, neither was to leave Harvard Yard.[53] Back in Washington he piled on John: "I found your standing in a class of about 85 [*sic*] students in point of scholarship at number 45. . . . To express to you the mortification with which I made the discovery . . . I could feel nothing but sorrow and shame in your presence [and will not see you] until you should have not only commenced but made larger progress in redeeming yourself from that disgraceful standing."[54] John was crushed; a sociable young man, he had been looking forward to Washington's holiday society with great anticipation. He wrote begging his father's indulgence. If John Quincy would relent and let him come, he would out of gratitude work diligently and relentlessly on his studies. "Gratitude!" John Quincy wrote back. "It is to your country, to mankind, to your God that you are answerable for the use of the blessing entrusted to you." Believe me, he declared, "you will be grateful to me for [not] indulging you with dissipated vacations and winter frolics . . . [in] Washington, but for the sterner kindness of having roused you from the nerveless slumbers and indolence."[55] Why exactly the banishment of fourteen-year-old Charles was necessary is unclear.

The forced absence of her two younger sons devastated Louisa. Upon learning of her husband's diktat, she confided to her diary, "This day has blasted my hopes, and I am absolutely refused the sight of my children—I must submit because I have no recourse, but it grieves me to the soul."[56] "Your father has adopted the opinion that severity is necessary to promote the education of his sons," she subsequently wrote John, "and suddenly from some unaccountable but concealed influence which must emanate from the College itself, [he] has changed altogether the plans which he pursued for years of general confidence and indulgence."[57] Not surprisingly, she fell ill. "My old friend erysipelas seizes on me with more than usual violence," she recorded in her journal. Soon most of her face and head were covered with the painful rash. So swollen were her hands and feet that she could barely arise from her bed. Finally, the accomplished, attractive hostess developed a ridge across her forehead.[58] Louisa was convinced, moreover, that at age forty-six, she had become pregnant once again. Certain that she could not survive another birth, Louisa began to prepare for the worst. "Should it please the Almighty disposer of events that I may never see them [John and Charles], may their father make up to them by redoubled tenderness the loss they will sustain in an affectionate mother."[59]

Once George had graduated, his father seems to have forgiven him his sins. He arranged for his eldest to study law under his direction for two years and then a spend a third with a noted jurist. While studying with his father, George would also serve as his faithful assistant and companion. He did his best to comfort his mother over the 1821–1822 Christmas holiday, accompanying her when she was healthy enough to various balls and soirees. Louisa expressed her appreciation, but George was not the warmhearted convivial individual that Charles was.[60]

Charles, as it turned out, hated Harvard. He found the faculty cold and uninspiring, and failed to develop any meaningful relationships with other members of the student body. He spent his freshman year, he later wrote, in "dissipation, melancholy, and waste of time"; his command of "money and dash" made him the envy of his classmates. Like his mother, Charles considered himself a Southerner. He found New Englanders cold and distant.

Charles did not really look like an Adams; even at fourteen, he was tall and thickly built. During his extended stay in Washington in 1819, Louisa and he had grown close. She later confided that she found him a charming companion. He was romantic like his mother and so enamored of the romantic poets and novelists that his grandfather had to warn: "Mathematics and law are the true rocks on which men of business may surely found his reputation. . . . It is not novels or poetry. It is neither Scott nor Lord Byron who make useful men."[61] "I do not hesitate to say that you suit me better than either of your brothers as your manners are more like my own," Louisa would later write him. Like his father, Charles Francis would often wear a protective mask of stiffness and indifference, but he observed that "people never made such a mistake in the world as when they judge me cold or naturally grave. I am the creature of inclination."[62] As he matured, Charles would reveal an emotional resiliency and degree of self-possession that would save him. Again, he was the only son not abandoned during his parents' St. Petersburg years.

In December 1821, John Quincy learned that at the close of his first term at Harvard, Charles ranked near the bottom of his class. But having heard from Kirkland and friends in Cambridge and Boston that Charles appeared to be a sober, even studious, young man, his father chose not to savage him as he had George and John. "I am convinced that you had not been properly prepared for admission to the University and that you should have had at least one year more of previous study before you entered," he wrote. "You would even then have been a full year in advance of the age at which either of your brothers entered."[63] Why didn't he consider dropping out for a year of independent study or, at the close of his freshman year, moving down a class? When subsequently Charles wrote that he did not believe he was cut out for college, his father remained conciliatory.

Noting that Charles had always been enamored of the navy, John Quincy observed that that career also required an education. Just finish your freshman year and then propose an alternative life plan if you so desire.[64] Charles did indeed persevere. Both he and John, whose rank in his class had risen to twenty-fourth, were welcomed for the 1822–1823 Christmas season.

The previous spring, Louisa's brother, Thomas Baker Johnson, had arrived in Washington from New Orleans, where he had been postmaster since 1808. He was suffering terribly from hemorrhoids and severe constipation (dyspepsia); the conditions were, of course, mutually reinforcing. In June, Louisa gathered up her brother and their fifteen-year-old niece, Mary Hellen, and departed for Philadelphia to seek treatment from the pioneering physician Dr. Philip Syng Physick. The practice of medicine had not kept up with other developing technologies; engineering had given the world steamboats and the power looms of the New England textile mills. Physicians were still applying leeches and prescribing emetics. Only one in ten possessed a degree in medicine or its equivalent in training. The germ theory was still in the future. Instruments were crude—the stethoscope and the oral thermometer were yet to be invented. Bleeding was considered the remedy for virtually all diseases and illnesses. Physicians believed that bloodletting induced sleep, prevented hemorrhages, and eased pain. Before being bled, patients were usually given emetics to purge their bowels, and administered a dose of mercury. Thus poisoned, the individual might then be blistered.[65] Louisa's and Abigail's home remedies were more effective than those offered by licensed practitioners. When yellow fever swept New York and Philadelphia in 1817 and 1819, medical men knew that it was contagious and warned their patients to avoid contact with those suspected of having the illness. Illiberal ministers, however, told their flocks that sin, especially debauchery, was responsible for their maladies. Some of those caught in the midst of the fever believed that smoke was a deterrent; it was not unusual to see women and even children smoking cigars. Others hung garlic around their necks or put it in their shoes, burned gunpower, or sprinkled vinegar on their walls.[66]

Philip Physick was considered one of the top surgeons in America in 1822. He had studied medicine in London, Edinburgh, and Philadelphia. At the time Louisa and her brother arrived in the City of Brotherly Love, Physick was professor of surgery and chairman of the anatomy department at the University of Philadelphia and chief of surgery at Pennsylvania Hospital. In those days, lacking anesthesia, successful surgeons had to have quick hands, sharp instruments, and thorough knowledge of the human body. Unlike one of his Philadelphia colleagues, who, in his haste to amputate a patient's leg at the hip, cut off one of his testicles and two of his assistant's fingers, Physick possessed all of the attributes of a successful surgeon. During his career, he operated on virtually every part of the human body and won international notoriety as an ophthalmic surgeon. He was among the first modern physicians to surgically remove a cataract.[67]

Louisa had of course written ahead. Dr. Physick recommended a boarding-house, Mrs. Purdon's, situated on South Sixth Street between Chestnut and Walnut directly opposite the State House Garden. "[He] says he never knew it to be unhealthy in this part of the city," Louisa wrote John Quincy.[68] In due course Louisa and Thomas called on Physick at his offices on Mulberry Street. The man they encountered was of medium height with a high forehead, his hair clubbed and powdered. His manner was formal, even cold, but he was thorough in his examination, both verbal and physical. The physician found Thomas's condition serious but not hopeless. "The Dr. says he looks at him with astonishment for his sufferings are beyond description. All . . . complaints, he says, should be attended to early and that he can assure me that nothing will do but the knife, and it is only deceiving patients and prolonging their misery to pretend otherwise." He found Louisa's hemorrhoids (what childbearing woman of that era did not suffer from them!) less serious but recommended surgery for her as well. "This morning Dr. Physick to whom I have submitted myself," she wrote her husband, "informed me . . . that nothing could be done for me unless I would undergo an operation which . . . cannot be performed until cool weather; after which he will ensure me better health than I have had for years."[69]

And so, Louisa, Thomas, and Mary retired to Mrs. Purdon's to wait. Her brother was miserable, Louisa wrote John Quincy. "[T]he Dr. yesterday informed him that though the operation would relieve it [the hemorrhoids], it could not cure the dyspepsia which so terribly afflicts him—I am much afraid from his prescriptions that he considers it of the nature of a paralysis of the bowels."[70] Thomas could eat little else but "Icelandic seaweed," which had to be boiled all day and which Louisa found nauseous to the smell and taste. Humiliated by his physical condition, Thomas avoided society and began to obsess on his coming operation with a combination of hope and dread.[71]

While they waited, Louisa became immersed in Philadelphia society, where the Adamses had numerous friends and supporters. Robert Walsh and former congressman Joseph Hopkinson were in almost constant attendance. Through them she was introduced to the city's political and social elite. The city was all abuzz over the Adams–Russell contretemps, which was just reaching its peak. Both Walsh and Louisa declared John Quincy the victor, but it seemed that in the weeks that followed, the victor could not resist pummeling the vanquished. "The poor worm must crawl on his belly for the rest of his days," Louisa wrote her husband "and it would be degrading to trample on him and crush him lower—When a man handles his pen with so much vigor [as you], he leaves his enemy powerless to harm, but if he push that enemy too hard he excites a feeling of pity towards him which raises him and elevates him into consequence."[72]

John Quincy accepted her advice and praised her for her good judgment. But that was not his reaction when Louisa chastised him for refusing to campaign even to the point of avoiding common society. "Mr. Walsh is very desirous of seeing you here; he says he has much to say to you and wishes you could come and stay a week."[73] "You must pillow yourself upon his support which is promised with much energy and endeavor to improve your manners by imitating the fascinations of Mr. Calhoun and avoiding the 'vegetable plant' immobility of your great Master [Monroe] who you are too much inclined to resemble."[74] As she continued to prod him, he lost his temper. He would not journey to Philadelphia "to show how much I long to be president." But the office would go to another by default. "Well and what then?" he wrote Louisa. "There will be candidates enough for the presidency without me." He quoted from *Macbeth*: "'If chance will have me King, why, chance may crown me, / Without my stir.'"[75]

In truth, Louisa the politician was of two minds concerning her husband's reclusiveness and obstinacy. It was costing him dearly, but he was so sensitive to any criticism, no matter how frivolous, that he seemed bound to overreact and lose his temper when mixing in society. In mid-August the *Columbian Observer* declared that the secretary of state had abandoned all propriety, having shed his cravat and waistcoat and even appearing in church barefoot. When John Quincy wrote denouncing these "liars" and "back-biters," she tried to give him some perspective. When several persons attending one of her salons had asked if her husband really attended Sunday services without shoes, "I replied that I had once heard you rode to your office with your head to your horse's tail, and that the one fact was as likely as the other. . . . Put a little wool in your ears and don't read the papers."[76]

On August 7, Dr. Physick operated successfully on Thomas Johnson. There was, Louisa wrote, "great hopes of the recovery of our poor patient." The procedure had taken surprisingly little time. Indeed, the good doctor had been gone from the boardinghouse for fifteen minutes before she realized the operation was over. Thomas suffered little during the operation, but his first night was spent "in anguish."[77] Several tumors remained, and Physick operated again on the seventeenth, again successfully. Thomas's night after was eased by several drops of laudanum. Within a week, Thomas was able to socialize and even ride a gentle horse.

Louisa's letters to her husband during her extended stay in Philadelphia were witty, vivid descriptions of life and politics in Philadelphia similar to those she wrote to her father-in-law. She repeated gossip that Dr. Physick's wife had drunk herself to death. "[O]ne of the great causes of complaint on the part of the lady was that the Doctor would always sleep in gloves and stockings and never would allow the window to be opened in summer. . . . [He] assigned as a reason for it that it rendered his hand more susceptible and increased the delicacy of his touch, perhaps an additional cause of complaint to his lady."[78] Philadelphia was a strange mix of saints and sinners, she reported: "Five young ladies of respectable families it is said are obliged to go into retirement for some time, access having been found too easy to their chambers from the windows." At the same time, the city brimmed with pious Quaker abolitionists.[79] Like his father, John Quincy reveled in Louisa's missives. "Whatever the cause of the confidence which you say you have but recently acquired of writing to me whatever comes into your head is, I am the principal gainer by the acquisition. I hope it will be permanent."[80] His letters in turn were frank and affectionate. On July 26 the couple had separately celebrated their twenty-fifth anniversary. "With the dawn of this morning I awaked and ejaculated [!] a blessing to heaven upon the semi-jubilee of our marriage," he wrote. "More than half of your life and nearly half of mine [we] have traveled hand-in-hand in our pilgrimage through this valley not alone of tears."[81]

The discovery in June 1822 of an alleged plot by a free Black carpenter named Denmark Vesey to foment a massive slave rebellion in South Carolina presented Louisa with the opportunity to express her views on race relations in America. "When we see the thousands of Blacks padding the streets of every city in the Union," she wrote her husband, "and witness the insolence and extravagance of their manners and appearance, we have indeed reason to tremble for the future; and they cannot be too strongly impressed with the ideas of their own weakness, and the dreadful punishments which they must be exposed to if they rise upon the whites whose interest it must be from one end of the union to the other to guard against them, either as free men or slaves."[82] But then, writing some days later: "Black insurrections will I fear teach the South that on their part it [slavery] is unanswerable—It is an evil of awful magnitude which will fall on and crush a future generation and thus do we see 'the sins of the fathers visited upon the children unto the third and fourth generation.'"[83] Louisa was opposed to the institution in the abstract, but her beloved father had owned slaves in Maryland and had still owned four when the family returned to the United States. Louisa's brother-in-law Nathaniel Frye owned two. Johnson Hellen, Walter and Nancy's son, who lived with the Adamses, kept two bondsmen as well. In her diary, Louisa took great pains to convince her readers that her family members were the kindliest of masters.

Louisa took advantage of her brother's improving health to accept an invitation to visit Joseph Hopkinson's summer home situated in Bordentown, New Jersey, on the banks of the Delaware River. The picturesque village dated back to 1682; its mineral waters had turned it into one of the most popular spas in the Northeast. Hopkinson and other Philadelphia grandees had built homes on the bluffs overlooking the river; his, a spacious redbrick mansion with large shuttered windows was located at 101 Farnsworth Avenue.[84] The month that followed was like a dream for Louisa—the women fished, picnicked, played whist, and "had as noisy a party as you can possibly imagine, absolutely shouting with laughter at every *jeu d'esprit* and puns which were uttered, and which fell with copious abundance from our lips."[85] Louisa could forget about Thomas's ailments, her misanthropic husband's political career, and her struggling children.

Just upriver from Bordentown was the magnificent fifteen-hundred-acre estate of Joseph Bonaparte, Napoleon's brother and the exiled king of Spain. There he lived in a sprawling mansion filled with priceless art and surrounded by gardens and parks. The Frenchman had arrived with only his daughter at his side, his wife having refused to come to America. He kept a mistress, Annette Savage, tucked away in a separate residence in Trenton. "The Count" invited Louisa and several of her female companions to dine at his estate. Louisa and Joseph hit it off immediately: "He is very handsome," Louisa gushed, "very much like Napoleon but the whole countenance expressing benevolence. . . . There is so much easy good humor about him, and he looks so much like a good, fat substantial farmer that were we not pre-acquainted with his history, no one would suspect he had ever filled a throne. In this little village he is adored for he has made the widows' hearts to sing with joy and has been a father to the fatherless; and though a king, has showered blessing around him, thus proving himself far more than a king—a good man."[86] Both Joseph and his daughter were equally taken with Louisa. At several breakfasts, teas, and dinners, they discussed politics, society, and art in French. One of Joseph's treasures was a Titian nude of Venus, which hung in his bedroom. "I would not affect modesty as I said that I had seen a number of fine pictures in Europe," she wrote John Quincy.[87]

Her spirits buoyed, Louisa returned to Philadelphia to take her turn at surgery under the skilled supervision of Dr. Physick. On the eve of the operation, Louisa found that "stern and cold almost callous . . . our good Dr. possesses the great gift of the most unbending firmness from which . . . he never was known to flinch. . . . It is said that it takes him several days to brace his feelings or his nerves [to] his duty but that once done, he is immoveable . . . but his heart is full of sensibility and his manner during an operation soothing and kind . . . ," and he was careful never to appear "alarmed or intimidated by the cries and groans of his agonized patients."[88] So prominent was his patient in this instance that Physick described the operation in a subsequent memoir. He had Louisa's hands and feet tied, rolled her over on her left side, and placed a pillow under her hip. The process was fairly simple: Physick applied a soft wire snare to each of her two large hemorrhoids and tightened the snares. "This gives momentary pain," he wrote, "but is not in all cases so severe as might [be expected]."[89] Typically, the physician left the wire noose in place for up to twenty-four hours. He did so with Louisa, and when the tumors dropped off, he stitched the wounds and applied a caustic that caused more discomfort than the wire snares. Within forty-eight hours Louisa was on the mend, and as Physick promised, she would enjoy great relief from a condition that dated back to her early pregnancies.

27

The Monroe Doctrine

I N 1823 THE ISSUE of whether the Holy Alliance would come to the rescue of Spain and restore its rebellious colonies would finally be resolved. In May a French army commanded by Louis XVIII's nephew, the Duke d'Angoulême, crossed the Pyrenees Mountains and occupied Madrid. The duke declared Ferdinand to be once again an absolute monarch and then proceeded to overwhelm constitutionalist forces holed up in Cádiz. Rumors then circulated that the French, perhaps in harness with one or more of the other members of the Holy Alliance, would sail to the New World and through force of arms restore Spain's and Portugal's former colonies to their respective monarchs. The Holy Alliance did in fact discuss such a scheme, but the French and Spanish were divided. Louis's chief minister, the Count de Villèle, preferred to avoid all-out warfare by leaving the newly declared republics their independence while installing members of the Spanish royal family as heads of their governments. Ferdinand insisted on complete capitulation.[1] What seemed certain to the rest of the world, however, was that there would be some effort by the Holy Alliance to restore the principles of the ancien régime to the New World. The overriding question as far as the United States was concerned was, what would Great Britain do?

In the summer of 1822, Lord Castlereagh suffered a mental breakdown and somehow managed to cut his own throat with a penknife. "It required great anatomical skill to do what he did so effectually with the instrument," Lord Bathurst subsequently commented to an acquaintance.[2] For several weeks following his death, the members of the cabinet were unable to name a successor. They finally settled on the veteran diplomat George Canning, even though he was anathema to the conservative wing of his party and to the king. The new foreign minister was much too liberal for the Crown's taste. As a youth, Canning had been an ardent Whig, but the excesses of the French Revolution turned him into a moderate

Conservative. Politically, he was a man of the future who believed that public opinion ought to be courted and mobilized to support policy decisions. The transition from Castlereagh to Canning had absolutely no effect on Anglo-American relations or on British policy toward the Holy Alliance and the independence of Latin America, however. In 1817, Castlereagh had informed the French minister that although Britain was considering mediation between Spain and its rebelling colonies, "H.R.H. cannot consent that his mediation shall under any circumstances assume an armed character."[3] Following the fall of Cádiz, some Conservatives in the Liverpool government applauded the return of legitimacy, but like most other Britons, the prime minister and Canning sympathized with the constitutionalists.

On March 31, 1823, Canning issued a formal warning to the French through the British ambassador in Paris, Sir Charles Stuart. The message to Louis and his ministers was clear: "Disclaiming in the most solemn manner any intention of appropriating to himself the smallest portion of the late Spanish possessions in America, His Majesty is satisfied that no attempt will be made by France to bring under her dominion any of those possessions, either by conquest or by cession from Spain."[4] Shortly thereafter, Stratford Canning wrote his cousin that "the course which you have taken in the great politics of Europe has had the effect of making the English almost popular in the United States . . . even Adams has caught something of the 'soft infection.'"[5] Why not, thought the foreign minister, cap the First Rapprochement that had been building between the two countries since the signing of the Treaty of Ghent with a joint policy statement warning France, and by inference the other members of the Holy Alliance, to let matters between Spain and the emerging republics take their course? London and Washington would at the same time reassure the Continental powers that neither the United States nor Great Britain sought a foot of territory for itself. In a casual conversation with Richard Rush, the U.S. minister, Canning asked, "What do you think your government would say to going hand in hand with England in such a policy?"[6] There would be little or no risk, no action to be taken. "[T]he simple fact of our two countries being known to hold the same opinions would, by its moral effect, put down the intention on the part of France. . . . I base this belief upon the large share of the maritime powers of the world which Great Britain and the United States share between them."[7] Rush was guardedly encouraging.

Adams would not learn the specifics of the Canning–Rush negotiations until October, but they came as no surprise. He had continued to base his foreign policies during his second term as secretary of state on the premise of an ongoing Anglo-American rapprochement. In 1821, Alexander had issued a ukase claiming all of the coast of northwest America down to the fifty-first parallel and forbidding any approach by foreign nationals to the coast of Russian North America closer than a hundred nautical miles. During the next year and a half, in conversations with the Russian minister, Baron van Tuyll, and through the U.S. minister in St. Petersburg, Henry Middleton, Adams tried to persuade the Russians to negotiate a compromise similar to that provided in the Anglo-American Convention of 1818. He got nowhere. In July 1823, with Monroe's approval, the secretary of state summoned van Tuyll to the State Department. "I told him specially that we should contest the right of Russia to any territorial establishment on this continent and that we should assume distinctly the principle that the American continents are no longer subjects for any new European colonial establishments."[8] Throughout these negotiations, the secretary of state had taken care to keep London informed. When Christopher Hughes, headed for his post as minister to Sweden, had stopped off in London, Canning assured his American guest that his government and the Monroe administration continued to see eye to eye on the issue of Russian expansion in North America. "The only question to settle," he said, "is how moderately we shall let them down or let them off, or what shall be the nature of the atonement we shall consent to receive for their folly."[9]

On June 24, Stratford Canning, the British minister, made his last call on the secretary of state. He had been summoned to London for consultations and would presumably be reassigned. Did Adams think the United States and Great Britain were headed toward an alliance? Canning asked. Not a formal one, the secretary of state replied. In his diary, John Quincy wrote, "This coincidence of principle connected with the great changes in the affairs of the world passing before us seems to me a suitable occasion for the United States and Great Britain to compare their ideas and purposes together with a view to the accommodation of great interests upon which they had heretofore differed."[10]

In October, Monroe called the cabinet together to discuss Canning's proposal. Adams remembered that the president was immensely flattered by the offer because it seemed to establish the United States as one of the world's great powers.[11] Canning's suggestion had its attractions, Adams declared, but there were issues to be addressed. Making common cause with Britain against the Holy Alliance could be seen as a violation of the two-spheres and no-entangling-alliances principles laid down in Washington's Farewell Address. And what if Canning's offer was a trap to enlist the United States in an initiative in which it would surely be seen as a junior partner?

At this point Monroe decided to consult his mentors, Jefferson and Madison. Jefferson was enthusiastic, Madison less so. The Sage of Monticello, the former bête noire of the Federalist Party, wrote, "Great Britain is the nation which can do us the most harm of anyone on all earth and with her on our side we need not fear the whole world."[12] Accept Canning's offer; the United States could then fish in the troubled international waters and perhaps land Cuba, a prize Jefferson had long coveted. Madison also urged Monroe to accept but to do so in a way not to sacrifice U.S. interests to John Bull. Although Canning's proposal was "made with an air of consultation as well as conceit," he wrote, "[it] was founded on a predetermination to take the course marked out whatever might the reception given to his invitation."[13] Monroe showed the missives to John Quincy on October 30. "Mr. Madison," Adams confided to his diary, "thinks as I do."[14]

The first week in November, the cabinet met again to discuss Canning's offer in light of Russia's ongoing intransigence regarding its claim to the Pacific Northwest. On October 16, Baron van Tuyll had informed Adams that the tsar had no intention of recognizing the independence of the Latin American republics and he expected the United States to continue its policy of neutrality in the contest between Spain and its rebelling colonies. Calhoun subsequently led the way in arguing that Washington should embrace Canning's proposal even if it should commit the United States never to seize Cuba or Texas. It would not only deter the French and the Russians, but the self-denial pledge would keep Cuba from falling into the hands of the British, "their power . . . being greater than ours to seize upon them." Adams disagreed across the board. "We have no intention of seizing either Texas or Cuba," he declared. "But the inhabitants of either or both of them may exercise their primitive rights and solicit a union with us. They will certainly do no such thing to Great Britain."[15] What was needed, he insisted, was a unilateral declaration by the United States. "It would be more candid, as well as more dignified, to avow our principles explicitly to Russia and France, than to come in as a cock-boat in the wake of the British man-of-war." Here was an opportunity to assert the principles that had been guiding U.S. foreign policy since the founding of the republic. "The answer to be given to Baron van Tuyll, the instructions to Mr. Rush . . . , those to Mr. Middleton at St. Petersburg, and those to the Minister who must be sent to France must all be parts of a combined system of policy and adapted to each other."[16] The perfect vehicle would be the president's upcoming annual address to Congress scheduled for December 2.

On November 13, the secretary of state delivered a draft of the passages on foreign policy to the president. "I find him yet altogether unsettled in his own mind as to the answer to be given to Mr. Canning's proposal and alarmed far beyond anything that I could have conceived possible with the fear that the Holy Alliance are about to restore immediately all South America to Spain. Calhoun stimulates the panic."[17] Following a meeting on November 15, Adams recorded, "Mr. Calhoun is perfectly moon struck by the surrender of Cadiz and says the Holy Allies with ten thousand men will restore all Mexico and all South America to the Spanish dominions."[18] Even if that were so, Adams observed, it would not hold. The urge of peoples to control their own destinies, the desire of the republics for independence, would in the end prove too strong. Indeed, movements for national self-determination were more powerful than even democracy itself. Should it not be the policy of the United States to respect the sovereignty of all nations, especially those in close physical proximity? "Considering the South Americans as independent nations, they themselves, and no other nation had the right to dispose of their condition. We have no right to dispose of them either alone or in conjunction with other nations. Neither have any other nations the right of disposing of them without their consent."[19] This had been the driving force behind the American Revolution; it was the notion sure to garner the support of every American, Adams insisted.

Then, on the seventeenth, Rush from London reported that Canning seemed much less worried about the possibility that the Holy Alliance would dispatch an armada to the New World and was suddenly indifferent as to whether the U.S. accepted his proposal for a joint policy statement. He speculated that the British had extracted some concessions from France following the fall of Cádiz. The secretary of state agreed. "My own opinion is confirmed that the alarm was affected," Adams wrote. "That the object [of Canning's proposal] was to obtain by a sudden movement a premature commitment of the American government against any transfer of the island of Cuba to France or the acquisition of it by ourselves." In truth, Canning had on October 9 compelled the French minister to Britain, the Prince de Polignac, to sign a written pledge that the government of Louis XVIII considered Spain's efforts to regain control of its rebelling colonies as hopeless, and that France would neither send an armed expedition to restore Spain's colonies to it nor "appropriate to herself any part of the Spanish possessions in America."[20] Canning did not show a copy of the Polignac Memorandum to Rush until November 24, eight days before Monroe delivered his famous message. Nevertheless, with his diplomatic intuition, John Quincy had seen the Polignac Memorandum coming since his conversations with Castlereagh when he was minister to the Court of St. James's.

On the afternoon of the eighteenth, van Tuyll called at the State Department with some alarming news. Count Nesselrode, the Russian foreign minister, had issued a circular in which he announced the tsar's enthusiastic approval of the Holy Alliance's recent success in putting down revolutionary movements in Spain, Piedmont, and Naples. It was his intention to guarantee the tranquility "of all the states of which the civilized world is composed."[21] Does this mean that Alexander supports the restoration of Spain's rule of its New World colonies? Adams asked. Yes, van Tuyll replied. But, as Adams well knew, Alexander possessed no navy of any consequence; the Polignac Memorandum, in binding France, blocked the entire Holy Alliance. But the Russian threat could be used as a basis for the United States making its own stand separate from Great Britain.

On the twenty-first the cabinet met yet again to go over a draft of Monroe's message to Congress. Before it could proceed, Adams brought up his conversation with van Tuyll. He declared that it was his intention to make the administration's position crystal clear: "My purpose would be in a moderate and conciliatory manner but with a firm and determined spirit, to declare our dissent from the principles avowed in those communications. To assert those upon which our own government is founded and while disclaiming all intention of attempting to propagate them by force and [while renouncing] all interference with the political affairs of Europe, to declare our expectation and hope that the European powers will equally abstain from the attempt to spread their principles in the American hemispheres or to subjugate by force any part of these continents to their will."[22] Here was the heart of what would become known as the Monroe Doctrine. The president and the rest of the cabinet expressed their hearty approval.

But the cabinet debate over Monroe's forthcoming message to Congress was not over. The sections on foreign policy including the notion of the two spheres, the noncolonization principle, and the concept of mutual noninterference were all included in the draft. But Monroe had added some material; two sections particularly alarmed Adams. "Its introduction was in a tone of deep solemnity and of high alarm," he subsequently recorded in his diary, "intimating that this country is menaced by imminent and formidable dangers such as would probably soon call for their most vigorous energies and the closest union."[23] Monroe's draft denounced France's subjugation of Spain and Portugal and the principles that underlaid the invasion. He not only expressed support for Greece's ongoing rebellion against Turkish rule but declared it his intention to recognize Greek independence. At the time, the Greek struggle to escape the shackles of the Ottoman Empire was even more popular with the American public than the Central and South American revolutions.

In private conversation, Adams pleaded with the president to reconsider. His opening remarks hinted at war with the Holy Alliance; peaceful coexistence must be the great desideratum of the United States, short of an armed invasion of the Americas. And this the Royal Navy would not allow. Formal recognition of the Greek revolutionary government could be regarded in and of itself a casus belli with the Holy Alliance. Recognition would contravene the principle of the two spheres, Adams observed, and run the risk of alienating Great Britain, which still presided over the world's most extensive empire. Were we indirectly inciting India and Britain's other dependencies to rise in revolt? Canning might justly ask. "The ground that I wish to take is that of earnest remonstrance against the interference of the European powers by force with South America but to disclaim all interference on our part with Europe," he declared, "to make an American cause and adhere inflexibly to that." If the Holy Alliance truly intended to dispatch an armada to the New World, "we shall have as much as we can do to prevent them without going to bid them defiance in the heart of Europe."[24]

Monroe relented. His address of December 2 expressed the country's sympathy and support for the Greek revolution but went no further. The aggressive rhetoric regarding the Holy Alliance was toned down. America and Europe were culturally, politically, and historically two separate entities and would remain so. Their two systems were incompatible but could readily coexist. To this end the United States promised not to interfere in the affairs of Europe and expected Europe to follow suit in regard to the New World. Henceforward, North and South America would be considered off-limits to further European colonization. The United States would not force itself on its neighbors, nor interfere with existing colonies, but it would not turn its back on spontaneous movements among people presently colonized to break away and join the United States.

What the Monroe Doctrine did not include was the no-transfer principle. Adams had argued long and hard for it in various cabinet meetings, but his colleagues were unanimous in their opinion that it not be included. It was, however, part of Adams's subsequent response to van Tuyll. Not only would the United States act to prevent further European colonization of the Americas—another rejection of the emperor's ukase of 1821 claiming the Northwest Territory down to fifty-one degrees—but it would also not stand by and see Spain cede any of its existing New World empire to a third party.[25]

The Monroe Doctrine was at one and the same time a reaffirmation of American isolationism and American expansionism. At this point, Adams did not foresee the emergence of a hemispheric community rooted in common principles. "As to an American System," something both Henry Clay and the Abbé Correa were then urging, he had declared to Monroe in 1820, "there is no community of interests or of principles between North and South America."[26] What Adams proposed was to erect a fence around the Western Hemisphere that would prevent further European colonization, a fence that would allow the United States to dominate Spanish and Portuguese America, politically and economically. The United States would inevitably expand into borderlands and islands vital to its security, but it would participate in a confederation of New World states only to the extent necessary to prevent European interference.

Throughout the making of the Monroe Doctrine, the secretary of state's genius at reading the international tea leaves proved crucial. No one knew Europe better than Adams. Calhoun and Attorney General Wirt had expressed some misgivings at the warning Adams had delivered to van Tuyll. Would it not make Russia more militant, more likely to support a French-led invasion of the New World? Not at all, Adams had observed. He knew Alexander intimately. "[T]he Emperor Alexander did not mean to include [the United States] . . . in his invectives against revolutions. . . . [H]e was honestly wedded to his system . . . he was profoundly penetrated with the conviction that he was laboring for the good of his people and for the welfare of mankind." But Adams knew from his conversations with the tsar that he recognized and respected the American Revolution and the republic it had produced. Alexander understood that like any other nation, the United States had the right to secure its frontiers.[27] And in this, of course, Adams was right. Alexander would subsequently come to an agreement on the Northwest Territory that recognized American claims, and he refused to support armed intervention in the Americas by the Holy Alliance.

Adams perceived correctly that Great Britain would not permit the Holy Alliance or any member of it to restore Spain's New World empire. The only thing the Continental powers could tempt London with was Cuba. But Madrid would never agree to part with the Ever-Faithful Isle; the Spanish were at least realistic enough to realize that they had best keep what they had. If the Royal Navy was in fact going to deter the Holy Alliance from invading the Americas, why not just remain silent? Wirt had asked. Because John Bull would get all the credit, Adams declared. "It would throw them [the Latin Americans] completely into her arms, and in the result make them her colonies instead of those of Spain."[28] The Holy Alliance did in fact stay its hand, and in 1824 the Liverpool government formally recognized the independence of Buenos Aires. The other republics would soon be accorded the same status.

The Monroe Doctrine was widely applauded in the United States. Kentuckian John J. Crittenden was typical in his praise. "It has given us a more dignified and heroic attitude," he wrote Monroe. "It has made us the protector of the free governments of South America and arrayed us boldly against any attempts on the part of the Holy Alliance to extend to this hemisphere that despotism and slavery which it has fastened on Europe."[29] Those Latin American officials and newspapers that took notice commented favorably, although it was clearly understood that for the foreseeable future, the Monroe Doctrine would be enforced by the Royal Navy. Public and press opinions in Britain were generally favorable. The *Chronicle* declared Monroe's message "worthy of the occasion and of the people who seem destined to occupy so large a space in the future history of the world."[30] Only George Canning seemed miffed. In 1824 he would see to it that the Polignac Memorandum was published, and he would, during the remainder of his tenure in office, fight tooth and nail to limit Washington's influence with its neighbors to the south.

JOHN ADAMS THE YOUNGER continued to be a cause of concern to his parents throughout 1822 and 1823. Unfortunately, John Quincy and Louisa's middle son, charming and vivacious though he might have been, was headstrong and impressionable. The notorious class of 1823, of which he was a member, continued to make history. In the fall of 1819, President Kirkland had decreed an end to the tradition of holding an off-campus celebration the night before the "Annual Examination." At this point juniors, the class of '23, ignored the order and retired to the Neponset Hotel, situated several miles away from the campus, for an evening of drinking, billiards, bowling, and singing; two days later Kirkland suspended the organizers. Then John and his surviving classmates, infuriated by this perceived injustice and what they considered to be the tyrannical behavior of their tutors, lit a bonfire in Harvard Yard. Shortly afterward, the rebels "met at the 'sign of the golden eagle' on the common at midnight, formed themselves into separate parties, armed themselves with *clubs* and *stones*, and broke [two tutors'] windows and then the windows of the president's study."[31] Not all of John's classmates were born to rebellion. A small group, subsequently named the "Blacks," informed on their peers. Several of the ringleaders, including John, were compelled to appear before a disciplinary committee that penalized them.

"It has given me great pain to learn that you have in the course of the present term exposed yourself to the censure of the government and received a public admonition," John Quincy wrote his son in May 1822. Accusing John of "dissipation and extravagance," he canceled his son's planned summer vacation. "I have made up my mind not to be present at your commencement if at the settling of the lists last before that time, your name shall stand lower than N. 5 in your class."[32] As it turned out, there would be no commencement to attend. In the spring of 1823, the feud between the Blacks and the insurgents came to a head. One of the snitches, coveting the position of Latin orator at the fall commencement ceremonies, informed on his chief rival, a popular young man and a superior scholar. The administration censured the student, whose name was Robinson, and barred him from any place in his class's commencement ceremonies. John and his fellows proceeded to harass and torment the informer, Woodbury by name, and announced that they would boycott classes and continue to demonstrate until justice was done. Thereupon, President Kirkland expelled thirty-seven members of the class of 1823, including young Adams.[33]

It took more than a month after he learned of his son's expulsion from Harvard for John Quincy to gather himself and write. By the time he did, his anger had subsided. "I have written to President Kirkland [pleading for leniency] and hope to hear soon from him in reply—in the meantime I wish to spare you and myself the pain of expressing my feelings on this occasion."[34] When the administration refused to relent, John Quincy invited his errant son to come and live with his family in Washington and act as his personal secretary. In this case, proximity led to fondness. Their shared love of poetry drew them together. John presented his father with a new edition of Lord Byron's *Don Juan*. Inspired, John Quincy, while on board a steamboat to visit his father, wrote a brief poem in the epic mode and dedicated it to John.[35]

So EVENTFUL WERE THE days of John Quincy's second term as secretary of state that he began to worry about his spiritual life. I am "too much absorbed by the world for due devotion to the Lord's Day," he confided to his diary. "I carry too much of the week into the Sabbath and too little of the Sabbath into the week."[36] Exacerbating the problem was the absence of a proper Congregationalist church in the capital. Washington was a Southern city. When the House dared to elect a Unitarian as its chaplain, Episcopal ministers called for a boycott of the man's prayers and sermons. Adams experimented. Episcopalian theology he found tolerable; the church's rituals he did not. He attended a Quaker meeting, which he found to be at the other end of the spectrum. "We sat nearly two hours in perfect silence," he recalled. "No moving of the Spirit, and I seldom in the course of my life passed two hours more wearily. . . . I found myself quite unable to reduce my mind to that musing meditation which forms the essence of this form of devotion."[37]

Neglecting his spiritual life was one thing; abandoning his physical well-being was quite another. Weather permitting, John Quincy accompanied by his long-time manservant, Antoine Guista, continued to bathe at dawn in the Potomac and its tributary Tyber Creek. By this point in his life—Adams turned fifty-six in 1823—he had come to regard swimming as the ultimate form of physical exercise. "The art of swimming ought in my opinion to be taught as a regular branch of education," he wrote. Ever the experimenter, he abandoned his normal attire, which consisted of nothing more than a skullcap and goggles, to swim in various forms of dress. "I went into the river half-clad with pantaloons, drawers, and stockings— by way of experiment. In a swimming school the practice should be taught of swimming entirely clad—of diving and of bearing burdens in the water."[38] As he had in his walks during his earlier years, he stretched himself to the limit, swimming anywhere from thirty minutes to an hour and a half. "Dr. Huntt [the

Adamses' family physician] and all my friends think I am indulging it to excess."[39] In truth, the tide, current, and beds of grass made swimming in the river difficult. In August 1823, John Quincy opted to swim across the Potomac and back. To be on the safe side, Adams decided Antoine would accompany him in a canoe. After being immobilized by seaweed several times, Adams climbed into the boat, and the two found a clear area in which to bathe. "It sometimes occurs to me that this exercise . . . I am now indulging myself in . . . is with the constant risk of life. Perhaps that is the reason why so few persons ever learn to swim."[40]

JOHN QUINCY KNEW INSTINCTIVELY that his wife and political advisers were right; his refusal to actively campaign would probably cost him the presidency. With the contest at a fever pitch in the summer of 1823, Adams began to look to a future outside politics.[41] In July, George Johnson, one of Louisa's cousins, came calling with a business proposition. Johnson was then proprietor of Columbia Mills, a flour mill situated on Rock Creek on the northern outskirts of Washington. Times had recently been hard, he told John Quincy, so much so that he had had to mortgage the property. He owed twenty thousand dollars to the Bank of Columbia; the note was now due, and if he could not come up with the money, he, his wife, and their three young children would be thrown into the street. What Johnson proposed was that John Quincy buy Columbia Mills; all he would have to do was pay off the mortgage and invest ten to twelve thousand dollars in needed renovations. Louisa's cousin asked that he be retained to manage the mill and that he reserve the right to buy back half ownership when he got back on his feet.

Adams was both attracted and repelled by the proposal. A flour mill seemed a safe investment; there would always be a market for the product. When the operation was up and running, it could produce a hundred barrels a day of milled wheat that could then be transported up and down the East Coast. But he would have to sell off a substantial portion of his stock portfolio and mortgage the house on F Street. "I cannot accept [Johnson's proposal] but at great hazard and with deep stakes to myself and my family," he wrote. "But man must trust. Of my motives, I am sure." The latter observation indicated that John Quincy was acting as much out of humanitarian considerations as out of business ones. He, Louisa, George, and Johnson rode out to inspect the property and its machinery. "They are in rather a neglected condition but appear to be a valuable property." As it turned out, Columbia Mills actually belonged to Roger Johnson, George's father. At John Quincy's urging, the Johnson family got its act together, and on August 11, the sale was completed.[42] It would turn out that the secretary of state had acquired a white elephant whose plight was only magnified by George Johnson's continued mismanagement.

In August, John Quincy, Louisa, and George departed for their annual visit to Quincy. They reveled in the modernity of the steamboats that bore them most of the way on their journey. From Boston they made the trip to Quincy by carriage. "[W]e arrived at my father's house, and I was deeply affected at meeting him," Adams recorded in his diary. "Within the last two years since I had seen him, his eyesight has grown dim and his limbs stiff and feeble. He is bowed with age and scarcely can walk across a room without assistance."[43] Buoyed by the reunion, however, John was able to join his son in the days that followed in gamboling over the family's considerable property. Life as a gentleman farmer might not be so bad, John Quincy thought as they walked. His dreams of planting and managing fruit orchards were reawakened.

In Boston, John Quincy arranged for George to complete his third year of legal studies in the offices of Daniel Webster. Significantly, he appointed George as manager of all his property in the Commonwealth of Massachusetts except Quincy—which included a house in Court Street, one in Hancock Street, and three properties on Nassau Street—and various investments, chief of which were in the Mutual Insurance Company, the Neponset Bridge, and the Braintree and Weymouth Turnpike.[44] Among George's instructions was an order to donate a thousand dollars to Harvard toward the construction of an observatory.[45] John Quincy's eldest son would be admitted to the bar in Boston in November 1824.

The Adamses were invited to a magnificent ball at the Waltham estate of China merchant Theodore Lyman. "Miss Lyman is the beauty of this region and her father one of the wealthiest men of Massachusetts or of the Union," John Quincy subsequently wrote in his diary. "It is said he has spent 150,000 dollars upon this country seat which is a little palace; the party was very numerous; the dancing elegant; the music charming; the supper sumptuous." But it was "all magnificent and more princely than Republican," he sniffed.[46]

Back in Washington, John Quincy's rivals for the presidency and their supporters continued to pound him. In early 1824 the ambitious senator from Missouri, Thomas Hart Benton, a rising star in the West, joined with Massachusetts congressman Daniel Webster, still a Federalist at heart, to accuse the secretary of state of thwarting America's manifest destiny.[47] He had abandoned Texas and was then in the process of giving away the Northwest Territory, they charged. Meanwhile, some of Crawford's acolytes had succeeded in uncovering a secret correspondence written in 1804 and 1809 between John Adams and his confidant William Cunningham. The letters comprised a scathing denunciation of Jefferson, Madison, and "American Jacobinism" in general. Did the Republican Party really intend to nominate a member of the Adams tribe to be president of the United States? a pro-Crawford newspaper asked rhetorically.[48] John Quincy had hoped that his famous diatribe against John Bull of July 4, 1821, had put to rest for once and for all the notion that he was still a closet Federalist. The publication of the Cunningham correspondence was a bitter blow.

28

The Election of 1824

B ETWEEN NOVEMBER 1822 AND January 1823, the legislatures of Missouri, Kentucky, and Ohio placed Henry Clay's name in nomination for the presidency. On the opening day of the Eighteenth Congress, the House elected Clay Speaker over the Crawfordite Philip Barbour of Virginia by a vote of 139 to forty-two. Harry of the West voiced his support for the Monroe Doctrine, but together with Congressman Daniel Webster, he lambasted the Monroe administration and especially its secretary of state for not supporting Greek independence. When Webster introduced a resolution calling for recognition of the Greek rebels, the Speaker rose to give it his support. "Sir, has it come to this?" he declared. "Are we so humble, so low, so despicable that we dare not express our sympathy for suffering Greece, lest, peradventure, we might offend some one or more of their imperial and royal majesties? In Greece a million free men were ready to give their lives to throw off the yoke of oriental despotism."[1] Shortly thereafter, the Speaker ran into the Adamses at a Washington social function. "Mr. Clay almost overpowered me with compliments," Louisa subsequently recorded in her diary. "He seems inclined to play the courtier this winter notwithstanding the slander and insidious attacks which appeared a short time previous to his visit."[2] Louisa, still her husband's political hotspur, was moved to disgust. "How much discretion and discernment it requires to be the wife of a great man, and how very difficult to avoid irritating enmity without an appearance of fawning and intrigue which is despicable to the soul of a proud and virtuous woman."[3]

Initially, all of the Republican candidates presented themselves as nationalists—supporters of the Bank of the United States, a moderate tariff, internal improvements, continental expansion, and a strong military. But then, in order to separate himself from the field, William H. Crawford assumed leadership of the Old Republicans—John Randolph of Roanoke, John Taylor of Caroline, and their philosophical descendants. Incredibly, the eccentric Randolph was still a voice in American politics. "Asking one of the states to surrender part of her sovereignty," he declared, "is like asking a lady to surrender part of her chastity."⁴ Crawford touted the virtues of state sovereignty, economy in government, and strict construction of the Constitution. His stance not only reassured the slaveholding South, still alarmed by the restrictions imposed on the expansion of slavery by the Missouri Compromise, but appealed also to Martin Van Buren's version of Northern Republicanism. The New Yorker had successfully assembled a coalition of extreme laissez-faire businessmen, artisans, small farmers, and shop owners of the Northeast who blamed the federal government, and the Bank in particular, for the Panic of 1819. In his role as treasury secretary, Crawford, with the help of his allies in Congress, had cut the budget of Calhoun's War Department to the bone; they even succeeded in ending funding for the system of government-owned and -operated trading posts spreading across the trans-Mississippi West.

Calhoun—dour, cerebral, and intense—represented Republican nationalists in the South. His biggest handicap was his age, then forty-one. Adams was the candidate of the East—New England with some support in states to the south, such as New York and Pennsylvania. Clay, of course, presented himself as the candidate of the West. Like Calhoun and Adams, he was all for an active federal government that would promote the development of a national economy, continue to expand the nation's frontiers, and pursue a strong foreign policy.

The wild card in the campaign was the Hero of New Orleans. Like Adams, Jackson assumed the persona of a devoted public servant who would not actively seek the presidency. "I have no desire, nor do I expect ever to be called to fill the Presidential chair," he declared, but "should this be the case, contrary to my wishes or expectations, I am determined it shall be without any exertion on my part."⁵ In January 1822, the Tennessee General Assembly had voted unanimously to place the general's name in nomination for the presidency. The following year his "friends" secured his election to the U.S. Senate in order for him to be near the center of action. Old Hickory arrived in Washington bearing a special grudge against Crawford and Calhoun for their efforts to have the Monroe administration disown him during his Florida exploits. At this point, Jackson had no formal political organization, but he appealed to a new breed of American voter—the common man. Between 1816 and 1824, a number of states had entered the Union with constitutions providing for adult male suffrage. Several of the older states then followed suit, thus vastly expanding the franchise. For the newly empowered, Jackson—a man of action, a soldier, a leader who made his own rules, an outsider who claimed to stand above political intrigue and special interests—had great appeal. Not surprisingly, the prospect of a Jackson presidency sent shudders through the political elite, whether nationalists or states' righters. "He is one of the most unfit men I know for such a place," Thomas Jefferson observed.[6]

As 1823 drew to a close, Louisa seemed ready to throw in the political towel. "In the eight years of Mr. A's service as Secretary of State, independent of all his former public services, he has done more to establish his fame and to deserve the gratitude of the nation than any man in the country," she wrote George. "In this respect he has little, in fact nothing, to gain [from becoming president] and should he lose the election, which is most likely from present appearances, the disgrace will [fall not on him but] the very enlightened country and people who couldn't discriminate between sterling worth and base intrigue."[7] John Quincy's diary was full of the same pessimism and self-pity. He heaped scorn on his rivals; their intrigues were beneath them. Never would he lower himself to trade favors, flatter, or deceive. Yet he was obsessed with the presidency: the highest office in the land was his destiny; his election would redeem his father and George Washington, both of whom had accepted the call to office from a grateful nation that recognized their selfless service. "Were it possible to look with philosophical indifference to the event [the election], that is the temper of mind to which I should aspire," he confessed to his diary. "But who can hold a fire brand in his hand by thinking of the frosty Caucasus? To suffer without feeling is not in human nature, and when I consider that to me alone of all the candidates before the nation, failure of success would be equivalent to a vote of censure by the nation upon my past service."[8]

As the election year dawned, not many in positions of authority or influence took Andrew Jackson's candidacy seriously. Thus did John Quincy and Louisa, at the urging of young John, decide to try to hitch the general's star to Mr. Adams's wagon by giving a grand ball in honor of his victory at New Orleans. Louisa was at first intimidated by the task that lay ahead; she would have only nineteen days to prepare. John Quincy, who was then thinking of asking Jackson to serve as his running mate, was as enthusiastic as his general disdain for social events would allow. Louisa immediately ordered five hundred invitations from the printer, and she proceeded to personalize them. Word quickly spread through the city that "Mrs. Adams's Ball" would be the event of the social season. Those not on the invitation list besieged the secretary of state and his staff. Eventually upward of a thousand invitations were sent. All members of Congress, excepting two from the House who had abused John Quincy so severely that the Adamses could not tolerate their presence, were included. Adams called upon Monroe personally to invite him and his lady. Monroe, who had scrupulously avoided taking sides in the campaign, declared that he would have to think about it.[9] Louisa had as much of the furniture as possible removed from the house on F Street and relegated John Quincy's study to a closet in the rear of the house. She summoned carpenters to remove all of the interior doors and to erect a series of temporary pillars to support the weight of guests who would congregate on the second floor. John, Mary Hellen, and any friend Louisa could enlist were put to work weaving wreaths and garlands of roses, wintergreen, laurel, and cedar.[10] Louisa even went so far as to hire a Baltimore craftsman to chalk the floors with spread eagles, American flags, and the motto "Welcome to the Hero of New Orleans."

On the evening of January 8, the ninth anniversary of the Battle of New Orleans, the festivities got underway. "We were so busy . . . as to be almost exhausted by the time our company arrived which they began to do at about seven o clock," Louisa later recorded; "during the first hour there came only four ladies, and Mr. A, who is apt to take alarm, began to be uneasy and anxious."[11] He need not have worried. A New York reporter who covered the gala described the scene: "I mingled in the multitude who were literally thronging to Mrs. Adams' party. The city was at that hour in commotion. Carriages were rolling through every street, and the sidewalks were covered with gentlemen on foot all hastening to the same. The street opposite the Secretary's mansion was completely blocked up with carriages waiting their turn to drive to the door." John Quincy, dressed in his daily business attire, and Louisa, in an elaborate gown of her own design, met guests at the door. Company flocked in in such numbers, Charles wrote in his diary, "that they could hardly get through. . . . And it was not till the upper rooms were crowded to suffocation almost, that the lower ones were thrown open."[12] The women of Washington were attired in their best ball gowns and the men in uniforms or evening dress. Adams's spacious office had been cleared for dancing, with music provided by the Marine Band. Louisa was the belle of the ball, moving easily through the crowd, chatting and laughing. "In her manner she unites dignity with an unusual share of ease and elegance," the journalist wrote, "and I never saw her appear to greater advantage than promenading through the rooms winding her way through the multitudes."[13]

The guest of honor arrived around nine. He and the Adamses chatted briefly, and Louisa then proceeded to lead him through the house. "At the approach of such a couple, the crowd involuntarily gave way as far as practicable and saluted as they passed."[14] Shortly thereafter an elaborate supper featuring "natural and candied fruits, pies, sweetmeats, tongues, game . . . prepared in the French style and arranged in the most exquisite taste was served."[15] Jackson departed soon afterward, but the festivities continued well into the wee hours of the morning "Mr. A was so pleased with my success," Louisa celebrated in her diary, "that he joined in a reel with the boys and myself, and you [her grandchildren] would have laughed heartily to see the surprise of our people and the musicians who were the only witnesses of the sport."[16]

In the wake of the fete honoring Old Hickory, one of Adams's supporters asked if the secretary of state was not promoting a rival, a man whose vanity and growing popularity would not permit him to accept second place on the ticket. John Quincy admitted that this was so but declared that it was worth the gamble. Hopefully, the nation would follow the lead of a Savannah, Georgia, paper that called for the election of "The People's Ticket: For President—John Quincy Adams, who can write. For Vice President—Andrew Jackson, who can fight."[17] There needed to be a Westerner on a ticket if it was to be headed by a New Englander. Adams observed in his diary, "If by voting for him as Vice-President my friends should induce others to vote for him as President, they and I must abide by the issue."[18] Jackson and Adams took a hit when it was revealed that the Hero had declared in a letter to a friend that had he been in a position to do so, he would have hanged the organizers of the Hartford Convention. Though he privately agreed, Adams had to protect his home base. The general had spoken in the heat of the moment, Adams declared. "The Vice Presidency is a station where the General can hang no one," Adams told a concerned supporter, "and in which he would need to quarrel with no one. His name and character will serve to restore the forgotten dignity of the place, and it will afford an easy and dignified retirement to his old age."[19]

Adams continued to view Crawford as his principal rival for the presidency. The Georgian's alliance with Van Buren appeared to give him control of Congress. The Treasury's vast patronage, and Crawford's relentless campaign to undermine the Monroe administration and especially its secretary of state from within seemed to place him in an impregnable position. But then the president came within a hair of dismissing his secretary of the treasury after a blowup between the two late in 1823. Incensed that Monroe would not name more of his supporters to government positions, Crawford stormed into the president's office. Secretary of the Navy Samuel L. Southard was present and recorded the scene that followed. "I wish you would not dilly-dally about it any longer," Crawford declared, "but have some mind of your own and decide it so that I may not be tormented with your want of decision." Did you come here to disrespect me? Monroe asked indignantly. "Mr. C. then raised his cane and said—You damned infernal old scoundrel! Mr. M. seized the [fireplace] tongs and ordered him instantly to leave the room" or he would have the servants come and throw him out. Crawford attempted to apologize as he departed, but Monroe would have none of it. The two men never met again during the remainder of Monroe's term, but the president refused to dismiss Crawford from his cabinet.[20]

In September 1823, at the age of fifty-one, Crawford suffered a severe stroke. While he lay partially paralyzed, family and colleagues labored successfully to hide his illness from the public. The Georgian recovered slowly and incompletely. When he felt strong enough to appear in public, he was unable to recognize his friends and colleagues, so impaired was his vision. "He walks slowly, & like a blind man," reported William Plumer. "His feet were wrapped up with two or three thicknesses over his shoes—& he told me they were cold and numb."[21] Despite Crawford's infirmity, the Georgian's friends and supporters carried on with their plans to elevate him to the presidency. On February 24, confident of their control of Congress, they went ahead with plans to convene a congressional caucus in which presumably the majority would nominate Crawford. "The organization of his party is stronger than that of any other candidate," Adams noted in his diary; "there is now the greatest probability that his caucus will succeed."[22]

In January 1824, several Crawfordites had called on Adams: their man was certain to win the approval of the caucus and subsequently the presidency. If the secretary of state would jump on the bandwagon, Crawford would endorse him for the vice presidency. From this vantage, Adams was sure to be next in line to be chief magistrate. Adams strung the Crawford people along even though he subsequently learned that the Georgian's men were offering the same deal to Clay.[23] Then, several days later, one of Calhoun's emissaries proposed an arrangement "by which I should be president, General Jackson as vice president; Clay to be secretary of state, and he himself [Calhoun] secretary of the treasury. . . . It discloses the forlorn hope of Calhoun which is to secure a step of advancement to himself and the total exclusion of Crawford," John Quincy reported to his diary.[24] In many ways Adams's political intuition was as strong as his diplomatic instincts. By early February he had concluded that all of this maneuvering by both Calhoun and Crawford was a sign of desperation rather than strength. Congressman John W. Taylor of New York, an Adams confidant and go-between, met with the secretary of state the last week in January. "I told Taylor that my mind was made up," Adams recorded in his diary. "I was satisfied there was at this time a majority of the whole people of the United States and a majority of the states utterly averse to a nomination by congressional caucus, thinking it adverse to the spirit of the Constitution and tending to corruption. I thought it so myself and therefore would not now accept a congressional caucus nomination even for the presidency. And, of course, a nomination for the vice-presidency in co-operation with one for Mr. Crawford as President have no charms for me."[25] When the congressional caucus convened on February 24, only sixty-six of the two hundred forty congressmen and senators showed up, thus dispelling the myth that Crawford's forces controlled the legislative branch. This would be the last presidential caucus held in the United States.[26]

The presidential election of 1824 took place in the midst of a radical change in the way Americans (that is, white male Americans) elected their chief executive. Initially, presidential electors had been chosen by state legislators, but the move toward greater democracy changed that. By 1824, eighteen of the twenty-four states had decreed that their electors had to be chosen by popular vote. With this change came the custom that electors declared their preferences for president and vice president ahead of time rather than reserving their rights of personal judgment. Nineteen states had decided to cast their electoral votes as a block, but five, including New York, had opted for a proportional system whereby a candidate would receive the vote of the elector who had been chosen by his congressional district (electoral votes were then allotted on the number of congressional districts in a given state).[27]

Adams and the other candidates recognized early on that with so many aspirants in the field, the election was likely to be thrown into the House of Representatives, where each state delegation would have one vote. As Jackson's campaign took off in late 1823, this became an ever-more-certain possibility. In 1824 it was still considered unseemly for presidential candidates to make speeches, appear at rallies, or participate overtly in other ways in their own campaigns. But the five horses in the race differed widely in what they considered acceptable. For most, Crawford's machinations, especially his use of federal patronage and his favor trading, seemed beyond the pale. But political organization, in and of itself, passed the respectability test, and the Adams machine was one of the most active and effective. The secretary of state was one of the first to employ the device of a campaign biography. In 1819, John Quincy's friend Joseph Hall, editor of the *Port Folio*, published an admiring sketch of the nation's chief diplomat. The piece had actually been written by John Quincy with the help of his father. In 1824 the admiring account of Adams's life was printed in the *Baltimore American*.[28] The secretary of state, with a limited number of positions at his command, played the patronage game as best as he could, offering diplomatic posts abroad to Calhoun and Clay, both of whom politely refused. He suggested dangling an ambassadorship before Jackson, but Monroe initially balked. He would have the United States embroiled in a feud with the country to which he was accredited within weeks. But the president eventually relented. Old Hickory was offered Mexico but turned it down.[29] Adams told DeWitt Clinton, still a powerful force in New York politics, that in his opinion Clinton was fit to fill any foreign post to which he might aspire. One thing was certain, John Quincy declared: if he were elected, the continued support of the Empire State "would be so vitally necessary to me that my course must be shaped by that consideration."[30]

A group of Adams supporters, including port collectors, postmasters, state legislators, lawyers, judges, and editors, established a committee of correspondence to coordinate their activities. The bulk came from Massachusetts, New York, and Pennsylvania, but there were Adams activists in all of the states. The machine succeeded in having three state legislatures—Massachusetts, Maine, and Rhode Island—place Adams's name in nomination.[31] The author of "the Macbeth Policy" ("If chance will have me King, why, chance may crown me / Without my stir") established a press network that rivaled that of any of his competitors.[32] His friends purchased the *Washington National Journal*, which covered the secretary of state's activities and passed on glowing accounts to the *New York American*, the *Philadelphia National Gazette*, and the *Baltimore American*. Defending Adams became a kind of campaign in itself, an endeavor in which John Quincy participated personally with gusto, most notably in his confrontation with Jonathan Russell. The previously retiring secretary of state became a virtual social butterfly, attending three different church services every Sunday, accepting numerous ball invitations, and receiving hundreds of visitors both at the State Department and on F Street.[33]

In June 1824 supporters of Adams and Crawford decided to stage a seagoing race that would begin at the northernmost tip of Maine and end at New Orleans. A reporter from the *Boston Patriot* described the scene. "The *Adams* was a barge beautifully adorned with paintings emblematical of the wars and successive victories of the United States. . . . John Quincy Adams was [depicted] presenting the treaty of Ghent to John Bull. The vessel was propelled by eight banks of oars. The Stars and Stripes waved from the stern while on the prow Neptune was portrayed calming his minions. An old patriot of '76 [was] seated as cockswain with a merchant and farmer on his left and right." The *Crawford* was a gigantic barge carved in the image of an Indian war canoe. It featured twenty-four banks of oars. From its prow hung a standard with the motto "States' Rights" emblazoned in Latin. "Her prow was a double-faced image half Indian and half white woman. . . . William H. Crawford [was depicted] seated on a pile of deer skins and worn-out moccasins."[34] Needless to say, the elaborate campaign vessels never cleared the coast of New England.

A New England Federalist called to inform Adams that Crawford was courting him and his fellows with a vengeance and that he was succeeding because Federalists there and everywhere feared that they would be totally excluded from power if Adams were elected. "Personally the Federalists had done me wrong," John Quincy declared, but "if it should be the pleasure of the people of the United States that I should serve them as their president, I should be the president not of a section, or of a faction, but of the whole Union." However, if the burgeoning Federalist opposition to his candidacy did not stand down, it would be almost impossible to ask his Republican supporters to acquiesce in the appointment of any of their number to high office should he be elected.[35] None other than Daniel Webster called on Adams, seeking assurance that Federalist luminaries like Jeremiah Mason would be given their due. Adams assured Webster that he thought well of Mason but that it was not his practice to "sell the skin before the animal was taken."[36] "My own hopes, at present, are strong that Mr. Adams will pursue an honorable, liberal, magnanimous policy," Webster subsequently wrote Mason.[37]

On the issues, Adams took care to have it known that he was an early and consistent supporter of internal improvements. When Pennsylvania manufacturers and South Carolina planters asked his position on the tariff (the former supported taxes on imports; the latter did not), Adams declared that he favored a moderate tariff—one that would protect American manufacturers but not cripple producers of raw materials. When pressed by Northern Free-Soilers and Southern and Western slave owners to state his position on the institution of human bondage, he evaded. When pressed to the wall, Adams told a Western slave state politician that he "had been against the proposed restriction [of slavery] in Missouri as contravening both the Constitution and the Louisiana Treaty."[38] It was his position that the citizens of the individual states and territories ought to be able to decide whether to be free or slave without the interference of the federal government.

Despite his paean to state sovereignty, Adams was the only alternative for antislavery activists. During his second term as secretary of state, he had given them some reason for hope. On December 21, 1822, in the wake of the Denmark Vesey slave uprising, the South Carolina legislature had passed the Negro Seamen's Act. It stipulated that those Black sailors working on commercial vessels entering Charleston or any other of the state's ports had to be imprisoned during the vessel's stay. The captain of the ship on which they served would be forced to pay for their upkeep; if they did not, the Black seamen would be sold into slavery. The slave power in South Carolina was convinced that free Blacks by example and action were provoking their enslaved brethren to rebel. They considered visiting mariners of color—worldly, independent, and prosperous—as a special threat. In the wake of passage of the Negro Seamen's Act, the Monroe administration was deluged with howls of protests from domestic and foreign shipowners and their governments. If enforced against free Blacks of other states, the Seamen's Act would have violated the equal protection clause of the Constitution. If against British shipowners and sailors, it would have contravened the Anglo-American commercial agreement of 1815, which guaranteed unrestricted access to each nation's ports by the other.

Adams was appalled on both moral and diplomatic grounds. The measure, he argued to the cabinet, was clearly unconstitutional, and the Justice Department must intervene. He applauded when a shipowner sued on behalf of one of his imprisoned sailors and won his case. The presiding federal district judge did in fact rule the measure unconstitutional. State authorities, however, declared that the court had no jurisdiction: the matter was for state and local authorities to decide. Visiting Black seamen continued to be jailed.[39] Following his election as president, John Quincy would openly condemn the Negro Seamen's Act. When one of South Carolina's two senators approached him to request that he say something "soothing" to the state, Adams replied that "the Legislature of South Carolina itself had put it out of my power to say anything soothing to the South . . . by persisting in a law which a Judge of the Supreme Court of the United States, himself a native and inhabitant of South Carolina, had declared to be in direct violation of the Constitution."[40]

Antislavery forces were interested in the rights of free Blacks but still more concerned with the burgeoning international slave trade. When George Canning became foreign minister in 1822, he had taken up his predecessor's crusade on behalf of an international convention authorizing the warships of the signatories to seize slavers wherever they were to be found on the high seas. Adams had been adamant: "Unless Britain will bind herself by an article as strong and explicit as language can make it never again in time of war to take a man from an American vessel, we never for a moment can listen to a proposal for allowing for such a search in time for peace."[41]

In 1824, John Quincy still believed that his lifelong defense of neutral rights, especially his opposition to impressment, was one of his strongest political credentials. But the tide was beginning to turn. Anti–slave trade sentiment had always been strong in parts of the North and the East; a pact outlawing the international commerce in chattel also appealed to some Southerners hoping to salve their consciences. A slave trade convention had the indirect support of members of the American Colonization Society, including William Crawford. The ACS had acquired Liberia to provide a haven for both free Blacks in the United States and chattel seized aboard slave ships. In April 1822 a committee of the House of Representatives had passed a resolution urging the administration to negotiate with one or more of the maritime powers a slave trade treaty that allowed a restricted and reciprocal right of visit and search for the sole purpose of suppressing the slave trade. Then, on February 28, 1823, the House had voted 131 to nine to recommend to the executive negotiations with the maritime powers "for the effectual abolition of the African slave trade and its ultimate denunciation as piracy under the law of nations."[42]

What was Adams to do? In a letter to George, he recalled advice his father had given him when he, John Quincy, was serving in the Senate: "Your intention to act and vote according to your own sense of right even at the hazard of losing your popularity is right, but you must also be careful to avoid taking the side which is both unpopular and wrong; and if the popular sentiment be strong and urgent, you should reconsider your own impressions whether they may not be erroneous."[43] The slave trade was manifestly wrong and now apparently its abolition was more popular than the age-old U.S. campaign against the practice of visit and search. But for Adams a reversal of such a long-taken and fervently held course was not easy. He needed a way out. He found it in the notion that the slave trade should be labeled as piracy, which was already universally outlawed, its perpetrators subject to execution. Pirates were the enemies of all nations, miscreants with whom they were at perpetual war. A limited right of visit and search would therefore be exercised in a time of war, not peace. Adams and defenders of neutral rights could have their cake and eat it too.

Matters quickly moved to a resolution—or so it seemed. In London, U.S. minister Rush and William Huskisson, president of the Board of Trade, concluded the Slave Trade Convention of March 13, 1824. Both signatories agreed that the citizens and subjects of their respective nations caught participating in the slave trade were to be deemed pirates, and that the Royal Navy and U.S. warships had the right to stop and search suspicious vessels. If they were found to be slavers, the ship, captain, and crew would be sent to the country of their flag to be tried. The officers of both navies should go to every length to see the practice of search and seizure would be conducted with the utmost care.[44] Adams and Monroe were virtually certain of Senate approval, given its previous resolutions. But suddenly Crawford turned into a champion of free ships make free goods and the archenemy of impressment. Southern Senators and Crawford's Northern allies did not have the votes to defeat the treaty outright, so they amended it to death. An embittered Adams concluded that the whole affair had been a scheme by Crawford to deny him the presidency. In his diary: "The eager lookout of my political opponents at this moment [is] for anything that may serve as a missile weapon against me."[45]

THE ADAMS CAMPAIGN TOOK another hit in the summer of 1824. John B. Colvin, a disgruntled former State Department employee who had been dismissed some years before, published an article in the *Washington City Gazette* chastising John Quincy for his role in the "Moulton affair." Unable to pay her rent, Mary Moulton, Louisa's hatmaker, had gone to the Adamses for help. Her furniture had been seized by her landlord, and she faced eviction. John Quincy agreed to sign a note promising to make good if Mrs. Moulton was not able to make her next payment. When she could not, the landlord came to F Street and presented Adams with a bill, not for the fifteen dollars Mary said she owed but for $187.50. John Quincy lost his temper and kicked the man out of his house. That worthy then went to the press. Responding to inquiries, Adams denounced the man as a liar and a cheat. The *City Gazette* declared that the secretary of state's behavior was "highly immoral, if not positively dishonest," and that he proved on that occasion that "he is a man of an arrogant and quarrelsome temper, prone to altercations, and vehement and intemperate in his discourse upon little or no provocation." Anti-Adams papers all across the country joined the chorus.[46] Particularly galling to Louisa was the implication in some press accounts that her hatmaker and her husband were having an affair. "Mrs. Moulton is said to be a bad character, and it is thought that there is a desire to make it appear that your father did 'not give the note for nothing,'" she complained to Charles.[47]

One of the advantages that John Quincy had over the other candidates in the 1824 election was that he was both the son of a Founding Father and, arguably, a Founding Father himself. He would benefit immensely, although indirectly, from a fourteen-month-long visit by the Marquis de Lafayette that began in the late summer of 1824. The Hero of Two Revolutions came at the invitation of both houses of Congress. The "Guest of the Nation" had just been ousted as a member of the Chamber of Deputies by an ultraroyalist candidate, and he had fallen on hard times. Lafayette, whose son was named after George Washington, was greeted as no other foreign guest had ever been. Citizens of every faction, section, and class turned out to welcome him. After attending dinners at the White House and other venues in Washington, the general, his son, and his private secretary set out on a tour of the Northern and Mid-Atlantic states, where he was wined and dined by state and local officials. While the marquis was in Washington, the Adamses were constant guests at functions honoring him; at each, the Revolutionary War hero paid the secretary of state marked attention. Returning from a visit to Quincy, Adams encountered the famous Frenchman in Philadelphia. "Called this morning before breakfast again upon General La Fayette," he recorded in his diary on October 2. "He had not risen but a few minutes after sent me word he was rising and wished to see me. I went immediately and found him in his bedchamber, dressing."[48] During the Frenchman's visit, America seemed to momentarily forget its divisions and animosities, and reveled in memories of the glorious birth of the nation. Here was a political vein that Adams supporters could tap into, and they did so with gusto.[49]

The final stages of the 1824 presidential campaign focused on which of the five candidates would secure enough electoral votes to be one of the three presented to the House of Representatives. In those days the Electoral College convened not in Washington to cast their ballots but in their respective state capitals. As news of outcomes in various states trickled in during the winter of 1824, it eventually became clear that Andrew Jackson had won both the popular and the electoral votes. Jackson's tally stood at 152,901 (42.5 percent), Adams 114,023 (31.5 percent), Clay 47,217 (13 percent), and Crawford 46,979 (13 percent). The electoral vote stood at Jackson ninety-nine, Adams eighty-four, Crawford forty-one, and Clay thirty-seven. Jackson had denied Clay his beloved West, and his support in the South cut into Crawford's standing with the Old Republicans. But Jackson owed his victory to the three-fifths clause in the Constitution. If the general hadn't had the "slave vote," Adams would have won with eighty-three electoral votes to Jackson's seventy-seven.[50] But none of the candidates had garnered a majority, so the election was thrown to the House of Representatives to decide among the top three vote getters.

The Congress that would elect the next president of the United States convened in December 1824. Because he controlled the votes of at least three states—Kentucky, Missouri, and Ohio—and because he was Speaker of the House, Clay saw himself, with some justification, as kingmaker. In letters written a year before the election, Harry of the West had made it clear that if he were not one of the final three, he would support Adams. Jackson was out of the question, with Crawford only a little less so. Despite their past differences, Clay considered the New Englander by far the most meritorious of the three finalists—by experience, by judgment, and by vision. In truth, Clay and Adams saw eye to eye on nearly all of the major issues of the day—internal improvements, the tariff, an active and powerful federal government, future continental expansion, and even U.S. policy toward Latin America.[51] But the Kentuckian was determined to have assurances on both policy matters and his own future role in government.

On December 17, Robert P. Letcher, a congressman from Kentucky and an intimate of Henry Clay, called upon the secretary of state. Following some small talk, Letcher asked Adams bluntly what his sentiments toward Clay were. Adams responded that he was certain that the Speaker had been the driving force behind Jonathan Russell's attacks, but as they had been thoroughly discredited, Adams bore the Kentuckian no animosity. Most of Clay's supporters, Letcher asserted, believed that the Russell affair had been a mistake and that Clay now regretted it. The gist of the congressman's message, Adams later recalled in his diary, was "that Clay would willingly support me if he could thereby serve himself, and the substance of his meaning was that if Clay's friends could know that he would have a prominent share in the administration, that might induce them to vote for me even in the face of instructions [from their state legislatures not to support Adams]."[52] In a subsequent encounter, Letcher informed Adams that instructions had come from the Kentucky legislature to cast the state's vote for Jackson, but that would not matter. The Kentucky congressional delegation would do what Clay told them to do.[53]

At a congressional dinner to honor Lafayette held in early January at Williamson's Hotel, virtually every one of political importance was a guest, including Monroe and the three candidates. During the festivities, Clay spied the two chief rivals for the presidency sitting near the fireplace with a single chair separating them. Adams was his usual dour self and Jackson seemed ill at ease. Harry of the West took the intervening seat and declared in a loud voice, "Well, gentlemen, since you are both so near the chair, but neither can occupy it, I will slip in between you and take it myself!"[54] Neither the soldier nor the diplomat joined in the general laughter that followed. Later Clay pulled Adams aside and told him "that he should be glad to have with me soon some confidential conversation upon public affairs. I said I should be happy to have it whenever it might suit his convenience," Adams recorded in his journal. On January 8, Clay wrote Francis Blair, a Kentucky friend, that he realized that many of his constituents favored Jackson because he was a Westerner, but that "the election of the General would give to the military spirit a stimulus and a confidence that might lead to the most pernicious results." By contrast in "the election of Adams we shall not by the example inflict any wound upon the character of our institutions."[55]

Clay called at F Street on the evening of January 9, and the two men got down to business. He had, since his arrival in Washington, been besieged by supporters of the three candidates to be voted on in the House, Clay said. While Adams's supporters went out of their way to make it clear that they were acting on their own, friends of Mr. Crawford had been so blatant in offering bribes "that it disgusted him." The Speaker declared that his preference was for the secretary of state but that he "wished me as far as I might think proper to satisfy him with regard to some principles of great public importance but without any personal considerations for himself."[56] Several days later Missouri congressman John Scott, who would alone cast his state's vote in the House, visited Adams. "He spoke of himself as being entirely devoted to Mr. Clay and of his hope that he would be a member of the next administration." Adams replied that he could not be specific, but that if he were elected with the aid of the West, the preeminent representative of that region would surely be entitled to a powerful place.[57]

News that Kentucky would cast its vote for John Quincy Adams broke on January 24, 1825, throwing Congress into an uproar. Representative Robert Y. Hayne of South Carolina declared, "We are in commotion about the monstrous union between Clay & Adams for the purpose of depriving Jackson of the votes of the Western states where nine tenths of the people are decidedly in his favor."[58]

(Not true.) Clay was committing political suicide, Martin Van Buren declared. "I received this morning an anonymous letter from Philadelphia threating organized opposition and civil war if Jackson is not chosen," Adams confided to his diary.[59] Daniel P. Cook, the House's sole member from Illinois, knew that his constituents were leaning toward the Hero, but he was a protégé of Adams. In early February two pro-Jackson congressmen called on Cook. "It's time for you to make your stand," declared George McDuffie of South Carolina. "If you do so, you can settle the question in Jackson's favor. There is no doubt that an arrangement has been made between Mr. Clay and Mr. Adams to transfer Clay's influence to him. Clay to be made secretary of state for doing so. It is in your power to defeat it."[60] Cook refused to commit, and when the final vote came, he went for John Quincy in what would be the last act of his public career.

Adams would need Missouri to win; he thought Clay could deliver, but John Scott wanted something for himself. "An application has been made to the President," Scott told the secretary of state, "for the removal of my brother as Judge in the Territory of Arkansas because he killed his colleague . . . in a duel."[61] Adams let Scott know that Monroe would not take any action during the few days he had left in office. Scott voted for Adams. After he became president, John Quincy submitted Judge Scott's name to the Senate for another four-year term. That body turned it down, but Adams had paid his debt.

The vote to elect the next president of the United States was scheduled for the second Wednesday in February. As the final hours before the tally ticked away, it appeared that Adams's fate lay with New York. Stephen Van Rensselaer, an old Federalist and relative by marriage of Alexander Hamilton, had been chosen to cast the state's vote in the House. He disliked Adams personally and had promised Van Buren he would support Crawford. But on the day he arrived in the capital, Webster and Clay cornered him. Adams would not persecute former Federalists, Webster declared. Jackson's election would create political and social chaos, an appeal that resonated with Van Rensselaer, whose estate was one of the largest in New York. The old gentleman swung back and forth. A colleague found him "in tears literally."[62] According to Van Buren's *Autobiography*, while the tally was underway, Van Rensselaer laid his head on his desk and mouthed a brief prayer, a request for a sign. When he opened his eyes, there on the floor lay a ballot with Adams's name on it. Joyfully he picked it up and put it in New York's ballot box.

At high noon the members of the Senate assembled to count the electoral ballots. As expected, John C. Calhoun was chosen vice president, but neither Crawford, Jackson, nor Adams had a majority. Attention then turned to the House. Clay took the Speaker's chair and ordered a roll call. State delegations seated themselves in the order in which they would be called, north to south along the Atlantic Seaboard and then south to north along the Mississippi. John Quincy Adams was elected on the first ballot with thirteen votes to Jackson's eleven and Crawford's four. The New Englander had carried his native region plus Missouri, Ohio, and Kentucky—all delivered by Clay—and Louisiana, Maryland, and Illinois, which Adams had pried away from Crawford.[63] With the tally completed, Clay turned to the assembled legislators and declared, "John Quincy Adams of Massachusetts, having received a majority of the votes of all the states of this Union, was duly elected President of the United States for four years to commence on the fourth of March, 1825."[64] Adams's supporters erupted in applause while the Jackson and Crawford men sat in stunned silence. "May the blessing of God rest upon the event of this day!" John Quincy exclaimed in his diary.[65]

All of Massachusetts, which had gone overwhelmingly for its second-favorite son, had been waiting expectantly for news of the election. It arrived by mail around midnight on February 13. Boston erupted; citizens poured into the streets and organized an impromptu torchlight parade. News reached Quincy around three in the morning. John Adams at once took pen in hand: "Never did I feel so much solemnity as on this occasion. The multitude of my thoughts and the intensity of my feelings are too much for a mind like mine in its ninetieth year," he wrote his son. "May the blessing of God Almighty continue to protect you to the end of your life as it has heretofore protected you in so remarkable a manner from your cradle!"[66]

The evening of the election, the Monroes held their last drawing room. All of the candidates and most of Congress were in attendance. All eyes turned to Old Hickory. As the people's choice and the House's choice approached each other, the assembled guests held their collective breath. The general had a lady on his arm. "How do you do, Mr. Adams?" Jackson asked with equanimity. "I give you my left hand for the right, as you see, is devoted to the fair. I hope you are very well, sir."

"Very well, Sir," responded Adams. "I hope General Jackson is well."[67] Clay was also in attendance, parading about with a fashionable lady hanging on each arm. "The villain," exclaimed one Jacksonian. Another pointed out Adams and declared, "There is our 'Clay President,' and he will be molded at that man's will and pleasure as easily as clay in a potter's hands."[68]

The day following, a congressional committee headed by Daniel Webster called at F Street and officially informed John Quincy of his election. According to one bystander, Adams was sweating profusely and trembling noticeably. He had reason. He was, setting aside the three-fifths clause, a minority president. In his written reply to the committee, Adams declared that "could my refusal to accept the trust thus delegated to me give an immediate opportunity to the people to form and to express with a nearer approach to unanimity the object of their preference, I should not hesitate to decline the acceptance of this eminent charge. . . . But the Constitution itself has not so disposed of the contingency which would arise in the event of my refusal."[69]

Adams sensed that the political tide in the country over which he was to preside was turning. It was no longer a nation that would defer to its natural aristocracy. The new chief executive believed that the "people," most of whom were uneducated and uninformed, were ripe for political demagogues—descendants of the American Jacobins—who would resort to any tactic, tell any lie in their obsession to overthrow the established order. His son Charles was astounded that a man like his father could win the presidency in 1825. "The people are more judges of external than internal merit and more led by the winning graces of a flattering demagogue than by the more esteemed and severe character of the unbending statesman," he observed in his diary.[70] In the wake of Adams's election, Kentuckian Richard M. Johnson, a Jackson supporter, confided to the editor of the *National Intelligencer* that "as for this administration, we will turn them out as sure as there is a God in heaven. . . . By the eternal if they act as pure as the angels that stand at the right hand of the throne of God, we'll put them down."[71] Samuel Ingram, a Calhoun-turned-Crawford supporter, predicted that Adams's election "would produce two parties in this country," one supporting the administration and another born out of Southern distrust of the New Englander on the slavery issue, Western anger at Jackson's defeat, and the ambitions and machinations of Martin Van Buren.[72] He proved to be prescient.

29

"Liberty Is Power"

A T AROUND ELEVEN THIRTY on March 4, inauguration day, John Quincy left his house on F Street. Accompanied by several companies of militia and a crowd of citizens, he proceeded to the Capitol. In his carriage were Secretary of the Navy Southard and Attorney General Willard Wirt, a clear indication that the two men would be kept on in their posts. Following behind were President Monroe and his entourage. The once and future presidents arrived at the Capitol and entered the Senate Chamber, where John C. Calhoun was presiding. He immediately adjourned the body; he, his colleagues, and the members of the Supreme Court then retired to the House, where John Quincy was sworn in. His inaugural address was relatively free of the rhetorical flourishes so beloved by the former Boylston Professor. It was a dignified call for national unity; the "baneful weed of partisanship" had died out in America, Adams proclaimed. The nation's first half century had been "a time of trial," but it had survived and thrived. "We the People" faced a rare opportunity in which citizens north, south, east, and west had an opportunity to reconcile their differences under a government devoted to national unity. If the nation continued its westward expansion, continued to support internal improvements, and committed itself to public education and scientific research, America's greatness would know no bounds. He acknowledged that he was a minority president, which, he said, made it even more incumbent on him to govern on behalf of all the people. Andrew Jackson was among the first to step forward and offer his hand.[1]

CHARLES ADAMS WAS PLEASED with his father's election, not only because he thought it was deserved, but because it meant the family would be based in the capital—the South—for at least four more years. His greatest fear in the run-up was that he might "lose sight of Washington for years and perhaps for life. I may never see more [of] that place in which I have spent the very happiest passages of my youthful years . . . it appears more like the fairy land to me in which so many of our pleasant dreams are situated."[2] So much a warm-blooded Southerner did Charles consider himself that he would adhere to the code duello under certain circumstances. "My passions are not things . . . to be trifled with," he declared, "for if excited to a very high degree, it might cost my antagonist and myself our life."[3]

Following an unsuccessful first two years at Harvard, Charles would settle down and earn a respectable rank in his class by the time he graduated. During his last two years, his dissatisfaction with Harvard was rooted in educational rather than in cultural or social concerns. It seemed that Kirkland and the Board of Overseers could not decide, Charles observed, whether the college would continue to be a training school for young boys or a genuine institution of higher learning.[4]

Surveying his family in 1824, Charles recognized that if any of the Adams boys were going to carry on with the family tradition of distinguished public service, it would probably be him. John he continued to find charming and entertaining but as substantial as a leaf in a strong wind. George drove him to despair. While Charles was at Harvard and George was studying law in Boston in Daniel Webster's office, the two saw much of each other. "I cannot think as highly of him as I do of John," Charles confided to his diary. "I cannot but despise the weak points in his character. . . . I wish him a happy life and a distinguished course, but I fear for him. He is not swayed by that high and immutable sense of pride and honor which ought to be the first characteristic of a great man."[5] Grudgingly, Charles acknowledged that his father was the family sun around which all other planets revolved, and this seemed to be a special problem for his elder brother. "George knows nothing of the character of my father," he wrote. "He does not appreciate it and cannot look upon him with anything but fear."[6]

For his part, Charles was not intimidated by his father, but he struggled to understand him. That John Quincy in his private life could be as impetuous, passionate, and romantic as Charles's grandfather seemed to have escaped him. "He is the only man, I ever saw, whose feelings I could not penetrate. . . . I can study his countenance forever and very seldom can find any sure guide by which to move. . . . He makes enemies by perpetually wearing the Iron Mask." Charles would be the only one of the three brothers whose ego would be able to withstand the expectations of their father. "I rather think that he does not understand me and that he underrates me," he confided to his diary. "To myself, I can speak with freedom, and as it is useless for me to try to persuade myself that I am destitute of abilities." He was not, he promised, going to drive himself to distraction trying to prove that he was someone he could never be.[7]

In August 1824, while Charles was trying resolutely to apply himself to his studies, he received letters from his mother and his brother John that alarmed him. "There is something going on at Washington to the bottom of which I cannot see. And I receive dark and mysterious hints about the matter in every letter upon the subject of family affairs."[8] At issue was the fickleness of the teenage siren who lived with the Adamses, Mary Catherine Hellen, Louisa's niece. In 1823 she had become betrothed to George, but when John was kicked out of Harvard and came to live with the family in Washington, she transferred her affections to him. Then, when Charles visited during the winter break of 1823–1824, Mary began flirting with him. He was not impressed. "She has some alluring ways which are apt to make every man forget [himself], but she is not what she was, and I have had too hard a trial to think of ever wishing to endure the same [an attachment to Mary]. George . . . fortunately . . . is not with us. . . . [He] would be in a perfect fever and sickness if he was to imagine that she had encouraged me in the least."[9]

In truth, by this point, George Washington Adams was languishing for a variety of reasons, only one of which was his betrothed's fickleness. In 1825 he had finished reading law in the offices of Daniel Webster. Though he dreamed of writing a great epic poem, the eldest Adams son dutifully opened a law office at 10 Court Street; he continued to board with the Welshes. That year, at his father's insistence, George began to keep a diary. It would, John Quincy admonished him, bring a sense of order and discipline to his life. Alas, the journal, which spanned just three months, did not accomplish that goal. Gorge idled away his time in Quincy with his grandfather, whom he continued to adore. He neglected his law practice; the simplest tasks seemed insurmountable. A trip to the bank proved impossible. He forgot the form he needed, returned to his office, and on the way back to the bank got a cinder in his eye. Instead of proceeding, he returned home and took a two-hour nap. George's diary reveals a sensitive, gentle soul proceeding through life without direction, a prisoner of his parents' expectations. On one occasion, as George returned to Boston from Quincy, his carriage horse went lame, not an unusual occurrence. The young man slowed the pace, but the beast's suffering troubled him. "It was impossible," he wrote "to witness the animal suffering without becoming deeply depressed."[10]

Like most young men, George fantasized about women; unfortunately, he lacked his brother John's self-confidence. During his visits to Washington, George convinced himself that the flirtatious Mary Hellen and he were meant for each other. In 1823, he asked for his father's permission to propose. He assured John Quincy that the marriage would not take place until his law practice flourished.

Reluctantly, his father gave his consent. But during the next three years, George visited Washington only intermittently, and he wrote infrequently. Meanwhile, Mary openly flirted with John and then Charles. When the family gathered in September 1824 for dinner at Peacefield, Louisa urged Charles to help terminate the engagement. In his conversation with his brother, Louisa instructed, he should give the connection a "preposterous and ridiculous turn"—the relationship was without substance and should be ended.[11] And so it was that George and Mary's nuptials died aborning. In August 1825 the eldest son ceased keeping his diary. "I close the year in melancholy feeling," he wrote. "Its course cannot meet approval from a strict and scrutinizing conscience."[12]

ON FEBRUARY 18, 1825, Clay formally accepted President Adams's invitation to be his secretary of state. By this point Jackson's supporters had convinced him that he had been cheated out of the election. "So you see," the Hero of New Orleans declared, "the Judas of the West has closed the contract and will receive the thirty pieces of silver; his end will be the same. Was there ever witnessed such a bare faced corruption in any country before?"[13] The emerging anti-Adams coalition smelled blood. "The . . . profligacy with which this second Burr [Clay] sells himself and attempts to dispose of the people of the West like a drove of swine has excited contempt as well as abhorrence and disgust," opined the *Columbian Observer*.[14] "They will abuse me for it [accepting State]," Clay had observed to a friend. "They would have abused me more if I had declined it." The appointment was natural and expected; if he had said no, Clay asserted, it would leave the impression that he had something to feel guilty about; having contributed significantly to Adams's election, how could he refuse to be part of his administration? His presence would provide "balance."[15] In truth, the partnership was more than personal and philosophical; it was meant to signify a new ruling alliance between the East and the West.

Still determined to be seen as the president of the whole people, Adams chose his cabinet to reflect various sections and philosophies, including those diametrically opposed to his own. He first offered the Treasury Department to Virginian James Barbour, a Crawfordite who opposed both the tariff and internal improvements. Fortunately, he turned down the post, and Adams then convinced Richard Rush of Philadelphia, a longtime supporter who was then serving as minister to the Court of St. James's, to take the job. Adams had already made it clear that he intended to keep Monroe loyalists Southard and Wirt on. Incredibly, Adams elected to retain John McLean as postmaster general. He was the opposite of Wirt, every inch an aspiring and conspiring politician. An active partisan of

Crawford and then Jackson, McLean would use his control over a vast patronage network to appoint to office the personal and political enemies of the president. When presented with evidence of McLean's perfidy, Adams responded, "I see yet no reason sufficient to justify a departure from the principle with which I enter upon the Administration," Adams declared, "of removing no public officer for merely preferring another candidate for the presidency."[16]

Adams, like Monroe abhorred the whole notion of patronage, but he was swimming against the tide. States such as New York and Pennsylvania had been moving toward a "spoils system" (to the victor belong the spoils) for some time. In 1820 Congress had attempted to nationalize the practice by passing the Tenure of Office Act, which limited the terms of most middle- and upper-level federal officials. Adams stubbornly renominated virtually every individual who had held office under his predecessor. The new chief executive declared that "the principle of change or rotation in office at the expiration of these commissions . . . would make the Government a perpetual and unremitting scramble for office."[17] Clay thought the president naive: "[N]o officer depending upon the will of the President for his place should be permitted to hold . . . [office] in open and continual disparagement of the administration and its head."[18] Unfortunately, Adams's devotion to the notion of continuity in office degenerated into a policy by which virtually no one was dismissed for any cause.

John C. Calhoun was part of the Adams administration in name only. The morning following the election, George Sullivan, longtime friend and confidant of both men, had called on the president-elect. "The Calhounites say," he reported, "that if Mr. Clay should be appointed secretary of state, a determined opposition to the Administration will be organized from the outset." If Adams wanted to keep the vice president-elect from joining the opposition, he would have to agree to name the South Carolinian's own supporters to key cabinet positions: Joel Poinsett to be secretary of state; Langdon Cheves as secretary of the treasury (both Poinsett and he were from South Carolina); and Calhoun's longtime friend John McLean to be secretary of war. Adams asked Sullivan with whom he had had these conversations. With Mr. Calhoun himself and Poinsett, Sullivan replied. "I told Sullivan that I would someday call on him testify to these facts in a Court of justice. . . . At least I am forewarned," the president noted in his diary.[19]

In the wake of the Denmark Vesey uprising, moderation and nationalism became increasingly unpopular in America. By the time of his inauguration, John Quincy Adams had come to represent all that was evil, politically, to South Carolinians. When he was Secretary of State Adams, he had angered citizens of the Palmetto State when he opposed the Negro Seamen's Act. In 1825, the price of cotton plummeted from thirty-two cents a pound to thirteen. Instead of blaming booming production in the new Gulf States, South Carolinians faulted the tariff. Adams hailed from New England, perceived to be a hotbed of antislavery sentiment. His seeming sympathy for the Cherokees, who were in the process of being dispossessed of their land in Georgia and Alabama, and his reputation as a free-soiler were also damaging him politically south of the Mason–Dixon Line.

During a prolonged visit to his home state in 1823, Calhoun had decided that he would have to convert from a nationalist to a staunch states' righter if he were to have any political future at all. In June 1826, in hopes of retaining the vice presidency into the next administration, Calhoun would offer his unequivocal support for Andrew Jackson for president in the next election.[20] In the fall of 1825, the South Carolinian wrote a friend, gloating over Adams's inability to placate either his Southern or Western critics. "The folly of Mr. Adams begins to be manifest to the South. The attempt to secure Mr. C-d [Crawford] and his partisans in Virginia and the Southern states had wholly failed. They are deadly hostile to him and his administration almost to a man." This from an individual who had wanted to disavow Jackson over his Florida exploits and who had in his preelection maneuvering tried to form a coalition that would have completely excluded Crawford.[21]

The new president wholeheartedly embraced the ideals stated in the Declaration of Independence. He believed in the notion that all men were created equal and endowed with inalienable rights. But with those rights came responsibilities. "If you infringe the right of any other man," he declared in a speech to the Cincinnati Astronomical Society in 1843, "you place yourself at war with your brother, and in assailing one of his rights, you make him the master of your own."[22] But, like his father, he believed that God had endowed mankind with free will and so made him subject to evil as well as good. He believed that individuals were born with a moral component, at the heart of which was the capacity for public virtue—that is, a willingness to sacrifice individual interests to the welfare of the whole. But there were no guarantees. The keys to a healthy republic, Adams was convinced, were property and education. "The right of property is a natural right as much as the right of life . . . the earth was given by the creator to mankind in common," he wrote historian George Bancroft; "the distribution of property in it is left to be settled among the human race by physical force or by agreement, compact, covenant. This I take to be the origin of government . . . if democracy is founded exclusively on persons and not on property, I fear it will follow the tendency of its nature and degenerate into ochlocracy [mob rule]."[23] In order to understand his rights and obligations, the citizen of a virtuous republic must have the capacity to think historically and abstractly, to learn the lessons of the past, and to understand the ideas and institutions that were the cornerstones of a vig-

orous republic. Consequently, in John Quincy's mind, not all individuals living in
the United States were entitled to citizenship. Property and education were the
qualifiers, but in a liberal society rife with opportunity, the door was open to all
free males. Like his father, John Quincy still embraced the notion of the family as
a voting unit with the male head of household being the decider. He was ambivalent about whether free Blacks and members of the "Five Civilized Tribes" were
capable of seizing the ring, but they were entitled to make the attempt.[24]

Of one thing Adams was certain: in a virtuous republic, the national government ought to exist solely for the benefit of the people, and it was under a moral
obligation to provide them with security, opportunity, and the example of good
government. Indeed, the sixth president's nationalism went beyond that of Jefferson and Madison, who wanted to make America strong in order to ensure that the
rights of the individual and the states were protected, and beyond Alexander
Hamilton's nationalism, which envisioned America as an oligarchy dedicated to
protecting property and capitalism. He was an "improver," one who defined the
rights of those living in a republic in positive as well as negative terms. The national government was under a moral and philosophical obligation to make better
the lives of its citizens. Representative government and a system of checks and
balances benefited all citizens. So did federally funded roads, canals, and ports.
Internal improvements, including the promotion of exploration and scientific inquiry, were just the public policy iteration of enlightened individuals' efforts to
improve themselves through reading and cultivated conversation.[25]

Like his father, John Quincy was a lifelong student of the Scottish Enlightenment. He believed that the search for the optimal form of government was an
ongoing experiment, and that America was its latest and most fruitful laboratory.
The future of Western civilization, indeed of all mankind, depended on the survival of that laboratory. Consequently, what Adams feared most was the breakup
of the Union. "Union is to me what the balance is to you," he had written his father, "and without this there can be no good government among mankind in any
state . . . without that [union] there can be no good government among the people
of North America in the state in which God has been pleased to place them."[26]

As he prepared his annual message to Congress, which was scheduled to be
delivered on December 6, 1825, President Adams decided on boldness and vision
rather than caution. He had had little patience with Monroe's hidden agenda, in
which the Virginian had sought to implement his nationalist program through
behind-the-scenes negotiations. Topping John Quincy's wish list was a massive
program of internal improvements. Perhaps the new chief executive's favorite
Scottish Enlightenment author was Adam Smith, who in his *Wealth of Nations*
argued that in a country's early development, it was imperative that its govern-

ment provide aid to private enterprise by funding infrastructure projects. Adams looked forward to the time when "the swelling tide of wealth" generated by the sale of public land—the acquisition of which the former secretary of state had made his early life's work—"may be made to reflow unfailing streams of improvement from the Atlantic to the Pacific."[27] Federally funded infrastructure would enhance the price of public lands, generating revenue that would be plowed back into internal improvements, thus alleviating the need for taxes. But there was more. Long a champion of trade agreements based on reciprocity and the most-favored-nation principle, he promised to sign such pacts with as many nations as possible. America's rapidly modernizing economy and massive merchant marine meant that it would best any competitor on a level playing field. As a further aid to business, Adams proposed a federal bankruptcy law and the adoption of a metric system that he predicted would become the international standard. It should be noted that in his day capitalism was generally equated with political and economic liberalism. Americans, whether nationalists or states' righters, did not view free enterprise as inherently exploitive, and they could not envision a planet where natural resources would not be perpetually abundant.

A new Department of the Interior would oversee everything from land sales to conservation to infrastructure. A strong navy would protect American commerce and defend the nation's coastlines. What excited Adams the most, however, were proposals for federally funded programs in science, exploration, and education. He would recommend to Congress the creation of a national university in Washington, DC. Closest to his heart was a national observatory; Europe, Adams declared, boasted a hundred thirty of these "lighthouses of the skies," the United States none.[28]

"Liberty is power," Adams declared in his proposed address. "The nation blessed with the largest portion of liberty must in proportion to its numbers be the most powerful nation upon earth." But Americans were also people of a covenant with their God. "[T]he tenure of power by man is, in the moral purposes of his Creator, upon condition that it shall be exercised to ends of beneficence, to improve the condition of himself and his fellowmen. While foreign nations less blessed with that freedom which is power than ourselves are advancing with gigantic strides in the career of public improvement, were we to slumber in indolence or fold up our arms and proclaim to the world that we are palsied by the will of our constituents, would it not be to cast away the bounties of Providence and doom ourselves to perpetual inferiority?"[29]

In November the president read the entire five-thousand-word message to his assembled cabinet. All but Rush recoiled at one section or another. "I wish the whole concluding part respecting internal improvements could be suppressed,"

Barbour, a states' righter, declared. Even Clay, the author of the American System, had cold feet. "I am for discarding the National University and perhaps some other objects," he argued. "Let us not recommend anything so unpopular as not likely to succeed. The University is certainly hopeless. . . . It does not rest on the same principle as internal improvement or the bank." Adams took no offense at his cabinet's qualms. "It's like the man with two wives. One is plucking out his white hairs, the other the black till none are left," he joked.[30]

More cabinet meetings ensued. Wirt, who had been absent from the first, declared the speech to be "excessively bold . . . [but] there was not a line in it that he did not approve." The problems he envisioned from it were political. Such a massive enhancement of the federal power would set off alarms in Virginia and the other Southern states. "Patrick Henry's prophecy would be said to have come to pass: that we wanted 'a great, magnificent Government.'"[31] Adams said that he understood that there would be opposition in Congress and that some, if not most, of his proposals would lie dead in the water, but he intended to move forward: "I agree that no absolutely impracticable projects ought to be recommended, but I look to a practicability of long range [rather] than a simple session of Congress . . . the plant may come late though the seed be sown early."[32]

As his department heads had predicted, Adams's first annual message created a firestorm in and out of Congress. Its expansive vision and call for an active, interventionist government played right into his enemies' hands. The slaveholding South viewed any enhancement of federal power and diminution of states' rights as an ipso facto threat to their institution. But there were other issues as well. Adams's sweeping proposals came at a time when distrust of the federal government was rampant, fallout from the Panic of 1819. The downturn had been the product of a number of factors. European agriculture had fully recovered from the Napoleonic Wars, and bumper crops there had driven down food and raw material prices in the United States. The Transcontinental Treaty had spawned a massive wave of western immigration; tens of thousands of frontier farmers and a handful of speculators bought public land on credit offered by the country's more than four hundred state banks. In addition, these institutions had issued millions of dollars in paper money without the specie to back it up. Late in 1818, British banking houses had begun calling in their loans; the Bank of the United States followed suit. Panic ensued. State banks had been forced to close their doors; tens of thousands of farmers had seen their property foreclosed on; unemployment had spread like wildfire. This was the first of a series of boom-and-bust cycles that would come to characterize America's unregulated capitalist economy. No precedents existed to enable the county to place the crash in context. The Panic of 1819 exacerbated class and sectional differences, pitting farmers and artisans of the

South and the West against the creditors of the Northeast. The calling in of loans by the Bank of the United States created a steady flow of specie out of the South and the West and into the financial centers of Boston, New York, Philadelphia, and other Eastern metropolises. In the areas hardest hit by the depression, fierce battles broke out between creditors and debtors. State legislatures, controlled primarily by working- and middle-class voters, passed debt relief laws that forced creditors to extend payment periods or accept worthless state banknotes at face value. The unemployed and debt-ridden blamed the federal government in general and the B.U.S. specifically for their plight.[33]

In Congress speaker after speaker rose to denounce the Adams administration. There was no provision in the Constitution for federally funded internal improvements, declared Martin Van Buren. Back in Congress, John Randolph railed against the president's speech for hour after incoherent hour. To many radicals, Adams's declaration that "liberty is power" seemed an oxymoron. The objective of power, they insisted, was to encroach on liberty. Was that not the lesson of the Panic of 1819 and its aftermath? The duty of every true republican, they declared, was to wage continual war against the concentration of federal authority. If there had ever been any doubt that John Quincy Adams was an aristocrat to the bone, his reference to the "palsied will" of the American electorate ended it, his critics declared.

Old Hickory joined the chorus. He had just resigned his seat in the Senate and been renominated by the Tennessee legislature for the presidency in the next election. Of Adams's speech, he wrote: "When I view the splendor & magnificence of the government embraced in the recommendations of the late message . . . together with the declaration that it would be criminal for the agents of our government to be palsied by the will of their constituents, I shudder for the consequence—if not checked by the voice of the people, it must end in consolidation & then despotism."[34] Throughout the remainder of Adams's term, Congress would ignore, when it could, every initiative included in the first annual message. The Senate approved the establishment of a naval academy, but the House, with a Jacksonian majority following the midterm elections, voted the measure down; the cost, seven thousand dollars a year for six faculty members, was extravagant, it declared. Such an institution would serve as a "vast source of promotion and patronage" and would threaten the democratic virtues of the republic by fostering the creation of an educated elite in the armed forces.[35] What internal improvements that were funded were given over to local and state governments to operate.

In truth, the Adams administration was not nearly as unpopular as its political opponents would have their fellow Americans believe. Without the three-fifths clause, the New Englander would have won both the popular and the electoral votes. It was true that on domestic matters, the body politic was inclining toward state sovereignty and particularism but not in foreign affairs. Manifest destiny was still a powerful phenomenon; Lafayette's prolonged tour of the United States had fueled the country's already strong sense of mission. America's favorite Frenchman had taken every opportunity to laud Monroe and Adams. Following his election as president, John Quincy received Lafayette at the White House and toured with him as time allowed. The evening before the general's departure, Adams presided over a farewell banquet during which he heaped praise on the Hero of Two Revolutions. Lafayette reciprocated and embraced the president with tears running down his cheeks.[36]

MANY STUDENTS OF FOREIGN affairs speculated as to how Adams and Clay, who had differed openly concerning U.S. recognition of Spain's revolted colonies, would fashion a coherent foreign policy. They need not have worried. In their preelection discussions, the two men had had a meeting of the minds. By 1824, Henry Clay was espousing the merits of two American Systems, one domestic and one foreign. The first consisted of the nationalist views of Monroe and Adams and the second an inter-American association of nations. He looked forward to the creation of a U.S.-led confederation of the Americas that would act collectively to resist future European interference and promote popular sovereignty, free trade, and republicanism throughout the hemisphere. Though Adams had initially dragged his feet on the question of recognition and in particular on the creation of an inter-American federation, by 1825 he had apparently caught "the Spanish American fever." As one observer noted, "He [the president] had started from a caution cold as marble but was, following his election, uttering phrases such as 'the fraternity of Freedom . . . sister Republics . . . nations of this hemisphere . . . [and] Powers of America.'"[37] Aware that U.S. participation in a Pan-American union would be criticized on the grounds that it violated the no-entangling-alliances declaration in Washington's Farewell Address, the president insisted that the Americas were far different places in 1825 from what they had been in 1796. They were then colonial appendages of Europe; now they were independent states, "seven of them republics like ourselves." Their "political principles and systems of government . . . must and will have an action and counteraction upon us . . . to which we cannot be indifferent if we would."[38]

Despite their differing personalities, Clay and Adams not only worked harmoniously together during the latter's presidency but developed a deep respect and even affection for each other. The Kentuckian told a friend that "an entire harmony as to public measures exists between Mr. Adams and me."[39] Clay's tenure as secretary of state was marred by personal tragedy and ill health. He was sometimes so incapacitated that the president had to visit him at his home—a three-story brick residence on F Street between Fourteenth and Fifteenth Streets—to discuss foreign affairs. In August 1825, the Clays' twelve-year-old daughter, Eliza, died of a mysterious malady. Two months later his eldest daughter, twenty-year-old Susan Clay Duralde, who lived in New Orleans, succumbed to yellow fever. Clay buried himself in his work, which made his several chronic maladies worse.[40]

Adams and Clay were concerned not only about European intervention in the Americas but also armed aggression by one American state against another. During Spanish rule, the six provinces of Central America had been joined together in the Captaincy General of Guatemala. Weaker than their fellow colonies to the north and south, the Central Americans were among the last to break their colonial bonds. Finally, in 1821, they had declared their independence, only to see it threatened by Augustín de Iturbide, the Mexican general who had himself proclaimed emperor in May 1822. With Mexican troops massed to invade, Guatemala, Honduras, and Nicaragua agreed to annexation, but Costa Rica and San Salvador held out. In March 1823 the government of San Salvador dispatched an emissary to Washington seeking annexation to the United States.

Both as secretary of state and president, Adams took an active interest in developments in Central America; so did Clay when he was in the House and after he became the United States' chief diplomat. With Iturbide's overthrow in 1823 and the emergence of a constitutionalist regime in Mexico City, pressure on the Central American republics slackened. In July 1823, San Salvador and Guatemala confederated as the United Provinces of Central America; Honduras, Nicaragua, and Costa Rica subsequently joined the two founding provinces. The United States in 1825 signed a commercial treaty with the United Provinces that became the model for all subsequent U.S. trade pacts, based as it was on reciprocity and the most-favored-nation principle. Shortly thereafter, Antonio José Cañas, the United Provinces minister to Washington, proposed a U.P.–U.S. agreement for the construction of a canal connecting the Atlantic and the Pacific. Due to British opposition and the engineering difficulties involved, nothing came of the project. But in his instruction to the U.S. minister to the United Provinces, Clay declared that the "circumstances of its origin and subsequent conduct" entitled that nation "to the interest and regard of the United States, perhaps even superior to that which they have ever felt in any of the other Southern republics."[41]

On December 7, 1824, Simón Bolívar, Liberator of the North, invited the newly independent republics of the Americas to attend the Congress of Panama, scheduled to open October 1, 1825. There were those in power in the capitals of Latin America, including Bolívar, who did not want to invite the United States.

Presciently, they saw in the Monroe Doctrine not only a warning against European intervention but a portal through which the United States could establish its
hegemony throughout the hemisphere. Others, however, believed that it would be
counterproductive not to invite the United States, a burgeoning power whose very
physical proximity to Latin America guaranteed that it would be a major player in
hemispheric affairs. With Bolívar away campaigning, the government in Bogotá
ordered its minister in Washington to sound out the Adams administration on the
possibility of sending a plenipotentiary to the upcoming gathering. Among the
issues to be discussed were the Monroe Doctrine, a hemisphere-wide trade treaty,
a statement of principles outlining the rights of belligerents and neutrals in time
of war, abolition of the African slave trade, and future relations with Haiti.[42] In
February 1825 a translation of Bolívar's invitation appeared in the *National Intelligencer*. The Liberator, the article declared, expected the states represented at the
congress would combine into an amphictyonic (league of neighbors) body or assembly with a charter resembling bilateral treaties signed between seven of the
republics earlier in the decade. The treaties guaranteed the political independence
and territorial integrity of the signatories; there were to be reciprocal rights of
citizenship and an inter-American organization.[43] An entangling alliance if there
ever was one.

   Adams and Clay had come to view inter-American relations as an opportunity
to establish precedents that would affect the United States' relationships with
other members of the international community. The liberal trade pact with the
United Provinces was one example. There was another that was particularly compelling to the president. Adams had for some time dreamed of an international
convention embracing the Plan of '76—that is, free ships make free goods and
all that that entailed, plus a proviso that would outlaw both impressment and
privateering. In 1823, he had drafted such a scheme: "My plan involves nothing
less than a revolution in the laws of war," he wrote in his diary, "a great meliora-
tion in the condition of man; Is it the dream of a visionary? Or is it the great and
practicable conception of a benefactor of mankind?"[44] Calhoun, then still his
friend and colleague, had been skeptical; John Bull would never go for it. Perhaps
not, Adams replied, but his intention was to go ahead and propose it to France,
Russia, Britain, and all of the great maritime powers. It would plant a seed that
just might bear the fruit of peace. "I feel that I could die for it," he subsequently
confided to his diary. "I could go before the throne of omnipotence with a plea for
mercy and with a consciousness of not having lived in vain for the world of mankind."[45] As Calhoun had predicted, the British government denounced Adams's
scheme and let it be known that it would use the leverage of its maritime and naval
power to keep the other seafaring nations from signing on. If not the Old World,

then the New could serve as a laboratory in which Adams could plant and grow his seeds of peace. In listing the reasons that the United States should attend the Congress of Panama, President Adams emphasized the great importance of the opportunity "to establish American principles of maritime, belligerent, and neutral law . . . an additional interest of infinite magnitude."[46]

The cabinet approved the dispatch of emissaries to Panama, although not without voicing some entangling-alliance concerns and predicting, correctly, that the slaveholding states would raise some major objections. So enthused was Clay, however, that he proposed nominating Albert Gallatin, dean of the U.S. diplomatic corps, to join with minister to Colombia Robert C. Anderson as delegates to the congress. When Gallatin declined, Clay notified Congress that he intended to nominate John Sergeant of Pennsylvania and Anderson as ministers plenipotentiary, with William B. Rochester of New York to act as their secretary. Meanwhile, in Bogotá, Bolívar had sent an invitation to Great Britain to attend the conference as an observer. George Canning readily agreed and subsequently advised his emissary that "any project for putting the United States of North America at the head of an American Confederacy against Europe would be highly displeasing to your government."[47]

The Panama conference invitation was the opportunity that the anti-administration coalition had been waiting for. The attack was launched from the Senate Foreign Relations Committee, all of whose members had been appointed by Calhoun. That august body issued a report blasting the administration for not consulting Congress before agreeing to attend the Panama gathering. The report, authored by Littleton W. Tazewell of Virginia, warned that the very act of the United States agreeing to discuss the slave trade and the future of Haiti was an affront to the slaveholding states and would set a dangerous precedent. When Washington had said no entangling alliances, he meant to include the entire world. Issues arising between the United States and Latin America should be dealt with as they arose on a nation-by-nation basis. Matters relating to trade and the rights of nations during wartime should be settled through bilateral agreements. The report was stoutly defended on the floor of the Senate by Van Buren, Jacksonian Thomas Hart Benton of Missouri, and Calhoun disciple Robert Y. Hayne of South Carolina. Hayne declared that "the question of slavery is one, in all its bearings, of extreme delicacy. . . . It must be considered and treated entirely as a DOMESTIC QUESTION."[48]

In that same speech, the South Carolinian attacked the American System. Adams and Clay's notions "when applied to our domestic policy, [are] mean[s] restriction and monopoly." Remnants of Old Republicanism egged them on. John Randolph used the occasion to express his disgust with the "corrupt bargain" that had brought Adams and Clay to power and created a "combination of the Puritan with the black-leg—a coalition of Blifil and Black George" (two villains in the popular novel *Tom Jones* by Henry Fielding). On the matter at hand, "this Panama mission is a Kentucky cuckoo's egg laid in a Spanish-American nest."[49]

But the anti-Adams coalition had badly miscalculated. The Congress of Panama was quite popular with public and press. On March 14, 1826, the Senate approved Anderson's and Sergeant's nominations by a vote of twenty-four to fourteen. A month later the House voted 132 to sixty to appropriate funds for the mission. Adams and Clay had no intention of entering into a treaty guaranteeing the sovereignty and independence of their neighbors to the south. The gathering was to be treated as a diplomatic and not a legislative conclave, Clay subsequently instructed the U.S. emissaries: "It should be considered as merely consultative." Under no circumstances should the United States join a pact that was capable of "binding a minority to agreements and acts contrary to its will."[50] The ministers were authorized to press the representatives of the other republics to endorse the noninterference and noncolonization principles of the Monroe Doctrine. It was all for naught. Sergeant insisted on delaying his departure until autumn, when the pestilence that usually accompanied summer weather had died out. When the time came for him to depart, he suddenly resigned. Anderson died in Cartagena of yellow fever on July 24, 1826. When the Congress of Panama finally opened, no representative of the United States was in attendance.

FOR HENRY CLAY, JOHN Randolph's referral to him and Adams as "Blifil and Black George" was something not to be tolerated. It was a gross insult, and though Clay opposed dueling in principle, he issued a written challenge to the Virginian in late March 1826. Randolph accepted. The evening before the face-off, Thomas Hart Benton, a cousin of Clay's wife, Lucretia, paid a visit to the secretary of state's home. Mrs. Clay had recently lost two of her children; a surviving son lay asleep on the couch. Benton found the Clays calm and composed. He was not sure, he later wrote, whether Lucretia was aware of what was to transpire on the field of honor the next day. From there Benton called on Randolph and described the scene he had just witnessed. "I shall do nothing to disturb the sleep of the child or the repose of the mother," the Virginia firebrand assured Benton. The two antagonists met on Saturday, April 8, near Little Falls Bridge on the Virginia side of the Potomac. This was at Randolph's insistence. If his blood were to be shed, he wanted it to be on "the sacred ground of Virginia."[51] The two men fired simultaneously; Clay's bullet struck a stump behind the Virginian while Randolph's dug harmlessly into the dirt in front of Clay. Harry of the West insisted on another exchange. He missed again, whereupon Randolph pointed his pistol to the sky and fired. "I do not fire at you, Mr. Clay," he exclaimed, and rushed to offer his hand. Clay accepted it, and shortly thereafter, the two men exchanged cards.[52]

IN HIS INSTRUCTIONS TO the ill-fated American delegation to the Congress of Panama, Clay told them to make it clear to the other delegates that the United States "could not, with indifference see it [Cuba] transferred from Spain to any other European Power" and likewise was "unwilling to see its transfer or annexation to either of the new American states." At the time, both Mexico and Colombia were formulating plans to "liberate" both Cuba and Puerto Rico from Spanish rule.[53] Adams and Clay were confident that they could protect the islands from Central or South American aggressors; what they were really concerned about were Spain and Britain. The secretary of state instructed the U.S. minister in Madrid, Alexander H. Everett, to inform his host government that the United States "would entertain constant apprehension" should the island pass into the hands "of some less friendly sovereignty."[54] As it turned out, London was as worried about a U.S. takeover of Cuba as Washington was about British ambitions there. Canning suggested to Madrid that it officially end hostilities with the American republics in return for a British guarantee of Spanish sovereignty over Cuba and Puerto Rico.

No one, especially the government in Madrid, doubted that the ultimate goal of U.S.–Caribbean policy was the annexation of the two very rich and strategically important Caribbean islands. Presidents from Jefferson to Adams had made no secret of their county's desire for Cuba in particular. But timing was everything. In 1826, Europe was not ready to allow the United States these prizes, and Brother Jonathan was not yet strong enough to seize them with impunity. But Captain David Porter of the United States Navy, an ardent expansionist, had plans of his own.

Porter had earned his spurs attacking British shipping in the Pacific during the War of 1812. From 1815 to 1822, he had served on the Board of Navy Commissions, but bored with bureaucratic red tape, he requested and was granted command of the United States' West Indian squadron. The principal task of that force was to find and destroy the region's numerous pirates, many of whom were operating out of Cuba and Puerto Rico. Porter's orders in regard to these operations were unequivocal: he was to "observe the utmost caution not to encroach upon the rights of others," and he was to notify Spanish authorities of his approach and seek their "favorable and friendly support."[55] Governor-General Francisco Dionisio Vives of Cuba, whom Adams as secretary of state had gone to great lengths to cultivate, offered every cooperation. Not so the authorities in San Juan.

In November 1824, Captain Porter learned that two of his officers while in search of stolen American property had been arrested in the Puerto Rican port of Fajardo (or Foxardo). He immediately set sail and, arriving off the coast of the offending city, laid siege. At the head of two hundred men, he landed and headed for government headquarters, destroying several artillery batteries en route. After extracting apologies from the local authorities, Porter reported his escapades to Washington, expecting to be hailed as a hero of the republic. In this, he was to be sadly disappointed. Indeed, Porter's raid on Foxardo came at the worst possible time as Clay and Adams were then working feverishly to convince Spain and the rest of Europe that the United States had no designs on the two islands. Porter's assault, Adams declared, was "one of the most high-handed acts . . . ever heard of."[56]

At the president's behest, Secretary of the Navy Southard ordered Porter to return to Washington to face court-martial. The commander obeyed but protested mightily, even publishing a pamphlet comparing his actions to those of General Jackson in invading the Floridas. Several pro-Jackson newspapers blasted the administration. Porter, one declared, was a "faithful servant" who had "devoted the morning and noon of his years to the public weal"; he was being persecuted by men who were petty, vindictive, and insolent toward the nation's heroes.[57] Porter was duly tried and found guilty of insubordination and disobedience of orders. His penalty was a six-month suspension with pay. He promptly resigned his commission and joined the Mexican Navy.[58] Porter subsequently established a base of operations at Key West, from which he raided Spanish shipping with a view to embroiling the United States and Spain in a war.

There was a final threat to the status quo in the Caribbean—the Cubans themselves. During the early 1820s, sentiment for annexation to the United States increased markedly on the Ever-Faithful Isle. Creole plantation owners feared the growth of British influence primarily because of mounting abolitionist sentiment in Parliament. Antislavery sentiment was also widespread among the emerging republics in the rest of Latin America, making independence and confederation with them impractical. The entrenched power of the slave states and access to the internal slave trade in the United States made the idea of annexation attractive to slaveholding Cubans. In 1822 a representative of the Cuban planters had actually proposed annexation to the Monroe administration. It had firmly rebuffed him. Any move to acquire Cuba at that point would have torpedoed the Monroe Doctrine, then in the making. Britain would certainly have intervened, and as Adams, then secretary of state, observed to a cabinet colleague, the United States "would not and could not prevent by war the British from obtaining possession of Cuba."[59]

In 1825 the U.S. minister in Madrid reported to Washington that the status quo in Cuba could not be sustained for more than two or three years. Ongoing hostilities between Spain and the Latin American republics coupled with annexationist sentiment in Cuba rendered the situation precarious. In 1825 and then again in 1826, Washington dispatched secret agents to the island to report on conditions there. The Spanish and the Creoles hated one another, they informed Adams and Clay. A civil war would "be attended with dreadful consequences."[60] The losing side would inevitably turn to the free Black population or even unleash Cuba's slaves, in which case the world would witness the birth of another Haiti. There was still a chance that either Colombia or Mexico would invade and either annex Cuba or facilitate its independence. In view of Washington's opposition to annexation, the Creoles would accept aid from virtually any quarter.

In the summer of 1825, President Guadalupe Victoria of Mexico founded the Junta Promotora de la Libertad Cubana, a political and paramilitary organization comprised of Cuban exiles and Mexican volunteers whose purpose was to liberate Cuba from Spanish rule. Rumors were still emanating from Bogotá that Bolívar would lead an invading army that would not only free Cuba but, in the process, abolish slavery. "A military despot of talent and experience at the head of a black army is certainly not the sort of neighbor whom we should naturally wish, if we had the choice, to place upon our southern frontier," Everett observed.[61] Adams and Clay heartily agreed. When later that year Madrid granted Governor-General Vives dictatorial powers that he employed to impose martial law in Cuba, the Adams administration breathed a sigh of relief. The administration's secret emissaries inquired if the governor had enough force at hand to either repel an invasion or put down an insurrection. For the time being, he replied, he was well prepared. So it was that during his administration that for geopolitical reasons, John Quincy Adams threw his and his country's support behind a Spanish colonial regime in Cuba that brutally suppressed any hint of dissent.

By the time he became president, John Quincy was finally willing to strike a blow for Greek freedom. Support for the ongoing Greek insurrection against the Ottoman Empire had become so strong in the United States that if Adams had any hope for a second term, he would have to climb aboard the bandwagon. In the fall of 1825, he dispatched to the Near East a secret envoy, William C. Somerville, a Marylander who had fought in the War of 1812, toured Europe extensively, and served as minister to Sweden. Go to Athens, he was instructed. Furnish aid to American ships and seamen trapped in Greek ports by the war with Turkey. Make it clear to American citizens who were furnishing aid to the Ottomans that their conduct was "unworthy of American citizens, and . . . contrary to their duty, as well as their honor." Most important, try to determine the Greeks' ability "to prosecute the war and to sustain an independent government." Assure them, Somerville's orders stated, "that the people of the United States and their government, throughout the whole of the struggle of Greece, have constantly felt an anxious desire that it might terminate in the reestablishment of the liberty and independence of that country."[62] Unfortunately, Somerville died en route.

In his annual message to Congress in December 1827, Adams expressed sympathy for the suffering of the Greeks, a people who had shown the way for the United States in its quest for liberty and democracy; he expressed the fervent hope that they would succeed in their struggle for independence. In this, the president was hardly going out on a diplomatic limb. In July 1827, Great Britain, France, and Russia had signed the Treaty of London, which gave the Ottoman Empire one month to end hostilities against the Greeks. Both parties would then have to accept mediation by the three powers, a step that everyone knew would end with Greece receiving its independence. In the ensuing Russo-Turkish War of 1828–1829, Istanbul was forced to grant Greece its unconditional freedom while also ceding large swaths of territory bordering on the Black Sea. "I expected and hoped great things from [the] Emperor Nicholas for the benefit of mankind," John Quincy subsequently wrote in his diary. "Hoped he would expel the Turks from Russia and at least make great advances towards the extinction of the mahometan imposture [Sultan Mahmud II]—I regretted he had now stopped short of Constantinople."[63]

JOHN QUINCY ADAMS SPENT much of his time as secretary of state and president wrestling with the problem of frontiers, both internal and external. Cordoning off in the New World what belonged to the United States and preventing the European powers from hijacking the independence of the Latin American republics were relatively straightforward matters of diplomacy among nation-states. Establishing a boundary between whites and Native Americans proved more problematical. Throughout the history of the Early Republic, the powers that ruled the nation were conflicted. Should the United States, as Washington had thought, treat the various tribes as sovereign nations; negotiate trade and territorial treaties with them; and view them as would-be Europeans who, if they adopted the ways of the white man, could be assimilated? Or should they write the tribes off as unregenerate savages who were beyond the pale? John Quincy did not share Thomas Jefferson's interest in and affinity for the Indians of North America, but he sympathized with them as fellow human beings. Adams was an assimilationist through and through. When push came to shove, he would treat indigenous peoples who did not embrace Christianity, farming, and trousers as no less a threat to the United States' manifest destiny than the Spanish or the British.

In his second annual message to Congress, President Monroe had recommended that the United States stop dealing with the various Indian tribes as sovereign entities, and place them under a set of federal laws that would offer grants of land as inducements to settle down and embrace the "civilized" ways of the white man. The problem was that whites living in states where Native Americans resided did not want them to assimilate; they wanted to cast the Indians into the wilderness of the trans-Mississippi West and confiscate their lands. And in the end, it was the frontier farmers, merchants, traders, land speculators, and railroad entrepreneurs who called the shots. After all, America was not only a republic but also the most capitalistic nation the world had yet produced. By the end of his second term, Monroe could read the handwriting on the wall. In a special message to Congress delivered in January 1825, just prior to his leaving office, he declared, "Any attempt to remove them by force would, in my opinion, be unjust."[64] But he also admitted that it was probably impossible for the country's indigenous peoples to continue to live on their tribal lands within the states. They should be removed to "lands equally good and perhaps more fertile west of the Mississippi but only with their consent."[65]

In truth, removal, engineered by territorial governments and corrupt Indian agents, had been going on for years. By the early 1820s, Ohio, Indiana, and Illinois had disgorged their indigenous peoples. The Cherokees of Georgia and Alabama—most of whom had taken up farming while at the same time preserving their tribal culture, including institutions of governance—had managed to hold on. "Since [1802] . . . many treaties have been made and many millions of miles purchased . . . [with] the state of Georgia continually pressing to obtain more. At last, the Cherokees have come to the determination that they will on no considerations part with any more of their lands, and their delegation now here have most explicitly so declared," John Quincy noted in his diary in March 1824.[66] At that point secretary of war, Secretary of State Calhoun was charged with the administration of Indian affairs. When he notified Congress of the Cherokees' position, the Georgia delegation responded angrily, charging the Monroe administration with "fraud and hypocrisy."[67] The legislative delegation was then in thrall to Governor George M. Troup, whose position in state politics rested on his promise to drive the Cherokee completely and finally out of Georgia.

During the waning days of the Monroe administration, Indian agents employed by the federal government had signed the Treaty of Indian Springs with a faction of the Creek Nation who agreed to sell all Creek lands to the state of Georgia for four hundred thousand dollars and move west of the Mississippi. The Indians were given eighteen months to pack up and clear out; there were to be no state surveys of the ceded lands prior to September 1, 1826. It quickly became apparent that the treaty did not have the support of the vast majority of Creeks. Indeed, it had been negotiated by William McIntosh, principal chief of the Lower Creek tribes, and seven lesser chiefs representing only eight of the forty-six Creek settlements in Georgia. McIntosh was a longtime ally of Andrew Jackson. It was the Lower Creeks who had been Old Hickory's Indian auxiliaries in the Battle of New Orleans and his subsequent invasion of East Florida. Nevertheless, the permanent United States Indian agent in Georgia, Colonel John Crowell, had advised the Creeks not to sign the Treaty of Indian Springs.[68] By the time the pact had been ratified by the Senate, John Quincy had become president, and he duly signed it, something he would forever regret. Chiefs representing the majority of Creeks declared the pact null and void. Four hundred enraged Upper Creeks surrounded McIntosh's house, set it afire, and shot him dead as he attempted to flee.[69] Adams subsequently confided to George Hay that the pact should never have been signed, much less ratified. The two Indian agents who had represented the United States were both Georgians who had directly disobeyed their instructions. "[B]ut when the treaty came here, the President [Adams] could not withhold it from the Senate, and when before the Senate, no one would take the invidious task of expressing its injustice. . . . I had no practicable alternative but to ratify it."[70]

Regretful though he was, the president desperately wanted to avoid a situation in which his administration would have to choose between justice for the Creeks or armed conflict with the state of Georgia. In September both Creek factions sent delegations to Washington to appeal to the "Great White Father." One was headed by McIntosh's eldest son, Chilly, who had barely escaped the flames and gunfire. He and his colleagues defended the Treaty of Indian Springs and bore with them a letter from Governor Troup declaring that he was ordering Indian lands to be surveyed immediately. Hostilities seemed inevitable. "I told Chilly that I was deeply distressed at these melancholy tidings and would do all that would be in my power for him," Adams wrote in his diary. Later in the day, he called at Secretary of War Barbour's house "and found him at home deeply affected at the intelligence from Georgia, thinking Governor Troup a madman."[71]

Shortly thereafter, President Adams dispatched a special agent, Timothy P. Andrews, together with General Edmund P. Gaines to Georgia to investigate and report on the true state of affairs. If they found the anti-McIntosh faction armed and organized, they were to order them to disperse. If they had already decided to stand down (which in fact, they had), Andrews and Gaines were to request that they convene a tribal council and ratify the Treaty of Indian Springs. Gaines was to inform Governor Troup that under no circumstances would Georgia be allowed to begin surveying Indian land prior to September 1826 as provided for in the treaty.[72] Troup responded by issuing a statement calling for Gaines's "immediate recall, arrest, trial, and punishment, under the articles of war." But in the end, he caved. "The Governor was full of guns, drums, trumpets, blunderbuss, and thunder," John Quincy declared, but he did not proceed with the survey.[73]

Meanwhile, a delegation from the mainstream Creek faction, led by Opothle Yoholo, principal chief of the Upper Creeks, had arrived in Washington. As he had with the McIntosh faction, Adams welcomed them. "We should all meet in friendship," he said. "We are glad to be here," replied Yoholo, a noted orator and defender of Creek tribal customs. "Things have happened which have frightened us. We hope now that all will be well."[74] Yoholo and his comrades refused to accept Indian Springs, but said they would consider ceding all lands east of the Chattahoochee River, an area that composed about two-thirds of the whole of Creek lands in Georgia.

Adams and his cabinet met in almost continuous session during the crisis. There seemed to be no clear path forward. "We ask of Congress to annul the treaty or to furnish means to compel the execution of it by the Indians," Adams declared. "Congress does nothing. We consider the treaty as binding, but the Indians refuse to comply and [intend to] remain on the lands after September 1826. We have no means to compel their compliance and therefore do nothing."[75] What was to prevent war between the Creeks and the state of Georgia? The assimilationist Barbour declared that the federal government ought to stop negotiating treaties with the Indian tribes; they should be declared citizens of the United States, subject to the laws of the nation. Clay disagreed. "It was impossible to civilize Indians," he declared; "there never was a full-blooded Indian who took to civilization. It was not in their nature." He believed that Native Americans were doomed to extinction, as Adams remembered him saying, "and although he would never use or countenance inhumanity towards them, he did not think they, as a race, worth preserving. . . . They were not an improvable breed, and their disappearance from the human family will be no great loss to the world." Barbour was thoroughly shocked, but Adams was not. "I fear there is too much foundation" in what Clay said, he confided to his diary.[76] In cabinet, the president broke off the debate. The future would define itself; they must deal with the present crisis.

It was decided to sound out the members of the Georgia delegation to see if their state would accept the line of the Chattahoochee. If we must, replied Senator Thomas W. Cobb, but you know, he told Barbour, Georgia will necessarily be driven to support General Jackson in the next election. Barbour then conveyed this news to the cabinet and suggested, given Clay's previously stated views, that if removal was inevitable, why not give way to Troup? The administration could at least keep the friends that it had in Georgia. But Adams said, "We ought not to yield to Georgia because we could not do so without gross injustice. And . . . as to Georgia's being driven to support General Jackson, I feel little concern or care for that."[77] On January 18, 1826, Barbour presented the draft of a new treaty that would supplant Indian Springs. In it the Creeks would agree to deed to Georgia all of their lands east of the Chattahoochee. The Upper Creeks resisted, and the talks were broken off. "Opothle Yoholo attempted last evening to commit suicide," Adams noted in his diary. But by the end of the week, he and his fellow chiefs had agreed to sign the Treaty of Washington.[78]

When the September 1, 1826, deadline for surveying Creek lands for sale to the public arrived, Troup chose to ignore the Treaty of Washington and ordered his men to measure all Indian lands in the state. After Creek officials arrested several of the surveyors, the governor dispatched a troop of cavalry to protect them. "Georgia," he proclaimed, "is sovereign on her own soil."[79] The cabinet voted to use force if necessary. "[T]he President will feel himself compelled to employ, if necessary, all means under his control to maintain the faith of the nation by carrying the treaty into effect," the administration declared. Troup remained undaunted. "From the first decisive act of hostility, you will be considered and treated as a public enemy," he retorted, "and, what is more, the unblushing allies of the savages whose cause you have adopted."[80] To Adams's mind the nation teetered on the brink of civil war: "To send troops against them [the surveyors and the state militia] must end in acts of violence." He would have to make a stand and ask for Congress's support, he decided. "This is the most momentous message I have ever sent to Congress. . . . Well may I say, 'Cast me not away from Thy presence and take not Thy Holy Spirit from me.'"[81]

Adams's address to the House and Senate, delivered in February 1827, stated his determination to enforce the terms of the Treaty of Washington, whatever the cost. But the Van Buren–Jackson–Benton coalition would have none of it. The Treaty of Indian Springs, declared the Missouri senator, had been duly signed and ratified. It was the law of the land. The survey was completed, and the Creeks evicted. In 1837, looking back over these events and ensuing injustices committed against Native Americans, John Quincy would observe, "We have done more harm to the Indians since our Revolution than had ever been done to them by the French and English nations before. . . . These are crying sins for which we are answerable before a higher jurisdiction."[82]

30

Under Siege

WHEN THE ADAMSES TOOK up occupancy in March 1825, the President's House—just beginning to be called the White House—was complete except for the North Portico. In the back were stables, workshops, and a dairy. Flanking the mansion were the War Department and Navy Department buildings on one side with Treasury Department and State Department on the other. Directly across from the mansion was President's Square, soon to be known as Lafayette Park. At the far edge sat St. John's Episcopal Church. From the front of the White House, or the South Portico, the Adams family had a view of the Potomac. The First Lady was charged with managing a household staff of sixteen, including a butler, a steward, a housekeeper, a porter, scullion maids, two boys who carried wood and waited on table, cooks, and coachmen. The white servants resided in attic rooms in the West Wing. The Blacks (free) lived in the basement in small rooms white or yellow washed, and with dirt floors. Those rooms had previously housed domestic slaves kept by the members of the Virginia dynasty. White House servants began and ended every day. In the mornings they lighted fires, furnished water for washbasins, and served breakfast; they cleaned and cooked—the kitchen, with its perpetual fire, was an oven in itself in the summertime; they served meals, waited on visitors, and cleared tables following family meals and banquets. The White House coachmen rode on the outside of their carriages in all weather. At day's end, the servants doused the lamps and locked the doors.[1]

The White House had been built with public monies, and the Adamses inherited the custom by which any person with stated public business could visit at virtually anytime. Congressmen and senators regularly brought by out-of-town guests. When they were in the capital, the Adamses presided over the president's weekly reception. Guests began arriving around eight o'clock in the evening;

most were gone about ten. Arrivals made their way to the Oval Room or official drawing room, there to be greeted by the president and the First Lady. Liveried waiters moved through the crowd, serving tea, coffee, liqueurs, wine, and cake. There was no music or dancing. Every New Year's Day the presidential mansion turned into the people's palace. Anyone and everyone could call, and they did. Adams estimated that the first family received between two and three thousand people on New Year's Day 1826 and around twelve hundred the following year.[2]

For a portion of each working day, the White House resembled a scene from the Middle Ages in which each and every citizen was entitled to an audience and a request for relief. In 1828 a Mrs. O'Sullivan came calling. She was attired in men's clothing and peddling a book she had authored. If only the president would provide a bit of relief, she could obtain some suitable female garments. He gave her five dollars and told her to do just that. "It is a difficult thing to persevere in kindness with a half-insane man," John Quincy wrote in his diary, "with a half-insane woman, impossible."[3]

Adams's day began between five and six. In winter and autumn, he took a four-mile hike: "I walk by the light of moon or stars, or none . . . usually returning home in time to see the sun rise from the eastern chamber of the House." The president would then make his own fire and read three chapters of the Bible. Then it was newspapers till nine. After breakfast, John Quincy settled himself in his office for a day of visitors and business. The evening meal was served between four and five. On nights when there was no reception, he chatted with Louisa and other family members and enjoyed an occasional game of billiards. Then it was back to his office, where he wrote on foreign and domestic matters and signed papers. There was, he lamented, no time for intellectual pursuits.[4] As he had when he was secretary of state, Adams continued bathing in the summers with Antoine Guista. The men would walk down to a spit of land, later the site of the Washington Monument. Situated where Tyber Creek, formerly known as Goose Creek, emptied into the Potomac was a large rock shaded by a sycamore tree. The bathers used it as a base of operations, laying out their clothes and then sunning themselves dry when they had finished. Unless he was experimenting with some article of clothing, the president continued to swim naked except for goggles and skull-cap, the latter donned after he severely sunburned his bald pate.

One morning in June 1825, John Quincy Adams nearly drowned. On the ill-fated day, he decided to cross to the far side of the Potomac and then swim back. There was a weathered dinghy moored at the jetty near the poplars on the Van Ness family's property, at the mouth of the Tyber, and Adams decided that it was capable of transporting them to the far shore. John, who had decided to join the party, and Guista did not like the looks of the boat. John chose to jump off the leaky vessel at their familiar rock, where he could swim, sunbathe, and wait for his companions to return. "I thought the boat safe enough, or rather persisted carelessly in going without paying due attention to its condition," the president later recalled. He gave John his watch and then bundled his coat and waistcoat, which, together with his shoes, he put in the boat. Antoine, who was completely naked, began paddling them across the river. By the time they were midway across, the ramshackle dinghy was half full of water. "Just at that critical moment, a fresh breeze from the northwest blew on the river as from the nose of a bellows. In five minutes time it made a little tempest and set the boat to dancing till the river came in at the sides."[5] Both men jumped overboard, with Antoine hanging on with one hand. He soon lost his grip, and the little craft, nearly swamped, drifted away. They decided to try swimming to the opposite bank; the servant made it easily, but Adams, still wearing his bulky long-sleeved shirt and pantaloons, nearly went under. Eventually he too made it to the far shore, but the president was near exhaustion. After catching his breath, Adams instructed Guista to cross the river bridge, proceed to the White House, and return with a carriage. On his way he should look for the boat; perhaps some of their clothing could be salvaged. The president removed his shirt and pants and wrung them out. At that point, John arrived, having swum all the way across the Potomac expecting to meet his father and Antoine somewhere along the way. Antoine found some of his clothing and one of his master's shoes on his way back to the White House, but nothing else. Eventually he returned with the carriage, and the bedraggled members of the party made their way home. They had been gone five hours.[6]

By this point rumors were circulating that the president had drowned, several passersby having witnessed the commotion from the riverbank. Louisa was not pleased: "The affair is altogether ridiculous," she declared.[7] The First Lady summoned the family physician, who attempted to convince John Quincy that swimming in fresh water was injurious to the liver. The president was properly chastised. "Among my motives for swimming, that of showing what I can do, must be discarded as spurious, and I must strictly confine myself to the purposes for health, exercise, and salutary labor."[8]

JOHN ADAMS FERVENTLY HOPED to live to see the fiftieth anniversary of the founding of the republic, July 4, 1826. On his visits to Peacefield during his second term as secretary of state, John Quincy had noted his father's increasing physical feebleness. Yet through 1824 John's correspondence and conversation remained vigorous, full of observations and inquiries. But then in 1825 the senior Adams's condition began to deteriorate. A frequent visitor noted that the former president seemed to have lost interest in conversation. By May 1826, John Adams was bedridden and experiencing difficulty in swallowing. Stubbornly, he clung to life. Several hundred miles to the south, Thomas Jefferson, eighty-three—seven years younger than Adams—also lay on his deathbed. His health had been in sharp decline since 1825. By the spring of 1826, the Sage of Monticello was consuming large doses of laudanum to relieve pain from a urinary tract infection. On the morning of the Fourth, he roused himself enough to confirm that it was Independence Day. Jefferson breathed his last at twelve fifty p.m. On the second, a visitor from Quincy's Independence Day celebration committee called at Peacefield and asked the aged Adams for a comment. "Independence Forever," he declared. On the morning of the Fourth, John Adams drifted in and out of consciousness. George arrived from Boston and remained with his beloved grandfather until the end. Around noon he raised himself and declared, "Thomas Jefferson survives." At six in the evening, John Adams—architect of the Constitution, negotiator of peace with both Great Britain and France, and second president of the United States—expired.[9]

On July 8, John Quincy received a packet of letters from Quincy. One was from his niece Susanna Clark, warning that his father's end was fast approaching. It was dated the second. A note from Thomas written two days later declared that their father would not live out the day. Gathering up John, the president boarded a coach-and-four and set out for Peacefield. Stopping for breakfast just outside Baltimore, John Quincy and John received word of the patriarch's death. "From the letters which I had yesterday received, this event was so much expected by me that it had no sudden and violent effect on my feelings," Adams wrote in his diary. "The time, the manner, the coincidence with the decease of Jefferson are visible and palpable marks of Divine favor for which I would humble myself in grateful and silent adoration before the Ruler of the Universe."[10]

John Quincy and John the younger reached Quincy on the morning of the twelfth. There they embraced George, Thomas, and other members of the extended family. "Everything about the house is the same. I was not fully sensible of the change till I entered his bed-chamber, the place where I had last taken leave of him . . . that moment was inexpressibly painful and struck me as if it had been an arrow to the heart." Not surprisingly, his father's death led John Quincy to consider his own mortality. "My attachment to it [Peacefield] and to the whole region is stronger than I ever felt it before. I feel it is time for me to begin to set my house in order and to prepare for the church-yard myself."[11] Two months would pass before the president could tear himself away from Mount Wollaston and resume his official duties.

A seemingly endless round of memorial services, testimonials, and eulogies commenced. Among the most moving was the service at the Unitarian church of Quincy, John and Abigail's church. John Quincy had attended but never became a member. But it was John's youngest grandson who would deliver the most telling eulogy. Of the patriarch, Charles Francis wrote: "My grandfather was always personally kind to me. I revered his character. There was something in it calculated to stir a youthful mind. Bold, energetic, ardent, he was ignorant of the power of self-restraint. This worked him evil for it made him sincere. Falling into the hands of artful adversaries and ambitious friends, he has been a martyr to their intrigues." John Adams—whose character was "the boldest, the most enthusiastic, the most passionate in its support of liberty of all those who figured in the history of the American Revolution—has been handed to us with more of odium attached to it than any other. But the country will still do him justice; she has begun, and I trust in God she will continue to so to do."[12]

John Adams had named his eldest son, together with Josiah Quincy, executors of his estate. John Quincy was to serve as trustee, supervising the distribution of funds to the many inheritors. In his will the patriarch had deeded Peacefield and ninety-three acres of land surrounding it to John Quincy on the condition that he pay Thomas ten thousand dollars as compensation.[13] The will named a dozen other beneficiaries, including the town of Quincy. Their inheritance would come from the sale of the rest of John's property plus the family home's household items. John Quincy, increasingly consumed with what he believed was his inevitable exit from public life, could not bear to part with anything. Thus, he took out two large loans to buy the undeeded lands his father had owned, the sale of which was required to pay the other beneficiaries. Louisa protested; the Columbia Mills, Mount Wollaston, and Penn's Hill mortgages were already threatening the financial security of the family. Now her husband was borrowing again in order to acquire "a large, unprofitable, landed estate which has nearly ruined its last possessor." Did he wish, like Jefferson, to die penniless? "[I]t is impossible, utterly and decidedly impossible," she wrote her husband, "for you to do strict justice to them [the various claimants] and to your own children and, were you an angel, to give satisfaction to relatives who for years have been jealous both of your talents, your station, and your fortune."[14] But Louisa complained in vain. Her husband seemed consumed with nostalgia. "My design is to remain here in all possible retirement until my return to Washington shall become indispensable; if agreeable to you, I wish you to come here with Charles . . . as soon as you can," he wrote his wife.[15]

Following the final tribute and church service, John Quincy decided to personally lead a team of surveyors to establish the exact dimensions of the property he owned. He persuaded George and John to go along. "We march over tangled brakes and rattlesnakes and have everything of heroic fatigue but the glory," he wrote Louisa. He found the trek through the rough countryside—the weather alternating between thunderstorms and extreme heat—exhilarating. His sons did not. "George after one half-day found he had business in Boston; John discovered that he was of no use in the survey and takes a dispensation of attendance for the future."[16] That was hardly the whole story.

Returning to Boston, where his mother was in temporary residence, George, on the verge of a nervous breakdown, took to his bed. Louisa was furious. She poured out her anger and frustration in a letter to Charles: "The scenes in which he [George] has been called upon to become the principal performer, the great responsibility he incurred [George was then managing his father's property and had during the past year been elected to the Massachusetts General Court], the . . . irritating sensibility . . . of the women who surrounded him, and the dreadful exhibition on the day of your G.F.'s death and the two succeeding days, in addition to the unusual fatigue which he had to undergo, prostrated his strength which had already been impaired by a long indisposition; and to crown the climax, he was . . . laughed and sneered at because he was not able to bear the exposure to rain and every species of bad weather . . . all these circumstances added to harshness and severe mortification in the presence of strangers, have produced a state of painful dejection [and] have impressed him with an idea that he is unfit for the society or the duties for which other men are born."[17] Apparently John Quincy's frustration with his eldest had boiled over. In front of the survey team, he had ridiculed George for his weakness, self-indulgence, and failure to live up to the Adams name. John had somehow escaped his father's wrath. In the letter to Charles, Louisa recommended *Vivian Grey* as a cautionary tale. "Let me hope if in *yourself* you see any resemblance to the cold, calculating, selfish . . . Vivian Gray [*sic*], that you will set to work immediately to destroy the likeness."[18] A commentary, perhaps, on her husband?

"I cannot bear to stay at Quincy a day [longer] as it is more uncomfortable than ever and there is more hypocrisy and canting than I have ever been used to," Louisa subsequently wrote Mary Hellen, "and there always was quantum sufficient."[19] Louisa departed Quincy for Boston, where she rented a suite at Hamilton's Exchange Hotel; there she could be near her ailing son and far from her husband. In September, she took George on an outing to Nantasket Beach; John Quincy remained in Quincy. Shortly thereafter, with John in tow, Louisa departed for parts unknown. As was usual with her, emotional stress had led to physical illness. She sent John back to Quincy with a note asking her husband where he thought she should go. Tell her, he said to John, "that I wished her to go wherever she thought it would be most conducive to her health and comfort, and if she would let me know anything she wished me to do, I would do it."[20]

Ill and depressed, Louisa returned to Boston to be under the care of the family physician. "I enquired of him what he thought of the state of my wife's health," John Quincy wrote in his diary. "He said he believed there was disease in the right ovarium, but he did not consider it as dangerous to life. . . . It [her illness] was the occasion of great nervous irritability and excitement but transient in its paroxysms."[21] Louisa wrote in her diary, "Like a bird in a cage struggle as I will, there is an overbearing and preponderating influence which I cannot shake off in both my husband and my children that only make my exertions futile and destructive to my peace of mind and to my health. Thus, sickness passes for ill temper and suffering for unwillingness, and I am deemed an encumbrance unless I am required for any special purpose for a show or for some political maneuver."[22] As Louisa lay abed in Hamilton's Exchange Hotel, John Quincy came and visited her. "She conversed with me on family subjects of painful interest," he subsequently wrote in his diary. "I told her my dispositions for the future after my seclusion from public life." She later wrote in her own chronicle that "his plans had the approbation of my own heart."[23] By October, John Quincy and Louisa were back in Washington. "Let us mutually obliterate this summer from our memory," Louisa wrote George "or rather let it be stamped on our minds as a warning for the future."[24]

In truth, Louisa Catherine Adams was miserable in the White House. When John Quincy and she moved in, they had found that the Monroes had left the mansion with its vast chambers and hallways in a state of disrepair. Furniture was mismatched or missing. The new First Lady set workmen to replastering, painting, and applying new wallpaper. She scoured the capital for furniture that was attractive but not too expensive. Her husband was obsessed with economy and recordkeeping, lest his political enemies should accuse him of betraying the public trust. To her, the President's House seemed impersonal, institutional, devoid even of the amenities "any private mechanic's family" enjoyed. Her husband's office, lined with towering bookshelves containing his abundant library, reinforced the notion. "There is something in this great unsocial house which depresses my spirits beyond expression," Louisa wrote Charles, "and makes it impossible for me to feel at home or to fancy that I have a home anywhere."[25]

The sterility of the White House aside, life during the 1820s was hard in general for women, even one of Louisa's standing. Those of her gender were treated by men and society in general largely as ornaments, keepers of the hearth, and little else. Women's lives were restricted, confined physically by the whalebone corsets that they were compelled to wear and intellectually by their limited education and the denial of economic and political power. John Quincy had reached the pinnacle of his ambition, but what of Louisa? Because she was socially isolated and in desperate need of understanding and affection—of which she apparently had very little—her health, predictably, deteriorated. She became obsessed with chocolate, gorging on it, obsessing on its "thick, dark, melting deliciousness."[26] She was, as her son Charles observed, still an attractive woman, petite with fine features, light brown hair speckled with gray. Louisa's only apparent physical flaw was her teeth. By this point she had none, and she carried her dentures around with her in a bottle when she traveled.[27]

Louisa was ambivalent concerning the men in her family. She wrote Charles asking if he knew of a good book in French which she could translate. I am "almost a prisoner in my own house; the habit of living almost entirely alone has a tendency to render us [women] as savages," she wrote her youngest. He could not think of an appropriate French volume, Charles wrote back, and observed that hers "was the lot of every woman after she has attained a certain age in life."[28] In 1827, Louisa would warn her future daughter-in-law, Abigail Brooks [then engaged to Charles], that in their treatment of women, "the Adams family are one and all peculiarly harsh and severe . . . There seems to exist no sympathy, no tenderness for the weakness of the sex."[29]

In 1825, Louisa began her *Record of a Life, or My Story*, an account of her early years, her marriage to John Quincy, and her time in Berlin. Large portions were devoted to defending her family and herself against imagined charges of having deceived and defrauded the Adams family. Writing soon became her only solace. She penned a few stylistically simple poems, "To My Mother," "The Silken Knot," and others. There were one-act plays; melodramas were popular at the time. Her most telling composition, aside from her diary, was a play entitled *The Metropolitan Kaleidoscope, or Varieties of Winter*. The central characters were Lord and Lady Sharpley and their three sons. Of the offspring nothing revealing was said, but the portrait of the lord was John Quincy himself. He was a man of great accomplishments and a brilliant mind, absolutely devoted to the interests of his country. His knowledge of the human psyche was massive, but that knowledge was gained primarily through books and not experience. The lord of the manor practiced his virtues—"morality in conduct, sobriety, unceasing industry, and endless application"—to such excess that he neglected human relationships, including those with members of his own family. He exhibited a "natural coldness and reserve." (At this point Louisa had access to her husband's diaries. Could this have been quoted directly?) Beneath this front of rationality and self-control, however, lay an "ardent and impetuous" spirit and a volcanic temper that, though seldom vented, was terrible to behold. "He was full of good qualities, but ambition absorbed every thought of his soul . . . and to the attainment of this object no sacrifice would have been deemed too great."[30]

Of Lady Sharpley, Louisa wrote that, spoiled as a child, she would grow to be a woman of "strong affections and cold dislikes, of discretions and caprice, of pride and gentleness, of playfulness and hauteur." Lady Sharpley possessed "a too warm heart not understood by the cold and calculating world in the midst of which she lived." Life in the great Sharpley mansion was lonely and tedious, causing her to neglect and even abuse herself. "With a temper soured, bad health, and an almost total indifference to life or death, she was seldom roused to exertion, and knew little of enjoyment."[31]

In truth John Quincy's misogyny was complex and not unrelieved. His intolerance of human foibles included men as well as women. He was enthralled with female beauty, especially when combined with intellect and wit. Adams admired actresses not just for their beauty and sexuality but also for their deep understanding of the dramas in which they performed and for their interpretation of roles. He sought out and enjoyed conversation with women like Madame de Staël. Adams would recognize the central role that women were playing in the burgeoning reform movement, which focused on prisons, orphanages, insane asylums, and particularly slavery. "Elizabeth Robson, the female Quaker preacher . . . came on the morning visit," he recorded in his diary in September 1826. "After the usual salutations, Elizabeth sat some time with her hand covering her face as in deep meditation and then addressed me in a formal religious exhortation of about a quarter of an hour concerning the cares and duties of the ruler of a nation; but particularly upon the condition of the poor oppressed colored people in this country."[32] He was both impressed and moved.

John Quincy loved and admired his sometimes humorless mother, and he loved Louisa passionately, especially after he came to recognize the qualities of her mind. One of the things that bound Louisa, John the elder, and John Quincy together was their curiosity about and insights into human psychology. "My poor father used to tell me when I was a girl," Louisa wrote in her diary, "that I should defeat my own happiness in this world in consequence of my anxiety to trace even the commonest actions to their motives."[33] Both Louisa and John Quincy were discerning believers in a merciful God who had granted human beings free will— with all that that implied—and a creation that invited rational inquiry and moral behavior. After she and her sons attended a church service in Washington where they were treated to "a violent and threatening sermon from Mr. McIlvaine, full of bitter denunciations and punishment leaving little hope for either sinner or penitent," she vented to her diary that such men were not worthy of the cloth. Denial of the possibility, nay the certainty, of confession and forgiveness was nothing less than heresy.[34] Her husband could not have agreed more. "There is . . . in man a spirit," he wrote, "and the inspiration of the Almighty giveth him understanding. It is the duty of man to discover the vicious propensities and deficits of his heart, to control them. This, with the grace of God, a large portion of the human race in Christian lands do accomplish. It seems, therefore, to be worse than useless of preachers to declare that mankind are universally depraved. It takes from honest integrity all its honors; it degrades men in their own estimation."[35]

When all is said and done, the Quincy Adamses suffered from the same dysfunctions that plague families whose patriarchs serve for most of their lives in high public offices. As John Adams had warned his son as he undertook his first diplomatic mission, your country is destined to be your true mistress.

THE NEXT PRESIDENTIAL ELECTION would not take place until 1828, two years hence; consequently the anti-administration coalition that would morph into a new political party—the Democratic-Republicans—focused on winning control of Congress in the 1826 midterm elections. Its headquarters in Washington, known as the "house of Southern resort," was Mrs. Ann Peyton's boardinghouse situated at Pennsylvania Avenue and 4½ Street. Littleton Tazewell of Virginia and James K. Polk and John Bell, both of Tennessee, resided there. Calhoun, Jackson, and Thomas Hart Benton were frequent visitors.[36] But the architect and real leader of the anti-Adams movement was Martin Van Buren of New York. His political exploits had already earned him the sobriquets "the Little Magician" and "the Sly Fox." He was a brilliant, calculating, dispassionate operator whose goal was the re-creation of a two-party system in America. Clearly, the new party would serve as a vehicle for his personal ambitions, but he argued that the resurrection would do nothing less than save the nation from disunion and civil war. In order to succeed in a two-party system, the winner would have to have national appeal, hopefully in the North, West, and South, but at a minimum two regions out of the three; for that to happen, the issue of slavery would have to be finessed.

Martin Van Buren was born and raised in the village of Kinderhook, some twenty miles south of Albany. His father, a Revolutionary War hero, operated a tavern there, a cultural crossroads where young Martin was able to learn about the various foibles and motives of his fellow human beings. He studied law and was elected to the state legislature, identifying as a Jefferson–Madison Republican. In New York he championed the expansion of the franchise and created a powerful political faction including artisans and farmers, laissez-faire businessmen, and denizens of Tammany Hall, the political machine that would come to control

New York City. Van Buren's election to the U.S. Senate in 1821 placed him in a position to realize his dream of a new party, combining, improbably, the plantation owners of the South and the states' rights, democratic coalition he had forged in New York, New England, and Pennsylvania.[37] "Political combinations between the inhabitants of the different states are unavoidable," Van Buren wrote "and the most natural and beneficial to the country is that between the planters of the South and the plain Republicans of the North."[38]

With slavery temporarily off the board as topic of public debate, the anti-administration coalition focused on states' rights; the concept could be used to indict the administration on a number of issues: the Congress of Panama, internal improvements, Indian removal, the Second Bank of the United States, and the proposed creation of new national institutions. The slave power was obsessed with its institution while the South's yeomen farmers were focused on cheap land and debt relief, which in turn linked them to the "plain republicans" of the West and the North. The only fly in the ointment—a large one—was the tariff, over which North and South were irreconcilably split. What the burgeoning Democratic-Republican Party needed above all was a face, an avatar. One was at hand: Andrew Jackson, a vessel into which all of this discontent could be poured. He was, to boot, everything that John Quincy Adams was not.

In 1823, Tennessee senator John H. Eaton, in a series of letters signed "Wyoming," portrayed Jackson as the archetypal "Man of the People." Of the leading political figures of the country, only Old Hickory had achieved distinction as a private citizen, unsullied by ties of party, system, prejudice, or intrigue, Eaton wrote. "On nothing is he committed and to no one is he under obligation. . . . No parasite claims rest against him; he will be left free to administer the government as his judgment and prudence may direct."[39] So it was that Jackson was to be the anointed one for the Democratic-Republicans, but in truth many members of the Southern elite shared Clay's concerns about the Hero. Jackson seemed to many to be a man on horseback, unscrupulous and uneducated, who might very well lead a rabble army to overthrow the republic Jefferson and Madison had worked so painstakingly to establish. A Virginia journalist who eventually threw his support behind Jackson's candidacy remained uneasy, confiding to Van Buren that he rarely went to bed "without apprehension that he would wake up to hear of some *coup d'état* by the General which he would be called upon to explain or defend."[40]

Before departing for Tennessee in the spring of 1825, Old Hickory had voted against Clay's nomination to become secretary of state. The Kentuckian's letter to Francis T. Brooke in which he declared Jackson to be nothing more than a "military chieftain" had been published in the Washington newspapers shortly before. Actually, the Hero was content to be identified primarily as a soldier; he wrote

Samuel Swartwout of New York insisting that his military record was his principal recommendation. "It is very true that early in life . . . I contributed my mite to
shake off the yoke of tyranny and to build up the fabric of free government. . . .
Mr. Clay never yet has risked himself for his country, sacrificed his repose, or
made any effort to repel an invading foe . . . even Washington might be so considered [a military chieftain] because he dared to be a virtuous and successful
soldier, an honest statesman."[41] Recognizing the letter's value as a campaign document, Swartwout had it published.

As he made his way back to the Hermitage, Jackson took every opportunity
to denounce the "corrupt bargain" that had brought his rivals to power. On October 6 the Tennessee state legislature nominated him to run for president, and he
accepted eight days later. At the same time, that body debated a constitutional
amendment providing for direct election of chief executives in order to "preclude
all idea of fraud and combination in these elections." Shortly thereafter, Jackson
once again resigned from the Senate, a place "where temptation may exist and
suspicions arise in relation to the exercise of an influence tending to my own aggrandizement."[42]

By the fall of 1825, Van Buren's putative vessel was spouting criticism of the
administration. Instead of building lighthouses of the skies, establishing national
universities, and making explorations around the globe, the Adams administration ought to be looking after the interests of the common man, he proclaimed.
His charges that the administration was ignoring the popular will and creating a
federal colossus that would oppress its citizens and favor the East over the South
and the West struck a chord with many Americans. He decried the president's
plan to continue to sell the public lands of the West to the highest bidder, and to
use the proceeds to pay off the national debt and fund internal improvements.
Thomas Hart Benton, now Jackson's staunch ally, introduced a series of bills that
would cheapen public lands to the point that they would be given away to those
with the gumption to move in and occupy them. Adams, of course, was not unaware of all this. "Van Buren is now the great electioneering manager for General
Jackson as he was before the last election for Mr. Crawford," he noted in his diary.
"He is now acting . . . the part in the affairs of the Union which Aaron Burr performed in 1799 and 1800; and there is much resemblance of character, manners,
and even person, between the two men."[43] The comparison was, of course, strained
to say the least.

Like his father, John Quincy Adams knew how to write and think about governing other men, but he seemed incapable of actually walking the walk. It was
not that he lacked popular support. In October 1827 the Adamses made their
annual pilgrimage to Quincy. "At ten we landed at Philadelphia. A very great

crowd of people were assembled on the wharf, who, as I passed through them, greeted me with three hearty cheers. Great numbers of them followed me to the United States Hotel where, upon my entering the house, the cheering was repeated."[44] The outpouring of support continued throughout their stay. As the president prepared to depart by steamboat for New York, he was almost overwhelmed. "On the wharf a crowd of several thousands of persons were assembled, many of whom followed me into the boat, and thronged the deck till it became almost impassable; between two and three hundred of them shook hands with me."[45] Adams was hardly powerless to foil the machinations of his political enemies. He was president of the United States; he was the son of a Founding Father, an empire builder par excellence. The network of supporters that had labored to get him elected stood ready not only to help him govern but to get reelected. But the candidate would have to consult with them, plot strategy with them, empower them, and reward them. Up until the very end of his administration, Adams would have none of it. He still clung to the notion that the federal government ought to be run by nonpartisan experts dedicated to the public welfare. Surely Congress and the voting public would see the virtue in such an arrangement.

The Senate, dominated by Calhoun, was, of course, hopeless from the beginning, but not the House, where the National Republicans, as the Adams–Clay faction came to be called, held a majority. The administration failed in its efforts to have its candidate, John W. Taylor, elected Speaker of the House—by a margin of two votes. Taylor had made a name for himself as a hard-line restrictionist during the Missouri Compromise debate. He was also one of the handful of politicians who had helped swing the majority of New York's electoral votes to Adams in 1824. As such he was anathema to both Southerners and Van Buren's supporters in the House. Taylor would be swept out of office in 1826 in the wake of Democratic-Republican electoral successes. Another acolyte in waiting was Congressman Daniel Webster of Massachusetts, who had also played a prominent role in Adams's election. A former Federalist, he supported the American System and was daily gaining influence as a speaker and writer.[46] John Quincy had briefly considered naming the New Englander minister to the Court of St. James's, a post that Webster would covet throughout his career, but decided against it. It would, Adams and Clay feared, add fuel to the "corrupt bargain" flames. Throughout 1826 and 1827, Webster toured the Northeast and the Mid-Atlantic states, reporting to the president on political conditions and urging him to leap into the fray. Adams ignored him.[47]

But what of individuals like Walsh and Hopkinson, journalists and men of affairs who were in a position to shape public opinion? Early in 1826 a New Yorker named William Morgan attempted to publish a book revealing the secrets of Freemasonry. He soon afterward disappeared; his corpse was subsequently discovered floating in Lake Ontario some fifteen months later. The consensus was, of course, that the Masons had kidnapped and killed Morgan.[48] Shortly thereafter a rising young New York politico named Thurlow Weed called at the White House. Weed was then in the process of building an Anti-Masonic political party with which he hoped to challenge Van Buren's control of the Empire State. Adams received Weed cordially but absolutely refused to talk politics.

In June 1827 a supporter in the Keystone State wrote begging the president to attend the opening of the Pennsylvania Canal, where he could shake hands, slap backs, and speak to the German farmers in their own language. He was "highly obliged to my friends for their good purposes," Adams wrote back, but declared that "this mode of electioneering suited neither my taste nor my principles."[49] Weed would later write that the Adams administration had failed "owing to Mr. Adams's political impracticality. He was able, enlightened, patriotic, and honest . . . [but] he disregarded or overlooked what Monroe, Madison and Jefferson had deemed essential, namely, political organization and personal popularity. Mr. Adams, during his administration, failed to cherish, strengthen, or even recognize the party to which he owed his election. Nor . . . with the great power he possessed, did he make a single influential political friend."[50] Not only that, but the president refused to expel enemies within the gates who were working to undermine him and his administration.

When a friend of the administration complained to the president that the deputy collector of customs in Philadelphia was rewarding his enemies and punishing his friends to the point where it seemed in the Adams supporters' interest to switch parties. Adams replied, let them do so, and good riddance. By this point, it was clear that Postmaster McLean was an active and open supporter of the Jackson–Calhoun faction. He proceeded to use the massive patronage at his command to reward enemies of the administration. In 1826, John Binns, a Philadelphia newspaper publisher, wrote John Quincy complaining that McLean had taken away his government printing contract and given it to Richard Bache, an avid Democratic-Republican. The president summoned McLean and asked for an explanation. On what grounds should he punish Bache? the postmaster general asked; the man had done nothing illegal. Adams accepted this explanation, and Bache kept his government contract while printing one scurrilous attack after another on the administration and Adams personally.[51] Late in 1827, with Clay and Webster ready to pull out their collective hair, Adams summoned McLean, who vehemently denied supporting the Jackson–Calhoun faction. "As he is an able and efficient officer, I have made every allowance of the peculiarity of his situation and have not believed him willfully treacherous," John Quincy recorded in his diary.[52]

* * *

ALTHOUGH ANDREW JACKSON HAD explicitly endorsed the terms of the Transcontinental Treaty, including accepting the Sabine River as the boundary between Louisiana and Texas, he and his supporters hammered Adams during the run-up to the election of 1828 for "giving away" the valuable territory that lay west of the Sabine. The Jacksonian attacks were all the more hypocritical in that John Quincy had been the last of Monroe's cabinet to agree to the Sabine rather than a boundary that lay farther to the West. Thus, for political and strategic reasons, Adams and Clay hoped to renegotiate the Transcontinental Treaty so as to incorporate all or part of Texas into the Union. The slavery issue be damned.

Clay instructed the administration's ambassador to Mexico, Joel Poinsett, to acquire as much of Texas as possible through persuasion and purchase, and to establish a new boundary at the Río Colorado or even the Río Grande. When he arrived in Mexico City, Poinsett found the British emissary entrenched and well along in negotiating with Mexico a trade treaty that would grant British citizens preferential treatment. When Poinsett approached the Mexican foreign minister, Lucas Alamán, about renegotiating the Transcontinental Treaty of 1819, he readily agreed. Why don't we start with the Mississippi as the proper boundary between the United States and Mexico? Alamán suggested. In effect, this would have given to Mexico all the territory the United States had acquired from Spain. Infuriated, Poinsett began to plot a regime change. He helped a group of wealthy businessmen obtain a charter from the York, England, or York rite, branch of Masons. Scottish rite Masons—featuring many of Mexico's most influential landowners, clergymen, and former Spanish officials—had long been a powerful political presence in Mexico; it was a mainstay in the ruling Conservative party. With Poinsett's aid, the new Liberal party managed to overthrow the pro-European, anti-American regime, but the new government proved no less willing to part with Texas than its predecessor. Upending friendly governments with which the United States had formal relations was not yet part of the republic's repertoire, and Clay suggested Poinsett's recall. Adams insisted that they wait until there was a formal request from Mexico City; it came in due course.[53]

IT WAS NOT UNUSUAL for presidents to receive death threats, but in the spring of 1826, John Quincy was confronted with a situation that he had to take seriously. In May the family physician, Dr. Henry Huntt, called at the White House and informed the president that he had learned from an acquaintance, a lawyer named Colonel Thomas Randall, that a client of his, Dr. George Todson, intended to assassinate the chief executive. Todson, previously the assistant surgeon general in the Army, had been court-martialed and cashiered for embezzling funds. He swore his innocence and insisted that he was the victim of a cabal of which the president was a part; Todson was, Randall had assured Huntt, determined to take his revenge, salvage his honor, and suffer the consequences. Randall had offered to meet with the president and brief him. Adams agreed but observed to Huntt "that [in the meantime] I knew not anything that I could do by way of precaution."[54]

Sometime later the attorney came calling. "He said Todson had avowed to him his determination to assassinate me," John Quincy subsequently recorded in his diary, "and that he believed it was no idle menace; that the man was desperate, and upon this subject perfectly mad. Randall is a phrenologist, [and] with the utmost seriousness avowed that his apprehension arose in part from Todson having a most extraordinary organ for destructiveness. The tendency of this observation was to throw an aspect of ridicule upon the whole affair." Adams had indeed refused to renominate Todson to his army medical post; reviewing the findings of the court-martial, he had found nothing amiss. Nevertheless, the president was concerned. Phrenology aside, Randall had a reputation for honesty and integrity. "I am in the hands of a Higher Power," Adams wrote in his diary.[55]

A month later the physician-cum-assassin called at the White House, and the president received him. Todson demanded to be restored to office. Leave and only return in company with your lawyer, the president admonished him. Todson duly reappeared with Randall in tow an hour later. Adams informed them both that he had painstakingly reviewed the legal proceedings against the doctor and stood by his decision. If the two could come up with any solid evidence of partiality by the court, he would reconsider. They, of course, could not. Several days later Todson came round again and asked Adams to pay for his room and board in Washington since his dismissal and cover the expenses of his return to New Orleans, his home. "I told him that, whatever I might have done under other circumstances, he had rendered it impossible [by threatening Adams's life] for me to afford him any relief."[56] This would not be the last that Adams would hear of the good doctor.

ON MAY 5, 1827, Andrew Stevenson of Virginia, an outspoken Jacksonian, was elected Speaker of the House of Representatives, cementing the Democratic-Republicans' control of both chambers of Congress. Six days later, Adams observed in his diaries, "My own career is closed. My hopes such as are left me, are centered upon my children. My capacity to write fails me from day to day. My duties are to prepare for the end with a grateful heart and unwavering mind."[57] He tried to distract himself with swimming, but the sense of adventure had waned in the wake of his near drowning. "My confidence in the celebrity of the river-bath and swimming is greatly shaken, and yet not wholly gone," he wrote in his diary. "I have bathed less than any preceding summer, usually diving from a boat [sea-worthy, presumably] and swimming to the shore not less than ten nor more than twenty minutes in the water."[58] The chief executive sought refuge in a new hobby: "enquiries relating to the production and growth of fruit and forest-trees . . . I have Loudon's *Encyclopaedia of Gardening* . . . an octavo volume of twelve hundred and forty pages; and his *Encyclopaedia of Agriculture* . . . a similar volume of twelve hundred and twenty-four pages. I find a wide field opened before me."[59] He had during previous vacations in Quincy attempted to raise fruit trees—with disastrous results.

In the summer of 1827, the president and the White House gardener planted Spanish cork, walnuts, shagbark hickory, persimmons, tulip trees, and those fruit trees that had some hope of surviving the Washington climate. Within a year, the White House grounds boasted seven hundred trees of numerous varieties. The president had Clay instruct American consuls abroad to send seeds of native plants for possible inclusion in his outdoor herbarium.

But nothing seemed to work; the black dog of depression continued to stalk Adams. "My health has been languishing, without sickness," he recorded in his diary, "from four to five hours of sleep not of good repose; a continued habit of costiveness, indigestion, failure of appetite, uncontrollable dejection of spirits . . . a sluggish carelessness of life, an imaginary wish that it were terminated with a clinging to it as close as it ever was in the days of [my] most animated hopes."[60]

Adams's relationships with his sons during this period were a mixed bag. Despite their best efforts, John Quincy and Louisa could not end the budding romance between Mary Hellen and John. When their middle son informed his parents on February 1, 1828, that Mary and he would wed in three weeks, the two were understandably incredulous. "I have declined having anything to do with it, therefore can give you no further information," Louisa wrote Charles. And then again, a few days before the scheduled nuptials: "[Y]ou could never imagine that anything of the sort was dreamt of and strange to say neither by word or look has your father intimated the idea of such an event taking place. . . . He had never said a kind word to the young Lady to give her courage for the occasion."[61] But John Quincy and Louisa reconciled themselves to the union, and the couple was married quietly at the White House on February 25, 1828. Thirty-one guests attended, but Charles and George were not among them. After cake and copious amounts of champagne, the president actually danced a Virginia reel. Nine months later the newlyweds presented the president and First Lady with a granddaughter, Mary Louisa, who would become the apple of her grandparents' eyes.

The marriage, not surprisingly, delivered another blow to George's self-esteem. When he had been in St. Petersburg in the midst of a lengthy separation from his two elder sons, John Quincy had written his mother that he had read a passage from Adam Smith's *Theory of Moral Sentiments* that had "smote him to the heart." Smith had observed, "A father is apt to be less attached to a child who, by some accident, has been separated from him in its infancy and who does not return to him till it is grown up to manhood. The father is apt to feel less paternal tenderness for the child; the child less filial reverence for the father."[62] In truth, this seemed to be exactly the case with John Quincy and the children he had left behind in America. He would never forgive John for his expulsion from Harvard, but at least the second son was able to fill the role of faithful personal secretary and dogsbody. A glimmer of hope appeared in Adams's relationship with George when the latter had been elected to the Massachusetts General Court in the spring of 1826. "I congratulate you upon this early and honorable token of the confidence of your fellow-citizens," father wrote son. But do not let your election go to your head. "Consider the station to which you are called as a post of danger and of duty . . . prepare and discipline your mind for disappointment."[63]

But then, not long after, John Quincy learned that his eldest was wallowing in debt, and this at a time when unpaid bills could land one in debtors' prison. Dr. Thomas Welsh reported that for many months, George had not paid for his room and board in order to cover his drinking and gambling debts. In addition, George had borrowed a thousand dollars from Henry Wood, a Quincy coffin maker. "What is Henry Wood?" Adams wrote his son. "And what are you? By what properties was it that he had superfluity of 1,000 dollars to put out at interest while you was plunging up to the ears in consuming debt . . . and was running in arrears for your daily bread besides?"[64] But he could not help but bail George out. He wrote proposing that George sell his library to his father for two thousand dollars. Make a list and paste John Quincy's name in each to prove ownership, the president instructed. George could then keep the library. This would give George a fresh start and, John Quincy hoped, free him to live on the two-hundred-fifty-dollar quarterly allowance he regularly received. But the benefactor would have his pound of flesh. John Quincy implored his son "nevermore to burden yourself with shameless expenses and senseless debts.—As to books—debts for books! Of what earthly use to you are . . . books with such life as you have led? . . . May a merciful God redeem you from the very verge of ruin."[65] But George never compiled a list, nor did he paste his father's name in his books. There was no proof that the two thousand dollars had righted the ship; George's correspondence to his parents subsequently dwindled to almost nothing.

How different was John Quincy's relationship with his youngest child. In 1825, Charles had graduated from Harvard in the middle of his class but with no history of rebellion. Like his brother George, he studied law in the offices of Daniel Webster. In October 1827, Charles wrote asking his father to provide advice and guidance as he prepared to enter the next stage of his life. "I ask you . . . to write me every week, and as far as I am able, [I] will answer your letter," his father wrote back.[66] Not surprisingly, John Quincy began his "Plan for Success for Charles" with an admonition to rise early, preferably between five and six. "One hour of the morning lamp is better than three of the evening taper." The extra time would prove beneficial in every way; remember, "Genius is the child of toil." He sent his son a ditty: "Six hours to sleep and six to law / And four devote to prayer / Let two suffice to fill the maw / and six the muses share."[67] To John Quincy's amazement and amusement, Charles stood up to him. I can never rise before seven and never will, he replied. You may rise at six but frequently you fall asleep at the dinner table. His father decided to drop the issue. Of course, there was the drumbeat of advice to read the classics—especially Cicero in Latin—plus Voltaire, Pascal, the Scottish philosophes, and history. Charles largely complied but dared to challenge his father's adulation of Cicero, charging that "the individual whom you have pronounced your favorite" was lacking in "firmness of character," and was, therefore, "inferior to Cato."[68] Charles dared another heresy. The Tory version of the events leading up to the American Revolution made more sense to him than the Whig: Parliament had had every right to tax the colonies; in this, he was challenging both his father and grandfather. Louisa advised her youngest to ease off: "even if his [John Quincy's] deductions are not entirely like yours in points of moral character, respect prejudices acquired by favorite studies and . . . do not harshly and positively condemn them."[69]

Charles loved and respected his father, but the growing awareness that he would be the son called upon to carry on the family tradition of public service weighed heavily upon him. "I do not expect to make a very great figure in the world," he wrote his father. "I cannot get over my dislike of the idea of a political existence. It shackles the independence of mind and feeling which I have always perhaps extravagantly admired, and in this country it destroys all social ties, all the finer but less intense enjoyments of existence." John Quincy was offended: "If you prefer to remain in private life, stand aloof—you may be sure not to be disturbed in your privacy."[70] But Charles's tone was generally respectful and even loving. As was true of husband and wife, father and son could achieve an intimacy on paper that they found difficult in person. "Your letters are becoming a necessary of life to me," John Quincy wrote Charles. "I have not in seven years read so much of classical literature as since I began these letters to you. And I might add I have not in seven years enjoyed so much luxurious entertainment."[71]

The correspondence was cathartic for both men. Charles's letters were a declaration of independence. I respect and admire you, he was telling his father, but I am your equal and will not be held prisoner to your expectations. I will have my own values and standards for myself and will sink or swim by them. Initially offended and hurt by his son's implied criticism, John Quincy was in the end relieved. He sensed that Charles, unlike his brothers, would be whole, with a chance to become self-sufficient and live life on his own terms.

In 1826, Charles Francis fell deeply in love with Abigail Brooks, the daughter of Peter Chardon Brooks, the wealthiest man in New England. He met her at a ball in New York given by the French ambassador. She was charming, intelligent, and modest. Abby lived with her family in Medford, outside Boston, but traveled to Washington frequently to visit her sister, who was married to Congressman Edward Everett, an intimate of the Adamses. In view of Miss Brooks's many suitors, Charles had to court her assiduously.[72] A year after they first met, Charles, at another ball, made his intentions known in the customary way. He danced every dance with Abigail, and she reciprocated by taking his arm and parading around the room. He asked if she would permit him to pay her further attentions; flustered, Abigail declared that she would have to consult her father.[73]

Peter Brooks hesitated; Abigail was only eighteen, Charles nineteen. Like Joshua Johnson had with Louisa, he hoped to keep his favorite daughter at home for a bit longer. Moreover, Charles was just beginning his law studies; it would be years before he could support a family. Desperate, the young man informed his parents of his intentions and appealed for their support. John Quincy and Louisa were delighted with his choice. "Miss Brooks is a great belle here and a wonderful favorite with the family," Louisa wrote George.[74] John Quincy agreed to write a letter of recommendation to Peter Brooks. His son was "sedate and considerate—his disposition studious and somewhat reserved—his sense of honor high and delicate, his habits domestic and regular, and his temper generous and benevolent. An early marriage is more congenial to a person thus constituted than to youths of more ardent passions and of more tardy self-control." Why not allow the couple to announce their engagement but postpone marriage until Charles had reached his twenty-first birthday? Money would not be a problem. Abby was promised a dowry of twenty thousand dollars. "Both her fortune and my own prospects," declared Charles, "are such as to prevent any uneasiness as to our condition in life."[75] Brooks, who greatly admired the Adams family, gave in.

In the wake of his engagement to Abigail Brooks, Charles faced the daunting task of breaking up with his mistress. He had begun the affair eighteen months earlier. It was obviously more than a tryst with a servant girl; his consort, never named, could have been the daughter of a middle-class family or an older unattached woman.[76] Boston was a small town, full of gossip. Continuing the liaison would have threatened his engagement and the lifestyle it promised. On April 24, 1827, Charles recorded the breakup in his diary: "In the evening I went through one of those disagreeable scenes which occur sometimes in life. No man of sense will ever keep a mistress. For if she is valuable, the separation when [it] comes is terrible, and if she is not, she is more plague than profit. Ever since my engagement, I have been preparing for a close of my licentious intrigues, and this evening I cut the last cord which bound me." Abigail Brooks was in many ways similar to Charles's mother: well-bred, skilled at music and conversation, a charming social partner, tolerably well-read, and never vain. The one glaring difference was the size of their dowry. But Charles did not marry for money. "I do love this girl as I think a woman ought to be loved," he wrote. "Sincerely, fervently, and yet with purity and respect."[77]

But a two-year engagement was a long one and, for Charles, expensive. John Quincy had been subsidizing his youngest to the tune of eight hundred dollars a year. In November 1827, Charles wrote asking for an increase. When he was in Boston, he had to bear "the whole care of her [Abby] in going to evening parties," and when she was in Medford, he was obliged to rent a horse and gig to make his frequent visits.[78] John Quincy raised the allowance to a thousand dollars, but Charles was still not satisfied. In August 1828, while at Peacefield visiting his father, he asked for yet another increase. John Quincy exploded. The two argued and parted in anger. Adams subsequently wrote his son accusing him of "being unearthly extravagant" and reminding him that he was after all "a beggar, living on charity." Charles confided to his diary that his feelings "were cruelly hurt and in a manner which no subsequent kindness can remedy."[79] Young Adams then took the unusual step of appealing to Abby's father to shorten the engagement. "He was short," Charles noted in his diary, "merely saying that he wished it [the marriage] deferred for a year until he might build another house for his daughter, that I was young and next autumn would be time enough. This was an unexpected blow and prostrated my spirits."[80] He subsequently informed Abby of her father's decision; they had no choice but to acquiesce. She wept bitter tears and promised that come what may, they would be betrothed the coming October.

During a subsequent visit to Washington, John Quincy called Charles into his quarters and gifted him shares of the Middlesex Canal Company. "This was meant as kindness, and I received it as well as I could," Charles recorded in his diary, "but nothing like this can efface the effect of the conversations of last August."[81] To be fair, the president was at the time quite concerned about his ability to support his family if, as was almost certain, he would lose the presidential election. When one of his supporters came round requesting that the president personally contribute to his own election campaign, Adams told him that "the expenses of my family and the support of my three sons now absorb very nearly the whole of my public salary; that all my real estate in Quincy and Boston is mortgaged for the payment of my debts; that my income of my whole private estate is less than six thousand dollars a year; and that I am paying at least two thousand of that for interest upon my debt. Finally, that upon going out of office in one year from this time . . . it will only be by the sacrifice of that which I now possess that I shall be able to support my family."[82]

31

The Election of 1828

THE PRESIDENTIAL ELECTION OF 1828 would prove to be one of the most
bitterly fought, most rancorous in American history. By 1828 the Jacksonian machine had erected a powerful press network that bombarded Adams and Clay on a weekly basis. In Washington the administration could count
on the support of Peter Force's *National Journal* and the *National Intelligencer* edited by Joseph Gales and William Seaton. But they were no match for the *United
States Telegraph*. The ardent Calhounite Duff Green had been brought to the capital from St. Louis, where he had edited the *Enquirer*. Green, a skilled propagan-
dist, made no attempt at objectivity. Except for a few excerpts from congressional
debates, the articles in the paper were screeds written by Green or harvested from
the Jacksonian papers around the country. At the height of the campaign, the
Telegraph claimed a circulation of forty thousand, with another twenty thousand
for special editions.[1] In 1827 the paper published "An Exposition of the Political
Character and Principles of John Quincy Adams." The essay, purportedly a description and analysis of John Quincy's speeches and public statements, insisted
that he, like his father, was at heart a monarchist, a man who believed that the
common man was not fit to govern himself, much less others. According to the
article, Adams, deeply impressed by his years in Europe, saw the American chief
executive as just another king. "The people themselves, if uncontrolled, will never
long tolerate a freedom of inquiry, debate, or writings," Adams was quoted as
saying. "What a libel on the principles of free government," Green exclaimed.[2]
Most of the quotes were fabricated; those that were not had been taken from John
Quincy's commentaries on the French Revolution.

Van Buren's mouthpiece was the *Albany Argus*, and it proved second only to the
Telegraph in scourging the president. In a series of editorials in 1828, the *Argus*
repeated the charge that the Adamses were royalists. Far from being the defender

of George Washington and the architect of American foreign policy, John Quincy Adams was a parasite on the body politic, having been only once elected to office (false) while spending the bulk of his career in appointive offices, growing fat off public funds. "You have made no sacrifices for a country from whose treasury you have been supported through life," the *Argus* opined. "The nation has gained nothing from your experience."[3] Recall that the Adamses, father and son, had been the authors of the anti-republican Alien and Sedition Acts. The *New York Evening Post*, another Jackson sheet, accused the president of being the driving force behind the Hartford Convention! The *Argus* declared that Clay was nothing less than a reincarnation of Aaron Burr.[4]

One of the charges leveled against the Adamses was that Louisa was an Englishwoman, not even a citizen of the United States. The accusation prompted her to write a mini autobiography that was published in the *Philadelphia Evening Post*. The essay was a disaster. Her father, she wrote, had risked life and limb to aid American agents in Europe during the Revolutionary War. For his trouble he had been cheated by his business partners and forced to return to the United States, penniless and unappreciated. She then described her time as the wife of a U.S. minister abroad, unwisely highlighting her warm reception and intimate relationships with the crowned heads and noble born in Berlin and St. Petersburg. There was a brief description of her winter journey from St. Petersburg to Paris. Louisa denied that she was a liability to her husband's campaign; rumors that the Johnson family had "palmed" her off on the Adamses were untrue.[5]

Green and the *Telegraph* rushed through the door that Louisa had opened. The First Lady was putting on airs, trying to prove that she was above Rachel Jackson, the Hero's wife, and attempting to "demonstrate how much better qualified she was to discharge the duties of the drawing room than the unassuming, plain, old housewife of the Tennessee farmer."[6] Louisa's trip across Europe had been funded with taxpayer money. Her efforts to appear "unassuming" were the height of hypocrisy. Then the crowning blow. The *Telegraph* claimed to be privy to the real "truths" concerning Louisa's background—"what is known to the boys in the streets of this city." The paper had no intention "to trace the love adventures of the Chief Magistrate, nor to disclose the manner, nor the time, at which he, his brother-in-law, and his father-in-law before him led the blushing brides to the hymenal altar." Green, of course, had heard rumors that Joshua and Catherine had not been married at the time of Nancy's birth and that Louisa's sister Adelaide had given birth to a daughter long after her husband, Walter Hellen, had died. "The effect on her [Louisa] was like electricity," Green wrote Jackson. "The whole Adams corps were thrown into consternation."[7]

By 1828 a number of administration supporters were talking about running

Clay against Jackson instead of Adams. But Harry of the West refused to jump ship. "We are both guilty or both innocent of the calumnies which have been propagated against both," he wrote a supporter. "By their calumnies they have completely identified us, and I hope every friend I have will see in Mr. Adams' re-election my interests as much involved as if . . . [my] name were directly held up for the presidency."[8]

Riding the rising tide of anti-intellectualism in the nation, the *New York Enquirer* asserted "that no person can have a correct knowledge of mankind who has led a life of entire abstraction from the great body of the people and who relies for his information on the books he has read and the scholastic theories that he taught."[9] In truth, the Adams–Clay people generally turned up their noses at the idea of appealing to the common man. They acknowledged that "the ignorant and degraded class of our population"—as they put it—"are all against us." They contented themselves with the knowledge that their ranks included "all the merchants and nearly all the principal mechanics . . . mostly quiet moral people—men of wealth and influence." Isaac Russell of Cincinnati and an intimate of Clay reported that "there was a great stir or fuss here a few days ago; carriages gratis, filled with the halt, the lame & the blind; nearly all drunk, to vote for Jackson."[10]

While the president fiddled, Clay, Rush, and Southard worked the electioneering circuit as best as they could, writing letters to doubters, making appearances, and giving stump speeches. Even this boomeranged. The Jackson sheet the *United States Telegraph* blasted Adams for allowing his lieutenants to quit their official posts and neglect the business of the nation. Clay's and Southard's illnesses during the summer of 1828, the editors claimed, were faked in order to give them time away from Washington to pound the campaign trail.

In truth Clay was ill to the point of resigning. Please don't, Adams pleaded with him. Go home, rest, and recuperate. He and Daniel Brent could run the State Department. "I told him it was my wish to set aside all consideration of political effect in this matter," Adams recorded in his diary. "His life and his health should be paramount to all other considerations. . . . It would be exceedingly painful to me to part with him, as I had fondly hoped we should continue together at least until the close of my present term of service."[11] The Kentuckian was moved to tears.

The political coup de grâce, if one were needed, was delivered by the Democratic-Republicans when they secured passage of the "Tariff of Abominations" in 1828. Though a free trader in theory, Adams was committed to a modest tariff that would help protect the country's "infant industries" from the import of more cheaply produced foreign products and from discriminatory tariffs imposed on U.S. exports.[12] But the issue was a tricky one. The people of Southern states like

South Carolina, which exported cotton and other raw goods (upon which there were no duties) to Europe, were generally free traders. More important, the slave power saw the tariff as part of a nationalist conspiracy to crush states' rights. If, John Randolph and others argued, the federal government could impose a protective tariff on the South, it could do anything, even abolish slavery. But protectionism was strong in New England and some parts of the West, in transmontane Virginia, and in southwest Pennsylvania. Manufacturing was on the verge of replacing shipping as the economic mainstay of New England. Daniel Webster, who had voted against the Tariff of 1824, had been converted by the industrial revolution in his native region into a staunch protectionist. John C. Calhoun, the nationalist turned states' righter who had also voted for the 1824 measure, had become an ardent opponent of protection. Slavery aside, Southern planters feared that Britain and other nations would retaliate against U.S. protective tariffs by taxing their cotton, sugar, and indigo. Moreover, high tariffs on imported manufactured items meant that raw material producers would have to pay higher prices for their finished goods.[13]

Nevertheless, Adams and Clay believed that they could craft a tariff measure that would appeal to protectionists in New England, Pennsylvania, and New York and to Westerners who hoped to profit from internal improvements. The South they considered a lost cause. Van Buren and the Jacksonians had other ideas. A newspaper friend of Clay's warned the secretary of state in August 1828 that Van Buren and his allies were "resolved to support a tariff such as one as no sensible man can support, and hope[d] to throw the blame of rejecting it on the North."[14] The bill that the Democratic-Republicans introduced in Congress in the fall of 1828 raised duties on almost every product, both finished goods and raw materials. Duties were particularly high on raw materials, upon which New England depended. Jackson supporters planned to then vote down the very measure they had crafted. "The Jackson party is playing a game of brag on that subject," Clay wrote a friend. "They do not really desire the passage of their own measure"; it "was the vilest of cheats."[15] The coalition that Adams and Clay had envisaged held together and voted for the measure; the House passed the Tariff of Abominations by a vote of 105 to ninety-four, and the Senate by a tally of twenty-six to twenty-one. Adams dared not veto it. Thus, the measure, which raised rates on both imported manufactured goods and raw materials, become law to the glee of the Jacksonians and the despair of the administration.

In April 1828, Russell Jarvis, a journalist in the employ of the *United States Telegraph*, a man who pilloried and slandered the president on a weekly basis, had the audacity to show his face at one of Louisa's drawing rooms. John, then acting as his father's personal secretary, spied the journalist and declared in a loud voice that if Jarvis "had the feelings of a gentleman, he would not show himself here."[16] When subsequently Jarvis learned of the remark, he wrote a note to John demanding satisfaction. The young man ignored him. A week later John was delivering some papers to a congressional committee. Jarvis followed him out of the House and into the Capitol rotunda, called his name, and asked if he had given his final answer. When Adams said yes, Jarvis punched him. John attempted to retaliate but was restrained by onlookers. When Edward Everett subsequently reported the incident to John Quincy, the president's inclination was to stay out of the argument. John had been assaulted in the midst of performing a public duty. If there was to be an investigation, Congress should initiate it. When the matter came up at the next cabinet meeting, Calhoun was adamant: the chief executive should demand a congressional investigation. "The act was of the most dangerous character as an example," Adams recorded him as saying. "It had a tendency to introduce assassination into the Capitol." If left to its own devices, the House, dominated by Jacksonians, would have done nothing. "The other members of the Administration concurred in these views, and I acquiesced in them," the president wrote.[17]

The House did indeed investigate; John testified at length; Jarvis declined an invitation to appear; and in the end, nothing was done. In an editorial in the *Telegraph*, Duff Green blasted the president for bringing "a private affair before Congress." Jarvis, he declared, "could not have anticipated that the baby, who was considered old enough to take charge of the contingent fund [that covered White House expenses] and deliver messages to Congress, would run blubbering to tell his daddy that he had had his nose pulled and his jaws slapped for his impudence."[18] The incident did lead to the establishment of the United States Capitol Police.

In July 1828 the president was invited to attend the groundbreaking for the Chesapeake and Ohio Canal. To the two thousand assembled souls who could hear him, Adams declared, "May the use to which it is about to be devoted prove the precursor to our beloved country of improved agriculture, of multiplied and diversified arts, of extended commerce and navigation."[19] Needless to say, the crowd was less than inspired. The president of the Chesapeake and Ohio Canal Company handed Adams a shovel to perform the groundbreaking. "It happened that at the first stroke of the spade it [hit] immediately under the surface a large stump of a tree," as John Quincy would describe the incident; "after repeating the stroke three or four times without making any impression, I threw off my coat, and resuming the spade, raised a shovelful of the earth at which a general shout burst from the surrounding multitude." Adams was taken aback. "It [the demonstration of his physical determination] struck the eye and fancy of the spectators more than all the flowers of rhetoric in my speech."[20] By the time it was completed, the Chesapeake and Ohio, like John Quincy Adams, was an anachronism, one overtaken by the railroad and the other by popular politics.

Though it repelled him, John Quincy stooped to campaign personally during the waning days of the election, although he typically confined himself to trying to persuade influential fence-sitters among the political elite. His supporters in the press, in Congress, and around the country took off the gloves. Jackson was an unlettered frontiersman, they declared, a tool of Machiavellian politicians who pulled his strings. The alliance between the "plain republicans" of the North and the slaveholding aristocracy of the South was absurd on its face. Jackson was a drunkard, impious, and a duelist, opined the *Rhode Island American*, which then proceeded to publish John Quincy's letters to his son George on the Bible.[21] It was true that Adams and Clay wanted to consolidate power in Washington, but it was to advance the common good; Jackson, like Napoleon, would consolidate power in himself and tyranny would be the result, the Adams camp declared. States' rights, particularism, and laissez-faire were a formula for national weakness, not national greatness.

Adams's supporters declared that Jackson and his wife, Rachel, had lived together in sin for years before she obtained a divorce from her first husband. Jacksonians announced that Adams, when minister to Russia, had pimped Louisa's beautiful young maid to Tsar Alexander. The first charge was true; the second was not. In 1790, Jackson had moved in with Rachel Robards, who at the time was married to another man. In 1794, Rachel's husband, Lewis Robards, managed to obtain a divorce on the grounds of abandonment and adultery. As soon as they learned of the decree, Rachel and Jackson married. In 1827, when the story broke, the couple insisted that they had secretly married in 1791, but there was no evidence to support their claim. Old Hickory never forgave Adams and blamed his wife's death on the campaign slander of 1828.[22] Martha Godfrey, Louisa's maid and Charles's nanny, was indeed a beautiful girl. In St. Petersburg she had written her mother describing the tsar's "amours and gallantries." She was unaware that all letters passing through the Russian post office were opened and read. Her stories came to the eye of the emperor and the empress, who were much amused. They asked to meet Martha, and she, Louisa, and baby Charles paid a brief visit to the imperial palace.[23] It was, of course, Louisa's sister Kitty whom the tsar had had his eye on, but his hot pursuit of her had proved fruitless.

The presidential election of 1828 took place in different states on different days between October 31 and November 5, 1828. Jackson and Calhoun captured 73 percent of the popular vote in the South and the West. They also won in New York and Pennsylvania. Adams and his running mate, Richard Rush of Pennsylvania, carried New England, New Jersey, Delaware, six out of eleven electoral votes in Maryland, but only sixteen out of New York's thirty-six. Because of his efforts to defend the Creeks, Adams did not receive a single vote in Georgia. The electoral vote was 178 to eighty-three and the popular tally 647,276 to 508,264.[24]

Was Andrew Jackson's victory in 1828 the herald of a return to Jeffersonian democracy? In a sense, no, in that the Old Republicanism that Van Buren, Calhoun, and Duff Green espoused was a sham. Without the three-fifths clause, the Jefferson–Jackson "revolution" could never have taken place. The four hundred thousand popular votes Jackson garnered in the North brought him only seventy-three electoral votes while the two hundred thousand he racked up in the South produced 105. The vast majority of the adult males who voted in 1828 were farmers; Adams prospered among those living along commercial routes while Jackson did well in economically undeveloped areas. Old Hickory fared well among non-English-speaking and first-time voters. But most of the counties that Adams carried in the North were more democratically run than those he lost in the South. Jackson benefited from an emerging political machine that was able to arouse and manipulate public opinion. Nevertheless, the election of 1828 sounded the death knell of a nationalist political philosophy of planned improvement and the fostering of a diversified economy that had the potential to wean the country from dependence on the export of slave-grown staples.[25]

Adams's epitaph for the election of 1828 was not far off the mark: "When I came to the presidency, the principle of internal improvement was swelling the tide of public prosperity till the Sable Genius of the South saw the signs of his own inevitable downfall in the unparalleled progress of the general welfare of the North and fell to cursing the tariff and internal improvement and raised the standard of free trade, nullification and states' rights. I fell, and with me fell, I fear never to rise again, certainly never to rise again in my day, the system of internal improvement by national means and national energies. The great object to my life heretofore as applied to the administration of the government of the United States has failed. The American Union as a moral peon in the family of nations is to live from hand to mouth, to cast away, instead of using for the improvement of its own condition, the bounties of Providence." His successors, Adams predicted, would "rivet into perpetuity the clanking chain of the slave, and . . . waste in boundless bribery to the West the invaluable inheritance of the public lands."[26]

On a personal level, John Quincy and Louisa were filled with a sense of relief; it was as if a great burden had been lifted. "Your father is well and growing very fat," Louisa wrote Charles. "It is impossible to behave with more real dignity than he does amidst trials which are sufficient to shake the nerves of a Pallas."[27] Adams even permitted himself a bit of magnanimity. "The condition of the Union at home and abroad is upon the whole more prosperous than it has ever been before at any period of its existence," he wrote Jeremiah Condy. (That was true. During the Adams administration the national debt had been reduced by seven million dollars; both agriculture and manufacturing were booming.) "The symptoms of disaffection to the Union which have recently been exhibited in its Southern section, having produced the effect for which they were gotten up, will subside when no longer necessary for the purposes of those for whose benefit they were excited." Protectionists and antitariff men would "like the lamb and the lion" lie down together. "We have abundant evidence that the popularity of General Jackson is of a character not easily shaken . . . and as there is in his own character a fund of genuine public spirit, . . . we have every reason to hope that his administration will be successful not only to himself but to the general welfare of the Union."[28] At one of the last White House receptions, the Adamses were seen to be "social, gay, frank, and cordial." Louisa had hired a band, and there was dancing. The ladies of the cabinet showed up "in new dresses just arrived from Paris."[29] What a change! exclaimed Margaret Bayard Smith, an acute observer of Washington life and frequent critic of the president and the First Lady. Feelings of satisfaction and optimism soon passed, of course, Adams being Adams and Jackson being Jackson.

President-elect Jackson—tall, thin, and hawk faced, with his trademark shock of white hair—slipped unobtrusively into town. He let it be known that in memory of his beloved Rachel, who had just died in December, he wanted to be inaugurated with a minimum of pomp and splendor. John Quincy sent word that he and his family would vacate the White House by March 4 in order that the new chief executive could receive his friends and supporters there. Old Hickory replied cordially enough, thanking Adams and expressing the wish that the Adamses would not inconvenience themselves; stay another month if you so desire.[30] John Quincy and Louisa had no desire to linger and were out by the fourth. The president-elect asked Adams's longtime manservant, Antoine Guista, and his wife to stay on at the White House, and they agreed. "This separation from domestics who have so long lived in the family is among the painful incidents of the present time," Adams lamented in his diary.[31]

Henry Clay paid a farewell visit; Adams informed him that "after the 3rd of March I should consider my public life as closed and take for that time as little part in public concerns as possible."[32] But what will you do with yourself? Clay asked. Read and write, Adams replied. The life of an intellectual had always attracted him. But Adams found it not so easy to go into that good night. One morning during the interregnum between his defeat and Jackson's inauguration, he rose early as usual to write. Louisa had spent an uncomfortable night, and it promised to be a cold, gloomy day. "[A]s I began to write my shaded lamp went out, self-extinguished. It was only for lack of oil, [but] the notice of so trivial an incident may serve but to mark the present temper of my mind."[33]

As Jackson awaited his coronation day, thousands of people, many of them working-class, began pouring into Washington; they came by wagon, on foot, on mules, in carriages, and in boats. They filled the city's rooming houses and hotels, and spilled over into Georgetown and across the Potomac into Arlington. They had come to see "their" president.[34] An estimated twenty thousand persons surrounded the Capitol on inauguration day. Departing his hotel, Jackson together with his entourage made his way slowly up the hill. Chief Justice John Marshall administered the oath of office. Following a brief address, Old Hickory was mobbed by those seeking to shake his hand. With some difficulty, the Hero escaped through the rear of the building.

The scene that ensued at the White House was even more chaotic. Jackson had decreed that one and all were welcome at his postinaugural reception. He was, after all, the people's president. Men, women, children, shopkeepers, mechanics, farmers, and common laborers pressed upon the new chief executive. Shielded by a phalanx of supporters, Jackson was finally able to beat a retreat to Gadsby's Hotel. After the crowd rushed through the front door and climbed in through the windows of the White House, they pulled down curtains, stood on furniture, and toppled china cabinets. Servants attempted to draw them away by setting up punch bowls and tables laden with food on the White House lawn but with little success. Henry Clay was a witness to the scene: "Orange punch by barrels full was made, but as the waiters opened the door to bring it out, a rush would be made, the glasses broken, pails of liquor upset, and the most painful confusion prevailed. . . . Wines and ice creams could not be brought to the ladies, and tubs of punch were taken from the lower story into the garden to lead off the crowd from the rooms . . . it was mortifying to see men, with boots heavy with mud, standing on the damask satin chairs."[35]

John Quincy Adams did not attend the inauguration, one of only two outgoing presidents who failed to do so, the other being his father. The fact that Jackson had not called or invited him to be part of the ceremonies stung. Duff Green blamed Old Hickory's cold shoulder on his anger at the slanders flung at his beloved Rachel. "I have not been privy to any publication in any newspaper against either himself or his wife," Adams protested in his diary.[36] In truth, he had polled his cabinet, asking whether he should attend the inauguration. All but Rush advised against it. The ex-president was, no doubt, deliciously gratified by the mayhem that occurred on inauguration day. While publicly he remained silent on the new administration, privately to his family, he vented his spleen. When Jackson named the feckless John McLean to the Supreme Court and Kentucky spoilsman William T. Barry to be postmaster general, Adams observed, "The General Post Office . . . and all the post offices are to be subjected to its patronage. Memorable reform. The next step will be to turn it into a police department and to take the fingering of all the letters into Executive hands . . . the composition of the cabinet is not sufficient to the Heroite party itself . . . the dictation of caucuses and central committees, the conflicting puppets of Van Buren and Calhoun . . . feed the ravening of hungry and prostituted partisans."[37]

In truth, Andrew Jackson had at his disposal some eleven thousand jobs. The Jacksonians were determined that all should be filled by their partisans. "A clerk in the War Office named Henshaw who was a strong partisan for Jackson's election, three days since [has] cut his throat from ear to ear from the mere terror of being dismissed," Adams reported to his diary. "Linnaeus Smith, of the Department of State, one of the best clerks under the government, has gone raving distracted and others are said to be threatened with the same calamity."[38]

For a variety of reasons, not the least of which was Louisa's fragile health, John Quincy decided to delay the family's annual retreat to Quincy. He rented from the wife of Commodore David Porter their mansion on Meridian Hill. The lovely estate, a mile and a half north of the White House, sat astride the meridian line of seventy-six degrees, fifty-three minutes, which bisected the city of Washington. There was room not only for John Quincy and Louisa but for John, Mary Catherine, and their two young children as well. Amidst a steady stream of visitors and well-wishers, the former president busied himself preparing a response to the "Thirteen Confederates" in Massachusetts, who were insisting that he name those "traitors" who in 1808 and then again in 1814 had allegedly plotted secession from the Union. Most of the thirteen were longtime personal friends of John Quincy. Adams confided to his diary that he had shared many of the concerns of Harry Otis, Theophilus Parsons, and other Federalists about Jefferson and his policies. "The disunion project of 1804 cannot be fully exposed without developing the causes of dissatisfaction with Mr. Jefferson's administration," he confided to his diary. "Most of these were well founded. I felt them deeply myself."[39] But there was no excuse for plots to dismember the Union.

Adams's *Reply to the Massachusetts Federalists*, dated December 31, 1828, was designed to vindicate himself before the bar of public opinion. He would not name the original conspirators (of 1804–1805) but assured Otis and the others that their names were not among them. But many of the thirteen had participated in the Hartford Convention. "I . . . hold it as a principle without exception that whenever the constituted authorities of a state authorize resistance to any act of Congress, or pronounce it unconstitutional, they do thereby declare themselves and [the] state *quoad hoc* out of the pale of the Union. . . . [T]here is no supposable cause in which the people of a state might place themselves in this attitude. Those who think that each state is a sovereign judge not only of its own rights but of the extent to [which] power [is] conferred upon the general government by the people of the whole Union" were sadly mistaken. Adams ended by imploring Otis and his friends, "Here if you please, let our joint correspondence rest."[40] But the thirteen would not; they came back with the public *Appeal to the Citizens of the United States*, published on January 28, 1829. They charged Adams with sullying the reputation of his home state of Massachusetts without a shred of evidence. In the end, Adams decided not to publish his massive *Reply to the Appeal of the Massachusetts Federalists*, a rare act of restraint on his part. As Charles put it, the document "told the truth far too violently to be useful."[41]

In the weeks following Jackson's inauguration, the only member of the cabinet to reach out to Adams was Martin Van Buren. He called at Meridian Hill and asked to discuss past U.S. relations with the Ottoman Porte. The meeting was cordial enough. "He pursues enmity," wrote Adams, "as though it might be one day his interest to seek friendship."[42] "He has played over again the game of Aaron Burr in 1800 with the addition of political inconsistency in transferring his allegiance from Crawford to Jackson—He sold the state of New York to them both—His pale and haggard looks show that it is already a reward of mortification."[43] Shortly afterward, Van Buren attempted to effect reconciliation between Adams and Jackson. He urged the president to approach his predecessor and shake hands at the next public venue at which both should be in attendance. Remember the New Englander's defense of you following the Florida affair, he reminded Jackson. Old Hickory agreed, but when an occasion arrived—the funeral of Philip Doddridge, a congressman from Virginia—he could not bring himself to do it. "I approached Mr. Adams with a *bona fide* intention to offer him my hand," Jackson later sheepishly explained, "but the old gentleman, observing the movement, assumed so pugnacious a look that I was afraid he would strike me if I came nearer."[44]

MEANWHILE, ALARMING REPORTS REGARDING George Adams were emanating from Boston. His brother was living "like a pig," Charles reported; his room was dirty and cluttered, and he seldom showed his face at his law office (the brothers had rented rooms in the same building). In his diary Charles referred with disgust to his brother's "[i]ndolence and inactivity, mental and bodily." He reported to his mother that George was suffering from "dejection, low spirits, and inability to occupy himself—and this acts upon reflections of a melancholy kind in regard to father and himself."[45]

Louisa could hardly have been surprised. She knew her eldest—how sensitive, how romantic, he was; how so often detached from reality, so fearful of his father. She decided that a change of scenery and closer proximity to family would remedy the situation. In April 1829 she wrote George suggesting that he come to Washington "to escort your father and myself on our way home." Then, pathetically: "You know that we are neither of us famous travelers, and your assistance for me will be absolutely necessary." Your father has mellowed, she wrote. Once they were all back in Quincy, John Quincy would keep a horse and gig, "and you will always command the use of it. P.S. If you come you will see our pretty baby."[46]

Louisa's call terrified George. He would have to face his father again. He was deeper in debt than ever, and his law practice was at best inconsistent. He had begun drinking heavily and neglecting his personal appearance. And as for viewing a baby, he had fathered his own, born out of wedlock, in December 1828. The mother was a young servant girl, Eliza Dolph, employed by the Welshes, with whom George had continued to board.[47] George had retained a physician, Dr. David Humphreys Storer, to care for Eliza during the pregnancy and deliver the baby when the time came. In February 1829, George arranged with one Miles Farmer to take Eliza and the child into his household "to restore the mother to her friends and society again." Farmer managed the extensive real estate holdings of the Amherst entrepreneur Martin Thayer. As compensation, Farmer, his wife, and their four children were then living rent-free in one of Thayer's houses in Hanover Street.[48] Presciently, George told Charles that he had tucked away in his clothes trunk a letter of great importance, and if he should die sometime in the near future, the letter should be retrieved and its instructions followed.

Early on Wednesday morning, April 29, George Adams boarded the stage that would bear him from Boston to Providence. There he took passage aboard the luxurious new steamship *Benjamin Franklin*, under the command of Captain T. S. Bunker and headed for New York. He seemed well and in good spirits, but as the day wore on, he complained to a fellow passenger of a severe headache and declared that he wished that the ship would either slow down or speed up so that he could be really seasick. That evening George began to hear voices. He went to bed but could not sleep; the ship's engines seemed to intensify his auditory hallucinations. George rose and, in the hallway, accused a fellow passenger of spreading false rumors about him, which, of course, the man denied. He returned to his berth but rose again and dressed around three a.m. on the morning of the thirtieth. Climbing the ladder to the bridge, George confronted Captain Bunker and demanded to be put ashore. The *Franklin* was then cruising through Long Island Sound at sixteen knots. "Why?" Bunker asked. "There is a combination among the passengers against me," the young man replied. "I heard them talking and laughing at me." The captain dismissed him. Minutes later, George encountered a fellow Bostonian, John Stevens; the two men held a brief conversation after which Stevens ascended to the upper deck. Shortly thereafter he spied George's hat lying on the lower deck near the stern rail. Stevens sounded the alarm, and Bunker had the ship searched. But all that was found was George's cloak lying near his hat. John Quincy and Louisa's tortured son had either jumped or fallen overboard.[49]

Two days later John Quincy and Louisa spied a carriage coming up the road from Washington to Meridian Hill. It must be George, they thought, but it was instead Nathaniel Frye, Louisa's brother-in-law, with a notice from the *Baltimore American* declaring that George Washington Adams had gone missing. John Quincy and Louisa hoped for the best, but shortly thereafter Judge William (Billy) Cranch arrived with letters confirming George's disappearance. The New York firm of Davis and Brooks, undertakers, had taken possession of George's trunk. There had been a thorough but fruitless search. George was presumed dead. "God be merciful to him and to his wretched parents—the condition of his mother from the time I informed her of the event is not to be described," John Quincy noted in his journal.[50] Louisa and John Quincy were overcome not only with grief, but with guilt, hers interspersed with fits of rage at her husband for what she considered his heartless and unrealistic expectations. To his credit, John Quincy did not attempt to defend himself. "Deep has been her afflictions heretofore," he wrote. "But this! Stay thy hand God of Mercy—Let she not say—My God! My God! Why hast thou forsaken me?"[51]

Charles, in Boston, learned of his brother's demise the same day as his parents. "I was totally unprepared for such a shock, and it seemed to turn the current of my blood," he confided to his diary. "I felt no other emotion excepting the chill under the skin." His inclination was to rush to Washington to console his parents, but Dr. Welsh and his soon-to-be father-in-law urged him to remain in Boston to clear up his brother's affairs. The next morning Charles began to go through George's belongings. "Poor fellow, he [George] complained to Dr. Welsh before he went, but I never suspected alienation of mind, or he should never have gone."[52] Leafing through his brother's correspondence, Charles found three or four letters that he decided ought not to see the light of day. "George had an extremely amiable disposition, but he was the creature of impulse and frequently gave way to the seduction which an ill regulated imagination excited. My father almost lived in him." Charles recalled George's request that in case of his demise, his younger brother should look for a letter of instructions. He found it. "The paper . . . was in the shape of a request in case he died that his debts should be paid and the balance given to a little girl whom he had seduced and who was then pregnant by him."[53] There would be nothing to bestow on Eliza and her child, however, because, as Charles recorded, his brother's debts to his father would consume whatever assets he possessed. He destroyed the letter but promised himself that he would do what he could for those George had left behind.

On the morning of May 28 as he worked in his office, Charles received a visit from Miles Farmer, Eliza's caretaker. He had since lost his position as Thayer's agent, and it was all George's fault, Farmer declared. George had kept coming around to see Eliza, causing Farmer's other renters to gossip. Rumors that Farmer was harboring the liaison had cost him his job (which was not true). He demanded compensation, or he would tell all. "I will make some provision probably similar to what it [the child] would be entitled to by law," Charles replied, but he would not be blackmailed. "I certainly will be forced to do nothing," he wrote Farmer. "You are welcome to all the benefit a disclosure will give you," but he warned Farmer that he had discovered a large unpaid debt Farmer had owed George, and that would certainly be collected. Farmer immediately backtracked.[54]

George could do in death what he could not do in life—bring his parents closer together. Moved by John Quincy's remorse over his harsh treatment of their eldest, Louisa forgave him. She begged her husband to ignore whatever accusations might spring from her lips in the midst of her ravings. They prayed for him and for each other. At her request John Quincy read to the assembled family the service for the dead from the Episcopal *Book of Common Prayer*: "I am Resurrection, and I am Life, says the Lord." Adams wandered through Rock Creek Park, grieving and praying. "May we humble ourselves in the dust," he exclaimed, "and be conscious that thy chastisements have been deserved."[55] During one of his strolls, a summer shower doused him; but then came a rainbow, which the father took as a sign of hope and a gentle command to get on with his life. John Adams and his cousin William Steuben Smith journeyed to New York to recover George's trunk and whatever other possessions of his that were left aboard the *Franklin*. As John Quincy and Louisa planned their funerary trip, she shrank from the task. Friends, family, Peacefield, all the memories—she feared they would overwhelm her. She announced that she must stay behind in Washington to care for Mary Catherine and her baby.

John Quincy and John departed Washington and traveled by canal boat to Philadelphia. There they boarded the steamboat *Swan*, destined for New York. Aboard the vessel, the elder Adams read in the *Morning Herald* that George's body had washed up on City Island in the sound some sixteen miles north of Manhattan. "May it sooth you to learn," he wrote Louisa upon deboarding in

New York, "that the person was entire without mark of violence or contusion— His watch and small pocket book were still in their places and his name was legible within his boots."[56] From his friends, John Quincy learned that his son's body had been temporarily entombed in Eastchester. John and he rode out to the churchyard where the crypt lay. The grieving father could not bring himself to unlatch the cover and view George's corpse. John arranged for the body to be shipped to Quincy to await a formal funeral scheduled for the fall. In his hotel room, John Quincy spread the contents of his son's pockets on his bed—there were several five-dollar bank bills, a penknife, pocket change, a watch, a comb, and ornamental sleeve buttons that John Quincy had given George four years earlier as a token of his affection.[57]

Charles wrote his own epitaph for his brother: "Poor George. Much merit as he had for his spirit of literature and his generosity of heart, he was eminently unfitted for the duties and common occurrences of life. His mind was throughout speculative, at times philosophical, but always unequal to what the world terms common sense. With a keen sense of right, he was unable to resist wrong in an alluring shape, and with a bitter recollection of the past, he could not turn to improvement for the future. Thus, his life was a continued scene of virtuous resolutions, and vicious transgression, of violent repentance and passionate repetition."[58]

From New York John Quincy made his way to Quincy. It was time to prepare for retirement and the few short years the former president believed God had allotted him. Peacefield had been the showplace of Quincy since John and Abigail had improved it upon their return from Europe in 1788. An imposing two-story frame house, the structure was sided with brick on each end and topped with a mansard roof. Visitors approached the house from the south along a flagstone walkway leading to the front door. On the left as one entered was the famous West Room, paneled in rich mahogany. To the right was a spacious dining room. On the second floor were the two principal bedchambers.

But by 1829, Peacefield had fallen on hard times. Charles had ridden out to the family home shortly before his father's arrival and was appalled: "The sight of the old house and its condition made me sick," he recorded in his diary. "I felt disgust at its extremely dismal appearance. The nursery looks miserably and everything bears powerful marks of utter want of attention."[59] During John the patriarch's last years, when he had lived there with his wife's spinster sister, Louisa Smith, the house and grounds had begun to deteriorate. Thomas had lived on the premises from 1826 to 1829 but had done nothing to arrest the decline. The farmer Isaac Farrar and his wife occupied a small tenant house on the edge of the grounds; he worked the nearby fields but was under no obligation to care for the Adams family's house. When John Quincy arrived, he found Peacefield almost devoid of furniture, the floors without carpets, and the wallpaper peeling. Almost all of the fruit trees that his father and he had planted had withered and died.[60]

That first night Adams spent in the Old House (his birthplace) was filled with memories. Overwhelmed, he turned to prayer: "Almighty God bestow upon me a spirit of gratitude, of humility, of cheerfulness, and of resignation. . . . Grant me health, peace of mind, the will and power to employ the remaining days which thou hast allotted me on earth to purposes approved by thee."[61] The following Sunday he attended services at the new stone church erected by the townspeople of Quincy, paid for by a bequest from John Adams's estate. It was a gracious and elegant building referred to as "the Temple" by parishioners. The church had disinterred John's and Abigail's remains from their resting places in the churchyard and placed them in a special crypt beneath the nave.

Peacefield was in such wretched condition that John Quincy considered erecting a new stone house near the Temple and a planned school for teaching the classics, also funded by John Adams's bequest. Louisa objected. If you are going to build anything new, build two frame houses so that your surviving sons will have residences close by.[62] In the end, John Quincy was unable to come up with the funds to do either. And so, in the summer and fall of 1829, he set about restoring Peacefield. He hired Louisa Smith to be his housekeeper and employed a local carpenter. Charles came out frequently from Boston. Thomas lived nearby in the Old House, and his son Lieutenant Thomas B. Adams. Jr., on leave from Fort Pickens, Florida, spent much of the summer there. John Quincy retrieved from storage in Boston some furniture that he and Louisa had brought back from Europe. But what was he to do with his six-thousand-volume library, the finest private collection in America? His dream was to build a separate library building on the grounds, but for the present, they were stored on makeshift bookshelves built in rooms throughout the house.[63]

John Quincy, of course, merely supervised the renovations on Peacefield. There was much time left for reading, writing, and exercise. In the summertime heat, he resumed swimming. Several times each week, he, in company with one or more of his nephews, gathered at Daniel Greenleaf's wharf, where Black's Creek flowed into Quincy Bay. They covered the half-mile round trip from the upper wharf to the lower wharf in approximately thirty minutes. Charles had been urging John Quincy to write a biography of his father; he began the task, going through family papers and local historical records. He delved into various histories of colonial America and the American Revolution but soon found composing the life of John Adams so daunting that he put down his pen.

The social climate was warm in Quincy, but it remained frosty in Boston. There were no public fetes for the ex-president; the Athenaeum attempted to cancel his membership but could not, as he was an original proprietor. The American Academy of Arts and Sciences removed him as president, an honorary post he had held for the previous twelve years. Harrison Gray Otis, who had been elected mayor of Boston—as a Jacksonian!—ignored him. There was an invitation to the July 4 celebration, but it was perfunctory.

Meanwhile, in Washington, Louisa was dismayed to learn that the Porter mansion had been sold out from under her and her family. Forced to vacate the premises on August 1, she had no choice but to take up residence in John's as-yet-unfinished house. Louisa quickly decided that she, Mary Catherine, and the little one would repair to Quincy. After all, Peacefield was to be her permanent home, and she wanted to be on hand for Charles and Abby's wedding, which was scheduled for September. It was decided that John would escort them as far as New York, where Charles would meet them. On his way south Charles traveled from Providence to New York aboard the *Benjamin Franklin*, the very vessel that had been the scene of George's demise. After he informed Louisa that she too would be traveling on the ghost ship, she collapsed. "It was just after the clock struck twelve," Charles recorded in his diary, "that my brother's wife burst into my room in the utmost alarm and roused me from a sound sleep by telling me that my Mother had been taken excessively ill. . . . She was lying under one of those violent attacks which she is subject to with all the family and servants up and trying to assist her in her distress. . . . Suffering was dreadfully stamped . . . on my memory. I had never seen anything like this before, and it affected me to the soul."[64] Reluctantly, Charles agreed that Louisa, Mary, and her baby, who had also become ill, should return to Washington.

Charles and Abigail married on September 3, 1829. The ceremony at the Brooks home in Medford was modest with only twenty-one guests in attendance. At midnight, Charles recorded in his diary that "we were on our road to town, took possession of our house [a gift from Peter Brooks] and there consummated the marriage."[65]

The last week in November, George's remains finally arrived in Boston. "Mr. Hubbard the sexton of the parish at Quincy came and I accompanied him to the vessel where I saw the remains of my poor brother transferred to his wagon and on their road to their final resting place," Charles recorded in his diary. "It gave me at the moment a strong feeling of melancholy, for I knew him well and was witness to much of the latter part of his feverish dream."[66] When the body reached Quincy, John Quincy, a neighbor friend, and the Reverend Peter Whitney conveyed it to the churchyard, where it was interred in the family sepulcher. That evening he poured out his grief. "In this journal was recorded on the 12th of April

1801 the birth of this my first-born son. Desired how long, how anxiously! Granted to fervent prayers after frequent disappointments. With what earnestness of hope, with what anguish of fear have we followed the course of his short career! How small a portion of his life was passed under the paternal roof! . . . Heavenly Father, let it have mercy before thee, and in the day of retribution let not my errors be visited upon my child!"[67]

ADAMS DEPARTED QUINCY FOR the capital in early December 1829. For much of the way, he found himself in the company of Daniel Webster, whom he described as "averse to conversation."[68] Arriving at John's house in Washington, the former president found, to his relief, all of his family well. John's residence, built with the help of his parents, was a comfortable frame abode situated on the west side of Sixteenth Street between I and K Streets, less than two blocks from President's Square. The elder Adams quickly resumed old habits. Each morning, early, he rose and walked to and around Capitol Hill, frequently in the company of Chief Justice John Marshall. He began making notes for a history of political parties in America. And he reread Cicero, which delighted him in yet a new way. He believed he could see in the orator-statesman's life a strong parallel to his own. "I feel the agitation of his pulse, not for himself but for his son [who had died], for his Tulia [Cicero's daughter who was ill], for his country [the Roman Republic was facing destruction]. There is sometimes so much in it of painful reality that I close the book. . . . My morning always ends with a hearty execration of Caesar [Jackson] and with what is perhaps not so right, a sensation of relief at the 23 stabs of the Ides of March, and the fall at the feet of Pompey's statue."[69]

Upon George's death, John Quincy had begun reading the Bible again, taking the full tour from Genesis to Revelation. He agreed to pen some articles on the Russo-Turkish War for Joseph Blunt's *American Annual Register*. Like his father, John Quincy had always been an avid student of history. Now began the study of the craft of historical writing. He understood clearly the difference between primary and secondary sources.[70] He lamented the dearth of primary sources not necessarily because they would provide a clearer, more accurate picture of the past, but because, as he believed, they would shed light on the fundamentals of moral and ethical philosophy.

For Adams the function of the historian was not simply to lead the reader through a historical landscape but to use the past to make him/her a better person. This is why in 1822 he had urged Charles to make the Bible the center of his historical reading.[71] It was the moral "lessons" that history had to teach that were important. The other "legitimate purpose" of writing history was to vindicate oneself or a family member and/or to indict a political enemy. Throughout his life Adams had had a tendency to associate the sins of the subjects being written about with the historians who were chronicling them. All of this was unbelievably archaic for a man of Adams's intelligence. Perhaps he believed he could control history as he thought he could control everything else.

On his way back to Washington, John Quincy had conferred with the artist Thomas Sully concerning his full-length portrait of the sixth president. The portrait had been commissioned by Ward Nicholas Boylston, Adams's patron, to be painted by his friend Gilbert Stuart. Stuart had begun the project, but he had completed only John Quincy's head when he died in 1828. The commission then passed to Sully. One of the reasons Stuart had not finished was a disagreement with John Quincy concerning the costume in which he would appear. Stuart had favored the full court dress in which Adams had appeared when minister to the Court of St. James's. For one reason, he wanted it to match the painting of John Adams completed in 1783 by John Singleton Copley, in which the second president appeared in formal dress. But John Quincy was determined that he should be presented in the costume of a plain American: "I have confirmed myself in the opinion that the portrait should be painted in plain black pantaloons and boots under them—A round hat should be also introduced, whether in one hand or on a table."[72] The portrait was completed as John Quincy directed. It went to hang with his father's likeness in the halls of Harvard College.

As was true of his predecessors, the former president faced an uphill battle financially. When he left office, Adams was worth around a hundred thousand dollars. There were sundry properties in Quincy, Boston, and Washington as well as stock in the Bank of the United States and shares in assorted canal and turnpike companies. But his liabilities were daunting. He had to make interest payments on mortgages stemming from the implementation of his father's will as well as payments to Thomas Boylston and John's other heirs. Then there was Columbia Mills, the grain processing operation he had purchased when secretary of state. The mill on Rock Creek bought wheat and corn from nearby farms and milled it into flour to be sold in and around Washington or shipped to cities up and down the Atlantic Seaboard. By 1829, Columbia Mills was producing only a hundred barrels a week instead of the anticipated hundred a day. There was George Johnson's mismanagement, but other factors figured in as well. Flash floods from spring rains damaged or destroyed part of the mill's equipment. Local crop yields were unpredictable, and the East Coast was then being flooded with Western flour shipped in over the recently completed Baltimore and Ohio Railroad.

John Quincy worried constantly that the business would become a stone tied around his—and his family's—neck, reducing him to the virtual state of penury that had overtaken Jefferson and Madison.

ADAMS COULD NOT HELP obsessing on the new administration. In truth Andrew Jackson and his governing methods and public policies provided much food for thought—and criticism. The new president was accustomed to command rather than governing in a democracy, which required, among other things, consensus building. He had grown up on the American frontier, on the border between North Carolina and South Carolina in a log cabin, the son of Scots-Irish itinerants. Left to his own devices by the early deaths of his parents, Jackson had made his own way in the world, buying land and slaves and acquiring enough education to enable him to practice law. A Tennessee militia commander, he fought and dueled throughout his early manhood, killing one man in 1806 and subsequently suffering a life-threatening wound in a barroom brawl with the future senator Thomas Hart Benton and his brother. In between his military exploits in the War of 1812 and the invasion of Florida in 1817–1818, Jackson built a magnificent estate in Tennessee, the Hermitage. The Hero of New Orleans bought and sold slaves on a large scale, at one point selling some forty human chattel to Edward Livingston for twenty-four thousand dollars.[73]

Like Adams, Jackson was an empire builder. The New Englander and he had worked hand in glove to expand the nation's western frontier. But there were far more differences than similarities between the two men. Jackson was a democrat in that he believed in equal opportunity for every white male American regardless of social class or education. He was also a thoroughgoing racist. Indians who were loyal to him were his children; those who were not were savages fit only for extermination. Jackson had ridden into power on a horse groomed by Martin Van Buren and, ironically, Thomas Hart Benton. The steed breathed the fire of righteous indignation against the corruption of financial and political elites and harnessed itself to the Old Republican doctrines of states' rights and minimal government. But soon after his inauguration, Old Hickory made it clear that he was the rider, and the horse was the horse, and no one should ever get them confused.

Previous presidents had viewed their cabinet members as colleagues, frequently making decisions and issuing policies only after a consensus emerged. Not Jackson. The secretaries and postmaster general were convened primarily to receive their marching orders. What advice the Hero took came from an informal "kitchen cabinet" made of journalists and political hacks. The new administration applied the spoils system with a vengeance and largely without regard to merit. In his message to Congress of December 1829, Jackson famously declaimed: "The duties of all public offices are, or at least admit of being made, so plain and simple that men of intelligence may readily qualify themselves for their performance."[74] One spoilsman, Samuel Swartwout, a crony whom the president personally selected for the post of collector of customs for the port of New York, absconded in 1839, having embezzled more than one million dollars from the port's accounts. But Jackson not only survived; he thrived. "General Jackson rules by his personal popularity which his partisans in the Senate dare not encounter by opposing anything that he does," John Quincy observed, "and while that popularity shall last, his majorities in both houses of Congress will stand by him for good or evil."[75]

Vice President Calhoun had jumped on the Jackson bandwagon certain that he would succeed the president after he served two terms. That was not to be. In the spring of 1831, the perpetually ambitious William H. Crawford, who hated Calhoun, wrote the president and confided to him that during the brouhaha over the general's invasion of Florida, the South Carolinian, then secretary of war, had demanded that the Monroe administration disown Jackson. Immediately thereafter, Jackson demanded an explanation from the vice president. Calhoun, of course, was not able to come up with a satisfactory response.[76]

Adams wanted to make public the records of conversations showing that Crawford had been as willing to repudiate Jackson as Calhoun. He told William Wirt that he owned nothing to either man. "Both of them had treated me with base and gratuitous ingratitude. But Calhoun was a drowning man and now stretched forth his arms imploring us to save him. . . . Upon mere principles of humanity I would save Mr. Calhoun—extricate him from the deep waters into which he is sinking."[77]

Calhoun was grateful for Adams's willingness to stand up for him. He called on his former friend to pay his respects. "I meet Mr. Calhoun's advances . . . because I cannot reject them," Adams recorded in his diary. "I once had confidence in the qualities of his heart. It is not totally destroyed, but so impaired that it can never be fully restored."[78]

One of the issues Adams and Calhoun had seen eye to eye on was Indian removal. When one was secretary of state and the other secretary of war in the Monroe administration, both had insisted that the Cherokee, Chickasaws, Creeks, Choctaws, and Seminoles—the so-called Five Civilized Tribes—not be coerced into parting with the lands they had occupied since before the nation's founding. This should be accomplished only voluntarily through the treaty-making process. During the presidential campaign of 1828, Jackson had equivocated on internal improvements and the tariff, but he was explicit on the Indian question: all had to be removed beyond the Mississippi posthaste. Indeed, removal lay at the very core of Old Hickory's plans for national development. Not only did the Indians occupy hundreds of thousands of acres of valuable land, but their continued existence as sovereign peoples within the borders of the United States also constituted a threat to the nation's sovereignty and to white supremacy. In December 1828, shortly after Jackson's election, the state of Georgia declared that as of June 1830 all members of the Cherokee Nation would be subject to state law, notwithstanding the provisions of virtually all of the treaties signed between the tribes and the federal government since 1785. At Governor John Forsyth's request, the Jackson administration withdrew federal troops from the state, leaving law enforcement to the Georgia Guard. Under state law, the Cherokee would not be able to vote, sue, own property, or testify in court against a white person. Alabama and Mississippi would soon follow Georgia's lead. When Congress convened in December 1829, Jackson introduced the Indian Removal Bill, which declared that the federal government had the right to remove through financial inducement or by force if necessary all members of the five tribes to lands west of the Mississippi.

The removal bill stirred up a storm of protest among feminists, abolitionists, and spiritual leaders, especially in the free states. The American Board of Commissioners for Foreign Missions organized letter-writing campaigns and financed antiremoval speakers and editorials. Even the former skeptic Henry Clay signed on to defend the indigenous peoples he had once declared to be beyond the pale. The Indian Removal Bill passed the Senate in a straight party vote twenty-eight to nineteen, but the tally in the House was close: 102 for and ninety-seven against. Twenty-four Jacksonians voted no.[79] John Quincy was, predictably, disgusted. "[T]he bullies of Georgia have succeeded in the project of extirpating the Indians by the sacrifice of the public faith of the Union and of all our treaties with them," he wrote in his diary.[80]

Adams saw Georgia's defiance of the federal government and the treaties that it had made with the Indians as part of a larger and much more dangerous assault on the powers that had been vested in the federal government by the Constitution. Western settlers and Eastern speculators wanted to be able to buy public lands from the federal government as cheaply as possible—the settlers because they were generally poor and the speculators because they wanted to hold and then sell dear when land became scarce. Their champion was Senator Thomas Hart Benton, who sponsored bill after bill reducing the price of Western lands as they were surveyed and put up for sale. Eventually Benton and other Westerners would go a step further and insist that public lands belonged to the states and not to the federal government. Nationalists like Adams had opposed cheapening the public lands and were adamantly opposed to ceding them to the states. They looked to the proceeds from the regulated sale of the vast, unsurveyed territories west of the Mississippi to fund internal improvements, public education, and other projects of benefit to the nation as a whole. Benton denounced the nationalists as pawns of Northeastern merchants and industrialists who feared losing a source of cheap labor as working people migrated westward. The policies advocated by the National Republicans posed a threat not only to the West but to the South, the Missourian declared. Would not that region join with his in a South–West alliance dedicated to states' rights and all the benefits that would stem from it?

Yes, declared Senator Robert Y. Hayne of South Carolina, a disciple of Calhoun's who had embraced the particularism of the Old Republicans. His state was then considering ordinances declaring the Tariff of Abominations unconstitutional and insisting that South Carolina had a right to interpose its authority between its citizens and the federal government. The several states, he declared, should indeed control the sale of lands within their borders, decide the constitutionality of federal laws for themselves, and halt any attempt to interfere with the institution of slavery in its tracks. "Benton and Hayne," John Quincy wrote in his diary, "by a joint and concerted attack upon the Eastern portion of the Union propose to break down the union of the Eastern and Western sections [personified by his partnership with Clay], and of [*sic*] restoring the old joint operation of the West and the South against New England. Benton's object is personal advancement and plunder; Hayne's, personal advancement by the triumph of South Carolina over the tariff and internal improvement and Calhoun's succession to the presidency."[81]

To the delight of Adams and other National Republicans, Daniel Webster rose to defend the Constitution and the Union that it had created. The federal compact, the nation itself, had been established by the people as a whole and not by the several states, he declared. It was they who had apportioned the various powers between the states and the federal government. The Constitution made it clear that in every instance of ambiguity, national power was supreme. The notion of absolute state sovereignty had been rejected when the Founding Fathers replaced the Articles of Confederation with the U.S. Constitution. Webster, a former sympathizer with the Hartford Convention and a free trader, had made a philosophical switch that was the mirror image of that of Calhoun—the former nationalist turned states' righter. Webster was a rising star, the most famous trial lawyer in America, a man of letters, and one of the great orators of his time. The language of his "Second Reply to Hayne" would be recited by schoolchildren for generations: "When my eyes shall be turned to behold for the last time the sun in heaven, may I not see him shining on the broken and dishonored fragments of a once glorious Union; on states disserved, discordant, belligerent; on a land rent with civil feuds, or drenched, it may be, in fraternal blood."[82]

"Mr. Webster has attained the station which you assign to him," John Quincy wrote Charles, a great admirer of his law tutor, "by two splendid speeches."[83] If Benton, Calhoun, and Hayne were to prevail, Adams subsequently observed to Richard Rush, the federal government would be rendered prostrate. "[W]e agreed that the Indians are already sacrificed; that the public lands will be given away; that domestic industry and internal improvement will be strangled; and when the public debt will be paid off and the bank charter expired, there will be no great interest left upon which the action of the general government will operate."[84]

But where was Old Hickory in all of this? On April 13, both Jackson and Calhoun attended the first of annual Jefferson Day dinners. The gathering rang with toast after toast lauding the principles expressed by Hayne. Then it was the president's turn. He lifted his glass and declared, "Our Union—it must be preserved."[85] Jackson's support for states' rights and particularism went only so far; after all, he was the nation's chief executive. The Hero was not going to stand by and see Calhoun and his cohorts neuter him by reducing the federal government to a nullity. It soon became clear that Jackson had stolen the show at the Jefferson–Jackson dinner. Calhoun was cast into the political wilderness, at least as far as succeeding to the presidency was concerned.

IN AUGUST 1830, John Quincy, Louisa, Mary Catherine, and her two-year-old departed the capital for Quincy to escape the sweltering, miasmatic swamp that was Washington, DC, in the late summer. The weeklong journey by carriage, stage, and steamboat proved arduous and depressing. The family made the trip from New York to Providence aboard the *President*, commanded by Captain Bunker, the same officer who had been in charge of the *Benjamin Franklin* when George met his death. En route they encountered the *Benjamin Franklin* itself. The *Franklin*, trailing a black plume of smoke, reminded Louisa and John Quincy of a funeral barge.[86]

In Quincy the gloom persisted. Louisa took to her bed while John Quincy attempted to divert himself with the Bible, Cicero, and gardening. The birth of John and Mary's second child, Georgianna Frances Adams, in September was a ray of sunshine but provided only a brief respite. "At a little before one I went for my wife and we rode to Quincy to reach their dinner hour," read the entry for Charles Francis's diary for Monday, June 14. "Found my mother better but still quite sick. My father full of care and much depressed."[87] John Quincy had become obsessed with death. He read Cicero's *Tusculan Disputations*, in which the sage meditated on the end of one's physical existence. Was it a good or was it an evil? Like all animals, Adams observed, human beings feared death; it marked the end of suffering but the beginning of the great unknown. "The sincere believer in Christianity longs for death but dares not hasten to it; and in spite of all belief, he dreads and shrinks from it." As for himself, "I have no plausible motive for wishing to live." His hopes for the future, both for himself and his nation, seemed dashed. He was sixty-three. But, he confessed to his diary, he was not ready for the end: "[T]he love of life and the horror of dissolution is as strong in me as it ever was at any period of my existence."[88] The actor longed for a stage, the performer for an audience.

32

Thwarted Ambitions

THE FIRST WEEK IN September 1830, the editor of the *Boston Courier* published an anonymous letter proposing John Quincy Adams as a candidate
for the U.S. House of Representatives from the district of Plymouth, to
which the town of Quincy had recently been added. Adams did not think much
of it because the *Courier* was a staunch supporter of Henry Clay. The object of the
exercise, observed Charles, was to get his father out of the way to ensure that he
would not compete with the Kentuckian for the National Republican nomination
for president in 1832. But then, while attending the Boston bicentennial celebration on September 17, Adams was approached by the congressional incumbent,
the Reverend Joseph Richardson, and Representative John Davis of the Norfolk
District. Could they call on him the following day to discuss a political matter?
Adams assented. Richardson, whose parishioners were complaining of neglect,
and Davis duly appeared at Peacefield the following morning. Sometime earlier
a fellow National Republican had written Davis, "We think him [Adams] a good
rallying point for those who wish to throw off the incubus of Jacksonianism, to
send an able man to Congress, and at the same time to compliment an abused
patriot."[1] Richardson made the offer. He assured the former president that he
would be elected. Both newspapers in the district, the *Hingham Gazette* and the
Old Colony Memorial, would be supportive. The Federalists and Democratic-
Republicans were certain to nominate candidates. John Quincy was the only sure
bet the National Republicans had. Think of the good of the state. Anticipating
an obvious objection, Richardson observed that the election of a former president
to Congress would not degrade the individual but exalt the House. "I said I had
in that respect no scruple whatever," Adams wrote of his reply. "No person could
be degraded by serving the people as a representative in Congress. Nor, in my
opinion, would an ex-President of the United States be degraded by serving as

Selectman of his town. . . . But age and infirmity had their privileges and disqual-ifications."[2] He then voiced a familiar mantra: he would not consent to be a candidate—that would be too much like courting the vote—and he reserved the right to decide if elected whether to accept. "Mr. Richardson said this was suffi-cient and he would go to work."[3]

As his supporters began canvassing, the former president remained madden-ingly coy. If he were elected, would he accept? John Bailey asked him. I wouldn't go that far, Adams replied. Another supporter came calling and asked him if he considered himself a citizen of Quincy. I said certainly—Adams reported to his diary. "If not an inhabitant of Quincy, I was an inhabitant of nowhere." Finally, on October 15, Adams responded in the *Boston Daily Advertiser* to a notice of his nomination: "If my fellow-citizens of the district should think proper to call for such services as it may be in my power to render them by representing them in the Twenty-Second Congress, I am not aware of any sound principle which would justify me in withholding them."[4]

Louisa and Charles were aghast at the prospect of John Quincy returning to Washington as a mere congressman. Think of the indignities he would face. There was a clear Democratic-Republican majority in the House. The former chief mag-istrate and the greatest secretary of state in the nation's history would be subject to being overruled by the Speaker, to receiving insults from colleagues, and to being called to order; he would even be exposed to the risk of censure and expul-sion. All former chief executives had retired to their respective estates to receive distinguished visitors and offer sage advice when called on to do so, Louisa and Charles pointed out. Personally, Louisa was horrified at the prospect of returning to a life of political intrigue, innuendo, and insult. Charles let his father know that he was "disappointed" in him. To his diary, he confided, "His is not the highest kind of greatness. As much as he may try to conceal his feeling under the cloak of patriotic inclination . . . my eye is a little too deep to be blinded. I regret the de-cision on his account. I regret it upon my own."[5] It was particularly unseemly, the family argued, for a traditionalist to break tradition. "His course . . . has not been calculated to raise him in the judgment of the public," Charles complained. "The examples of Washington, Jefferson, and Madison have produced so strong an ef-fect that a departure from their line of policy is considered as a departure from true dignity."[6]

John Quincy attempted to defend himself. "My election to Congress was a call . . . from the dwellers of my native land," he wrote Charles. "From the scenes of my childhood—almost from the sepulchers of my fathers." Don't speak to me of our forefathers, Charles Francis retorted. Was this call "so imperious as to put in the background other calls which perhaps are not less urgent[?]"[7] "Does my grandfather's reputation stand so high that it will need no mending or restoring? . . . Even at this moment a deliberate attempt is made to rob him of all credit. . . . If this [a biography of John Adams] is an important duty, which you and you only can perform," why is it that you are prepared to abandon it for the "exhausting political warfare of a seat in the House of Representatives?"[8]

John Quincy learned on the evening of November 6 that he had won election to Congress, garnering three out of every four votes cast. The totals were 1,817 for Adams (National Republican), 373 for Arad Thompson (Democratic-Republican), and 279 for William Baylies (Federalist). "And so again I am launched upon the faithless wave of politics," the newly elected congressman exulted.[9]

Adams's decision to stand for Congress was, of course, deeply personal. He faced retirement not with a sense of satisfaction with the expectation that he would be honored by the country as an elder statesman, another Washington, Jefferson, or Monroe. He was acutely aware that he had been elected as a minority president and then turned out of office after one term. He could not even expect warmth and comfort from the people of Boston. Following his retirement, Jacksonians and Federalists alike had continued to rain blows upon his head. It made him think, he recorded in his diary, of the French opera of *Richard Coeur-de-lion*, in which the minstrel Blondel stood before the gates of the prison in which his hero was incarcerated and sang, *"Oh! Richard! Oh! Mon Roi / L'univers t'abandonné."*[10] But then came redemption: election to office by a spontaneous, overwhelming majority of the people of Plymouth. It was an Adams dream come true. "My election as President of the United States was not half so gratifying to my inmost soul," he confided to his diary. "No election or appointment conferred upon me ever gave me so much pleasure."[11]

Ego aside, Adams really thought he could make a difference at a crucial time in the nation's history. "There is no harmony in the government of the Union. . . . The whole head is sick and the whole heart faint," he lamented. "This example of the state of Georgia will be imitated by other states and with regard to other national interests. Perhaps the tariff—still more probably the public lands . . . The Union is in the most imminent danger of dissolution from the old inherent vice of confederacies [and] anarchy in the members. To this end, one third of the people is perverted—one third slumbers—and the rest wring their hands with unavailing lamentations."[12] He had played as important a role as anyone in the Early Republic in combating disunion and the causes underlying it. He had known in his heart of hearts that freedom and slavery could not dwell together in the same house forever. Adams's goal as a diplomat had been to safeguard the republic and make it strong enough to address and resolve its great contradiction. Perhaps civil war could be avoided; perhaps it could not, but it was impossible for John Quincy to stand idly by and see his country die a slow, agonizing, and perhaps violent death. Your country is your mistress, John Adams had told his son at the dawn of his diplomatic career, and she will never let you rest.

To her family's consternation, Louisa declared that she would not be accompanying John Quincy to Washington. Her husband resigned himself to his fate as a solitary man, instructing his son John to advertise his two houses in F Street for sale for twenty thousand dollars. "Whether you will deem it advisable to remain at Washington for the sale of the business of the Mills is for your consideration."[13] Charles quailed at the prospect of having to care for his hypochondriac mother while she was residing in a part of the country that she had always detested. Perhaps his disapproval of his father's decision to return to political life, he wondered, had exacerbated his mother's discontent. He wrote Louisa asking her to reconsider, and urged his brother to do likewise.[14] John complied, but Louisa remained adamant. You argue that the New England winter will be damaging to my health, she wrote John. "The climate will never prove half so deleterious to me as a house which will become the focus of intrigue and to which all those feelings of deep mortification and agony already so painfully endured will be aroused anew in a heart already half broken by its former sufferings." Where was the hope, the compensation for all that and what the family had endured so far? "Is it in the grave of my lost child? . . . is it in the advantages resulting to any of our connections of either side? Or is it in the grasping ambition which is an insatiable passion swallowing and consuming all in its ever-devouring maw?"[15] But in the end, she relented.

Louisa departed Quincy for Washington the last week in November 1830. John Quincy, delayed by a driving snowstorm, followed several days later. He tarried in New York, visiting old friends and colleagues. In company with Dr. Jonathan Wainwright and Albert Gallatin, the newly minted congressman attended a national convention to promote the liberal arts. He was chosen presiding officer and named to a committee to draw up plans for a national library and scientific institution. Shortly after he departed the city, the *New York Whig* commented on the "moral grandeur" of an ex-president preparing to take a seat in the lower house of Congress. "Where but in our own free land could such an event take place?"[16] Adams caught up with Louisa in Philadelphia, where more socializing and reminiscing ensued. Judge Joseph Hopkinson, Charles J. Ingersoll, and Robert Walsh embraced the Adamses warmly; opinion on the wisdom of the former president's decision to stand for Congress was divided, however.

At Baltimore the proprietor of a newly built railroad line connecting that city to the capital persuaded John Quincy and Louisa to come aboard for the last leg of the trip. As one of the country's leading advocates of internal improvements,

Adams could hardly refuse. An unfortunate decision, as it turned out. Heavy rains made it difficult for the train to remain on the tracks. Louisa eventually became so frustrated that she disembarked and hired a carriage. John Quincy stuck with it and reached Washington an hour ahead of her. On New Year's Day 1831, the congressman and his wife entertained three hundred guests at John and Mary Catherine's house, their temporary home in the capital.[17]

It would be eleven months before the Twenty-Second Congress convened. Predictably, John Quincy decided to busy himself with literary endeavors. But suddenly, in early February, the inflammation of the eyes that had plagued him off and on since his observation of a solar eclipse with the naked eye in Boston in 1791 returned. At times he had to retire to his chamber and lie in total darkness. His mind turned once again to rhyming. He summoned Louisa and dictated a poem on his condition: "Of my two orbs of vision one / Has caught fire; and while it burns / Swollen, bloodshot, for the blessed sun / And Heaven's faint light it turns."[18] Because he knew the Bible almost by heart, he began rewriting the psalms. The previous fall, he had perused several biographies of Lord Byron; Adams admired the man's literary skills but abhorred his morals. When, at last, his vision cleared, he began rereading some of Byron's epic poems including *Beppo*, written in Boccaccio's ottava rima (a form of poetry consisting of eight-line stanzas composed of ten or eleven syllables, rhyming *abababcc*). Perhaps, he thought, he should try his hand at an epic poem himself.

While in St. Petersburg as a youth, John Quincy had read David Hume's eight-volume *History of England*. Recent events in American politics and his own fortunes had brought to mind the portions dealing with the English conquest of Ireland by King Henry II in the twelfth century. A principal figure in Hume's account was an Irish prince named Dermot MacMorrogh, who after cuckolding a fellow prince, Orrick by name (the lady in question was named Dovergilda), bolted from the country and joined the English army. At the head of Henry's forces, MacMorrogh then invaded his native land and slew the reigning king before being murdered himself. To Hume, the Irish prince was not a traitor but a true patriot who had served his king faithfully and well. Adams deplored both Dermot and Henry II; for him, inevitably, the story became a morality play demonstrating the noxious effects of licentiousness, blind ambition, and armed aggression. Here was the perfect subject for an epic poem. Hopefully, readers of *Dermot MacMorrogh* would identify the legitimate rulers of Ireland with the Adamses, father and son, and the British invaders aided by an Irish traitor with Jefferson and Jackson. Perhaps thinking of his own ill-fated presidency, John Quincy described the deposed king of Ireland, Roderick O'Conner, as "ill obeyed, even within his own territory," observing that he "could not unite the people in any measures either for the establishment of order or for the defense against foreigners."[19] Both of Adams's current antiheroes—Jackson and MacMorrogh—had corrupted another man's wife.

Adams had planned an epic running to fifty stanzas, a story filled with drama but also humor and irony in keeping with Byron's *Beppo*. But he could not restrain himself either in the matter of length or tone. He had fallen prey to a "rhyming fit," he recorded in his diary. "I write every morning one stanza of paraphrase from the Bible and, in my morning walk, from two to three stanzas of a tale which I have undertaken . . . so totally does it absorb my attention . . . that in my morning walk round the Capitol Square I go out and return almost without consciousness of the passage of time—the melancholy madness of poetry."[20] Soon *Dermot* was approaching two hundred stanzas—two thousand lines. Not only had the epic becoming overly long; it was ponderous as well. "All my attempts at humor evaporated in the first canto," he confessed. On April 16, the former president put down his pen. He was conflicted and considered burning the manuscript. He knew good poetry when he read it; *Dermot* was at best mediocre. "I want a faculty of inventing and delineating character, of naturalizing familiar dialogue, and of spicing my treat with keen and cutting satire. I want the faculty of picturesque description, of penetrating into the inmost recesses of human nature, of passing from grave to gay, from lively to severe; of touching the cords of sympathy with the tender and sublime."[21]

In truth, John Quincy had too much of the Puritan in him to become a genuine "man of literature." He was at times like the apocryphal Calvinist minister who, upon experiencing an impure thought, slammed his arm down on a studded belt he had hidden beneath his waistcoat. Adams continued to be simultaneously attracted to and repelled by the poet he had chosen as a model for *Dermot*. He was entranced by the rhythm and grace of Byron's verse, but he thought him immoral and a panderer to the crowd. "[H]is libertinism [is] so shameless, his merriment such grinning of a ghastly smile, that I have always believed his verses would soon rank with forgotten things. The author keeps his reader forever in sight of himself [that is, pandering]. Such writers must always be vicious and miserable."[22]

Dissatisfied though he was with Byron and himself, John Quincy found it impossible to abandon his epic. It was his creation, and the process of writing had taken him out of himself. "It has amused and occupied two months of my life," he wrote in his diary, "and leaves me now like a pleasant dream to dull and distressing realities." He was left with "a sense of wasted time and the humility of enterprise ashamed of performance, yet, at the same time with an insatiate thirst for undertaking again higher and better things."[23] *Dermot MacMorrogh* was published in 1832—a thousand copies for a royalty of one hundred dollars. He sent copies to friends who raved, but in truth, *Dermot* was ignored by the most prominent journals and newspapers in the United States and Great Britain. Charles was its most brutal reviewer: "There is vigor in the lines and occasionally a high order of poetry. But as a whole, the work wants invention and imagination. It is totally deficient in descriptive imagery and leans, as almost all my father's poetry does, too much to the didactic style."[24]

DESPITE THE "OUR UNION—IT must be preserved" toast, Jackson, in John Quincy's eyes, remained in tacit alliance with the states' righters, with the slave power, with the nullifiers. He had sided with Georgia over Indian removal. In May 1830 he had vetoed legislation providing federal subsidies for the Maysville Road, a turnpike linking Lexington, Kentucky, and Maysville, Kentucky. Old Hickory was getting ready to make war on the Bank of the United States and he stood idly by as the governor of South Carolina urged the state legislature to call a convention that would declare the Tariff of Abominations null and void.

Appalled by these developments, John Quincy set about demonstrating that Jacksonism was nothing less than the flowering of the poisonous seed planted by Jefferson and Madison. After he finished work on *Dermot*, Adams began reading the recently published letters and memoirs of the Sage of Monticello. The Jefferson–Jackson philosophies and policies—American Jacobinism—had menaced the United States since its birth, he was convinced. The Jeffersonians and Jacksonians were democratic anarchists, demagogues who catered to the prejudices of the masses. Like Robespierre, Danton, and Camille Desmoulins, they were licentious and immoral. There was no doubt that Jefferson was an atheist, Adams wrote Alexander Everett in late May. "He never examined the evidence of Christianity," he declared. "He rejected it as an imposture." Rather than perusing the many gifted defenders of the faith, Jefferson had "rejected it . . . under the influences of the infidel school of his own and the immediately preceding age— Bolingbroke, Hume, Voltaire, Diderot, and the rest of that gang." (Earlier in his life, of course, John Quincy had expressed admiration for the writings of both Bolingbroke and Hume. But all was fair in love and politics.) Not surprisingly, "the nullification doctrine which may shiver this union to atoms is the child of his own conception. . . . Mr. Jefferson's infidelity, his anti-judicialism, and his nullification were three great and portentous errors . . . that should be probed to the bottom and exposed in their naked nature."[25] Gone were the fond memories of the days in Paris when John Quincy described the Virginian as a second father. Gone were the days when he, like his father, supported Jefferson, an honorable man dedicated to the interests of his country, over Aaron Burr. Ignored were the genial and thoughtful letters his father and Jefferson had exchanged after their retirement. In truth, Jefferson was no more a freethinker than the Unitarian John Adams. While John Quincy fretted and fumed, in England the *Westminster Review* declared Jefferson's *Memoirs and Correspondence* as one of the most significant meditations on history and political thought ever offered to the world.[26]

Everett had just bought control of the *North American Review* from Jared Sparks. He notified his mentor and friend, John Quincy, that he was going to strive to inculcate in his readers "correct principles in taste, politics, morals, and religion." Everett invited the former president to be a regular contributor and to begin with an essay on the Webster–Hayne debates. Here was an opportunity for Adams to air his views on "American Jacobinism" past and present. But Adams knew that the Jacksonians would throw the Hartford Convention in his face, so he stayed his hand. He agreed to submit an occasional piece, but the broadside he had in mind exposing the "nefarious conspiracy" that was afoot in the land would have been too strong for the *Review*. He had to admit that the Kentucky and Virginia Resolutions and the Hartford Convention were "all chips off the same block and there is no great political party in this country but at some time or other has made itself a god of this 'inutile lignum.'"[27] (From Horace's "Eighth Satire": "Once upon a time I was the trunk of a fig-tree, wood good for nothing, and the carpenter, uncertain whether to make of me a stool . . . decided I was to become a god.")

In truth, Adams did not want to comment on the speeches and writings of others but to deliver an address for others to comment upon. Throughout 1830 and into the spring of 1831, he had been gathering his thoughts for a defense of the Constitution and popular sovereignty in America. Like other nationalists he was a great admirer of Chief Justice John Marshall. The Virginian had, Adams observed in his diary, "done more to establish the Constitution of the United States on sound construction than any other man living."[28] Adams also respected Associate Justice Joseph Story, the newly named Dane Professor of Law at Harvard. Marshall was then in poor health and Adams hoped upon hope that Story would replace him as head of the court. He feared the worst, however, shuddering to think of the consequences if a states' righter like Philip Barbour of Virginia, a "shallow-pated wildcat," were chosen instead.[29] A frequent correspondent, Story sent John Quincy a copy of Nathan Dane's recently published *Appendix* to his voluminous *General Abridgement and Digest of American Law*. Dane was a former Hartford Convention enthusiast turned nationalist. An original member of the Continental Congress, he was in a position to comment firsthand on the intentions of the Founders. In his *Appendix* Dane cited the calling of the First Continental Congress as the ultimate justification for the primacy of popular sovereignty. The colonists, acting as individuals rather than as members of a province, had convened both the First and Second Congresses. Sovereignty, Dane wrote, transcended the Constitution, tracing its roots to the people from whom it had grown. The Declaration of Independence was the fundamental and perfect statement of this intent. And popular sovereignty most certainly trumped state sovereignty. "Those who can," John Quincy wrote Story, acknowledging receipt of Dane's *Appendix*, "will find great and decisive consequences for that simple historical reminiscence of Mr. Dane. . . . The sovereignty of each state was the child and creature of the Union."[30]

How could Thomas Jefferson and John Quincy Adams, both defenders of and advocates for the notion of absolute popular sovereignty, come to such different conclusions concerning the relative powers of the national government as opposed to those of the several states? It depended upon time and circumstance and whom one considered "popular." The Constitution of the United States—the charter meant to implement the will of the people—was an imperfect thing, the product of political compromise between large and small colonies, slave and free. It was designed to reflect the will of the majority and to protect the rights of the minority simultaneously. In a sense John Quincy was the more direct democrat, but his view of who was entitled to citizenship was more restricted than Jefferson's. In reality, Adams's 1831 indictment of Jefferson had much more to do with his desire to discredit Jackson and Van Buren, whom he considered beyond the pale of moral philosophy, than to discredit Thomas Jefferson.

JOHN QUINCY AND LOUISA departed Washington in midsummer for their annual retreat to Quincy and Boston. On the way, they stopped in New York City to visit James Monroe, who lay on his deathbed.

Almost as soon as the Adamses reached Peacefield, John Quincy received an invitation from the citizens of Quincy to deliver the annual Fourth of July oration. Here was his chance to make a statement. His 1821 Independence Day speech had anticipated the Monroe Doctrine. Now he would focus on the vision outlined in the Declaration of Independence and the charter that sought to give substance to that vision, the Constitution of the United States. As the day approached, the former president struggled. "Why is it that I feel more anxiety and more apprehension of failure on this occasion than I ever did in youth," he speculated in his diary. He then proceeded to answer his own question. "I fear the exhibition of faculties in decay. I fear a severity of judgment of the hearer and yet more of the readers. I experienced this on my second Fourth of July oration delivered at Washington ten years since, at the meridian of my life." But there could be no retreat.

"I shall now assail passions and prejudices as earnestly as then, deeming it now, as I deemed it then, my duty."[31]

On the appointed day, the newly completed Quincy meetinghouse, built with the support of the second president, was filled to overflowing. Following a choral song, a blessing by Reverend Whitney, and the reading of the Declaration of Independence, the man of the hour stepped to the podium. Echoing Dane, John Quincy declared the notion of absolute state sovereignty and the right of interposition "absurd." Nowhere in the Constitution was the power to nullify an act of Congress or an edict of the executive granted to the states. Any attempt by a single state or a group of states to block enforcement of federal law was "neither more nor less than treason skulking under the shelter of despotism." Echoing Dane again, Adams pointed out that the Declaration of Independence made no reference either to individual colonies or future states. It was, John Quincy declared, "a social compact by which the whole people covenanted with each citizen of the United Colonies, and each citizen with the whole people, that the United Colonies were and of right ought to be free and independent states. To this compact union was as vital as freedom or independence."[32] As the speech neared its climax, Adams was interrupted by bursts of applause. Then came the finish. He was nearing the end of his life, the former Boylston Professor declared, but most of his auditors would, he hoped, live long and fruitful lives, as would their descendants for ages to come. "[W]ere the breath which now gives utterance to my feelings the last vital air I should draw, my expiring words to you and your children should be, INDEPENDENCE AND LIBERTY FOREVER!"[33] Exhilarated, the crowd escorted the speaker to the town hall for a banquet and numerous toasts. A Boston publishing house printed two thousand copies of the oration and, after they were gobbled up, two thousand more. Led by John Marshall, prominent nationalists sent their congratulations.

WITH HIS CHANCES FOR the presidency seemingly doomed, John C. Calhoun felt free at last to sound the trumpet of states' rights, including nullification and interposition, without reservation. On July 26, from his plantation at Fort Hill, the South Carolinian penned an essay entitled "On the Relation which the States and General Government Bear to Each Other." It repeated the principles broached in *South Carolina Exposition and Protest*, written anonymously by Clay in 1828, with what Calhoun declared to be an important modification—the doctrine of "concurrent majority." According to this notion, a single state or several states could declare an act of Congress null and void and refuse to enforce it until and unless three-fourths of the states of the Union voted that it must be enforced. This was a significant retreat from the notion of absolute state sovereignty. Upon learning of Calhoun's broadside, John Quincy sent him a copy of his Fourth of July address "with ever friendly recollections." "I present it with the single [simple] assurance of my regret that upon topics of transcendent importance our opinions should be so much at variance with each other." Calhoun responded graciously. It pained his heart as well that they should differ. "Whatever may be the final disposition of the people . . . I hope the Union will be safe."[34]

There was no chance that the National Republicans were going to choose John Quincy as their standard-bearer in 1832. Despite the growing strength of the Jacksonians in Kentucky, Henry Clay managed to have himself elected to the U.S. Senate in 1831. He had run at Daniel Webster's urging. "I speak in unaffected sincerity & truth," he wrote Clay in October 1831, "when I say that I should rejoice, personally, to meet you in the Senate . . . the cause would under present circumstance be materially benefitted by your presence there . . . we need your arm in the fight."[35] John Quincy was of the same opinion. He still felt gratitude and affection toward the Kentuckian for his loyalty and considered him a fellow laborer in the anti-nullification vineyard. We have something ironically in common, Adams wrote Clay in September 1831. Sending him a copy of his Independence Day remarks, Adams observed wryly that "you will have seen that among the states which I have charged with directly asserting or imprudently giving countenance to it [nullification] is your beloved state of Kentucky [the Kentucky and Virginia Resolutions] as with my own Massachusetts [the Hartford Convention]." But past threats to the Union were mild compared to the present ones. "We the People" and the Union they had formed were under attack. "The doctrine [interposition and nullification] in all its parts is so averse to my convictions that I can view it in no other light, than as *organized civil war.*"[36]

But when it became known that Henry Clay was a prominent Mason, his presidential candidacy and John Quincy's support for it were thrown into doubt. Before 1828, being a Mason was generally considered a plus for aspiring American politicians. The Royal Arch Masons, a secret fraternal society dedicated to serving God and their fellow man, could trace their origins back to early-eighteenth-century London. During the later Enlightenment, Masonic gatherings attracted freethinkers and reformers of various stripes. Washington was a Mason. So was the Adams family's hero, Dr. Joseph Warren. Franklin and Lafayette were Masons; so were Henry Clay and Andrew Jackson. Members were initiated in robed, candlelit ceremonies and sworn to absolute secrecy. Those who took the oath for the first degree of Masonry pledged "that I will always hail, forever conceal, and never reveal, any of the secret or secrets of Masons or Masonry . . . under no less penalty than to have my throat cut across from ear to ear, my tongue plucked out by the roots, and buried in the rough sands of the sea a cable's length from shore."[37] Masons swore never to betray a fellow member no matter what his transgressions. Those who chose to take the rites of the Fifth Libation drank wine from a human skull as a tribute to the immortality of the soul and the temporariness of the body. The Masonic rituals and oaths were simultaneously weird and adolescent, but the only people who paid any attention to the order were kings and popes who saw the organization as politically subversive. In the United States, no one paid attention.

But then came the mysterious disappearance in 1826 of one William Morgan, a Freemason living in upstate New York. He claimed to have become a Mason while living in Canada, and he briefly attended lodge meetings in Rochester. When he disappeared, Anti-Masons spread the rumor that members of the secret society had drowned Morgan in the Niagara River. In October 1827, the remains of a body washed ashore on Lake Ontario. Critics of the order declared the corpse to be that of Morgan.

Led by crusading newspaper editor Thurlow Weed, outraged New Yorkers decried the Masons as a secret order made up of privileged elites who were conspiring to gain control of the political and economic life of the country—a nineteenth-century version of the deep state. When attempts to bring the alleged Morgan abductors to justice ended in mistrials and the leaders of the order closed ranks, the notion grew legs. In February 1828 in upstate New York, Anti-Masons founded a political party. To Van Buren and other Democratic-Republican leaders, the Anti-Masonic Party seemed to pose a particular threat because the Democrats' avatar, Andrew Jackson, was a high-ranking Mason. The anti-elitist appeal of the new organization seemed likely to resonate with members of the party's core constituency—mechanics, artisans, and small farmers.[38] The National Republicans were no more enthusiastic about the new party than the Jacksonians. Clay made no attempt to deny his membership in the order; he would not and, indeed, could not repudiate it. But the growing popularity of the Anti-Masons would cost him more dearly than it would Jackson.

Neither John nor John Quincy had ever considered joining the Royal Arch Masons; they were opposed to secret societies in principle and in practice because they viewed most of them as hotbeds of Jacobinism. But they were elitists and close friends with many prominent Masons. In 1804 in Quincy, the younger Adams had attended ceremonies celebrating the formation of a chapter of Freemasons.[39] In 1822, Louisa and her brother were received and feted by the Philadelphia chapter of the Royal Arch Masons. "Having had the honor of being seated in this Chair [the grand master's], I shall claim the right of being at least an honorary member of this society without aiming at a knowledge of their secret mysteries," she wrote John Quincy.[40] But then in 1831, as he planned his assault on Jackson and the Democratic-Republicans, John Quincy took a sudden interest in the Anti-Masonic Party. "I . . . received a letter from Mr. Abner Phelps informing me that an Anti-Masonic State Convention would assemble at Faneuil Hall on the 19th and 20th instant [May 1831]," he confided to his diary, "and inviting my attendance at the meeting. I saw no good reason for declining to go and went with Charles in his chaise."[41]

The Anti-Masons treated the former president like royalty, and, flattered, he decided to take up their cause. "Charles is afraid of the consequences of my expressing an opinion upon the Masonic controversy supposing it will be imputed to selfish motives," Adams subsequently observed. "But this [assumption] is the vital essence of all political collusions. No man can escape them, and a man susceptible of being intimidated by them is not fit for any useful agency in public affairs. I have for nearly five years abstained from taking part in the Masonic controversy" but "there is a time when it becomes the duty of a good citizen to take his side."[42] Principle notwithstanding, by the end of July, Adams had become convinced that the Anti-Masonic Party was his only political refuge. "There is a combination of parties against me including almost the whole population of the country," he lamented, "and of which my former supporters are the most inveterate—the Clay Masons and so-called National Republicans."[43] This, of course, was not true.

Like his predecessors Jefferson and Adams, James Monroe breathed his last on July 4. John Quincy was asked to deliver a eulogy at Old South Church in Boston, which he did to a large and appreciative audience. The house was filled to capacity, the overheated air stifling. Still the people came, crowding at the church door and struggling to get in. As Adams spoke, wagonloads of people could be heard rolling down the streets outside. The sun went down, and John Quincy had to finish, speaking from memory because it was so dark.[44] He had initially considered his tribute to the fifth president as an opportunity to declare war on the Masons, but he decided, probably wisely, against it. A second opportunity came in August, when a defender of the Masons, John H. Sheppard, published an essay insisting that John Adams had been a patron of the order and included passages from a friendly letter that the former president had written to the grand master of the Massachusetts lodge. John Quincy responded with a letter to Stephen T. Bates, the publisher of the Anti-Masonic Boston *Free Press*. His father's note, he wrote, had been "a complimentary answer to a friendly and patriotic address of the Grand Lodge to him . . . he knew nothing of their secrets, their oaths, nor their penalties." Had he lived to witness the abduction and murder of William Morgan, the nation's second president would have denounced the order in no uncertain terms. Warming to the task, John Quincy observed that the Masons had always claimed adherence to the highest principles of Christianity and enlightened moral philosophy, but so had the Jesuits. "In the Inquisition itself whose ministers in the very act of burning the body of the heretic to death were always actuated by the tenderest and most humane regard for the salvation of his soul."[45]

NOT COINCIDENTALLY, AT THE time Adams came out of the closet in regard to his views on the Masons, the Anti-Masonic Party had become a major player in the politics of New England and the Mid-Atlantic states. From its origins in the "Burned-Over District" of western New York—the birthplace of evangelical religious movements and utopian social schemes—it spread northward through Massachusetts, Rhode Island, and Connecticut, and southward into Pennsylvania, its principles appealing especially to the latter state's Quakers. In New York Thurlow Weed and William H. Seward and in Pennsylvania Thaddeus Stevens dreamed of merging their organization with the National Republicans, reinvigorating the party, and creating a populist alternative to Jackson and the Democratic-Republicans. Though unorganized in states like Ohio, Delaware, New Hampshire, Maryland, and Maine, Anti-Masonry had its disciples. Even in the South, there were those who objected to the order on moral grounds. In the elections of 1830, the Anti-Masons captured the governorship and lieutenant governorship of New York.

In September 1831 the party would convene in Baltimore, holding what was the first national presidential nominating convention. Their top choice was Henry Clay, the favorite to garner the National Republican nomination. Combining the American System with Anti-Masonry, party leaders believed, would create a political machine that would be more than a match for the Jacksonians. When Clay demurred, party leaders focused on Richard Rush of Pennsylvania, distinguished diplomat and Adams's secretary of the treasury, but he made it clear that he thought John Quincy Adams, coauthor of the American System and now an avowed Anti-Mason, ought to be the nominee. Adams pressed his protégé to reconsider: "It may become your indispensable duty" to run, he wrote.[46] But Rush, who still felt a strong sense of loyalty to his former chief, would not.

In late August, Abner Phelps and another Boston Anti-Mason, George Odiorne, rode out to Quincy and inquired if John Quincy would accept the nomination of the Baltimore convention if it were proffered. "I neither desire it nor even the office of President of the United States itself," he told them. "I will give no pledge nor make any promise to any man or body of men to obtain it." That, of course, was Adams for yes. "If they propose my name," Adams declared, "my only entreaty is that they shall not pass it one instant after ascertaining that any other name would be likely to receive a more unanimous vote."⁴⁷ (This last was a reveal-ing oxymoron.) It was the old John Quincy Adams one-two punch: he was and would remain above the fray, but if called, he would serve. All the while he was secretly working to persuade the leaders of the National Republican Party to dump Henry Clay.

Throughout September and October John Quincy focused on establishing his credentials as an ardent Anti-Mason. In September 1831, Edward Ingersoll of Philadelphia, a longtime Adams friend and an intimate of both Clay and Rush, wrote to him appealing to him to separate his morals from his politics. He under-stood that Adams deplored Masonry for its secret oaths, its attempts to position itself above the law, and the alleged murder of Morgan, but could he not at the same time throw his support behind a political alliance between the National Republicans and the Anti-Masons? If none could be achieved, the Jacksonians in all their vileness would certainly be returned to office in November 1832. The Masonic Order included some of the most upstanding and patriotic individuals in the country; they should not be held responsible for the activities of a few bad apples.

John Quincy responded in three letters, which found their way into the press. Perhaps so, Adams declared, but he could not remain silent in the face of the re-fusal of the Royal Arch chapters to denounce Morgan's kidnapping and murder, and the conspiracy to obstruct justice that had followed. Indeed, with that event, "it became the solemn and sacred, civic, and social duty of every Masonic Lodge in the United States either to dissolve itself or to discard forever . . . all oaths, all penalties, all secrets and all fantastic titles, exhibitions and ceremonies hitherto used in the institution."⁴⁸

As a diplomat and a statesman, John Quincy Adams had never been willing to sacrifice the good for the perfect. But in 1831 he was neither a diplomat nor a statesman but a first-term congressman with lingering ambitions for greater things. Both Clay and Jackson were Masons. By attacking the order, he could, he hoped, weaken his enemy, Jackson, and his rival, Clay. He hoped, of course, that the Anti-Masons and National Republicans would rally around him, form an alliance, and defeat Jackson and the Democratic-Republicans. As far as Clay was concerned, what was friendship compared to power and fame.

Lest future generations should accuse him of political opportunism and hy-pocrisy, Adams penned a searing indictment of Masonry in his diary. "That it is a most pernicious institution I am profoundly convinced. . . . In principle it is un-just, but in power it is great. . . . Religion-charity-pure benevolence and morals mingled up with superstitious rites and ferocious cruelty. Their forerunner, the

Knights Templar—they governed during the crusading ages—were responsible both for the 'Mahometan religion' and the Jesuits."[49]

Ten days prior to the Baltimore convention, William H. Seward traveled to Quincy to confer with the ex-president. By then the leading candidate for the party's nomination was Associate Justice John McLean. When the New Yorker arrived at Peacefield, Adams descended the stairs to meet him. "He was bald, his countenance was staid, sober, almost to gloom or sorrow, and hardly gave indication of his superiority over other men," Seward would later recall of their encounter. "His eyes were weak and inflamed. He was dressed in an olive frock-coat, a cravat carelessly tied and old-fashioned, light-colored vest and pantaloons. It was obvious that he was a student just called from the labors of his closet. . . . Our interview lasted over three hours; he was all the time plain, honest, and free, in his discourse but with hardly a ray of animation or feeling in the whole of it. In short, he was just exactly what I before supposed he was, a man to be respected for his talents, admired for his learning, honored for his integrity and simplicity, but hardly possessing traits of character to inspire a stranger with affection."[50] John Quincy, of course, evidenced little enthusiasm for McLean, the enemy within his presidency's gates. He did not want to be president again, he informed his visitor. "I know its duties, privations, enjoyments, perplexities and vexations, but if the Anti-masons think my nomination would be better than any other, I will not decline." The main thing, Adams told Seward, was for the party to be united in its choice. "I think we'll be able to agree on a candidate all right," Seward replied noncommittally, and departed.[51]

Meanwhile, in Baltimore, McLean appeared to be a shoo-in for the nomination, but spooked by the certainty of Clay's anointment by the National Republicans, who were to gather in Baltimore the following month, he withdrew at the last minute. The aged Marshall flatly refused to be nominated. That left Adams, but in the end the conventioneers decided that he was a sure loser; he had been a minority president after all, and Clay's supporters would, not without cause, accuse Adams of ingratitude and disloyalty. In desperation, the Anti-Masons turned to William Wirt. He, a former Mason, issued a statement declaring that he had never been an active member and denouncing the current order as a threat to freedom and democracy.

"I am very highly delighted with this," Charles Francis wrote in his diary, "and both from my father's not being named and Mr. Wirt being the man."[52] Indeed, Charles had been opposed from the outset to his father's candidacy and made no secret of his feelings. The previous July, following the Anti-Masonic gathering in Boston that he and his father had attended, he had tried to dissuade Phelps from encouraging his father. "Whatever he [John Quincy] might reply would of course be to me very right. But that his family felt, and I felt, as if it was hard that the last days of his life should be molested by attacks more bitter even than any he had yet experienced. That this [the presidential campaign] would be a war of great violence and its result would undoubtedly be defeat."[53]

In October 1831 a committee from the Massachusetts Anti-Masonic state convention called on John Quincy to inform him that the body had voted unanimously to nominate him for governor. He was flattered, he replied, but the National Republican candidate who was running for reelection, Levi Lincoln, was an old and dear friend who had made his views on the evils of Masonry public. Hopefully, the Anti-Masons would see clear to throw its support to him.[54] The committee made no reply, but the Anti-Masonic Party would refuse to follow Adams's advice. Lincoln and the National Republicans had failed to remove Masonic members from various offices and had refused a political alliance.

33

Congressman Adams

JOHN QUINCY ADAMS WAS sworn in as a member of the House of Representatives at eleven thirty on the morning of December 5, 1831. He was one of ninety freshmen and, at sixty-four, by far the oldest. The House then occupied two stories of one wing of the Capitol. Members were seated in semicircular rows facing the elevated Speaker's chair. Each occupied a modest chair in front of a mahogany desk with drawers for pens, ink, and paper. The Speaker occupied a veritable throne, backgrounded by crimson drapery hung from the chandelier situated directly overhead. There were spacious galleries for visitors, and as in the past, ladies and gentlemen, particularly the former, came to listen to orations on important subjects by important people.[1] In the 1830s and 1840s, Congress received the lion's share of attention from those interested in public affairs. It was there, in the cloakroom and the basement committee chambers, as well as in the city's boardinghouses, that legislation was conceived, deals cut, and promises made.

Fittingly, Adams entered the House at a time when oratory was king; the speeches of Webster, Clay, Calhoun, and Adams were printed in newspapers and in pamphlet form to be read and reread throughout the nation. The *National Intelligencer* published congressional debates verbatim. At the end of marathon sessions, which were frequent given the compelling issues of the day, decorum tended to break down with members abandoning their seats to gather in knots or take naps on the divans ringing the chamber. Frequently the sergeant at arms had to send his minions out to scour the boardinghouses and bars for enough members to make a quorum.[2]

Charles Dickens visited the Capitol in 1842, and he was appalled by what he witnessed. It was "remarkable . . . to say the least to see so many honorable members with swelled faces carving new plugs [of tobacco] to insert in their cheeks and expelling old ones from their mouths. God help anyone who dropped something on the tobacco juice splattered floor."[3] And in truth, the more than one hundred spittoons scattered across the House Chamber were largely ignored. Many members appeared more or less inebriated much of the time. There was a bar in the lobby, but Daniel Webster felt compelled to install his own near his office on the second floor. Drinking was not the only vice. Visiting the halls of Congress in 1825, the American writer Anne Royall was impressed by the architecture but repelled by the wantonness of the Capitol. "[O]f all sights that ever disgraced . . . a house of Legislation . . . is the number of abandoned females which swarm in every room and nook in the capitol even in daylight. I have seen these females with brazen fronts seated in the galleries listening to the debates. They used to mix promiscuously with the respectable class of females until Mr. Clay assigned them a place by themselves."[4]

Adams's family and friends feared that he would be disrespected, the butt of jokes and insults leveled by uncouth Jacksonians and closet Federalists. But he was received as a senior statesman, the son of a Founding Father.[5] John Quincy benefited from a movement then afoot to burnish his father's reputation. A review in the *American Quarterly Review* of Jared Sparks's recently published *Diplomatic Correspondence of the American Revolution* heaped praise on Adams the diplomat: "Every sentiment, erroneous or not, on the subject of the French connection expressed in this correspondence [with Vergennes], seems to have been the result of cautious deliberation and patriotic impulses . . . he was not willing to sacrifice much to obtain what he knew his country could do without."[6]

It was then the prerogative of the Speaker of the House to make all committee assignments. What to do with a former president? A natural choice would have been the Committee on Foreign Affairs, but instead Andrew Stevenson, a Jackson loyalist, named Adams to chair the Committee on Manufactures. The post was sure to be a hot seat because that body would initiate new tariff legislation at a time when South Carolina was threatening secession over enforcement of the Tariff of Abominations. John Quincy approached his friend Edward Everett, the second-ranking member on the Foreign Affairs Committee, and asked him to exchange places. Everett readily agreed but expressed doubt whether the Speaker would approve. He proved correct. Adams visited Stevenson in his chamber following the House's adjournment to plead his case. The Speaker would not relent. The House had already approved all committee assignments, and its decision could not be appealed. When subsequently pressed again on the matter, Stevenson remarked that the gulf that then separated Mr. Adams and President Jackson would not permit the close working relationship that the post required.[7]

And so John Quincy accepted his fate and turned to the task at hand, drafting new tariff legislation that would simultaneously please free traders and protectionists. Though Adams would never admit it, Old Hickory and he held almost identical views on the issue. Both were moderate protectionists who hoped conciliation would appease various regions and interests, thus preserving the Union. "The mission of the tariff is not now wanted for revenue," Adams had written Robert Walsh in 1824; "our existing revenue exceeds our expenditures and a few more years of peace could extinguish our debt without needing to add a dollar of new taxation. The revival of the tariff is for protection of domestic manufacturing, and I believe it to be necessary. Yet it ought to be done with great caution; with a tender and sincere regard to the agricultural interests of the South and the commercial interests of the North."[8] Jackson's message to Congress on the tariff delivered in December 1831 echoed these sentiments precisely.

The problem for Adams was that his middle-of-the-road position on the tariff placed him at odds with the new head of the National Republican Party, Senator Henry Clay. The party's leadership, which included John Quincy as chair of the Committee on Manufactures, gathered at Edward Everett's lodgings to decide on the position it would take. "How do you feel upon turning boy again to go into the House of Representatives?" the Kentuckian teased his old boss. "I find the labor light enough," replied the new member, "but the House has not [yet] got to business."[9] Their conversation then turned to the tariff issue.

George McDuffie of South Carolina, chair of the Ways and Means Committee, had introduced a measure that would reduce the tariff on protected articles from a high of 40 percent to 18.75 percent over a three-year period. The protective system, his committee declared, was proving utterly ruinous to the planting states, injurious to the Western states, and of benefit exclusively to the manufacturing states. Though a Westerner, Clay was determined to preserve the American System, which included protection for "infant industries." Clay declared it his intention to counter McDuffie with a motion to reenact the protectionist Tariff of 1824. As for Adams, no matter how much he favored setting aside federal revenues for internal improvements and opposed giving away public lands, he could not support the Clay measure. There was no way the Jacksonian majorities in Congress were going to support such a bill. It would hurl defiance at the South, the president, and the Democratic-Republicans, the newly minted congressman declared. "I do not care who it defies," Clay declared. "To preserve, maintain, and strengthen the American System, I would defy the South, the President, and the devil. If the Committee on Manufactures has committed itself as you have stated [to the McDuffie measure], they have given a very foolish and improvident pledge."[10]

In March, Adams asked the House to be relieved of the chairmanship of the Committee on Manufactures, his reason being that he had just been named a member of a select committee to investigate the Bank of the United States.

During the ensuing debate, member after member representing all regions of the country rose to praise the New Englander as uniquely able to resolve the sectional conflict over the tariff because he more than any of his colleagues enjoyed the confidence of all sections and interests.[11] "It was ridiculous," Everett wrote his brother, "to hear men who but three years ago were abusing Mr. Adams with all their might . . . now suddenly impressed with the belief that he is the only man who can save the Union."[12]

The Tariff of 1832, which the press would refer to as the Adams Tariff, reduced rates from an average of 42 percent to 35 percent on enumerated manufactured products. It was still a protectionist measure and did nothing to satisfy South Carolina. But Southern congressmen cast thirty-two yeas and thirty-six nays; the bill was supported overwhelmingly by those representing the Northeast and the West. The vote was a clear rejection of South Carolina and its doctrines of nullification and interposition.

In March, Colonel Richard M. Johnson, then a member of Congress from Kentucky and an intimate of the president's attempted to negotiate a rapprochement between Old Hickory and Adams. One day at the close of business, Johnson asked Adams to walk with him. The president bore Mr. Adams no ill will and was open to reconciliation; Johnson and other administration supporters would like to facilitate it. The New Englander observed that the interruption in their social intercourse, he believed, was due to the president's conviction that Adams had slandered Rachel Jackson in the newspapers. He had had absolutely nothing to do with that, John Quincy declared. "Colonel Johnson said he had always been sure it was so; that General Jackson had come here with dispositions entirely friendly to me and intending to call upon me; that his mind had been poisoned here by scoundrel office-seekers; that he was a warm-tempered, passionate man, and had been led to believe that I was the cause of those publications against his wife."[13] He now knew that it was not true and appreciated that Adams had supported him during his incursion into Florida in 1817 and 1818. Jackson was ready to make the first move. What would satisfy Mr. Adams?

The freshman congressman, veteran diplomat/politician that he was, sensed that he had been placed upon a razor's edge. "The old Federal party now devoted to Mr. Clay have already more than once tried their hands at slandering me," he confided to his diary. "They have drawn the sword and brandished it over my head. If I set my foot in the President's house, they will throw away the scabbard."[14] Johnson asked if Adams would accept an invitation to dine with the president. No, responded the congressman, such favors were extended to all members of Congress. What about "a small, select party of friends"? Same objection. What, then, would Mr. Adams accept? "I said that it was not for me to prescribe." Frustrated,

Johnson abandoned his attempt at reconciliation. Adams to his diary again: "[T]he path is narrow to avoid on the one hand the charge of an implacable temper, and on the other of eagerness to propitiate the dispenser of power [Jackson]."[15]

In addition to the tariff, Congressman Adams found himself in the middle of the burgeoning conflict between Andrew Jackson and the Bank of the United States, the so-called Bank War. In 1816, during the latter stages of the second Madison administration, Congress had chartered the Second Bank of the United States for a twenty-year period. It was modeled on Hamilton's institution—the bank's stock privately held but with board members chosen both by stockholders and the federal government. In 1832 the bank was the largest corporation in the country, indeed, its only national business. It held the tax receipts collected by the Treasury and managed the federal government's financial transactions. Like other banks, the B.U.S. could issue paper money; unlike them, its paper was legal tender and could be redeemed for silver or gold. The bank loaned money to state institutions and to an extent could control credit by calling in these notes and demanding that they be redeemed in specie. It also loaned money to private businesses and individuals including powerful political figures. Clay had been its representative in Kentucky and Ohio; Webster was its attorney in 1832.

Andrew Jackson disliked banks in general, and the Bank of the United States in particular, referring to it throughout his presidency as "the Monster." Early in life he had speculated in land and promissory notes; many had gone bad, and he had barely escaped bankruptcy. But he also saw opposition to the bank as a major political card to play. By decrying the B.U.S. as an unfettered monopoly preying on the common man, the president could appeal to small farmers, artisans, mechanics, and shopkeepers, some of whom still remembered the bank's role in the Panic of 1819. In his annual message to Congress in 1829, Jackson questioned whether the institution's charter should be renewed.[16]

But the bank had its champions, the most notable and formidable of whom was its president, Nicholas Biddle. The scion of a prominent Philadelphia family, Nicholas was something of a child prodigy who had studied at the University of Pennsylvania and Princeton between the ages of ten and fifteen. His twentieth birthday found him serving as the private secretary to the U.S. minister to England. After returning to Philadelphia, Biddle edited the nation's foremost literary magazine, the *Port Folio*, for a time. He was an avid patron of the arts and a noted intellectual who wrote the first history of the Lewis and Clark expedition. As a member of the Pennsylvania State Senate during the War of 1812, Biddle helped the Madison administration float war loans and encouraged the establishment of the Second Bank of the United States. When Congress rechartered the B.U.S., Madison named the Pennsylvanian one of its five public board members. In 1823 the board elected him president. Biddle was to the Jacksonian era what Albert Gallatin had been to the Early Republic; no one could match his knowledge of economics and finance, and especially political economy. Bon vivant, public intellectual, and friend to the rich and powerful, Biddle was a formidable figure.[17]

After consulting with Henry Clay—the presidential nominee of the National Republican Party—Biddle decided to preempt an anticipated Jacksonian attack on the Bank of the United States and ask for its recharter four years ahead of time. Biddle and Clay were convinced that the bank enjoyed widespread support; Jackson, they believed, would either duck the issue in an election year or veto legislation rechartering "the Monster," thus gifting the National Republicans a winning issue. In June 1832, Pennsylvania members in both houses of Congress introduced legislation rechartering the bank for another twenty years. At that point the House, acting on a motion by Augustin Smith Clayton of Georgia, an avid opponent of the institution, voted to appoint a committee of seven to go to Philadelphia and "investigate" the B.U.S. Speaker Stevenson packed the delegation with anti-bank members; one of two exceptions was ex-president Adams.

Both John and John Quincy Adams were Hamiltonians when it came to the protection of private property rights and the power and duty of the federal government to regulate the economy in the national interest. This included the authority to impose some sort of order on the nation's otherwise chaotic banking system. John Quincy was an early supporter of imprisonment for debt. When in 1831 reformers pressed him to relent, he would consent only on the condition that they offer an appropriate substitute. Without a deterrent, debtors would run rampant, he argued, and the economy would collapse.[18] Since his days in the Senate, John Quincy had been a steadfast supporter of the bank. Like Hamilton, he viewed it as a vital instrument of state, necessary to conduct and oversee the business of the nation and its government. Most important, however, was his conviction that the institution was an indispensable safeguard against the excess of state banks and a check on the irresponsible debtor classes. "It is my firm belief," he had observed to Monroe in the aftermath of the Panic of 1819, "that this Union cannot hold together while every state exercises an unlimited power of making paper money under the pretense of incorporating banks unless the general government by such a bank substantially under its control . . . could preserve the obligations of contracts and give security to property against the frauds of paper swindling."[19]

Adams and Nicholas Biddle had long been friends. They had struck up a correspondence shortly after the Philadelphian became president of the bank, and they discussed literature, art, and moral philosophy. Adams found the educated, cosmopolitan, and congenial Biddle a delight. Whenever Louisa and he were in Philadelphia, Biddle acted as their host. "There is except for my own son," John

Quincy wrote his friend, "not a man living with whom I could open in such un-limited confidence all my impressions of public duty . . . as I [on one of his visits] did with you."[20] Unlike some of Adams's other Philadelphia friends, Biddle supported John Quincy's decision to run for Congress. After Adams was elected, the financier continued to cultivate him. The congressman was not unaware of the possible appearance of a conflict of interest. In November 1831, passing through Philadelphia, he called on his friend at the offices of the B.U.S. "I left with Mr. Biddle my certificate of stock to be sold," he recorded in his diary, "and the proceeds to be remitted according to such directions as I may give. I told him that, as I might be called to take a part in public measures concerning the bank, and was favorable to it, I wished to divest myself of all personal interest in it."[21] While the congressional investigating committee was in the City of Brotherly Love, Adams was careful to avoid all social contact with Biddle.

Not surprisingly, given its Jacksonian majority, the committee issued a sweeping indictment of both Biddle and the bank. It accused the institution of usury, of manipulating stock markets for the benefit of its governors and their friends, of abusing its authority over state banks, and of making donations to public subscriptions to support the building of canals and roads. Adams and the other National Republican on the committee were incensed. The members who dredged up the charges were ignorant and incompetent when it came to matters of finance, they charged. Adams and his colleague drafted a minority report that refuted each charge made in the majority's document. The usury accusation was particularly outrageous, it declared. Adams and his minority colleague accused the majority of violating the privacy of Biddle and other directors by snooping without permission through their private papers; they had had no more authority do so, Adams declared, than they had to enter "the dwelling-house, the fire-side, or the bed chamber of any one of them."[22] So pleased was Biddle with the Adams minority report that he had six thousand copies printed and distributed:

In July 1832, Congress voted to extend the charter of the Bank of the United States for another twenty years when the current authorization expired in 1836. Old Hickory, however, had other ideas. Just returned from England, Martin Van Buren called at the White House to find the chief executive gravely ill but full of steely determination. "The bank is trying to kill me," Jackson told his political comrade, "but I will kill it!"[23] In his famous veto message, Jackson focused more on political and class considerations than on economics or law. Anticipating that his critics would argue that the Marshall court had on several occasions upheld the constitutionality of the bank, the president made the dubious claim that each of the three branches of the federal government had the power to decide what was constitutional and what was not. "[T]he rich and powerful too often bend the acts of government to their selfish purposes," he declared. When an instrument of the federal government facilitated "artificial distinctions" and "grant[ed] titles, gratuities, and exclusive privileges, to make the rich richer and the potent more powerful, the humble members of society . . . have a right to complain of the injustice of their government."[24] After a rancorous debate, Congress sustained Jackson's veto. Of Jackson's veto message, Nicholas Biddle said that "it has all the fury of a chained panther banging the bars of his cage" and called it a "manifesto of anarchy."[25] The institution still had four years remaining on its original charter, and for Biddle and his friend John Quincy Adams, the Bank War was far from over.

Adams found the struggles over the tariff and the bank invigorating, probably because he was at the center of the first drama and a player in the second. On July 9 a letter from a "New England Man . . . and a sojourner in Washington" was printed in the *Boston Daily Advertiser*: "I have never seen Mr. Adams look so well these ten years. He was much indisposed about the third year of his presidency which his friends thought was in a great measure owing to his habit of cold bathing. . . . Everybody, ladies and all, say he looks younger and sprightlier than when he stood at the head of nation. . . . [T]his delicate and ungrateful business [the bank investigation and the tariff] he conducted with a steady calmness and coolness that I hardly expected, but, at the same time with a promptness and decision characteristic of his patriotic predecessor of the same name. . . . He certainly at this time stands on an eminence deservedly high."[26]

HIS WORK COMPLETED FOR the time being, John Quincy fled Washington's sweltering heat for the cooler climes of New England. Louisa had preceded him in May. When he reached New York, he found the city in the grip of a cholera epidemic that was claiming a hundred lives a day. The port was quarantined, the *Benjamin Franklin* tied up at dock. The congressman took a small boat from Hoboken up the Hudson to Kingston; from there it was a bone-jarring three-day ride to Quincy by stage. Reunited with his family, he began again his country strolls, wharf bathing, and classics reading. And as always there was politics; the presidential election of 1832 lay just around the corner. "Your father," Louisa wrote John, "is in high spirits dabbling as usual in public affairs while fancying he has nothing to do with them. His mind must be occupied with something, and why not this?"[27]

The previous March, Thomas Boylston Adams had died, impoverished and alcoholic. On several occasions he had been returned home "raving" drunk by a friend in his chaise. His family had become afraid of him and sought shelter at Peacefield. By 1831, Louisa was reporting to her diary that Thomas was "with an almost constant delirium," a skeleton of a man shaken by continual spasms.[28] John

Quincy would remember his brother fondly. Tom's passing had caused him "deep affliction," he wrote in his diary, and recalled "how dear and how affectionate he has been to me through a long life."[29] Charles Francis, who of course had not known his uncle in his youth, was less generous. "If I was disposed to moralize, this event [Tom's death amidst poverty and dissolution] would easily afford matter for it. But it would be at the expense of a man now beyond the reach of reproach or benefit, of a man who paid little penance for his follies and left his children to share the shame as his only legacy."[30]

Shortly after John Quincy arrived in Quincy, Louisa, in company with Abigail Brooks Adams and her children, was involved in a near disastrous carriage accident. "As we were ascending Penn's Hill one of the horses got his leg over the [center] pole and Kirk [the family coachman] being alone could not dismount so as to assist him," Louisa subsequently reported to Charles. "[F]ortunately a man came up and opened the door of the carriage. When we got the children out Mrs. Charles [Abigail] caught your Louisa, and I just cleared the step when the horses, becoming entirely unmanageable, upset the carriage; and poor Kirk has broken one of his ribs, and the horse is much hurt. We are all well."[31]

THE ONLY NOTICE THE National Republicans and the Democratic-Republicans took of the Anti-Masonic Party in 1832 was to embrace its pioneering notion of a national nominating convention. The National Republicans had selected Clay and adopted a platform attacking Jackson over Indian removal and his opposition to internal improvements. The Democrats subsequently met in Baltimore and renominated Old Hickory by acclamation. Jackson let it be known that he wanted Van Buren as his running mate, and the delegates complied. This first Democratic nominating convention adopted the two-thirds rule, which would give the South a veto over the party's candidate for the next hundred years.[32]

The only hope for the National Republicans and Henry Clay was to fold the Anti-Masonic Party in with them. Clay refused to renounce his Royal Arch oath, although he made no attempt to defend those involved with William Morgan's disappearance.[33] Edward Ingersoll, still laboring to unite the National Republicans and Anti-Masons, once again appealed to John Quincy to be pragmatic. He was not an expert on the order, Ingersoll wrote; could not Adams inquire further of William Wirt, the Anti-Masonic candidate for president, or Colonel William L. Stone, editor of the *New York Commercial Advertiser*, a Mason but a critical one? Adams duly contacted Stone, who agreed to defend the order, which he did in June 1832 in *Letters on Masonry and Anti-masonry, Adressed to the Hon. John Quincy Adams*. Stone's principal defense was more of an apologia. The ceremonies, oaths, tokens, and grips were harmless exercises that Masons used to identify and greet one another, he declared. It was not fair to hold the generally honest and upright majority responsible for the excesses of a few. Adams replied politely but unrelentingly. He focused on the "Oaths, obligations, and penalties" that were binding on an apprentice Mason. They were, he insisted, "[c]ontrary to the laws of the land—extra-judicially taken and administered . . . [and] in violation of the positive precepts of Jesus Christ." The penalties to be imposed for violation of the Masonic code involved "a mode of death, cruel, unusual, unfit for utterance from human lips."[34] If he was not going to benefit from the proposed alliance between the National Republicans and the Anti-Masons, apparently, Adams was going to do nothing to facilitate it.

The presidential election of 1832 was no contest: Old Hickory garnered 219 electoral votes and 54.2 percent of the popular vote to Clay's abysmal forty-nine electoral votes and 37.4 percent of the popular vote. With seven college tallies, and 7.9 percent of the popular vote, Wirt was not a factor. In truth, by election time, the Masons were in steep decline and with it the Anti-Masonic Party. Jackson proved more popular than the Bank of the United States, carrying even Pennsylvania. The pillars of the Democratic Party—Indian removal and white supremacy, opposition to federally funded internal improvements as signified by the Maysville veto, and opposition to the Bank of the United States articulated so eloquently in Jackson's veto message—remained intact.[35]

DURING THE TARIFF DEBATES, Edward Everett had written his brother, "It is the decided opinion of many persons here that if the Tariff [of 1828 and subsequently 1832] is not modified to suit the Southern states, South Carolina will proceed to nullify the law. . . . [Senator John] Forsyth and some others have told me that Virginia and the other Southern states will soon be ready to join her. I have replied . . . that if S. Carolina alone nullifies, it will be an abortive act. If Virginia and the other Southern States go with her, it will be a separation of the Union."[36] Everett, as it turned out, was prescient. In the elections of 1832 in the Palmetto State, where only 11 percent of the population was eligible to vote, the nullifiers won a large majority in the state legislature, which proceeded to call a special convention to devise a response to the Adams Tariff. That body voted on November 24, 1832, to declare all protective tariffs null and void, without legal status, and thus not binding on the state's citizens and officials. South Carolina would take up arms if the Jackson administration attempted to use the U.S. Army to enforce the nation's tariff laws. The legislature voted to send copies of its nullification decree to the other slave states.

With nothing now to lose, Calhoun rode the crest of the nullification movement. He had sealed his political fate with the National Democrats by casting the tiebreaking vote against Martin Van Buren's confirmation as minister to Great Britain. He had resigned the vice presidency only to be elected by his native state to the Senate. His hope after 1832 was to build a political coalition consisting of extreme states' righters, disappointed office seekers, followers of ex-governor De-Witt Clinton, and Old Republicans.[37] He issued a call to all the states of the Union to attend a constitutional convention that would presumably affirm a state's right to interpose its will between its citizens and the federal government.

To John Quincy, the Ordinance of Nullification was blackmail pure and simple. South Carolina was threatening disunion to get its way. "They must rule or ruin," he declared in his diary.[38] He believed that President Jackson would do nothing. He had removed the Indians, vetoed the bank, and blocked the Maysville Road project. Adams was convinced that the Palmetto State had dared to act so audaciously only when it was apparent that Old Hickory was going to win the presidential election. When Adams was back in Washington for the convening of the second session of the Twenty-Second Congress on December 3, his fears seemed confirmed when he read Old Hickory's annual message to Congress. The nation's coffers were filled to overflowing, the president declared; the tariff should be modified to meet the objections of those states that believed that they were being penalized by a protectionist policy. He proposed reducing levies on foreign products to levels that would meet the minimal needs of the federal government. With a balanced budget in sight, there was no need to charge more than a token amount for the sale of public lands. In fact, Jackson declared, they ought to be turned over to the states.[39] Not surprisingly, Adams despaired. In their rush to appease the slave power, the newly victorious Jacksonians were destroying every edifice he had fought to erect and repudiating every nationalist principle his father and he had stood for. Jackson's message, Adams declared in his diary, revealed once and for all the conspiracy by the South and the West to subjugate and exploit the Eastern and Mid-Atlantic states.

John Quincy's dislike and distrust of Jackson, Van Buren, and the Democrats blinded him. Andrew Jackson had no intention of countenancing nullification, interposition, and especially armed rebellion against the government of the United States. On December 10, 1832, Old Hickory issued his justly famous Nullification Proclamation. He warned the citizens of his "native state" not to lend themselves to an act of disunion; they did so under penalty of treason. Then, echoing John Quincy's Fourth of July oration, he declared, "I consider, then, the power to annul a law of the United States, assumed by one state, incompatible with the existence of the Union, contradicted expressly by the letter of the Constitution, unauthorized by its spirit, inconsistent with every principle on which it was founded, and destructive of the object for which it was founded."[40]

Writing to his father from Boston, Charles Francis reported that the proclamation "has produced an electrical effect here. . . . The first general impression . . . which found its way into the newspapers was that you wrote the paper. The singular coincidence in its opinion with those expressed in your 4th of July address certainly gave color to such a suspicion."[41] (In truth, the author was Secretary of State Edward Livingston, a distinguished New York lawyer who had written treatises against the Kentucky and Virginia Resolutions.) Even the "moldering relics of the Hartford Convention" had rallied to the administration, Charles wrote his father.[42] No less a personage than Harrison Gray Otis hailed the Nullification Proclamation, insisting that the resolutions passed by the Hartford Convention in 1814 had been a plea for concessions and not a statement of defiance. For his part, Adams was willing to concede that the proclamation contained much sound constitutional doctrine, but, he wrote Charles, Jackson was probably just making a show. The nullifiers still ruled in Washington, and it was his prediction that the administration would capitulate. Besides, if Congress acted as Jackson wished and did away with the protective tariff, the source of South Carolina's discontent would be removed.

Meanwhile, the House Committee on Ways and Means introduced a new tariff measure that would cut the prevailing rates in half during the next two years. Congressman Augustin Smith Clayton of Georgia rose to defend the proposed new measure. The Adams Tariff was a protective tariff, and it penalized the planters and farmers of the South who would have to pay a premium for the manufactured goods they required. Slavery was a national institution that benefited the entire economy, he declared. "Our slaves sail the Northern ships and run the Northern spindles. . . . Our slaves are our machinery, and we have as good a right to profit by them as do the Northern men to profit by the machinery they employ."[43]

Adams could remain silent no longer. Human beings; machinery! The manufacturing states' machinery was not sentient beings with beating hearts. Protection! No region of the country enjoyed more protections under the Constitution than the slaveholding states; the three-fifths clause gave to the South twenty more representatives than its voting population entitled it to. As to the North, "I believe that their looms and factories have no representative in Congress." The free states had accepted the three-fifths bargain; were they not entitled to protection? And if they did not receive it, why should they, like South Carolina, not threaten nullification and interposition?[44] The South could not have it both ways, declared the New Englander—enjoying the protection afforded by the army and the navy while refusing to pay for that protection. Who had shielded the frontier farmers of the Southeast against marauding Indians? Who would protect the slave states in case of a massive slave uprising? William Drayton of South Carolina leapt to his feet: "The member from Massachusetts" he shouted, "has thrown a firebrand into the Hall."[45]

And indeed, Adams had touched a very sore spot. On August 21, 1831, a group of bondsmen in Southampton County had staged an armed insurrection. Their leader, Nat Turner, was an enslaved preacher and prophet. After experiencing a vision of white and Black angels wrestling in heaven, he became convinced that he had been appointed by God to lead a rebellion that would free America's slaves. Moving from plantation to plantation, he recruited followers who murdered their masters and their families, seizing arms as they went. Turner and his band succeeded in killing sixty whites—men, women, and children—before a contingent of U.S. Marines supported by the local militia overwhelmed them. Those who survived, including an unrepentant Turner, were hanged, as were dozens of other slaves suspected of aiding or even knowing of the conspiracy. In a number of areas, especially South Carolina, Blacks outnumbered whites. Would militia suffice if there were a "servile war"? Congressman Adams asked his colleagues. "It is not I who have thrown the 'firebrand,'" Adams replied to Drayton. "The Nullification Ordinance is the firebrand."[46]

Congress subsequently passed the Force Bill, authorizing the commander in chief to use the military might of the nation to quash the nullification movement in South Carolina. The president began moving troops into forts bordering the Palmetto State and issued a call for volunteers for the anticipated fight. He declared that if it came to it, he would lead U.S. troops into battle personally. The firebrands in Charleston began to quail and the unionists to take heart. In the Senate Clay and Calhoun agreed on a compromise. Congress would replace the Adams Tariff with a new bill that would over the following ten years reduce the tax on imports to a level of 20 percent, in effect severely eroding protection for Northern manufacturers. In return South Carolina would revoke its Ordinance of Nullification. The measure passed the House on February 26, 1833, by a vote of 119 to eighty-five, with John Quincy voting no. Two weeks later the Senate approved the bill twenty-nine to sixteen. In South Carolina, the legislature voted to accept the Tariff of 1833, but then nullified the Force Bill, which of course had become moot.

Adams was not finished, however. During the debate over the administration's new tariff bill, he had attempted to persuade his Committee on Manufactures to rise in revolt as a matter of jurisdiction if nothing else. He got nowhere. The Speaker had packed the committee with anti-protectionists. In desperation, Adams drafted and submitted to the House a minority report. Not surprisingly his missive was far more than a dispassionate analysis.[47] "The Report of the Minority of the Committee of Manufactures Submitted in the House of Representatives February 28, 1833" would be one of John Quincy Adams's most significant state papers. For the first time, he turned his guns directly on the slaveholding South, on its undemocratic grip on the Congress and federal policy, and on those in the West who allied with them. He began by quoting Jackson's annual message: "The wealth and strength of a country are its population, and the best part of that population are cultivators of the soil."[48] That contention was debatable on its face, Adams declared. The United States would still be weak and dependent on one European power or another if it were not for its merchants, shipowners, and manufacturers. But what really angered Adams was the implication that Jackson was speaking for the nation's yeomen farmers—the heroes of Jefferson's imagination— when it was the feudal aristocracy of the South, a tiny percentage of the nation's population, whom the president was really representing. Jackson had declared his intention to reduce the federal government to "a simple machine." Simplicity, Adams declared, was the salient characteristic of slavery, in which all men were either masters or slaves.

The United States was a vast republic founded and fueled by immigrants; it was comprised of different sections with differing interests, Adams declared. If the nation was to prosper, it required an active federal government capable of weaving those interests into a whole, resilient fabric. The proposed Tariff of 1833 was a surrender to South Carolina and nullifiers in general. Jackson, Clay, and Calhoun were doing nothing less than conspiring to make the federal government the servant of the slave power. They attacked internal improvements that would benefit the nation as a whole because they would do anything to weaken the national government. For what, he asked, was this unholy alliance, "this enormous edifice of fraud and falsehood erected? To rob the free workingman of the North of the wages of his labor—to take money from his pocket and put it into the hands of the Southern owners of [human] machinery." He suggested that the terms of the bargain that had produced the three-fifths clause were broken. Adams ended by comparing his vision of an America strengthened and enriched by an activist government, harnessing "national energies and resources to great undertakings," to Jackson's imagined future "impending with universal ruin, draining all the sources of fertility from the fountains of internal national improvement, shaking to its foundations all commercial confidence by the determined annihilation of the Bank, and wresting forever from the people of the United States and from their posterity for unnumbered ages the inestimable inheritance of the public lands."[49]

Adams subsequently wrote his friend William Plumer that he had been motivated to write the report because he was no longer willing that the nation should continue in thrall to the tyranny of a minority, especially when that minority consisted of holders of human chattel. Continued acquiescence in the ongoing corrupt bargain between the South and the West would not only threaten the prosperity of the country but produce "the most fatal of catastrophes—the dissolution of the union by a complicated, civil, and servile war."[50] What America was witnessing was "an entire new system for the government of the Union . . . the free industry of the whole subservient to that of the slave holders and pampering the South and bribing the West for the depression of the North, and above all of New England."[51]

This latter notion was a seed that would take root in the Northern and Mid-Atlantic states and grow relentlessly, eventually transcending the fears of free whites concerning the consequences of disunion, civil war, and emancipation.

Adams initially thought his riposte would never see the light of day. Anti-protectionists on the committee had done their best to keep his broadside from being presented to the House. It had barely made its way into the record on the eve of adjournment. Charles subsequently contracted with a Boston publisher to have five thousand copies printed; most major newspapers reproduced Adams's missive either in whole or in part. "The Report," editorialized the *Philadelphia National Gazette*, "is the product of his athletic and capacious mind . . . the performance is altogether one of extraordinary strength and momentum. . . . Mr. Adams . . . [reveals] . . . all the spuriousness and evil tendencies of the claim of nullification."[52]

WITH THE ADJOURNMENT OF the second session of the Twenty-Second Congress in March 1833, the Adamses retreated to Quincy. Two hours a day were spent tending his orchard and another two on correspondence. When John Quincy was reminded that it had been fifty-four years since he had first set foot on European soil with his father, memories flooded his mind, not only of public affairs but of the joys of British and French culture, especially the theater.[53]

As chance would have it, the famous British writer and actress Fanny Kemble and her equally renowned father, Charles, made their first stage appearances in Boston while the Adamses were in residence. The adults went to see her play the roles of Bianca in the tragedy of *Fazio* and of Belvidera in *Venice Preserv'd*, an English Restoration play by Thomas Otway. Fanny took the town by storm. A member of the audience for the latter performance later recalled, "When [Miss Kimble] as Belvedira [*sic*], shrieking, stares at her husband's ghost, I was sitting in front in her line of vision, and I cowered and shrank from her terrible gaze."[54] John Quincy observed in his diary: "Fanny Kemble [passes here] for a great beauty and a great genius, both of which with the aid of fashion and fancy, she is."[55] Charles thought her a great actress but not so much a beauty. She was "an ugly, bright looking girl," he wrote but admitted that "her eyes have great power."[56] On May 2, Dr. George Parkman, who was hosting the Kembles, called on the former president and requested his presence at a dinner to honor the actors. "He said the young lady was desirous of being introduced to me," John Quincy noted in his diary. "And I could but say that it would be very pleasing to me. . . . As a sort of personage myself of the last century, I was flattered by the wish of this blossom of the next age . . . , and I answered Dr. Parkman accordingly."[57]

John Quincy and Fanny were, of course, seated next to each other. "I had much conversation with Miss Kemble, chiefly upon dramatic literature. . . . I spoke to her of some of her own poetical productions. . . ." The conversation turned to Shakespeare. "Presently, [Mr. Adams] began a sentence by assuring me that he was a worshipper of Shakespeare," Fanny subsequently wrote in her journal, "and ended it by saying that Othello was disgusting, King Lear ludicrous, and Romeo and Juliet childish nonsense whereat I swallowed half a pint of water and nearly my tumbler too and remained silent; for what could I say?"[58]

That portion of the Kemble journal subsequently found its way into the papers. Parkman persuaded Adams to publish a reply. "I said that my admiration of him [Shakespeare] as a profound delineator of human nature and a sublime poet was little short of idolatry, but that I thought he was often misunderstood as performed on the stage. In the original of Romeo and Juliet, the heroine is aged 14 but in recent stage productions in London, her nurse declared her to be nineteen. 'Nineteen!' In what country of the world was a young lady of nineteen ever be constantly attended by a nurse? . . . Take away the age of Juliet and you take away from her all . . . all that childish simplicity which blended with the fervor of her passion constitutes her greatest charm. . . ."[59] *King Lear* and *Othello* were great plays, Adams had observed to Fanny, but he found both characters unsympathetic: "The lady was little less than a wanton, and the old king nothing less than a dotard . . . the dotage of an absolute monarch may be a suitable subject for a tragedy, and Shakespeare has made a deep tragedy of it. But as exhibited upon the stage, it is turned into a comedy." Fanny, who would write disparagingly of America and its culture in 1835, must or should have known that "improving" Shakespeare onstage had been and still was a subject of much criticism in British literary and theatrical circles. John Quincy's contention that "the great moral lessons of the tragedy of Othello is that black and white blood cannot be intermingled in marriage without a gross outrage upon the law of nature" drew no comment from either the Kembles or the readers of his defense because it represented the opinion of the vast majority of white Americans, whatever their views on slavery.[60]

By this point twenty-six-year-old Charles Francis had assumed the role of Adams family heir apparent. His law practice and investments were both flourishing. "My worldly prosperity so far as it depends upon pecuniary matters had increased again in a most extraordinary . . . degree," he confided to his diary. "The causes of my anxiety upon this subject are now to a considerable extent removed."[61] In August Charles and Abby presented their parents with another grandchild, a son they named John Quincy. On the day of the child's baptism, the elated grandfather turned over to Charles Francis the seal—*Piscemur, Venemur ut Olim*—used by John Adams when he signed the final treaty of peace between America and Britain in 1783.

By contrast John, then still struggling to keep Columbia Mills' head above water, was slipping into decline and drinking as his personality deteriorated. That summer he and Mary Catherine made a trip to Quincy to see their daughter and reunite with the rest of the family. The visit did not go well. Given to braggadocio and exaggeration, John irritated his brother to the point at which at dinner one evening, Charles exploded. "In conversation a remark together with a gesture of my brother at table produced in me an excessive burst of passion and a scene ensued which was quite of an unpleasant character."[62] Such incidents, Charles observed, inevitably occurred when the two were under the same roof for very long.

John Quincy's principal feelings toward John continued to be affection and concern, toward Charles respect and admiration. "Charles . . . gave me his own candid opinion of *Dermot MacMorrogh* [soon to see its third edition]. That it excited no interest. The freedom with which he expresses this opinion deserves my respect and is a pledge of the goodness of his heart as well as of the firmness of his temper and the sincerity of his filial affection."[63]

In June, Harvard invited President Jackson to attend graduation ceremonies, during which he would be awarded an honorary Doctor of Laws. Shortly after the invitation had been extended, President Josiah Quincy called upon John Quincy and asked if he would attend the occasion. "I said that the personal relations in which President Jackson had chosen to place himself with me were such that I could hold no intercourse of a friendly character with him [which, of course, was Adams's and not the president's fault]. And independent of that, myself an affectionate child of our alma mater, I would not be present to witness her disgrace in conferring her highest literary honors upon a barbarian who could not write a sentence of grammar and hardly could spell his own name."[64] To the congressman's disgust, not only did Harvard welcome Jackson and confer the degree, but Boston and all of Massachusetts threw out the welcome mat; the city staged a ceremony on Bunker Hill, where Edward Everett delivered a complimentary address and presented the Old Hero with two cannonballs from the famous Revolutionary War battle. The ceremony and other fetes in neighboring communities had to be delayed because of the president's ill health. "I believe much of his debility is politic," Adams sneered in his diary. "He is one of our tribe of great men who turn disease to commodity like John Randolph who for forty years was always dying."[65] But this was not only unkind but unfair. The president was at the time suffering from severe dysentery and coughing up blood from an old dueling wound. At Concord he collapsed and had to be rushed back to Washington.

In the wake of the Baltimore national nominating convention in the fall of 1831, Massachusetts Anti-Masons had offered their gubernatorial nomination to John Quincy. He had refused because he did not want to run against the incumbent, his longtime friend Levi Lincoln. But in 1833 Lincoln decided to step down to run for the House. That August, a month before the Massachusetts Anti-Masonic state convention, two party leaders visited Peacefield and asked Adams if he would accept the gubernatorial nomination this time around. He again declined, declaring that his election could result only in "a turbulent administration and a furious renewal of the contest at the end of the year."[66] Shortly afterward, Charles visited and found John Quincy despondent: "My father has been drooping for some time past. His health is bad, and his spirits are worse. The great misfortune of his life, I still continue to believe, was his return to public life."[67]

The Anti-Masons caucused on Thursday morning, September 12, in Faneuil Hall. Charles attended. The delegates quickly divided between the city faction and the country party "when a private current was set in motion in favor of the nomination of my father which very soon took the place of every other sentiment," Charles wrote, "and I left the Hall to start for Quincy and announce to him the state of the case previous to the arrival of the committee who were to announce it."[68] John Quincy assured his son that he would not accept, but the Anti-Masons knew their man. The resolution of nomination read: "We recognize as a sound republican principle, which ought to govern nominations and acceptances of nominations for office, that in a free government no citizen standing prominent for public service is at liberty to reject a nomination upon personal considerations alone when tendered to him by a large body of his fellow citizens." Adams could not resist. His letter of acceptance made no mention of Masons or National Republicans. His goal, he wrote, was to "merge all party spirit and feeling in the great interests of the whole Commonwealth."[69]

Adams's great hope was that the National Republicans would second his nomination, but there was no chance of that. That party included a number of Masons and old Federalists who had never forgiven him for his "apostasy." On September 30 the *Columbia Centinel* published a letter from a prominent National Republican calling upon all party members to reject Adams if his name should be put forward.

He was, the missive declared, "the most unpopular man that could be mentioned in the whole state of Mass[achusetts]. . . . If there is anyone among your number who means to support him at the convention, he has no right to go there."[70]

The National Republicans nominated John Davis of Worcester, a former colleague of Adams in the House. Though his prospects for election to the governorship were more than bleak, John Quincy would not abandon the field until the people had spoken. "The plot thickens," Charles wrote, "but nearly all my father's political friends have deserted him. And the fire of Masonic hatred is opened upon him with a fury that baffles conception."[71] The vote, held in October, showed Davis with 25,149, Adams, 18,274, and Marcus Morton (Democrat) with 15,493. But John Quincy was still a member of the House of Representatives, and as he well knew, office was what one made of it, particularly if you were the greatest secretary of state in the nation's history, the son of a Founding Father, and a man with an eye for causes that stirred men's souls.

The congressman nearly did not live to take the public stage again. He departed Boston on November 6, Louisa and the rest of the family having preceded him by several days. It was overland by stage to Providence and from thence to New York aboard the steamboat *Boston*. "The boat was crowded almost to suffocation, and people of every land and language seemed congregated in it," Adams recorded in his diary; "among the rest, a whole tribe of wild Irish whose language I now heard for the first time spoken."[72] Two trains were waiting for the nearly two hundred passengers who disembarked. Each was comprised of a locomotive pulling two passenger cars—B and then A—followed by a baggage car. John Quincy boarded coach B on the second train. Ticket holders sat on benches running along the sides of the car and facing each other. En route Adams and a fellow passenger timed their progress. "We had gone about five miles . . . and had traversed one mile in one minute and thirty-six seconds when the front left wheel of the car in which I was [sitting], having taken fire and burned for several minutes, slipped off the rail." On this particular train, the iron hub of the wheel was connected to the iron rim by wooden spokes, and the friction of the rim against the rail had created sparks that set the wheel on fire. "The pressure on the right side of the car, then meeting resistance, raised it with both wheels from the rail, and it was oversetting on the left side but the same pressure on the car immediately behind raised its left side from the rail till it actually overset to the right, and, in oversetting brought back the car, in which I was, to stand on the four wheels and saved from injury all the passengers in it." But coach A came crashing down on its side. The locomotive dragged the overturned coach some two hundred yards before it could stop. "Men, women, and a child scattered along the road, bleeding, mangled, groaning, writhing in torture, and dying," Adams subsequently recorded in his diary.[73] What if his wife and grandchild had been in the coach behind him? was John Quincy's first thought. The injured were transported on cushions to Bordentown. John Quincy and the able-bodied followed; shaken, the congressman continued his journey.

WHILE JOHN QUINCY AND Louisa were in Massachusetts during the congressional recess, the Bank War had heated up again. Angry over the role that Biddle and bank supporters had played in the election of 1832, Jackson polled his cabinet in March on whether the federal government should withdraw its deposits from the institution—some ten million dollars representing half the bank's capital. Only Amos Kendall, postmaster general, and Roger B. Taney, attorney general, were in favor. Secretary of State Edward Livingston and, most important, Secretary of the Treasury Louis McLane were opposed. Because the bank's charter was due to expire in 1836, the move would appear petty and gratuitous, they argued. It was a maxim with Old Hickory that if he did not like the vote of his cabinet, he would change the voters. He dispatched Livingston to England as the new U.S. minister and moved McLane to the State Department; to be the new secretary of the treasury, the president named William J. Duane, an outspoken critic of the bank. Nevertheless, when Jackson ordered him to withdraw federal monies from the Bank of the United States, Duane refused; the institution, he declared, was on sound footing with $79 million in assets and $37 million in liabilities. Thereupon, Old Hickory fired Duane and replaced him with the ever-pliable Roger Taney. The administration did not suddenly withdraw all of its funds but simply stopped deposits and began placing its monies in selected state banks ("pet banks" Jackson's critics called them).[74]

Upon his return to Washington in December 1833, Adams immediately huddled with other friends of the bank. They all agreed that the decision to withdraw federal funds from the institution was clearly an abomination—petty, vindictive, unnecessary, and ultimately a threat to the economic health of the nation. But what to do? Removal was accomplished through an executive order making it hard for the legislative branch to gain procedural purchase. Adams got around the problem by introducing in the House a resolution passed by the Massachusetts legislature voicing its opposition to removal. He had prepared a comprehensive defense of Biddle and the bank to accompany the resolution. His old enemy Speaker Stevenson cut him off, however, by recognizing a previous question. Undeterred, Adams persuaded the *National Intelligencer* to publish his broadside on April 12 under the title "Speech (Suppressed by the Previous Question) . . . on the

Removal of the Public Deposits."[75] In it Adams scourged the administration. Taney's justification for the removal order was specious. The bank was not only solvent, but it was the glue that held the national financial system together. The decision to deposit the public monies in selected state banks proved once again that the Jacksonians were nothing more than political grafters. Nicholas Biddle, Adams declared, was both able and honorable, a man whom he was proud to call a friend.[76] Biddle conveyed his profound thanks to the congressman and paid to have fifty thousand copies of the "Suppressed Speech" printed and distributed.

The decision to withdraw federal funds from the Bank of the United States proved a turning point in American politics. Martin Van Buren had stayed clear of the Bank War; he feared that Jackson's unwillingness to support rechartering and especially his removal order would divide the Democratic Party—and he was right. Jackson's obsession with destroying "the Monster" led a number of prominent Democrats to leave the party. Not only were the business and financial communities alienated, but Southern planters who appreciated and depended on a national banking entity were as well. Henry Clay smelled blood. He led the way as the Senate passed a vote of censure against the president twenty-six to twenty, the only such event in American history. In April 1834, National Republicans, Anti-Masons, and other discontented factions joined together to form the Whig Party. The name was universally recognized as referring to those in British political history who were critical of executive usurpation. "[T]he Whigs of the present day," declared Clay, were just reincarnations of the Revolutionary War heroes who had risen up against the tyranny of George III.[77]

The Whigs and the Democrats became the two major components of what historians refer to as the Second American Party System. There was during this period and into the 1840s a strikingly even balance between the two. Business and professional men gravitated to the Whigs, who were especially strong in southern New England and in parts of the country such as Ohio and eastern Tennessee that favored internal improvements. Congregationalists, Unitarians, and "New School" Presbyterians voted Whig in disproportionate numbers, as did people of higher social standing, larger income, and greater education. Jacksonian Democrats were laissez-faire in their approach to government and economics. The perpetuation of democracy, they argued, depended on strong local and state governments and a minimum of regulation and intervention by Washington. Whigs tended to be Protestant and Anglo while the Democrats were strong among people of German and Dutch descent and among Catholics. Whigs thought of themselves as sober, industrious, and morally upright—the guardians of middle-class values in a liberalizing society. They were unambiguous supporters of the Clay–Adams American

System, believing that social improvement would not just occur automatically; if the common good was to be advanced, the forces of progress would have to be actively managed.[78] But the Whigs, unlike the Democrats, were unable to successfully finesse the slavery issue. The party was born in the midst of an ever-widening chasm on the subject.

34

The Great and Foul Stain on the Union

URING THE 1830S AND 1840s, the United States was swept by a reform movement of major proportions. Much of the energy was supplied by the Second Great Awakening, a Christian interdenominational evangelical movement that began in New York's Burned-Over District and swept through the upper Midwest. Its chief proselytizer was Charles Finney, who declared that the newly reborn Christians of the awakening should "aim at being useful in the highest degree possible."[1] It differed from Jonathan Edwards's Great Awakening in many ways, but especially in the prominent role afforded to women and the linking of salvation to works. Finney's movement spawned or nourished a number of reform movements—communitarianism, women's rights, the temperance movement, prison and insane asylum reform, but especially abolitionism.

In April 1829 there appeared in Boston the most inflammatory pamphlet to be published in America since Thomas Paine's *Common Sense*. It bore the ponderous title "An Appeal to the Colored Citizens of the World, but in Particular, and Very Expressly, to Those of the United States of America." Its author was a self-educated free Black named David Walker, who operated a used-clothing shop near the waterfront. Walker was a devotee of the Reverend Richard Allen, the prominent Black cleric and civil rights leader. His screed was triggered perhaps by the abuse of a Black man near Boston's Park Street Church that he had witnessed. Did not the Declaration of Independence proclaim the equality of all men? Walker asked. Did not the New Testament preach the universal brotherhood of all men? The notion that people of color were innately inferior went hand in hand with slavery; one could not exist without the other. Educated freemen like himself had an obligation to stand up for the race and denounce the South's "peculiar" institution for what it was—an abomination. But that would not be sufficient unto the day, he acknowledged. The enslaved themselves must rise up, cast off their chains, and take vengeance upon their oppressors. If God—this time the God of the Old Testament, who smote the wicked—were good, He would come to their aid.[2] If the day of racial reckoning did not come, then there was no God. "I say that if these things do not occur in their proper time, it is because the world in which we live does not exist, and we are deceived with regard to its existence."[3] Walker and those whom he inspired worked to have the "Appeal" reprinted and distributed as widely as possible. They were remarkably successful. In the months that followed, Georgia, Virginia, the Carolinas, and Louisiana ordered the confiscation of every copy and stipulated harsh punishments for anyone found in possession of the incendiary sheet.

SHORTLY THEREAFTER, A WHITE version of David Walker appeared on the national scene. William Lloyd Garrison had grown up poor; his father deserted them when he was two, and his mother, a cleaning woman, struggled to make ends meet. She did provide her son with a Baptist upbringing at a time when the denomination was caught up in the Second Great Awakening. Garrison grew to manhood impoverished but lettered, on fire with a determination to set the world aright before Christ's Second Coming. Leaving his birthplace, Newburyport, he traveled to Baltimore to work for a time for the Quaker Benjamin Lundy on an antislavery sheet entitled the *Genius of Universal Emancipation*. Returning to Massachusetts, Garrison, with the support of Boston's Black community, began publishing the *Liberator* in January 1831. It was uncompromising in its call for immediate, uncompensated emancipation. Because the Constitution condoned slavery, Garrison declared, it was a mere piece of paper to be ignored by the righteous. God's law demanded abolition. "I will be as harsh as truth and as uncompromising as justice," he promised in the first issue.[4] Within months the *Liberator* was circulating regularly in Black neighborhoods throughout the North. When Lewis and Arthur Tappan, two wealthy New York businessmen who had supported Charles Finney's work, began subsidizing the *Liberator*, it went national. Walker's and Garrison's work helped pave the way for the formation of the American Anti-Slavery Society in Philadelphia in 1833. By 1835 the AASS could boast some two hundred local chapters and by 1838 some thirteen hundred fifty comprising two hundred fifty thousand members.

Adding fuel to the flames was the rapid progress of abolitionism in Great Britain. Parliament began debating the issue in 1830, and in 1833 it would outlaw slavery in British colonies including the West Indies, Africa, and a remnant in Canada. Some eight hundred thousand souls were affected. During the debate, British abolitionists had sent pamphlets and spokespersons to America to attract Britain's former colonists to the cause. They found many ready converts. "Let us imitate our British brethren and open the flood gates of light on this dark subject," the *New York Evangelist* editorialized.[5]

With his aspirations for higher office seemingly at an end, John Quincy would seem to have been free to speak out in favor of abolition. "[T]he result of the Missouri question and the attitude of parties have silenced all the declaimers for the abolition of slavery in the Union," he had written in 1831. "The state of things, however, is not to continue forever."[6] But he hesitated. There was no question that Adams abhorred the institution. "Slavery," he had written in his diary during the debate over the Missouri Compromise, "is the great and foul stain upon the North American Union. . . . This object [emancipation/abolition] is vast in its compass, awful in its prospects, sublime and beautiful in its issue. A life devoted to it would be nobly spent or sacrificed."[7] In the wake of his defeat for a second term as president, he had begun a history of political parties in the United States. In it he had listed six causes for the rise of partisanship and burgeoning sectionalism in the United States. He made it clear that slavery ranked first among equals, exacerbating every other source of division, including unequal wealth distribution, ethnicity, religion, and culture. It was the persistence of the barbaric institution above all else that had led to his defeat and the rise of Jacksonism.[8] Yet before 1833, he and his had remained largely silent on the issue in public speech and in policy. More than that, as a diplomat, John Quincy had faithfully represented the interests of the slave power.

As ambassador to Great Britain and secretary of state, Adams had made every effort to obtain indemnity for Southern slaveholders whose human property had been carried off by the British. He had shown little enthusiasm for joining a British-led effort to hammer out an agreement outlawing the slave trade, preferring to privilege America's lifelong crusade against impressment. During the Missouri statehood debate, Adams had told Governor Jonathan Jennings of Indiana that the status of slavery where it was established must be left entirely to the people of the state in question. Although it became clear in the Missouri Compromise that further continental expansion would facilitate the survival and spread of human bondage, John Quincy continued to serve as a high priest to manifest destiny. "Oh, the time will come," prophesied an anonymous correspondent at the beginning of his presidency, "when reflection on this neglect will blister your very soul as it comes over you. Fatal, fatal deference to proud oppressors!"[9] What kept Adams's mouth shut and his public pen still were his nationalism, his political ambition, and his innate conservatism.[10]

John and John Quincy Adams strove to make a more perfect union, but not to kill the good for the perfect. Their goal was to strengthen the United States, to make it so powerful and independent that it could afford to confront its great contradiction. Unity is to me what balance is to you, John Quincy had remarked to his father. His experience with the Federalist secessionist plot culminating in the Hartford Convention had instilled in him a deep abhorrence of sectionalism. Prior to the Missouri Compromise, the younger Adams had believed that the best and brightest among America's reformers and political theorists could manage and eventually solve the problem of slavery. Were not the members of the Virginia dynasty pioneering republicans who, despite owning human chattel, had spoken out against slavery? Had not John Randolph of Roanoke and John Taylor of Caroline provided for the emancipation of their slaves in their wills?

In the context of his day, John Quincy was not a racist. He believed that Blacks and Native Americans were fully human, equal at birth to Anglo-Saxons. But he was convinced of the cultural, if not the moral, superiority of the white race. His defense of the Cherokees and the Creeks during his stint in the White House, though fruitless, was heartfelt, but only if Native Americans embraced the ways of the white man. Blacks, like Indians, were fully capable of assimilation. Education and property trumped color. He had no problem in hosting the Reverend Richard Allen at the White House.[11] Adams endorsed the ideas expressed by his protégé and friend Alexander Everett in *America: Or, A General Survey of the Political Situation of the Several Powers of the Western Continent*. The history of civilization was cyclical not evolutionary, Everett wrote. In the ancient world, the Egyptians—non-whites—had ruled the world and been the bearers of civilization. "As respects the immediate question it would seem . . . that the blacks (whether of African or Asiatic origin) would have not only a fair right to be considered as naturally equal to men of any color but are even not without some plausible pretensions to a claim of superiority."[12] The education and general improvement of free Blacks, declared Everett, was the best bet for promoting emancipation.

Adams was at once more radical and more conservative than Everett. He could not quite conceive of Africans, particularly former slaves, ever being able to participate fully in a republic such as the United States. Indeed, his opposition to the institution, despite his poems and diary lamentations, were philosophical and political rather than humanitarian. In 1829, Elliott Cresson, a proponent of the American Colonization Society, had called on John Quincy. "He has a profound horror of the condition of the slaves in our Southern States," Adams subsequently wrote of their conversation. "There is, I believe in this respect some misapprehension and much prejudice—There are no doubt cases of extreme oppression and cruelty, and the impunity for them is complete; but I believe them to be very rare and that the general treatment of slaves is mild and moderate."[13]

In 1831, Alexis de Tocqueville—who would later author *Democracy in America*—and his companion, Gustave de Beaumont, visited Boston. Alexander Everett hosted a dinner, the primary objective of which was to have them meet and converse with the former president. "Do you regard slavery as a great evil for the United States?" de Tocqueville asked. Yes, indeed, Adams replied, the greatest. "It's in slavery that are to be found almost all the embarrassments of the present and fears of the future." In reconciling themselves to the institution, Southerners, even now the best of them, the most educated and intelligent, had corrupted their minds and principles, Adams observed. "Every white man in the South is a being equally privileged whose destiny is to make the negroes work without working themselves." Slavery's existence demeaned the workingmen of the free states. "Do you think it is really impossible to get along without Blacks in the South?" the Frenchman continued. "I am convinced of the contrary," Adams replied. "The Europeans work in Greece and Sicily; why should they not in Virginia and the Carolinas? It's no hotter there." But the former president had little positive to say concerning the victims of slavery. "I know of nothing more insolent than a black," John Quincy declared, "when he is not speaking to his master and is not afraid of being beaten. It is not even rare to see negroes treat their masters very ill when they have to do with a weak man. The negresses especially make frequent abuse of the kindness of their mistresses. They know that it isn't customary to inflict bodily punishment on them."[14]

On Haiti, Adams was ambivalent. He had heard much of the Black kingdom-cum-republic when he was minister to the Court of St. James's and entertained Prince Saunders, the Black American educator hired by King Henri Christophe to create a national school system for the island nation. Like Alexander Everett, who had praised Haiti, Adams welcomed a successful experiment in Black self-government, but he also believed that its example might possibly encourage a "servile war" in the United States. When in 1833 the British freed their West Indian slaves, he expressed apprehension that the entire Caribbean would become not only an example for American Blacks but a seedbed of revolution that might spread throughout the Western Hemisphere. "The abolition of slavery will pass like a pestilence over all the British Colonies in the West Indies; it may prove an earthquake upon this continent."[15] No longer could the slave power in the United States afford to depict the institution as a necessary evil, to be regretted perhaps, but an inevitable and permanent necessity. At this point John Quincy was clearly worried more about the sanctity of the Union than about the welfare of Black bondsmen. But that would change.

Virginia responded to Nat Turner's rebellion in two very divergent ways. The governor asked for and received legislation designed to prevent future uprisings—prohibiting unsupervised slave gatherings, further restricting the activities of free Blacks, strengthening laws prohibiting the education of slaves, and the like. At the same time, with the General Assembly flooded with emancipation petitions, that body embarked on a yearlong debate on the wisdom of freeing the state's bondsmen. Antislavery sentiment was strong in the Virginia piedmont and in Richmond, but the slave-owning coastal areas held the power. In the end, the General Assembly passed an impotent resolution denouncing slavery as an evil but declaring its abolition to be impractical at the present time.

In 1833, Congressman Adams read "A Review of the Debates in the Legislature of 1831 and 1832" by Thomas Dew, who would become president of William and Mary. His essay was a ringing defense of slavery on moral, economic, and political grounds. Like other apologists, Dew argued that whites and free Blacks could never live in harmony together. Blacks were racially inferior, naturally dependent, and possessed of low self-control and a debased nature. He denounced the schemes of the American Colonization Society in no uncertain terms. Returning freed Blacks to Africa was logistically impossible and prohibitively expensive. Emancipation in Virginia would, among other things, prevent the commonwealth from profiting as "a negro raising state for other states of the South."[16] Dew was greatly respected in the South, his writings widely distributed. Defenders of slavery ranked him with Samuel A. Cartwright, the Southern surgeon who had invented the "diseases" of drapetomania (the "madness that made slaves want to run away") and dysaesthesia aethiopica (rascality), both of which were cured by beatings.

John Quincy perused Professor Dew's essay with great interest: "It is a monument of the intellectual perversion produced by the existence of slavery in a free community," he wrote. "To the mind of Mr. Dew slavery is the source of all virtue in the heart of the master." That his essay passed among the South's elite for authentic scientific and social observation was a sign of how morally and intellectually corrupt the slave power had become. For this reason, if for no other, "A Review of the Debates" was worthy of serious study by opponents of the barbaric institution. Know thy enemy.[17] But when the congressman's nephew John Quincy approached him about subscribing to the journal of the American Anti-Slavery Society, Adams declined.[18] His reticence stemmed from a number of motives.

In 1833 abolitionists, led by Garrison's *Liberator* in Boston and the *Emancipator* in New York, began bombarding the South with antislavery literature; so angered was the slave power that it placed a two-hundred-thousand-dollar bounty on Arthur Tappan's head. In Charlestown abolitionist pamphlets were set aflame in the city square. At this point, Garrison, Walker, and the Tappans were regarded by most Northerners as a lunatic fringe; anti-abolitionists in Boston, New York, and other cities attacked antislavery speakers, broke up meetings, and destroyed presses. When, two years later, Jackson's postmaster general Amos Kendall ordered postal officials to seize abolitionist mailings, the Anti-Slavery Society began flooding Congress with petitions. Under the rules of the House, during the first thirty days of each congressional session, an hour a day was devoted to petitions; thereafter petition submissions were limited to one hour every other Monday.[19]

In December 1831, in one of his first acts as a congressman, Adams had presented fifteen petitions from citizens of Pennsylvania begging for the abolition of slavery in general but especially for ending the slave trade in the District of Columbia. He made it clear that he did not agree with the portions concerning the slave trade in the capital. The New Englander also requested that the petitions be laid on the table and not discussed in the House. Shortly afterward, a Quaker friend asked him why. He detested slavery as much as any other sane man, Adams said; he was proud of the fact that in the first census in 1790, Massachusetts had been the only state not listing human chattel. But he added that he "believed discussion would lead to ill will, to heart-burnings, to mutual hatred where the first of wants [in Congress] was harmony; and without accomplishing anything else."[20] Later, Moses Brown, another Quaker and a Rhode Island philanthropist, also inquired of Adams his reasons for not speaking out. As to the slave trade in the district, Adams replied, it was unconstitutional for the citizens of one state to petition Congress to seize the property of another. "Suppose the inhabitants of the City of Washington . . . should petition the Legislature of Rhode Island to take away from the inhabitants of Providence their land titles or to eject them from their houses?" There were also compelling political considerations. "The great mass of the people, though averse to slavery in the abstract, are altogether unwilling to meddle with it in the Southern states." That was certainly true of his constituents in Plymouth. "The remedy must arise in the seat of the evils."[21] If the South were to be redeemed, Southerners would have to make it happen.

WHILE JOHN QUINCY WAS in Massachusetts during the long interim between the first and second sessions of the Twenty-Second Congress, Charles Francis and he were on hand in Boston to witness three balloon ascents by the aeronaut C. F. Durant. The flights were for notoriety and profit rather than for science. It had been nearly a half century since John Quincy and his father had witnessed the pioneering efforts of the Montgolfier brothers in Paris. For Durant's liftoffs, a large amphitheater had been erected on Charles Street at the lower end of the common.

Several thousand Bostonians paid fifty cents to see the balloon ascend to the accompaniment of band music and cannon fire. The Adamses viewed the first liftoff from the roof of Dr. George Parkman's house. "He rose from the bottom of the Common at about 6 o'clock and moved rapidly to the Northeast gradually rising until he appeared like a mere speck in the horizon," Charles recorded. "The day was so clear that it was a beautiful spectacle."[22] Durant landed safely in the sea off Cape Ann, following a flight of an hour and ten minutes. "I rejoice to hear that Durant was saved," John Quincy commented. "It made my heart ache when I saw him suspended between earth and heaven, to think how needlessly men will be prodigal of life, and how wanton they will defy the laws of nature."[23]

IN FEBRUARY 1834, WITH the House once again in session, Congressman T. T. Bouldin of Virginia, a fellow laborer with Adams in the struggle over the fate of the Bank of the United States, rose on the floor of the House to speak. Just as he began, Bouldin shook, staggered, and fell. Members rushed to his side, lifted him up, and carried him to lay him underneath an open window. The Senate physician was summoned; Bouldin was bled but died within fifteen minutes. His wife was present in the gallery and rushed to his side, but it was too late. "As I walked home," John Quincy subsequently wrote in his diary, "I mused on the frailty of human life, and the vicissitudes of human passions and fortunes, but especially on the tenderness with which the feelings and judgments and motives of others ought to be treated in political debate."[24]

Indeed, debate in the House of Representatives could be vicious, personal, and emotionally corrosive. In April, Congressman James Blair of South Carolina, a notorious alcoholic, shot himself in his Washington boardinghouse. "Blair was a man of amiable natural disposition, of excellent feelings, of sterling good sense, and of brilliant parts," John Quincy lamented to his diary, "irredeemably ruined by the single vice of intemperance which had crept upon him insensibly to himself till it had bloated his body to a mountain, prostrated his intellect, and vitiated his temper to madness." Blair had been fined three hundred dollars for beating Duff Green unconscious because the journalist had charged the unionist party in South Carolina, of which Blair was a member, with being Tories; he had fired a pistol at an actress from one of the boxes in a Washington theater; and he regularly brought a loaded firearm onto the floor of the House. "The chances were quite equal that he should have shot almost any other man than himself," Adams observed. "Yet he was one of the most kind-hearted men in the world, a tender and affectionate husband and father, and has left a wife devoted to him."[25]

Adding to the congressman's melancholy was news of his son John's physical and mental decline. In 1829, John had taken over management of Columbia Mills and somehow had managed to keep the operation solvent. By 1833, however, despite his modest success at running the flour mill, John despaired of his future and, like so many other Adams men, had taken to the bottle. Over the years John's alcoholism had worsened; he suffered increasingly from fevers, stiffness in his joints, loss of memory, and diminished eyesight. Before leaving Washington for Quincy in the spring of 1834, Louisa observed in her diary, "Poor John is seldom able to get out of bed until twelve o'clock and then shuffles about the house wrapped in his wadded coat." In July, Louisa journeyed to Washington to check on her middle son and his family. What she found alarmed her in the extreme and prompted a detailed report and harsh rebuke to her husband. "John has again been sorely threatened with loss of sight, and I am convinced that it is entirely owing to the dreadfully debilitating effect of this climate," she wrote John Quincy. "Would to God we could find some lucrative and advantageous scheme of business" that would allow him to escape the swamp of Washington. "[A]ssuredly there has been great want of judgment in all our plans which has caused great disappointment, and I fear serious if not irredeemable evils. . . . In no way, as you know, have I ever been consulted or have I even participated in the settlement of my children, but it is impossible for any longer to remain a silent spectator when I think timely and judicious exertion might save them from years of misery. . . . Let me entreat you carefully to deliberate on these suggestions as I really think that the perfect nonchalance exhibited by you as it regards your own affairs has had most fearful effect upon your sons."[26]

Surprisingly, John Quincy chose not to take offense and reached out to John with compassion and generosity. Come home to Quincy, he wrote; I will put you in charge of the family's property and pay you a handsome commission. "A large portion of it [the property] I intend shall pass to you or your children." Receiving no response, John Quincy wrote again. "You have had many severe disappointments but let them not overcome your resolution or your perseverance. There are prospects incomparably more favorable for you [here] than any that it is possible should arise for you in Washington."[27] But it was too late.

In mid-October Charles Francis received an alarming letter from his cousin Walter Hellen Jr. in Washington. John had taken to his bed and could not rise. The doctors spoke of "bilious fevers" and other ailments. But he was not fooled, Charles wrote in his diary; like George and his uncle Tom, his brother had succumbed to the drink. Charles boarded his carriage and rode to Quincy to prepare his parents for the worst. Louisa, who was just recovering from a serious illness, insisted on going to Washington at once. He would go, John Quincy declared, but she must not. "Dr. Holbrook . . . assured my wife that . . . the attempt would be at the hazard of her life," Adams recorded in his diary. "She became herself convinced it would be so and was partially tranquilized."[28] Louisa penned a note of love and compassion for her husband to deliver to John.

The distraught father left on the eighteenth and arrived in Washington on the twenty-third, only to find his second son some four hours dead. The former president sat beside John's corpse, kissing his "lifeless brow" and observing that at least his countenance was placid. He assured Mary Catherine that she and the children would always find a home at Peacefield.[29] "A more honest soul or more tender heart never breathed on the face of this earth," the bereaved father wrote in his diary.[30] Word of John's death reached Quincy on the twenty-sixth. William and Kitty Smith, who had been alerted, arrived shortly after and began consoling Louisa. "Dr. Holbrook . . . gave her an opiate under which she soon became quiet and found relief in tears and in conversation."[31] "My dearest, best beloved friend," John Quincy wrote his wife. "Your message to our dear departed child was faithfully retained by me, to be delivered in all its tenderness and affection so far as a father's lips can speak the words of a mother's heart."[32] He had not been in time, he said, but he was sure that John had heard her.

Upon examining his middle son's affairs, John Quincy found that he was some fifteen thousand dollars in debt. He summoned Charles to Washington to help dispose of the family property there in order to pay what John owed. Charles resented it. "The family of my father must assume a new [financial] position and upon that position will depend very much its future happiness," he lamented in his diary. "Knowing as well as I do the particular characters of its members, I cannot say that I have any great hope in futurity."[33] Then, bitterly: "I cannot regard the loss of either of my brothers as a calamity either to their families or to themselves."[34] Would he have to sacrifice his prosperity to support his parents and the large brood of children gathered under their roof? More worrying was the feeling that upon him would rest the reputation of the Adams clan for distinguished public service. Charles chafed at his perceived fate. "My habits are too speculative, my feelings not at all inclined to court the public."[35]

Charles and Louisa arrived in Washington in mid-November. "We reached the door of my late brother's house [at 1601 I Street NW], and my father came out full of anxiety and distress," Charles wrote. Louisa consoled Mary Catherine and prepared to take her and her children back to Quincy. Charles and John Quincy discussed financial matters. The former observed that the sale of the Adamses' property in Washington would not begin to cover John's personal debts and those incurred by Columbia Mills. He would have to sell some of the family estate at Quincy. John Quincy rebelled but then gave in. He would turn everything over to Charles's management; do what you must even to selling Peacefield, he said. His son agreed but complained bitterly to his diary: his father had been a fool to run for Congress, unkind and unthinking as usual concerning his own affairs and the future of his wife and family.[36]

During his four-day stay in Washington, Charles paid a visit to Antoine Guista and his wife, Hellen. They discussed John's decline, and Charles mentioned the financial straits in which his brother had left the family. Antoine immediately offered to help. His and Hellen's Washington tavern and restaurant were prospering. Reluctantly, the Adamses agreed, and during the next several years, John Quincy's former manservant extended several thousand dollars of interest-free loans. Charles returned to Boston determined to wipe out the family debt; he sold the family's houses at 103 and 105 Tremont Street for thirty thousand dollars and raised several thousand more dollars by auctioning off his father's shares in the New England Insurance Company.[37]

THE MARQUIS DE LAFAYETTE died on May 20, 1834, and Congress voted to ask John Quincy Adams to prepare a eulogy. He labored all summer on his oration, relying on his own memories, his father's papers, and documents provided by Lafayette's son. At high noon on December 31, Adams stood before a joint session of Congress, the president and his cabinet, and members of the diplomatic corps. The galleries were packed. For two and a half hours, the congressman from Massachusetts harangued his audience on the Frenchman's exploits, declaring him to have been a vessel bearing notions of freedom and democracy from the Old World to the New.

The speech was delivered in the midst of the worst crisis in Franco-American relations since the Napoleonic Wars. Impressment aside, French warships and privateers had wreaked almost as much havoc with the U.S. merchant fleet as had the British during that upheaval. When the Bourbons finally finished paying indemnities to the members of the Holy Alliance, the American minister Albert Gallatin approached the government of Charles X and submitted a claim for $7.75 million on behalf of American citizens or their heirs who had suffered from French deprivations. The Quai d'Orsay procrastinated. The issue carried over into the Adams administration, but the president and his secretary of state contented themselves with periodic appeals for justice. Andrew Jackson's reputation as a man of action reawakened hope in the breasts of American claimants, and they flooded the administration with petitions. The new U.S. minister to France, William C. Rives, advised Jackson to make compensation for damages a matter of national interest and honor. Otherwise, there would be no action from the Tuileries or the National Assembly. When in July 1830 Louis-Philipe overthrew the

Bourbons, Americans seemed to have another reason for optimism. The new king was committed to providing France with a liberal monarchy; he had, while in exile in the United States, gained respect for its republican institutions. The American minister and he quickly concluded a treaty in which France agreed to pay $5 million to settle all outstanding claims and the U.S. agreed to pay three hundred thousand dollars to settle counterclaims. The U.S. Senate voted unanimously to ratify the treaty, but the French National Assembly refused to appropriate the necessary funds.

Many observers expected Adams to address the current state of Franco-American relations in his tribute to Lafayette, but he chose not to. Shortly afterward, however, he assumed center stage in the claims issue in a most political and perverse way. In January 1835 the Massachusetts legislature met to fill the Senate seat just vacated by Nathaniel Silsbee. Their choice would join Daniel Webster as Massachusetts's representative in the upper house. On Thursday, February 5, Charles learned that the state senate had voted to offer the post to his father. "This is one of the most singular political results that has occurred within my remembrance of political affairs. The present Senate of Massachusetts consists of forty men not one of whom stands in any political relation with him [John Quincy]. It consists of a large proportion of the old Federal spirit which is as well as Masonry [is] adverse to him. And yet the reputation of my father is too strong for them to resist."[38] But Adams's ascent to the Senate did not suit Daniel Webster. He wrote his supporters in the General Assembly urging them to act quickly to subvert John Quincy's selection. He suggested moving Davis from the governorship to the Senate and electing Edward Everett governor. Everett would unite the Anti-Masons and the Whigs. "Be sure to burn this letter," Webster concluded. Both Everett and Davis, of course, were pledged to support Webster's aspirations to be elected president in 1836. "Mr. Webster knows very perfectly what he is about in all this," Charles noted in his diary. "The presence of my father in the Senate would hardly be agreeable to him."[39]

At this point the scene of the drama switched back to Washington. In his annual message to Congress, Jackson declared, "After the delay on the part of France of a quarter of a century in acknowledging these claims by treaty, it is not to be tolerated that another quarter of a century be wasted in negotiating about the payment."[40] Old Hickory recommended retaliatory measures, such as nonimportation of French goods, exclusion of French vessels from American ports, and increased military appropriations. In the Senate, Clay and Webster counseled caution. The Kentuckian was then chair of the Senate Committee on Foreign Affairs. "Nothing should be done to betray suspicion of the integrity of the French Government," its report on the matter read. Webster intended to run as the peace candidate against the allegedly irresponsible and jingoist Jackson. "It seems to me that our course is peace, and that determination should be expressed in the fewest words," he declared.[41]

Incredibly, Congressman Adams leapt to Old Hickory's defense. "Let the House be put in possession of the subject," he urged, "and let them say to the nation and to the world whether they will sustain the President in the spirit of the proposition he has made for maintaining the rights, interests, and honor of the country."[42] The House subsequently passed a resolution declaring that the executive should insist that France meet its obligations under the 1831 treaty but without threatening reprisals. The real fireworks came in the wake of the president's request for an appropriation of $423 million to bolster the nation's defenses. In the Senate, Webster declared that he would not vote for the appropriation even if "the guns of the enemy were battering against the walls of the Capitol."[43]

John Quincy smelled blood. "Sir, if we do not unite with the President of the United States in an effort to compel the French Chamber of Deputies to carry out the provisions of this treaty, we shall become the scorn, the contempt, the derision and the reproach of all mankind! Re-open negotiations, Sir, with France? Do it, and soon you will find your flag insulted, dishonored, and trodden in the dust by the pigmy states of Asia and Africa—by the very banditti of the earth."[44] He then called out Webster by name.

Adams's bellicose statements created a brief though intense war scare up and down the Eastern Seaboard, with financial markets going into steep decline. "A single individual connected with no party, expressing only his single opinion of the necessity of action and not even pledging himself to any course of action," Charles observed in his diary, "sets the House of Representatives in a blaze and spreads a panic through all the commercial cities. Few men attain such power in a nation."[45] Perhaps so, but John Quincy's declaration in support for Jackson and an ultimatum to France dashed, once again, any chance he had for higher office. "He [John Quincy] has the instinct of those animals which, when enraged, turn upon their keepers, & mangle those who have showed him most kindness," the treacherous Webster wrote his wife.[46] "Mr. Adams, whose ill-starred fortunes we have labored so hard to uphold," he complained to Edward Everett, "has gone completely over to the adversary." The entire Massachusetts delegation was up in arms. Conversely, the Jackson–Van Buren machine was certainly not going to embrace him, Webster declared. "He is likely to become a political vagrant seeking for a settlement from party to party."[47]

In the wake of the mini panic and Webster's admonitions, the Massachusetts Senate offered the Senate seat to Governor Davis, and he accepted. The House of Representatives subsequently passed a moderate resolution urging the president to press on with negotiations but recommending against belligerent actions that might risk war. Adams claimed victory and martyrdom. "I obtained in the House of Representatives of the United States a triumph unparalleled in the history of the country while at the same time, it was the immediate cause of my exclusion from the Senate of the United States."[48] An exaggeration, but Adams, who probably knew that his elevation to the Senate was dead from the outset, had had his revenge. Following his patriotic oration, the member from Plymouth received a standing ovation; Webster's declaration that he would not vote for the fortifications bill even if the Capitol were under attack would cost him the presidency. Following some diplomatic pushing and shoving, the French National Assembly funded the treaty, and payments began in early 1836.

CHARLES CONTINUED TO PROSPER but grumbled about his father's perceived political perversity. He complained that John Quincy had managed to alienate virtually every person of any interest or influence in Boston—Webster, Otis, Everett, the Masons, the Whigs, and, of course, the Democrats. "It is a matter of regret to me here to see the extent of the prejudices existing against you— prejudices inherited from father to son." Privately, to his diary: "It is plain to me that after the session of Congress is over, it will be better for me to reside out of the town for a year or more."[49] John Quincy responded by boasting of his accomplishments. His decision to return to public life was benefiting both him and the nation. Consider, he wrote Charles, "the Bank investigation report of 1832, the reports of the Committee of Manufactures of 1832 and 1833, the suppressed deposit speech, and the La Fayette Oration of 1834, and the unanimous vote of March 1835 [in support of continuing to demand payment of the French claims]. . . . The interest which I have taken in the transaction of the public business has contributed much to the enjoyment of my life and has served in some degree to assuage the sense of the repeated and heavy calamities with which it has pleased heaven to afflict me."[50] As to Boston and his son's future, you are master of your own fortunes, the elder Adams declared. "If you are frightened or disheartened by the turbulence and dangers and disasters of all political adventure . . . Turn your attention to making money. Get rich, apply all the faculties that God has given you to hoarding up treasures."[51] Charles was, not surprisingly, outraged.

Louisa feared an irreparable split. Your father's mind is much agitated, she wrote Charles. "Be soothing in your answers . . . for his mind is too much engrossed by self to remember or to enter into the feelings of others." Not a chance. You think, Charles wrote his father, that your sacrifice of family and fortune for what you believed to be the greater good is commendable; it is despicable, particularly your decision to run for Congress after a long and productive career in politics and diplomacy. I do not question your motives, only your values. "But you say if I dislike political affairs, let me turn my attention to making money . . . the spirit of the whole sentence betrays as it seems to me an erroneous idea of the purpose of life." Money is not to be valued for itself but for the independence it brings and the freedom of one's family from fears and anxiety. "To be a slave to a game of chance would be as bad as to be a slave to a game of reputation. They are both and equally contrary to the injunctions of the gospel and the doctrines of all enlightened philosophy. . . . Can you say it . . . pays off all your sufferings [and those of your family] by a little breeze of popular favor upon the eulogy of La Fayette?"[52]

Here was as savage and telling a rebuke as John Quincy Adams had ever or would ever experience. The master of self-justification and self-delusion concerning the hold that his vanity and lust for fame had on him was at a loss. The elder Adams responded not by striking out but by sidestepping the issue. Conceding Charles's point concerning financial security, he suggested to his son a life in literature or science. "I am aware of the danger of self-delusion even in the estimate of one's own motives, but in a public life of more than fifty years' duration I am not conscious of having done wrong to any one man." Irrelevant, of course. As to ambition: "I have never sought public life or any one of its numerous stations which I have occupied. It has always come and offered itself to me."[53] The leopard did not show its fangs nor did it change its spots.

This bitter exchange seemed to bring father and son closer together rather than driving them apart, however. When Charles and family visited Quincy in June, he found his father "exceedingly kind to me," informing him of a forthcoming gift of coins and medals. "This is a present of high value to me as some of the pieces are reminiscences of the public services of my parents." Later, to his diary: "Thinking him sometimes wrong in judgment as I have occasionally taken the liberty to do, I have yet experienced too much kindness from him to allow my opinions ever seriously to affect my conduct. I am indebted to him and to God for his signs of parental affection [and] personal esteem."[54]

"THERE IS A GREAT fermentation upon the subject of the slaves in the parts of the Union," John Quincy noted in his diary in August 1835.[55] There was indeed. In Charleston slaveholding "gentlemen" besieged post offices, seizing abolitionist literature and burning it. "The accounts of riots in Baltimore continue," Adams recorded. "In the State of Mississippi mobs are hanging up blacks suspected of insurgency and whites suspected of abetting them."[56] And in the nation's capital, "a slave of Mrs. Thornton made an attempt to murder her and her mother with an axe in the night—He was prevented from accomplishing his purpose by his own mother and in revenge for this, mobs of white people at Washington have destroyed sundry Negro houses, school-houses, and a church."[57]

Feeling against abolitionists ran almost as high in the North as in the South. When in July 1834 Black citizens of New York gathered to celebrate the seventh anniversary of the end of slavery in the Empire State, a huge mob gathered and assaulted them. For three days and nights, vigilantes burned, looted, and murdered in the free Black communities of the city. More than sixty structures were destroyed, including six African American churches.[58] Boston, that seedbed of liberty, was not immune. Following the announcement that the British abolitionist George Thompson would speak on October 21 at the offices of the local chapter of the Boston Female Anti-Slavery Society, leading citizens of the city, including Harry Otis and Charles's father-in-law, Peter Chardon Brooks, called for a public protest.[59] On the day of the address, a mob of some two thousand Bostonians besieged the building. Inside were William Lloyd Garrison and a group of female abolitionists. The goal of the crowd, declared the *Columbia Centinel*, was to stop a "foreigner" from attacking one of "our national institutions." Fortunately, the mayor and the police intervened and escorted the women out of the building. They "marched downstairs in couples, black and white arm in arm," an observer recorded. Fearing the worst, Garrison jumped from a window in the rear of the building but was seized by the crowd. He was saved from lynching at the last second by the police, who put him in jail for his own protection. Even Charles was outraged at the abolitionist gathering. "The tendency of the labors of such men is to convert this land into scenes of blood and carnage."[60]

The breaking of abolitionist waves on the shore of the slave power divided innumerable families, including the Adamses. Both William Steuben Smith and Nathaniel Frye were slave owners. "Every friend is turned into an enemy," Louisa lamented, and "now the prospect terminates with the fear of losing the love, the friendship, and the society of my own nearest and dearest connections. Are we to go on forever bartering away every portion of happiness remaining to us—My God, my God have mercy on me . . . look down with pity upon the pangs of a broken heart and guide my beloved husband on his way that he may know and adore thee in purity and meekness of spirit."[61]

When Congress reconvened in December 1835, the antislavery forces were ready to take the offensive. Denied use of the mail by Jackson's postmaster general, Amos Kendall, they were poised to again flood Congress with antislavery petitions. This time the slave power was ready. "The peculiar institution of the South," Senator John C. Calhoun declared, "that on the maintenance of which the very existence of the slaveholding states depends, is pronounced to be sinful and odious in the eyes of God and man, and this with a systematic design for rendering us hateful in the eyes of the world—with a view to a general crusade against us and our institutions. . . . The subject is beyond the jurisdiction of Congress; they have no right to touch it in any shape or form or to make it the subject of deliberation or discussion."[62] Antislavery spokesmen admitted that the Constitution prohibited Congress from interfering with slavery in the states where it existed—that is, the thirteen original states—but not in the states that were admitted afterward. As for the Federal district, it had not even existed at the time the Constitution was written. Surely Congress—which had been given the sole power of making rules and regulations for Washington, DC, and which represented the nation as a whole—had the right to abolish commerce in human chattel there.

John Quincy was still conflicted. "Debate . . . has been all on one side. The voice of freedom has not yet been heard, and I am earnestly urged to speak in her name. She will be trampled underfoot if I do not, and I shall be trampled underfoot if I do."[63] So, then, what was to be done? He grudgingly agreed with the young congressman Henry A. Wise recently elected from Virginia. "Sir," Wise had declared to the House, "slavery is interwoven in our political existence, is guaranteed by our Constitution, and its consequences must be borne by our Northern brethren as resulting from our system of government. They cannot attack the institution of slavery without attacking the [other] institutions of our country, our safety and welfare."[64] Adams had just read William Ellery Channing's essay on slavery and abolitionism, in which the prominent Unitarian minister had condemned both. "How slavery shall be removed is a question for the slaveholder and one which he alone can fully answer. . . . [I wish only] that the slaveholding states would resolve conscientiously and in good faith to remove this greatest of moral evils and wrongs and would bring immediately to the work all their intelligence, virtue and power."[65] All well and good, Adams observed, but how was the slave power to be brought around without its feet being held to the fire?

35

The "Gag Rule"

IN JANUARY 1836, CONGRESSMAN Thomas Glascock of Georgia insisted that antislavery petitions were in fact abolitionist propaganda, no different from the pamphlets and broadsides that had been banned by the postmaster general. He offered a resolution declaring that "any attempt to agitate the question of slavery in this House is calculated to disturb the compromises of the Constitution, to endanger the Union, and if persisted in, to destroy by a servile war the peace and prosperity of the country."[1] The following May the select committee that was headed by Henry Laurens Pinckney of South Carolina and to which all resolutions were referred presented three resolutions to the House for its approval. The first affirmed that Congress had no power to interfere with the institution of slavery in any of the states of the Union; the second declared that Congress "ought not" to interfere with slavery in the District of Columbia; and the third declared that "all petitions, memorials, resolutions, propositions, and other papers relating in any way to the subject of slavery or the abolition of slavery should . . . be laid on the table [without discussion]."[2] With Tennessee congressman and slave power advocate James K. Polk in the Speaker's chair, the House voted to approve the first resolution. Polk recognized several Southern members, but when Adams rose to speak, he ignored the former president and then called on George W. Owens, a unionist from Savannah, Georgia, who moved the previous question, thus shutting off debate. John Quincy would not be silent. "Am I gagged or am I not?" he shouted. "Order, order," screamed members of the Democratic majority. Adams appealed the ruling but lost by a vote of 109 to eighty-nine.

Before the vote on the second resolution, the House went into the Committee of the Whole—where the previous question rule did not apply—to consider another matter. Adams gained the floor and went on the attack. Texas was then in the midst of its war for independence from Mexico, a war applauded and supported by the slaveholding South and clandestinely aided by the Jackson administration. One of the principal causes of the revolution was Mexico's decree of 1829 abolishing slavery throughout all of its provinces, Adams pointed out. The congressman from Plymouth accused the slave power and its Democratic supporters in the North and the West of plotting to steal Texas from Mexico and have it admitted to the Union as a slave state. He predicted that the scheme would result in wars both foreign and domestic.

Adams went on to link the Texas controversy to the so-called Second Seminole War, which had begun in 1835 when the federal government had attempted to move the Creeks, Choctaws, Alabamas, and other tribes off their reservation in central Florida to the trans-Mississippi West. As had happened during the first Seminole conflict, the Indian insurgents were aided by runaway slaves. "Mr. Chairman," Adams declared, "are you ready for all these wars? A Mexican war? A war with Great Britain, if not with France [to prevent the annexation of Texas]? A general Indian war? A servile war? And as an inevitable consequence of them all, a civil war?" Did the slave power understand that if such conflicts did unfold, it would mean the end of its despicable institution forever. "From the instant that your slaveholding states become the theatre of war—civil, servile, or foreign— from that instant the war powers of Congress extend to interference with the institution of slavery in every way by which it can be interfered with."[3]

Members from the South and the West roared like wounded animals while antislavery representatives from the North and the Mid-Atlantic states rose to applaud. Charles J. Ingersoll of Pennsylvania asked the New Englander if he was saying that a slave uprising would bring an end to the Constitution. Adams replied, if "the people of the free states were called on by the President to suppress it, they would have the perfect right to dictate the terms on which peace should be restored. If the free portion of the Union were called upon to expend their blood and treasure to support that institution which had the curse and displeasure of the Almighty upon it, the subject itself would come within the constitutional power of Congress, and there would be no such objection as that *Congress had not the right to interfere*."[4] "I shall henceforth speak in the House of Representatives at the hazard of my life," John Quincy subsequently confided to his diary.[5]

On the second resolution before the House, the one expressing its option that slavery in the federal district ought not to be interfered with, Adams remained silent, in part, perhaps, out of deference to his divided family. It passed. But when the third proposal, prohibiting debate on antislavery petitions, was introduced, Adams once again rose to speak. "I hold this resolution to be a violation of the Constitution of the United States, of the rules of this House, and of the rights of my constituents."[6] Calls for order rang out; Adams requested that his statement be printed in the record of the House. Polk ignored him. The third resolution passed by a vote of 117 to sixty-eight.[7]

Adams's remarks in the House—subsequently elaborated on in "Speech of John Quincy Adams, of Massachusetts, upon the Right of the People, Men and Women, to Petition"—attracted American abolitionists to him like bees to honey. "Benjamin Lundy came at six," John Quincy recorded in his diary on July 11, "and I walked with him to the house of his friend James Mott . . . where the[re] was a large tea and evening party of men and women, all of the Society of Friends—I had free conversation with them 'til between ten and 11 O'clock upon slavery—the abolition of slavery. . . . Lucretia Mott, the mistress of the House . . . is sensible and lively and an abolitionist of the most intrepid school."[8] In many ways, Adams found these reformers—Christian evangelicals, many of them intellectuals—irresistible. But when Lundy solicited a contribution to support the *Genius of Universal Emancipation*, Adams refused.[9]

Later, a young man from Philadelphia would write Adams asking his advice about joining an antislavery society for people of his age. Adams advised against it. "In this our beloved country," he wrote, "all associations of men are concentrations of power, more power. That power may be exercised for good or for evil, but political associations for the purpose of promoting specific measures . . . are subject to so many sinister influences and in the exercise of their power are apt to [infringe on] the rights of others, that I have never felt myself warranted to join . . . not even when I have heartily approved the . . . objects for which it was formed . . . including the Colonization, Anti-Masonic, Temperance and Anti-slavery Societies."[10]

Adams was and would remain a fellow traveler with the abolitionists—conferring with them, strategizing with them, encouraging them, but refusing to become one of them. As of 1836 and for the foreseeable future, he took the position that emancipation could occur only if voluntary and compensated for by the federal government in case of a servile war. In conversation with Channing, in many ways a like-minded soul, Adams observed that "it is absurd to make a test question upon immediate abolition. There is something captious about it because it is notoriously impracticable. There is in the present House of Representatives a majority of nearly two-to-one opposed to the consideration or discussion of the subject, and if the proposition should be made, they would refuse to consider it." If he were to have any influence, Adams declared, he must keep channels of communication open with at least some Southerners. How do they treat you? Channing asked. "They all treat me as gentlemen," he replied, "and most of them with kindness and courtesy. . . . I have thought it apparent that they generally hold in contempt the Northern members who truckle to them, [those] such as John Randolph has called 'dough-faces.'"[11]

His Southern colleagues' constituents were not so well-disposed toward the former president. "Congress cannot get on with its business of the American people owing to your damned abolition petitions," wrote a Virginian who claimed to have once voted for Adams. "Some gentlemen in this section of the country are ready and anxious to pay a large premium for the head of J.Q. Adams," a Georgian wrote. "You should be ashamed of yourself to try to disgrace our country as to wish a Big Black, Thick lipped, Cracked Heeled, Woolly headed, Skunk smelling, damned Negro, alias Whig, to be seated in Congress." An Alabama correspondent was more succinct: "On the first Day of May next I promise to cut your throat from ear to ear."[12]

Despite John Quincy's constant complaints to his diary about being a political outcast and an object of abuse from people of virtually every region and inclination, he continued to be regarded as a national icon. He was the son of a Founding Father, an architect of American empire, an avowed enemy of partisanship, and a nationalist. As a nationalist, he had been joined once upon a time by a number of prominent Southerners, including John C. Calhoun. He was, no matter how vitriolic his rants against slavery, a man devoted to the Union. In 1835, when a border dispute between Ohio and Michigan, then applying for statehood, threatened to erupt into armed conflict, it was Adams that the House chose to head a select committee to investigate, report, and conciliate. And in the end, the waters were calmed.[13]

In 1836 the citizens of Boston asked Adams to eulogize former president Madison for their Fourth of July celebrations. In delivering his tribute to Madison, whom he clearly favored over Jefferson as an intellectual and patriot, "Old Man Eloquent," as some of his admirers had taken to calling him, was reminded of his age. "Forty-three years and more have passed away since I first spoke to a crowded audience in Boston. My voice is gone; my eyes are in no better condition." The day was stormy. While he spoke, heavy showers broke over the meetinghouse. The only illumination came from a skylight, so at times Adams had to recite from memory. However, he noted, the crowd gave its "uninterrupted and fixed attention" and he was repeatedly interrupted by cheering and applause.[14]

IN SPITE OF HIS ego and love of power, Andrew Jackson decided to honor the two-term tradition established by George Washington. His handpicked successor was Martin Van Buren, who somehow had managed to stay in Old Hickory's good graces during the eight years of his presidency. A slight, dapper, ingratiating man who achieved his goals through intrigue and manipulation rather than through power plays, he was as unlike Jackson as a man could be. His enemies,

John Quincy among them, declared him to be unprincipled. "Pragmatic" would have been a better term. Unlike the Adamses, Van.Buren believed that political parties were essential to the proper functioning of a democracy. In a vast republic like the United States, there had to be mechanisms to represent various sections and interests, to form them into coalitions, to organize and propagandize and thereby offer the American people a clear choice come election time. Or so he said. In truth Van Buren was not so much interested in a clear choice as in building a lasting national coalition that could retain power. In combining the "plain democrats" of the North with the slaveholders of the South around Jeffersonian principles, he had seemingly achieved just that.

Van Buren easily won the presidential poll at the Democratic national nominating convention. His running mate, Richard M. Johnson—a Jackson favorite, a former Indian fighter, and the father of two acknowledged mulatto children—barely squeezed by. The Whigs did not convene, something of which they boasted—no political caballing—but in truth, they were so disunited that a convention would have been an impossibility. Instead, there emerged several regional candidates, some running as Whigs, some not. There was William Henry Harrison, the former governor of the Indiana Territory and victor over Tecumseh's Indian confederation. He had the support of most Whigs in the North and the West; he campaigned against executive usurpation and in favor of internal improvements and revenue sharing. Hugh Lawson White of Tennessee, a former Jackson protégé who had turned against his mentor over his alleged abuses of power, threw his hat in the ring. He promised a return to public morality. Representing Southern outrage over Jackson's Nullification Proclamation was Willie P. Mangum of North Carolina. Last and probably least was Daniel Webster.

John Quincy himself played almost no role in the election. If Van Buren won, it would mean the perpetuation of Jacksonism—the "corrupt" deal between South and West in which Westerners were provided cheap public land and Southerners received continuing support for slavery. The preamble to the Constitution, Adams wrote Alexander Everett, set out the six principal objectives of that document: to form a more perfect union; to establish justice; to insure domestic tranquility; to provide for the common defense; to promote the general welfare, and to secure the blessings of liberty to ourselves and our posterity. Of these, John Quincy declared, perhaps the most important was the fifth, and it had been not only abandoned but made war upon by the Jacksonians, that despicable coalition of "plain republicans" and slaveholders. Of the four Whig candidates, Adams wrote, "Not one of them [has] substance or shadow or has one steadfast principle . . . which his friends or supporters could hold up as a recommendation of him to the people for their suffrage." Two of them carried the anti-general-welfare system quite as far as Andrew Jackson. In truth, the whole Whig Party was a farce: "The principle of whigism . . . opposition to the executive . . . is not and cannot be a principle of administration," Adams observed to Alexander Everett.[15]

By the end of November, it was clear that the Whigs, collectively, had fared better than Clay had individually in 1832. Van Buren carried just 50.9 percent of the popular vote but polled a hundred seventy electoral tallies to his opponents' combined one hundred twenty-four. The Bank War hurt him in the North and the West, and a number of Southerners were reluctant to vote for a candidate from a free state. But the Democrats had a platform, an organization, and Old Hickory.

BY THE TIME THE second session of the Twenty-Fourth Congress opened in December 1836, not only was John Quincy Adams's conscience bothering him; he had begun to worry about the fate of his immortal soul. His abolitionist friends were not loath to confront him. If slavery were a sin, its immediate abandonment was a duty, they declared. In September 1837, a young Quaker activist named Mary L. Cox came to see Adams. She was an abolitionist and had been moved, she said, "to address a discourse to me if I had no objection."[16] Following a short sermon, Cox prayed for the congressman's soul. He was moved by her commitment and genuine concern for him. Abolitionist Sarah Grimké subsequently expressed her gratitude to Adams for his support of the right of petition but chafed at his unwillingness to go further. "I regretted it because it appeared to me to be a surrender of moral principle to political expediency," she wrote.[17] "The object [abolition] is noble," Adams declared, "the motive pure—but the undertaking is of such tremendous magnitude, difficulty, and danger, that I shrink from the contemplation of it."[18] On New Year's Day 1837, he listened to a hell-and-damnation sermon at a Presbyterian church in Washington; it both repulsed and frightened him. "I know that I have been, and am, a sinner," he subsequently wrote in his diary, "perhaps by the depravity of the human heart, an unreclaimable sinner." But was it not God who had created man with all of his flaws? Surely the Maker would not punish those who are "passive instruments in his hands. He will not suffer us to do evil, and then sentence us severely for what He has suffered us to do."[19]

Louisa urged him to keep his distance from the abolitionists, but in her heart, she knew that slavery was an abomination before the Lord. The notion, espoused by the slave power, that slavery was sanctioned by scripture was wrong, the argument nothing less than heretical, she declared. Slavery had existed in the land of the Israelites but was "never sanctioned by any law emanating from the highest tribunal," Louisa observed in her diary. Christ did not have to single out human bondage as a sin. The institution was so contrary to the "practical principles of the Christian creed" that it required no specific prohibition.[20]

Perhaps Adams, by focusing on the gag rule and the threat that it posed to the constitutionally guaranteed right to free speech, could resolve both the moral and the political dilemmas he faced. The right to petition could be portrayed as a universal good, an umbrella under which abolitionists, Free-Soilers, advocates of women's rights, and the "plain republicans" of the North—worried about their liberty, their rights, and the threat posed to the sanctity of free labor by slavery—could rally.

Despite the gag rule, the second session of the Twenty-Fourth Congress was inundated by antislavery petitions: one hundred thirty thousand for the abolition of slavery in the District of Columbia; thirty-two thousand for the repeal of the gag rule; twenty-one thousand two hundred for legislation forbidding slavery in the territories.[21] Adams was heartened by the willingness of the members of the Massachusetts congressional delegation—anti-abolitionists almost to the man—to speak out in favor of the right to petition. In January 1837, before the House had a chance to renew the gag rule, John Quincy presented scores of petitions, many of them from women. A class of "pure and virtuous citizens" had appealed to him and through him to Congress, he declared, to bring about "the greatest improvement that can possibly be effected in the condition of the human race—the total abolition of slavery on earth."[22]

One of the petitions Adams submitted was on behalf of a group of women from Fredericksburg, Virginia. John Mercer Patton of that state rose to remonstrate with the gentleman from Massachusetts. He hailed from Fredericksburg, Patton declared, and he could assure the House that there was not a respectable name on the petition; they were all free Negroes or mulattoes, one of whom he knew to be "infamous." Debating John Quincy Adams was a dangerous business, as Patton soon learned. The member from Plymouth rose; the right of petition should be denied to no human being. Had the gentleman from Virginia called one of the petitioners a "prostitute"? "[I]f they were infamous women," the New Englander declared, "then who is it that had made them infamous? Not their color, I believe, but their masters! . . . I am inclined to believe it is the case that in the South there existed great resemblances between the progeny of the colored people and the white men who claim possession of them." Infamous, indeed! "Order, Order . . . He has insulted the South; he is threatening the Union," declared representatives of the slave power. But the gentleman from Massachusetts was just beginning.[23]

On February 7, with the gag rule still in effect, Adams addressed the chair:

"Mr. Speaker, I have in my possession a petition of a somewhat extraordinary character; and I wish to inquire of the chair if it be in order to present it." What was the nature of the request? Well, Adams replied, it appeared to be from eleven slaves living in and around Fredericksburg. The request itself was in plain English but many of the signatures were x's or scratches. "I will send it to the Chair." Polk was taken aback; never before had the House had to deal with a petition from bondsmen. Sensing that the representative from Plymouth was up to something, the Speaker declared that he would have to take the sense of the House. Dixon Lewis of Alabama—a mountain of a man, a stalwart of the slave power, and a person with a reputation for violence—demanded to know what was in the petition. Polk replied that it appeared to be a plea of some sort from slaves. "By God, sir, this is not to be endured any longer!" Dixon declared. "Treason, Treason," shouted some of his fellow Southerners. "Expel the old scoundrel: put him out; do not let him disgrace the House any longer!"[24]

Congressman George C. Dromgoole of Virginia introduced a resolution declaring that whereas the Honorable John Q. Adams of Massachusetts in offering up a petition submitted by bondsmen was "giving color to an idea" that a slave was entitled to such a right, it was "resolved that he be taken to the bar of the House and be censured by the Speaker thereof." At this point Adams rose to his feet and declared that his accusers had best be certain that they knew what they were charging him with; he then pointed out that the petition was in favor of maintaining and sustaining the "peculiar institution." "[M]y crime has been for attempting to introduce the petition of slaves that slavery should not be abolished."[25] There followed an even greater eruption. But Adams had the bit in his teeth and didn't intend to let go of it. "Where is your law which says that the mean and the low, and the degraded shall be deprived of the right of petition? . . . Where in the land of free men was the right of petition ever placed on the exclusive basis of morality and virtue? Petition is a supplication—it is entreaty—it is prayer. . . . Where is such a law [banning petition] to be found? It does not belong to the most abject despotism! . . . The Sultan of Constantinople cannot walk the streets and refuse to receive petitions from the meanest and vilest of the land. This is the law even of despotism."[26]

Thereupon, the air began to go out of the pro-slavery balloon; shouts and screams became grumbles. The South presented three resolutions: first, that any member who should in the future present a petition from bondsmen would be considered as hostile to the South and the Union itself; second, that slaves did not have the right to petition Congress; third, that John Quincy Adams, having declared that he did not mean to insult the House, ought to be left in peace. Gleefully, Adams insisted that he be allowed a full defense. He read back to the House a passage in the debate in which South Carolina firebrand Waddy Thompson had called for Adams to be subject to criminal prosecution. Pocketing the transcript, the former president declared, "If he thought to frighten me from my purpose . . . if that, sir, was his object, he mistook his man! I am not to be intimidated by the gentleman from South Carolina nor by all the grand juries in the universe." Henry Wise, a pro-slavery warrior from Virginia, entered the House. He sensed that matters were getting out of hand. What was the issue? he inquired of the Speaker. After Polk described the debate, Wise declared, "And is that all? The gentleman from Massachusetts had presented a petition signed by slaves! Well, sir, and what of that? Is anybody harmed by it? Sir, in my opinion, slaves are the very persons who should petition. . . . Sir, I see no danger—the country, I believe is safe."[27]

The first resolution failed to pass by a vote of ninety-two to 101, the second passed 163 to eighteen; the third—after Adams requested that it be defeated, as it exonerated him from a crime he had not committed—lost twenty-one to 205. The editor of the *Boston Advertiser* had been in the galleries to witness the events. He subsequently wrote that "the effect of [Adams's] speech has been rarely if ever exceeded by the influence of any speech on any assembly." The American Anti-Slavery Society reprinted the debate in pamphlet form. Newspapers across the country carried accounts. Later, a fellow toiler in the field, Joshua Giddings of Ohio, wrote that "this defiance of the slave power was unexpected. The oldest member of the body had never witnessed such boldness, such heroism, on the part of any Northern member."[28]

John Quincy would write in his diary that he had been traumatized by the rhetorical combat. Nothing could have been further from the truth! One observer declared that witnessing the slave power attacks on the member from Plymouth had been like seeing "the sting of so many mosquitoes upon the hide of a rhinoceros." Ralph Waldo Emerson saw to the heart of the man. "When they talk about his old age and venerableness and nearness to the grave, he knows better. . . . He is like one of those old cardinals, who, as quick as he is chosen Pope, throws away his crutches and his crookedness and is as straight as a boy. He is an old roué who cannot live on slops, but must have sulfuric acid in his tea."[29]

ACCORDING TO HIS DIARY, John Quincy Adams, if denied a career in public service, wished to be a literary man, and if not that, a man of science. On December 21, 1835, President Jackson sent to Congress a message informing it that an Englishman named Smithson had bequeathed a sizable sum of money for the establishment of a learned institution in the United States. No one paid particular attention except the former president. Sensing an opportunity to advance the position of the United States in the Republic of Letters, Adams moved that a committee of the House be established to supervise use of the funds. According to custom, he, as the author of the motion, was appointed chair.[30]

In comparison to Europe, America had a lot of ground to make up in the scientific field. France and Germany were far advanced in terms of government support for scientific inquiry. This coupled with liberal patronage from royalty and the nobility led to cutting-edge advances in geology, chemistry, physics, and astronomy. Sir Joseph Banks—the famed English botanist, founder of the Royal Botanical Gardens at Kew, and twenty-first president of the Royal Society—had at one time sat at the center of an international network of scientists that exchanged information, collaborated on learned papers, and promoted scientific inquiry in general. At the turn of the nineteenth century, there were no professional scientists in the United States, only learned gentlemen like Franklin, Jefferson, and Adams who dabbled in the field. America lacked a monarch and the nobility who could serve as patrons. Nevertheless, the country's burgeoning market economy thirsted for the technical knowledge that would enhance infrastructure, promote manufacturing, and increase agricultural production. It quickly became apparent to John Quincy that only an activist federal government with a commitment to scientific inquiry could fill the void. To Adams, the Smithson bequest seemed like the key to a long-locked door.

Sir Hugh Smithson, who became the first Duke of Northumberland in 1766, was one of the richest men in the United Kingdom; his annual income was estimated at fifty thousand pounds. His wife, Elizabeth Seymour Percy, was even wealthier. A notorious philanderer, Sir Hugh took a mistress while living in Bath. His paramour, Elizabeth Hungerford Keate Macie, was no chambermaid but rather a member of the powerful Hungerford clan. When the affair produced a child, James Louis Macie, Elizabeth took herself and her offspring off to Paris in 1765 and from thence to London.[31]

At age seventeen, James Macie enrolled at Pembroke College, Oxford, and was immediately attracted to chemistry and geology. Macie and his mentor, James Hutton, were empiricists, shunning theory and received truth and accepting only formal evidence provided by fieldwork. In the spring of 1787 members of the Royal Society gathered for their regular meeting. Its chief presided over the induction of James Macie, at twenty-two the youngest member ever elected.[32] Macie had grown close to his maternal half brother, Henry Dickinson, who at sixteen had joined the Royal Horse Guards in Northumberland. In May 1800, Elizabeth Hungerford Keate Macie died, leaving the bulk of her considerable estate to her

son James. Shortly thereafter he changed his name to Smithson, his father's original surname. On October 23, 1826, James Smithson, his health in decline, made
out his own will. He bequeathed his fortune to his half brother's illegitimate son,
Henry James Dickinson. If his heir died without any heirs, what was left of the
inheritance was to be donated to the government of the United States "to found at
Washington, under the name of the Smithsonian Institution, an Establishment
for the increase & diffusion of Knowledge among men."[33]

Smithson died in Genoa in 1829, and his estate went to his nephew, who by
this time was living under the name Baron Henri de la Batut. (Following his father's death, Dickinson's mother had married a French ne'er-do-well named Theodore de la Batut.) When the self-styled young baron died six years later, the
remainder of his inheritance, still considerable, went to the United States.[34] But
the drama was just beginning. When the White House learned that his will was
tied up in the Court of Chancery, Jackson appointed Richard Rush, a former
ambassador to Great Britain and an intimate of John Quincy Adams, as a special
emissary to cut away the red tape. Upon arriving in London, Rush retained the
law firm of Clarke, Fynmore and Fladgate to advise him. He was told that "a
Chancery suit is a thing that might begin with a man's life and its termination be
his epitaph."[35]

Meanwhile, John Quincy had seized on the bequest like a dog with a bone. As
none of his colleagues seemed to take an interest, he was left to proceed with his
report alone. No one seemed to know anything about the donor. He called on the
British chargé d'affaires in Washington and Colonel Thomas Aspinwall, then
U.S. consul in London who was home on leave, to see if they could be helpful.
Apparently, James Smithson was the "antenuptial" son of the first Duke and
Duchess of Northumberland, Adams subsequently reported to his diary. "But
how he came to have a nephew named Hungerford, son of a brother named Dickinson and why he made his contingent bequest to the United States of America,
no one can tell. . . . But certainly in the bequest itself there is a high and honorable
sentiment of philanthropy, and a glorious testimonial of confidence in the institutions of this Union." Just think of it! The heir of a British noble family, members of
whom had fought on the British side during the Revolutionary War, had donated
to the republic that they tried to strangle a half million dollars for the diffusion of
knowledge! It "is an event in which I see the finger of Providence compassing
great results by incomprehensible means."[36]

In the Senate, the matter of the Smithson bequest was referred to the Judiciary
Committee, which duly recommended that the gift be accepted. The House chose
to appoint a select committee and named Congressman Adams as its chair. It also

recommended acceptance, and during the debate, Adams took the opportunity to make a compelling case for federal support for the diffusion of knowledge: "The attainment of knowledge is the high and exclusive attribute of man. . . . It is by this attribute that man discovers his own nature as the link between earth and heaven. . . . To furnish the means of acquiring knowledge is therefore the greatest benefit that can be conferred upon mankind."[37] In the Senate, Calhoun and other representatives of the slave power argued against accepting the bequest. It would lead to further unconstitutional enhancement of federal power, they insisted. But the Senate voted overwhelmingly to accept the bequest, and both houses voted to approve Adams's report.

On May 12, 1838, nearly two years after his arrival in England, Rush was able to inform President Van Buren that the American claim had cleared the Court of Chancery. He collected £104,960 in gold coins; chests containing the treasure were loaded aboard the packet ship *Mediator*, and Rush set sail. The vessel reached port on September 4, and with a great sigh of relief, the American emissary delivered the gold to the U.S. Mint.[38]

While Rush and the money were still at sea, Adams had set about ensuring that the bequest would be spent for the purposes Smithson had intended. Ah, but there was the rub. It was not exactly clear from the terms of the gift what the donor had envisioned. Adams was determined to step into the breach and present his interpretation. The House select committee of which he was chair still existed, providing him with a platform. In late June, John Quincy called on Van Buren at the White House. He urged the president to present a plan to the next session of Congress, and suggested that it should include a national observatory and a course of lectures on natural, moral, and political science. "Above all, no jobbing, no sinecures—no monkish stalls for lazy idlers!"[39] Van Buren expressed support for Adams's proposals but decided to leave the matter to Congress. Before the next session opened in December 1838, he had Secretary of State Forsyth solicit suggestions from a list of learned Americans, among whom was the congressman from Massachusetts. There were three principles that should be observed above all else, Adams subsequently proposed: first, only the interest from the endowment could be spent; second, none of the money should be used to educate the youth of the country or be linked to any religious institution; and third, the first moneys earned by the endowment should go toward establishing a national observatory along the lines of the Royal Observatory in Greenwich. He anticipated a struggle once the matter was before Congress. "[T]he great object of my solicitude," he confided to his diary, "would be to guard against the sops for hungry incapacity. Not so easy will it be to secure, as from a rattlesnake's fang, the fund and its income forever from being wasted . . . in bounties to feed the hunger or fatten the lead idleness of mountebank projectors and shallow and worthless pretenders to science."⁴⁰

During the following year, Congress received petitions from a variety of interested parties; among the projects suggested were a national university, a national agricultural institution, a professorship in German, a national library, and prizes for literary and scientific competitions. As the debate dragged on, John Quincy became increasingly discouraged. "The apparent total indifference of Mr. Van Buren to the disposal of the money . . . the assentation [insincere declarations of support] of all the heads of Department without a particle of assistance from any one of them . . . the opposition, open and disguised, of Calhoun, [congressman from South Carolina William C.] Preston and Waddy Thompson even to the establishment of the Institution in any form; the utter prostration of all public spirit in the Senate proved by the encouragement which they gave to the mean and selfish project of Asher Robbins [senator from Rhode Island] to make a university for him to be placed at the head of it . . . are all so utterly discouraging that I despair of effecting anything for the increase and diffusion of knowledge among men."⁴¹

Then, in 1841, the Smithson endowment vanished, the victim of a corrupt deal between Jackson and Van Buren's secretary of the treasury, Levi Woodbury, and stockjobbers. No sooner had Rush notified the president that the Smithson bequest had cleared the Court of Chancery than a group of "interested" congressmen attached a rider to a bill appropriating funds for West Point and requiring that the Smithson gift be invested in state bonds. Then Woodbury placed in the *Washington Globe* an announcement that a half million dollars would soon be available for investment in state paper. To oversee the sale, he turned to the prominent broker William W. Corcoran, founder of the Washington banking firm Corcoran & Riggs. Corcoran in turn bought 523 Arkansas state bonds and eight pieces of Michigan paper. The promised return was 6 percent. Adams alone had objected to the West Point rider. State bonds were notoriously unreliable. And sure enough, in 1841, Arkansas defaulted. Adams demanded explanations from Woodbury, but none were forthcoming. Then President John Tyler ordered the Treasury to make good on the lost money and to pay 6 percent interest on it.⁴² John Quincy breathed a sigh of relief, but there was still the issue of what uses the bequest would be put to.

In 1840, Adams had acquired a powerful ally in the person of Joel Poinsett, member of Congress from 1821–1825 and Van Buren's secretary of war from 1837–1841. Born to a wealthy and influential South Carolina family, Poinsett was educated, cultured, and, surprisingly enough, an avid opponent of slavery and nullification. He had studied medicine at the University of Edinburgh and was an ardent botanist. He understood the symbiotic relationship between cotton and slavery. After touring France and other parts of Europe, Poinsett became convinced that the South could grow other staples such as grapes, silkworms, olives, and flax. In 1840 he and a group of other scientifically minded gentlemen, including Adams, established the National Institution for the Promotion of Science in Washington; it proposed to build and combine botanical gardens with laboratories, a library, and a publishing house.[43] For a time Adams considered recommending that proceeds from the Smithson endowment be used to fund the institution, but Arkansas's default on its bonds and the refunding effort intervened. By the time the smoke cleared from that fire, the institution was foundering.

Less helpful to Adams was Congressman Robert Dale Owen of Indiana, the son of the Welsh industrialist and communitarian Robert Owen. Robert Dale was born in Glasgow in 1801 and raised in the shadow of his father's experimental mill. Imbued with the elder Owen's universalist vision, Robert Dale immigrated to America and taught school for a period at New Harmony, the famous Indiana commune. In Congress he campaigned for the Smithson fund to be used to support communitarianism, its principles and practices.[44] Adams thought Owen and his fellow universalists untethered from reality and blocked them at every turn. "Robert Owen and Fanny Wright have now come again to this country," John Quincy noted in his diary in December 1844, "and they are apparently as crafty and crazy as ever."[45] Though he had dismissed Robert Owen's communitarian ideas some twenty-five years earlier, he politely granted the son several interviews. "Mr. Owen came this morning . . . with a farrago of confused, indefinite ideas, the only clear and distinct proposition in which is the formation of a community in or near Washington to revolutionize the world—from a world of wretchedness and bad principles to a world of wealth . . . of peace, of plenty, and of love, without religion."[46] Adams could afford to patronize Owen. Both the Whigs and the Democrats thought his ideas subversive and a threat to their interests.

The fate of the Smithson bequest was not settled until April 1846. Because the Democrats were then a majority in the House, Adams was no longer chair of the select committee, but he approved of the charter. The Smithsonian Institution was to be a collection of museums and research centers focusing on science, technology, and natural history. John Quincy succeeded in having the amount of interest on the bequest lost between the Arkansas default and the passage of the final bill added to the endowment; it came to an additional $242,129.[47]

36

Texas

The firestorm that followed in the wake of John Quincy Adams's spontaneous outburst regarding a slave power plot to annex Texas—with the inevitable consequence of war with both Mexico and Great Britain—had both excited and alarmed him. Annexationist diplomacy had added millions of acres to the public domain, some of which had formed into free states and some into slave states. Up until this point he had never publicly voiced opposition to further westward expansion. The problem that John Quincy faced was that geopolitically he remained an expansionist. He could not simply abandon his dream of an American empire stretching from coast to coast just because the slave power was succeeding in co-opting manifest destiny. Indeed, when in May 1836, during a debate in the House on an appropriations bill for the defense of the western frontier, the New Englander had been accused of giving away Texas during negotiations over the Transcontinental Treaty, he could not remain quiet. The exact opposite was true, he declared. Of all Monroe's cabinet, he had been most adamant about demanding that the Spanish cession include Texas to the Colorado River. But the president and his colleagues had deemed the territory between the Sabine and the Colorado not worth risking the entire treaty for. Not only that, Adams declaimed, but General Jackson had explicitly approved the Sabine as the southwestern boundary of the U.S. claim. "With his cane, sir, he pointed to the boundaries, as they had been agreed upon by the parties; and sir, with a very emphatic expression, which I need not repeat, he affirmed them."[1]

When transcripts of the exchange on the floor of the House were reprinted in the newspapers, Jackson replied, also in print, that the gentleman from Massachusetts must have be mistaken; he had not even been in Washington at the time. Thereupon, Adams produced the relevant pages from his diary, with precise dates and transcripts of conversations and meetings. To a visitor, Jackson subsequently remarked, "His diary! Don't tell me anything more about his diary! Sir, that diary comes up on all occasions—one would think that its pages were as immutable as the laws of the Medes and Persians! Sir, that diary will be the death of me!"[2] At the time the Transcontinental Treaty was signed, Adams declared, the question of the extension of slavery into the trans-Mississippi West had yet been to be settled. Indeed, there had been every reason to believe that slavery was on its deathbed. He was of course being disingenuous; at the time, Monroe and he had agreed that slavery was very much an issue and that for the administration to demand and receive Texas might very well split the Union.

But Adams was right about one thing: matters were far different in 1836 from what they had been in 1819. The Missouri Compromise had guaranteed the expansion of slavery into at least parts of the trans-Mississippi West. In the case of Texas, Adams observed in his journal, the slave power had actually occupied the territory before seeking its annexation to the Union.

The first Americans began filtering across the Sabine into Texas between 1800 and 1820 while Mexico was still part of Spain. The province boasted more cattle than people, and Spanish authorities welcomed the immigrants. The door was opened even wider following Mexico's successful bid for independence in 1821. Two years later Mexico City confirmed a prerevolutionary grant made to Moses Austin and his heirs in which he was authorized to settle three hundred families in central Texas. In 1825 the state of Coahuila and Texas opened the province to those enterprising Christians who would swear allegiance to Mexico. All but a few of the immigrants from the United States were Southerners who were shocked when in 1829 the Mexican national legislature outlawed slavery throughout the country. Differences over religion further exacerbated tensions between American settlers and native Mexicans. As early as 1826, *federales* clashed with bands of armed Texas immigrants.

Efforts to acquire Texas during this period by the government of the United States convinced Mexico that it was about to become another victim of manifest destiny. It was in fact the Adams administration that had made the first move. In 1825, John Quincy had instructed Joel Poinsett, then his ambassador to Mexico, to negotiate a new western boundary extending U.S. territory from the Sabine to the Río Colorado; in 1827 the Adams administration offered a million dollars for Texas, but Mexico would not sell. The Jackson administration—committed as it was to building a South–West political coalition based on slavery expansion and abundant, cheap public land—was determined to have Texas by hook or by crook. For six years, Jackson's unscrupulous ambassador to Mexico, Anthony Butler, tried first to force an unrepayable loan on Mexico City, then attempted to bribe Mexican officials into selling the province, and finally urged President Jackson to seize East Texas by force. His efforts came to naught.

In 1830, the Mexican Congress appropriated funds to strengthen federal military garrisons in Texas and passed a law prohibiting further immigration from the United States. But the flood continued, and by 1835 there were thirty thousand Americans living in Texas, compared to a mere three thousand Mexicans. When violence broke out anew, the Mexican president-cum-dictator, General Antonio López de Santa Anna, announced that he would personally lead an army into the province and crush the brewing insurgency. The Texans set up a provisional government in San Felipe de Austin in November 1835 and six months later declared independence. By then full-scale war had erupted in the territory north of the Río Grande. Then followed the massacres at the Alamo and Goliad. The bulk of the Texan militia, under the command of Jackson's longtime friend and comrade in arms Sam Houston, remained intact, however. In April, just west of the San Jacinto River near Galveston Bay, Houston's men surprised Santa Anna during siesta and routed his army. The war for independence was over, but the struggle for annexation of a now independent Texas to the Union had just begun.

In truth, Adams had been looking for another path to attack and undermine Northern support for, or at least acquiescence in, the continuance of slavery; the gag rule and its threat to free speech had opened a breach, but it might take years for it to widen significantly. A theme that ran throughout his speeches during the Twenty-Fourth and Twenty-Fifth Congresses was that the slave power was dictating to the free states and their representatives in Congress just as a master would to a slave. The alliance between the "plain republicans" of the North and the slaveholding South in every instance had favored the South, as the brouhaha over the bank and the tariff indicated. Van Buren and his Quid doctrines ran counter to the interests of the free states. It was with gusto, then, that Adams turned his attention to the Texan war for independence and the Jackson–Van Buren administration's role in facilitating it.

In May 1836, Jackson invited the House and the Senate Committees on Foreign Affairs to consider a resolution approving recognition of the Republic of Texas. The House report, written by Southerners, so moved and lobbied for passage. "It [the report] represents the Texans as a people struggling for their liberty and therefore entitled to our sympathy," John Quincy wrote in his diary. "The fact is directly the reverse—they are fighting for the establishment and perpetuation of slavery. . . . Can this fact be demonstrated to the understanding and duly exhibited to the sentiment of my countrymen? With candor, with calmness, with moderation . . . Alas! no!"[3] It would have to be with fire and brimstone and warnings of the coming apocalypse. Following the lead of the Senate, the House voted for recognition. John Quincy was among the small minority who voted nay. Just before he left office on March 4, 1837, Jackson received Texas's first ambassador to the United States, Memucan Hunt. Meanwhile, Texas's provisional government had held a plebiscite on the question of annexation to the United States. The republic voted almost unanimously in favor, and on August 4, 1837, Hunt submitted a formal proposal to the Van Buren administration.

By this point the American Anti-Slavery Society was up in arms, peppering Congress with anti-Texas petitions, some of which were presented by the congressman from Massachusetts. Adams had been kept abreast of events in Texas by his abolitionist friend Benjamin Lundy. Like Poinsett, Lundy hoped to prove that sugar, cotton, and rice could be produced profitably in the South and the Southwest by free labor. To this end he made two trips to Texas, the first in 1830–1831 and the second in 1834–1835, in an effort to persuade Mexican authorities to allow him to establish experimental farms manned by free labor. The turmoil in Texas pitting pro-slavery American settlers against the abolitionist Mexican government spoiled Lundy's scheme. He did secure a grant of a hundred thirty-eight thousand acres from the state of Tamaulipas, south of the Río Grande. He returned to Philadelphia to recruit settlers, but by that time, the war of Texan independence had broken out. Lundy then turned his attention to arousing Northern opposition to annexation.

In a series of nine articles published in Robert Walsh's *Philadelphia National Gazette*, Lundy described a nefarious plot in which slaveholders in the United Stated working through the Jackson administration and the Democratic majorities in Congress had schemed to simultaneously flood Texas with pro-slavery Americans and trick or bully Mexico into ceding Texas to the Union. The newspaper pieces, soon published in pamphlet form as the "Origins and True Causes of the Texas Revolution Commenced in the Year 1835," became the bible of the antislavery forces and an opening wedge for the concerns of free white Northerners in general. "People of the North!" Lundy cried. "Will you permit it? Will you sanction the abominable outrage; involve ourselves in the deep criminality and perhaps the horrors of war for the establishment of slavery in a land of freedom and thus put your necks and the necks of your posterity under the feet of the domineering tyrants of the South for centuries to come?"[4] Lundy mailed copies of his broadside to John Quincy, who was busy conducting his own inquiry into the Texas "conspiracy." "In 1829, the year of our Jackson's election to our Presidency," he wrote William Ellery Channing, "[the] President of the Mexican Confederacy issued a decree of universal emancipation throughout the whole republic from which time the conspiracy to sever Mexico [along the line of] the Rio del Norte from its mouth to its source and to unite it with our Southern states has been in active operation between the slave holding states leagued with the banks, land and stock jobbers, and editors of popular newspapers in the North and North-west."[5]

FOLLOWING CONGRESS'S ADJOURNMENT, JOHN Quincy and Louisa set out for New England and the haven that Peacefield had become. They longed to be surrounded by friends and family, to forget if possible the new and terrible crisis that the further expansion of slavery into the trans-Mississippi West was bringing about. On July 11, the elder statesman celebrated his seventieth birthday, and two weeks later, he and Louisa observed the fortieth anniversary of their nuptials. The citizens of Newburyport, once the scene of such heartache for John Quincy, invited him to deliver their annual Fourth of July speech, which he did, speaking for ninety minutes on the Declaration and its promise. The event was held in the open air; hundreds attended, with many more being turned away. Charles noted with amusement how his father's natural aloofness and formality melted away amidst the adulation of the crowd. He thought the address much too Whiggish. "The prospect in the United States is certainly not favorable to the perfection of the race of man nor to the duration of the good institutions we live under. . . . I defer more to the authority of my grandfather [than to John Quincy]. . . . He saw no cessation of war, still less much perfectibility while man is constituted as he has been known to be since the world began."[6]

The abolitionist Grimké sisters—Sarah and Angelina—paid a visit to "Old Man Eloquent," as his admirers had taken to calling him, and the inhabitants of Quincy held public meetings to express their support for his opposition to the annexation of Texas. Perhaps, Adams thought, the threat to freedom of speech posed by the gag rule, coupled with the prospect of being overwhelmed by ever-expanding slave power, was moving the free states to action. In August he and Louisa set off for Washington to begin the next session of Congress.

When the Adamses arrived back in the capital, they sensed a change in attitudes toward them. John Quincy was no longer a pariah in his own state delegation. "By the continual evolution of political opinions and passions," he rejoiced in his diary, "I happen at this moment to be again upon terms of good understanding and good fellowship with them all."[7] On New Year's Day, President Van Buren, as was the custom, opened the White House to visitors. "I was not among them," Adams recorded in his diary. "I have found it necessary to assume a position in public towards him and his administration which forbids me from any public exhibition of personal courtesy."[8] The Adamses held their own reception, however, and more than three hundred of Washington's dignitaries attended. Whatever changes in opinion were occurring in the North and the Mid-Atlantic, however, the slave power still controlled Congress.

On September 16, 1837, John Quincy presented a batch of anti-Texas petitions to the House and then offered a resolution that declared that "the power of annexing the people of any independent State to this Union is a power not delegated by the Constitution of the United States to their Congress or to any department of their government but reserved to the People."[9] (The Louisiana Purchase and Transcontinental Treaty notwithstanding!) The Speaker refused to receive the resolution and would not even allow it to be read. "In the present composition of Congress," John Quincy observed in December 1838, "I can bring forward no public measure of probable utility with the remotest hope of success."[10] But this did not mean that he should abandon the fight. "Measures may fail in Congress and yet make a salutary impression upon the public mind. . . . The question, whether and when to bring them forward, is of great difficulty and requires the coolest self-scrutinizing exercise of the judgment . . . the thought occurred to me while at church this morning that I needed a lamp and a key."[11] He was of a mind with the abolitionist Elizur Wright, who wrote Theodore Dwight Weld, "There will be, indeed is, a tendency in some parts to build hope too much on political measures. We ought all to understand each other on this point and be made to feel that our business lies with the heart of the nation, not its fingers and toes."[12]

HER SON JOHN'S DEATH in October 1834 launched Louisa Catherine Adams on a spiritual and intellectual journey that would place her squarely in the middle of both the movement to abolish slavery and the campaign for women's rights. In the wake of her son's demise, she sought solace in the Bible but initially went unrewarded. She was mad at her husband, mad at Andrew Jackson and Martin Van Buren, and mad at God. The first week in November 1835, a year following John's passing, she attended church with her daughter-in-law Mary and her sister Caroline. They were shocked when she did not go forward to receive communion. "I said that I felt afraid to present myself at the Lord's table as there was still a livid spot in my heart."[13] That very day she began writing her memoir *Mélanges d'une Déclassée,* or "Miscellaneous Writings of One Who Is Refreshed." The early passages were anguished. Never had she felt more inadequate. "O my wracked conscience," she wrote, "night and day I reproach myself for my passiveness, and never shall I cease to regret the past for I was a—Mother."[14] She felt inadequate because of her "feminine" education. But at last, she—the daughter-in-law of Abigail

Adams—bridled, both at her own feelings of inferiority and at the male-dominated society that instilled feelings of inadequacy in all women. She suddenly recalled with pride her thousand-mile journey from St. Petersburg to Paris, undertaken in the dead of winter in 1815. Thereupon, Louisa began writing a detailed narrative of her adventure with a view to publishing it as an inspiration to others of her sex. "Under all circumstances," she declared, "we must never desert ourselves."[15]

Women's rights had advanced hardly at all since Abigail wrote her "Remember the Ladies" letter to John when he was a delegate to the Continental Congress in 1776. Educational opportunities were still quite limited; access to higher education did not exist. Women were to express their views on politics only within the home, if at all. A married female could not inherit property, sue, or be sued. As late as 1850, the *Public Ledger* of Philadelphia published an article ridiculing women's rights advocates. "A woman is a nobody," it declared. "A wife is everything. A pretty girl is equal to 10,000 men, and a mother is, next to God, all powerful. The ladies of Philadelphia therefore . . . are resolved to maintain their rights as wives, belles, virgins, and mothers and not as women."[16] But American women like Abigail Adams had been corresponding, forming educational self-help circles, and conducting charitable operations since before the Revolution. Philanthropy was one of the few public activities that were condoned. Women in New York, Philadelphia, Baltimore, and Charleston met in homes and churches to organize fund-raising campaigns on behalf of widows, orphans, and the poor. Typical was the Washington Orphans' Society, to which Louisa belonged, or the Female Missionary Society, which as of 1818 boasted chapters in forty-six New York towns. Some of the participants were social conservatives but some were not. Most important, these philanthropic enterprises taught women organization, fund-raising, and strategic planning, just the skills required by the burgeoning abolitionist movement.

Deeply rooted notions of gender roles made it difficult for men and women to belong to the same organizations. In the City of Brotherly Love, Lucretia Mott and twenty other women formed the Philadelphia Female Anti-Slavery Society to parallel the American Anti-Slavery Society. As of 1837, of the hundred thousand abolitionists active in New England and the Midwest, half were women.[17] Were females any less worthy than slaves? many began to ask. Were not men and women created equally by God—at least in spiritual, intellectual, and emotional terms? Were women not entitled to realize and enjoy all of the promises contained in the Declaration of Independence? Gradually, the drive for emancipation and for women's rights became inextricably intertwined.

Late in the day on February 6, 1837, Louisa and her niece Elizabeth Adams decided to pay a visit to the House of Representatives. The session was supposedly nearing adjournment. The two women loitered in the Rotunda, where the walls were adorned with John Trumbull's patriotic paintings—the signing of the Declaration of Independence, the surrender of the British at Yorktown, Washington resigning his commission. This was the same Colonel Trumbull who had taught Louisa how to paint, who had so admired her singing, and who had introduced her to her husband. With the House still not adjourned, Louisa and Elizabeth decided to go sit in the galleries to wait for John Quincy. But they required a member to escort them; spotting George Lay, a young congressman from New York, they approached him, but he warned that "the House was in a state of prodigious excitement, Mr. Adams being the principal actor."[18] The women decided to press on; as they entered the chamber, John Quincy was just taking his seat, having presented the antislavery petitions from various women of Fredericksburg, Virginia, and in the process accusing the slaveholding gentlemen of the South of mass rape. As enraged Southern congressmen took turns berating Adams and calling for his censure, they noticed that a small woman dressed in black had entered the galleries. The uproar briefly ceased. "I found myself," Louisa subsequently wrote proudly, "in the brunt of the fight."[19]

As hundreds of antislavery petitions, the majority signed by women, poured into the F Street residence, John Quincy set Louisa and Mary to cataloguing them. Louisa read many and was moved. She continued to visit the House gallery to see her husband do battle. "The platoons [of pro-slavery congressmen] came swift and thick while I was present," she wrote in her diary. "Instead of dampening my spirit they seemed to produce a contrary effect and inspired a degree of ardor to my hotspur head fully equal in force and energy to their own." Had she had "the privilege of speech," she continued, she would have "overmastered them by dint of words, notwithstanding the miserable deficiency of ideas which they so handsomely displayed."[20] Like other antislavery women, Louisa began to make connections between the campaign for emancipation and women's rights. During the summer of 1837, while the family was vacationing in Quincy, she read Abigail's letters on feminism; they resonated deeply. She was struck, she wrote, "by the vast and varied powers of her mind; the full benevolence of an excellent heart; and the strength of the reasoning. Her letters are treasures richer than the Mines of Golconda" and will "shed a luster upon her race."[21] She subsequently read Mary Wollstonecraft's *Vindication of the Rights of Women* and Sarah Grimké's *Letters on the Equality of Sexes and the Condition of Women*. To Charles shortly thereafter: "I cannot believe that there is any inferiority in the sexes, as far as mind and intellect are concerned."[22]

Coincidentally Sarah and Angelina Grimké visited the Adamses in Quincy that summer. The sisters were on their famous tour of New England, on which they described to overflow crowds the evils of slavery that they had witnessed firsthand growing up in South Carolina. In February 1838, Angelina would speak before the Massachusetts General Court, the first woman in American history to address such a body. Her sister was no less vehement in her demand that political rights be extended to women. "Men and women were CREATED EQUAL," Sarah had written in "On the Province of Women"; "they are both moral and accountable beings, and whatever is right for a man to do is right for women."[23] In February 1838, Louisa Adams and Sarah Grimké began a correspondence that would continue sporadically for several years. The Quaker abolitionist and female rights advocate was just another of the strong, independent-minded women who had attracted Louisa throughout her life. Both lamented the cultural stereotypes that had been imposed on females. Deficits in their education had caused Louisa to doubt her intellect throughout her life, she wrote. "We have aimed to be the idol of man's worship rather than the companion of his heart," Sarah wrote. "With a mind like thine, my sister, I feel persuaded that had not the trammels of education fettered thee, thy pursuits would have been far different."[24]

But Grimké was more interested in converting Louisa—and through her, John Quincy—to the cause of abolitionism than anything else. The former First Lady confessed that she distrusted free Blacks and feared that abolition would unleash a mass of ignorant, rootless, and ultimately dangerous people on the country. "Please inform me whether thy opinion of them is founded on actual and extensive knowledge or whether it is the result of hearsay evidence," Grimké wrote.[25] Visit the slave auctions and see for yourself. Visit the numerous slave quarters in and around Washington. Have you "cried with the widow torn from her husband, the mother sold from her children, the thousands of slavery's victims who pass through Washington & moisten the soil with their blood & their tears? . . . Can we feel the wrongs of women & not deplore a system which degrades her to the level of a beast?"[26] Louisa could not bring herself to go that far. Like other Southern cities, Washington was rife with rumors of slave insurrections. During a visit with his parents in Washington in May 1838, Charles Francis wrote in his diary: "Much talk of an insurrection of the blacks supposed to be about to break out at 11 o'clock this night and instigated by an abolitionist from New York or elsewhere. The alarms of the whites sufficiently show the horrors of the slavery system without the need of exaggeration. Their fears magnify their own danger, and this produces all the violence they dread. . . . My mother and the family are always apprehensive at such times of the possible direction of the public feeling against my father for having taken so much part in the matter."[27]

But slavery was a human institution that brought slave and freeman face-to-face, and the humanity of the bondsman could not be denied. In October 1837 the Adamses had been moved by the plight of Dorcas Allen and her family. Dorcas had been the slave of the wife of Gideon Davis, an employee of the War Department. On her deathbed, Gideon's wife had made him promise to free Dorcas, which he subsequently did. Dorcas lived free for more than a decade, during which time she married a free Black named Nathan Allen and bore him four children. Gideon Davis had subsequently remarried, and when he died, his widow married one Rezin Orme, who in August 1837 rounded up Dorcas and her children and sold them to the slave trading firm of Birch and Dyer for seven hundred dollars. Certain that they were going to be sold into the Deep South to see their lives drained away on a cotton or sugar plantation, Dorcas, then in a slave prison in Alexandria, cut the throats of her two youngest children—one a boy four years old and the other a girl less than one. She then tried unsuccessfully to cut her own throat but was prevented when her two older children raised a hue and cry. Dorcas Allen was charged with murder, tried, but then acquitted by reason of insanity. When asked why she had taken her children's lives, Dorcas replied that they were now safe in heaven.

John Quincy was alerted to the case by an article in the *National Intelligencer*. He immediately intervened, inquiring about Dorcas Allen and her circumstances at the offices of the *Intelligencer*, of the district attorney Francis Scott Key, and of Birch and Dyer. He managed to hammer out an agreement between Key and the slave traders in which Dorcas would be freed but her two surviving girls, ages twelve and nine, would remain in captivity and sold. In the days that followed, Nathan Allen tried desperately to raise the $475 purchase price for his children. John Quincy promised Allen fifty dollars, but Key then informed Adams that even if the money were raised, the children were still slaves and would remain so. "Such is the condition of things in these shambles of human flesh that I could not now expose this whole horrible transaction but at the hazard of my life," Congressman Adams confided to his diary.[28] Louisa was at first sympathetic, seeing Dorcas Allen primarily as a mother, but when the Black woman showed up at the Adams house dressed in her best finery, Louisa had her sent away for showing a lack of respect for her dead children.

ANTISLAVERY AND ANTI-TEXAS PETITIONS continued to pour into Congress throughout late 1837 and early 1838. During the congressional session that spanned those years, there were delivered four hundred twelve thousand slave-related petitions, including a hundred thirty thousand calling for the extinction of slavery and the slave trade in the District of Columbia, thirty-two thousand demanding a repeal of the gag rule, and a hundred eighty thousand opposing the annexation of Texas. This in a nation of sixteen million people.[29] "I received this day thirty-one petitions and consumed the whole evening in assorting, filing, endorsing, and entering them on my list," John Quincy recorded in his diary for January 28, 1838. "With these petitions I receive many letters. . . . Most of them are so flattering and expressed in terms of such deep sensibility that I am in imminent danger of being led by them into presumption and puffed up with vanity." They were almost compensation for the flood of hate mail he was receiving from the South. "My duty to defend the free principles and institutions is clear; but the measures by which they are to be defended are involved in thick darkness."[30]

In his private correspondence to his abolitionist friends, Adams seemed to have joined their ranks. In a letter to Channing, he railed against Northern doughfaces, who continued to cower before the slave power. "Even now our boldest statesmen of the North scarcely dare avow an opposition to the annexation of Texas . . . *for fear they should be taken for Abolitionists!* Abolitionists? Not they! They think the annexation of Texas would be impolitic and unfavorable to Northern interests, but heaven forbid they should ever be suspected of Abolitionism! No! No!"[31] And then the former scourge of the Essex men, the spoiler of the New England–New York secessionist plot of 1804–1805, the saboteur of the Hartford Convention, declared that if Great Britain should undertake the universal emancipation of slaves, New England should break away from the Union and fight alongside her. "[I]f Britain accomplishes her internal reform without festering into Civil War," he wrote in his letter to Channing, "she will before long lead in a war for the express purpose of abolishing slavery in this hemisphere. Our Confederation then, if not sooner, will fall to pieces, and our posterity will, I trust, be found braving the battle and the breeze in the cause of human freedom."[32] This to a man with whom he had previously agreed that slavery could be expunged from the South only voluntarily through the conversion of white Southerners to the cause. By the fall of 1837, slavery and Texas, it seemed, had driven Adams to countenance the great Satan of disunion.

But John Quincy was soon made to realize that he was in danger of getting ahead of his constituents. In November 1837 in Alton, Illinois, a pro-slavery mob attacked and killed Elijah P. Lovejoy, a prominent abolitionist who had been in the process of establishing a newspaper. They surrounded the warehouse where the sheet was to be published and demanded possession of the offending press. When Lovejoy refused, the crowd set fire to the building housing his press and shot him dead. Adams was horrified, outraged. He would later publish a laudatory obituary. But shortly after Lovejoy was killed, an anti-abolitionist meeting convened in Boston at Faneuil Hall during which speakers praised those who had committed the crime. "The course of the abolition party," declared one speaker, "was like that of a man who should insist upon the liberation of the wild animals of a menagerie."[33] Widespread opposition to the annexation of Texas did not mean that white citizens of the free states had been converted to the cause of emancipation. "In the North, the people favor the whites and fear the blacks of the South," John Quincy observed in his diary. "Upon this subject of anti-slavery my principles and my position make it necessary for me to be more circumspect in my conduct than belongs to my nature."[34] "I am heartily glad that you have kept yourself entirely aloof from this abolition and Anti-Slavery excitement," he wrote Charles in late January 1838. "Keep yourself still aloof from it as long as you possibly can. . . . I think you are not ready to carry out in their necessary consequences the self-evident truths of the Declaration of Independence."[35]

So it was back to the drawing board—free speech, free press, and protection of the nation's free white workingmen. At times, like William Lloyd Garrison, John Quincy seemed ready to abandon the Constitution, with its three-fifths clause. "[I]f you will marry into a family afflicted with Scrofula," he wrote a friend, "you must not expect that the blood of your children will escape infection from the disease. We have bound up our destinies in community with the people of states encumbered with slavery . . . and by the bond covenanted to tolerate, to defend, to protect that institution."[36] Elimination of the three-fifths clause by constitutional amendment was, of course, statistically impossible. But Adams continued to reject the central argument of the South and its supporters—namely that the federal government did not have the right to interfere with the institution of slavery. "What was the recommendation of President Jackson to Congress to enact laws to suppress the conveyance of incendiary publications by the mail but interference with the institution of slavery . . . ? What was the bill . . . turning every postmaster throughout the Union into a catchpoll and spy . . . but interferences with the institution of slavery in the states? What has been the whole history of the Colonization Society?"[37]

CONGRESS, LIKE THE NATION as a whole, was a volatile place in the 1830s and 1840s. Bullying, or "crowding," as it was called at the time, was a common practice in both the House and Senate, primarily employed by Southerners against their Northern colleagues. Solons appeared on the floor of debate with pistols on their hips and Bowie knives in their belts. In June 1838, a dispute between two Tennessee congressmen, Hopkins Turney and John Bell, a former Speaker, erupted into fisticuffs. Bell accused Turney of being "the scavenger of all the filth raked up" by his political rivals and that he and they were "men equally destitute of public principle and private worth." Whereupon Turney, "who was sitting within arm's reach of Bell," rose and struck him in the face. Bell retaliated and the two men traded blows until the sergeant at arms intervened.[38] That same spring, as Adams was leaving the chamber, an acquaintance approached him and warned him that Congressman Ratliff Boon, with whom the New Englander had just had a heated exchange, intended to assault him at the first opportunity.[39] During one vitriolic exchange between Adams and Henry Wise, the Virginian burst out, "If the member from Massachusetts had not been an old man, protected by the imbecility of age, he would not have enjoyed, as long as he has, the mercy of mere words." That evening Adams wrote in his diary, "Wise then replied to me in his own way, closing with a threat of murdering me in my seat."[40]

Among gentlemen, matters of honor were still settled on the dueling grounds at Bladensburg, Maryland. When unwritten but generally agreed-upon lines of etiquette were crossed, the insulted party would have an associate deliver a note demanding an explanation. If an apology were not forthcoming, a challenge would be issued. A gentleman challenged only a person considered his social equal. Caning and nose tweaking were reserved for inferiors.[41]

In February 1838, the code duello claimed its first congressional victim. The principals in the dispute were Jonathan Cilley, a Democratic congressman from Maine, and Henry Wise, a Whig. Cilley was slight in stature but intense, abrasive, and ambitious. Wise, a nullifier and ardent defender of slavery, was a strange mixture of firebrand and hail-fellow-well-met. As one observer put it, "Wise was the virtual epitome of a Virginia gentleman . . . a man of extremes: blustering, flamboyant, impulsive, high-strung, even violent, yet a remarkably genial jokester when he wanted to be."[42] By the opening of the Twenty-Fifth Congress, the Virginian had fought a duel, engaged in a fistfight, and threatened a colleague with his pistol during a committee meeting. The Democrat and the Whig first crossed rhetorical swords in January 1838 over the Bank of the United States and the Second Seminole War. In an effort to provoke Cilley into a duel, Wise became increasingly abusive. The dispute went national with various partisan newspapers taking sides. James Watson Webb, editor of the *New York Courier and Enquirer*, accused Cilley of graft; when the Maine Democrat revealed that it was Webb and not he who was on the take, Webb descended on Washington, determined to extract an apology or, failing that, gain satisfaction. On the floor of the House, Webb approached Congressman William J. Graves, a Kentucky Whig, and asked him to deliver his challenge to Cilley. Graves, a large, good-natured man, agreed. Cilley refused to accept the letter, which was considered a dueling matter in itself. Graves challenged the Mainer, and he accepted. The two men with their seconds met on the dueling field at Bladensburg on February 24. The weapons of choice were long rifles at eighty yards. In the first exchange, both men missed; Wise, who was acting as Graves's second, insisted on a second round. Both men fired almost simultaneously. Cilley was struck in the leg, the bullet severing an artery. He bled out in minutes.[43]

Adams was appalled, especially at Wise's role. As Graves's second, he should after the first volley have declared that there had been a misunderstanding between the two men and that any offense taken had been settled on the field of honor. Instead, Wise had insisted on another round and declared that if that one failed to draw blood, the distance between the duelists should be shortened. John Quincy rose to his feet in the House in the wake of Cilley's killing to declare that it was Henry Wise rather than William Graves, the man who had pulled the trigger, who was responsible for Cilley's death.[44]

For the previous several months, John Quincy Adams had been laboring to convince Congress and the American people that the violence sweeping the land was a by-product of slavery. Inhumanity bred more inhumanity. The domination and exploitation of their fellow human beings had transformed white Southerners into barbarians; their "code of honor" was but a fig leaf. In February 1838, to shouts of "Order! Order!" he produced letters and broadsides in which Southern "gentlemen" promised to hang any abolitionist who dared cross the Mason–Dixon Line.[45] The Cilley–Graves duel—both men had been on the most cordial of terms personally—and the public revulsion it provoked offered a chance to beard the lion in his den, argued many of Adams's antislavery friends. In the weeks following Cilley's death, he pored over the anti-dueling debates that had taken place in the British House of Commons and the Virginia General Assembly. His reading strengthened his conviction that "private war [dueling]" was not only barbarous and unchristian but an "appendage of slavery."[46] He joined with Senator Samuel Prentiss of Vermont in sponsoring a bill prohibiting the delivery or acceptance of a challenge to a duel within the District of Columbia. Penalties were to be ten years' imprisonment if one of the parties was killed, five years if wounded, and three years for assaulting a person for refusing a challenge. The Adams–Prentiss Anti-dueling Bill passed both houses of Congress in February 1839.

During a floor debate in 1841, Henry Wise would bemoan the passing of the code duello. Members of Congress could say anything they wanted about one another with no consequences. Adams rose to his feet. That had been going on for many years, he declared. Because Northerners abhorred dueling and refused to engage in it, Southern members had felt free to bully and slander their colleagues. I am not willing to sit here any longer and see other members from my own section of the country, or those who may be my successors here, made subject to any such laws as the law of the duelist. The anti-dueling law, he insisted, was necessary to "maintain the independence of this House . . . for the independence of the members of the Northern section of this country who not only abhor dueling in theory but in practice."⁴⁷

MEANWHILE, THE STRUGGLE OVER Texas between antislavery forces and pro-annexationists continued apace. Crippled by the Panic of 1837 and the depression that followed in its wake, Van Buren decided to postpone the question of annexation for as long as he could. But matters were moving beyond his control. In the process of trying to wrest the province from Mexico, Anthony Butler had pressed the claims of U.S. citizens for reimbursement for damages to the persons and property of Americans resulting from the unrest in Texas. In December 1837, under pressure from the claimants—and annexationists in general—the president invited Congress to decide how the United States would go about obtaining redress. At that point Congressman Adams was in the process of presenting a new batch of anti-Texas petitions; he moved immediately to expose Van Buren's "war-whoop" for what it was. "The annexation of Texas and the proposed war with Mexico are all one and the same thing."⁴⁸ The claims issue was a fabricated issue designed to be an excuse for a declaration of war on Mexico with Texas as the prize.

Throughout 1837 and 1838, Adams had continued to correspond with Benjamin Lundy, whose investigation of the Texas "conspiracy" was still ongoing. As the abolitionist fed John Quincy information, he also massaged his ego. "The eyes of millions, my dear and honored friend," Lundy wrote Adams, "are turned to thee. No mortal ever held a part of greater usefulness—more enviable distinction—or higher moral responsibility than is thine at the present moment."⁴⁹ But then Adams's source suddenly dried up. Lundy was in the process of turning over the editorship of the *National Enquirer* in Philadelphia to John Greenleaf Whitter and transferring his operation to Illinois. In the interim he stored his papers in a room in Pennsylvania Hall, which the city's reform community had recently built at a cost of forty thousand dollars. It included meeting rooms on the first floor and a large convention hall and gallery on the second and third. In May 1838 the Anti-Slavery Convention of American Women gathered there to make speeches and draft petitions. The Grimké sisters were, of course, prominent in the proceedings. To much notoriety Angelina had just recently wedded Theodore Weld. Broadsides declaring that the object of the convention was to promote the "amalgamation" of the races had been posted around the city. While Angelina was speaking to a crowd of some three thousand, a mob broke down the entry doors to the hall and shattered its windows. White and black women, arm in arm, exited through the crowd amidst curses and spitting. The evening after, the mob returned and set fire to the building. City fireman doused neighboring structures but did nothing to save Pennsylvania Hall. Lundy's papers went up in flames.[50]

For the time being, Adams and his compatriots had foiled plans to add Texas to the Union by means of a war with Mexico, so the South and the West refocused their efforts on annexation by means of a treaty with the new republic. Significantly, the anti-Texas petition drive had evolved from pleas from individuals and societies to requests from state legislatures, including those of Rhode Island, Michigan, Ohio, and Massachusetts. What's sauce for the goose is sauce for the gander, the South decided. Immediately following the introduction of the state-driven anti-annexation petitions, the legislatures of Alabama and Tennessee presented resolutions calling for the annexation of Texas. John Quincy sensed that an opening for an end run around the gag rule was in the making. The House, still dominated by slave representatives and their doughface collaborators from the North, could not very well table the pro-annexationist petitions. But if they were accepted for debate, the whole slavery question would once again be up for discussion on the floor of the House. The New Englander smelled blood.

John Quincy's opportunity came in mid-June as Congress was preparing for adjournment early the following month. All of the state resolutions—pro and con—had been referred to the House Committee on Foreign Affairs. Speaking for the committee, George C. Dromgoole of Virginia reported to the House that as no motion calling for the annexation of Texas was currently before the House, the issue was moot, and all of the petitions would be laid on the table without debate. Thereupon, Adams rose and asked Dromgoole if the thousands of petitions the committee had received relating to Texas "had ever received five minutes of consideration." The Virginian replied by denying that any member of the House had the right "to catechize the committee as to its actions." In a fury Adams shouted, "That is enough, Sir! That, Sir, is enough for this House and this country. The committee refuses to answer?"[51] He demanded that the petition from his home state of Massachusetts be treated with respect.

The following day Benjamin Howard of Maryland, chair of the committee, tried to finesse the issue, but Adams would have none of it. Did not one member have the right to ask another whether he had read a particular document? No, not in his opinion, Howard replied. But then the congressman from South Carolina, Hugh Legaré, a member of the committee, interjected: "For myself I have no hesitation in admitting that I have not read the papers or looked into them, nor was I bound to do so."[52] Gleefully, Adams cited the seventy-sixth rule of the House, which required that the Committee on Foreign Affairs must "take into consideration all matters concerning the relations of the United States with foreign nations."[53] At this point Waddy Thompson moved that the committee's report be amended to recommend to the president the annexation of Texas. Adams then proposed an amendment to the amendment declaring that neither Congress nor the executive had the authority to take such action. The congressman from Massachusetts had the annexationists by the parliamentary throat. House rules permitted an amendment to an amendment and prohibited further action until the latter had been voted upon. On the morning of June 16, Adams stepped forward to present arguments on behalf of his motion. By tradition an hour each morning was devoted to "committee business"; for fifteen straight sessions until July 9, the old man would hold the floor for an hour each day.

Adams excoriated the Van Buren administration for not providing the correspondence between the State Department and Anthony Butler, which, he declared, would clearly reveal the nefarious plot to convert Texas into one or more slave states. The free men of the North would not fight in a war with Mexico and possibly Great Britain to facilitate the spread of slavery. In excruciating detail Adams described the moral, political, and economic evils that human bondage and its supporters had wrought upon the nation. The gag rule, he added, was undermining democracy at home and ruining its reputation abroad. He praised the virtue, patriotism, and high-mindedness of the thousands who had presented antislavery and anti-Texas resolutions. When Benjamin Howard lamented the fact that many of the Texas petitions had originated with women and insisted that the weaker sex should confine their activities to "their duties to their fathers, their husbands, and their children . . . instead of rushing into the fiery struggle of political life," Adams added the abuse of the rights of women to his indictment of the slave power. The gentleman from Maryland had insulted not only the 238 women of Massachusetts who had signed the first anti-Texas petition he had presented to the House, but females everywhere. "Are women to have no opinions or actions on subjects related to the general welfare?" He proceeded to list those of the "weaker sex" who had throughout history stepped forward to mold the destinies of mankind, from Esther in the Old Testament, to Queen Isabella of Castille, to the heroines of the American Revolution, including his own sainted mother. The right of petition was open to all human beings. What about Jesus raising Lazarus from the dead? "[T]he Savior performed this stupendous miracle *at the petition of a woman!*"[54] In their sensitivity, in their heightened sense of right and wrong, in their compassion, women were particularly well positioned to denounce the sin of slavery. Do you object to their begging the attention of Congress because they cannot vote? he asked Howard. And then a most extreme declaration: "Is it so clear that they have no such right as this last?" The slavery issue, it seemed, was radicalizing John Quincy Adams on a number of issues.

During his defense of the fairer sex, Adams, of course, brought up the Grimké sisters of Charleston. South Carolina congressman Francis Pickens interrupted to declare that the writings and speeches of these two notorious females were nothing but a tissue of lies. Really? declared Adams. No doubt the gentleman was "a kind and indulgent master" and thus was unaware of "the cruel, the tyrannical, the hard-hearted master" who "procreates children from his slave, and then sells the children as slaves." He then related the wrenching tale of Dorcas Allen and her benighted offspring. When another South Carolinian rose to declare that the abolitionists were causing a great change in the hearts and minds of Southerners and creating a siege mentality and an iron determination to defend the "peculiar institution," Adams turned on him: "I am well aware of the change that is taking place in the political philosophy of the South. I know well that the doctrine of the Declaration of Independence that 'all men are created equal' is there held as an incendiary doctrine and deserves lynching; that the Declaration is a farrago of abstractions. . . . Sir, this philosophy of the South has done more to blacken the character of this country in Europe than all other causes put together. They point to us as a nation of liars and hypocrites who publish to the world that all men are born free and equal, and then hold a large portion of our own population in bondage."[55]

When Congress finally adjourned on July 9, John Quincy's diatribe came to an end. His speech, running to 112 pages with an eighteen-page introduction added after the fact, was printed in pamphlet form by Joseph Gales and William Seaton, then reprinted again and yet again. Van Buren decided that annexation was not possible at that point, and in October, Texas withdrew its offer to join the Union.[56]

Adams sensed the beginning of a sea change. Remarkably, attempts to halt his fifteen-day speech had failed. Every motion to move the previous question went down to defeat. When he began to stray from the substance of his amendment and there were calls for order, various Southern congressmen, including Howard and Thompson, defended him: "Let him speak!" Despite his scathing attack on slavery and the "conspiracy" to annex Texas, John Quincy continued to make it clear that he regarded the institution as a national problem, not just a sectional one. He was, at this point in his life and the life of the nation, unique—an architect of American empire, a relentless opponent of secessionist movements, a protector of American independence, a man above party, and a living link between the Revolutionary Era and the Early Republic. For better or worse, his was a voice that would be heard.

In truth the pro-slavery camp was almost as complex and paradoxical as the antislavery community. Of course, there were rabid racists, soulless exploiters of other human beings. Some representatives of the slave power in Congress who now proved willing to let John Quincy speak, such as Henry Wise, were tired of parliamentary maneuver and wanted the merits of the issue openly debated because they thought they could prevail. But there were also educated, sensitive men and women who were conflicted concerning Black enslavement. And the South had produced outright abolitionists like the Grimké sisters and Joel Poinsett. Moreover, at this point, the vast majority of Southerners were unionists. Witness the lack of success that South Carolina nullifiers had had in rallying their neighboring states.

IT WAS WITH THE usual sense of relief and anticipation that the Adamses departed Washington in mid-July, headed for Quincy. John Quincy was there when Ralph Waldo Emerson delivered his famous commencement address to the Harvard Divinity School, in which he introduced the world to transcendentalism. Emerson's vision was an extension of Unitarianism, with its concept of a kind and gracious "oversoul"—the notion that the divine could be experienced best in communion with nature, and a belief in the power of individual discernment. The transcendentalists would campaign for social and economic justice and would question received wisdom, such as the sanctity of property and marriage. Adams read the speech, which was printed in the Boston newspapers. Publicly he said nothing, but privately he was appalled, referring in his diary to that "crazy address and oration" and observing that Emerson was "ambitious of becoming the founder of a sect and thinks there is an urgent necessity for a new religion. . . . The deadly sophistry of the transcendental school consists in the alliance of atheism with hypocrisy. We are to argue pro and con whether parricide [in this case, mercy killing] be a crime or a virtue; whether property be by the law of nature or the mere creature of conventional law; whether the contract of marriage constitutes an obligation of duty restrictive of promiscuous social intercourse; in short, whether justice or force is at the root of all human institutions . . . the transcendentalists not only dig up the corner-stones of human society but pronounce them decayed, rotten and worthless."[57] Emerson's address, of course, would come to be regarded as an American classic in literature and philosophy.

Adams's defense of women's rights in his "Speech . . . upon the Right of the People, Men and Women, to Petition" had earned him plaudits throughout the nation but particularly in his home state. In August and September 1838, while Congress was in recess, the congressman was treated to two tributes, one by the ladies of Hingham and the other by the women of Quincy. Some five hundred gathered at Tranquility Grove outside Hingham on August 2. Tables were set up and stocked with coffee, tea, and various delicacies. Thomas Loring, a local dignitary, welcomed Adams on behalf of the ladies, declaring that it was their wish "to express their heart-felt gratitude for the eminent services which [he] had rendered to the cause of humanity and justice in defending the sacred right of petition." The former president, beaming, stepped forward and delivered brief remarks: "I consider the ladies of this Congressional District as much my constituents as their relatives by whose votes I was elected. . . . I know that it is asserted that women have no political rights. The petitions had been treated . . . as if they had none. But all history refuted this position."58

During his lifetime, Adams had grown used to doing battle with the citizens of Boston over a variety of subjects. He enjoyed Quincy, but the state capital had been just as much a battlefield for the old warrior as Washington, DC. Even when treated to the adulations of the crowd over his defense of the right of petition, he remained skeptical. His fellow citizens' "anxious desire to see and hear me," he observed sourly, was like "the passion of a crow to see an execution." And again "there is no good will to me in any part of Boston." I am "doomed to the last gasp of my life . . . to hold my course in opposition to them all."59 But gradually, he began to let his guard down. On this visit the capital seemed genuinely to revere him. The staid Massachusetts Historical Society invited him to chair a meeting. The city fathers paid to have him sit for a portrait by William Page that would, when finished, adorn a gallery in Faneuil Hall. For perhaps the first time, John Quincy found himself reluctant to leave New England. He called his stay "this delightful dream." Sensing his euphoria, Louisa urged him to prolong his vacation, which he did. She returned to Washington ahead of him and managed by the time he arrived to have moved their household from her daughter-in-law's residence to their old commodious abode on F Street. Adams was much pleased.

ON JANUARY 21, 1839, with the Twenty-Fifth Congress back in session, Adams rose on the floor of the House and asked the Speaker for permission to explain his position on the question of when and how slavery should be done away with. "I further ask the courtesy of the House because I have received a mass of letters threatening to assassinate me for my course. My real position has never been understood by the country."60 While he had presented petitions calling for the abolition of slavery in the nation's capital, he would never vote for such a measure, he declared. Congressman William Slade of Vermont, a friend and fellow crusader against slavery, was aghast. Would the gentleman from Massachusetts care to explain himself? He would explain in a public letter to his constituents, John Quincy replied curtly. In the meantime, to make his position perfectly clear on the question of emancipation, he was proposing three amendments to the Constitution of the United States: first, from July 4, 1842, hereditary slavery in the United States was to be abolished—following that date, every child born in the United States or its territories was to be free; second, with the exception of Florida, no new slave state would be permitted to join the Union; and third, after the date in question, neither slavery nor the slave trade would be permitted in Washington, DC. Given the ratio of slave states to free and the three-fourths requirement, these amendments would never be adopted, as Adams well knew. His intention, it seemed, was to reveal the futility of the abolitionist movement.

The proposed amendments, coupled with Adams's declaration that he would personally never vote for emancipation in the District of Columbia, seemed to many a cynical abandonment of the field. Abolitionists were predictably furious. "If you had been as explicit in your declarations at the time your election was pending as you now are," wrote William Lloyd Garrison, "a majority of your constituents would have cast their votes for some other candidate."[61] The *Emancipator* published a bit of doggerel: "He that played Sir Pander / While wages were to be had / And saved slave-trading Andrew / Now rails at them like mad / And turning to us says modestly / 'Your language is too bad.'"[62]

In a long letter to abolitionist Joshua Leavitt and others, Adams expressed his sympathy with those who were seeking to strike the shackles from the nation's three million bondsmen but accused them of being willing to burn down the barn to get rid of the rats. He found the reference to "man stealing" in the American Anti-Slavery Society's declaration of purpose especially offensive, he said. The term came from the sixteenth verse of the twenty-first chapter of Exodus, if he were not mistaken: "And he that stealeth a man, and selleth him, or if he be found in his hand [in his possession], he shall surely be put to death." "May I be permitted to say it is unjust to the whole free population of the slave holding states. It charges every slave holder with a capital crime of which he is not guilty. Slaveholding is not man stealing."[63] (This despite the fact that Adams had repeatedly cited the same chapter and verse when confronting the British over impressment.) The slaveholders were their fellow countrymen, kinsmen, neighbors—Christians who needed to be recalled to the path of righteousness through persuasion, not through the threat of death. Southerners, he wrote, were unique but not beyond the pale.[64]

Why, seemingly, had the fire died in the furnace? In part it was personal. The newly formed Liberty Party had fielded a candidate against Adams in the November 1838 congressional elections, splitting the Whig vote and nearly leading to a Democratic victory. "The moral principle of their interference to defeat elections when they cannot carry them appears to me to be vicious," Adams sniffed.[65] But, in addition, he was still a republican and a unionist. "I am not for the immediate abolition of slavery in the District of Columbia or the Territory of Florida," he subsequently wrote Charles P. Kirkland, "but I am for the abolition of slavery in both; and throughout the United States," but only if it could "be accomplished without injustice to white inhabitants . . . and without violation of the faith pledged in the Constitution" to the property rights of all citizens. The Constitution was what it was and must be obeyed until and unless it was altered through amendment. He would continue to work for emancipation "by all lawful means in my power when the wrongs of one portion of mankind may be redressed without inflicting wrongs not less deplorable upon the other."[66] To another, he declared that while he shared with Christ and his disciples a dedication to "the cause of human freedom," he had learned from him to render to God what was God's and to Caesar what was Caesar's.[67]

Mr. Adams's face was becoming alarmingly doughlike, his abolitionist friends must have thought. John Quincy kept coming back to the reality that abolition forced on the South would inevitably mean the breakup of the Union and civil war. "It was one of the purposes of the divine mission to proclaim peace on earth as the law of nature and of God between man and man," he wrote a cleric friend. "All war therefore is a violation of the law of nature and of God."[68] But were not slavery and the slave trade a kind of war, and of the most vicious variety, waged by white men against Black? the minister responded. Adams did not answer.

Among other things, Adams was troubled by the uncertainty that would surely follow in the wake of abolition. What would America look like? In truth, most antislavery crusaders—the Quakers excepted—did not envision full citizenship for newly freed slaves. One of Theodore Weld's fellow crusaders outlined his and his fellows' plans for the post-emancipation Black. "I . . . stated that we did not claim for the slave the right of voting immediately or eligibility to vote. Also, that we did not wish them turned loose having the possession of unlicensed liberty; nor even to be governed by the same code of laws which are adapted to intelligent citizens. That on the contrary, we believed that it would be necessary to form a special code of laws restricting them in their freedom upon the same general principles that apply to foreigners, minors, etc."[69] The Adams family, lifelong advocates of the notion that a virtuous republic could survive and thrive only with an educated electorate, agreed wholeheartedly. The Declaration of Independence declared all men to be free and equal—equal at birth, perhaps, but thereafter? It would take decades for men kept in subjugation and ignorance to be able to exercise full citizenship. Consequently, even with the chains of slavery broken, the United States would continue to be a land part free and part unfree. Was this really worth civil war?

It must be remembered that Adams valued property rights almost as much as he did union. His heart thirsted for emancipation but his mind quailed at the prospect of the massive, unlawful seizure of property that forced abolition would involve. As Congress was adjourning, the former president received and accepted an invitation from the New-York Historical Society to deliver an address on the fiftieth anniversary of George Washington's inauguration to be held on April 30, 1839. As usual he obsessed on the task and complained how onerous it was and at his age how unfit he was to prepare for it. "My reputation, my age, my decaying faculties, have all warned me to decline," he complained to his diary, but he had accepted. "Such is my nature, and I shall have no quiet of mind till it is over."[70] The speech turned out to be a great success, delivered over two hours to a packed house. Afterward a dinner was held in Adams's honor; three hundred of the state's political and literary elites attended.

The address, subsequently dubbed the "Jubilee of the Constitution," was one of his most remarkable, and it was widely reprinted and cited. In it he seemed to embrace the "Jacobin" principles espoused during the Revolutionary Era by Thomas Jefferson and Thomas Paine. "Democracy, pure democracy," the former Federalist declared, "is founded on the natural equality of mankind. It is the corner stone of the Christian religion. It is the first element of all lawful government upon earth." The Declaration of Independence was "the ark of your covenant." All men were born equal, with natural rights, entitled to a government based on the consent of the governed, grounded in the rule of law. It called out to present-day America for emancipation. The Founders, including Washington and Jefferson, Adams declared, had all been abolitionists, "in the most extensive sense of the term."[71]

Adams gloried in the speech's fame, which he helped to promote by providing the publisher of "Jubilee" with an extensive list of notables to whom the printed version should be mailed. But close readers of the text noted that while the Jubilee speech was a call for emancipation, it was also a ringing endorsement of the rule of law and the rights of property. If both the dream of the Declaration and the preservation of the Union were to be achieved, abolition could occur only with the acquiescence of the South. But Adams had the sense that he was riding the wind: "the conflict between the principle of liberty and the fact of slavery is coming gradually to an issue; . . . the conflict will be terrible, and the progress of improvement perhaps retrograde before its final progress to consummation."[72]

From New York Adams moved on to Quincy for his annual vacation from the rigors of the gag rule and the Texas debates. Both Louisa and Charles chastised him for continuing to neglect the biography of his father. "Let me implore you to commune with your own heart and do justice to yourself as well as to them [John Quincy's parents] and to redeem the past in exertion for the future," Louisa wrote.

The biography, she declared, was "too sacred to be trifled with under any pretensions whatever."[73] Adams dutifully set aside an hour a day to work on the project, but he was soon distracted by correspondence with the British actor James H. Hackett on the merits of *Hamlet*. "I think upon the tragedy of Hamlet as the masterpiece of the drama—the masterpiece of Shakespeare—I had almost said the masterpiece of the human mind," Adams exulted. The Bard's protagonist was John Quincy's idea of the perfect man—educated, sensitive, perceptive, devout, full of filial piety, the perfect blend of "intelligence and sensibility." The command of his murdered father to take revenge on Claudius, Hamlet's uncle, who not only killed his father, the king, but married his mother, sets the stage for the perfect tragedy—the story of a good man led to murder and mayhem by a universal virtue: filial piety. As Hamlet plots revenge for his slain father, he grossly mismanages his love affair with Ophelia. He searches for meaning in the world, for justification, but is doomed to disappointment and disillusionment.[74] Of course, John Quincy saw himself in Hamlet—educated, rational, yet full of sensibility. He had spent much of the first half of his life taking vengeance on his father's enemies, seeking justice for a slain reputation. The second half was the tale of a virtuous man—himself—having inadvertently done a great evil—promoting and sustaining slavery in the process of building an empire of liberty. He identified completely with Shakespeare's fallen angel and thought the play the perfect cautionary tale for his country. Hamlet's story was in a sense a refutation of Whiggery, the notion that human society was evolving into an ever-higher order of civilization. Despite his paean to the Declaration and to the Founding Fathers in the Jubilee speech, Adams was becoming profoundly disillusioned with the republic he had done so much to nurture. The impending presidential election of 1840 featured two prominent military men—Winfield Scott and William Henry Harrison. "[T]he direct and infallible path to the presidency is military service coupled with demagogue policy," Adams observed bitterly in his diary.[75]

Whatever the case, Adams was thrilled by the critical acclaim that followed in the wake of the publication of his correspondence with Hackett. "This extension of my fame is more tickling to my vanity than it was to be elected President of the United States." And then, always in character: "I pray God to forgive me for it, and to preserve me from falling in my last days into the dotage of self-adulation."[76]

Death, it seemed, was never far from the Adams family's doorstep, perhaps no closer than for any other in that day and time, but no less agonizing. John Quincy and Louisa had come to dote on their granddaughters, Georgianna Francis (Fanny) and Mary Louisa. Louisa was particularly fond of Fanny, a lovely and vivacious eight-year-old. The child had suffered from poor health since her birth, and in the summer of 1839, she came down with an unidentifiable malady that grew increasingly worse. By November she was in crisis. "I have long been afflicted with an apprehension that this poor child was destined to a short life," John Quincy recorded in his diary. "I have watched the symptoms of her disease with a trembling heart and with sinking hope."[77] On November 4, Fanny's doctors treated her with stramonium, a narcotic derived from a poisonous weed usually used in the treatment of bronchial conditions. It was no use. The child expired shortly thereafter. "This poor little one has no memory to leave behind her," Charles lamented, "but a pleasing one to her friends as she was lovely in her youth and innocence and simplicity beyond most children of her age."[78] When Mary Louisa began displaying some of the same symptoms, the family braced itself for yet another tragedy. But she recovered and lived to adulthood, during which she married and bore three children.

THE TWENTY-SIXTH CONGRESS OPENED in chaos in December 1839. At the beginning of each new session, the clerk from the previous session presided while the chamber set about electing a Speaker and a new clerk. The problem was that there were two competing delegations from New Jersey, both demanding to be seated. It was the custom for the clerk to call the roll state by state. When the sitting clerk reached New Jersey, he refused to proceed any further and would not entertain motions from the floor to resolve the imbroglio; shouts from members demanding to be heard were ignored. This continued for three days; on the fourth, the congressman from Massachusetts spoke. "I rise to interrupt the Chair [clerk]," he declared. "[H]ear him, hear him!" various members shouted. "Hear John Quincy Adams!" "It was not my intention," Adams said, "to take part in these extraordinary proceedings. But what a spectacle we here present! We degrade and disgrace ourselves . . . we do not, and cannot organize; and why? Because the Clerk of the House, the mere Clerk, whom we created, whom we employ . . . usurps the throne and sets us, the representatives, the viceregents of the whole American people at defiance, and holds us in contempt!" This was not the time nor the place to debate the merits to the two contending New Jersey delegations, he declared. "That should occur following the organization of the House." A member interrupted to say that the clerk had declared he would rather resign than call the name of New Jersey. "Well, let him resign," declared Adams; he thereupon submitted a motion requiring the pretentious official to call the roll, but the man refused to accept it. "Several voices in unison: Who will put the question?" Adams: "I will put the question myself!" At this point, Richard Barnwell Rhett of South Carolina leapt up on one of the desks and exclaimed, "I move that the Honorable John Quincy Adams take the chair of the Speaker of this House and officiate as presiding officer 'til the

House be organized by the election of its constitutional officers. As many as are agreed to this will say aye; those—" Before he could finish, there was a resounding, unanimous shout of approval. Whereupon Lewis Williams of North Carolina and Rhett escorted John Quincy to the dais. None other than Henry Wise would declare, "Sir, I regard it as the proudest hour of your life. If and when you shall be gathered to your fathers . . . I would inscribe upon your tomb this sentence, 'I will put the question myself.'"[79]

37

The *Amistad* Affair

W HILE HE WAS IN Quincy tending his garden during the late summer of 1839, Adams read an indignant letter in Joshua Leavitt's *Emancipator* from William Jay, son of John Jay, the first chief justice and one of John Quincy's early role models. The younger Jay was on the cutting edge of the evangelical reform movement spawned by the Second Great Awakening. He was a relentless advocate for Sunday schools and Bible societies, an anti-duelist, a temperance supporter, and, of course, an abolitionist. Jay reported that in the spring of 1839, an American cutter operating off the coast of Connecticut had come upon the *Amistad*, a Spanish-owned slave ship that had been forcibly taken over by its Black cargo. In violation of the Anglo-Spanish Treaties of 1817 and 1835, which had outlawed international traffic in human beings, the Van Buren administration was plotting to bypass the American judicial system and return the slaves to their Spanish owners. Both the United States and Great Britain had branded trade in slaves as piracy and prohibited their citizens from engaging in it upon penalty of death, Jay pointed out. The Africans were free men and entitled to treatment as such by the American government. Adams wrote Jay a sympathetic note. No grand jury of free men, he hoped, could be found to indict the Africans for mutinying against the pirates who had illegally abducted them from their homeland and sold them into slavery.[1] Adams could not foresee that he would become a principal actor in the affair of the *Amistad*, one of the most dramatic and significant court cases of the antebellum period.

Early in 1839, some two hundred Mende tribesmen living in Sierra Leone had been captured by African slave traders. They were taken to Lomboko, south of Freetown, and imprisoned in barracoons (holding pens) behind the walls of a well-guarded stockade. A Portuguese slave trader named Don Pedro Blanco subsequently sold all the captives to Don Pedro Martinez and Company of Havana.

The Africans were stowed in the stifling hold of the *Tecora*, a Portuguese slaver, to endure the infamous Middle Passage. The survivors landed at Havana and were immediately put on the auction block. José Ruiz, a Cuban plantation owner, purchased forty-nine of the captives for four hundred fifty dollars each. If he could smuggle them into the United States, he could sell them for twice that; if not, they could be employed at his plantation at Puerto Principe, Cuba.[2] One of his associates, Pedro Montes, bought three more, including two little girls. The two men bribed local Spanish officials at the rate of fifteen dollars a head to look the other way and subsequently to issue documents declaring the captives ladinos—a term used to describe individuals who had been in country long enough to learn the Spanish language and Cuban customs. It was a sham, of course. The Africans could speak not a word of Spanish, and all were obviously too young to have been born before the signing of the Anglo-Spanish Treaty of 1835. They were clearly *bozales*, meaning new to the country and thus illegally enslaved.

Ruiz and Montes persuaded Captain Ramón Ferrer, of the schooner *Amistad*, to take them and their slaves aboard and transport them to Puerto Principe, some three hundred miles distant from Havana. Because the ship was delayed by strong headwinds, the captain cut the Africans' already meager rations in half. Further exacerbating the captives' discontent and anxiety was a conversation they had with the ship's cook, Celestino, as to what the future held for them when they landed. The white men will eat you, he insisted. On the third night out, led by one of their own, Cinque, the Africans broke their shackles and snuck into the cargo holds, where they found several heavy machetes used for sugarcane cutting. When dawn broke, the captives stormed the main deck. They killed Ferrer and the cook but not until after a struggle during which four surviving crewmen escaped in a longboat. Ruiz and Montes were spared when the latter, a former ship's captain, promised to sail the *Amistad* back to Sierra Leone.

By day the *Amistad* headed east, but by night while the Africans could not see the sun, Montes sailed it north and west, keeping just out of sight of the U.S. coastline. Weeks passed, food and fresh water threatened to give out, and the ship's sails began to rot. Outside New York Harbor, the *Amistad* encountered the *Blossom*, an American merchantman, which provided the former slaver with some food and water. The *Blossom* subsequently reported to the port authority the fantastical sight it had come across—a barnacle-covered, rotting schooner full of armed Africans. The collector of customs dispatched a revenue cutter to investigate; word spread up and down the Eastern Seaboard to be on the lookout for the *Amistad*. By this point Cinque realized that Montes had deceived him, but there was no one else capable of navigating the ship. He ordered the Spaniard to steer close enough to shore to allow a ship's boat to land and search for provisions.

Montes complied, and several of the Africans were able to go ashore near Culloden Point on Long Island and purchase food and water. They returned only to discover that the U.S.S. *Washington,* a survey brig commanded by Lieutenant Commander Thomas R. Gedney and Lieutenant Richard W. Meade, had arrived on the scene. Gedney and his men seized the ship and brought it into the nearest port, New London, Connecticut.[3]

American authorities were understandably in a quandary as how to proceed. The situation was unique. Federal district court judge Andrew T. Judson boarded the *Washington* and convened a hearing to decide the fate of the Africans and the *Amistad.* Ruiz and Montes described the mutiny and "murder" of the captain and the cook. According to the ship's papers, the Blacks on board the *Amistad* were slaves, all certified by Cuban authorities as having lived in Cuba since 1820. At the request of the district attorney, William Holabird, Judson charged Cinque and his compatriots with piracy and murder and ordered them bound over until further guidance could be gained from the U.S. circuit court. At the same time, Gedney and Meade filed suit in admiralty court declaring that the *Amistad* and its human cargo were prizes of war (pirates then being considered permanent enemy combatants), thus entitling them to prize money. Meanwhile, the prisoners were transported to the county jail in New Haven. In a subsequent proceeding, Supreme Court Justice Smith Thompson, acting as U.S. circuit court judge, upheld the charges against the Africans and ordered them tried in Judson's court in November.

Capture of the *Amistad* Africans made headlines up and down the Atlantic Seaboard. The *New London Gazette* took a particular interest in Cinque, a young man who was approximately twenty-six, "well built and active . . . a match for any two men on board the schooner . . . [possessing] a composure characteristic of true courage and nothing to mark him as a malicious man. . . . He expects to be executed but nevertheless manifests a *sang froid* worthy of a stoic."[4] Meanwhile, Ruiz and Montes had set out first for New York to plead their case before the Spanish consul there and then to Washington to appeal to the Spanish minister, Ángel Calderón de la Barca. The two slave traders had little trouble bringing Calderón de la Barca around to their side. The minister dispatched to Secretary of State John Forsyth a note demanding that as shipwrecked property as defined in Pinckney's Treaty, the vessel and its Africans must be restored to their true owners. Forsyth, a Georgia slave owner, was sympathetic but told Calderón de la Barca that the matter had been introduced into the judicial system of United States and would be hard to extract.

When news of the *Amistad*'s capture reached New York City, Lewis Tappan convened a meeting of prominent abolitionists, who voted to create a committee of three—Tappan to be chair—to raise funds and mount a legal defense for Cinque and his compatriots. The other two members were Joshua Leavitt, a graduate of the Yale Divinity School and editor of the *Emancipator*, and Simeon S. Jocelyn, a fellow Yale graduate and former pastor of a Black church. All three were friends of John Quincy Adams. Tappan immediately filed suit against Montes and Ruiz, charging them with assault and battery and false imprisonment. They were duly arrested and imprisoned. Ruiz made bail but Montes remained in jail under a three-hundred-dollar bond.[5]

A few days following their initial arraignment, the *Amistad* Africans had been transported by canal boat to Farmington, Connecticut, and from thence by stage to Hartford, where they were jailed while awaiting trial. During their first three days in the Hartford lockup, more than three thousand curiosity seekers paid twelve and a half cents each to view the exotic prisoners. Crowd favorites were Cinque and Konoma, whom the papers nicknamed "the Cannibal" for his sharply filed teeth. His intention, Konoma managed to convey to reporters, was to make himself more attractive to Mende women rather than to consume human flesh. Visitors to the New Haven jail included a Yale Divinity School faculty member who set about teaching the Africans to read and write English; his students led them in prayer each morning. In New York, wax effigies of the mutineers appeared in Peale's Museum. In New Haven an artist mounted a 135-foot painting depicting the uprising on the *Amistad*. In New York's Bowery Theater, a production entitled *The Black Schooner* proved a great success.[6]

The legal team assembled by the Tappan committee—which was headed by Roger Sherman Baldwin of New Haven, grandson of the Founding Father Roger Sherman—visited their clients at the Hartford jail. Communication proved an insurmountable problem until Joshua Gibbs, one of its members, managed to locate two men who knew the Mende dialect: James Covey and Charles Pratt, crewmen aboard the British warship *Buzzard*. Both were former slaves. The trial date was set for November 19, 1839, in New Haven.[7]

The trial took place in circuit court with Judge Judson presiding. Attorneys for the defense invoked habeas corpus for the three children, who were being held as witnesses to the uprising, and Thompson granted it. Two Connecticut attorneys appeared for the Spanish Crown. District Attorney Holabird put the question squarely to the court. Were the *Amistad* Africans slaves, and if so, should they be delivered up to Spanish authorities as provided under the treaty of 1795? Or were they free men and women unlawfully seized and taken to Cuba, where they had been illegally sold? If the former, they should be turned over at once to the new

Spanish minister, the Chevalier Pedro Alcántara de Argáiz. If the latter, they should be remanded to the president of the United States, who would provide for their safe return to Africa.

Like Secretary of State Forsyth, President Van Buren had initially hoped that the *Amistad* mutineers could be quietly turned over to Spanish authorities and through them returned to their "rightful" owners. But his hands were tied. Alcántara de Argáiz asked him why he could not simply issue a decree. Because we are a republic and not a monarchy, Van Buren replied. "[T]he judiciary is, by the organic law of the land, a portion, though an independent one, of that government."[8] But anxious to please his slaveholding political partners during the run-up to the 1840 presidential election, the president ordered the U.S.S. *Grampus* to New Haven to be ready to whisk Cinque and company away to Havana if the verdict went against them. Somehow Lewis Tappan gained access to Van Buren's orders and had them published in the newspapers. The abolitionists countered the president by hiring their own ship to stand by to transport the Africans back to Sierra Leone if the court decided in their favor.

When the judicial proceedings reconvened, Judge Smith ruled that the Circuit Court had no jurisdiction, whereupon his associate, Judge Judson, convened the district court. Van Buren and the Spanish were hopeful; Judson had an established track record as a racist. Both sides presented their arguments. The most telling testimony came from Dr. Richard R. Madden, a British scholar and a consultant to the Foreign Office who was an expert on the Cuban slave trade. Each year between twenty thousand and twenty-five thousand Africans were illegally imported into Cuba and sold, their owners bribing the local authorities to declare the Blacks to be either ladinos or Creoles—native-born Cubans. Madden testified that the *Amistad* mutineers were clearly *bozales*—they knew not a word of Spanish—who had been unlawfully abducted and illegally sold into slavery.[9] Judson stunned both the prosecution and the defense when he ruled that the Africans had been born free, kidnapped, and illegally sold into slavery. In mutinying against their captors—mere pirates—they had been perfectly within their rights. They were to be turned over to the executive, which was to provide safe passage back to Sierra Leone. Circuit judge Thompson upheld Judson's decision, but the Justice Department subsequently appealed to the Supreme Court, which agreed to hear oral arguments when it next convened in Washington in early 1841.

Adams had followed the *Amistad* case with great interest. Ellis Gray Loring, a prominent Massachusetts lawyer and antislavery activist, provided him with details of the proceedings. The New Englander hit the books: *Blackstone, Bacon's Abridgement, Wheeler's Law of Slavery*, notes on the *Antelope* case, and others.[10] Loring put all the principal questions to him. Could Van Buren turn the Africans over to the Spanish under Spanish laws not recognized within the jurisdiction of American courts? Were the Africans slaves or free men? Were the Anglo-American slave trade agreements applicable in this case? "The time has not come," Adams told himself following an extended discussion with Loring, "when it would be proper for me to give an opinion for publication. Prudence would forbid my giving an opinion upon it at any time; and if I ever do, it must be with great consideration and self-control."[11] As usual, John Quincy failed to heed his own advice. When Congress reconvened, he introduced a resolution in the House protesting the continued imprisonment of the *Amistad* Africans. When rumors spread that the Van Buren administration was withholding vital documents bearing on the case, the Speaker of the House named a five-man committee, with Congressman Adams as its chair, to investigate.[12]

Meanwhile, Tappan and his fellow abolitionists searched for a national figure who would lend an aura of gravitas to the defense team. Still angry with John Quincy over his refusal to support abolition of the slave trade and/or slavery in the District of Columbia, they turned first to Daniel Webster, who begged off, and then the prominent Boston attorney Rufus Choate, who also declined, claiming ill health. In truth neither wanted to be linked to the abolitionist cause. The defense team then approached Adams, who hesitated, citing his age (seventy-three), his absence from the courtroom for more than thirty years, and his congressional duties. "With a shaking hand, a darkened eye, a drowsy brain, and with all my faculties dropping from me one by one and the teeth . . . dropping from my head," he was genuinely intimidated.[13] But once again plagued by his conscience and tempted by fame, he agreed to participate in defense of the *Amistad*s.[14] Adams first offered to provide advice and assistance to Roger Baldwin. But we want you to do more than that, Loring and Tappan declared; we want you to argue the case. "It is a case of life and death for these unfortunate men," they declared. At last Adams gave in. That evening he prayed: "I implore the mercy of God so to control my temper, to enlighten my soul, and to give me utterance, that I may prove myself in every respect equal to the task."[15]

John Quincy's family was once again aghast at what they considered his impetuousness and thirst for glory. Charles had just been elected as a Whig to the Massachusetts House of Representatives. "This will be productive of results unpleasant to myself," he observed in his diary, "for it must greatly embarrass the political party with which I have undertaken to act."[16] The congressman tried to explain to his son that as a republican and a defender of the rule of law, he had no choice. He recalled to Charles that when he had been in London in 1783, he had visited the British Museum and viewed the Magna Carta, a signer of which was one Saer de Quincy, an Adams ancestor. At the very heart of that document was the concept of habeas corpus, "to give up the body"—that is, to release jailed persons who had not been legally and reasonably charged with a crime.[17]

In November 1840, Adams departed Boston for New Haven to confer with Baldwin and visit the incarcerated Africans. The trip was by train via Springfield and it consumed a mere two and a half hours. Baldwin called on John Quincy, who was staying at the Tontine Hotel. They discussed a motion to the court to dismiss without oral arguments, and then proceeded to the jail. "There are thirty-six men confined all in one chamber perhaps thirty feet long by twenty wide sleeping in eighteen crib beds in two rows, two deep on both sides, the length of the chamber," Adams recorded in his diary. The men were short, some no taller than John Quincy himself. They ranged in color from black to "almost mulatto bright . . . Cinque and Grabow, the two chief conspirators, have very remarkable countenances." Three of the captives read from the New Testament "very indifferently."[18]

After Adams reached Washington, he received letters from two of the incarcerated Africans, Ka-le and Kinna. "Dear Friend Mr. Adams," began Ka-le, "I want to write a letter to you because you love Mendi people and you talk to the Great Court." Please tell the judges that Ruiz and Montes are liars. The *Amistad* prisoners were born in Sierra Leone, not Cuba. None of them knew a word of Spanish. They had killed the cook because he had told the Africans that white men would eat them. "[T]ell American people to make us free," Kinna wrote. "We want to go home to Mendi and see our fathers and mothers, and brothers and sisters." Tappan would swear that the two Africans, and they alone, had written the letters. The missives were more likely dictated by one of the abolitionists. "Have the goodness to inform Ka-le and Kinna," John Quincy wrote their jailers, ". . . that I think of them, hope for them, and pray for them, night and day."[19]

For a variety of reasons, the *Amistad* hearing was postponed until February 22, 1841. Adams thought it a good omen. It was the anniversary of both George Washington's birthday and the signing of the Transcontinental Treaty. The Supreme Court was then comprised of Chief Justice Roger Taney, Philip Barbour, James Moore Wayne, John Catron, John McKinley, Henry Baldwin, John McLean (Adams's treacherous treasury secretary), Smith Thompson (the New Haven circuit judge), and Joseph Story. Only McKinley, Smith, and Story were not Jackson appointees. Taney of Maryland, former attorney general and secretary of the treasury under Jackson, was a slaveholder who would eventually emancipate his human chattel. Like Adams, Taney was a former Federalist who had broken with the party over the War of 1812. Adams had thought him a Jacksonian lackey when he had been part of the administration, but as chief justice, he had proven himself evenhanded and judicious. Baldwin was a Connecticut native, a devout unionist who wanted to push the slavery issue down the road. Moore was a Georgia slaveholder who had studied law at the College of New Jersey (now Princeton University). Story was a Harvard graduate and a noted legal scholar. His *Commentaries on the Constitution of the United States* was the gold standard for American legal scholars. Adams respected Story the most of all the Supreme Court justices.

The chamber of the high court was a cramped, pie-shaped affair located beneath the Senate. The justices sat on a raised podium and overlooked a railing from which contending attorneys could address them. Along the sides, galleries rose from floor to ceiling, and a limited number of spectators could view the proceedings.

There had been a presidential election in 1840; the Whig candidate William Henry Harrison had handily defeated Martin Van Buren. Upon his arrival in Washington, Adams had paid a visit to Henry Gilpin, the new attorney general, and appealed to him to drop the case against the *Amistad* mutineers. Gilpin refused to intervene. John Quincy later observed that he did not seem to understand the complexities of the case. And indeed, Gilpin's opening presentation to the court was a mess. The Golden Rule should apply to international relations as well as to private intercourse, the attorney general declared. The United States should treat Spain as it would have Spain treat the United States. The *Amistad* Africans were property and should be restored to their rightful owners. Gilpin seemed unaware of the contradiction when he proceeded to indict Cinque and company as criminals and pirates.[20] Property could hardly commit crimes whether on land or sea.

It was then Adams's turn. He confessed a "great agitation of nerves" before rising to speak, but once he had begun, the butterflies disappeared. For four and a half hours, he harangued the court. Were the *Amistad* mutineers property under the laws of Spain? That was indeed the question. Given Spain's anti–slave trade treaty with Great Britain and Madrid's subsequent orders to enforce it, they were clearly not. Adams denounced the Van Buren and Harrison administrations for conspiring to make slaves out of free men. The justices seemed spellbound. "Extraordinary," wrote Judge Story. "Extraordinary for its power and its bitter sarcasm, and its dealing with topics far beyond the record and points of discussion."[21]

John Quincy was scheduled to finish his arguments the next day, but that evening Justice Philip Barbour died in his sleep. The hearing was delayed while the Virginia lawyer, politician, and slaveholder was buried. The court resumed its deliberations on March 1. By what right had Commander Gedney and Lieutenant Meade boarded, overpowered, and disarmed a group of free men on their way to their homeland? Adams asked. By what law had these officers of the United

States the right to imprison and transport the *Amistad* Africans from New York to Connecticut? What right had the circuit and district courts of Connecticut to indict and try the captives? "[O]ne of the grievous charges brought against George III was that he had made laws for sending men beyond [the] seas for trial."[22] Cinque and his fellows had been illegally abducted from their homeland, unlawfully sold into slavery, and illegally detained by U.S. authorities. They were Mende, residents of the sovereign state of Sierra Leone, which was subject to and a beneficiary of the law of nations, the aged statesman declared. Ruiz, Montes, and company were pirates who were subject to that same law of nations. "Say it was a Baltimore clipper fitted for the African slave trade and, having performed a voyage, had come back to our shores with fifty-four African victims on board and was thus brought into port . . . the captain would be seized, tried as a pirate, and hung."[23]

In his appeal to the court, Adams charged, the secretary of state had been acting as an agent of a foreign power in his effort to have the United States contravene its own laws, to contravene even the laws and treaty obligations of Spain itself! Lawyers for the Harrison administration had cited the case of the *Antelope*, which had been decided during John Quincy Adams's administration; they pointed out that the courts had ordered the slaves who had been seized by an American war vessel be returned to their owners. Adams pointed out that the seizure was in 1819 when the Spanish prohibition of the slave trade had applied only to territory above the equator (the *Antelope* had been taken off the cost of Brazil). By 1839 decrees of the Spanish government had outlawed the slave trade throughout the globe.

The court set March 9 for announcement of a verdict in the case of the *United States v. Cinque and Others, Africans*. Adams, who arrived early at the court's chambers, was on tenterhooks. The justices filed in and donned their robes. The clerk declared that Judge Story, the longest-serving justice, would present the opinion—a good sign, Adams thought.[24] "There does not seem to us to be any ground for doubt," Story declared, "that these Negros ought to be deemed free; and that the Spanish treaty interposes no obstacle to the just assertion of their rights."[25] The opinion reaffirmed the Connecticut district court's order to the executive to provide the means for the safe return of the Africans to Sierra Leone. "The captives are free!" John Quincy wrote jubilantly to Lewis Tappan. "Not unto us! Not unto us! but thanks, thanks in the name of humanity and justice to you [God]."[26]

Adams's role in the *Amistad* affair returned him to the good graces of all but the most hard-core abolitionists. "Some of us," wrote John Greenleaf Whittier, "may have at times done thee injustice in our regret and disappointment at thy expressed sentiments in regard to the District of Columbia, but I believe we now all appreciate thy motives, and while we regret that there should be any difference of opinion between us, we feel that thou are entitled to our warmest gratitude as abolitionists."[27] From Boston, Charles Francis sent his congratulations. His father proved most ungracious in victory. "The agony of soul that I suffered from the day that I pledged my fealty to argue the cause of the Africans before the Supreme Court," he wrote back, "till that when I heard Judge Story deliver the opinion . . . of the Court was chiefly occasioned by the reprobation of my own family . . . and their terror at the calamities which they anticipated they would bring upon *them*."[28]

When it became clear that the Harrison administration would not lift a finger to help the *Amistad* mutineers return to their homeland, Tappan and the other committee members arranged a fund-raising tour for Cinque and his fellows during which they displayed their newly acquired skills in writing and reading, particularly from the Bible. John Quincy received a quarto Bible dedicated to him with an inscription by Cinque, Kinna, and Ka-le. "Mr. Lewis Tappan has been extremely desirous of having this done [the presentation] by a public exhibiting and ceremony which I have speedily and inflexibly declined for a clear conviction of its impropriety [and] an invincible repugnance to exhibiting myself as a public . . . show."[29] In fact, the New Englander was ambivalent about what should have been done with the *Amistad*s. "I have not been without apprehension that you might have trouble with some of your 33 freemen when in full possession of their liberty," he wrote Tappan and company. "It is hardly to be expected that they will all be regular and orderly in their conduct or able or willing to support themselves honestly and reputably in this country." But if they, as they wished, were returned to "their barbarous and savage land," what was to prevent them from being sold back into slavery? Had not one of the young girls been "pawned by her own father for a debt"?[30] By November 1841 the abolitionists had raised enough money to buy a ship and provision it. On the twenty-fifth, the thirty-five surviving *Amistad*s, including the three children, sailed from New York aboard the *Gentleman* and reached Sierra Leone fifty days later.[31]

38

The Censure Fight

WHILE THE *AMISTAD* CASE played out, Adams continued his war on the gag rule. On January 28, 1840, the House adopted the most restrictive version yet. It declared that any and all petitions calling for the abolition of slavery or the slave trade in the District of Columbia, in the territories of the United States, or in the states where it existed should be laid on the table without debate. The motion called for making this version a standing rule of the House, eliminating the need to repass it every session. "The difference between the resolution of the four preceding sessions of Congress and the new rule of the House," John Quincy wrote in his diary, "is the difference between petty larceny and highway robbery."[1] "You seem to feel sore upon the vote adopting the gag rule excluding petitions," remarked Edward Stanly of North Carolina as he passed Adams's seat. "I do," replied the member from Plymouth, "but the mortification that I feel is not of mere defeat; it is the disgrace and degradation of my country, trampling in the dust the first principle of human liberty. This is the iron that enters into my soul."[2]

Whittier wrote Adams that the proposed standing rule was so extreme that it would ultimately turn all free men against both the gag rule and slavery. The New Englander wrote back saying that he doubted it, but Whittier was right. The standing gag rule was passed with just a majority of six votes, 114 to 108, with only twenty-six of the 128 free state congressmen voting aye. At the opening of the special session in the summer of 1841, Adams moved to rescind the gag rule; the House first supported him 112 to 104 but then on reconsideration reversed itself. The pendulum was swinging.

Adams rejoiced that the political coalition that Martin Van Buren had so meticulously put together seemed to be falling apart. "Mutual [con]gratulation [among Whigs] at the downfall of the Jackson–Van Buren Administration is the universal theme of conversation. One can scarcely imagine the degree of detestation in which they are both held."[3] The effects of the Panic of 1837 still lingered. Friends of the Bank of the United States had deserted ship. The "plain republicans" of the North were beginning to doubt that an alliance with the slave power was in their interests. And then there was the Second Seminole War.

In 1832 the United States had forced the Treaty of Payne's Landing on the Indians of Florida. They were given three years to move their families and possessions west of the Mississippi, where they were to be merged with the Creeks. Those affected included Choctaws, Creeks, Alabamas, Yamasees, and assimilated runaway slaves. As the end date for their departure approached, the Indians, collectively referred to as Seminoles, took up arms. Local militia joined with a contingent of regulars commanded by Generals Winfield Scott and Edmund P. Gaines and went on the attack. Their campaign immediately bogged down. By 1840 the seemingly never-ending struggle was a hot topic in Congress. Adams, whose nephew Thomas Boylston Adams Jr. would die in the conflict, led the way. "The wrong of the war is on our side," he declared. "It depresses the spirits and humiliates the soul to think that this war is now running into its fifth year, has cost thirty millions of dollars, has successively baffled all our chief military generals . . . and that our last resources now are bloodhounds and no quarter. Sixteen millions of Anglo-Saxons unable to subdue in five years by force and by fraud, by secret treachery, and by open war, sixteen hundred savage warriors!"[4] He proceeded to home in on the army's use of bloodhounds procured from Cuba, demanding a report from the secretary of war "showing the peculiar fitness of that class of warriors [the dogs] to be the associates of the gallant army of the United States, showing the nice discrimination of his scent between the blood of the freeman and the slave, between the blood of the armed warrior and that of women or children, between the blood of the black and the white."[5]

In 1841, the Speaker moved to appoint Adams chair of the House Committee on Indian Affairs. He declined. "The policy from Washington to myself . . . had been justice and kindness to the Indian tribes—to civilize and protect them. With the Creeks and Cherokees it had been eminently successful." But then with Jackson overseeing, the slaveholding states led by Georgia had defrauded these worthies, confiscated their property, and shipped them off to the Western wilderness. "The Florida War is one of the fruits of this policy. . . . It is among the heinous sins of this nation for which I believe God will one day bring them to judgment. I refuse, he declared in his diary, to have anything to do with "this sickening mass of putrefaction."[6]

* * *

CONGRESSIONAL LIFE HAD BECOME brutal by the early 1840s. The sessions seemed to drag on forever. "I walked home and found my family at dinner," John Quincy lamented to his diary. "From my breakfast yesterday morning 'til one this afternoon, twenty-eight hours, I had fasted. My carriage had been waiting for me four or five hours last evening till Thomas, the coachman, could hold out no longer and came home sick and faint." Congressmen Jesse Bynum and Rice Garland engaged in fisticuffs on the floor of the House. A terrific storm broke one of the arms off the statue of Justice that sat atop the pediment fronting the entrance to the House. "Ominous," commented Congressman Adams.[7] In May 1841, Adams tripped over newly installed carpeting, fell hard, and dislocated his right shoulder. "Several of the members who remained in the House came immediately to my assistance and attempted to set the bone without success. I was taken to Mr. Monroe's lodgings where in about half an hour the bone was set by Drs. Thomas and May, Jr."[8] May asked Adams if he had ever dislocated that shoulder before. He replied that he seemed to recall his mother telling him that when he was two or three, he had wandered into the street and a nursery maid had jerked him out of danger displacing his shoulder. Whatever the case, the old man observed, he had had trouble with his right arm and hand all his life.[9] Not enough, though, to prevent the production of a seven-thousand-page diary and thousands more letters, reports, and broadsides.

BACK IN NEW ENGLAND for the summer break, the former president and his son embarked on a nineteen-day tour of Nova Scotia and New Brunswick. The pair journeyed to Halifax aboard one of the new transatlantic steamships, which, after depositing them in Canada, set out for Liverpool. John Quincy was wined and dined, acclaimed as one of the great men of his day. Charles and he departed Canada by stagecoach and made several stops in Maine and Vermont. In Bangor he was a guest at a dinner and ball given in his honor. Urged on by the guests, of whom there were several hundred, Adams was persuaded to make a few remarks. He stood on a sofa and spoke for ninety minutes.[10]

While in Quincy, Congressman Adams decided to take on the transcendentalists publicly. He viewed the ideas espoused by Emerson and his fellow believers as existential threats to the notion of a virtuous republic and to the American experiment. If God was not the God of the Old Testament and his son the Christ of the New Testament, if Jesus's call on the powerful and privileged to use government for the benefit of all, if morality and politics were separated, there could be naught but autocracy or chaos. To make his case, Adams chose to challenge the social and theological writings of the transcendentalist Orestes Augustus Brownson. Brownson was a Presbyterian-cum-Unitarian. He had founded his own church and published *New Views of Christianity, Society, and the Church* in 1836. In his book, the cleric railed against inequalities of wealth and status and espoused the communitarian views of Robert Dale Owen and Fanny Wright. Brownson and the "Marat democrats" had to be confronted, Adams announced in his diary.[11] He began work on his address, which was to be entitled "Faith," but was plagued with self-doubt. "Can I take it [the subject] up without encroaching upon the province of the pulpit? Can I touch it without getting entangled in the theological snarl between salvation by faith and by works? Can I trace and unfold to demonstrate the indissoluble union between religious and moral faith?"[12] Judging from the warm reception of "Faith," he was successful. The speech, which ran to seventy minutes and was later published in pamphlet form, was a reiteration of the Adams family's worldview of a transcendent, loving, merciful God whose son through the Sermon on the Mount had called human beings to a life of charity and self-sacrifice, and whose followers had conceived the ideal Christian form of government, a virtuous republic dedicated to the welfare, moral and material, of its constituents. John Quincy delivered the lecture to audiences in Quincy and Boston and then, on his way back to Washington, in Hartford and New York, where an audience of four thousand gathered to listen.[13] "The outward marks of respect which I have received on the delivery of these lectures for the last five weeks are too [effusive] and more than my honest nature can endure," Adams wrote in his diary. "It augurs some deep humiliation awaiting me to teach me in the last state of my existence upon earth what I am."[14]

As JOHN QUINCY AND Louisa approached Washington, the member from Plymouth's mood grew foul. The Massachusetts legislature had again refused to elect him to the Senate to replace John Davis, who had resigned at the close of the Twenty-Sixth Congress. It would pass him over again when Daniel Webster was named secretary of state in President-elect Harrison's cabinet. Adams did not quite know what to expect from the new administration. He was delighted that the Jackson–Van Buren "edifice has crumbled into ruin by the mere force of gravitation and the wretchedness of their cement." The Whigs had captured majorities in both houses of Congress. Adams detested Webster personally but regarded him as knowledgeable and probably capable when it came to foreign affairs. However, Harrison had chosen as his running mate John Tyler of Virginia, a slaveholder and a nullifier.

Although by custom all ex-presidents were invited to join the inaugural procession to the Capitol, Adams remained at home. Joshua Leavitt and he were conferring on the *Amistad* case in Adams's study on the second floor of the F Street house. From there they could observe the parade. "General Harrison was on a mean-looking white horse in the center of seven others in a plain frock-coat," John Quincy subsequently wrote snidely in his diary.[15] The hero of Tippecanoe, hatless and coatless in subfreezing temperatures, addressed the throng from the East Portico of the Capitol. His speech was full of platitudes, and he promised not to interfere with slavery in the states and territories where it existed, or with the slave trade in the District of Columbia. Adams, who had once declared that "the greatest beggar and the most troublesome of all the office seekers during my administration was General Harrison," certainly had no reason to expect favors from the new chief executive.[16] But then, a week after taking the oath of office, President Harrison appeared unexpectedly on the Adamses' doorstep. While John Quincy and Louisa were being summoned from upstairs, the hero of Tippecanoe chatted amiably with twelve-year-old Mary Louisa. The congressman and his wife greeted Harrison warmly. When Adams leaned in to ask if they could have a private conversation sometime in the near future, the president replied, "Come when you please as often as you please, or drop me a line, for I shall at any time be happy to take your advice and counsel as that of a brother."[17]

For the sixty-eight-year-old Harrison, the inauguration proved fatal. He had contracted a severe cold as a result of his lengthy address delivered in the open air. "The condition of the President's health is alarming," John Quincy noted in his diary on April 2. "He was seized last Saturday with a severe chill, and the next day with what his physicians called a bilious pleurisy. Since that time he has been very ill, with symptoms varying from day to day, and almost hour to hour."[18] Shortly after midnight on April 4, 1841, the ninth president expired. On the sixteenth, Adams called at the White House, despite the fact that he objected to John Tyler calling himself "President of the United States, and not Vice-President acting as President. . . . He received me very kindly and apologized for not having visited me without waiting for this call."[19] Adams had no illusions concerning Tyler, however. The slave power was back in control and with it the ongoing Jefferson–Jackson assault on the powers of the executive branch. "[T]he improvement of the condition of man will form no part of his policy, and the improvement of his country will be an object of his most inveterate and inflexible opposition."[20]

On the morning of February 18, John Quincy's carriage delivered him to the Capitol. As the coach was leaving the yard, a contingent of soldiers gave a demonstration of Colt's new repeating rifle; the shots caused the horses to bolt, overturning and wrecking the chaise. Adams's coachman, Jeremy Leary, a longtime employee and favorite of the family, was thrown from the box and grievously injured. "He was taken into one of the lower rooms of the Capitol, where as soon as I heard of the disaster, I found him in excruciating torture." The wounded man asked for a priest; one was summoned, and he administered the last rites. Leary died the next day. "The arrangements had been made for the funeral of my poor, humble, but excellent friend Jeremy Leary at three o'clock this afternoon. I walked to the Capitol this morning with a spirit humbled to the dust with a heart melted in sorrow."[21]

During the summer and fall of 1841, Adams's ever-present martyr complex was particularly evident. Despite decreasing support for the gag rule and the addition to Congress of antislavery figures like Congressman Joshua Giddings of Ohio, Adams continued to think of himself as a solitary warrior fighting the good fight but besieged on all sides. In March, Adams had learned that Nicholas Trist, the U.S. consul in Havana, had not only been turning a blind eye to the illegal importation of slaves into the United States but had been aiding and assisting it. The former president demanded an investigation, but the Tyler administration ignored him. The struggle to abolish the slave trade, much less the institution, seemed hopeless. "[N]o one but a spirit unconquerable by man, woman, or fiend can undertake it but with the heart of martyrdom. The world, the flesh, and all the devils in hell are arrayed against any man who now in this North American Union shall dare to join the standard of Almighty God to put down the African slave-trade."[22] Adams, of course, believed himself possessed of "a spirit unconquerable."

When slave state congressmen brought up the *Antelope* case in the midst of the *Amistad* controversy, the member from Plymouth rose to smite the slave power. "I then took my turn for an hour, and arraigned before the committee, the nation, and the world, the principles avowed by Henry A. Wise, and his three-colored standard, of overseer, black, [and] dueling, blood-red, and dirty, cadaverous, nullification, white," he recorded in his diary.[23] Adams had a knack for getting under the Virginian's skin. "Wise began [his reply] in a tone, which I saw would break him down—loud—vociferous—declamatory—furibund—he raved about the hell-hound of abolition, and at me as the leader of the abolitionists throughout the Union, for a full hour till his voice had broken into childish treble . . . his tone suddenly fell, he became bewildered . . . his voice failed him, he became ghastly pale . . . sank into his chair and fainted." Wise recovered sufficiently, however, to continue his rant the following business day. "[H]e immediately bowed down over his desk till his head and chest became horizontal, his mouth pouring out all the time his words in a whisper. Abolition—abolition—abolition—was the unvarying cry."[24]

Back in Quincy for his annual vacation, John Quincy paid particular attention to Harvard, dining frequently with his cousin Josiah Quincy, the controversial president. He launched a fund-raising campaign for the construction of an observatory and a new library building designed to hold a hundred fifty thousand volumes. Harry Otis and his wife had him to dinner in October and urged him to return for Thanksgiving. The invitations "are tenders of reconciliation which I am bound to meet in the same spirit," he wrote in his diary.[25] Adams was reunited with members of his old Wednesday Evening Club, where the conversation focused on science and literature rather than on politics. Later that fall, Adams would publish a bit of doggerel entitled "The Wants of Man."

As the congressman prepared to return to Washington for the opening of the new session of Congress, he was afflicted with boils, which covered his bald head and his loins. "[T]he crown of my head is hideous to behold," he confided to his diary. Invitations to dinners and public events continued to pour in. The member from Plymouth could not restrain himself; he attended every one, wearing a white turban or a silk cap with a tassel. Charles reported to his mother that her husband's costumes were creating quite a stir. She wrote John Quincy wryly, "I wish you would do as other people do." But in truth she missed him. They had been separated too long; she expressed hope for his "speedy return to be scolded by your wife."[26]

Back in Washington, Adams girded his diseased loins for another skirmish in the war against the gag rule. In an effort to divert him, perhaps, the Speaker named him chair of the Foreign Affairs Committee. By this point, Anglo-American relations had once again reached a flash point. There was the ongoing Northeast boundary dispute. The map used to establish the boundary between Canada and the United States in the Treaty of 1783 had been flawed, resulting in rival claims by Maine and Nova Scotia to some 7,600,000 acres. In 1838–1839, militias from both sides had faced off on the banks of the Aroostook River, which ran through the middle of the disputed territory. Hostilities had narrowly been averted.

In 1837, one William L. Mackenzie had led an armed insurrection in southern Canada in an attempt to throw off the British yoke. The rebellion proved immensely popular on the American side of the border. Ever since the treaty of 1783 establishing American independence, there had been lust in the hearts of many Northerners for Canadian territory. The Panic of 1837 had thrown large numbers of lumberjacks, rivermen, artisans, and small farmers out of work. Some of them, lured by promises of anywhere from ten to three hundred twenty acres of Canadian land, rushed to enlist in the rebel cause. British regulars and militia had little trouble crushing the uprising, however, and Mackenzie and the remnant of his force were compelled to remove their headquarters to Buffalo, New York. The Canadian adventurer was far from finished, however.

With red-blooded Americans continuing to volunteer their services and their money, Mackenzie established an encampment on Navy Island on the Canadian side of the Niagara River. A small American steamer, the *Caroline*, ferried supplies and troops from Buffalo. On the night of December 29, 1837, a contingent of Canadian soldiers rowed across the river, boarded the *Caroline*, and overpowered its crew. They set the craft afire and cut it loose from its moorings. The *Caroline* sank just before plunging over Niagara Falls. The assault on an American vessel in American waters with the killing of at least one U.S. citizen set the border aflame. Broadsides depicting the burning steamer laden with shrieking souls plunging over the falls were widely distributed. Van Buren dispatched General Winfield Scott to the scene to appeal for calm, but there was none to be had. In May 1838, a group of patriotic Americans boarded and sank the *Sir Robert Peel*, a Canadian vessel plying its trade in the St. Lawrence River. War seemed but a matter of time. The apparent straw that broke the camel's back was the arrest in Buffalo in 1840 of one Alexander McLeod, a Canadian deputy sheriff suspected of participating in the *Caroline* affair. State prosecutors charged him with murder and arson, and a trial date was set. The British Foreign Office declared that McLeod was part of an authorized military expedition and threatened war if he was not released. The Van Buren administration wanted desperately to comply, but the U.S. Constitution gave the State of New York sole jurisdiction. The trial got underway in September 1841, just as Adams was taking his seat in the new Congress.

"All the newspapers have been full of reports of the progress of the trial which involves at once a question of peace and war with Great Britain and of civil war [New York versus the United States]," John Quincy noted in his diary. "This is one of the consequences naturally flowing from the Jeffersonian doctrine of nullification and of states' rights . . . the case of McLeod, and the burning of the *Caroline* is complicated with the convulsive condition of Canada . . . the sympathies and antipathies, always existing between the bordering populations of rival nations, and the reckless spirit of adventure, avarice, and ambition burning in the bosoms of multitudes, especially of young men having little or nothing to lose and, in imagination, everything to gain by war and confusion."[27] Adams was adamant in his support for Maine's boundary claims against Nova Scotia and equally insistent in his conviction that Deputy Sheriff McLeod ought to be freed.

On September 4, with the attention of the nation riveted on Utica, New York— the scene of McLeod's trial—the House was considering a resolution advising the Tyler administration to reject the most recent British demand for McLeod's unconditional release. You are playing with fire, Adams warned his colleagues. You are going to sacrifice an issue on which Great Britain is entirely wrong—the Maine–Nova Scotia boundary dispute—for an issue on which the United States was entirely in the wrong—trying McLeod for participating in the *Caroline* affair. Mackenzie and his American followers had been in violation of U.S. neutrality laws. The British had every right to seize and destroy the *Caroline*. "I say that in the judgment of all impartial men of other nations we shall be held as a nation responsible; that the *Caroline* . . . was in a state of war against Great Britain for the purposes of war, and the worst kind of war, to sustain an insurrection."[28] On more practical grounds, Adams declared, not only the right was on Britain's side but the might. "She has stationed there [along the border] in military array an army nearly double in number to the whole army of the United States . . . who at a signal from their commander could sweep through a thousand miles of your country with fire, and sword, and desolation."[29] Fortunately the jury in Utica deliberated less than an hour before voting to acquit McLeod. The Maine–Nova Scotia boundary dispute would be brought to an end by the Webster–Ashburton Treaty of 1842.

ON NEW YEAR'S DAY 1842, John Quincy and Louisa, as was their wont, held an open house. Among their visitors were Generals Winfield Scott and Edmund P. Gaines. Gaines "said to me that he came to see the only president of the United States that he ever saw," Adams recorded in his diary. "He said there had been other presidents of the United States [but] the rest had all been presidents not of the United States but of a party."[30] Next came the noted abolitionists Joshua Giddings, Joshua Leavitt of the *Emancipator*, and another man John Quincy did not recognize. "Is it Mr. Theodore D. Weld?" the former president asked.[31] It was. Giddings had invited the noted evangelist to come to Washington to serve as secretary and researcher for the newly formed Select Committee on Slavery, an abolitionist lobbying group.

Weld was the son and grandson of Congregationalist ministers. While a student at Hamilton College, situated near Oneida, New York, the young man had fallen under the spell of the great evangelist Charles Finney. Weld moved west to attend Oberlin College in Ohio, where he embraced abolitionism and women's rights. He then answered a call from the Tappan brothers to devote his life to the cause of emancipation. In 1839, Weld had published the monumental *Slavery as It Is*, which documented in excruciating detail the brutality of the institution. In 1838, he had famously married Angelina Grimké.

John Quincy and Louisa were immediately taken with Weld, a charming, unpretentious man with a will of iron. The abolitionist was equally impressed with the Adamses. "Found him and his wife living in a plain house," he wrote his wife, "plainly furnished and themselves plainly dressed—the old gentleman very plainly."[32] A week later Weld and several of his colleagues had dinner at the Adamses'. "It was a genuine abolition gathering and the old patriarch talked with as much energy and zeal as a Methodist at a camp meeting. Remarkable man!"[33] The only drawback for Adams the wine connoisseur was that his company was all teetotalers.

John Quincy's rapprochement with the abolitionists enabled him to enter the political fray refreshed and renewed. "More than sixty years of incessant active intercourse with the world," he noted in his diary, "has made political movement to me as much a necessary of life as atmospheric air."[34] The third week in January, he presented a petition from certain citizens of Georgia demanding that he be removed as chairman of the Committee on Foreign Affairs on the grounds that he was "possessed of a specie of [sympathetic] monomania on all subjects connected with people as dark as a Mexican" and therefore unfit to play a role in U.S.–Mexican relations. "It is a hoax!" exclaimed Richard Habersham of Georgia. I don't care if it is, Adams retorted. "I demand the right to be heard in my defense."[35] Sensing correctly that the New Englander was once again hatching a scheme to circumvent the gag rule, Southerners cried, "Order, order." The House tabled Adams's request for the privilege to defend himself, ninety-four to ninety-two. But he still had the floor when Congress reconvened the following day. John Quincy declared that he intended (after being heard in his own defense) to move that the petition be referred to the Committee on Foreign Affairs with instructions to elect another chairman if they thought proper.

The House then voted to reconsider the question of privilege, thus allowing Adams to continue holding the floor. He presented a petition calling for the recognition of Haiti and provoked a crescendo of denunciations from Southern members. Giddings, Slade, and Seth Gates of New York encircled the old man protectively while Wise, Waddy Thompson, and others stood nearby braying at him. Then came the coup de grâce. Turning to the Speaker, Adams declared, "I hold in my hand the memorial of Benjamin Emerson and forty-five other citizens of Haverhill in the state of Massachusetts praying Congress to adopt immediate measures for the peaceful dissolution of the Union of these States."[36] They no longer wanted to be made to sacrifice their interests to those of the slave power. George Washington Hopkins of Goochland County, Virginia, rose and asked the Speaker, "Is it in order to burn the petition in the presence of the House?" Then it was Henry Wise's turn: "Is it in order," he asked, "to move to censure any member presenting such a petition?" "Good," Adams exclaimed. Thomas Walker Gilmer of Albemarle County, Virginia, then offered a motion: "Resolved, that in presenting to the consideration of this House a petition for the dissolution of the Union, the member from Massachusetts has justly incurred the censure of this House." Bedlam ensued. When cries of protest and support died down, Adams resumed. "I hope this resolution will be received and debated," declared the former president, "and that I shall have the privilege of again addressing the House in my own defense."[37]

That evening the members of the Select Committee on Slavery called on Adams at his F Street residence, expressing their admiration and declaring their intention to stand by him during the ordeal to come. "The aged statesman listened attentively," Giddings subsequently wrote, "but for a time was unable to reply laboring under great apparent feeling. At length he stated that the voice of friendship was so unusual to his ears that he could not express his gratitude."[38] He then provided them with a list of books he would need to prepare his defense.

The leaders of the Whig party were furious with Adams. Like the Van Burenites before them, they depended on a tacit alliance between portions of the slaveholding South and various factions in the North to sustain the national majority they had only recently constructed. Led by Henry Wise, Southern Whigs gathered to plot their strategy while their Northern brethren looked on approvingly. Adams had burned his opponents during their previous attempt at censure when he had presented a petition purportedly from slaves. This time they were determined to proceed more carefully. The Whigs selected as their point man Thomas F. Marshall, just recently elected to Congress from Kentucky. A nephew of the great chief justice, Marshall had distinguished himself as a member of his state legislature, in which he had earned a reputation for thoughtfulness and judiciousness. When Congress resumed, the House galleries were packed with expectant spectators, journalists, and members of the diplomatic corps. Marshall rose to present a substitute resolution for the one offered by Gilmer the previous day:

> Whereas the Federal Constitution is a permanent form of government and a perpetual obligation until altered or amended in the mode pointed out in that instrument, and the members of this House deriving their political character and powers from the same, are sworn to support it . . . A proposition to the Representatives of the people to dissolve the organic law . . . is a high breach of privilege, a contempt offered to this House, . . . and . . . in its execution and its consequence, the destruction of our country and the crime of high treason . . . Resolved therefore, that the Hon. John Quincy Adams in presenting . . . a petition praying the dissolution of the Union has offered the deepest

indignity to the House . . . [He might] well be held to merit expulsion from the national councils, and the House deems it as an act of grace and mercy when they only inflict upon him their severest censure. . . .[39]

Adams got to his feet and asked the clerk of the House to read he first paragraph of the Declaration of Independence. He obeyed: "When in the course of human events . . ." Then he slowed, unsure as to how far he should go. "Read on! Read on!" exclaimed Adams. "Down to the right and the duty." The clerk: ". . . that whenever any form of government becomes destructive of these ends, it is the right of the people to alter or abolish it . . . and organizing its [a new government's] powers in such a form as to them shall seem most likely to effect their safety and happiness." It was not he who was trying to destroy the Union, John Quincy declared. It was the slave power that was waging war on free speech, the right to petition, and the hallowed principle of habeas corpus. Georgia was then trying to force slavery on Maine, Virginia, and New York by coercing them into returning runaway slaves, Adams pointed out. "If the right of habeas corpus and the right of trial by jury are to be taken away by this coalition of Southern slaveholders and Northern democracy, it is time for the Northern people to see if they can't shake it off; it is time to present such petitions as this. I can say it is not yet time to do this [dissolve the Union]. . . . I say that if the petition is referred and answered, it will satisfy the petitioners."[40]

At this point Henry Wise asked the Speaker if the Marshall resolution censuring Adams was open for debate. Yes, the chair declared. The Haverhill petition asking for the dissolution of the Union had apparently driven the Virginia hotspur near to distraction. The member from Massachusetts was nothing more than a British agent, he proclaimed. Had not Adams blocked the annexation of Texas to the Union, thus serving both the geopolitical interests of Great Britain and abolitionism in general? Wise would, he declared, fight to the death against the "British-abolitionist-dissolutionist" conspiracy. "The principle of slavery," he insisted, "is a leveling principle; it is friendly to equality. Break down slavery and you would with the same blow destroy the great democratic principle of equality among men."[41] Derisive laughter sounded from the galleries and portico of the House, but Wise continued undeterred. "The gentleman [Adams] is politically dead; dead as Burr—dead as Arnold. The people will look upon him with wonder, will shudder, and retire."[42]

Following Wise's rant, Theodore Weld called at F Street and offered his services as Adams prepared his defense. The old man gratefully accepted. The abolitionist noted that the former president seemed to have regained much of his vitality. Following a six-hour rehearsal of Adams's speech of rebuttal, Weld said,

"I am afraid you are tiring yourself out." "No, no, not at all. I am all ready for another heat." Adams continued at full voice accompanied by theatrical gestures. "Stop," cried Weld. "You will need all your strength for the next day," but Adams continued for another hour.[43]

John Quincy took the floor on January 27. Turning to face his accusers, he declared, "If they say they will try me, they must try me. If they say that they will punish me, they must punish me. If they say that in grace and mercy, they will spare me expulsion, I disdain and cast their mercy away." Let them expel me. "I defy them. I have constituents to go to who will have something to say if this House expels me. Nor will it be long before gentlemen will see me here again!" At this point William Cost Johnson of Maryland intervened: "I demand Mr. Speaker that you put him down. I demand that you shut the mouth of that old harlequin."[44] But Adams was allowed to continue. Wise had accused him of supporting assassins and murderers, referring to the *Amistad* and *Creole* mutinies. (In November 1841, 128 slaves abroad the American coastal trader *Creole* had seized the ship. They sailed it into the British West Indian port of Nassau, where they were awarded their freedom, slavery having been abolished throughout the British Empire in 1833.) It was the honorable member from Virginia who was the assassin and murderer, Adams declared. Had he not instigated the Cilley–Graves duel and urged it to its tragic conclusion. Wise had come fresh from the killing field into the House "with his hands and face dripping—when the blood spots were yet visible upon him. . . . It is very possible that I saved this blood-stained man from the censure of the House."[45]

With Wise spluttering with rage, Adams turned his guns on Marshall. Sir, Adams asked rhetorically, what is high treason? "The Constitution of the United States has defined high treason . . . and it was not left for the gentleman from Kentucky, nor his *puny mind*, to define that crime, which consists solely in levying war against the United States, or lending aid and comfort to their enemies. I . . . have presented a respectful petition from my constituents, I have done so in an orderly manner. . . . Were I the father of that young man . . . I would advise him to return to Kentucky and take his place in some law school and *commence* the study of that profession which he has so long disgraced."[46]

Theodore Weld was in the galleries and he subsequently described the scene to Angelina. One half of the slave state congressmen had massed in the vicinity of Adams's desk, menacing him while he spoke. "Old Nestor lifted his voice like a trumpet," Weld wrote, "'til slaveholding, slave trading, and slave breeding absolutely quailed and howled under his dissecting knife. . . . Lord Morpeth, the English abolitionist, was present and sat within a few feet of Mr. A., his fine, intelligent face beaming with delight as the old man breasted the storm and dealt his blows upon the head of the monster."[47]

With petitions condemning the attempt to censor Adams pouring in, and the former president delivering one rhetorical blow after another, the slave power and its allies had begun to believe that they had once again erred in trying to bring Adams to heel. The Whig leadership sensed that the "plain republicans" of the North were beginning to rally around Adams's banner. Gilmer offered to withdraw his resolution if Adams would withdraw his petition. "No! No! I cannot do that," declared the member from Massachusetts. "That proposition comes to the point and issue of this whole question—that is to say the total suppression of the right of petition."[48] On February 7, John Quincy informed the House that he would need another week to complete his defense, but if his colleagues would vote to table the resolution of censure, he would stand down. Thereupon, John Minor Botts, a Virginia Whig, so moved, and the House approved 106 to ninety-three. "I would rather die a thousand deaths than again to encounter that old man," Marshall subsequently moaned.[49] He would not have to; this would be Marshall's first and last session in Congress. Henry Wise would later refer to Adams as the "acutest, the astutest, the archest enemy of Southern slavery that ever existed."[50] Theodore Weld declared the censure vote to be the first significant defeat of the slave power in Congress since the founding of the republic. Adams understood that the battle was far from its climax, but he was nevertheless exultant going to bed that evening, as he recorded in his diary, with the strains of *Io Triumphe* ringing in his ears.

In truth it would be more than twenty years before civil war destroyed the "peculiar" institution, but opinion in the North was beginning to shift. On January 28, 1842, Faneuil Hall in Boston was the scene of a massive antislavery rally presided over by William Lloyd Garrison. This was the same man who only a few years earlier had had to flee for his life as a mob of "gentlemen" threatened to lynch him. The gathering passed a resolution thanking John Quincy Adams for his "bold, faithful, and indefatigable advocacy of the right of petition under circumstances of great difficulty and peril."[51]

JOHN TYLER HAD BEEN placed on the Whig ticket in 1840 to ensure that the slave power and the nullifiers would not bolt from the party. With Harrison's demise and Tyler's succession to the presidency, that branch of the party became ascendant. Tyler wanted to do nothing less than reestablish the old political alliance between the South and the West that had been the backbone of Jacksonism.

When Congress in 1842 passed a tariff measure not to his liking, Tyler vetoed it. In the House, Adams denounced the Virginian as a tyrant and a betrayer of the national trust. He proposed a constitutional amendment giving Congress the power to override a presidential veto by a simple majority vote of both houses rather than the prevailing two-thirds. The anti-Tyler faction could not, of course, muster the two-thirds majority necessary even to submit such an amendment to the states. Henry Clay, who had been hopeful of reviving the American System within the Whig Party, despaired and resigned his seat in the Senate. He called on John Quincy to take up the banner. Writing from Ashland, his plantation, he declared, "My hopes [are] concentrated more upon you than on any other man. In the dispensations of an all-wise Providence, it has hitherto so happened in our country, that upon every great emergency, some man appeared who was adequate to the service of conducting us in safety through the impending danger. Upon the present occasion that noble office is yours."[52] Adams responded warmly but replied that at seventy-five, he was too old. The Whigs would never nominate him for the highest office in the land; he would devote what energies he had to seeing the gag rule abolished.

In the wake of the censure fight, the slaveholders in the House were determined to have their pound of flesh, and if it could not be from John Quincy Adams, they would take it from someone else. Joshua Giddings, the antislavery congressman from Ohio, had been something of an Adams acolyte since he took his seat in Congress. He had been particularly interested in the New Englander's views on the issue of congressional jurisdiction over slavery and the slave trade.[53] The *Creole*, whose slave cargo had mutinied and fled to the safety of the British West Indies, and Britain's refusal to return it had infuriated the slave power and particularly the state of Virginia, from whence the *Creole* had sailed. Richmond demanded that the Tyler administration compel Britain to disgorge the ship and its mutineers. In November 1842, Giddings, after consulting with Adams and Weld, submitted a resolution declaring that by the terms of the Constitution, the states had ceded all power over commerce and navigation on the high seas to the federal government. Virginia had ceased to have dominion over the *Creole* and its human cargo once the vessel reached international waters. The resolution was, of course, tabled, whereupon Giddings's colleague from Ohio, Democrat John Weller, moved that he be censured for condoning mutiny and murder. Weller then moved the previous question, in effect denying Giddings the opportunity to defend himself. Adams and other antislavery congressmen looked on in disgust as the zealous antislavery advocate was forced to stand before the Speaker and listen to the charges against him read. The House then voted not only to censure but to expel him.[54] "I can find no language to express my feelings at the consummation of this act," Adams subsequently wrote in his diary.[55] Giddings's constituents promptly reelected him, and he returned to Washington to continue to twist the slave power's tail.

The censure battle might have invigorated John Quincy at the time, but its conclusion left him exhausted and depressed. "I was roused twice in the night by severe cramps in the legs," he noted in his diary the first week in August, "and feel that my body and mind are rapidly falling into decay. The position that I have taken is arduous enough to crush any man in the vigor of youth; but . . . with failing senses and blunted instruments, surrounded by remorseless enemies and false and scary and treacherous friends, how can it end but in my ruin?"[56] His thoughts turned to death. Perhaps it would be a release, he speculated, freeing him from the trap he had laid for himself by commingling ambition and conscience. He loved popularity but continually took positions that made him unpopular. "John Quincy Adams was BORN TO BE THE FRIEND OF HIS ENEMIES AND THE CURSE OF HIS FRIENDS," observed one letter to the editor in the *Eastern Argus*.[57] But there were still comforts and consolations.

When the congressman returned to Quincy that summer, it was into the open arms of his townsmen. Local dignitaries arranged for a welcoming reception at the Braintree village church. As the old man entered, the capacity crowd rose. Lining the sides of the building were banners praising the native son for his efforts on behalf of freedom of speech. Adams reveled in his six grandchildren—John's daughter Mary Louisa and Charles and Abby's five offspring. He instinctively tutored them—in French, mathematics, and the classics—in the book-lined library at Peacefield. Henry, one of the five, recalled an incident that began with his "standing at the house door one summer morning in a passionate outburst of rebellion against going to school."[58] Hearing the commotion from his bedroom, his grandfather descended the stairs and without a word donned his hat and coat, took Henry by the hand, and led the lad, who was "paralyzed by awe," to his school. He did not release Henry's hand until the boy was seated at his desk. When Adams became so enfeebled that he could no longer write, Mary Louisa served as his transcribing secretary. Writing fifty years later, Charles Francis II—Charley to his grandfather—recalled: "I can see him now seated at his table . . . a very old-looking gentleman with a bald head and white fringe of hair . . . [and] a perpetual ink stain on the forefinger and thumb of the right hand."[59]

Eighteen forty-two was a congressional midterm election year. Following the census of 1840, the Twelfth District—John Quincy's—had been greatly altered, eliminating some areas of Plymouth County and more of Norfolk near Boston.

Although the Whig Party seemed to be falling apart, both he and Charles—standing for reelection to his seat in the state legislature—ran under its banner and won, although by much-reduced margins. There had been an influx of Irish immigrants into Boston and its environs. John Quincy uncharacteristically stooped to gratify them, declaring that in the age-old dispute between the Irish and the British, he had always favored the former. If in doubt, read *Dermot Mac-Morrogh*. Doubtless many of his Irish constituents could not read and would not have opened *Dermott* if they could, but they voted for him.[60]

The Price of Empire

B Y THE TIME JOHN Quincy returned to Washington for the opening of the Twenty-Eighth Congress, much of the nation was afflicted with the Texas fever. Antislavery forces were of course immune, but manifest destiny still held great appeal for Americans of all regions and political affiliations. The accession of John Tyler, a Virginia slaveholder, to the presidency had reopened the door to acquisition that had been temporarily closed during the Van Buren administration. He had appointed the South Carolina pro-slavery stalwart Waddy Thompson as his minister to Mexico. Adams thought Thompson worse than Anthony Butler, Jackson's unscrupulous ambassador. In November and December 1841, articles demanding the "re-annexation" of Texas—to take back what John Quincy Adams had "ceded" to Spain in 1819—began to appear in Democratic newspapers. One New York sheet went so far as to argue that abolitionists ought to support annexation. With the opening of millions of acres of fertile territory, the remnant of the Old South's slaves would be sold to the West, allowing states such as Virginia and South Carolina to abolish the institution. That impossible scenario might have appealed to lesser minds, but not to Adams, Weld, and the Tappan brothers. Slavery was so interwoven in the fabric of politics and culture in the Old South that it was unlikely that the region would ever voluntarily declare emancipation. Adams seemed to be in the process of giving up the battle for the hearts and minds of his countrymen south of the Mason–Dixon Line.

The Tyler administration argued that annexation of Texas was absolutely essential on national security grounds. It was indeed true that Great Britain was doing everything in its power to sustain an independent Texas, which would, London was convinced, act as a barrier to further westward expansion by the United States and relieve Britain's textile mills of their dependency on the slave-grown cotton of the American South. British abolitionists dreamed of a slave-free

Texas, which would sell cotton raised by free labor to Britain in return for British
manufactured goods that would not have to bear the burden of U.S. tariffs. As
long as Daniel Webster was secretary of state, there was little possibility that the
United States would risk war with Mexico—and probably Great Britain—by
forcibly annexing the Republic of Texas. There was, however, still a chance that
the administration could persuade Mexico to part with its rebellious province
voluntarily in return for forgiveness of the $8.542 million in debts still claimed by
U.S. citizens.

The administration's chief advocate on the Texas question in the House was,
not surprisingly, Henry Wise. He at first downplayed the significance of slavery.
Great Britain was out to get not only Texas but California and Cuba as well. "Let
her obtain Cuba, and she will command the Gulf of Mexico and the Mississippi,
and nothing will prevent her from making that sea a *mare clausum* to the people
of the West. Let her obtain California and establish a naval base there, and she at
once controls the whole trade of the Pacific Ocean."[1] Why, none other than John
Quincy Adams when he was president had instructed his minister to Mexico, Joel
Poinsett, to purchase Texas from Mexico. Adams rose to reply. Yes, he said, but
at that time Santa Anna's proclamation outlawing slavery throughout Mexico,
including Texas, had been in force. Charles Ingersoll, another Southern fire-
breather, accused Adams of being willing to abandon America's historic opposition to the practice of visit and search; the British "confiscation" of the *Creole* was
a classic example. Southern Congressmen and their doughface lackeys were not
worried about America's strategic security or freedom of the seas, Adams declared. They were as usual scheming to spread slavery into as much of the West as
possible and to circumvent the constitutional prohibition on the external trade in
human chattel.

At the beginning of the opening session of the Twenty-Eighth Congress, the
New Englander as usual moved to amend the rules of the House eliminating the
twenty-first—the gag—rule. The ensuing debate, which stretched over two
weeks, was typically rancorous. As he passed by Adams's desk one morning,
Joshua Giddings stopped to chat. He found the old man uncharacteristically depressed. Although his "hand was palsied and trembling [and] his voice was somewhat feeble and broken," Adams declared that it was not his physical health that
was bothering him. He despaired of ever having the gag rule repealed, observing
to Giddings that "our Government had become the most perfect despotism of the
Christian world."[2] During the debate, one of Adams's detractors quoted from a
message John Quincy had sent to a group of African Americans in Pittsburgh:
"We know that the day of your redemption must come. The time and manner of

it's coming we know not: It may come in peace, or it may come in blood; but, whether in peace or in blood, LET IT COME." Did he not realize that such a conflict would shed the blood of thousands of white men? To which Adams responded: "Though it cost the blood of millions of white men, LET IT COME: Let justice be done though the heavens fall."[3] Giddings recalled that the House was struck dumb until at last the Speaker declared the gentleman from Massachusetts out of order.

Shortly afterward, congressmen from Alabama and Mississippi again presented petitions from their respective state legislatures calling for the annexation of Texas. Adams reintroduced his two resolutions of 1838: one prohibiting Congress or the executive from annexing "any foreign State or people to this Union" and the other declaring that any attempt through the executive's treaty-making power or by act of Congress to annex Texas was a violation of the Constitution—"null and void, and to which the free States of the Union, and their people, ought not to submit."[4] American politics had produced some remarkable philosophical reversals, but none quite so dramatic as this. John Quincy Adams—denouncer of the Kentucky and Virginia Resolutions, scourge of the Hartford Convention, archenemy of South Carolina nullifiers—was suggesting that the free states not only had the right but the duty to ignore policies and decisions of the federal government. The old man, it seemed, was at last moving to embrace Armageddon. Adams's anti-expansionist resolutions were, of course, laid on the table.

With the gag rule fight once again lost, Adams, Weld, and other members of the Select Committee on Slavery spent their time and energy trying to alert the public to the ongoing conspiracy hatched by Andrew Jackson, his friend Sam Houston, and now the Tyler administration to foment a war with Mexico, the fruits of which would yield not only Texas but California as well. By 1840 several hundred Americans had migrated to California, which had become a province of Mexico after that country gained its independence in 1821. California, with its magnificent port of San Francisco, was about as remote from Mexico City as a place could be. Few of the province's Spanish residents felt any real fealty to their national government. Jackson had tried to purchase San Francisco from Mexico but failed. The Van Buren administration had shown little interest, but Tyler and his advisers proved even more excited about California than Jackson and his kitchen cabinet. "I am profoundly satisfied," Tyler's ambassador to Mexico, Waddy Thompson, wrote, "that in its bearing upon all the interests of our country, agricultural, political, manufacturing, commercial, and fishing, the importance of the acquisition of California cannot be overestimated."[5]

While stationed off the coast of Peru, Commodore Thomas ap Catesby Jones, commander of the U.S. Pacific Squadron, heard that Mexico and the United States had gone to war. Jones, an enthusiastic agent of manifest destiny, immediately set sail for California. On October 18, 1842, he entered Monterey Bay, occupied the town—the provincial capital—and raised the Stars and Stripes. Two days later Jones learned that he had erred, apologized to the Mexican authorities, and departed. Adams and his colleagues, of course, believed that Jones had been acting on secret orders from the War Department.[6] In March 1843, Adams called at the State Department and questioned Webster about the Tyler administration's foreign policy. Had Waddy Thompson been instructed to purchase California? Had Jones been acting at the behest of the War Department? An embarrassed silence followed. It's all right, Adams remarked; I do not expect you to divulge administration secrets, but he told his fellow Bay Stater, "I considered all the questions about the right of search. . . . Captain Jones's movement on California, and all the movements for the annexation of Texas, were parts of one great system, looking to . . . a war with England and alliance with France."[7]

Later, musing in his diary, Adams wrote: "The root of the danger is in the convulsive impotence of Mexico to maintain her own integrity, geographical, political or moral, and the inflexible perseverance of rapacity of our South and West, under the spur of slavery, to plunder and dismember her."[8] In 1817 and 1818, Secretary of State Adams had invoked Spain's impotency to separate that nation from Florida, which had been certain to become a slave state. He had, moreover, been willing to employ the rapacity of the South and the West to achieve his objective. To be fair, at that point in the nation's history, Adams had believed that he had to privilege the strategic and economic well-being of the republic over the evils of an expanding slave power. But still . . .

During the early days of the republic, John Quincy had railed against both Britain and France for directly interfering in American politics in an effort to bend the United States to their will. He had been especially outraged by their American accomplices—Timothy Pickering for the British, for example, and Thomas Paine and James Monroe for the French. But by 1843, Adams was willing to act more or less as an agent for the British government, at least in so far as it was attempting to abolish slavery in Texas and/or keep it out of the hands of the United States. Adams would have preferred the former but was willing to accept the latter. When the congressman returned to Quincy in the spring of 1843, he found Lewis Tappan and Stephen P. Andrews waiting for him. Andrews was a Massachusetts abolitionist who had dared to go to Texas to agitate for emancipation; the two were preparing to depart for London to attend the General Anti-Slavery Convention. "I believed the freedom of this country and of all mankind depended upon the direct, formal, open, and avowed interference of Great Britain" to see that Texas remained independent and a home to free labor, Adams told them.[9] Tappan and Andrews subsequently conveyed this message to Lord Peel, the prime minister. From London, Andrews wrote Adams: "I have been from the first, received and treated with the utmost courtesy and my suggestions seem to have made all proper impression on the ministry."[10] The Peel government planned to approach Santa Anna—once again in power in Mexico—and try to convince him to accept abolition as a condition for recognition of Texan independence. What better way for the general to gain revenge against the Southern slave owners who he believed had engineered the Texas Revolution?

It seemed then that one of America's great nationalists, John Quincy Adams, was willing to sacrifice his principles—not only for a strong, activist federal government, but for a vigorous and independent foreign policy—in his war against the slave power. But Adams was willing to serve Britain's interests only if and when worldwide emancipation became the cardinal principal of that nation's foreign policy. In a conversation with Joshua Leavitt, also a delegate to the world convention, he confessed that he did not trust the Peel ministry. There were those in the British government and press who so hated America that they would sell out both Texas and Mexico in order to strengthen the slave power and thus facilitate the United States' inevitable decline.[11]

DURING THE LONG CONGRESSIONAL break from April to December 1843, the country that Adams loved, loved him back. Before he left Washington, the former president received an invitation from his daughter-in law Abigail Brooks Adams to join her, her father, and her son John Quincy Adams II for a trip to view Niagara Falls. John Quincy gratefully accepted.

The Adams–Brooks party departed Boston for New York aboard a Western Railroad train in July. The countryside, Adams subsequently recorded in his diary, was resplendent, a "Garden of Eden." "Fields of Indian corn, rye, potatoes, and oats, interchangeably [mixed] with pastures covered with grazing cattle, neat and comfortable houses, and kitchen-gardens, and orchards laden with ripening fruit."[12] The party overnighted in Springfield, where Adams received a tour of the vast Springfield Armory. "[W]e saw the various processes of making the gun-barrels and the black walnut gun-stocks." The armory was then in the midst of abandoning the old flintlock rifles and moving to the more efficient percussion lock and pan. Then it was time to board their rail coach to start the journey northward. As the train passed from Massachusetts to New York, the terrain became rougher—"a wild region of dark forests and stupendous rocks." The party stopped at Lebanon Springs to take the baths. Adams was enchanted with the setting: "For three-quarters of an hour the peaks of the mountains were taking one after another the golden tinge, before the sun became visible from the piazza on which I was walking and listening to the morning concert of the birds."[13]

On the twenty-fourth, the Adams–Brooks party arrived at Niagara Falls. They first approached the roaring cataract from above. John Quincy got to see Navy Island and Goat Island, the settings for the infamous *Caroline* affair. On Goat Island a tower from which tourists could look over the falls had been erected. From there it was on to Buffalo, Batavia, and Rochester. As Adams and his companions were entering Rochester, they were met by a company of militia and hundreds of well-wishers whose carriages formed a procession stretching more than a mile. At Utica a delegation of free Blacks paid their respects, thanking the old man for his efforts on behalf of the right of petition and the abolition of slavery. Adams replied, telling them that "I had performed no more than my indispensable [duty] . . . and that I should still and ever be happy to serve them to the utmost extent of my power." The next day, escorted by Joshua Spencer, the U.S. attorney for northern New York, the travelers visited the Utica Female Seminary. As part of a tribute to the former president, Spencer read from some of Abigail Adams's letters to him and his father written in 1778. "I actually sobbed as he read," John Quincy later recorded in his diary, "utterly unable to suppress my emotion."[14]

While he was on his New York jaunt, Adams received an invitation from the Cincinnati Astronomical Society inviting him to lay the cornerstone of an observatory that it proposed to erect. Of all the sciences, that of observing and mapping the heavens had been John Quincy Adams's favorite. "To me," he wrote in his diary in 1838, "the observation of the sun, moon, and stars has been for a great portion of my life a pleasure of gratified curiosity, of ever returning wonder, and of reverence for the creator and mover of these unnumbered worlds . . . the rising of the whole Constellation of Orion . . . and his ride through the Heavens with his belt, his nebulous sword, and his four corner stars . . . are sources of delight to me which never tire."[15] In hopes that Harvard would become the site of America's first observatory, he had in 1823 donated a thousand dollars to the institution for that purpose. As president, in his first annual address, Adams had famously called for federal funding for "lighthouses of the skies." In a republic of educated and virtuous men, the government had a duty to promote the study of science, he believed. "The people of this country do not sufficiently estimate the importance of patronizing and promoting science as a principle of political action; the slave oligarchy systematically struggles to suppress all . . . progress of the mind. Astronomy has been specially neglected and scornfully treated."[16]

So it was that in October 1843, accompanied by a single servant, Benjamin Andrews, John Quincy departed for what would be a monthlong trek to Cincinnati. He was at once excited and apprehensive. He had never seen the West, and he anticipated that the crowds he encountered along his route would be friendly, but he could not be sure. And at seventy-six, he was frail, reduced, as he put it, almost "to the nervous affections of second childhood."[17] His family had been uniformly opposed to the trip. But the old gentleman had already prepared his fifty-four-page address. "My task," he wrote, "is to turn this transient gust of enthusiasm for the science of astronomy at Cincinnati into a permanent and preserving national pursuit which may . . . make my country instrumental in elevating the character and improving the condition of man upon earth."[18] Adams was not in general an admirer of Niccolò Machiavelli, but perhaps he recalled the Italian's famous invocation: "Make no small plans for they have no power to stir the soul."[19]

The two men traveled by train to Springfield. From there it was on to Albany and a night's rest in a hotel. Adams rose to find the town covered in snow and ice. When he and his valet boarded the train to Buffalo, its wheels were frozen to the tracks. It took a team of horses an hour and a half to pull the train free and another half hour for the locomotive to get up a head of steam.[20] The former president proceeded on his journey almost unnoticed. At Buffalo Andrews and he boarded the steamer *General Wayne* for the trip across Lake Erie. The unusual October winter storm intensified, compelling the vessel to spend a day and a half in a sheltered cove under Point Albino on the Canadian side. In Cleveland someone recognized the aged statesman, and a reception was hastily arranged. For their four-day journey southward to Columbus, Adams chose to travel down the Ohio and Erie Canal aboard the canal packet *Rob Roy*. It proved an unfortunate choice. Twenty passengers and four horses were bedded down at night in overheated compartments on the eighty-foot-long, fifteen-foot-wide craft. "So much humanity crowded into such a compass was a trial such as I had never before experienced," Adams recorded in his diary, "and my heart sunk within me when, squeezing into this pillory [the overcrowded packet], I reflected that I am to pass three nights and four days in it."[21]

There was a welcome respite at Akron; at a reception, a "very pretty" woman kissed Adams on the cheek. "I returned the salute on the lip, and kissed every woman that followed, at which some made faces, but none refused."[22] At Columbus the governor greeted the former president, and he was feted at a large banquet; two days later he and his manservant set out for Dayton, escorted by two companies of militia. On the way he was met by a welcoming committee that offered him "an elegant open barouche in which I took a seat, and thus in triumphal procession we entered the city."[23] As he neared Cincinnati, Adams found the road packed with Ohioans anxious for a glimpse of the great man. Mayor Henry Spencer came out to meet him at Mount Auburn, and a cannonade announced his entrance into the city. On the day appointed for the laying of the cornerstone and Adams's address, Cincinnati experienced a deluge of rain. The honoree made a few remarks to a sea of umbrellas. Those in charge of the festivities decided to postpone the address until the next day, when it would be delivered at the Wesley Chapel. Once again, Adams had mercy on his audience, and he delivered but half of the fifty-four-page address, which consumed some two hours. It comprised a history of astronomy and a paean to government support for scientific inquiry.[24] Henry Clay invited Adams to visit Kentucky, but the exhausted septuagenarian politely refused.[25]

On November 18, Adams and Andrews started their return journey to Washington, traveling by steamer up the Ohio River. Traversing Pennsylvania from west to east, Adams was treated to an endless stream of parades, testimonial dinners, laudatory speeches, and receptions. At Cumberland he and his servant boarded a train and made their way more speedily to Washington. When he reached his house on F Street, the old man was exhausted and seriously ill. It would be some weeks before he recovered his strength. "[H]e will do nothing and take no care of himself," Louisa wrote Charles, "but lives in a state of perpetual excitement."[26]

AT THE OPENING OF Congress in December 1843, John Quincy simultaneously offered his usual resolution to adopt rules of the House excluding the twenty-fifth (gag) rule, and a petition offered by the Massachusetts legislature calling for a constitutional amendment repealing the three-fifths clause. Bedlam, predictably, ensued. The House voted to retain the gag rule, but by the slimmest margin to date. When Adams proposed that the Speaker name a select committee of nine to consider the Massachusetts petition, Henry Wise, to everyone's surprise, rose to support the motion. He was tired of using parliamentary tactics to defeat the congressional "war against Southern rights." Let the committee be established; let John Quincy Adams chair it; and let its members all be like-minded. Let each of the abolitionist petitions previously presented to the House by Adams and his cohorts be received and let the committee report as it chose. At last, Wise declared, the nation would see clearly the massive conspiracy that was abolitionism.[27] The committee was formed, but the Speaker stocked it with defenders of slavery. With the gag rule still in effect, there was no discussion of the petitions calling for the abolition of slavery. In March 1844 the select committee would recommend that the House take no action on the three-fifths clause, and the motion was approved by a vote of 153 to thirteen.[28]

In February 1844, the president, his cabinet, and members of the Senate and House were invited to Greenleaf Point at the confluence of the Potomac and Anacostia Rivers to visit the newly completed warship, the U.S.S. *Princeton.* The huge vessel, powered by both sail and steam, featured twelve forty-two-pound carronades and two superguns mounted on her main deck. These last two enormous cannon, named the Peacemaker and the Orator, were wrought iron monsters whose mouths measured twelve inches in diameter; they each packed forty pounds of powder to propel a 225-pound ball.[29] With his nephew Isaac Hull Adams in tow, the member from Plymouth rowed out to inspect the *Princeton.* With visitors on board, the vessel sailed twelve miles downriver, fired its two great guns, and returned to Greenleaf Point. Several days later news reached the House that the Peacemaker had burst, killing Secretary of State Abel Upshur, Secretary of the Navy Thomas Gilmer, and several other people. For Adams, the explosion was doubly a disaster; not only had it killed some of his fellow human beings, but it also paved the way for Tyler to name John C. Calhoun secretary of state.

When Calhoun arrived at his new post, he found on his desk a treaty of annexation Upshur had secretly been negotiating with the government of Texas. He had also been in the process of concluding a definitive agreement with Great Britain setting the northern boundary of the Oregon Territory at the Columbia River, which would have placed the Olympic Peninsula and the Strait of Juan de Fuca in Canadian hands. This concession, Upshur had believed, would perhaps persuade London to acquiesce in the annexation of Texas to the Union as a slave state. The South Carolinian was enthusiastic about both projects, but he rather obtusely intended to justify the Texas treaty as a measure to ensure the perpetuation of slavery rather than as a strategic and economic boon to the nation.

Calhoun submitted the treaty of annexation to the Senate together with a letter that Lord Aberdeen, the British foreign secretary, had written to Richard Pakenham, his minister to the United States. The latter admitted that Britain had been exerting itself diplomatically to ensure that Texas remained independent but observed that the government would accept annexation to the United States if the republic abolished slavery. What more proof could America have that abolitionists controlled British foreign policy and that annexation was absolutely necessary to protect the "peculiar" institution? Calhoun asked. "What is called slavery is in reality a political institution essential to the peace, safety, and prosperity of those states in the Union in which it exists."[30] Adams, predictably, was beside himself. If Texas were annexed to the Union, "aggrandizement will be its [the United States] passion and its policy. A military government, a large army, a costly navy, distant colonies . . . will follow, of course, in rapid succession. . . . A Captain General for life and a Marshal's truncheon for a scepter will establish the law of arms. . . . War and slavery will stalk unbridled over the land—Blessed God deliver us from this fate."[31]

The congressional debate over the Texas treaty got underway as the national nominating conventions of the Whig, Democratic, and Liberty (abolitionist) Parties were preparing to convene. Each of its candidates would have to take a stand. Clay, a sure bet to be the Whigs' choice, came out strongly against annexation. The North would not stand for it, thanks in no small part to Adams's campaign to convince the free laboring men of that region that the slave power was an enemy of the industries and businesses that employed them.[32] In effect, the election provided Southern Whigs with their last chance to choose the American System over slavery expansion. Van Buren was the early favorite for the Democratic nomination, but with the North, and especially his home state of New York, dead set against annexation, he had no choice but to oppose ratification of the treaty. Thus ended his carefully but awkwardly constructed political alliance between the planters of the South and the "plain republicans" of the North. Tyler was unable to amass a two-thirds majority at the Democratic convention, so the delegates turned to Jackson protégé James K. Polk of Tennessee, an ardent annexationist. In hopes of seeing manifest destiny trump the slavery expansion issue, the party's platform called for the annexation of Texas and the negotiation of a new treaty with Britain that would bring all of the Oregon Territory up to fifty-four degrees, forty minutes into the Union—"fifty-four forty or fight." The Liberty candidate, James G. Birney, whom Adams detested for leading an abolitionist movement in Massachusetts to oust him from Congress, came out against annexation of Texas and for emancipation but only as permitted by the Constitution. Because of Samuel Morse's telegraph, Washington learned of these developments almost as soon as they transpired. "By the new invention of the electro-magnetic telegraph of Professor Morse," Adams noted in his diary, "the proceedings of these bodies through the day were made known here at the Capitol, and announced as soon as received, in manuscript bulletins suspended to the wall in the rotunda."[33]

On June 9, 1844, following an impassioned speech by Thomas Hart Benton of Missouri, the Senate voted to reject the treaty annexing Texas to the Union. Benton was a Van Buren loyalist who was determined to save the New Yorker and the political coalition he had constructed. Nine of twenty Southern senators voted no. "I record this vote," Adams exulted in his diary, "as a deliverance, I trust, by the special interposition of Almighty God, of my country and of human liberty from a conspiracy comparable to that of Lucius Sergius Catilina. . . . Moloch and

Mammon have sunk into temporary slumber."[34] The debate in the house was not without incident. After Congressmen George Rathbun of New York and John White of Kentucky traded insults, violence erupted. "Rathbun, sitting near where [White] spoke, started up, and, in a transport of rage, turned upon him and struck him. A short fight ensued—a rush of members over the tables and chairs to part them . . . A pistol-ball was fired at McCausland, a member, by a Kentuckian named Moore . . . the ball missed him, but passed through the door and wounded an officer of the police."[35]

The drama playing out over the annexation of Texas and Adams's ongoing fight against the gag rule left him sleepless and spent. He turned once again to exercise, both walking and a renewed attempt at swimming. "I have for a full month [been] longing for a river bath without taking it," he wrote in his diary on June 27. "This morning at five I went in the barouche to my old favorite spot . . . all my standard rocks were occupied by young men except one. I had some difficulty to undress and dress but got my bath; swam about five minutes and came out washed and refreshed."[36]

The following month, Louisa and he suffered a near-death experience as they traveled by train from Baltimore to Boston. At midnight in Jersey City, the passengers disembarked to change trains. John Quincy and Louisa in pitch-darkness exited onto a raised platform without railings. The old gentleman stepped over the edge, tumbling head over heels and carrying his wife, who was on his arm, with him. "While falling, I had the distinct idea that I was killed," he later recalled. "A shriek from my wife and the consciousness that she too was killed had in it a thrill of horror of which I knew not that the human frame was susceptible."[37] Fortunately Adams suffered only a badly bruised hip and Louisa a contusion on her breast.

The Adamses were in Quincy when in November they learned of Democrat James K. Polk's triumph. John Quincy was buoyed somewhat by his own reelection to Congress from the Eighth District. Both the Democratic and Liberty Parties ran candidates, but the former president polled eight thousand votes to their combined six thousand.[38]

Adams returned to a Congress more fluid than anyone he had yet experienced. On December 3, 1844, as expected, the congressman from Massachusetts proposed the repeal of the gag rule; the opposition countered by moving to lay it on the table. The latter motion was defeated 104 to eighty-one, paving the way for the House to decide the question. With nine Southerners voting in favor, Adams's proposal passed 108 to eighty. The gag rule was dead. "Blessed, forever blessed, be the name of God!" John Quincy exulted in his diary.[39] A year earlier a group of antislavery supporters had presented him with a three-foot-long ivory cane topped

with an American eagle fashioned out of gold; his name had been inscribed and a
blank space for the date of repeal of the gag rule. Adams had it so inscribed and
then turned it over to the Patent Office for posterity to admire.[40] The vote, of
course, did not indicate any slackening of the determination of the slave power to
defend its defining institution, but rather, as Wise had signaled, a willingness to
see the battle fought out in the open. With Polk's election, the slave power believed that time was on their side.

Abrogation of the gag rule opened the way for debate on slavery and all of the
concomitant issues. Not surprisingly, the level of violence on the floor of the house
increased. As Joshua Giddings was making his customary speech denouncing the
slave power, Congressman Edward J. Black crossed behind the Speaker's platform and approached the Ohioan from the rear. As he raised his cane to strike,
however, one of Giddings's friends "threw his arms round him and bore him off
as he would a woman from a fire."[41] The following year, as Giddings was once
again holding forth, Congressman John Bennett Dawson of Louisiana, whom
Adams had described as a "drunken bully," drew his pistol and declared that he
intended to kill Giddings. Several Southern congressmen joined him with weapons drawn. But then a group of armed antislavery solons surrounded the Ohioan,
and the standoff ended peaceably.[42] In December, shortly after the gag rule was
voted down, a page came to John Quincy's desk on the floor and informed him
that a man named Sangster wanted to speak with him in the lobby. As Adams
exited the chamber, the man approached him, declaring, "'You are wrong, you are
wrong, and I will kick you.'"[43] As he drew back to strike, the former president
seized him by both wrists until bystanders came and subdued the man.

JOHN TYLER'S DREAM OF being elected president in his own right had gone up in
smoke; he was determined, as a lifelong servant of the slave power, to leave the
annexation of Texas as his legacy. The soon-to-be ex-president knew that he did
not have the two-thirds vote in the Senate necessary for ratification of a treaty, so
he proposed annexation through a joint resolution, which required only a simple
majority in both houses. Adams and his fellow Whigs cried foul, but administration supporters were in the majority. The House passed a resolution approving
annexation on January 25, 1845, by a vote of 120 to ninety-eight. All but two
Whigs voted against it. A month later the Senate followed suit by a tally of
twenty-seven to twenty-five. Hardly a sweeping mandate, but the deed was done.
Under the terms of the joint resolution, which Texas would accept in July, the
newly acquired territory could be divided into as many as four slave states if Tex-

ans so decided. "The Constitution is a menstruous rag, and the Union is sinking into military monarchy," Adams lamented in his diary.[44]

During the Early Republic, John Quincy Adams had gloried in the westward march of his strapping young nation. Yeomen farmers, mechanics, miners, trappers, explorers, and canal and turnpike builders were spreading the glories of American civilization into a howling wilderness. Slavery, he convinced himself, would die its own death in its own time. Were not the members of the Virginia dynasty opposed to the institution? But at that time, the New Englander had not anticipated the rise of Jacksonian democracy, with its unholy marriage of the slave power to the "plain republicans" of the North—or perhaps he had shut that possibility out of his mind; the independence and strength of the Union and his own political career were more important. But the unimaginable alliance had been forged, corrupting the moral fiber of the nation and converting westward expansion into a vehicle for the extension and perpetuation of slavery. "The tendency of our government," he wrote in the wake of the annexation of Texas, "is to an elective monarchy of Olympiads and combining with a permanent system of annexations and a regular increase of Army and Navy appropriations." American frontiersmen he now declared to be riffraff with "nothing to occupy their restless and [enterprising] nature, but tilling, trapping, mining, and exploring."[45] Quincy Adams appeared ready to give up on his dream of gradual voluntary emancipation. "I have concluded," Adams wrote Lewis Tappan, "that no action of mine can in the present state of things contribute . . . to the abolition of slavery; I feel the finger of Heaven pressing upon my lips and dooming me to silence and inaction."[46] Only in God's time would justice be done, it seemed.

In the meantime, Adams would expend what little energy he had left in seeing that the United States acquired as much of the Oregon Territory as possible in order to balance the increase in the number of slave states with free ones. The influx of American settlers into the Willamette Valley crescendoed in 1843 and 1844. These frontiersmen petitioned Congress to allow them to claim their farms under the public land acts of the United States. This would require termination of the joint occupancy agreement of 1818—renewed by the Adams administration in 1827—and a subsequent Anglo-American treaty establishing a permanent boundary. Though Southern congressmen and senators ware not enthusiastic, Polk, in hopes of preserving the new South–West alliance that had brought him into office, was ready to make the move. When the Twenty-Ninth Congress convened in December 1845, the Tennessean requested authorization to give the British notice that the United States was terminating the joint occupancy agreement. The Democratic platform of 1844 had committed Polk to "fifty-four forty or fight," but he had no intention of standing that ground. Mexico was threatening war over the annexation of Texas, and the United States' claim to anything north of the forty-ninth parallel in the Oregon Territory was very weak. In his first annual message to Congress, Polk told Congress that he would have been willing to demand "fifty-four forty," but that his predecessors—Monroe and John Quincy Adams—had prejudiced America's case by offering forty-nine degrees to the Strait of Juan de Fuca.

John Quincy proved to be a hard-liner on Oregon. He actually advocated for the "fifty-four forty or fight" plank in the Democratic platform. His motives were several. He was flattered that Polk, in his address requesting the power to give Britain notice, cited the Monroe Doctrine, especially the noncolonization principle, which Adams alone had authored. He wanted to add as much free territory to the Union as possible. And he was furious with the British for their abandonment of Texas to the slave power. Clearly, the Peel government had no intention of leading an international crusade to abolish slavery beyond the boundaries of the British Empire; it had maneuvered to keep Texas independent solely for geopolitical reasons—to block the further expansion of U.S. power. In the debate over notification, Southerners balked, especially at demanding fifty-four degrees, forty minutes. They were apparently ready to risk war with Mexico over Texas but not with Great Britain for all of Oregon.[47] Thomas Butler King of Georgia confronted Adams directly. Do you, sir, believe that the United States claim to fifty-four forty to be "clear and unquestionable?" Adams asked the clerk of the House to read the eighth verse of the second chapter of Psalms. He complied: "Ask of me, and I shall give thee the heathen for thine inheritance and the uttermost parts of the earth for thy possession."[48] It was no less America's destiny to occupy all of North America in 1845 than it had been in 1783, Adams insisted. "I want the country for our western pioneers . . . for them to go out and make a great nation that is to arise there, and which must come from us as a fountain comes from its source, of free, independent sovereign republics instead of hunting grounds for the buffaloes, braves, and savages of the desert."[49] Apparently, American frontiersmen were riffraff when colonizing Texas, but noble patriots when moving into the Oregon Territory.

In private conversation, Adams predicted correctly that Polk would settle for the forty-ninth parallel and that he would maneuver Britain into offering what it had previously rejected.[50] The House passed a notification resolution 163 to fifty-four, with Adams in the affirmative, but it included a conciliatory preamble inviting Britain to come and reason together. When one of his English abolitionist friends admonished him for his aggressiveness, the New Englander refused to back down. "We want to fulfil the commands of Almighty God, to increase and multiply, and replenish and subdue the Earth," he replied. "Britain wants them [Oregon territories] for no honest purpose of her own. She wants them to check, and control and defeat the progress of our prosperity, to stunt our natural growth."[51]

John Bull had his own jingoes of course. Lord George Bentinck rose in the House of Commons to denounce the United States in general and John Quincy Adams in particular: "[W]hen America is arming her seaboard, and Mr. John Quincy Adams impiously and blasphemously calls to his aid the word of God as a justification for lighting up the firebrands and unleashing the hell-hounds of war . . . I shall meekly and humbly appeal to the government to address America not in the language of purchase but the thundering broadsides of line-of-battle ship."[52]

The Peel government had no intention of going to war for the territory north of the Columbia—its version of "fifty-four forty or fight." The Hudson's Bay Company had trapped out the area south of the Strait of Juan de Fuca. The Polk administration was preparing to pass a for-revenue-only tariff that would open up American markets to all sorts of British commodities. The State Department intimated to the British Foreign Office that if it would propose a line of forty-nine degrees to the Strait of Juan de Fuca and from thence to the Pacific Ocean, the United States would accept. Lord Aberdeen, the foreign secretary, did just that, and on June 12, 1846, the U.S. Senate voted thirty-eight to twelve to ratify the Oregon Treaty of 1846.

SUMMER AND FALL 1845 in Quincy passed pleasantly enough for John Quincy and Louisa. On the twenty-sixth of July, the couple celebrated their forty-eighth anniversary. "A small remnant [of life] only can be before us," Adams noted in his diary. "A merciful Providence has hitherto conducted us along the path of life. We have enjoyed much. We have suffered not a little."[53] For her part, Louisa had come to accept her lot as the wife of John Quincy Adams. In her letters to Charles, she felt free to praise him. "The only thing that distresses me," she wrote her son, "is that he expends much of the strength of his great mind upon the butterfly race." Lesser men hovered about him "as the moth round the candle and would consume themselves if he would let them alone."[54] She felt increasingly comfortable with her husband's leadership of the antislavery movement. Over time her own views had matured, and she, like John Quincy, no longer felt isolated. In 1843, Louisa's brother Thomas—he of the hemorrhoids and constipation—had died and left her ten thousand dollars. There were still coverture laws on the books that gave domain to a husband over his wife's property. Fortunately, in 1842, the Massachusetts legislature passed a law allowing wives to make out their own wills, which Louisa immediately did. The law required the permission of the husband, but for one reason or another, Louisa neglected to consult John. The inheritance allowed her to buy her grandchildren presents. The money was liberating, wiping out whatever vestiges of guilt she suffered for not having brought a dowry to her marriage.[55]

John Quincy's sympathies for the free Black population in America remained consistent. The census of 1840 had caught the attention of the Select Committee on Slavery. Russell Jarvis and others noted a disproportionate number of free Blacks listed as insane. They investigated and uncovered evidence that the State Department— the appointees of which were Democrats—had falsified the records in an attempt to discredit emancipation. On behalf of the committee, Adams presented to Congress a memorial demanding a revision of the census.[56] It failed. While Adams was in Boston during the 1845 congressional recess, a free Black man named Joseph P. Humphries came to ask his advice. Humphries was literate and trained as a tailor. He had fled South Carolina—"that glorious exemplification of democracy," as Adams put it—for obvious reasons. He had encountered some prejudice in Boston, Humphries told the former president; would it not be better to settle in some country village to ply his trade? I think not, observed Adams. You are likely to find more discrimination there than in the city, where there was a large number of respectable free Blacks whose society and protection Humphries and his family could enjoy. Sage advice that the South Carolinian took.[57]

The old gentleman had resumed his practice of rising at four a.m.—"commenced in the summer of 1796, at the Hague"—to read write, meditate, and watch with awe as the sun illuminated the horizon. The practice, observed off and on for nearly fifty years, had provided him with "the most contented, the most active and efficient hours of the day," and still did. Beginning in 1843, he enhanced the experience by rubbing his body with a horsehair strap and mitten.[58] Not surprisingly Adams's thoughts began to focus on the life he had led and the death that he faced. "With regard to what is called the wheel of Fortune, my career in life has been, with severe vicissitudes, on the whole highly auspicious. With advantages of education perhaps unparalleled, with principles of integrity, of benevolence, of industry and frugality, and the lofty spirit of patriotism and independence taught me from the cradle, with the love of letters and the arts, useful and ornamental, and with aspirations of science, . . . [my life has] been much more successful than I deserved." But then inevitably a note of self-pity: "I have enjoyed a portion of the favor of my country . . . but have suffered, and yet suffer, much from that slander which outvenoms all the worms of the Nile."[59]

The aged statesman dwelled on sin and atonement. The latter concept troubled him deeply because it implied original sin. How could God in His endless goodness create beings who were inherently tainted and then sacrifice His son to relieve them of their eternal burden? "I reverence God as my creator," he wrote in his diary. "As creator of the world, I reverence him with holy fear. I venerate Jesus Christ as my redeemer; and, as far as I can understand, the redeemer of the world. But this belief is dark and dubious."[60] Adams seemed unaware of the teaching that God was all powerful, all knowing, and all loving. But love trumped everything. As a result, He chose to limit His power, giving human beings free will. Without the capacity to choose between good and evil with the accompanying consequences, there could be no faith, and men and women would be mere animals or mannequins. At church Adams prayed for mercy and, with the Lord's Prayer in mind, pledged to divest himself "of every sentiment of animosity, anger, and resentment against any and every fellow creature of the human family."[61] But then, of course, having done so, he would no longer be an Adams.

Among his most treasured legacies to his family and posterity in general, John Quincy believed, would be his diary, which he had begun at age twelve. It was an exceptional document, he observed toward the close of that same journal, but not what it could have been, had his Creator endowed him with "the conceptive power of mind." Had he been better equipped with literary talent and prescience, "my diary would have been, next to the Holy Scriptures, the most precious and valuable book ever written by human hands. . . . I would . . . have banished war and slavery from the face of the earth forever."[62] Was this claim just the product of a senile elderly man, or did John Quincy Adams truly believe that he had lived his life on the edge of immortality? Whatever the case, the diary would become one of the two most famous chronicles written in the English language (the other by Samuel Pepys); Adams's belief that the written and spoken words—his in particular—were capable of bringing peace and freedom to the world was a testimony to his faith in the power of rhetoric and a lasting monument to his enormous ego.

In October 1846, the Whig Party of Massachusetts renominated John Quincy for another term in Congress. In the November elections, he bested his two opponents combined by three to one. On the morning of November 20, the former president rose, breakfasted with his family at Charles's house in Boston, and then departed in company with Dr. George Parkman to visit the newly reestablished Medical College at Harvard. "I suddenly found myself unable to walk, and my knees sinking under me," the aged statesman later recalled.[63] Parkman helped him back to Charles's abode, where he was put to bed; for days he moved in and out of consciousness while Dr. Jacob Bigelow and a nurse, a Mrs. Fader, attended to his needs. Upon learning of her husband's illness, Louisa rushed back from Washington. She would sleep in his room on the floor or in a trundle bed during his illness. News of his "sudden and extraordinary seizure" was announced in newspapers across the land. When he was awake, John Quincy convinced himself that he had taken to his bed for the last time. He—in perhaps the ultimate act of a controlling mind—wrote his own obituary, including the circumstances of his death. "From that hour [when he was stricken] I date my decease, and consider myself, for every useful purpose to myself or to my fellow-creatures, dead; and hence I call this [a letter to Charles postdated to January 1, 1848] what I may write hereafter as a posthumous memoir."[64]

The old gentleman surprised Dr. Bigelow by not only surviving but regaining some of his strength. Adams suggested to friends that he had merely suffered a bout of vertigo, but when he tried to walk, he could only drag his right leg behind him. Louisa noted that his memory was slipping and that he drooled like a baby and wept at the slightest provocation. Nevertheless, by the dawning of the New Year, the aged statesman was able to ride in a carriage and two months later take short strolls. On February 8, John Quincy, his nurse, Louisa, and Charles set out for Washington. They arrived on the twelfth, and the former president announced that he was going to take his seat in the House the following morning. He was as good as his word, and as he entered the chamber, members of all regions and convictions rose to applaud him.[65]

As JOHN TYLER DURING the dying days of his presidency was pushing Congress toward a joint resolution inviting Texas into the Union, the Mexican minister to the United States notified the administration that his country would consider annexation to be an act of war. When Congress passed the joint resolution, he asked for his passports and withdrew from the country. James K. Polk did not want war with Mexico, but he wanted California and its crown jewel, the port of San Francisco, and if that required a war, he was willing to fight it. In 1845 he dispatched John Slidell to Mexico City to either bully or bribe Santa Anna's government into accepting the annexation of Texas and selling California. Following a year of fruitless negotiations, Slidell returned to Washington. Nothing but force, he reported, would move these people. Thereupon, Polk decided to goad Mexico into war.

At the time, General Zachary Taylor was stationed with a substantial force at Corpus Christi, just southeast of the Nueces River. For as long as anyone could remember, the Nueces had been considered the southern boundary of Texas. Polk ordered Taylor to move southward and take up a position on the north bank of the Río Grande. Meanwhile, in Washington, Polk was losing patience. Then, in the midst of a meeting with his cabinet to discuss whether he should go to Congress and ask for a declaration of war, he received word that on April 25, as Taylor was approaching the Río Grande, his forces had come under attack from Mexican troops; in the ensuing skirmish, the Americans had lost sixteen men. With a sense of relief, the president sent to Congress a message requesting that it recognize that a state of war existed between Mexico and the United States.

Needless to say, these developments left John Quincy distraught. By an act of aggression, his beloved country had initiated war with a much weaker country. "[H]is [Taylor's] position at Corpus Christi itself was an act of flagrant war," he wrote Albert Gallatin.[66] The Constitution gave to Congress and Congress alone the power to declare war. But Polk had presented the House and the Senate with a fait accompli. *Hail Caesar!* wrote Adams.

Like Adams, other members of Congress had deep reservations concerning the origins of the war with Mexico, but once the blood of American soldiers had been shed, it was virtually impossible politically for a senator or a congressman to vote against a declaration of war. The House approved a war resolution 174 to fourteen with thirty-five abstentions, with Adams voting no; the Senate followed suit forty to two. The former president did support the military appropriations bill that followed. Look not abroad for monsters to slay, John Quincy Adams had warned his country a quarter century earlier. Now it seemed that the United States had in its own right become a monster. In devouring its prey, Adams predicted, the republic was ingesting the seeds of its own destruction.

As was true for most men of his age and condition, Adams had his good days and his bad ones. Louisa recorded that an evening of brilliant conversation was followed by a day in which he could "barely crawl." In June it was time for his and Louisa's annual sojourn in New England. Charles was shocked when he saw his father. "He is now a feeble old man. . . . I feel sad when I look at him."[67] John Quincy could no longer write for any length of time—he had abandoned his diary following his first stroke—but he could read, which he did with pleasure: Milton, Herodotus, and the English poet Samuel Rogers, whose "Pleasures of Memory" (1792) he had declared to be the best poem of the age. The family hoped he would stay put, but at his insistence, it was back to Washington the first week in November. "It seemed to me on leaving home as if it were upon my last great journey," he wrote.[68] The old gentleman took his seat in the House; he was no longer strong enough to torment his enemies, which seemed to endear him to one and all. "The world seems to idolize him," Louisa noted in her diary.[69]

On Sunday, February 20, 1848, the former president attended two worship services; that evening he had Louisa read Bishop Wilberforce's sermon on "Time." The next morning John Quincy mounted his carriage as usual and proceeded to the

Capitol. He took his seat and as was his wont conversed with nearby colleagues. The first order of business was a resolution thanking the American generals who had so decisively defeated the Mexican Army at the battles in Monterrey and Mexico City. Congressman Adams wanted no part of it. As he cast his no vote, he rose to address the chair. He opened his mouth but could not speak. With his temple and cheeks blushing bright red, he gripped the corner of his desk with his right hand. Congressman David Fisher of Ohio, whose desk was next to John Quincy's, caught him before he could hit the floor. "Mr. Adams is dying! Mr. Adams is dying!" cried out several members.[70] Colleagues rushed to his side and laid him on the carpet; a couch was produced, and the stricken man was carried to the Speaker's chamber. The House moved to adjourn, and as soon as they received word, both the Senate and the Supreme Court rose.

Access to the dying man was denied to all but the physicians who had been summoned and his closest colleagues. Adams revived long enough to ask for Henry Clay. His old nemesis turned compatriot appeared and, weeping, held Adams's hand for a few moments before taking his leave. Shortly afterward, Louisa and her friend Mary Elizabeth Cutts arrived. John Quincy's wife of fifty years knelt over him, but he did not recognize her. In the late afternoon, friends persuaded the two women to go home to get some rest. Louisa returned the next day, and accommodations for her were set up in a committee room.[71]

When Adams had collapsed at one o'clock on Monday the twenty-first, his longtime friend John G. Palfrey, a Unitarian minister from Boston and a member of the House, immediately sent a messenger to the Washington telegraphy office. Lines connected the capital to Baltimore, Philadelphia, New York, and Boston. Palfrey's first message was to Charles. "Dear Adams," he wrote, "your father fainted half an hour ago" and is still unconscious.[72] Charles rushed to be with John Quincy, while Abby stayed behind in Boston to tend to the children. Palfrey then began to telegraph messages to newspapers up and down the East Coast, reporting on the former president's condition. Attending physicians had rubbed brandy on the old man's feet and applied suction cups to his temples but to no avail.

Throughout the twenty-second and the twenty-third, Adams lay mostly senseless, occasionally attempting to speak. The Senate met briefly to ratify the Treaty of Guadalupe Hidalgo, ending the war with Mexico, and in the process bringing into the Union not only Texas and California but all the territory in between. The pact fulfilled John Quincy Adams's dream of an American republic stretching from sea to shining sea, but alas, it also facilitated the spread of slavery. On the evening of February 23, 1848, John Quincy Adams breathed his last, his final words reportedly being, "This is the end of the earth, but I am content."[73] Among those in the room who witnessed his demise was the young antislavery congressman from Illinois, Abraham Lincoln. Louisa was at home on F Street with Mary Catherine, several of her grandchildren, and friends. Palfrey reported that she took the news calmly and slept well that night.[74]

John Quincy Adams's death seemed as cathartic for the nation as his father's and Jefferson's simultaneous demises on July 4, 1826. On the twenty-fourth of February, the Speaker announced Adams's passing to the assembled House. Charles Hudson, now the senior member of the Massachusetts delegation, gave a brief summary of his colleague's remarkable career and then moved for the establishment of a committee of thirty to oversee services and tributes to be held in the Hall of the House. Before the body could act, Isaac E. Holmes, a Democrat from Charleston, South Carolina, rose and declared, "When a great man falls, the nation mourns; when a patriarch is removed, the people weep."[75] The House passed Hudson's resolution and another appointing a congressman from each state to accompany Adams's remains to their final resting place. It was Thomas Hart Benton, John Quincy's old nemesis, who had the final word that day: "Wherever his presence could give aid and countenance to what was useful and honorable to man, there he was . . . where could death have found him but at the post of duty."[76]

Adams's body lay in state for two days in a House committee room. Thousands of mourners passed by his silver-topped casket, the lid inlaid with an American eagle. Charles arrived too late to witness his father's passing, so when he arrived, the room was cleared to allow him a few minutes alone. John Quincy's funeral began at ten minutes before noon in the House. President Polk headed the procession of cabinet members, justices of the Supreme Court, and members of the corps diplomatique. Charles Francis, Mary Catherine, and finally Louisa entered and seated themselves.[77] The chaplain of the House, the Reverend R. R. Gurley, delivered the official eulogy, his most memorable words a quote from Job, chapter eleven, verses seventeen and eighteen: "And thine age shall be clearer than the noonday; thou shalt shine forth, thou shalt be as the morning. And thou shall be secure because there is hope."[78]

Shortly after the service, the Committee of Thirty escorted the former president's body home to Quincy, traveling by steamboat and train. Along the route flags were flown at half-mast, and mourners lined the way. When the entourage reached Boston, Adams's body was placed in a hearse pulled by six black horses, their heads adorned with black plumes, and carried to Faneuil Hall, on whose steps John Quincy had first entered American politics. From there it was on to

Quincy. As the hearse entered the town, two small cannons situated atop Penn's Hill fired a salute. Adams was then interred in the Stone Temple alongside his father, mother, sister, and son George.

In death John Quincy Adams perhaps experienced the peace he had never known during his life. He was at last free from himself, his family's ambitions, and the paradox of a nation that he loved and served and that at times had bound him hand and foot.

Bibliography

Adams Papers, Founders Online, National Archives.

Adams Family Papers: An Electronic Archive, Massachusetts Historical Society.

Charles Francis Adams, ed., *Memoirs of John Quincy Adams*, 12 vols. (Philadelphia, 1874–77).

John Quincy Adams, Diaries, 1789–1841 (raw transcripts), Massachusetts Historical Society.

———, Papers. L. Dennis Shapiro Collection, Huntington Library, San Marino, CA.

———, "Speech of John Quincy Adams, of Massachusetts, upon the Right of the People, Men and Women, to Petition on the Freedom of Speech and of Debate in the House of Representatives of the United States: on the Resolutions of Seven State Legislatures, and the Petitions of More than One Hundred Thousand Petitioners, Relating to the Annexation of Texas to this Union" (Washington, DC, 1838).

Thomas B. Adams, Diary, Adams Papers, Series II–IV, microfilm, Massachusetts Historical Society.

David Grayson Allen et al., eds., *Diary of John Quincy Adams, November 1779–December 1788*, 2 vols. (Belknap Press, Harvard University, 1982).

Catherine Allgor, *Parlor Politics: In Which the Ladies of Washington Help Build a City and a Government* (University of Virginia Press, 2002).

Harry Ammon, *James Monroe: The Quest for National Identity* (University of Virginia Press, 1990).

Gilbert H. Barnes and Dwight L. Dumond, eds., *Letters of Theodore Dwight Weld, Angelina Grimké Weld, and Sarah Grimké, 1822–1844*, 2 vols. (New York, 1970).

Samuel Flagg Bemis, *John Quincy Adams and the Foundations of American Foreign Policy* (New York, 1949).

———, *John Quincy Adams and the Union* (New York, 1956).

H. W. Brands, *Andrew Jackson: His Life and Times* (New York, 2005).

Nina Burleigh, *The Stranger and the Statesman: James Smithson, John Quincy Adams, and the Making of America's Greatest Museum: The Smithsonian* (New York, 2003).

L. H. Butterfield et al., eds., *Adams Family Correspondence*, 15 vols. (Belknap Press, Harvard University, 1963–2022).

Lester J. Cappon, ed., *The Adams–Jefferson Letters: The Complete Correspondence Between Thomas Jefferson and Abigail and John Adams* (University of North Carolina Press, 2012).

Stephen Chambers, "'No Country but Their Counting-Houses': The U.S.–Cuba–Baltic Circuit, 1809–1812," in *Slavery's Capitalism*, edited by Sven Beckert and Seth Rockman (University of Pennsylvania Press, 2017).

Alfred W. Crosby Jr., *America, Russia, Hemp, and Napoleon: American Trade with Russia and the Baltic, 1783–1812* (Ohio State University Press, 1965).

Alexander DeConde, *A History of American Foreign Policy, Vol. I: Growth to World Power (1700–1914)*, 3rd ed. (New York, 1978).

Robert Divine et al., *America Past and Present*, 2 vols. (New York, 1987).

Aida DiPace Donald et al., eds., *Diary of Charles Francis Adams*, 8 vols. (Belknap Press, Harvard University, 1964).

William Doyle, *The Oxford History of the French Revolution* (New York, 2002).

Richard Drinnon, *Facing West: The Metaphysics of Indian-Hating and Empire-Building* (University of Minnesota Press, 1980).

Jonathan R. Dull, *A Diplomatic History of the American Revolution* (Yale University Press, 1985).

Charles N. Edel, *Nation Builder: John Quincy Adams and the Grand Strategy of the Republic* (Cambridge, 2014).

Joseph J. Ellis, *Founding Brothers: The Revolutionary Generation* (New York, 2002).

———, *First Family: Abigail and John Adams* (New York, 2011).

Melvin Patrick Ely, Jennifer R. Loux, and *Dictionary of Virginia Biography*, "Thomas R. Dew (1802–1846)," in *Encyclopedia Virginia* (Charlottesville, 2020).

John Ferling, *John Adams: A Life* (New York, 2010).

Robert Pierce Forbes, *The Missouri Compromise and Its Aftermath: Slavery and the Meaning of America* (University of North Carolina Press, 2009).

Worthington Chauncey Ford, ed., *Writings of John Quincy Adams*, 7 vols. (New York, 1968).

Joanne B. Freeman, *Affairs of Honor: National Politics in the New Republic* (Yale University Press, 2002).

———, *The Field of Blood: Violence in Congress and the Road to Civil War* (New York, 2018).

Joshua R. Giddings, *History of the Rebellion: Its Authors and Causes* (New York, 1864).

Judith S. Graham et al., eds., *Diary and Autobiographical Writings of Louisa Catherine Adams*, 2 vols. (Belknap Press, Harvard University, 2013).

Charles Wilson Hackett, "The Development of John Quincy Adams's Policy with Respect to an American Confederation and the Panama Conference, 1822–1825," *The Hispanic American Historical Review* 8, no. 4 (November 1928): 496–526.

Mary W. M. Hargreaves, *The Presidency of John Quincy Adams* (University Press of Kansas, 1985).

Margery M. Heffron, *Louisa Catherine: The Other Mrs. Adams* (Yale University Press, 2020).

Charles Herbermann et al., eds., "Jean-Baptiste Massillon," in *Catholic Encyclopedia*, 16 vols. (New York, 1913).

George C. Herring, *From Colony to Superpower: U.S. Foreign Relations Since 1776* (New York, 2008).

Peter P. Hill, "An Expedition to Liberate Venezuela Sails from New York, 1806," *The Historian* 78, no. 4 (2016): 671–89.

Woody Holton, *Abigail Adams* (New York, 2009).

James F. Hopkins et al., eds., *The Papers of Henry Clay*, vols. I–II (University Press of Kentucky, 1959–63).

Daniel Walker Howe, *The Political Culture of the American Whigs* (University of Chicago Press, 1984).

———, *What Hath God Wrought: The Transformation of America, 1815–1848* (New York, 2008).

Nancy Isenberg and Andrew Burstein, *The Problem of Democracy: The Presidents Adams Confront the Cult of Personality* (New York, 2019).

Margaret C. Jacob, *The Enlightenment: A Brief History with Documents* (New York, 2016).

Howard Jones, *Crucible of Power: A History of American Foreign Relations to 1913*, vol. I (Wilmington, 2002).

———, *Mutiny on the* Amistad: *The Saga of a Slave Revolt and Its Impact on American Abolition, Law, and Diplomacy* (New York, 1987).

Fred Kaplan, *John Quincy Adams: American Visionary* (New York, 2015).

Ralph Ketcham, *James Madison: A Biography* (University of Virginia Press, 1990).

Jill Lepore, "The Strange and Twisted Life of *Frankenstein*," *New Yorker*, Feb. 5, 2018.

Phyllis Lee Levin, *The Remarkable Education of John Quincy Adams* (New York, 2015).

James E. Lewis Jr., *The American Union and the Problem of Neighborhood: The United States and the Collapse of the Spanish Empire, 1783–1829* (University of North Carolina Press, 1998).

David F. Long, *Nothing Too Daring: A Biography of Commodore David Porter, 1780–1843* (Annapolis, 1970).

Benjamin Lundy, "A Citizen of the United States," *The War in Texas* (Philadelphia, 1836).

Daniel McCarthy, "Liberty and Order in the Slave Society," *American Conservative*, Aug. 1, 2005.

James P. McClure and J. Jefferson Looney, eds., *The Papers of Thomas Jefferson*, digital edition (Charlottesville, 2009–24).

David McCullough, *John Adams* (New York, 2001).

Jon Meacham, *Thomas Jefferson: The Art of Power* (New York, 2012).

Thomas J. Meyer, "The Great Rebellion of 1823," *Harvard Crimson*, Feb. 17, 1982.

William Lee Miller, *Arguing About Slavery: The Great Battle in the United States Congress* (New York, 1996).

Samuel Eliot Morison, *Harrison Gray Otis, 1765–1848: The Urbane Federalist* (Boston, 1969).

Michael A. Morrison, *Slavery and the West: The Eclipse of Manifest Destiny and the Coming of the Civil War* (University of North Carolina Press, 1997).

Paul C. Nagel, *John Quincy Adams: A Public Life, a Private Life* (New York, 1997).

Allan Nevins, ed., *The Diary of Philip Hone*, 2 vols. (New York, 1936).

Gregory H. Nobles, *American Frontiers: Cultural Encounters and Continental Conquest* (New York, 1998).

John T. Noonan Jr., *The Antelope: The Ordeal of the Recaptured Africans in the Administrations of James Monroe and John Quincy Adams* (University of California Press, 1977).

Michael O'Brien, *Mrs. Adams in Winter: A Journey in the Last Days of Napoleon* (New York, 2010).

R. R. Palmer and Joel Colton, *A History of the Modern World* (New York, 1992).

Lynn Hudson Parsons, *John Quincy Adams* (Madison, WI, 1998).

Bradford Perkins, *Castlereagh and Adams: England and the United States, 1812–1823* (Berkeley, CA, 1964).

George W. Pierson, *Tocqueville and Beaumont in America* (New York, 1938).

Marlana Portolano, *The Passionate Empiricist: The Eloquence of John Quincy Adams in the Service of Science* (State University of New York Press, 2009).

Daniel Preston, ed., *The Papers of James Monroe*, digital edition (University of Virginia Press).

William H. Rehnquist, *Grand Inquests: The Historic Impeachments of Judge Samuel Chase and President Andrew Johnson* (New York, 1992).

Robert V. Remini, *Andrew Jackson and His Indian Wars* (New York, 2001).

———, *Henry Clay: Statesman for the Union* (New York, 1991).

Adam Rothman, *Slave Country: American Expansion and the Origins of the Deep South* (Harvard University Press, 2007).

Robert A. Rutland et al., eds., *The Papers of James Madison: Presidential Series*, 11 vols. (University of Virginia Press, 1984–2020).

Simon Schama, *Patriots and Liberators: Revolution in the Netherlands, 1780–1813* (New York, 1977).

William H. Seward, *Life of John Quincy Adams* (New York, 1849).

Jack Shepherd, *Cannibals of the Heart: A Personal Biography of Louisa Catherine and John Quincy Adams* (New York, 1980).

Noah Shusterman, *The French Revolution: Faith, Desire, and Politics* (New York, 2014).

Joel H. Silbey, *Martin Van Buren and the Emergence of American Popular Politics* (Lanham, MD, 2002).

Albert Soboul, *The French Revolution, 1787–1799: From the Storming of the Bastille to Napoleon* (New York, 1975).

Anders Stephanson, *Manifest Destiny: American Expansion and the Empire of Right* (New York, 1996).

William L. Stone, *Letters on Masonry and Anti-Masonry Addressed to the Honorable John Quincy Adams* (New York, 1832).

Richard B. Strothers, "The Great Tambora Eruption in 1815 and Its Aftermath," *Science* 224 (1984): 1191–98.

Edward H. Tatum Jr., ed., "Ten Unpublished Letters of John Quincy Adams, 1796–1837," *Huntington Library Quarterly* 4, no. 3 (1941): 369–88.

Louisa Thomas, *Louisa: The Extraordinary Life of Mrs. Adams* (New York, 2017).

James Traub, *John Quincy Adams: Militant Spirit* (New York, 2016).

United States Congress, *Congressional Globe*, 36 vols. (Washington, DC).

Martin Van Buren, *The Autobiography of Martin Van Buren*, edited by John C. Fitzpatrick (New York, 1920).

William Preston Vaughn, *The Anti-Masonic Party in the United States, 1826–1843* (University Press of Kentucky, 1983).

David Waldstreicher, ed., *A Companion to John Adams and John Quincy Adams* (New York, 2013).

———, ed., *John Quincy Adams: Diaries, 1779–1848*, 2 vols. (New York, 2017).

——— and Matthew Mason, eds., *John Quincy Adams and the Politics of Slavery: Selections from the Diary* (New York, 2016).

Steven Watts, *The Republic Reborn: War and the Making of Liberal America, 1790–1820* (Johns Hopkins University Press, 1987).

William Earl Weeks, *John Quincy Adams and American Global Empire* (University Press of Kentucky, 1992).

Joseph Wheelan, *Mr. Adams's Last Crusade: John Quincy Adams's Extraordinary Post-Presidential Life in Congress* (New York, 2008).

Charles M. Wiltse, ed., *The Papers of Daniel Webster*, digital edition (University of Virginia Press).

Gordon S. Wood, *Empire of Liberty: A History of the Early Republic, 1789–1815* (New York, 2009).

Notes

CHAPTER 1

1. Quoted in Ferling, *John Adams*, 11.
2. Ibid., 14.
3. Bernstein, "John Adams," in Waldstreicher, *Companion*, 6.
4. Quoted in Staloff, "John Adams and Enlightenment," in Waldstreicher, *Companion*, 40.
5. Ferling, *John Adams*, 18.
6. Ibid., 22–23.
7. Ibid., 29–30.
8. Quoted in ibid., 31.
9. Quoted in Holton, *Abigail Adams*, 6–7.
10. Ibid., 4–5.
11. Ibid., 10.
12. Quoted in ibid., 15.
13. Quoted in ibid., 18.
14. Quoted in Ferling, *John Adams*, 32.
15. Quoted in Isenberg and Burstein, *The Problem of Democracy*, 7–8.
16. Quoted in Holton, *Abigail Adams*, 34.
17. Ibid., 36.
18. Ibid., 37.
19. JA to R. Cranch, Sept. 23, 1767, Fam. Cor., I.
20. Ferling, *John Adams*, 42–44.
21. Ibid., 57.
22. Holton, *Abigail Adams*, 49.
23. Quoted in ibid., x.
24. Ibid., 51.
25. Quoted in ibid., 60.
26. AA to Mercy Warren, Jan. 1777, Fam. Cor.
27. Quoted in Holton, *Abigail Adams*, 60.
28. Quoted in ibid., 69.
29. JA to AA, Sept. 8, 1774, Fam. Cor., I.
30. Quoted in Barzilay, "John Adams in the Continental Congress," in Waldstreicher, *Companion*, 80–81.
31. AA to JA, Aug. 19, 1774, Fam. Cor., I.
32. JA to AA, Aug. 28, 1774, ibid.
33. JQA to JA, Oct. 13, 1774, ibid.
34. Quoted in Divine et al., *America*, 134.
35. CFA, *Memoirs of JQA*, VII, 325.
36. JQA to Joseph Sturge, April 1846, Adams Papers, II, reel 155.
37. Holton, *Abigail Adams*, 74–75.
38. Ibid., 78–79.
39. AA to JA, June 18, 1775, Fam. Cor., I.
40. Quoted in Divine et al., *America*, 134.
41. JQA to Joseph Sturge, April 1846, Adams Papers, II, reel 155.
42. Holton, *Abigail Adams*, 74–75.
43. Ibid., 78–79.
44. Barzilay, "John Adams in the Continental Congress," in Waldstreicher, *Companion*, 87–88, and Bemis, *JQA and the Foundations*, 6.
45. Barzilay, "John Adams in the Continental Congress," in Waldstreicher, *Companion*, 90–91.
46. Staloff, "John Adams and Enlightenment," in Waldstreicher, *Companion*, 36–38.
47. Quoted in ibid., 40.
48. Quoted in ibid., 41.
49. Quoted in ibid., 43.
50. Quoted in ibid.
51. Quoted in Watts, *Republic Reborn*, 34–35.
52. Quoted in ibid.
53. "Some Books the Adams Family Read During the Revolution," Fam. Cor., II, xii.

54. Barzilay, "John Adams in the Continental Congress," in Waldstreicher, *Companion*, 90.

55. Siemers, "John Adams's Political Thought," in Waldstreicher, *Companion*, 110–11.

56. Quoted in Holton, *Abigail Adams*, 71.

57. AA to JA, March 31, 1776, Founders Online.

58. JA to AA, April 14, 1776, ibid.

59. AA to JA, May 7, 1776, Fam. Cor., I.

60. Cotton Tufts to JA, Aug. 6, 1776, ibid.

61. AA to JA, July 29, 1776, ibid.

62. Quoted in Holton, *Abigail Adams*, 113.

63. Quoted in Meacham, *Thomas Jefferson*, 102–3.

64. Quoted in McCullough, *John Adams*, 121–22.

65. Quoted in Barzilay, "John Adams in the Continental Congress," in Waldstreicher, *Companion*, 95.

66. JA to AA, Dec. 3, 1775, Fam. Cor., I.

67. Quoted in Levin, *Education of JQA*, 25.

68. JA to AA, April 18, 1776, Fam. Cor., II.

69. JA to JQA, July 28, 1777, ibid.

70. JQA to JA, March 23, 1777.

71. Quoted in ibid., 186.

72. Waldstreicher, *JQA Diaries*, II, 214–15.

73. JQA to JA, March 1777, ibid.

74. Ibid.

CHAPTER 2

1. Herring, *Colony to Superpower*, 14–17.

2. Ibid., 19, and Ferling, *John Adams*, 185.

3. Quoted in Ferling, *John Adams*, 285.

4. AA to John Thaxter, Fam. Cor., II.

5. Ibid.

6. Ibid.

7. Butterfield et al., *Adams Family Correspondence*, II, 269.

8. Ibid., 272.

9. Ibid., 276–77.

10. Ibid., 285.

11. Samuel Tucker to James Hove, Aug. 26, 1826, in ibid., 286.

12. Ibid.

13. Ibid., 292.

14. Ibid., 295–96.

15. Ibid., 298.

16. JA to AA, April 19, 1778, Fam. Cor., II.

17. Nagel, *John Quincy Adams*, 14.

18. JQA to AA, April 20, 1778, Fam. Cor., II.

19. JQA to Lucy Cranch, June 1, 1778, ibid.

20. Butterfield et al., *Adams Family Correspondence, Diary of JA*, 306.

21. JA to AA, April 12, 1778, Fam. Cor., II.

22. JA to AA, April 25, 1778, ibid.

23. Isenberg and Burstein, *The Problem of Democracy*, 484, nt. 7.

24. AA to John Thaxter, Feb. 15, 1778, Fam. Cor., II.

25. AA to JQA, June (10?), 1778, ibid.

26. CFA, *Memoirs of JQA*, V, 143.

27. Quoted in Drinnon, *Facing West*, 71.

28. JA to AA, April 19, 1778, Fam. Cor., II.

29. Quoted in Holton, *Abigail Adams*, 146–47.

30. Ibid.

31. Butterfield et al., *Adams Family Correspondence*, II, 304–5.

32. Ferling, *John Adams*, 198.

33. Quoted in ibid., 196.

34. Quoted in Butterfield et al., *Adams Family Correspondence*, II, 311.

35. Ferling, *John Adams*, 196.

36. Ibid.

37. Quoted in Isenberg and Burstein, *The Problem of Democracy*, 69.

38. Quoted in Ferling, *John Adams*, 203.

39. Isenberg and Burstein, *The Problem of Democracy*, 44.

40. JQA to AA, Sept. 27, 1778, Fam. Cor., III.

41. JQA to TBA and CA, Oct. 2, 1778, ibid.

42. JA to AA, Nov. 27, 1779, ibid.

43. Butterfield et al., *Adams Family Correspondence*, II, 359.

44. JA to AA, May 14, 1779, Fam. Cor., III.

45. Levin, *Education of JQA*, 41.

46. JA to AA, May 24, 1779, Fam. Cor., III.

47. Butterfield et al., *Adams Family Correspondence*, II, 367.

48. Ibid., 369.

49. Ibid., 370.

50. Ibid.

51. Ibid., 385.

52. Ferling, *John Adams*, 212.

53. Quoted in Levin, *Education of JQA*, 42.

54. Ibid.
55. Quoted in Bemis, *JQA and the Foundations*, 11.
56. Quoted in Levin, *Education of JQA*, 43.
57. Ibid.
58. JA to AA, Nov. 13, 1779, Fam. Cor., III.
59. Ibid.
60. Butterfield et al., *Adams Family Correspondence*, II, 418.
61. Diary entry, Nov. 1779, JQA Diaries.
62. Quoted in Levin, *Education of JQA*, 47–48.
63. Ibid., 48, and Ferling, *John Adams*, 219.
64. JQA to AA, Jan. 16, 1780, Fam. Cor., II.
65. Diary entry, Dec. 8, 1779, JQA Diaries.
66. Butterfield et al., *Adams Family Correspondence*, II, Dec. 6, 1779.
67. Allen et al., *Diary of JQA*, I, 113. The knight Hudibras and his squire, Ralpho, are the principal characters in Samuel Butler's mock-heroic poem, *Hudibras*.
68. Butterfield et al., *Adams Family Correspondence*, II, 409.
69. Allen et al., *Diary of JQA*, I, 15.
70. Butterfield et al., *Adams Family Correspondence*, II, 412–15.
71. Ibid., 416.
72. Allen et al., *Diary of JQA*, I, 25.
73. Ibid.
74. Butterfield et al., *Adams Family Correspondence*, II, 433, and Ferling, *John Adams*, 219.
75. Allen et al., *Diary of JQA*, I, 34.

CHAPTER 3

1. Ferling, *John Adams*, 221.
2. Ibid., 220.
3. Fam. Cor., III, 272.
4. JQA to AA, Feb. 17, 1780, ibid.
5. JQA to JA, March 16, 1780, ibid.
6. Allen et al., *Diary of JQA*, I, 35.
7. AA to JQA, March 20, 1780, Fam. Cor., III.
8. Ferling, *John Adams*, 228–31.
9. Isenberg and Burstein, *The Problem of Democracy*, 74–75.
10. Allen et al., *Diary of JQA*, I, 62–64.
11. JA to AA, Sept. 25, 1780, Fam. Cor., II.
12. Fam. Cor., III, 425.
13. Quoted in Levin, *Education of JQA*, 54.
14. Quoted in ibid., 55.
15. JQA to JA, Dec. 21, 1780, Fam. Cor., IV, and Ford, *Writings of JQA*, I, 12–13.
16. JQA to AA, Dec. 21, 1780, Fam. Cor., IV.
17. Butterfield et al., *Adams Family Correspondence*, II, 451.
18. Allen et al., *Diary of JQA*, I, 75.
19. Quoted in Ferling, *John Adams*, 217.
20. Quoted in ibid., 234.
21. AA to JA, Dec. 25, 1780, Fam. Cor., IV.
22. Quoted in Holton, *Abigail Adams*, xii.
23. Quoted in ibid., xiv–xv.
24. Levin, *Education of JQA*, 57–58.
25. Allen et al., *Diary of JQA*, I, 91–92.
26. Ibid., 59.
27. Quoted in Levin, *Education of JQA*, 590.
28. Francis Dana to JA, Aug. 28, 1781, Papers of John Adams, II, Digital Edition, MHS.
29. JQA to AA, Aug. 21, 1781, Adams Papers, IV, reel 355.
30. Ibid.
31. Levin, *Education of JQA*, 62.
32. Quoted in ibid.
33. Francis Dana to JA, Aug. 28, 1781, Papers of John Adams, II, Digital Edition, MHS.
34. See, for example, Allen et al., *Diary of JQA*, I, 104ff.
35. Quoted in Levin, *Education of JQA*, 63.
36. Francis Dana to JA, Aug. 28, 1781, Papers of John Adams, II, Digital Edition, MHS, and Allen et al., *Diary of JQA*, I, 107.
37. JQA to JA, Oct. 23, 1782, Fam. Cor., IV.
38. Allen et al., *Diary of JQA*, I, 102, and JQA to JA, Feb. 21, March 4, 1782, Fam. Cor., V.
39. JA to JQA, Feb. 5, 1782, Fam. Cor., IV.
40. AA2 to JQA, May 3, 1782, ibid.
41. Ferling, *John Adams*, 239.
42. JQA to AA, Sept. 10, 1783, Fam. Cor., V.
43. JA to JQA, Dec. 15, 1781, Adams Papers, IV, reel 355.
44. Quoted in Levin, *Education of JQA*, 69.

45. JQA to AA, July 23, 1783, Fam. Cor., V.

46. Quoted in ibid., xv.

47. Quoted in Levin, *Education of JQA*, 70.

48. Allen et al., *Diary of JQA*, I, 170.

49. JQA to AA, July 23, 1783, Fam. Cor., V.

50. JA to JQA, Feb. 18, 1783, ibid.

51. Ferling, *John Adams*, 239.

52. Ibid., 240, 243.

53. JA to AA, Oct. 12, 1782, Fam. Cor., V.

54. JA to AA, Dec. 4, 1782, ibid.

55. Quoted in Isenberg and Burstein, *The Problem of Democracy*, 83.

56. Quoted in Levin, *Education of JQA*, 76.

57. Quoted in Allen et al., *Diary of JQA*, I, 174.

58. Ibid., 175.

59. JA to JQA, May 19, 1783, Fam. Cor., V.

60. JA to AA2, Aug. 13, 1783, ibid.

61. Levin, *Education of JQA*, 77, and JA to JQA, May 19, 1783, Fam. Cor., V.

62. Allen et al., *Diary of JQA*, I, 181.

63. Traub, *John Quincy Adams*, 32.

64. Ibid., 187.

65. Ibid., 187–88.

66. AA to JQA, Nov. 20, 1783, Fam. Cor., V.

67. Quoted in Nagel, *John Quincy Adams*, 31.

CHAPTER 4

1. Elbridge Gerry to AA, April 16, 1784, Fam. Cor., V.

2. JA to AA, Sept. 7, 1783, ibid.

3. AA to Elbridge Gerry, Oct. 15, 1783.

4. JA to AA, June 19, 1783, ibid.

5. JQA to Elizabeth Cranch, April 18, 1784, ibid.

6. Quoted in Levin, *Education of JQA*, 90–91.

7. Allen et al., *Diary of JQA*, I, 198.

8. Ibid., 203.

9. Levin, *Education of JQA*, 90–91.

10. Butterfield et al., *Adams Family Correspondence*, II, 152.

11. Ibid., 152–54.

12. Ibid.

13. AA to JQA, April 25, 1784, Fam. Cor., V.

14. Quoted in Levin, *Education of JQA*, 92.

15. Ibid., 93.

16. JQA to JA, June 15, 1784, Fam. Cor., V.

17. JQA to W. V. Murray, Jan. 27, 1801, Adams Papers, II, reel 134.

18. AA to JA, May 25, 1784, Fam. Cor., V.

19. AA to JA, July 30, 1784, ibid.

20. Quoted in Holton, *Abigail Adams*, 200.

21. JA to AA, July 26, 1784, Fam. Cor., V.

22. Ibid., 385.

23. JQA to JA, July 30, 1784, Adams Papers, IV, reel 363.

24. JA to JQA, Aug. 8, 1784, Fam. Cor., V.

25. Levin, *Education of JQA*, 95.

26. AA to Elizabeth Cranch, Sept. 5, 1784, Fam. Cor., V.

27. Quoted in Holton, *Abigail Adams*, 205.

28. Quoted in Levin, *Education of JQA*, 104.

29. Ibid., 109.

30. Allen et al., *Diary of JQA*, I, 216.

31. Ibid., 225.

32. Ibid., 232.

33. Ibid., 240.

34. Ibid., 237.

35. Ibid., 226.

36. Ibid., 243.

37. Quoted in Ferling, *John Adams*, 273.

38. Meacham, *Thomas Jefferson*, 8.

39. Ibid., 28–29.

40. Ibid., xxi–xxxiii, xxvi.

41. Allen et al., *Diary of JQA*, I, 218, 220.

42. Ibid., 233.

43. Ibid., 262.

44. AA to Mary Smith Cranch, Dec. 9, 1784, Fam. Cor., VI.

45. Allen et al., *Diary of JQA*, I, 256.

46. Elizabeth Smith Shaw to AA, May 20, 1787, Fam. Cor., VI.

47. Allen et al., *Diary of JQA*, I, 256–57.

48. Quoted in Fam. Cor., V, 484–85.

49. Quoted in Levin, *Education of JQA*, 117–18.

50. Quoted in Fam. Cor., V, 484–85.

51. AA to Mary Smith Cranch, April 15, 1785, Fam. Cor., VI.

52. AA to Cotton Tufts, May 2, 1785, ibid.

CHAPTER 5

1. Allen et al., *Diary of JQA*, I, 274, 278.
2. CFA, *Memoirs of JQA*, IX, 353–54.
3. JQA to AA, Oct. 1, 1815, Founders Online.
4. Ferling, *John Adams*, 275.
5. Quoted in Ketcham, *Madison*, 120.
6. Quoted in ibid., 122–23.
7. Fam. Cor., VI, 264.
8. Ferling, *John Adams*, 280.
9. Quoted in Holton, *Abigail Adams*, 219.
10. JQA to AA2, May 11, 1785, Fam. Cor., VI.
11. AA2 to JQA, July 4, 1785, ibid.
12. Quoted in Ferling, *John Adams*, 262.
13. Thomas Jefferson to AA2, Jan. 15, 1787, Fam. Cor., VII.
14. Ferling, *John Adams*, 381–82.
15. Quoted in Levin, *Education of JQA*, 126.
16. Ibid., 130, and Ferling, *John Adams*, 283–84.
17. Quoted in Holton, *Abigail Adams*, 184.
18. Elizabeth Smith Shaw to AA, April 25, 1785, Fam. Cor., VI.
19. Quoted in Levin, *Education of JQA*, 118–19.
20. AA to CA, Feb. 16, 1785, Fam. Cor., VI.
21. Allen et al., *Diary of JQA*, I, 289–93, 300.
22. Ibid., 303–8.
23. JQA to AA2, Aug. 19, 1785.
24. Quoted in Nagel, *John Quincy Adams*, 38.
25. Allen et al., *Diary of JQA*, I, 309–10.
26. Ibid., 112–13.
27. JQA to AA2, Aug. 26, 1785, Fam. Cor., VI.
28. Quoted in Isenberg and Burstein, *The Problem of Democracy*, 99.
29. Elizabeth Smith Shaw to AA, Sept. 1, 1785, Fam. Cor., VI.
30. Mary Smith Cranch to AA, Aug. 14, 1785, ibid.
31. AA to Cotton Tufts, May 2, 1785, ibid.
32. Quoted in Levin, *Education of JQA*, 138.
33. Allen et al., *Diary of JQA*, I, 335, 339.
34. Elizabeth Smith Shaw to AA2, Feb. 14, 1786, ibid.
35. Mary Smith Cranch to AA, Feb. 9, 1786, Fam. Cor., VII.
36. JA to JQA, Sept. 9, 1785, ibid.
37. Quoted in Nagel, *John Quincy Adams*, 43.
38. Ibid., 321.
39. Quoted in ibid., 338.
40. Quoted in ibid., 435.
41. Ibid., 346.
42. Quoted in ibid., 351.
43. Quoted in ibid., 356.
44. Quoted in ibid., 368.
45. Quoted in ibid., 387.
46. Quoted in ibid., 44.
47. AA2 to JQA, April 25, 1786, Fam. Cor., VII.
48. Quoted in Levin, *Education of JQA*, 114.
49. Allen et al., *Diary of JQA*, I, 400–1.
50. Fam. Cor., VIII, 55.
51. JQA to AA2, March 15, 1786, Fam. Cor., VII.
52. Ibid., 374.
53. Elizabeth Smith Shaw to AA2, Feb. 14, 1786, Fam. Cor., VI.
54. Elizabeth Smith Shaw to AA, March 18, 1786, ibid.
55. Allen et al., *Diary of JQA*, II, 1.
56. JA to JQA, May 26, 1786, Fam. Cor., VII.
57. Allen et al., *Diary of JQA*, II, 2.
58. JQA to AA2, March 15, 1786, Fam. Cor., VII.
59. Richard Cranch to AA, July 5, 1786, ibid.
60. Mary Smith Cranch to AA, March 22, 1786, ibid.
61. JQA to JA, April 12, 1786, ibid.
62. JQA to AA2, April 1, 1786, ibid.
63. JQA to JA, May 21, 1786, ibid.
64. Allen et al., *Diary of JQA*, II, ix–x.
65. JQA to AA2, May 18, 1786, Fam. Cor., VII.
66. JQA to AA2, April 29, 1786, ibid.
67. Allen et al., *Diary of JQA*, II, 29.
68. Quoted in Levin, *Education of JQA*, 159.
69. Heffron, *Louisa Catherine*, 58.
70. Allen et al., *Diary of JQA*, II, 32, 54–55, 88.
71. Ibid., 84–86.

72. Quoted in Holton, *Abigail Adams*, xv.

73. Allen et al., *Diary of JQA*, II, 167.

74. Ibid., 13.

75. JQA to JA, Aug. 30, 1786, Fam. Cor., VII.

76. Allen et al., *Diary of JQA*, II, 150.

77. JQA to AA2, May 19, 1786, Fam. Cor., VII.

78. Allen et al., *Diary of JQA*, II, 234.

79. JQA to AA2, June 17, 1786, Fam. Cor., VI.

80. AA2 to JQA, July 22, 1786, ibid.

81. Quoted in Levin, *Education of JQA*, 157.

82. Allen et al., *Diary of JQA*, II, 78–79.

83. Divine et al., *America*, 166.

84. Allen et al., *Diary of JQA*, II, 91–92.

85. Ibid., 93.

86. Ibid., 133.

87. CFA, *Memoirs of JQA*, X, 111.

88. See Cotton Tufts to AA, Feb. 6, 1787, Fam. Cor., VII.

89. AA to JQA, Nov. 28, 1786, ibid.

90. Quoted in Levin, *Education of JQA*, 156.

91. See, for example, JQA to AA, Nov. 22, 1786, Fam. Cor., VII.

92. JQA to AA2, Jan. 14, 1787, ibid.

93. Ibid.

94. Mary Smith Cranch to AA, April 22, 1787, ibid.

95. AA to JQA, Jan. 17, 1787, ibid.

96. Allen et al., *Diary of JQA*, II, 205.

97. See JA to CA, June 5, 1793, Fam. Cor., VII.

98. Quoted in Houpt, "John Adams and the Elections of 1796 and 1800," in Waldstreicher, *Companion*, 154.

99. Ibid., 103, 51–53, Siemers, "John Adams's Political Thought," 103, and Staloff "John Adams and the Enlightenment," 51–53.

100. Quoted in Ferling, *John Adams*, 288.

101. Fam. Cor., VII, 378.

102. Ferling, *John Adams*, 288–90, and Siemers, "John Adams's Political Thought," in Waldstreicher, *Companion*, 103.

103. Quoted in Isenberg and Burstein, *The Problem of Democracy*, 115.

104. Elizabeth Smith Shaw to AA, May 20, 1787, Fam. Cor., VIII.

105. Allen et al., *Diary of JQA*, II, 223.

106. Ibid., 226.

107. Quoted in Holton, *Abigail Adams*, 245.

108. Allen et al., *Diary of JQA*, II, 255–63.

109. Mary Smith Cranch to AA, Aug. 19, 1787, Fam. Cor., VIII.

110. Allen et al., *Diary of JQA*, II, 265.

CHAPTER 6

1. Allen et al., *Diary of JQA*, II, 243.

2. Ibid., 253.

3. Traub, *John Quincy Adams*, 51.

4. Allen et al., *Diary of JQA*, II, 275–76.

5. JQA to AA, Dec. 23, 1787, Fam. Cor., VIII.

6. Quoted in Heffron, *Louisa Catherine*, 59.

7. Allen et al., *Diary of JQA*, II, 319.

8. Isenberg and Burstein, *The Problem of Democracy*, 117.

9. Allen et al., *Diary of JQA*, II, 281.

10. Ibid., 302–3.

11. Ibid., 303.

12. Ibid., 357.

13. Ibid., 297.

14. Ibid., 303.

15. Ibid., 333.

16. AA to JQA, Feb. 28, 1787, Fam. Cor., VIII.

17. Allen et al., *Diary of JQA*, II, 339.

18. Ibid., 343.

19. AA2 to JQA, Feb. 10, 1778, Fam. Cor., VIII.

20. Allen et al., *Diary of JQA*, II, 373.

21. Quoted in Holton, *Abigail Adams*, 241.

22. Ferling, *John Adams*, 296.

23. Ibid.

24. Allen et al., *Diary of JQA*, II, 393–94.

25. Quoted in Levin, *Education of JQA*, 14.

26. Allen et al., *Diary of JQA*, II, 420.

27. Ibid., 447–52.

28. AA to JQA, March 15, 1784, Fam. Cor., VIII.

29. Elizabeth Smith Shaw to AA, Sept. 21, 1788, ibid.

30. Elizabeth Smith Shaw to AA, Oct. 3, 1788, ibid.

31. Quoted in Nagel, *John Quincy Adams*, 61.

32. AA to Mary Smith Cranch, Nov. 24, 1788, Fam. Cor., VIII.

33. Ferling, *John Adams*, 298–99.

34. Allen et al., *Diary of JQA*, II, 338.

35. Fam. Cor., VIII, 362.

36. Traub, *John Quincy Adams*, 55.

37. AA2 to JQA, June 6, 1790, Fam. Cor., IX.

38. Quoted in Nagel, *John Quincy Adams*, 65.

39. Quoted in ibid.

40. JA to JQA, July 9, 1789, and JQA to JA, June 28, 1789, Fam. Cor., VIII.

41. AA to Elizabeth Smith Shaw, Sept. 27, 1789, and xiv–xv, ibid.

42. Ibid., IX, xxvi–xxvii.

43. AA to JQA, Sept. 12, 1790, ibid.

44. AA2 to JQA, Dec. 26, 1790, ibid.

45. Quoted in Levin, *Education of JQA*, 186–87.

46. JQA to AA, Dec. 5, 1789, Fam. Cor., VIII.

47. JQA to William Cranch, April 7, 1790, Fam. Cor., IX.

48. Ibid., JQA to JA, March 19, 1790, and Ford, *Writings of JQA*, I, 44.

49. Quoted in Nagel, *John Quincy Adams*, 66.

50. AA to JQA, Aug. 20 and Nov. 7, 1790, Fam. Cor., IX.

51. JQA to William Cranch, May 27, 1790, Fam. Cor., VIII.

52. JQA to AA, Nov. 20, 1790, Fam. Cor., IX.

53. Quoted in Nagel, *John Quincy Adams*, 68.

54. Quoted in ibid., 69.

55. JQA to William Cranch, July 12, 1790, Fam. Cor., IX.

56. JA to JQA, April 1, 1790, ibid.

57. JQA to JA, Sept. 21, 1790, ibid.

58. Quoted in Levin, *Education of JQA*, 199.

59. JQA to AA, Oct. 17, 1790, Fam. Cor., IX.

60. Nagel, *John Quincy Adams*, 71.

61. AA to AA2, March 12, 1791, Fam. Cor., IX.

62. Quoted in Levin, *Education of JQA*, 201.

63. Diary entry, April 17, 1791, JQA Diaries.

64. Ibid.

CHAPTER 7

1. See Doyle, *Oxford History of the French Revolution*; Palmer and Colton, *History of the Modern World*; Schama, *Patriots and Liberators*; and Soboul, *French Revolution*.

2. Wood, *Empire of Liberty*, 89–90.

3. Quoted in Divine et al., *America*, 185.

4. Quoted in ibid., 188.

5. Quoted in Isenberg and Burstein, *The Problem of Democracy*, 130.

6. Ferling, *John Adams*, 103–4.

7. Staloff, "John Adams and Enlightenment," in Waldstreicher, *Companion*, 45.

8. Quoted in Ketcham, *Madison*, 34.

9. Quoted in Ferling, *John Adams*, 307.

10. Fam. Cor., XI, 33.

11. Quoted in Ferling, *John Adams*, 309.

12. Quoted in ibid.

13. JQA to JA, Oct. 1790, Fam. Cor., XI.

14. Quoted in Meacham, *Thomas Jefferson*, 221.

15. Quoted in ibid., 234.

16. Bemis, *JQA and the Foundations*, 7–8, and Ferling, *John Adams*, 314.

17. Wood, *Empire of Liberty*, 479.

18. Freeman, *Affairs of Honor*, 124.

19. Quoted in Howe, *What Hath God Wrought*, 225.

20. Diary entry, Sept. 7, 1790, JQA Diaries.

21. Ford, *Writings of JQA*, I, 65.

22. Ibid., 70.

23. Ibid.

24. Ibid., 75.

25. Ibid., 83.

26. JA to CA, June 5, 1793, Fam. Cor., IX.

27. Thomas Jefferson to James Monroe, July 10, 1791, Preston et al., *Papers of James Monroe*, II.

28. Quoted in Bemis, *JQA and the Foundations*, 27.

29. McClure and Looney, *The Papers of Thomas Jefferson*, Digital Edition.

30. Ibid.

31. Diary entry, April 13, 1792, JQA Diaries.

32. Quoted in Nagel, *John Quincy Adams*, 72.

33. Diary entry, July 21, 1792, JQA Diaries.

34. Ibid., diary entry, Sept. 3, 1792.

35. Ibid., diary entry, Oct. 8, 1792.

36. Ibid., diary entry, June 28, 1793.

37. JA to TBA, Oct. 18, 1793, Fam. Cor., IX.
38. See Morison, *Harrison Gray Otis*, 41.
39. Quoted in Levin, *Education of JQA*, 217.
40. Ibid., 216–17.
41. JQA to JA, Dec. 16, 1792, Fam. Cor., IX, and Ford, *Writings of JQA*, I, 123.
42. JQA to JA, Dec. 8, 1792, Fam. Cor., IX, and Morison, *Harrison Gray Otis*, 60–61.
43. Family Cor., IX, 260.
44. Ibid., xv.
45. See Shusterman, *French Revolution*, 187–221.
46. AA2 to AA, Sept. 13, 1792, Fam. Cor., IX.
47. Ibid., JQA to TBA, Sept. 2, 1792.
48. Quoted in Meacham, *Thomas Jefferson*, 266.
49. Ferling, *John Adams*, 316.
50. CA to JQA, July 29, 1791, Fam. Cor., IX.
51. "Marcellus," in Ford, *Writings of JQA*, I, 136–45.
52. Quoted in DeConde, *History*, I, 59.
53. Ibid., 60.
54. Cappon, *Adams–Jefferson Letters*.
55. Ford, *Writings of JQA*, I, 149.
56. Ibid., 150–51.
57. See "Columbus," in Ford, *Writings of JQA*, I, 159.
58. JA to JQA, Jan. 5, 1794, Fam. Cor., IX, and Ford, *Writings of JQA*, I, 176.
59. Ford, *Writings of JQA*, I, 177.
60. JA to AA, Dec. 19, 1793, Fam. Cor., IX.
61. JA to JQA, Dec. 14, 1793, ibid.
62. JQA to TBA, Feb. 13, 1794, ibid.

CHAPTER 8

1. Ford, *Writings of JQA*, I, 181.
2. JQA to JA, March 24, 1794, Fam. Cor., X.
3. Ford, *Writings of JQA*, 183.
4. JA to JQA, March 11, 1794, Fam. Cor., X.
5. JA to JQA, April 3, 1794, ibid.
6. Quoted in Levin, *Education of JQA*, 230.
7. Ford, *Writings of JQA*, I, 186.
8. JA to JQA, April 23, 1794, Fam. Cor., X.
9. JA to JQA, May 26, 1794, ibid.
10. Diary entry, June 3, 1794, JQA Diaries.

11. Ibid., diary entries, June 9–10, 1794.
12. Ford, *Writings of JQA*, I, 148.
13. JA to JQA, May 29, 1794, Fam. Cor., X.
14. AA to Martha Washington, June 20, 1794, ibid.
15. Levin, *Education of JQA*, 235–36.
16. Ibid., 257.
17. Diary entry, July 7, 1794, JQA Diaries.
18. JQA to JA, July 10, 1794, Fam. Cor., X.
19. Diary entry, July 11, 1794, JQA Diaries.
20. Siemers, "John Adams's Political Thought," in Waldstreicher, *Companion*, 117.
21. Quoted in Isenberg and Burstein, *The Problem of Democracy*, 128.
22. Diary entry, July 11, 1794, JQA Diaries.
23. JQA to JA, July 29, 1794, Fam. Cor., X.
24. JA to JQA, Aug. 24, 1794, ibid.
25. "Instructions," in Ford, *Writings of JQA*, I, 198–99.
26. JQA to JA, July 18, 1794, Fam. Cor., X.
27. Diary entry, Sept. 17, 1794, JQA Diaries.
28. Ibid., diary entry, Sept. 23, 1794.
29. Ford, *Writings of JQA*, I, 201–2.
30. Bemis, *JQA and the Foundations*, 43–49, and DeConde, *History*, I, 54–55.
31. Ford, *Writings of JQA*, I, 203.
32. Ibid.
33. Quoted in Ketcham, *Madison*, 357.
34. See DeConde, *History*, I, 550, and Divine et al., *America*, 194.
35. Nagel, *John Quincy Adams*, 85.
36. Diary of TBA, Oct. 1794, Adams Papers, III, reel 281, 10.
37. Ibid.
38. Diary entry, Oct. 27, 1794, JQA Diaries.
39. Ibid., diary entry, Oct. 29, 1794.
40. Diary of TBA, Nov. 1798, Adams Papers, III, reel 282, 23.
41. Ibid., 35–36.
42. See Schama, *Patriots and Liberators*.
43. Ford, *Writings of JQA*, I, 204–5.
44. Ibid., 227.
45. Fam. Cor., X, 258.
46. Ford, *Writings of JQA*, I, 205–6.
47. Ibid., 213.
48. Ibid., 247.

49. Quoted in Levin, *Education of JQA*, 255.
50. Ford, *Writings of JQA*, I, 262.
51. Ibid., 280–82.
52. Diary of TBA, Jan. 22, 1795, Adams Papers, III, reel 282, 80.
53. Ibid., 83–84.
54. Ford, *Writings of JQA*, I, 206.
55. AA to JQA, Jan. 10, 1795, Fam. Cor., X.
56. Bemis, *JQA and the Foundations*, 52, and Fam. Cor., X, xv.
57. Ford, *Writings of JQA*, I, 343, and JQA to CA, April 25, 1795, Fam. Cor., X.
58. Quoted in Nagel, *John Quincy Adams*, 89.
59. Jacob, *The Enlightenment*, 23–25.
60. Quoted in Nagel, *John Quincy Adams*, 89.
61. Diary entry, June 12, 1795, JQA Diaries.
62. Ibid., diary entry, Oct. 26, 1796.
63. JA to AA, June 23, 1789, Fam. Cor., X.
64. Ford, *Writings of JQA*, I, 154–55.
65. Diary of TBA, Adams Papers, II, reel 282, 86.
66. Ford, *Writings of JQA*, I, 370.
67. Quoted in Doyle, *Oxford History of the French Revolution*, 320.
68. Ford, *Writings of JQA*, I, 404.
69. Ibid., 356–60.
70. Ibid., 387–89.
71. JQA to JA, Oct. 31, 1795, Fam. Cor., XI.
72. JA to JQA, Aug. 25, 1795, ibid.
73. Quoted in Ford, *Writings of JQA*, I, 408–9.
74. Quoted in Levin, *Education of JQA*, 263.
75. AA to JQA, Oct. 8, 1795, Fam. Cor., XI.
76. Ammon, *James Monroe*, 119–20.
77. Quoted in Bemis, *JQA and the Foundations*, 60.
78. Ford, *Writings of JQA*, I, 424, and JQA to JA, Dec. 29, 1795, Adams Papers, II, reel 127.
79. Bemis, *JQA and the Foundations*, 73.
80. CFA, *Memoirs of JQA*, I, 139–41.
81. Ibid., 141–44.
82. JQA to CA, Dec. 30, 1795, Fam. Cor., XI.
83. Ford, *Writings of JQA*, I, 467.
84. CFA, *Memoirs of JQA*, 137–38.
85. Quoted in Bemis, *JQA and the Foundations*, 78.
86. CFA, *Memoirs of JQA*, I, 145–46.
87. Ford, *Writings of JQA*, I, 507.
88. JQA to JA, Dec. 29, 1795, Adams Papers, II, reel 127.
89. Bemis, *JQA and the Foundations*, 73.

CHAPTER 9

1. Fam. Cor., XI, xi.
2. JQA to AA, Nov. 7, 1795, Founders Online.
3. Levin, *Education of JQA*, 264.
4. *Record of a Life*, in Graham et al., *Diary and Autobiographical Writings*, I, 37.
5. Heffron, *Louisa Catherine*, 7–9.
6. Ibid., 9–10.
7. *Record of a Life*, in Graham et al., *Diary and Autobiographical Writings*, I, 19.
8. Quoted in Heffron, *Louisa Catherine*, 11.
9. Quoted in ibid., 12.
10. Ibid., 14–15.
11. Ibid., 15–16.
12. *Record of a Life*, in Graham et al., *Diary and Autobiographical Writings*, I, 3–4.
13. Heffron, *Louisa Catherine*, 19.
14. Quoted in ibid., 21.
15. *Record of a Life*, in Graham et al., *Diary and Autobiographical Writings*, I, 6.
16. Ibid.
17. Quoted in Heffron, *Louisa Catherine*, 22.
18. *Record of a Life*, in Graham et al., *Diary and Autobiographical Writings*, I, 8.
19. Ibid., 6.
20. Ibid., 8.
21. Ibid., 9.
22. Ibid., 12.
23. Ibid.
24. Ibid.
25. Ibid.
26. Heffron, *Louisa Catherine*, 38.
27. Quoted in ibid.
28. Ibid., 42–43.
29. *Record of a Life*, in Graham et al., *Diary and Autobiographical Writings*, I, 22.
30. Quoted in Heffron, *Louisa Catherine*, 32.
31. Ibid.

32. *Record of a Life*, in Graham et al., *Diary and Autobiographical Writings*, I, 31.

33. Heffron, *Louisa Catherine*, 34–35.

34. *Record of a Life*, in Graham et al., *Diary and Autobiographical Writings*, I, 16.

35. Heffron, *Louisa Catherine*, 36.

36. *Record of a Life*, in Graham et al., *Diary and Autobiographical Writings*, I, 26.

37. Ibid., 33.

38. Heffron, *Louisa Catherine*, 41.

39. Ibid., 40.

40. *Record of a Life*, in Graham et al., *Diary and Autobiographical Writings*, I, 26.

41. Ibid., 30.

42. Heffron, *Louisa Catherine*, 66.

43. Diary entry, Jan. 27, 1796, JQA Diaries.

44. Ibid., diary entry, Feb. 2, 1796.

45. Ibid., diary entry, Feb. 12, 1796.

46. *Record of a Life*, in Graham et al., *Diary and Autobiographical Writings*, I, 37.

47. Ibid., 40.

48. Quoted in Heffron, *Louisa Catherine*, 68.

49. *Record of a Life*, in Graham et al., *Diary and Autobiographical Writings*, I, 41.

50. Ibid., 42.

51. Diary entry, Feb. 17, 1796, JQA Diaries.

52. Ibid., diary entry, Feb. 21, 1796.

53. *Record of a Life*, in Graham et al., *Diary and Autobiographical Writings*, I, 41.

54. Heffron, *Louisa Catherine*, 26–31.

55. Diary entry, March 2, 1796, JQA Diaries.

56. Quoted in Heffron, *Louisa Catherine*, 71.

57. Diary entry, March 13, 1796, JQA Diaries.

58. Ibid., diary entry, April 18, 1796.

59. Ibid., diary entry, April 10, 1796.

60. Ibid., diary entry, May 10, 1796.

61. *Record of a Life*, in Graham et al., *Diary and Autobiographical Writings*, I, 41.

62. Ibid., 41–42.

63. Ibid., 42.

64. Diary entry, May 11, 1796, JQA Diaries.

65. Quoted in Heffron, *Louisa Catherine*, 77.

66. JQA to AA, Feb. 28, 1796, Fam. Cor., XI.

67. AA to JQA, May 20, 1796, ibid.

68. Diary entry, May 27, 1796, JQA Diaries.

69. Ibid., diary entry, May 28, 1796.

70. Ibid., diary entry, June 1, 1796.

71. Ibid., diary entry, July 11, 1796.

72. AA to JQA, Feb. 29, 1796, Fam. Cor., XI.

73. JQA to AA, July 25, 1796, and JQA to AA, Aug. 16, 1796, ibid.

74. Ford, *Writings of JQA*, I, 494–95.

75. Heffron, *Louisa Catherine*, 77–78.

76. AA to JQA, July 11, 1796, Fam. Cor., XI.

77. JA to JQA, Aug. 7, 1796, ibid.

78. AA to JQA, Aug. 10, 1796, ibid.

79. JQA to LCA, June 2, 1796, ibid.

80. JQA to LCA, June 17, 1796, ibid.

81. Quoted in Heffron, *Louisa Catherine*, 80.

82. JQA to LCA, Aug. 13, 1796, Fam. Cor., XI.

83. LCA to JQA, Sept. 30, 1796, ibid.

84. JQA to LCA, Oct. 12, 1796, ibid.

85. *Record of a Life*, in Graham et al., *Diary and Autobiographical Writings*, I, 47.

86. Joshua Johnson to JQA, Sept. 30, 1796, Fam. Cor., XI.

87. *Record of a Life*, in Graham et al., *Diary and Autobiographical Writings*, I, 45.

88. LCA to JQA, Nov. 29, 1796, Fam. Cor., XI.

89. Ibid., JQA to LCA, Jan. 10, 1797.

90. Quoted in Heffron, *Louisa Catherine*, 82.

91. LCA to JQA, Jan. 17, 1797, Fam. Cor., XI.

92. Diary entry, Jan. 23, 1797, JQA Diaries.

93. AA to JQA, Nov. 11, 1796, Fam. Cor., XI.

94. Diary entry, Jan. 31, 1797, JQA Diaries.

95. Ford, *Writings of JQA*, I, 482.

96. Ibid., 44–45.

97. Ibid., 80–82.

98. Houpt, "John Adams and the Elections of 1796 and 1800," in Waldstreicher, *Companion*, 146–47.

99. Ferling, *John Adams*, 330.

100. Houpt, "John Adams and the Elections of 1796 and 1800," in Waldstreicher, *Companion*, 148.

101. Wood, *Empire of Liberty*, 212.

102. Quoted in Meacham, *Thomas Jefferson*, 301.

103. Ketcham, *Madison*, 367.

104. Ford, *Writings of JQA*, II, 60.

105. Fam. Cor., XII, 10–11.

106. AA to JQA, Jan. 23, 1797, ibid.

107. Ford, *Writings of JQA*, II, 164.

108. Ibid., 128.

109. Fam. Cor., XII, 27.

110. LCA to JQA, Feb. 28, 1797, Fam. Cor., XI.

111. Quoted in Heffron, *Louisa Catherine*, 83.

112. JQA to LCA, Feb. 12, 1797, Fam. Cor., XI.

113. JQA to LCA, Feb. 7, 1797, ibid.

114. LCA to JQA, Feb. 28, 1797, ibid.

115. JQA to LCA, March 14, 1797, Fam. Cor., XII.

116. LCA to JQA, March 27, 1797, ibid.

117. JQA to LCA, April 13, 1797, ibid.

118. Diary, in Graham et al., *Diary and Autobiographical Writings*, I, 85.

119. LCA to JQA, March 20, 1797, Fam. Cor., XII.

120. Quoted in Heffron, *Louisa Catherine*, 87–88, and JQA to LCA, April 13, 1797, Fam. Cor., XII.

121. Joshua Johnson to JQA, April 25, 1797, Fam. Cor., XII.

122. Quoted in Ford, *Writings of JQA*, II, 192.

123. Fam. Cor., XII, 173.

124. Quoted in Heffron, *Louisa Catherine*, 87–88, and JQA to LCA, May 12, 1797, Fam. Cor., XII.

125. Ford, *Writings of JQA*, II, 192, nt. 1.

126. Heffron, *Louisa Catherine*, 91.

127. *Record of a Life*, in Graham et al., *Diary and Autobiographical Writings*, I, 50.

128. Ibid.

129. Diary entry, July 26, 1797, JQA Diaries.

130. Ibid., diary entry, Aug. 6, 1797.

131. JQA and LCA to AA and JA, July 28, 1797, Fam. Cor., XII.

132. AA to LCA, Nov. 24, 1797, ibid.

133. TBA to AA2, Aug. 17, 1797, ibid.

134. Quoted in Levin, *Education of JQA*, 129.

135. *Record of a Life*, in Graham et al., *Diary and Autobiographical Writings*, I, 52.

136. Ibid.

CHAPTER 10

1. Diary entry, Sept. 6, 1797, JQA Diaries.

2. Ibid., diary entry, Oct. 18, 1797.

3. Thomas, *Louisa*, 83.

4. Diary, in Graham et al., *Diary and Autobiographical Writings*, I, 66.

5. Diary entries, Nov. 3–7, 1797, JQA Diaries.

6. Ibid., diary entry, Nov. 9, 1797.

7. Ibid.

8. *Record of a Life*, in Graham et al., *Diary and Autobiographical Writings*, I, 55. See also Thomas, *Louisa*, 90–92.

9. Diary entry, Nov. 5, 1797, JQA Diaries.

10. JQA to AA, Dec. 18, 1797, Fam. Cor., XII.

11. Diary entries, Nov. 2–5, 1797, JQA Diaries.

12. Ibid., diary entry, Nov. 8, 1797.

13. Ford, *Writings of JQA*, II, 232.

14. *Adventures of a Nobody*, in Graham et al., *Diary and Autobiographical Writings*, I, 68–69.

15. Isenberg and Burstein, *The Problem of Democracy*, 206–7.

16. Diary, in Graham et al., *Diary and Autobiographical Writings*, I, 69.

17. Quoted in Isenberg and Burstein, *The Problem of Democracy*, 199.

18. See Morison, *Harrison Gray Otis*, 87–99.

19. Ford, *Writings of JQA*, II, 344.

20. Ferling, *John Adams*, 340–43.

21. AA to JQA, June 23, 1797, Fam. Cor., XII.

22. Ford, *Writings of JQA*, II, 219.

23. Fam. Cor., XII, 105.

24. JA to William Stephens Smith, Feb. 16, 1798, ibid.

25. JQA to CA, Aug. 1, 1797, ibid.

26. Ferling, *John Adams*, 351.

27. Ford, *Writings of JQA*, II, 224.

28. Quoted in Jones, *Crucible of Power*, I, 42.

29. Fam. Cor., XII, 45.

30. JQA to the secretary of state, Jan. 15, 1798, Adams Papers, III, reel 129.

31. Heffron, *Louisa Catherine*, 109.

32. Diary, in Graham et al., *Diary and Autobiographical Writings*, I, 88–89.

33. Ibid., 77–78.

34. Ibid., 82.

35. Ibid., 84.

36. Quoted in Heffron, *Louisa Catherine*, 111.
37. Diary entries, July 17 and 18, 1798, JQA Diaries.
38. Nagel, *John Quincy Adams*, 117.
39. Diary entry, Dec. 30, 1798, JQA Diaries, and Bemis, *JQA and the Foundations*, 109.
40. JQA to AA, May 25, 1800, Fam. Cor., XIV.
41. Quoted in Nagel, *John Quincy Adams*, 120.
42. JA to JQA, Jan. 3, 1798, Adams Papers, II, reel 129.
43. Quoted in Levin, *Education of JQA*, 38.
44. Pinckney to King, April 15, 1798, Adams Papers, II, reel 133.
45. Ford, *Writings of JQA*, II, 277.
46. See Fam. Cor., XIII, 160.
47. Ford, *Writings of JQA*, II, 276.
48. AA to TBA, May 1, 1798 Fam. Cor., XIII.
49. Ibid., JQA to AA (forwarded to JA), May 4, 1798, Ibid.
50. Ford, *Writings of JQA*, II, 295.
51. JQA to W. V. Murray, June 23, 1798, Adams Papers, II, reel 133.
52. Ford, *Writings of JQA*, II, 309–10.
53. Ibid., 242–43.
54. Ibid., 398.
55. Ibid., 271–73.
56. Ibid., 336.
57. Ibid., 348.
58. Ibid., 351.
59. Ibid., 358.
60. Ibid., 367.
61. Ferling, *John Adams*, 382.
62. Fam. Cor., XIII, 160.
63. Quoted in Bemis, *JQA and the Union*, 1.
64. Ford, *Writings of JQA*, II, 335.
65. TBA to JA, Jan. 12, 1799, Fam. Cor., XIII.
66. Fam. Cor., XIII, 416.
67. JA to William Stephens Smith, Dec. 19, 1798, ibid.
68. JQA to AA, July 25, 1799, ibid.
69. JQA to TBA, around Oct. 1798, ibid.
70. AA to JQA, Nov. 19, 1798, ibid.
71. AA to JA, Feb. 14, 1799, ibid.
72. JQA to AA, Oct. 8, 1798, ibid.
73. LCA to TBA, Oct. 6, 1798, Founders Online.
74. Fam. Cor., XIII, xiv.
75. Ibid., xxi.
76. *Adventures of a Nobody*, in Graham et al., *Diary and Autobiographical Writings*, I, 105.
77. Ibid., 101.
78. Ibid., 131.
79. Ibid., 143–44.
80. Ibid., 106.
81. Ibid., 121.
82. JQA to W. V. Murray, July 26, 1799, Adams Papers, II, reel 134.
83. *Adventures of a Nobody*, in Graham et al., *Diary and Autobiographical Writings*, I, 115.
84. Ibid., 114.
85. JQA to JA, Jan. 3, 1798, Adams Papers, II, reel 129.
86. Ibid.
87. Fam. Cor., XIII, 478.
88. AA to TBA, June 2, 1799, ibid.
89. Ferling, *John Adams*, 383–84.
90. Ford, *Writings of JQA*, II, 439–40, and TBA to William Smith Shaw, Oct. 23, 1799, Fam. Cor., XIII.
91. Quoted in Ferling, *John Adams*, 385.
92. Fam. Cor., XIV, xxiv.
93. Ibid.
94. AA to Mary Smith Cranch, Dec. 18, 1799, ibid.
95. Ibid., 128–29.
96. JQA to AA, June 12, 1800, ibid.
97. Bradburn, "The Presidency of John Adams," in Waldstreicher, *Companion*, 176–77.
98. Quoted in Ferling, *John Adams*, 394.
99. Ford, *Writings of JQA*, IV, 25.
100. *Adventures of a Nobody*, in Graham et al., *Diary and Autobiographical Writings*, I, 130.
101. Diary entry, Jan. 23, 1800, JQA Diaries.
102. "A Tour of Silesia," Fam. Cor., XIV, 308.
103. Ibid., 308–9.
104. JQA to TBA.

CHAPTER 11

1. JQA to W. V. Murray, Dec. 16, 1800, Adams Papers, II, reel 134.
2. Fam. Cor., XIV, 437.
3. Houpt, "John Adams and the Elections of 1796 and 1800," in Waldstreicher, *Companion*, 156.
4. Quoted in Isenberg and Burstein, *The Problem of Democracy*, 227.
5. Burstein, *The Problem of Democracy*, 253.
6. Houpt, "John Adams and the Elections of 1796 and 1800," in Waldstreicher, *Companion*, 156.
7. AA to Catherine Nuth Johnson, May 8, 1800, and June 16, 1800, Fam. Cor., XIV.
8. JQA to JA, Nov. 25, 1800, Adams Papers, II, reel 134.
9. JQA to JA, June 19, 1800, Fam. Cor., XIV.
10. AA to Catherine Nuth Johnson, Aug. 20, 1800, ibid.
11. Ford, *Writings of JQA*, II, 489.
12. AA to TBA, Feb. 3, 1801, Fam. Cor., XV.
13. AA to Mary Smith Cranch, Nov. 10, 1800, ibid.
14. Quoted in Ferling, *John Adams*, 405.
15. Quoted in ibid., 406.
16. Ford, *Writings of JQA*, II, 485.
17. JQA to W. V. Murray, April 7, 1801, Adams Papers, II, reel 134.
18. Ford, *Writings of JQA*, II, 495.
19. Ibid., 444.
20. Ibid., 495.
21. *Adventures of a Nobody*, in Graham et al., *Diary and Autobiographical Writings*, I, 157. See also Thomas, *Louisa*, 113–18.
22. Quoted in Heffron, *Louisa Catherine*, 134.
23. *Adventures of a Nobody*, in Graham et al., *Diary and Autobiographical Writings*, I, 152.
24. Diary entry, April 12, 1801, JQA Diaries.
25. *Adventures of a Nobody*, in Graham et al., *Diary and Autobiographical Writings*, I, 154.
26. Ibid.
27. Diary entry, May 4, 1801, JQA Diaries.
28. Quoted in Diary, in Graham et al., *Diary and Autobiographical Writings*, I, 170.
29. Quoted in Levin, *Education of JQA*, 366.
30. Diary entry, June 24, 1891, JQA Diaries.
31. *Adventures of a Nobody*, in Graham et al., *Diary and Autobiographical Writings*, I, 158.
32. Ibid.
33. Ford, *Writings of JQA*, III, 1.
34. Diary entries, Sept. 12–21, 1801, JQA Diaries, and Levin, *Education of JQA*, 370.
35. Diary entry, Sept. 21, 1801, JQA Diaries.
36. Ibid., diary entry, Sept. 30, 1801.
37. Quoted in Levin, *Education of JQA*, 371.
38. Quoted in Heffron, *Louisa Catherine*, 131.
39. Quoted in ibid., 139.
40. Quoted in ibid., 140.
41. Quoted in Levin, *Education of JQA*, 373.
42. *Adventures of a Nobody*, in Graham et al., *Diary and Autobiographical Writings*, I, 164.
43. Diary entry, Nov. 25, 1801, JQA Diaries.
44. *Adventures of a Nobody*, in Graham et al., *Diary and Autobiographical Writings*, I, 164.
45. Quoted in Heffron, *Louisa Catherine*, 143.
46. *Adventures of a Nobody*, in Graham et al., *Diary and Autobiographical Writings*, I, 165–66.
47. Ibid., 166.
48. Ibid., 165–67.
49. Diary entry, Jan. 8, 1802, JQA Diaries.
50. Bemis, *JQA and the Foundations*, 111.
51. Quoted in Levin, *Education of JQA*, 30.
52. Diary entry, Jan. 31, 1802, JQA Diaries.
53. Ibid., diary entries, Jan. 7 and Feb. 12, 1802.
54. Quoted in Levin, *Education of JQA*, 367.
55. Quoted in Morison, *Harrison Gray Otis*, 246.
56. Morison, *Harrison Gray Otis*, 250–52.
57. Diary entry, Jan. 28, 1802, JQA Diaries.
58. Ford, *Writings of JQA*, III, 5.
59. Heffron, *Louisa Catherine*, 144–45.
60. Quoted in ibid., 145.
61. *Adventures of a Nobody*, in Graham et al., *Diary and Autobiographical Writings*, I, 172.

62. Ibid., 189.

63. Heffron, *Louisa Catherine*, 154.

64. *Adventures of a Nobody*, in Graham et al., *Diary and Autobiographical Writings*, I, 173.

65. Ibid., 173–75.

66. Quoted in Heffron, *Louisa Catherine*, 148.

67. Bemis, *JQA and the Foundations*, 113.

68. Diary entry, Nov. 3, 1802, JQA Diaries.

69. Ibid., diary entries, March 2–3, 1802.

70. Ibid., diary entry, April 2, 1803.

71. Ibid.; Bemis, *JQA and the Foundations*, 114–15; and Ford, *Writings of JQA*, III, 13–14.

72. *Adventures of a Nobody*, in Graham et al., *Diary and Autobiographical Writings*, I, 188.

73. Diary entry, July 4, 1803, JQA Diaries.

74. Quoted in Heffron, *Louisa Catherine*, 156.

75. Diary entries, Oct. 7–13, 1803, JQA Diaries.

76. Ibid.

77. *Adventures of a Nobody*, in Graham et al., *Diary and Autobiographical Writings*, I, 195.

CHAPTER 12

1. Quoted in Wood, *Empire of Liberty*, 308.

2. Wood, *Empire of Liberty*, 302.

3. JQA to Rufus King, Oct. 8, 1803, Adams Papers, II, reel 135.

4. See Wood, *Empire of Liberty*, 110.

5. Quoted in Levin, *Education of JQA*, 390.

6. Quoted in DeConde, *History*, I, 76.

7. Quoted in ibid., 76.

8. Quoted in Levin, *Education of JQA*, 394.

9. Diary entry, Jan. 7, 1804, JQA Diaries.

10. Ford, *Writings of JQA*, II, 26.

11. Ibid., 29.

12. Waldstreicher and Mason, *JQA and Slavery*, 15.

13. Diary entry, Nov. 15, 1803, JQA Diaries.

14. Quoted in Ford, *Writings of JQA*, III, 20.

15. Quoted in Bemis, *JQA and the Foundations*, 123.

16. Quoted in Ford, *Writings of JQA*, III, 30.

17. Ibid.

18. Quoted in Levin, *Education of JQA*, 397.

19. Diary entry, Jan. 27, 1804, JQA Diaries.

20. Quoted in Wood, *Empire of Liberty*, 289.

21. Quoted in Ketcham, *Madison*, 408.

22. See Nagel, *John Quincy Adams*, 143–44, and diary entry, Oct. 23, 1803, JQA Diaries.

23. JQA to LCA, April 9, 1804, Founders Online.

24. JQA to LCA, April 9 and 15, 1804, ibid.

25. LCA to JQA, May 3, 1804, ibid.

26. JQA to LCA, April 9 and 15, 1804, ibid.

27. Holton, *Abigail Adams*, 340.

28. Quoted in Ketcham, *Madison*, 107.

29. LCA to JQA, May 12, 1804, Founders Online.

30. JQA to LCA, May 20, 1804, ibid.

31. LCA to JQA, May 13, 1804, ibid.

32. JQA to LCA, May 25, 1804, ibid.

33. LCA to JQA, May 29 and Aug. 12, 1804, ibid.

34. Ibid., LCA to JQA, May 29, 1804.

35. Quoted in Heffron, *Louisa Catherine*, 160.

36. Ketcham, *Madison*, 446.

37. Diary entries, April 19 and 22, May 25 and 26, and Aug. 6, 1804, JQA Diaries.

38. See Nagel, *John Quincy Adams*, 150–51.

39. JQA to LCA, May 31, 1804, Founders Online.

40. LCA to JQA, July 4, 1804, ibid.

41. See JQA to William Plumer, March 21, 1829, Adams Papers, II, reel 149.

42. Quoted in Divine et al., *America*, 225.

43. JQA to LCA, July 26, 1804, Founders Online.

44. Quoted in Heffron, *Louisa Catherine*, 171.

45. Ibid.

46. JQA to LCA, Oct. 14, 1804, Founders Online.

47. Diary entries, March 2–12, 1804, JQA Diaries.

48. Quoted in Rehnquist, *Grand Inquests*, 52.

49. Quoted in Divine et al., *America*, 223.

50. Diary entries, Dec. 6 and 20–21, 1804, JQA Diaries.

51. Ibid., diary entry, Feb. 27, 1805.

52. Ford, *Writings of JQA*, III, 108.

53. Ibid.

54. JA to JQA, Feb. 7, 1805, Founders Online.

55. JA to JQA, Dec. 2, 1804, ibid.
56. Morison, *Harrison Gray Otis*, 270.
57. "Publius Valerius," in Ford, *Writings of JQA*, III, 70.
58. Ibid., 73.
59. Diary, in Graham et al., *Diary and Autobiographical Writings*, I, 218.
60. Ibid., 215–16.
61. Ibid., 204.
62. Ibid., 199.
63. Quoted in Heffron, *Louisa Catherine*, 163.
64. Diary entry, Aug. 15, 1804, JQA Diaries.
65. Ibid., diary entry, Aug. 23, 1804.

CHAPTER 13

1. *Adventures of a Nobody*, in Graham et al., *Diary and Autobiographical Writings*, I, 204.
2. Ibid.
3. Quoted in Ketcham, *Madison*, 446–47.
4. LCA to AA, Nov. 27, 1804, Founders Online.
5. Ibid.
6. Quoted in Heffron, *Louisa Catherine*, 173.
7. Quoted in ibid., 175.
8. Quoted in Nagel, *John Quincy Adams*, 152–53.
9. Diary entry, Jan. 4, 1805, JQA Diaries.
10. Quoted in Heffron, *Louisa Catherine*, 175–76.
11. Diary entry, March 25, 1805, JQA Diaries.
12. Quoted in Heffron, *Louisa Catherine*, 176.
13. Ibid., 176–77.
14. Diary entry, Dec. 31, 1804, JQA Diaries.
15. Ibid., diary entry, June 24, 1805.
16. Ford, *Writings of JQA*, III, 123–25.
17. Quoted in Heffron, *Louisa Catherine*, 178.
18. Diary, in Graham et al., *Diary and Autobiographical Writings*, I, 186.
19. Diary entry, Nov. 20, 1805, JQA Diaries.
20. Quoted in Levin, *Education of JQA*, 415.
21. Ibid.
22. JA to JQA, Feb. 5, 1806, Founders Online.
23. JA to JQA, Jan. 25, 1806, ibid.
24. Quoted in McCarthy, "Liberty and Order in the Slave Society," 6.

25. Diary entry, March 8, 1806, JQA Diaries.
26. JA to JQA, Jan. 29, 1806, Founders Online.
27. Quoted in Ketcham, *Madison*, 95.
28. Quoted in ibid., 107.
29. Quoted in Bemis, *JQA and the Foundations*, 136–37.
30. JQA to LCA, May 4, 1806, Founders Online.
31. See Hill, "Expedition to Liberate Venezuela Sails," 671–89.
32. JQA to LCA, July 13, 1806, Founders Online.
33. JQA to William Stephens Smith, April 16, 1806, ibid.
34. Quoted in Levin, *Education of JQA*, 421.
35. *Adventures of a Nobody*, in Graham et al., *Diary and Autobiographical Writings*, I, 190–91.
36. LCA to JQA, May 25, 1806, Founders Online.
37. JQA to LCA, June 29, 1806, ibid.
38. JQA to LCA, May 15, 1806, ibid.
39. Diary entry, June 30, 1806, JQA Diaries.
40. JQA to LCA, May 5, 1806, Founders Online.
41. Diary entry, June 5, 1805, JQA Diaries.
42. Ford, *Writings of JQA*, III, 145.
43. Diary entry, Jan. 15, 1805, JQA Diaries.
44. Ibid., diary entry, Aug. 24 and 25, 1806.
45. Portolano, *Passionate Empiricist*, 13.
46. Quoted in ibid., 12–13.
47. Quoted in Isenberg and Burstein, *The Problem of Democracy*, 182–83.
48. LCA to JQA, July 20, 1808, Founders Online.
49. Portolano, *Passionate Empiricist*, 21–2, 30–2.
50. Ford, *Writings of JQA*, II, 13–5, and JQA to Noah Webster, Nov. 6, 1806, Adams Papers, II, reel 135.
51. Diary entry, June 16, 1806, JQA Diaries.
52. LCA to JQA, July 6, 1806, Founders Online.
53. *Adventures of a Nobody*, in Graham et al., *Diary and Autobiographical Writings*, I, 238.
54. JQA to LCA, June 29, 1806, Founders Online.

55. Quoted in Heffron, *Louisa Catherine*, 182.

56. Diary, in Graham et al., *Diary and Autobiographical Writings*, I, 245.

57. Quoted in DeConde, *History*, I, 83.

58. Quoted in ibid.

59. Ford, *Writings of JQA*, II, 170.

60. Quoted in Divine et al., *America*, 225.

61. JQA to TBA, Jan. 3, 1807, Founders Online.

62. Quoted in Parsons, *John Quincy Adams*, 88–89.

63. JQA to LCA, Feb. 6, 1807, Founders Online.

64. Ibid., JQA to LCA, Feb. 16, 1807.

65. Diary entry, March 8, 1807, JQA Diaries.

66. Ibid., diary entries, March 21 and April 2, 1807.

67. Quoted in Nagel, *John Quincy Adams*, 171.

68. JQA to Ebenezer Storer, November 1, 1806.

69. Quoted in Emerson, Ralph Waldo, *The Complete Works of Ralph Waldo Emerson: Letters and Social Aims,* vol. 8 (Boston: Houghton Mifflin, 1909).

CHAPTER 14

1. Quoted in DeConde, *History*, I, 86.

2. Quoted in Bemis, *JQA and the Foundations*, 141.

3. Diary entry, July 11, 1807, JQA Diaries.

4. Bemis, *JQA and the Foundations*, 141.

5. "Letter from Certain Citizens of Massachusetts to JQA," Nov. 26, 1828, JQA Papers.

6. Morison, *Harrison Gray Otis*, 272.

7. Quoted in ibid., 270–71.

8. Diary, in Graham et al., *Diary and Autobiographical Writings*, I, 255.

9. Quoted in Nagel, *John Quincy Adams*, 173.

10. Diary entries, Aug. 10 and 12, 1807, JQA Diaries.

11. Ibid., diary entry, Sept. 2, 1807.

12. Ibid., diary entries, Oct. 5–9, 1807.

13. *Adventures of a Nobody*, in Graham et al., *Diary and Autobiographical Writings*, I, 259.

14. Diary entry, Oct. 30, 1807, JQA Diaries.

15. JQA to AA, Nov. 4, 1807, Founders Online.

16. Ibid.

17. Ford, *Writings of JQA*, III, 164–65.

18. JQA to TBA, Dec. 14, 1807, Founders Online.

19. Quoted in DeConde, *History*, I, 85.

20. Ford, *Writings of JQA*, III, 169.

21. Ibid., 171–72.

22. Diary entry, Jan. 30, 1808, JQA Diaries.

23. Ibid., diary entry, Jan. 23, 1808.

24. AA to JQA, Feb. 15, 1808, Adams Papers, II, reel 405.

25. Quoted in Parsons, *John Quincy Adams*, 91–92.

26. JA to JQA, Feb. 19, 1808, Founders Online.

27. Diary entry, Feb. 24, 1808, JQA Diaries.

28. Quoted in DeConde, *History*, I, 87.

29. See Meacham, *Thomas Jefferson*, 431.

30. Ford, *Writings of JQA*, III, 188.

31. Diary entry, Nov. 20, 1805, JQA Diaries.

32. Ibid., diary entry, May 8, 1808.

33. JQA to TBA, Feb. 6, 1808, Founders Online.

34. Diary entry, Feb. 1, 1808, JQA Diaries.

35. Ibid., diary entries, March 4 and 15, 1808.

36. Quoted in Isenberg and Burstein, *The Problem of Democracy*, 287.

37. Ibid.

38. See Bemis, *JQA and the Foundations*, 147.

39. Isenberg and Burstein, *The Problem of Democracy*, 288–89.

40. Ford, *Writings of JQA*, III, 190.

41. Ibid., 189.

42. Quoted in Isenberg and Burstein, *The Problem of Democracy*, 289.

43. Ford, *Writings of JQA*, II, 192.

44. "Timothy Pickering and John Quincy Adams," *Albany Gazette*, June 16, 1808.

45. Diary entry, March 31, 1808, JQA Diaries.

46. Ibid.

47. *National Intelligencer*, June 17, 1809.

48. Quoted in Morison, *Harrison Gray Otis*, 301.

49. *Adventures of a Nobody*, in Graham et al., *Diary and Autobiographical Writings*, I, 274.

50. Quoted in Traub, *John Quincy Adams*, 157.

51. Diary entry, April 23, 1808, JQA Diaries.

52. Ibid., diary entry, Sept. 5. 1808.

53. Ibid., diary entry, Aug. 23, 1808.

54. Ibid., diary entry, July 10, 1808.

55. Ford, *Writings of JQA*, III, 45.

56. Ibid., 251.

57. Ibid., 279.

58. Bemis, *JQA and the Foundations*, 150, nt. 54.

59. Diary entry, Sept. 26, 1808, JQA Diaries.

60. *Adventures of a Nobody*, in Graham et al., *Diary and Autobiographical Writings*, 278.

61. Diary entry, March 4, 1809, JQA Diaries.

62. JQA to LCA, March 5, 1809, Founders Online.

63. Diary entry, March 6, 1809, JQA Diaries.

64. Bemis, *JQA and the Foundations*, 151.

65. JQA to LCA, March 9, 1809, Founders Online.

66. *Adventures of a Nobody*, in Graham et al., *Diary and Autobiographical Writings*, I, 279.

67. Quoted in Bemis, *JQA and the Foundations*, 153.

68. Henry Dearborn to James Madison, June 11, 1809, Rutland et al., Papers of James Madison, Presidential Series, I, 216.

69. Quoted in Freeman, *Field of Blood*, 109.

70. Ibid., 112.

71. Ford, *Writings of JQA*, III, 317.

72. Diary entry, June 24, 1809, JQA Diaries.

73. Bemis, *JQA and the Foundations*, 151.

74. *Adventures of a Nobody*, in Graham et al., *Diary and Autobiographical Writings*, I, 283.

75. Quoted in Nagel, *John Quincy Adams*, 187.

76. See Ketcham, *Madison*, 469–70.

77. Quoted in Ford, *Writings of JQA*, III, 321.

78. Diary entry, July 5, 1809, JQA Diaries.

79. Quoted in Nagel, *John Quincy Adams*, 186.

80. Quoted in Levin, *Education of JQA*, 428.

81. Diary entry, July 7, 1809, JQA Diaries.

82. Bemis, *JQA and the Foundations*, 154.

83. *Adventures of a Nobody*, in Graham et al., *Diary and Autobiographical Writings*, I, 284.

84. Diary entry, Aug. 6, 1809, JQA Diaries.

85. Quoted in Levin, *Education of JQA*, 429.

86. Nagel, *John Quincy Adams*, 187, and diary entry, Aug. 5, 1809, JQA Diaries.

87. Ford, *Writings of JQA*, III, 331.

88. Diary entry, Aug. 6, 1809, JQA Diaries.

89. See Heffron, *Louisa Catherine*, 195.

90. Ford, *Writings of JQA*, 343.

91. JQA to TBA, Sept. 24, 1809, Founders Online.

92. Ibid.

93. Ibid.

94. Diary entry, Sept. 25, 1809, JQA Diaries.

95. Quoted in Heffron, *Louisa Catherine*, 195–96.

96. JQA to TBA, Nov. 16–28 and Dec. 14, 1809, Founders Online.

97. Ibid.

98. *Adventures of a Nobody*, in Graham et al., *Diary and Autobiographical Writings*, I, 291.

99. Ibid.

100. Quoted in Heffron, *Louisa Catherine*, 198.

101. Diary entry, Oct. 25, 1809, JQA Diaries.

102. Ibid., diary entry, Oct. 28, 1809.

CHAPTER 15

1. Diary entry, Nov. 4, 1809, JQA Diaries.

2. Ibid.

3. Ibid.

4. Ibid.

5. Ibid.

6. JQA to W. V. Murray, Nov. 25, 1800, Adams Papers, II, reel 134.

7. *Adventures of a Nobody*, in Graham et al., *Diary and Autobiographical Writings*, I, 73.

8. Diary entry, Nov. 15, 1809, JQA Diaries.

9. Crosby, *America, Russia, Hemp, and Napoleon*, 95.

10. Ford, *Writings of JQA*, VI, 370.

11. Crosby, *America, Russia, Hemp, and Napoleon*, 112–15.

12. Diary entry, Dec. 29, 1809, JQA Diaries.

13. Ibid., diary entry, Feb. 27, 1810.

14. *Adventures of a Nobody*, in Graham et al., *Diary and Autobiographical Writings*, I, 293.

15. Ibid., 295.

16. Quoted in Heffron, *Louisa Catherine*, 207.

17. Quoted in ibid.

18. *Adventures of a Nobody*, in Graham et al., *Diary and Autobiographical Writings*, I, 297–99, 302.

19. Diary entry, Dec. 4, 1809, JQA Diaries.

20. *Adventures of a Nobody*, in Graham et al., *Diary and Autobiographical Writings*, I, 303.

21. Ibid.

22. Diary entry, Nov. 22, 1809, JQA Diaries.

23. JQA to AA, May 2, 1811, Founders Online.

24. Bemis, *JQA and the Foundations*, 164.

25. LCA to her mother, May 13, 1810, Founders Online.

26. Heffron, *Louisa Catherine*, 211.

27. Quoted in Bemis, *JQA and the Foundations*, 166.

28. Diary entry, April 24, 1810, JQA Diaries.

29. Ibid., diary entry, March 3, 1812.

30. Ibid., diary entry, Dec. 22, 1810.

31. Ibid., diary entry, Oct. 11, 1810.

32. Quoted in Levin, *Education of JQA*, 447.

33. Quoted in ibid.

34. Quoted in Heffron, *Louisa Catherine*, 207.

35. Quoted in ibid., 201.

36. Quoted in ibid., 202.

37. *Adventures of a Nobody*, in Graham et al., *Diary and Autobiographical Writings*, I, 316.

38. Ibid., 318.

39. Quoted in Heffron, *Louisa Catherine*, 203.

40. Diary entries, Oct. 23–26, 1810, JQA Diaries.

41. Ibid., diary entry, March 28, 1810.

42. Ford, *Writings of JQA*, III, 542–43.

43. Diary entries, March 2–18, 1810, JQA Diaries, and *Adventures of a Nobody*, in Graham et al., *Diary and Autobiographical Writings*, I, 313, nt. 381.

44. Diary entry, Sept. 26, 1810, JQA Diaries.

45. See Herbermann, "Jean-Baptiste Massillon."

46. JQA to JA, July 7, 1814, Founders Online.

47. Fea, "John Adams and Religion," in Waldstreicher, *Companion*, 186–87, 190–92.

48. JA to JQA, Dec. 24, 1813, Adams Papers, IV, reel 416.

49. Ford, *Writings of JQA*, V, 433.

50. Ibid., 362.

51. Ford, *Writings of JQA*, IV, 135.

52. JQA to JA, July 7, 1814, Founders Online.

53. Diary entry, Nov. 4, 1810, JQA Diaries.

54. Quoted in Fea, "John Adams and Religion," in Waldstreicher, *Companion*, 194.

55. Waldstreicher, *JQA: Diaries*, II, 400.

56. Diary entry, April 11, 1812, JQA Diaries.

57. Ibid., diary entry, Aug. 15, 1811.

58. Ibid. diary entry, Nov. 17, 1816.

59. CFA, *Memoirs of JQA*, VIII, 353.

60. Ibid., 229.

61. Ibid., IX, 9.

62. Ibid., VIII, 176–77.

63. Quoted in Bemis, *JQA and the Union*, 106, nt. 42.

64. Diary entry, June 30, 1810, JQA Diaries.

65. Ibid., diary entry, Feb. 9, 1810.

66. Quoted in Nagel, *John Quincy Adams*, 196.

67. Ford, *Writings of JQA*, III, 522.

68. LCA to AA, Oct. 23, 1810, Founders Online.

69. AA to James Madison, Aug. 1, 1810, Rutland et al., *Papers of James Madison*, Presidential Series, III, 456.

70. Ford, *Writings of JQA*, III, 518.

71. Ibid., 528–29.

72. James Madison to JQA, Oct. 16, 1810, 582, ibid.

73. JA to JQA, Jan. 15, 1811, Founders Online.

74. Ford, *Writings of JQA*, IV, 18–19.

75. Quoted in Heffron, *Louisa Catherine*, 212.

76. Ibid., 213.

77. JQA to JA, July 21, 1811, Founders Online.

78. Diary entry, Jan. 25, 1811, JQA Diaries.

79. Ford, *Writings of JQA*, III, 465–66; Chambers, "'No Country but Their Counting-Houses,'" 200–1; C. L. Woodward to JQA, June 18, 1814, Adams Papers, IV, reel 418; and Ford, *Writings of JQA*, III, 520–21.

80. Bemis, *JQA and the Foundations*, 172.

81. Ford, *Writings of JQA*, III, 475–77, 486–88, and Albert Gallatin to James Madison, Sept. 5, 1810, Rutland et. al., *Papers of James Madison*, Presidential Series, II, 626–27.

82. *Adventures of a Nobody*, in Graham et al., *Diary and Autobiographical Writings*, I, 312–13.

83. Diary entry, Sept. 19, 1810, JQA Diaries.

84. Ibid., diary entries, May 14 and 14, 1814. In 1819, American merchant W. D. Lewis upon his return to America accused Harris of corruption. Harris sued him for libel, and the case eventually reached the Supreme Court of Pennsylvania. Harris insisted that his wealth came from his activities as a businessman and not as U.S. consul. The jury awarded him damages of a hundred dollars. See Bemis, *JQA and the Foundations*, 169.

CHAPTER 16

1. Ford, *Writings of JQA*, III, 479.

2. Ibid., IV, 65.

3. Diary entry, July 26, 1810, JQA Diaries.

4. Ford, *Writings of JQA*, IV, 51.

5. Crosby, *America, Russia, Hemp, and Napoleon*, 179, 183.

6. Ford, *Writings of JQA*, III, 554.

7. Crosby, *America, Russia, Hemp, and Napoleon*, 172–74, and Ford, *Writings of JQA*, IV, 34–35, 39.

8. Quoted in Crosby, *America, Russia, Hemp, and Napoleon*, 183.

9. Ford, *Writings of JQA*, III, 554.

10. Diary entry, March 7, 1810, JQA Diaries.

11. JQA to JA, May 25, 1813, Founders Online.

12. Ibid., and diary entry, April 18, 1813, JQA Diaries.

13. LCA to AA, June 2, 1810, Founders Online.

14. JQA to AA, May 2, 1811, ibid.

15. Diary entries, May 5, 1810, and May 7, 1812, JQA Diaries.

16. Ibid., diary entry, July 16, 1810.

17. *Adventures of a Nobody*, in Graham et al., *Diary and Autobiographical Writings*, I, 320.

18. Ford, *Writings of JQA*, III, 472.

19. Diary entry, Aug. 14, 1810, JQA Diaries.

20. JQA to AA, Dec. 19, 1804, Founders Online.

21. JQA to GWA, Sept. 12, 1812, ibid.

22. Ford, *Writings of JQA*, III, 529, 497.

23. JQA to TBA, Sept. 10, 1811, Founders Online.

24. See Ford, *Writings of JQA*, IV, 88.

25. Crosby, *America, Russia, Hemp, and Napoleon*, 187.

26. Ford, *Writings of JQA*, IV, 2–3.

27. Ibid., 149–50.

28. Quoted in Crosby, *America, Russia, Hemp, and Napoleon*, 222–23.

29. Diary entry, April 20, 1812, JQA Diaries.

30. Ford, *Writings of JQA*, IV, 147.

31. JQA to William Plumer, June 11, 1811, Adams Papers, II, reel 152.

32. Ford, *Writings of JQA*, IV, 127.

33. Ibid.

34. Diary entry, July 30, 1811, JQA Diaries.

35. Ibid., diary entry, May 6, 1811.

36. Ibid., diary entry, Oct. 9, 1810.

37. *Adventures of a Nobody*, in Graham et al., *Diary and Autobiographical Writings*, I, 338.

38. Ibid., 344.

39. Diary entries, May 23 and 25, 1811, JQA Diaries.

40. Ibid., diary entry, Feb. 15, 1813.

41. Ibid., diary entry, July 26, 1811.

42. Ibid.

43. Ibid., diary entry, July 13, 1811.

44. Quoted in Heffron, *Louisa Catherine*, 215.

45. Diary entry, July 21, 1811, JQA Diaries.

46. JQA to AA, Aug. 12, 1811, Founders Online.

47. JQA to TBA, Aug. 27, 1811, ibid.

48. JQA to AA, Sept. 10, 1811, ibid.

49. Diary entry, Oct. 17, 1811, JQA Diaries.

50. *Adventures of a Nobody*, in Graham et al., *Diary and Autobiographical Writings*, I, 351.

51. Ibid., 354.

52. Diary entry, Aug. 11, 1812, JQA Diaries.

53. Ibid., diary entry, Jan. 14, 1812.

54. Ibid., diary entries, Dec. 6, 1811, and Jan. 13, 1812.

55. Ibid., diary entry, Aug. 12, 1812.

56. Ibid., diary entry, Aug. 22, 1812.

57. Ibid.

58. Ibid., diary entry, Sept. 4, 1812.

59. Ibid., diary entry, Sept. 11, 1812.
60. Ibid., diary entry, Sept. 12, 1812.
61. Ibid., diary entries, Sept. 15 and 16 1812.
62. JQA to AA, Sept. 21, 1812, Founders Online.
63. Diary, in Graham et al., *Diary and Autobiographical Writings*, I, 359.
64. Lepore, "Strange and Twisted Life of *Frankenstein*," 86.
65. Diary, in Graham et al., *Diary and Autobiographical Writings*, I, 359–60.
66. Diary entry, Oct. 22, 1812, JQA Diaries.
67. Diary, in Graham et al., *Diary and Autobiographical Writings*, I, 358.
68. Quoted in Heffron, *Louisa Catherine*, 224.
69. Quoted in ibid.
70. Quoted in ibid., 227.
71. Quoted in ibid.
72. Holton, *Abigail Adams*, 366–68.
73. JQA to AA, Oct. 24, 1811, Founders Online.
74. JA to JQA, Feb. 19, 1812, ibid.

CHAPTER 17

1. Quoted in Crosby, *America, Russia, Hemp, and Napoleon*, 187.
2. Ford, *Writings of JQA*, IV, 251.
3. Ibid., 298.
4. CFA, *Memoirs of JQA*, VIII, 40.
5. Diary entry, March 19, 1812, JQA Diaries.
6. Ibid., diary entries, June 27 and 28, 1812.
7. JQA to JA, Nov. 15, 1812, Founders Online.
8. JQA to AA, Oct. 24, 1812, ibid.
9. Ford, *Writings of JQA*, IV, 412–13.
10. Ibid., 421–22.
11. Diary entry, Nov. 11, 1812, JQA Diaries.
12. Ford, *Writings of JQA*, IV, 285.
13. Ibid., 315.
14. Ibid., 368.
15. Ibid., 329.
16. Quoted in Ketcham, *Madison*, 517.
17. Quoted in Perkins, *Castlereagh and Adams*, 5.
18. Morison, *Harrison Gray Otis*, 331.
19. Ford, *Writings of JQA*, IV, 497.
20. See Jones, *Crucible of Power*, I, 79–80.
21. Diary entry, Oct. 27, 1812, JQA Diaries.
22. JQA to AA, June 30, 1813, Founders Online.
23. Ford, *Writings of JQA*, IV, 435.
24. JQA to AA, Feb. 18, 1813, Founders Online.
25. Ford, *Writings of JQA*, IV, 443.
26. Ibid., 415.
27. Ibid., 390–91.
28. Ibid., 417.
29. Ibid., 465.
30. Ibid., 468–69.
31. Waldstreicher, *JQA: Diaries*, I, 260.
32. Holton, *Abigail Adams*, 335.
33. Diary entry, Jan. 17, 1813, JQA Diaries.
34. Diary, in Graham et al., *Diary and Autobiographical Writings*, I, 367, and diary entry, Jan. 16, 1813, JQA Diaries.
35. AA to LCA, July 24, 1813, Adams Papers, IV, reel 416.
36. Diary, in Graham et al., *Diary and Autobiographical Writings*, I, 373.
37. Ibid., 367.
38. LCA to AA, April 13, 1813.
39. Diary entry, Dec. 18, 1812, JQA Diaries.
40. Ford, *Writings of JQA*, IV, 450–54.
41. Holton, *Abigail Adams*, 185–86.
42. AA to JQA, Aug. 30, 1813, Adams Papers, IV, reel 416.
43. Quoted in Holton, *Abigail Adams*, 388.
44. Thomas Jefferson to AA, Aug. 22, 1813, Adams Papers, IV, reel 416.
45. Ibid., AA to LCA, Dec. 6, 1813.
46. Ford, *Writings of JQA*, IV, 480–81, nt. 1.
47. Diary entry, July 22, 1813, JQA Diaries.
48. Ibid., diary entries, July 23–25, 1813.
49. Ibid., diary entry, Aug. 17, 1813.
50. Ibid., diary entry, Nov. 10, 1813.
51. Ibid., diary entry, Jan. 3, 1814.
52. Ibid., diary entry, Jan. 11, 1814.
53. Ibid.
54. Ibid., diary entry, Nov. 19, 1813.
55. Ford, *Writings of JQA*, IV, 533.
56. Ibid., V, 21.
57. Diary entries, Sept. 25, 1813, and Feb. 23, 1814, JQA Diaries.

58. Ibid., diary entry, Jan. 28, 1814, and Jérôme de Lalande's *Astronomie des dames* (1785).

59. Diary entry, May 5, 1814, JQA Diaries.

CHAPTER 18

1. Bemis, *JQA and the Foundations*, 190.

2. Remini, *Henry Clay*, 2–19, 66–67.

3. Ibid., 81–83.

4. Perkins, *Castlereagh and Adams*, 46–47.

5. Quoted in ibid., 45.

6. Ford, *Writings of JQA*, V, 14.

7. Ibid., 24, nt. 1.

8. Richard Rush to JA, April 17, 1814, Adams Papers, IV, reel 417.

9. Monroe to JQA et al., Jan. 28, 1814, ibid.

10. Ford, *Writings of JQA*, V, 22.

11. JQA to JA, May 8, 1814, Founders Online.

12. JQA to AA, May 12, 1814, Adams Papers, IV, reel 418.

13. Ford, *Writings of JQA*, V, 38.

14. Diary entry, April 27, 1814, JQA Diaries.

15. Ibid., diary entry, April 31, 1814.

16. JQA to LCA, May 3, 1814, Founders Online. See also diary entry, May 1, 1814, JQA Diaries.

17. JQA to LCA, June 12, 1814, Founders Online.

18. JQA to LCA, May 19–25, 1814, ibid.

19. Diary entries, May 25, 26, and June 1–7, 1814, JQA Diaries, and Ford, *Writings of JQA*, V, 47–48.

20. JQA to LCA, June 12, 1814, Founders Online.

21. JQA to LCA, June 14, 1814, ibid.

22. Ford, *Writings of JQA*, V, 40.

23. JQA to LCA, June 17, 1814, Founders Online.

24. Diary entry, June 22, 1814, JQA Diaries.

25. Ibid., diary entries, June 25–30, 1814.

26. Ford, *Writings of JQA*, V, 69.

27. Perkins, *Castlereagh and Adams*, 44.

28. Quoted in Ketcham, *Madison*, 571.

29. Quoted in ibid., 590.

30. Monroe to JQA, June 27, 1814, Adams Papers, II, reel 418.

31. Diary entries, July 7 and Sept. 4, 1814, JQA Diaries.

32. Quoted in Perkins, *Castlereagh and Adams*, 41.

33. Traub, *John Quincy Adams*, 188.

34. Diary entry, July 21, 1814, JQA Diaries.

35. Ford, *Writings of JQA*, V, 73.

36. Bemis, *JQA and the Foundations*, 193.

37. Diary entry, Aug. 13, 1814, JQA Diaries.

38. Quoted in Bemis, *JQA and the Foundations*, 193–94.

39. Quoted in Ford, *Writings of JQA*, V, 75, nt. 1.

40. Perkins, *Castlereagh and Adams*, 65–67.

41. See Ford, *Writings of JQA*, V, 85–86.

42. Bemis, *JQA and the Foundations*, 198.

43. Ford, *Writings of JQA*, V, 75–77, 85–87.

44. Perkins, *Castlereagh and Adams*, 78–80.

45. Ford, *Writings of JQA*, V, 104.

46. Ibid., 92–93, nt. 1.

47. JQA to LCA, Aug. 26, 1814, Founders Online.

48. Diary entry, Sept. 1, 1814, JQA Diaries.

49. Ibid., diary entry, Aug. 16, 1814.

50. Ford, *Writings of JQA*, VI, 145.

51. Diary entry, Sept. 29, 1814, JQA Diaries.

52. Ford, *Writings of JQA*, VI, 272–73.

53. Ibid.

54. Quoted in Heffron, *Louisa Catherine*, 234.

55. LCA to JQA, Aug. 7, 1814, Founders Online.

56. LCA to JQA, Oct. 23, 1814, ibid.

57. LCA to JQA, Aug. 2 and 15, 1814, ibid.

58. JQA to LCA, July 8, 1814, ibid.

59. LCA to JQA, July 28, 1814, ibid.

60. LCA to AA, July 10, 1814, ibid.

61. LCA to JQA, July 28, 1814, ibid.

62. CFA to JQA, June 10, 1814, Adams Papers, IV, reel 416. Charles misdated this letter. It was more likely written in November or December.

63. JQA to CFA, June 20, 1814, Founders Online.

64. JQA to CFA, Dec. 16, 1814, ibid.

65. LCA to JQA, July 6, 1814, ibid.

66. LCA to JQA, Aug. 7, 1814, ibid.

67. Ford, *Writings of JQA*, V, 189.

68. JQA to LCA, July 26, 1814, Founders Online.
69. Ibid.
70. Quoted in Heffron, *Louisa Catherine*, 236.
71. LCA to JQA, Sept. 4, 1814, Founders Online.
72. Quoted in Heffron, *Louisa Catherine*, 237.
73. Ford, *Writings of JQA*, V, 153, 155.
74. Quoted in ibid., 72–73, nt. 2.
75. Quoted in Perkins, *Castlereagh and Adams*, 108.
76. Quoted in Ford, *Writings of JQA*, V, 179–80, nt. 2.
77. Ibid., 235, nt. 2.
78. Diary entry, Nov. 25, 1814, JQA Diaries.
79. Ford, *Writings of JQA*, V, 239.
80. Quoted in Perkins, *Castlereagh and Adams*, 124.
81. Morison, *Harrison Gray Otis*, 358, 362–63.
82. Ford, *Writings of JQA*, V, 219.
83. Quoted in Heffron, *Louisa Catherine*, 239.
84. Nobles, *American Frontiers*, 121–23.
85. Quoted in Drinnon, *Facing West*, 92.
86. Herring, *Colony to Superpower*, 131–32.
87. Waldstreicher, *JQA: Diaries*, I, 306.

CHAPTER 19

1. Ford, *Writings of JQA*, V, 253–56.
2. LCA to JQA, Jan. 20, 1815, Founders Online.
3. LCA to JQA, Feb. 7, 1815, Founders Online.
4. Quoted in Heffron, *Louisa Catherine*, 240.
5. Ibid.
6. LCA to JQA, March 5, 1815, Founders Online.
7. Ibid., LCA to JQA, Jan. 31, 1815.
8. Diary, in Graham et al., *Diary and Autobiographical Writings*, I, 387–88.
9. Ibid., 382.
10. Ibid., 376.
11. LCA to JQA, Feb. 12, 1815, Founders Online.
12. See O'Brien, *Mrs. Adams in Winter*, 53–56.
13. Diary, in Graham et al., *Diary and Autobiographical Writings*, I, 377, and Heffron, *Louisa Catherine*, 246.
14. Heffron, *Louisa Catherine*, 247.
15. Diary, in Graham et al., *Diary and Autobiographical Writings*, I, 378.
16. Ibid.
17. Ibid., 379.
18. Ibid., 380.
19. Ibid.
20. Ibid., 381.
21. LCA to JQA, Feb. 17, 1815, Founders Online.
22. JQA to LCA, Feb. 4, 1815, ibid.
23. Diary entry, Feb. 6, 1815, JQA Diaries.
24. Ford, *Writings of JQA*, V, 523.
25. Diary entry, Feb. 12, 1815, JQA Diaries, and Traub, *John Quincy Adams*, 197.
26. Ford, *Writings of JQA*, VI, 291.
27. Diary entry, March 12, 1815, JQA Diaries.
28. Ibid.
29. Ford, *Writings of JQA*, V, 292.
30. Ibid., 300.
31. Diary, in Graham et al., *Diary and Autobiographical Writings*, I, 382–83.
32. Ibid.
33. Ibid., 384.
34. Heffron, *Louisa Catherine*, 251.
35. Ibid., 385–86.
36. Ibid., 255.
37. Quoted in Thomas, *Louisa*, 220.
38. Diary, in Graham et al., *Diary and Autobiographical Writings*, I, 388–89.
39. LCA to JQA, March 5, 1815, Founders Online.
40. Diary, in Graham et al., *Diary and Autobiographical Writings*, I, 392.
41. Ibid., 394–95.
42. Quoted in Heffron, *Louisa Catherine*, 259.
43. Diary, in Graham et al., *Diary and Autobiographical Writings*, I, 397.
44. Ibid.
45. See O'Brien, *Mrs. Adams in Winter*, 268–75.
46. Diary, in Graham et al., *Diary and Autobiographical Writings*, I, 399.
47. Quoted in Heffron, *Louisa Catherine*, 261.
48. Ibid.
49. O'Brien, *Mrs. Adams in Winter*, 271–74. O'Brien demonstrates that their route was

more likely through Velaines, Vitry-sur-Seine, and Port à Binson.

50. Diary, in Graham et al., *Diary and Autobiographical Writings*, I, 401.

51. Ibid., 402.

52. Ibid.

53. Ibid.

54. Ibid., 404.

55. Diary entry, March 24, 1815, JQA Diaries.

56. Quoted in Heffron, *Louisa Catherine*, 265.

57. Ibid., 267.

CHAPTER 20

1. JA to JQA, Feb. 25, 1815, Founders Online.

2. Quoted in Bemis, *JQA and the Foundations*, 223.

3. Diary entries, March 1 and 29, 1815, JQA Diaries.

4. JQA to AA, May 7, 1815, Founders Online.

5. Diary entry, May 15, 1815, JQA Diaries.

6. Ibid., diary entry, May 23, 1815.

7. Quoted in Nagel, *John Quincy Adams*, 272.

8. Ibid., 273.

9. Quoted in ibid., 272.

10. JQA to AA, Sept. 11, 1815, Founders Online.

11. Diary entry, May 29, 1815, JQA Diaries.

12. JA to JQA, May 14, 1815, Founders Online.

13. Quoted in Perkins, *Castlereagh and Adams*, 173.

14. Diary entry, June 11, 1815, JQA Diaries.

15. Ibid., diary entry, June 22, 1815.

16. JQA to AA, Feb. 1, 1817, Founders Online.

17. Quoted in Heffron, *Louisa Catherine*, 281 and Ford, *Writings of JQA*, V, 519.

18. Ibid., 160.

19. JQA to AA, July 6, 1817, Founders Online.

20. JQA to AA, July 17, 1815, ibid.

21. Quoted in Bemis, *JQA and the Foundations*, 228.

22. Quoted in ibid., 226–27.

23. Ibid., 230–32.

24. Ford, *Writings of JQA*, V, 51.

25. JQA to James Madison, Sept. 27, 1815, Kreider et al., *Papers of James Madison*, Presidential Series, IX, 658–59.

26. Ford, *Writings of JQA*, V, 385.

27. Ibid., 380.

28. Bemis, *JQA and the Foundations*, 234–35.

29. Perkins, *Castlereagh and Adams*, 166.

30. Ford, *Writings of JQA*, V, 349.

31. Perkins, *Castlereagh and Adams*, 166.

32. Ford, *Writings of JQA*, V, 457.

33. LCA to AA, July 8, 1815, Founders Online.

34. Diary entry, Aug. 1, 1815, JQA Diaries.

35. Ibid., diary entry, Aug. 2, 1815.

36. Quoted in Heffron, *Louisa Catherine*, 276.

37. Diary entry, Aug. 10, 1815, JQA Diaries.

38. Ibid., diary entry, Aug. 10, 1815.

39. Ibid.

40. Quoted in Heffron, *Louisa Catherine*, 280.

41. LCA to AA, Jan. 21, 1816, Founders Online.

42. Quoted in Heffron, *Louisa Catherine*, 280.

43. Diary entry, Oct. 13, 1815, JQA Diaries.

44. Ibid., diary entry, Oct. 25, 1815.

45. Ibid., diary entry, Oct. 27, 1815.

46. Ibid., diary entry, Oct. 29, 1815.

47. JQA to AA, June 30, 1815, Founders Online.

48. Nagel, *John Quincy Adams*, 229.

49. Diary entry, Dec. 2, 1815, JQA Diaries.

50. Ford, *Writings of JQA*, V, 341–42.

51. Waldstreicher, *JQA: Diaries*, I, 370–71.

52. LCA to AA, Nov. 11, 1816, Founders Online.

53. Diary entry, March 20, 1816, JQA Diaries.

54. Ibid., diary entry, Aug. 7, 1816.

55. Heffron, *Louisa Catherine*, 286.

56. Ford, *Writings of JQA*, V, 75–76.

57. Diary entry, Aug. 22, 1816, JQA Diaries.

58. Ibid., diary entry, June 27, 1816.

59. Ford, *Writings of JQA*, VI, 90.

60. See Strothers, "Great Tambora Eruption," 1191–98.

61. Diary entry, April 12, 1816, JQA Diaries.

62. Ford, *Writings of JQA*, VI, 94, nt. 1.

63. Heffron, *Louisa Catherine*, 288–89.

64. Ford, *Writings of JQA*, VI, 41.

65. Diary entry, Oct. 10, 1816, JQA Diaries.

66. Ibid., diary entry, Oct. 11, 1816.

67. Quoted in Heffron, *Louisa Catherine*, 291.

68. Diary entry, Oct. 19, 1816, JQA Diaries.

69. Quoted in Heffron, *Louisa Catherine*, 290.

70. Diary entry, Nov. 29, 1818, JQA Diaries.

CHAPTER 21

1. Ford, *Writings of JQA*, VI, 132.

2. Quoted in Divine et al., *America*, 258.

3. See Howe, *What Hath God Wrought*, 91.

4. Quoted in Ford, *Writings of JQA*, VI, 133–40, nt. 1.

5. Quoted in ibid.

6. Quoted in Seward, *Life of JQA*, 115.

7. Quoted in Ford, *Writings of JQA*, VI, 133.

8. Quoted in ibid., 165.

9. Diary entry, April 7, 1817, JQA Diaries.

10. Ford, *Writings of JQA*, VI, 177.

11. Quoted in Heffron, *Louisa Catherine*, 293.

12. Quoted in ibid., 294–95.

13. Waldstreicher, *JQA: Diaries*, I, 408.

14. Ibid., 415.

15. Ibid.

16. Ibid.

17. Diary entry, July 23, 1817, JQA Diaries.

18. Ibid.

19. Ford, *Writings of JQA*, VI, 271.

20. Diary entry, June 2, 1817, JQA Diaries.

21. Ibid., diary entry, July 21, 1817.

22. Ibid., diary entry, May 14, 1817.

23. Ibid., diary entries, May 13 and 15, 1817.

24. Ibid., diary entries, May 10 and 13 and June 13–15, 1817.

25. Ibid., diary entries, June 25–28, 1817, and LCA to AA, Aug. 14, 1817, Founders Online.

26. Diary entries, June 25 and July 23, 1817, JQA Diaries.

27. Ibid., diary entry, July 15, 1817.

28. Ibid., diary entry, Aug. 6, 1817.

29. Nagel, *John Quincy Adams*, 236.

30. Diary entry, Aug. 9, 1817, JQA Diaries.

31. Quoted in Bemis, *JQA and the Foundations*, 247.

32. Nagel, *John Quincy Adams*, 236.

33. Ford, *Writings of JQA*, VI, 113.

34. See Nagel, *John Quincy Adams*, 237.

35. Diary entries, Aug. 30 and Sept. 3 and 6, 1817, JQA Diaries.

36. LCA to AA, Sept. 13–16, 1817, Founders Online.

37. Heffron, *Louisa Catherine*, 298–99.

38. Quoted in ibid., 299.

39. See Ammon, *James Monroe*, 359, and Bemis, *JQA and the Foundations*, 252.

40. See Bemis, *JQA and the Foundations*, 252, and Ammon, *James Monroe*, 360.

41. Ammon, *James Monroe*, 363.

42. Quoted in ibid., 369.

43. Quoted in ibid., 362.

44. Remini, *Henry Clay*, 139–40.

45. Morrison, *Slavery and the West*, 4–5.

46. Bemis, *JQA and the Foundations*, 255–56.

47. Ford, *Writings of JQA*, VI, 228.

48. Quoted in Edel, *Nation Builder*, 112–13.

49. Diary entry, Nov. 7, 1817, JQA Diaries.

50. Quoted in Ford, *Writings of JQA*, VI, 250, nt. 1.

51. JA to JQA, Oct. 28, 1817, Founders Online.

52. See Heffron, *Louisa Catherine*, 303. For a comprehensive history of the etiquette wars and Washington society in general, see Allgor, *Parlor Politics*.

53. Ammon, *James Monroe*, 398.

54. Quoted in Heffron, *Louisa Catherine*, 302.

55. Diary entry, Jan. 5, 1818, JQA Diaries.

56. Quoted in Heffron, *Louisa Catherine*, 304.

57. Quoted in ibid., 306.

58. Quoted in ibid., 305.

59. Quoted in Nagel, *John Quincy Adams*, 246.

60. Diary, in Graham et al., *Diary and Autobiographical Writings*, II, 416.

61. Quoted in Heffron, *Louisa Catherine*, 205.

62. Quoted in ibid.

63. Quoted in Ford, *Writings of JQA*, V, 331.

64. Quoted in Seward, *Life of JQA*, 111.

65. Quoted in Heffron, *Louisa Catherine*, 306.

66. Ford, *Writings of JQA*, VI, 567–68.

67. LCA to JA, Dec. 8, 1818, Founders Online.

68. LCA to JA, Dec. 8, 1818, Founders Online.

69. Bemis, *JQA and the Union*, 174–75.

70. Diary entry, Sept. 14, 1820, JQA Diaries.
71. Diary, in Graham et al., *Diary and Autobiographical Writings*, II, 654.
72. Quoted in Heffron, *Louisa Catherine*, 320.
73. Ibid.

CHAPTER 22

1. Ford, *Writings of JQA*, V, 466.
2. Ibid., 189, nt. 2.
3. Quoted in Perkins, *Castlereagh and Adams*, 202–3.
4. Quoted in ibid., 204.
5. Diary entry, April 13, 1819, JQA Diaries.
6. Ford, *Writings of JQA*, VI, 203.
7. Diary entry, Nov. 24, 1818, JQA Diaries.
8. Quoted in Bemis, *JQA and the Foundations*, 279.
9. Bemis, *JQA and the Foundations*, 280, 291.
10. Weeks, *JQA and American Global Empire*, 49.
11. Bemis, *JQA and the Foundations*, 281–82.
12. Quoted in Weeks, *JQA and American Global Empire*, 54–55.
13. Ford, *Writings of JQA*, VI, 121–22.
14. Diary entry, Nov. 24, 1817, JQA Diaries.
15. On the question of British compensation for slaves seized during the War of 1812, the two parties agreed to ask Alexander I to arbitrate. In 1822 he awarded U.S. claimants $1.2 million. See Bemis, *JQA and the Foundations*, 290–98.
16. See Stephanson, *Manifest Destiny*, 8–12.
17. Quoted in Wood, *Empire of Liberty*, 171.
18. Quoted in Stephanson, *Manifest Destiny*, 19.
19. Diary entry, Nov. 16, 1819, JQA Diaries.
20. Weeks, *JQA and American Global Empire*, 97, and Lewis, *American Union and the Problem of Neighborhood*, 106.
21. Weeks, *JQA and American Global Empire*, 70–71.
22. JQA to LCA, July 8, 1814, Founders Online.
23. Ibid., 92–94.
24. Quoted in Remini, *Henry Clay*, 175.
25. Diary entry, Jan. 12, 1818, JQA Diaries.
26. Ibid., diary entry, Dec. 24, 1817.
27. Quoted in Weeks, *JQA and American Global Empire*, 89.

28. Ibid., 99.
29. JQA to TBA, April 14, 1818, Founders Online.
30. Diary entry, Sept. 19, 1818, JQA Diaries.
31. Ford, *Writings of JQA*, VI, 376.
32. Ibid., 379.
33. Ibid., 143.
34. Diary entries, Dec. 30, 1817, and Feb. 7, 1818, JQA Diaries.
35. Ammon, *James Monroe*, 412–13, and Ford, *Writings of JQA*, VI, 284–86.
36. Weeks, *JQA and American Global Empire*, 63–64.
37. Ammon, *James Monroe*, 413–14.
38. Diary entry, Jan. 5, 1818, JQA Diaries.
39. Ibid., diary entry, Jan. 27, 1818.
40. "Taking into view the peculiar position of Spain and her American provinces and considering the influence which the destiny of the territory adjoining the southern boundary of the United States may have upon the security, tranquility, and commerce . . . the United States cannot . . . without serious inquietude see any part of the said territory pass into the hands of any foreign power." Quoted in Bemis, *JQA and the Foundations*, 301.
41. Diary entry, Jan. 12, 1818, JQA Diaries.
42. Weeks, *JQA and American Global Empire*, 63–64.
43. Ford, *Writings of JQA*, VI, 142, nt. 1.
44. Diary entry, Jan. 9, 1818, JQA Diaries.
45. Ibid., diary entry, Jan. 13, 1818.
46. Quoted in Bemis, *JQA and the Foundations*, 313.
47. Quoted in ibid., 314.
48. Quoted in Ammon, *James Monroe*, 417.
49. Diary entry, Dec. 24, 1818, JQA Diaries.
50. Quoted in Remini, *Andrew Jackson and His Indian Wars*, 134–35.
51. Ibid., 139–40.
52. Drinnon, *Facing West*, 108.
53. Ibid.

CHAPTER 23

1. Diary entry, May 4, 1818, JQA Diaries.
2. Ford, *Writings of JQA*, VI, 384.
3. Diary entry, July 15, 1818, JQA Diaries.

4. Ibid., diary entry, July 13, 1818.

5. Ibid., diary entries, March 18 and 24, 1818.

6. See Lewis, *American Union and the Problem of Neighborhood*, 107–9.

7. Diary entry, July 28, 1818, JQA Diaries.

8. Ibid., diary entry, July 21, 1818.

9. Ibid.

10. Ibid., diary entries, July 15, 16, and 17, 1818.

11. Ibid., diary entry, July 30, 1818.

12. Ibid., diary entry, July 12, 1818.

13. Ibid., diary entry, Aug. 22, 1818.

14. Ford, *Writings of JQA*, VI, 444–46, and Bemis, *JQA and the Foundations*, 316.

15. Quoted in Ammon, *James Monroe*, 424.

16. Ibid.

17. Diary entry, Nov. 8, 1818, JQA Diaries.

18. Ford, *Writings of JQA*, VI, 476.

19. Ibid.

20. Ibid.

21. Ibid., 475, nt. 1.

22. Quoted in Bemis, *JQA and the Foundations*, 328.

23. Quoted in ibid.

24. Quoted in Perkins, *Castlereagh and Adams*, 289.

25. Ammon, *James Monroe*, 430–31.

26. Quoted in Remini, *Henry Clay*, 165.

27. Ford, *Writings of JQA*, VI, 528–29.

28. Quoted in Remini, *Henry Clay*, 167.

29. Diary entry, March 18, 1819, JQA Diaries.

30. Quoted in Weeks, *JQA and American Global Empire*, 72.

31. Quoted in Bemis, *JQA and the Foundations*, 318–19.

32. "I would henceforth never recede an inch from the Bravo," Adams wrote Joseph Hopkinson at the time. Ford, *Writings of JQA*, VI, 346.

33. Diary entry, April 14, 1818, JQA Diaries.

34. See ibid., diary entry, Dec. 24, 1818.

35. Bemis, *JQA and the Foundations*, 267.

36. Ford, *Writings of JQA*, VI, 547–48.

37. Diary entry, Dec. 28, 1818, JQA Diaries.

38. Quoted in Weeks, *JQA and American Global Empire*, 151.

39. Diary entry, Dec. 28, 1818, JQA Diaries.

40. Ibid., diary entry, Jan. 1, 1819.

41. Ibid., diary entry, Nov. 14, 1818.

42. Bemis, *JQA and the Foundations*, 329.

43. Diary entry, Oct. 26, 1818, JQA Diaries.

44. Quoted in Holton, *Abigail Adams*, 410.

45. Quoted in ibid., 411.

46. Diary entry, Oct. 26, 1818, JQA Diaries.

47. Ford, *Writings of JQA*, VI, 463.

48. JA to JQA, Nov. 10, 1818, Founders Online.

49. Diary entry, Nov. 1, 1818, JQA Diaries.

50. Ibid., diary entry, Jan. 14, 1819.

51. Ibid., diary entry, Feb. 5, 1819.

52. Ibid., diary entry, Feb. 3, 1819.

53. Ibid., diary entry, Feb. 14, 1819.

54. Quoted in Bemis, *JQA and the Foundations*, 338–39.

55. Diary, in Graham et al., *Diary and Autobiographical Writings*, II, 425.

56. Quoted in Weeks, *JQA and American Global Empire*, 167.

57. Ford, *Writings of JQA*, VI, 61–62.

58. Diary entry, Dec. 27, 1819, JQA Diaries.

59. Ford, *Writings of JQA*, VI, 62.

CHAPTER 24

1. Diary entry, Feb. 3, 1819, JQA Diaries.

2. Quoted in Remini, *Henry Clay*, 173.

3. Diary entry, Dec. 16, 1819, JQA Diaries.

4. Ibid., diary entry, Feb. 2, 1819.

5. Bemis, *JQA and the Foundations*, 336–37, and diary entry, March 15, 1819, JQA Diaries.

6. Diary, in Graham et al., *Diary and Autobiographical Writings*, II, 487.

7. Ibid.

8. Ford, *Writings of JQA*, VI, 278, nt. 1.

9. Quoted in ibid., 301, nt. 1.

10. Diary entry, April 10, 1819, JQA Diaries.

11. Ibid., diary entry, March 2, 1819.

12. Quoted in Heffron, *Louisa Catherine*, 340.

13. Ibid., 311.

14. Ibid., 320–21.

15. JQA to GWA, Dec. 26, 1817, Founders Online.

16. Ford, *Writings of JQA*, VI, 258.

17. Bemis, *JQA and the Foundations*, 350.

18. Diary entry, Aug. 4, 1819, JQA Diaries.

19. Ibid., diary entry, Aug. 10, 1819.

20. Ibid., diary entry, Nov. 5, 1819.

21. Ammon, *James Monroe*, 441.

22. Diary entry, Nov. 25, 1819, JQA Diaries.

23. Ibid., diary entry, May 26, 1819.

24. Ibid., diary entry, Jan. 8, 1820.

25. Ammon, *James Monroe*, 444.

26. Quoted in ibid., 444–45.

27. Diary entry, May 27, 1820, JQA Diaries.

28. Bemis, *JQA and the Foundations*, 352.

29. Diary entry, Feb. 21, 1821, JQA Diaries.

30. Rothman, *Slave Country*, 2–7.

31. Ibid., 31–32, 84–85.

32. Ibid., 195.

33. Quoted in Forbes, *Missouri Compromise*, 35–36.

34. Quoted in Howe, *What Hath God Wrought*, 148.

35. Quoted in Forbes, *Missouri Compromise*, 43–44.

36. See ibid., 29–30, 35–36.

37. Diary entry, July 5, 1819, JQA Diaries.

38. Diary, in Graham et al., *Diary and Autobiographical Writings*, II, 453, nt. 1.

39. Ibid.

40. Remini, *Henry Clay*, 178–79.

41. Diary entries, March 11 and 12, 1819, JQA Diaries.

42. Quoted in Noonan, *The Antelope*, 19.

43. Ibid., 25.

44. Quoted in Howe, *What Hath God Wrought*, 155.

45. Diary entry, Nov. 28, 1820, JQA Diaries.

46. Ibid., diary entry, Oct. 21, 1820.

47. Ibid., diary entry, Feb. 24, 1820.

48. Diary, in Graham et al., *Diary and Autobiographical Writings*, II, 444, nt. 10.

49. Ibid., 462, nt. 2.

50. Diary entry, Oct. 8, 1819, JQA Diaries.

51. Ammon, *James Monroe*, 460–61.

52. See Howe, *What Hath God Wrought*, 152.

53. Quoted in Waldstreicher and Mason, *JQA and Slavery*, 74.

54. Edel, *Nation Builder*, 155.

55. Quoted in Forbes, *Missouri Compromise*, 114.

56. Diary entry, March 3, 1820, JQA Diaries.

57. Quoted in Bemis, *JQA and the Foundations*, 419.

58. Diary entry, Feb. 11, 1820, JQA Diaries.

59. Diary, in Graham et al., *Diary and Autobiographical Writings*, II, 458–59.

60. Ibid., 450, and LCA to JA, Feb. 18, 1820, Founders Online.

CHAPTER 25

1. Ford, *Writings of JQA*, VI, 550.

2. Diary entry, Feb. 3, 1818, JQA Diaries.

3. Ford, *Writings of JQA*, VI, 377.

4. Diary entry, March 9, 1821, JQA Diaries.

5. "An Address Celebrating the Declaration of Independence," July 4, 1821, JQA Papers.

6. Ford, *Writings of JQA*, VI, 379.

7. Diary entry, March 17, 1818, JQA Diaries.

8. Quoted in Noonan, *The Antelope*, 9.

9. Ammon, *James Monroe*, 434–36.

10. Diary entry, Dec. 6, 1818, JQA Diaries.

11. Ibid., diary entry, March 18, 1819.

12. Ibid., diary entry, April 8, 1819.

13. Ibid., diary entry, Oct. 18, 1819.

14. Noonan, *The Antelope*, 9.

15. Diary entry, July 8, 1820, JQA Diaries.

16. Ford, *Writings of JQA*, VI, 523, nt. 1.

17. Diary entry, May 29, 1819, JQA Diaries.

18. Ford, *Writings of JQA*, VI, 442.

19. Diary entry, June 6, 1820, JQA Diaries.

20. Ibid., diary entry, Oct. 31, 1820.

21. Quoted in Burleigh, *The Stranger and the Statesman*, 218.

22. Diary entry, Dec. 25, 1820, JQA Diaries.

23. Quoted in Ford, *Writings of JQA*, VI, 519–20, nt. 1.

24. Diary, in Graham et al., *Diary and Autobiographical Writings*, II, 486.

25. CFA, Diary, I, xxvi.

26. Quoted in Nagel, *John Quincy Adams*, 323.

27. LCA to GWA, Nov. 17, 1818, Founders Online.

28. JQA to GWA, Dec. 6, 1818, ibid.

29. LCA to GWA, April 22, 1819, Founders Online.

30. Nagel, *John Quincy Adams*, 322.
31. LCA to JA2, May 9, 1819, Founders Online.
32. JQA to CFA, Nov. 30, 1818, ibid.
33. LCA to CFA, July 1, 1819, ibid.
34. Diary entries, Sept. 3 and 4, 1819, JQA Diaries.
35. Ibid., diary entry, Sept. 17, 1819.
36. CFA, Diary, I, xxiv.
37. TBA to LCA, March 15, 1819, Founders Online.
38. Diary entry, Sept. 18, 1819, JQA Diaries.
39. Ibid., diary entries, Sept. 22, 24, and 30, 1819.
40. LCA to JA2, Dec. 1, 1819, Founders Online.
41. Diary entry, Feb. 6, 1820, JQA Diaries.
42. Diary, in Graham et al., *Diary and Autobiographical Writings*, II, 542.
43. Ibid., 541.
44. Ibid., 555.
45. Diary entry, Jan. 24, 1821, JQA Diaries.
46. Ibid., diary entries, Jan. 13 and 24, 1821.
47. Ibid., diary entry, Dec. 7, 1820.
48. JQA to TBA, Sept. 12, 1820, Founders Online.
49. Quoted in Nagel, *John Quincy Adams*, 324–25.
50. LCA to JA2, Nov. 14 and 20, 1820, Founders Online.
51. Diary, in Graham et al., *Diary and Autobiographical Writings*, II, 519.
52. Diary entry, Aug. 12, 1819, JQA Diaries.
53. Diary, in Graham et al., *Diary and Autobiographical Writings*, II, 418.
54. Diary entry, July 12, 1820, JQA Diaries.
55. Diary, in Graham et al., *Diary and Autobiographical Writings*, II, 491–92.
56. LCA to JA, Nov. 22, 1820, Founders Online.

CHAPTER 26

1. Ammon, *James Monroe*, 459.
2. Diary entry, March 5, 1821, JQA Diaries.
3. Ibid., diary entry, March 8, 1821.
4. Ibid., diary entry, Oct. 23, 1821.
5. Quoted in Brands, *Andrew Jackson*, 359.
6. Quoted in ibid., 360.
7. Ibid.
8. Diary entry, Oct. 24, 1821, JQA Diaries.
9. Ibid., diary entry, Oct. 20, 1821.
10. Ibid., diary entry, March 9, 1821.
11. Quoted in Remini, *Henry Clay*, 195.
12. Diary entry, April 16, 1821, JQA Diaries.
13. Ibid.
14. Quoted in Remini, *Henry Clay*, 196.
15. Diary entry, May 2, 1821, JQA Diaries.
16. JQA, "An Address . . . Celebrating the Declaration of Independence," Teaching American History, https://teachingamericanhistory.org.
17. Ibid.
18. JQA, "July 4, 1821: Speech to the U.S. House of Representatives on Foreign Policy," Miller Center, University of Virginia, 1.
19. Quoted in Bemis, *JQA and the Foundations*, 357.
20. Margaret S. Boeringer, *Joseph Gales, Printer* (University of North Carolina Press, 1989), 302.
21. Diary entry, Oct. 2, 1821, JQA Diaries.
22. "John Quincy Adams," *St. Louis Enquirer*, Dec. 15, 1821.
23. Diary entry, Jan. 2, 1822, JQA Diaries.
24. Ibid., diary entry, Jan. 3, 1822.
25. LCA to JQA, Aug. 3, 1821, Founders Online.
26. Diary entry, Oct. 7, 1821, JQA Diaries.
27. Ibid., diary entry, April 22, 1822.
28. Ibid., diary entry, April 24, 1822.
29. Ibid., diary entry, April 26, 1822.
30. Quoted in Bemis, *JQA and the Foundations*, 503.
31. Diary entries, April 30 and May 1, 1822, JQA Diaries.
32. Ibid., diary entry, May 11, 1822.
33. Quoted in Bemis, *JQA and the Foundations*, 508.
34. Ibid., 506–7. See also Remini, *Henry Clay*, 212–13.
35. Bemis, *JQA and the Foundations*, 486.
36. See ibid., 483–84.
37. Ibid. 488.
38. Diary entry, Jan. 26, 1821, JQA Diaries.
39. CFA, *Memoirs of JQA*, V, 253.

40. Quoted in Bemis, *JQA and the Foundations*, 492–93.
41. Lewis, *American Union and the Problem of Neighborhood*, 165.
42. Bemis, *JQA and the Foundations*, 359–60.
43. *Boston Daily Advertiser*, Nov. 14, 1822.
44. Diary entry, April 29, 1819, JQA Diaries.
45. See, for example, ibid., diary entry, April 30, 1819.
46. Quoted in Nagel, *John Quincy Adams*, 323.
47. Diary entry, Aug. 27, 1821, JQA Diaries.
48. Ibid., diary entry, Aug. 29, 1821.
49. Ibid., diary entry, Sept. 2, 1821.
50. Ibid., diary entry, Sept. 28, 1821.
51. Ibid., diary entry, Oct. 1, 1821.
52. Ibid., diary entry, Sept. 30, 1821.
53. See Nagel, *John Quincy Adams*, 325.
54. JQA to JA2, Dec. 16, 1821, Founders Online.
55. Ibid.
56. Diary, in Graham et al., *Diary and Autobiographical Writings*, II, 618.
57. LCA to JA2, May 21, 1822, Founders Online.
58. Shepherd, *Cannibals*, 22.
59. Diary, in Graham et al., *Diary and Autobiographical Writings*, II, 614.
60. See diary entries, Oct. 3 and 18, 1821, JQA Diaries.
61. CFA, Diary, I, xxviii.
62. Ibid., xxvii.
63. JQA to CFA, Jan. 30, 1822, Founders Online.
64. Ibid., JQA to CFA, May 18, 1822.
65. See Shepherd, *Cannibals*, 222.
66. Ibid., 221.
67. Ibid., 229.
68. LCA to JQA, June 25, 1822, Founders Online.
69. Ibid., LCA to JQA, July 15, 1822.
70. Ibid., LCA to JQA, July 26, 1822.
71. Ibid., LCA to JQA, Aug. 2, 1822.
72. Ibid., LCA to JQA, July 19, 1822.
73. Ibid., LCA to JQA, June 28, 1822.
74. Ibid., LCA to JQA, July 31, 1822.

75. Quoted in Shepherd, *Cannibals*, 226.
76. Quoted in ibid., 227.
77. Quoted in ibid., 233.
78. LCA to JQA, Aug. 15, 1822, Founders Online.
79. LCA to JQA, July 19, 1822, ibid.
80. Quoted in Heffron, *Louisa Catherine*, 333.
81. Quoted in ibid., 334.
82. LCA to JQA, Aug. 18, 1822, Founders Online.
83. Ibid., LCA to JQA, Aug. 27, 1822.
84. Shepherd, *Cannibals*, 234.
85. LCA to JQA, Sept. 27, 1822, Founders Online.
86. Quoted in Heffron, *Louisa Catherine*, 335.
87. Quoted in ibid., 336.
88. LCA to JQA, Aug. 8, 1822, Founders Online.
89. Shepherd, *Cannibals*, 236–37.

CHAPTER 27

1. Perkins, *Castlereagh and Adams*, 314.
2. Quoted in ibid., 303.
3. Quoted in ibid., 299.
4. Quoted in Bemis, *JQA and the Foundations*, 371.
5. Quoted in ibid., 375.
6. Quoted in ibid., 376.
7. Quoted in ibid.
8. Diary entry, July 17, 1823, JQA Diaries.
9. Quoted in Bemis, *JQA and the Foundations*, 378–79.
10. Diary entry, June 20, 1822, JQA Diaries.
11. Ammon, *James Monroe*, 479.
12. Quoted in DeConde, *History*, I, 128.
13. Quoted in Ammon, *James Monroe*, 480.
14. Diary entry, Oct. 30, 1823, JQA Diaries.
15. CFA, *Memoirs of JQA*, VI, 177–78.
16. Ibid.
17. Diary entry, Nov. 13, 1823, JQA Diaries.
18. Ibid., diary entry, Nov. 15, 1823.
19. Ibid.
20. Quoted in Bemis, *JQA and the Foundations*, 381.
21. Quoted in ibid., 387.
22. Diary entry, Nov. 21, 1823, JQA Diaries.

23. Ibid.

24. Ibid., diary entry, Nov. 22, 1823.

25. Ammon, *James Monroe*, 486–87.

26. Quoted in Bemis, *JQA and the Foundations*, 366.

27. Diary entry, Nov. 25, 1823, JQA Diaries.

28. Ibid., diary entry, Nov. 26, 1823.

29. Quoted in Ammon, *James Monroe*, 490.

30. Quoted in Perkins, *Castlereagh and Adams*, 339.

31. Meyer, "Great Rebellion of 1823," 4–6.

32. JQA to JA2, May 6, 1822, Founders Online.

33. Meyer, "Great Rebellion of 1823," 4–6.

34. JQA to JA2, May 29, 1823, Founders Online.

35. Ibid., JQA to JA2, Oct. 13, 1823.

36. Quoted in Nagel, *John Quincy Adams*, 272.

37. Diary entry, March 25, 1821, JQA Diaries.

38. Ibid., diary entry, June 21, 1823.

39. Ibid., diary entry, June 19, 1823.

40. Ibid., diary entry, July 7, 1823.

41. Ibid., diary entry, July 12, 1823.

42. Ibid., diary entry, Aug. 11, 1823.

43. Waldstreicher, *JQA: Diaries*, I, 46–47.

44. JQA to GWA, Oct. 1, 1823, Founders Online.

45. Ibid., JQA to GWA, Oct. 4, 1823.

46. Diary entry, Sept. 5, 1823, JQA Diaries.

47. See "Col. Benton's Speech," *St. Louis Enquirer*, April 19, 1823.

48. Diary entry, Sept. 9, 1823, JQA Diaries.

CHAPTER 28

1. Quoted in Remini, *Henry Clay*, 223.

2. Diary, in Graham et al., *Diary and Autobiographical Writings*, II, 657.

3. Ibid., 658–59.

4. Quoted in Bemis, *JQA and the Union*, 26.

5. Quoted in ibid., 14.

6. Quoted in Howe, *What Hath God Wrought*, 205.

7. LCA to GWA, Dec. 12, 1823, Founders Online.

8. Diary entry, May 8, 1824, JQA Diaries.

9. Ibid., diary entry, Jan. 6, 1824.

10. CFA, Diary, I, 31–32.

11. Diary, in Graham et al., *Diary and Autobiographical Writings*, 457.

12. CFA, Diary, I, 33–34.

13. Quoted in Heffron, *Louisa Catherine*, 350.

14. Ibid.

15. Diary, in Graham et al., *Diary and Autobiographical Writings*, II, 681.

16. Ibid., 457. For a full account of the affair, see Allgor, *Parlor Politics*, 176–82.

17. Quoted in the *Columbia Centinel*, April 28, 1824.

18. Diary entry, March 11, 1824, JQA Diaries.

19. Quoted in Bemis, *JQA and the Union*, 28.

20. CFA, *Memoirs of JQA*, VII, 81.

21. Quoted in Remini, *Henry Clay*, 237.

22. Diary entry, Nov. 19, 1823, JQA Diaries.

23. Ibid., diary entry, Jan. 20, 1824.

24. Ibid., diary entry, Jan. 30, 1824.

25. Ibid., diary entry, Jan. 25, 1824.

26. Howe, *What Hath God Wrought*, 206.

27. See ibid., 208.

28. Bemis, *JQA and the Union*, 19.

29. Callahan, "John Quincy Adams and the Elections of 1824 and 1828," in Waldstreicher, *Companion*, 308.

30. Diary entry, April 17, 1824, JQA Diaries.

31. Callahan, "John Quincy Adams and the Elections of 1824 and 1828," in Waldstreicher, *Companion*, 307.

32. Quoted in Bemis, *JQA and the Union*, 20.

33. For a comprehensive review and analysis of the election of 1824, see Callahan, "John Quincy Adams and the Elections of 1824 and 1828," in Waldstreicher, *Companion*, 305–19.

34. *Boston Patriot*, June 19, 1824.

35. Diary entry, May 1, 1824, JQA Diaries.

36. Ibid., diary entry, April 17, 1824.

37. Wiltse et al., *Papers of Daniel Webster*, Daniel Webster to Jeremiah Mason, Feb. 14, 1825.

38. Diary entry, May 24, 1824, JQA Diaries.

39. Forbes, *Missouri Compromise*, 156–61.

40. CFA, *Memoirs of JQA*, VII, 57.

41. Quoted in Bemis, *JQA and the Foundations*, 425.

42. Quoted in ibid., 427.
43. JQA to GWA, July 5, 1826, Founders Online.
44. Bemis, *JQA and the Foundations*, 433.
45. Diary entry, May 7, 1824, JQA Diaries.
46. See for example the *Salem Gazette*, Oct. 14, 1824, and the *Richmond Enquirer*, Sept. 14, 1824.
47. Quoted in Heffron, *Louisa Catherine*, 352.
48. CFA, *Memoirs of JQA*, VI, 419.
49. For accounts of Lafayette's visit, see Ammon, *James Monroe*, 539–41, and Heffron, *Louisa Catherine*, 353.
50. Howe, *What Hath God Wrought*, 208.
51. Remini, *Henry Clay*, 239.
52. CFA, *Memoirs of JQA*, VI, 447.
53. Ibid.
54. Quoted in Remini, *Henry Clay*, 257.
55. Quoted in ibid., 258.
56. CFA, *Memoirs of JQA*, VI, 464–65.
57. Ibid., 474.
58. Quoted in Remini, *Henry Clay*, 260.
59. CFA, *Memoirs of JQA*, VI, 483.
60. Quoted in Bemis, *JQA and the Union*, 41.
61. CFA, *Memoirs of JQA*, VI, 42.
62. Quoted in Remini, *Henry Clay*, 263.
63. Bemis, *JQA and the Union*, 47.
64. Quoted in Remini, *Henry Clay*, 265.
65. CFA, *Memoirs of JQA*, VI, 501.
66. Ibid., 504.
67. Quoted in Bemis, *JQA and the Union*, 50. "General Jackson was . . . altogether placid and courteous," John Quincy subsequently recorded in his diary (CFA, *Memoirs of JQA*, VI, 502).
68. Quoted in Remini, *Henry Clay*, 266.
69. Quoted in *New Hampshire Sentinel*, Feb. 18, 1825.
70. CFA, *Diary*, II, 620.
71. Quoted in Forbes, *Missouri Compromise*, 190.
72. Hargreaves, *Presidency of JQA*, 44.

CHAPTER 29

1. Bemis, *JQA and the Union*, 52–53.
2. CFA, *Diary*, I, 89.
3. Ibid., xxviii.
4. Ibid., 10.
5. Ibid., 268.
6. Ibid., 314.
7. Ibid., 88.
8. Ibid., 32, nt. 4.
9. Ibid.
10. Quoted in Shepherd, *Cannibals*, 271.
11. Quoted in ibid., 273.
12. Quoted in ibid., 274.
13. Quoted in Remini, *Henry Clay*, 268.
14. "Antony and Caesar," *Columbian Observer*, Jan. 28, 1825.
15. Quoted in Hargreaves, *Presidency of JQA*, 47.
16. CFA, *Memoirs of JQA*, VII, 163.
17. Ibid., VI, 520–21.
18. Quoted in Remini, *Henry Clay*, 289.
19. CFA, *Memoirs of JQA*, VI, 506.
20. Howe, *What Hath God Wrought*, 249–50.
21. Quoted in Bemis, *JQA and the Union*, 60, nt. 21.
22. "An Oration Delivered Before the Cincinnati Astronomical Society," Nov. 10, 1843, JQA Papers, 13.
23. JQA to George Bancroft, Oct. 25, 1835, Adams Papers, II, reel 152.
24. Ibid.
25. For thoughts on "improvement," see Howe, *What Hath God Wrought*, 244–45.
26. Ford, *Writings of JQA*, VI, 267.
27. Quoted in Bemis, *JQA and the Union*, 62.
28. Quoted in Nagel, *John Quincy Adams*, 302.
29. Quoted in Bemis, *JQA and the Union*, 69. For the full text of Adams's address, see Seward, *Life of JQA*, 153–60.
30. Quoted in Bemis, *JQA and the Union*, 67.
31. CFA, *Memoirs of JQA*, VII, 64.
32. Quoted in Bemis, *JQA and the Union*, 67–68.
33. See Lewis, *American Union and the Problem of Neighborhood*, 129–31, and Ammon, *James Monroe*, 462–64.
34. Quoted in Remini, *Henry Clay*, 287.
35. Quoted in Hargreaves, *Presidency of JQA*, 167.

36. Seward, *Life of JQA*.

37. Quoted in Hargreaves, *Presidency of JQA*, 161.

38. Quoted in ibid.

39. Quoted in Remini, *Henry Clay*, 284.

40. Ibid., 282–83.

41. Quoted in Hargreaves, *Presidency of JQA*, 122.

42. Bemis, *JQA and the Foundations*, 543–45.

43. See Hackett, "Development of JQA's Policy," 505–26.

44. Diary entry, July 28, 1823, JQA Diaries.

45. Ibid., diary entry, July 31, 1823.

46. CFA, *Memoirs of JQA*, VI, 531.

47. Quoted in Hargreaves, *Presidency of JQA*, 115.

48. Quoted in Edel, *Nation Builder*, 222.

49. Quoted in Bemis, *JQA and the Foundations*, 553.

50. Quoted in Hargreaves, *Presidency of JQA*, 153.

51. Quoted in Remini, *Henry Clay*, 294.

52. Quoted in ibid., 294–95.

53. Quoted in Hargreaves, *Presidency of JQA*, 155.

54. Quoted in Remini, *Henry Clay*, 302.

55. Long, *Nothing Too Daring*, 214, 225–26.

56. CFA, *Memoirs of JQA*, VI, 453–54.

57. *Washington Gazette*, July 1, 1825.

58. See CFA, *Memoirs of JQA*, VII, 17, 19, 24, 115.

59. Ibid., VI, 138.

60. Quoted in Hargreaves, *Presidency of JQA*, 138.

61. Alexander H. Everett to Clay, Jan. 7, 1827, in Hopkins et al., *Papers of Henry Clay*, VI, 27.

62. Quoted in Hargreaves, *Presidency of JQA*, 119.

63. Waldstreicher, *JQA: Diaries*, II, 217.

64. Quoted in Ammon, *James Monroe*, 539.

65. Quoted in ibid.

66. Diary entry, March 12, 1824, JQA Diaries.

67. Ibid., diary entry, March 26, 1824.

68. Bemis, *JQA and the Union*, 8.

69. CFA, *Memoirs of JQA*, VII, 3.

70. Ibid., 12.

71. Ibid., 3.

72. Ibid., 12.

73. Ibid., 49.

74. Ibid., 87.

75. Ibid., 73–74.

76. Ibid., 90.

77. Ibid., 92.

78. Ibid.

79. Quoted in Bemis, *JQA and the Union*, 85.

80. Quoted in ibid.

81. CFA, *Memoirs of JQA*, VII, 221.

82. Quoted in Bemis, *JQA and the Union*, 87.

CHAPTER 30

1. See Bemis, *JQA and the Union*, 92–93, and Thomas, *Louisa*, 374–75.

2. Bemis, *JQA and the Union*, 97–98.

3. CFA, *Memoirs of JQA*, VIII, 56.

4. Ibid., 21, 28, 91.

5. Ibid., 27–28.

6. Ibid.

7. Quoted in Nagel, *John Quincy Adams*, 310.

8. CFA, *Memoirs of JQA*, VIII, 29.

9. See Ferling, *John Adams*, 443–44.

10. CFA, *Memoirs of JQA*, VII, 125.

11. Ibid., 129.

12. CFA, Diary, II, 66.

13. CFA, *Memoirs of JQA*, VII, 128.

14. LCA to JQA, July 18, 1826, Founders Online.

15. JQA to LCA, July 14, 1826, ibid.

16. JQA to LCA, Aug. 26, 1826, ibid.

17. LCA to CFA, Sept. 9, 1826, ibid.

18. Ibid.

19. LCA to Mary Catherine Hellen Adams, Sept. 12, 1826, ibid.

20. Quoted in Thomas, *Louisa*, 353.

21. Quoted in ibid.

22. Quoted in ibid., 356.

23. Quoted in ibid., 354.

24. LCA to GWA, Oct. 29, 1826, Founders Online.

25. Quoted in Shepherd, *Cannibals*, 260.

26. Quoted in ibid., 264.

27. LCA to Mary Catherine Hellen Adams, July 25, 1826, Founders Online.

28. Quoted in Shepherd, *Cannibals*, 263.

29. CFA, Diary, II, 155, nt. 1.

30. Quoted in Shepherd, *Cannibals*, 266.

31. Quoted in ibid.

32. CFA, *Memoirs of JQA*, VII, 148.

33. Diary, in Graham et al., *Diary and Autobiographical Writings*, II, 478.

34. Ibid., 639.

35. CFA, *Memoirs of JQA*, VII, 269.

36. Forbes, *Missouri Compromise*, 205.

37. See Silbey, *Martin Van Buren and the Emergence of American Popular Politics*.

38. Quoted in Forbes, *Missouri Compromise*, 214.

39. Quoted in Hargreaves, *Presidency of JQA*, 248.

40. Quoted in Forbes, *Missouri Compromise*, 215.

41. Quoted in Remini, *Henry Clay*, 270.

42. Quoted in Hargreaves, *Presidency of JQA*, 249.

43. CFA, *Memoirs of JQA*, VII, 272.

44. Ibid., 329.

45. Ibid., 332.

46. Wiltse et al., *Papers of Daniel Webster*, Daniel Webster to Isaac Parker, March 7, 1828.

47. Robert Walsh to Daniel Webster, Feb. 25, 1828, ibid.

48. CFA, *Memoirs of JQA*, VII, 45.

49. Ibid., 297.

50. Quoted in Edel, *Nation Builder*, 236.

51. Hargreaves, *Presidency of JQA*, 50–51.

52. CFA, *Memoirs of JQA*, VII, 275.

53. Remini, *Henry Clay*, 304–5, and Bemis, *JQA and the Foundations*, 562–63.

54. CFA, *Memoirs of JQA*, VII, 190.

55. Ibid., 193.

56. Ibid., 216.

57. Ibid., 273.

58. Ibid., 311.

59. Ibid., 261.

60. Ibid., 311.

61. Quoted in Shepherd, *Cannibals*, 307.

62. Quoted in Holton, *Abigail Adams*, 358.

63. JQA to GWA, May 25, 1826, Founders Online.

64. Quoted in Shepherd, *Cannibals*, 300.

65. Quoted in ibid.

66. CFA, Diary, II, 171, nt. 2.

67. Quoted in Shepherd, *Cannibals*, 296.

68. CFA, Diary, II, 171–72, nt. 2.

69. Ibid.

70. Ibid.

71. Ibid.

72. Ibid., 132, nt. 1.

73. Ibid., 104–5.

74. Quoted in Shepherd, *Cannibals*, 287.

75. Quoted in ibid.

76. As speculated in Shepherd, *Cannibals*, 288.

77. Quoted in ibid., 288–89.

78. CFA, Diary, II, 180, nt. 1.

79. Quoted in Shepherd, *Cannibals*, 298–99.

80. CFA, Diary, II, 307–8.

81. Ibid., 303.

82. CFA, *Memoirs of JQA*, VII, 470.

CHAPTER 31

1. Hargreaves, *Presidency of JQA*, 269.

2. Green, "An Exposition of the Political Character and Principles of JQA," 1827, JQA Papers, Huntington Library.

3. Quoted in Isenberg and Burstein, *The Problem of Democracy*, 376.

4. *New York Evening Post*, Dec. 8, 1828, and *Albany Argus*, Jan. 11, 1828.

5. Quoted in Thomas, *Louisa*, 360.

6. Quoted in ibid.

7. Quoted in ibid.

8. Clay to Peter B. Porter, May 13, 1827, in Hopkins et al., *Papers of Henry Clay*, VI, 549.

9. Reprinted in *United States Telegraph*, Sept. 10, 1828.

10. Quoted in Hargreaves, *Presidency of JQA*, 291–92.

11. CFA, *Memoirs of JQA*, VII, 521.

12. See JQA to Robert Walsh Jr., March 14, 1824, Adams Papers, II, reel 147.

13. See Howe, *What Hath God Wrought*, 273.

14. Quoted in Hargreaves, *Presidency of JQA*, 194.

15. Clay to John J. Crittenden, Feb. 18, 1829, in Hopkins et al., *Papers of Henry Clay*, VII, 136.

16. CFA, *Memoirs of JQA*, VII, 508.

17. Ibid., 510–11.

18. Quoted in Hargreaves, *Presidency of JQA*, 211.

19. Quoted in Seward, *Life of JQA*, 219.

20. CFA, *Memoirs of JQA*, VIII, 49–50.

21. *Rhode Island American*, Jan. 11, 1828.

22. See Howe, *What Hath God Wrought*, 277.

23. CFA, *Memoirs of JQA*, VII, 415–16.

24. Callahan, "John Quincy Adams and the Elections of 1824 and 1828," in Waldstreicher, *Companion*, 323–27.

25. See Howe, *What Hath God Wrought*, 282–83.

26. JQA to the Reverend Charles W. Upham, Feb. 2, 1837, in Tatum, "Unpublished Letters of JQA," 381–84, nt. 3.

27. Quoted in Thomas, *Louisa*, 375.

28. JQA to Jeremiah Condy, Jan. 24, 1829, Adams Papers, II, reel 148.

29. Quoted in Thomas, *Louisa*, 376.

30. CFA, *Memoirs of JQA*, VIII, 99.

31. Ibid., 103.

32. Ibid., 88.

33. Ibid., 89.

34. Quoted in Bemis, *JQA and the Union*, 152.

35. Quoted in Shepherd, *Cannibals*, 310–11.

36. CFA, *Memoirs of JQA*, VIII, 102.

37. Ibid., 78.

38. Ibid., 144.

39. Ibid., 115.

40. JQA to Messrs. H. G. Otis et al., Dec. 31, 1828, Adams Papers, II, reel 149.

41. Quoted in Nagel, *John Quincy Adams*, 329.

42. Quoted in Bemis, *JQA and the Union*, 157.

43. CFA, *Memoirs of JQA*, VII, 210–11.

44. Quoted in Van Buren, *Autobiography of Martin Van Buren*, 270.

45. CFA to LCA, April 4, 1829, Founders Online.

46. LCA to GWA, April 8, 1829, ibid.

47. CFA, Diary, II, 376.

48. Ibid., 382, nt. 1.

49. Ibid., 208, and Bemis, *JQA and the Union*, 179–80.

50. CFA, *Memoirs of JQA*, II, 207.

51. Waldstreicher, *JQA: Diaries*, II, 208.

52. CFA, Diary, II, 371–72.

53. Ibid., 376.

54. Quoted in Shepherd, *Cannibals*, 319.

55. Quoted in ibid., 321.

56. Ibid., 322.

57. CFA, Diary, III, 47.

58. Ibid., 384.

59. Quoted in Bemis, *JQA and the Union*, 185.

60. Ibid., 186.

61. CFA, Diary, II, 408, nt. 1.

62. Bemis, *JQA and the Union*, 188.

63. CFA, Diary, II, 423.

64. Quoted in Shepherd, *Cannibals*, 330.

65. CFA, Diary, II, 432.

66. CFA, Diary, III, 84.

67. Diary entry, Nov. 24, 1829, JQA Diaries.

68. Quoted in Nagel, *John Quincy Adams*, 332.

69. JQA to CFA, Feb. 21, 1830, Adams Papers, II, reel 157.

70. CFA, *Memoirs of JQA*, VIII, 196.

71. JQA to CFA, Feb. 18, 1822, Founders Online.

72. Ibid., JQA to Ward Nicholas Boylston, Nov. 8, 1828.

73. Howe, *What Hath God Wrought*, 328–29.

74. Quoted in ibid., 333.

75. Quoted in ibid., 334.

76. JQA to William H. Crawford, July 30, 1830, Adams Papers, II, reel 150.

77. CFA, *Memoirs of JQA*, VIII, 306.

78. Ibid., 331.

79. Ibid., 227.

80. Waldstreicher, *JQA: Diaries*, II, 227.

81. CFA, *Memoirs of JQA*, VIII, 190–91.

82. Quoted in Howe, *What Hath God Wrought*, 371.

83. Quoted in Bemis, *JQA and the Union*, 227, nt. 16.

84. CFA, *Memoirs of JQA*, VIII, 229.

85. Ibid., 229.

86. Bemis, *JQA and the Union*, 203.

87. CFA, Diary, III, 260.

88. CFA, *Memoirs of JQA*, VIII, 235.

CHAPTER 32

1. Quoted in Wheelan, *Mr. Adams's Last Crusade*, xiii.

2. CFA, *Memoirs of JQA*, VIII, 239–40.

3. Ibid., 240–41.

4. CFA, Diary, III, 333, nt. 1.

5. Ibid., 331.

6. Ibid., xxxvii.

7. Ibid., xxxiii.

8. Ibid., xxxvii.

9. CFA, *Memoirs of JQA*, VIII, 25.

10. Ibid., 237.

11. Ibid., 238.

12. Ibid., 262–63.

13. CFA, Diary, III, 348, nt. 1.

14. Ibid., 349.

15. Ibid., nt. 1.

16. Quoted in Bemis, *JQA and the Union*, 220.

17. Nagel, *John Quincy Adams*, 337.

18. Quoted in Traub, *John Quincy Adams*, 391.

19. Quoted in Edel, *Nation Builder*, 257.

20. CFA, *Memoirs of JQA*, VIII, 339.

21. Ibid., 340.

22. Ibid., IV, 218.

23. Ibid., VIII, 355.

24. CFA, Diary, IV, 391.

25. JQA to Alexander H. Everett, May 24, 1830, Adams Papers, II, reel 150.

26. Bemis, *JQA and the Union*, 216–17.

27. JQA to Alexander H. Everett, May 24, 1830, Adams Papers, II, reel 150.

28. CFA, *Memoirs of JQA*, VIII, 315.

29. Ibid.

30. Quoted in Bemis, *JQA and the Union*, 232.

31. CFA, *Memoirs of JQA*, VIII, 370.

32. Ibid., 375–76.

33. Ibid., 235.

34. Quoted in Bemis, *JQA and the Union*, 237.

35. Wiltse et al., *Papers of Daniel Webster*, Daniel Webster to Henry Clay, Oct. 5, 1831.

36. JQA to Henry Clay, Sept. 7, 1831, Adams Papers, II, reel 150.

37. Stone, *Letters on Masonry*.

38. See Vaughn, *Anti-Masonic Party in the United States, 1826–1843*.

39. JQA to LCA, Sept. 23, 1804, Founders Online.

40. Ibid., LCA to JQA, Aug. 2, 1822.

41. CFA, *Memoirs of JQA*, VIII, 363.

42. Ibid., 364.

43. Ibid., 389.

44. Ibid., 402.

45. Reprinted in the *Rhode Island American and Gazette*, Sept. 5, 1831.

46. Quoted in Bemis, *JQA and the Union*, 284.

47. CFA, *Memoirs of JQA*, VIII, 404.

48. JQA to Edward Ingersoll, Sept. 21 and 22, 1831, in "Letters and Opinions of the Masonic Institution," 1851, JQA Papers.

49. CFA, *Memoirs of JQA*, VIII, 277.

50. Seward, *Life of JQA*, 204–7.

51. CFA, *Memoirs of JQA*, VIII, 413.

52. CFA, Diary, III, 119.

53. Ibid., 120.

54. CFA, *Memoirs of JQA*, VIII, 414.

CHAPTER 33

1. Wheelan, *Mr. Adams's Last Crusade*, 67, and Shepherd, *Cannibals*, 334–35.

2. See Freeman, *Field of Blood*, 25–28.

3. Quoted in ibid., 3.

4. Quoted in Burleigh, *The Stranger and the Statesman*, 215.

5. See the *Richmond Enquirer* quoted in the *Indiana Democrat*, Jan. 24, 1832.

6. CFA, Diary, IV, 214–15, nt. 3.

7. CFA, *Memoirs of JQA*, VIII, 436–37.

8. JQA to Robert Walsh Jr., March 14, 1824, Adams Papers, II, reel 147.

9. Diary entry, Dec. 2, 1831, JQA Diaries.

10. CFA, *Memoirs of JQA*, VIII, 446–47.

11. CFA, Diary, IV, 265, nt. 1.

12. Quoted in Parsons, *John Quincy Adams*, 211.

13. CFA, *Memoirs of JQA*, VIII, 484.

14. Ibid., 486.

15. Ibid.

16. See Howe, *What Hath God Wrought*, 374–75.

17. Ibid., 373–74.

18. CFA, *Memoirs of JQA*, VIII, 27–28.

19. Ibid., IV, 499.

20. Quoted in Wheelan, *Mr. Adams's Last Crusade*, 76.

21. CFA, *Memoirs of JQA*, VIII, 425.

22. Quoted in Wheelan, *Mr. Adams's Last Crusade*, 76.

23. Quoted in Van Buren, *Autobiography of Martin Van Buren*, 625.

24. Quoted in Howe, *What Hath God Wrought*, 380.

25. Quoted in ibid., 381.

26. Quoted in CFA, Diary, IV, 327, nt. 2.

27. Quoted in Bemis, *JQA and the Union*, 258.

28. Quoted in Shepherd, *Cannibals*, 341.

29. Quoted in Nagel, *John Quincy Adams*, 342.

30. CFA, Diary, IV, 259.

31. Ibid., 330, nt. 1.

32. See Howe, *What Hath God Wrought*, 384.

33. JQA to Alexander H. Everett, Aug. 18, 1832, Adams Papers, II, reel 150.

34. JQA to William L. Stone, Aug. 29, 1832, in Stone, *Letters on Masonry*.

35. See Howe, *What Hath God Wrought*, 383–86.

36. Quoted in Bemis, *JQA and the Union*, 246, nt. 11.

37. See Forbes, *Missouri Compromise*, 256–57.

38. Diary entry, Nov. 15, 1832, JQA Diaries.

39. See Bemis, *JQA and the Union*, 261.

40. Quoted in ibid., 262–63.

41. CFA, Diary, IV, 419–20, nt. 1.

42. Ibid.

43. Quoted in Bemis, *JQA and the Union*, 266.

44. Quoted in Traub, *John Quincy Adams*, 404.

45. Quoted in Bemis, *JQA and the Union*, 267.

46. Quoted in ibid.

47. JQA to William Plumer, April 6, 1833, Adams Papers, II, reel 151.

48. Quoted in Traub, *John Quincy Adams*, 406.

49. Quoted in ibid., 407.

50. Waldstreicher, *JQA: Diaries*, II, 651.

51. JQA to William Plumer, April 6, 1832, Adams Papers, II, reel 151.

52. CFA, Diary, V, 51, nt. 3.

53. CFA, *Memoirs of JQA*, IX, 13.

54. CFA, Diary, V, 75, nt. 1.

55. Ibid., x.

56. Ibid.

57. Ibid., 84, nt. 1.

58. Ibid., 84–85.

59. Ibid.

60. Ibid.

61. Ibid., 150.

62. Ibid., 155.

63. Ibid., 193, nt. 3.

64. Ibid., 155–56.

65. CFA, *Memoirs of JQA*, IX, 5.

66. CFA, Diary, V, 145, nt. 2.

67. Ibid., 141.

68. Ibid., 168.

69. Bemis, *JQA and the Union*, 198.

70. Quoted in ibid., 182, nt. 1.

71. CFA, Diary, V, 187.

72. CFA, *Memoirs of JQA*, IX, 30.

73. Ibid., 31–32.

74. See Howe, *What Hath God Wrought*, 387–88.

75. CFA, Diary, V, 295, nt. 1.

76. Howe, *What Hath God Wrought*, 390.

77. Howe, *Political Culture of the American Whigs*, 12–18.

78. Ibid.

CHAPTER 34

1. Quoted in Wheelan, *Mr. Adams's Last Crusade*, 93.

2. See Howe, *What Hath God Wrought*, 423–24.

3. Quoted in Forbes, *Missouri Compromise*, 236.

4. Quoted in Howe, *What Hath God Wrought*, 425.

5. Quoted in Wheelan, *Mr. Adams's Last Crusade*, 93.

6. CFA, *Memoirs of JQA*, IX, 269.

7. Ibid., 531.

8. Waldstreicher and Mason, *JQA and Slavery*, 145–46.

9. Quoted in Bemis, *JQA and the Union*, 328.

10. Waldstreicher and Mason, *JQA and Slavery*, xiv–xxi.

11. Ibid., 194. See also Weeks, *JQA and American Global Empire*, 194.

12. Quoted in Forbes, *Missouri Compromise*, 200.

13. Waldstreicher, *JQA: Diaries*, II, 206.

14. Pierson, *Tocqueville and Beaumont in America*, 418–20.

15. CFA, *Memoirs of JQA*, IX, 269.

16. Quoted in Ely and Loux, "Thomas R. Dew."

17. CFA, *Memoirs of JQA* IX, 414.

18. Waldstreicher and Mason, *JQA and Slavery*, 168.

19. Wheelan, *Mr. Adams's Last Crusade*, 97–98.

20. CFA, *Memoirs of JQA*, VIII, 462.

21. JQA to Moses Brown, Dec. 9, 1833, Adams Papers, II, reel 151.

22. CFA, *Diary*, V, xix–xx.

23. Ibid., 353, nt. 1.

24. CFA, *Memoirs of JQA*, IX, 92.

25. Ibid., 119.

26. CFA, *Diary*, V, 348, nt. 2.

27. Ibid., 349, nt. 2.

28. Quoted in Nagel, *John Quincy Adams*, 346, and CFA, *Diary*, V, 405, nt. 2.

29. Quoted in Nagel, *John Quincy Adams*, 347.

30. Diary entry, Oct. 23, 1834, JQA Diaries.

31. CFA, *Diary*, V, 410.

32. Quoted in Thomas, *Louisa*, 407.

33. CFA, *Diary*, V, 410.

34. Ibid., 411.

35. Ibid., 351.

36. CFA, *Diary*, VI, 14.

37. Ibid., 24, nt. 1.

38. Ibid., 68.

39. Ibid.

40. Quoted in Bemis, *JQA and the Union*, 309.

41. Ibid.

42. Ibid., 313.

43. Quoted in Wheelan, *Mr. Adams's Last Crusade*, 81.

44. Quoted in Seward, *Life of JQA*, 265.

45. CFA, *Diary*, VI, 75.

46. Wiltse et al., *Papers of Daniel Webster*, Daniel Webster to Caroline LeRoy Webster, April 29, 1836.

47. Ibid., Daniel Webster to Edward Everett, Jan. 27, 1836.

48. JQA to CFA, March 5 and April 8, 1835, Adams Papers, II, reel 156.

49. CFA, *Diary*, VI, 117.

50. Ibid., 118–19, nt. 1.

51. Ibid., 121, nt. 1.

52. Ibid., 123–24, nt. 1.

53. Ibid., 130–31, nt. 1.

54. Ibid., 151, 300.

55. CFA, *Memoirs of JQA*, IX, 25.

56. Quoted in Waldstreicher and Mason, *JQA and Slavery*, 175.

57. Ibid., 464.

58. Howe, *What Hath God Wrought*, 433.

59. CFA, *Memoirs of JQA*, IX, 256.

60. CFA, *Diary*, VI, 248–49, nt. 2.

61. Diary, in Graham et al., *Diary and Autobiographical Writings*, II, 695–96.

62. Quoted in Bemis, *JQA and the Union*, 335.

63. CFA, *Diary*, VI, 296, nt. 1.

64. Quoted in Bemis, *JQA and the Union*, 336.

65. CFA, *Diary*, VI, 326–27, nt. 1.

CHAPTER 35

1. Quoted in Bemis, *JQA and the Union*, 336.

2. CFA, *Diary*, VI, 399, nt. 1.

3. Quoted in Bemis, *JQA and the Union*, 338.

4. Quoted in Giddings, *History of the Rebellion*, 156.

5. CFA, *Memoirs of JQA*, IX, 278.

6. CFA, *Diary*, VI, 339, nt. 1.

7. See Miller, *Arguing About Slavery*, 51–67.

8. Waldstreicher, *JQA: Diaries*, II, 387.

9. Waldstreicher and Mason, *JQA and Slavery*, 195.

10. JQA to Roland Johnson, Jan. 19, 1837, Adams Papers, II, reel 153.

11. CFA, *Memoirs of JQA*, X, 39–44. See also Waldstreicher and Mason, *JQA and Slavery*, 198–99.

12. Quoted in Bemis, *JQA and the Union*, 375–76.

13. CFA, *Memoirs of JQA*, IX, 214–15, 220–21, 223, 232–33.

14. Ibid., 308–9.

15. JQA to Alexander H. Everett, undated, Adams Papers, II, reel 152.

16. CFA, *Memoirs of JQA*, IX, 367.

17. Quoted in Bemis, *JQA and the Union*, 349.

18. Ibid.

19. CFA, *Memoirs of JQA*, IX, 340.

20. Diary, in Graham et al., *Diary and Autobiographical Writings*, II, 717.

21. Bemis, *JQA and the Union*, 340.

22. Quoted in ibid., 341.

23. Quoted in ibid., 344.

24. Quoted in Seward, *Life of JQA*, 286–87.

25. Quoted in ibid., 287, 289.

26. Quoted in ibid. See also, "JQA to Messrs. Green and Osborne, editors of the *Quincy Patriot*, March 18, 1837," Adams Papers, II, reel 153.

27. Quoted in Seward, *Life of JQA*, 290–91.

28. Quoted in Traub, *John Quincy Adams*, 446.

29. Quoted in Thomas, *Louisa*, 420.

30. Nagel, *John Quincy Adams*, 357.

31. Portolano, *Passionate Empiricist*, 1–2.

32. Burleigh, *The Stranger and the Statesman*, 60–62, 65–71.

33. Ibid., 82–87.

34. Quoted in ibid., 168.

35. Ibid., 178–79.

36. Quoted in ibid., 196.

37. Waldstreicher, *JQA: Diaries*, II, 374–75.

38. Bemis, *JQA and the Union*, 505.

39. Quoted in Burleigh, *The Stranger and the Statesman*, 200–4.

40. CFA, *Memoirs of JQA*, X, 25.

41. Quoted in Bemis, *JQA and the Union*, 508.

42. CFA, *Memoirs of JQA*, X, 139.

43. Burleigh, *The Stranger and the Statesman*, 221–22.

44. Ibid., 240.

45. Quoted in ibid., 240–41.

46. CFA, *Memoirs of JQA*, XII, 116.

47. Ibid., 141.

CHAPTER 36

1. Quoted in Seward, *Life of JQA*, 277.

2. Quoted in ibid., 278.

3. CFA, *Memoirs of JQA*, IX, 333.

4. Benjamin Lundy, "A Citizen of the United States," *War in Texas*.

5. JQA to William Ellery Channing, Nov. 21, 1837, Adams Papers, II, reel 153.

6. CFA, Diary, VII, 272.

7. CFA, *Memoirs of JQA*, IX, 363.

8. Ibid., 412.

9. Ibid., 461.

10. Ibid., 378.

11. CFA, *Memoirs of JQA*, X, 48–49.

12. Barnes and Dumond, *Letters of Weld, Grimké Weld, and Grimké*, I, 292.

13. Quoted in Thomas, *Louisa*, 408.

14. Diary, in Graham et al., *Diary and Autobiographical Writings*, II, 705.

15. Quoted in Thomas, *Louisa*, 411.

16. Quoted in Shepherd, *Cannibals*, 351.

17. See ibid., 351–52.

18. Quoted in Thomas, *Louisa*, 418.

19. Quoted in ibid., 421.

20. Quoted in ibid., 427.

21. Diary, in Graham et al., *Diary and Autobiographical Writings*, II, 713.

22. Ibid.

23. Ibid.

24. Quoted in Thomas, *Louisa*, 431.

25. Quoted in ibid., 430.

26. Quoted in Shepherd, *Cannibals*, 378.

27. CFA, Diary, VIII, 54.

28. CFA, *Memoirs of JQA*, IX, 421–29.

29. Traub, *John Quincy Adams*, 450.

30. CFA, *Memoirs of JQA*, XI, 479.

31. JQA to William Ellery Channing, Nov. 21, 1837, Adams Papers, II, reel 153.

32. Ibid.

33. CFA, Diary, VII, 358.

34. CFA, *Memoirs of JQA*, IX, 349.

35. For the time being, Charles was willing to take his father's advice. "I am . . . disposed to think well of the moral results which our abolition movements may unintentionally produce," he wrote Louisa, "but this is a very different thing from throwing oneself forever and aye, headlong into them." CFA, Diary, VII, 389–90, nt. 3.

36. JQA to Rich Bayley, March 27, 1837, Adams Papers, II, reel 153.

37. Ibid.

38. CFA, *Memoirs of JQA*, X, 4.

39. Ibid., IX, 523.

40. Quoted in Freeman, *Field of Blood*, 114–15.

41. See Freeman, *Affairs of Honor*, 168–78.

42. Freeman, *Field of Blood*, 80.

43. See ibid., 86–91, and CFA, Diary, VII, 406, nt. 1.

44. CFA, *Memoirs of JQA*, XI, 101.

45. Ibid., 497.

46. Ibid.

47. CFA, *Memoirs of JQA*, X, 413, and Bemis, *JQA and the Union*, 378.

48. Quoted in Bemis, *JQA and the Union*, 361–62.

49. Quoted in Traub, *John Quincy Adams*, 455.

50. Shepherd, *Cannibals*, 376–77.

51. Quoted in Traub, *John Quincy Adams*, 456.

52. Quoted in ibid.

53. Quoted in ibid.

54. JQA, "Speech . . . upon the Right . . . to Petition on the Freedom of Speech and of Debate," 67.

55. Ibid.

56. Quoted in Traub, *John Quincy Adams*, 459.

57. Quoted in Nagel, *John Quincy Adams*, 366.

58. Quoted in ibid., 367.

59. CFA, Diary, VIII, 87, nt. 2.

60. Waldstreicher, *JQA: Diaries*, II, 441.

61. Quoted in Nagel, *John Quincy Adams*, 369.

62. "Speech of John Quincy Adams," *Newburyport Herald*, Feb. 1, 1839.

63. Quoted in Nagel, *John Quincy Adams*, 382.

64. *Emancipator*, Sept. 26, 1839.

65. JQA to Joshua Leavitt et al., July 11, 1839, Adams Papers, II, reel 153, MHS.

66. CFA, *Memoirs of JQA*, XI, 295.

67. Quoted in Wheelan, *Mr. Adams's Last Crusade*, 159.

68. Quoted in Waldstreicher and Mason, *JQA and Slavery*, 221, nt. 4.

69. Quoted in ibid.

70. JQA to Reverend J. Edwards, Adams Papers, II, reel 153.

71. Quoted in Barnes and Dumond, *Letters of Weld, Grimké Weld, and Grimké*, I, 257.

72. Quoted in Nagel, *John Quincy Adams*, 371.

73. Quoted in Edel, *Nation Builder*, 282, 284–85.

74. CFA, *Memoirs of JQA*, X, 63.

75. Quoted in Nagel, *John Quincy Adams*, 373.

76. JQA, "On the Character of Hamlet," *Alexandria Gazette*, Dec. 5, 1839.

77. Waldstreicher, *JQA: Diaries*, II, 465.

78. CFA, *Memoirs of JQA*, X, 136.

79. Quoted in Seward, *Life of JQA*, 297–99. See also CFA, *Memoirs of JQA*, VIII, 146–47.

CHAPTER 37

1. Bemis, *JQA and the Union*, 394.

2. Wheelan, *Mr. Adams's Last Crusade*, 167.

3. Ibid., 7–9. For a comprehensive history of the *Amistad* affair, see Jones, *Mutiny on the Amistad*.

4. Quoted in Wheelan, *Mr. Adams's Last Crusade*, 169.

5. Ibid., 170.

6. Ibid., 172–73.

7. Ibid., 171, 174.

8. Quoted in ibid., 72.

9. Ibid., 171.

10. CFA, *Memoirs of JQA*, X, 112, 135. In 1820 a boatload of enslaved Africans had been captured off the coast of Georgia. U.S. participation in the slave trade had been outlawed since 1808. The U.S. federal district court judge for Georgia, William Davies, subsequently ruled that no matter how deplorable, the international slave trade had not been universally outlawed.

Spain in particular continued to condone the practice in regions south of the equator. Those Africans whom Spanish and Portuguese representatives could prove belonged to their citizens were to be restored to them. See Noonan, *The Antelope*.

11. Diary entry, Sept. 26, 1839, JQA Diaries.

12. Wheelan, *Mr. Adams's Last Crusade*, 80.

13. Quoted in Parsons, *John Quincy Adams*, 240.

14. Diary entry, Sept. 26, 1839, JQA Diaries.

15. CFA, *Memoirs of JQA*, X, 458.

16. CFA, Diary, V, Sept. 1839.

17. JQA to CFA, April 14, 1841, Adams Papers, II, reel 154.

18. CFA, *Memoirs of JQA*, X, 360.

19. JQA to Roger Baldwin, Jan. 24, 1841, Adams Papers, II, reel 158, and Bemis, *JQA and the Union*, 403.

20. See Wheelan, *Mr. Adams's Last Crusade*, 178–79.

21. Quoted in Bemis, *JQA and the Union*, 408.

22. "Argument of John Quincy Adams Before the Supreme Court of the United States in the Case of the *United States v. Cinque and Others, Africans*," JQA Papers, 16.

23. Ibid., 22.

24. See CFA, *Memoirs of JQA*, X, 431–37.

25. Quoted in Bemis, *JQA and the Union*, 410.

26. CFA, *Memoirs of JQA*, X, 441–42.

27. Quoted in Bemis, *JQA and the Union*, 411.

28. JQA to CFA, April 14, 1841, Adams Papers, II, reel 156.

29. Waldstreicher, *JQA: Diaries*, II, 519.

30. JQA to Lewis Tappan et al., April 3, 1845, Adams Papers, II, reel 154.

31. See Wheelan, *Mr. Adams's Last Crusade*, 185, and CFA, *Memoirs of JQA*, X, 446–47.

CHAPTER 38

1. CFA, *Memoirs of JQA*, X, 206.

2. Ibid., XI, 35.

3. Ibid., X, 366.

4. Ibid., 256.

5. Quoted in Seward, *Life of JQA*, 140.

6. CFA, *Memoirs of JQA*, X, 492.

7. Ibid., 219.

8. Ibid., 291.

9. Ibid., 293.

10. Nagel, *John Quincy Adams*, 376–77.

11. CFA, *Memoirs of JQA*, X, 145.

12. Ibid., 356.

13. Ibid., 365.

14. Diary entry, March 4, 1841, JQA Diaries.

15. Quoted in Bemis, *JQA and the Union*, 419.

16. Quoted in Traub, *John Quincy Adams*, 483.

17. Ibid.

18. CFA, *Memoirs of JQA*, X, 454.

19. Ibid., 463–64.

20. Ibid., 459.

21. Ibid., 427.

22. Ibid., 454.

23. Ibid., 413.

24. Waldstreicher, *JQA: Diaries*, II, 510–11.

25. Quoted in Nagel, *John Quincy Adams*, 383.

26. Quoted in ibid., 384.

27. Waldstreicher, *JQA: Diaries*, II, 517.

28. "Speech of Mr. John Quincy Adams on the Case of Alexander McLeod," 1841, JQA Papers.

29. Ibid.

30. CFA, *Memoirs of JQA*, XI, 48.

31. Quoted in Traub, *John Quincy Adams*, 486.

32. Quoted in Bemis, *JQA and the Union*, 424.

33. Barnes and Dumond, *Letters of Weld, Grimké Weld, and Grimké*, I, 889.

34. CFA, *Memoirs of JQA*, X, 451.

35. Quoted in Bemis, *JQA and the Union*, 426.

36. Quoted in Traub, *John Quincy Adams*, 488.

37. Nevins, *Diary of Philip Hone*, II, 582–85.

38. Giddings, *History of the Rebellion*, 161–62.

39. Quoted in ibid., 162–63.

40. United States Congress, *Congressional Globe*, XI, 170–72.

41. Ibid.

42. Quoted in Bemis, *JQA and the Union*, 432.

43. Barnes and Dumond, *Letters of Weld, Grimké Weld, and Grimké*, II, 905–6.

44. Quoted in Bemis, *JQA and the Union*, 434.

45. Quoted in ibid.

46. Quoted in Giddings, *History of the Rebellion*, 166–67.

47. Barnes and Dumond, *Letters of Weld, Grimké Weld, and Grimké*, II, 899.

48. Quoted in Bemis, *JQA and the Union*, 435.
49. Quoted in Traub, *John Quincy Adams*, 491.
50. Waldstreicher, *JQA: Diaries*, II, 532.
51. Quoted in Bemis, *JQA and the Union*, 437.
52. Henry Clay to JQA, July 24, 1842, Adams Papers, II, reel 154.
53. Waldstreicher, *JQA: Diaries*, II, 533.
54. Freeman, *Field of Blood*, 138–39.
55. Quoted in Waldstreicher and Mason, *JQA and Slavery*, 265.
56. CFA, *Memoirs of JQA*, XI, 241.
57. "Mr. Buckingham," *Eastern Argus*, Sept. 11, 1842.
58. Quoted in Nagel, *John Quincy Adams*, 388.
59. Quoted in ibid., 387.
60. See Bemis, *JQA and the Union*, 444–45.

CHAPTER 39

1. Quoted in Bemis, *JQA and the Union*, 451.
2. Quoted in Giddings, *History of the Rebellion*, 217.
3. Quoted in ibid., 218.
4. CFA, *Memoirs of JQA*, XI, 330.
5. Quoted in DeConde, *History*, I, 178.
6. CFA, *Memoirs of JQA*, XI, 348.
7. Ibid., 346.
8. Ibid., 351.
9. Ibid., 380.
10. Quoted in Bemis, *JQA and the Union*, 465, nt. 4.
11. CFA, *Memoirs of JQA*, XI, 374.
12. Ibid., 390.
13. Ibid., 391–93.
14. Ibid., 400.
15. Waldstreicher, *JQA: Diaries*, II, 443.
16. CFA, *Memoirs of JQA*, XI, 441.
17. Quoted in Nagel, *John Quincy Adams*, 395.
18. Waldstreicher, *JQA: Diaries*, II, 572.
19. See Wikipedia.
20. CFA, *Memoirs of JQA*, XI, 412.
21. Ibid., 419.
22. Ibid.
23. Quoted in Nagel, *John Quincy Adams*, 396.
24. See "An Oration Delivered Before the Cincinnati Astronomical Society," Nov. 10, 1843, JQA Papers.

25. CFA, *Memoirs of JQA*, XI, 410.
26. Quoted in Nagel, *John Quincy Adams*, 398.
27. Waldstreicher, *JQA: Diaries*, II, 580.
28. CFA, *Memoirs of JQA*, XII, 5.
29. Ibid., XI, 514.
30. Quoted in Bemis, *JQA and the Union*, 471.
31. Waldstreicher, *JQA: Diaries*, II, 593.
32. See JQA to Thomas Loring, Aug. 8, 1842, Adams Papers, II, reel 154.
33. CFA, *Memoirs of JQA*, XII, 35.
34. Ibid., 49.
35. Ibid., 16.
36. Bemis, *JQA and the Union*, 426.
37. CFA, *Memoirs of JQA*, XII, 64, 268–69.
38. See Nagel, *John Quincy Adams*, 401–2. See also CFA, *Memoirs of JQA*, XII, 97, 105.
39. CFA, *Memoirs of JQA*, XII, 116.
40. Ibid., XI, 543.
41. Ibid., XII, 162–63.
42. Freeman, *Field of Blood*, 70.
43. CFA, *Memoirs of JQA*, XII, 126.
44. Ibid., 171.
45. JQA to CFA, March 27, 1845, Adams Papers, II, reel 154.
46. Ibid., JQA to Lewis Tappan, July 15, 1845.
47. CFA, *Memoirs of JQA*, XII, 231–32.
48. Ibid., 243–44.
49. Ibid., 244.
50. Ibid., 221.
51. JQA to Joseph Sturge, April 1846, Adams Papers, II, reel 155.
52. CFA, *Memoirs of JQA*, XII, 259.
53. Ibid., 206.
54. Quoted in Thomas, *Louisa*, 445.
55. See ibid., 446.
56. Waldstreicher, *JQA: Diaries*, II, 573.
57. CFA, *Memoirs of JQA*, XII, 211.
58. Ibid., 213, 279.
59. Ibid., 205–6.
60. Quoted in Nagel, *John Quincy Adams*, 407.
61. Quoted in ibid.
62. CFA, *Memoirs of JQA*, XII, 277.
63. Ibid., 279.
64. Ibid., 279, 282.
65. Nagel, *John Quincy Adams*, 409.

66. JQA to Albert Gallatin, Dec. 26, 1846, Adams Papers, II, reel 155.

67. Quoted in Nagel, *John Quincy Adams*, 412.

68. Quoted in ibid.

69. Quoted in ibid., 413.

70. Quoted in Bemis, *JQA and the Union*, 535.

71. See Giddings, *History of the Rebellion*, 335–36.

72. John G. Palfrey to CFA, Feb. 21, 1848, Adams Papers, II, reel 158.

73. Quoted in Bemis, *JQA and the Union*, 537.

74. Ibid., 538.

75. See Shepherd, *Cannibals*, 403.

76. CFA, Diary, VIII, Feb. 26, 1848.

77. See Shepherd, *Cannibals*, 403.

78. Quoted in *JQA and the Union*.

Acknowledgments

Anyone attempting to write about a member of the illustrious Adams family must stand on the shoulders of many other scholars. This is certainly true of me. Without the biographers, historians, and editors who have labored so long and well in the Adams vineyard, *A Man for the Whole People* would not have been possible. And thanks to those who have chronicled and analyzed the momentous events of the late eighteenth and early nineteenth centuries, for when I began this project some seven years ago this was a new field for me.

As usual my harshest critic and biggest supporter has been my in-house editor, Rhoda Woods. Thanks also to my children and their spouses, Nicole and Thomas Olmstead and Jeff and Andrea Woods, for their suggestions. Then there are my grandchildren, Darcy and Avery Olmstead and Cullen and Abigail Woods, whose patience has been sorely tested by my obsessive diatribes on John Quincy Adams. I will forgive them for arranging a secret drinking game during this Christmas dinner past when they permitted themselves a draw every time I mentioned John Quincy's name.

I cannot say enough about the work that my agent, Susan Ginsburg, and her assistant, Catherine Bradshaw, have put into this project. I am also indebted to Brent Howard, Grace Layer, and John Parsley at Dutton for their belief in and commitment to such a vast project. Copy editor Frank Walgren saved me countless embarrassments. Sarah Martin and her staff at the Massachusetts Historical Society cheerfully fulfilled my every request. Research assistants Kyra Schmidt, James Cooke, Bonnie Barnes, Robyn Spears, Airic Hughes, Katlyn Rozovics, and Connor McGownd were my faithful hewers of wood and drawers of water. Finally, thanks to my mentor, Robert A. Divine, who first introduced me to John Quincy Adams.

Index

Note: The abbreviations "JA" and "JQA" refer to John Adams and John Quincy Adams, respectively.

About the Author

Randall B. Woods is the John A. Cooper Distinguished Professor of History at the University of Arkansas, where he has taught since 1971. In 2008 he was the Stanley Kaplan Distinguished Visiting Professor at Williams College and in 2013 the John G. Winant Visiting Professor of American Government at the University of Oxford. His books include *LBJ: Architect of American Ambition, Shadow Warrior: William Egan Colby and the CIA,* and *Fulbright: A Biography,* which won the Robert H. Ferrell Book Prize.